Hebrew Bible / Old Testament
The History of Its Interpretation

Volume I/1

V&R

Hebrew Bible / Old Testament
The History of Its Interpretation

Edited by
Magne Sæbø

VOLUME I
From the Beginnings to the Middle Ages
(Until 1300)

Göttingen · Vandenhoeck & Ruprecht · 1996

Hebrew Bible / Old Testament
The History of Its Interpretation

Volume I

From the Beginnings to the Middle Ages (Until 1300)

In Co-operation with
Chris Brekelmans and Menahem Haran

Edited by
Magne Sæbø

Part 1

Antiquity

Göttingen · Vandenhoeck & Ruprecht · 1996

Die Deutsche Bibliothek – CIP-Einheitsaufnahme

Hebrew Bible, Old Testament:
the history of its interpretation /
ed. by Magne Sæbø. –
Göttingen: Vandenhoeck und Ruprecht
NE: Sæbø, Magne [Hrsg.]

Vol. 1. From the beginnings to the Middle Ages (until 1300) /
in co-operation with Chris Brekelmans and Menahem Haran.
Pt. 1. Antiquity. – 1996
ISBN 3-525-53636-4

Financially supported by the
Förderungs- und Beihilfefond Wissenschaft der VG Wort, Munich
and by the Norwegian Research Council, Oslo

Manufactured by Hubert & Co., Göttingen

Johann Ernst Ludwig Diestel

(1825–1879)

in memoriam

Contents

Preface

The project of *Hebrew Bible / Old Testament: the History of Its Interpretation* stands in a tradition of similar works on the research history of the Hebrew Bible / Old Testament. Yet it has the intention of presenting something new and unprecedented. Since the planning of this HBOT Project started in the early eighties biblical research history seems to have come in vogue, and various new works on the subject have appeared. However, the need for a comprehensive research history in the field, written anew in the light of the current status in biblical as well as in historical disciplines, is still imperative. More will be said on this in the following Prolegomenon.

Linking back to two aged and renowned predecessors, namely LUDWIG DIESTEL's monumental *Geschichte des Alten Testamentes in der christlichen Kirche* (1869) and FREDERIC W. FARRAR, *History of Interpretation* (1886), the present history will pursue the best of their universal character; and at the same time it will attempt to overcome their limitations and deficiencies as well. Both DIESTEL and FARRAR, as most authors in this field, were representatives of modern European Protestantism, and the History of FARRAR, presenting the Bampton Lectures of 1885, had even an apologetic bias. But in a new history of biblical interpretation confessional as well as national or regional borders will be crossed, in accordance with the present situation of a worldwide biblical scholarship.

As for the practical accomplishment, DIESTEL completed his great work alone and after few years, as did also FARRAR. Today it would be hard to compete with their immense and laborious achievement – for which one can but express admiration. Instead a scholarly team-work seems now to give the most appropriate possibility of procedure, and even more so as in our time the mass of new data, insights and informations on the subject has increased immensely.

DIESTEL had the intention of giving a comprehensive historical description, but, for practical reasons, he also felt compelled to confine himself to the Christian side of the field, leaving mainly out the broad and significant Jewish biblical interpretation through the centuries as well as elements of Jewish-Christian interactions in this field at various times. Excusing himself for this "substantial loss", DIESTEL hoped for a "partition of work", *Arbeitstheilung,* with Jewish scholars (Geschichte, p. v); regrettably, however, that did not take place, at least not directly. Today it would be inconceivable not to include the Jewish side of the history of biblical interpretation. Therefore, Jewish scholars were integrated into the HBOT Project from the beginning; and one of my first steps in organizing the Project was – during the IOSOT Congress in Salamanca 1983 – to make contact with a Jewish Bible scholar, namely Professor Menahem Haran, of Jerusalem; during the same Congress also Professor Henri Cazelles, of Paris, consented to act as a Co-editor, taking special responsibility for matters related to Roman Catholic exegesis. In 1987, when Professor Cazelles, for personal reasons, had withdrawn from the Project, Professor Chr. Brekelmans, of Leuven, kindly replaced him (see, further, my Presentation of the Project in *Biblica* 1992).

Coming to the pleasant duty of *acknowledgements* I, first of all, should like to express my sincere gratitude to the distinguished Co-editors of this volume, especially Professor Haran, without whose guidance and manifold help I would not have managed a proper inclusion of the Jewish interpretation, and then, to my Catholic colleagues, Professor Cazelles, for the years 1983-86 that were so important for the establishing of the Project, and thereafter Professor Brekelmans. For valuable help I also wish to thank Professor Dr. Rudolf Smend DD, of Göttingen, and Professor Dr. Dr. Norbert Lohfink SJ, of Frankfurt/M.

Of vital importance for the propulsion of the Project was, from 1987 onward, the contact with Vandenhoeck & Ruprecht and its Publisher, Dr. Arndt Ruprecht, who has been most generous to the Project and to whom I am under deep obligation for all his help. Generous financial support from *Förderungs- und Beihilfefonds Wissenschaft der VG Wort GmbH*, of Munich, as well as from the *Norwegian Research Council*, during the years 1989-92, and from the *Norwegian Academy of Science and Letters*, in 1994, and *Fridtjof Nansens Fond,* in 1995, all of Oslo, has been of decisive significance for the Project; and I am deeply indebted to these institutions as well as to my own faculty, the *Free Faculty of Theology,* of Oslo. To them all I express sincere thanks. Also on this occasion, I should like to extend best thanks to my colleague of Church History, Professor Dr. Oskar Skarsaune, for a lot of good help and advice, as well as to cand. theol. Terje Stordalen, who served as Project Assistant in 1989-91 and built the Bibliographical Data base of the Project, paid by the *Research Council*, and, finally cand. theol. Richard Lee Blucher, cand. theol. Øystein Lund and Mrs. Marie Luise Diehl for indispensable assistance of various kind.

Last but not least, I am deeply obliged to the individual contributors of this first volume of HBOT, who not only have been loyal to its plan and specific character, but who also, in their respective contributions, for which they are responsible, have done considerable personal research; thereby they have fostered biblical and historical scholarship with new insight.

Oslo, in May 1995 M. S.

Historiographical Problems and Challenges
A Prolegomenon

By MAGNE SÆBØ, Oslo

General works, mainly on historiography: W. BODENSTEIN, *Neige des Historismus. Ernst Troeltschs Entwicklungsgang* (Gütersloh 1959); H. BUTTERFIELD, *Man on His Past* (Cambridge 1955); idem, "The History of Historiography and the History of Science", *L'aventure de la science* (FS A. Koyre; Paris 1964) 57–68; E. HALLETT CARR, *What is History?* (London 1961); R. G. COLLINGWOOD, *The Idea of History* (Oxford 1946); B. CROCE, *Theorie und Geschichte der Historiographie* (Tübingen 1930); O. DAHL, *Problemer i historiens teori* (Oslo 1986); R. C. DENTAN (ed.), *The Idea of History in the Ancient Near East* (New Haven [1955] 1967); W. DRAY, *Laws and Explanations in History* (Oxford 1957); A. DUNKEL, *Christlicher Glaube und historische Vernunft. Eine interdisziplinäre Untersuchung über die Notwendigkeit eines theologischen Geschichtsverständnisses* (FSÖTh 57; Göttingen 1989); H.-G. GADAMER, *Wahrheit und Methode. Grundzüge einer philosophischen Hermeneutik* (Tübingen [5]1986; ET: *Truth and Method*, New York 1984); P. GARDINER (ed.), *Theories of History. Edited with Introductions and Commentaries* (New York / London 1959); L. GOTTSCHALK (ed.), *Generalization in the Writing of History* (Chicago 1963); H. C. HOCKETT, *The Critical Method in Historical Research and Writing* (New York 1955); TH. S. KUHN, *The Structure of Scientific Revolution* (International Encyclopedia of Unified Science II/2; Chicago 1962); P. MEINHOLD, *Geschichte der kirchlichen Historiographie* I–II (Orbis Academicus III/5; Freiburg / München 1967); A. R. MILLARD / J. K. HOFFMEIER / D. W. BAKER (eds.), *Faith, Tradition, and History. Old Testament Historiography in Its Near Eastern Context* (Winona Lake, IN 1994); K. POPPER, *The Poverty of Historicism* (Boston 1957; [Routledge Paperbacks] London [3]1961); H. RICKERT, *Die Probleme der Geschichtsphilosophie* (Heidelberg [3]1924); CH. SAMARAN (ed.), *L'histoire et ses méthodes* (Encyclopédie de la Pléiade; Paris 1961); K. SCHMIDT-PHISELDECK, *Eduard Meyer og de historiske problemer* (Aarhus 1929).

General works on the history of study and interpretation of the HB/OT: The Cambridge History of the Bible (I. *From the Beginnings to Jerome,* ed. P. R. Ackroyd / C. F. Evans; Cambridge 1970; repr. 1980; II. *The West from the Fathers to the Reformation,* ed. G. W. H. Lampe; 1969; repr. 1980; III. *The West from the Reformation to the Present Day,* ed. S. L. Greenslade; 1963; repr. 1978); T. K. CHEYNE, *Founders of Old Testament Criticism* (London 1893); R. E. CLEMENTS, *A Century of Old Testament Study* (Guildford / London 1976); L. DIESTEL, *Geschichte des Alten Testamentes in der christlichen Kirche* (Jena 1869; repr. Leipzig 1981, "Mit einem Nachwort von Siegfried Wagner", 819–826); A. DUFF, *History of Old Testament Criticism* (London 1910); J. D. G. DUNN (ed.), *Jews and Christians. The Parting of the Ways A.D. 70 to 135* (The Second Durham-Tübingen Research Symposium on Earliest Christianity and Judaism; WUNT 66; Tübingen 1992); G. EBELING, "Kirchengeschichte als Geschichte der Auslegung der Heiligen Scrift", idem, *Wort Gottes und Tradition* (Göttingen 1964) 9–27; F. W. FARRAR, *History of Interpretation* (1886; repr. Grand Rapids 1961; 1979); R. M. GRANT, *A Short History of the Interpretation of the Bible* (Philadelphia 1963; 2nd rev. and enlarged edition, with D. Tracy, Philadelphia / London 1984); E. MCQUEEN GRAY, *Old Testament Criticism, Its Rise and Progress: From the Second Century to the End of the Eighteenth. A Historical Sketch* (New York / London, cr. 1923); H. F. HAHN, *Old Testament in Modern Research* (Philadelphia 1954; [2]1970, with a survey of recent lit. by H. D. Hummel); M. HARAN, "Midrashic and Literal Exegesis and the Critical Method in Biblical Research", *Studies in Bible* (ScrHier 31, ed. S. Japhet; Jerusalem 1986) 19–48; CH. KANNENGIESSER (ed.), *Bible de tous les temps* (1. *Le monde grec ancien et la Bible,* ed. C. Mondésert; Paris 1984; 2. *Le monde latin antique et la Bible,* ed. J. Fontaine / Ch. Pietri; 1985; 3. *Saint Augustin et la Bible,* ed. A.-M. la Bonnardière; 1986; 4. *Le Moyen Age et la Bible,* ed. P. Riché / G. Lobrichon; 1984; 5. *Le temps des Réformes et la Bible,* ed. G. Bedouelle / B. Roussel; 1989; 6. *Le Grand Siècle et la Bible,* ed. J.-R. Armogathe; 1989; 7. *Le siècle des Lumières et la Bible,* ed. Y. Belaval / D. Bourel; 1986; 8. *Le monde contemporain et la Bible,* ed. C. Savart / J.-N. Aletti; 1985); H. KARPP, *Schrift, Geist und Wort Gottes. Geltung und Wirkung der Bibel in der Geschichte der Kirche: Von der Alten Kirche bis zum Ausgang der Reformationszeit* (Darmstadt 1992); D. A. KNIGHT / G. M. TUCKER (eds.), *The Hebrew Bible and Its Modern Interpreters* (Philadelphia / Decatur, GA 1985); E. G. KRAELING, *The Old Testament since the Reformation* (London 1955; New York 1969); H.-J. KRAUS, *Geschichte der historisch-kritischen Erforschung des Alten Testaments* (3. erweit. Aufl.; Neukirchen-Vluyn 1982); idem, *Die Biblische Theologie. Ihre Geschichte und Problematik* (Neukirchen-Vluyn 1970); W. G. KÜMMEL, *Das Neue Testament. Geschichte der Erforschung seiner Probleme* (Orbis Academicus III/3; Freiburg/München 1958); O. LORETZ / W. STROLZ (eds.), *Die Hermeneutische Frage in der Theologie* (Schriften zum Weltgespräch 3; Wien / Freiburg 1968); H. DE LUBAC, *Exégèse médiévale. Les quatre sens de l'Ecriture,* 1–2 (Paris 1959–1964); W. MCKANE, *Selected Christian Hebraists* (Cambridge 1989); M. J. MULDER (ed.), *Mikra. Text, Translation, Reading and Interpretation of the Hebrew Bible in Ancient Judaism and Early Christianity* (CRINT II/1; Assen / Maastricht / Philadelphia 1988); H. GRAF REVENTLOW, *Bibelautorität und Geist der Moderne* (Göttingen 1980; ET by J. Bowden, *The Authority of the Bible and the Rise of the Modern World,* London 1984); idem, *Epochen der Bibelauslegung,* I. *Vom Alten Testament bis Origenes* (München 1990), II. *Von der Spätantike bis zum ausgehenden Mittelalter* (München 1994); J. B. ROGERS / D. M. MCKIM, *The Authority and Interpretation of the Bible: An Historical Approach* (New York / San Francisco 1979); J. ROGERSON, *Old Testament Criticism in the Nineteenth Century: England and Germany* (London 1984); J. ROGERSON / C. ROWLAND / B. LINDARS, *The Study and Use of the Bible* (The History of Christian Theology, ed. P. Avis, 2; Basingstoke / Grand Rapids 1988); H. ROST, *Die Bibel im Mittelalter* (Augsburg 1939); M. SÆBØ, "The History of Old Testament Studies: Problems of Its Presentation", *"Wünschet Jerusalem Frieden". Collected Communications to the XIIth Congress of the I.O.S.O.T., Jerusalem 1986* (ed. M. Augustin / K.-D. Schunck; BEATAJ 13; Frankfurt/M 1988) 3–14; idem, "Hebrew Bible / Old Testament: the History of Its Interpretation. Report on a New International Project", *Bibl.* 73 (1992) 137–143; R. SCHÄFER, *Die Bibelauslegung in der Geschichte der Kirche* (Gütersloh 1980); B. SMALLEY, *The Study of the Bible in the Middle Ages* (Oxford [1952], 1983, repr. 1984); R. SMEND, *Deutsche Alttestamentler in drei Jahrhunderten* (Göttingen 1989); idem, *Epochen der Bibelkritik. Gesammelte Studien Band 3* (BEvT 109; München 1991); H. F. D. SPARKS, *The Old Testament in the Christian Church* (London 1944); C. SPICQ, *Esquisse d'une histoire de l'exégèse latine au Moyen Age* (Bibliothèque thomiste 26; Paris 1944); B. UFFENHEIMER / H. GRAF REVENTLOW (eds.), *Creative Biblical Exegesis. Christian and Jewish Hermeneutics through the Centuries* (JSOTSup 59; Sheffield 1988). – R. J. COGGINS / J. L. HOULDEN (eds.), *A Dictionary of Biblical Interpretation* (London / Philadelphia 1990).

Every discipline of research that is of some age has its specific history, without which its identity would not be fully understood. It is, therefore, perceivable that the history of research, as a discipline of its own, in recent years has become an expanding scholarly matter of concern, both in science and in humanities, and not least in the field of biblical studies. It may be maintained that the writing of the history of studies increasingly seems to be regarded as a significant scholarly challenge.

1. In view of a broader context of the present new History of biblical studies two introductory remarks of a general character may be relevant.

First, historiography of research is, methodically, not different from any other kind of historiography, each kind having its distinct character according to its specific object and setting. A critical history of the study and interpretation of the Hebrew Bible / Old Testament through the centuries has definitely a most specific object of its own; at the same time, however, it will be but a part of cultural and social history in general as well as of ecclesiastical history and Bible studies in particular (cf. MEINHOLD; EBELING).

Second, the basic and partly philosophical questions of what 'history' and 'historiography' really might be cannot, for obvious reasons, be discussed as such or at any length on this occasion, and far less so as the opinions concerning these issues among historians and other scholars occupied with historiography are considerably divergent. This may be demonstrated quickly by reading the selected general works listed above, which may be regarded as representative today, not to speak of many others not listed.[1] But, on the other hand, it would be neither wise nor advisable, on this occasion, to avoid any discussion of methodological problems regarding 'history' and 'historiography', and even more so as existing histories of Old Testament studies apparently presuppose and involve, in this way or another, different methodical approaches. A brief presentation and discussion of some historiographical problems, related to present works in the field, might therefore be considered appropriate as a Prolegomenon. Possibly, it may even bring about some clarification of the task and methodical procedure lying ahead.

2. The histories and surveys of the study of the Hebrew Bible / Old Testament are of very diverse kind, differing from each other both in structure and content. Instead of going into a detailed discussion of the most outstanding histories – whereby a short history of research histories of the HB/OT might have been given – some main trends will be focused upon, primarily trends that may have an actual bearing on the question of what the character and function of a 'historiography' might be in this case.

When sorting the vast and variegated *literature* on the history of the study of the Hebrew Bible / Old Testament, including also the broader use of it through the ages, the literature may be categorized in most different ways. Here, some distinctions will be presented that have – *mirabile dictu* – been given little or no attention among scholars.

First, the literature may be divided into two groups related to two different aspects of the 'history of the Bible' that tend to go in opposite directions.

In *the one group,* the Bible may be said to be the influential *subject* or the 'motor' of the history. For, from the beginning, the Bible has been of great and varied influence and has had a complex *Wirkungsgeschichte,* in the proper sense of the word. The literature focusing upon this aspect may occasionally represent a kind of story-telling of how the Bible made its way under different conditions, from language to language, from people to people, through the centuries. In general, although varying in extent, one has here focused particularly upon the great impact of the Bible on Church life and theology, and beyond that, also on a people's culture, art and literature, and even on its social life and political laws.

Though, in all this, some *interpretation* of biblical texts normally has been involved, biblical interpretation is, however, first of all characteristic of *the other group* of literature, where the Hebrew Bible / Old Testament mainly

[1] The anthology edited by Gardiner, Theories of History (1959), may serve as an introduction to the subject, demonstrating well its deep complexity.

has been regarded as the *object* of an individual's or a group's scrutiny. In biblical studies, then, above all in their scholarly part, it is the interpretation, in the sense of hermeneutical and theological understanding as well as of methodical exegesis of the biblical text, that has been predominant. It has constituted another approach and 'history' than the first one; in addition, it may implicate the acceptance or refusal of the Bible as a *received* text. In this respect, the history has not least the character of being a theologically – and historiographically – significant *reception history*, especially as the Bible as *canon* of Holy Scriptures is concerned.

The distinction between these two aspects and groups of literature is surely not a question of right or wrong approach, because both aspects have their rights and merits in the history writing. Although being somewhat abstract and ideal, the distinction may, however, contribute to some clarification of the character and purpose of historical works and studies, especially of those that are combining both aspects in one survey.

Thus, for Diestel the scope of his History was threefold, comprising the history of exegesis and of the variegated theological assessment of the Old Testament and also of the impact of the Old Testament on the Church life in general as well as on the culture and art and even on the social order of 'Christian societies'. Paying due attention to this extensive influence of the Old Testament it was scarcely at random that he named his book *History of the Old Testament in the Christian Church.*[2] In recent times, the volumes of *The Cambridge History of the Bible* and of *Bible de tous les temps*, like the History of Diestel, combine these two different aspects; but to a greater extent they focus on a very broad range of various influences of the Bible – both the Old and the New Testament – upon the areas of practical and theological Church life, including the rich history of Bible translations,[3] as well as on cultural life in broadest sense.[4] Differently, Farrar concentrated his *History of Interpretation* explicitly on the history of scrutiny and varying exegesis of the Bible, mostly of the Old Testament. In this century, McQueen Gray and Kraus, for the time of the Reformation onward, and recently Graf Reventlow, have proceeded along the same line.

In the perspective of these two different aspects of history writing, having really a deep shift in approach between them, the present project of *Hebrew Bible / Old Testament: the History of Its Interpretation* definitely represents the latter approach that simply may be called 'History of the *study* of the Bible'; thereby 'history of study' is primarily seen as an interpretation and reception history.

Second, the literature on the study and interpretation of the Hebrew Bible / Old Testament may also be divided into two groups of another and more

[2] Geschichte, iii; at the same place he also says that his History is going to fill a gap in the scholarly literature by presenting "eine umfassende Darstellung der Art und Weise, wie das Alte Testament innerhalb der christlichen Kirche, von Beginn an bis auf die Gegenwart, wissenschaftlich behandelt, theologisch aufgefasst und practisch verwerthet worden ist".

[3] Cf. also D. F. Wright (ed.), *The Bible in Scottish Life and Literature* (Edinburgh 1988).

[4] Cf. Karpp, Schrift (1992) 1–7.

formal kind. For, on the one hand, there is a group of many and specialized studies and monographs, discussing primarily minor parts or special topics of this history; and this group is by far the greatest one. On the other hand, there is a relatively small group of books and works that cover the history at length, either the whole of it (like the Histories of DIESTEL, FARRAR and McQUEEN GRAY, up to their time, and later GRANT, in a popular manner) or some greater part of it (like CHEYNE and KARPP, KRAELING and KRAUS and, more recently, CLEMENTS and GRAF REVENTLOW who, moreover, is planning to cover it all).[5]

As already indicated, the present History of the HBOT Project may be reckoned to the latter group of literature, covering the whole history of study and interpretation of the Hebrew Bible / Old Testament, continuing in the traditional path of DIESTEL, FARRAR and McQUEEN GRAY, but now in view of the current situation. Only in this way, one may contend, will it be possible to do justice to the longer perspectives, to proper main proportions and to the inner dynamics of the complex history of biblical study and interpretation.

3. It is, first of all, in the latter group of historical literature that the fundamental problems of 'historiography' become importunate. When, as example, DIESTEL in the Preface of his History discusses the problem of an exclusion of the Jewish biblical interpretation from his historical discourse,[6] he also reflects upon the possible objection that he may have had many valuable studies, that he calls *Vorstudien,* at hand; but he responds that these studies are not capable of giving an 'overall picture', *ein Gesammtbild*.[7]

There may, in other words, exist a considerable distance and difference between historiographical *parts*, like studies and monographs, and what might be called a *historiography 'at large'*; that is 'historiography' in its strict sense, representing a general idea or construct and giving a comprehensive and coherent picture, for a longer period of time, focusing especially on the description of the longer lines and inner dynamics of the historical process.[8] Individual studies and monographs, brilliant and outstanding as they may be, cannot replace or 'compete' with historiography and history in this sense; although variously related they may be regarded as 'irreplaceable'.

The historiographical problem at this point, then, is another version of the general problem of the so-called 'hermeneutical circle', or, the problem of the reciprocal *relation between part and totality.*[9] As a 'totality', broadly speaking, historiography resp. history should be more than only an addition of individual historiographical studies. But, at the same time, there will be a relationship of mutual and necessary dependence between partial or topical studies,

---

[5] The grand volume of *Mikra* (1988), on the period of Antiquity, may be placed in both groups. As for older Histories cf. Farrar, History (1886) viii–ix, where he starts by saying: "There does not exist in any language a complete History of Exegesis".

[6] Geschichte, v–vi. On L. Diestel cf. A. JEPSEN, "Ludwig Diestel als Greifswalder Theologe", an (18 pages) offprint from *Bild und Verkündigung* (FS Hanna Jursch; Berlin 1962), Berlin 1963.

[7] "Allein sie liefern noch lange nicht ein Gesammtbild von so plastischer Klarheit, dass ihre grössere Verwerthung unsrer besonderen Aufgabe zu Gute kommen könnte", Geschichte, vi.

[8] This includes also elements of generalization; cf. Gottschalk, Generalization (1963).

[9] Cf. i. a. Gadamer, Wahrheit (1986) 178 f; 250 ff; 275 ff.

on the one hand, and a comprehensive historiography, on the other. The remaining challenge will be to find a proper historiographical balance between them.

4. In these perspectives, however, special aspects of the issue of 'totality' might be at stake when it comes to the specific kind of Research History that the HBOT Project now is presenting.

First, it may be recognized as a problem of *fragmentation* when the present History is written by many contributors, belonging to most different traditions; the more so, as in every work that is the result of an international team-work of scholars there is the risk of fragmentation. In this point, therefore, one has to consider seriously the problem of possible tension between fragmentation and 'totality', understood as the coherent whole of a history. But a risk of this kind may be limited, first of all, by detailed editorial plans and guidelines for the authors and also by some combining summaries in the History itself. Further, the fact that the contributing scholars, despite their differences, agree upon a critical historiography, in the framework of present scholarship, may have a restricting or at least reducing effect on a potential risk of fragmentation as well. That a history, on the other hand, is written by many and different authors – which is frequently the case today – should not merely be judged negatively, for it may imply an advantage for a history as a whole that authors of even opposite opinions are represented, mirroring, thus, the current situation of research.

Second, the problem of a potential fragmenting restriction of the 'totality' of a history may also be a question of content, or, by what might be called an 'intrinsic' fragmentation. For every writing of history has, of necessity, to make some selection of an often vast, or even boundless, source material and to set priorities. The 'totality' is, in other words, dependent on historiographical limiting, selection and preference of material.

This question is dealt with, in characteristic and most different ways, by DIESTEL and KRAUS, among others. DIESTEL clearly intended to present a History that was as comprehensive as possible with regard to periods covered and topics discussed in the history of the use and study of the Old Testament. Limiting the source material, however, he confined himself – as already mentioned – to the 'Christian side' of the history, leaving out the important Jewish one.[10] In addition, he divided his treatment into two types of historical description in order to cope with the practically infinite material on 'Christian side': for every period first is given a brief presentation of the general characteristics and main lines of the period; then follows a longer and strongly

---

[10] See sect. 2 above, and cf. Sæbø, (1988) 4–6; (1992) 140. Differently, both Farrar, History (1886) 47–107. 111–116, and Duff, History (1910) 83–106, described parts of the Jewish exegetical tradition, primarily with regard to the times of Antiquity and Middle Ages, whereas McQueen Gray, OT Criticism (1923) 62–64, had remarkably little and, unexpectedly, Kraus, Geschichte (1956 / 1982), nearly nothing in this respect. Recently, however, more attention has been paid to the issue, cf. CHB (II, 252–279), and in particular BTT (I, 19–54.107–125; IV, 233–260; V, 401–425; VI, 33–48; VII, 93–102.511–521.599–621) and, regarding the Antiquity, Mikra (1988) pass., as well as, most recently, Graf Reventlow, Bibelauslegung (I, 1990, 24–37.104–116; II, 1994, 231–258).

concentrated part with compendious comments on individual scholars and works. It may be said that DIESTEL, on the whole, managed to present a comprehensive and yet condensed History that is of considerable merit.

KRAUS, however, has strongly criticized the broad scope and specific procedure of DIESTEL, claiming that he presents "an incalculable number of names and titles" and that he fails "to draw the relations of the intellectual and theological history clearly and deeply enough".[11] For his own part, KRAUS reduced the 'Christian side' remarkably more than DIESTEL did, first, by starting with the Reformers and their theologically significant dictum of *sola scriptura*; second, by concentrating mainly on Protestant European, preferably German, scholars; third, by leaving out of his treatment the history of exegesis and of theological assessment; and fourth, by focusing primarily on some – certainly central – parts of the Old Testament, viz. the Pentateuch, the Prophecy and the Psalms. When, additionally, KRAUS brought the development of *modern* critical methods and specific theories and results strongly into focus, this preference together with the selected parts of the Hebrew Bible / Old Testament apparently was meant to represent the whole, the 'totality', of the history.[12] But, generally speaking, in instances like these there may be the risk that a 'history' simply is constituted by a series of independent 'case-histories', or, that a 'history' merely turns into an aggregate of *problem-histories*, where the historiographical value, in a strict sense and within a broader context, might be problematic.

By comparing the distinguished and different Histories of DIESTEL and KRAUS, in this way, a methodological focal point is brought into relief, viz. the question – and need – of an adequate *criterion,* or criteria, of limitation and selection of material. Reflection on this question will always be crucial for the historiography, and it will remain imperative for the historian to avoid priorities of issues that may be found to be but arbitrary. Although no one, presumably, would object to this theoretically, in practical performance the problem is undeniable anyway. Harking back to the issue of material selection, another observation may be worth due consideration as well: in spite of various reductions – like those made by DIESTEL and KRAUS – there seems to be a general historiographical tendency of expanding in content, seeking – at least idealistically – a *maximum* of themes and studies, both weighty ones and others of more peripheral character. But, methodically, the opposite direction should be considered more seriously, asking instead for the central *minimum* and moving from the variegated *multa* to the basic *multum.* For, just this movement towards the basic minimum may prove to be more adequate and

---

[11] Kraus, Geschichte (1982) 1 (cf. 4): "[die Arbeit Diestels] zeichnet die geistesgeschichtlichen und theologie-geschichtlichen Zusammenhänge nicht klar und tief genug. ... Eine unübersehbare Zahl von Namen und Titeln wird vorgeführt. Doch das aufgehäufte Material ist auf weite Strecken hin stumm. Die Quellen sprechen nicht".

[12] Cf. the detailed criticism by G. FOHRER, *ThLZ* 82 (1957) 682–684, and, especially, by W. BAUMGARTNER, "Eine alttestamentliche Forschungsgeschichte", *ThR* NF 25 (1959) 93–110. In response to the severe criticism from these and others, KRAUS expanded his book in its 2nd (1969) and 3rd (1982) edition. Regrettably, the last part of the title from 1956, "von der Reformation bis ...", that indicated an exact delimitation of the work, was then left out.

operative than the striving for maximum because it implies a *concentration of the scholarly concern around the very core of the subject matter*. Examining, more concretely, what seems to have been the central occupation and motivation in the study of Scriptures through the centuries, among Jews as well as among Christians, the result will, definitely and without much discussion, be that the *understanding of the Hebrew Bible / Old Testament expressed through interpretation and exegesis* is to be regarded as the very centre of the matter, through all diversities and controversies. This might appear to be a truism, but it is not.

Along a way of this kind went FARRAR in his *History of Interpretation,* concentrating his historical description around the history of interpretation and exegesis of the Holy Scripture, both the Jewish tradition and, particularly, the Christian one.[13] He selected and reduced the immense source material in another way than DIESTEL did shortly before him. Refusing to seek a maximum in discussing a plurality of scholarly names and phenomena he deliberately sought "to deal with the chief *epochs* in the progress of Biblical science", giving primarily account "of those who caused the chief moments of fresh impulse to the methods of interpretation". In other words, he left aside many persons and works that did not truly manage to renew the matter and method of interpretation, in order to focus more upon the real stepping-stones in the long history of interpretation, "the epoch-making events of Scriptural study",[14] by which the process and development of the history were brought forward.

Summing up so far, it may be assumed that the Hebrew Bible / Old Testament as Scripture is the essential subject matter, and that the variegated scrutiny of it constitutes the very core of the actual history. This study of the Bible may primarily be understood as *interpretation,* which includes both theological understanding, hermeneutical reflection and exegetical exposition of the biblical text, through the ages up to the present time. Further, the history of interpretation, in this sense, may also be regarded as the main criterion for the selection of source material and of leading historiographical priorities. Finally, it may even serve as the prime point of orientation for the presentation of this new History of the study of the Hebrew Bible / Old Testament.

5. When focusing on *the history of interpretation* as the very backbone of a critical history of the study of the Hebrew Bible / Old Testament another problem arises in all its gravity, namely the problem of determining the time or situation in which this history of interpretation supposedly started. The problem of a *proper starting-point*, however, seems not to be as simple as one

---

[13] KRAUS seems not to have known the History of FARRAR.

[14] Farrar, History (1886) viii. As for the key term of 'exegesis' he says, at the beginning: "I always mean the explanation of the immediate and primary sense of the sacred writings" (vii); and that seems to be the very point of orientation for him. Besides, the book was a publication of his Bampton Lectures and has, therefore, some apologetic flavour in its discussion, but not more than that he seems compelled to an apology for himself, saying: "I have never forgotten that the Bampton Lectures are meant to be apologetic", and showing in what ways he "desired to carry out the purposes of the Founder" (ix).

at first might think. It may be appropriate to reflect briefly on some aspects of it.

A. DUFF was indeed aware of this problem; but he took an extreme position when he opened his History by asking: "Where shall we begin with this History? At what date?" and answered these questions of method and procedure by starting his Research History with the first stages of the 'critical' *formation* of the Hebrew Bible itself. He dated the starting-point, in his own words, with the time of "the so-called 'Iahwistic' writers of 900 B.C.".[15] However, he was not followed by anyone in this. His position may partly be due to his somewhat peculiar understanding and use of the word 'criticism', mingling its historiographical and isagogical functions.

In sharp contrast with the view of DUFF, one may be inclined to state, as a *conditio sine qua non,* that biblical interpretation necessarily presupposes a standard biblical text to be interpreted, or, in other words, a *completed* – and mainly canonized – Hebrew Bible resp. Old Testament. It is, further, also most usual to start the historical account by the end of the first century CE, when the Hebrew text had been standardized and, mainly, the canon questions of the Hebrew Bible and to some extent also those of the New Testament were established. This is the position of DIESTEL and other scholars, and it may be an appropriate one.[16]

On closer investigation, however, the initial stage of the history of interpretation turns out to be far more complex than that; the crucial point in this connection is the *relationship between 'tradition' and 'interpretation'*. It may be adequate here to quote I. SEELIGMANN, saying: "Es ist nicht leicht, den Abschluss fest zu stellen von dem komplizierten und langwierigen Prozess des Werdens biblischer Literatur; in manchen Fällen lassen sich die Anfänge der Exegese geradezu bezeichnen als Ausläufer des Wachstums von biblischen Texten".[17] Also DIESTEL referred to the state of flux of the biblical text and canon, at the earliest period when Synagogue and the Early Church were still closely related to each other (Geschichte, 7–14). There was, indeed, no clear-cut border between Holy Writ and its interpretation, but rather a gradual transition from Scriptures to their various interpretations. This has recently been paid much attention by biblical scholars, not least Jewish ones; notably M. FISHBANE has in different ways highlighted elements of 'inner-biblical exegesis', at times also called 'midrashic' or 'rabbinic' glosses, in the Hebrew Bible.[18] This terminology is, to some extent, equivalent to what is otherwise

---

[15] Duff, History (1910) 1–10, esp. 1; 5, where he also says: "We are going to see how some literary men among the Hebrews in those far-away days examined, judged, criticised, rejected, and altered this or that in the writings that lay before them as inheritances from the past".

[16] Cf. Diestel, Geschichte (1869) 15f; McQueen Gray, Criticism (1923) 13ff; Grant / Tracy, Short History (1984) 8 ff; cf. also Graf Reventlow, Bibelauslegung I (1990) 11–49 and 50 ff (NT).

[17] I. L. SEELIGMANN, "Voraussetzungen der Midraschexegese", *Congress Volume: Copenhagen 1953* (VTSup 1; Leiden 1953; 150–181) 151; cf. M. SÆBØ, "Vom 'Zusammen-Denken' zum Kanon. Aspekte der traditionsgeschichtlichen Endstadien des Alten Testaments" (JBTh 3, 1988, 115–133) 119–128.

[18] Cf. i. a. M. FISHBANE, "Revelation and Tradition: Aspects of Inner-Biblical Exegesis", *JBL* 99 (1980) 343–361; first of all, his *Biblical Interpretation in Ancient Israel* (Oxford 1985, pass.); B. S. CHILDS, "Psalms, Titles and Midrashic Exegesis", *JSS* 16 (1971) 137–150; D. PATTE, *Early*

called 'tradition history', including elements of 're-interpretation', and 'redaction history', or also to what B.S. CHILDS has phrased as "the canonical process" – which in his opinion started relatively early and was not exclusively the same as the late stages of 'canonization'.[19] It would surely be desirable that scholars established a more homogeneous terminology in this point; but, be that as it may, it has still to be maintained that there, nevertheless, existed a considerable difference between the 'inner-biblical interpretation', on the one hand, and the interpretation made *after* the final stabilization of text and canon, on the other.[20]

In consequence, this will have an essential bearing on the plan of a new History of the study of the Hebrew Bible / Old Testament in general and on the question of its proper starting-point in particular. In order to combine the two aspects just described one may, first, agree on the traditional view, holding an established Hebrew Bible / Old Testament to be a basic premise for the history of Scriptural interpretation. But then, it may also be considered most important for the History as a whole to have a preceding part, starting with the inner-biblical interpretation and including the interpretative character of the Septuagint as well as of various contemporary literature excluded from the Hebrew Canon. A first part of this kind, describing the 'beginnings' of Scriptural interpretation, might also, with some right, be called a 'pre-history'. Anyhow, it may be of fundamental significance, both for the understanding of the traditio-historical relationship of Scripture and interpretation, and not least, as an influential background and partly even context, for the later and 'canonical' interpretation.[21]

6. These reflections on a proper starting-point for the history of biblical interpretation actualize, in another way, the aspect of history as a whole, as a 'totality', and the problem of its potential 'fragmentation' that were discussed above. For considering a division of history into specific *epochs*, which is both usual and essential, just this indispensable procedure might well have an effect of fragmentation. The crucial point, however, will be how a division into epochs is to be grounded theoretically and carried out practically.

DIESTEL has in his History divided the history mostly chronologically into three 'books' and seven 'periods', starting with the "time of the Fathers", ca. 100 to 250.[22] FARRAR has, likewise, divided the history into "seven main

---

Jewish Hermeneutic in Palestine (SBLDS 22; Missoula, MT 1975); G. VERMES, "Bible and Midrash: Early Old Testament Exegesis", CHB I (1980; 199–231); also J. WEINGREEN, "Rabbinic-Type Glosses in the Old Testament", *JSS* 2 (1957) 149–162.

[19] CHILDS, *Introduction to the Old Testament as Scripture* (London 1979) 49–68, esp. 59.

[20] Cf. G. VERMES, Bible and Midrash (1980) 199: "Post-biblical midrash is to be distinguished from the biblical only by an external factor, canonisation".

[21] Cf. Sæbø, 'Zusammen-Denken' (1988), see n. 17 above.

[22] The three 'books' refer to the longer periods of "die alte Zeit" (ca. 100–600), "die mittlere Zeit" (600–1517) and of "die neue Zeit", beginning with 1517, i.e. the Lutheran Reformation, whereas the 'periods' include more theological and ecclesiastical considerations, so i. a. the second period being "die Zeit der grossen Kirchenlehrer (250–600)", the fourth period "die Zeit der kirchlichen Macht (1100–1517)" and the sixth period "die Entstehung der Gegensätze unter der Herrschaft der Orthodoxie (1600–1750)", and, finally, the last period is the time of "Kampf und Lösung der Gegensätze (1750 bis zur Gegenwart)".

periods", but he also adds "systems of Biblical interpretation". Differently from DIESTEL, he begins with Ezra and *Rabbinic* exegesis and proceeds to the *Alexandrian* one as well as to the *Patristic* and to the *Scholastic* exegesis of "the Dark Ages" before coming to the *Reformation* and the *Post-Reformation* period and, at last, to "the Modern Epoch, which seemed for a time to culminate in widespread atheism".[23] As for his division of epochs, or, "main periods and systems", it may be said, first, that it is convential to some extent; second, that it seems to underestimate the border-setting function of canon and beyond that to be thematically rather than historiographically orientated; thirdly, that it is combined with a conspicuous apologetic and valuing character of style.[24]

A historiography will surely not be quite without presuppositions and a ferment of *Vorverständnis.* It should, however, be more neutral and objective in its historical description than is the case of the History of FARRAR. On the other hand, the notion of 'epoch' is supposed to mean something more than the chronologically neutral word 'period' seems to do, but its substantiation has to be of an intrinsic and historical, not of any dogmatic or personal character, on the side of the historian. Generally, it may be stated that a historiographical 'epoch' is supposed to qualify a particular period of time as distinct from the preceding one by a new coherence, caused by some memorable events or a radical "shift of paradigms".[25]

Not only in the Histories of DIESTEL and FARRAR but also in the History of KRAUS – and in that of KRAELING as well – there is a partly theologically determined division of epochs that may be found problematic in a broader historical context. For, making the Reformation not only a starting-point but also a fundamental point of orientation[26] KRAUS in his evaluation of the Reformation seems to be somewhat one-sided,[27] and even more so as he also pays all too little attention to the close relatedness of Humanism / Renaissance, originating in the late Middle Ages, on the one hand, and the Enlightenment, on the other. Only by due consideration of this arching perspective will also the Reformation be properly understood, both in its context, in view of its near relation to Humanism, and for its historical and theological uniqueness.

As for the plan of the present History, it may be briefly mentioned – and the reasons be given more fully later – that the *second* volume, then, is planned to cover the broad epoch reaching *From the Renaissance to the Enlightenment*, that is so heavily marked by Humanism. Around the year 1800, how-

---

[23] Farrar, History (1886) 12.

[24] See n. 14 above.

[25] On the scientific use of the concept of 'paradigm' see, first of all, Kuhn, Structure (1962) x; 43–51.

[26] With some right, this may certainly be done because of the important "shift of paradigms" that the Reformation caused.

[27] When KRAUS made the Reformers, especially the reformed theologians, even the 'pioneers' responsible for the later historical criticism of the Bible (Geschichte, 1982, 4), drawing, at the same time, attention also to the basic significance of Humanism (Geschichte, 1956, 21 ff; 1982, 24 ff), there is some ambiguity in his discussion of the modern historical process in this connection, as W. Baumgartner critically has shown, see n. 12 above, esp. p. 96.

ever, there seems to be another "shift of paradigms",[28] whereby the *third* and last volume may start here and is intended to describe the historical development of the Nighteenth and Twentieth Centuries, *From Modernism to Post-Modernism*.

7. Finally, related to the question of 'epochs', the key problem of what might be called 'personalism' in much historiography represents another aspect of historiographical 'fragmentation'. Thereby is not meant a separate writing of scholarly portraits, like the outstanding collection on *Deutsche Alttestamentler* by R. Smend, but what is meant is the main tendency of relating of the history writing, in a broader sense, to *persons*, mostly well-known scholars. A tendency of this kind may be found in various Histories like those of Kraus and Graf Reventlow,[29] or in the chapter on "The Bible in the Early Church" in *The Cambridge History of the Bible,* I, that is mostly taken up with portraits of Origen, Theodore of Mopsuestia, Jerome and Augustine as "biblical scholars".

The specific problem, in this respect, is, first, that the selection of persons described is but a part of the general problem of selection of historical source material, that was discussed in section Four above.

Second, the problem of a mainly *person-related type of historical description* might, at worst, be the risk that the History as a whole merely constitutes a collection of personal histories. In historiography, to be sure, there will always be a tensional reciprocity of personal and 'extra-personal', *überpersönliche,* aspects. However, a proper attention to the influence of the spiritual heritage of one epoch upon another should not be weakened, although it generally may be problematic to differentiate the epochs properly. The potential historiographical loss in a case like this may relate to the possible reduction or limitation of the longer lines of theological streams of tradition and of influential intellectual movements.

Third, the 'extra-personal' aspects also include social, socio-cultural and institutional aspects, like – as an example – the development of the school system in the Carolingian Era, in the Middle Ages and the Renaissance, from monastic to cathedral schools and further on to universities as the new and dominating institutions of learning.

The general problem of necessary relationship and due balance, then, between personal and 'extra-personal', between individual and 'collective' factors is most obvious, and its proper solution will be urgently essential. It will be a prime historiographical challenge.

[28] Cf. Smend, Epochen der Bibelkritik (1991) 19.
[29] Kraus, Geschichte (1982) *passim*; Graf Reventlow, Bibelauslegung II (1994).

A.
Beginnings of Scriptural Interpretation

Chapter One

Inner-Biblical Exegesis

By Michael Fishbane, Chicago

Bibliography: P.R. Ackroyd, "The Chronicler as Exegete", *JSOT* 2 (1977) 2; Ch. Albeck, *Das Buch der Jubiläen und die Halacha* (47. Bericht der Hochschule für die Wissenschaft des Judentums in Berlin; Berlin 1930); idem, *Mabo' la-Mishnah* (Jerusalem: The Bialik Institute 1959); R. Artzi, "The Glosses in the el-Amarna Documents", Bar Ilan Annual 1 (1963) 24-57 [Heb.]; R. Bach, "Gottesrecht und weltliches Recht in der Verkündigung des Propheten Amos", *Festschrift für Günther Dehn* (ed. W. Schneemelcher; Neukirchen Kreis Moers 1957) 23-24; W. Bacher, "The Origin of the Word Haggada (Agada)", *JQR* OS 4 (1892) 406-29; W.E. Barnes, "The Midrashic Element in Chronicles", *Expositor* 44 [5th Series, 4] (1896) 426-39; idem, "Ancient Corrections in the Text of the Old Testament", *JTS* 1 (1900) 387-414; J. Begrich, "Sōfēr und Mazkir", *ZAW* 58 (1940) 1-29; R. Bergen, *The Prophets and the Law* (MHUC 4, 1974); R. Block, "Écriture et tradition dans le Judaïsme. Aperçus sur l'origine du Midrash", *CS* 8 (1954) 9-34; B.S. Childs, "Psalm Titles and Midrashic Exegesis", *JSS* 16 (1971) 137-50; J.J. Collins, *The Apocalyptic Vision of the Book of Daniel* (HSM 16, 1977); D. Daube, "Zur frühtalmudischen Rechtspraxis", *ZAW* 50 (1932) 148-59; idem, *Studies in Biblical Law* (Oxford: The Clarendon Press 1947); idem, "Error and Accident in the Bible", *RIDA* [2nd ser.] 2 (1949) 189-213; idem, "Concerning Methods of Bible-Criticism", *ArOr* 17 (1949) 89-99; idem, "Rabbinic Methods of Interpretation in Hellenistic Rhetoric", *HUCA* 22 (1949) 239-64; idem, "Alexandrian Methods of Interpretation and the Rabbis", *FS Hans Lewald* (Basel: Helbing und Lichtenhahn 1953) 27-44; G.R. Driver, "Glosses in the Hebrew Text of the Old Testament", *L'Ancien Testament et l'Orient* (OBL 1, 1957) 123-61; Y. Elman, "Authoritative Oral Tradition in Neo-Assyrian Scribal Circles", *JANESCU* 7 (1975) 19-32; J.J. Finkelstein, "Ammiṣaduqa's Edict and the Babylonian 'Law Codes'", *JCS* 15 (1961) 100-104; M. Fishbane, "Varia Deuteronomica", *ZAW* 84 (1972) 349-52; idem, "Numbers 5:11-31: A Study of Law and Scribal Practice in Israel and the Ancient Near East", HUCA 45 (1974) 25-45; idem, "The Qumran Pesher and Traits of Ancient Hermeneutics", *Proceedings of the Sixth World Congress of Jewish Studies* 1 (Jerusalem 1977) 97-114; idem, "On Colophons, Textual Criticism and Legal Analogies", *CBQ* 42 (1980) 438-49; idem, *Biblical Interpretation in Ancient Israel* (Oxford 1985) [abbr.: BIAI]; idem, *The Garments of Torah. Essays in Biblical Hermeneutics* (Bloomington, IN 1989); M. Fishbane/S. Talmon, "The Structuring of Biblical Books, Studies in the Book of Ezekiel", ASTI 19 (1976) 129-53; G. Fohrer, "Gie Glossen im Buche Ezechiel", *ZAW* 63 (1951) 33-53; idem, "Tradition und Interpretation im Alten Testament", *ZAW* 73 (1961) 1-30; K. Freedy, "The Glosses in Ezekiel I-XXIV", *VT* 20 (1970) 129-52; H. Fuchs, *Pesîq, ein Glossengleichen* (Breslau: H. Fleischmann 1907); H.M. Gevaryahu, "Colophons in the Books of Proverbs, Job and Ecclesiastes", *Studies in the Bible and the Ancient Near East* (FS S. Loewenstamm 1; Jerusalem: A. Rubinstein 1978) 107-31 [Heb]; D.W. Gooding, *Relics of Ancient Exegesis. A Study of the Miscellanies in 3 Reigns 2* (Cambridge: Cambridge University Press 1976); B.S. Jackson, *Essays in Jewish and Comparative Legal History* (SJLA 10, 1975); J. Koenig, "L'activité herméneutique des scribes dans la transmission du texte de l'Ancien Testament", I, *RHR* 161 (1962) 141-74; idem, "Midrash and Mishna", *Rabbinic Essays* (New York: Ktav reprint 1973) 163-256; S. Lieberman, *Hellenism in Jewish Palestine* (New York: Jewish Theological Seminary 1962); C. McCarthy, *The Tiqqune Sopherim and Other Theological Corrections in the Masoretic Text of the Old Testament* (OBO 36, 1981); J. Milgrom, "Profane Slaughter and a Formulaic Key to the Composition of Deuteronomy", HUCA 47 (1976) 1-17; J.P.J. Oliver, "Schools and Wisdom Literature",

JNSL 4 (1975) 49–60; S. Paul, "Literary and Ideological Echoes of Jeremiah in Deutero-Isaiah", *Proceedings of the Vth World Congress of Jewish Studies* 1 (Jerusalem 1969) 102–20; G. von Rad, "The Levitical Sermon in I and II Chronicles", idem, *The Problem of the Hexateuch and Other Essays* (New York: McGraw-Hill 1966) 267–80; M. Sæbø, "Vom 'Zusammen-Denken' zum Kanon. Aspekte der traditionsgeschichtlichen Endstadien des Alten Testaments", *Zum Problem des biblischen Kanons* (JBTh 3, 1988) 115–133; J. Sanders, *Torah and Canon* (Philadelphia: Fortress Press 1972); idem, "Adaptable for Life: The Nature and Function of Canon", *Magnalia Dei, The Mighty Acts of God* (FS G. Ernest Wright, ed. F. Cross/W. Lemke/P. Miller; Garden City, NY: Doubleday 1976) 531–60; S. Sandmel, "The Haggadah Within Scripture", *JBL* 80 (1961) 105–22; N. Sarna, "Ps 89: A Study in Inner Biblical Exegesis", *Biblical and Other Studies* (ed. A. Altmann; Brandeis Texts and Studies; Cambridge, MA: Harvard University Press 1963) 29–46; G. Scholem, "Revelation and Tradition as Religious Categories in Judaism", *The Messianic Idea in Judaism* (New York: Schocken 1971) 282–303; I. L. Seeligmann, *The Septuagint Version of Isaiah: A Discussion of its Problems* (Mededelingen en Verhandelingen, no. 9, van het Vooraziatisch-Egyptisch Genootschap 'Ex oriente Lux'; Leiden: E. J. Brill 1948); idem, "Voraussetzungen der Midrasch-Exegese", VTSup 1 (1953) 150–81; idem, "Investigations on the Transmission of the Massoretic Text of the Bible, I", *Tarbiz* 25 (1955/6) 118–39 [Heb]; idem, "From Historical Reality to Historiosophical Apprehension in the Bible", *P'raqim* (*Yearbook of the Schocken Institute for Jewish Research*, II, ed. E. S. Rosenthal; Jerusalem 1969/74) 273–313 [Heb]; A. Toeg, "Num 15:22–31; Midrash Halacha", *Tarbiz* 43 (1973/4) 1–20 [Heb]; E. Urbach, "The Exegetical Sermon as the Source of Halakha and the Problem of the Scribes", *Tarbiz* 27 (1958) 166–82 (repr. in *Gershom Scholem Jubilee Volume, on the Occasion of his 60th Birthday*; Jerusalem: Magnes Press 1958) 40–56 [Heb]; G. Vermes, "Bible and Midrash: Early Old Testament Exegesis", CHB 1 (*From the Beginnings to Jerome*; ed. P. Ackroyd; Cambridge: Cambridge University Press 1970) 199–231; B. Z. Wacholder, "Chronomessianism. The Timing of Messianic Movements and the Calendar of Sabbatical Cycles", HUCA 44 (1975) 201–80; M. Weinfeld, *Deuteronomy and the Deuteronomic School* (Oxford: Clarendon Press 1971); J. Weingreen, "Rabbinic-Type Glosses in the Old Testament", *JSS* 2 (1957) 149–62; T. Willi, *Die Chronik als Auslegung. Untersuchungen zur literarischen Gestaltung der historischen Überlieferung Israels* (FRLANT 106; Göttingen: Vandenhoeck and Ruprecht 1972); W. Zimmerli, "Zur Sprache Tritojesajas", *Gottes Offenbarung. Gesammelte Aufsätze zum AT* (ThBü 19, 1963) 217–33. – Also, M. Fishbane, "Census and Intercession in a Priestly Text (Exodus 30: 11–16) and in Its Midrashic Transformation", *Pomegranates and Golden Bells* (FS J. Milgrom, ed. D. P. Wright/D. N. Freedman/A. Hurvitz; Winona Lake, IN: Eisenbrauns 1995) 103–111.

Special abbreviation:
BIAI = M. Fishbane, *Biblical Interpretation in Ancient Israel* (see above).

1. Introduction

Over the course of a millenium and one-half, ancient Israel was heir to the great civilizations of the ancient Near East and the source of its own creative patrimony. The Hebrew Bible (HB) is thus a thick texture of traditions received and produced over many generations. In the process, a complex dynamic between tradition (*traditum*) and transmission (*traditio*) developed – since every act of *traditio* selected, revised, and reconstituted the overall *traditum*. To be sure, the contrast between authoritative *traditum* and ongoing *traditio* is most clear at the close of ancient Israelite literature. It is here that one may observe (incipiently in Qumran texts and more elaborately in normative Jewish sources) a transition to two types: a body of Scripture and a corpus of Interpretations. Indeed the copying, citation, interpretation, and explanation of the sacred Scriptures gave ample opportunity for the reformulation of *traditum* in postbiblical *traditio*. But a long prehistory is preserved in the HB.[1] That is, the canonical corpus contains a vast range of annotations, adaptations, and comments on earlier traditions. We call this 'Inner-Biblical Exegesis'. With the close of the canon one could not add or subtract to these examples within Scripture itself.

The formal separation of a *traditum* and its exegetical *traditio* is not as neat within the HB as in subsequent stages. Appropriate methodological procedures must therefore be adduced to disentangle the *traditum-traditio* complex. These vary by genre, topic, and period. Overall, the most objective signs of a *traditum* subjected to *traditio* include citation formulary and verbal repetition in parallel or related genres; but close analysis is still required to isolate interpolations, changes or conflations.[2] Deictic markers and semantic redundancies are helpful indices in this process. The analytic effort is rewarded by insight into cultural processes of tradition and change in ancient Israel for which only the textual results survive. These processes bear on the scribal transmission of texts and the clarification of words; the adaptation, harmonization and revaluation of legal rules; the theological reuse of laws or historical themes; and the explication or reapplication of prophecies for new times. This emergent culture of interpretation drew upon distinct classes and groups, which overall anticipate the great scholastic and educational institutions of early Judaism. At the same time, ancient Israelite exegetical culture must be set within the wider framework of Near Eastern civilizations where scribal-lexical annotations, legal scholarship, and esoteric exegesis are attested in many periods and forms.[3]

2. Scribal Interpretation

While oral recitation, instruction, and repetition were basic carriers of earlier traditions to new generations, and a living context for their clarification and adaptation, our sole witness to this process is the written word of Hebrew scriptures. Indeed many of the examples to be considered below (in parts II–IV) – legal instructions and prophetic rhetoric of various sorts – were primarily verbal and only secondarily inscribed; other cases – like the legal codes or historical narratives – undoubtedly had their inception in written form. Either way, the scribal *traditio* transmitted each *traditum* to new groups and times. It was in the context of this copying that clarifications (of words and terms) and other considerations (bearing on theological tone or legal constistency) were often introduced. The class primarily responsible for such matters were the scribes – a title attested over centuries for different groups. Thus groups

[1] Overall, see Fishbane, *Biblical Interpretation in Ancient Israel* (BIAI), from which most examples are derived.

[2] See BIAI 41–43, 106, 144, 163–64, 187–88, 291, 460, and pass.

[3] See the discussion and references in BIAI 29–32, 39–40, 82, 233–34, 452–57; also S.J. Lieberman, "A Mesopotamian Background for the So-called *Aggadic* 'Measures' of Biblical Hermeneutics", HUCA 58 (1987) 212ff; and A. Livingstone, *Mystical and Mythological Explanatory Works of Babylonia and Assyrian Scholars* (Oxford 1986).

of scribes are frequently mentioned among prophetic and priestly circles (cf. 2 Kgs 25:19 and 1 Chr 4:6; 27:32); their formal procedures and technical terms are often remarkably similar to those of the other Near Eastern scribal schools whose products are more fully attested. Close study shows that legal, prophetic, liturgical and wisdom literature all (variously) indicate title-lines, colophons, comments on closure, or indications of collation.[4]

Such objective indicia demonstrate the anthological or combinatory character of much biblical literature. This is all the more marked where mini-series of subject matter are embedded in narrative complexes or where the colophons themselves betray the composite nature of the rules they tag.[5] Copying and collection are thus first-order features of the scribal *traditio*, the inevitable product of those entrusted with a *traditum.*

Biblical sources preserve various types of scribal annotation, marked and unmarked in the text. The clarification of words, places, or grammatical oddities are most common. Different deictic particles are used. Thus the term *hû'* ('it is') regularly marks changed toponyms due to renaming (cf. "Jebus *hû'* Jerusalem", 1 Chr 11:4), though sometimes only a translation is involved (e.g., "the Valley of the *šāveh* [King] *hû'* the Valley of the *melekh* [King]").[6] In such cases, the force of *hû'* is 'it is *now*' – a kind of double signpost preserving both the older and latter names. In such cases, it would be hard to determine whether the annotations are scribal additions in the strict sense or merely contemporizing adjustments by tradents of the narrative *traditum* itself – in the manner of the historical comment "and the Cannanite was *then* in the land" (Gen 12:6). The distinction between author and scribe is not apparent here, but also not consequential for the point that terms are clarified in the course of a *traditio.*

Annotative glosses are more intrusive, and betray a different cultural 'hand'. Often, the syntax is disrupted. In the case of Ezra 3:12, the phrase "*zeh* (this [refers to]) the Temple" sticks out. Its apparent purpose is to clarify the antecedent pronoun in the narrative (viz., "when *it* was built");[7] no further ideological end is served. Quite otherwise is the comment in Isa 29:10. Here the marker *'et* ('namely') introduces a tendentious respecification of the addressee. As is evident from the overall context (especially vv. 9, 11), the prophet condemned the people's obliviousness to the divine word. This rebuke is recast as a diatribe against false prophets: "For YHWH has poured over you a spirit of stupefaction; He has closed your eyes – *'et* the prophets – and cloaked your heads – *'et* the seers". With the respecification, the direct rhetoric is disrupted and a new word for different times is 'heard' from the text. The LXX and its Lucianic revisor regularized the awkward syntax witnessed by the MT.[8] Each textual level thus shows the power of *traditio* to transform

---

[4] See BIAI 24–37; also M. FISHBANE, "Law to Canon: Some 'Ideal-Typical' Stages of Development", *Minhah le-Nahum* (FS N. M. Sarna, ed. M. Brettler/M. Fishbane; Sheffield: JSOT Press 1993) 65–86.

[5] See especially Leviticus 11–16, discussed in Fishbane, ibid. 76–79.

[6] A. WIEDER, "Ugaritic-Hebrew Lexicographical Notes", *JBL* 84 (1965) 160–62; see BIAI 45.

[7] Full discussion in BIAI 52–54.

[8] Ibid. 50–51.

(and so reinvent) the *traditum*. Paradoxically, the tradents' interpretations have become scripture – even the (new) divine word.

Other examples occur in the laws, where ritual instructions would hardly have been phrased in deliberately difficult terms. In the course of time, however, obscurities could arise – either through disregard of the practice or its transmission to groups alien to the original rule and its traditional meaning. In such cases, the *traditio* (in oral or written form) would include a marginal gloss; and this would eventually become part of the transcribed *traditum*. The rule on forbidden mixtures is a case in point. In Lev 19:19 the law forbids mixed breeding, mixed sowing, and mixed weaving. The formulation is rhythmic and repetitive. In each case the prohibition is apodictic and (thrice) emphasizes the word *kil'ayim* ('mixtures'). The pattern suggests that earlier receivers of the rule knew exactly what was meant by *kil'ayim* in each case; but the stylistically intrusive term *šaʿaṭnēz* in the third case only suggests that the precise area circumscribed by the *kil'ayim* of woven garments needed clarity. The qualifying term (of apparent Egyptian origin)[9] eventually became obscure as well; and so in the more paraphrastic *traditio* of this rule in Deut 22:9–11 the term *kil'ayim* occurs only with regard to the prohibition of mixed seeds (in a vineyard), whereas in the case of woven garments the word *šaʿaṭnēz* is itself explained as "wool and flax" (v. 11). Conceivably, the question had arisen whether mixed garments might mean the hair or products of different types of animals (e. g., those whose mixed breeding was prohibited), and so the rule specifies that mixtures from the sphere of animals and seeds are meant (i. e., the two prior types; thus wool is exemplary of animal produce, flax of vegetable or sown substances). The line between a scholastic and scribal annotation is blurred here; but what is clear is that the written *traditum* anent the *kil'ayim* of woven garments (for clothes; cloths for use are unspecified) had a complex *traditio*. Whatever the living context(s) of the clarification – whether public or private study or preaching – it enters each stage of the *traditum* through scribal hands entrusted with its formal transmission.

Annotative supplementation is thus the exegetical procedure when tradents were faced with a fixed *traditum*. But where this was not the case, as in free variants of a rule, new terms were substituted. This process seems evident in Deut 22:12, where *gedilîm* ('twisted fringes') may merely be a layman's simplification of the priestly term *ṣîṣit* mentioned in Num 15:38. Similarly, in the narrative historical sources, there was little inhibition against replacing older words in their reworking. Thus terms like *ʿannôtô* (2 Sam 7:10), *ḥephṣekhā* (1 Kgs 5:22) and *muphāz* (1 Kgs 10:18) are replaced by *ballôtô* ("destroy him"), *ṣorkekhā* ("your requirements") and *ṭāhôr* ("pure") in 1 Chr 17:9 and 2 Chr 2:15 and 9:17, respectively. It would be gratuitious to claim that these substitutions are of a purely scribal nature, rather than features of the overall historiographical revision. For that reason the designation 'scribal' here must simply signify a type of exegetical feature characteristic of scribes who transcribed documents. The substitutions of new words in the Isaiah A scroll from

---

[9] Cf. T. O. Lambdin, "Egyptian Loan Words in the Old Testament", *JAOS* 73 (1953) 155; for the whole example, see BIAI 58–63.

Qumran is a parallel case in point.[10] But however labelled, it is vital to observe the inner-cultural processes of clarification and revision at work – processes which transform a *traditum* in the very course of its *traditio*.

Along with concern for the meaning of a word, 'scribes' also addressed fixed orthographic features or exceptional grammatical forms. It therefore became traditional to spell 'lass' *naʿar* ('lad'!), but pronounce it *naʿarah* (a *qre perpetuum*). By the same token, unusual spellings could occassion marginal (or interlinear) annotations which, in due course, might wander into the text itself. Such a situation helps explain the otherwise meaningless *mn* in Ps 61:8 ("grace and truth *mn* will protect him [*yinṣĕruhû*]"); for as compared with the same idiom in Prov 20:28 ("grace and truth will the king protect [*yiṣrû*]") the first case preserves the *prima-nun* in a closed, unaccentuated situation. This irregular articulation was marked by the acronym *mn*, which stands for *mālē' nûn* (viz., '*plene-nun*').[11] By contrast, in several striking cases theologically problematic formulations were revised. Thus the somewhat meaningless comment in 1 Sam 3:13, where God tells Samuel that Eli's priestly lineage was rejected "because his sons cursed *lāhem* (themselves)" is retrieved via the LXX and medieval rabbinic lists which indicate that the original reading *'elōhîm* ('God') was apocopated to 'correct' the offending phrase.[12] Such a scribal solution parallels the change of the apostasizing idiom ("your god*s* [*'elohêkhā*] who took you up [*heʿĕlûkha*] from Egypt"; Exod 32:4) into a theologically normative one ("your God [*'elōhêkhā*] who took you up [*heʿelkhā*]; Neh 9:18). The mere deletion of the letter *waw* [*û*] makes all the difference: the plural verb was thereby singularized and the result was a restoration of divine dignity to the *traditum*. As in other examples, the emergent tradition is the product of an attentive and invasive *traditio*. More than one jot and tittle was thus added or lost for the sake of an unfolding *traditum* – scribal witnesses to the paradoxes of 'faithful transmission'.

3. Legal Exegesis

The ideological and proclaimed center of the biblical covenant is the Law. This vast corpus embodies materials that purportedly extend from immediately after the exodus (Exod 15:25–26; 16:23) to the ordinances at the Sinai event (Exod 20–24; 25–40), and the sundry teachings given subsequently in the desert (Lev 1–6; 11–16; 18–25; Num 5–6; 9–10; 18–19; 27–30) – before the entrance into the Land and the grand review and explication of the Law by Moses before his death (Deut 1; 12–26). Critically viewed, these rules cover a millenium of growth and exemplify numerous types of lawgiving and legal tradition. Some rules derive from the legistic-scholastic orbit of ancient Mesopotamia (and reflect typical or traditional topoi); others seem to be

10 BIAI 57.

11 Following J. WEINGREEN, Rabbinic-Type Glosses, *JSS* (1957) 160; see BIAI 63–64 and n. 49.

12 BIAI 66–68, with references to the *tiqqûnê sôphĕrîm* in rabbinic literature and modern discussions (esp. nn. 1–3).

(ideal) formulations for Israelite jurists; and still others reflect the tangle of hard cases that might serve as theoretical precedents in problematic circumstances.[13] Their collation in corpora and case-histories around Sinai and its successive moments underscores the theological intention of the editors to teach that the Law is a series of revelations to Moses, whose voice alone (whether as conduit of the revelations or their sense) is authoritative. Accordingly, subsequent pronouncements by prophets and priests purport to transmit the words of Moses – even though analysis shows additions or changes; and later historians and legists also promote their understanding or revision of the Law as nothing but the old teachings of Moses. That is to say, the ongoing legal *traditio* was formulated as expressions of the formative *traditum*. The same is true for adjustments to the Sinaitic corpus itself. Here, too, the words of tradition are valorized as the (written) Torah of Moses. It is only critical study that reveals this faithful *traditio*.

Of particular pertinence is the ongoing explicit and implicit reflection on earlier scholastic or practical formulations – through adaptation, revision and harmonization. Thus within the multi-tiered corpus of legal topics and process in the HB, apparent repetitions or reticulations actually reflect types of exegesis practiced in pre- and post-exilic Israel. These indicate how certain rules were taken over and transformed; something of the forms of legal reasoning and interpretation; as well as patterns of legal discourse and authority.[14] Different aspects of legal exegesis are revealed in the different literary sources – legal corpora, historical narratives, and prophetic collections. Whether for theoretical, practical or potential purposes, the legal *traditio* has the effect of clarifying or closing-off ambiguities in the *traditum*; making the rules more practicable or protean as guides to action; and harmonizing or disambiguating problematic expressions in the light of ideological consensus (e. g., centralized worship) or outright contradiction (due to different centers of tradition). The latest sources (Ezra-Nehemiah), based on near-contemporary events, often presents in mimetic detail the circumstances that occasioned such processes (Torah recitation; polemics; textual difficulties), and the role of scholars in the teaching and interpretation of the Law (cf. Nehemiah 8).[15] In these contexts new covenantal forms developed which express exegetical solutions for emergent 'exegetical communities' (cf. the *'ămānāh* in Nehemiah 10).[16]

The *ambiguity* of a legal *traditum* was ever a source of exegetical energy. One may wonder whether rabbinic speculations concerning the phrase *'ebed 'ibrî* (either the slave of a Hebrew or a Hebrew slave) in Exod 21:2 was an old worry independent of comparison with the diverse terms of service mentioned in Lev 25:39-46.[17] But surely the question of whose field would be used for compensation where damage ensued from a destructive agent that

[13] For discussion and literature, see BIAI 91-97.

[14] See the full discussion in BIAI, Part II, and especially the Conclusions, 231-77.

[15] See BIAI 107-113.

[16] Ibid. 113-114, 213-216.

[17] Cf. *Mekilta de-Rabbi Ishmael, Massekhta' de-Nezikin* 1-2 (ed. J. Z. Lauterbach; Philadelphia: The Jewish Publication Society 1935; III, 3-18).

transgressed one's property was inherently necessary – for the formulation in Exod 22:4 leaves ambiguous whether payment from "the best of *his* field" refers to the property of the damageor or damagee.[18] Moreover, the word used to indicate the agent of destruction – the verbal stem *biʿer* – is uncertain: the term could refer either to wandering livestock or a fire (in either case culpability is limited to intention: one sends forth cattle to graze, and they wander; or one lights a fire, and it spreads). Since the penalty clause in v. 5 b repeats the ambiguous term(s) of v. 4, it is possible that the reference to damage by *'ēš* ('fire'; v. 5 a) was inserted for clarification. In the end, however, considerations of linguistic parsimony would yield a more differentiated and so more comprehensive rule: the case in v. 4 would then cover damage by animate agents; while v. 5 a would typify inanimate causes. Customary resolutions of the pronoun and technical terms have been incorporated into a Qumran version of the *traditum* and the Targumic *traditio*.[19]

In addition to the concern for clarity, the legal *traditum* shows a will to completion or comprehensiveness. This is expressed at various levels and through several technical means. Most simply, tradents introduce the new specifications with the term *'ô* ('or').[20] Thus in the case of accidental homicide, death caused by iron implement or a stone (held in the hand) are formulated in parallel casuistic forms to typify the two main categories: rough natural implements and wrought utensils (Num 35:16–17). The case of wooden objects (in similar terms, introduced with *'ô*) adds nothing a lawyer could not infer, and may be considered an 'empty phrase' supplemented to close-off a potential loophole (that of natural growths vs. minerals). Similarly, the additional clause "or a woman" in Num 6:2 adds nothing to the law of vows – which could be formulated without it (cf. Num 30:3) – and is an exception to the fixed (and comprehensive) formula "if one" (*'îš*; lit., 'a man'). A comparison of the rule of servitude in Exod 21:2 (referring only to an *ʿebed ʿibrî* ["Hebrew slave"; masc.]) with that of its repetition in Deut 15:12 (which adds "or an *ʿibrîyāh* [fem.]") shows a different instance of supplementation – for now complications unanticipated by the original *traditum* are elicited (e. g., can a woman bring her husband with her into servitude, and may the master breed her with his own male slaves for profit?). The clause "and you shall also (*'aph*) do the same (*taʿăśeh khēn*) to your bondswoman" at the end of this rule (v. 17 b) is another legal postscript. It too introduces more problems than it solves (e. g., is her case similar to the *ʿibrî* and *ʿibrîyāh* with respect to term of servitude and manumission; and does this *clausula finalis* abrogate the different rule in Exod 21:7–11?). The *traditio* undoubtedly developed solutions to these matters.

In other instances, the clause *we-khēn taʿăśeh* ("and act similarly") introduces more precise extensions.[21] Thus comparison shows that the rule on

---

[18] See BIAI 94–95, and the full discussion in A. Toeg, "Exod 22:4: The Text and the Law in Light of the Ancient Sources", *Tarbiz* 39 (1970) 226–28 [Heb].

[19] See previous note for sources.

[20] See BIAI 170–72 for examples and parallels.

[21] For examples, see BIAI 17–83.

returning other people's livestock in Exod 23:4 is taken-over in Deut 22:1-2—though now restricted to a compatriot's property, and with the added requirement to retain the object until claimed by the owner. Besides these changes, the new rule extends (in v.3, after the abovenoted formula) the examples to include garments and "any (*kol*) loss". In this case, the tradents did not presume that one would necessarily infer such matters from the reference to wandering livestock—and so exegetical specifications were added. Exod 23:10-11 is a parallel instance. Hereby, the rule of releasing the sabbatical produce of sown fields (so that the needy and thereafter field animals might eat thereof) is extended to vineyards and olive groves. But the case has further ramifications; for though the legal *traditio* is marked by the formula *we-khēn ta'ǎśeh*, in a later version of the regulation (Lev 25:3-7) its several details are paraphrastically explicated even as the addendum (anent vinyards, etc.) is incorporated (disjunctively and *minus the formula*) into the phrase concerning sown produce. Thus, in this sermonic elaboration an earlier *traditio* has become a *traditum* without any trace of its secondary origins.[22] The expansion of Lev 4:20b in Num 15:25-26 shows a similar homiletic structure,[23] though in this latter context the voice of the *traditio* is exposed—for the words in vv. 22-23, referring to God *and* Moses in the 3rd person, are manifestly those of the preacher of this rule about unintentional transgression.[24] Evidently the didactic sermon was an occasion for exegetical *traditio* from early times.

The *khēn ta'ǎśeh* formulary reveals other exegetical dimensions. For example, an ancient siege law stated that if a Canaanite city responds favorably to Israelite overtures of peace it may not be destroyed, though its population could be exploited for forced labor (Deut 20:10-12); whereas if the Canaanites choose to fight, then all males must be killed (v. 13). This rule plainly contradicts the later deuteronomic law of *ḥērem*, which envisaged no suit for peace and required death of the entire autocthonous population (see Deut 20:16-17 and 7:2, where it is a blatant interpolation). This clash required an exegetical reapplication of the first formulation to a different situation. The delimitation (introduced by the aforesaid formulary) determined that the prior (now contradictory) rule dealt with cities *outside* the borders of Canaan only.[25] This left the *ḥērem* rule intact and did not render the prior *traditum* null and void. The paradoxical result is that an older *traditum* functions as the exegetical *traditio* of a newer one which factually displaces it.[26] In other instances *harmonization* is not the dominant impulse, and distinct rules are compared for the purpose of *analogical deduction*. Thus with respect to the seizure and rape of betrothed virgins in the city (Deut 22:23-24) and country (vv. 25-26), the penalties differ. In the city the woman *and*

[22] Full discussion in BIAI 179-81.
[23] BIAI 190-193, and the comprehensive study of A. Toeg, Num 15:22-31 (1973/74) 1-20 [Heb].
[24] BIAI 193-94.
[25] See A. Biram, "The Corvée", *Tarbiz* 23 (1952) 138, and BIAI 199-201.
[26] For the further exegetical reworking of Deut 20:10-18 in Joshua 9, see BIAI 206-07.

the rapist are culpable if the woman did not cry for help; whereas in the field *only* the male is culpable, since there is no way to determine if the woman called out. In the absence of proof, the woman was presumed honorable; but the need for clarification led to a comparison of rape with premeditated violence pertetrated upon an unconsenting party (Deut 19:11). The interpolation of this latter case *into* the *traditum*—at 22:25b—is introduced by the exegetical formula *ka'ăšer ... khēn*, "just as ... so [also]". By this means the *traditum* is widened through the *traditio* of it, and later jurists are expressly informed that this case must not be regarded as a mere crime of passion (in which case the male might be excused by blaming the victim) but one of intentional and overbearing assault (in which case the female is *de facto* always helpless). In this reuse of a *traditum* as an exegetical *traditio* a precious moment of ancient legal reasoning is preserved.[27]

As the variety of traditions were gathered and compared, in exilic schools and thereafter, differences were correlated and resolved. Exemplary of the first solution is the combination in Neh 10:32 of the different formulations of sabbatical release mentioned in pentateuchal sources (produce, in Exod 23:11; loans, Deut 15:1–2). The specific terms make it certain that the older rules are combined, for the references to the "Torah of God" or the "commandments of the Lord" (vv. 29–30) are not sufficient to make that point. Quite different are those instances in the late sources which actually refer to the "Book of Moses" as a "written" text and attempt to blend contradictory rules in a lapidary way. Thus the remark that the people in the time of Josiah "*boiled* the paschal-offering *in fire*, according to the Law" is manifestly an irresolute harmonization of two pentateuchal rules: the one in Exod 12:9, which requires the offering to be "roasted by *fire*" and not "*boiled* in water"; and the other, in Deut 16:7, which directly enjoins the worshipper to "boil" it. Separate ritual traditions have been spliced to suggest an ancient *traditum*, which is actually their exegetical *traditio*.[28]

The occurance of *nomos* in the late historical narratives shows other exegetical dimensions. One of these is the resolution of contradictions between the ritual behavior of the ancients and the received Mosaic *traditum*. Since it was inconceivable that David did not observe the *ḥērem* regulation forbidding use of Canaanite booty (Deut 7:25), or that the builders of Solomon's Temple disregarded the prohibition of dressed stones in altar construction (Deut 27:5–6), the offending passages were deftly reinterpreted. In the first case, the apparent plain sense of the verb *wa-yiśśā'ēm* in 2 Sam 5:21, "he [David] bore them [the idols] off", was rendered in 1 Chr 14:12 by David's command that the troops "burn" the foreign gods in fire. This change repairs the 'faulty' *traditum* by using precisely the term required by deuteronomic norms (*śāraph*); but (as medieval exegesis suggests and old inscriptions confirm) the latterday tradent may have justifiably believed that he was merely making an uncommon meaning of the verbal stem *nāśā'* (as 'ignite'; not 'carry') explicit.[29]

---

[27] Discussion in BIAI 217–20.

[28] BIAI 134–38.

[29] See R. David Kimhi *ad* 2 Sam 5:1; he also adduces Nah 1:5 and Job 32:22. The noun *mas'et*

In the second instance the apparent breach of divine regulations (through use of dressed stones) in the construction of the Temple was exegetically resolved by the qualifying comment that iron implements were never employed inside the sacral area *while the building was going on (be-hibbānōtô;* 1 Kgs 6:7)—thus validating the quarrying and dressing of the hewn blocks outside it.[30] In this way, the old *traditum* was purportedly obeyed from earliest times.

Quite different is the exegetical reapplication of an old *traditum* to new circumstances. Such is the case in 2 Chr 30, where the *nomos* of a second Passover (Num 9:1–14) provided the precedent for a structurally similar situation. Thus whereas the pentateuchal rule is addressed to lay persons afflicted with corpse defilement or away from the holy land at the time of the paschal-offering, the later source applies it to a national ceremony when some priestly officiants remained defiled by idols and members of the laity were distant from the Temple at the requisite moment. The links to the Torah are assured by the close verbal correspondences between the sources; the exegetical aspect is dramatized by the role of a consultative body engaged by a king to resolve the dilemma.[31] With this we have moved to a different social realm, paralleling the public performance of ritual exegesis in Neh 8 and the active involvement of official interpreters. The engagement of exegetical groups for the purpose of eliminating unwanted persons is a more political expression of the same developments. This is fully documented in the use of pentateuchal texts (restricting contact with the autocthonous Canaanites) for the purpose of controlling inclusion in the post-exilic covenant community (see the reuse of Deut 7:1–6 and 23:4–7 in Ezra 9:1–2; cf. Neh 13:23–27).[32] Legal interpretation is thus constitutive of the emergent polity; indeed, it is the vital force in its exegetical construction of reality.

4. Aggadic Exegesis

Like the preceding, the following section deals with the reapplication of traditional materials; but unlike it the sources are drawn from the entire range of biblical texts (legal; cultic; moral), and the genres of the *traditio* are often quite distinct from the inspiring *traditum* (e.g., laws are reinterpreted in prophetic homilies). Moreover, the adaptation of a legal or ritual *traditum* into one or another rhetorical form with new theological purposes does not mean that the older *traditum* has been cancelled: the law or rite remains in effect whatever their transforming *traditio*. This is not necessarily so with respect to theologoumena or moral dicta, in which case the *traditio* often intends to transcend or replace the offending *traditum*. In the present discus-

as 'fire' occurs in Judg 20:38, 40 and Jer 6:1. For inscriptional evidence, cf. KAI I, no. 194 (Lachish). The meaning survives in rabbinic legal usage; note *maśśî'în maśśû'ôt*, 'ignite torches', *m. Rosh Hashanah* II: 2–3.

[30] See BIAI 159–62.

[31] Full discussion in BIAI 98–99, 154–59.

[32] See BIAI 123–29; also 138–43.

sion, the later term 'aggadah' indicates those cases of exegetical *traditio* which are neither legal or prophetic *sensu stricto*. As against the latter, aggadic *traditio* is less concerned with normative acts or great expectations than with understandings of a theological or historical nature.

On various occasions the prophet Jeremiah adapted legal traditions to his rhetorical purpose. In 2:3, for example, he proclaimed: "Israel is consecrated (*qōdeš*) to YHWH, the first fruit of his produce; whoever destroys him (*'okhlâw*) will be judged guilty (*ye'šāmû*), and evil will befall them: oracle of YHWH". The prophet's concern was to stress the special relationship between God and his people (complementing the marriage figures in v. 2), and thus Israel's protected destiny. To do so he draws from the cultic rule in Lev 22:14–16, where it is stated that if a layperson eats a consecrated (*qōdeš*) donation by accident he must pay a penalty over and above the cost of the desecrated foodstuff; there follows an exhortation to the priests to guard the *sacra* lest laypersons bear guilt (*'ašmāh*) by eating (*bĕ-'okhlām*) improper foods. Clearly, the old rule has undergone a metaphorical reconfiguration. Israel is now the sacred produce of God himself and the desecrators are the enemy which will be destroyed.[33] But in the process of infusing Israel with corporate sanctity the prophet drew on a notion which had already undergone an aggadic reworking in deuteronomic circles. Thus in an early proclamation the people are told that if they faithfully observe the commandments they will be "a kingdom of priests and a holy (*qādôš*) nation" (Exod 19:4–6). The preachers recorded in the book of Deuteronomy rejected this conditional holiness and reworked its assumptions. For them Israel *is*, unconditionally, "a nation holy (*qādôš*) to YHWH" and therefore has special covenantal obligations (Deut 7:6). This transformation of Israel's corporate being later served as the basis for the legal exegesis in Ezra 9:1–2, noted above, in which foreign women are dismissed from the restoration community out of a desire to preserve Israel as a "holy (*qōdeš*) seed".

The rhetorical reuse of priestly sources served other theological ends as well—as when the prophet in Isa 58:1–12 utilizes the terminology of Lev 16 in order to indicate that the fast which the Lord desires is not the public mortification of the flesh (*we-ʿinnîtem 'et naphšōtêkhem*, "you shall afflict your bodies"; Lev 16:31; cf. 23:24) but care for the "poor" (*ʿăniyyîm*) and "tormented" souls (*nepheš naʿănāh*) of the nation (Isa 58:5–8, 10).[34] As with the Jeremian example, here too (and elsewhere) the legal *traditum* is transfigured and developed—but in no way abrogated by aggadic *traditio*. The same holds true where the rule concerns civil or criminal matters (e.g., the uses of Exod 22:1–2 or Deut 24:1–4 in Jer 2:26 and 3:1–5, respectively). By contrast, concerns to override a *traditum* occur in matters of theology. Thus the theologoumenon of divinely deferred punishment (viz., the matter of vicarious punishment) in Exod 20:5 is forcefully rejected in Deut 7:9–10, where each individual is said to receive his own just deserts in his lifetime. This principle comports with the rejection in the deuteronomic laws of vi-

[33] BIAI 300–03.
[34] BIAI 304–06.

carious punishment (24:16) – formulated there with respect to capital punishment and fathers and sons (notably, nothing is stated regarding seizing a son for a dead father's debts; or substituting a slave in a case of stripes). But not all Israelites were convinced of this theological innovation, for in the experience of many the adage that "the fathers have eaten sour grapes but the teeth of (their) children are set on edge" remained valid. Accordingly, in his address to the exiles the prophet Ezekiel invoked this proverb (Ezek 18:2) and valiantly sought to rebut it (v. 3) through an aggadic reworking of the aforenoted legal principle (v. 4) – reinterpreted to mean (*inter alia*) that good sons of bad fathers are not punished: for God wants the life of the faithful and willingly foregoes punishment when a son is (or becomes) good. Notably, the legal norm is not rejected here either. It rather serves as the basis for an aggadic reinterpretation that even rejects the theologoumenon that a person is necessarily punished for his own sins. In fact, in Ezekiel's homily a bad son who repents and does good will not be punished (but the reverse also obtains; see 18:18–32).[35]

A different type of aggadic *traditio* occurs when the *traditum* pertains to an ancient worthy, whose actions are preserved in the old narratives. Using the model of Abraham, a late prophet exhorts his fainthearted people in God's name to "recall Abraham your father ... for he was one when I called him, but I blessed him and made him numerous" (Isa 51:2). Through this allusion to Gen 12:1–3 he hopes to encourage the people to return to their homeland. The rhetoric implies *a fortiori* reasoning: if Abraham, who was one, responded in faith and was blessed with a multitude, how much more will the exiles, being many, merit an even greater reward if they come back. No doubt there is an ideological counterpoint here to the smug assertion of those Judeans who did not go into exile, contending that "Abraham was but one and inherited the land, and we are many [so how much more so] is the land given us as an inheritance!" (Ezekiel 33:24). In this case, typological identification with the patriarch serves a presumptive self-confidence which Ezekiel cites in order to reject (vv. 25–29). In a different vein, the narrative *traditum* (in Gen 27:35–36) about Jacob (*yaʿăqōb*) who tricked (*yaʿqĕbēnî*) his brother (*ʾāḥ*) with guile (*mirmāh*) was utilized by Jeremiah (9:3–5) in a sardonic rebuke of the people, Jacob/Israel, who mendaciously (*mirmāh*) deceive (*ʿāqôb yaʿqōb*) their brethren (*ʾāḥ*) in social life. The aggadic *traditio* thus extends the characterization of the eponomous ancestor to the nation as a whole (cf. already Hos 12:8–9).

Verbal exhortations in the old traditions also evince aggadic modifications – in particular, the transformation of originally military charges of courage into statements advocating spiritual fidelity to the Torah. In such cases the *traditio* is not a verbal event *per se*, but the editorial reshaping of a quoted discourse. Typical of this procedure is the way that Moses' charge to Joshua to be "strong" and "fearless" in battle (Deut 31:4–6) is repeated in Joshua 1. Hereby, the precise language of the original command is split-up

[35] For a full discussion of these and other sources, with literature, see BIAI 337–45.

(vv. 5–6, 9) and *within it* (vv. 7–8) is embedded a call to piety and observance, for which sake (and it alone) the people will achieve victory.[36] A similar transformation of virtues occurs in David's final testament to Solomon (cf. 1 Kgs 2:1–2 + 5–9 *and* vv. 3–4).[37] Such processes were part of a comprehensive transvaluation of Torah-consciousness in the later period.[38] As part of this process, such venerable theologoumena as trusting or seeking God were applied to the Torah and its commandments (cp. Ps 16:8 and 115:9 with Ps 119:30 and 42; or Lam 2:19 with Ps 119:48).[39] In these cases, the aggadic *traditio* transfigures belief itself.

Without being comprehensive, the foregoing examples demonstrate the diversity of sources from which aggadic *traditio* could draw; the varied genres in which it was realized; and the many new dimensions of Israelite culture thereby revealed. At the most textual level, this material shows the emerging canon; viz., the authoritative traditions which could be culled and quoted by later tradents (the fact, e.g., that Jeremiah uses materials from the patriarchal narratives, the Covenant Code, the priestly laws and Deuteronomy is remarkable). In addition, aggadic *traditio* demonstrates features of rhetorical strategy whereby living audiences were confronted with older teachings or memories for the purpose of eliciting new behavior. And finally, the preceding cases reveal ongoing transformations in cultural and religious consciousness in ancient Israel – and how this was achieved through texts and traditions. In its canonical shape, this complex *traditio* has also been preserved as a *traditum* for new generations.

5. Mantological Exegesis

In contrast to the present-day immediacy of legal and aggadic *traditio*, prophecy is a word for the future. Expectation and its tensions surcharge each pronouncement. Accordingly, oracles must make sense and project a conceivable future. For that reason, ambiguities of formulation require new explanations. As to onset: prophecies of doom arise from the people's failure to heed the law and its aggadic challenge, whereas prophecies of hope predict an end to sorrow. Both types are thus situated 'in the middest' – in a time of expectation, before the present condition will be changed by divine action. As a result, the unexpected deferral of fulfillment also elicits reinterpretation of the *traditum*. A rhetoric once thought to be immediate and clear is now mediated by exegetical *traditio*. Both earthly tradents and heavenly beings have a share in this process. Paradoxically, the original *traditum* is disambiguated by a *traditio* which much first apprehend ambiguities in its formulations.

Paralleling lexical clarifications, specifications of a generalized oracle could

[36] BIAI 384–85.

[37] Ibid. 385.

[38] For full discussion with examples, BIAI 385–92.

[39] See Fishbane, Garments of Torah (1989) 70–71.

be introduced by deictic particles. Thus the doomsday prediction that "YHWH will cut off from Israel head and tail, palm branch and rush" (Isa 9:13) is immediately applied to distinct classes: "the elder and haughty one: *hû'* (this is) the 'head'; and the prophet [and] false teacher: *hû'* the 'tail'" (v. 14). While the relationship between the general word and its specification may be concurrent here (and not the work of later tradents), the difference between an encoded *traditum* and its interpretation is maintained. This form (with and without deictics) is similar to reports of dreams, visions, or conundrums and their interpretation (cf. Gen 41:26–30; Zech 4:2–6a, 10b–14; Dan 4:17–23; 5:25–27);[40] and it was utilized by later-day prognosticators of future events believed to be mysteriously sealed in Israelite prophecies (cf. the *pešer* to Habakkuk from Qumran). Significantly different is the paraphrastic reworking of earlier rhetoric. The long castigation in Ezek 22:25–28, as compared with the concision of Zeph 3:3–4, is exemplary. In this case, the development is in the direction of rhetorical elaboration rather than the decoding of symbols.[41] It also points to the existence of formal tropes which were learned and variously applied by prophets in the exigencies of the moment and divine inspiration.

Apart from clarifications or elaborations, it was also necessary to up-date or reapply oracles whose sense once seemed certain. Thus in Isa 16:13 the prophet refers to a "former prophetic word" (*zeh ha-dābhār*) against Moab which is now (*we-ʿattāh*) reissued (v. 14). In a similar way, Ezekiel refers to an unfulfilled prophecy about Nebuchadnezzer (29:17–18) and goes on to respecify it for a future king (vv. 19–20). As in the previous case, the older *traditum* is revised by a new oracle. A similar strategy of authority was adopted by Jeremiah in his reworking of Jer 25:9–12. This latter forecasts a 70-year period of ruin for the land of Judea, and subjugation of the people to the king of Babylon – after which a reversal of fortune is anticipated. The prophet subsequently refers to this oracle but changes it strategically. Originally the oracle predicted that YHWH would "visit" (*'ephqōd*) punishment on the oppressor; but in 29:10 it is reworked to suggest that in time YHWH would "remember" (*'ephqōd*) his oppressed people and save them. Hereby, the old word of doom is reformulated to stress compassion. In a later guise, the oracle appears in 2 Chr 36:19–21. This *traditio* cites Jeremiah's words and adds phrases from Lev 26:34–35 in order to suggest that the land would lie waste in recompense for Israel's desecration of the sabbatical years (this version further implies that the *traditum* in Jer 25:9–12 is in fact a fulfillment of the prophetic warning in Lev 25:41–45). Such a move is significant, for the connection between 70 years and sabbatical cycles underlies the decoding of the old *traditum* in Dan 9 to mean a desolation of 490 years – or 10 Jubilees. The exegetical process is significant. At the outset, Daniel "investigates" (*bînōtî*) the written *traditum* of Jeremiah – but without success. After

---

40 Full discussion in BIAI 447–57.

41 See D. H. Müller, "Der Prophet Ezechiel entlehnt eine Stelle des Propheten Zephania und glossiert sie", idem, *Komposition und Strophenbau* (Wien: A. Hölder 1907) 30–36; see BIAI 461–63.

a ritual of prayer and penance, however, he received an angelic revelation of the true meaning of the original words (together with further allusions to Lev 26).[42] In related developments, fragments of many other older oracles are studiously combined and reinterpreted throughout Dan 10–12.[43]

But for all its remarkable character, such studious attention to older oracles does not begin in the Hellenistic period. It is rather part of a scholasticism which enters prophecy most noticably in early exilic prophecy—especially the way the oracles of Isaiah (of Jerusalem) were reworked by his inheritors. In numerous cases, the master's voice reappears in a new guise. For example, the doomsdays words of Isa 1:7 recur in 62:4, even as the prediction of hope (through images of light) in 9:1–3 are recapitulated in the more euphoric setting of 60:1–2. Similarly, all the terms of the great oracle of universal reunion in 2:1–4 are echoed in enlarged ways in 60:3,5,14,17. Clearly the times seemed ripe for fulfillment, and induced a searching of scriptures. In this effort, latterday students of Isaiah also studied pentateuchal materials, quoted as *pî YHWH* ("the word of YHWH"; cp. Isa 58:14 with Deut 32:9, 13); the very same formula was used by Obadiah (17–18) in his own studious *traditio* of Balaam's ancient word (in Num 24:17).[44] Fatefully, the prophetic future is variously unsealed by interpretation. At the close of ancient Israelite literature, this development is a turning point in the history of prophecy.

The final phase of mantological exegesis thus parallels the endpoint of legal and aggadic interpretation. In each sphere study of the written *traditum* has become the true means of piety and knowledge of God's will. Technical terms underscore the connection. Just as the understanding of Torah for legal exegesis and theological piety are expressed by the verb *haśkîl* (Neh 8:13; Ps 101:2), its nominal form (*maśkîlîm*) refers to those who are the "enlightened [interpreters]" of prophecy (Dan 11:13; 12:3, 10). Similarly, the verb *bîn/hābîn* not only indicates true legal (Neh 8:13) and theological understanding (cf. Ps 119:27, 34, 144, 169), but comprehension of the secrets of prophecy as well (Dan 9:2). This overall move to a text culture based on interpretation on written sources, is equally a shift from the ear of the people (which receives legal, homiletic, and prophetic address) to the eye of the interpreter (of an authoritative *traditum*). The choice of sources for reflection, study, and interpretation reveals, moreover, something of the canon-in-formation; of the move from scriptures to Scripture. The prayer in Ps 119:18 is indicative of these developments. *gal ʿênay wĕʾabbîṭāh niphlāʾôt mittôrātekhā*, says the Psalmist: "Unveil my eyes that I may perceive wonders from (out of) Your Torah". The perception that the written and received *traditum* (as a whole) depends upon ongoing and transforming *traditio* was shared by the various heirs of ancient Israel. Its roots are in the Hebrew Bible itself.

---

[42] Detailed discussion of all these texts is given in BIAI 479–89.

[43] See BIAI 489–94.

[44] For discussions, see BIAI 477–79.

Chapter Two

The Interpretative Significance of a Fixed Text and Canon of the Hebrew and the Greek Bible

2.1. The History and Significance of a Standard Text of the Hebrew Bible

By Emanuel Tov, Jerusalem

Bibliography: B. Albrektson, "Reflections on the Emergence of a Standard Text of the Hebrew Bible", VTSup 29 (1978) 49–65; W. F. Albright, "New Light on Early Recensions of the Hebrew Bible", *BASOR* 140 (1955) 27–33; B. Chiesa, "Appunti di storia della critica del testo dell'Antico Testamento ebraico", *Hen* 12 (1990) 3–14; idem, "Textual History and Textual Criticism of the Hebrew OT – Some Reflections upon 'A Modern Textual Outlook Based on the Qumran Scrolls'", in: *The Madrid Qumran Congress – Proceedings of the International Congress on the Dead Sea Scrolls – Madrid, 18–21 March 1991* (ed. J. Trebolle Barrera/L. Vegas Montaner; Studies on the Texts of the Desert of Judah 11; Madrid/Leiden 1992) 257–272; F. M. Cross, "The Contribution of the Qumrân Discoveries to the Study of the Biblical Text", *IEJ* 16 (1966) 81–95; idem, "The Evolution of a Theory of Local Texts", in: *Qumran and the History of the Biblical Text* (ed. F. M. Cross/S. Talmon; Cambridge, MA/London 1976) 306–320 [= QHBT]; G. Gerleman, *Synoptic Studies in the OT* (Lund 1948); R. Gordis, "Prolegomenon" to the reprinting of idem, *The Biblical Text in the Making – A Study of the Kethib – Qere* (Philadelphia 1937; repr. New York 1971) xi–lvi; M. H. Goshen-Gottstein, "Hebrew Biblical Manuscripts: Their History and Their Place in the HUBP Edition", *Bib.* 48 (1967) 243–290; repr. in QHBT 42–89; M. Greenberg, "The Stabilization of the Text of the Hebrew Bible Reviewed in the Light of the Biblical Materials from the Judean Desert", *JAOS* 76 (1956) 157–167; A. F. J. Klijn, "A Library of Scriptures in Jerusalem?" *Studia Codicologica* 124 = TU 124 (1977) 263–272; S. Lieberman, *Hellenism in Jewish Palestine* (2nd ed.; New York 1962) 20–27; J. Olshausen, *Die Psalmen* (KeH; Leipzig 1853) 17–22; M. Sæbø, "From Pluriformity to Uniformity. Some Remarks on the Emergence of the Massoretic Text, with Special Reference to Its Theological Significance", ASTI 11 (1977–1978) 127–137; M. Z. Segal, "ltwldwt msyrt hmqr'", *Mnḥh ldwd, spr hzkrwn ld' ylyn* (Jerusalem 1935) 1–22, 254–255; idem, "The Promulgation of the Authoritative Text of the Hebrew Bible", *JBL* 72 (1953) 35–47; A. Sperber, *A Historical Grammar of Biblical Hebrew – A Presentation of Problems with Suggestions to Their Solution* (Leiden 1966); S. Talmon, "The OT Text", in: CHB I (1970) 159–199; idem, "Tn"k, nwsḥ", EncBib 8 (Jerusalem 1982) 621–641; E. Tov, *Textual Criticism of the Hebrew Bible* (Minneapolis/Assen-Maastricht 1992) [= TCHB]; idem, "The Textual Base of the Corrections in the Biblical Texts Found at Qumran", in: *The Dead Sea Scrolls – Forty Years of Research* (ed. D. Dimant/U. Rappaport; Leiden/Jerusalem 1992) 299–314; E. Ulrich, "Horizons of Old Testament Textual Research at the Thirtieth Anniversary of Qumran Cave 4", *CBQ* 46 (1984) 613–636; A. van der Woude, "Pluriformity and Uniformity – Reflections on the Transmission of the Text of the Old Testament", in: *Sacred History and Sacred Texts in Judaism* (ed. J. N. Bremmer/F. García Martínez; *Contributions to Biblical Exegesis and Theology* 5; Kampen 1992) 151–169.

Special abbreviations:

QHBT = *Qumran and the History of the Biblical Text* (see above);
TCHB = Tov, *Textual Criticism of the Hebrew Bible* (see above).

1. The Prehistory and History of a Standard Text

1.1. The History of Research

A description of the development of the biblical text must be based on solid evidence relating to textual witnesses and the relation between them. Too often, however, scholars take as their point of departure only abstract assumptions and preconceived ideas.

Such preconceived ideas find acceptance by all scholars, and certainly, this chapter is not free of them. Positions taken with regard to the composition of the biblical books and their copying, the issue of the *Urtext*, and the development of textual traditions have all been influenced by abstract assumptions and prejudices. When speaking of the latter type of approach, we refer to those scholars who describe the development of several texts in a similar way, even though each text probably developed according to different internal dynamics. For example, DE LAGARDE[1] described the development of the biblical text in general as well as that of the LXX and MT in particular along the same lines, while for KAHLE (see 1.1.3 below), the Targumim served as the model for describing the development of all other texts.

Taking the influence emanating from these preconceived ideas into consideration, we now turn to a description of the development of the biblical text. In this description, we first review the opinions expressed in the research and afterwards present our own views.

The reader will find only partial answers to the questions relating to the development of the biblical text in the following pages, for, in the past, scholars usually referred only to limited aspects of the development of the text, even though they themselves often thought that their views pertained to all aspects. A posteriori, one could say that occasionally their opinions were correct for their time only, since the discoveries of texts from the Judean Desert, which completely altered the face of research, were not known at the time. Furthermore, one should note that many scholars described the history of the research schematically in terms of a thesis (usually: the views of DE LAGARDE), antithesis (usually: the views of KAHLE), and occasionally, even synthesis. However, on closer examination of the details of this presentation, such a schematic presentation is found to be untenable.

One should remember that the following description pertains to the biblical text in its entirety and the MT is only one component within this framework. Scholars did not always make a clear distinction between these two levels, as can be seen, for example, from their approach to the view of ROSENMÜLLER (see section 1.1.1 below), which in fact pertains only to MT.

---

[1] P. DE LAGARDE, *Anmerkungen zur griechischen Übersetzung der Proverbien* (Leipzig 1863) 4.

1.1.1. The first theoretical statements about the development of the biblical text were by EICHHORN (1781 and later),[2] BAUER (1795),[3] and ROSENMÜLLER (1797)[4] – in modern research Rosenmüller is often credited with the priority rights for this view, but CHIESA (1990) has shown that he was actually preceded by EICHHORN and BAUER. All three dealt solely with the manuscripts of MT from the Middle Ages, and not with the biblical text as a whole. On seeing that these manuscripts agree even in the minutest details, these scholars determined that all manuscripts of MT reflect one textual recension, a recension which was different from the "recension" of the LXX (see the discussion of Rosenmüller's opinion *apud* GOSHEN-GOTTSTEIN (1967), TALMON (1970), and CHIESA (1990)). This view remains valid even today, except that one should substitute *recension* with a term that is less definitive, such as *group* or *family*. Beyond EICHHORN (n. 2) and BAUER (n. 3), ROSENMÜLLER (n. 4) claimed that all Hebrew manuscripts derived from "one source" (ibid.).

1.1.2. In concise, abstract terms, DE LAGARDE (1863) proposed that all manuscripts of MT derived from one source which served as an archetype of what he called the "recension" of MT.[5] The brief, pertinent formulations of DE LAGARDE, though having great influence, did not break completely new ground since they continued the line of thought of EICHHORN, BAUER, ROSENMÜLLER (all these as quoted above), and OLSHAUSEN (1853) in their research on the Hebrew Bible, and of K. LACHMANN in the field of NT study.[6] DE LAGARDE resorted principally to abstract reasoning with regard to textual development but also added a concrete argument pertaining to MT: in his opinion, the identical transmission of even small details, such as the *puncta extraordinaria*, in all manuscripts of MT proves that they were all copied from one source (the presumed *archetype* of MT). This claim, without argumentation, was also applied to the manuscripts of the LXX, all of which, in his opinion, also derived from one archetype. Moreover, DE LAGARDE claimed that it was possible to reconstruct the original form of the biblical text from the reconstructed first copies of MT and the LXX. This original text was not described by him; later it was depicted in general terms by BUHL, who also claimed that it had authoritative status.[7]

This proposition became known in scholarly literature as the *Urtext* theory of DE LAGARDE. One should note that DE LAGARDE's statements were very succinct and that more than what he actually said was attributed to him, partly due to a confusion of his views with those of ROSENMÜLLER and others (see 1.1.1 above), who ascribed all the manuscripts of MT to one recension.

---

[2] J.G. EICHHORN, *Einleitung ins AT*, II (Leipzig 1781; Leipzig ²1787 and Reutlingen 1790; Leipzig ³1803; Göttingen ⁴1823) 129 in the first edition, and more clearly in the second edition, 111, 113, 203.

[3] G.L. BAUER, *Salomonis Glassii Philologia sacra his temporibus accomodata* ... (Leipzig 1795) 396 ff.

[4] E.F.C. ROSENMÜLLER, *Handbuch für die Literatur der biblischen Kritik und Exegese*, I (Göttingen 1797) 244.

[5] See n. 1 and further *Mittheilungen* I (Göttingen 1884) 19–26.

[6] On the relation between the views of these scholars, see especially Goshen-Gottstein (1967) and Chiesa (1990).

[7] F. BUHL, *Canon and Text of the OT* (trans. J. MacPherson; Edinburgh 1892) 256.

De Lagarde's intuitive views have been accepted by many scholars even though we do not possess the tools necessary for reconstructing the original biblical text from MT and the LXX in accordance with his opinion. Similarly, De Lagarde's view that the manuscripts of the LXX derived from one source is generally accepted, although for different reasons: the translation is conceived of as a single act even if it later passed through a process of revision, especially correction towards the changing Hebrew text.

1.1.3. In a series of studies Kahle dealt with the original form of both the individual textual witnesses and the biblical text in its entirety. In his opinion none of these textual witnesses were created in a single act, but rather through a process of editing and revising. Basing himself, on the one hand, on the internal differences between the medieval manuscripts of MT and, on the other hand, on the variants contained in the Cairo Genizah texts and the biblical quotations in the Talmud, Kahle stressed, against de Lagarde, the difficulty in assuming one original text for MT. Similarly, he claimed that the LXX did not originate in a single act of translation but rather, that various translations were originally attempted, which only at a later stage were revised into the form now known to us through the uncial manuscripts of this translation. With regard to the Hebrew Bible in its entirety, Kahle did not in fact reject the assumption of one original text, but emphasized that the textual sources known to us were created from an intermediary source which he at first (1915) named *Vulgärtext* ("vulgar" text), and later (1951), in the plural *Vulgärtexte*, that is, texts created to facilitate the reading (see p. 59 below).[8] He described both the Sam. Pent. and the LXX as such texts and also MT, although, in his opinion, it passed through a stage of refinement in approximately 100 CE.

According to Kahle, these texts thus developed from a textual plurality into a unity, whereas de Lagarde had maintained that the unity preceded the textual plurality. Kahle's approach is in many aspects opposed to that of de Lagarde, but one cannot appropriately define the differences between them, since de Lagarde's exposition was very concise and also, the textual information on which Kahle based his opinions was not known in the time of de Lagarde.

The following points may be raised against Kahle: 1) Although there were undoubtedly texts which facilitated reading ("vulgar" texts in the terminology of Kahle), to be described on pp. 59–60 below, these did not have the central status that Kahle attributed to them, and there is also no proof of their early date as Kahle has supposed. 2) Kahle's claim that both the LXX and 1QIsa^{b} (belonging to the family of MT) were "vulgar" texts is unfounded. 3) Even in Kahle's time there was no justification for his claim that MT was a text that had been edited at a later period, how much more so at the present time,

---

[8] See P. Kahle, "Untersuchungen zur Geschichte des Pentateuchtextes", *TSK* 88 (1915) 399–439 = idem, *Opera Minora* (Leiden 1956) 3–37; idem, *Die hebräischen Handschriften aus der Höhle* (Stuttgart 1951); see further the three editions of his book *The Cairo Geniza* (Oxford 1947, ²1959; *Die Kairoer Genisa*, Berlin 1962).

after the discoveries of Qumran when many proto-Masoretic texts from the third century BCE onward have become known, among which are those written in the "early" Hebrew script that were apparently based on even more ancient scrolls. 4) Although MT, like any other text, contains deliberate changes, there is no reason to assume that it was created by textual revision. 5) The texts from the Cairo Genizah, from which KAHLE drew his theory of textual multiplicity, are late and do not even pertain to the situation in the Second Temple period, much less the First Temple period. 6) Criticism of the approach which sees the ancient texts as recensions was discussed in TCHB, 155–158.

1.1.4. Those who accepted the rather extreme opinions of KAHLE are few in number. Among them one should mention in particular GERLEMAN (1948) and A. SPERBER. The latter scholar reduced the textual multiplicity to two principal traditions: northern – the Sam. Pent. and LXX^B – and southern – MT and LXX^A.[9] In his *Grammar* of 1966 SPERBER collected internal differences both within the MT group (parallel texts, *Ketib-Qere*, etc.) and between certain manuscripts of the LXX, as well as between MT on the one hand and the Sam. Pent. and transliterations of names in the Greek and Latin traditions on the other.

Various scholars accepted from KAHLE's writings the concept of "vulgar" texts, albeit with certain changes. NYBERG,[10] LIEBERMAN,[11] GERLEMAN (1948), GREENBERG (1956), and KUTSCHER ("vernacular and model texts"),[12] posited in their descriptions the "exact" tradition of MT alongside the "vulgar" texts. These texts are in essence what their name describes, that is, texts whose writers approached the biblical text in a free manner inserting changes of various kinds, including orthography. While accepting the plausibility of this opinion, we presuppose different proportions for the "vulgar" texts and use a different terminology and formulation (below, pp. 59–60).

1.1.5. In the wake of a brief article by ALBRIGHT (1955) a new view developed, mainly in the United States, according to which all Hebrew textual witnesses were divided into groups, which were at first described as "recensions" and, later, "families".[13] These groups were linked to particular areas: Babylon (MT), Palestine (the Sam. Pent., MT of Chronicles, several Qumran texts), and Egypt (the Hebrew *Vorlage* of the LXX). This view was developed in particular in the articles of CROSS (1966; see the latest formulation in QHBT).

---

[9] A. SPERBER, *Septuaginta-Probleme* (Texte und Untersuchungen zur vormasoretischen Grammatik des Hebräischen; BWANT 3, 13; 1929); idem, "New Testament and Septuagint", *JBL* 59 (1940) 193–293.

[10] H.S. NYBERG, "Das textkritische Problem des ATs, am Hoseabuche demonstriert", *ZAW* 52 (1943) 254.

[11] Lieberman, Hellenism (1962) 20–27; see also p. 59 below.

[12] E.Y. KUTSCHER, *The Language and Linguistic Background of the Isaiah Scroll* ($1QIs^a$) (Studies on the Texts of the Desert of Judah VI; Leiden 1974) 77–89.

[13] A similar view had been expressed previously by H.M. WIENER, but his views did not receive much attention: "The Pentateuchal Text – A Reply to Dr. Skinner", *BSac* 71 (1914) 218–268, esp. 221.

The principal argument in favour of such an assumption is an abstract and logical one, which posits that texts developed in different ways and directions in the different locations in which they were preserved and/or copied.[14] According to this view, the lack of contact between the centers in which the three recensions/families were developed, created different textual characteristics. For example, the Palestinian recension is held to be expansionistic and full of glosses and harmonizing additions (cf. the features of the Sam. Pent.), the Egyptian recension is considered to be full, whereas the Babylonian recension is conservative and short.[15] The three families developed during the fifth to third centuries BCE.

The assumption of local textual families uses the argumentation that, in the absence of close contact between remote centers, each text developed its own form. Even if the characterizations mentioned above do not appear convincing, other features of the textual witnesses do indeed fit the theory. Thus, it would seem that the editorial differences between MT and the Hebrew source of the LXX described in TCHB, chap. 7, could well have been preserved (rather than created) in Egypt on account of its distance from Palestine. Apparently the Greek translation was made from ancient manuscripts, which had been replaced by a new edition (MT) in Palestine. This reasoning also pertains to the preservation in Qumran of a different edition of Jeremiah, contained in 4QJer^{b,d} (see TCHB, 325–327). Geographical (the LXX) or sociological (Qumran) distance from the influential circles in Palestine must have been determinative in the mentioned instances.

On the negative side, one should note that there is no possibility of verifying the details of this theory of local textual families as proposed by CROSS, and it appears to lack plausibility in its present form: 1) The textual characterization is too general and cannot be proven; only the description of the Palestinian group can be supported with solid evidence, i.e., the typological characteristics of the Sam. Pent. (see TCHB, 85–97, 161). 2) The reconstructed Hebrew *Vorlage* of the LXX does not reflect any proven Egyptian characteristics; rather, it is more likely that the LXX was translated from Palestinian texts, as claimed by the Epistle of Aristeas. 3) The discovery of Hebrew texts in Qumran (such as 4QJer^{b,d}; see TCHB, 325–327), which are very close to the LXX contradicts the theory which connects them to the Egyptian local text. 4) Finally, in Qumran, located in Palestine, a mixture of texts, said to reflect all three local textual groups, has been found, and this fact actually contradicts the logic of the theory of local families.

---

[14] In addition, Albright (1955) mentioned a few assumed Egyptian characteristics of the Hebrew *Vorlage* of the LXX as well as some Babylonian features found in MT, but his examples are unconvincing and have not even been discussed in the literature.

[15] See Cross (1966) 86. The discussion in QHBT provides more details on the characterization of the individual witnesses in the various biblical books. For the most detailed analysis according to this system, see P.K. MCCARTER, *Textual Criticism, Recovering the Text of the Hebrew Bible* (Guides to Biblical Scholarship, OT Series 11; Philadelphia 1986) 87–94.

1.2. A New Description

In this section readers will find less information than they would like, since we do not (yet?) possess sufficient knowledge to be able to give this topic a full description. The theories and descriptions discussed in the preceding section clarify the subject from one angle only and are often too dogmatic. Since a textual theory which could explain the development of the biblical text in its entirety does not exist, one must be content with partial descriptions of limited phenomena.

The first question in any discussion on the development of the biblical text is that of its chronological framework. The lower limit for the period of the development of the biblical text can be fixed at the end of the first century CE, for the biblical text did not change greatly beyond this point in time. At that time, the texts had become firmly anchored in various socio-religious frameworks and did not continue to develop to a great extent. On the other hand, the upper period began at the moment the compositions contained in the biblical books had been completed since, from this point in time on, they were copied many times over. Limited copying had, however, already begun at an earlier stage. Segments of the books existed in writing even before the process of the composition was complete, i.e., at a stage prior to that reflected in MT. In other words, a description of the development of the biblical text begins with the completion of the literary compositions and, to a certain extent, even beforehand.

The Hebrew Bible itself occasionally contains explicit evidence of the writing of segments of the books prior to the writing of the biblical books as they are now known to us. Thus the Ten Commandments were inscribed on the stone tablets of the Covenant (Exod 34:1). Exod 24:4 states that "Moses then wrote down all the commands of the LORD". This statement probably refers to the "Book of the Covenant" (Exodus 21–23). Finally, Jeremiah dictated to his scribe Baruch the scroll containing "all the words that I have spoken to you – concerning Israel and Judah and all the nations – from the time I first spoke to you in the days of Josiah to this day" (Jer 36:2). Similarly, it appears that the editorial process, assumed for most biblical books, presupposes previously written texts. It is reasonable to assume that editors who inserted their words into an earlier formulation of a composition had to base themselves on written texts. We refer in particular to the revision by the deuteronomistic editor(s) of Joshua-Kings and Jeremiah. It thus follows that the editors of the final stage in the composition of the biblical books acted as both authors and copyists, since in the course of their editing, they copied from earlier compositions. The same applies to the author of Chronicles who, in the process of rewriting, copied considerable portions of Genesis and Samuel-Kings, either as known to us or a similar form of these books, as well as limited sections of other compositions. A comparison of Chronicles with its sources and, likewise, a comparison of the pairs of parallel psalms 2 Samuel 22 // Psalm 18, Psalm 14 // Psalm 53, and, like them, other parallel texts, points to many scribal differences (for examples see TCHB, chap. 4 c) which were perhaps created at a very early stage, before these units were integrated into the complete compositions now known to us.

At some stage, the literary growth was necessarily completed. It is possible that at an early stage there existed different early compositions that were parallel or overlapping, but none of these have been preserved. At a certain point in time the last formulations were accepted as final from the point of view of their content and were transmitted and circulated as such. But sometimes this process recurred. Occasionally a book reached what appeared at the time to be its final form, and as such was circulated. However, at a later stage another, revised, edition was prepared, which was intended to take the place of the preceding one. This new edition was also accepted as authoritative, but the evidence shows that it did not always succeed in completely eradicating the texts of the earlier edition which survived in places which were geographically or socially remote. So it came about that these earlier editions reached the hands of the Greek translators in Egypt and remained among the scrolls at Qumran. This pertains to many of the examples analyzed in TCHB, chapter 7, especially the shorter text forms described there (pp. 319–336).

The aforementioned acceptance of the final form of the books can, in retrospect, also be considered as the determining of the authoritative (canonical) status of the biblical books. This process took place by degrees, and it naturally had great influence on the practice and procedures of the copying and transmission of the biblical books.

Since we describe the development of the biblical books in this section, it is important to connect our survey with the discussion of the original form of the biblical text. According to our view (see TCHB, 164–180), the biblical books in their final and canonical edition (as defined in the preceding paragraphs) are the objective of textual criticism. From this point of view it seems that the opinion of de Lagarde, who posited an *Urtext* for all the biblical books, is acceptable, even if several details of his view are not plausible. Our description corresponds, therefore, for it takes into account the possibility of earlier, written stages. It is an ancient text such as this, or various pristine texts, that scholars have in mind when they speak of the original form of the Hebrew Bible or, in a less abstract way, when they compare and evaluate readings.

The period of relative textual unity reflected in the assumed pristine text(s) of the biblical books was brief at best, but in actual fact it probably never even existed, for during the same period there were also current among the people a few copies representing stages which preceded the completion of the literary composition, as described above. It is possible that parallel literary compositions were also current, as mentioned above, although no remnants of these have been preserved. If this situation could be described as one of relative textual unity, it certainly did not last long, for in the following generations it was soon disrupted as copyists, to a greater or lesser extent, continually altered and corrupted the text. It is possible that there were mutual influences between the different stages of the literary composition or between parallel literary compositions, if such existed. The lack of unity was also due to changes that occurred in the transmission of the text in various areas, among them word division, final forms of letters, script, and orthography.

Many scribes took the liberty of changing the text from which they copied, and in this respect continued the approach of the last authors of the books. Several scholars even posit a kind of intermediary stage between the composition and the copying of the books, a stage which one could call compositional-transmissional or editorial-scribal. This free approach taken by the scribes finds expression in their insertion of changes in minor details and of interpolations. Although many of these changes also pertain to content, one should draw a quantitative and qualitative distinction between the intervention of the authors-editors before the text received its authoritative (canonical) status and the activity of the copyists which took place after this occurred. The latter made far fewer and smaller changes and were less free in their approach than the former—as can be seen from most of the Qumran texts.

At this stage many significantly different texts were circulating such as MT, the Sam. Pent., the LXX, and some of the Qumran texts. These texts are probably genetically related in such a way that they derive from one common ("original") text (see TCHB, 164–180). At the same time it is now impossible to relate the surviving data to one common stemma, such as is often done with manuscripts in a medieval text tradition, partly due to a lack of information, and partly because there is no certainty that these texts indeed derived from one common text.

Given the fact that different copies of the biblical text were circulated, it is possible that a certain tendency developed to compare texts or even to revise or correct some texts according to others. It is therefore relevant to note that there is little evidence that such a process took place. For one thing, there is no evidence that non-Masoretic texts were corrected to a form of the proto-Masoretic text (which according to our knowledge was the majority text from the last centuries BCE onwards) or any other text. There is, however, some evidence of the comparison of texts within the group of MT. Thus the so-called *maggihim*, "correctors, revisers", were involved in safeguarding the precision in the writing and transmission of specific texts, within the family of proto-Masoretic texts. Furthermore, it is possible that the Talmudic sources preserve a tradition suggesting a conscious effort to limit the range of variation within the proto-Masoretic group of texts, but the evidence is not sufficiently clear.[16]

It is possible that all scribes initially approached the text freely in the manner described above. It is also possible that even then there were those who did not adopt this free approach and refrained from changing the text transmitted to them. In any case, the earliest Qumran finds dating from the third pre-Christian century bear evidence, among other things, of a tradition of the exact copying of texts belonging to the Masoretic family, that is, the proto-Masoretic texts. However, it is difficult to know whether this approach

[16] The texts from the Judean Desert are often taken as reflecting evidence of revisional activity because they contain many instances of corrections, additions, and omissions. However, most of these are corrections of mistakes by the first scribe (or a subsequent one). Some of the texts thus corrected with a high frequency are proto-Masoretic (MurXII, 4QJer[a], 1QIsa[b]), that is, the corrections are within the proto-Masoretic family, so to speak, while other frequently corrected texts are written in the Qumran practice (4QSam[c], 1QIsa[a], 11QPs[a]).

was characteristic of this textual tradition from its earliest times. One should note that even these texts occasionally reflect the intervention of scribes, although to a limited extent.

In this survey we have not yet referred to absolute chronological data. Although the evidence does not allow precision, in the wake of the discoveries of the scrolls from the Judean Desert it is now possible to express a sufficiently well-founded opinion on the textual developments in the last three centuries BCE. During this period several of the biblical books developed in different ways – if we are not misled by the evidence – and among the various groups within Judaism, the approach to the biblical text was not a unified one. The extant discoveries only allow for a discussion of MT, the LXX, the Sam. Pent., and the Qumran scrolls. The latter give a good reflection of the period from the mid-third century BCE to the year 68 CE for Palestine in general, and not necessarily only for the Qumran sect. It appears that during the last three pre-Christian centuries many different texts were current in Palestine; in other words, this period was characterized by textual plurality.

Although this textual plurality was characteristic for all of Palestine, it appears that in temple circles there existed a preference for one textual tradition, i.e., the texts of the Masoretic family. In this connection one should mention that all the texts found at Masada – dating up till the year 73 CE – reflect MT.

The Qumran discoveries bear evidence of the various texts that were current during this period. These have been described as texts produced by a school of Qumran scribes, proto-Masoretic and pre-Samaritan texts, texts close to the Hebrew *Vorlage* of the LXX, and non-aligned texts which are not exclusively close to any one of these groups.[17] Because of the existence of this latter group of texts, it would appear that for every biblical book one could find an almost unlimited number of texts, differing from each other, sometimes in major details.

In the past scholars regarded such textual variety as evidence of proximity to the so-called "main" texts, sometimes called recensions or text-types, that were known before the Qumran discoveries. This method of describing the Qumran scrolls is, however, a mere convention deriving from the chance situation that for several centuries no Hebrew texts earlier than the medieval manuscripts of MT and the Sam. Pent. were known. Because of this unusual situation, the data were described inversely, that is, in recent generations texts from Antiquity were compared to medieval ones. The new discoveries, however, now enable a correct description of the relations between the texts. This means that today one should not emphasize the proximity of the proto-Masoretic texts to the much later MT, but rather, place the early texts at the center of the description. Similarly, one should not stress the proximity between the pre-Samaritan texts to the later the Sam. Pent., but rather, the opposite. Thus, the way in which MT developed from ancient texts which are now called proto-Masoretic and the way in which the Sam. Pent. was based

[17] Thus TCHB, 107–110, and the literature mentioned there.

on one of the so-called pre-Samaritan texts can be understood more easily (cf. TCHB, 29–36, 97–100).

The textual variety which is characteristic of the entire corpus of the sacred writings did not exist to the same extent for every book. This is due in no small degree to the randomness of the textual transmission. That is to say, scribes who left their mark on the character of a specific text (book) by means of expansion, abridgement, rewriting, by modernizing the orthography, or by changing linguistic features probably did so in an inconsistent manner for certain biblical books which they happened to copy, so that it is impossible to draw an analogy between the specific textual development known from one book and the rest of the biblical books.

Within this textual plurality two principal textual approaches which gave rise to different texts are recognizable: less precise texts, usually and somewhat mistakenly named "vulgar", in general use by the people, and texts which were not "vulgar". The latter usually bore a conservative character and some of them were preserved with great caution by specific groups who also used them in the liturgy. Extant discoveries do not permit us to distinguish three types of texts as Lieberman (1962) has claimed. This scholar distinguished between "inferior" (φαυλότερα) texts which were used by the populace, texts which were used for purposes of instruction and learning (κοινότερα, "widely circulated"), and "exact copies" (ἠκριβωμένα) which were fostered by the temple circles. Although this assumption appears logical, there is not, as stated above, the evidence to support it. Therefore it seems that one should think in terms of only two approaches to the text. However, although the latter assumption is more straightforward, it is still difficult to know under which circumstances and in which social circles the two groups of texts were created, perpetuated, and used. It stands to reason that the vulgar texts were not used for official purposes, such as the liturgy, but one cannot be sure of this with regard to the Qumran community. Among the nonvulgar texts the group of MT stands out. This group was circulated widely, but apparently not exclusively, by a central stream in Judaism.

Vulgar texts – these texts are known from various places in Palestine. Their copyists allowed themselves the freedom of inserting many changes and corrections into the text and even of introducing an idiosyncratic orthographic and morphological practice, such as found in many Qumran texts. Vulgar texts contained also many simplified readings, as was claimed at the time by Kahle (see p. 52). Typical representatives of this group are the majority of the texts written in the Qumran practice (see TCHB, 108–110). These texts are sometimes written with a great degree of carelessness and contain many erasures and corrections. From a textual point of view, their secondary nature is recognizable in orthographic and morphological alterations and innovations and in the insertion of changes in keeping with the context. It appears that the Severus Scroll and R. Meir's Torah (see TCHB, 119–120) also contained many secondary readings of this type, in particular, phonetic ones.

To this group also belong the pre-Samaritan texts and the Sam. Pent. Although these texts are certainly not written negligently and do not contain the unusual orthography and morphology of the Qumran practice, their scribes did permit themselves great freedom in intervening in the text. The harmonizing additions, the linguistic corrections, and contextual changes in these texts are very clearly non-original, and this secondary nature is also characteristic of the vulgar texts. The Nash papyrus, though not a biblical text in the usual sense of the word, also belongs to this group.

By definition, the vulgar texts contain many secondary variants, but they also contain original readings which may have been preserved in them just as in any other text. Thus, both the Qumran scrolls written in the special Qumran practice and the Sam. Pent. whose content is sometimes very artificial, occasionally contain ancient readings which are superior to all other texts, that is MT, the LXX, Targum, Peshitta, and Vulgate.

Nonvulgar texts – Alongside the vulgar texts another relatively large number of texts lacking signs of secondary nature have become known. These are described here as nonvulgar texts and are usually conservative in nature, that is, they disallowed changes more than the other texts. Each one contains original elements which were altered in the other texts, but it is difficult to decide which text contains the greater number of such elements.

Among the nonvulgar texts those best known to us are the proto-Masoretic texts (see TCHB, 27–33), from which MT developed in the early Middle Ages. Despite the scrupulous care taken in the transmission of these texts, changes and corrections such as the "corrections of the scribes" (TCHB, 64–67) and other corrections (TCHB, 213–216, 285) were inserted into them and they also were corrupted (see, for example, the text of Samuel extant in the MT, Targum, Peshitta, and Vulgate). This text is attested among the Hebrew scrolls from Qumran beginning from the third century BCE.

Another text of this category is reflected in the LXX. By chance a few Hebrew texts containing a text similar to that which stood before the Greek translators were preserved at Qumran.

Also belonging to this category are some of the non-aligned Qumran texts, defined as being texts which are not exclusively close to any one of the other texts.

All of the texts described here as vulgar and nonvulgar were current in ancient Israel during the last three centuries BCE and the first two centuries CE. It is not clear what the situation was in earlier periods and it is not known which texts were most widely circulated, for the archeological evidence is liable to be random. If one can regard the evidence from Qumran as providing a reliable picture for all of Palestine, a specific pattern emerges from it, namely, the relatively large representation of MT: some 40 percent of the Qumran manuscripts reflect this text. It is not clear whether the preponderance of the proto-Masoretic texts visible in the collection of texts found at Qumran and dating from the mid-third century BCE onwards is indeed representative for all of that period. For it is not impossible that the preponderance of the proto-Masoretic texts started only in the later part of the period covered by the Qumran finds, that is, in the first century BCE, or the first century CE. The preponderance of the proto-Masoretic texts should probably be traced to the influence of a central stream in Judaism which impelled the copying and circulation of these texts.

After several centuries of textual plurality, a period of uniformity and stability can be discerned at the end of the first century CE. This situation was not a consequence of the processes of textual transmission, but was rather due to political and socio-religious events and developments. By the end of the first century CE, the LXX had been more or less accepted by Christianity and rejected by Judaism. Copies of the Sam. Pent. were in use within the Samaritan community, but since that community had become a separate religion, its biblical text was no longer considered Jewish. The Qumran community, which preserved a wide variety of texts, had ceased to exist after 70 CE. Consequently, the main copies of the text of the Hebrew Bible found in that period were those which were copied and circulated by the central stream of Judaism. Thus, the texts from the Bar-Kochba period, found in Naḥal Ḥever and Wadi Murabbaʿat, reflect only MT, although the evidence could be misleading.[18] These data relating to the post-70 CE period in the past have led to the questionable conclusion that MT had replaced the remaining texts, but such a construction is reminiscent of a modern cultural struggle and does not necessarily reflect the situation as it actually was. There probably was no stabilization (this term is mentioned frequently in the professional literature) or standardization bringing about what is often called the "victory of the proto-Masoretic family". The situation was probably an outcome of political and socio-religious factors (thus in particular ALBREKTSON, 1978). It is not that MT triumphed over the other texts, but rather, that those who fostered it probably constituted the only organized group which survived the destruction of the Second Temple. Thus, after the first century CE a description of the transmission of the text of the Hebrew Bible actually amounts to an account of the history of MT. The Torah scroll from the synagogue of Severus and R. Meir's Torah (see TCHB, 119–121) probably are an exception to this situation.

We do not possess evidence on whether during this period some sort of official meeting took place during which a decision was reached on the authoritative status of the twenty-four books of the Hebrew Bible according to MT. Various scholars have mentioned in this context a meeting or council that was held at *Jabneh*, Jamnia, between the years 75 and 117 CE.[19] In the ancient texts, however, we find only references to a *beth din*, "law court", a *metibta'*, "academy", a *yeshivah*, and a *beth midrash* ("school" or "college") at Jabneh. There is no reference to any convention or council. In addition to this, according to LEIMAN,[20] the only decision reached at Jabneh was that "the Song of Songs and Ecclesiastes render the hands unclean" (*m. Yad.* 3:5). No decision was taken on the authoritative (canonical) status of all of the biblical

---

[18] Possibly the evidence does not give a correct representation of the situation in all of Palestine at the time of the Bar Kochba revolt. The documents found at Naḥal Ḥever and Wadi Murabbaʿat were left there by Bar Kochba's warriors, and since the revolt was supported by various Rabbis, the scrolls probably were representative only for the mainstream in Judaism.

[19] See J.P. LEWIS, "What Do We Mean by Jabneh?" *JBR* 32 (1964) 125–132.

[20] S. LEIMAN, *The Canonization of Hebrew Scripture – The Talmudic and Midrashic Evidence* (Transactions of the Connecticut Academy of Arts and Sciences 47; Flamden, CO 1976) 120–124.

books and it is hard to know whether the activities of the Rabbis at Jabneh had any influence on the position of the text during that period.

The above survey has dealt with the Hebrew Bible as an entity, but one should remember that each of the biblical books had a separate history – each one developed in a different way and received canonical status at a different time. The number of variant readings that one might expect fo find in a particular book is a direct result of the complexity of its literary development and textual transmission.

Within this framework, one should pay attention to the Torah, which had a history of development as complex as the rest of the biblical books, but which also had a distinctive status and on account of this, might be expected to have a special position from a textual point of view. The evidence does not, however, support such an assumption. While on the one hand, the orthography of the Torah in MT is usually more conservative than that of the rest of the biblical books, on the other hand, the quantity of variant readings that it contains was not less than that of the other books. The LXX also reflects in the Torah as wide a range of variant readings as in the other books and the pre-Samaritan texts and the Sam. Pent. also exhibit extensive editorial intervention in the Torah. At the same time, there is one area in which a special approach to the Torah may be detected. Some readers and scribes of the Torah were more sensitive to divergencies in narratives between the books of the Torah and to "inconsistencies" within stories than to similar features in the other biblical books. Therefore, with some exceptions, textual developments such as those known for the Torah in the Sam. Pent. and the pre-Samaritan texts are less in evidence for the other biblical books.

One should always remember that it is the random preservation of evidence that determines the character of a description such as the one given here. Moreover, the textual nature of the books included in MT and the LXX has been determined by the selection of ancient scrolls from which these texts were composed. This selection has also come about to a great extent by chance. For example, the somewhat corrupt nature of the book of Samuel in MT was apparently due to the copy of this book that was entered into MT and which, by chance, had become corrupted to a certain extent at an earlier stage. Accordingly, the distinctive state of Samuel does not reveal anything of the history of the book's transmission or the approach of the early copyists towards it. It only shows something of the nature of MT in this book alone. Similarly, it was only by chance that important data on the development of the book of Jeremiah were discovered in Qumran and have been preserved in the LXX (see TCHB, 325–327), and it is quite probable that other books also passed through a similar process of editing.

2. The Nature and Significance of a Standard Text

For the text of the Hebrew Bible, a standard text developed at an earlier stage than for other writings, including most sacred texts. An extreme case is the New Testament for which such a stabilization took place only in recent centuries, and not even as an integral development of the history of the text, but as a result of scholarly endeavors.[21] Two stages are discernible in the development of a standard text of the Hebrew Bible, at first relating to one of its textual families, the Masoretic Text, and secondly with regard to the Hebrew Bible as a whole.

The development of a standard text of the Hebrew Bible which was binding in all its details for ancient Judaism was enabled only after the contents of the Hebrew sacred Scripture had been determined, stage by stage. Thus, when the contents of the third section of Hebrew Scripture, that of the Hagiographa had yet to be determined, detailed care had already been taken of the text of the two other sections of the authoritative writings of the Hebrew Scriptures, the Torah and Prophets. The exact dates of the acceptance of an authoritative (canonical) status of the three segments of the Hebrew canon are not known, nor of the beginning of the concept of a standard text in Judaism.

From the very beginning of the period of transmission many different texts of the Hebrew Bible circulated in ancient Israel, most of which probably had an equal claim of authority in the circles in which they were circulated. In other words, since these early texts differed from each other in many details, the very differences between them probably did not disturb their authoritative status,[22] although for some texts an inferior status was recognized. The assumption of an equal status for most early texts cannot be proven, but it can be made likely by the fact that different texts of the Hebrew Bible were used in ancient Israel, as can be seen from the differences between the copy of the Hebrew Bible used by the LXX translators in Alexandria in the third and second centuries BCE, and the various copies of the proto-Masoretic text, the pre-Samaritan text, and various Qumran texts, in the Qumran caves. There is no evidence that a standard text developed anywhere in Palestine in the pre-Christian era, except for the pharisaic and possibly sadducean circles. Certainly in Qumran such a standard text is not recognizable at a time when the concept of a standard text must have been in existence for centuries in the circles which produced MT.

The earliest evidence for the existence of a standard text is connected with the early copies of MT, or as they are usually named, the proto-Masoretic texts, as known mainly from Qumran from the period of the mid-third century BCE until the mid-first century CE. Further copies of the proto-Masoretic text are known from other places in the Judean Desert: Masada (evidence preceding 73 CE) and Naḥal Ḥever and Wadi Murabbaʿat (evidence preceding 135 CE). These copies differ little from each other and from the medieval text of MT with regard to the latter's consonantal text. The very existence of many copies closely related to each other must point to the existence of a textual family consisting of closely related copies. This assumption is strengthened

[21] These efforts started with Erasmus in the sixteenth century.

[22] Van der Woude (1992), 167–168 addresses this issue when claiming that this situation was possible only "as long as there was an authoritative body within his – i.e., the believer's – circle which, besides Scripture, decides on doctrine and life".

by the fact that the great majority of the Qumran texts (some 60 percent according to our calculation) reflect this proto-Masoretic text, a situation which leads one to believe that these texts, which were probably brought from outside to Qumran, were more numerous in Israel than other texts. Thus while a textual variety is clearly visible in the Qumran finds, beyond that variety one discerns the existence of a single textual family which probably reflected the standard text of the Pharisees.

The Qumran evidence from the third pre-Christian century onwards leads us to believe that from that period onwards there existed an entity that may be named the proto-Masoretic text family. That was a tight family, in a way a standard text for a certain group in Judaism. But we do not know from which time onwards the proto-Masoretic text family constituted such a standard. Nor do we know much about the origin of that family. One can only conjecture on the origin of the proto-Masoretic text family since there is no evidence which points clearly in any one direction. An elucidation of the origin of MT must involve an analysis of its nature. As a rule, the scribes treated MT with reverence, and they did not alter its orthography and morphology as did the scribes of the Sam. Pent. and of many of the Qumran scrolls. Since MT contains a carefully transmitted text, which is well-documented in a large number of copies, and since it is reflected in the rabbinic literature as well as in the Targumim and many of the Jewish-Greek revisions, it may be surmised that it originated in the spiritual and authoritative center of Judaism (that of the Pharisees?), possibly in the temple circles. It was probably the temple scribes who were entrusted with the copying and preserving of MT. Though this assumption cannot be proven, it is supported by the fact that the temple employed correctors (מגיהים, *maggihim*) who scrutinized certain scrolls on its behalf. It is further supported by the existence of a *sefer haʿazarah* (a book of the temple court). The fact that all the texts found at Masada (dating until 73 CE) reflect MT is also important.

But there is a snag in this description. While on the one hand it is claimed that those involved in the transmission of MT did not insert any change in MT and as a result its inconsistency in spelling as well as its mistakes have been preserved for posterity, on the other hand, there never existed any one single text that could be named *the* (proto-)Masoretic Text. In fact, at a certain stage there was a *group* of Masoretic texts and obviously this situation requires a more precise formulation. Although at one time an attempt was made not to insert any changes in MT, at that time the texts within the group of Masoretic texts already differed internally one from another. In other words, although there indeed existed the express wish not to insert any changes in the Masoretic texts, the reality was in fact paradoxically different, since the texts of the MT group themselves already differed one from the other. There thus existed a strong desire for textual unity and standardization, but this desire could not erase the differences already existing between the texts. The wish to preserve a unified textual tradition thus remained an abstract ideal which could not be accomplished in reality.[23] More-

[23] Thus especially M. COHEN, "h'ydy'h bdbr qdwšt hnwsḥ l'wtywtyw wbyqwrt hṭksṭ", *Deoth* 47 (1978) 83–101, reproduced in: *The Bible and Us* (ed. U. Simon; Heb.; Tel Aviv 1979) 42–69.

over, despite the scribes' meticulous care, changes, corrections, and mistakes were added to the internal differences already existing between the members of the MT group.

Because of the meticulous care of those who were involved in the copying of MT, the range of the differences between the members of the MT group was from the outset very small. One should remember that the temple employed professional *maggihim*, "correctors" or "revisers", whose task it was to safeguard precision in the writing and transmission of the text: "*Maggihim* of books in Jerusalem received their fees from the temple funds" (*b. Ketub.* 106 a). The Talmud also uses the term *sefer muggah*, "a corrected/revised scroll": "and when you teach your son, teach him from a corrected scroll" (*b. Pesaḥ.* 112 a). Likewise one finds the term *sefer še-'êno muggah*, "a book that is not corrected" (*b. Ketub.* 19 b). Furthermore, it is not impossible that an effort was made to limit the range of differences between early texts for a Talmudic tradition reports on the limiting of the differences between three specific texts by comparing their readings in each individual instance of disagreement. Apparently this was done in order to compose from them one single copy which would reflect the majority readings (the agreement of two sources against the third one). Although such a procedure seems to be the implication of the *baraita* to be quoted below, the procedures followed are not sufficiently clear.

Three scrolls of the Law were found in the temple court. These were the *ma'on* ("dwelling") scroll, the *za'ᵃṭuṭê* ("litte ones") scroll, and the *hy'* scroll. In one of these scrolls they found written, "The eternal God is your dwelling place (מעון, *ma'on*)" (Deut 33:27 where MT reads מענה). And in two of the scrolls it was written, "The eternal God is your dwelling place (*mᵉ'onah* ‹that is, referring to מעונ›)". They adopted the reading found in the two and discarded the other. In one of them they found written, "He sent the little ones (*za'ᵃṭuṭê*) of the sons of Israel" (Exod 24:5). And in the two it was written, "He sent young men (*na'ᵃrê*) of the sons of Israel". They adopted the two and discarded the other. In one of them they found written הוא, *hw'* (= הִוא), nine times, and in two, they found it written היא, *hy'*, eleven times. They adopted the reading found in the two and discarded the other (*y. Ta'an.* 4:68a).[24]

Scribal activity involving the correction of the base manuscript of MT according to another source seems also to be at the base of the omission of some words in MT indicated in the Masorah with the so-called "extraordinary points" (see TCHB, 55–57).

The meticulous care taken in the transmission of MT is also reflected in the words of R. Ishmael: "My son, be careful, because your work is the work of heaven; should you omit (even) one letter or add (even) one letter, the whole world would be destroyed" (*b. Soṭ.* 20 a). This precision even pertained to matters of orthography, since various *halakhot*, "religious instructions", were, as it were, fixed on the basis of the exact spelling of words. For example, the number of the walls of the *sukkah* (four) is determined according to the spelling סֻכֹּת (*b. Sukk.* 6 b), thus excluding a spelling סוכות with five letters.[25] Some of the examples of this type actually were formulated in a later period.

---

[24] For a thorough analysis of this tradition, see S. TALMON, "The Three Scrolls of the Law That Were Found in the Temple Court", Textus 2 (1962) 14–27.

The processes described above show the meticulous care taken in the textual transmission. At the same time, it is not clear whether we should actually speak about a process of standardization, and certainly not of stabilization. Both of these terms imply active involvement in textual activity according to modern critical principles. In actual fact we only know that the processes and procedures such as described above produced a stable or standard text, but that text may have been created by careful transmission rather than by a conscious standardization or stabilization.

It is not known to what extent the existence of this standard text influenced the approach to the Bible in non-textual issues. As mentioned above, some of the *halakhot* were determined on the basis of exact spelling of words in the Bible which would have been created only with the existence of a standard text. In other words, the existence of a standard text of MT, seems to have been a *conditio sine qua non* for the development of the type of halakhic interpretation such as found in the Talmud. This seems to be logical for some elements of that exegesis, but not for all. For most components of the biblical exegesis reflected in the Talmud and midrash the dependence on a standard text is not a necessary precondition. By the same token, the Qumran *pesharim* do not presuppose such a standard text, which has indeed not been instituted by the Qumran community. As mentioned above, in the name of VAN DER WOUDE (n. 22), believing communities often developed their ideas and literature without a standard text.

In Israel of the last three centuries BCE and the first century CE textual uniformity and pluriformity coexisted, as pointed out by VAN DER WOUDE (1992): pluriformity relating to different textual traditions in all of Israel, and uniformity (relating to the Masoretic family) in the temple circles (Pharisees). There is no evidence concerning the situation before the third century BCE. At that time many different textual traditions were in vogue, but whether at the same time a standard text was used within the temple circles is not known.

After the destruction of the Second Temple the sole texts to be used by Jewish communities were the proto-Masoretic texts, so that at that time the existence of a standard text for the proto-Masoretic textual family was carried over to the text of the Bible as a whole. This stability was not achieved by any change of approach in Judaism, but by the fact that no Jewish communities had survived which carried a rival biblical text, such as was the case in the previous centuries. Since the central stream in Judaism was already used to a standard text, the new situation did not herald a new approach to the text of the Bible.

---

[25] For further examples, see Y. Y. YELIN, *Hdqdwq kystwd bhlkh* (Jerusalem 1973) 336–356.

2.2. The Significance of a Fixed Canon of the Hebrew Bible

By John Barton, Oxford

Bibliography: P. R. Ackroyd, "The Chronicler as Exegete", *JSOT* 2 (1977) 2–32; idem, "Original Text and Canonical Text", *USQR* 32 (1977) 166–73; G. W. Anderson, "Canonical and Non-canonical", CHB I (ed. P. R. Ackroyd/C. F. Evans; Cambridge 1970) 113–59; J. Barr, *Holy Scripture: Canon, Authority, Criticism* (Oxford/Philadelphia 1983); J. Barton, *Oracles of God: Perceptions of Ancient Prophecy in Israel after the Exile* (London 1986; New York 1988); idem, *People of the Book? The Authority of the Bible in Christianity* (London 1988; [2]1993); R. T. Beckwith, *The Old Testament Canon of the New Testament Church* (London/Grand Rapids, MI 1985); J. Blenkinsopp, *Prophecy and Canon: A Contribution to the Study of Jewish Origins* (Notre Dame, IN 1977); B. S. Childs, "The Exegetical Significance of Canon for the Study of the Old Testament", VTSup 29 (1978) 66–80; idem, *Introduction to the Old Testament as Scripture* (Philadelphia/London 1979); E. E. Ellis, *The Old Testament in Early Christianity: Canon and Interpretation in the Light of Modern Research* (WUNT 54; Tübingen 1991); M. Fishbane, *Biblical Interpretation in Ancient Israel* (Oxford 1985); D. N. Freedman, "Canon of the OT", IDBSup (Nashville, TN 1976); idem, "The Formation of the Canon of the Old Testament", *Religion and Law* (ed. E. B. Firmage et al.; Winona Lake, MI 1990) 315–31; M. Haran, "Problems of the Canonization of Scripture", *Tarbiz* 25 (1956) 245–71; idem, "Archives, Libraries, and the Order of the Biblical Books", *Comparative Studies in Honor of Yochanan Muffs* (*JANES* 22, 1993) 51–61; H. Hübner, "Vetus Testamentum et Vetus Testamentum in Novo receptum. Die Frage nach dem Kanon des Alten Testaments aus neutestamentlicher Sicht", *Zum Problem des biblischen Kanons* (JBTh 3; 1988) 147–62; E. Jacob, "Principe canonique et formation de l'Ancien Testament", VTSup 28 (1975) 101–22; J.- D. Kaestli/O. Wermelinger (eds.), *Le canon de l'Ancien Testament. Sa formation et son histoire* (Geneva 1984); P. Katz, "The Old Testament Canon in Palestine and Alexandria", *ZNW* (1956) 191–217; S. Z. Leiman (ed.), *The Canon and Masorah of the Hebrew Bible: An Introductory Reader* (New York 1974); idem, *The Canonization of Hebrew Scripture: The Talmudic and Midrashic Evidence* (Hamden, CT 1976); G. Maier, *Der Kanon der Bibel* (Gießen 1990); J. Maier, "Zur Frage des biblischen Kanons im Frühjudentum im Licht der Qumranfunde", *Zum Problem des biblischen Kanons* (JBTh 3; 1988) 135–46; R. A. Mason, *Preaching the Tradition: Homily and Hermeneutics after the Exile* (Cambridge 1990); D. Monshouwer, "The Reading of the Bible in the Synagogue in the First Century", *Bijdragen* 51 (1990) 68–84; M.- J. Mulder (ed.), *Mikra: Text, Translation, Reading and Interpretation of the Hebrew Bible in Ancient Judaism and Early Christianity* (CRINT II/1; Assen/Philadelphia 1988); R. C. Newman, "The Council of Jamnia and the Old Testament Canon", *WTJ* 38 (1976) 319–49; R. H. Pfeiffer, "The Canon of the Old Testament", IDB I (Nashville, TN 1965) 510–11; M. Sæbø, "Vom 'Zusammendenken' zum Kanon: Aspekte der traditionsgeschichtlichen Endstadien des Alten Testaments", *Zum Problem des biblischen Kanons* (JBTh 3; 1988) 115–33; A. J. Saldarini, *Kanon: von den Anfängen bis zum Fragmentum Muratorianum* (HDG I; Freiburg 1974); J. A. Sanders, *Torah and Canon* (Philadelphia 1972, [2]1976); idem, "Adaptable for Life: the Nature and Function of Canon", *Magnalia Dei: the Mighty Acts of God* (New York 1976) 531–60; idem, "Text and Canon: Old Testament and New", *Mélanges Dominique Barthélemy. Études bibliques* (OBO 38, ed. P. Casetti/O. Keel/A. Schenker; Fribourg/Göttingen 1981) 373–94; N. M. Sarna, "The Order of the Books", *Studies in Jewish Bibliography, History and Literature in Honor of I. Edward Kiev* (ed. C. Berlin; New York 1971) 407–13; G. Stemberger, "Jabne und der Kanon", *Zum Problem des biblischen Kanons* (JBTh 3; 1988) 163–74; A. C. Sundberg, *The Old Testament of the*

Early Church (Cambridge, MA/London 1964); idem, "The 'Old Testament': a Christian Canon", *CBQ* 30 (1968) 143–55; G. Vermes, "Bible and Midrash: Early Old Testament Exegesis", CHB I 199–231; J. Weingreen, "Oral Torah and Written Records", *Holy Book and Holy Tradition* (ed. F. F. Bruce/E. G. Rupp; Manchester 1968) 54–67.

1. The Concept of Canon and the Question of Date

The term 'canon' is part of the standard vocabulary of religious discourse in Christianity and, to a considerable extent, in Judaism. It denotes a number of the following ideas about Scripture: that its limits have been fixed, either by God himself or by competent religious authorities; that all the books within it are divinely inspired, authoritative, and edifying; that the books form a unity among themselves, are mutually consistent or mutually illuminating; that there are no generic differences among the different books; that scriptural books are to be interpreted differently from other books.

Many of these various implications of calling Scripture 'canonical', while compatible, could exist in isolation from the others. For example, it would be logically possible to think that a book was divinely inspired without supposing that no other books could be, or to revere particular books without thinking that their holiness required special kinds of interpretation. But in practice 'canonicity' tends to be a loose concept, in which such distinctions are not drawn or are not sharply in focus. There is now a wealth of literature about the formation of the canon of the Hebrew Bible, but it has tended to be bedevilled by a failure to define the concept of 'canonicity' with which this or that scholar is operating. As a consequence, although there are many real disagreements among scholars, there are also times when they seem rather to be at cross-purposes. Indeed, both agreements and disagreements are sometimes more apparent than real. This problem has a direct bearing on the significance of the canon for interpretation.

On the face of it there is agreement among scholars on only one matter concerning the canonization of the Hebrew Scriptures: that the present threefold division into Law (*tōrâh*), Prophets (*nbî'îm*) and Writings (*ktûbîm*) provides a rough guide to the *relative* date at which these collections were regarded as 'canonical scripture'. The Law was already a fixed entity at the time when the later books of the Prophets were still being composed, and the Prophets were complete at the time when the last of the Writings were taking shape. It is commonly suggested, for example, that Daniel failed to become one of the prophetic books in the Hebrew canon (whereas it is so in the Greek) simply because the Hebrew prophetic canon was already closed.

Now it is initially puzzling that such a simple consensus turns out to conceal very wide divergences of opinion, once we move from relative to *absolute* dating. For example, Leiman[1] argues that the whole Bible must have been complete ('closed') by about 150 BCE, that is, not long after the composition of Daniel, while Vermes[2] pushes this back by a further fifty years, claiming that Daniel was added to a collection all of whose other contents were agreed by 200

[1] Leiman, Canonization (1976).

[2] Vermes, Bible and Midrash (1970) 199–231.

BCE. So far as the Law and the Prophets are concerned, it is possible to go back still further and hold, with FREEDMAN[3], that both collections were compiled and canonized soon after the return from Exile – say about 500 BCE; and LEIMAN tends to concur with this, arguing that Chronicles would have been added to the Prophets (since it is similar in genre to the Deuteronomistic History or 'Former Prophets') if it could have been. Hence the Prophets were 'closed' before Chronicles was written (perhaps as early as the beginning of the fifth century BCE).[4]

At the other extreme, SUNDBERG[5] argued that in the first century CE the Writings were still open. This, in his view, is the only satisfactory way of explaining the difference between the Hebrew Bible and the Old Testament canon of the Greek Bible. The longer Greek selection of books is not evidence, as was once thought, for an 'Alexandrian' Jewish canon of Scripture which existed in parallel with the shorter Hebrew canon of Palestinian Jews.[6] Rather, the third division of the canon was still 'open' throughout the first (and possibly into the second) century CE, and Jews and Christians made different selections from the considerable corpus of 'holy books' available in Hebrew and Greek. The Greek (LXX) canon never had a Jewish existence, but is a Christian list from the beginning, even though of course all the individual books in it are Jewish in origin. Equally, there was never a time (until the Reformation!) when Christians recognized only the shorter Hebrew list which Jews now share with Protestant Christians, despite Jerome's attempts to argue for excluding the 'Greek' books. This means that the canon did not exist in any of the forms we know it until a century or more into the Christian era.

The present writer has sought to extend SUNDBERG's argument a little further, and to argue that even the Prophets did not yet form a closed canon in New Testament times.[7] The separate Christian and Jewish decisions about canonization did not, after all, affect only the contents of the biblical text, but also its ordering. The Greek canon does include Daniel among the Prophets, and inserts the Hebrew wisdom books (augmented by the addition of Sirach and the Wisdom of Solomon) between the 'Former' and 'Latter' Prophets. So it might seem reasonable, following SUNDBERG's argument to its logical conclusion, to say that what was 'closed' around the turn of the era was the Torah; the rest was still fluid.

Thus there is a potential disagreement about the fixing of the canon involving a difference of as much as four or five centuries for some sections. This could hardly fail to have implications for the interpretation of the scriptural texts. The 'lower' dating for the Prophets and Writings preferred by SUNDBERG, for example, would mean that canonicity, or the existence of a fixed canon, could have had no significance in respect of those books until well into the Christian era. On the other hand, if LEIMAN and VERMES are right, it was already a highly significant factor for much of the Second Temple period. How people interpreted at least Pentateuchal and Prophetic texts, and quite possibly those in the Writings too, is likely to have been influenced considerably by their canonical status. One example for many might be the interpretation of Jer 25:11 in Dan 9:1–2, 24. Jeremiah is here being treated as

---

[3] Freedman, Canon of the OT (1976).

[4] Leiman, Canonization (1976) 28.

[5] Sundberg, Old Testament of the Early Church (1964); idem, The 'Old Testament' (1968) 143–55.

[6] The 'Alexandrian canon' hypothesis goes back to Francis Lee in the early eighteenth century: see J. E. GRABE/F. LEE, *Vetus Testamentum iuxta LXX interpretes* II (Oxford 1719; chap. 1, §§ 75–7). There is a straightforward account of it in Pfeiffer, The Canon of the Old Testament (1965) 510–11. See also Katz, The Old Testament Canon (1956) 191–217.

[7] Barton, Oracles (1986/1988) 35–95.

a holy book of prophecy, and it is precisely because it is authoritative that its prediction of a (no more than) seventy-year exile is a problem.

However, as already suggested, at least some of the disagreement here can be traced back to different understandings of what it is for texts to be 'canonical'. The crucial element is the question of *closure.* Some scholars regularly use 'canonical' of any texts that are regarded by a community as authoritative: thus LEIMAN defines a canonical book as "a book accepted by Jews as authoritative for religious practice and/or doctrine, and whose authority is binding upon the Jewish people for all generations".[8] For SUNDBERG, on the other hand, canonicity has to do with inclusion in a list – this is indeed probably the original sense of *kanon.*[9] A 'canon' is thus by definition a way of setting *limits* to the books recognized as holy. Lists may, indeed, be lengthened; but the question whether or not a book is on the list matters. In SUNDBERG's terminology, there were many holy books in the first century CE, which constituted "a wide religious literature without definite bounds".[10] Though at least some of them were every bit authoritative enough to be what LEIMAN calls 'canonical', from SUNDBERG's point of view they constituted 'scripture' but not yet 'canon'. The point may be put simply by saying that books are scriptural if they deserve reverence and are not merely ephemeral: *at least* such books ought to be studied and treated as sacred. But for books to be canonical some authority must have decided that these books and no more (*at most* these books) are scriptural. The establishment of a canon does not merely recognize some books, it excludes others.

Once this distinction is recognized, there is clearly more common ground between proponents of an early and a late canon than at first appears. SUNDBERG, a proponent of a 'late' canon, never denied that many of the books now in both Hebrew and Greek canons had possessed an authoritative status from very early times. Indeed, he would have stressed that the Pentateuch, and certain other texts such as Isaiah or the Psalms, did not owe their authority to a formal decision to venerate them. If they were not 'canonized', that was not because people questioned their authority, but because it was so obvious as not to need any official endorsement. This means that many such books were indeed 'canonical' *in LEIMAN's sense* as early as he and other supporters of an 'early' canon argue. Conversely, it would probably be agreed by many who believe in early 'canonization' that there was as yet little sense of exclusiveness about the collections of holy texts available even as late as the first century BCE. Even if they still wish to speak of the Prophets, for example, being 'closed' by this period, such scholars would not mean to imply that Scripture as a whole had by this time acquired hard edges – only that particular *collections* of scriptural books were already in some sense finished.

On the other hand, scholars of both types are agreed that Hebrew Scripture did eventually become 'canonical' in the exclusive sense, particular books

---

[8] Leiman, Canonization (1976) 14.

[9] See Anderson, Canonical and Non-canonical (1970) 113–59.

[10] Sundberg, Old Testament of the Early Church (1964) 102.

being treated as different in kind from the general run of human writings. Differences remain, but the edges of the two opposing points of view are softer than they seem.

To speak of the significance of a *fixed* canon implies, strictly speaking, that we are using the 'exclusive' model of canonicity. Only when an exclusive list of books has been agreed can there be said to be a 'fixed canon'. But in practice the distinction is blurred in most scholarly writing about the growth of Scripture, where 'canon' tends to mean the generally accepted corpus of holy books that was widely regarded as authoritative and whose authority put that of other, less widely accepted writings in the shade. By the first century CE there is not much doubt which books formed the core of this 'canon': more or less the books that are now in the Hebrew Bible. There may have been a little doubt about a few of them, such as the Song of Songs and Ecclesiastes. *M. Yadaim* 3:5 reports that some authorities denied that these two books could 'defile the hands', and some scholars think that 'defiling the hands' is synonymous with 'being canonical' – LEIMAN, in fact, takes this for granted. But it is not obvious that this is so. The disputes may well have been literally about the treatment to be accorded to these two books, considered as physical objects; and the question may have arisen precisely because of the high ('canonical') status they were agreed to have, which apparently conflicted with some other characteristic we can no longer identify. (One possibility is that these were the only two scriptural books which did not contain the tetragrammaton.)[11]

On the other hand, a few books now reckoned deutero-canonical, apocryphal, or even pseudepigraphical may have enjoyed a status they subsequently lost in Judaism. The Wisdom of Solomon and 1 Enoch may be examples of the latter category. But it was not an open question for anyone whether Genesis or Isaiah had religious authority, or whether some much more recent book should be accorded an equal status with them. In that sense the canon was, if not literally 'fixed', then at any rate stable. Nevertheless, the distinction between 'inclusive' and 'exclusive' canonicity is a useful one, because it points us to two different kinds of effect or implication that derive from the existence of a Scripture.

1.1. The first implication has to do with the value or importance of the texts that are being accorded 'canonical' or 'scriptural' status. Such works are perceived, not as human documents arising out of particular historical circumstances that simply happened to move an author to write in a certain way, but instead as divine oracles, deliberately created through the power of God and intended to provide spiritual nourishment to successive generations of his people. 'Scriptural' books contain no error, nothing accidental or casual, nothing irrelevant or meaningless. They are not to be read as any other books are read, but require their own special hermeneutic. This implication begins to operate as soon as a corpus of writings are regarded as 'scripture', irrespective of whether this is a closed or open class.

[11] See Barr, Holy Scripture (1983) 50–51; and Barton, Oracles (1986/1988) 68–72.

1.2. The second implication is likely to operate only when the canon has begun to be in some sense 'closed'. It has in turn two aspects. The first is a sense that the texts in the canon are a unique, and uniquely authoritative, compendium of the teachings of the religion to which they belong. Any thoughts or ideas that conflict with what is in this authoritative collection must be false. Secondly, and closely linked with this: all the writings that make up this unique Scripture must be consistent with each other. Since they are not an adventitious but a divinely ordained collection, they must create a harmony among themselves. Important truths may even follow from the way in which they are arranged: the *order* of the books, or their grouping into sections, may be seen as significant.

All these features can be detected in the way the Hebrew Bible was interpreted in the Second Temple period and in the first centuries of our era. They will be examined under the two headings just suggested.

2. Implications of the Growth of 'Scripture'

2.1. The recognition that certain books were 'Scripture' – not necessarily as part of an exclusively defined 'canon', but at least as belonging to a corpus of writing that ought to be revered – had as one consequence an expectation of meaningfulness and significance. By the end of the Second Temple period, it was not a serious option to read one of the 'core' holy books of Judaism as meaningless or incoherent, nor to think of its meaning as trivial or ephemeral. In both Jewish and early Christian interpreters we find an insistence that Scripture can contain no errors, and that any apparent error or self-contradiction must be a pointer to a more profound meaning.

Philo handles the Greek Bible in this way. For example, Ps 75:9 (LXX 74:9) says

ποτήριον ἐν χειρὶ κυρίου οἴνου ἀκράτου πλῆρες κεράσματος

"In the hand of the Lord there is a cup of unmixed wine, full of mixture". Philo takes the contradiction here to refer to an ambivalence in the 'powers' that govern the world. "The powers which God employs are unmixed in respect of himself, but mixed to created beings" (*quod deus immutabilis sit* 77–78). The particular interpretation here depends on Philo's own mystical theology; but any other interpreter of his day would have been equally certain that there was no *real* contradiction in the Psalm, and would have sought some solution to the difficulty.

It is said (*b. Shabb.* 30 b) that early Rabbis discussed the status of Proverbs, the problem being that it was felt to be self-contradictory. In due course they managed to resolve the contradictions and so save the book's place in Scripture. It is not known what the alleged contradictions were, though possibly 26:4–5 was one: "Answer not a fool according to his folly, lest you be like him yourself; answer a fool according to his folly, lest he be wise in his own eyes". If such disputes really occurred, we could interpret them in one of two ways. We might take them at face value, and say that contradictions were shown to be only apparent, and the scriptural status of the book was saved. But on the other hand we might say that a prior conviction on the part of some that Proverbs was divinely inspired – and therefore incapable of containing contradictions – led to its being read as satisfactorily self-consistent. It is very unlikely that readers in the Second Temple period really supposed any of their holy books to contain error or self-contradiction, for recognition of a text as holy implies a hermeneutical imperative: Read this book as consistent and true. At all events the report about Proverbs shows that canonicity and consistency were felt to go together.

The meaningfulness of the sacred texts did not reside only in the whole sense of large passages, but also in minute details of the verbal form. Pressing precise details of wording in the quest for meaning is, in many cultures, a mark of the interpretation of 'official' or authoritative texts over against more everyday writings. Sacred and legal texts are the two sorts of text commonly subjected to such interpretation. Paul famously presses the wording of Gen 12:7 in Gal 3:16, where he argues that "the promises were made to Abraham and to his offspring. It does not say, 'And to offsprings', referring to many; but, referring to one, 'And to your offspring', which is Christ". In fact the word in Gen 12:7 (*zarʿô*, 'his seed') would normally be taken to imply many descendants; but whether or not Paul knew that, he is not unusual in treating the grammatical form of the word as bearing a theological significance. This helps to undergird something of which he is convinced on other grounds anyway, namely that Christ is the inheritor of the promises to Abraham. Non-Christian Jews would have disputed his interpretation in this case, but the *manner* of argumentation was not in itself controversial.

Paul also supplies an example of the hermeneutical insistence that biblical texts are not trivial, but deal always with weighty matters. In 1 Cor 9:9 he cites Deut 25:4, "You shall not muzzle an ox when it treads out the grain". This might be hailed today as a rare ancient example of a recognition of the rights of animals; but Paul takes it for granted that God is not particularly interested in oxen. This makes the law *prima facie* trivial. The principle that there is no triviality in Scripture requires the interpreter to find a 'deeper' or 'higher' meaning in terms of *human* rights, and conveniently allows Paul to argue that the right of ministers of the gospel to be paid by their converts is grounded in the Torah.

None of these examples of exegesis would be found in the case of non-'canonical' texts: it is the texts' authoritative status that both enables and requires them. At the same time as such interpretations are explained by the canonical status of the biblical books cited, so they are in turn evidence for that status. Where we find interpreters proceeding in this way, we can be sure that the books they are interpreting were seen as holy texts.

2.2. A second feature of sacred texts in most cultures is that they are assumed to be relevant to the concerns of the reader. Perhaps this is true of all texts that are regarded as 'classics': a classic is, precisely, a text whose significance is not exhausted by what it had to say to its original audience, but which goes on illuminating each successive generation. All the books now in the Hebrew canon had this kind of status for the Judaism of their day.

The historical books of the Hebrew Bible, for instance, were treated as collections of what in the Middle Ages would be known as *exempla* – stories with a moral. They held up models of good or bad conduct for, respectively, imitation or avoidance; they promised rewards or punishments to those who acted in one way or the other. The biblical characters were seen as typical of various human virtues or vices.

This process can already be seen at work, well before the canon was closed in any sense, by noticing how the laws and stories of the Pentateuch have been combined to produce *tôrah*. Just as the laws in the Pentateuch are to be obeyed, so the narratives too are to be consulted as sources of ethical guidance. The tales of Abraham or of the sons of Jacob may originally have been recorded to glorify great ancestors, to explain the origins of the nation, or even just for entertainment. But as part of the finished Pentateuch they have to be seen as guiding the reader through example, just as the laws guide him through admonition and exhortation. Only so can the books of Moses be read in a unitary way; and there is no doubt that they were so read in the Second Temple period. People read about Abraham to learn about the life of faithfulness to the covenant.

The same was true of the 'Former Prophets' (Joshua-Kings). As M. NOTH put it, "When this community preserved and maintained the ancient narrative tradition of the history of Israel along with [the Law], it was understood as a collection of historical examples of the attitude of man to the law and its consequences".[12] This is exactly how Chronicles already sees the history which its author is rewriting. As the prophet Azariah ben Oded says to Asa (2 Chr 15:2–7), "The LORD is with you, while you are with him. If you seek him, he will be found by you. For a long time Israel was without the true God, and without a teaching priest, and without law; but when in their distress they turned to the LORD, the God of Israel, and sought him, he was found by them".

This tradition of seeing the history of Israel as a collection of examples of good and bad conduct was thus rooted in the way earlier biblical material was treated in later biblical books, well before there was a formal 'canon'. It is clearly one of the interpretative procedures that is naturally adopted once stories from the past, originally told for their particularity, indeed for their *non*-typical character, come to be regarded as 'Scripture' and hence as having a universal meaning and importance. Treating them as *exempla* and looking for the 'moral' of the tale is one of the most obvious answers to the question "Why are we reading this story?" Josephus regularly treats characters in the biblical narrative as examples – most oddly, perhaps, the witch of Endor, whom he sees as an example of generosity and unselfishness (1 Sam 28; *Antiquities* 10. 260–2).

---

[12] M. NOTH, "The Laws in the Pentateuch: their Assumptions and Meaning", *The Laws in the Pentateuch and Other Essays* (Edinburgh/London 1966) 87; (from *Die Gesetze im Pentateuch. Ihre Voraussetzungen und ihr Sinn*, SKG.G 17; Halle 1940; repr. in idem, *Gesammelte Studien zum Alten Testament*, München ³1966, 9–141).

Thus particular narratives are generalized – interpreted so as to stress their general applicability. But this is not true only of the human conduct recorded in the histories, it applies equally to what the biblical accounts reveal about the nature of God. The scriptural status of these books meant that whatever they said about God had to be taken as having universal relevance. Anything true of God at one point in Israel's history must be true of him at all times. Thus the passage quoted above from 2 Chron 15 not only sets out how Israel should behave; it also derives from the older histories a picture of how God acts in response to Israel's conduct: "when [ever] in their distress they turned to the LORD, he was found by them". The general applicability of canonical texts means that from them one can discover truths about God valid in all generations. One common implication thought to be inherent in the existence of perennially relevant 'holy books' was a scheme for human history as directed or guided by God. Prophetic writings (and in the Second Temple period all the sacred writings tended to be seen as prophetic) were important because they outlined God's plans for the future of Israel and, indeed, of the world. They showed that he would act purposefully, justly, and in an ordered way. The book of Tobit, for example, already reads the prophetic scriptures in this way (Tob 14). And if prophetic scriptures were interpreted like this, that means they were being read with an eye to long-term or permanent applicability; which in turn means that they were at least incipiently 'canonical'.

But the relevance of sacred texts to the reader's own day may also have a different meaning from this. It may mean, not that sacred writers correctly perceived the whole sweep and shape of divine activity in history, but that they foretold quite specific events, and that these events are about to occur in the reader's lifetime.[13] Both at Qumran and in the early Church it was normal to take particular chapters or verses of biblical books and explain them as referring to events which were far distant for the writer, but either imminent or even already discernible for the community reading the text in the light of its own experience. Isaiah had spoken of "an acceptable time", a "day of salvation" (Isa 49:8); Paul can reveal that "now is the acceptable time ... now is the day of salvation" (2 Cor 6:2). If the texts Judaism had come to revere as its sacred books were still, indeed were supremely, of relevance to the new Christian community, that might be because these texts revealed very precisely the circumstances in which the first Christians were living.

The community at Qumran, *mutatis mutandis*, felt the same. 1 Peter sums up the matter (1 Pet 1:10–12): "The prophets who prophesied of the grace that was to be yours searched and inquired about this salvation ... It was revealed to them that they were serving not themselves but you, in the things which have now been announced to you by those who preached the good news to you". The Qumran Habakkuk commentary (1 QpHab) registers the same sense every time it takes a piece of the text and alleges that it really refers to events in the life of the Dead Sea community. Such ideas were

---

[13] For this distinction see Barton, Oracles (1986/1988) 214–26.

infinitely remote (as a modern reader would see it) from anything that could have been in the mind of the prophet, but entirely credible, of course, once it was granted that Habakkuk was no more than the mouthpiece for a divine prediction. The more 'strained' the interpretation, it may be said, the more 'canonical' the text being interpreted must have been – why should people trouble to extract improbable meanings from a text, unless that text is somehow a given for them?

This approach is sometimes called 'charismatic exegesis'.[14] It implies that the true meaning of Scripture is hidden except to those who have received a revelation of it – unlike readings that seek to show the relevance of Scripture by pointing to universal features of the text. Where the latter see the text's meaning as more general than the surface implies – e.g., Abraham stands for all who seek to obey God's call – charismatic exegesis sees it as more particular: Habakkuk was not talking generally about trends in future Jewish history, but about the Qumran community and its (very specific) troubles. Both approaches are united, however, in believing that the text has a meaning not exhausted by the circumstances of its own day: it is pregnant with future implications. This is a natural consequence of regarding the text as 'Scripture', and a confirmation for us that it was so regarded.

2.3. All the above represents the refusal to see anything contingent, time-bound, or (above all) trivial in texts that have a divine origin. A third aspect of this ascription of supreme value to Scripture is the belief that it contains *mysteries*. It is not surprising that texts like Ezek 1–2, the chariot-vision, should have been so interpreted, for on any showing it concerns a revelation to the prophet of more about the nature of God than had ever been known before. Even here, though, it would have been possible for the exegetical tradition to treat the text historically, as an account of an experience Ezekiel had happened to have, and which was not significant for anyone else: that, more or less, is how modern critical scholarship treats it. Instead, major exegetical currents in Judaism, which eventually produced the massive tradition of *merkabah* (chariot) mysticism,[15] saw Ezekiel's vision as something that could be replicated in the person who meditated on Ezekiel's description of it. The knowledge which Ezekiel had derived from his *vision* could be appropriated by people of later times by reflecting on the *text* in which that vision was described.

But this development was possible only because the idea that mysteries lay encoded in scriptural texts had become a commonplace of Second Temple Judaism. Philo regularly treats the essential core of scriptural teaching as the communication of divine mysteries. Though he was greatly influenced by Hellenistic mystagogy, he was not seriously out of step with the way biblical texts were interpreted by other Jews of his day. Taking seriously the scriptural ('canonical') status of these books meant turning to them for all important

[14] The phrase is used by D. Aune, *Prophecy in Early Christianity and the Ancient Mediterranean World* (Grand Rapids, MI 1983) 133.

[15] For a comprehensive guide to *merkabah* mysticism see C. Rowland, *The Open Heaven: A Study of Apocalyptic in Judaism and Early Christianity* (London 1982).

knowledge; that in turn encouraged an expectation that the knowledge they communicated was secret and divinely revealed, for Scriptures that communicated obvious or easily accessible information would hardly deserve the name.

We might say that Scripture as a whole began to function rather as 'wisdom literature' had functioned in earlier times, disclosing truths about 'the meaning of life' – but wisdom literature as produced in the post-exilic age, emphasizing the hiddenness of 'true' wisdom, not wisdom literature as seen in the aphorisms of Proverbs, where what is said is meant to be obvious to the sensible person. 'Wisdom' in the Second Temple period was often conceived of as the divinely given ability to plumb mysteries, as in Dan 2:20–1, where God is the one "to whom belong wisdom and might" ... who "reveals deep and mysterious things"; and one way in which he does so is through the Scriptures. Thus the non-triviality of canonical texts is construed to imply that they contain truth far above human imagination, but whose essence can be grasped by those to whom God reveals it.

A feature of particularly sacred texts is that meaning comes to be seen in aspects of the text that modern critical reading would regard as subsemantic. We have seen this already in the case of Paul's use of Gen 12:7. This is perhaps specially likely to be the case when readers are hunting for mysteries. One problem in rabbinic Judaism, which believed in the resurrection, was the paucity of references to any such thing within the Hebrew canon, and this generated considerable ingenuity in finding unpromising texts that could, none the less, be read as references to resurrection. A classic example in Ex 15:1, "Then Moses and the people of Israel sang this song to the LORD", where 'sang' represents a Hebrew *yiqtol* or imperfect form rather than a *qatal* (perfect). The Rabbis[16] regarded *yiqtol* as normally future in meaning, and argued that the text thus predicted that Moses and the people of Israel would in the future sing the Song of the Sea; in which case they must be meant to rise from the dead, otherwise they could not sing; and thus resurrection is proved from the Torah. One should not conclude from this that these exegetes did not realize that the verse was really a reference to the past (however the imperfect is to be explained). They saw *additional* possibilities of meaning in the strange syntax, possibilities which could be used to support an important doctrine. The capacity for many layers of meaning is one significant, perhaps indeed defining, characteristic of canonical Scripture. Mysteries lie encoded in its pages.

2.4. There is a fourth, and on face of it surprising, implication of canonicity. A community that acknowledges certain texts as 'scriptural' tends to be unwilling, or even unable, to read them as contradicting what it considers to be true or important. One might think that 'canonization' would imply that the texts being canonized took on a regulative function which they formerly lacked. Such is, perhaps, the Protestant theory of the subordination of the Church to the canon of Scripture, so that the Church's beliefs must be adjusted to bring them into line with Scripture. But this does not usually seem

[16] See for example *Mekilta,* ad loc.

to be how matters turn out in practice – not even in Protestant churches with a high doctrine of Scripture. For the most part religious communities interpret their Scriptures in the light of the doctrine and practice they have come, by custom and usage, to regard as correct. Thus any conflict there may be between Scripture and doctrine is masked, and is deprived of its power to threaten.

This can be seen very clearly in early rabbinic judgements, in the Mishnah for example. If a scriptural text appears to forbid what in rabbinic Judaism was not forbidden, or to command what is not part of Jewish practice, the solution is neither to change the custom nor to deny the canonicity of the text, but to *reinterpret* the text so that the conflict is removed. And the higher the status of the text, the more likely it is to be reinterpreted in this way. This in turn provides a test of whether a given text is canonical; if a text is treated in this way, then it is likely to have scriptural status. If the text were less authoritative, people would not bother to reinterpret it.[17]

3. Implications of the Closing of the Canon

All of the consequences of regarding certain texts as scriptural outlined so far are neutral with respect to the *closing* of the canon. They apply to any text which is sufficiently revered, and in some cases certainly operated before anyone had had the idea of excluding books from the category of 'Scripture'. For example, the way the Chronicler treats the narratives of Kings probably implies that he regarded Kings as an ancient and holy text, but few people would suggest that the Hebrew Bible was already a *closed* corpus in the Chronicler's day. We now turn to implications specifically of closure. As we have seen, there is wide disagreement about when the whole Bible, or the three divisions of it, became finished entities to which nothing might legitimately be added. But there are certain interpretative procedures that do seem to presuppose this kind of closure, and which can in turn serve as evidence for the advent of an 'exclusive' understanding of Scripture.

3.1. If by calling books canonical we mean that they are divinely sanctioned, and so have a high claim on the reader's attention, then the 'closure' of the canon must imply that *no other* books have this status. What is outside the canon is, comparatively, unimportant. A very early manifestation of this tendency can be seen in the 'decision' (or unconscious consensus) that only two blocks of narrative material belonged in the first two parts of the canon. The whole of history to the death of Moses has pride of place, being found in the Torah; and then the subsequent history from Joshua to the Exile forms the first half of the Prophets. There are thus two 'ages' in the history of Israel (or of the human race), and narrative accounts of any events that occurred after the second age have less than 'canonical' status.

---

[17] See Barton, People of the Book? ([2]1993) 19–20.

This position is modified by the work of the Chronicler and by the authors of Ezra and Nehemiah (who may or may not have belonged to the same school), who continue the post-exilic history into the Persian period. But, as Josephus rightly says in *Contra Apionem* 1.37–43, "From Artaxerxes to our own times the complete history has been written, but has not been deemed of equal credit with the earlier records". Josephus says that this is "because of the failure of the exact succession of prophets"; but that is his own interpretation, and has no 'official' status. The fact he is interpreting, however, is indeed a fact. Jewish historiography dealing with the period after Ezra and Nehemiah never became canonical, whereas entirely fictitious accounts of events allegedly before them often did: Daniel, for example, in the Hebrew Bible, Judith and Tobit in the Greek.

It should be observed that the principle of canonicity implied by Josephus uses the age of a document as the criterion for deciding whether it should be revered – its age, not its inclusion in, or exclusion from, an official list. There is no evidence that Judaism had any such a list in his day. Nevertheless there is a *principle* of closure at work here. It is no longer the case that absolutely anything could in principle have been a candidate for canonicity. When Christians decided that all canonical New Testament books must go back to an apostle or an associate of an apostle, they were applying a similar criterion to the one Josephus reports as the Jewish way of determining the Hebrew canon.

3.2. Once a sense developed that the canon – or the collections that would eventually come to form it – was a unity, then it would have to be susceptible of a unitary interpretation, much as an individual book would be. It is difficult to know how soon the idea developed that the Hebrew Bible was a single, unified 'work'. In the case of the Christian Bible this may have been facilitated by the use of the codex, from a comparatively early period. In a codex all the books of the Bible could appear between two covers. But Judaism did not adopt the codex for writing the Scriptures until much later – indeed, for the most solemn use of the Pentateuch, its liturgical reading, it has still not done so. The scroll was assumed by everyone in the Second Temple period, and well into the present era, to be the normal vehicle for a biblical book. A collection of individual scrolls obviously cannot form a coherent whole in quite the same way as the sections of a codex. One cannot guarantee that they will always be together; some collections might lack one or more of them, possibly even without this being realized; and cross-reference from one to another is far more difficult and laborious than in a codex. Nevertheless, once an author such as Josephus can be found asserting that the Scriptures consist of "only twenty-two books" (whichever exactly these were),[18] and "no-one has ventured either to add, or to remove, or alter a syllable" of them, and furthermore that this is a corpus of books which are not "inconsistent ... conflicting with each other", unlike the books of the Greek philosophers –

---

[18] Leiman, Canonization (1976), discusses fully the problem of reconciling Josephus's twenty-two books with the twenty-four of the Hebrew canon as we now have it. The question is whether there is a difference in the actual books involved, or merely in the way they are counted.

then it can fairly be said that internal consistency has become a salient feature of the canon and in principle a criterion for canonicity. Just as there can be no inconsistency within a scriptural book (see 2.1 above), so there can be none among the different books that comprise a closed canon.

Once again this criterion, which in principle sounds as if it would have made it possible to evaluate books that were candidates for inclusion in the canon, in practice probably operated as a hermeneutical imperative: Interpret all the canonical books as consistent with each other. It is possible that the disputes about whether certain books "defiled the hands" (*m. Yad.* 3:5) in the first century CE had a bearing on questions of canonicity (though see above). If so, then the reason why Ecclesiastes (Qoheleth) is one of the books about which there was disagreement could be the perception that this book challenges or even contradicts the teaching of other wisdom books (e.g. Proverbs) or of the Torah. But why should all the scriptural books say the same thing? The idea that they should seems to assume that they ought to form part of a coherent collection. So at least it might be argued.

It is striking that some of the most obvious examples of inconsistency in Scripture do not in fact seem to have worried readers in this period. No attempt was made, apparently, to reconcile Chronicles with Kings, and neither work was apparently of doubtful canonicity on this or any other account. Probably the concern for consistency was stronger in matters of halakah than of historical narrative. It is not surprising to find that in the first century CE there was a proposal to 'store away' (*gnz*) the book of Ezekiel – the exact meaning is uncertain, but at any rate it implies some uncertainty about its suitability for general circulation, even if not 'decanonization'. Hananiah b. Hezekiah is said to have consumed three hundred barrels of oil, sitting up into the night to reconcile it with the Torah, so successfully that the proposal was dropped.[19] Probably the difficulty concerned inconsistencies between Ezekiel and the Pentateuch on matters of the priesthood and the ordering of the cultus. These were areas in which Judaism could not tolerate divergent texts, whereas historical details perhaps mattered less. Certainly there is an assumption here that sacred texts will not conflict in areas of significance.

3.3. The division of the sacred books into the three categories of Law, Prophets, and Writings could be expected to have had some interpretative implications, though it is not easy to track them down. It has been argued[20] that the decision to make a decisive break between Deuteronomy and Joshua – the last book of the Torah and the first book of the Prophets – was not an arbitrary one, but was full of hermeneutical significance. Especially if there had once been a Hexateuch, which ended on a note of triumph with the conquest under Joshua, the Pentateuch as we now have it must have seemed quite a downbeat work: it ended with the death of Moses, who was allowed to see the land but not to enter it, and with the people of Israel still in Moab. One might see it as the Scripture of a people who had received great promises,

---

[19] *b. Shab.* 13b.

[20] See Sanders, Torah and Canon (1972).

but had not yet received them; in other words, a people in exile from their land. This might (extending the speculation further) make sense if the decision to have a Pentateuch and Former Prophets, rather than a Hexateuch plus a few 'histories', was made by the Jewish community in exile. It would also make sense if it was either made, or endorsed, by the post-exilic community, physically back in Jerusalem but 'spiritually' in exile because it no longer owned the land it inhabited. It would not be surprising if such an attitude continued through the long years of foreign domination, and was still present at the turn of the era; so that the very division of the Hebrew canon expressed a particular style of Jewish theology, a sense of being always *in via*, of never having arrived. For all its profundity, however, it is hard to find historical evidence of theological reflection on the division between Deuteronomy and Joshua. A more prosaic suggestion would be that the Pentateuch or Torah is to be seen as a complete collection of the works of Moses, and and accordingly ends with his death, just as the Psalms are the complete works of David.

The Prophets/Writings division is equally mysterious. To some extent the Writings are later works than the Prophets – later in point of composition (like Daniel) or in terms of their inclusion in the canon (Chronicles, perhaps). But this is certainly not the whole story. The Psalms, for example, are now usually thought to contain much pre-exilic material, and the same may very well be true of Proverbs. Nor is the distribution of books between Prophets and Writings a question of importance. The Psalms are far more central to Judaism than some of the Twelve Prophets or most of Kings. We may speculate that some message was being conveyed by assigning texts to the third rather than the second division of the canon. But none of the Jewish or Christian texts that use these works seem to throw any light on what this significance might be.

3.4. The use of scrolls for individual biblical books, rather than of the codex which became standard in Christian practice, means that in antiquity there was no strong sense that the books were arranged in a particular order. There is an obvious (chronological) sense in which Kings follows Samuel, or Exodus follows Genesis. But Proverbs 'follows' Psalms only if these books are written successively in a single document; so long as they are two separate scrolls, the idea of order has little meaning. Nevertheless, there were discussions about the order (*seder*) of the books of the Hebrew Bible in ancient times, and it is possible that the order was significant for their interpretation. The Talmud (*b. B. Bat.* 14 b–15 a) reports both a general consensus, and detailed points of disagreement, among rabbinic authorities as to the order of the books. Interestingly, its order does not correspond precisely to any other known to us. The order of the Latter Prophets is given as Jeremiah, Ezekiel, Isaiah, the Twelve. This unusual order is justified on the basis of the books' *content.* Kings (the last of the Former Prophets) ends, it is said, with words about destruction; Jeremiah speaks of destruction throughout; Ezekiel begins with destruction but moves on to promises of consolation; and Isaiah is pure consolation. Thus these books are seen as communicating an important theological message, about the way judgement is followed by mercy, and communicating it *through the order in which they are arranged.*

Such an argument certainly requires a fixed canon, in which it is known for certain which books are included; but ideally it also requires a consensus about the way the individual books are ordered within it. As it is, it is uncertain whether the Talmud is reasoning that we can learn the truth about God's way of dealing with Israel (viz. that judgement is always followed by mercy) from the very ordering of the Bible; or that because we know God's judgement is always followed by his mercy, we ought to order the canon in such a way as to bring this out. The former seems more convincing, but given the evident lack of an agreed order in antiquity, the latter is perhaps what the argument really amounts to. It remains unclear what purpose, other than such an interpretative one, the discussion of 'order' in the canon could have had in Judaism. The best suggestion is probably that of SARNA,[21] that there was some concern for the correct way to store scrolls in a bookroom. That, like library classifications today, could have implications for how the books were perceived and interpreted.

3.5. Questions such as the arrangement of scrolls in a library have not traditionally belonged to the study of the canon. But in fact physical aspects of books can be very important in assessing the degree of honour in which they were held, and how they were interpreted. A brief example will form our last point. Judaism developed a complex code of practice for copyists of biblical scrolls, culminating in the so-called 'Minor Tractate' of the Talmud, Sopherim, perhaps in the eighth century CE. Provision is made for preparing the writing-materials, ruling the page, and arranging the text. It is not known how early such practices are, but at least in one case, the writing of the divine name YHWH, there is manuscript evidence from early times. In some Qumran texts the Tetragrammaton is written in old Hebrew characters rather than in 'square script'; and rabbinic texts often attest the idea that it is the presence of the Name that makes a text holy. As so often in this article, we have to note here a certain reciprocity: it is in canonical texts that special care is taken over such matters as the Name; conversely, books in which the Name appears may have had a *prima facie* claim to canonical status. Applying special rules to the copying of Scripture does, however, presuppose an agreement about which books belong in Scripture, and thus in principle a closed canon, however much it may be wishful thinking to imagine that all Jewish communities in the Second Temple period had an exact knowledge of what the limits were, and could not have been deceived by a non-canonical book written in the 'correct' way.

The potential interpretative significance of a fixed canon is easy to see, and we have looked at some examples of it. But in practice there is much less evidence that Jews at the turn of the era believed in the closure of Scripture than there is for the existence of Scripture as such, and correspondingly it is a good deal harder to find examples where significance is accorded to the canon as a bounded corpus. Modern movements such as 'canonical criticism'[22]

---

21 Sarna, The Order of the Books (1971) 407–13; see also Haran, Archives (1993) 51–61.

22 See Childs, Introduction (1979); idem, *Old Testament Theology in a Canonical Context* (Philadelphia/London 1985); Sanders, Torah and Canon (^{2}1976); idem, Adaptable for Life

have sought to make the canonicity of Scripture – the codification of exactly these books – important for theological interpretation. This is an important line of argument in a modern theological context, but there are few signs that it was very significant in antiquity. The 'inclusive' sense of 'canon' mattered a great deal: scriptural, authoritative, in this sense 'canonical', books were interpreted very differently from profane ones. But the 'exclusive' idea of a canon – 'these books and no others' – seems weakly attested, and is a comparatively minor factor where interpretation is concerned. Reflection on the fact that particular books are *not* canonical, or on those that are as a kind of *maximum* that may be believed in or interpreted, seems on the whole alien to Judaism in ancient times. For the most part the canon was 'fixed' in the sense that there were certain books which no-one would doubt were in it, but not in the sense that all other books were known in advance to be definitely outside it. It was fixed, but not closed. The evidence of scriptural interpretation bears this out as strongly as do the occasional overt discussions of the issue in ancient writers.

(1976) 531–60; and compare the discussion in Sæbø, Vom "Zusammendenken" zum Kanon (1988) 115–33, for an assessment of how far this theological programme accords with what is known of the history of the formation of the canon.

2.3. The Interpretative Character and Significance of the Septuagint Version

By JOHN WILLIAM WEVERS, Toronto

Editions and texts: Z. ALI, *Three Rolls of the Early Septuaqint: Genesis and Deuteronomy: A photographic edition with preface, introduction and notes by* L. KOENEN (PTA 27; Bonn: Rudolf Habelt 1980); A. E. BROOKE/N. MCLEAN (and H. ST. J. THACKERAY, beginning with Vol. I, 4), *The Old Testament in Greek.* Parts I, II and III, 1 comprising *Genesis, Exodus, Leviticus, Numbers, Deuteronomy, Joshua, Judges and Ruth; I and II Samuel, I and II Kings, I and II Chronicles, I Esdras, Ezra-Nehemiah; Esther, Judith, Tobit* (Cambridge: Cambridge University Press 1906–1940); M. L. MARGOLIS, *The Book of Joshua in Greek* (Parts I–IV Paris: Paul Geuthner 1931; Part V Philadelphia: Annenberg Research Institute 1992); A. RAHLFS (ed.), *Septuaginta: id est Vetus Testamentum Graece iuxta LXX Interpretes* (Stuttgart: Privilegierte Württembergische Bibelanstalt 1935); *Septuaginta Vetus Testamentum Graecum: Auctoritate Academiae Scientiarum Gottingensis editum* (Göttingen: Vandenhoeck & Ruprecht 1931–): I. *Genesis* (ed. J. W. WEVERS, 1974); II, 1. *Exodus* (idem, 1991); II, 2. *Leviticus* (idem, 1986); III, 1. *Numeri* (idem, 1982); III, 2. *Deuteronomium* (idem, 1977); VIII, 1. *Esdrae liber 1* (ed. R. HANHART, 1974); VIII, 3. *Esther* (idem, 1966); VIII, 4. *Judith* (idem, 1979); VIII, 5. *Tobit* (idem, 1983); IX, 1. *Maccabaeorum liber I* (ed. W. KEPPLER, [2]1967); IX, 2. *Maccabaeorum liber II* (ed. R. HANHART, 1959); IX, 3. *Maccabaeorum liber III* (idem, 1960); X. *Psalmi cum Odis* (ed. A. RAHLFS, 1931); XI, 1. *Iob* (ed. J. ZIEGLER, 1982); XII, 1. *Sapientia Salomonis* (idem, 1962); XII, 2. *Sapientia Jesu Filii Sirach* (idem, 1965); XIII. *Duodecim Prophetae* (idem, 1943); XIV. *Isaias* (idem, 1939); XV. *Ieremias, Baruch, Threni, Epistulae Ieremiae* (idem, 1957); XVI, 1. *Ezechiel* (idem, 1952); XVI, 2. *Susanna, Daniel, Bel et Draco* (idem, 1954); E. TOV, *The Greek Minor Prophets Scrolls from Naḥal Ḥever (8 Ḥev XII gr)*, DJD VIII (Oxford: Clarenden Press 1990).

General introductions: N. FERNÁNDEZ MARCOS, *Introduccion a las Versiones Griegas de la Biblia* (TyE; Madrid 1979); M. HARL/G. DORIVAL/O. MUNNICH, *La Bible grecque des Septante: Du Judaïsme hellénistique au Christianisme ancien* (Paris: Éditions du Cerf 1988); S. JELLICOE, *The Septuaqint and Modern Study* (Oxford: Clarenden Press 1968).

Collections of essays: G. J. BROOKE/B. LINDARS, *Septuagint, Scrolls and Cognate Writings: Papers Presented to the International Symposium on the Septuagint and its Relations to the Dead Sea Scrolls and Other Writings* (SCS 33; Atlanta: Scholars Press 1992); P. CASETTI/O. KEEL/A. SCHENKER (eds.), Mélanges DOMINIQUE BARTHÉLEMY: *Études bibliques offertes à l'occasion de son 60e anniversaire* (OBO 38; Fribourg: Éditions universitaires/Göttingen: Vandenhoeck & Ruprecht 1981); C. E. COX (ed.), *VI Congress of the International Organization for Septuagint and Cognate Studies: Jerusalem 1986* (SCS 23; Atlanta: Scholars Press 1987); idem, *VII Congress of the International Organization for Septuagint and Cognate Studies: Leuven 1989* (SCS 31; Atlanta: Scholars Press 1991); N. FERNÁNDEZ MARCOS, *La Septuaginta en la Investigacion Comtemporanea: V Congreso de la IOSCS* (TyE; Madrid 1985); D. FRAENKEL/U. QUAST/J. W. WEVERS (eds.), *Studien zur Septuaginta – ROBERT HANHART zu Ehren; aus Anlaß seines 65. Geburtstages* (Göttingen: Vandenhoeck & Ruprecht 1990); M. HARL, *La Langue de Japhet: Quinze Études sur la Septante et le Grec des Chrétiens* (Paris: Les Éditions du Cerf 1992); S. JELLICOE (ed.), *Studies in the Septuagint: Origins, Recensions and Interpretations.* Selected Essays (New York: Ktav Publishing House 1974); G. J. NORTON/S. PISANO, *Tradition of the Text: Studies offered to* DOMINIQUE BARTHÉLEMY *in Celebration of his 70th Birthday* (OBO 109; Freiburg: Universitätsverlag/Göttingen: Vandenhoeck & Ruprecht 1991); A. PIETERSMA/C. COX, *De Septuaginta: Studies in honour of* JOHN WILLIAM WEVERS *on his sixty-fifth birthday* (Mississauga: Benben Publications 1984); J. SCHREINER (ed.), Wort,

Lied und Gottesspruch: *Beiträge zur Septuaginta. Festschrift für Joseph Ziegler* I (Würzburg: Echter Verlag 1972); I. Soisalon-Soininen, *Studien Zur Septuaginta-Syntax* (AASF, B 237; Helsinki: Suomalainen Tiedeakatemia 1987); J. Ziegler, *Sylloge: Gesammelte Aufsätze zur Septuaginta* (MSU 10; Göttingen: Vandenhoeck & Ruprecht 1971).

Text-critical studies: D. Barthélemy, *Critique textuelle de l'Ancien Testament.* 1. *Josué, Juges, Ruth, Samuel, Rois, Chroniques, Esdras, Néhémie, Esther;* 2. *Isaïe, Jérémie, Lamentations;* 3. *Ezéchiel, Daniel et les 12 Prophètes* (OBO 50/1-3; Fribourg: Éditions universitaries/Göttingen: Vandenhoeck & Ruprecht 1982, 1986, 1992); D. Barthélemy/J. Lust/E. Tov/D. W. Gooding, *The Story of David and Goliath: Textual and Literary Criticism* (OBO 73; Fribourg: Éditions universitaires/Göttingen: Vandenhoeck & Ruprecht 1986); W. R. Bodine, *The Greek Text of Judges: Recensional Developments* (HSM 23; Chico: Scholars Press 1980); R. Hanhart, *Text und Textgeschichte des 1. Esrabuches, ... des Buches Judith, ... des Buches Tobit* (MSU 12, 14, 17; Göttingen: Vandenhoeck & Ruprecht 1974, 1979, 1984); idem, *Zum Text des 2. und 3. Makkabäerbuches* (MSU 7; Göttingen: Vandenhoeck & Ruprecht 1961); J. G. Janzen, *Studies in the Text of Jeremiah* (HSM 6; Cambridge, MA: Harvard University Press 1973); A. Pietersma, *A Textual-Critical Study of Genesis Papyri 961 and 962, Chester Beatty Biblical Papyri IV and V* (ASP; Toronto: A. M. Hakkert 1977); S. Talmon, "The Textual Study of the Bible: A New Outlook", *Oumran and the History of the Biblical Text* (ed. F. M. Cross, Jr./S. Talmon; Cambridge, MA: Harvard University Press 1975) 321-400; E. Tov, *The Text-Critical Use of the Septuagint in Biblical Research* (Jerusalem Biblical Studies 2; Jerusalem: Simor 1981); J. C. Trebolle-Barrere, *Sálomón y Jeroboán: Historia de la recensión y redacción de 1 Reyes 2-12:14.* (Salamanca/Jerusalem: Universidad Pontificia 1980); A. van der Kooij, *Die alten Textzeugen des Jesajabuches: Ein Beitrag zur Textgeschichte des Alten Testaments* (OBO 35; Freiburg: Éditions universitaires/Göttingen: Vandenhoeck & Ruprecht 1981); P. Walters, *The Text of the Septuagint: Its Corruptions and their Emendation* (ed. D. W. Gooding; Cambridge: University Press 1973); J. W. Wevers, *Text History of the Greek Genesis, ... Exodus, ... Leviticus, ... Numbers, ... Deuteronomy* (MSU 11, 21, 19, 16, 13; Göttingen: Vandenhoeck Ruprecht 1974, 1992, 1985, 1982, 1978); J. Ziegler, *Beiträge zum griechischen Iob* (MSU 18; Göttingen: Vandenhoeck & Ruprecht 1985); idem, *Beiträge zur Jeremias-Septuaginta* (NAWG. PH 1958, Nr. 2; Göttingen: Vandenhoeck & Ruprecht 1958).

Selected bibliograpby: L. C. Allen, *The Greek Chronicles: The Relation of the Septuagint of I and II Chronicles to the Massoretic Text* (VTSup 25, 27; Leiden: E. J. Brill 1974); J. Barr, *The Typology of Literalism in Ancient Biblical Translations* (MSU 15; Göttingen: Vandenhoeck & Ruprecht 1979); D. Barthélemy, *Les Devanciers d'Aquila* (VTSup 10; Leiden: E. J. Brill 1963); E. Bickerman, "The Septuagint as a translation", *PAAJR* 28 (1959) 1-39. Reprinted in *Studies in Jewish and Christian History* (Leiden: E. J. Brill 1967) 167-201; S. P. Brock, "Aspects of Translation Technique in Antiquity", GRBS (1979) 69-87; idem, "The Phenomenon of the Septuagint", OTS 17 (1972) 11-36; J. R. Busto Saiz, *La traducción de Símaco en el libro de los Salmos* (TyE 22; Madrid: Instituto «Arias Montano» 1985); M. Cimosa, *Il vocabolario di preghiera nel Pentateuco greco dei LXX.* Quaderni di «Salesianum» 10 (Roma: Libraria Ateneo Salesiano 1985); J. Coste, "La première expérience de traduction biblique", *La Maison Dieu* 53 (1953), 56-88; C. Dogniez/M. Harl, *Le Deutéronome* (La Bible d'Alexandrie 5; Paris: Les Éditions du Cerf 1992); Z. Fraenkel, *Über den Einfluß der palästinischen Exegese auf die alexandrinische Hermeneutik* (Leipzig: J. A. Barth 1851); D. W. Gooding, "Problems of Text and Midrash in the Third Book of Reigns", Textus 7 (1969) 1-29; idem, *Relics of Ancient Exegesis: A Study of the Miscellanies in 3 Reigns 2* (SOTS 4; Cambridge: University Press 1976); idem, *The Account of the Tabernacle: Translation and Textual Problems of the Greek Exodus* (Cambridge: University Press 1959); P. Harlé/D. Pralon, *Le Lévitique* (La Bible d'Alexandrie 3; Paris: Éditions du Cerf 1988); M. Harl, *La Genèse* (La Bible d'Alexandrie 1; Paris: Éditions du Cerf 1986); H. Heater, *A Septuagint Translation Technique in the Book of Job* (CBQ Monograph Series 11; Washington DC: The Catholic Biblical Association of America 1982); A. Le Boulluec/P. Sandevoir, *L'Exode* (La Bible d'Alexandrie 2; Paris: Éditions du Cerf 1989); R. Le Déaut, "La Septante, un Targum?", *Études sur le Judaïsme Hellénistique.* Congrès de Strasbourg (1983), publié sous la direction de R. Kuntzmann et J. Schlosser (*Lectio Divina* 119; Paris: Éditions du Cerf 1984) 147-195; J. A. Lee, *A Lexical Study of the Septuagint Version of the Pentateuch* (SCS 14; Chico: Scholars Press 1983); O. Munnich, "Contribution à l'étude de la première révision de la Septante", ANRW II, 20/1; Berlin: De Gruyter 1987) 190-220; K. G. O'Connell, *The Theodotionic Revision of the Book of Exodus* (HSM 3; Cambridge, MA: Harvard University Press 1972); H. M. Orlinsky,

"The Septuagint as Holy Writ and the Philosophy of the Translators", *HUCA* 46 (1975) 89-114; L. Prijs, *Jüdische Tradition in der Septuaginta* (Leiden: E. J. Brill 1948); C. Rabin, "The Translation Process and the Character of the Septuagint", Textus 6 (1968) 1-26; A. Rahlfs, *Septuaginta-Studien* I-III (Göttingen: Vandenhoeck & Ruprecht ²1965); I. L. Seeligmann, "Probleemen en perspectieven in het Septuaginta-onderzoek", JEOL (1941) 359-390; idem, *The Septuagint Version of Isaiah: A discussion of its Problems* (Leiden: E. J. Brill 1948); J. D. Shenkel, *Chronology and Recensional Development in the Greek Text of Kings* (HSM 1; Cambridge, MA: Harvard University Press 1968); E. Tov, *The Septuagint Translation of Jeremiah and Baruch. A Discussion of an Early Revision of Jeremiah 29-52 and Baruch 1:1-3:8* (HSS 8; Missoula, MT: Scholars Press 1972); J. W. Wevers, *Notes on the Greek Text of Exodus* (SCS 30; Atlanta: Scholars Press 1990).

0. Terminology

The term 'Septuagint' has been used by scholars in three senses. In its broadest sense it refers to the Alexandrian canon, and included not only the Greek version of the Hebrew Scriptures, but also the so-called deuterocanonical books; these are 1 Esdras, Ecclesiasticus, Wisdom of Solomon, Judith, Tobit, Baruch, Epistle of Jeremiah, and the books of the Maccabees. The historical relations between this canon and the Hebrew canon is complex and not at all clear; these texts will not be dealt with in this essay, nor will the problem be discussed.

The term is also used to include the translation of the Hebrew canon into Greek, and might better be called Old Greek (OG) to distinguish it from the third and original sense of the term, the translation of the Hebrew Torah into Greek in Alexandria in the first half of the third century BCE. Only in this third sense do we have historical information about its origin in the so-called Letter of Aristeas to Philocrates. The letter is apocryphal, an apologetic story created to defend the validity of the Greek Torah, probably to be dated cir. the middle of the second century BCE. The term "Septuagint", i.e. "70", probably refers to the 72 translators who according to this story came to Alexandria from Jerusalem at the request of Ptolemy Philadelphus to the Jerusalem high priest in order to translate the Hebrew Torah. The text used was a Palestinian copy of the Law which the 72 brought along with them. From internal evidence it is credible that the Septuagint originated in Alexandria and that it dates from the time suggested, but that it was based on a copy brought from Jerusalem and executed by translators, six from each of the twelve tribes of Israel, is pure propaganda meant to withstand Palestinian critics of a Greek Translation made in the diaspora. (For further discussion of the Letter see F. Siegert, below chapter 4.2.)

1. The Question of 'Interpretative Character'

The topic assigned this essay is the interpretative character and significance of the Septuagint Version, presumably for the understanding of the Hebrew Bible/Old Testament. It will be noted that its 'interpretative character' precedes its 'significance', which fact itself creates a problem of interpretation.

Does the significance of the Septuagint (hereafter LXX) flow from its interpretative character? If that is the case, the use to which the LXX has chiefly been put by students of the Hebrew Bible since the days of Reuchlin at the beginning of the 16th Century[1] and continuing down to the present[2] has in the main misrepresented this significance. The LXX has principally been used to emend the Hebrew text, particularly in places where the text is difficult to understand. By retroversion from Greek into Hebrew scholars have proposed changes to the Hebrew text on the understanding that the Masoretic Text (MT) has been corrupted from a presumed original 'pure' text.

1.1. It is of course obvious that speaking of the interpretative character of a translation presupposes a text which is being translated. But MT itself was the end result of a long process of development, a development which continued some centuries beyond the translation of the Hebrew Scriptures into Greek. In other words, the textual form of the parent text of the various books of OG is considerably earlier than the consonantal text of MT, and at times is clearly divergent from it.

What then does 'interpretative character' mean? It is a truism that any translation is an interpretation, but surely the term must mean more than that. To put the question bluntly, does the term refer to the interpretation by OG of its parent text, or to its relation to MT? Does the significance of the Greek version lie chiefly in its value in reconstructing an earlier (or at least another) text than that of MT?

1.2. This raises a further question: What is this presumed original text of the Hebrew? Was there ever such a text, i.e. precisely where in the long history of the development of an ancient text, a text rooted in oral traditions and gradually evolving and in its evolution being copied with the inevitable lure of human error; is this the text which is being reconstructed? Is it not preferable to consider both OG and MT canonical texts in their own right? In that case OG would serve as another, and at times earlier, text interesting for its own sake.

2. Differences in Length of Some Hebrew and Greek Texts

2.1. That the text of OG was at times quite different from our MT is clear.

The Greek book of Esther is over twice the length of its Hebrew counterpart. The story has been amplified by six lengthy additions, usually dubbed A through F. The A text precedes 1:1 and relates the dream by which God led Mordecai to a favored position in the court. Since 3:12–13 refer to a letter sent by Artaxerxes throughout the empire ordering the destruction of

---

[1] His *De Rudimentis Linguae Hebraicae* which appeared in 1506 made it possible for Western Scholars to compare the LXX with the Hebrew text.

[2] Early works using LXX extensively for the interpretation of the Hebrew text include A. Masius, *Josuae imperatoris historia illustrata atque explicata* (1574), J. Drusius, *In Psalmos Davidis veterum interpretum quae extant fragmenta* (1581), and his *Veterum interpretum graecorum in totum VT fragmenta* (1622), L. Capellus, *Critica sacra* (1651), I. Vossius, *De LXX interpretibus* (1661–1663), and J. Morinus, *Exercitationum biblicarum de hebraei graecique textus sinceritata* (1669).

the Jews, Section B details this letter. At the end of ch. 4 Section C presents the prayers of Mordecai and Esther. D relates Esther's approach to the king. The subsequent letter of the king to the Jews throughout the empire ordering them not only to defend themselves but actually to go on the offensive is given in E after 8:12. The Greek text ends with Section F recounting Mordecai's testimony to God's protection of his people and its institutionalized memorial in the feast of Purim.

These long pluses are haggadic amplifications of the story, but they also change the book from a secular story to one in which God's direction of world affairs to the benefit of his people is emphasized; in fact, only in Section B is God not referred to. It is obvious that the Greek extended version made it easier to regard the book as a canonical text.

2.2. By contrast the Greek Text is at times considerably shorter than MT. The Greek Job is only five sixths the length of the Hebrew text.

The poetic material from 3:1–42:8 consists of 2200 strophes in the Ziegler text, of which 383 are secondary, i.e. added by Origen from the first century revision by Theodotion. It might be noted that of these 383 strophes 318 are concentrated in chapters 21–42. This bizarre conflate text became the ecclesiastical text used by the church; in fact, it is attested in all extant witnesses except the Sahidic version which has omitted all the strophes under the asterisk, the sign which marked the Origenian additions in his Hexapla. Origen tried to repair the shorter text by filling in the lacunae, but unfortunately this resulted at times in a bizarre and barely comprehensible text. After all, the styles of the two renderings were completely different. One example should suffice. At 28:3–9 the OG has (a) τάξιν ἔθετο σκότει· (b) οἱ ἐπιλανθανόμενοι ὁδὸν δικαίαν ἠσθένησαν ἐκ βροτῶν· (c) κατέστρεψεν δὲ ἐκ ῥιζῶν ὄρη. "He has set order for darkness. Those who have forgotten the right way have been weakened by reason of (their) mortality, and he overturned mountains by (their) roots". Then the ecclesiastical text has inserted between (a) and (b) a literal rendering of vv. 3b–4a and between (b) and (c) a word for word translation of vv. 5–9a. Just what the three clauses of OG were supposed to communicate to a reader may not be all that clear, but Origen's insertions from Theodotion made that which was not clear something totally opaque.

On the other hand, most scholars are agreed that the shorter text of OG was not based on a shorter parent text, but that the translator himself tried to present an abridged text for the Greek reader, particularly in the second half of the book. The shorter text should then not be used for text critical purposes.

2.3. The Greek Jeremiah is also much shorter than MT, but here the reason is textual. Furthermore, the materials are presented in a different order;[3] the oracles against the nations (chs. 46–51 in MT) have been rearranged and placed between 25:13 and 15,[4] i.e. these oracles are placed in the middle of the book on the analogy of Isaiah and Ezekiel. The abridgement of text is also considerable; approximately one-eighth to one-nineth of the Hebrew text has no counterpart in OG.[5] That this shorter text was based on a Hebrew parent text is now certain in view of Qumran text 4QJer[b] which basically represents this same shorter text. Most scholars believe that this text was an earlier and superior form of the Hebrew Jeremiah, and therefore the textual witness of OG Jeremiah is of primary importance.

---

[3] For the details on the reordering see the tables on p. 147 of the Ziegler text.

[4] V. 14 is absent in the Greek.

[5] For a recent discussion of the problem see J. G. Janzen, *Studies in the Text of Jeremiah* (HSM 6; Cambridge MA: Harvard University Press 1973).

3. Different Translators and Recensions

3.0. It has long been known that the four books of Reigns, which constitute the Greek translation of 1–2 Samuel and 1–2 Kings, is not the product of a single translator. Already in 1906 THACKERAY had noted that sections βγ (2 Sam 11:2-1 Kgs 2:11) and γδ (1 Kgs 22:1–2 Kgs 25) were the work of a translator other than that of the rest of the Sam-Kgs complex.[6] This remained a puzzling fact until the discovery of the Nahal Hever Minor Prophets Scroll. It was clear that this text, likely copied in the late first century BCE,[7] was an extensive revision of the OG text. The scroll was sufficiently extensive to enable BARTHÉLEMY[8] to describe this text as a careful recension of OG based on the Hebrew (a Hebrew almost identical with the consonantal text of MT). The regular rendering of וגם/גם by καίγε in the Minor Prophets Scroll, usually rendered in OG simply by καί, was also characteristic of sections βγ and γδ of Reigns (= Sam–Kgs), and the term *kaige recension* was soon used regularly to designate texts in the Greek OT which followed this practice.

But BARTHÉLEMY also found other recensional traits in the text of the Scroll: the replacement of ἕκαστος by ἀνήρ for איש; the rendering of מעל by ἐπάνωθεν/ἀπάνωθεν rather than by ἀπό or ἐπάνω; the translation of יצב - נצב by στηλόω to agree with the usual equivalent of στήλη - מצבה; the distinction of שופר and חצצרה, both rendered by σάλπιγξ in OG, but in the recension by κερατίνη and σάλπιγξ resp.; the elimination of the historical present in favor of a past tense; the intemporality of the particle אין, i.e. instances in which OG used οὐκ ἦν were changed to οὐκ ἔστιν; the rendering of אנכי by ἐγώ εἰμι so as to distinguish it from אני - ἐγώ, even where the presence of εἰμι created nonsense Greek, and the rendering of לקראת by εἰς συνάντησιν or εἰς ἀπαντήν. By these criteria sections βγ and γδ of Reigns were classified as part of the *kaige* group as well.

3.1. Meanwhile other books of the Greek OT were also seen to show some of these same characteristics, and the net was extended to include the B text of Judges, Ruth, Canticles, Lamentations, and the work of Theodotion, as well as the Quinta revision cited by some of the early Church Fathers.[9]

3.2. This Palestinian recensional activity was stimulated by the rabbinic insistence on closer literal translations, and was particularly influenced by the exegetical methods of the School of Hillel, though it must be said that not all scholars find this influence compelling.[10] Other scholars have studied the B text of Judges,[11] the Theodotion text of Exodus,[12] as well as that of Joshua,[13] and have in turn added new characteristics to this group. In fact, the list has now grown to 96![14] It must be stressed that not all of these 96

[6] H. ST. J. THACKERAY, «The Greek Translators of the Four Books of Kings», *JTS* 9 (1906–07) 262–278.

[7] See P. J. PARSONS, «The Script and their Date», in E. Tov's official edition of the scroll, 19–26.

[8] In his *Les Devanciers d'Aquila.*

[9] Notably Justin, Origen and Jerome.

[10] E. g. O. Munnich (see Bibliography).

[11] W. Bodine.

[12] K. O'Connell.

[13] L. J. GREENSPOON, *Textual Studies in the Book of Joshua* (HSM 28; Chico CA: Scholars Press 1983).

[14] Ibid., 270–276.

are convincing. E.g. thirty of these are to be found in the Theodotion text of Exodus; most of them are technical terms connected with the tabernacle account. Their designation as characteristic of the *kaige* group begs the question; all that is certain is that they are used in the pluses attributed to Theodotion in Exodus.

This *kaige* group is not a single recension, but was rather part of a Palestinian trend towards revising at least parts of OG in the direction of MT.[15] This tendency became more and more compelling and culminated in the revision of Aquila in the second century CE, a revision in which the demands of the source language far outweigh those of the target language, in fact to such an extent that it could only be understood by a reader equally at home in both languages. Ecclesiastes, the Greek translation of Qoheleth, is almost certainly the product of Aquila.

3.3. Another factor that must not be overlooked is the poor state of the Hebrew text of Samuel. The discovery of substantial fragments of the Sam text at Qumran has produced texts which are at times closer to OG than to MT, texts which can sometimes be used to repair the bad state of MT. This in turn gives the Greek text of Sam a great deal of textual value.

3.4. The Greek translation of 1 and 2 Kings presents quite a different problem. In a number of places doublet accounts dealing with the reigns of Solomon, Jeroboam I, Jehoshaphat and Joram ben Ahab occur. In ch. 2 of 3 Reigns (= MT 1 Kings) two such accounts dealing with Solomon's reign obtain. Vv. 35 a–k is an amalgam of materials illustrating Solomon's wisdom with respect to his building activities. It corrects any impression which OG gave that Solomon might not have finished building the temple before engaging on his own house, his wife's dwelling, and a number of cities. A second doublet occurs to illustrate his wisdom in the conduct of his reign at vv. 46 a–l. Gooding in a detailed study of these two accounts[16] considers them the midrashic product of early Jewish exegesis emphasizing Solomon's wisdom. Similar doublets obtain at 3 Reigns 12:24 a–z, 16:28 a–h as well as at 4 Reigns 1:18 a–d.

The reign of Jehoshaphat is also doubly related, but in much briefer fashion. The doublet occurs in 3 Reigns 16:28 a–h; this parallels that of 1 Kgs 22:41–51. Presumably it was retold in ch. 16 so as to precede the account of the reign of Ahab over the ten tribes. A similar impulse explains the virtual repetition of the account of Joram's reign in 2 Kgs 3:1–3 at 4 Reigns 1:18 a–d. Joram's reign followed the two year reign of his brother, Ochoziou; the archival summary of his reign and his death are recorded in 1:17–18. The doublet account from 3:1–3 records the succession here as well.

---

[15] See the writer's «Barthélemy and Proto-Septuagint Studies», *BIOSC* 21 (1988) 23–34, especially the concluding paragraph.

[16] D.W. Gooding, Relics of Ancient Exegesis.

4. Different Groups of Renderings

By now it will be clear that general statements on the interpretative character of the Septuagint need a great deal of propaedeutic investigation of the particular texts which served as parent texts for the translators. When OG differs considerably from MT this could theoretically be due to the translator's freedom in the translation process, i. e. the translator might simply be putting the general content of the source language into the target language, and therefore very little if anything can be inferred about the exact nature of the parent text.

It must then be accepted as a truism that the texts of OG and LXX have textual significance, i. e. they can at times help one reach an earlier, and at times better, form of the Hebrew text than MT, an understanding that has long been taken for granted in the history of scholarship,

4.1. It is now also fully clear that the terms OG and LXX not only include different translations and translators, but also different conceptions of what the translation process consists of.

This process of translating a substantial document into the Greek language was highly unusual, if not unique, when it was first attempted by the Jews of Alexandria; the first translators (i. e. of the Pentateuch) had to proceed on an ad hoc basis. How should one translate a Semitic document into Greek?[17] Did the fact that what was being translated was a holy book, a canonical text, make any difference to the art of translation?[18] It must not be forgotten that these translators had no patterns to follow. Not that the phenomenon of translation had not obtained prior to the LXX translation, but Sumerian texts into Akkadian or Pali translations of the Buddhist Scriptures were certainly unknown to the Alexandrians. In fact, there is no extant evidence of any translated materials into the Greek language as early as the early third century BCE in Egypt, or for that matter elsewhere in the Hellenistic world.

How then should the translators proceed? Later in the Roman period translation from Greek into Latin was a common-place.[19] In Classical times two types of translations were common: literary texts which were rendered into Latin in paraphrastic fashion on the one hand, and translations of legal, governmental and commercial texts on the other, which were rendered word for word. Cicero spoke scornfully of such translations as *interpretes indiserti*, whereas his own translating was done *ut orator*, i.e. he was an *expositor*, not an *interpres*. Jerome apparently approved of the *expositor*, speaking of Cicero's rendering *sensus de sensu* rather than *verbum e*

[17] For a discussion of these grammatical categories for the two languages and their translation equivalences see the discussion in J. W. Wevers, "The Use of Versions for Text Criticism: The Septuagint", *La Septuaginta en la Investigacion Contemporanea (V Congreso de la IOSCS*; editado por N. Fernández Marcos; TyE, Madrid 1985) 15–24, but especially 15–19.

[18] See J. W. Wevers, "Translation and Canonicity: A Study in the Narrative Portions of the Greek Exodus", *Scripta Signa Vocis:* Studies about Scripts, Scriptures, Scribes and Languages in the Near East presented to J. H. Hospers by his pupils, colleagues and friends (ed. H. L. Vanstiphout/K. Jongeling/F. Leemhuis/G. D. Reinink; Groningen: E. Forsten 1986) 295–303.

[19] For this section see the articles of S. P. Brock, To Revise or not to Revise, and The Phenomenon of the Septuagint, as well as J. Barr, *The Typology of Literalism in Ancient Biblical Translations* (see Bibliography).

verbo with approval, and insisting that he himself normally translated *de sensu* with the single exception of the Scriptures, which he translated literally.[20]

It might be argued that LXX translators were in the main *oratores* rather than *interpretes*. Even in relatively free renderings there are cases of literal renderings, often side by side with free ones. Thus Prov 1:12 reads נבלעם כשאול חיים ותמימים כיורדי בור "Let us swallow them alive like Sheol, wholly like those who descend into the Pit". The first line becomes καταπίωμεν δὲ αὐτὸν ὥσπερ ᾅδης ζῶντα. Except for the singular pronoun αὐτόν and the change in word order this renders the Hebrew adequately. The second line, however, reads καὶ ἄρωμεν αὐτοῦ τὴν μνήμην ἐκ γῆς "And let us remove his memory from the earth". The second stich has completely abandoned the figure of swallowing whole those going down into the Pit.

In fact, one can distinguish OG translations as ranging from free, at times paraphrastic, translations to the slavishly literal. In the former the demands of the target language will override those of the source language. In such cases the stress is on the *signifiant* rather than on the *signifié* to use a happy distinction coined by F. DE SAUSSURE.[21] By contrast the literal accents the *signifié*, i. e. the demands of the source language are made paramount.

4.1.1. The distinction can best be seen from a few examples. The Greek Job is often quite different from MT. At 20:2–4 MT reads לכן שעפי ישיבני ובעבור חושי בי מוסר כלמתי אשמע ורוח מבינתי יענני הזאת ידעתי מני עד מני שים אדם עלי ארץ "Therefore any anxious thoughts give me answer, and because (of this) my excitement is with me. A reproof which insults me I hear, and the spirit of my understanding makes me give answer: 'Do you know this from of old, from (the time that) mankind was put upon the earth?'" OG has only three stichs: οὐχ οὕτως ὑπελάμβανον ἀντερεῖν σε ταῦτα, καὶ οὐχὶ συνίετε μᾶλλον ἢ καὶ ἐγώ· ἀφ' οὗ ἐτέθη ἄνθρωπος ἐπὶ τῆς γῆς "Not thus was I thinking that you would gainsay these things. And don't you understand better than I do: From where was man placed on the earth?" In spite of the condensation of the text the Hebrew source is apparent; the translator has rendered the text without attempting to imitate the grammatical structure of the parent Hebrew.

The Greek Proverbs also often renders its Hebrew counterpart in free fashion. At 11:25 נפש ברכה תדשן ומרוה גם הוא יורא (for יורה) "A prosperous person will become wealthier, and one who waters will himself be watered". OG has ψυχὴ εὐλογουμένη πᾶσα ἁπλῆ ἀνὴρ δὲ θυμώδης οὐκ εὐσχήμων "A blessed person is fully straightforward, but a man of passion is not a gentleman". Regardless of the difficulty of the second stich[22] it is clear that the Greek does not translate the Hebrew text.

At 23:27–28 MT reads כי שוחה עמקה זונה ובאר צרה נכריה אף היא כחתף תארב ובוגדים באדם תוסף "A harlot is a deep pit, and a deep well is an adulteress; indeed she lies in ambush like a robber (?), and the deceitful among mankind she increases". The Greek reads πίθος γὰρ τετρημένος ἐστὶν ἀλλότριος οἶκος καὶ φρέαρ στένον ἀλλότριον· οὗτος γὰρ συντόμως ἀπολεῖται καὶ πᾶς παράνομος ἀναλωθήσεται "For a perforated cask is a strange house, even a strange narrow well; for this one will perish straightaway and every transgressor shall be destroyed". Again the translator has abandoned the Hebrew proverb in favor of an analogous Greek one,[23] and has also added a moral application, an assurance that such evildoers will die.

---

20 That one should take this distinction with a grain of salt is clear from J. W. WEVERS, "The Attitude of the Greek Translator of Deuteronomy towards his Parent Text", *Beiträge zur alttestamentlichen Theologie:* Festschrift für WALTHER ZIMMERLI zum 70. Geburtstag (ed. H. Donner/R. Hanhart/R. Smend; Göttingen: Vandenhoeck & Ruprecht 1978) 498–505 in which the styles of the Vulgate and LXX of the opening verses of Deuteronomy are contrasted. The rendering of Jerome is hardly *verbum e verbo*!

21 In his *Cours de Linguistique Générale* (Paris: Payot 1916).

22 For v. 25b LAGARDE says "da grundtext und übersetzung verderbt sind". P. DE LAGARDE, *Anmerkungen zur griechischen Übersetzung der Proverbien* (Leipzig: F. A. Brockhaus 1863) 38.

23 The phrase πίθος τετρημένος is, according to LAGARDE, found in Aristotle and quoted by Erasmus, ibid. 75.

Or note the difference between the Hebrew and the Greek at v. 31 b. Referring to wine and its dangers MT has כי יתן בכוס עינו יתהלך במישרים "for its sparkle (עינו) is in the cup; it goes down smoothly". Once again the Greek interprets for a Greek speaking audience with its ἐὰν γὰρ εἰς τὰς φιάλας καὶ τὰ ποτήρια δῷς τοὺς ὀφθαλμούς σου, ὕστερον περιπατεῖς γυμνότερος ὑπέρου "for if you gaze (literally, put your eyes) into goblets and cups you will afterwards walk about more naked than a pestle".[24]

Translations which are free can be used for text critical purposes only with much caution. The translation may partially reflect the Hebrew as in the case of the last example where δῷς τοὺς ὀφθαλμούς σου is related to עינו, and εἰς τὰς φιάλας καὶ τὰ ποτήρια reflects בכוס, but it would be impossible to determine the exact form of the parent text. On the other hand, such translations are most useful for demonstrating how the translator understood the text.

4.1.2. At the other extreme is the work of Aquila, as e. g. in Ecclesiastes (= Qoh). Here the translator/reviser has tried to reproduce the structures of the original Hebrew by strict equivalences in the Greek, at times resulting in strange Greek.

This is well-illustrated by the well-known Aquila reading for Gen 1:1: ἐν κεφαλαίῳ ἔκτισεν θεὸς σὺν τὸν οὐρανὸν καὶ σὺν τὴν γῆν. Its character is immediately evident when it is contrasted with LXX: ἐν ἀρχῇ ἐποίησεν ὁ θεὸς τὸν οὐρανὸν καὶ τὴν γῆν. Instead of ἀρχῇ Aquila used ἐν κεφαλαίῳ, not because κεφαλαίῳ better reflected the meaning of ראשית, but because the root of the Hebrew word is ראש, for which he used the root κεφαλ-. The LXX's ἐποίησεν was rejected because this was reserved for עשה. The article before θεός was also abandoned because אלהים is not articulated, even though Greek usage normally articulated θεός. And finally, the two accusatives are preceded by σύν to reflect the את of the Hebrew. It has at times been defended as possible Greek by declaring σύν to be an adverb. Nonetheless it is highly unusual and a Greek reader who knew no Hebrew would make little sense out of Aquila's translation.

It is this kind of odd Hebraic Greek which is found in the OG of Qoheleth. Thus 8:17 a reads καὶ εἶδον σὺν τὰ ποιήματα τοῦ θεοῦ, ὅτι οὐ δυνήσεται ἄνθρωπος τοῦ εὑρεῖν σὺν τὸ ποίημα τὸ πεποιημένον ὑπὸ τὸν ἥλιον but this would be more intelligible in the MT form: וראיתי את כל מעשה האלהים כי לא יוכל האדם למצוא את המעשה אשר נעשה תחת השמש. The modifier of εἶδον is σύν – θεοῦ, the σύν reflecting את and מעשה necessarily being understood as plural in view of כל.

Note the use of ποιήματα rather than the more usual ἔργα of the Greek; Aquila reserved the root ποιε- for עשה, and consequently uses ποίημα for מעשה. Since האלהים is articulated, τοῦ θεοῦ is used. Within the object clause the verb δυνήσεται is future so as to reflect the prefix inflection of the verb יוכל, even though the present tense might well fit the intent of the Hebrew much better. Note that ἄνθρωπος is unarticulated, which does not reflect האדם; one can in view of Aquilanic literalness be fairly certain that the parent text read אדם. The complementary infinitive in MT is marked by ל, and this is reflected by the marker in OG as well, i. e. in τοῦ εὑρεῖν. Its modifier is again a σύν construction to reflect the Hebrew את, and τὸ ποίημα for המעשה is now singular because it has no כל modifying it. And finally note that the relative clause modifying it, אשר נעשה, has become τὸ πεποιημένον, the perfect passive participle reflecting the Niph'al perfect, the root ποιε- again being used for עשה.

---

[24] For further analysis of the Greek Proverbs see G. Gerleman, *Studies in the Septuagint* III. *Proverbs* (LUÅ N. F. Avd. 1. Bd. 52, Nr. 3; Lund: C. W. K. Gleerup 1956).

4.1.3. At 3.2. the *kaige group* was said to reflect exegetical tendencies towards revision whose literalness culminated in the work of Aquila. That Aquila was related to those tendencies is clear from Qoh 9:6a which reads καί γε ἀγάπη αὐτῶν καί γε μῖσος αὐτῶν καί γε ζῆλος αὐτῶν ἤδη ἀπώλετο. Its equivalent in MT is גם אהבתם גם שנאתם גם קנאתם כבר אבדה. The characteristic rendering of גם (or וגם) in the *kaige group* was καί γε, and Aquila adopts this throughout. Actually, it is quite likely that the Greek OT text that he revised was not OG but the text of Theodotion which also uses καί γε in this manner. It might be noted that the particle כבר occurs only in Qoheleth and is regularly rendered by ἤδη. Compare also the last line of v. 7: ὅτι ἤδη εὐδόκησεν ὁ θεὸς τὰ ποιήματά σου for כי כבר רצה האלהים את מעשיך. Though the modifier of the verb in MT is an את phrase, Aquila does not use σύν, which he omits whenewer the noun it governs has a pronominal suffix. But if the word כל intervenes, σύν is used, as e.g. at 2:18 σύν πάντα μόχθον μου for את כל עמלי. On the other hand, if the כל has the suffix Aquila also has no σύν; see 9:11 τοῖς πᾶσιν αὐτοῖς for את כלם.

Under Sect. 3 above it was noted that a number of books or parts of books were part of the *kaige group*. Two parts of the Sam-Kings complex, 2 Sam 11:2-1 Kgs 2:2 and 1 Kgs 22:1–2 Kgs, were identified as being part of this group. Both parts do indeed use καί γε extensively. In the first section καί γε occurs 26 times, and in all but two cases MT has either גם or וגם. The two cases, 14:6 and 18:27, have *waw* in MT. The second section has 18 instances of καί γε, and all but one, 10:18, represent גם or וגם.

To test the consistency of this membership one might note how אנכי is translated over against אני. Barthélemy had given ἐγώ εἰμι as calque for the long form of the pronoun as characteristic of this group as well. This is only problematic when it is also accompanied by a verb inflected in first person. In the first section this impossible Greek occurs 10 times; these are 12:7 ἐγώ εἰμι ἔχρισά σε and ἐγώ εἰμι ἐρρυσάμην σε; 13:28 ἐγώ εἰμι ἐντέλλομαι; 15:28 ἐγώ εἰμι στρατεύομαι; 18:12 ἐγώ εἰμι ἵστημι; 20:17 ἀκούω ἐγώ εἰμι; 24:17 ἐγώ εἰμι ἠδίκησα and ἐγώ εἰμι ... ἐκακοποίησα and 1 Kgs 2:2 ἐγώ εἰμι πορεύομαι. In each of these cases MT had an אנכי. In four of these the predicate was a participle. One case obtained in which ἐγώ was used to render the long form; at 14:18 ἐγὼ ἐπερωτῶ stood for אנכי שאל.

The second section has only four cases of καί γε, but one of these was modified by a predicate nominative (for a Hebrew nominal clause), ἄνθρωπος τοῦ θεοῦ ἐγώ εἰμι at 1:12, but MT does not have אנכי but אני. Only one case followed the expected pattern; at 4:13 אנכי ישבת is translated by ἐγώ εἰμι οικῶ. At 10:9 ἐγώ εἰμι συνεστράφην had אני קשרתי in MT, and similarly at 22:20 ἐγώ εἰμι ἐπάγω represented אני מביא. In v. 19, however, אנכי שמעתי occurs in MT, but the Greek has ἐγὼ ἤκουσα. It is obvious that these two sections, though both of the word for word type of translation, are not recensionally the same. It might also be noted that the second section, as a mark of considerable freedom, has a doublet account about Joram ben Ahab's reign at 1:18 a–d; cf. 3.4. above.

4.2. In contrast to the free translations (see 4.1.1.) literal, particularly slavishly literal, translations are useful for text critical purposes. Should האדם be rendered by ἄνθρωπος it is reasonable to assume that the parent text read אדם, i.e. without an article. It is conversely much more difficult to speak of the interpretative character of such translations, if all they do is reflect the Hebrew as precisely as possible – even to the extent of violating the rules of the Greek language.

5. The General Interpretative Character of Greek Pentateuch

By now it is obvious that it would be foolhardy to attempt to describe the interpretative character of such a diverse group of renderings as OG represents. In fact, it would only make sense to take each work separately and describe its character, a task far beyond the scope of this essay. Accordingly this essay will limit itself to LXX, i.e. to the Greek Pentateuch.

A discussion of the interpretative character of books of the Greek Pentateuch is based on four presuppositions, ones which have been outlined elsewhere.[25] The first one is obvious but relevant, viz. that the translators were aware that they were translating a canonical text, and so took their work very seriously. They were actually creating a canonical text, the word of God in Greek.[26] Secondly, it is presupposed that the parent text was in the main much like the consonantal text of MT. This is a reasonable assumption, and it suggests that textual criticism should only be based on textual evidence and not on emendations which originate in modern minds; only emendations which are acceptable to all reasonable minds should be proposed, and even then with hesitation. A third presupposition made is that the Alexandrian translators of the Pentateuch made sense. They did not produce gibberish, and when the modern reader has difficulty with their translation it is not the translator but the reader whose Greek is deficient. And finally, it is suggested that the Greek Pentateuch is a humanistic document of interest by and for itself, i.e. without reference to its parent text. It is not just a source for interesting emendations, but gives us an insight into the faith and attitudes of Alexandrian Jewry of the third century BCE.

6. The Specific Character of Genesis in the Septuagint

To illustrate how LXX constitutes an interpretation of the Hebrew Bible the remainder of this essay will deal only with the book of *Genesis*. Since individual translators may reflect individual ways of translating, or have individual approaches to a source text, such a limitation is sensible; it is based on the unproven but reasonable assumption that Greek Genesis is the work of a single translator. Furthermore, it is an equally reasonable but demonstrable assumption that the five books of the Greek Pentateuch reflect the work of at least five individuals.[27]

6.0. In contrast to Exodus the Greek Gen regularly translates ויהי "and it happened (that or when)" by καὶ ἐγένετο or ἐγένετο δέ. A good example is 27:30 καὶ ἐγένετο μετὰ τὸ παύσασθαι Ἰσαάκ ... καὶ ἐγένετο ὡς ἐξῆλθεν ... . LXX similarly renders והיה throughout Genesis by καὶ ἔσται except at 46:33

[25] In J.W. Wevers, *Notes on the Greek Text of Exodus* (SCS 30; Atlanta GA: Scholars Press 1990) xiv–xvi.

[26] See Aristeas 308–311.

[27] For a possible sixth translator see J.W. Wevers, *Text History of the Greek Exodus*, chapter 6 "The Composition of Exod 35 to 40", 117–146; see especially 145–146.

where for ויהי כי יקרא LXX simply has ἐὰν οὖν καλέσῃ. Also characteristic of LXX is its disregard of Masoretic vocalization of מצרים "Egypt" when a vocalization as "Egyptians" seemed sensible to the translator, e.g. 47:20 τὴν γῆν τῶν Αἰγυπτίων and οἱ Αἰγύπτιοι, both for מצרים "Egypt".

Both the tetragrammaton and אדני are rendered by κύριος, but אדני can refer either to God or to a human master. LXX keeps the renderings of the two names rigidly apart, however, by articulating κύριος when it represents אדני. In chapter 24 κύριος occurs 43 times, 19 of which represent יהוה, and κύριος is always unarticulated. The other 24 all refer to Abraam and κύριος is always articulated except at v. 18 where the vocative κύριε obtains, where an article would be inappropriate.

Occasionally Genesis can be distinguished from the rest of the Pentateuch. Thus παιδίσκη is generally used to render שפחה (e.g. at 16:1), but in the other books παιδίσκη is only used for אמה. Also characteristic of Genesis is the use of μετὰ σωτηρίας for לשלום/בשלום found at 26:31 28:21 44:17; in fact, it is unique in the entire OT. Elsewhere εἰρήνη is used.

6.0.1. Characteristic of Genesis is the translation of a number of proper nouns, mainly place names. Such translations are: Ur of the Chaldees as τῇ χώρᾳ Χαλδαίων at 11:28; cf also v. 31 and 15:7; Mamre and (land of) Moriah both as τὴν ὑψηλήν at 12:6 and 22:2 resp. based on a false etymology from רום; (towards the) Negeb as (ἐν) τῇ ἐρήμῳ at 12:9; cf also 13:1, 3; the Rephaim as γίγαντες possibly based on Josh 12:4 13:12, and see also Deut 3:11; Beersheba as τὸ φρέαρ τοῦ ὅρκου at 21:14 and as Φρέαρ ὁρκισμοῦ at v. 31; cf also 26:33; Gilead as Βουνὸς μάρτυς at 31:47 (taken as גל עד); Mizpah as (ἡ) ὅρασις at 31:48; Mehanaim becomes Παρεμβολαί at 32:2(3); Peniel is translated as Εἶδος θεοῦ at 32:30(31); Succoth becomes Σκηναί at 33:17; Kiriath Arba is rendered as πόλιν τοῦ πεδίου at 35:27, and On is realized as Ἡλίου πόλεως at 41:45.

6.1.0. One can only understand the translator as interpreter from such renderings which do not reflect the parent text exactly. One dominating characteristic of the Genesis translator is the tendency to level out or harmonize the text. Should a similar statement recur Genesis often disregards differences and repeats the earlier statement, i.e. does not retranslate. A few examples out of many will suffice to illustrate this common tendency. At 6:20 MT says: And they came in to him להחיות, for which LXX has τρέφεσθαι μετὰ σοῦ ἄρσεν καὶ θῆλυ. This is simply taken over from v. 19 for להחית אתך זכר ונקבה. At 7:2 MT refers to the animal pairs entering the ark as איש ואשתו, but LXX continues to use ἄρσεν καὶ θῆλυ throughout. At 7:13 MT has: And the three wives of his sons אתם, but LXX has μετ' αὐτοῦ, which harmonizes with the singular at 6:18 8:16, 18.

6.1.1. Such leveling sometimes takes place where the source is later, i.e. it is based on the translator's excellent knowledge of the Hebrew text. Thus at 8:7 MT simply has: And he sent out the raven, to which LXX adds τοῦ ἰδεῖν εἰ κεκόπασεν τὸ ὕδωρ. This reflects the longer text of v. 8 where MT has: And he sent out the dove from him לראות הקלו המים. At 24:4 LXX adds καὶ εἰς τὴν φυλήν μου after "you shall go to my land where I was born", which levels with the parallel in v. 38. Similarly at v. 14 after "and your camels I will water" LXX adds ἕως ἂν παύσωνται πίνουσαι, which reflects the עד אם כלו לשתת of v. 19. That this is based on the translator's knowledge of the Hebrew of v. 19 is clear, since that is rendered freely by ἕως ἂν πᾶσαι πίωσιν.

At 27:43 after ἀπόδραθι LXX added εἰς τὴν Μεσοποταμίαν, which reflects MT of 28:2: לך פדנה ארם. An interesting instance of leveling obtains at 30:5. Rachel has given her handmaid Balla to Jacob as wife "and she shall give birth on my knees and I shall produce children, even I, out of her". As a result v. 5 states that בלהה conceived and bore a son, to which LXX adds ἡ παιδίσκη Ῥαχήλ, which does occur in v. 7 for שפחת רחל; cf also vv. 3 and 4. It is, however, also important that it is as Rachel's handmaid that she consorts with Jacob. At 42:27 Joseph's brothers stopped at a lodging, and one of them opened his sack and saw את כספו, but the Greek has τὸν δεσμὸν τοῦ ἀργυρίου αὐτοῦ. Loose silver lying about in a sack is not overly practical, and LXX has leveled with v. 35 where each one found צרור כספו in his sack.

6.1.2. This same kind of leveling occurs based on parallel accounts. At 20:2 "Abraam said concerning Sarah ... (she) is my sister". MT continues with: "And Abimelech sent ... and took Sarah". In the parallel story of Isaak and Rebekka at 26:7 the reason for the deception is given as ἐφοβήθη γὰρ εἰπεῖν ὅτι Γυνή μού ἐστιν μήποτε ἀποκτείνωσιν αὐτὸν οἱ ἄνδρες (τοῦ τόπου περὶ Ῥεβέκκας). LXX has taken this over at 20:2 adapting the last part in parentheses as τῆς πόλεως δἰ αὐτήν.

At 21:19 Hagar saw a באר מים which LXX renders by φρέαρ ὕδατος ζῶντος. Wells are also referred to in ch. 26 and at v. 19 the well dug by Isaak is actually called a באר מים חיים – φρέαρ ὕδατος ζῶντος. And at 21:22 Abimelech and Picol the commander-in-chief of his army speak to Isaak. But LXX included after Abimelech καὶ Ὀχοζὰθ ὁ νυμφαγωγὸς αὐτοῦ (so too at v. 32b). This is simply lifted from the account at 26:26 where ואחזת מרעהו is one of the three who visit Isaak.

6.1.3. LXX tends to straighten out inconsistencies in the Hebrew text. Thus at 11:31 inconsistency of number creates some confusion: And יקח Terah ... ויצאו אתם ... ויבאו to Haran וישבו. Particularly unclear is the meaning of "and they went out with them". LXX makes a simpler and consistent narrative by making all verbs singular and translating אתם by αὐτούς. At 12:3, the first of the patriarchal promises, נברכו occurs. Is the Ni to be understood in a passive or a reflexive sense? The same problem occurs at 18:18 28:14, but at 22:18 26:4 the Hithp obtains. LXX decided for the passive throughout, and uses ἐνευλογηθήσονται, i. e. "they (the nations) shall be blessed". In the account of the three visiting Abraam in ch. 18 verbs relating to the visitors are at times in the plural and at times singular. LXX has created a reasonable pattern; except for v. 5 where simple concurrence to Abraam's proposal by the three is involved verbs involving dialogue are placed in the singular (there is only one who speaks), but wherever the visitors are physically concerned, i. e. in standing, resting, inclining, eating, the plural is used. MT lacks this consistency; cf v. 9. At 48:20 MT has an inconsistent text. It says: And he blessed them (i. e. Ephraim and Manasseh) in that day saying בך יברך Israel saying. The Masoretes have vocalized the verb as Pi, thus "Israel shall bless", but the real problem is the singular בך. LXX straightens it out by understanding the verb as a passive and changing the phrase to a plural ἐν ὑμῖν.

6.1.4. That the translator does not simply render the Hebrew in a word for word fashion, but thinks about the meaning of the text is clear from numerous instances in which he rationalizes the text.

At 2:3 MT has the rather difficult אשר ברא אלהים לעשות, but LXX has ὧν ἤρξατο ὁ θεὸς ποιῆσαι "which God had begun to do". Note that the words ברא אלהים reflect the beginning of the account; this was modified by בראשית – ἐν τῇ ἀρχῇ, and the use of ἤρξατο forms a type of inclusio pattern. After all, the word ברא also begins בראשית! At 4:26b MT has: Then invoking the name Yahweh was begun. But this is contradicted by Exod 3:14 6:3. LXX voided the contradiction by vocalizing הוחל as a Hi meaning "await, expect, hope for". Then instead of אז

he contextualized the statement by a pronoun referring to Enosh. LXX has οὗτος ἤλπισεν ἐπικαλεῖσθαι τὸ ὄνομα κυρίου τοῦ θεοῦ "this one hoped (but did not actually do so) to invoke the name of the Lord God".[28]

The Flood Story is also dealt with in independent fashion. At 7:11 LXX delays the start of the flood by ten days, i.e. "on the 27th of the month" rather than the 17th day of MT. The flood ended according to 8:14 exactly one year later, i.e. on the 27th day of the month as well. This must have been intentional. Then in v.13 Noah and his family enter the ark. V.15 reads ויבאו אל נח "they came in to Noah", the compound subject being given in v.14. But that compound subject begins with המה ו referring to Noah and his family. How could they come in to Noah when he and his family were already in the ark? LXX rationalized the text by omitting המה ו.

The Joseph story also shows numerous cases of rationalization of its text. At 40:3 Pharaoh put his two servants במשמר בית of the prison governor, which is then defined as "in prison". But the prison would hardly be the home of the governor, and LXX changes the collocation to ἐν φυλακῇ παρά "in custody with". At 45:6–7 Joseph is speaking to his brothers. At v.5 he had said that God had sent him on before you למחיה – εἰς ζωήν. Furthermore (v.6) this is the second year of famine בקרב הארץ. But the famine was not just within Egypt, it also covered Canaan, and LXX translates by ἐπὶ τῆς γῆς. V.7 continues with: And God sent me before you לשום לכם שארית בארץ, at best a difficult phrase: "to set for you a remnant in the land", which LXX interprets by ὑπολείπεσθαι ὑμῶν κατάλειμμα ἐπὶ τῆς γῆς. The prepositional phrase was also used in v.5, and this ties the two verses together; Joseph becomes "your remnant", i.e. your agent. Coordinate with the infinitival construction is a second difficult construction ולהחיות לכם לפליטה גדלה. This becomes καὶ ἐκθρέψαι ὑμῶν κατάλειψιν μεγάλην "and to nourish your large posterity". So Joseph is your agent in Egypt, and his efforts have prepared the way for the emerging possibility of an Israelite people in Egypt.

6.2.0. What appears as a somewhat difficult construction in Hebrew is at times simplified by LXX. E.g. at 18:19 the collocation כי ידעתיו למען אשר probably meaning "For I have designated him that he should" is much easier in LXX: ᾔδειν γὰρ ὅτι "For I know that (he will)". In the story of Lot's escape from Sodom MT says at 19:26: His wife looked מאחריו with its awkward masculine suffix. LXX smoothes out the text by its εἰς τὰ ὀπίσω. At 20:16 Abimelech ends his statement to Sarah with the difficult ואת כל ונכחת possibly meaning "and as to everything you are an upright woman". LXX is much simpler; by disregarding the conjunction and vocalizing נכחת as a verb the Greek becomes καὶ πάντα ἀλήθευσον "And speak the full truth", i.e. do tell the whole story!

At 24:10 Abraam's servant took ten camels from his master's camels וילך וכל טוב אדניו בידו, i.e. "and he went and all the goods of his master were in his hands", which fits badly into the context. LXX disregarded the verb and has καὶ ἀπὸ πάντων τῶν ἀγαθῶν τοῦ κυρίου αὐτοῦ μετ' ἑαυτοῦ; this makes excellent sense – he took all the provisions with him that he needed.

---

[28] This was suggested by M. Harl, Genesis, ad loc.

Jacob bargains for his wages at 30:33; about his proposal he says כי תבוא על שכרי לפניך. LXX's statement is much simpler: ὅτι ἐστὶν ὁ μισθός μου ἐνώπιόν σου "because my wages are before you", i.e. you can see them for yourself.

The Joseph story also shows evidence of an intelligent translator at work simplifying the story. At 42:25 Joseph gives instructions and the servants fill their bags ... and provide provisions for the journey ויעש להם כן. The singular verb is difficult; it seems to say that Joseph himself did all this thus for his brothers. LXX simplifies by: καὶ ἐγενήθη αὐτοῖς οὕτως. In 49:28 the narrator subscribes Jacob's blessing as איש אשר כברכתו. LXX has simplified the text by its (He blesssed them) ἕκαστον κατὰ τὴν εὐλογίαν αὐτοῦ.

6.2.1. Occasionally LXX has rearranged a text into a more sensible order. A number of such reorderings obtain in ch. 31, and well illustrate such reordering. At vv. 26–27 a MT has: (What have you done) ותגנב את לבבי and you carried off my daughters as captives by the sword; why did you hide yourself by fleeing ותגנב אתי? LXX has no doublet, having omitted ותגנב את לבבי; it then transposed the rest of v. 26, i.e. "and you carried ... sword" to the end. Thus it reads "Why did you run away secretly and steal from me and led off my daughters as captives by the sword?" At vv. 47–48 a LXX transposes the two; thus: (48 a) And Laban said to him, This hill shall be a witness between me and you today. (47) And Laban called it Hill of witness, but Jacob called it A hill is witness, admittedly a more logical order of events. Furthermore, v. 48 b: על כן קרא שמו גלעד has vv. 51–52 a transposed before it: "And said Laban to Jacob Behold this hill and the stele which I have set between me and you; this hill shall witness and this stele shall witness". Only then according to LXX can it legitimately be said: Therefore its name was called A hill bears witness.

6.2.2. At times the Greek is more specific or detailed than MT. Thus at 6:3 Yahweh says לא ידון רוחי באדם לעלם. The verb is a hapax legomenon, and its meaning is uncertain. LXX interprets it as καταμείνῃ "remain", thus "my spirit will not remain on mankind for ever", and a limitation of a lifetime of 120 years is imposed. But LXX translated באדם by ἐν τοῖς ἀνθρώποις τούτοις, "on these men", i.e. on the product of the sons of God and the human daughters, i.e. the γίγαντες of v. 4. In Abraam's plea before Yahweh at 18:25 he says: Will not the one judging the whole earth יעשה משפט? LXX makes the remark even more pointed by putting the verb in second person: ποιήσεις.

At 24:14 amd 34:3 (ה)נער is applied to Rebekka and Dinah resp., both unmarried lasses. LXX specifies their unmarried state by translating as ἡ παρθένος. Even the choice of preposition can be a more specific statement. At 28:13 MT says that Yahweh had set himself עליו. This is ambiguous, since it could mean "beside Jacob" or "upon the stairway", since both יעקב and סלם are masculine. LXX removes all possible doubt by its ἐπ' αὐτῆς which can only refer to κλίμαξ.

At 31:41 Jacob accuses Laban תחלף (my wages ten times), but in LXX he accuses him of falsifying them – παρελογίσω. Then in the Dinah story of ch. 34 she goes out in v. 1 to become acquainted with בנות הארץ, but LXX specifies that these are τὰς θυγατέρας τῶν ἐγχωρίων, i.e. daughters of the inhabitants. LXX also makes the dream character of Pharaoh's dream more apparent by adding ᾤετο at the introduction in 41:1, i.e. "he thought" that he was standing by the river.

6.3.0. LXX tends to make what MT says somewhat clearer, and to that end often makes explicit what is already implicit in the text. A few examples of this common practice should suffice. At 9:22 it is said that Ham informed his two brothers outside. LXX introduces this by the participle ἐξελθών. Of course, he went out, so as to inform his brothers outside! At 19:15 the angels urge Lot: Take your wife and your two remaining daughters פן תספה בעון העיר. This abrupt clause naturally presupposes the order "leave" or "hurry up", and LXX makes this clear by its καὶ ἔξελθε.

At 41:13 MT states "As he (i.e. Joseph) interpreted to us, so it happened; me השיב into my position and him תלה". Common sense dictates that the subject changes for these verbs; it was not Joseph but Pharaoh who acted, and so LXX renders the verbs by passives: ἐμέ τε ἀποκατασταθῆναι ... ἐκεῖνον δὲ κρεμασθῆναι.

6.3.1. The LXX translator was intent on producing a text which would make clear what he believed MT meant. Thus at 1:2 the terms תהו ובהו are translated by ἀόρατος καὶ ἀκατασκεύαστος "invisible and unstructured", describing the character of the chaos before light and a structured universe had been made. At 4:1 the difficult קניתי איש את יהוה is clarified in the Greek by ἐκτησάμην ἄνθρωπον διὰ τοῦ θεοῦ "I have acquired a man through God", i.e. the experience of reproduction is a divine gift; God makes it possible for mankind to reproduce. At 6:12 Yahweh God saw ... that all flesh had corrupted את דרכו on the earth. Does the suffix here refer to God or to flesh? LXX makes it clear that its antecedent is not σάρξ but κύριος ὁ θεός by the masculine pronoun in τὴν ὁδὸν αὐτοῦ.

At 22:13 Abraam saw a ram caught by his horns בסבך "in a thicket". The translator knew that it was some kind of bush, but he had no specific Greek word for it, so he has ἐν φυτῷ σαβέκ, i.e. "in a sabek bush". At 24:55 the phrase ימים או עשור is not clear; LXX is a real help with its ἡμέρας ὡσεὶ δέκα. At 25:22 Rebekka says אם כן למה זה אנכי a cryptic statement probably meaning "If it is thus why is it that I?" Again LXX makes it much clearer with εἰ οὕτως μοι μέλλει γίνεσθαι ἵνα τί μοι τοῦτο "If thus it is going to happen to me why is this to me", a fitting reason for going to inquire of the Lord. An interesting case of elucidation obtains at 31:7, 41. Jacob accuses Laban of having changed his wages עשרת מנים. LXX makes this more concrete by its τῶν δέκα ἀμνῶν. The wages would be changed at the time of the lambs being born; what LXX says is that Laban changed the nature of the lambs assigned as Jacob's wages on ten occasions. At 31:13 God says to Jacob in a dream אנכי האל בית אל "I am the God, Bethel", which is not immediately sensible. Certainly LXX's insertion of ὁ ὀφθεὶς σοι ἐν, so that it reads "I am the God who appeared to you in τόπῳ θεοῦ" is clear. At 32:13 (14) Jacob יקח from what he carried, gifts לעשו which LXX understood as a zeugma, and so realized it as ἔλαβεν ... καὶ ἐξαπέστειλεν Ἠσαύ (τῷ ἀδελφῷ αὐτοῦ). And at 38:28 it is said about Tamar that when she was giving birth ויתן יד which seems rather mysterious. Since there were twins in her womb, it must mean that one of them put out a hand. This is made clear by LXX ὁ εἷς προεξήνεγκεν τὴν χεῖρα.

A few examples of such clarification may be given for the Joseph story as well. At 40:14 Joseph pleads with the butler to remember him so that he may be released מן הבית הזה; "this house" is identified in the Greek as (ἐκ) τοῦ ὀχυρώματος τούτου. Then at 44:4 Joseph's servant is told to rail against the brothers with: Why did you repay evil for good? Then v. 45 continues with "Is not this that cup with which my master drinks?" But no reference to any cup had occurred, so LXX clarifies this by inserting at the end of v. 4 ἵνα τί ἐκλέψατέ μου τὸ κόνδυ τὸ ἀργυροῦν. And at 48:6 Jacob refers to children which might come to Joseph after Manasseh and Ephraim who will be called by the name of their brothers בנחלתם. Unclear is the antecedent of the pronoun; is it the future children or is it Manasseh and Ephraim? LXX makes a clear choice with its ἐν τοῖς ἐκείνων κλήροις.

6.3.2. Sometimes MT uses a word more than once, and LXX distinguishes them semantically. Thus at 11:7 שפה occurs twice. Yahweh says: Let us confuse their שפתם so that they won't understand each שפת רעהו. LXX makes a fine distinction; the first one is αὐτῶν τὴν γλῶσσαν (their language), and the second is spoken – τὴν φωνὴν (τοῦ πλησίον), i.e. speech. In 13:10 צער is mentioned as being on the border of Egypt. Then in the Lot story of ch. 19 צער is given as the place to which he and his daughters fled for safety. But LXX keeps them rigidly apart; the first one is ζόγορα, and the second is Σήγωρ. At 14:19 אברם is declared ברוך and in v. 20 אל עליון is also called ברוך. But LXX distinguishes the two: Abram is εὐλογημένος "was made blessed", but God Most High is εὐλογητός as a statement of fact. At 22:5 the same word is used for Abraam's servants נעריו and for his son Isaak הנער, but LXX distinguishes them by τοῖς παισὶν αὐτοῦ vs τὸ παιδάριον.

At 45:2 the verb שמע occurs twice. The reference is to Joseph's weeping. MT says וישמעו מצרים וישמע בית פרעה. LXX rightly distinguishes the two. The first is rendered by ἤκουσαν, but the second one, by ἀκουστὸν ἐγένετο. In the second case the sound was physically audible, whereas in the first it obviously was not. And in 50:8 בית is twice used of those accompanying Joseph to bury his father: all בית of Joseph … and all בית of his father. The first of these LXX translates by ἡ πανοικία, i.e. the full household, but the second by ἡ οἰκία, i.e. the household in the narrower sense.

6.3.3. Passages in MT which betray some obscurity and so give trouble to a translator are interpreted by LXX contextually. E.g. at 4:7 the Hebrew is quite obscure. Cain is warned: Is it not so that if you do good, there is a lifting up, but if you do not do good sin is crouching at the door? Since in the Cain and Abel story various sacrifices are involved LXX interpreted this cultically: (οὐκ) ἐὰν ὀρθῶς προσενέγκῃς ὀρθῶς δὲ μὴ διέλῃς ἥμαρτες ἡσύχασον "If you sacrifice correctly but do not divide correctly you have sinned. Be quiet".

In the instructions concerning the ark LXX had trouble with the hapax legomenon צהר at 6:16. Since the next clause reads "to a cubit you shall finish it upwards" the translator contextualized with ἐπισυνάγων "bring (it) together", i.e. the ark gradually narrows in an upwards direction. At 14:14–15 LXX apparently did not understand ירק "to empty (i.e. the scabbard)", but since 318 people were involved he guessed with ἠρίθμησεν. At 15:2 the translation τῆς οἰκογενοῦς μου for ביתי (as modifying the strange משק) means that Μάσεκ is understood as a woman, i.e. as Eliezer's mother. LXX took ביתי as in apposition with משק. Note that in v. 3b בן ביתי, referring to Eliezer, is translated by ὁ οἰκογενής μου.

LXX tried to make some sense out of Jacob's genetic engineering hocus pocus at 30:37 by interpreting the stripping of the rods by ἐφαίνετο δὲ ἐπὶ ταῖς ῥάβδοις τὸ λευκὸν ὃ ἐλέπισεν ποικίλον, "the white which he had peeled appeared dappled (i.e. both white and bark-colored)"; the ποικίλον has no equivalent in MT. And at 31:25 MT has Jacob תקע his tent, whereas Laban תקע his brothers, which is odd indeed. LXX made sense by translating the first instance by ἔπηξεν "pitched", but the second one by ἔστησεν "established".

In Joseph's interpretation of the butler's dream he predicts at 40:13 that ישא פרעה את ראשך, and this is carried out in v. 20 using the same idiom. LXX clearly takes ראש not as "head" but as ἀρχή meaning "top, first, beginning", but it can also mean "office". The phrase is translated by μνησθήσεται Φαραὼ τῆς ἀρχῆς σου. Then the noun recurs for the construction כמשפט הראשון as κατὰ τὴν ἀρχήν σου τὴν προτέραν. But at v. 19 in the explication of the baker's dream the idiom ישא פרעה את ראשך is translated by ἀφελεῖ Φαραὼ τὴν κεφαλήν σου (ἀπὸ σοῦ). The translator does not translate thoughtlessly.

At 43:11 Jacob instructs his sons to take מזמרת הארץ in your vessels. זמרת is an unknown word, and from the context καρπῶν is a reasonable, in fact, almost certainly correct, rendering. At v. 18 the brothers were brought to Joseph's house, and they were scared להתגלל עלינו ולהתנפל עלינו. The first infinitive is difficult. The root means "to roll", and its meaning is not at all clear. The next infinitive means "to attack", i.e. "to make oneself fall (upon)". LXX has a clear translation: τοῦ συκοφαντῆσαι ἡμᾶς καὶ ἐπιθέσθαι ἡμῖν "to denounce us and arrest us". And at v. 30 Joseph's reaction to seeing Benjamin is described as ימהר and his inwards churned ... and he wanted to weep. But "hurried" does not suit the context, whereas LXX's ἐταράχθη "he was overcome with emotion" does.

6.4.0. There are times that LXX simply shows a different point of view from that of MT. At 2:4 אלה תולדות, which is usually translated by αὗται αἱ γενέσεις, becomes, however, αὕτη ἡ βίβλος γενέσεως as at 5:1 where MT has זה ספר תולדת. The two do contrast; at 2:4 it concerns "heaven and earth", whereas at 5:1 it is אדם – ἀνθρώπων "mankind". The change seems intentional, since these two contrast with γενέσεις which refer to specific people. And at 2:23 MT has a word play: She shall be called אשה because from איש she was taken. LXX could hardly reproduce the pun, but by translating מאיש by ἐκ τοῦ ἀνδρὸς αὐτῆς "out of her husband" this is tied to the statement on marriage in v. 24.

At 26:35 the wives of Esau are described as being מרת רוח to Isaac and Rebekka, i.e. "a bitterness of spirit". But LXX presupposes the root מרה "be contentious", and has ἦσαν ἐρίζουσαι, i.e. they were quarreling with Isaac and Rebekka. At 32:20 (21) Jacob says concerning Esau: I will propitiate him by במנחה "the gifts" ההלכת לפני "which are preceding me", but LXX refers to the gifts as τοῖς προπορευομένοις αὐτοῦ "those passing in front of him", i.e. Jacob is trying to overwhelm his brother by visible gifts. At 33:10 Jacob is pressing Esau to accept those gifts because ראיתי your face ... ותרצני "I have seen your face ... and you have accepted me". But LXX understands this differently; it makes the second verb future καὶ εὐδοκήσεις με, i.e. coordinate with the imperative δέξαι rather than with εἶδον – ראיתי. And at v. 18 Jacob is said to arrive שלם (safely) at the city of Shechem, but LXX took this to be a place name, thus "he came to Salem, a city of the Sikimites".

When Joseph was released from prison at 41.14 MT has ויריצהו "they hurried him" from the prison ויגלח ויחלף his garments ויבא, "he shaved and changed ... and he came". But LXX has ἐξήγαγον αὐτὸν ... καὶ ἐξύρησαν αὐτὸν καὶ ἤλλαξαν τὴν στολὴν αὐτοῦ καὶ ἦλθεν. Those who hurried him from prison also shaved him and changed his outer garment, after which he came in to Pharaoh. At 47:31 the aged Israel bowed down על ראש המטה "upon the head of the bed". LXX understood a different vocalization for מטה as meaning "staff", which understanding is confirmed by adding a pronoun: ἐπὶ τὸ ἄκρον τῆς ῥάβδου αὐτοῦ.

6.4.1. On occasion LXX makes up a different total of numbers than MT. Chapter 5 constitutes a genealogy beginning with Adam and ending with Noah, but the chronological system underlying the two differs. In MT the years from creation to the flood constitute 1656, whereas in LXX it is a span of 2242. The system underlying LXX is not sui generis, since it agrees in the main with the chronology of Demetrius the Historian as well.[29] In general

[29] For Demetrius see C. R. HOLLADAY, *Fragments from Hellenistic Jewish Authors*, vol. I: *Historians* (Chico CA: Scholars Press, 1983).

the long chronology adds a hundred years to the age of these worthies at the time of the birth of their firstborn in view of their overall longevity.

Another genealogy in which LXX differs considerably from MT is that of Shem in 11:10–25, i.e. from Shem to the birth of Abram. If one examines the age of this group when they became parents the two lots agree on Shem at 100 years and on Terah at 70. In MT there are seven intervening with a total of 220 years, whereas LXX has added an extra in Kainan who was 130 years old when his son Salla was born. The total for the eight men is 1000 years, clearly an intentional change. Furthermore, by adding Kainan to the list the total genealogy constitutes ten generations, which parallels the ten generations of the genealogy of Adam in ch. 5. There is obviously a thought-out system underlying the LXX chronology.

One further instance of fiddling with numbers obtains at 46:27. MT informs us that two sons were born to Joseph in Egypt; all the persons belonging to Jacob's household entering Egypt were seventy persons. But the numbers differ in LXX. The total entering Egypt was 75. This new number was the result of adding (from v. 20) not only Joseph's two sons, but also the three grandchildren, to the 70 entering with Jacob, thus a total of 75. But according to v. 26 the descendants of Jacob entering Egypt were 66, a number probably derived from 70 minus Jacob, Joseph and his two sons. LXX noted that to grow to 75 from 66 Joseph must have had a total of nine sons.

6.4.2. Occasionally LXX 'corrects' MT so as to agree with the context. This context may not be an immediate one at all; e.g. at 7:3 MT simply says: From the birds of the sky by sevens male and female. But the distinction between clean and unclean creatures as applied in v. 2 to cattle also applied according to Lev 11 and Deut 14 to birds. Accordingly LXX applies this only to birds τῶν καθαρῶν, and then adds καὶ ἀπὸ τῶν πετεινῶν τῶν μὴ καθαρῶν δύο δύο ἄρσεν καὶ θῆλυ.

At 24:18 Rebekka hurried and lowered her (water) jug על ידה. The translator knew better than that; women carried such jugs on their head, but then lowered them ἐπὶ τὸν βραχίονα. At 25:10 MT refers to השדה אשר Abraham bought ... there Abraham was buried. But this was not factually exact; he and Sarah were buried in the cave in the field, and LXX thus translates τὸν ἀγρὸν καὶ τὸ σπήλαιον ὅ, the relative pronoun referring to the cave, not to the field.

A pedantic exactitude at 28:4 propelled the translator to a shorter text. There Isaac pronounces a farewell blessing on Jacob, viz. לרשתך the land of your sojournings which God gave to Abraham. But technically it would only be Jacob's descendants who would inherit Canaan, so by omitting the suffix, i.e. κληρονομῆσαι, the subject automatically refers to the compound σοὶ καὶ τῷ σπέρματί σου (μετὰ σέ) which precedes. At v. 14 God promises Jacob ופרצת to the west and east and north and south. But this was not quite accurate; it was not Jacob who would spread out in all directions but rather his seed, and LXX translates by a third person verb πλατυνθήσεται referring to τὸ σπέρμα σου.

And at 41:34 Joseph advises Pharaoh to appoint overseers over the land וחמש את ארץ מצרים in the seven years of plenty. But Pharaoh would hardly collect the fifth himself, nor would he take over a fifth of the land of Egypt. By translating the verb in the plural, ἀποπεμπτωσάτωσαν, the toparchs become responsible for the collection, and by changing the modifier to πάντα τὰ γενήματα τῆς γῆς Αἰγύπτου what is collected is the produce of the land.

6.4.3. Sometimes one suspects the translator of intentionally changing the narrative. At 22:14 Abraham named the place יהוה יראה "Yahweh will see (to it)", of which it is said in explanation: בהר יהוה יראה "on the hill where Yahweh will appear (Ni)". LXX applies this only to Abraam and changed the tense accordingly, i.e. κύριος εἶδεν and ἐν τῷ ὄρει κύριος ὤφθη resp., so not a promise but a past event.

At 24:26 the servant יקד and worshipped Yahweh and at v. 48 he reports the event to Rebekka's relatives similarly but in first person אקד. In both cases LXX has εὐδόκησας, thus not "bowed down" by "being content, pleased". That this was an intentional change is clear from v. 27 where instead of אנכי בדרך נחני יהוה "as for me Yahweh led me on the way", LXX ties the clause to v. 26 by his ἐμὲ εὐόδωκεν κύριος, a fine literary word play.

At 26:34 one of the wives of Esau was את יהודית the daughter of Beeri the Hittite, but LXX calls her 'Ιουδὶν. This does not presuppose a different parent text; by changing the ending to *-in* the translator avoids calling the daughter of a Hittite 'Ιουδίθ "Jewess". At 35:5 God's protection of Jacob and his household is described by "and the terror of God came on the cities ... and they did not pursue בני יעקב". But LXX renders this using Jacob's new name, thus τῶν υἱῶν 'Ισραήλ. This allowed for a double meaning, a literal reference to Jacob's household, and in midrashic fashion so that "When Israel moved ... they (the cities) did not pursue the Israelites".

At 46:5 reference is made to the wagons which פרעה has sent to carry him (i.e. Jacob). In fact, Pharaoh had given the order in 45:17, but it was Joseph who actually gave his brothers the wagons (45:21), and so LXX makes 'Ιωσήφ the subject. At 48:15 in the context of Jacob's blessing of Joseph's two children by crossing his hands MT says ויברך את יוסף, which seems out of place, so LXX changed it to "and he blessed αὐτούς". And at v. 20 LXX makes an interesting change. The Hebrew says בך יברך ישראל לאמר. The Masoretes vocalized the verb as Pi: "by you (singular) Israel shall bless, saying". LXX not only changes בך to the plural ἐν ὑμῖν, and the verb to the passive: In you (i.e. Ephraim and Manasseh) Israel shall be blessed, but also rendered the direct speech marker by the plural λέγοντες; the Alexandrian makes the blessing refer to Israel as a nation rather than as a person.

6.5. On rare occasions one of the patriarchs is presented in a slightly different light than in MT. At 17:27 it is said of the entire household of Abraam that נמלו אתו "they were circumcized with him". In LXX Abraam plays an active role περιέτεμεν αὐτούς. And in MT at 18:19 God speaks in glowing terms of Abraham "in order that Yahweh" might bring upon Abraham what he had said עליו "concerning him", but in LXX this is πρὸς αὐτόν; after all Yahweh had just been speaking to him. In 34:7 there are slight differences in the two accounts of the reaction of Jacob's sons to the rape of Dinah. In MT יחר להם מאד "it angered them exceedingly", but in LXX their rage is somewhat softened: λυπηρὸν ἦν αὐτοῖς σφόδρα "it was very painful to them". Over against this the rape is called נבלה "a foolish thing" in MT, but ἄσχημον "a shameful matter" in LXX, a somewhat stronger term. At 35:22 Reuben's incest with Bilhah, Jacob's concubine, has the single reaction on his father's part: וישמע ישראל. This was hardly adequate for the Alexandrian who added καὶ πονηρὸν ἐφάνη ἐναντίον αὐτοῦ.

At 45:8 Joseph tells his brothers *inter alia* that he is a משל בכל ארץ מצרים "a ruler in all the land of Egypt". LXX avoids any notion of Joseph being but one among the nomarchs of Egypt by its ἄρχοντα πάσης γῆς Αἰγύπτου. And in 49:9 Judah is spoken of as a lion, but in the second hemistich MT describes him in a somewhat savage light: מטרף בני נעלית "from tearing prey, my son, you have gone up". LXX avoids this entirely by changing the figure to the plant world: ἐκ βλαστοῦ υἱέ μου ἀνέβης "from a sprout, my son, you have gone up", i.e. from a small beginning you have grown to full stature.

6.6. Particularly noteworthy are instances reflecting the times and place of the translator. Thus at 9:21 Noah is said to have undressed himself אהלה "in his tent". But tents were hardly common in Alexandria, and the translator updated this by his ἐν τῷ οἴκῳ αὐτοῦ. So too the reference to "the tents of Shem" in v. 27 appears in LXX as ἐν τοῖς οἴκοις τοῦ Σήμ; see also 24:67 and 31:33–35. In 23:16 Abraam according to MT ישקל את הכסף to Ephron as payment, i.e. "he weighed out the silver", but that is not how payment was made in third century Egypt. In LXX ἀπεκατέστησεν τὸ ἀργύριον, "he handed over the money", which is what one does with coins. So too at 24:22 to speak of נזם זהב "nose rings of gold" made little sense in Alexandria where such were not worn, so LXX substituted ἐνώτια χρυσᾶ "golden earrings". The Greek of 36:16 shows a contemporary political situation where בארץ אדום becomes ἐν γῇ 'Ιδουμαίᾳ. Idoumea was its contemporary identification by the Alexandrian, though the literal ἐν τῇ γῇ 'Εδώμ could also be used (v. 21). At 37:28 the price paid the Ismaelites for Joseph was בעשרים כסף "for twenty (shekels) of silver", but LXX has εἴκοσι χρυσῶν; twenty (didrachms) of gold was a more rational price for a slave in third century Alexandria. Note also the same change at 45:22, thereby heightening Joseph's generosity to his brothers.

At 41:34 Joseph advises Pharaoh to appoint פקדים "overseers" over the land. These overseers are given a contemporary Egyptian title τοπάρχας. And at 43:23 the terrified brothers are assured by Joseph's steward: כספכם בא אלי "your money came to me", which LXX interprets in a third century context by τὸ δὲ ἀργύριον ὑμῶν εὐδοκιμοῦν ἀπέχω "your money I received in genuine fashion" (i. e. it was not counterfeit) reflecting an age when coinage was the medium of exchange. In 45:10 Joseph tells his brothers: And you will dwell בארץ גשן "in the land of Goshen", which LXX locates more precisely both here and at 46:34 as being ἐν γῇ Γέσεμ 'Αραβίας. 'Αραβίας was one of the nomes of the delta in Ptolemaic times; LXX makes the text more understandable for the Alexandrian Jews.

6.7.0. The treatment in LXX of the divine names אלהים and יהוה is complex;[30] though the former requires ὁ θεός and the latter κύριος (unarticulated) LXX is not consistent, and the raison d'être for the inconsistency is not readily apparent. Occasionally, however, some kind of pattern appears. Thus in ch. 13 יהוה is used throughout, but only in vv. 4 and 18 is κύριος used, and in vv. 10, 13, 14 ὁ θεός is substituted. What distinguishes vv. 4, 18 from the rest is that the divine name is used in a cultic context. The situation is complicated by the fact that κύριος is also equivalent for אדון. When אדני refers to God as well LXX distinguishes in ordinary narrative by articulating κύριος, thus πρὸς τὸν κύριον at 18:27, 31 occurs for אדני, though when the Lord is addressed only κύριε obtains; cf 18:30, 32 20:4. But in 15:2, 8 the double vocative אדני יהוה occurs. At v. 8 δέσποτα κύριε constitutes LXX's solution, whereas at v. 2 only δέσποτα obtains.

The divine name אל שדי occurs five times in Genesis, and it is always translated by ὁ θεός plus either σου (17:1 35:11) or μου (28:3 43:14 48:3). The word שדי was apparently analyzed as consisting of ש plus די, i.e. a relative particle plus an Aramaic particle meaning "of, belong to", so the name is either "my God" or "your God" depending on the context. And at 16:13 Hagar called the name of Yahweh who was speaking to her אל ראי "God of vision"; the second word is interpreted as a participle plus a suffix, and the name becomes ὁ θεὸς ὁ ἐπιδών με. And at 21:33 it is said that "Abraam there invoked the name of Yahweh, eternal God". LXX understood the idiom קרא ב not as "invoke" but as ἐπεκαλέσατο (τὸ ὄνομα), i.e. "he named the name of Yahweh Eternal God".

---

[30] See J. W. Wevers, «An Apologia for LXX Studies», *BIOSCS* 18 (1985) 32–33.

6.7.1. Finally some renderings of LXX may be impelled by theological concerns. At 6:6–7 God's reactions to sinful humanity are narrated. MT says Yahweh ינחם "repented" that he had made mankind ויתעצב in his heart. Furthermore, he is determined to wipe out his sentient creation "because נחמתי that I made them". That Yahweh should repent was an overly daring way of describing God's state of mind, and LXX says that God ἐνεθυμήθη "was angry" that he had made mankind ... ἐθυμώθην "I was provoked" that I made them. And rather than "he was grieved in his heart" the Greek has διενοήθη "he pondered" (presumably what he would do). But to Noah who was a righteous man God said at v. 18 "I will establish את בריתי אתך (my covenant with you)". But such a covenant is not between equal partners; in fact, it is unidirectional as well; this covenant is then God's testament, his διαθήκην, which is not with you, but πρὸς σέ. God is the only actor in this covenant.

At 9:2 God describes man's dominion over the sentient world by בידכם נתנו "into your hand (i. e. power) they have been placed". But it is God who gives this authority, upon which LXX insists with its ὑπὸ χεῖρας ὑμῖν δέδωκα "into your power I have put (them)". At v. 14 MT says "and הקשת will appear in the cloud". But this is the sign of the divine covenant with Noah; it belongs to God and hence it appears in LXX as τὸ τόξον μου.

At 15:1 in MT God identifies himself in a vision to Abram as: I am a מגן for you. LXX verbalizes this by ὑπερασπίζω σου "I am covering you over with a shield"; in this way the translator avoids calling God a shield. But at 16:13 the translator interprets more daringly. Admittedly the Hebrew is obscure: הגם הלם ראיתי אחרי ראי possibly "have I here seen behind the one seeing me"? LXX makes a clear but theologically daring translation: καὶ γὰρ ἐνώπιον εἶδον ὀφθέντα μοι "For I have even seen before me one who appeared to me".

When MT says that God spoke אתו LXX avoids a literal μετ' αὐτοῦ except at 35:13–15 for the collocation מקום אשר דבר אתו. Otherwise, as at 17:3 the translator insists on the dative αὐτῷ or a πρὸς αὐτόν. God does not converse with man; he addresses him. At 18:25 Abraam twice uses the strong oath formula חללה לך (literally "profanation be to you") in addressing God. LXX tones this down by its μηδαμῶς "by no means". The formula also occurs at 44:7, 17 though not addressed to deity; there it is rendered by μὴ γένοιτο.

At 30:8 Rachel etymologizes on Naphthali in the difficult נפתולי אלהים נפתלתי "with the wrestlings of God I have wrestled" (?). The notion of "wrestlings of God" was neatly avoided by LXX's rewriting of the text as συνελάβετό μοι ὁ θεὸς καὶ συνανεστράφην "God helped me and I competed (i. e. with my sister)". God is actively helping in Rachel's rivalry with Leah. At 31:44 Laban proposes to Jacob that they should make a covenant between them "and it will become a witness between me and you". But how this is to be a witness is left up in the air, so LXX added an explanation: εἶπεν δὲ αὐτῷ Ἰδοὺ οὐθεὶς μεθ' ἡμῶν ἐστιν, ἴδε ὁ θεὸς μάρτυς ἀνὰ μέσον ἐμοῦ καὶ σοῦ i. e. there are no human witnesses, so God will serve as witness. The subject of εἶπεν is left unstated.

At 33:20 Jacob erected an altar ויקרא לו אל אלהי ישראל. LXX avoids giving a divine name to the altar by omitting לו אל, i. e. καὶ ἐπεκαλέσατο τὸν θεὸν

Ἰσραήλ "and he invoked the God of Israel", a fine sentiment, but it does not equal MT. Similarly at 35:7 giving a divine name to a cult place is avoided. In MT Jacob built an altar and he called the place אל בית אל "God, Bethel", but LXX simply disregarded אל; the name was Bethel. At 35:4 Jacob is said to have hidden the strange gods and the earrings under a terebinth at Shechem. This was not sufficient for LXX which added καὶ ἀπώλεσεν αὐτὰ ἕως τῆς σήμερον ἡμέρας, thereby assuring readers that they remained destroyed for all time.

And finally at 50:19 Joseph comforts his brothers with the assurance: Do not fear כי התחת אלהים אני "for am I in the place of God"? This could be taken as somewhat irreverent, and LXX changes it into a statement of faith: τοῦ γὰρ θεοῦ εἰμι ἐγώ, "For I belong to God".

6.8. The query as to the interpretative character of the Septuagint has been resolved by a practical demonstration. Its character can only be understood case by case through a detailed study of differences, often slight and sometimes meaningless, of the work of a single translator over against his parent text. The Greek Genesis is the earliest commentary extant for any biblical book, and as such repays close attention, both for an understanding of how the Jews in the third century BCE of Alexandria understood their Bible as well as a humanistic document in its own right.

Chapter Three

Early Jewish Biblical Interpretation in the Qumran Literature

By Johann Maier, Cologne

Bibliography: Archaeology and History in the Dead Sea Scrolls (ed. L. H. Schiffman, JSP Suppl. series 8; Sheffield: JSOT Press 1990); M. Baumgarten, *Studies in Qumran Law* (SJLA 24; Leiden: Brill 1977); M. J. Bernstein, "Introductory Formulas for Citation and Re-citation of Biblical Verses in the Qumran Pesharim: Observations on a Pesher Technique", *Dead Sea Discoveries* 1 (1994) 30–70; D. I. Brewer, *Techniques and Assumptions in Jewish Exegesis before 70 CE* (Texte und Studien zum Antiken Judentum 30; Tübingen: Mohr 1992); G. J. Brooke, *Exegesis at Qumran. 4Q Florilegium in Its Jewish Context* (JSOT Suppl. Series 29; Sheffield: JSOT Press 1985); F. F. Bruce, *Biblical Exegesis in the Qumran Texts*, (Exegetica III/1; Den Haag: Van Keulen 1959); M. Fishbane, *Biblical Interpretation in Ancient Israel* (Oxford: Univ. Press 1985); H. Gabrion, "L'interprétation de l'Écriture dans la littérature de Qumran", in: ANRW II,19/1 (Berlin 1979) 779–848; M. Gertner, "Terms of Scriptural Interpretation. A study in Hebrew Semantics", *BSOAS* 25 (1962) 1–27; M. D. Herr, "L'Herméneutique juive et chrétienne des figures bibliques à l'époque du deuxième temple, de la Mishna et du Talmud", *Messiah and Christos. Studies in the Jewish Origins of Christianity, presented to David Flusser* (ed. I. Gruenwald/S. Shaked/G. G. Stroumsa; Tübingen: Mohr 1992) 99–110; *Mikra* (ed. M. J. Mulder/H. Sysling, CRINT II/1; Assen; Van Gorcum 1988); D. Patte, *Early Jewish Hermeneutics in Palestine* (SBL Diss. Series 22; Missoula: Scholars Press 1975); L. H. Schiffman, *The Halakhah at Qumran* (SJLA 16; Leiden: Brill 1975); idem, *Sectarian Law in the Dead Sea Scrolls* (Brown Judaic Studies 33; Chico: Scholars Press 1983); idem, *The Eschatological Community of the Dead Sea Scrolls* (SBL Monograph Series 38; Atlanta: Scholars Press 1989); idem, *Law, Custom and Messianism in the Qumran Sect* (Jerusalem: Z. Shazar Centre 1993; in Hebrew); E. Slomovic, "Toward an Understanding of the Exegesis in the Dead Sea Scrolls"; *RevQ* 7 (1969/70) 3–15; *Temple Scroll Studies* (ed. G. J. Brooke, JSP Suppl. ser. 7; Sheffield JSOT Press 1989); G. Vermes, "The Qumran Interpretation of Scripture in its Historical Setting"; idem; *Post-Biblical Jewish Studies* (Leiden: Brill 1975) 37–49; idem, "Bible Interpretation at Qumran", *Er.Isr* (Y. Yadin Memorial Volume) 20 (1989) *184–*191.

1. Introduction

1.1. 'The Bible and Qumran'

Most authors of publications on early Judaism and the Qumran texts employ the terms 'Scripture' or 'Bible' in connection with 'interpretation' or 'exegesis' precisely as biblical scholars are used to doing.[1] A glimpse into the microfiche

---

[1] See in the bibliography the publications of Gertner, Vermes, Patte, Gabrion, Slomovic, Fishbane, Brooke, Herr and Brewer. A more differentiated view may be found in: J. Trebolle-Barrera, La biblia judía y la Biblia cristiana (Madrid: Trotta 1993).

edition of the Qumran texts edited by E. Tov (1993) illustrates this state of affairs: Non-biblical texts are frequently defined according to their relationship to the 'canonical' Scriptures and, consequently, labelled as 'apocryphal', 'pseudepigraphical', 'biblical paraphrase', 'expanded biblical text', 're-written Bible', 'pseudo-xy' etc. This presupposes for early Judaism the concept of written documents defined or at least accepted as authoritative in the sense of the Jewish Scriptures of the Talmudic period or even of the 'Old Testament' canon of the Christian Bible.

Another reason is a more or less implicit tendency to stress the continuity between a so-called 'mainstream Judaism' before 70 CE and rabbinic Judaism, antedating characteristics of the Talmudic literature and defining all other groups as 'sectarian', and at the same time stressing the significance of the 'Bible' so dear to Christian readers. A special relationship between established biblical text and interpretation or commentary is, indeed, characteristic of later Jewish tradition in general, but this does not justify presupposing the usual concept of 'the Bible' for such early times. Symptomatic is also the frequent but nevertheless anachronistic use of the terms 'canon' and 'canonical' which should be applied only as far as a corpus of authoritative texts had been formally defined in this sense and in the period in question.[2]

What is important is that the Christian view of the 'Bible' and the Jewish evaluation of the Hebrew Scriptures rest on fundamentally differing concepts of 'canon', and imply, therefore, also different hermeneutics. Differentiated hermeneutic approaches existed already within Judaism itself according to the fundamentally different evaluation of the traditional parts of the Hebrew Bible as: "Torah", *N^e^bî'îm*/"Prophets", and *K^e^tûbîm*/"(other) Scriptures".[3] Only the "Torah" represents the absolutely authoritative revelation of God to Israel by Moses. The prophetic revelation is of a less obligatory quality and contains no Torah. Exactly according to this traditional graduation and evaluation the Pentateuch emerged as a first Biblical corpus of authoritative Scriptures, in a secondary stage supplemented by that of the "Prophets", and in part by the Psalter as a kind of prophetic poetry composed by King David[4]. This graduation led to a corresponding practice of public reading: the "Torah" is read as a whole in a cycle of pericopes, the "Prophets" only partially as selected supplementary readings, with no liturgical readings from the "other Scriptures" at all.[5] Finally, the Rabbis also developed exactly defined and differentiated scribal prescriptions for each part of the *TN"K*. The interpretation of "Torah", "Prophets" and "other Scriptures" has, therefore, to be treated separately, the Psalter representing a special case because of the inspired character attributed (also by the early Church) to the liturgical poetry of David.

---

[2] See HBOT 2.1 the contribution of E. Tov.

[3] J. MAIER, *Zwischen den Testamenten* (NEchtB, Erg.-Bd. AT III; Würzburg 1990) 15–22.

[4] See particularly 11QPs[a] 27:2–11.

[5] J. MANN/I. SONNE, *The Bible as Read and Preached in the Old Synagogue*, I (New York: Ktav [2]1971), II (Cincinnati: HUC 1966); P. Grelot, La lecture de la Bible dans la Synag*ogue* (Hildesheim: Gerstenberg 1973); idem, "La lecture de la Bible dans la diaspora hellénistique", *Études sur le judaïsme hellénistique* (Paris 1984) 109–32.

This presupposed, it is rather misleading to speak in view of the period in question and in view of the Qumran community in particular about 'Bible interpretation' and 'the Bible' at all[6]. It is true that fragments of almost all the biblical books have been identified among the Qumran texts. The number of exemplars for each biblical book and its significance as attested by use, citations and interpretation, are however considerably different. Even regarding "Torah" the situation is by far more complicated than usually presupposed. Torah authority was not only a question of religious and liturgical definitions of texts, it was closely connected with claims to power within a community or group, between groups, and in Jewish society as a whole.

1.2. Research on the Subject

Biblical texts or at least traditions similar to biblical contents constitute remarkable components of the Qumran literature,[7] and this not only in 'exegetical' writings.[8] Apart from the treatment of the biblical texts themselves it was their use and interpretation which soon became the subject of scholarly research, in most cases with a special interest in the bearing on NT scholarship. Of the edited texts during these early years 1QpHab provided the basis for the first publications on the subject.

W. F. Brownlee, the first to treat 'biblical exegesis' at Qumran in a systematic manner,[9] established on the basis of 1QpHab thirteen principles,[10] much discussed during the following years, particularly by K. Elliger[11] and F. F. Bruce[12]. D. Patte realized in his study of early Jewish hermeneutics the significance of the tripartite Jewish Bible. Relying, however, rather heavily on later rabbinic sources he presupposed a traditionalist scheme, comparing in an anachronistic manner an alleged "classical Judaism" (attested by rabbinic literature) with "Sectarian Judaism" (before 70 CE), thus blurring some important historical facts.[13] His presupposition of the liturgical significance of the 'Bible' was certainly exaggerated, and it was this tendency together with a modern (but never exactly defined) concept of 'identity' which led him back to speak again about one 'Scripture'. His description of Qumranic exegesis (209–308) contains a lot of important observations in details. His evaluation of its place within the ancient Jewish evidence is, however, not convincing. In any case it is a surprise to read there that contrary to "classical Judaism" (distinguishing between a halakhic and haggadic level) the Qumran community integrated its use of Scripture on one, the haggadic level (309, 311–14). It seems that Patte's term "liturgical" had a misleading effect, for at stake was in reality the question of authority in connection with a massive priestly tradition. G. J. Brooke embedded his detailed treatment of 4Q174 (4QFlor)[14] also in a general frame of ancient Jewish exegesis and employed for the rules of Brownlee

---

[6] J. Trebolle Barrera, La Biblia judía (1993) 481–489.

[7] M. Fishbane, "Use, Authority and Interpretation of Mikra at Qumran", *Mikra* (1988) 339–377.

[8] For orientation: D. Dimant, "Qumran Sectarian Literature", *Jewish Writings of the Second Temple Period* (ed. M. E. Stone, CRINT II/2; Assen: Van Gorcum 1984) 483–550.

[9] W. F. Brownlee, "Biblical Interpretation among the Sectaries of the Dead Sea Scrolls", *BA* 14 (1951) 54–76; idem, "The Background of Biblical Interpretation at Qumran", *Qumran* (ed. M. Delcor; Paris 1978) 183–193.

[10] W. F. Brownlee, *The Midrash pesher of Habakkuk* (Missoula: Scholars Press 1979).

[11] K. Elliger, *Studien zum Habakkuk – Kommentar* (Tübingen: Mohr 1953).

[12] F. F. Bruce, Biblical Exegesis (1959).

[13] D. Patte, Early Jewish Hermeneutics (1975).

[14] G. J. Brooke, Exegesis at Qumran (1985).

rabbinical terms. This was useful for illustrating the common presuppositions and techniques but less helpful for an understanding of the Qumranic peculiarities, for the common features are for the most part general features of hermeneutics and not characteristics of a certain group.

Rather theologically accentuated and written from a Christian point of view is the sketch of H. Gabrion (1979).[15] From a traditional Jewish point of view, evaluating and labelling all Qumran traditions as "sectarian" and, in any case secondary to biblical and rabbinical evidence, M. Fishbane presented an otherwise instructive overview.[16] Like Patte, D. I. Brewer tried to describe in a recent publication ancient Jewish Bible exegesis as a whole.[17] He, too, followed the traditionalist scheme. In chronologically reverse sequence a description of the "Scribal traditions" (rabbinical exegesis) appears as the first part of his book, and a second part (177ff.) is devoted to "non-Scribal traditions". Brewer treats here – after Josephus! – Qumran only on a few pages (187–198). Except for Patte and Fishbane almost all of the mentioned authors have ignored the significance of the differentiation between Torah and non legal traditions.

As regards publications on Second Temple Judaism it is also characteristic for the history of Qumran research that legal texts and contents remained for a long time among the neglected subjects. This state of affairs changed with a series of relevant publications, particularly by L. H. Schiffman (see below). And of the more recent shorter publications attention should be paid to a paper by D. Dimant on the Damascus Document with informative remarks about Qumran exegesis in general.[18]

2. Torah

2.1. Torah and Pentateuch

The Qumran community did not restrict "Torah" to the legal contents of the Pentateuch and some texts contain Torah material in no way related to Pentateuchal laws.[19] Some cases however, are ambiguous because of a more or less similar wording. In some cases this may be the result of interpretation of Pentateuchal laws. In other cases the 'citations' or presupposed text passages may have been taken as well from a book which among other materials contained laws which are known to us from the Pentateuch. And finally, we cannot presuppose that a Qumran passage resembling some verses or words in the Books of Exodus, Leviticus, Numeri or Deuteronomy, has been cited and has to be regarded as a citation of the Pentateuch as a corpus. And unless believing in a "Written Torah" transmitted to Moses at Sinai we cannot assume that the legal materials contained in the books of the Pentateuch did not exist in independent collections before and after the redaction of the Pentateuch. Finally, it is obvious that a Jewish Commonwealth in any case could not be organized only on the basis of pentateuchal laws. Consequently,

---

[15] H. Gabrion, ANRW II,19/1 (1979) 779–848.

[16] M. Fishbane, Use, Authority and Interpretation, *Mikra* (1988) 339–377.

[17] D. I. Brewer, Techniques (1992).

[18] D. Dimant, "The Hebrew Bible in the Dead Sea Scrolls: Torah Quotations in the Damascus Covenant", *"Sha'arei Talmon". Studies in the Bible, Qumran, and the Ancient Near East Presented to Shemaryahu Talmon* (ed. M. Fishbane/E. Tov; Winona Lake: Eisenbrauns 1992) 113*–122*.

[19] About Qumran texts of the Pentateuch, similar works and Torah collections see G. J. Brooke, "Torah in the Qumran Scrolls", *Bibel in jüdischer und christlicher Tradition. Festschrift für Johann Maier zum 60. Geburtstag* (ed. H. Merklein/K. Müller/G. Stemberger, BBB 88; Frankfurt a. M. 1993) 97–120. He, too, uses designations as "excerpted texts", "paraphrases", or "re-written Torah".

there must have been legal regulations practised as Jewish law during the Persian and Hellenistic periods, of which the relationship to the "Torah" of Moses is not known, and which to some extent have fallen into oblivion because later Judaism had no use for them. As it seems impossible to register today the full extent of "Torah" or Jewish law of such remote days, we should be careful in treating "the law" as a theological issue. Judaism was not a uniform unit but rather a conglomerate of different social, political, and religious tendencies, more or less organized as groups, all of them with their own concept of "Torah" and authority, presupposing, of course, a common basis.

Modern research presupposes, however, for almost every case a one way street of interpretation from one or two biblical passages to a new formulation, and scholars scarcely asked for eventual cases of a different or even reverse procedure, which should have in any case been checked too. The fact that non-biblical laws are formulated in the form of Torah related to Moses and in many cases also with God as speaking in the first person as in 11Q19 and 11Q20 (11Q Temple) and in so-called "Pentateuchal paraphrases", demonstrates sufficiently that the Qumran people never ascribed to the written legal texts in the Pentateuch a kind of exclusive or higher ('canonical') authority. A difficult question to be answered is: What of all the legal materials in Qumran texts has to be regarded as "Torah of Moses"? Much of the contents of (unfortunately only fragmentarily preserved) scrolls as 2Q25; 4Q159; 4Q185; 4Q229; 4Q251; 4Q256–265; 4Q274–283; 4Q294–298; 4Q394–399(4QMMT); 4Q512–514(4QOrd); 4Q523–524; 5Q11–13 had evidently the quality of "Torah", and the same is without doubt true for 11Q19–11Q20 (11QTemple). In many cases, however, this quality cannot be verified. The same problem exists regarding legal materials in 1QS and CD, in part collected in *s^erakîm*, in part defined as *midraš hat-Tôrah* (see below). Evidently two levels existed: one for commandments or laws formally defined and enacted as Torah and a second level for regulations of more or less organizational and disciplinary significance.[20] It has been assumed that a *serek* contained written regulations on both levels, while a *midraš hat-Tôrah* (as in 1QS 8:15), however, contained only defined and enacted Torah, whether in detail derived from extant written laws (not necessarily Pentateuchal ones) or not. But *midraš* appears 4QS (4Q256, 5; 4Q258 1,i) simply in place of *serek* ("written order") in 1QS 5:1! Regarding the Pentateuch it should be taken into account that it is not the only basis from which all other similar texts have to be derived. The MT text of the Pentateuchal books may in some cases well be the result of processes similar to those which on the basis of older traditions resulted in certain Qumran texts or in certain Samaritan textual features.

Astonishingly, also Jewish Qumran scholars are used to speaking about "the Bible or the Scripture(s) and Qumran" without differentiating between Torah, Prophets and other Scriptures. And this in spite of contributions which improved the state of research considerably due to a

[20] J. M. Baumgarten, "The Laws of the Damascus Document in Current Research", in: M. Broshi, *The Damascus Document Reconsidered* (Jerusalem: IES 1992) 51–56.

profound knowledge of later Judaism and particularly of the history of Jewish law. J. Milgrom wrote several articles on cultic/ritual items,[21] and L. H. Schiffman treated whole thematic complexes, concentrating on 1QS and CD.[22] This helped to change the situation but also enforced in effect the 'biblicistic' line as far as they tried to prove that almost everything in the legal traditions in Qumran has to be regarded as the result of 'biblical exegesis'. J. M. Baumgarten, however, underlined the fact that some of the legal materials have no biblical background at all.[23] Schiffman finds non Pentateuchal Torah essentially only in 11Q19 (11QTemple) and considers this text as an exceptional source. Even Baumgarten remained under the influence of rabbinic concepts, translating like Schiffman the verb *drš* in some cases with "to study", or "to expound".[24] The understanding and respective translation of this term plays, indeed, a key function for the issue in general.

2.2. *The Verb* drš *and the* Midrash

In scholarly literature "Torah" has been frequently regarded as identical with the "Pentateuch" or, more precisely as a term for the legal traditions within the Pentateuch, thus identical with the "Written Torah" of Rabbinic Judaism. Due to this presupposition certain rabbinic hermeneutic concepts have also found their way into the treatment of early Jewish literature, particularly the rabbinic concepts of *drš* and *Midrash*; during the last decades, this has become a kind of fashion in NT scholarship.[25]

In spite of the prevalent view and the lexicographical practice, scarcely sufficient evidence exists for a connotation of the verb *drš* like 'to interpret' or 'to expound' in early Jewish literature. This statement has been made already by I. Heinemann.[26] L. H. Schiffman, however, tried to maintain in his publications the opposite view and assumed that *midraš* "is an exegesis in which a corroborative passage in Scripture plays a part".[27] Concerning the Qumran procedures of Torah definition he wrote: "The legal materials of the Dead Sea Sect are the result of sectarian biblical exegesis. This exegesis, described in the *Manual of Discipline*, took place in regular sessions which were part of the life of the sect at its main center. The results of the decisions reached at such sessions were assembled into lists (serakhim), and it is in these lists of sectarian legal statements that many of the component parts of the *Manual of Discipline* and the *Zadokite Fragments* had their origin. ... The usual technique was to take words and expressions of the biblical verses as the basis of the legal derivation and to weave these into legal statements. Only through textual study, therefore, it is possible to unravel these statements and

---

[21] J. Milgrom, "The Qumran Cult: Its Exegetical Principles", *Temple Scroll Studies* (1989) 165–180; idem, "The Scriptural Foundations and Deviations in the Laws of Purity in the Temple Scroll", Archaeology and History (1990) 83–99.

[22] L. H. Schiffman, The Halakhah (1975); idem, Sectarian Law (1983). A revised version of both studies appeared together with The Eschatological Community (1989) in a Hebrew edition, see: Law, Custom (1993).

[23] M. Baumgarten, Studies (1977).

[24] Baumgarten, Studies (1977) 31 f.

[25] A. G. Wright, *The Literary Genre Midrash* (Staten Island: 1967); G. Porten, "Palestinian Jews and the Hebrew Bible in the Greco-Roman Period", ANRW II,19/2 (1979) 103–138.

[26] See I. Heinemann's Hebrew articles: "Lhtpthwt hmwnhym hmqṣw'ym lfrwš hTwrh", *Leshonenu* 14 (1945/6) 182–189; idem, "Mdrš", EncBibl 4 (1962) 695–701.

[27] The Halakhah (1975) 9.

to uncover their Scriptural basis. Almost never do we find an explicit proof text for a law".[28] The wording of SCHIFFMAN exhibits, particularly in his last sentence a certain uneasiness. It rests almost totally on his translation of the verb *drš* in the sense of 'to study' and in the sense of exegesis, a connotation which cannot be proved in lexicographical terms. The same is true for SCHIFFMAN's statement (ibd.): "The sect believed that its interpretations were arrived at under some form of Divine inspiration by which God's will would be discovered. According to the Qumran sect, the Law fell into two categories, the *nigleh* ("revealed") and the *nistar* ("hidden"). The *niglot* are those laws rooted in Scripture whose interpretations are obvious to anyone. The *nistarot*, on the other hand, are those commandments the correct interpretation of which is known only to the sect. The sectarian interpretation of the *nistarot* is the result of a process of inspired Biblical exegesis, a sort of divinely guided *midrash*. Study sessions were regarded as a medium through which God made known to the sect the correct interpretations of His commandments". This statement is formulated in a very convincing manner but it implies a series of imputed items not to be corroborated, such as (a) exclusive relationship of the *niglôt/nistarôt* to biblical Scripture, (b) inspiration for legal interpretation, and (c) *mdrš* in the sense of study or interpretation.

The decisive passage is 1QS 6:6–8. The context 1QS 6:3–8 concerns the smallest unit within the communal organization, the group of ten men. The first statement concerns the indispensable presence of a priest and his precedence. Not every priest is necessarily also an expert in Torah matters[29]. The following statement wants, therefore, to ensure the presence of an expert in law: "In the place where these ten (members) are (living) must not be missing a man *dôreš ba-tôrah*, day and night, *'l ypwt* each one with his companion". The concluding statement concerns a third matter: "The full members shall remain awake one third of all nights of the year in order to read in the (a ?) book and *lidrôš mišpaṭ* and to praise in company". The last statement includes three subjects: (1) To read, and this means probably also to study, (2) *lidrôš mišpaṭ*, a juridical term: to "seek" a juridical decision, to decree a verdict. It is not likely that the second statement concerns a subject contained in the third. The usual translation is: "In a/the place where (the) ten are (present/living) must not be missing a man studying the Torah day and night". Most translators felt, however, that the following concluding words do not fit this translation, and they emended the text of *'l ypwt* and translated "alternating each one with his companion" or similar. G. VERMES translated the first part "a man who shall study the law continually, day and night", the last phrase, however, without emendations of the text as: "concerning the right conduct of a man with his companion".[30] F. GARCÍA MARTÍNEZ preferred in his new Spanish translation: "un hombre que interpret la ley día y noche, siempre,

---

[28] Sectarian Law (1983) 14–17.

[29] This does not affect his prerogatives, cf. CD 13:1–7.

[30] G. VERMES, *The Dead Sea Scrolls in English* (Sheffield: JSOT Press [3]1987) 69.

sobre las obligaciones (?) de cada uno para con su prójimo".[31] The present author totally revised his German translation of 1960[32] in view of the new evidence and formulated for the new edition of 1995: "Und nicht weiche von einem Ort, wo sich die Zehn befinden, ein Mann, der in bezug auf Torah Anweisung(en) erteilt, (und zwar) tagsüber und nachts (7), ständig, bezüglich des guten (Verhaltens) eines jeden zu seinem Nächsten".[33]

The idea that in each group of ten all the members were organizing an alternating, continuous study of Torah fascinated in particular readers who regarded Qumran as a kind of a monastery. But "day and night" refers rather to "not missing", and from a practical point of view it is evident that the group needed an expert for advice in practical matters of Torah. And this expert has as a rule also to be a priest. This is explicitly stated in a similar passage about the "camps" CD 13:2–6. There we find these advising and commanding functions clearly distinguished from certain ritual acts which have to be performed by a priest anyway, versed in Torah (here: in the Book *Hhgj*) or not. The meaning of *dôreš* is here unequivocally 'advising', 'instructing', 'enacting', and certainly not 'interpreting' or 'studying', and this is also true for other references of that kind.

Particularly, it is significant that the Greek Bible translations did not employ verbs for interpretative procedures for Hebrew *drš*, and that even the Targumim still consistently translated it by forms of the verb *tbʿ* ('to demand', 'to summon').

The concrete meaning of *drš* is like that of *drs* and *dwš* 'to tread', with the basic connotations: 'to keep step by step close to', 'to follow close behind', 'to seek (and find)'. M. GERTNER was obviously mistaken by assuming for *dwš* a concrete meaning 'to thresh out' which, however, already denotes an effect of 'to tread (on the corn)'.[34] Originally a term of the shepherd's language, *drš* developed the prevalent general meaning: to seek, to take care of, to call for, to summon. And it became a religious *terminus technicus* particularly in connection with oracles: to demand an oracle by a priest or prophet who demands it for him from a Divinity and transmits to him the message (an action usually also designated by *jrh* Hifʿil), *drš* thus designating both parts of the procedure, asking and finding/answering/instructing. In juridic contexts it became a term for 'to summon for interrogation'. The semantic horizon of the verb in question covers a number of connotations well attested in biblical and non-biblical literature:

(a) Non technical use: To seek, to demand, to care for, to call for, to be intensively and practically concerned with. Sometimes also for a religious attitude: "to seek God" (in a general sense).

(ba) Mantic usage (cf. *šʾl*) with accusative and with particles b^e and *ʾel*: to ask for an oracle or a prophetic statement.

(bb) *drš* l^e: specific religious/cultic practice.

[31] F. GARCÍA MARTÍNEZ, *Textos de Qumran* (Madrid: Trotta 1992) 56.

[32] J. MAIER, *Die Texte vom Toten Meer,* I. *Übersetzung* (München: Reinhardt 1960) 154.

[33] J. MAIER, *Die Qumran Essener. Die Texte vom Toten Meer* I (UTB 224; München: Reinhardt 1995) 182.

[34] M. Gertner, "Terms of Scriptural Interpretation".

(c) Juridical usage, of particular relevance here:

(ca) to apply for binding advice or a verdict.

(cb) to summon in order to investigate, inquire and decree (Deut 13:15 (followed by *ḥqr* and *š'l*); Deut 17:9–12; Ezra 10:16).

(cc) To look for and to give (to mediate) binding advice; to pronounce a verdict, to enact a law. Isa 16:5 describes the task of the Davidic king as follows: "Through gracefulness a throne will be established and on it will take place a man ...judging and proclaiming *(dôreš)* judgement". In a more general sense Isa 1,17 says: look for *(dršw)* judgement (LXX: *ekzêtêsate krisin*; Tg: *tb'w dyn')*.

Isa 34:16 (not in LXX): "Look for it (Tg: *tb'w)* from *(dršw me'al)* the book/scroll of YHWH".

(cda) to be concerned with, to procure (justice / judgement), to proclaim, to enact (law). 1 Chr 28:8: "*šmrw wdršw*: Observe carefully and be (practically) concerned with all commandments of YHWH, your God". Ezra 7:10, frequently quoted for *drš* in the sense of "to study, to expound", presupposes exactly the same sense: "For Ezra had devoted his heart (*lidrôš*, LXX: *zêtêsai*) to be concerned with (or: to enact) the Torah of YHWH and to practice and to teach in Israel prescription and law".

(cdb) To find and formulate the wording of an advice or a verdict, the procedure being called *midraš*. Such juridical procedure is presupposed in 1QS 6:24: "These are the laws by which they shall judge ⟨in common *midraš*/lawsuit⟩[35] according to the facts of the case". Or 1QS 8:25–26: "If his conduct turns out as perfect (26) ⟨among them, then he returns⟩[36] to *midraš* /lawsuit and to council according to the decision of the full members ...".

(cdc) To formulate and mediate an advice, a verdict or the results of the *midraš* procedure (eventually in written form), its result being called *midraš*, in written form a record, a book, as in CD 20:6: "and if his practice proves to be in accordance with the record of the Torah, in which the men of perfect holiness should walk ...". Or 1QS 8:15: "This is the record of the Torah [which] He commanded through Moses to do ⟨according to⟩[37] all the revealed for each time and as the prophets revealed by His holy spirit".

(cdd) In a generalized sense: To formulate in written form (a record of something), as in 2 Chr 13:22; 24:27 (LXX: *biblion*!). This meaning probably underlies also 4Q174 (Flor) 1:14 frequently cited as example of a pre-rabbinic use of *midraš*: "A record from (*m*[*id*]*raš min*)". The use with "*min* /from" is exceptional and the correct translation seems to be: "a copy/extract from", i.e. a certain book. The translation "exposition" presupposed, and neglecting the problem of *min*, the expression may be perceived as "*midraš* out of Ps 1:1". But what follows is Pesher – interpretation of Ps 1:1 and Ps 2:1, and it has to be underscored that as *pêšer* never concerns a legal tradition, *drš* never occurs in the juridic sense in connection with non legal traditions.

The procedure of *drš* in connection with Torah was bound to the old priestly monopoly concerning Torah. The priestly claims rest on ancient priestly privileges, for instance attested by Deut 17:8–12, a passage concerning the central court of appeal, and instructive concerning the relevant terminology. The issue is also attested in the Temple Scroll 11Q19 56:1–11.

Deut 17:8	*11Q19*
If something is too difficult	[...
for you for judgement	
concerning	
any case of bloodshed	
or any case of lawsuit	
or any case of leprosy	
causing dispute in	
your local courts,	

[35] ⟨⟩ Read in place of *bmwšb* ("in the session") with M. KISTER/E. QIMRON: *bm wšb*; cf. 4Q258 = 1QS^{d}.

[36] ⟨⟩ Not in 4Q258 = 4QS^{d}.

[37] ⟨⟩ Not in 4Q261 = 4QS^{g}.

you should go up	...]*they*[shall go u]p
to the place	to the [place
which *YHWH* your God	which *I*
will elect	will elect]
Deut 17:9	
and you should come	
before the priests,	
the Levitical ones,	
and before the judge,	
who will be (officiating)	
at that time	
Deut 17:10	
and you shall *(tdrš)* demand	and you shall demand
(a verdict)	(a verdict)
and they will	and [they] will
communicate to you	comm[unicate to you]
	the word(s)
	which concern it
	in/by[....]
	they[did communic]ate
	to you
the word(s of the verdict).	the word(s of the verdict).
And you shall act	And you shall act
according to the *word(s)*	according to the *Torah*
which they will	which they will
communicate to you	communicate to you
	and according to the word(s)
	which they will
	say to you
	from the book of the Torah
	in truth
from that place	from that place
which *YHWH*	which *I*
will choose.	will choose
	to let dwell
	my name on it.
And you shall be careful	And you shall be careful
to act according	to act according
to everything	to everything
what they will	what they will
direct to you *(ywrwk)*.[38]	direct to you
Deut 17:11	
According to	*and* according to
the *Torah*	the *verdict (mišpaṭ)*
which they will	which they will
direct (yrh) to you	*say* to you
and according to the verdict	
which they will say to you	
you shall act;	you shall act;
do not turn aside	Do not turn aside
from the *word*	from the *Torah*
which they will	which they will
communicate to you	communicate to you

[38] LXX: *nomothetêtê soi.*

to the right	to the right
or to the left.	or to the left.
Deut 17,12	
And the man	And the man
	who does not listen and
who acts on purpose	who acts on purpose
in order not to listen	in order not to listen
to the priest	to the priest
in service there	there in service
of YHWH, your God,	*before me,*
or to the judge,	or to the judge,
this man shall *be dead*	this man shall *die*
and you will	and you will
(thus accomplish to) purge	(thus accomplish to) purge
the evil from Israel	the evil from Israel.
further.	

This is not only a case of changing the positions of textual passages, of expanding the text of Deuteronomy, and of its interpretation.[39] There are two different wordings of the legal subject at stake, each one from a different point of view, the one in 11Q19 being eventually older than the wording (avoiding the first person) in Deut 17. A Qumranic re-writing of Deut 17 would certainly have underlined the priestly prerogative which appears in 11Q19 (Temple) as a matter of fact and not subject to dispute. Deut 17 displays, however, a less rigid formulation concerning the authoritative basis for judgement. The *Sefer ha-Tôrah* mentioned in 11Q19 is certainly not the Pentateuch but a Book of Law proper. Another challenging treatment of the subject of Deut 17 appears in Josephus, *Antiquities* 4:216–218. In his more detailed description of the judicial organization, one item in §218 is particularly noteworthy for the context of this paper: Josephus mentions explicitly the High Priest (in place of the "judge" as king?), a prophet (!) and the *Gerusia* as members of the court of appeal. This is scarcely the result of Josephus' fantasy, but is rather a reflex of an historical institution or a programmatic device also apparent in 1 Macc 14:41 and 1 Macc 4:46. This torah-prophetic office formed part of a constitutional scheme, and 1QS 8:13 mentioning a prophet beside the two Anointed ones (High Priest and King) is probably to be understood in this sense.

As for *midraš* the lexicographical evidence is rather simple because of its unequivocally attested meaning in late biblical literature as 'record' or 'book'. The correct translation of *midraš hat-tôrah* is, consequently, 'account/record of the Torah' as enacted under the guidance by the (Zadoqite) priests in the respective sessions of the full members of the community, as L. H. SCHIFFMAN has pointed out.[40] But first of all, the procedure was of a legislative or enacting character, not exclusively bound to biblical written law, and not requiring a special form of inspiration. Certainly, such procedures could include acts of interpretation on a preliminary level, but they were never called *midraš*.

---

[39] As suggested by G. GRIN, "Hmqr' bmgylt hmqdš", *Shenaton* 4 (1980) 182–225 (184–185).

[40] L. H. Schiffman, Law, Custom (1993) 71 ff.

The Zadokite tradition and under its influence also the Qumran community claimed that the actually effective Torah (*nigleh*) can only be found under the guidance of priestly/Zadokite mediation. Not necessarily thanks to their textual transmission of laws or by their exegesis of written laws, but just like an oracle attained by *drš*, meaning both the applying and responding procedures as well, denoting thus a mediating function; it is a process of continuous revelation of a Torah, essentially already given as a whole to Moses, but not accessible in its entirety. The priests/Zadokites are, however, able to decide, to define and to enact what of the "hidden" Torah has to be practised as "revealed" Torah.[41] Certain aspects correspond to the relationship between deposited exemplar and published exemplar of a document. In the case of Torah, however, "the hidden" becomes "the revealed" not by publication of the whole, nor primarily by exegesis, but by acts of proclamation of the respective binding norms and their registering in a *midraš hat-Torah*. Analogy as well as difference in relation to later rabbinical "halakhah (from Sinai)" are evident: the Rabbinic Sages took the functional position of the priests/Zadokites, the rabbinical schools replaced the priestly institution; but their method to proclaim what the actual Halakhah is, was not less authoritative, it became, however, restricted to the "Oral Torah", also not necessarily derived by exegesis (rabbinic Midrash). The function of the *Môreh ha-ṣedeq* was not that of an exegete nor that of a teacher, it was a personally monopolized version of that priestly monopoly that later (transferred to the Sages) has been ascribed to a *Môrêh h^alakhah* – a Torah adviser. In Greek Hebrew *môreh* corresponds to *nomothetês* in LXX Ps 9:21, while in Deut 17:10 *nomothetêtê soi* represents Hebrew *ywrwk*. In any case the term *hôrôt* or *môreh* is closely related to concrete cases of Torah and jurisprudence. Moses is regarded as the *Môreh* kat exochen, more or less the type according to which the priestly as well as the laic Sages modelled their claims. The key text in this sense is Exod 18:15–16: The people come to Moses *lidrôš* God – to demand (Tg: *ltb'*) Divine advice or a verdict (Tg: *'wlpn mn qdm YY*; LXX: *ekzêtêsai krisin*) by Moses. And Moses says to Jethro: "Whenever they have a dispute it is brought before me and I decide and I make known the prescriptions of God and His tôrôt". And Jethro says v. 20: "And you shall admonish them concerning the prescriptions and the tôrôt and make known to them the way in which they shall walk, and the practice which they shall perform". There is no place for interpretation, it is a procedure of jurisdiction in the sense that Moses – or his successors, the priests, are performing an essentially Divine action.

Consequently, there is no reason to assume for Qumran *drš/mdrš* a connotation like "to expound" or "to derive from scripture".[42] Some of the her-

---

[41] Cf. the blessing for the Zadokite priests in 1Q28b (1QS^b) 3:22–25: "... whom God has chosen to enforce His covenant [for ever and to scr]utinize all His laws in the midst of His people, and to advise (*l^e-hôrôt*) them as He commanded and who shall establish ...[......] and in justice take care of all His prescriptions, and walk a[s] He has chosen".

[42] E. Qimron, *The Hebrew of the Dead Sea Scrolls* (HSS 30; Atlanta: Scholars Press 1986) 92: "exposition", following R. Polzin, *Late Biblical Hebrew* (New Haven 1976) 141–42.

meneutical devices ascribed to the Qumran community do not fit the Qumranic concept of revelation and authority at all, but correspond more or less to Christian or/and orthodox Jewish Biblical canon theology and hermeneutics.

2.3. *Priestly Authority*

According to the community's own historical outlook as attested particularly in CD and 1QS, the institutionalized group in charge of Torah are the priests, and in particular the Zadokite priests. The prominent position of the latter has already been a request of the Book of Ezekiel (Ezek 40:46; 44:15; 48:11), and in Qumran their exclusive right of Torah disposal is stressed in an unequivocal way, as for instance 1QS 5:1–4: "This is the rule for the men of the *yahad* who are ready to turn back from all evil and to stick to everything which He had commanded according to His will, to separate themselves from the community of the men of evil, to form a *yaḥad* in Torah and goods, obedient to the Sons of Zadok, the priests, the guardians (!) of the Covenant, and to the majority of the men of the *yaḥad*, who stick to (!) the Covenant. On their authority passes the decision about the rank of status (of everyone) concerning Torah, goods, and jurisdiction, to perform faithfulness, *yaḥad*, humility, justice and law, charity and regardful behaviour in all their ways". And, further, 5:7–9: "Everybody who enters the corporation of the *yaḥad* shall enter the Covenant in the presence of all the wilful ones, and impose upon himself by a binding oath to return to the Torah of Moses according to everything which He had commanded, with all his heart and with all his soul, according to all which is revealed from it to the Sons of Zadok, the priests, the guardians of the Covenant, and the mediators of His will (*dôr^{e}šê r^{e}ṣônô*), and to the majority of the men of their (!) Covenant ...".

1QS 8:15 formulates as a résumé of the activity of the *yaḥad*: "This is the midraš (record, account) of the Torah which He has commanded by Moses, in order to practise according to all the 'revealed' from time to time, and as the prophets revealed by His holy spirit". This sentence exhibits three aspects, (a) the Torah of Moses and (b) its application to the respective "time", (c) as revealed by the prophets, but not directly, for according to other passages the respective "time" has to be defined by Pesher interpretation (s. below chapter 3.2).

1QS 9:12–15 illustrates the practical significance for the community's particular organization: "These are the commandments for the Maskil in order to apply them in (their relationship) to every living, according to the order of precedence of every time and (according to) the reputation of each person, to do the will of God according to all the 'revealed' for each (period of) time, and the learning of all the knowledge which results according to the times, and the prescription of the time, to distinguish and weigh the sons of justice according to their spirit, and the elect of the time to ...".

3. The Teacher of Righteousness and the Qumranic Claims to Authority

3.1 "Enactor of Justice" and "Prophet like Moses"

In addition to this Zadokite privilege the Qumran people claimed a unique form of double authority for the *Môreh ha-ṣedeq*, usually translated as "Teacher of Righteousness". A more precise translation is: "Adviser" or "Enactor of Justice".

1QpHab 7:1–8 explicitly presupposes that God revealed to the "Teacher (Enactor) of Justice" by His holy spirit also the actual meaning of the prophetic texts so as to establish the respective "time" in the course of history and the period of the end of days. The prophet himself did not realize the actual meaning, his words are something like a riddle or a dream which has to be solved. Consequently, the verb for dream interpretation, *ptr/pšr*, also became the *terminus technicus* for this kind of actualizing eschatologization (Pesher-interpretation) of prophetic texts[43] while it never appears in a context concerning Torah contents, which are subject to *drš*. The "Teacher (Enactor) of Justice" and his followers after him claimed for themselves, therefore, two different kinds of disposal of revelation: (a) Torah revelation *(mdrš)* and (b) inspired interpretation of prophetic texts each of them with its own hermeneutics. The combination of both leads to the provocative claim that the Teacher and his followers were able to determine the respective moment in its relation to the course of history in the imminent end of days and to proclaim *(drš)* the Torah or prescription "of the time" as the "revealed" one. While the eschatological interpretation and application of prophetic texts was a common practice also in rabbinic (and, of course, Christian) circles without, however, using the term *pšr*, the ultimate step of Qumran claims to Torah authority has no parallel in Rabbinic Judaism. It is represented by the designation of the "Teacher/Enactor of Justice" as "a prophet like Moses" (Deut 18:18).

Since the Torah as revelation of God's will has been bound to the name of Moses the latter appears in Jewish literature as a prophet of unique quality. To call somebody a prophet like Moses would mean not less than to announce his official appointment to this function with its unique relationship to God and to the Torah, and thus to claim the highest possible degree of human authority – "like Mose". The Christians claimed it for Jesus Christ, but in Rabbinic and later Judaism such claims rarely appeared, the Mosaic authority being divided among the Rabbis. Towards the end of the second century BCE, however, the Hasmonean propaganda tried to make the people believe that John Hyrcanus displayed three qualities: that of a military leader, that of a statesman and that of a prophet – like Moses (Josephus, *De bello Iudaico* 1.68). The more or less chronological coincidence with similar claims for the Qumranic "Teacher (Enactor) of Justice" is scarcely incidental. Among the Qumran texts the prophet of Deut 18:18 appears twice in characteristic contexts. In 4Q158,6 the concept is directly connected with the revelation at Sinai by formulations as in Exod 20:19–22 and Deut 5:28f, in 4Q175 (4QTest) the polemical note is much more perspicuous: The chain of sentences resemble Deut 5:28f, Deut 18:18; Num 24:15–18 (eschatological prophecy about a ruler!), Deut 33:8–11 (prophecy about Levi, and Josh 6:26, a

[43] M. Fishbane, "The Qumran Pesher and Traits of Ancient Hermeneutics", *Proceedings of the Sixth World Congress of Jewish Studies* I (Jerusalem 1977) 97–114.

polemic against Jericho. Jericho was an important priestly settlement, to a large extent a royal domain with strongholds in its vicinity, and at the same time a Hasmonean (and later on Herodian) winter residence. The combination of the situation in Exodus 20 with sentences also included in Deuteronomy corresponds to a broader tradition, it is also attested in the Samaritan Text tradition. And in the Samaritan Targum to the Pentateuch. The whole issue needs critical investigation.

As a consequence of these disputes about Torah authority it became necessary to define, a) what institutions or functionaries are to be regarded as in charge of "the Torah", and b) what "Torah" should or could mean in a concrete situation, in the language of the Qumran texts: What has to be acknowledged on what personal or institutional authority as "Torah of the time"? Consequently, we have to realize that "Torah" at Qumran is not at all restricted to the Pentateuch and, in further consequence, that legal developments were not necessarily dependent on exegesis but on juridical reasoning which may become part of exegetical procedures. Even the rabbinic hermeneutical *middôt* reflect in their oldest strata juridical methods.

3.2. Torah and Prophets

The Prophets ("His servants") in the Qumran texts are representatives of a kind of revelation secondary to the Torah (1QS 8:15f.), not yet in the sense of an already defined literary corpus. Texts from Isaiah and Ezekiel are frequently cited and interpreted, but from the Minor Prophets only in some cases to the same extent. As seen above in connection with the "Teacher (Enactor) of Justice" the Qumran community presupposed that Prophetic texts (the Psalms of David included) require like dreams an additional step of revelation by *pesher* interpretation. They serve as basis for the definition of the stage of time within the course of "history" or more accurately: the end of days. This renders it possible to proclaim the respective "prescription of the time", the *Midraš hat-Torah* revealing the "hidden" precepts and making them into "revealed" ones. This presupposes, that the Torah itself comprises all the will of God for all times, but that the whole Torah is not "revealed" for each period. The Prophetic texts are of substantially different character than the legal Torah traditions. No Qumran text would insinuate that Moses did not know the sense of a Torah regulation. The prophets, however, did not know the whole and accurate meaning of their words aiming at a certain point of final history, a riddle to be resolved by *pesher* method, a hermeneutic device of totally different character.

In a tradition shared also by the Qumran community an essentially elitist and conservative Zadokite group merged with clear cut claims to priestly privileges with radical eschatologists, thus combining the priestly privilege of Torah disposal (or: enacting) and a cultic world view with apocalyptical-prophetical speculations about history.

According to these presuppositions the Zadokites could not have been interested in a definition of a 'canon'. A defined canon would have changed their Torah enacting privilege or *Midraš hat-Torah* in its character as *revelatio continua* into interpretation of revealed 'canonical' texts. Precisely this change took place on the line which led to Rabbinic Judaism as soon as the "Written Torah" became restricted to the Pentateuch. The quest for a definiton of "Torah" authority was not only a religious issue, it was also a question of power.

4. Questions Regarding the Chronological Relationship of Torah Traditions

An investigation of the story of the flood in Gen 6–9 and its underlying calendrical conceptions by U. GLESSMER suggests that a solar calendar as attested in the *Book of Jubilees* and its account of the flood seems to fit the chronological scheme more than the lunar calendar in the text form of MT.[44] In this case the question is not how the author of the *Book of Jubilees* interpreted the "biblical" story of the flood but in reverse: how the redactors of the pre-MT text form eliminated on the basis of the new lunar calendar an older tradition which has been retained by the author of the *Book of Jubilees* and others.

The Pentateuch contains no regulations for the temple. This is astonishing in face of the number of laws concerning the situation in the land of Israel. There are, of course, passages and laws in connection with the tabernacle or the "camp" but from a historical point of view it is evident that they reflect circumstances during the time of the late first and early second temple. Regulations concerning the sanctuary at Jerusalem must have been extant since its earliest days – for instance regulations concerning persons not entitled to enter its precincts as in 11Q19 45:7–18. Does it really make sense to assume that the latter has been formulated and derived from pentateuchal passages? More likely, the authors of P formulated their text for the tabernacle on the basis of existing regulations for the temple, and they did so already facing conflicting views as already reflected in many respects in the pentateuchal sources P and H.[45]

As a rule, and really with only a few exceptions, scholars labelled Qumran practice or Qumran law as "sectarian" presupposing thus a) a chronological sequence, and b) a qualification in the sense of mainstream Judaism versus sectarian deviation. The "sectarian" point of view reflects, however in many cases an older practice, and the innovation appears as non-"sectarian" only because of the circumstances of power. 11Q19 (Temple) has been usually qualified as a sectarian product in spite of some evidence that it contains regulations of older origin; so too for instance concerning the hides of (clean) animals slaughtered outside Jerusalem 11Q19 47:7–15. The issue had been introduced in a less stricter formulation (concerning only hides of unclean animals) among the decrees of Antiochus III (Josephus, *Antiquities* 12.146) which indicates that at that time a strict tendency prevailed which represented traditions also contained later in Qumran writings, where, however, the ritual aspects appear even more stressed. The mere fact that it seemed necessary to engage the king in such a measure attests to already existing disputes and

---

[44] U. GLESSMER, "Antike und moderne Auslegungen des Sintflutberichtes Gen 6–8 und der Qumran-Pesher 4Q252", *Theologische Fakultät Leipzig. Forschungsstelle Judentum. Mitteilungen und Beiträge* 6 (Leipzig 1993) 3–79.

[45] I. KNOHL, *Mqdš hdmmh* (Jerusalem: Magnes Press 1993).

differing practices. At the time of Antiochus the mentioned practice was not a "sectarian" one, at least in this instance.

A fascinating example of juridical reasoning combined with interpretation of written laws is provided by 11Q19 (Temple) 66:11–17, an unfortunately incomplete account of incest laws. The passage may be conceived as composed of biblical components and expanded by exegetical and juridical argumentation to avoid the impression that certain prohibitions hold true only concerning relatives explicitly mentioned. The known biblical laws in Lev 18:6–18; Lev 20:19–21; Deut 27:22 are in this respect not complete, and on their basis alone the status of a niece remains an open question. This is a juridical problem which needs clarification for the practice. On the basis of logical reasoning it would be a matter of course according to the legal system if the daughter of the brother or sister of the father and likewise of the mother were regarded on one level, and, consequently forbidden for marriage. 11Q19 draws this conclusion, a polemical passage in CD (5:6–11) attests, however, that others avoided this consequence. CD cites 5:8 f. Moses: "But Moses had said: 'Do not approach your mother's sister, she is your mother's near kin'." This is only partially the wording of Lev 18:13 and not necessarily a variant text of Lev 18:13 but rather a citation from some other source. In addition, a juridical reasoning follows: "It is true that the laws concerning incest are written in respect to men but in analogy to them they apply also to the women. If, therefore, a brother's daughter enters sexual relations with the brother of her father she is (to be regarded) surely (as) his near kin!" This law is logically derived. The opponents were in this case 'exegetes' insisting on the exact wording of extant texts which did not mention the niece. Now, what was the older practice or opinion? Due to the circumstances of power the logical solution in this case became a "sectarian" point of view.

Not in every instant but probably in many cases a more strict regulation has to be regarded as older than a liberal one. The tendency to formulate less stricter norms out of practical reasons and group interest is a normal phenomenon. In the eyes of the apocalyptically motivated lawyers in Qumran this meant enacting "smooth rulings" *(lidrôš ḥ^a^laqôt)* and contrary to the character of the situation immediately prior to the end of days. Consequently they felt themselves bound to maintain a conservative attitude. But an eschatological outlook of this kind was certainly likely also to stimulate a more strict legislation and in which case an innovative practice. The consequence is that Qumran laws cannot be classified according to either attitude alone.

It is evident that 11Q19 is not only the product of Qumran scribes who far abroad from temple practice began to reorganize the whole cultic organization by theoretical exegetical procedures and derivations, creating a "sectarian" cult order.[46]

Even more important is another point of view. 11Q19 represents in spite of its composite character (including sources of probably much older origin) a work with clear marks of a systematic composition, a first step in the direction of a code, here organized according to the concept of concentric graduated areas of holiness. This is, in first circle a juridic/legislative achieve-

[46] For the opposite view cf. for instance J. Milgrom, "The Scriptural Foundations and Deviations in the Laws of Purity in the Temple Scroll", *Archaeology and History* (1990) 83–99.

ment presupposing the faculty of systematic reasoning, provoked by real existing problems, for instance in the case of disputed practices, as a rule connected with concrete interests within the various circles and layers of the priestly society.

In the second circle certainly the question emerged, of how existing regulations and practices could be harmonized with extant written regulations as far as they enjoyed the acknowledgement of revealed Torah. Harmonizing was, therefore, not restricted to pentateuchal laws. It was a necessary procedure in any case of contradicting wordings of extant laws whether in the Pentateuch or not. To use similar wordings or identical phrases for the formulation of laws concerning related subjects should not be mistaken in an exclusive manner as exegesis of the one text known to us from the Pentateuch, presupposing at the same time the later 'canonical' significance of the Pentateuch.

Probably only in the third circle did the problem of the relationship of existing disputed practices or regulations to laws in the Pentateuch emerge, and this to the degree as the Pentateuch gained the prestige of a document acknowledged by all parties involved, thus providing arguments which could been accepted by the rival party too.

5. Interpretation of Non Legal Texts

Interpretation of Scriptures may be found in many text passages but not in the form of running commentaries, and in most cases it is difficult to distinguish from certain kinds of text use for various purposes. All the materials which frequently have been labelled as "rewritten Bible", "expanded Bible" or with similar designations, and even the Aramaic translation of the Book of Job, are not to be regarded as interpretation of text but rather as reworking of subjects (in German: 'Stoff').

In CD for instance some biblical passages serve with their peculiar interpretation as polemical instruments in the admonition parts. In the frame of an 'historical' retrospective, biblical passages are interpreted in a typological way: for instance 1:13–20 (Hos 4:16; 10:11 or 13); 4:10–20 (Isa 24:17; Ezek 13:10); 6:2–11 (Num 21:16–18; Isa 54:16); 7:9–8:19 (Isa 7:17; Zech 6:8; Am 5:26; 9:11; Num 24:17; Hos 5:10; Deut 32:33; Ezek 13:10; Mic 2:11; Deut 9:5). This typological exegesis refers events of the past to current events and corresponds in this respect to Pesher interpretations. The difference consists in the hermeneutical device; the sporadic interpretations including such of typological character, do not exhibit a consistent hermeneutical line.

M. FISHBANE[47] mentioned as an example for "paraenetic or liturgical reapplication" 1QS 2:2–10 with its peculiar form of the priestly blessing. FISHBANE

---

[47] *Mikra* (1988) 372.

assumes as basis Num 6:24–26, but this is not necessary as the priestly blessing formula seems to have been in use from early on in a number of variations.[48] It is a dogmatic presupposition that a pentateuchal text has in all cases to be regarded as prior to all other text forms and as the only possible basis for 'interpretation'.

6. Pesher

All research on Qumran exegesis focused for a long time on Pesher interpretation.[49] The formula is a stereotype. An interpretation of a passage is introduced by *pšr hdbr* ("the interpretation of the word …"), or by *pšrw* ("its interpretation is …"), subsequent interpretations are introduced by *hw'* ("this is"). There seems to be a formal difference between "thematic Pesharim" and Pesharim as running commentaries like 1QpHab. The formulations correspond in general to an already fixed conventional terminology and procedure which, however, has not been applied in all instances in a strictly identical way.

The number of extant testimonies for this kind of exegesis is in spite of the fragmentary character of the most texts, impressive. But all these commentaries are of a relatively late date and only in extant one copy. The concentration on certain books, particularly Isaiah, is puzzling, for Jeremiah and others are missing. Ezechiel has been of great interest, but evidently more in the sense of 'Stoff' (content) than text or for Pesher-interpretation.

Isa	3Q4 (?)	Isa 1:1
	4Q161	Isa 10:20–22, 24–28.34; 11:1–5
	4Q162	Isa 5:5–6, 11–14, 24–25, 29–30; 6:9?
	4Q163	Isa 8:7–9?; 9:11?, 14–20; 10:12–13, 19(?), 20–24
	4Q164	Isa 54:11–12
	4Q165	Isa 1:1?; 40:12; 14:12; 15:4–6; 21:2(?), 11–15; 32:5–7
Hos	4Q166	Hos 2:8–14
	4Q167	Hos 5:13–15; 6:4, 7, 9–10; 8:13–13
Hab	1QpHab	Hab 1:1–2:20
Mal	5Q10 (?)	
Micah	1Q14	Mic 1:2–9; 4,13; 6,14–16; 7:6, 8–9, 17
	4Q168	Mic 4:8–12
Nah	4Q169	Nah 1:3–6; 2:12–14; 3:1–12, 14
Zeph	1Q 15	Zeph 1:18–2:2
	4Q170	Zeph 1:12–13
Ps	1Q16	Ps 57:1,4; 68:12–13, 26–27, 30–31
	4Q171	Ps 37:7–26, 28–40; 45:1–2; 60:8–9
	4Q173	Ps 127:2–3, 5; 129:7–8; 118:26f.

[48] B. BARKAI, "The Priestly Benediction on Silver Plaques from Ketef Hinnom in Jerusalem", *Tel Aviv* 19 (1992) 139–192.

[49] Recent publications: P. HORGAN, *Pesharim. Qumran Interpretations of Biblical Books* (CBQ Suppl. Series 8; Washington 1979); B. NITZAN, *Pesher Habakkuk* (Jerusalem: Bialik Institute 1986); H.-J. FABRY, "Schriftverständnis und Schriftauslegung der Qumran-Essener", *Bibel in jüdischer und christlicher Tradition* (see n. 19) 87–96.

Smaller literary units including Pesher interpretations are rather common, for instance CD 4:10–20; 4Q174 (= 4QFlor) and 4Q177 (4QCatena^{a});[50] 4Q181; 4Q239; 4Q252 (4QpGen^{a}); 4Q253 (4QpGen^{b}) and 4Q254 (4QpGen^{c}). Sometimes a citation of or an allusion to a passage presupposing a certain meaning appears in texts of a different literary genre. Some cases may be regarded as "hidden interpretations" but not necessarily always as a Pesher interpretation.[51]

Characteristic is a lack of consciousness concerning the difference between finding out the meaning of the text and an interpretation aiming at a different meaning than the obvious one. 1QpHab 7:1–2 presupposes that the text itself and its prophetic author cannot provide the real meaning of the prophecy. This real meaning or the message of God as transmitted by the words of this prophecy remained unknown even to the prophet until the establishment of a specific hermeneutical device combined with the claim to inspired interpretation by "the Teacher of Justice, whom God made has known all the mysteries of the words of the prophets, His servants". The hermeneutical device consists in the claim to dispose of a secret apocalyptical knowledge.[52] Characteristic for most Pesher texts are consequently, references to current events, introducing frequently typological interpretations of earlier historical events, all in the light of the imminent "end of days". A Pesher passage displays in many cases already in the form of the citation a pre-existent interpretation. The authors looked for text passages and ('atomizing' the text) even for rather small parts of them, to find the passage or word fit to serve as vehicle for the message to be presented as result of Pesher interpretation, and as the message which God really had in mind. The respective actual situation of the community, on the verge of the "end of days", or historical events with some meaning for the present situation of the community, provided the criteria for this apparently arbitrary treatment of the prophetic texts.

One of the consequences was that, in spite of a presupposed and not contested revelatory authority of the prophet in question, it was not the prophetic text itself which constituted the decisive factor and the real basis of the message. It was the pre-conceived message of the *pesher*, the "biblical text" being rather an instrument to arrange and to set forth what the author already had in mind, presupposing that his interpretation is the message of God hidden in the vessel of prophetical speech. The analogy to dreams and dream interpretation is clear. The same procedure, however, focussed on christological issues, has been applied by the Christians. The concentration of all exegetical endeavours on the christological purpose provided, however, a rather coherent hermeneutical device in which typological christology prevailed.

---

[50] A. Steudel, "Eschatological Interpretation of Scripture in 4Q177 (4QCatena^{a})", *RevQ* 14 (1989/90) 473–481.

[51] M. Kister, "Biblical Phrases and Hidden Biblical Interpretations and Pesharim", *The Dead Sea Scrolls. Forty Years of Research* (ed. D. Dimant/U. Rappaport; Leiden: Brill 1992) 27–39.

[52] J. A. Sanders, "Habakkuk in Qumran, Paul and the Old Testament", *JR* 39 (1959) 232–244.

Also the emergence of commentaries to prophetic books as 1QpHab in Qumran seems to have been the consequence of the development of a hermeneutical device initiated by the claim of the "Teacher/Enactor of Justice" and his followers to know the real eschatological bearing of prophetic Scriptures in general. This implies that in earlier stages the application of the Pesher interpretation has been only a more or less sporadic one, in the frame of diverse literary genres and not in form of running commentaries. This fits the literary evidence for Pesher interpretations in various contexts and the relatively late appearance of Pesher commentaries within the Qumran literature proper. The Pesher commentaries were apparently the work of individual authors and (contrary to texts extant in a number of exemplars) not written for use on a wider scale. Writing of *pesher* commentaries on prophetic texts was a kind of professionalization based on an older tradition of sporadic Pesher interpretation. The single, sporadic Pesher seems to have been still nearer to the patterns of oracle or dream interpretation, and was therefore open to a variety of uses. In any case, Pesher application was already in these earlier stages not a question of real interpretative undertaking in the first instance, but a fictitious interpretation to transmit a certain pre-conceived content as in the case of pre-meditated oracles with oracle interpretations. As soon as actual oracles were replaced by the use of a selected written text passage of an alleged prophetic quality, the respective text became exposed to adaptations matching the pre-conceived message, the text itself being only of instrumental significance. The text critical value of such passages in Pesher contexts is, consequently, a rather restricted one[53], because it was not the text itself which formed the point of departure nor its original meaning. The issue of correct textual transmission and real interpretative activity emerged when dissenting readers began to compare text and Pesher message, and when the question of the correct wording of a text and the plausibility of its interpretation became subject to dispute. This does not presuppose text critical activities in a modern sense, for the crucial question was first of all: who disposes of acknowledged standard text exemplars? It is clear that for Torah texts the priestly privilege has to be taken into account and that, on this basis, the master exemplars at the temple of Jerusalem had their special significance independent from the question of a philologically 'correct' text. We know practically nothing about similar claims to a textual monopolization concerning prophetical Scriptures. But it seems very likely that the disputes during the decisive stages of the Qumran community caused among certain groups involved a new sensitiveness for the text's wording as well as for the task of interpretation.

Among the groups that most likely developed new outlooks of this kind were the Pharisees, in a special situation in between the extremes concerning the relationship between Torah and Pentateuch, as well as concerning text and meaning of prophetical Scriptures. As a predominantly laicistic movement they could not claim to dispose of the master exemplars of the temple. They

---

[53] Cf. G.J. Brooke, "The Biblical Texts in the Qumran Commentaries: Scribal errors or exegetical variants?", *Early Jewish and Christian Exegesis. Studies in Memory of W.H. Brownlee* (ed. C.A. Evans/W.F. Stinespring; Atlanta: Scholars Press 1987) 85–100.

had, consequently, to look for arguments not connected with institutional prerogatives: arguments of text transmission leading finally to the MT, and arguments of logical hermeneutics leading to a principal priority of the obvious (usually but not necessarily literal) meaning. Regarding Torah they created their own mechanism of authoritative claims: reducing the written Torah to the laws in the Pentateuch they achieved three aims:

(a) The replacing of the old institutionalized priestly Torah monopoly by the monopoly of their own Sages and their institutions.

(b) An enhanced significance of interpretative juridic procedures for which they finally and consequently developed specific rules (*middôt*). According to Josephus (*De bello Iudaico* 1.110; cf. *Vita* 191) the Pharisees distinguished themselves by their *akribía* regarding the Torah.

(c) A relatively free disposal of legal traditions with the possibility of defining them as part of authoritative "traditions (or customs) of the fathers" and later on as "Oral Torah", and to enact them as *h*[a]*lakah*, eventually (and this was done increasingly) but not necessarily looking for some support in the "Written Torah" and introducing thus the exegetical procedures regarding the Written Torah into the realm of the Oral Torah.

Concerning use and interpretation of "Prophets" and "other Scriptures" the space for free disposal remained by far more extensive, contrary to the claims to monopoly and inspired exegesis in the Qumran community. But this did not exclude similar procedures (without, however, using the term *pšr*).

In face of Qumran Pesher exegesis, however, a crucial question arises: What sense and what authority remains for the prophetic text beyond the meaning pretended by the Pesher? Evidently none except by a new Pesher in a changed situation. However, the Pesher interpretation implicates a temporal limit by pretending to concern "the end of the days", for how long was a community able to endure under the rigid conditions of the *yaḥad* the continuous delay of the end, trusting nevertheless unswervingly that all the dates of God's mysterious plan of history will come true (1QpHab 7:9–14)?

CHAPTER FOUR

Early Jewish Interpretation in a Hellenistic Style

By FOLKER SIEGERT, Münster

1. Homer and Moses. Hellenistic Art of Interpretation and the Jewish Bible

Sources: CORNUTUS: *Theologiae Graecae compendium* (ed. C. Lang; Leipzig 1881; Teubner). HÉRACLITE (Heraclitus Stoicus): *Allégories d'Homère* (ed. F. Buffière; Paris 1962; Budé; cited as *Quaestiones Homericae*). PLUTARQUE (Plutarch): *Œuvres morales* I/1 (Paris 1987; Budé; relevant for *De audiendis poetis*, ed. A Philippon, and for its "Introduction générale", by R. Flacelière); idem, V/2 (*De Iside et Osiride*, ed. C. Froidefond); ⟨Plutarchus⟩, *De Homero* (ed. J. F. Kindstrand; Leipzig 1990; Teubner); Plutarch, *Moralia* (ed. F. C. Babbitt et al.; LCL, 15 vols. in 16, 1927–1976; vol. 1, 72–197: *De audiendis poetis;* vol. 5, 1936, 3–197: *De Iside et Osiride*); M. STERN (ed.), *Greek and Latin Authors on Jews and Judaism* I–III (Jerusalem 1976–84).

Bibliography: G. DELLING, *Bibliographie zur jüdisch-hellenistischen und intertestamentarischen Literatur* (TU 106, 2; Berlin ^{2}1975) 20–53.

General works: F. BUFFIÈRE, *Les mythes d'Homère et la pensée grecque* (Paris 1956; 1973); D. DAWSON, *Allegorical Readers and Cultural Revision in Ancient Alexandria* (Berkeley 1992); H. DÖRRIE, "Zur Methodik antiker Exegese", *ZNW* 65 (1974) 121–138; A.-J. FESTUGIÈRE, *La révélation d'Hermès Trismégiste* II. *Le dieu cosmique* (Paris 1949; Ebib); G. GLOCKMANN, *Homer in der frühchristlichen Zeit bis Justinus* (TU 105; Berlin 1968); M. HENGEL, *Judaism and Hellenism: Studies of their Encounter in Palestine in the Early Hellenistic Period*, I–II (London 1974; esp. ch. II, sect. 2); idem, *The 'Hellenization' of Judaea in the First Century after Christ* (London/Philadelphia 1989); J. C. JOOSEN/J. H. WASZINK, Art. "Allegorese", RAC 1 (1950) 283–293; R. LAMBERTON, *Homer the Theologian* (Berkeley 1986); J. LEIPOLDT/S. MORENZ, *Heilige Schriften. Betrachtungen zur Religionsgeschichte der antiken Mittelmeerwelt* (Leipzig 1953) 129–140; H.-I. MARROU, *Histoire de l'éducation dans l'antiquité* (Paris ^{2}1950; ET: *A History of Education in Antiquity*, London 1956); J. PÉPIN, *Mythe et allégorie* (1958; Paris ^{2}1976; esp. 125–242); idem, *De la philosophie ancienne à la théologie patristique* (London 1986; esp. ch. 9); R. PFEIFFER, *History of Classical Scholarship* (Oxford 1968; esp. Part II, ch. VII); E. SCHÜRER, *The History of the Jewish People in the Age of Jesus Christ* ⟨175 B. C.–A. D. 135⟩. *A New English Version* (rev. and ed. by G. Vermes and F. Miller), III/1-2 (Edinburgh 1986-87) [abbr. Schürer/Vermes, History]; F. SIEGERT, *Drei hellenistisch-jüdische Predigten* II (WUNT 61; Tübingen 1992) 55–91; N. WALTER, *Der jüdisch-hellenistische Thoraausleger Aristobulos* (TU 86; Berlin 1964) 124–149.

1.1. Classical Texts Outdated

Hellenistic culture falls within the scope of the present study because of its clear and early awareness of problems of interpretation. It first gave birth to the art of hermeneutics. Scholarly interpretation is a product of the Greek mind.

To its inventors it was not just an intellectual game but a response to necessity. Homer's epics had become the basis of Greek culture. Since classical times they were everybody's schoolbook (to be more or less retained by memory) and companion for life. Grammar school began with memorizing lines from Homer and learning grammar from him. High school (the Greeks spoke of the γραμματικός as opposed the γραμματιστής)[1] consisted largely of interpretation of Homer and of finding in him examples bearing on every domain of learning.

In the Hellenistic period this meant that any schoolboy from Marseille to Seleucia on the Tigris started his education by copying down and memorizing hundreds and hundreds of Homeric verses. By then the religious and moral contents of the *Iliad* and the *Odyssey* had become more and more questionable. They showed the 'Father of the gods' courting earthly women and even boys, his wife becoming jealous, and so on. The same criticism applied to Hesiod. It was told that Pythagoras on his descent to Hades saw the souls of Hesiod and of Homer being tormented for what they had said about the gods.[2] Would not the education of the youth require some poetry of higher religious and moral standards?[3]

1.2. Plato's Ban of Homer and the Uses of Allegorical Interpretation

Plato, therefore, banned the Homeric epics from his utopian Republic.[4] He strongly objected to the common practice whereby the Greek national epic was regarded as a storehouse of information about things human and divine, including medicine, warfare, politics, education, and law.[5]

In the intellectual circles of the Greco-Roman period, a harsh critique of religion in general,[6] and of myth in particular,[7] bore heavily on any exegete. Interpretation became a kind of apologetic. The term ἐξηγεῖσθαι which once had applied to a priestly activity, namely the interpretation that gives sense to an oracle (λόγιον),[8] ended up designating some kind of demythologization according to the epoch's intellectual standards. In Artemidorus' book on dreams (2nd cent. CE) Endymion's intercourse with Selene (the Moon) means,

---

[1] See Marrou, Histoire de l'éducation (1950), part II, chs. 2 and 5–6.

[2] Diogenes Laërtius 8.21, in the name of the 3rd-cent. BCE Peripatetician Jerome of Rhodes.

[3] Criticism of archaic Greek epics is as old as the pre-socratic philosophers Heraclitus (frg. 56, concerning Homer's pretention to encyclopedic knowledge) and Xenophanes of Colophon (frg. 11, blaming Homer for his immorality; cf. Heraclitus, frg. 42). For discussions in the Roman period, see also 1.5 below.

[4] Plato, *Republic* 377 C ff.; 368 A ff. (cf. Josephus, *Ap.* 2.255–257) and mainly 598 D–599 D.

[5] The same opinion may be found, without irony, in Greek literature from Xenophon, *Convivium* 4.6 to Artemidorus, *Onirocriticon* 1.2 p. 10 (cf. n. 9) and later on. No wonder that the Greek magical papyri offer a collection of Ὁμηρομαντεῖα (Homeric verses used as oracles): nos. 7.1–52 (Preisendanz). Ps.-Plutarch, *De Homero* 218 mentions the phenomenon of magical use; it has a parallel in the ancient and medieval reception of Vergil.

[6] See e.g. Lucian's *De sacrificiis*. Josephus gives a summary of the most relevant Greek arguments in *Ap.* 2.238–249. Christian apologists, like Aristides 8–11, and Minucius Felix 22 f. seem to draw upon the same tradition.

[7] H. D. Betz, *Hellenismus und Urchristentum. Gesammelte Aufsätze* I (Tübingen 1990) 200, n. 111: critiques and defenses of myth in Plutarch. As to Strabo's attitude, see 1.5, below.

[8] F. Büchsel, art. ἡγέομαι, ἐξηγέομαι, TWNT II (1935) 910.

"if interpreted" (ἐξηγούμενα), astrology.[9] We shall see that more than one term of scholarly exegesis derives from Greek religion.[10]

So far we have spoken of Stoic rationalism. The Platonists were less drastic. Plato himself had sometimes spoken in mythical form; and this form seemed to be inseparable from certain contents. Plutarch's interpretation of myths is more careful and avoids anatomizing (see 1.6). An extreme position was represented in the 4th cent. BCE by the Cynic Zoilus who dismissed all modernizations of ancient myths. The Byzantine Homer commentator Eustathius, archbishop of Thessalonica, still distinguishes the λυτικοί (exegetes seeking 'solutions' of Homeric riddles) from the ἐνστατικοί, 'those who insist' on the difficulties.[11] Other opponents known by name are Ariston of Chios (an early Stoic), and Seneca. Plutarch also may join them: in *De audiendis poetis* (*Mor.* 19 E) he rejects λύσεις τοῦ ποιητοῦ of the 'physical' type (see below) and proposes ethical considerations instead. To his mind, Homer deliberately gives examples not only of good but also of bad behaviour.

We know from Plato's writings that efforts to save Homer's fame through skillful interpretation were already going on in his day. In one of the passages prohibiting Homer's works he argues that it is wrong to have the gods fight against each other, "be it ἐν ὑπονοίαις, be it ἄνευ ὑπονοιῶν" (*Rep.* 378 D), using the very term on which the allegorists rested their case.[12]

In a much disputed passage of the *Iliad* (8.10–27) the angry Zeus threatens the other gods with casting them down to Hades so that even a chain of gold would not draw him nearer to them. Plato (*Theaetetus* 153 C/D) has Socrates say that this 'golden chain' is nothing else than the Sun whose revolution guarantees the existence (εἶναι) and the survival (σῴζεσθαι) of gods and men. This somewhat biased interpretation is also recorded in the manuals of Homeric interpretation of the Imperial period (see 1.5, below), and it has even been used by the Neoplatonists (Proclus).[13] In other words, it was classical for nine centuries.

Tatian, *Oratio ad Graecos* 31, names Theagenes of Rhegium (6th cent. BCE) and many others as inventors of, and authorities on, allegorical interpretation of Homer. His mention of Theagenes seems to be confirmed by a note in Porphyry[14] by which we also learn that Theagenes used both 'physical' and 'ethical' allegorical explanations (see 1.3, below).

A curious document of Greek endeavour to modernize ancient poetry through allegorization is the Derveni papyrus,[15] dating from the 4th cent. BCE. It contains one of many known texts of the Orphic cosmogony, adding to each verse several lines of commentary. It clearly formulates and uses the hermeneutic maxim that Orpheus' poem was meant to be an allegory.[16] Thus, philosophically minded readers became free to adapt the words of the text to

---

[9] Artemidorus, *Onirocriticon libri V* (ed. R. Pack; Leipzig 1963; Teubner) 4.47 end.

[10] The same holds for 'hermeneutics'; see below, 1.3.

[11] See Liddell/Scott/Jones s.v. ἐνστατικός. An example may be Apollodorus (1.4/5, below).

[12] See below, 1.5, Glossary. In Plato, cf. further *Phaedrus* 229 C–E.

[13] Siegert, Hellenistisch-jüdische Predigten II (1992) 74f. (with reference to Philo, *De Deo* 5).

[14] See Pépin, Mythe et allégorie (1976) 97–99, with critical doubts in the footnote.

[15] It was found in 1962 in Derveni, near Thessalonica. For a provisional publication, see *ZPE* 47 (1982) a 12-page appendix after p. 300.

[16] col. 9, 1. 5 f.: ὅτι μὲμ πᾶσαν τὴμ πόησιν περὶ τῶμ πραγμάτων αἰνίζεται καθ' (sic) ἔπος ἕκαστον ἀνάγκη λέγειν. A late form of this poem has been interpolated into Aristobulus, frg. 4 § 5. – To us, of course, this poem is a pseudepigraphon.

their conception of the subject matter; in extreme cases they entirely exchanged the subject matter in order to retain the words as a kind of riddle.

The Homeric poems thus retained their status as a kind of Scripture.[17] Readers "turned them and turned them for everything was in them", as did Ben Bag-Bag later on with the Tora.[18] Opposition was rare and restricted to intellectual circles; occasionally Josephus may join them.[19]

Being newcomers on the Greek cultural scene, the Stoic philosophers needed to prove the antiquity of their doctrines. They were eager to use the classical epics as well as the 'obscure' Heraclitus to make their point. Their answer to Plato was that Homer actually did know more than he was able to tell a large audience. He left it to his interpreters to figure out his hints (αἰνίγματα) and his beautiful, though enigmatic expressions (ἀλληγορίαι).[20]

A centre for Stoic interpretation was the so-called Pergamene school. It had very little in common with Alexandrine philology (see 1.4, below). Its beginnings lay in the early 2nd cent. BCE when Crates of Mallos, the first head of the newly founded library at Pergamum and a contemporary of Aristarchus, became renowned for extensive use of Homeric 'allegories'.

1.3. The Theological Basis of the Stoic Interpretation of Homer

The pre-Socratic philosopher Xenophanes, whose criticism of Homer may have stimulated other scholars to preserve Homer's standing, opposed one God, "the greatest among gods and men", to the Homeric polytheism (frg. 21 B 11). Homer's Stoic exegetes respond to this postulate by distinguishing Zeus, the divine fire, from minor cosmic agents which are part of this fire.

We may rightly speak of a 'theological' basis because *theology* is a Greek word which has no counterpart in the Bible. In Imperial times, it meant nearly what it means in modern languages, i.e. the coherent presentation, in discursive form, of religious doctrine.[21] The Greeks started it, and the Jews who spoke Greek took it over from them. For understandable reasons they rarely called Moses' wisdom a θεολογία.[22] Only Philo claims Moses to be "the

---

[17] Dörrie, Zur Methodik (1974) 122; Buffière, Les mythes d'Homere (1956) 10–13 ("Homère, Bible des Grecs"); Leipoldt/Morenz, Heilige Schriften (1953) 130; Stanley, *NovT* 1990 (see below, n. 35), 51. Thus the Jewish Bible did not compete with the ἱεροὶ λόγοι of the period (which were not published), but with the greatest of poets.

[18] *'Abot* 5:25.

[19] Josephus, *Ap.* 2.255, at the end of his (or his source's) rendering of Greek critique of religion, claims that the true philosophers always avoided polytheism, "nor were they ignorant of the insipid pretense of expressing oneself allegorically (οὔτε τὰς ψυχρὰς προφάσεις τῶν ἀλληγοριῶν ἠγνόησαν — ψυχρός being a rhetorical term meaning something of bad taste). They despised them rightly and agreed with us (i.e. the Jews) about the true and befitting opinion about God".

[20] See Dörrie, Zur Methodik (1974) 124ff. and below, 1.5, for Greek exegetical terminology.

[21] R. Flacelière rightly proposes to render οἱ θεολόγοι (poets such as Homer and Hesiod) by *les théologues*, whereas the same word used in Plutarch's times for those who interpret ancient myths ὁσίως καὶ φιλοσόφως (so Plutarch's words in *Mor.* 355 C) should be translated by *les théologiens.* See his general introduction to Plutarch: *Œuvres morales*, I/1 (1987), p. clxi, n. 3.

[22] The word stem is absent from the LXX and from the Pseudepigrapha even in the largest definition; see Denis, Concordance grecque des Pseudépigraphes (see sect. 2, below) and the English index in Charlesworth, OTP. Some centuries later Eusebius of Cesarea was less hesitant:

Theologian" (see 4.2–3, below). Josephus once extols the σεμνότης τῆς ἡμετέρας θεολογίας (*Ap.* 1.225), and he once uses the verb θεολογεῖν to refer to the Essenes' speculations about the immortality of the human soul.

Paradoxically, Stoic materialism was instrumental in saving ancient mythical poetry from the charge of impiety. The Stoics viewed the divine as a kind of fire or material energy. They called it by the Aristotelian term *ether*[23] (on the surface) or *pneuma* (penetrating the cosmos). The cosmos was surrounded by a fiery globe of ether called Zeus, of whose splendour the heavenly bodies were only a part (but more than a symbol). Thus it became possible to explain the quarrels of the Homeric gods as antagonisms between the elements of the cosmos. In its classical form attested by Cornutus, Zeus is the origin of the world as well as its periodical end (in the ecpyrosis); he is its force of life (Ζεύς – ζῆν) and of self-rejuvenation as well as the one through whom (Δία – διά τινος) all beings exist. Hera was identified with the upper air (Ἥρα – ἀήρ, Homeric acc. ἠέρα), Hades with the lower air,[24] Poseidon with water, and so on.

This kind of theology was part of the second section of Stoic philosophy called 'physics'. (According to the Stoics, philosophy consists of logic, physics and ethics.) Accounting for the gods, therefore, was part of the task of explaining the cosmos. A.-J. Festugière describes this phenomenon in much detail in his second volume to which he gave the appropriate sub-title *Le dieu cosmique*. We may wonder how Jewish theologians managed to replace the Stoics' presuppositions with the very different ones required by the biblical God. Here lies one of Philo's great merits.

It goes without saying that the 'divine' Poet, 'the' Poet (Homer) was thought to be inspired by (a) God. Hesiod makes this claim for himself (*Theogonia* 22 and 35 f.); it was all the more readily granted to the great Homer.[25] Platonism with its theory of divine 'frenzy' (*Ion* 534 C–E; *Phaedrus* 244 A–245 B) had prepared the way, and the Stoic doctrine of *pneuma* as a divine element penetrating the cosmos with different degrees of intensity provided 'scientific' answers to sceptical questions.[26] In Antiquity, generally speaking, poets were a kind of prophet. In Latin, *vates* has both meanings.

---

in his *Praeparatio evangelica* 15.1.4 where he summarizes the Jewish material of bk. 7–9 he calls it τὰ Ἑβραίων λόγια and speaks of the δογματικὴ θεολογία which they contain. Cf. n. 205, below.

[23] Homer could be quoted as well, since in the *Iliad* and in the *Odyssey* Zeus is qualified as αἰθέρι ναίων: *Iliad* 2.412; 4.166; *Odyssey* 15.523. There was only one step to his identification with that fire.

[24] A common opinion in late Antiquity locates the spirits and the souls of the dead not below the earth, but in the air.

[25] Heraclitus the Stoic, *Quaestiones Homericae* 53.2; 76.1 (Homer as ἱεροφάντης), etc. Homer's being blind may have supported (or been supported by) the acknowledgement of his inner sensorium. – A negative proof is Lucian's ridiculing of Homer's alleged inspiration in *De sacrificiis* 5.

[26] See Posidonius' theory about three degrees of "the gods' impulse" (*deorum adpulsus*) on prophesying persons: 1st, the common *logos* "which is held by the gods' thinking"; 2nd, some spirit coming from the element of air, 3rd, when "the gods themselves speak with those asleep" (frg. 108 [Edelstein/Kidd] taken from Cicero, *De divinatione* 1.64). – Since its founder, Zeno of Citium, Stoicism provided a theory of oracles (μαντική): see I. ab (H. von) Arnim, *Stoicorum veterum fragmenta* I (Leipzig 1905) nos. 173 f., and Chrysippus, ibid. II (1903), nos. 1187–1216.

The Stoic Cornutus sums up his handbook of Greek theology by stating that his purpose was to lead young people to piety (εὐσεβεῖν) and to save them from superstition (δεισιδαιμονεῖν, chap. 35, end). The Stoic Heraclitus ends his book on the solution of Homeric problems in even stronger terms with the claim (79.12) that all his readers and all readers of Homer are "priests and temple guardians of his godly words".[27]

We may conclude this short lesson on Hellenistic theology with a philological remark about *hermeneutics*. To a Greek ear, this word is automatically understood in reference to Hermes, the god of communication (also, of commercial exchange, of theft, and of deceit).[28] Now the Stoics held Hermes in great esteem because of his status as mythical representative of the cosmic *logos*.[29] Not only did he promote efficient communication between men, but he also gave them divine knowledge. The Stoics had formal theories about this process (see n. 26) which left a mark on Philo (see 4.2).

1.4. A Note on Alexandrian Homeric Philology

Prior to the Pergamene School, Alexandrian philology had become known for a rather different approach to classical texts: Aristarchus, one of the Museum's first librarians, and others had the merit of laying down the basis of textual criticism. They emended Homer's epics on the basis of dialectological studies and of intra-Homeric analogy; they proceeded to conjectures (without deleting anything of the transmitted text) and they discarded (ἀθετεῖν) numerous verses by critical signs. Up to recent editions such verses are put into brackets as spurious, whereas in the handbooks of Homeric interpretation (see 1.5) they may be used without distinction.

Josephus occasionally tells us interesting details of ancient Homeric critique. His remark in *Ap.* 1.12 has been the basis of F. A. Wolf's hypothesis (1795) concerning the composite nature of the Homeric poems. Josephus also speaks of divergencies in the texts of Homer, and in 2.256 he mentions Plato's ban of the Poet.[30] Nevertheless no Jewish author, even among those who lived at Alexandria, ever got infected by this critical spirit. Even though the text of the Septuagint never was uniform, no attempt to apply Alexandrian criticism to the Bible is known before Origen. Hellenistic Jewish authors always regarded the LXX copies as textually identical even where they are not.[31]

---

[27] Ἱερεῖς δὲ καὶ ζάκοροι τῶν δαιμονίων ἐπῶν αὐτοῦ πάντες ἐσμὲν ἐξ ἴσου.

[28] *Wo getauscht wird, da wird auch getäuscht* (German proverb). – The verb ἑρμηνευειν (there is also the noun, ἑρμηνευτικὴ [τέχνη], Plato, *Politicus* 260 B), means 'to translate', 'to interpret', but also 'to express' (one's own thoughts). Hermes was the god of all of these. The ambiguity of the term has remained up to this day.

[29] Cornutus, *Theologiae Graecae compendium* 16; Heraclitus, *Quaestiones Homericae* 55; 59.9; 67.5; 72.5.

[30] Another detail, namely the remark that Homer does not know the word "law" (νόμος) (*Ap.* 2.155), has its parallel in *De Homero* 175.

[31] See Ps.-Philo, *De Sampsone* 41: in the context of a literal exegesis the author switches from LXX cod. A (etc.), used so far, to cod. B. The interpretation rests on a detail only found in cod. B, See below, 5.4.

The *Epistle of Aristaeus* whose author is immune to contemporary philological science is representative of this dogmatic choice (see 2.2 and 2.7, below). He knows the term ἀντιβολή (*collatio*), but misuses it in § 302. From Philo's writings many traces of critical discussions may be gathered,[32] but he always takes the apologetic stance. As D. DAWSON[33] puts it,

> Jewish reading of Scripture in Ptolemaic Alexandria does not appear to have been significantly influenced by the interests and practices of the Alexandrian grammarians and editors. This is initially surprising since the high point of Alexandrian philology coincided with the emergence of creative and interpretative literature written in Greek by Alexandrian Jews of significant social, intellectual, and political status. But Jewish interpreters were engaged in an enterprise fundamentally different from that of the scholars of the Museum and Library. Alexandrian editors of the Greek poets, determined to salvage the remains of a quickly receding classical heritage, sought to purify ancient texts by assessing passages whose authenticity could no longer be taken for granted. But Alexandrian Jews were not preoccupied with authentication of an authoritative text that was believed to have become corrupted. Rather than attempting to edit old classics for a new age, they were seeking to interpret the new age in light of their own old classic – the Septuagint version of the Pentateuch.

Ancient quotations from Homer are remarkable for a number of conventional elements which make Homer come close to the Bible:

First of all, there is a kind of canon which singles out the Homeric epics from all other Greek literature. Nothing can be added to the *Iliad* and the *Odyssey.* If any later verses found their way into the manuscripts or (rather) into quotations, they were liable to be discarded by the critique. Homer was 'the Poet' *par excellence.*[34] Later on the Pharisees, Scribes and Rabbis (not the Essenes) regarded Moses as 'the Prophet' *par excellence.* In the same sense, medieval scholastics cited Aristotle as 'the Philosopher'.

In quoting Homer or other classical authors there was no freedom to alter the text, except for stylistical reasons determined by the new context. As a rule, in Hellenistic and Imperial times the wording of an author was faithfully retained in quotations, more so than in the Qumran texts or in the Pauline letters. The original context was usually respected.[35] The only liberty consisted in the fact that writers quoting from the classics took care to create smooth transitions. The stereotyped repetition of three or four introductory formulae, as is familiar to readers of Paul or of the Rabbis, was avoided.

The practice described above was exceptionally and perhaps unconsciously neglected in cases involving the use of source books or *florilegia.*[36]

---

[32] See the well-informed, but rare article by E. STEIN, "Alttestamentliche Bibelkritik in der späthellenistischen Literatur", *Collectanea Theologica* 16 (Lwów 1935) 38–82.

[33] Dawson, Allegorical Readers (1992) 74 f.

[34] Strabo (quoted below); Ps.-Plutarch, *De Homero* 213, 217 f.; Artemidorus, *Onirocriticon* 1.1, etc.

[35] C. D. STANLEY, "Paul and Homer: Greco-Roman citation practice in the first century CE", *NovT* 32 (1990) 48–78.

[36] Cases are known, e. g. from Plutarch. See A. PHILIPPON in his introduction to *De audiendis poetis* (Plutarque I/1), p. 71. – Much has been speculated on this kind of instrumentary. By its very nature it is unlikely to survive the situation for which it had been created. The *Florilegium* contained in the writings of Cyprian of Carthage gave its name to the whole *genre;* the earliest surviving specimen seems to be *4QFlor.* Philo, *De aeternitate mundi* is of similar nature; it is a kind of notebook or doxography, citing many names.

Due to the composite character of the Homeric epics and their quasi-liturgical use in public recitals, it was usual to cite them by pericope: in the *Iliad* there was an ἀριστεία (heroic action) of Diomedes (= bk. 5), one of Agamemnon (= bk. 11) and another of Menelaus (= bk. 17). Referring to the *Odyssey*, ὁ 'Αλκίνου ἀπόλογος meant bks. 9–12, ἡ Νέκυια bk. 11 alone. The Alexandrian Homer critic Apollodorus of Athens wrote twelve books *On the catalogue of ships* (i. e. *Iliad* 2. 484–877). Porphyry's allegorical treatise *De antro nympharum* is an allegorical exegesis of *Odyssey* 13. 102–112. Other passages are named by Strabo, e. g. *Geography* 1. 2. 4.[37]

A general hermeneutic rule of the Alexandrian philologists consisted of "explaining Homer by Homer".[38] This programme somehow anticipates the protestant maxim *Sacra Scriptura sui ipsius interpres*. The copious *scholia* to Homer and to the dramatists as well as the surviving fragments of commentaries suggest that the Alexandrian approach was close to what we call 'historical' and 'critical' exegesis. There were even cases of hyper-criticism (e. g. Apollodorus, see next section). This approach was typical for an intellectual *élite*. The efforts of vulgarization of which we now must speak were of a different, and less academic, character.

1.5. Homer at School. Greek Handbooks of Interpretation and Their Terminology

Whereas no handbook of biblical exegesis was ever composed by a Jewish writer in Antiquity,[39] we possess three handbooks of Homeric exegesis, all in Greek, which provide us with an excellent, though little used, documentation. As to the *Sitz im Leben* of this specialized literature, the handbooks obviously served high school teachers (γραμματικοί) in the preparation of their lessons. Since they do not engage in critical inquiries nor in promoting philosophical reflection they have been mostly neglected, especially in modern times.[40] These handbooks are:

– Ps.-Plutarch, *De Homero* (the book has no authentic Greek title): a miscellaneous work containing materials from all centuries of Stoic Homeric scholarship including additions of a more Platonic nature. After an introduction (§§ 1–6) the book describes Homer's rhetoric and poetic (§§ 7–90), his theoretical philosophy (§§ 91–160) and his practical philosophy (§§ 161–199). The philosophical sections consist of a long series of physical and ethical solutions of

---

[37] Strabo, *Geography* (ed. H. L. Jones; LCL, 8 vols.; 1917 ff.); Strabon, *Géographie* (ed. F. Lasserre et al.; Paris 1966 ff.; Budé; 9 vols so far published). Older examples of this method of quoting may be found in Herodotus, Plato and others.

[38] Ὅμηρον ἐξ Ὁμήρου σαφηνίζειν: N. G. Wilson, "An Aristarchean maxim", *The Classical Review* 21 (1971) 172; Pépin, Mythe et allegorie (1976) 170. On the disputed authorship of this maxim and its fate until Luther's *Sacra Scriptura sui ipsius interpres* see B. Neuschäfer, *Origenes als Philologe* I–II (Basel 1987), I, 276–85; notes in II, 481–87, and C. Schäublin, "Die antiochenische Exegese des Alten Testaments", *L'Ancien Testament dans l'Eglise* (Chambésy 1988) 115–128. – See also below, Procopé, chap. 12, sect. 3.5.

[39] A modest exception to this are the 'high priest Eleazar's' hermeneutical rules, see below, 2.5. Of Philo's *Quaestiones* we cannot tell whether they were ever complete in the sense of Heraclitus' *Quaestiones Homericae*, i. e. whether they included a methodological or literary framework.

[40] There are praiseworthy exceptions, like Buffière, Les mythes d'Homère (1956) esp. 45–78.

Homeric 'riddles' (αἰνίγματα): Homer 'hints at' (αἰνίττεται) such and such scientific doctrine or practical wisdom.

– Heraclitus 'the Stoic' (also called 'the Rhetor' because, in fact, he is more a rhetor than a philosopher), Ὁμηρικὰ προβλήματα (*Quaestiones Homericae*): a somewhat polemical defence of Homer's dignity against some philosophers' accusations, to be dated approximatively in the 1st cent. CE. Its basic postulate is stated in 1.1: πάντα γὰρ ἠσέβησεν, εἰ μηδὲν ἠλληγόρησεν, Homer "would have impiously spoiled everything, if he had not spoken in allegory". The book's structure is particularly interesting as it follows the order of the difficult passages of the *Iliad* (chaps. 6–59) and the *Odyssey* (60–75), being framed by an introduction (1–5) and a conclusion (76–79). This is a selective commentary, the main parts of which belong to the same literary *genre* as Philo's *Quaestiones in Genesin* and *in Exodum*. It seems that this type of text has been created for exegetical purposes, long before it came to serve the needs of medieval Christian dogmatics. The presumably earlier date of Philo's works does not entail that Philo was the creator of the *genre*, as the art of interpreting Homer is much older than its surviving handbooks. – Of lesser interest, finally, is

– Cornutus: Ἐπιδρομὴ τῶν κατὰ τὴν Ἑλληνικὴν θεολογίαν παραδεδομένων, conventionally called *Theologiae Graecae compendium*. The author, a Stoic, was Persius' teacher in Rome in the 1st cent. CE. It contains interpretations of the Greek gods' names and myths, beginning with a somewhat systematical arrangement. Chap. 1 contains generalities (on Uranos, cosmos, the ether, the term 'gods'); chap. 2 is on Zeus, 3 on Hera, 4 on Poseidon, 5 on Hades, 6 on Rhea, 7 and 8 on their interactions. Chaps. 9 and 11 deal with Zeus again; on the whole there are 35 chapters. The evidence is borrowed from Homer, Hesiod, and others. Therefore the book is rather a doctrine about gods than a manual of exegesis.

Besides these technical treatises, apologies of Homer and reflections about the right way to understand his verses may be found elsewhere. The *Geography* of Strabo (Augustan age)[41] opens with an 80-page defence of the Poet's authority in geographical matters (1. 1–2). The whole work is full of Homeric quotations, to which are joined references to Greek myth criticism, and apologetic procedures in favour of the truth of 'the Poet' (e. g. 7. 3. 3–7; 8. 6. 5–10).[42] Strabo puts into practice a very clear definition of the difference between historical truth and poetic fiction (cf. note 48, below, and 1. 2. 16; 1. 2.19; 1. 2. 35; 7.3. 1). His rejection of the exaggerated criticism of the Poet by his commentator Apollodorus (worked in 2nd cent. BCE Alexandria)[43] in 7. 3. 6 and elsewhere (esp. in bk. 8) anticipates much of the discussions aroused by modern biblical criticism.

Strabo's main rule is to interpret the Poet to his favour: as long as there is no evidence to the contrary, one should suppose that the author knows what he is talking about. As long as his words admit of an understanding which is consistent with available information, a favourable understanding is justified. The opposite stance has to be proved, not Homer's. Thus in case of critical doubt the burden of proof is not his, but his critics'.

From the common vocabulary of the handbooks and the discussions cited so far we may extract a short *hermeneutical glossary*:

---

41 See n. 37. In vol. I/1 (1969) of the Budé edn. of Strabo, pp. 11–23, there is a good survey of ancient historico-critical discussions of Homer.

42 Cp. Buffière, Les mythes d'Homère (1956) 229 f. ("les principes de l'exégèse historique"), also on Strabo's predecessors (notably Polybius) and his followers.

43 For bibliographical information on Apollodorus' fragments, see the Budé edn. of Strabo, vol. 5 (= bk. 8) (ed. R. Baladié 1978) 20–23.

αἴνιγμα, αἰνίττεσθαι 'riddle': the assumption that the words do not mean what they seem to mean, but are there for the sake of a hidden meaning to be found through some art of decoding, e.g. etymology.

ἀλληγορία, ἀλληγορεῖν, ἀλληγορικῶς 'saying one thing, but meaning another'. Absent from Cornutus, this term is used in *De Homero* (70, 96, 102) and clearly defined in Heraclitus the Stoic.[44] Since ancient exegetes tend to play down their own contribution (and their licence), they always assign to the classical author himself the intention of meaning something other than what he seems to say. The term, first attested by Cicero (in Greek), is relatively young.[45] Plutarch, *De audiendis poetis* (*Mor.* 19 E) remarks that earlier authors only used ὑπόνοια (q.v.).

ἀτοπία, ἄτοπον 'pointless(ness)'. This gives the exegete the leeway to do anything about it. A semantic opposite is θεοπρεπές 'befitting God (or: a god)', e.g. Plutarch, *Mor.* 727 C; 729 D.

διάνοια see below s.v. τὸ ῥητόν.

ἐτυμολογία 'giving account of the truth (τὸ ἔτυμον)'. This term rarely refers to the evolution of a natural language, but exploits all kinds of assonances.[46] Examples borrowed from an oriental language (Egyptian, in the given case) can be found in Plutarch, *De Iside* 355 A; 362 B–E; 375 C–376 A, etc.

ἠθικῶς 'ethically' meant, i.e. with a deeper meaning belonging to human conduct. Alternative: φυσικῶς.

λύσις 'solution' of a riddle encoded by the ancient author in his text.

μεταφέρειν ἐπί 'to transpose' the figurative content of a metaphor to its proper meaning. The counterpart of the trope called μεταφορά is the κύριον ὄνομα.

μῦθος, μυθώδης 'myth', 'mythical': whereas Platonic writers use this term in a neutral sense,[47] Stoic interpreters may attach to it a pejorative accent. It now refers to something said very naively and improperly. To men of letters, the opposite is λόγος; to Strabo, the Stoic philosopher and geographer, it is ἱστορία.[48]

τὸ ῥητόν / ἡ διάνοια 'what is said', the literal meaning as opposed to 'the (author's) thought', cp. Lat. *mens auctoris*, a term of rhetoric as well as of law.

σύμβολον may be a synonym of αἴνιγμα (e.g. in Cornutus 35, p. 46 l. 4 f.).

ὑπόνοια refers to 'what is hinted at, a suggestion'. On the other hand, ἁπλῶς λέγειν refers to 'plain talk'.

φυσικῶς: being said with a deeper meaning belonging to natural science. Other possibility: ἠθικῶς. See above on the three parts of Stoic philosophy. The remaining one, logic, was not capable of being illustrated by ancient authors.

The only criterion of the allegorists' intelligent guesswork seems to have been consistency within a given system of knowledge. In the Hellenistic period this system was defined in philosophical terms based on Stoic physics and ethics, and could be dressed in a more or less Platonic fashion. Later on, in Christian use, allegory was subordinated to theological dogmatics. As Judaism never developed dogmatics in the proper sense, Hellenistic Jewish exegesis floats, as it were, in a void between these two points.

---

[44] Ὁ γὰρ ἄλλα μὲν ἀγορεύων τρόπος, ἕτερα δὲ ὧν λέγει σημαίνων, ἐπωνύμως ἀλληγορία καλεῖται (5.2).

[45] R. P. C. HANSON, *Allegory and Event. A Study of the Sources and Significance of Origen's Interpretation of Scripture* (London 1959) 37–41, also discusses seemingly older references, none of which can be taken for authentic.

[46] It is not possible to discuss here the Stoic theory of (Greek) language which supports this device.

[47] Satorninos Saloustios, an apologist of pagan religion writing under the Emperor Julian (4th cent. CE), excuses the castration of Attis (which he interprets cosmologically) by an intelligent definition of myth: ταῦτα δὲ ἐγένετο μὲν οὐδέποτε, ἔστι δὲ ἀεί; Saloustios, *Des dieux et du monde* (ed. G. Rochefort; Paris 1960; Budé) ch. 4, § 9.

[48] In his *Geography* 1.1.10 and elsewhere Strabo excuses Homer for having attached μυθώδη τινά to his ἱστορικῶς καὶ διδακτικῶς λεγόμενα. His motif for defending Homer is that the Poet serves him to defend Geography as a respectable part of philosophy.

1.6. Alternatives to Allegorism: A Note on Platonic Symbolism and on Vergilian Typology

At the end of a previous section (1.4) we already noted that Alexandrian philology, as an academic activity, could not compete with the allegorical method in terms of popularity. Firmly established in secondary schools, the latter method imposed itself on any intelligent Jew who read his holy book in Greek.

Maybe Jewish scholars made a conscious choice in preferring the 'Pergamene' method to the 'Alexandrian' one, as the latter is hardly adapted to apologetic demands. As is well known, this situation occurred again some centuries later in the Christian antagonism between 'Alexandrian' (by then, allegorical) and 'Antiochian' (historical) exegesis.

There were also other ancient alternatives to allegorism. They were not necessarily opposed to it,[49] but they allowed for a 'multiplicity of approaches' to ancient texts.

The Middle Platonists' readiness for allegorical explanation of myths was rather limited, as is shown by Plutarch.[50] He does not share the Stoic optimism, whereby a large audience is thought capable of understanding the plain meaning of a symbol or a myth about the gods (or the one God, as he philosophically believed). He kept to the famous verdict of Plato's *Timaeus* (28 C).[51] To him myth remains a necessary vehicle for conveying (and protecting) sublime truths.

This is not to say that an author like Plutarch refrains from proposing allegorical interpretations. His *De Iside et Osiride* is one of the lengthiest and most elaborated examples to be found in Greek literature. But his method is somewhat different from that of the Stoics. Instead of boldly replacing symbols with something 'really meant', he tries to find analogies fitting to the general outline of a myth.[52] The relationship between Isis/Osiris and their negative counterpart Typhon, e. g., is similar to (and not just 'means') the relationship between eternal Being and the Hades in Greek thought. Thus, the details remain a myth and need not be replaced by explanations, whereas the whole tale and its general content is regarded as philosophy. It seems that

---

[49] On radical opposition against allegorical exegesis, see sect. 1.2, above.

[50] Cf. above, 1.2, and A. BATES HERSMAN, *Studies in Greek Allegorical Interpretation* (phil. diss. Chicago 1906; mainly on Plutarch, *De Iside*). Cp. also H. D. Betz, "The problem of apocalyptic genre ...", in: idem, Hellenismus und Urchristentum (1990) 201–06. – We may refer to Plutarch in the present chapter even though the dates of his life (ca. 45 to nearly 125 CE) are at the very limit of the period under consideration. But there is general agreement about treating him still as a representative of 'Middle' Platonism.

[51] τὸν γὰρ Πατέρα καὶ ποιητὴν τοῦδε τοῦ παντὸς εὑρεῖν τε ἔργον καὶ εὑρόντα εἰς ἅπαντας ἐξειπεῖν ἀδύνατον, "the maker and father of this universe it is a hard task to find, and having found him it would be impossible to declare him to all mankind" (trans. F. M. CORNFORD, *Plato's cosmology: The* Timaeus *of Plato translated with a running commentary*, London 1937, 22).

[52] The logical basis of this operation belongs to the universals of human thought; it has been called the 'symbolic link' (*liaison symbolique*) by C. PERELMAN/O. TYTECA, *The New Rhetoric: A Treatise on Argumentation* (Indiana/London 1969 [French edn. 1958]) § 75. It is defined as follows: things which have something in common are *ipso facto* a reference to each other.

Jewish exegetes, even Philo, were not so Platonic as might be expected from this point of view.

Another contrast is worth noticing. All hermeneutical methods described so far have one thing in common: the more or less complete loss of the historical content of the text. Space and time are forgotten; eternal truth is looked for. The contrary of this attitude, the so-called Euhemerism, never made its way into Jewish exegesis.[53] Until Christian times there was rarely anything in between 'non-historical' (allegorical) and 'over-historical' (euhemeristic) exegesis. Josephus may be an exception, Paul another one;[54] both think in terms of universal history, as does Strabo (1.5, above).

In this context it may be interesting to note that the poet and 'chief ideologist' of Roman power, Vergil, wrote his epic in a kind of typological exploitation of Homer. Belonging himself to the nation which dominated the course of events in his time, he actualized Homer in his *Æneid* in a way which may be called typological.[55] Whereas the speculations of Alexandrian Jews sought an eternal meaning in the past, and apocalyptists announced a totally different future, this author presents the genesis of the Roman nation and of Roman power in the tradition of Homer's *Odyssey*. Æneas is a new Odysseus; he eludes the envy of Juno, the protectress (not of Troy but) of Carthage, and so on.

This is to say that even typology is based on universals of ancient thought. *There is no hermeneutics which could be considered specifically or exclusively biblical.*

1.7. The Jews' Situation in a Greek World. Their Apologetic Interests

When Plutarch was in Rome, in the 90s, he met at a party a Pythagorean from Etruria. Somebody asked him why Pythagoreans never let swallows build their nests around their houses, and why they always shake their beds when they get up. He answered by claiming that in Etruria Pythagoreans observe the sect's specific customs (σύμβολα) most strictly. He left it to other members of the party to contrive reasons for them, showing his disapproval of their speculations concerning a hidden ethical meaning (ἠθικαὶ λύσεις) through 'Pythagorean' silence.[56]

---

[53] Euhemerus (ca. 300 BCE) taught that the gods originally were exceptional men. His book bears the curious title *Sacred writing* (Ἱερὰ ἀναγραφή). A certain type of literature περὶ ἀπίστων maintained his approach well into Byzantine times. Palaephatus, e.g., in his *De incredibilibus* explains the sea-monster (κῆτος) killed from inside by Heracles as a confusion with the barbarian king Keton, and so on. In Jewish literature, one may compare to some extent the critique of idolatry (e.g. Wis 13–14).

[54] The term τυπικῶς used in 1 Cor 10:11 to serve as a hermeneutical device seems to be an innovation in Paul's day. 'Theological' interpretation was to become the model of much of the Church Fathers' and the Protestant Reformators' exegesis.

[55] G. N. KNAUER, *Die Aeneis und Homer* (Göttingen 1964; 1979) 332ff., esp. 345–359; cf. idem, "Vergil and Homer", ANRW II 31/2 (1981) 870–918. Of course, Vergil as a poet uses no technical term for his hermeneutical procedure. The apostle Paul (see preceding note) is more explicit than he is.

[56] Plutarch, *Quaestiones convivales* 8.7–8 (*Mor.* 727 A–730 F; esp. 727 C–D).

This episode highlights the problems of any observant Jew. The very detailed nature of the Mosaic law did not fit with general and philosophical notions[57] – not to mention the countless theoretical and practical difficulties which lay in these details. Philo's *Quaestiones* tackle them by the very methods with which Homeric *quaestiones* were discussed in schools.

Our Pythagorean's reaction seems to imply that giving reasons (λύειν) for σύμβολα leads to the danger of abandoning the literal meaning and the concrete observance. There are fragments of corpora of Pythagorean *Laws* with initial summaries enjoining annual reading in front of the citizens assembly.[58] We do not know which communities ever respected such a prescription and whether this kind of literature differs in nature from the ideal and utopic Νόμοι by Plato; as far as the Jews are concerned, we do know. The apologetic demand for them was all the more urgent.

In Antiquity the Jews were often blamed for keeping themselves apart. In the great Mediterranean community of peoples created by Hellenism, the Jews – and the Pythagoreans[59] – refused to mix with other people. They had their own cult holidays and customs and kept themselves 'pure'[60] with regard to marriages and food, and observed different taboos. Moses, their lawgiver, was therefore accused of misanthropy.[61] There are clear traces of mockery of Jewish Scriptures in Philo's day.[62] It is not without interest for our understanding of the genesis of scriptural hermeneutics to know that Homer, too, was accused of misanthropy.[63]

On the other hand, the strength of the Jewish attitude rested on the custom of reading over and over again the *Laws*[64] in their assemblies and explaining them.

The synagogue service, be it by chance or not, fitted very well with Pythagorean and Stoic concepts of 'pure' and 'unbloody' worship which had developed out of philosophical criticism of religion and sacrifice. It was nonviolent, bloodless and λογικόν in every sense of the term: a cult based on *verbal* utterance, with *reasonable* meaning. It consisted of learning and prayer. The Pythagoreans, who categorically refused to kill animals, and the Stoics, who were conscious of the divine *logos* within them, were longing for such a perfect way for a community to communicate with the divine. But since

[57] See Y. Amir, "Der jüdische Eingottglaube als Stein des Anstoßes in der hellenistisch-römischen Welt", JBTh 2 (1987) 58–75.

[58] Ps.-Zaleukos and Ps.-Charondas; see Stobaeus, *Anthologium* 4.2.19 and 24; for their authors' legends, Diodorus of Sicily, *Bibliotheca historica* 12.20f. and 12.11–19.

[59] See Plutarch's report, *Mor.* 730B.

[60] The concept of a 'purity of race' seems to be of Jewish origin. Ezra was the first to put it into practice (Ezra 10).

[61] E.g. Hecataeus of Abdera, Apollonius Molon, Tacitus, and others. See Stern, Authors (1976–84), nr. 11, 49, 63, 281. On pagan polemics and Jewish apologetics, Schürer/Vermes, History III/1 (1986) 594–616.

[62] See his *QG* 3.3.43; 4.168; G 15.2f. etc. (cf. n. 32, above); Ps.-Philo, *De Sampsone* 26.

[63] Ps.-Plutarch, *De Homero* 213; cf. his apology of Zeus in 116. A Jewish counterpart is present in all of Ps.- Philo's *De Jona*.

[64] Apart from the LXX translation, the plural νόμοι, being more Greek, was mostly preferred.

traditional cults were open to interpretation but not to innovation, they had to resort to more private forms of prayer and contemplation.

The Jews, on the other hand, built synagogues where services were accessible to everybody. Thus they created the necessary conditions for Moses's wisdom and doctrines to reach a large audience. The presence of heathen 'God-fearers' who even took over honorary (and paying) offices testifies to the success.[65]

Yet we do not hear of any attempts to avoid contact with pagan myth and theology by founding Jewish schools.[66] To do so, it seems, would have had the consequence of cultural inferiority. Be that as it may, it is remarkable that for five centuries at least pagans and Jews (later on also Christians) sat side by side listening to the same teachers, who spoke mainly on Homer, later on also on the dramatists. In the gymnasia they honoured Heracles and Hermes,[67] and open-minded intellectuals such as Philo attended performances in the theatre,[68] even though they were connected with the cult of Dionysus and the Muses.

On the following pages our interest will focus on Alexandria as a unique centre of Jewish contact with, and emulation of, Greek culture. (Egyptian culture, as far as remains of it were still alive, was of little interest to the Jews.) One of Alexandria's five quarters was settled by Jews; and the largest synagogue known in Antiquity was located there.[69] It is assumed that readers are aware of the precarious situation in which the Alexandrian Jews lived: wanting to pass for Greeks, they claimed equal rights with the privileged Macedonian settlers.[70] While unable to prove their case, they infuriated the Egyptian population of the city. Racial riots linked to recurrent messianic insurrections put an end to Alexandrian Jewish culture in 115 CE.

Thus, from the 3rd cent. BCE to the 1st cent. CE, the necessity of coming to a practical arrangement with Hellenistic culture set the frame for theoretical compromises, one of which is the art of interpreting Scripture.

---

[65] See, e.g., Acts 10:1,22; 13:16,26; 16:14; 18:7, etc.; Schürer/Vermes, History III/1 (1986) 150–176. Our evidence has been enriched by the recently found synagogue inscription at Aphrodisias; see Schürer/Vermes, l.c., 25 f., 166.

[66] All we know about Jewish schools (see Hengel, Judaism and Hellenism [1969] chap. II, sect. 3) does not lead us to think that there ever was a primary school where Homer was dethroned in favour of the Septuagint. There was no Jewish Greek text appropriate for primary teaching.

[67] Inscriptions found in Cyrenaica gave name lists of *ephebes*, among which are unambiguous Jewish names. Nevertheless the inscriptions begin with the standard dedication Ἑρμᾷ, Ἡρακλεῖ.

[68] Philo, G 13.177; *Quod omnis probus liber sit* 141; cf. *QG* 4.201 (p. 494 Marcus) and Schürer/Vermes, Histoy III/2 (1987) 819.

[69] See *t. Sukk.* 4:6. In Jerusalem synagogues were numerous, but not large. To look for an example in Palestine, in Tiberias existed "the largest synagogue in Palestine, presumably modelled on the famous synagogue in Alexandria" (Hengel, 'Hellenization' of Judaea [1989] 39).

[70] Philo, *In Flaccum* 53; *Legatio ad Gaium* 194; 353 f., Josephus, *Ap.* 2.36–41. The Roman administration knew of no such arrangement, as is evidenced by the letter of Claudius to the Alexandrians (41 CE), P. Lond. 1912 (CPJ 153 = A. S. Hunt/C. C. Edgar (eds.); *Select Papyri* 2 [1934; 1956] LCL nr. 212; esp. lines 73 ff.). Cf. next note.

2. The *Epistle of Aristaeus:* A Hermeneutic Programme

Editions and translations: Lettre d'Aristée à Philocrate (SC 89; ed. A. Pelletier; Paris 1962; Greek text with French tr. and commentary); ET: *Aristeas to Philocrates* (ed. M. Hadas; New York 1951); R. J. H. SHUTT in: Charlesworth, OTP II 12–34 (hereafter quoted); N. MEISNER, JSHRZ II/1 (1973) 35–87 (Germ. tr.). The numbering of paragraphs is that of the Teubner edition (1900), retained since.

Indexes: Pelletier 261–319; A.-M. DENIS (ed.), *Concordance grecque des Pseudépigraphes d'A. T.* (Louvain-la-Neuve 1987; siglum *Arist.*).

Bibliographies: G. Delling, Bibliographie (see sect. 1) 97–98; Hadas (see above) 84–90; Schürer/Vermes, History III/1 (1986) 676 f.

General works (cf. sect. 1): J. R. BARTLETT, *Jews in the Hellenistic world: Josephus, Aristeas, The Sibylline Oracles, Eupolemus* (Cambridge Commentaries on Writings of the Jewish and Christian World 200 BC to AD 200, I/1; Cambridge 1985) 11–34; D. Dawson, Allegorical Readers (see sect. 1) 74–82; D. W. GOODING, "Aristeas and Septuagint Origins", *VT* 13 (1963) 357–79; Schürer/Vermes, History III/1 (1986) 677–87; N. WALTER, "Jüdisch-hellenistische Literatur vor Philon von Alexandrien", ANRW II 20/1 (1987) 67–120, esp. 83–85; G. ZUNTZ, "Aristeas Studies" I. II; idem, *Opuscula selecta* (Manchester 1972) 110–43.

Turning now to Hellenistic Jewish exegetes, we may observe at first that they used neither a 'Hebrew Bible' nor an 'Old Testament'. The name 'Bible' has its very origin in the period under review (see below, 2.4), but it applied first to the Pentateuch. Paradoxically, the Greek wording of the sacred text was the first to be regarded as inalterable and verbally inspired (see 2.6). Apart from etymologies of Hebrew names, the Hellenistic Jewish exegetes never refer to the Hebrew text as something distinct from the Greek text which had become customary to them.

Geographically the scene – or, at least, the centre – of all which follows was Alexandria, a Greek city on Egyptian soil, its peculiarity having been recalled in the preceding section.[71] It was composed of three cultures and three social strata: Greek, (Hellenistic) Jewish, and Egyptian. As we know through Philo,[72] the first known Jewish ghetto came into being in Alexandria.

The earliest Jewish texts which contain hermeneutical reflexions are the Fragments of Aristobulus and the pseudepigraphical *Epistle of Aristaeus.* As it is impossible to assertain a relationship of dependence between the two,[73] we may conveniently begin our reading of Hellenistic Jewish exegetes with the latter. The *Ep. Arist.* is a programmatic pamphlet, and it has the advantage of having been transmitted in its entirety. So we may use it as an initiation to Hellenistic Jewish exegesis, even though the Aristobulus fragments may well be older by one generation, and even though it has been claimed that they represent a more primitive stage in the application of Hellenistic hermeneutics to the Jewish holy books.[74]

---

[71] Cf. n. 70. In Ptolemaic and Roman times, Alexandria was not a part of Egypt, but a separate political entity: *Alexandria ad Egyptum.* Immigrants from Egypt, just as the Jews, would not have civic rights. For detailed information, see A. KASHER, *The Jews in Hellenistic and Roman Egypt* (TSAJ 7; Tübingen 1985).

[72] See his *In Flaccum* 55–57, referring to events of the 4th decade of the 1st cent. CE.

[73] Ancient authors, of course, regard Aristobulus as the younger because they believe in the ficticious story of the *Ep. Arist.* and because they assume that Aristobulus got it from there. But the legend of the 'Septuagint' may well have circulated orally before and outside the *Ep. Arist.*

[74] Walter, Aristobulos (1964) 35 ff. Some of WALTER's Arguments are based on silence, esp.

2.1. *Author, Place, Date, and Nature of the Epistle*

The author is not Aristeas, the Jewish exegete of whom we have one fragment (see below, 5.1), but a ficticious person named Aristaeus.[75] He purports to be an Alexandrian Greek and a high official at Ptolemy II's court. Modern critique, however, dates this pseudepigraphical work a century later, at the mid-2nd or near the end of the 2nd cent. BCE. As its narrative frame is largely ficticious,[76] a date can be based only on indirect evidence.

Josephus paraphrases the *Ep. Arist.*, except its section on hermeneutics (sect. 128–171), in *Antiquities* 12.12–118.[77]

The text bears the superscription Ἀριστέας[78] Φιλοκράτει, as if it was a letter. But it comprises 70 pages of Greek text, and in the very first phrase its author calls it a 'report' (διήγησις). This comes a bit closer to the truth. Other *genres* have also been used, viz. the 'diatribe', the 'banquet of sages', etc. In short, the text is a miscellany.

2.2. *The Contents. Hellenistic and Jewish Components*

By the narrative *framework* (sect. 1–82 and 301–322), the author of the *Ep. Arist.* tries to give the etiological legend of the Greek Pentateuch a historical setting. The legend itself may well be older.[79] Unfortunately, the compiler's knowledge of 3rd cent. history is not sufficient to avoid blatant anachronisms.[80]

In its narrative parts the Epistle contains some political propaganda which highlights Jewish aspirations of the time. It claims for the Alexandrian and Egyptian Jews the role of an *élite*. It extols their military merits under Ptolemy I and assigns to the Alexandrian Jewry the rank of a *politeuma* (sect. 310).[81]

on the absence of Hellenistic exegetical terms or of their specifically technical meaning. Such an argumentation is particularly uncertain in dealing with fragments. Meisner, JSHRZ II/1 (1973) 42, judiciously refrains from drawing chronological conclusions from a comparison of the two documents. One more reason for being cautious lies in the different nature (legal or not) of the biblical texts; they call for different approaches. See 2.2. below.

[75] This is the spelling of his name in the best testimonies, including Josephus. The manuscripts of the Epistle, however, prefer the form 'Aristeas'. See W. Schmidt (next note), 21 f (following G. Zuntz). The same confusion of Ἀρισταῖος and Ἀριστέας is found in Pausanias 1.24.6–5.7.9 (concerning a certain Aristeas of Chersonesus).

[76] W. Schmidt, *Untersuchungen zur Fälschung historischer Dokumente bei Pseudo-Aristaios* (Bonn 1986). Some details which are historically attested (see, e.g., Pelletier's note on sect. 9, 36, 115, 201 and Bartlett's note [*Jews* 17] on sect. 12–27) have been tainted with anachronisms and grotesque exaggerations (e.g., sect. 177 and 317) which make it hard to learn anything historical from the Epistle.

[77] For a detailed comparison, see A. Pelletier, *Flavius Josèphe adaptateur de la Lettre d'Aristée* (Etudes et commentaires 45; Paris 1962).

[78] Thus the manuscripts. See n. 75.

[79] Aristobulus (mid-2nd cent. BCE) knows it; and there is no need to assume that he had read it in the *Ep. Arist.* (see n. 72).

[80] See Pelletier's note on sect. 9, 115, 201.

[81] Cf. 2 Macc 12:7 for the case of Joppe, where the Jewish population was no part of the *politeuma*. A *politeuma* may be defined as an autonomous national group dwelling in a Hellenistic *polis*.

Ptolemy's embassy, which is headed by 'Aristaeus', treats the Jerusalem High Priest Eleazar[82] as a king.

– *Passages referring to the translation* proper are relatively short. Sect. 9–11, 28–33, and 301–16 describe the preparation of the work and its realization by seventy-two Palestinian Jewish elders (six[83] from each tribe). No details are given on the philological aspect of the translators' work, except that they worked as a group.[84] In sect. 302 they are represented as ἕκαστα σύμφωνα ποιοῦντες πρὸς ἑαυτοὺς ταῖς ἀντιβολαῖς – "reaching agreement among themselves on each by comparing versions" (cf. sect. 32). The word ἀντιβολή, a term originally belonging to Alexandrian textual criticism and designating a *collation*, is incorrectly used in this context. Differences of texts are only stated (in somewhat ambiguous terms) in relation to the Hebrew texts (sect. 30).

– Sect. 83–120 present a panegyric *description of Jerusalem*, its Temple, its priests. Its basis is a detailed reading of the Pentateuch, esp. of Exodus 28, rather than personal acquaintance with the place.

– The *High Priest Eleazar's farewell address* to the 72 Elders (sect. 121–127) sketches the ideal of an observant and educated Jew: each one of the Elders is an expert in Jewish (i.e. Hebrew) as well as in Greek literature.[85] Eleazar uses some terms of Aristotelian ethics (sect. 122: the *aurea mediocritas*) in giving the Elders his advise. He states the general thesis: τὸ καλῶς ζῆν ἐν τῷ τὰ νόμιμα συντηρεῖν εἶναι.

– After a transition formula, the author lets the High Priest give a concise *lesson on interpretation* (sect. 128–171): how to understand the Law and to use it, and why it is reasonable for the Jews to keep apart from all other people. Sect. 139 philosophically links Jewish elitist behaviour and self-consciousness with the affirmation of universal validity of its values. On this very interesting section, see below, 2.5.

– The arrival of the Elders carrying the scrolls incites Ptolemy to a kind of *Simhat Tora* feast (sect. 172–186). In a lengthy *Banquet* (sect. 187–300) the king receives a lesson in political ethics which is reminiscent of a Hellenistic περὶ βασιλείας or *Fürstenspiegel*. This may seem bold because no Jew of the diaspora was ever in the position to teach a pagan monarch. The passage may be understood as a request, addressed to some Ptolemy in the 2nd cent. BCE, to treat the Jewish race according to humanitarian values like the Hellenistic concept of *philanthropy*.

During the table talks (while eating *kasher*), the Elders do not quote Moses' Law. Their answers are made up by commonplaces of Hellenistic thought[86] followed by a reference to God:

---

[82] A person not known otherwise. Schürer/Vermes, History III/1, 474, 678 f, dispenses with any attempt at identification. No mention is made of the Leontopolis temple. It is absent from all of the literature to be reviewed in this chapter.

[83] The number of a week's working days.

[84] See below (2.6) for a contrast: Philo's and the Christians' theory of personal and verbal inspiration.

[85] Cf. sect. 287 and 321, paying respect to the Hellenistic ideal of παιδεία. Elsewhere in the Epistle the sense of παιδεία is rather similar to that of ἀγωγή = הלכה: sect. 8, 43, 124, 246, 280.

[86] E.g. sect. 256 (Aristotelian), 290 (political philosophy of the day), 259 and 263 (some basic

καὶ γὰρ Θεός ... These references may often seem biased and unnecessary; obviously they are meant to substantiate the claim made in sect. 139 that the values of Jewish religion[87] are universal ones. The (heathen) ruler's behaviour is to be an imitation of God (sect. 188, 190, 192, 205, 210, etc.) who is the Creator, the giver of all things, and a lover of mankind.

For our inquiry the author's theory of ethical motivation is of particular interest: "It is God's gift to be a doer of good works and not of the opposite" (sect. 231; cf. 272, 274). Likewise, righteousness (δικαιοσύνη) is a gift of God (sect. 280). His work consists in directing a man's mind: Θεὸς δὲ τὴν διάνοιαν ἄξει σοι, βασιλεῦ, πρὸς τὰ κάλλιστα (sect. 247).[88] The "dynamic" of piety is "love (ἀγάπη), a divine gift" (sect. 229). Another gift of God, an extrinsic one, is the completion of a man's deeds (sect. 195, 239, 255, 265).

All this may be taken as a kind of instruction concerning God's will even though there is no mention of Moses' Law. Implicitly it may be there. Ptolemy's question in sect. 240 how he might "avoid doing anything contrary to the law (μηθὲν παράνομον)" is incomprehensible to anyone who shares the Pharaonic and Ptolemaic ideology whereby royal will and law are the same thing. In his answer the Jewish sage states that "God has given to legislators the purpose (τὰς ἐπινοίας) of saving men's lives".[89] This answer is a compromise with Hellenistic political theology and even a more favourable one than Paul's opinion in Rom 13:1–7.

The propaganda of the *Ep. Arist.* vindicates no uniqueness for Moses. The Epistle does not claim that other peoples should follow his prescriptions. But it does claim that Moses is in no way inferior to other lawgivers in Antiquity.[90]

– Taking up the narrative thread of the LXX legend, sect. 301–3 mention the translators' work (see above). The finale of sect. 304 ff is a glorification of the Mosaic Law. Sect. 310–11 assert the absolute accuracy of the wording of the Greek Pentateuch and condemn anyone who changes the slightest detail of the text. This might be an interior Jewish apology for the LXX Pentateuch as against other translations or total rejection of such an endeavour. The legends told in sect. 312–316 tend to neutralize an attitude which considers any vulgarization as sacrilegous.

In sum, the interests of the *Ep. Arist.* are clearly Jewish and discredit totally the assertion that it was written by a pagan.[91] Its contents, however, bear witness to the author's intimate acquaintance with Hellenistic culture. To his mind, the Jewish people keeps apart in practice, but is entirely open in its theoretical exploits.

---

doctrines of Stoicism). The two Stoic etymologies of the name of Zeus (cf. 1.3) are already used in sect. 16, and Judaism is identified with universal (philosophical) religion.

87 The term used in the text is εὐσέβεια. 'Religion' is a rather modern term having its precursor in a generalized meaning of θρησκεία present, e.g. in Wis 14:18 and in Josephus. Cf. εὐσεβεῖν in 1.3, above (Cornutus).

88 On διάνοια, cf. sect. 237, 238, 243, 268, 270, 282, 292, and 2.5, below.

89 Cf. sect. 279: even the king is bound by the law, i.e. by God's command (θείῳ προστάγματι).

90 In an anonymous source used by Josephus this argument is expanded and Lycurgus, Solon, Zaleucus, and Minos are explicitly named (Josephus, *Ap.* 2. 151–63).

91 Theoretically, he might have been a God-fearer, but there is no evidence of God-fearers in so early a period. Furthermore, how could a God-fearer argue for ritual purity when he was living in a situation that prevented him from respecting purity?

2.3. *The Epistle's Theological Basis for the Interpretation of Scripture*

To begin with the framework, there is a positive reception of the Hellenistic critique of religion and sacrifices. Even though the Jerusalem Temple with its cult is given the highest honours (sect. 84–99), the theological basis of the Epistle consists of a rather metaphorical understanding of sacrifices.[92] "The man who offers", sect. 170 states, "makes an offering of every facet of his soul" (τῆς ... ἑαυτοῦ ψυχῆς τοῦ παντὸς τρόπου τὴν προσφοράν). A psychological bias such as we analyzed in the Banquet recurs in all of Hellenistic Jewish interpretation of Scripture as one of its most characteristic features. Again and again we find in the *Ep. Arist.* the terms διάθεσις ('mental disposition')[93] and διάνοια (see above); God is τῆς διανοίας ἡγεμών. As the latter term is also known as a hermeneutical one (see above, 1.5) we may presume that through interpretation the διάνοια or 'intention' of the Law is transferred into the observant reader's διάνοια or 'mind'.

The pedagogy of the Epistle aims at an intrinsic motivation through interiorizing of values. The constraint of conformity which is exercised in the Pentateuch's text as well as it was in Judaean society is superseded by an ethic based on abstract values. Thus the condition of Jewish life in the diaspora, even though it was bitterly deplored by others (3 Macc 6:9–11), became an incentive to interprete the Law in a scholarly and educational way.

Even the animals serving for sacrifices at Jerusalem are meant to express a truth about the person offering them (sect. 161–71). This provides plausible reasons for apparently ridiculous or shocking details of ritual Law. We may smile at this High Priest's way of reasoning; yet, it is remarkable that the question 'why' is never dismissed, as it may be in Rabbinic jurisprudence. Anyway, the glory of God is not enhanced by the smoke of burned meat,[94] but, as sect. 234 states, consists "in purity of soul and of devout conception (of God)" – ψυχῆς καθαρότητι καὶ διαλήψεως ὁσίας.[95]

In sect. 132 the High Priest states his credo "that God is one, that his power is shown in everything, every place being filled with his sovereignty, and that none of the things on earth which men do secretly are hidden from him". Sect. 133 adds that the High Priest was able to demonstrate the might of God throughout the Law (διὰ πάσης τῆς νομοθεσίας). This is a hint as to the interpreter's theological and apologetic interests. He looks for cosmological proofs such as corresponded to the taste of the epoch. God's historical action in favour of Israel carries little weight as an argument. The historical meaning of a text has no convincing power like the symbolic meaning has.

---

[92] Cf. H. Wenschkewitz, "Die Spiritualisierung der Kultusbegriffe: Tempel, Prieter und Opfer im Neuen Testament", *Angelos* 4 (1931/32) 70–230. A good example is found in the *Ep. Arist.* itself, where the manumission of Jewish slaves is described as χαριστήριον ἀνατιθέναι (sect. 19, 37).

[93] Sect. 1, 2, 4, etc. An synonym is κατασκευή in 236.

[94] The aesthetic problem, i.e. the bad smell of hecatombs and of continuous animal sacrifices, is politely hinted at in the praise of the canalization system of Jerusalem (sect. 89–91).

[95] For a 'devout' or 'pure' or 'sound' idea about God as part of a hermeneutic programme, see Aristobulus, frg. 4 § 7. Cf. sect. 2.5, on terminology, and 3.3, on Aristobulus' principles.

2.4. The Author's Bible and the Texts Referred to

In dealing with the *Epistle of Aristaeus* we have so far avoided speaking of the 'Septuagint'. This name and its reference to a large canon of sacred texts is only known from Christian sources. In fact, it is a label that simplifies[96] and transforms the legendary content of the *Epistle* into an automatic vindication of perfection for the whole of the Greek Old Testament.

The concern of the Epistle, however, is only with the Pentateuch. We may conveniently use this late and ecclesiastical term because, in fact, there were five scrolls of the Law in Hellenistic-Jewish custom,[97] and not just one. Even though תורה (i.e. Mosaic Law) in the Greek Pentateuch is always rendered by νόμος in the singular, there are no traces of a material symbol like the bulky leather scroll (be it contemporary or later) of the Hebrew Tora.

Mosaic Law is mostly cited as ἡ νομοθεσία (sect. 5, 15, 31, 128 f, 133, 147, 176, 313). For the first time we find also ἡ Γραφή 'Scripture'[98] (sect. 155, 168), and ἡ Βίβλος 'the Book, the Bible' (sect. 316). These occasional singulars are all the more remarkable as the Epistle normally speaks of "the books" or "the volumes", as we have seen. On the other hand, what is not fixed by a Mosaic prescription is ἄγραφον (sect. 56).[99]

The lawgiver (ὁ νομοθέτης, sect. 131, 148, 161; the verb νομοθετεῖν 144) is Moses, not God himself, as in Rabbinic exegesis. Nevertheless the contents of the Law are qualified as 'philosophical' and 'pure', because they are 'divine' (φιλοσοφωτέραν εἶναι καὶ ἀκέραιον τὴν νομοθεσίαν ταύτην, ὡς ἄν οὖσαν θείαν, sect. 31). Sect. 138 states that the Lawgiver was "divinely endowed with omniscience".[100] In sect. 177 Ptolemy himself bows seven times before the scrolls that contain the 'oracles' (λόγια) of God.[101] In sect. 158 the Law quotations fixed on Jewish doorposts (the *mezuzot*) are likewise called τὰ λόγια.

Philologically speaking, we are dealing with the LXX Pentateuch, as has been proven from details of the descriptions of the Table of the showbreads (sect. 51–72) and of the High Priest's garment (sect. 96–99). In sect. 160, some words of Deut 6:7 LXX are cited in an interesting context which is the oldest literary testimony of the use of *tefillin* and of Deut 6:4b ff. as a kind of credo.

Sect. 155 cites a conflation of Deut 7:18 and 10:21 which clearly depends on LXX wording. The conflation (probably a citation from memory) suggests that there was already a common use of this text. In sect. 135 critics found a trace of LXX Hebraism.[102] No direct use is made of the Hebrew text.

---

[96] The number 72 is made round to 70 since Josephus, *Ant.* 12.57 and 86.

[97] In the *Ep. Arist.* this is explicity stated in sect. 175; cf. 310: τὰ τεύχη, 317: τὰ βιβλία.

[98] γραφή means rather a drawing or a painting. Referring to something written, it means a pamphlet, e.g. an apology, as in Josephus, *Ap.* 2.146.

[99] See Pelletier's note *ad loc.*

[100] Sect. 240 states that all lawgivers receive their ideas (ἐπίνοιαι) from God, which was indeed a Greek belief.

[101] This term may not only be reminiscent of 'sayings' of Jesus, but also of Rom 3:2 (Israel is the depositary of the λόγια τοῦ Θεοῦ) and Hebr 5:12.

[102] In ἐκ λίθων καὶ ξύλων the καί stands for a Hebrew ו meaning 'or'. See Pelletier's ed., pp. 39 and 59 f.

Texts referred to are Exodus (mainly chap. 28), Leviticus, and Deuteronomy.[103] There are further allusions to, or influences from, the Former Prophets (Josh 3:15 in sect. 116), the Latter Prophets (Isa 2:2 and Mic 4:1 in sect. 84; Ezek 47:1 in sect. 89 – cf. also the contexts) and the Hagiographa. This distribution is typical of Hellenistic Jewish exegetic literature.[104]

2.5. The High Priest Eleazar's Hermeneutical Rules

Sect. 128–171 are one of the earliest hermeneutic programmes known from ancient literature. Critics have regarded this passage as a document in its own right which the Epistle just cites. Stylistically, however, there is no difference.[105] The fact that Josephus' paraphrase skips this section in *Ant.* 12. 85 is inconclusive; the context does not call for a lesson in hermeneutics. Whatever position one might adopt on this question, two things seem clear: (1) not all the various ideas the author incorporated in his work have sprung from his own mind; (2) the materials combined in the *Ep. Arist.* are sufficiently compatible to give a representative picture of how Alexandrian Jewish sages handled their (Greek) Scriptures for themselves and for outsiders. The higher attention given to the holy text in sect. 128–171 is due to the particular audience. Whereas most of the Epistle purports to be a heathen's information given to another heathen, in sect. 130–169 we hear the Jewish High Priest[106] speaking to a Jewish *élite*, namely the elders appointed to be translators. He gives them instructions; the narrator only 'witnesses' the scene.

In the narrative introduction (sect. 128–9) of this section the author first states the problem: *hoi polloi* (whoever they may be) take some of the prescriptions concerning food, drink, and unclean animals as περιεργία, i. e. something exaggerated or frivolous and superfluous (these are all meanings of the Greek term). The elders (whose company the narrator joins) ask the High Priest the question 'why' (διὰ τί, sect. 129), a question well known to readers of Aristotle. "Why, since there is one creation only (μιᾶς καταβολῆς οὔσης), are some things considered unclean for eating, others for touching?" Why is the Law so utterly scrupulous (or superstitious – δεισιδαίμων)? Again, the Greek term has more than one meaning, and its use appears to be deliberate.

In his answer (sect. 130–169) the High Priest immediately calls attention to the behaviour (τὰς ἀναστροφὰς καὶ τὰς ὁμιλίας, later on also τρόπος) of the animals concerned. They do something which, if it were imitated by humans, would be very immoral: violence, theft, and sexual abuse.[107] E. g.:

---

[103] See the list in Meisner's translation, JSHRZ II/1 (1974) 87. It may be expanded, as to the Hagiographa, by an allusion to Ezra 1:7–11, sect. 52. Resemblances with contemporary texts (Sir and Wisd; sect. 133, 135) bear witness to a common intellectual background.

[104] From this observation, the exceptional character of the sermons discussed in sect. 5, below, becomes all the more obvious.

[105] Some differences in vocabulary will be mentioned at the end of this section; they may be easily explained by the different contents. Prose rhythms *(versus Cretici)* are present everywhere in passages that called for rhetorical emphasis.

[106] Being a part of the Epistle's fictitious framework and placed in the obscure 3rd cent. BCE, this 'Eleazar' defies any attempt at historical identification.

[107] In the latter case (sect. 165) the author is not aware that he is confounding a myth with

> As to the birds which are forbidden, you will find wild and carnivorous kinds, and the rest which dominate by their own strength, and who find their food at the expense of the aforementioned domesticated birds – which is an injustice; and not only that, they also seize lambs and kids and outrage human beings dead or alive. By calling them impure, he [Moses] has thereby indicated that it is the solemn binding duty of those for whom the legislation has been established to practice righteousness and not to lord it over anyone in reliance upon their own strength, nor to deprive him of anything, but to govern their lives righteously, in the manner of the gentle creatures ...[108]

Nothing is impure by nature, sect. 143 concedes.[109] Ritual prescriptions are rationalized by assigning them a moral aim which can properly be called their *sensus plenior.* The argument rests entirely on analogy. The one-sided ethical bias of the explanations given by the High Priest is due to the fact that the given text is not poetry, but legislation. We are no longer dealing with Homer, but with Moses. Curiously, the narrative postscript tells that the φυσικὴ διάνοια of the text has been enucleated (sect. 171). The author seems not to distinguish between the two levels. In Aristobulus, though, we shall find clear evidence of the other level; and in Philo we shall find both.

The anthropomorphism inherent in the procedure of moralizing ritual matters is not regarded as a problem. The opinion that the animals and all other things are there for human utility had long been vulgarized by the Stoics. One may ask, however, how a man like Aristobulus would have answered the initial question (sect. 129, quoted above). Aristobulus speaks programmatically against anthropomorphical conceptions, at least about God. But he also agrees that "our Law" has been made "for piety, righteousness (δικαιοσύνη), chastity and the other true goods (values, ἀγαθά)".[110] So his answer might have been similar to that of the *Ep. Arist.* His words on the deeper meaning of Sabbath observance in frg. 5 come close to the *Epistle of Aristaeus*, and the ὅσιαι διαλήψεις of frg. 4 § 8 are paralleled by the metaphorical use of ἁγνός "(ritually) clean", which in sect. 144, cf. 31, 292 is applied to thoughts about God.

In Eleazar's speech Moses is formally acquitted of περιεργία. He did not bother with trifles such as mice and weasels[111] (as it seems, e.g., in Lev 11:29); but "everything has been solemnly set in order for unblemished investigation and amendment of life for the sake of righteousness (δικαιοσύνη)" – thus sect. 144; cf. 131, 151, 159, and again the conclusion, 169, on δικαιοσύνη.[112] There is no haphazard element in Mosaic Law and nothing associative or 'mythical'.[113] Everything is stated πρὸς ἀλήθειαν καὶ

---

scientific knowledge. Nor were Ælian, *De natura animalium* 2.55, Barn. 10:8 (depending on *Ep. Arist.*), the *Physiologus* 21 (ditto), and others.

108 Sect. 146 f. (Shutt's trans.).

109 Cf. Rom 14:14 οὐδὲν κοινὸν δι' ἑαυτοῦ.

110 Frg. 4 § 8.

111 Cf. 1 Cor 9:9, the only hermeneutical rule expressly adduced by Paul.

112 This term which refers to one of the four Greek cardinal virtues is a slight anthropomorphism in itself: in LXX language and ever since in biblical tradition it replaces the Greek terms for divine 'justice' and social order, δίκη and θέμις.

113 In the author's psychology, 'what comes to mind' is synonymous to 'the mythical', as is shown by the parallel between sect. 161 and 168. The identical term associated with these words is εἰκῆ, 'haphazard'.

σημείωσιν ὀρθοῦ λόγου, "bound up with truth and the expression of the right reason" (sect. 161).

Thus, even if a metaphoric meaning is supposed to lie behind the words, the literal sense is never abandoned, and literal obedience is never dismissed. This rule holds for all authors discussed in this chapter, at least as regards the exegesis of commandments.

The *hermeneutical terminology* used in *Ep. Arist.* 128–171 includes:

διάληψις (sect. 160): 'conception'. This notion is coupled with that of 'purity' which formerly belonged to the vocabulary of cult and sacrifice.

ἐνδεικτικῶς, opp. to ἀπαγορευτικῶς (sect. 131; cf. ἐνδείκνυσθαι sect. 33): 'by way of indication/probation'. Even negative commandments do not just forbid, but 'point to' a deeper (moral) meaning.

λόγος: ὀρθὸς λόγος (sect. 161, cf. 244) is 'sound reason', as opposed to what is said at random (εἰκῆ) or by myth (μυθωδῶς). Criteria are not specified, but are provided by common sense. Cf. φυσικὸς λόγος 'natural reasoning' and λόγος βαθύς 'profound reason' in sect. 143.

μελετᾶν (sect. 160): 'to exercise'. This refers to an exercise which is practical and theoretical at once, namely observing commands while being aware of their deeper sense.

σεμνῶς (sect. 144), σεμνότης (sect. 171): 'solemnity' as opposed to frivolity (περιεργία). The passages refer to a text of venerable content, to something worthy of being worshipped (σέβεσθαι). Cf. ἁγνὴ ἐπίσκεψις ('pure contemplation') in sect. 144.

σημείωσις (sect. 170) with the complement: τοῦ διατάξαντος: what the Lawgiver 'wanted to say'. In sect. 161, this is a σημείωσις ὀρθοῦ λόγου (q. v.). Cf. σημειοῦσθαι (sect. 151).[114]

τροπολογεῖν (sect. 150): 'to speak improperly', by a trope. Note that the subject of the utterance is the Legislator, not his interpreter. Cf. above, 1.5 s. v. ἀλληγορία.

φυσικὴ διάνοια (sect. 171), φυσικὸς λόγος (sect. 143); justifying an explanation referring to general world knowledge, see above in the text.

The other portions of the Epistle, which are less explicit in hermeneutical matters, fit in with the above sketch. The mind (διάνοια) as the center of human motivation must be pure (ἁγνή) in sect. 292; and in sect. 312 Ptolemy admires the Lawgiver's mind (τὴν τοῦ νομοθέτου διάνοιαν). Moses' Law is 'venerable' (σεμνή) and 'divinely mediated' (διὰ Θεοῦ γεγονέναι, sect. 313). The concept of 'sound reasoning' is present in sect. 267 (Θεοῦ σοι διδόντος εὖ λογίζεσθαι). Sound reasoning is regarded as a gift of God, as is the art of speaking (λόγος) and of persuading (πείθειν, πειθώ) in sect. 266.

All this is slightly more Greek than Eleazar's address to the seventy-two translators and their companions, and it seems that it is deliberately so. The term φιλοσοφία and φιλόσοφος, absent from the High Priest's language, are used in sect. 256 (definition of 'philosophy')[115] and 296 (the seventy-two elders are admired by the Alexandrine court's philosophers); and in sect. 31 the Law is qualified as 'very philosophical' (φιλοσοφωτέρα).[116]

---

[114] In contrast to this, παράσημον (sect. 147, 158) is a material sign, an emblem, namely the *mezuzah*.

[115] It is composed of logic and ethics (καλῶς διαλογίζεσθαι, μετριοπάθεια).

[116] 4 Macc 1:1, reflecting a more advanced stage, puts this term programmatically and without hesitation at its very beginning.

2.6. *The Reception of the* Epistle of Aristaeus

Josephus' rewriting of the *Epistle* has already been referred to (see 2.1); it includes a mention of Aristaeus' name. In the prologue to his *Antiquities* (1.10–12) Josephus stresses the fact that Ptolemy did not receive the whole Scripture (πᾶσαν τὴν ἀναγραφήν), but "only the (books) of the Law".

Nevertheless, the LXX legend, in the course of its transmission by Philo, Justin Martyr, Pseudo-Justin and others, received increasingly dogmatic augmentations until it became the assertion of the miraculous, verbally inspired identity of seventy-two individual translations of the whole Old Testament.[117] In the Latin Church Jerome forcefully opposed these accretions.[118]

The *Ep.Arist.*'s moralizing exploitation of 'symbolic links' between various ritual regulations concerning human conduct coincided with the *Zeitgeist*, as may be judged from Philo's allegorical exegeses, most of which are of the 'ethical' type. In a more general sense, the *Ep.Arist.* testifies to the common sense of an epoch, as is confirmed by the teaching of Jesus (Mark 7:17–23 par.).

Eusebius, *Praep. evang.* 8.2–5, 8.9 and 9.38, quotes long passages from the Epistle.[119] His interests focus on the LXX legend, on the description of Jerusalem, and on the hermeneutical section.

The text of the Epistle has come down to us in numerous manuscripts, all in Greek, all attached as an appendix to a catena on the Octateuch.[120] There is no ancient translation.

2.7. *Results and Questions*

Taken as a hermeneutical programme, the *Epistle of Aristaeus* has the historical merit of formulating what was to become common sense in interpreting Scripture during one and a half millennia – as far as Greek culture served as a model. It has succeeded in establishing a synthesis between biblical tradition and Greek philosophy, saving the former in the frame of the latter.

A genuinely biblical or Jewish element may be seen in the Epistle's insistence on *memory*. To take alimentary prescriptions as an example: ruminants are allowed to eat because they "express the phenomenon of memory" (τὸ τῆς μνήμης, sect. 153). The *mezuzot* are in use "that there may be a remembrance of God" (πρὸς τὸ μνείαν εἶναι Θεοῦ, sect. 158). And the High Priest, even though his discourse tends to assign metaphorical meanings to concrete texts, asserts the principle that the whole Law aims at demonstrating God's power (sect. 133).

---

[117] For all details, see Pelletier's ed., 78–98: *Le développement de la légende.*

[118] *Apologia adversus libros Rufini* 2.25 (PL 23, 2nd ed., 470 A/B) and other texts referred to by Pelletier, 89 f. The limits of Jerome's success may be judged from other sections of this handbook.

[119] They are dealt with in Pelletier's ed. of the *Ep.Arist.*, pp. 22–41.

[120] Pelletier, p. 9, surmises that one single copy which once pertained to the episcopal library at Caesarea is the common source of the entire transmission, be it direct or indirect.

But it is not clear from the text where this power becomes evident. There is some reference to God's action in history contained in the account of the liberation of the Jewish slaves in sect. 19–21; but 'classical' salvation history (the Exodus, etc.) is not referred to. Did the author avoid giving offense to his Egyptian readers? Anyway, in writings such as the *Ep. Arist.*, Aristobulus, and the *magnum opus* of Philo, it never becomes quite clear whether theological argumentation is founded in history (as is the case in much of the OT) or tends to make an abstraction from history. This problem will be highlighted by what follows:

– Taken as a historical document, the *Epistle* is a very questionable product. Even though it asserts its historical reliability in the very strongest terms (sect. 296–300), its narrative contents are as far from history as are those, say, of 3 Maccabees. The author's boundless naïveté, not to say his lack of sincerity, in reporting 'past' events and citing would-be documents marks a stupendous contrast with the sophisticated nature of the composition as a whole and of its hermeneutic programme in particular.

This observation may be combined with a fact already stated (1.4), that the Jews of Alexandria were never penetrated by the spirit of the Museum's historical and critical philology. The *Epistle* uses some of its terms, but it does so in an improper and metaphorical way (2.2).[121] Dogmatic postulates, such as the uniformity of the Greek Pentateuch text, override the factual substructure they would logically require.

– As a document of theological dogmatics, the *Epistle* mirrors a *bourgeois* position by its attempt to present a 'philosophy' and by the absence of eschatology, esp. of Messianism.[122] Salvation (σωτηρία) is achieved by the divinely inspired (Ptolemaic) king (sect. 18, 21). All these observations qualify the Epistle as the effort of a certain intellectualism – defying (in theory) the populace's fables, but keeping aloof from the critical spirit of the Alexandrian Museum.

3. Aristobulus

Editions and translations: A. M. Denis, PVTG I (1970) 217–202;[123] ET: A. Yarbro Collins in: Charlesworth, OTP II 831–842 (quoted hereafter).

Indexes: A.-M. Denis (ed.), *Concordance grecque des Pseudépigraphes d'A. T.* (Louvain-la-Neuve 1987; siglum *L. Ari* [sic]).

---

[121] This problem recurs in Philo's use of Greek philosophical terminology.

[122] As M. Hengel has shown, Messianic expectations are typical of the lower classes' disappointment with the ruling class and with current politics. See his essay "Messianische Hoffnung und politischer 'Radikalismus' in der 'jüdisch-hellenistischen Diaspora'", *Apocalypticism in the Mediterranean World and the Near East* (ed. D. Hellholm; Tübingen 1983) 633–686, esp. 666 f. In our text, sect. 133 contains only a faint hint at God's judgment.

[123] His text is based on the Eusebius editions of E. Schwartz (*Historia ecclesiastica*, 1903–09; GCS) and K. Mras (*Praeparatio evangelica*, 1954–56; GCS). The main transmission is:
for frg. 1: Eusebius, *H. e.* 7. 32, 17–18 (with a preceding summary in § 16);
for frg. 2: Eusebius, *Praep. evang.* 8. 10. 1–17;
for frg. 3: ibid. 13. 12. 1–2;
for frg. 4: ibid. 13. 12. 3–8;
for frg. 5: ibid. 13. 12. 9–16.

Bibliographies: N. Walter, Aristobulos (1964; see sect. 1) xi–xix; idem, JSHRZ II/1 (1973) 267 f; Schürer/Vermes, History III/1 (1986) 586–87.

General works: D. Dawson, Allegorical Readers (1992; see sect. 1) 74–82; M. Hengel, Judaism and Hellenism (1974; see sect. 1) I 163–69; 265–267 (notes in II 105–10; 176 f); N. Walter, Aristobulos (1964); idem, ANRW II 20/1 (1987; see sect. 2) 79–83.

The *numbering* of fragments (1–5) follows N. Walter (1964).

Aristobulus needs little comment, since everything is plain in his texts. Of all Jewish exegetes, Aristobulus is the most explicit about the theoretical basis of his work. There are no mysteries and no contradictions.

Nothing is known about his person. He may be identical with the Aristobulus mentioned in 2 Macc 1:10; but the 'document' in which his name occurs is suspected of being a 1st cent. BCE forgery. Therefore, we can only rely on what we learn from the fragments themselves.

The surname 'the Peripatetician' (= Aristotelian) which Aristobulus sometimes bears is of dubious authenticity; it unduly narrows down Aristobulus' philosophical spectrum. It is true that he once refers to "some of the αἵρεσις of the Peripateticians" (frg. 5 § 10) in order to promote a rather trivial truth; but he does so without involving himself.

3.1. Place, Date, and Character of Aristobulus' Work

Aristobulus' Ἐξηγήσεις τῆς Μωυσέως γραφῆς or Βίβλοι ἐξηγητικαὶ τοῦ Μωυσέως νόμου,[124] also cited as Πρὸς Πτολεμαῖον τὸν βασιλέα or Πρὸς Φιλομήτορα according to their dedication, is a work in several volumes addressed to Ptolemy VI (ca. 180–145 BCE). This monarch favoured the Jews in his country during a crisis concerning the High Priests' succession. He allowed them to construct a (schismatic) Jewish temple at Leontopolis.[125]

In the transmitted texts Aristobulus refers to his own writing by the term ζητήματα ('questions', frg. 2 § 1), which might well imply a kind of scholarly book such as the work of the Stoic Heraclitus: *Homeric Questions* (see sect. 1.5). As to its style, it is less rhetorical than the *Epistle of Aristaeus*, and prose rhythms are rare.[126] There is something timid and tentative about Aristobulus' style (e.g. optatives with ἄν)[127] which may win him the sympathies of some readers, at least modern ones. Before inferring that the methods of exegesis Aristobulus recommends had not yet been established for the Jewish Scriptures and that he marks the very first stage in experimenting with them,[128] we should take into consideration that it is one of the Ptolemy's Jewish subjects who dares to speak to him (be it fiction or fact), and not

---

[124] The former title is found in Eusebius' *Chronicles, anno Abrahae* 1841; for the latter see his *H. e.* 7.32.16.

[125] On his political motifs see below, 3.3, n. 143.

[126] Examples are frg. 5 § 12 (3 Cretic verses) and 13 (one and a half). But many ends of paragraphs lack them.

[127] In the κοινή this was an extremely distinguished means of expression, a kind of lingustic coquetry. Cf. Acts 5:24; 17:18.

[128] See sect. 2, above, on the relative chronology of Aristobulus and the *Ep. Arist.*

Jerusalem's High Priest giving instructions to the seventy-two elders. There once was a king who became interested in biblical exegesis ...[129]

The five fragments we possess from Aristobulus' work are all found in Eusebius (see n. 123), with occasional parallels in Clement of Alexandria. Although Clement wrote one century earlier he provides a less accurate text; often, he does not quote literally, but with stylistic alterations. Eusebius, on the other hand, is known for a high degree of reliability.

3.2. The Contents of Aristobulus' Fragments

Frg. 1 is of lesser interest for our purpose since it deals with chronological matters, giving astronomical details relevant to the Passover date. Its preservation is due to the quartodeciman controversy in 2nd and 3rd cent. Christianity. Eusebius' introduction to the fragment mentions a list of Hellenistic Jewish authors who made efforts "to solve (ἐπιλύειν) the questions concerning Exodus", one of which was the problem of the correct Passover date.

– Frg. 2 answers the question[130] how God may have 'hands', why he may 'stand', 'go down' to Mt. Sinai, and so on. This is the question of the so-called anthropomorphisms in Scripture. This Greek term[131] had already been used in the 3rd cent. BCE by Hecataeus of Abdera when he spoke of Judaism: Moses forbids images of Gods, he says, διὰ τὸ μὴ νομίζειν ἀνθρωπόμορφον εἶναι τὸν Θεόν.[132]

In his answer Aristobulus first asserts that one must not always take Moses' words at face value (κατὰ τὴν ἐπιφάνειαν), since he may speak of other things (ἐφ' ἑτέρων πραγμάτων) than what the words seem to mean. He blames those who just "cling to what is written" (τῷ γραπτῷ μόνον προσκείμενοι) and do not care whether there is anything admirable (= divine) in it.

Then he proceeds to name the things Moses must have had in mind. God's 'hands' are his forces (§ 7) or his achievements (§ 9). Aristobulus' argument based on everyday language may remind us of Aristotle's method of inquiry[133] as well as of modern Ordinary Language Philosophy. God's 'standing' is the establishment of the cosmos (ἡ τοῦ κόσμου κατασκευή, ibid.; cf. frg. 4 § 4). His 'descending' to Mt. Sinai with fire and trumpet blasts "was not local" (§ 15) since it did not burn anything and yet could be seen as far away as five days' travel; it was the manifestation of divine fire (= ether) which burns by itself without fuel.[134]

– Frg. 3 claims that Plato "closely followed our Legislation" (§ 1; cf. frg. 4 § 4 and frg. 5 § 13 on Homer and Hesiod). This was to become a stock

---

[129] *Ep. Arist.* 283 recommends good reading for a king's spare time.

[130] Eusebius' introduction supposes that the question was posed by Ptolemy VI himself; but this may be an inference from Aristobulus' dedication.

[131] It is found already in Epicurus and has also been used by Cornutus, *Theologiae Graecae compendium* (see sect. 1.5), ch. 27 (p. 49, l. 7; Lang), but not in a critical sense.

[132] We know this fragment through a historian who was writing in the time of Cesar: Diodorus of Sicily, 40.3. Cf. M. Stern, Authors (see sect. 1) I (1976), no. 11 § 4.

[133] So do also § 10–11 where Aristobulus argues by means of Aristotle's first category.

[134] On this doctrine, which is a Stoic development of Aristotelian cosmology to yield a materialist conception of Zeus or God, see Philo, *De Deo* (4.1, below, G 20 a; cf. 1.3, above). The way in which Aristobulus wants to associate to this sublime fire the sound of trumpets (§ 17) is not clear.

argument of Jewish and Christian apologetics.[135] In support of this thesis Aristobulus purports that there were partial Greek translations or paraphrases of the Jewish Law even before Demetrius of Phaleron had a complete translation made.[136]

– Frg. 4 programmatically converts anthropomorphisms into philosophical statements:

> It is necessary to take the divine 'voice' not as a spoken word, but as the establishment of things (οὐ ῥητὸν λόγον, ἀλλ' ἔργων κατασκευάς). Just so has Moses called the whole genesis of the world words of God in our Law. For he continually says in each case, "And God spoke and it came to pass" (§ 3, trans. Yarbro Collins; see Gen 1:3, 6 etc.).

Aristobulus continues by claiming that Pythagoras, Socrates, Plato and even Orpheus got their cosmology from Moses. As more recent evidence he cites the beginning of the astronomic poem of Aratus (*Phaenomena* 1–9)[137] and justifies the correction of 'Eκ Διός into 'Eκ Θεοῦ by claiming that the intention (διάνοια, see below, 3.5) underlying these words is to make a reference to God.[138] He continues:

> For it is agreed by all the philosophers that it is necessary to hold holy opinions concerning God (δεῖ περὶ Θεοῦ διαλήψεις ὁσίας ἔχειν), a point our philosophical school (ἡ καθ' ἡμᾶς αἵρεσις) makes particularly well. And the whole constitution of our Law is arranged with reference to piety and justice and temperance and the rest of the things that are truly good (§ 8).

– Frg. 5, again, proposes the metaphorical understanding of a difficult Scriptural passage. How can the Law say that God 'rested' on the seventh day (§ 11, referring to Gen 2:2)? Aristobulus first states that God "gave us the seventh day as a rest because life is troublesome for all".[139] He thus starts with a comment about the concrete and literal sense of the Sabbath command; he provides it with a rational incentive. But then he adds in somewhat metaphorical language that the 'seventh' day may well (φυσικῶς; see below, 3.5) be called the 'first' because it is the origin of the 'light' by which the universe is contemplated (§ 9, a clear allusion to the Jewish sabbath service). From there he proceeds to say that "the same thing might be said metaphorically (μεταφέροιτο δ' ἄν) about wisdom also, because all light has its origin in it" (§ 9–10). Aristobulus thus proposes to understand the term 'light' in this biblical context as a metaphor. The same language, Aristobulus says, has also

---

[135] Josephus, *Ap.* 2.168 cites it from an anonymous source; cf. 257, Philo, *QG* 4.167; Justin, *Apology* 1.59 f, etc. Logically, this claim seems to follow from Moses' chronological priority; but the hermeneutics which make 'Moses' speak like a philosopher are certainly not due to him. This makes the argument circular.

[136] This is a reference to the legend told also in the *Ep. Arist.* For the postulate that Greek authors had some knowledge of Moses' Law before the LXX translation was made, see there §§ 312–16.

[137] This poem was the text through which astronomy was taught to, and memorized by, schoolboys. See Marrou, Histoire de l'éducation (see sect. 1), part II, chap. 8.

[138] Cf. Philo, G 13.150, changing θεοί in a famous line by Hesiod into θεός. This procedure is not restricted to Jewish monotheism. Cornutus 11 (p. 11, lines 18 ff; Lang) corrects Homer in exchanging the Name of Helios with that of Zeus, the universal god: now it is Zeus who "oversees everything". Philo cites the same Homeric locution, in the same sense, in L 24.265.

[139] διὰ τὸ κακόπαθον εἶναι πᾶσι τὴν βιοτήν. This cliché, which was to become frequent in Philo, is hermeneutically important because it supports the interpreter's efforts to leave behind social life (including history) and to speculate about abstract truths instead.

been used by Peripateticians and, above all, by "one of our ancestors, Solomon" (§ 10, alluding to Prov 8:22–31).

God does not cease to be active, as "some"[140] would understand it. Instead, ἀποπεπαυκέναι said about God "means that, after he had finished ordering all things, he so orders them for all time" (§ 11). Or, as § 12 repeats it in citing Exod 20:11, "having set all things in order, he maintains and alters them so (in accordance with that order)". He thus formulates a fundamental dogma of Jewish Hellenistic theology.[141]

The seventh day, Aristobulus continues, is "legally binding for us as a sign" (ἔννομος ἕνεκεν σημείου); and he goes on to expound the symbolism of the number seven with numerous quotations from Homer, Hesiod, and "Linus". Associating the Sabbath with wisdom, he has Greek poets say that the number seven is typical of cosmic phenomena in that it corresponds to a universal rhythm (§ 13–16). The seventh day, therefore, prevents its observers from "the forgetfulness and evil of the soul" (ἀπὸ τῆς κατὰ ψυχὴν λήθης καὶ κακίας, recalling a platonic formulation) and allows "us" (the Jews) to receive knowledge of the truth (γνῶσιν ἀληθείας).

Aristobulus' proofs from classical pagan writers are revealing in more than one respect.

First, the use of apocryphal Homeric and Hesiodic verses (one in § 13 and all of § 14 are apocryphal) proves that Aristobulus is not a partisan of Alexandrian critical philology, as is true of the *Epistle of Aristaeus* and all of the "Pergamene" school of interpretation (see 1.2, end).

Second, the text of a quotation may be altered without warning. § 14 changes in *Odyssey* 5.262 the word 'four' into 'seven', thus introducing the very point on which the argument rests.[142]

Third, the poets may 'mean' (σημαίνειν, § 15) something much more global than the context would have us think. There is a surplus of meaning, a *sensus plenior*, which becomes independent from the context; the kind of quotations used proves this. This is indeed the starting point of the hermeneutics of multiple meanings as observed also in the threefold exposition in §§ 9–10.

Fourth, an easy means to extract a possible deeper meaning from a banal passage is to speculate about numbers. In most of Aristobulus' quotations the number seven does not bear the weight of the phrase; it is the interpreter who makes it do so. From here there is only a short step to transfer this truly allegorical hermeneutics to Scripture. We do not know whether Aristobulus himself ever went so far; Philo did. In his exegesis the most concrete phrase may acquire the most abstract meaning by virtue of its numerals.

3.3. Aristobulus' Theological Basis for the Interpretation of Scripture

Moses, Aristobulus says, possessed admirable wisdom and τὸ θεῖον πνεῦμα; that is why he is called a prophet (frg. 1 § 4).

Yet, historically speaking, there is also another kind of inspiration at work. The "holy opinions concerning God" required in frg. 4 § 8 avowedly have a philosophical origin. Aristobulus somehow justifies this duplicity by claiming (§ 7) that the philosophers' Zeus and God are identical. This was a contro-

---

140 These τινὲς, of course, are those who merely "cling to what is written" (frg. 2 § 5).

141 See Philo, G 5.87; Josephus, *Ap.* 2.190–192; the sermon *On Jonah* 1–4, etc.

142 One may suppose that Aristobulus here and in the context depends on a Jewish *florilegium*. At any rate, he did not use a critical edition of the poet.

versial thesis indeed. The same idea had been the centre of argument in the tumultuous events which took place in Jerusalem around 175 BCE.[143]

At any rate, Aristobulus' conception of God is very close to that of the Stoics, as is evident from his quotation of the opening verses of Aratus (in frg. 4 § 6; cf. Acts 17:28). God is ubiquitous, he penetrates all things; as humans, we are his offspring (by being able to use the *logos*), and he has arranged for every event to occur at the appropriate place and time (the Stoic dogma of providence).

For Aristobulus, as for a Stoic, God is narrowly linked with the cosmos. His 'standing', frg. 2 states, is "the establishment of the cosmos". In order to avoid anything like an identification of God with the cosmos, as was current in Hellenistic philosophy, the author hurries to add that "God is over all things and all things have been subordinated (to him)" (§ 10); they are "subjected to God" (§ 12). Speaking of God is not just an indirect way of speaking of the cosmos, as it was in Stoic teaching.

Taking God's words as deeds, as does frg. 4, corresponds entirely to the Greek intellectuals' conception of revelation. "God executes everything silently", Menander said.[144] The Stoics were convinced that the structure of the cosmos reveals the nature and activity of God (Zeus) and the gods to every attentive mind. Philo has reformulated Aristobulus' philosophical maxim time and again: *Opif.* 13; G 6.65; G 21.182; L 25.283; L 27.47.

In the Pentateuch, on the other hand, God speaks to Moses "face to face" (Deut 5:4; cf. 34:10),[145] or, in an oracular way during sacrifice, "between the two Cherubim" (Exod 25:21 [22];[146] Num 7:89; cf. 9:6–14; 11:25, etc.). The corresponding oracular practice, however, had ceased in Aristobulus' day. Even though the "breastplate", which was a decorated bag hanging on the High Priest's chest, is called 'oracle' (λόγιον) in the LXX (Exod 28:15–30; in Philo: λογεῖον), neither the *Ep. Arist.* 97 nor Josephus (*Ant.* 3.163–171) give any hint as to the actual use of the *urim* and *tummim* it once contained. Philo uses their names to refer to the λόγος ἐνδιάθετος resp. προφορικός of the Stoics (*QE* 2.116),[147] and Josephus speculates on the symbolism of the twelve stones.

3.4. *Aristobulus' Bible and the Texts Referred to*

The sacred text is called 'our Law' (ὁ νόμος ὁ παρ' ἡμῖν, frg. 2 § 1), or 'the Law' (frg. 4 § 8), or 'the Legislation' (ἡ νομοθεσία, ibid. §§ 8, 13, frg. 3 § 1) and 'our Legislation' (also frg. 3 § 1), or ἡ γραφὴ τοῦ νόμου (ibid. § 12). The

---

[143] Ptolemy VI's reception in Egypt of the legitimate High Priest in order that he may conduct a schismatic Temple service may well have been a clever move meant to undermine the Hasmoneans' position. Thus political and theological decisions were closely linked.

[144] Ἅπαντα σιγῶν ὁ θεὸς ἐξεργάζεται (frg. 462 in Stobaeus, *Anthologium* 1.1.11).

[145] Alluded to, in an eschatological context, by Paul in 1 Cor 13:12.

[146] A saying much commented upon by Philo. See below, 4.3.

[147] There seems to be a strong contrast between Israelite and Jewish mythical conceptions of revelation and the silently penetrating divine Logos of Greek religious philosophy. But the idea that God's words are deeds (*Maiestatis dicere est facere*, Luther says in commenting Ps 2:5, WA 40/2, 231, 5f) is foreshadowed not only in Gen 1 (Aristobulus' text in frg. 4) but also in Deut 8:3 (see Philo's comment in G 4.174–176), Deut 32:47, Isa 40:5, and 51:20.

text quoted is the Septuagint, with one exception: the wording of Exod 3:20 in frg. 2 § 8 comes closer to the MT.[148]

Its author is "our lawgiver Moses" (frg. 1 § 3, cf. §§ 6, 8, 13). In citing Proverbs, it is "one of our ancesters, Solomon" (frg. 5 § 11). We do not know whether Aristobulus had a theory on inspiration. Perhaps it did not exceed contemporary commonplaces (1.3).

The texts dealt with include:
Gen 1:3, 6 etc.; 2:2
Exod 3:9, 20; 13:9; 17:6; 19:11, 18, 20; 20:4; 24, 16
Deut 4:11 etc.
Prov 8:22–31,
i. e. the books of the Law which may receive some support from elsewhere.

Aristobulus' quotations are not necessarily literal (see frg. 1 § 8), and they are always short. He writes, after all, for a Greek reader, and his work is not meant to be a commentary. In citing pagan authors, his freedom is even greater, see the comments on frg. 4 § 6 and frg. 5 § 14.

3.5. Aristobulus' Hermeneutical Rules

It may be misleading to call Aristobulus an 'allegorist'. He does not discard the literal meaning of a problematic passage. But the literal meaning, he claims, may be a trope. It may be the interpreter's task to make plain a metaphor (frg. 5 § 9).

Besides, a text may call for another metaphorical activity or 'transfer'. Just as the term 'light' may *also* mean 'understanding', a Mosaic prescription may have an additional meaning. That Jews keep the sabbath is not just to enjoy rest but also to engage in learning (ibid. § 10). In looking for reasons for a given injunction one may thus find more than one. This is the origin of the hermeneutics of multiple meanings. In (later) Hebrew terminology this was the דרש as opposed to the פשט.

Historically, it is still later than the hermeneutics of *double entendre* which the Greeks had developed for their poets. Aristobulus himself uses it directly in frg. 5, §§ 13–14.

Even though the meaning of Scripture is (potentially) multiple, metaphoric understanding does not dispense with literal compliance. Nor does it in the *Epistle of Aristaeus.* There is no trace of ethical laxity, as there was later among some of Philo's all too liberal contemporaries (see below, 4.5). The Jewish sacred text continues to be a law; it does not become poetry.[149]

---

[148] The origin of this variant remains an open question. It may well be that the efforts of the *Ep. Arist.* tended to eliminate an original variety of renderings by establishing a Greek standard text, cf. 2.7. – A gloss translating σάββατον by ἀνάπαυσις in frg. 5 § 13 seems to be another evidence to the awareness of the existence of different Bibles. But as this gloss is misplaced (it comes rather late) it is subject to the doubts of literary criticism.

[149] See I. Heinemann, "Die Allegoristik der hellenistischen Juden außer Philon", *Mnemosyne*, ser. 4, 5 (1952) 130–38. Walter, Aristobulos (1964) 129 remarks: "Als Jude stand er in einem ganz anderen Verhältnis zur Tora als jeder Grieche zum Homer, nämlich in dem voller innerer Abhängigkeit".

Aristobulus' *exegetical terminology* includes:

ἀλογία 'want of reason, folly': the very thing Moses has to be excused from (frg. 1 § 6). For an opposite, cf. καλῶς and λόγος.

ἀφορμή 'starting point, stimulus': Moses' veiled words make his readers reflect and become philosophers and poets by formulating them otherwise (frg. 1 § 4) – just as do Homer's readers in Heraclitus, *Quaestiones Homericae* 68.9 and in Ps.-Plutarch, *De Homero* 6.115, 122, 214 etc.

τὸ γραπτόν 'the text': it may be opposed to what the author 'wants to say' (frg. 1 § 3 and 5), his 'thoughts' (νενοημένα, ibid. § 6).

διαλήψεις ὅσιαι 'holy opinions/conceptions' (frg. 4 § 8): thus, in consulting an oracle, you were required to "think holy thoughts and to speak words of good omen" (ὅσια φρονεῖν, εὔφημα λέγειν).[150] Likewise, ἡ ἁρμόζουσα ἔννοια περὶ Θεοῦ is 'a conception which befits God'. Greek philosophers had developed the idea of θεοπρεπές, meaning the same thing: avoiding anthropomorphisms and avoiding attributing evil qualities or actions to the divine. Philo uses this term expressly. Josephus demands of his readers a δόξα ... σεμνὴ περὶ Θεοῦ (*Ap.* 2.221). The opposite would be a περὶ Θεοῦ πλημμέλεια (ibid. 250).

διάνοια: what an author 'had in mind'; the (true) 'intention' of his words (frg. 4 § 7: a Poet naming Zeus 'meant' God). Cf. βούλεσθαι λέγειν (of Moses) in frg. 2 § 3.

ἔννοια: see διαλήψεις ὅσιαι.

ἔννομος: 'being encoded in the Law' (frg. 5 § 12). An opposite would be ἄγραφος (see above, 2.5).

ἐξηγεῖσθαι 'to interpret': Aristobulus does so "wishing to guard the right opinion about God (τὸν περὶ Θεοῦ λόγον)", frg. 2 § 12.

ζήτημα 'question, problem': this implies that it is legitimate to ask *why*; see above, 3.1–2.

καλῶς: 'well' thought or said (frg. 2 § 9 two times; 3 § 8; cf. frg. 1 § 4). This is what fits – after due interpretation – the common sense of educated people. Also frequent elsewhere in citation formulae,[151] this adverb praises an author, thereby concealing the interpreter's efforts. Philo frequently enhances it to παγκάλως, mainly in introducing "literal" explanations which are not as literal as they purport to be.

λόγος 'reason' implicitly refers to the interpreter's philosophical training; cf. ἔννοια, ἐξηγεῖσθαι.

μεταφέρειν 'to transfer', i.e. to understand a metaphor's meaning (frg. 1 § 8; frg. 5 § 9). This is not allegorization, but the solution of a trope.

σημεῖον, σημαίνειν in frg. 5, §§ 12 and 15, refers to an extended meaning, a *sensus plenior.*

φυσικῶς λαμβάνειν: 'to understand in a physical (or just: reasonable) sense'; opp. μυθωδῶς (frg. 2 § 2; cf. above, 2.5). In frg. 5 § 9 φυσικῶς may have been reduced already to a banalized meaning like 'naturally' or 'plausibly'.[152] Cf. φυσικὴ διάνοια in *Ep. Arist.* 171, where in fact an ethical meaning is referred to.

3.6. The Reception of the Fragments

A list of testimonies is given by Walter, Aristobulos (1964) 9–26, 33–35, with comments. On the Latin side, only Jerome is named (*De viris illustribus* 38.4).

Origen is one of the last authors to have access to Aristobulus' work. He relies on it (unfortunately without quoting it) in his answer to Celsus' mockery of Jewish efforts to rescue myth through allegory (*Contra Celsum* 4.51). After Eusebius, all references to Aristobulus depend on his (and Clement's) quotations.

---

[150] Cf. Plutarch, *De Iside et Osirde*, *Mor.* 378 C/D. Plutarch goes on to complain that on religious feasts this rule is little respected. On this score synagogue services may have been impressive to pagan intellectuals.

[151] Philo, *QG* II.61.62 (trans. παγκάλως), etc.; G 8.19; G 17.86; G 19.159; L 27.48 (παγκάλως), etc., Cornutus, *Theologiae Graecae compendium* 28 (p. 55, l. 17, Lang); Barn 10:11. The case of Acts 28:25 is somewhat different; here the adverb expresses Paul's anger.

[152] In Heraclitus the Stoic, who uses it frequently, cf. 16.5; 25.1.12 (here the "physics" are made more explicit); 66.10.

3.7. *Results*

Comparing Aristobulus with the *Epistle of Aristaeus* (see above, 2.5, for details), we may state that these documents are complementary. Aristobulus is as explicit on a 'physical' deeper meaning as is the *Epistle* on the ethical one. The king's questions exemplify a different interest from that of the Israelite High Priest. There is no need, either historically or logically, to see them as an alternative. In Philo we will find both interests at work in interpreting the same Mosaic sayings.

Aristobulus is more of an intellectual than is the compiler of the *Epistle of Aristaeus.* This is not to say that his arguments are beyond critique.[153] His importance consists in allowing Jewish intellectuals to take a clear stance vis-à-vis two different apologetic fronts: pagan accusations of "impiety",[154] and Jewish determination to "cling to the letter".

4. Philo of Alexandria

Editions and translations: A) The *Quaestiones*: *Philonis Judaei paralipomena Armena* [sic] (ed. J.B. Aucher [Awgerean]; Venice 1826; repr. Hildesheim 1988) 1-548 (Armenian with Latin trans.); ET: R. Marcus in *Philo, Supplement* I.II (LCL; 1953); French trans.: *Les Œuvres de Philon d'Alexandrie* (ed. R. Arnaldez/J. Pouilloux/C. Mondésert [the 'Lyon edition']; 36 vols. [vol. 34 in three]; Paris 1961 ff; vol. 33-34 C, 1971-92); J. Paramelle/E. Lucchesi/J. Sesiano, *Philon d'Alexandrie, Questions sur la Genèse II 1-7: Texte grec, version arménienne, parallèles latins* (Genève 1984); J.R. Royse, "Further Greek Fragments of Philo's *Quaestiones*", *Nourished With Peace* (1984; see final section of this bibl.), 143-53.[155]

B) Treatises 1-38: *Philonis Alexandrini opera quae supersunt* I-VI (ed. L. Cohn/P. Wendland [vol. 6 also: S. Reiter]; Berlin 1896-1915; Greek text, basis also for LCL and the 'Lyon edition'); *Philo in Ten Volumes,* (Greek text, with an Engl. trans. by F.H. Colson/G.H. Whitaker; LCL; 1929-1962); *Les Œuvres de Philon d'Alexandrie* [see A], 1-32; 36-7 (Greek with French trans.); Filone di Alessandria: *La filosofia mosaica* [= treatise 1-4]/ *Le origini del male* [= 5-10]/ *La migrazione all'eterno* [=11-16]/ *L'erede delle cose divine* [= 17]/ *L'uomo e Dio* [=18-22] (ed. C. Kraus Reggiani/R. Radice/G. Reale et al., Milan 1987/84/88/81/86; Italian trans. and comm.); *Obras completas de Filón de Alejandría* I-V (ed. J.M. Triviño; Buenos Aires 1975-76; Spanish trans.); פילון האלכסנדרוני, כתבים (ed. S. Daniel-Nataf; vol. 1 [of 5 vols. planned]; Jerusalem 1986; Heb. trans.); For other partial editions, see the bibliographies listed below.

C) Other writings: *Philonis Judaei sermones tres* (ed. J.B. Aucher [Awgerean]; Venice 1822; Armenian text of *De providentia* I.II and *De animalibus* with Latin trans.); Latin and French trans.: *Les Œuvres de Philon d'Alexandrie* 35-36 (1973, 1988); *Philonis Alexandrini De animalibus: The Armenian text with an introduction* (trans. and comm. by A. Terian; Chico, CA 1981) – Vol. 37 of the 'Lyon' Philo is to contain the *Hypothetica.*

Indexes: For A) none, except for biblical references (see below); for B) I. (H.) Leisegang, *Indices ad Philonis Alexandrini opera* I-II (Berlin 1926-30; = vol. VII/1.2 of the Berlin edition); G. Mayer, *Index Philoneus* (Berlin 1974; complete Greek index, except for the fragments); for

---

153 A circular argument in frg. 3 has been pointed out in n. 135.

154 In Aristobulus' fragments it can only be found 'between the lines'; but we know from Josephus, *Ap.* 2.6 ff (cf. 2.125 ff; 2.291 ff), and from other sources the calumnies on the Jews that circulated in the ancient world, especially in Egypt. Cf. n. 32.

155 A complete edition of Philo's fragments by J.R. Royse is in preparation. For questions of authenticity, cf. idem, *The Spurious Texts of Philo of Alexandria: A study of Textual Transmission and Corruption with Indexes to the Major Collections of Greek Fragments* (ALGHJ 22; Leiden 1991).

C), see the single editions. *Index of biblical quotations:* J. ALLENBACH/A. BENOÎT et al. (eds.), BPSup; Paris 1982.

Bibliographies: Delling, Bibliographie (see sect. 1) 56–80; E. HILGERT, "Bibliographia Philoniana 1935–1981", ANRW II 21/1 (1984) 47–97; R. RADICE/D. T. RUNIA, *Philo of Alexandria: An Annotated Bibliography 1937–1986* (Leiden 1988; 1992), continued in the "Bibliographical Section" of each issue of Studia Philonica Annual 1 ff (1989 ff); Schürer/Vermes, History III/1 (1987) 809–812; F. SIEGERT, "Der armenische Philon: Textbestand, Editionen, Forschungsgeschichte", *ZKG* 100 (1989) 353–369.

General works (post-1950): Y. AMIR, *Die hellenistische Gestalt des Judentums bei Philon von Alexandrien* (Neukirchen 1983); idem, "Authority and Interpretation of Scripture in the Writings of Philo", Mikra (1988) 421–453; R. ARNALDEZ, "Introduction générale", *Les Œuvres de Philon d'Alexandrie* (see above) I, 17–112 (survey of research) esp. 22–42; 70–96; P. BORGEN, "Philo of Alexandria: A Critical and Synthetical Survey of Research since World War II", ANRW II 21/1 (1984) 98–154; D. I. BREWER, *Techniques and Assumptions in Jewish Exegesis Before 70 CE* (Tübingen 1992) esp. 198–212; H. BURKHARDT, *Die Inspiration heiliger Schriften bei Philo von Alexandrien* (Gießen 1988); J. CAZEAUX, "Philon d'Alexandrie, exégète", ANRW II 21/1 (1984) 156–226 (and other articles in the same volume); J. DANIÉLOU, *Philon d'Alexandrie* (Paris 1958) esp. 102–142; Dawson, Allegorical Readers (1992; see sect. 1) 73–126; E. R. GOODENOUGH, *An Introduction to Philo Judaeus* (Oxford ²1962); R. P. C. HANSON, *Allegory and Event: A Study of the Sources and Significance of Origen's Interpretation of Scripture* (London 1959) esp. 9–64; V. NIKIPROWETZKY, *Le commentaire de l'Ecriture chez Philon d'Alexandrie* (ALGHJ 11; Leiden 1977); *Nourished With Peace: Studies in Hellenistic Judaism in Memory of Samuel Sandmel* (ed. F. E. Greenspahn/E. Hilgert/B. L. Mack; Chico, CA 1984); *Philon d'Alexandrie, Lyon 11–15 Septembre 1966* (Colloques Nationaux du CNRS; Paris 1967); D. RUNIA, *Exegesis and Philosophy: Studies on Philo of Alexandria* (Aldershot 1990) esp. chaps. I–VI, IX; S. SANDMEL, *Philo of Alexandria: An Introduction* (New York/Oxford 1979); idem, "Philo Judaeus: An Introduction to the Man, his Writings, and his Significance", ANRW II 21/1 (1984) 3–46; R. WILLIAMSON, *Jews in the Hellenistic World: Philo* (Cambridge Commentaries on Writings of the Jewish and Christian World 200 BC to AD 200, I/2; Cambridge 1989) esp. 144–200.

Numbering of treatises and abbreviations: see below 4.1. Paragraphs are those of the Cohn/Wendland edition, retained since. For texts only transmitted in Armenian, the paragraphs of the first edition have been numbered.

4.0. *Introductory*

As far as exegetical method is concerned, readers of the previous sections will not find much that is new in Philo. This holds true even though between Aristobulus, the *Epistle of Aristaeus*, and Philo a whole century of documentation is lacking.[156] Philo is not an innovator; his works are the rich harvest from two centuries of exegetical work.

This treasure would have been entirely lost had he not become a classic for the Christian Church. The readiness of Christians from the 2nd cent. CE onwards to assimilate his views[157] and his methods should not have us forget that in his lifetime his scholarship was an authentic expression of Jewish deference to the Law.[158] Philo was one of the Sages of the Jewish community

[156] There are, to be sure, Jewish writings in Greek that can be dated in the 1st cent. BCE. But their nature and contents do not fit with references such as "some have said", "excellent men have said" etc. in Philo; see n. 167.

[157] Christian legends make him a convert to Christianity. This opinion is based on the assumption that the Essene community described in his *De vita contemplativa* was a Christian monastery; see below, 4.7.

[158] See A. MENDELSON, *Philo's Jewish Identity* (Atlanta 1988) esp. 29–49 (on theoretical beliefs) and 51–75 (on practices).

of Alexandria.[159] There were others, too, and their style may have been different (see sect. 5, below). This did not prevent the Alexandrian Jewish community from choosing him as their representative. They appointed him to head an embassy (winter 39/40 CE) to the Emperor's court.

The purpose of this embassy highlights Philo's situation. Flaccus, a Roman governor in Egypt, had allowed the Alexandrian Egyptians to insult the Jews of that city, to destroy most of their synagogues and drive them back into a kind of ghetto.[160] The embassy's mission, which was balanced by a pagan counter-embassy, was to claim recognition of the Jews' rights which, in their eyes, amounted to Alexandrian citizenship.[161]

Apart from this fact and the account he gave in his *In Flaccum* and *Legatio ad Gaium*, little is known of his life.[162] His family most probably held Roman citizenship. His brother Alexander was a banker to King Herod Agrippa I and a trustee of Claudius' mother. This gave Philo Roman connections which he was to exploit during his embassy. Alexander's nephew Tiberius Iulius Alexander, a successful Roman offical and apostate from Judaism, is the absent partner of the dialogues *De providentia* and *De animalibus*.

Philo's Greek education was vast, except in exact sciences and critical philology. He knows Plato as thoroughly as the Mosaic laws, but he does not participate in Alexandrian empirical and critical scholarship – no more than any other educated Jew of that city. Philo's education is a literary one, and his Greek style is impeccable. The 'Asianic' exuberance of his writing which might bewilder modern readers is due to the general taste of the time. He uses an enormous vocabulary. He occasionally went to the theatre;[163] he also visited Jerusalem as a pilgrim.[164]

Philo has become the classical author for the hermeneutics of multiple meanings. In his day this was already a well-established methodology. Philo need not justify it, as did the *Epistle of Aristaeus* and Aristobulus.

Philo's hermeneutics is exactly the same as observed in Aristobulus' frg. 5 (see 3.2 and 3.5, above) except for the following points:

– Long quotations from pagan authors are avoided. Philo speaks mainly to Jews, and he cites mostly from the LXX Pentateuch.

---

159 Ancient sources – they are exclusively Christian – cite him as Philo "the Jew" in order to distinguish him from other authors bearing the same name. He is not even the only Jewish writer to bear this name: Eusebius in his *Praep. evang.* 9.20.1; 24.1, and 37.1–3 quotes some hexametrical verses of a certain Philo (now called "Philo the epic poet") who wrote a poem in Greek hexameters "On Jerusalem". On Philo the Elder see below, 5.1.

160 Philo, *In Flaccum* 55–57. This is the first ghetto known in history.

161 On this problem, see above, 1.7. Only the assassination of Caligula prevented the Jewish embassy from ending in a failure. The arguments of the counter-embassy may be gathered from the *Acta Alexandrinorum* (ed. H. Musurillo; Leipzig 1961; Teubner). The famous rescript of Claudius dated 41 CE (see n. 70) tries to settle matters by way of a compromise.

162 Josephus, *Ant.* 18.259f mentions him briefly. To Christian writers no further evidence was available. The Rabbis never mention his name.

163 See above, 1.7, n. 68. In G 13.20–29 and L 29.230 Philo recommends participation in (pagan) cultural life and in sports.

164 *De providentia* 2.107: he went there "to pray and to sacrifice" (εὐξόμενός τε καὶ θύσων).

- The 'deeper meaning' is given much more attention than the 'literal meaning'. In rare cases it may even be discarded.[165] Literal observance of the Law, however, is never discarded.[166]
- Philo uses elaborate theories about the mediating agents between God and the cosmos and concerning the 'ascent' of the human soul as it understands revelation.

Philo often hints at his Jewish predecessors. L25.4, e.g., places the "holy books" and "some elders of (our) people" side by side as his sources of information.[167] But he never mentions Jewish scholars by name and never quotes them expressly; so nothing concrete can be said about them.[168] Moses, David, Solomon, and the prophets Isaiah and Jeremiah are the only authors of his people whom he cites by name. As to other written sources, the only safe assumption is that he drew upon *Onomastica* of Hebrew terms and names.[169]

As to pagan culture, Philo names and sometimes quotes Homer, Pindar, the "most holy Plato",[170] Euripides, and others. Greek myths are alluded to as well as current allegorizations of these myths.[171] There is no great mystery as to whence Philo got his hermeneutics. It was the Greek art of rescuing myths, especially those of Homer; and he learned it from Greeks and Jews alike.

---

165 Examples see below, 4.5 (end), 4.8, and N. Walter, Aristobulos (1964) 141 f, with reference to the biblical passages discussed by Aristobulus. Philo denies a literal meaning of God's 'descent' to Mt. Sinai (Aristobulus, frg. 2 Philo, *QE* 2.45 and G 15.134–141); in interpreting the 'days' of Creation, he rightly observes (G 2.2 f) that time does not belong to the conditions, but to the consequences of Creation.

166 See G 16.89 f; cf. above, 2.5 and 3.5 for *Ep. Arist.* and Aristobulus.

167 Cf. *QG/QE* constantly; G 259; G. 12.51, 70, etc.; L23.99; L24.151; L25.4; L27.115; L28.8, etc.

168 Most of the more or less speculative literature concerning this question (see a review by R. H. Hamerton-Kelly, *StudPhil* 1 [1972] 3–26, and another one by B. L. Mack, ANRW II 21/1 [1984] 227–271) is hampered by an ignorance of the pagan manuals of (Homeric) interpretation that did exist (cf. sect. 1, above). It goes without saying that Philo does not refer to them. No philosopher ever mentions his grammar school teachers and the primitive manuals they worked with.

169 On the issue of this anonymously circulating literature see Schürer/Vermes, History III/2 (1987) 869 f; Brewer, Techniques (1992) 207 f. A list of this kind was attributed to Philo, used by Origen, and supposed to have been translated by Jerome. For a reconstruction, see L. L. Grabbe, Etymology in Early Jewish Interpretation: The Hebrew Names in Philo (Brown Judaic Studies 115; Atlanta 1988) 225–231. F. Wutz, *Onomastica sacra* I–II (TU 41, 1–2; Leipzig 1914–15) shows that the transmission of this material is complicated: the 'Philo' and 'Origen' lists are pseudepigrapha, and Jerome's *Liber interpretationis nominum Hebraicorum* is a rather independent work, based on his own knowledge of Hebrew (I 203, 241, 290). That is to say that the few linguists among the Biblical scholars of Antiquity, as far as they wrote in Greek, have remained anonymous.

170 κατὰ τὸν ἱερώτατον Πλάτωνα: *Quod omnis probus liber sit* 13.

171 Thus *QG* 2.82; G 7.178; G 12.127–130; G 15.2–5; G 22.70; L 27.54, etc. See Y. Amir "The transference of Greek Allegories to Biblical Motifs in Philo", in: Nourished With Peace (1984) 15–25; P. Boyancé, "Echo des exégèses de la mythologie grecque chez Philon", Philon d'Alexandrie (Congress Volume; 1967) 169–188; J. Dillon, "Ganymede as the Logos: Traces of a forgotten allegorization in Philo", *StudPhil* 6 (1979/80) 37–40 (including a list on pp. 37–39). Leisegang, Indices I (1926) 1–26 is a useful index of names and quotations.

Like Aristobulus, Philo has to defend himself against Jews who dismiss any quest for a 'deeper meaning' in Scripture.[172] To him these are 'provincials' (μικροπολῖται), whereas he himself is conscious to be the citizen of a "greater country" (μείζων πατρίς). Their views seem to be considerably narrower than those of the authors to be reviewed in the next section (5).

To sum up this preface, Philo represents much, but not all, of Alexandrian Jewish biblical scholarship.

4.1. *Place, Date, and Classification of Philo's Writings*

Philo's exegetical tractates are conventionally grouped according to their literary *genres.*[173] As attempts at a relative chronology did not reach a consensus,[174] we may safely place all of Philo's writings in the first half of the 1st cent. CE, without much distinction.

For reasons of convenience we shall begin our presentation of Philo's exegetical writings with those which are methodically the most explicit and the most transparent: the *Quaestiones* on Genesis and on Exodus (henceforth: *QG/QE*). The further distinction between an "Allegorical Commentary on Genesis" (G) and an "Exposition of the Law" (L)—both titles are modern—does not mean that the latter is less allegorical. Allegorical method is used throughout all of Philo's exegeses. There is only a difference in the ways of referring to the biblical text. The *Questions* always begin with a lemma, to which are added one or more explanations, one after the other; G also opens its argument with a quotation, but then it proceeds more freely and interweaves further quotations; L may fail to quote its text at all.

The following list is meant to give an orientation to Philo's copious work. Philo's treatises preserved in Greek are cited by number, as it is in G. Mayer's Index Philoneus, with the addition of an initial which refers to the different groups of writings just mentioned. For more detailed information, expecially on the kinds of exegesis found in Philo, see sect. 4.4–7, below.

A) The *Quaestiones* (preserved in Armenian and partly in Latin; Greek original mostly lost):[175]

Questions on Genesis (*QG*) (on Gen 2:4–28:9 with lacunae, e.g. Genesis 11–14 and 21–22) in four (originally: six) books;[176]

---

[172] See M.J. Shroyer, "Alexandrian Jewish Literalists", *JBL* 55 (1936) 261–284.

[173] The establishment of several series of Philonic treatises is one of the merits of Thomas Mangey's edition of 1742.

[174] There is a marked difference, e.g., between the opinions on the *Quaestiones.* The collective work edited by D.M. Hay (see n. 233, below) takes them to be relatively late, thus contradicting an opinion that was dominant before. As to G, themes poorly developed, e.g., in G 5 (the Cherubim allegory), reappear in an elaborate state in the same series, G 21. Nothing justifies the assumption that Philo finished one *genre* of writing before using another. It rather seems that Philo worked on more than one of these series at the same time.

[175] The fragments are found in *QE* (ed. Marcus) pp. 179–275; a more complete collection is the vol. 33 (1978) of the 'Lyon' Philo (F. Petit).

[176] They have been transmitted by different ways for each half. The second half, comprising the original books IV–VI, has come down *en bloc* as bk. IV. The Lyon edition follows Marcus' proposal to identify *QG* IV to sect. 1–70, V to sect. 71–153, and VI to sect. 154–245 of the transmitted bk. IV.

Questions on Exodus (*QE*) (incomplete; preserved for Exodus 12, Exod 20:25, and 22:21–28:38) in two books (of original five).

B) Exegetical treatises 1–33 (preserved in Greek):

1 *De opificio mundi* (*Opif.*) (on Gen 1:1–2:9; also 3). This programmatic treatise in which Philo states his Platonic credo seems to resist a close affiliation with one of the other series. In a self-reference (L 23.258) he calls it ἡ Κοσμοποιία. It is the ancestor of the Christian *Hexaëmeron* literature.

The "Allegorical Commentary on Genesis" (= G):
= vols. 1–3 (Cohn/Wendland), vols. 1–5 (Loeb), vols. 1–19 (Lyon).
G 2–4 *Legum allegoriae* I-III (on Gen 2–3)
G 5 *De Cherubim* (on Gen 3:24; 4:1)
G 6 *De sacrificiis Abelis et Caini* (on Gen 4:2–4)
G 7 *Quod deterius potiori insidiari soleat* (on Gen 4:8–15)
G 8 *De posteritate Caini* (on Gen 4:16–26)
G 9 *De gigantibus* (on Gen 6:1–4)
G 10 *Quod Deus sit immutabilis* (on Gen 6:4–12)
G 11–14 *De agricultura, De plantatione, De ebrietate, De sobrietate* (on Gen 9:20–27)
G 15 *De confusione linguarum* (on Gen 11:1–9)
G 16 *De migratione Abrahami* (on Gen 12:1–6)
G 17 *Quis rerum divinarum heres sit* (on Gen 15:2–18)
G 18 *De congressu eruditionis gratia* (on Gen 16:1–6)
G 19 *De fuga et inventione* (on Gen 16:6–12)
G 20 *De mutatione nominum* (on Gen 17:1–5 and 15–22)
G 20a: There follows a lacuna of at least three tractates. The fragment *De Deo*[177] (on Gen 18:2) most probably is a part of one of them.
G 21 *De somniis* I (originally bk. II [?], of five), (on Gen 28:11–15; Genesis 31)
G 22 *De somniis* II (originally bk. III), (on Gen 37:5 ff; 40:5 ff; 41:1 ff).

The "Exposition of the Law" (= L) by thematical treatises:
= vols. 4–5 (Cohn/Wendland), vols. 6–8 (Loeb), vols. 20–27 (Lyon).
L 23 *De Abrahamo* (selected from Gen 4:25–26:11)
L 24 *De Josepho* (selected from Genesis 37–50)
L 25 *De Vita Mosis* I (selected from Exodus 1–9; 12–17; Numbers 13–14; 20–25; 31–32)
L 26 *De Vita Mosis* II (selected from Exodus 25–32; Numbers 16–17; 27; Deuteronomy 33–34; also Numbers 15; Exodus 16)[178]
L 27 *De Decalogo* (selected from Exodus 20)
L 28–31 *De specialibus legibus* I–IV (no biblical thread)
L 32 *De virtutibus* (texts taken from Genesis 3 to Deuteronomy 33; no biblical sequence)
L 33 *De praemiis et poenis* (eschatological finale, on Gen 4:26; 15:6; Numbers 16, etc.; Deuteronomy 28 and 30).

C) Other thematic writings

partly extant in Greek: = vol. 6 (Cohn/Wendland), vols. 9–10 (Loeb), vols. 28–32 (Lyon). These are treatises of philosophical interest, illustrating or refuting Stoic doctrines of their day:
34 *Quod omnis probus liber sit* (containing in § 75–91 a description of the Palestinian Essenes);
35 *De vita contemplativa* (a panegyric of the Essene community near Alexandria);
36 *De aeternitate mundi* (a notebook on a much disputed theme; unfinished).

[177] F. Siegert (ed.), *Philon von Alexandrien. Über die Gottesbezeichnung "wohltätig verzehrendes Feuer" (De Deo): Rückübersetzung des Fragments aus dem Armenischen, deutsche Übersetzung und Kommentar* (WUNT 46; Tübingen 1988). For detailed criticisms of this reconstruction, see the review by D. Runia, *VC* 43 (1989) 398–405 (= idem, Exegesis and philosophy [1990] ch. XIII), and another one by J. Royse, Studia Philonica Annual 5 (1993) 219–22.

[178] Both these writings, which originally were one single tractate, are somewhat different from the rest of the L series; see Schürer/Vermes, History III/2 (1987) 854 f. On this problem, see below, 4.6.

Treatises of historical and/or apologetic character are:

37 *In Flaccum* (a polemic against a deceased Roman official who had allowed persecutions of the Egyptian Jews – see above);

38 *Legatio ad Gaium* (on the Alexandrian Jews' embassy to Caligula which was headed by Philo himself);

De providentia I-II (preserved in Armenian, fragments in Greek), a tractate lacking any biblical reference;

De animalibus[179] (a refutation of the Stoic doctrine of the animals' λόγος, in favour of the biblical uniqueness of man – Genesis 1-2).

Fragments of one or two apologetical treatises are cited by Eusebius, *Praep. evang.* 8.6–7 and 8.11[180] under the puzzling title *Hypothetica* (in the first case) or *Apology on behalf of the Jews* (in the second).[181] A list of Philo's entirely lost works, as far as there is some trace of them, is found in Schürer/Vermes, History III/2, 868.

In the present inquiry this last group will only occasionally be referred to. Yet, the presence of historical writings in the Philonic *corpus* is hermeneutically significant, as it proves that the author is able to refer to history if he is called upon to do so. This will prevent us from one-sided interpretations.

4.2. *Philo's Theological Basis for the Interpretation of Scripture*

Philo finds the true name of God in Exod 3:14 (LXX): ἐγώ εἰμι ὁ Ὢν. God 'is' (*Opif.* 170), he is 'the Being One' and 'being' (τὸ ὄν) at once. The fusion of LXX language with Platonic concepts becomes evident. Both qualifications, the masculine (= personal) one of the Bible and the neuter one of philosophy, occur with equal frequency.

This does not mean that Philo's God is beyond gender: He is 'male' in the sense of 'active', 'creative'; matter (ὕλη) is female and passive.[182] Thus the whole system of cross-references[183] between the world of ideas and the material cosmos, which is the basis of Philo's allegorical interpretations, relies on naturalistic pre-conceptions of an extreme kind.

In the realm of epistemology Philo's statements are paradoxical. Philo's Old Testament roots become obvious in a particularly strong accent on the transcendence of God. Εἶναι πέφυκα, οὐ λέγεσθαι God says in G 20.1 ("I've got to be, not to be spoken of" - cf. L 25.75). In the extreme neither the Tetragrammaton nor its most subtle Greek replacement, ὁ Ὢν, apply.[184] Nevertheless, the "truly being God" is regarded as a μάθημα ('object of learning',

[179] This tractate is also called *Alexander*. On its addressee, who is the same as the one of *Prov.* I. II, see 4.0, above.

[180] They are counted as nr. 39 in Mayer's Index Philoneus.

[181] This seems not to be an exact title, since it is contained in a remark addressed to one of Eusebius' secretaries (8.10. 19 end) which inadvertently has not been deleted from the final copy. The rubic prefixed to 8.11 gives instead: *On the virtuous life of the ancient philosophers among the Jews.* Conventionally, this fragment is cited as part of the *Hypothetica.*

[182] E.g. *QG* 3.3; G 20a.3. Sophia may become a kind of mother: G 7.54.

[183] See 1.6, above, on the 'symbolic link'.

[184] This might call to mind Plato's much quoted verdict, *Timaeus* 28 C (cited in n. 51, above). Surprisingly, Philo makes little use of this passage. See D. T. Runia, *Philo of Alexandria and the Timaeus of Plato* (Philosophia antiqua 44; Leiden 1986) 111–13.

L28.332).[185] Time and again Philo describes the ascent of "the soul" (scil. of a person meditating Moses' Law) as a comprehension of God which, of course, goes far beyond words.

Philo parades the vocabulary and imagery of contemporary mystery religions to illustrate this point. His language has led modern readers to believe that his theology presupposes experiences similar to those of the initiates of Isis, the Great Mother, and so on. But Philo never calls the Jewish cult – be it in the Temple, be it in the synagogue – a μυστήριον, but restricts this term to mean the felicitous event of understanding Scripture. Thus, none of his strong expressions can be taken in a concrete sense,[186] as is especially shown by the oxymoron μέθη νηφάλιος ('sober ebriety'):[187] its paradoxical nature indicates that Philo did *not* drink wine to reach some state of mental elevation, nor need his modern readers. The only initiatory practice required is obedience to the Mosaic commandments including participation in Sabbath service and teaching. In this sense his words on the "parts of exercise" (μέρη τῆς ἀσκήσεως) in G4.18 can finally be understood in their concrete meaning.

Thus Philo is quite explicit on the prerequisites for understanding Scripture. He speaks of the preparation of the reader's mind (διάνοια)[188] in a language reminiscent of the *Epistle of Aristaeus.* With Aristobulus he agrees in taking God's words for deeds: ὁ γὰρ Θεὸς λέγων ἅμα ἐποίει (L28.65).[189] In a similar way his theory of prophetic inspiration (see below) reduces the receiver's intellectual activity to little or nothing.

Like Aristobulus, Philo takes care to avoid anthropomorphisms.[190] His key to partial and less-than-perfect truths about God consists in distinguishing the 'Being (one)' from 'God' (Θεός) – a word that just names his power, but not himself – and from 'the Lord' (Κύριος), another name for a supreme power. The 'wrath' of God, and evils inflicted by the Lord (punishing sinners) now become just *God's* (or *the Lord's*) acts which do not necessarily qualify the Being one. Ὁ Ὢν is beyond motion and emotion, beyond evil, and beyond any contact with matter.

In L30.1–6 Philo presents the hermeneutical key of the two Powers as a revelation he personally received. In the historian's eyes this personal element can be quite accurately assessed.[191] Comparison with other sources suggests

---

[185] Cf. G20a.3 and μαθηταί (of God) in G6.7, 64, 79.

[186] D.M. Hay, "Philo's References to Other Allegorists", *StudPhil* 6 (1979/80) 41–75 shows that the metaphors Philo uses were already part of the tradition. Moreover, metaphors taken from mystery cults are also found in pagan Homeric exegesis; see 1.3 above (Heraclitus 79, 12). As to Philo's very negative judgment on mystery religions, see L28.319–323 where he denies the very principle of secrecy.

[187] See H. Lewy, *Sobria ebrietas: Untersuchungen zur Geschichte der antiken Mystik* (BZNW9; Giessen 1929), repr. in: L. Tarán (ed.), *Greek and Roman philosophy: A fifty-two volume reprint set*, vol. 28: *Philo of Alexandria* (New York/London 1987) ch. 3.

[188] See this term in *Opif.* 146; G10.45, etc.; Leisegang, Indices 180–85.

[189] Cf. *Opif.* 13; G6.65; G21.182; L25.283; L27.47, etc.

[190] He frequently quotes Num 23:19 "God is not like a man", in order to discard the contrary affirmation in Deut 1:31 and 8:5: see *QG* 1.55; 2.54; G10.52–54, 69; G21.237.

[191] The following paragraphs are a complement to D.M. Hay, "Philo's view of himself as an exegete", Studia Philonica Annual 3 (1991) 40–52. This article, as well as the works to which it refers, are an attempt at approaching Philo's thought from a psychological point of view.

that Philo only introduced a small, but important, element. The Pseudo-Aristotelian treatise *De mundo*, an eclectic text belonging to the 2nd or 1st cent. BCE, speaks on pp. 397b 9–398a 10[192] of the κόσμου κυριώτατον ("which dominates the cosmos"), called θεός, "out of whom and because of whom the universe came to be". He is the Creator (γενέτωρ) and Saviour (σωτήρ) of the world. As he is "established beyond heaven" (ἐγκαθιδρυμένος οὐρανοῦ), one might ask how this transcendent God – to put it in modern terms – may have an impact on the cosmos. This implicit question is explicitly answered by saying that God's power (δύναμις, sg.) acts on his behalf. This answer is not far from the cosmological interpretation of Homer's Golden Chain (see 1.2, above).

Such are the components of Philo's cosmological doctrine by which he accounts for God's simultaneous transcendence and immanence. His eclecticism consists in being *a Platonist about transcendence, and a Stoic about immanence.* The only element Philo introduces is the dualism of 'Powers' which agree or oppose each other, as the case requires, and their association with some peculiarities of the sacred text. This possibility may well have been a revelation to him, since it helps to account for many details in the Mosaic Law, including some of the most problematic ones.

In G 5.27–39 Philo explains this personal revelation in detail and brings it in accordance with the (traditional, Stoic) doctrine of the divine Logos as mediator. The Powers are identical to the Logos; their duality or even antinomy comes under consideration whenever a limited action is meant.[193]

To readers of rabbinic literature the two Powers are well known under the (less metaphysical) appellation of מדות ('measures') of YHWH. In Philo, however, the names of the two powers stand in reverse order. To the Rabbis, אדני stands for grace and אלהים for judgment. Philo, as a reader of the Septuagint, derives Κύριος from κυριεύειν, which implies some deployment of force, and θεός from τιθέναι,[194] which means a creative activity. And since Creation as a whole is a grace bestowed upon the creatures,[195] Θεός becomes the name of Grace. Astonishingly, this hermeneutical tool works quite well for him even though it only exploits a particularity of the Septuagint (cf. 4.8, below).

In terms of space, Philo's physical representation of the world is somewhat 'hanging'.[196] His world does not stand but is held from above. The Being (one) outside the world is the only 'standing one'.[197] This implies that a revelation coming from such an unimaginable distance is nothing less than

[192] All editions count the pages and lines of the Berlin Aristotle. For a scholarly presentation of this text, see Festugière, La révélation d'Hermès Trismégiste (1949) 460–520. Cf. the following essay: "Tradition scolaire et personnalité chez Philon", ibid. 521–554. FESTUGIÈRE thinks that Philo is one of the first readers of *De mundo.*

[193] For further details, see *QE* 2.68.

[194] On this etymology in pagan exegesis, see Cornutus, *Theologiae Graecae compendium* 1 (p. 3, l. 1; Lang): θεοὶ θετῆρες.

[195] G 5.127; G 20a.3, etc.

[196] Cf. Job 26:7 κρεμάζων γῆν ἐπ' οὐδενός (LXX). The verb κρέμασθαι is current in Orphic, middle Platonic, Philonic, and Neoplatonic cosmology.

[197] G 20.54, 57, 87; G 20a.2; G 21.246; 22.226.

sensational. Biblical revelation is identical with the acting of the Powers which guarantee the duration and conservation of the cosmos. Unlike the desperate Dr Faustus, Philo was confident that he knew from his Bible "what holds the world together".[198]

As regards *inspiration*, Philo's views seem heterogeneous.[199] In the first instance, the author of the Pentateuch is Moses. He is Israel's lawgiver (νομοθέτης). This seems to differ from the Rabbi's conception where YHWH speaks immediately in the Torah. But we shall soon see that in some contexts Philo's supernaturalism is in no way inferior to theirs. He makes an apologetic concession to Hellenistic culture in which a hero of the past and a great author is more credible – and no less venerable – than a voice from heaven.[200]

But Moses is more than a legislator; he is a prophet, and even the greatest of the prophets. Sometimes, and not indeed rarely, Moses is the recipient of a prophetic gift that outweighs any activity of his own. Moses is in a trance when the Lord speaks through him in the first person. In handing over the Decalogue and on other occasions Moses is in mechanical resonance with the divine Power that sets him in movement.[201] At this level the Philonic (and Platonic) concept of 'inspiration' excludes any intellectual activity on the side of humans; and it includes a kind of mechanical causation mediated by the material pneuma of Stoic cosmology. Like a stringed instrument struck by a plectron, Moses just utters sounds.[202] The meaning of these sounds is another thing; it is left to the exegete to determine it. There never was a more exaggerated theory of inspiration; and there could not be a stronger justification for the interpreter's license.

Thus every sentence of the Pentateuch may be regarded as an oracle (χρησμός, λόγιον).[203] Moses is the initiating priest (ὁ ἱεροφάντης): G 4.173; G 6.94; G 8.16, 173, etc.[204] He is "the prophetic *logos*" (G 18.170) and "the theologian" (L 26.115; P 33.53; *QG* and *QE* frequently),[205] which to Greek

---

198 See, e.g., *Opif.* 3, an influence of which may be seen in Josephus, *Ant.* 1.24.

199 Burkhardt, Inspiration (1988) 152–171, proves that Philo's somewhat contradictory theory of three stages of inspiration is based on a conflation of Posidonius' threefold theory of dreams (reported in Cicero, *De divinatione* 1.64) with Plato's notion of poetic 'frenzy', esp. in *Ion* 533 D-534 D.

200 See Amir, Die hellenistische Gestalt (1983) 40, 59, 77.

201 *QG* 3.10; 4.196; *QE* 2.44; G 20.139; L 25.274; L 31.49. – In Stoic theory, *pneuma* was energy, not communication. Modern Christian fundamentalism is hardly aware that 'inspiration' in its most drastic sense derives from Stoic materialism.

202 G 20.139; L 25.274; L 28.65 = 31.49. Burkhardt, Inspiration (1988) 171 ff, 211, 221–223, tends to play down this aspect of Philo's thought. For the present purpose, however, Philo needs no excuses and no modernization. His ancient (Christian) readers, at least, received and generalized his theory of inspiration just in its most exaggerated form; see below, 4. 9. A very accurate assessment of Philo's platonic theory of inspiration is found in H. Kraft, *Die Kirchenväter bis zum Konzil von Nicäa* (Bremen 1966) 94–104.

203 Numerous references in Burkhardt, Inspiration (1988) 112–122. The Greek terminological difference by which a λόγιον is spoken in prose and a χρησμός in hexameters, of course, does not apply to Philo's Bible.

204 In G 21.3 f Philo invokes him in the same way as Homer invokes the Muses, and as Aratus invokes Zeus.

205 *QG* 2.33, 64, 81; 3.5, 21, 38; 4.137; *QE* 2.37, 74, 87, 88, 108. His activity is called θεολογεῖν in *Opif.* 12.

ears means a kind of Jewish Homer. He is "the prophet" (*QG* 4.27; *QE* 1.11; 2.52; G4.173; G6.130; G17.262, etc.; L25.57; L26.187, 280, etc.).[206] But despite the seeming exclusivity of this singular, the whole people of Israel somehow participates in his role: in G19.47 Moses is a symbol for the "prophetic race". The Jewish people, L29.163 states, are priests of the whole habitable globe.[207] This is an implicit reference to the Sabbath service as a public event in which revelation takes place.

On the receptive side, Philo does not shun generalizations either. What happened with Moses also happens time and again with his readers (G17.264f):

> When the light of God shines, the human light sets; when the divine light sets, the human dawns and rises. This is what regularly befalls the fellowship of the prophets. The mind is evicted at the arrival of the divine Spirit,[208] but when that departs the mind returns to its tenancy. Mortal and immortal may not share the same home. And therefore the setting of reason and the darkness which surrounds it produce ecstasy and inspired frenzy (θεοφόρητον μανίαν).

Thus Philo's hermeneutics of understanding is the strongest possible supernaturalism – whereby *supra* not only has a qualitative but also a spacial meaning:[209] *pneuma* is the material link with the Being (one) outside the material cosmos.

How does God 'speak'? Philo often quotes the promise that the Being one gave to Moses: "I shall speak to thee from between the two Cherubim" (Exod 25:21[22]; 56 etc.).[210] We already saw (3.3) that the corresponding oracular practice had ceased long before Philo's day. Indeed we learn from Philo that the gilded sculptures in the Temple at Jerusalem are only the symbols of the two cosmic Powers: knowing them and knowing their activity in the cosmos (history is not the issue) *is* the act of revelation. Likewise, the Greek names of the *urim* and *tummim*, namely δήλωσις and ἀλήθεια, are taken by Philo to refer to the λόγος ἐνδιάθετος and προφορικός of the Stoics (*QE* 2.116).[211] Knowledge consists in knowing the structure of the cosmos as it was premeditated by its Creator.

4.3. Philo's Bible and the Texts Referred to

As in the *Epistle of Aristaeus*, there are five sacred books[212] and not just one. Philo's references to the Mosaic laws are stylistically variegated: ὁ Νόμος, οἱ Νόμοι,[213] ἡ νομοθεσία, ὁ ἱερὸς λόγος, ὁ θεῖος λόγος, τὰ ἱερὰ γράμματα (rarely:

206 Cf. *QG* 1.86 *naxamargarēn* = ὁ πρωτοπροφήτης (Moses).

207 Cf. Heraclitus the Stoic 79,12, referred to in sect. 1.3 and in n. 186, above.

208 ἐξοικίζεται μὲν γὰρ ἐν ἡμῖν ὁ νοῦς κατὰ τὴν τοῦ θείου πνεύματος ἄφιξιν. Cf. L 25.283; L 31.48; Plato, *Ion* 534 C–E, speaking of poets.

209 Interpreting Philo today, we would leave out this aspect; but to Philo himself it was of crucial importance: it garanteed the coherence of his views on inspiration with his knowledge in natural science (i.e., philosophy of nature).

210 A saying much commented upon by Philo. See *QE* 2.62–8; G 17.166; G19.100–105.

211 We already noted (1.3) that the Stoics demythologized Hermes, the messenger of the gods, to become the *logos* accessible to everybody. The content of the message, then, was supplied by Stoic philosophy. Philo is not far from this practice.

212 Cf. 2.4 with Philo, L 23.1: "the holy laws which are written down in five books".

213 A title dignified by Plato and the Pythagoreans. Cf. 1.7, above.

τὸ ἱερὸν γράμμα, τὸ ἱερώτατον γράμμα), αἱ ἱεραὶ βίβλοι, and so on.[214] They differ considerably from the monolithic νόμος in the Septuagint and from תורה in rabbinic literature.

Yet there is no doubt that Philo views the Pentateuch as a unity, because it has one author. In *QG* 3.3 he states programmatically: "The Legislation is in some sense a unified animal,[215] which one should view from all sides in its entirety". Divine Scripture, *QG* 1.12 states, is "wholly veracious".[216] Philo appears to be the first fundamentalist.

How can Moses have written the last chapter of Deuteronomy which relates his death? P 26.290–292 purports that he himself wrote the end of the holy writings (τὸ τέλος τῶν ἱερῶν γραμμάτων – the canon evidently stops at this point): "he prophesies aptly, as may happen with a person who is dying".

In L 33.1-2 Philo distinguishes three species of Mosaic oracles. One is concerned with *creation*, the next with *history*, and the third with *Law*. The third one may be further divided into the ten κεφάλαια (the Commandments) and special laws; hence the sequence L 27/L 28–31. If *Opif.* may be counted with the L corpus, then L comprises all three kinds of Scripture (cf. 4.6).

In Moses' Law, ἡ ῥητὴ γραφή is the wording as opposed to the allegorical meaning (L 23.131). The same holds for αἱ ῥηταὶ γραφαί (L 23.236; L 33.65). Book titles explicitly given are Γένεσις, Ἐξαγωγή, Λευιτικόν, Ἀριθμοί[217] Δευτερονόμιον or (imitating a title occuring in the Platonic corpus) Ἐπινομίς.[218] Following titles are: "Book of Judgments" (G 15.128), "Royal Books" (G 10.136; G 15.149 – 1–4 Kingdoms, LXX), " Hymns" (Psalms) and "Proverbs". Pericope titles occur like "the Curses" (G 17.250 – Deuteronomy 28), "the Assembly in Exodus" (G 17.251 – Exodus 19), "the Great Song/the Greater Song" (frequently – Deuteronomy 32),[219] and, outside the Pentateuch, "The song of Grace, i.e. of Hannah" (G 20.143 - 1 Samuel 2).

Philo's text is of course the Septuagint. He has the very highest opinion of its reliability (cf. above 2.2, and below 4.8). Philo's only link with the Hebrew text consists in the use of Hebrew-Greek onomastica.[220]

It is not our purpose to inquire into the peculiarities of Philo's LXX text.[221] Philo – as far as he is responsible[222] – is not aware of them. He is simply no

---

[214] For a detailed account see Burkhardt, Inspiration (1988) 75–134.

[215] The Greek text, preserved in a fragment (*QE*, ed. Marcus; p. 207), has ζῷον ἡνωμένον. This is reminiscent of the Stoic view of the cosmos as an animal (ζῷον).

[216] In Armenian, *yamenaynin ansowt* = πάντως ἀψευδής. Cf. L 23.258 ἐν ταῖς ἱεραῖς βίβοις ..., ἃς οὐ θέμις ψευδομαρτυριῶν ἁλῶναι, and *Quod omnis probus liber sit* 46: Νόμος δὲ ἀψευδὴς ὁ ὀρθὸς λόγος (referring to natural revelation).

[217] If L 26.115 may be so interpreted.

[218] References in Burkhardt, Inspiration (1988) 73 f. They are about three for each book of the Pentateuch, which is to say that Philo rarely quotes by title.

[219] References in Burkhardt, Inspiration (1988) 74; add G 20a.11.

[220] See n. 169, above.

[221] The reader may be referred to ch. 2.3 of the present work. Cf. P. Katz, *Philo's Bible: The Aberrant Text of Bible Quotations in some Philonic Writings and its place in the textual history of the Greek Bible* (Cambridge 1950), to be amended by more recent inquiries. See the references in Brewer, Techniques (1992) 210.

[222] Cf. D. Barthélemy, "Est-ce Hoshaya Rabba qui censura le 'Commentaire allégorique'?", Philon d'Alexandrie (Congress Volume, 1967) 45–79.

philologist in a modern sense, even though there were some in his very city (cf. 1.4 and 1.7, above). As D. Dawson puts it,[223]

> Philo is certain that the Septuagint translators, by sacrificing style to substance, have preserved scripture's true meaning, handing down their Adamic-Mosaic hermeneutical heritage intact. Because they were not mere word-changers but "prophets and priests of the mysteries" who consorted with "the purest of spirits, the spirit of Moses", they were able to select just the right Greek equivalents for the original Hebrew words.
>
> Philo seems certain that these scripturally rendered correspondences ultimately go back to the perfect perceptions and names of Adam, the originator of all language. The making of the Septuagint – aided by an inspired original author (Moses) and inspired translators – is a virtual extension of Adamic naming. We have the following representational chain:
>
> *Essences of Things*
> ↓
> Adamic Names
> ↓
> Hebrew Language
> ↓
> Inspired Moses
> ↓
> Hebrew Scripture
> ↓
> Inspired Translators
> ↓
> Septuagint
> ↓
> *Essences of Things*
>
> Apparently lacking the linguistic skill as Hebraist to judge the matter for himself, Philo reports the conclusions of those fluent in both Hebrew and Greek: reading the new Greek translation is just as good as reading the Hebrew original because the Greek and the Hebrew texts are "one and the same, both in subject matters (πράγματα) and words (ὀνόματα)".

There remains the problem of Mosaic metaphors and tropes of all kinds. Why doesn't he just stick to Adamic simplicity? The obvious answer is: because mankind lives outside of Eden. The Serpent first misused language in repeating God's command wrongly to Eve (*QG* 1.34, on Gen 3:1). The ambiguity of Hebrew as well as of Greek syntax somehow mirrors Eve's and Adam's fall. Dawson acutely observes:[224]

> The move from Adamic naming to scriptural language is a move from single names to complete statements or propositions, from nouns that supposedly reproduce the natures of things to syntactical units that make affirmations about things. Semantic and referential certitude seems to have suffered in this move; the ambiguity of the serpent's words is an ambiguity of syntax rather than of names.

Moses, to be sure, received perfect Adamic knowledge through revelation (G 11.1 f). But "even so, Moses is forced to use ordinary language to express his extraordinary insights. As a result, his message is always clear and deter-

[223] Dawson, Allegorical Readers (1992) 86 f, referring to L 26.40.

[224] Dawson, Allegorical Readers (1992) 89. There are more nuances to this which cannot be discussed for want of space. We have skipped the statement made on p. 88: "Philo's account of ideal Adam, the model for material Adam, suggests that material Adam may not have had the capacities necessary to create a perfectly mimetic language, even though the scene of Adamic naming follows shortly upon his creation" – and precedes the fall.

minate once it is perceived, but it lies hidden in very indirect linguistic expressions marked by various forms of semantic indeterminacy".[225]

As might be expected, there is also the 'pedagogical' excuse of indirect language in Scripture. E.g., *QG* 2.54:[226]

> All such forms of words (in Scripture) are generally used in the Law rather for learning and aid in teaching than for the nature of truth. For as there are two texts which are found in the Legislation, one in which it is said, "Not like man (is God)", and another in which the Eternal is said to chastise as a man (chastises) his son, the former (text) is the truth.[227] For in reality God is not like man nor yet like the sun nor like heaven nor like the sense-perceptible world but (only) like God, if it is right to say even this.

So much for Philo's theory. As to practice, Philo's unwarranted optimism concerning the Septuagint has led him to interpretations which would not have been possible with the original text. One example was his theological evaluation of the duality of divine names, 'God' and 'the Lord' (see 4.2, above). There are many others. The half shekel due by each Israelite to the Temple (Exod 30:13) had been correctly converted into a *didrachmon*. Now Philo in his interpretation (G 17.186) relies on the "double" nature of this tribute in order to justify the obligation to pay taxes to the Romans as well. – The misspelled word τραφείς ('nourished' – for ταφείς 'buried', Hebr. root קבר) in all manuscripts of Gen 15:15 LXX is the origin of a lengthy explanation whose 'truth' just rests on that erroneous letter (G 17.284–292).[228]

Texts referred to in Philo nearly always belong to the Pentateuch. In his exegetical writings Philo is nothing else than a commentator on the Law. The question of Philo's 'canon' thus receives a first and simple answer. His canon – if we mean by this term a collection of writings that are authoritative from the first word to the last – is the Law as it is laid down in the five scrolls of Moses.

This does not exclude quotations from other books of the collection which later became known as the "Septuagint". In two of the (rare) quotations from the Prophets Philo praises Isaiah's and Jeremiah's inspiration in the strongest terms, no less than he had extolled the entranced Moses as a receptacle of the Decalogue. This concerns Isaiah in G 20a.6 (Isa 6:1 f.)[229] and Jeremiah in G 5.49 (Jer 3:4). From Hosea he takes a χρησμός (G 12.138; G 20.139 – Hos 14:9 f.), as he is wont to do from the Pentateuch.

As to the Former Prophets of the Hebrew canon, Samuel, whose name occurs about eight times, once is qualified as "the greatest of kings and

---

[225] Dawson, Allegorical Readers (1992) 92. See Philo's *De confusione linguarum* (G 15), esp. §§ 55, 134 ff, 190 f.

[226] Cf. *QG* 1.55; G 10.60–64.

[227] This contrast between Num 23:19 and Deut 8:5, including the decision in favour of the former, is frequent in Philo. The decision itself parallels rabbinical procedures; see N. A. DAHL, "Contradictions in Scripture", idem, *Studies in Paul: Theology for the Early Christian Mission* (Minneapolis 1977) 159–177, esp. 168.

[228] For more examples see Sandmel, Philo's Place (1971 – see n. 278, below) 180, 183, 199 f, 203.

[229] Isaiah 6 is the *Haphtarah* associated with Exodus 18–20: this places both events of revelation at a similar level. But Philo's practice confirms the attitude of the Rabbis who generally do not estimate the prophets' inspiration as high as the inspiration of Moses.

prophets" (G 13.143) – to be sure, with the exception of Moses, since Philo is not likely to set him higher than the author of the Pentateuch. Philo then cites 1 Sam 1:11 with the formula ὡς ὁ ἱερὸς λόγος φησίν.

All this yields an impression that Philo's Bible is larger than the Pentateuch. In *Cont.* 25 he expressly enumerates "laws and oracles delivered through the mouth of Prophets, and hymns (ὕμνους) and everything else which fosters and perfects knowledge and piety". This seems to be a clear reference to the tripartite canon of the Hebrew Bible. However, Philo's use of historical, prophetic and poetic writings pertaining to the Jewish heritage is scarce. Greek poets and dramatists are more often cited (by name) and quoted (with texts). The rare use of Jewish writings outside the Pentateuch does not accord them a specific importance. In a most significant way, historical writings, Greek or Israelite, are the least cited.

There is more than one reason against assuming that the tripartite canon is Philo's canon. First, concerning the Hagiographa: Sirach und Wisdom of Solomon are also quoted,[230] which weakens the case of a third section of the canon identical to the Hebrew כתובים. More important, David and Solomon are never cited as inspired authors.[231]

This weighs all the more as inspired authority, in Philo, rests with persons, and not with writings. Inspired persons include Moses – in 99% of all cases – and some of the (Former or Latter) Prophets. Independently from this restriction there are instances where Philo mentions "holy scriptures" outside the Pentateuch – the book of Joshua as ἱεραὶ ἀναγραφαί (*Hypothetica* 8.6.5), and the ἱερὸς λόγος (1 Samuel 1) referred to above. But this does not amount to a proof of "canonicity" for the writings concerned.

In other words, Philo does not deal with the (ultimately Christian) question of a canon. In this respect he is not different from all the other Jewish Sages and Rabbis.

The attention Philo gives to Jewish writings outside the Pentateuch is somewhat similar to the attention Luther gave to the Epistle to the Hebrews: he viewed it as an instructive and edifying reading,[232] but not as a basis of an unfailing knowledge of God. In Philo's view revelation made no progress after Moses.

Philo's quoting habits, if nothing else, show him as a Torah teacher, which was perhaps his formal position in the Jewish community of Alexandria. He never chooses a *Haphtarah* (as in Ps.-Philo's *De Iona* and *De Sampsone*) as an object of his interpretations. In all of his preserved works he merely teaches Mosaic "philosophy" or wisdom – and some lessons from contemporary history, to which we shall return for a theological evaluation (see 4.10).

---

[230] For a complete list of Philo's biblical quatations and allusions, see BPSup (1982). *Contra* Burkhardt, Inspiration (1988) 73–146.

[231] Both names occur only once. David (G 15.149) is "the one who sang hymns on God"; and Solomon (G 18.177), being cited as the author of Proverbs, is "one of the followers of Moses".

[232] See his preface to Hebrews in the German Bible of 1546, WA, *Deutsche Bibel*, 7,345. – There remains an important difference: Philo does not criticize his source.

4.4. *The* Questions on Genesis *and* Questions on Exodus (QG, QE)[233]

They are of the *genre* of ζητήματα (or ἀπορίαι) καὶ λύσεις (Lat. *quaestiones*) known to us through Heraclitus the Stoic (see 1.5, above). Philo cites difficult passages, one by one, in the form of a question, and proceeds to give one or more possible solutions. He resorts first to literal and then to allegorical exegesis, both of which may yield a plurality of solutions. Philo thus cultivates a "multiplicity of approaches" – more clearly so in *QG/QE* than in G and even more so than in L.[234] Readers of the *Quaestiones* become aware of how much Philo may be a literalist. He rarely dismisses the literal, i.e. non-metaphorical or non-allegorical meaning.

Unfortunately, *QG* and *QE* are both mutilated. No trace of a literary framework has remained,[235] the text now just begins with the first question. The structure has also been disturbed: *QG* 4 now covers the rest of ancient *QG* 4–6. At least three books of *QE* are missing.

QG/QE are related to a concrete use of Scripture. Their arrangement by books and sections conforms to the pericopes of the annual cycle.[236] They are indeed the oldest evidence for this cycle.

The arrangement of *QG* and *QE* by biblical references makes their use easy to modern readers. The only problem is the lack of most of the original Greek text. Readers of English, however, are well served with MARCUS' excellent rendering of the Armenian translation that has survived.

Let us take an example, *QG* 2.9.[237]

> [1] Why does (Scripture) say, "Whatever is on earth shall die" (Gen 6:17), for what sin did the beasts commit?
> [2.1] In the first place, just as when a king is killed in battle, his military forces also are struck down together with him, so He decides now too that when the human race is destroyed like a king, other beasts should be destroyed together with it.
> [2.2] Second, just as when the head is cut off, no one blames nature if so many other parts of the body also die together with it, so also no one will now condemn (this).
> [2.3] Third, ...
> [3] But as for the deeper meaning, ...

In this section, the following elements can be discerned [numbering added]:

(1) the question, containing a quote from Scripture;

(2) one or more literal explanations, this first of which, in the given case, is a משל (rather rare in Philo); and

(3) one or more allegorical explanations (in the given case, only one).

---

[233] A recent monograph on this neglected corpus is D. M. HAY (ed.), *Both Literal and Allegorical: Studies in Philo of Alexandria's Questions and Answers on Genesis and Exodus* (Brown Judaic Studies 232; Atlanta 1991). The bibliography (227–236) lacks W. WIEFEL, "Das dritte Buch über 'Mose'", *ThLZ* 111 (1986) 865–882, an article holding the (traditional) opposite view concerning chronology.

[234] "It is best to ascribe the difference in emphasis to the fact that in the *Quaestiones* Philo wanted to present all the options, whereas in the Allegorical Commentary [= G] he wrote from a definite perspective" (G. E. STERLING in Hay [ed.], Both Literal and Allegorical [1993] 123).

[235] For a complete book of this kind, see Heraclitus the Stoic in sect. 1.5 above.

[236] See MARCUS' preface to *QG* (1953), x–xv, which is confirmed by J. R. ROYSE, "The original structure of Philo's Quaestiones", *StudPhil* 4 (1976/77) 109–139.

[237] Quoted with some omissions.

Whereas literal explanations use a great variety of arguments without any *a priori* system, allegorical explanations more or less follow a recurring pattern. Let us take one of the more elaborate examples, *QG* 2.35:

[1] Why did (Noah) first send the raven? (Gen 8:7)
[2] As for the literal meaning (τὸ ῥητόν),[238] the raven is said to be a sort of heralding and fulfilling creature. Wherefore down to our own time many observantly attend to its flight and its voice when it caws (as though) indicating something hidden.[239]
[3.1] But as for the deeper meaning (τὸ πρὸς διάνοιαν), the raven is a blackish and reckless and swift creature, which is a symbol of evil, for it brings night and darkness upon the soul, and it is very swift, going out to meet all things in the world at one time.
[3.2] In the second place, (it leads) to the destruction of those who would seize it, and is very reckless, for it produces arrogance and shameless impudence. And to this is opposed virtue, (which is) luminous and steady and modest and reverent by nature. And so it was right to expel beyond the borders whatever residue of darkness there was in the mind which might have led to folly.

In this *quaestio*, the 3rd (allegorical) section is made up of the following elements:
(3.1) a kind of "physical" explanation;
(3.2) an "ethical" explanation.
The difference between "physical" and "ethical" allegories does not mean much to Philo, no more than in the *Ep. Arist.* (see 2.5, glossary). He may retain it formally, as e.g. in QG 3.3 (p. 182 Marcus). But when he promises to examine Noah's ark φυσικώτερον (*QG* 2.1), he states the hermeneutic thesis that we "will find the construction of the human body" in it—which is the point of departure for a variety of moral teachings.

In the given example, both allegorical explanations are based on animal symbolism, as is frequent in Philo. They could as well be based on etymology, etc. Other *quaestiones* add a third element (which may also be the dominating or even the only one): arithmology;[240] e.g. 1.83; 1.91, etc.

To sum up this section, we observe that "Philo has produced two unequal series, distinct from one another and different in kind, in the sense that the *Quaestiones* does not claim do be a 'definite work' or 'discourse', whereas the Treatises are both things because the discourse technique raises them to the higher level".[241]

4.5. The 'Allegorical Commentary' on Genesis (G)

We may begin our survey of Philonic treatises with the longest of all series that can be distinguished: G. An account of its contents is found in Schürer/Vermes, History III/1 (1987) 830–839. It treats at length selected

[238] The original Greek formulae, which are very constant, may be gathered from the extant fragments of *QG*/*QE*.

[239] This is an allusion to bird oracles (Lat. *augurium, auspicium* < **avi-spicium*; Greek οἰωνισμός). Philo was very sceptical about oracles, since his only oracle is the Logos speaking through Moses' writings.

[240] See K. Staehle, *Die Zahlenmystik bei Philon von Alexandreia* (Leipzig/Berlin 1931) repr. in: L. Tarán (ed.), Greek and Roman philosophy (see n. 187), ch. 4. A related phenomenon is speculation on the letters of the alphabet, e.g. *QG* 3.43 on the added α in Ἀβραάμ.

[241] A. Méasson/J. Cazeaux in: Hay (ed.), Both Literal and Allegorical (1993) 224.

passages from the Law which are always quite short. Treatises may abruptly start wih a biblical quotation, e.g. the last ones of the series and the very first, G2.1: "And [!] the heaven and the Earth were finished, and the host of them ...". Alternatively they may begin with just one or two introductory phrases before the first quotation comes. The whole series is obviously a kind of scholarly or technical literature (*Sachprosa*), which does not exclude passages of a highly rhetorical nature like G6.20–51 (32!); G11.167ff; G12.72; G15.3, 116–119; G17.207–214; G19.8–18, etc. The work sometimes seems to echo the service in the Alexandrian synagogue with its lessons from the Septuagint and the more or less rhetorical expositions which would follow. Other passages seem to herold what the Christian Catechetic School of Alexandria was to become later on. To put it in rabbinic terms, no Philonic text, as it stands, fits the בית קנסת (Synagogue, place of cult) as a sermon, but they all fit the בית מדרש or place of (advanced) study.

The two levels of exegesis – literal and symbolical – are theoretically maintained;[242] but Philo's interest clearly aims at finding the 'deeper meaning'. Let us take, as an example, G22.8. Philo, having called to mind the literal explanations of Joseph's dreams which are already found in the biblical text (Gen 37:7–9), continues: "So much by way of foundation (θεμέλιος). As we go on to build the superstructure (ἐποικοδομεῖν) let us follow the directions of Allegory, that wise Master-builder, while we investigate the details".

Sometimes Philo's allegorizing becomes so radical that he *denies the literal sense*. A case where this happens with a legal regulation will be discussed later (4.8); it is a rare exception. But consider a passage like this (G18.43f):[243]

> Nahor, the brother of Abraham, has two wives, Milcah, and Reumah (Gen 22:23f). Now let no sane man suppose that we have here in the pages of the wise legislator an historical pedigree. What we have is a revelation through symbols of facts which may be profitable to the soul. And if we translate the names into our own tongue, we shall recognize that what is here promised is actually the case. Let us inquire into each of them ...

4.6. *The 'Exposition of the Law' (L)*

This series has only a loose link, if any, with particular texts. It is about persons (L23–26) and contents or ideas (L27–33). As to the persons, they are ἔμψυχοι νόμοι (living laws, impersonated laws). Exodus 20ff. just codifies their way of life. This is Philo's way of accounting for the fact that the "Law" of Moses contains much non-legal material.[244]

Thus, formal quotations from Scripture are comparatively rare in L. Programmatical statements are made e.g. in L23.1–6 (the beginning), L27.1 (the

---

[242] As is programmatically stated, e.g., in G15.190; L23.52, 236.

[243] Quoted with some omissions.

[244] Y. AMIR in: Mikra (1988) 424: The texts relating to the Creation and to the Patriarchs left Philo with the literary critical question, "Do such non-legislative elements have a legitimate place in a lawbook?" The answer, according to Philo, is: Just as Moses' lawbook has its proem (dealt with in *Opif.*), so it also includes other didactic material, namely the stories of the Patriarchs. "These he integrates into the law code with the help of the concept of 'unwritten law', which, according to a Hellenistic theory, is present als 'embodied law' in a perfect human being and precedes the written law as its archetype". AMIR's reference is R. HIRZEL (cf. below, n. 250).

transition to the second part), and L 33. 52 ff. (here Philo includes the *Life of Moses* in the series as its most prominent part). The last reference is important since the double treatise L 25–26 does not wholly fit into what is introduced by L 23–24 and is summarized in L 33.1–2.[245] It seems that Philo had written the *Life of Moses* before he conceived the plan of L and that he felt no need to re-write it[246] when he incorporated it afterwards into the series.

The case of *Opif.* may be similar: even though it is different in kind, namely exegetical like the G series, Philo (L 33. 1–2) gives it the role of an introduction to L.[247] The introductory statements of L 33 propose a division of the Mosaic oracles into three parts or species: cosmogony, history, and 'legislation' proper, each of which are claimed to have been dealt with παγκάλως καὶ θεοπρεπῶς, i. e. by way of allegorical interpretation. Now the only Philonic tractate explaining the Mosaic cosmogony is *De opificio mundi.* L thus is made up of a cosmological book, four historical ones (with their own prologue, L 23.1–6), and seven legal ones, again with a particular prologue (L 27.1–17). The last of these seven tractates, *De praemiis et poenis*, serves as an eschatological finale.

In L Philo's intention is clearly to teach the Law in a framework of universal history from Creation to the *eschaton.*[248] History – esp. the life of Moses and of the other Patriachs – illustrates the Law, and the Law illustrates history. The *Life of Moses* (L 25–26) which is introduced in L 25.1–5 as a fullfledged biography (in the large meaning the term once had) exemplifies the kind of life which is meant by his Law. So also do the lives of Moses' predecessors *Abraham* (L 23) and *Joseph* (L 24).[249] All these heroes were observers of the Law even before it was given. They are ἔμψυχοι νόμοι, as we said above. They illustrate the "unwritten legislation" (ἄγραφος νομοθεσία, L 23.5) which simultaneously is the (Stoic) law of nature (§ 6).[250]

A typical reading may be L 27.1, the beginning of *De Decalogo*:

> Having related in the preceding treatises the lives of those whom Moses judged to be men of wisdom, who are set before us in the Sacred Books as founders of our nation and in themselves unwritten laws, I shall now proceed in due course to give full descriptions of the written laws. And if some allegorical interpretation should appear to underlie them, I shall not fail to state it. For knowledge loves to learn and advance to full understanding and its way is to seek the hidden meaning rather than the obvious.

---

[245] Arguments for and against the affiliation of *De vita Mosis* I–II to L are summarized in: Schürer/Vermes, History III/1 (1987) 854 f. The Jerusalem edition groups this double treatise among the historical writings.

[246] There are no traces of double editing in Philo, except for some late manipulations: see n. 222.

[247] See C. Kraus Reggiani (ed.), *Filone Alessandrino, De Opificio Mundi – De Abrahamo – De Iosepho, Analisi critiche, testi tradotti et commentati* (Bibliotheca Athena 23; Roma 1979).

[248] See Dawson, Allegorical Readers (1992) 122–125. For another account of form and contents of L, see Schürer/Vermes, History III/1 (1987) 840–856, where *Opif.*, too, is included.

[249] The intermediate treatises on Isaac and Jacob are lost.

[250] This seems to be rather different from the "unwritten Law" (תורה שבעל פה) of the Sages and Rabbis. On the issue of *halakhah* in Philo, which cannot be discussed here, see, e. g., G. Alon, *Jews, Judaism and the Classical World* (Jerusalem 1977) 89–137 ("On Philo's halakha"). On ἄγραφος νόμος, an expression which has been coined independently from Judaism, see R. Hirzel, Ἄγραφος νόμος (Leipzig 1900). Philo's endeavour to found Mosaic legislation in the Law of Nature is too large a topic to be dealt with here. See the excellent presentation by J. W. Martens, "Philo and the 'Higher' Law", *SBL Seminar Papers* 127 (1991) 309–322.

The hermeneutical programme is put forward in the *Life of Joseph*, L 24.28: "After this literal account of the story, it will be well to explain the underlying meaning, for, broadly speaking, all or most of the law-book is an allegory".

Yet the historical perspective of L, nearly forgotten during long discussions of legal matters (L 27–32), is reaffirmed in the eschatological finale *De praemiis et poenis* (L 33). Of all Philo's treatises this one contains the most explicit expression of an eschatological hope within this world (L 33.97–117, 164).[251]

4.7. Other Treatises

The place of the first tractate, *De opificio mundi*, with regard to the series G and L is not clear. It was written in a manner like G, but (later?) included in the L series as its first element (see 4.6). It treats scriptural texts much as G; but it is referred to by a redactional statement contained in L (namely L 33.1–2). It stands somewhat apart, like the *Life of Moses*, and is of equally programmatical nature. Whereas the *Life of Moses* may convey the basic tenets of Judaism to pagan minds,[252] *De opificio mundi* does the same for the Jews; it tries to deepen the understanding of a well-known text.[253] It explains the co-existence of two creation stories in Genesis 1–2 by a Platonic duplication: there were two worlds created, an ideal one and a material one. This gives Philo the hermeneutical opportunity of similar dissociations elsewhere. The Ark of the Covenant, e.g., exists in Heaven before its imitation is used in Israel's cult (G 4.95, 102, etc.). Thus he overcomes the imperfections of what is concrete and historical. – This treatise may have founded Philo's fame as a Platonist,[254] whereas his Stoic rudiments, which are more concealed, are often underestimated.

De vita contemplativa is the panegyric on an Essene community living near Lake Mareotis. Surprisingly, these Essenes do not live in an eschatological tension – according to Philo's representation. The Sabbath service of this ideal community comprises hymns, lessons from the Law, and a lengthy sermon which does not seek rhetorical effects (δεινότης λόγων), Philo says (§ 31, § 75), but an interpretation δι' ὑπονοιῶν ἐν ἀλληγορίαις. The speaker inquires into the "symbols" and goes beyond the wording of the injunctions (αἱ ῥηταὶ διατάξεις) to find their "invisible mind" (ἀόρατος νοῦς, § 78; cf. L 23.119–121, etc.). There follows a common meal which is reminiscent of the rites of the Jewish חברים as well as of the Christians' weekly eucharist.[255]

---

[251] §§ 93–97 even promote a kind of Messianism, based on Num 24:7 LXX. On the Judgment, cf. also *De Providentia* 1.34–36.

[252] We probably shall never know whether Philo had pagan readers and whether he even aspired to have some; but he clearly engages in teaching the arguments necessary for a dialogue with pagans.

[253] On this treatise, see Schürer/Vermes, History III/1 (1987) 844 f; T. H. Tobin, *The Creation of Man: Philo and the History of Interpretation* (CBQMS 14; Washington 1983).

[254] Jerome, *De viris illustribus* 11.7 etc.: ἢ Πλάτων φιλωνίζει, ἢ Φίλων πλατωνίζει.

[255] In Antiquity Christian readers took this tractate as a description of a monastery and as a document of Christian origins in Egypt (Eusebius, *H. e.* 2.16 f, followed by Jerome, *De viris illustribus* 8.4; 11.6). Both report the legend that Philo became a Christian.

However, the Alexandrian Jewish community in which Philo lived was much less 'contemplative'.[256] His *historical writings*[257] bear witness to the fact that the situation dramatically changed for the worse. This is theologically important because it made Philo think of history, of politics and of concrete troubles. He did so in a prolific way. Eusebius tells that Philo's *In Flaccum* and *Legatio ad Gaium* were part of a five-volume work Περὶ ἀρετῶν (sc. Θεοῦ), a kind of historical aretalogy of the Jewish God.[258] Such a writing required considerable courage in a period of increasing persecution.

Thus the moralizing generalities which make the bulk of Philo's preserved exegeses reflect 'normal' circumstances. They should not make us forget that the same author is able to be a theologian of history. We may wonder what Philo's exegeses would have been had he written after the experiences which were the lot of subsequent generations.

4.8. Philo's Rules of Literal and Allegorical Interpretation

Philo's exegetical technique is already highlighted by his quotation habits. He very often introduces his (literal and mostly correct) quotations from the Septuagint with the adverbs καλῶς or παγκάλως ('well' or 'very well' said). This vindicates the interpreter's high, if not superior, standpoint.[259]

As a literalist, Philo may respect the meanest detail. In Gen 31:13 he observes a difference between ὁ θεός (the one God) and θεός (generic).[260] Arguments from silence may easily be drawn (G7.178), just as in rabbinic exegesis. There are no random details in Scripture. D. I. Brewer has pointed out how much this kind of philology – which automatically leads to allegorism – depends on an irrationalist concept of inspiration (cf. above, 4.2):

> Irrational prophetic messages in the pagan world could be recognised by mistakes in grammar, superfluous words and contradictions, and therefore Philo may have used the 'rules' [of allegorism, see below] to highlight similar elements in the Scriptures. Whenever unacceptable nonsense such as mythological elements, anthropomorphisms, contradictions, grammatical difficulties, such as spelling errors, strange sentence constructions or even poor style, such as needless repetition occurred in Scripture, they indicated to Philo that prophetic irrationality was involved at this point and therefore that allegory had to be used in order to extract the inspired but obscure message.[261]

It is not rare that Philo's interpretations apply only to details peculiar to the Septuagint. In checking the *Legum allegoriae* (G2–4), R. Arnaldez has

---

[256] Philo seems to complain of this fact in G4.18 f; L27.2.

[257] See Schürer/Vermes, History III/1 (1987) 542–43; cf. 4.0 above.

[258] Eusebius, *H.e.* 2.6.3; 2.18.8; on problems of textual and literary criticism, see Schürer/Vermes, History III/2 (1987) 859–864 f. – Cf. H. Lewy (trans.), *Philon von Alexandrien, Von den Machterweisen Gottes: Eine zeitgenössische Darstellung der Judenverfolgungen unter dem Kaiser Caligula* (Berlin 1935).

[259] *QG/QE* constantly; G 8.19; G. 17.86; G 19.159 etc. See H. Thyen, *Der Stil der jüdisch-hellenistischen Homilie* (Göttingen 1955) 56–58, citing also Barn 10:11. – Cf. Cornutus, *Theologiae Graecae compendium* 28 (p. 55, 1. 17; Lang) and εὐλόγως, ἀληθῶς, δικαίως, πιθανῶς etc. in the Stoic Heraclitus, most of which occur also in Philo, and 3.5, above, on Aristobulus, with n. 151.

[260] Justin Martyr, *Dialogus cum Tryphone* 56.4, 10 and 60.1–5, adapts this distinction to Christian use.

[261] Brewer, Techniques (1992) 209.

found a dozen cases.[262] In *QG* 1.4 Philo transforms a duplicity of expressions into the Platonic duplicity of worlds.

A curious, but revealing case is Gen 2:15: "And the Lord God took the man [whom he had formed], and put him into the garden of Eden". The relative clause is a LXX gloss referring back to v. 7. Philo's copy, however, did not read ὃν ἔπλασεν (as it is printed in Rahlfs), but happened to present the rare variant ὃν ἐποίησεν, referring farther back to Gen 1:27. Philo is puzzled because this confounds the two Creation stories, the first of which, to Philo's mind, speaks of the 'creation' (ποιεῖν < ברא) of the heavenly Adam, whereas the second is about the 'forming' (πλάσσειν < יצר) of the earthly man. The reader of G 2.53–55 may admire the artistry by which Philo manages to get a good sense out of a bad reading. Yet he might have had a better time by taking into account the possibility, or even the existence, of variant readings – had he not excluded them dogmatically.

It may happen that the text does not match at all with Philo's hermeneutical preconceptions. Take his dissociation of the two divine names 'God' and 'Lord'. In G 20a.7 he quotes Deut 4:24: "The Lord, your God, is a burning fire", tacitly altering the text in two respects: first, he leaves off (as does Heb 12:29) what follows: "a zealous God"; second, in his commentary he takes his quote as if it said: "*Kyrios* and *Theos* are burning fire". In G 20.12 Philo declares that "the Lord, your God" is a catachresis – because for him these are two distinct Powers.

Methodically this is not very far from Heraclitus' alteration of a Homeric verse, or Aristobulus' alteration of a verse of Aratus (see 3.2, above). In G 5.128 Philo finally takes the step toward a dogmatical alteration of the text. The interpretation of dreams, he says, does not come 'through' God (διὰ τοῦ Θεοῦ, as is stated in Gen 40:8) but from (ὑπό) him.[263] A similar case is *QG* 1.86 (end).

Philo exploits the details of his text by a variety of methods derived from contemporary theories on (Greek) grammar, rhetoric, and dialectic. A detailed survey of these has been given by J. Cazeaux.[264] Similarities with some of Hillel's *middot* have been examined by D. I. Brewer.[265] It does not seem useful to reduce this variety to a list.

Philo's *allegorical interpretations*,[266] on the other hand, are quite homogeneous and can be systematized in some way. We may begin with some

---

[262] See R. Arnaldez, "L'influence de la traduction des Septante sur le commentaire de Philon", in: R. Kuntzmann/J. Schlosser (eds.), *Etudes sur le Judaïsme hellénistique: congrès de Strasbourg* (LD 119; Paris 1984) 251–266. Texts concerned are Gen 2:4, 19, 21, 23; 3:14–16; 49:17; Exod 33:13; Lev 1:9; 7:34; 8:29; 9:14; Num 6:12.

[263] G 20.19 further attenuates in saying κατὰ Θεόν. – The MT has לאלהים.

[264] J. Cazeaux, Philon d'Alexandrie, exégète (1984) 156–226.

[265] Brewer, Techniques (1992) 211; result: "Both Palestine and Alexandria learned from each other".

[266] In addition to the chapters on this topic found in any introduction to Philo, cf. I. Christiansen, *Die Technik der allegorischen Auslegungswissenschaft bei Philon von Alexandrien* (Tübingen 1969) (on philosophical and logical procedures); H.-J. Klauck, *Allegorie und Allegorese in synoptischen Gleichnistexten* (NTA NS 513; Münster 1978) esp. 32–115; J. Pépin, "Remarques sur la théorie de l'exégèse allégorique chez Philon", *Philon d'Alexandrie* (Congress Volume; 1967) 131–167; Walter, Aristobulos (see sect. 1) 141–146; Brewer, Techniques (1992) 22 f (absence or infrequency of Hebrew parallels in Philo's time), 198–212.

borderline cases, comparable to Aristobulus' problem in frg. 4. There may be phrases in Scripture, the literal meaning of which cannot be accepted for various reasons:

QG 2.28 (against common sense); cf. G 7.94 f; G 18.44;
Opif 13.26 f. (anthropomorphisms); cf. G 8.1–4; G 10.21 f;
G 3.13 (dogmatic objections); cf. *QG* 3.13 and G 17.300–306;
G 21.102 (a trifle unworthy of divine attention; cf. 1 Cor 9:9); etc.[267]

Discussions of this kind seem to be particularly frequent in G.

In the last quoted passage Philo advocates avoiding unworthy ideas about God by "following the law of allegory". He replaces the poor man's cloak (Exod 22:25 f) by the *Logos* claiming that one is the symbol of the other. Unfortunately he does not formulate the "law" by which he abides, nor does he so in other places where he uses a similar language (G 21.73; G 22.8; L 23.68; L 28.287: οἱ τῆς ἀλληγορίας κανόνες / νόμοι / παραγγέλματα).[268] The reason may be that these 'canons' had long become trivial, i. e. a well-known element of school teaching. Definitions of the term 'allegory' may indeed be found elsewhere,[269] and not in Philo's exegesis. Besides generic definitions and a host of examples, formal 'canons' seem not to exist in ancient literature. In Philo they are obviously identical with the normative notions, positive or negative, which we recorded in the above list and in the glossaries of sect. 1. 5, 2. 5, and 3. 5. In addition, elements of a theory of allegorical interpretation may be gathered from passages like *QE* 2.52, L 23.119–121; *Cont.* 78, etc.[270] Philo gives his art a more philosophical touch in claiming that his distinctions follow the Λόγος τομεύς ('cutting Logos') which is at work since the Creation (G 7.110; G 17.130, 132 etc.).[271] Its symbol are the Cherubims' swords (G 5.28).

Thus allegorical understanding may be inevitable in some cases; in all others, it is at least allowed and even recommended as if it were a meritorious work – like the Sages' edifying talks in the Passover night.[272] One might say, allegorical understanding is to literal obedience what the soul is to the body. Philo even goes beyond the limits of "physical" and "ethical" allegory in adding a third kind of explanation which has been called "mystical".[273] Aristobulus' frg. 5 may be the earliest known example of this species. It consists of a series of efforts to obtain a true and even intimate knowledge of God. There is a formal theory about this, and a specialized literature.[274]

---

267 The last text quoted in 4.5, above, may imply this rule.

268 See, e.g., Thyen, Der Stil (see n. 259, above) 82–84; Brewer, Techniques (1992) 199–202.

269 See n. 44, above.

270 See E. Osborn, "Logique et exégèse chez Clément d'Alexandrie", Cahiers de Biblia Patristica 1 (1987) 169–190, esp. 169 (trans.): "He (Clement) has inherited from Philo the canons of allegorical exegesis: there is nothing superfluous in Scripture; its repetitions are significative; its doublets are not redundant; and its silences are full of meaning. ... All nuances in the meaning of a term are possible. Numbers, things and names have symbolic meanings".

271 Christiansen, Die Technik (see n. 266, above) 29 ff, 99 ff. much elaborates this point which she traces back to Platonic *dihairesis*.

272 See the long haggadic expansions on Deut 26:4–6 in the Passover Haggadah, or the High Priest's night-long entertainment in *Yoma* 1:6 f.

273 Daniélou, Philon (1958) 116 f, 135 ff. (his examples do not always apply); M. Harl, Philon d'Alexandrie (Congress Volume; 1967) 193; Williamson, Jews (1989) 150 f; 163 f.

274 See the three stages of perfection (= knowledge of the Being one) in 20a.1 etc. As to its

Philo likes to associate this kind of mystical epistemology to passages speaking of divine "light", e.g. G21.118f. (Gen28:11), L23.107–132 (Gen18:1f.), and the whole of G20a (*ditto*). In *QG* 1.10 a five-step climax leads from biblical quotation and literal interpretation via a variety of allegories to mystical understanding. In the latter case Philo adds that all these explanations have already been elaborated by "some", resp. by "worthy and pious men".

Nevertheless, Philo belongs to the first witnesses of what has been called "Hellenistic mysticism".

A *hermeneutical glossary* like those included in former sections (1.5, 2.5, 3.5) would be repetitious; Philo is not original in this respect. It is more promising to draw up a *list of persons* in whom, Philo says, the basic concepts of Mosaic wisdom and legislation are incorporated.[275] This list is likely to contain at least some original thoughts, even in comparison with Palestinian Jewish *haggadah*.[276] As to the method of taking persons as symbols, there is nothing specifically Jewish about that. Greek interpretation of Homeric and other myths had done so independently. Thus Athena was associated or even identified with prudence (φρόνησις), Hermes with the *Logos*, Ares with courage, Aphrodite with lust, the Muses with the arts, and so on.[277] Anyway, Philo's use of *biblical persons as symbols for abstract ideas* is remarkable for its riches and its consistency throughout his work.[278]

Adam: the (human) mind (νοῦς)	e.g. G2.90f.
Eve: sense-perception (αἴσθησις)	G5.57
Cain: possession, selfishness	G16.74
Abel: piety, holiness	ibid.
Seth: ποτισμός: the soul being "irrigated" by wisdom	G18.124f.
Enos: hope	L23.7
Enoch: grace; repentance (and other nuances)	L23.17f.

anthropological basis in Philo (which has been echoed in the distinction between three stages of salvation made by Egyptian Gnostics), the classical presentation is W. Völker, *Fortschritt und Vollendung bei Philo von Alexandrien: Eine Studie zur Geschichte der Frömmigkeit* (TU 49/1; Leipzig 1938).

[275] See 4.6, above.

[276] On similarities of these "living laws" with the *haggadah*, see E. Stein, *Die allegorische Exegese des Philo aus Alexandreia* (BZAW 51; Giessen 1929) 15ff, and idem, *Philo und der Midrasch: Philos Schilderung der Gestalten des Pentateuch verglichen mit der des Midrasch* (BZAW 57; Giessen 1931), esp. the summary on pp. 50–1. He points out that the haggadic elements in Philo's writings correspond much more to a coherent βίος than the *ad hoc* statements found in the Midrashim, and that Philo avoids painting in black and white. – On recent discussion, see L.L. Grabbe, "Philo and Aggada: a Response to B.J. Bamberger", Studia Philonica Annual 3 (1991) 153–166, esp. his very short list of possible "examples of aggada in Philo", pp. 159–61, and Brewer, Techniques (1992) 203f. For the case of Abraham, Sandmel (see n. 278, below), too, confirms Philo's relative independence from Palestinian *haggadah* (201–211).

[277] See Cornutus, *Theologiae Graecae compendium* as a whole. Plutarch, *Mor.* 757 B, whence the above examples are taken, objects against this (Stoic) method which seems to him too mechanical.

[278] The following list follows the examples of S. Sandmel, *Philo's Place in Judaism: A study of conceptions of Abraham in Jewish literature* (New York 1971) 100f, and J. Cazeaux, *Philon d'Alexandrie: De la grammaire à la mystique* (Cahiers Evangile 44, supplément; Paris 1983) 77–80. References abound: see Cazeaux, op. cit., and Leisegang's Indices I 1–26 under the proper names and the siglum 'All'.

Noah:[279] rest (ἀνάπαυσις); the righteous one	G 4.77
Abraham:[280] ἡ διδασκομένη ἀρετή (the ability to be taught); the sage; mind (νοῦς)	G 21.160 f.
Lot: indecision	G 16.148 f.
Hagar: provisional sojourn; the encyclical studies	G 18.20
Ishmael: sophistry	G 5.8
Sarah: virtue (ἀρετή); wisdom (σοφία)[281]	G 18.1–13
Isaac:[282] "laughter" (joy); ἡ φυσικὴ ἀρετή (natural virtue); intuition of truth; perfection	G 4.219; L 23.52
Rebeccah: constancy (ὑπομονή)	G 6.4
Jacob: the ascete; ἡ ἀσκητικὴ ἀρετή (the perfection attained through practice)	G 16.26–30
Israel: "the man who sees God"	G 16.25–52
Esau: stupidity (ἀφροσύνη); Edom: what is earthly	G 18.62
Laban: brightness, colour, illusion	G 18.208 f.
Leah: virtue attained through toil	G 17.45 f.
Rahel: stupidity of (mere) sense-perception	G 17.43 f.
Reuben: good shape (εὐφυΐα)	G 22.33
Simeon: hearing, learning	G 16.224
Levi: (as Simeon, or) attendance (θεραπεία)	G 6.120
Judah: confession (ἐξομολόγησις)	G 2.79 f.
Tamar:[283] victory, invincible virtue	G 19.149
Issachar: reward (μισθός)	G 22.33
Dan: judgment (κρίσις); the same holds for Dinah	ibid.
Gad: attempt, risk	ibid.
Asser: blessing; wealth	ibid.
Naphthali: peace (εἰρήνη)	ibid.
Joseph:[284] increase, bodily health, prosperity; the politician	L 24.28
Ephraim: wealth of fruits (καρποφορία)	G 18.40
Menasseh: remembrance (ἀνάμνησις)	ibid.
Benjamin: being young/being old	G 22.36
Moses: the prophetic *Logos*; also: the prophetic race (Israel)	G 4.43; 19.147
Miriam: hope;[285] purified sense-perception	G 4.103
Zipporah: being winged, the prophetic race	G 5.47
Pharaoh: perversion of mind	G 19.124 f.
Aaron: the advancing learner (ὁ προκόπτων): the *Logos*	G 4.132
Bezalel: who produces shadows	G 21.206 ff.
Bileam:[286] foolish people	G 16.133
Hannah: grace.	G 20.143

[279] J. Cazeaux, *La trame et la chaîne* II: *Le cycle de Noé dans Philon d'Alexandrie* (ALGHJ 20; Tübingen 1989); L. R. Bailey, *Noah: The Person and the Story in History and Tradition* (Studies on Personalities of the O.T.; Columbia 1989).

[280] See Sandmel (n. 278); G. Vermes, *Scripture and Tradition in Judaism* (SPB 4; Leiden 1962) 67–126.

[281] Women symbolizing something positive are not as rare in Philo as it is sometimes said. He does not fail to note, however, that in ἀρετή the grammatical gender is feminine, whereas the quality referred to is rather masculine (G 19.51; L 23.54).

[282] Vermes, Scripture and Tradition (1962) 127–177.

[283] M. Petit, "Exploitations non bibliques des thèmes de Tamar et de Genèse 38", in: ΑΛΕΞΑΝΔΡΙΝΑ: *Hellénisme, judaïsme et christianisme à Alexandrie. Mélanges offerts à C. Mondésert* (Paris 1987) 77–115.

[284] M. Niehoff, *The Figure of Joseph in Post-Biblical Jewish Literature* (AGJU 16; Leiden 1992) 54–83.

[285] G 22.142: so say "we, the allegorists".

[286] Vermes, Scripture and Tradition (1962) 129–163.

In all of these cases (this is not a complete list) Philo's Platonism leads him to represent the plural (Israel) in the form of a singular (an exemplary person). Other symbols taken from biblical history include:

Eden: τρυφή (luxury), as in LXX;[287] also, wisdom	G 16.37
The Serpent: lust	G 11.97
Egypt: the vices of the body	G 16.16
Canaan: restlessness, the vices of adolescence.	G 14.44 ff.

These symbolisms normally rely on Hebrew (or Greek)[288] etymologies, be they genuine ones or mere associations.

To sum up, Philo's use of "literal" and allegorical interpretations represents an extreme exploration of what we called the 'symbolic link' (1.6). The basic rule is: things which have something in common are *ipso facto* a reference to each other. Thus the whole cosmos becomes a universe of cross-references.[289] For modern readers wanting to understand Philo it is crucial *to free themselves from the monopoly of causal thinking* which has become undisputed since the great successes of experimental science. But in ancient thought — and in poetry of all times — things may be interconnected by a relationship of meaning without acting on each other.

4.9. *The Reception of Philo's Works*

Josephus briefly mentions Philo in connection with his embassy to Rome. He seems to have read his *De opificio mundi.*[290] The Rabbis, on the other hand, do not even record his name. In discussions of Palestinian Jewish Sages and Rabbis there may be found parallels of Alexandrian Jewish hermeneutics[291] and theology in general.[292] But the Targumic מימר, e.g., has little in common with the Philonic *Logos*;[293] and when Origen set out to verify what he had read in Celsus's *True Discourse* on a Jewish *Logos* theology, his Jewish partners said that there was never a Jewish authority who called the *Logos* the "Son of God"[294] (as Philo had done).

In pagan literature including Hermetism there are no traces of Philo.[295] Apparent similarities can be accounted for by reference to a common cultural context. As for the Gnostics, their way of appropriation, i.e. negation of

---

[287] The Gnostics turned this symbol into negativity, as they did with many others: see *Ap. John*, NH III 27,7 ff.

[288] Some examples are listed in Stein, Die allegorische Exegese (see n. 276) 60 f.

[289] This method of reasoning distinguishes Antiquity and Middle Ages from modern times. Before Galilei, Newton, Linné etc., examples are legion: take Isidorus' *Etymologies*, a Medieval cathedral, a baroque book of emblems, etc. — not to mention magic, alchemy, and occult 'sciences'.

[290] See above, n. 162.

[291] See Brewer, Techniques (1992) esp. 11–23 and 199–212. The later דורשי חמורות are sometimes considered as an independet phenomenon, but they may well have been influenced by Alexandrian Judaism (Brewer, 22).

[292] Mainly in utterings attributed to Hoshaya Rabba; cf. n. 222, above.

[293] See H. Bietenhard, "Logos-Theologie im Rabbinat. Ein Beitrag zur Lehre vom Worte Gottes im rabbinischen Schrifttum", ANRW II 19/2 (1979) 580–618.

[294] Origen, *Contra Celsum* 2.31.

[295] Festugière, La révélation d'Hermès Trismégiste II (1949) 521, n. 5.

Jewish theology is of a kind that precise statements seem impossible.[296] The *Exegesis on the Soul* from Nag Hammadi, e.g., uses the same techniques as those adopted by Philo, sharing also his 'psychological' interests; but there is much less respect for the biblical text. Philo's theological bases are denied.

Leaving aside the vexed question of similarities between Philo and the New Testament,[297] we may state Philo's immense impact on Christian exegesis and even on dogmatics immediately after the period of early Christianity.[298] Philo soon became one of the Church Fathers. Clement of Alexandria,[299] Origen,[300] and others read and imitated him; Eusebius recommends him at length (*H. e.* 2.4–6; 2.16f, etc.; *Praep. evang.* 7.12.14ff.) and gives a list of his writings in *H. e.* 2.18.[301] Greek exegetical catenae cite him among Cyril, Chrysostom, and all the others, sometimes even under the rubric Φίλωνος ἐπισκόπου.

In Latin Christian literature Ambrose is known to have translated whole pages of Philo without citing his name.[302] His influence on Augustine and the latter's influence on Latin theology, again, are immense.[303] Jerome enumerates Philo among the "illustrious men" on whom Christian literature depends (*De viribus illustribus* 11).

4.10. Results

It has become a standard criticism of Philo to say that he lacks any sense of history.[304] This is true for the kind of "deeper meanings" Philo looks for. For

[296] On Philo and Gnosticism, see R. McL. Wilson, "Philo of Alexandria and Gnosticism", *Kairos* 14 (1972) 213–19; B. A. Pearson, "Jewish Sources in Gnostic Literature", M. E. Stone (ed.), *Jewish Writings of the Second Temple Period* (CRINT II/2; Assen 1984) 443–481; J. Ménard, *La gnose de Philon d'Alexandrie* (Paris 1987). The question remains open whether the fall of Jerusalem and the catastrophe of messianism belong to the causes of Gnosticism as a kind of renegate Judaism. The Gnostics, who felt a strong contempt of history, do not inform us about their origins.

[297] This question has received a negative answer (and rightly so) in the monograph by R. Williamson, *Philo and the Epistle to the Hebrews* (ALGHJ 4; Leiden 1970). Of the first Christians, few are likely to have engaged in reading anything like Philo's works.

[298] D. T. Runia, *Philo in Early Christian Literature. A Survey* (CRINT 3,3; Assen 1993). An example has been discussed by Siegert, Philon von Alexandrien (1980; see above 4.1, note on G 20a) 73–85: Philo's hermeneutic key of distinguishing the Being one from two of his principal Powers has helped the Church to express her doctrine about the Trinity.

[299] A. van den Hoek, *Clement of Alexandria and His Use of Philo in the* Stromateis (VC Suppl. 3; Leiden 1988); J. C. M. van Winden, "Quotations from Philo in Clement of Alexandria's Protrepticus", *VC* 32 (1978) 208–13.

[300] See, e.g., J. Laporte, "Models from Philo in Origen's Teaching on Original Sin", *Laval Théologique et Philosophique* 44 (1988) 191–205.

[301] On the legend of Philo's becoming a Christian, see above, 4.7, on *Cont.*

[302] The Cohn/Wendland edition quotes such passages in its second apparatus, since they may help in controlling the text. They have been increased by specialized inquiries, e.g., E. Lucchesi, *L'usage de Philon dans l'œuvre exégétique de Saint Ambroise: Une "Quellenforschung" relative aux commentaires d'Ambroise sur la Genèse* (ALGHJ 9; Leiden 1977). Ambrose said of his Jewish predecessor what Luther later said of Scholastic theology: *Philo autem, quoniam spiritualia Iudaico non capiebat affectu, intra moralia se tenuit* (*De Paradiso* 4.25). To him as a Christian, the mystical side of Philo's thought did not mean much.

[303] Cf. J. Pépin, *La tradition de l'allégorie de Philon d'Alexandrie à Dante* II (Paris 1987 – no more published) esp. 187–294.

[304] E.g. Daniélou, Philon (1958) 119: "il est totalement dépourvu du sens de l'histoire". Cf. Dawson, Allegorical Readers (1992) 98: "Philo evades the temporal character of historical events

him, as for Lessing in his famous critique of biblical revelation, truths are eternal truths and not contingent ones recorded in history. In Philo, the event of the exodus (which has become a pivot of present-day theology) is not the basis of Israel's identity.

Yet, we should be careful in making negative statements. In an earlier section (4.7) attention has been called to the fact that under certain circumstances Philo could be a theologian of history. Situations of crisis became more and more intense toward the end of his life. In his apologetical treatise *Hypothetica*, which may be late, Philo gives an account of the exodus (cited in Eusebius, *Praep. evang.* 8.6) that is significantly different from his other exegeses. Here God takes care of his people in a visible way, and Israel's particular link with God is proven by its survival in disastrous situations.

With respect to the *Legatio ad Gaium* DAWSON says: "Philo may well intend his account of his embassy to the emperor Gaius Caligula to be a serious warning to the Romans to join the winning side of history".[305] – Two generations later Josephus found himself in the reverse situation.

This last remark makes it understandable that it is not Philo, the theologian of history, but Philo, the allegorist and philosopher of eternal ideas, who has been copied down and imitated by Christians. They appreciated in him one kind of 'edifying' use of Scripture; but he himself does not ignore the other.

Another negative statement, however, may well serve to characterize Philo's exegesis. Philo was no jurist, as were the authorities of Palestinian or Babylonian *halakhah*. In his attempt to be a moral philosopher, he has not enriched the Oral Torah. It is true that Philo's account of Mosaic prescriptions often tends to aggravate them,[306] but he (happily) never participated in any kind of formal legislation. There was no Jewish body of legislation in Alexandria. We do not know what Philo's exegesis would have been if it had mattered for a Jewish law court (בית דין). It was not just for his deference to Hellenism that he chose to be a philosopher. One of his reasons for doing so was his loyalty to Jerusalem.[307]

5. Alexandrian Jewish Non-Allegorists

Sources: A) for sect. 5.1: C. R. HOLLADAY (ed.), *Fragments from Hellenistic Jewish Authors* I. *Historians* (Chico, CA 1983 [Gk. and Engl., with notes]); Charlesworth, OTP II 843–903 (Engl. translations). B) for sect. 5.2–7: *Philonis Judaei paralipomena Armena* [sic] (ed. J. B. Aucher [Awgerean]; Venice 1826; repr. Hildesheim 1988) 549–628; F. SIEGERT, *Drei hellenistisch-jüdische Predigten: Ps.-Philon, "Über Jona", "Über Simson"*, I. *Übersetzung aus dem Armenischen und sprachliche Erläuterungen*; II. *Kommentar nebst Beobachtungen zur hellenistischen Vorgeschichte der Bibelhermeneutik* (WUNT 20; 61; Tübingen 1980, 1992); the two volumes are cited as Siegert I

---

in order to interpret both the exodus and its annual remembrance at Passover as an ever-present process of the sanctification of the human soul".

305 Dawson, Allegorical Readers (1992) 124.

306 E.g., *Hypothetica* (Eusebius, *Praep. evang.* 8.7.1–9) claims death penalty for any sexual act that does not aim at procreation.

307 Once more it may be called to mind that he does not mention the Temple and the High Priests of Leontopolis.

and II. *Numbering* of paragraphs (in *De Jona*) according to H. Lewy, numbering of chapters (in *De Sampsone*) according to the first edition. There is no English translation. A French one is to appear in SC.

Bibliographies: G. Delling, Bibliographie (1975; see sect. 1) 53–55, 175; Holladay, Fragments (see above) 25–46; P. W. van der Horst, Interpretation (see below) 545 f.

General works: I. Heinemann, "Die Allegoristik der hellenistischen Juden ausser Philon", *Mnemosyne*, ser. 4, 5 (1952) 130–138; P. W. van der Horst, "The Interpretation of the Bible by the Minor Hellenistic Jewish Authors", Mikra (1988) 519–546, esp. 528–545; Schürer/Vermes, History III/1 (1986) 509–17, 521–26; N. Walter, "Jüdisch-hellenistische Literatur vor Philon von Alexandrien ⟨unter Ausschluss der Historiker⟩", ANRW II 20/1 (1987) 67–120, esp. 77–79, 98 f.

In Alexandrian Judaism there were always interpreters of Scripture who avoided or even refused the idea that Moses had spoken in allegories. They are known to the reader of Philo as the σοφισταί who only elaborate the literal meaning of the text. Since Aristobulus' defence against "those who only cling to the letter" (frg. 2), the situation had not changed. It remained the same in the three centuries in which Alexandria was a centre of Jewish culture.

There are three principal sources of information: (1) numerous allusions in Philo,[308] (2) some names and fragments preserved by Eusebius (*Praep. evang.* 9.17–39) who quotes them from the pagan ethnographer Alexander Polyhistor (wrote in the mid-1st cent. BCE),[309] and (3) the Pseudo-Philonic sermons.

5.1. The Fragments of Demetrius, Aristeas, Artapanus, and Others

The authors to be mentioned in this section are generally cited as 'historians', because they dealt with biblical history; but they may quite as well have been exegetes who cultivated a literal approach. They try to answer critical questions about biblical history. The fragments are either short, or have been rewritten by Polyhistor, or both. This does not permit us to determine the exact nature of the writings of persons like Demetrius, Eupolemus, Artapanus, Aristeas "the exegete", Philo "the Elder", Cleodemus/Malchas and others—we do not mention those who wrote in verses (which is not typical for exegesis) or who were Samaritans.

Three of these names are of some interest for the present work. Demetrius "the Chronographer" (modern surname; wrote ca. 200 BCE) is "the earliest Jewish writer in Greek whom we know".[310] His calculations of biblical chronology rely entirely on the Septuagint; he is indeed the first datable reader of the LXX books he cites. His efforts tend to solve the problem of historical improbabilities in the sacred text. One of his merits consists in

[308] Daniélou, Philon (1958; see sect. 4.) 110–112; M. J. Shroyer, "Alexandrian Jewish Literalists", *JBL* 55 (1936) 261–284.

[309] On his Περὶ 'Ιουδαίων, see Holladay, Fragments (1983) 7 f; Walter, ANRW II 20/1 (1987) 71 f. There are independent references to some of these authors in Josephus (*Ap.* 1.218), but he surely did not know their writings from his own reading since he believed they were pagans.

[310] E. J. Bickerman, "The Jewish historian Demetrios", J. Neusner (ed.), *Christianity, Judaism and Other Greco-Roman Cults: Studies for Morton Smith at Sixty* III (Leiden 1975) 72–84; cited: p. 77.—Cf. Holladay, Fragments (1983) 51–91; Charlesworth, OTP II 843–54.

avowing them: "Demetrius is perhaps the first Jewish author who systematically engaged in biblical criticisim".[311]

Artapanus (a Persian name), another Jewish writer quoted by Polyhistor, is the author of a fanciful romance on Moses and on Israelite history. He embellishes the biblical account by many details. He excuses Moses' killing of an Egyptian as an act of self-defence; he claims that Moses and Musaeus are the same person, that Moses was the teacher of Orpheus, and that he was the inventor of nearly everything: a Hellenistic hero and a Jewish Homer at the same time. There is no fear of contamination with paganism in Artapanus' fragments; and sometimes he even comes near to Euhemerism.[312] We may evaluate the fragments as a witness to a naive appropriation of Hellenistic culture; after the Jerusalem drama of 175, this naiveté seems no longer possible.

Aristeas "the exegete" (modern surname) is known by one fragment, a midrashic expansion of the Book of Job similar to Job 42:17b–e LXX.[313] He links the heathen Job to the descendance of Abraham.

Such embellishments of, and narrative additions to, biblical history have not much in common with what we called 'exegesis' in the preceeding sections. They belong to the wide realm of *midrash*. Yet they have no similarity in literary *genre* with what we shall call a specifically 'Hellenistic Jewish midrash' (see 5.6). Let us now shift our attention to another set of texts, the *Pseudo-Philonic sermons*. Each of these comprises some forty pages of printed text, the Jewish authenticity of which has never been questioned.

5.2. *The Sermons* On Jonah *and* On Samson

The Hellenistic Jewish sermons On Jonah, another fragment bearing the same name, and *On Samson* would be a downright sensation, had the Greek originals survived. Now they are only preserved in a 6th cent. Armenian translation which groups them among the works of Philo. This translation is so slavishly literal that it cannot be understood by readers of Armenian either, except if they guess the underlying Greek.

There exist two translations of the Armenian text, one into Latin and one into German. In both of them the orality of the text becomes evident: this is a full-fledged *encomium*, a period piece of 'Asianic' oratory. It testifies to the ancient Jewish art of preaching at its very peak. There is nothing comparable in Christian sources down to the highly rhetorical "homilies" by the early Gnostic Valentinus and the Passah encomium by Melito of Sardis.

The fragment on Jonah, which consists of just one page, was added to the sermon *On Jonah* probably as an alternative to sect. 59 which is theologically objectionable.[314] It seems to come from another author. The question whether

---

311 Holladay, Fragments (1983) 53.

312 See 1.6, above. – Holladay, Fragments (1983) 189–243; Charlesworth, OTP II 889–96.

313 Holladay, Fragments (1983) 261–71; Charlesworth, OTP II 855–58.

314 It had represented Jonah's leap into the sea monster as a self-sacrifice, which made it appear like a suicide.

the authors of *De Iona* and *De Sampsone* are identical or not remains undecided.

The sermons prove that the art of public preaching, i.e. of applying rhetoric to scriptural explanation, had been developed before the Church adapted it to her needs. It was a Jewish innovation. Pagans never did their Homer exegesis in public; they taught it to schoolboys. In *De Iona* and *De Sampsone*, however, we hear a Hellenistic Jewish scribe or sage playing an orator's role and explaining a biblical text to a large audience. In order to find a plausible historical setting, we may think of the giant synagogue at Alexandria mentioned above (sect. 1.7), and of the time of Philo.[315]

There are interesting differences between the Sermons and Philo's writings:

- they are not 'literature' and not courses addressed to students, but speeches;
- they do not exemplify Law teaching, but are expansions of texts pertaining to other parts of the tripartite Bible;
- the austerity and constant recommendation of ascetism in Philo receive a counterpart in a marked sense of humour (*De Iona* 32f, 203, etc.) and a vivid imagination.

The Sermons are obviously meant to entertain a larger assembly, including women, perhaps on a Sabbath afternoon. We may even know their precise *Sitz im Leben*. In the rabbinical calendar of pericopes the Book of Jonah is the Haphtarah of the Day of Atonement, which fits the contents of *De Iona* very well. *De Sampsone*, in its turn, treats the Haphtarah linked with Num 6:1–21 (the law of Nazirites), which was read on a less important Sabbath. Its sub-title claims – and its rather loose structure confirms – that it was an improvised speech, an αὐτοσχέδιος (or αὐτοσχεδίαστος) λόγος.

5.3. *The Theological Basis for the Interpretation of Scripture in the Sermons*

The preacher's popular, non-technical language conceals that he is intimate with Greek culture as well as with the subtleties of theological discussions between the Jewish Sages.[316] *De Iona* shuns using the words 'God' or 'the Lord'; it mostly prefers a large variety of circumlocutions and qualifications.[317] This seems to be the author's way of respecting transcendance.

The preacher knows Homer and Plato.[318] His intellectual habits are impregnated with Stoicism. The duplicity of Old Testament and Stoic roots is best seen in the author's use of the term 'salvation' (σωτηρία). It often refers to the preservation of the established order in the cosmos and in society, a view which the preacher shares with contemporary upper-class philosophy

[315] For questions of literary *genre*, place and date, see Siegert II 1–52.

[316] For the latter, see *De Sampsone* 19 and 23f, referred to below, 5.6.

[317] The index in Siegert I marks them in italics.

[318] *De Iona* 18 makes an allusion to *Iliad* 18.104 (*Odyssey* 20.379); these verses were a proverb among the educated, as is attested by its use in Plato and in Philo. On a reminiscence of Plato's *Laws*, see below.

and politics. Yet this term also applies to God's particular action by which he 'saves' the Ninivites from sin (*De Iona* 6, etc.). The composite term σωτηρία ψυχῶν, on the other hand, derives its content from Plato: the sea monster is Jonah's prison in which he is re-educated, much as in Plato's *Laws* (909A) where this very term is used.

The preacher rationalizes mythical elements such as Samson's hair (*De Sampsone* 13) and moralizes ritual such as the ransoming of a newborn child by sacrifice (*De Iona* 124). His God is the 'overseer' and 'pilot' of the cosmos; he governs it by his 'providence'. But there is no theory about intermediaries, even though the two kinds of God's activity (cf. Philo's 'Powers') may be distinguished in *De Iona* (see 5.6, below).

Instead, the Sermons abound with psychological observations and subtleties such as we observed in the *Epistle of Aristaeus* (see 2.2–3). *De Iona* is occupied with motivating Jonah (i.e. the Jewish hearer) to engage in the salvation of a heathen society,[319] and *De Sampsone* explains psychologically many details, such as the effect of the angel's promise to Samson's mother (sect. 5, 8), the seemingly magical impact of Samson's long hair (sect. 13), his finding and communicating the riddle (sect. 29–32), and the Philistines' reaction (sect. 36 ff.).[320]

As to mystical elements, they are scarce but may show up unexpectedly. It seems that the preacher was bound to make this tribute to contemporary taste at least once: see the "light" in *De Iona* 94 and the "heavenly talks" in *De Sampsone* 15. As regards eschatology, *De Iona* 95–98 explores the similarity between Jonah's fate in the monster and human death in order to affirm individual survival (see below).

5.4. The Preacher's Bible and the Texts Referred to

De Iona recounts the whole Book of Jonah with few omissions. Sometimes the text is quoted, and a reference in sect. 67 implies that it had been read entirely. The psalm of Jonah 2, however, is replaced by a 'prayer' in which Jonah tells of his adventures in the sea monster in a most curious science-fiction style (sect. 69–98). – Other texts quoted or alluded to are:[321]

Genesis 6–9; 10:11
Exod 14:26, 21 f; 20:7
Isa 48:13 (quotation formula: "have you not read in *the Law*: …?")
Joel 1:14
Qoh 7:26
Dan 2:21; 6

The fragment on Jonah elaborates Jonah 1:8, 11, 12 in the style of a running homily, without further quotations.

The sermon *De Sampsone* expands Judg 13:2–14:9 with an anticipation of Judg 16:16 f. at the beginning (chap. 1). In chap. 15 he seems to allude to the

[319] See sect. 9, 21–23, 26 ff, 100, 182 ff, 215.

[320] As in LXX, the name 'Philistines' does not appear but is replaced by ἀλλόφυλοι, i.e. by a generalization.

[321] For references, see Siegert I 97.

author of the Book of Judges (Samuel?) by the term 'the prophet'. The following texts are quoted or alluded to:

Gen 1:26 f; 15:6; 18:2 ff; 34; 38; 39:7–20
Exod 33:20 (formula: "Scripture has: ...")
Isa 11:2
Qoh 10:8 (formula: "according to the will of the Holy Writ; because Scripture somewhere says expressly: ...").

This happens to conform perfectly with the Hebrew canon. Nothing is cited that is outside it,[322] and all parts are cited as 'Scripture' or (in the case of Isaiah)[323] as 'the Law'. God is "the Lord of the Law" (*De Iona* 115). The terms 'Scripture' and 'Law' are used as in the New Testament; there is much less variety than in Philo.

The text used is the Septuagint. The preacher is not aware of variants even where he switches between them. *De Sampsone* 41, a literal exegesis of Judg 14:18, makes a switch from LXX cod. A (etc.), used so far, to cod. B. The argument then rests on a detail only found in the cod. B version.

The apologetic front against "detractors of Holy Scripture" (thus *De Sampsone* 26, cf. 24) is as obvious as in Aristobulus and in Philo, and even more so. The preacher engages in a rhetorical dialogue with them.

5.5. *Literal Methods*

There is no allegorizing in the Sermons. The biblical book or pericope is taken as history in both cases, which necessitates apologies for the incredibility of the Jonah story and for the bad habits of the hero in the Samson narrative.[324] The texts need no transformation into general (philosophical) theories in order to become relevant for the audience. Being taken as history, they illustrate the saving action of Providence by examples. Lists (or 'catalogues') of other examples or counter-examples are contained in all three sermons (*De Iona* 91–94; the fragment at its end; *De Sampsone* 25); their roots may be seen in the aretalogies or 'historical' prayers of the synagogue.[325]

The preacher can dispose of allegorism as he is not concerned with updating the 'scientific' content of his text. This is not to say that his exegeses are naive or simple. They may be as sophisticated as the 'literal' exegeses proposed by Philo in his *Quaestiones*. In *De Iona* 192–94 the 'catastrophe' of Nineveh assumes the meaning of a 'conversion' by an elaborate play on words. *De Sampsone* gives an apology of Samson's *pneuma* by distinguishing six kinds of 'spirits' two of which were only Samson's gift. This is a Greek διαίρεσις using an element of Jewish *midrash* (on Isa 11:2, see below).

In *De Sampsone* 23 f. we participate in an inner-Jewish discussion on the issue of theodicy in the Samson cycle. The preacher combats the thesis that

---

322 Except one profane citation in *De Sampsone* 18 introduced by "Someone has said ...".

323 *De Iona* 146 ("Have you not read in the Law ...?") is paralleled by John 10:34 and 1 Cor 14:21.

324 *De Iona* 94–98; *De Sampsone* 24–26.

325 Cf. the presumably Jewish prayers in the pseudepigraphical *Apostolic Constitutions* 7.33, 37, 38, 39; 8.5, and 12; Charlesworth, OTP II 678, 684–5; 687–8, 693–4.

God induces Samson to evil – which was claimed by "some of the Sages" as the literal meaning of Judg 14:4 (ὅτι παρὰ Κυρίου ἐστίν). Just as he does – or as his colleague does – in *De Iona*, the preacher justifies the vicissitudes of the hero's life by the *topos* of finality: God did achieve his aim (which in *De Iona* is the salvation of heathens, and in *De Sampsone* the punishment of heathens). Thus any responsibility for the evil and any self-contradiction on God's side are avoided, as in Aristobulus and Philo.

In *De Sampsone* 7, 11, 14, 24, 38 f, and 41 the words of the text are forced to yield an answer to a question not envisaged by the biblical author. These artifices of interpretation are reminiscent of what Greek orators and advocates (which is the same thing) did in order to make a law say what they wanted it to say. Jewish law experts seem to have learned from them.

5.6. *Hellenistic Jewish* midrash

All three sermons are examples of 'narrative theology', i.e. the expansion of a biblical text by telling it in more detail and by interspersing reflections of various kinds, speeches, dialogues, etc. In *De Iona* 92, 101, and elsewhere, narrative details are added which recur in Hebrew sources. In *De Sampsone* 19 the preacher hints at other teachers who enriched the Samson narrative before him. The affinity with the *midrash* is obvious; but it is limited by the much more rhetorical nature of the Sermons. In *De Iona* 183–219 the preacher personifies God in attributing to him a lengthy speech – again, a rabbinical בת קול would be much more laconic, but would occur more frequently.

Thus the similarities with Hebrew *midrash* consist of many material details and they are restricted to them. One of the most interesting items is in *De Sampsone* 24 f. the use of Isa 11:2 (the list of the spiritual gifts of the Messiah) to found a kind of pneumatology. It has not been taken up in rabbinic literature, but it is present, in a slightly expanded variant, in 2nd cent. Christology (Irenaeus etc.). Here we have the oldest, purely Jewish form of the theorem. On the other hand, *De Sampsone* obviously exploits Hellenistic Heracles myths in order to extol Samson all the more.[326]

Turning our attention from details to structure, we become aware of a difference in kind between Greek and Hebrew *midrashim*. It is such that it may be useful to coin a term: *Hellenistic midrash*, for the kind of expansion of a biblical text which is represented by *De Iona* and *De Sampsone*. They do not consist of a chain of associations like the Hebrew *midrashim*; they are founded on a rhetorical matrix which gives them an overall structure.[327] They are not linear, as it were, but are constructed on a plane.

In *De Iona* the preacher organizes his materials around two basic concepts. They are developed and illustrated by way of narration, dialogue and various monologues of the judicial, deliberative, and epidictic kind. These basic concepts are: God is φιλάνθρωπος on one hand, ἄφυκτος on the other. God loves

---

[326] See Siegert II 269–272.

[327] The structures underlying *De Iona* and *De Sampsone* are graphically represented in Siegert II 92 f, 230 f.

Mankind; but nobody can flee from his orders. By an *inclusio* in the disposition of the sermon the first aspect frames and dominates the second. This reminds us of Philo's two Powers, of which the beneficient one was the more important. But the preacher does not use Philo's technical language.

De Sampsone is a specimen of what has been called a 'biographical encomium'.[328] This *genre* is the precursor of all Jewish and Christian hagiography. The structure and the sequence of biographical *topoi* in *De Sampsone* matches rhetorical convention as it is codified, e.g., in Theon's *Progymnasmata*.[329]

Another difference from Hebrew *midrashim* consists in the reluctance to invent names. There is no speculation about Jonah's ancestors and identity or about the localization of Tarshish, and none about the name of Samson's mother or the name of the angel who bears the promise of his birth.[330]

5.7. *Typology*

Literality does not exclude the 'symbolic link' between details of the narrative and elements of the interpreter's world. The Ninivites' sinfulness was already death (*De Iona* 152; cf. 13–81). Jonah's rescue from the dangers of the ocean was a resurrection (ibid. 95). Now every childbirth is in some way a rescue from the water and a grant of being able to breathe: by this analogy and some others taken from biblical history the interpreter establishes multiple interconnections (ibid. 91–98):

God saved Noah's family from the Flood (Genesis 6–9)
↓ ↑
God saved Abraham from a burning furnace (*midrash* element)
↓ ↑
God saved the Hebrews when they passed through the sea (Exodus 14)
↓ ↑
God saved "righteous men" from wild beasts (cf. Daniel 6)
↓ ↑
God saved Jonah from dying in the ocean and from dying in the monster
↓ ↑
Jonah has been physically and morally reborn
↓ ↑
In every childbirth God gives life and saves life
↓ ↑
God will save (the souls of the righteous) from dying with the body.

Each item in this system of cross-references serves to back up the others. The preacher, wanting to make plausible the story of Jonah in the sea monster, teaches at once biblical history, creationism (regarding the origin of individual human life), soteriology, and individual eschatology.

As much as the interconnections can be situated in the time axis, the argument may be called a *typology* proper. Philo, as is well known, mostly

---

[328] A. MOMIGLIANO, *The Development of Greek Biography* (Cambridge, MA/Leiden 1971) 82f; cf. the enumeration of ancient kinds of biography by R. HAMERTON-KELLY, *StudPhil* 1 (1972) 11.

[329] See Marrou, Histoire de l'éducation (1948) 274f, and Siegert II 233f.

[330] See, for the last and most elaborated detail, *De Sampsone* 15f.

exploits the interconnections on the 'vertical' axis: eternal idea – temporal realization. In the Sermons, much as in the New Testament (especially Hebrews), historical typology tries to make evident a temporal sequence of two or more comparable events. Given a prophetic testimony which qualifies at least one of them as a divine act, the others will be regarded so, too.

Theology is about God's action in the cosmos (so Philo, mostly) and/or in history (so the Sermons). The fact that the examples illustrated by the Sermons are of a questionable historicity (Jonah, Daniel)[331] does not invalidate the *form* of the argument.

So much for the origin of typology and for its logical and historical bases. Historically, it belongs to the common achievements of Antiquity (sect. 1.6 for Vergil). The merit of Jewish and of Christian theologians lies in the fact that they developed it to its clearest form.

5.8. *Epilogue: Hellenistic Jewish Hermeneutic and the Church. An Art Exchanges Its Masters*

All texts dealt with in this fourth chapter owe their preservation to the Christian Church. This does not testify against their Jewish authenticity, but to the Church's willingness to learn from her elder sister. We may sum up the intellectual achievements which Alexandrian Jewish masters handed over to their Christian pupils as follows. Alexandrian Judaism had developed:

– a large choice of methods of literal, allegorical, and typological exegesis, and
– oral and literary forms of expression appropriate to convey the results of exegesis to a given audience, whether small or large.

Thus the two options later known as 'Alexandrine' (allegorical) and 'Antiochene' (historical) exegesis were already there in Alexandrian Judaism. Both profited from a theology which was made

– to reconcile belief and reason;
– to overcome the particularity of ancestral religion in a world that had become one universe and one city.

Theology in the sense of 'accounting for God's action in the world/in history' had become more concrete and more coherent than it ever was before. There was nothing that could have served better to frame the message of God's acting in Jesus Christ.

On the level of the history of culture, Homer and Moses continued to be rivals for several centuries. The history of their precarious relationship, which had begun in the 2nd cent. BCE, continued down to the 3th and 4th cent. CE, when Porphyry and Julian the Apostate contested the appropriateness of searching for "profound" αἰνίγματα in Moses.[332] Nevertheless, for many centuries allegorical reading of Scripture dominated within the Christian Church.

---

[331] For a historical survey on this problem, see Siegert II 136–141.

[332] See Eusebius, *H.e.* 6.19.4. The emperor Julian, *Against the Galileans* 134 D–148 A refutes the very kind of exegesis we find in Philo (G 15.1–9), where Philo contrasts the confusion of

Speaking of the 'sense of history' in Jewish exegeses, we remarked already (4.7 and 10) that even Philo did not lose touch with the present or the past. To emphasize this point, we may call attention to the fact that Hellenistic diaspora Judaism in general retained a higher historical awareness than the Sages of the Land of Israel. If confessing the "God who acts in history" is a mark of biblical faith and of authentic Judaism, then 'authentic' Judaism was surely not absent in Alexandria.

The Pseudo-Philonic sermons are an attempt to interpret history, even if modern research would not qualify the Samson story and the Jonah story as good examples. We know the names of some persons – Philo and Josephus are the most prominent among them – who engaged in writing history. On the other hand, the Jewish communities who spoke a Semitic language have no historian, not even one.[333]

Yet, there remains one thing that has to be reserved for the Jewish homeland: the *halakhah* with all its techniques. The authors we dealt with in this fourth chapter do not engage in formulating or developing the *halakhah*. This simply was not their job. On the other hand, the rules of Hillel, being adapted to the needs of jurisprudence, did not mean a thing to the Christian Church.

The liberties of allegorical explanation were tolerable in Judaism on the basis of practical compliance with the literal meaning; they only added pious thoughts to a defined practice. In Christianity, the liberties of allegorism persisted while changing their *raison d'être*. Fidelity to the Mosaic law was replaced by faith in Christ. And as Christian faith could be formulated in well-defined terms (which, of course, were to be taken literally), any typological and allegorical explanation of Scripture was legitimate which expressed that faith.

During this process of Christian self-definition Justin, Clement, Origen, and countless others learned from Alexandrian Judaism how to exploit the Bible in order to sustain a given belief. They appropriated as much as they could from Alexandrian Jewish hermeneutics in a period when the masters of this art disappeared in the catastrophe of their communities.

The Hebrew speaking Jewish scholars, who were now called Rabbis, rejected the Greek heritage. Surviving Judaism effected a profound break with the Alexandrian tradition. An art exchanged its masters.

Manuscript finished 17 Dec. 1993, the first section partly revised 25 May 1995. Thanks are due to Prof. Dr. Nikolaus Walter (Jena/Naumburg) who checked the manuscript as to content, and to Mr. Jean-Jacques Aubert (Lausanne), Mrs. Marion Salzmann (Kassel), and to the editor of this volume, who corrected grammar and style.

---

language (Genesis 11) with the Homeric myth of the Aloadae in order to show that Moses is less 'mythical'. Julian reverses this argument.

333 It seems to be symptomatic that of Josephus' first, Aramaic, edition of his *Jewish War* not even a quotation has survived. It has not been received, nor has any other historian been received, if there was one who wrote a Semitic language. This holds true until the Yosippon, a 10th cent. Hebrew adaptation of the writings of Josephus.

Chapter Five

Scripture and Canon in the Commonly Called Apocrypha and Pseudepigrapha and in the Writings of Josephus

5.1. Scripture and Canon in Jewish Apocrypha and Pseudepigrapha[1]

By Robert A. Kraft, Philadelphia
(University of Pennsylvania)

Bibliography: R. Beckwith, *The Old Testament Canon of the New Testament Church and its Background in Early Judaism* (London: SPCK 1985); G. Boccaccini, *Middle Judaism: Jewish Thought, 300 BCE to 200 CE* (Minneapolis, MN: Fortress 1991); idem, *Portraits of Middle Judaism in Scholarship and Arts: a Multimedia Catalog from Flavius Josephus to 1991* (*Quaderni di Henoch* 6; Turin: Zamorani 1993); idem, "Middle Judaism and its Contemporary Interpreters (1986–1992): Methodological Foundations for the Study of Judaisms, 300 BCE to 200 CE", *Henoch* 15 (1993) 207–233; R. H. Charles, *The Book of Enoch or 1 Enoch* (Oxford: Clarendon 1912); M. de Jonge (ed.) *The Testaments of the Twelve Patriarchs: a Critical Edition of the Greek Text* (*Pseudepigrapha Veteris Testamenti Graece* 1.2; Leiden: Brill 1978); M. R. James, "Introduction" to R. Bensly's edition of *The Fourth Book of Ezra* (*Texts and Studies* 3.2; Cambridge: University Press 1895); P. Katz (Walters), *Philo's Bible: The Aberrant Text of Bible Quotations in Some Philonic Writings and its Place in the Textual History of the Greek Bible* (Cambridge: University Press 1950); R. A. Kraft, *Barnabas and the Didache* (*The Apostolic Fathers: A New Translation and Commentary* 3, ed. by R. M. Grant; New York: Nelson 1965); idem, "Reassessing the 'Recensional Problem' in Testament of Abraham", G. Nickelsburg (ed.), *Studies on the Testament of Abraham* (*Septuagint and Cognate Studies* 6; Missoula, MT: Scholars Press 1976) 121–137; idem, "Christian Transmission of Greek Jewish Scriptures: a Methodological Probe", *Paganisme, Judaisme, Christianisme: Influences et affrontements dans le Monde Antique* (*Melanges M. Simon*, ed. A. Benoit et al.; Paris: De Boccard 1978) 207–226; idem, "Enoch and Written Authorities in the Testaments of the Twelve Patriarchs" (Report Delivered to the SBL Pseudepigrapha Symposium in Washington DC, November 1993; available on the CCAT Gopher as part of the data collection on which this summary is based); idem, "The Pseudepigrapha in Christianity" (print version in *Tracing the Threads: Studies in the Vitality of Jewish Pseudepigrapha*, ed.

[1] This is a distillation of some of the detailed information found in the electronic file "Apocrypha, Pseudepigrapha, and Scripture", available on the ccat.sas.upenn.edu gopher (access through gopher.upenn.edu: Penn Gophers: Center for Computer Analysis of Texts: Electronic Publications: Kraft) or on the URL: http://ccat.sas.upenn.edu/rs/rak/kraft.html. Contributors to this collection of data include the following members of my 1993–94 Advanced Graduate Seminar at the University of Pennsylvania: Maxine Grossman [*Joseph and Aseneth*, *Judith*], Bradford Kirkegaard, Sigrid Peterson [*1–2 Maccabees*], David Sandmel [*Jubilees*], William Stroup (Westminster Theological Seminary) [*Apcl. Abr.*, *T. Abr*, *T. Sol*].

John C. Reeves [*SBL Early Judaism and its Literature* 6; Atlanta: Scholars 1994] 55–86; updated version on CCAT Gopher [Electronic Publications: Kraft]); J. Kugel, "Early Interpretation: The Common Background of Late Forms of Biblical Exegesis", Kugel/Greer (eds.), *Early Biblical Interpretation* (Philadelphia: Westminster 1986); M. E. Stone, "Categorization and Classification of the Apocrypha and Pseudepigrapha", *Abr-Nahrain* 24 (1986) 167–177; idem, *Fourth Ezra: A Commentary on the Book of Fourth Ezra* (*Hermeneia* Series; Minneapolis, MN: Fortress 1990).

Standard abbreviations for this section (see also note 5):

AJS = P. Riessler, Altjüdisches Schrifttum ausserhalb der Bibel (Heidelberg: Kerle 1928);

CCAT = Center for Computer Analysis of Texts at the University of Pennsylvania (see n. 1, on the CCAT Gopher);

CRINT 2.1 = M. J. Mulder (ed.), Mikra: Text, Translation, Reading, and Interpretation of the Hebrew Bible in Ancient Judaism and Early Christianity (CRINT 2.1; Philadelphia: Fortress 1988);

CRINT 2.2 = Michael E. Stone (ed.), Jewish Writings of the Second Temple Period: Apocrypha, Pseudepigrapha, Qumran Sectarian Writings, Philo, Josephus (CRINT 2.2; Philadelphia: Fortress 1984);

EJMI = Robert Kraft & George Nickelsburg (eds.), Early Judaism and its Modern Interpreters (Atlanta: Scholars Press 1986);

IOUDAIOS = the electronic discussion list on early Judaism, ioudaios-l, located on the listserv@lehigh.edu.

1. Introduction

The study of the awareness, impact, and interpretations of 'scriptures' in early Judaism and early Christianity remains a very popular subject[2] but is extremely difficult to pursue with any confidence for a variety of reasons:

(1) Identification of the target period for examination presents a minor problem, although its larger dimensions usually seem to be defined in relationship to the Jewish "second Temple" in Jerusalem (roughly late 6th century BCE through mid 2nd century CE), with a primary focus on the 3rd/2nd century BCE through the 2nd century CE (from the Maccabean crisis through Bar Kochba, more or less), from which most of the preserved evidence is alleged to derive.[3]

(2) The blocks of evidence from the known and suspected sources are usually treated in relative isolation from each other, often in arbitrary and artifical groupings (e. g. Qumran, 'extracanonical early Jewish writings', New Testament, 'extracanonical early Christian materials', etc.), with only sporadic attempts to juxtapose similar materials or gain an overview of the larger pattern of relationships, or of differences, from a historical and/or literary perspective.[4]

---

[2] The specific reasons for this popularity are manifold, but in general reflect an overriding interest in evidences of continuity and/or discontinuity in the traditions that have come to be associated with the survival of classical Judaism and/or classical Christianity. See Kraft, "Bibliography on Ancient Uses of Jewish Scriptures", on the CCAT Gopher (Electronic Publications: Kraft – see n. 1 above).

[3] On the labels and periodization, see Boccaccini, Foundations (1993) 207–233; see also his *Portraits* (1993) IX–XXIX ("Introduction"); and *Middle Judaism* (1991). Boccaccini's decision to champion the label "middle Judaism" seems unfortunate to me, given the current state of research on the period that I still prefer to call, with studied vagueness, "early Judaism(s)" (post-exilic, pre-rabbinic). The difficulties of dating the supposed sources are notorious; see further below.

[4] Hopefully, the larger project of which this essay is a part will help spell an end to such

(3) Especially with reference to default categories such as 'extracanonical', it is virtually impossible in the current state of scholarship to define with precision the corpus of materials to be examined (extent), much less to agree on exactly what text forms are appropriate representations of the sources pertinent to the period under examination (transmission). This is particularly true for that body of materials conveniently called 'pseudepigrapha', which sometimes overlaps with (or is treated synonymously with) the writings called 'apocryphal', and which represents modern collections drawn from primarily Christian copies of works suspected of having a Jewish origin.[5] In most instances it is not clear whether a particular writing derives from or is representative of any known group in the early Jewish or early Christian worlds, where or when the writing originated, or how many stages of significant retouching lie between the original production and the form(s) available to us.[6]

Furthermore, it is not always clear what would constitute firm evidence of 'scriptural consciousness' – that is, of special reverential attitudes towards the localization and preservation of traditional authoritative materials in fixed written format ('book' in some sense, whether roll or codex or even inscribed ["heavenly"] tablets). We are not speaking here of reverence to traditional law and/or laws, or to its/their formulation as "covenant", or to familiarity with certain traditional stories or hymns/prayers or phrases that we find as part of what has come to be known as "Jewish Scriptures" (Hebrew Bible, TaNaKh, OT, etc.). The 'scriptural consciousness' question focuses on the extent to which authoritative law and/or tradition had come to be explicitly associated with identifiable books and writings, or perhaps vice-versa.

---

practices by providing a sufficiently nuanced survey of the atomized materials to encourage reorganization and broader syntheses to take place. Isolated treatments of the Qumran evidence or of other writings (whether canonical or not) from the same periods of Jewish history makes little sense, historically or literarily. Partial and tentative moves in more synthetic directions, especially with reference to "genre", can be seen in various works from the last two decades: e.g. CRINT 2.2 (Stone), EJMI (Kraft-Nickelsburg), OTP (Charlesworth). On the complexity of the issue, see also Stone, Categorization (1986) 167–177.

[5] Modern collections that tend towards inclusivity are well represented by Riessler's AJS (61 works) and Charlesworth's OTP (63); much more limited in scope are Kautszch's APAT (13), Charles' APOT (17) and Sparks' AOT (26 works; in Sparks, the title "apocryphal" is used for texts elsewhere usually called "pseudepigraphical"). Traditionally "the Apocrypha" refers to a collection of Jewish sources included in the Roman Catholic and Eastern Orthodox Bibles, but not in Jewish or Protestant Christian canons – some works raise particular problems: *3–4 Maccabees* and *Psalms of Solomon* are included by Eastern Christendom, but not by the Roman Catholic Church; the Latin materials gathered under the rubric "*2 Esdras*" (*5, 4* and *6 Ezra*) in the AV/(A)SV/RSV/NRSV tradition are considered as an "appendix" in the Latin Apocrypha; two forms of *Tobit* are known in Greek, and various forms of *Psalm 151*; etc.

[6] For some aspects of these issues, see Kraft, Pseudepigrapha (1994) 55–86 and also Recensional Problem (1976). In general, see EJMI and the materials discussed there. The problem of assigning precise dates to the sources is well illustrated by a glance at the summary lines in the headers and table of contents in Charlesworth's OTP, which tends to be quite optimistic about the age of the materials. The evidence from Qumran has helped to locate some of the sources more firmly in pre-Christian times (e.g. some *Enoch* materials, *Jubilees*, early forms of the *Testaments of the 12 Patriarchs* traditions, *Tobit*), although the fragmentary nature of this evidence is not always able to clarify specific problems relating to the development and transmission of the texts.

A further stage in this attempt to understand the development of text-related ideas of authority could be called 'canonical consciousness'. Under what circumstances and in what formulations does the awareness of authoritative writings ('Scripture consciousness') come to exhibit itself in terms of collections (extension) and even a limited collection (exclusion) of writings invested with special authority ('canon consciousness')?[7] It is to such issues that we turn in the following attempt at a survey of the data and attitudes presented by the surviving miscellany of allegedly Jewish texts collected under the somewhat vaguely defined rubrics of 'apocrypha and pseudepigrapha'.

It is also worth noting at the outset that textual fidelity in the treatment of 'scriptural' quotations and allusions and references during the process of textual transmission is especially subject to suspicion. As materials are copied and recopied in the context of communities in which scriptural and canonical consciousness are increasingly seen as of central importance, passages pertinent to these concerns are especially vulnerable to 'correcting' and 'harmonizing' modification. There are some interesting test cases: in the manuscript transmission of Philo's works, the texts of the biblical quotations in one set of manuscripts are radically different from those in other manuscripts of the same Philonic passages;[8] the three recensions of the epistles of Ignatius show far greater and more precise attention to 'Scripture' materials and issues in their 'longer' form than in the presumably earlier forms; similarly the form of the *Didache* that is now embedded in the *Apostolical Constitutions* exhibits a tendency to increase its 'scriptural' components in comparison to the separate form of *Didache* that was discovered 1873.[9]

The identification and exploration of such 'control' cases is an area that deserves closer attention, and the current essay will touch upon, if only marginally, some directions pertinent to such an investigation (e.g. the pos-

7 In some instances, the difficulty of making a clear distinction between 'Scripture consciousness' and 'canonical consciousness' may be present – most notably with respect to the Mosaic Pentateuch, which can be considered both as a single scriptural work and as a canonical collection (of multiple works and/or scrolls) in itself. A similar situation may have existed with reference to other multi-volumed works (e.g. Samuel-Kings, Chronicles) or single volume anthologies (e.g. the Minor Prophets, collected Psalms, collected Proverbs). The issues involved have received little attention. Part of the need for distinguishing, it seems to me, relates to the effect on perceptions that must have been caused by the development of technology from scrolls (of limited length) to small codices (similarly limited; 2nd and 3rd centuries CE) to the full-blown codices of the 4th century CE. The ability to house and access a canonical collection of Scriptures between one set of codex covers surely inspired different perceptions from those depending on the transmission of 'canonical lists' (or possibly on access to local depositories) of necessarily distinct and separate 'book' entities. Failure to distinguish interest in 'Scripture' from interest in 'canon' may produce seriously misleading results.

8 For a detailed discussion, see Katz, Philo's Bible (1950).

9 See Kraft, Barnabas (1965) 58. It should be noted that some scholars have traced the longer version of the Ignatian corpus to the same general Christian context as is supposed for the compilation of the *Apostolic Constitutions* (4th century western Syria). Studies of the development of the Jesus traditions (e.g. especially the crucifixion narratives) also tend to support this suggestion/suspicion about the growing interest in 'scriptural' warrants – one form of accretion involves the identification of supposedly relevant 'scriptural' predictions and/or models. Similarly, studies of the textual variants in quotations from Jewish Scriptures found in early Christian writings (including NT) attest much 'harmonization' to presumably more familiar wording.

sible significance of textual and/or recensional variants). But the potential obstacles presented by this phenomenon for the subject of the current essay is serious – to what extent can the evidence from a 10th century copy (for example) of a presumably early source be trusted for its evidence concerning the attitudes of the original author or editor towards Scripture/canon?[10]

With such caveats in the background, the attitude with which we have determined to pursue these related questions of 'Scripture consciousness' and 'canon consciousness' in the 'pseudepigrapha' broadly attributed to early Judaism(s) (with an eye to the preservation of most of these materials in early Christianity), then, is to be as unassuming as possible with regard to the statements and conduct of the various sources. 'Law (or covenant) consciousness' will not be considered *automatically* as 'Scripture consciousness', nor will the mention of personal names and stories and phrases that we can find in our biblical materials be taken for granted as indicators of conscious dependence on *written* formulations that were at that time considered *authoritative*.[11] It is entirely possible that for some authors, every reference to Jewish law is automatically a reference to fixed Scripture and even to a canonical collection; it is, indeed, highly probable that later readers and copyists took such connections for granted. But to assume that such was true from the outset, without firm supporting evidence, is to preclude the possibility that other perspectives may be at work. Thus we will begin with an atomistic and minimalist approach to the available evidence.

---

[10] On the general reliability of Christian copying of Jewish Scriptures, see Kraft, Transmission (1978). Whether and to what extent the same attitudes would carry over to the 'apocrypha' and 'pseudepigrapha', however, is not easy to determine or to generalize. Presumably, that which is considered scriptural and canonical received more careful treatment than other materials that were considered less authoritatively 'fixed'. There is no question that clearly Christian comments can be found in many, perhaps most, of the preserved 'pseudepigrapha', however one chooses to interpret that phenomenon ('Christian interpolation' is a favorite explanation). An interesting illustration of aspects of the situation can be seen in the *Testament of Jacob* material, which in its body evidences the usual conglomorate of presumably Jewish traditions with suspiciously Christian elements (e.g. 8:4–8), but also includes a postscript in which quite explicit scriptural and canonical references are found (11:2–3). Less dramatically, the preface to the sister document, *Testament of Isaac*, offers an explicit quotation from *Qohelet*, despite the general absence elsewhere in these texts of such biblical awareness. On the other hand, the possibility that Christian editors might sometimes *remove* 'Christian' elements from texts that they considered basically 'Jewish' should not be ingnored; see James, Introduction (1895).

[11] The relatively recently emphasized category of 'rewritten Scriptures' (or similarly), which once seemed to me appropriate (see EJMI, Charlesworth OTP, CRINT 2.2, etc.), has probably rather quickly outlived its usefulness. It assumes both the existence of particular 'Scriptures' in roughly the forms that have been transmitted in our Bibles, and the presence of developed attitudes to those materials that roughly approximate 'Scripture consciousness'. Neither of these assumptions are necessary for understanding the phenomenon, and the assumptions may discourage the possibility of asking other types of questions about the transmission and use of materials that we now find embedded in the received biblical compilations. If a new label is needed for these works, I would suggest something like 'parallels to scriptural traditions', without prejudicing the question of whether the materials in question were dependent upon or drawn directly from accounts that were already accepted as 'scriptural'. Beckwith, Canon (1985) 45–46, avoids this type of simplification by distinguishing Biblical Exposition (Midrash), Halakic Narrative, History, and Edifying Narrative (Haggadah), among others, but it is not clear that this solves the problem of prejudging the situation.

2. Categorizing the Evidence

The materials we have examined tend to fall into four separable, although sometimes somewhat overlapping, groups. (1) On the one hand, there are texts that clearly exhibit a conscious valuation of materials that have come to be called 'Scripture', and may even have a well-defined collection (canon) in view – for example, the letter of *Aristeas*, the prologue to the translation of *Sirach*, *4 Ezra* (esp. ch. 14), the (clearly Christian) *Ascension of Isaiah*, or *1–2* and *4 Maccabees*.[12] (2) At the other extreme, there are texts that provide no clear evidence for such an outlook – e.g. *Apocalypse of Elijah*, *Psalms* and *Odes of Solomon*.[13]

In between these extremes, (3) there are sources that seem to have very close connections to the content and/or the wording of what became traditional canonical Scriptures, without making any *explicit* claims about those materials (perhaps *2 Baruch* would fit here, with other works such as *Joseph and Aseneth* and Ezekiel the tragedian), and (4) sources that include a very high estimation of authoritative books and related materials, often including themselves,[14] although the items in question seldom are identified with any of the Scriptures judged to be 'canonical' in the continuous Jewish and Christian traditions.[15] It is to this last category that we turn first.

---

[12] Applying this category more broadly than only to 'apocrypha and pseudepigrapha', we would want to distinguish between 'commentary' type usage, which presents (or assumes) a continuous scriptural text that inspires comments (as, e.g., in Qumran's "Pesharim", or Philo's "*Questions*" and most other Philonic treatises, or, in a somewhat different sense, Josephus'self-consciously biblically based *Antiquities* 1–11 [compare Ezekiel the tragedian, whose fragments and chosen genre do not betray the same sort of selfconsciousness; similarly, pseudo-Philo, *Biblical Antiquities*, and the Qumran *Genesis Apocryphon*]), 'prooftexting' collections (with or without attendant comments; see Qumran's *Testimonia* and *Florilegia* fragments), formula quotations from Scriptures (employed in various ways and various connections, as in some Qumran writings, Philo, Josephus, Paul, etc.), and explicit references to scriptural writings (without necessarily including the contents), such as lists and descriptions. All these constitute conscious and explicit evidence. For a more extensive, and somewhat differently focused, breakdown of the "sources of evidence", see Beckwith, Canon (1985) 45–46 (and above, n. 11).

[13] In general, 'poetic' and 'wisdom' type of writings tend to display less obvious Scripture consciousness or parallels than most other genres (obvious exceptions include *Wisdom of Solomon* and *Sibylline Oracles*). To some extent this may be due to the difficulty of isolating characteristically scriptural poetic language as somehow distinguishable from more 'ordinary' forms of prayer or praise. On the relatively ahistorical perspectives of Jewish 'wisdom' in our period, see the comments of Kugel, Interpretation (1986), esp. 48–49.

[14] Not unexpectedly, this sort of claim predominates among the "apocalypses". Works that refer to themselves as writings to be read and/or preserved include:
Enoch's First Book (*1 Enoch* 14:1); *Enoch's Similitudes* (*1 Enoch* 37:1); *Astronomical Enoch Book* (*1 Enoch* 72:1, 81–82); *Enoch Dream Visions* (*1 Enoch* 83:1 [implicit]); *Enoch's Testament* (*1 Enoch* 92:1); *Enoch to Methusaleh* (*1 Enoch* 108:1); *2 Enoch* 1 a [AOT], see 36:1f[long], 54:1 [= AOT 13:76], 68:1f [long] – on chapter and verse divisions in *2 Enoch*, see below, n. 18; *Testament of Isaac* (1:1, 2:11, 3:10, 10:8–9, etc.); *Testament of Jacob* (1:2); *Assumption [Testament] of Moses* (1:16, 10:11); *Testament of Solomon* (15:4); *Ascension of Isaiah* (1:3 ff, but see 11:39 ff); *Baruch* (1:14); *2 (Syriac Apocalypse of) Baruch* (77:12 ff, 77:78 ff); *3 (Greek Apocalypse of) Baruch* (1:1); *4 (Latin Apocalypse of) Ezra* (12:37); *6 Ezra* (15:2); *Greek Apocalypse of Ezra* (7:9 ff); *Sirach* 50:27–29; (see also *Life of Adam & Eve* 50 and the NT *Apocalypse/Revelation* 22:10 and 18–19).

[15] Interestingly, parts of the Enochic materials were included among 'Scriptures' for some ('marginal') early Christian representatives such as Tertullian (*De Cultu Feminarum* 1.3) and Mani

3. A Starting Point: Scripture before Moses' Scriptures (Or, In the Beginning God Inscribed the Heavenly Tablets)

Sparks' AOT includes twelve entries that claim to deal with persons and events in the period prior to the Sinai revelation, including two in which Moses also is a key participant.[16] From the viewpoint of the respective story settings, we would not expect Adam or Enoch or Abraham or the Patriarchs or even the early Moses to refer to the written Torah of Moses as a present reality, although they might sometimes be depicted as expecting its arrival in the future. Nevertheless, some of them do show a strong 'Scripture consciousness', in which 'Scripture' begins with, or is coextensive with, the "heavenly tablets" that are, sometimes, made known to God's select agents (human or angelic).[17] Indeed, one of the key issues in the book of *Jubilees* is the extent to which Moses is viewed as a conduit for exposing the preexisting tablets and their contents.

3.1. *The Situation in* Jubilees

Jubilees ties a number of related threads together as Moses prepares to receive Torah on Sinai. Not only do the "heavenly tablets" appear frequently as the locus of authority for a variety of matters – for what is destined to happen, past or future (16:3; 32:20–26; 23:32), but also as a record of what does happen (19:9; 30:5), especially for reference in future judgment situations (5:13; 16:9; 24:33; 30:18–23; 31:32; 36:10), and as a firm deposit of legal/liturgical law (3:10; 3:31; 4:5; 4:32; 6:17; 6:23–35; 16:28; 18:19; 28:6; 32:10;

(if his *Book of Giants* was of Enochic origin, as it seems), but these decisions were not accepted more generally by those whose influence determined what became 'canon'. In the early third century CE, both Tertullian and Origen comment, without necessarily agreeing, on Jewish rejection of the Enoch materials as authoritative, and most extant Christian commentators from the fourth century onward are suspicious of those who use writings identified with Enoch. For a convenient, if sometimes overzealous, catalog of "The Influence of Enoch on Patristic Literature", see Charles, 1 Enoch (1912) lxxxi–xcv.

[16] More than a dozen separable sources are covered by this group, since "*1 Enoch*" is a library of at least six distinct writings (see n. 14 above). The entries in Sparks are: *Jubilees*, *Life of Adam and Eve*, *1 Enoch*, *2 Enoch*, *Apocalypse of Abraham*, *Testament of Abraham*, *Testament of Isaac*, *Testament of Jacob*, *Laddar of Jacob*, *Joseph and Aseneth*, *Testaments of the 12 Patriarchs*, *Assumption of Moses*.

[17] Apart from *Jubilees*, the "heavenly tablets" are mentioned as directly available to Enoch (e.g. *1 En.* 103:2), Jacob (*Pr.Jos* B.1 = C), the patriarch Asher (*T.Asher* 7:5), and also to the angels (*1 En.* 108:7, cf. 93:1). (Later they are known also to Isaiah [*Asc.Isa.* 9:22]). They can be transcribed and transmitted to other humans (e.g. *1 En.* 81:1, 82:1–2). In *2 En.* 22:12 [= AOT 10:1] the recording angel Vreveil dictates heavenly books to Enoch who produces 360 [or 366] books (23:6; see 68:1–2). The contents of the tablets are described variously: they hold information about the future (*Pr.Jos.* B.1 = C), and record events that happen (*T.Levi* 5:4), but are especially relevant for judging human activities (*1 En.* 107:1, *Asc.Isa.* 9:22; see *1 En.* 106:19, 108:3–10, and possibly *T.Judah* 20:3f). It is a short step in some of the literature from these tablets to the "book(s) of life" by which human actions are judged – in *T.Abr.* 13:21ff, it is Enoch who serves as "scribe of righteousness" for this purpose.

33:10–12) – but the line between those tablets and the ones Moses receives is rather blurred (see, for example, the opening reference in 1:27–29 and the closing passage in 50:13, where the tablets that are written out are placed into Moses' hands). It is not entirely clear whether or to what extent the heavenly tablets are considered preexistent to the historical occurrence of the information they contain (as in "predestination") or whether, especially with regard to human history, they function primarily as repositories of accurate information on what takes place in human history. In any event, the authority of Moses' tablets and records seems clearly dependent on the heavenly tablets.

It is also noteworthy that in *Jubilees*, reference is made to various other early materials preserved in writing from various sources: Enoch is shown everything and writes it down (4:17–24, see also 21:10), the Watchers leave astrological inscriptions discovered by Cainan that lead him to sin (8:2–4), Noah/Shem produce and transmit written material (10:12–14 [on cures], 21:10, see also 8:11), Abraham is enabled to read and transcribe the Hebrew books of his fathers (12:25–27, see also 21:10 [on eating restrictions]), Jacob sees in a dream seven tablets from heaven with information about the future which he then transcribes from memory (32:20–26).

In this context, the treatment of Moses' role as a recipient and transmitter of authoritative written material is interesting. God (or his angelic agent) writes the "book of the first law" for Moses, including ancient calendric instructions that had been forgotten in more recent times (6:19–22). Similarly, in 30:11–12 Moses is told to give commands prohibiting marriage to gentiles, for which reason "I have written for you in the words of the law" details about Dinah and the Shechemites (see Gen 34). Formulas such as "it is written and ordained" (5:17; 49:17), or similar indirect statements (e.g. 3:14; 4:30; 6:12; 30:17), occur with some regularity. Except for a few general statements (1:5, 7, 26 "write everything I tell you on this mountain;" 2:1 "write the complete history of the creation", [but see 1:27 "write for Moses from the beginning of creation"!]), Moses is not usually depicted as independently involved, and the impression is that everything is tightly controlled by the heavenly authorities and tablets (see 23:32; 50:13), which are reflected in the instructions given to humans. All the more noteworthy, then, is 33:13–20, where Moses is told to establish an irrevocable law concerning incest (based on the Reuben-Bilhah story; see *T. Reuben* 3:10ff, Gen 35:22; 49:4), for which a consistent law had not formerly been revealed (see Lev 18:8; 20:11; and Deut 22:30; 27:20, for relevant laws).

Thus *Jubilees* is clearly conscious of the role of Moses as recipient and restater of authoritative heavenly instructions, and many events found in the biblical Pentateuch appear as well in *Jubilees*, but often with somewhat different details. Nevertheless, Moses functions in the shadow of the "heavenly tablets", and there are various indications that other ancient revelational sources are also at least theoretically known and/or available. 'Canon' does not seem to be an issue, and 'Scripture' is far from being well defined.

3.2. Production and/or Transmission of Earthbound Books: Other Scriptures before 'the Scriptures'

The transfer of the contents of the heavenly tablets to earthly books, as described in *Jubilees*, is a fairly widespread theme in this body of texts (see also n. 17 above). The Enochic *Astrological Book* has Enoch producing books on the basis of what he has learned and understood from the heavenly tablets (81–82), and in 81:6 he is instructed to use the last year of his earthly presence to teach his children ("another law" in MS B) and write things down for them. While the content of these books includes astrological mysteries and secrets, it seems to focus just as much on how to walk righteously.

Similarly, the *Testament/Miscellany* near the end of the "*1 Enoch*" corpus has Enoch writing another book (92:1) and then reading from the presumably earthly books produced (by him?) on the basis of the heavenly (e.g. 93:1 ff, cf. 103:2), with special focus on promoting righteousness. It is interesting to note in passing that in the text's perceived future, "law (or perhaps "covenant") for sinners" is associated with the cryptic Noah (93:4), and a "law (or "covenant") with a fence for all generations" seems associated with Moses (93:6). Reference is also made to an "eternal law" that sinners distort (99:2), although it is not clearly identified with any "book". In 104, there appears to be some confusion about what is written by and for whom – at very least, some record concerning the righteous (104:1) and concerning sinners (104:7; see 98:8) is made, presumably in the heavenly tablets, but there is also a warning not to alter the words of truth by writing false books (104:9 ff, see 98:15; 99:2). In contrast, the righteous and wise will be given "books" (104:12–13) from which to learn the ways of truth.

2 Enoch has its share of references to important earthly books associated with Adam, Seth (var. Joseph), and Enoch (33:1–12 [= AOT 11:22–29][18]; the longer version also includes Enosh, Kainan, Maleleil and Arad), and itself (1a:1[short]). Other Enochic compositions (numbered at least 360 or 366 in 23:6 [= AOT 10:7] and 68:1–2[long]) are mentioned in 36:1 [= AOT 11:35] and 47:1–2 [= AOT 13:49–50] (derived from the Lord's lips; the Lord also produces books in 33:3 var), with the emphasis on handing them down to posterity (see also 48:6–8 [= AOT 13:53–55]; 54:1 [= AOT 13:76]; 68:2[long]); and Enoch also seems to be depicted as the recorder of people's acts and words, presumably for reference at the judgment (50:1 [= AOT 13:57]; 53:2 [= AOT 13:74]). The mention of a large number of books is reminiscent of the passage in *4 Ezra* 14 (see below), although the details differ considerably.

---

[18] There are two major recensions of *2 Enoch*, to which APOT and OTP assign coordinated chapter and verse divisions to facilitate referencing. APOT calls the generally longer version "A" and the generally shorter "B", while OTP calls the former "J" and the latter "A". AOT, on the other hand, includes only the shorter version and gives it different chapter and verse divisions. AJS also seems to follow the shorter version, for the most part, but with the APOT(-OTP) chapters. In the present essay, the more standard chapter and verse divisions are given from OTP, with AOT divisions in brackets where appropriate, and "long" used to denote the relatively longer version.

There are a number of references to book(s)/scripture of Enoch in the *Testaments of the Twelve Patriarchs*, none of which can be located with confidence in the preserved Enochic materials. The overriding theme of these passages is the predicted moral failures of the generations to come:

T. Simeon 5:4 (warnings about envy and sexual promiscuity), *T. Levi* 10:5 (prediction about the naming of God's house in the context of the wickedness of Levi's descendants), *T. Levi* 14:1 (a "scripture" of Enoch predicts impious acts), *T. Levi* 16:1 f. (predicts period of straying from truth), *T. Judah* 18:1 (evil actions in the last days), *T. Zebulon* 3:4 (reference to a "scripture" of a law of Enoch on levirite marriage; see Deut 25:5–10), *T. Dan* 5:6 (on sexual evils), *T. Naphthali* 4:1 (after a reference to the fall of the watchers), *T. Benjamin* 9:1 (in the context of warnings against sexual misconduct), see also *T. Naphthali* 5:8 (refers to "a holy scripture" appearing, using formulae familiar from the Enoch and heavenly tablets passages).

Furthermore, there is clearly a battle over the presence or absence of explicit references to Enoch, and also to the heavenly tablets, in the background of the preserved texts of the *Testaments.*[19] Manuscript c and its allies (hij) are the most obvious 'anti Enoch' witnesses, relative to the main stream of textual attestation, and the same group avoids identifying the tablets as "heavenly".[20] Why this should be can only be conjectured. It seems less likely that the Enoch references are additions to an earlier text that made little or no reference to Enoch, than the opposite. Factors that could contribute to the demise of Enoch include the failure to find appropriately corresponding passages in the preserved Enoch literature, and the hesitation to use 'Scripture' language in connection with Enoch materials. Perhaps a general distancing from certain forms of apocalyptic traditions also played a role (as, e. g. with suppression (?) of references to the formerly "heavenly" tablets?), although much apocalyptic influence remains in all full texts of the *Testaments.* Possibly the change from "Enoch" in the Greek manuscripts of *Barnabas* 4:3 to the more familiar "Daniel" in the Latin version of that passage reflects the same sort of motivation.

3.3. Conclusions Regarding Pre-Scriptural 'Scriptures'

This emphasis on instructive, presumably authoritative, earthbound books is much wider than simply Enoch and his pre-deluvian associates or the literature associated with them. As we have already seen, Noah and Shem, then Abraham and Jacob, and finally Moses function in *Jubilees* as transcribers and conveyers of the truths of the heavenly tablets. In the *Life of Adam and Eve* 50, the widowed Eve instructs her children to write what their parents have told them on tablets of stone and clay, for preservation through any future calamaties, and Seth does this (51:3; on Adam's revelation to Seth see also the *Apocalypse of Adam*, start and finish). *4 Ezra* 3 mentions Abraham as a special recipient of secret knowledge about the last days, and *2 Baruch* 57:2 identifies Abraham with knowledge of the then unwritten law. In the

[19] For details, see Kraft, Written Authorities (1993). The textcritical data is available conveniently in de Jonge, Testaments (1978).

[20] The main passages are: *T. Levi* 5:4; 14:1; 16:1; *T. Judah* 18:1; *T. Zebulon* 3:4; *T. Naphtali* 4:1; *T. Asher* 2:10; 7:5; see also *T. Dan* 5:6.

Prayer of Joseph fragments, Jacob transcribes the heavenly tablets he has seen; he is also the speaker in the patriarchal *Testaments*, with their several allusions to the heavenly tablets (above, n. 17).

Moses, as would be expected, is frequently associated with the delivery and transmission of divine law, although it is remarkable how infrequently this is spoken of in terms of books or writings. *Jubilees* sees the work of Moses against the background of the heavenly tablets, as has been noted. But even in the *Testament [Assumption] of Moses*, set after Sinai and focusing on the legacy left by Moses, the references to writings appear to concern predictive/apocalyptic themes as found in this book (e.g. 10:11; 11:1; see also 1:16; 3:11–13), not to anything recognizable as scriptural Torah – Moses is mainly an apocalyptic revealer and an intercessor, within the context of God's oft mentioned covenant and commandments.[21]

A brief note is in order at this point concerning the *Sibylline Oracles*, a variegated body of literature that can make its own claim to "prophetic" authority (e.g. 3:809 ff)[22] while at the same time occasionally showing knowledge of Jewish scriptural materials (e.g. prologue: 24; 3:246, 257, 284). But the *Oracles* contain such a mixture of materials (Jewish, Christian, and other), from various periods and dealing with a wide range of themes, that they deserve more detailed attention than can be given here. Doubtless various portions of this anthology would fit into different categories treated in the present essay.

4. Works Showing Explicit Knowledge of what Comes to Be Canonical Scriptural Literature

The Latin apocalypse of *4 Ezra* (= *2 Esdras* 3–14) provides an interesting transition to this category of literature. In *4 Ezra* 14, Moses is depicted as having received from God on Sinai "words" to be made public and others to remain secret (14:6). Ezra knows, as he is about to end his earthly work, that God's "law has been burned"[23] so that guidance for humans is lacking, and asks to be given the spirit to enable him to "write everything that has happened in the world from the beginning, the things which were written in your law" (14:21–22). Permission is granted, and Ezra becomes a new Moses,

[21] The materials in 5:3 ff. deserve special mention, since the emended introductory formula (see Charles, APOT ad loc.) could be seen as suggesting a string of quotations here, although the contents suggest a summary of aspects of degeneration in the last times, similar to what is present elsewhere in this book, as well as in other works such as the *Testaments*.

[22] "The Sibyl" is indeed treated as of special authority by some Christian authors (e.g. Justin Martyr *Apol.* 44.12, Lactantius), although it is not always clear exactly what materials are in view in those instances. They are not likely to have been identical to the texts preserved for us.

[23] It is striking that in the various descriptions of the destruction of the first temple in 'early Jewish' literature, mention is seldom made of the destruction of scriptural books. Even in the detailed description in *4 Ezra* 10:21–23, it is not explicitly mentioned, unless in the general reference to the plundering of the ark or the concluding reference to the loss of "the seal of Zion".

taking five trained scribes for 40 days to restore the public and private books "in characters that they [the scribes] did not know" (14:42) – a total of 94, with 24 public but 70 restricted "for the wise" (14:44–45). Thus we have here a canon of sorts, or two canons, with sufficiently ambiguous description to embrace both the traditional canon of Judaism (although no real details are given in *4 Ezra*) and other esoteric literature such as was encountered above (note especially *2 Enoch* 23:6, etc., above).[24]

The thematically similar apocalypse known as (Syriac) *2 Baruch* seems to have a concept of authoritative written materials but does not draw much attention to them, unless the "two tablets" that an angel rescues from the threatened Temple in 6:7 are an exception. *2 Baruch* is replete with references to "law", which is unambiguously central to its message and is connected with the figure of Abraham, who already had this law while it was yet unwritten (57:2), and of Moses, on Sinai (e.g. 4:5; 59:4 ff). The readers are exhorted to transmit the traditions of the law to their children, just as they themselves received these traditions from their own fathers (84:2–9). Thus although the author seems to conceive of the law as written, it is not normal for *2 Baruch* explicitly to identify the law as a written "scriptural" record or to quote from it in that format.[25] "The law" frequently is found in association with references to wisdom, understanding, the covenant, and commandments, but not books. Even in the accounts of the histories of Moses (59) and of Josiah (66), there is no mention or focus on books; perhaps it is taken for granted – or perhaps the author does not habitually conceptualize things in this manner.[26] The revelation to Moses is broader even than the revered law, including various secrets of the universe (59:7 ff). Baruch's ability to receive and understand the secrets is also presented as special (e.g. 56:2; 81:4), and may reflect a similar vision of the reconstitution of (destroyed) revelation, as spelled out more explicitly in *4 Ezra*.

Much more straightforward, less ambiguous, regarding the presence and symbolic value of 'Scriptures' is the evidence from the *Epistle of Aristeas*, on the translation of the book or books of Jewish law (see 10, 15, 28, 30, 38,45, 144 [Moses], 176 [on fine skins], 312 [works], 316 f. [biblos, books]) – material very similar to passages in Philo and Josephus, some 200 years later –

---

[24] For more extensive discussion of this material, see Stone, Fourth Ezra (1990) ad loc. The author of *4 Ezra* seems to know some passages from what comes to be Scripture, in addition to events such as the general history of Israel (e.g. 3:4 ff) and the story of Moses as reflected here – e.g. 12:11 refers to Daniel's vision.

[25] In 4:2, the Lord refers to what he "said" about Jerusalem, with a passage echoing Isa 49:16, and also speaks about revelations to Adam, Abraham and Moses concerning the (new) Temple.

[26] *2 Baruch* 85 also makes reference to righteous ones and prophets who are important in the history of the people addressed. But their importance is as intercessors for the sins of the people, not as producers of scriptural materials. When *2 Baruch* reports on traditions that are also found in what developed into the Jewish Scriptures, there does not seem to be any characteristic borrowing of words or specific details. Indeed, such accounts as the angelic consorting with human women (see Gen 6:1–4) and the fate of Jeremiah after the fall of Jerusalem are significantly different from what come to be the biblical versions. The role of prediction of the future is present, but focuses on the contents of this very book. Similarly, Baruch is seen as one who writes exhortation and instruction to the exiles (77:12 ff), but this is not presented as anything particularly special or unusual.

although Aristeas provides no evidence of knowledge of other early Jewish scriptural works (unless they are hinted at in 28 and 30).

The prologue to the Greek translation of *Sirach*, on the other hand, makes specific reference to books of "the law, the prophets, and the others" as the source of great "instruction and wisdom", but does not name (or number; compare the similar passage in Josephus) the books as such, although the author seems to know that they exist in Greek translation as well as in presumably Hebrew originals, like his grandfather's book that he is translating. The body of the book of *Sirach*, however, gives no explicit references to scriptural passages, although in wisdom's paean of self-praise "the law which Moses commanded us" is identified with "the book of the covenant" (24:23), and elsewhere various biblical people and events are mentioned especially in the "praise of the famous" section (44–49/50).

Thus a core 'canon' of sorts can be said to exist in the form of the Mosaic book(s) in the 2nd century BCE, in at least some Jewish circles in Palestine/Israel and in Egypt/Alexandria, and from about that time we find at least one person also associating other books with "the law". There is no indication in the prologue to *Sirach* that its vague list of three categories of writings represented a closed collection. How the translator related his grandfather's "instruction and wisdom" to the aforementioned books is not clear, nor how the grandfather himself might have viewed these issues (50:27–29 makes no comparisons; but see 24:33).

From about the same general period, or slightly later, we find a much briefer "praise of ancient zealous heros" in *1 Macc* 2:51–60, vaguely tied to language about "the law" (2:50, 64, 67–68). No mention of books or writings occurs in this context, but it is clear that the traditions preserved in what came to be "Bible" are in view – on Abraham, Joseph, Phinehas, Joshua, Caleb, David, Elijah, the three Israelites in the flaming furnace, and Daniel. Elsewhere in *1 Maccabees*, the "books of the law" and "the book of the covenant" are mentioned (1:56–57; are they the same?), and in 3:48 "the book of the law" functions as something to consult about important matters, as when the gentiles consult their idols! In 7:17, a quotation from a written source is provided (see Ps 79:2b–3) in good formulaic style.

The work known as *2 Maccabees*, purportedly written by Judean Jews to their Egyptian co-religionists (1:1), also knows "the records" and "the writing" about Jeremiah (2:1 and 4, but these traditions are not in the 'biblical' materials as we know them) and "the records and memoirs" of Nehemiah, who collected various books about "kings and prophets, and the writings of David", etc. (2:13) – an activity emulated by Judas Maccabeus (2:14). There is a reference to the song of Moses (7:6), and as preparation for battle, Judas has Eleazar "read aloud from the holy book" (8:23). Clearly there is "Scripture consciousness" here, but exactly what it denotes as "the holy book" and how far it extends to the various written materials that are mentioned is not clear.

With *4 Maccabees*, we have probably moved into the first century of the common era, working with similar perspectives, or at least some of the same traditions, as are found in the two aforementioned *books of the Maccabees.*

But in *4 Maccabees*, "Scriptures" play a much more obvious role, even when the same story is told regarding the widow and her sons (*2 Macc* 7). The exhortations in *4 Macc* 13:9–17 and again in 16:16–21 (see also 16:3) recount stories of steadfastness, especially Isaac, Daniel, and the three Hebrews in the fiery furnace, while in 18:10–19, the list is expanded and specific scriptural books are mentioned by name or in groups: Law and Prophets, the scripture of Isaiah, a psalm of David, a proverb of Solomon, a word of Ezekiel, and the song of Moses. Moses is also explicitly quoted in 17:19 (from Deut 33:3). We are clearly viewing here a perspective conscious of a wide array of scriptural writings, although the evidence is insufficient to demonstrate more than a vague nod in the direction of what will become 'canon'.

Although it is not directly focused on the same developments, the work known as *3 Maccabees* deserves mention here as well. It is aware of many of the scriptural traditions of Judaism, and refers to the law being read to Ptolemy (1:12) as well as quoting a word of the Lord from Lev 26:44 (6:15). That Jews celebrated with "thanksgiving and psalms" (6:36) is probably not a reference to 'scriptural' texts.

In the apocryphal *Book of Baruch*, Moses is commanded to write the law (2:28), and there is reference to fulfilment of what was written in the law of Moses (2:2). In the appended section, probably originally from another source, wisdom is identified with law as the book of God's commands (4:1).

A number of 'pseudepigraphic' writings with strong evidence of Christian reworking (if not composition) deserve brief mention in this category.

The *Ascension of Isaiah* reflects a very interesting jumble of interests, motivations and material. At one level, secrecy and private transmission (not in writing) of visionary materials is the theme (esp. 5–11). This may be in conflict with the opening section that talks of the recording and transmitting of the visions of Hezekiah and Isaiah. At least 4:19 ff. is explicit in its awareness of public written authoritative materials, especially focusing on visions, parables, proverbs and psalms—with the twelve minor prophets named,[27] along with David and Solomon (compare *4 Macc* 18:10 ff, noted above). In 2:6, there is also explicit reference to the "book of the kings of Judah and Israel". But note the conspicuous absence throughout of references to Moses or his law/covenant. Earlier righteous persons are mentioned in 9:7 ff. (Adam, Abel, Enoch) and 9:27 f. (Adam, Abel, Seth), and Isaiah is even said to have seen the heavenly tablets regarding human deeds (9:22). But except for general references to Manasseh's repudiation of "commands and precepts/words" associated with Hezekiah and Isaiah (1:7; see 2:1), there is little "nomic" consciousness (2:5 lists some sins).

The following three works that associate themselves with Ezra/Esdras or Sedrach are clearly interrelated. Their main focus is the revelation they pro-

[27] The category of 'prophets' receives occasional mention elsewhere in this literature, but not usually explicitly with reference to writings, unless the idea of the "words of the prophets" is stretched in that direction (see e.g. *T. Levi* 16:1)—in *2 Baruch* 85 the prophets are noted as intercessors for the sins of the people (see also *4 Ezra* 7:106 ff) while in *Apocalypse of Elijah* 3:52, the deeds of the prophets are the focus.

vide, especially in the form of a narrative about angelic-guided trips to heavenly and nether regions. The human hero constantly questions the divine judgments and asks for leniency for humankind.

The *Greek Apocalypse of Ezra* contains an explicit reference to "the scriptures" (2:22) and in that passage seems to want to quote God's word to encourage leniency in God's actions. Otherwise, there are the expected references to God's covenant and commandments (5:18–20), and to a variety of 'biblical' personages and events (2:10f. [Adam]; 2:19f. [Sodom; also 7:12]; 3:10 [Abraham, with a reference to God's promise to him]; 5:22 [Enoch, Elijah, Moses, Patriarchs]; 7:6 [Elijah]), but no preoccupation with the 'writtenness' of such materials. The apocalypse itself is referred to as a "book" to be transcribed and believed (7:9–12).

The *Apocalypse of Sedrach* is somewhat more overtly oriented to 'scriptural' authority in that it considers inattention to God's word "in the gospels" to be a reason for punishment (14:10), and it quotes "Scripture" in various ways (14:9; 15:2; 15:6; compare 7:7–8). Law and commandments, apart from the disobedience of Adam and of the Angels in not worshipping Adam (4:4–6; 5:2), receive little attention beyond the comment that gentiles without the law can keep the law (14:5; 15:6). Fewer references to Jewish biblical stories or persons are found in this short work.

The even shorter *Vision of Ezra* shows none of these particular features that have been identified in its sister texts regarding 'Scripture' and Jewish scriptural traditions, although it does have one atypical condemnatory reference to Herod's killing of the infants in Christian tradition (37–39) – the reference to "doctors of the law" who don't practice what they teach (46) does not seem particularly relevant.

The *Testament of Solomon* contains apparent allusions to ideas and events that are present in both the Jewish and Christian Scriptures, and in the apocryphal and pseudepigraphic literatures. But the only explicit reference to a written source is the quotation from "Scripture" (Ps 118:22, often found in Christian texts) in *T. Sol.* 23:4. In general, the language of law, promises, covenant or commandments is not used in this writing.

5. Other Materials Reflecting Traditions that Come to Be Scriptural, without Focusing Explicitly on 'Scripture'

There are numerous writings, including some that locate themselves in pre-Sinai settings, that could be said to parallel or reflect what came to be scriptural traditions, without betraying any awareness of such a connection or consciousness. It would be difficult to draw any general conclusions from the evidence of this relatively undigested miscellany.

Probably the most comprehensive of these sources is the *Biblical Antiquities* associated with the name "Pseudo-Philo". This fascinating alternative version of most of the traditions of Israel from Adam through Saul does not seem to rely on any explicit 'Scripture consciousness' to tell its story, although it is filled with what we could call 'scriptural content'. The same sort of things can be said for the *Joseph and Aseneth* story, which does talk about heavenly books in connection with the recording of Aseneth's name in them (15:3 f) and the transmission of heavenly truths through Levi (22:8 f), but otherwise is relatively unconcerned about such things. Passing reference to the marriage of Joseph and Aseneth is found in Gen 41:45 (see 41:50; 46:20), without any elaboration.

In the *Apocalypse of Abraham*, the parallels with traditions reflected in Jewish scriptures are strong but are never presented as dependent on written documents, or as reflecting their authority, although there are some indications of awareness (if not dependence) of written material. Similarly with the *Testament of Abraham*, which has no explicit reference to authoritative Scripture.

The *Lives of the Prophets* clearly presupposes a wealth of information and respect for the various persons it eulogizes, but it's approach to the subject is not explictly 'book' oriented, and indeed, some of its stories are not to be found in the surviving "Scriptures" of Judaism.

The *Paraleipomena of Jeremiah* also tells of Bible related episodes, and does show some concern for written instructions and commands, such as the roll carried by the eagle to Babylon and back (6–7), which includes the words of the Lord (6:20) – with similarities to *2 Baruch*. The text also refers to Isaiah as a speaker of a remembered revelatory saying (9:20), and to the failure of the people to keep God's precepts (6:21). But there is no evidence of an awareness or focus on 'Scripture', much less on a scriptural collection.

The fragmentary *Apocalypse of Zephaniah* and *Anonymous Apocalypse* preserved in Coptic add nothing significant to the picture. The latter contains several references to writing and scrolls in the context of the angels and the Lord and the adversary recording the good and bad deeds of humans (1:9–10; 2:15; 3:2; 3:9). There are several allusions to 'biblical events' and persons (2:9; 3:10), but without any hint that these are Scripture based materials. One concrete reference to those who are punished for hearing "the word of God" but not observing it adequately (3:16) could be relevant for the question of 'Scripture consciousness'. The Greek Apocalypse *3 Baruch* is similarly conversant with some themes and figures found in traditional Scriptures, without showing any significant book consciousness.

Judith is a story that only very remotely parallels the Jewish scriptural tradition, but does mention some relevant events (chap. 5, Dinah in 9:2) and reveals an understanding of Jewish law: one must not eat (or even touch) the first fruits. But even when Sinai is mentioned, there is no explicit mention of law or commandments or Scripture. In *Tobit*, the situation is somewhat similar, although more clearly focused on obeying the traditional laws and customs (e. g. 4:5–19; 12:7–10) in a Jerusalem centered context (see 1:4–6; 13:8 f; 14:5). There are passing allusions to the ancients (4:12; 8:6) and the 'appendix' in chapter 14 speaks explicitly of Jonah's prediction about the fall of Nineveh. But the only clear references to written materials are the angel's command that Tobit write this story "in a book" (12:20) and Tobit's subsequent writing of the concluding prayer in chapter 13.

More extensive in its scriptural parallels, and quite different in format is *Wisdom of Solomon*, which especially in its latter half includes poetic 'homiletic' sections on various related themes such as the foolishness of idolatry (13–15), which transitions into a treatment of the exodus setting (16) that highlights the ten plagues and deliverance (17–19). But for all of its obvious concern for matters that we would describe as 'biblically related', there is no explicit reference to books or writings as sources of the information.

6. Writings in which the Scriptural Traditions Play no Obvious Role

The line between general knowledge of the events, persons, and themes that we find in Scripture, and no significant awareness of the same is difficult to draw. The *Apocalypse of Elijah*, which is clearly Christian in its preserved form, is a case in point. It knows about God's law and the covenant and even the "glorious promises" (1:13–14), and the Lord as creator of the heavens (1:15), and mentions the deeds of the prophets (3.52), but in general it is much more interested in its end-time themes, and presents no concentration of pertinent evidence.

Also concerned with God's impending judgment and his "word" about it (16:35) is the brief 'prophecy' known as *6 Ezra* (= *2 Esdras* 15–16), which is to be spoken and also written as trustworthy and true (15:1–2). There is no way to assess this author's knowledge of or attitude towards other writings, including those we call Jewish scriptures.

Similarly, *Psalms of Solomon* 4 does refer positively to lawkeeping and lawknowing, but otherwise there is little of relevance for our purposes in that collection. Nor is there anything in the patently Christian collection of *Odes of Solomon* (which in general want to sing the praises of the indwelling God and God's Son) to suggest any attitude of authority towards any scriptural writing or corpus, with the possible exception that the "letter" "written by God's finger" of Ode 23 seems to be an authorization for divine rule (like a stele set up in public) and reflects the idea that God instructs in writing.

7. Conclusions and Prospects

The main interest of this sketchy essay has been to explore the extent to which the miscellany of 'apocryphal and pseudepigraphical' sources show an awareness of or interest in authoritative written materials, and when such is found, the focus of such awareness. As would be expected from the nature and extent of the materials examined, there is no single pattern. There are several sources that are clearly directly relevant for discussions of the development of scriptural and even canonical consciousness as traditionally conceived. Detailed references in these sources are heavily weighted towards the Pentateuch, with a smattering of quotations from or statements about extrapentateuchal literature. A few other sources seem largely irrelevant or unrewarding for such discussions at any controlled level.

Otherwise, many of these sources see the pre-Moses era as an active period of transmission of heavenly knowledge and direction. Some of them connect the early revelations with the work of Moses, including the two tablets of law. Many sources show a central interest in God's law and covenant with Israel, but these are seldom connected explicitly with transmitted writings. Similarly, many sources connect to themes and stories that parallel the contents of what have become traditional Scriptures, without showing awareness of the latter as written authorities.

Whether this sort of evidence is adequate to recreate an ancient Jewish (and later, Christian) mentality that is less concerned with 'scriptural' and 'canonical' issues than we have become accustomed to think is difficult to determine, but the possibility deserves further exploration. It is not difficult to conceive of situations in which the transmission of these 'scriptural' materials is not connected to writings at all, but takes place in contexts of instruction, exhortation, and praise that are unaware of, or even antithetical to, the developments of literature as authoritative. Progress in the understanding and appreciation of properly 'scriptural' orientation and interpretation, with its 'canonical' offshoots, cannot afford to ignore investigating such possible alternatives.

5.2. Josephus on Canon and Scriptures

By STEVE MASON, Toronto
(York University)

with ROBERT A. KRAFT, Philadelphia
(University of Pennsylvania)[1]

Bibliography: P. R. ACKROYD/C. F. EVANS, *From the Beginnings to Jerome* (CHB 1; Cambridge: Cambridge UP 1970); H. W. ATTRIDGE, *The Interpretation of Biblical History in the Antiquitates Judaicae* (Missoula: Scholars 1976); idem, "Josephus and his Works", *Jewish Writings of the Second Temple Period: Apocrypha, Pseudepigrapha, Qumran Sectarian Writings, Philo, Josephus* (CRINT 2.2, ed. Michael E. Stone; Philadelphia: Fortress 1984) 210–227; D. E. AUNE, *Prophecy in Early Christianity and the Ancient Mediterranean World* (Grand Rapids: Eerdmans 1983); J. BARTON, *Oracles of God: Perceptions of Ancient Prophecy in Israel after the Exile* (New York: Oxford UP 1986); R. BECKWITH, *The Old Testament Canon of the New Testament Church* (Grand Rapids: Eerdmans 1985); P. BILDE, *Flavius Josephus Between Jerusalem and Rome: His Life, his Works, and their Importance* (Sheffield: JSOT 1988); H. BLOCH, *Die Quellen des Flavius Josephus in seiner Archäologie* (Leipzig: B. G. Teubner 1879); M. BRAUN, *Griechischer Roman und hellenistische Geschichtsschreibung* (Frankfurt: V. Klostermann 1934); J. BLENKINSOPP, "Prophecy and Priesthood in Josephus", *JJS* 25 (1974) 239–262; N. G. COHEN, "Josephus and Scripture: Is Josephus' Treatment of the Scriptural Narrative Similar Throughout the Antiquities I–XI?" *JQR* 54 (1963–64) 311–332; S. J. D. COHEN, *Josephus in Galilee and Rome: His Vita and his Development as a Historian* (CSCT 8; Leiden: E. J. Brill 1979); idem, "History and Historiography in the *Against Apion* of Josephus", in *Essays in Jewish Historiography* (ed. A. Rapoport-Albert; *History and Theory* 27, 1988); E. E. ELLIS, *The Old Testament in Early Christianity* (WUNT 54; Tübingen: J. C. B. Mohr 1991); L. H. FELDMAN, *Josephus and Modern Scholarship (1937–1980)* (Berlin: W. de Gruyter 1984) 121–191; idem, "A Selective Critical Bibliography of Josephus", in Feldman/Hata, Josephus (1989) 352–366; idem, "Use, Authority and Exegesis of Mikra in the Writings of Josephus", *Mikra: Text, Translation, Reading and Interpretation of the Hebrew Bible in Ancient Judaism and Early Christianity* (CRINT 2.1, ed. M. J. Mulder/H. Sysling; Minneapolis: Fortress 1988); idem, *Jew and Gentile in Antiquity: Attitudes and Interactions from Alexander to Justinian* (Princeton: Princeton UP 1993); L. H. FELDMAN/G. HATA, *Josephus, the Bible, and History* (Detroit: Wayne State UP 1989); T. W. FRANXMAN, *Genesis and the Jewish Antiquities of Flavius Josephus* (Rome: Biblical Institute Press 1979); R. GRAY, *Prophetic Figures in Late Second Temple Jewish Palestine: the Evidence from Josephus* (Oxford: Oxford UP 1992); B. HELLER, "Grundzüge der Aggada des Flavius Josephus", *MGWJ* 80 (1936) 237–246; G. HÖLSCHER, "Josephus", PW 18 (1916) 1934–2000; J. JEREMIAS, *New Testament Theology* I: *The Proclamation of Jesus* (New York: Charles Scribners Sons 1971); H. KRÄMER, "Προφήτης", TDNT 6, 783–796; R. LAQUEUR, *Der jüdische Historiker Flavius Josephus: ein biographischer Versuch auf neuer quellenkritischer Grundlage* (Darmstadt: Wissenschaftliche Buchgesllschaft 1970 [1920]); S. Z. LEIMAN, *The Canonization of Hebrew Scripture: the Talmudic and Midrashic Evidence* (Hamden CT: Archon

[1] This is a condensed and edited form of STEVE MASON's essay on "Scriptural Interpretation in the Writings of Josephus" (December 1993), which is available electronically on the IOUDAIOS-L listserv@lehigh.edu or from sxm42@psu.edu or kraft@ccat.sas.upenn.edu.

1976) 32; idem, "Josephus and the Canon of the Bible", in Feldman/Hata, Josephus (1989) 55; H. Lindner, *Die Geschichtsauffassung des Flavius Josephus im Bellum Judaicum* (AGJU 12; Leiden: E.J. Brill 1972); S. Mason, "Priesthood in Josephus and the Pharisaic Revolution", *JBL* 107 (1988) 657-661; idem, *Flavius Josephus on the Pharisees: A Composition-Critical Study* (SPB 39; Leiden: E.J. Brill 1991); idem, *Josephus and the New Testament* (Peabody, MA: Hendrickson 1992); idem, "Josephus, Daniel, and the Flavian House", in *Josephus and the History of the Greco-Roman Period: Essays in Memory of Morton Smith* (ed. F. Parente/S. Sievers; Leiden: Brill 1994); idem, review of Schwartz in IOUDAIOS REVIEW 2.008 (April 1992; this electronic review is available as SCHWARTZ MASON IOUD-REV from listserv@lehigh.edu, or from the "Electronic Publications" section of the ccat.sas.upenn.edu gopher at gopher.upenn.edu.); R. Mayer/C. Möller, "Josephus – Politiker und Prophet", in *Josephus-Studien: Untersuchungen zu Josephus, dem antiken Judentum and dem Neuen Testament* (FS O. Michel, ed. O. Betz/M. Hengel/K. Haacker; Göttingen: Vandenhoeck & Ruprecht 1974); R. Meyer, "Προφήτης", TDNT 6, 812-828; idem, "Bemerkungen zum literargeschichtlichen Hintergrund der Kanontheorie des Josephus", in *Josephus-Studien* (FS O. Michel; 1974); H. R. Moehring, *Novelistic Elements in the Writings of Flavius Josephus* (diss.; University of Chicago, 1957); J. G. Müller, *Des Flavius Josephus Schrift gegen den Apion* (Hildesheim: Georg Olms 1967 [1877]); S. Rappaport, *Agada und Exegese bei Flavius Josephus* (Vienna: A. Kohut Memorial Foundation 1930); S. Schwartz, *Josephus and Judaean Politics* (CSCT 18; Leiden: E.J. Brill 1990); J. A. Soggin, *Introduction to the Old Testament: From its Origins to the Closing of the Alexandrian Canon* (Louisville: Westminster/John Knox 1989); A. C. Sundberg, "The Old Testament: A Christian Canon", *CBQ* 30 (1968) 143-155; H. St. J. Thackeray, *Josephus: The Man and the Historian* (New York: Ktav 1967 [1928]) 75-99; W. C. van Unnik, *Flavius Josephus als historischer Schriftsteller* (Heidelberg: Lambert Schneider 1978).

Supplementary bibliography on Josephus (chronological): M. Olitzki, *Flavius Josephus und die Halacha* (Berlin: H. Iskowski 1885); A. Pelletier, *Flavius Josephe, adapteur de la lettre d'Ariste* (Paris: Klincksieck 1962); D. Goldenberg, "The Halakha in Josephus and in Tannaitic Literature: A Comparative Study", *JQR* 67 (1976) 30-43; E. C. Ulrich, *The Qumran Text of Samuel and Josephus* (Missoula: Scholars 1978); H.-F. Weiss, "Pharisäismus und Hellenismus: zur Darstellung des Judentums im Geschichtswerk des jüdischen Historikers Flavius Josephus", *OLZ* 74 (1979) 421-433; D. Daube, "Typology in Josephus", *JJS* 31 (1980) 18-36; D. Satran, "Daniel: Seer, Prophet, Holy Man", J. J. Collins/G. W. E. Nickelsburg (eds.), *Ideal Figures in Ancient Judaism: Profiles and Paradigms* (Chico CA: Scholars 1980) 33-48; B. H. Amaru, "Land Theology in Josephus Jewish Antiquities", *JQR* 71 (1980-81) 201-229; J. L. Bailey, "Josephus' Portrayal of the Matriarchs", L. H. Feldman/G. Hata, Josephus (1987) 154-179 and 180-197; G. Hata, "The Story of Moses Interpreted Within the Context of Anti-Semitism", L. H. Feldman/G. Hata, Josephus (1987) 154-179 and 180-197; C. A. Brown, *No Longer Be Silent: First Century Jewish Portraits of Biblical Women* (Louisville: Westminster/ John Knox 1992); G. E. Sterling, *Historiography and Self-Definition: Josephos, Luke-Acts and Apologetic Historiography* (NovTSup 44; Leiden: E.J. Brill 1992); C. T. Begg, *Josephus' Account of the Early Divided Monarchy (AJ 8.212-420): Rewriting the Bible* (Leuven: University Press/Peeters 1993).

1. Introduction

For the study of Scripture in early Judaism the writings of Josephus are an obvious reference point. His extensive biblical paraphrase in the *Judean Antiquities* has invited a massive amount of careful study;[2] the main results of which are readily available in recent surveys.[3] Thus this essay will focus on

---

[2] In general, see Thackeray, Josephus (1928) 75-99; Rappaport, Agada (1930); Braun, Geschichtsschreibung (1934); Heller, Grundzüge (1936) 237-246; Moehring, Novelistic Elements (1957); N. G. Cohen, Josephus (1963-64) 311-332; Attridge, Interpretation (1976); and Feldman, Mikra (1988) 455-518.

one passage and one issue: the shape of Josephus' 'Bible', or 'canon', and his most programmatic statement on that issue, *Against Apion* 1.37–43.

In the current debate over the shape of the first century Jewish canon(s), this passage must be dealt with by those who argue for whatever position – open or closed canon, tripartite or bipartite divisions.[4] Not surprisingly, perhaps, Josephus tends to support whomever is making the argument, and the debate provides a telling example of the observation that Josephus is extensively used but rarely understood on his own terms as an intelligent author.[5] This essay proposes to contribute to the discussion by looking carefully and contextually at the celebrated passage itself, which proves to be even less useful than has been feared for the scholarly canon quest, though it throws much light on his general outlook.

2. Context and Purpose of *Against Apion* 1.37–43

Josephus' last extant composition has a clear plan. He writes out of a perception that his magnum opus, the *Antiquities*, has provoked a chorus of detractors, who disbelieve what he says about Judean antiquity because of the lack of reference to Judeans in Greek literature (*AgAp.* 1.1–5).

The body of the work examines the evidence for Judean antiquity, both Oriental and Greek, and then argues the nobility of these ancient Judean traditions. Before he reaches the body, however, Josephus interjects a note of alarm that, in principle, Greek sources should be considered the final authority. The argument within this lengthy digression in 1.6–59 is also clearly structured with three main points: the lateness of Greek culture (1.6–14); the many contradictions among Greek accounts (1.15–18), which he attributes to a lack of "official records" (ἀναγραφαί, 1.19–22) and a preoccupation with

---

[3] Cf. Attridge, Works (1984) 210-227; Bilde, Josephus (1988) 80-104; Feldman, Modern Scholarship (1984) 121-191; Feldman, Critical Bibliography (1989) 352-366; Feldman, Mikra (1988); Mason, New Testament (1992) 64-73.

[4] For example, LEIMAN avers: "From Josephus' statement, it is evident that he recognized a tripartite canon..." (Canonization [1976] 32). In his later article "Josephus and the Canon of the Bible" 55, LEIMAN qualifies this position in deference to BECKWITH's proposal that the enumeration of *AgAp.* 1.37-41 is ad hoc and does not mirror a canonical arrangement. Still, LEIMAN seems to maintain (53-54), like BECKWITH (below), that the statement reflects an underlying tripartite canon. See Beckwith, Canon (1985) 79-80 [see below on the thirteen prophetical books and on the final fourbook section], 121-127 [125: Josephus' canon has three sections, but he has transferred the narrative books in the Hagiographa to join those in the Prophets]. This was the standard interpretation of the passage, summarized without further ado in Müller, Apion (1877) 99-103. More recently: Ackroyd and Evans, History (1970) 117, 136-137; Ellis, Old Testament (1991) 7. BARTON, however, contends: "At all events the primary idea to which Josephus is a witness is not that the books of Scripture were organized into a tripartite form, but that they derived from either of two sources: Moses and the prophets. ... Such evidence as we have from Hellenistic Judaism thus confirms the essentially bipartite character of Scripture ..." (Oracles [1986] 49).

[5] Van Unnik, Josephus (1978) 18. For a conspicuous example of the problem see Soggin, Introduction (1989) on Josephus and canon. Although LEIMAN and BARTON (above, n. 4) are at least somewhat sensitive to the particularity of Josephus' language and worldview they still end up drawing more or less direct support from him.

rhetorical competitiveness (1.23–27); and the superiority of Oriental (βάρβαροι, 1.58) recordkeeping (1.28–59).[6]

Within the subargument on Oriental recordkeeping, Josephus intends to show that the Judeans' measures for maintaining official records are even more rigorous than those of their more famous Eastern neighbours, which are in turn qualitatively superior to Greek practices. Whereas the Egyptians and Babylonians entrusted their records to priests and Chaldeans, the Judeans assigned theirs to chief priests and (corresponding to Chaldeans) prophets:[7]

1.29 But concerning our forebears, that they practiced ... even greater (care) than those mentioned, with respect to the official records, having assigned this matter to the chief priests and prophets, so that until our own times this charge has been cherished with all precision – and if it is not too bold to say, it will be (so) cherished (in the future also) – I shall try concisely to demonstrate.

Although Josephus is least clear about the role that Judean priests play in the keeping of records, it may be inferred from various bits of evidence that he sees the chief priests and their subordinates as preservers, executors, and philosophical expositors of the records, somewhat like the aforementioned Egyptian priests.[8] This is confirmed by his ensuing discussion of the prophets, for he leaves no doubt that it was the prophets who actually wrote the records:

1.37 Accordingly ... then, seeing that the writing (of the records) is not the personal prerogative of everyone, nor is there actual disagreement among any of the things written, but the prophets alone learned the highest and oldest matters by the inspiration of the God, and by themselves plainly recorded events as they occurred,

1.38 so among us there are not tens of thousands of discordant and competing volumes, but only twenty-two volumes containing the record of all time, which are rightly trusted.

1.39 Now of these, five are those of Moses, which comprise both the laws and the tradition from human origins until his passing; this period falls little short of 3000 years.

1.40 From Moses' passing until the Artaxerxes who was king of the Persians after Xerxes, the prophets after Moses wrote up what happened in their times [or, as they saw things] in thirteen volumes. The remaining four (volumes) comprise hymns toward the God and advice for living among men.

1.41 From Artaxerxes until our own time all sorts of things have been written, but they have not been considered of the same trustworthiness as those before them, because the exact succession of the prophets failed.

1.42 Now it is clear in practice how we approach our special texts: for although such an age has already passed [sc. since Artaxerxes], no one has dared either to add anything or to take away from them or to alter them. But it is innate among all Judeans from their very first moment

---

[6] That this outline is obvious is confirmed by the close but independent correspondence between my synopsis and that of Bilde, Josephus (1988) 117–118.

[7] All of the following translations, unless otherwise noted, are mine. They are deliberately wooden.

[8] *War* 2.411; 3.352; *Ant.* 4.304; *AgAp* 2.185–186, 188. Cf. Mason, Priesthood (1988) 657–661. Although in referring to the 2000 year genealogical succession of the chief priests in 1.36, Josephus uses the same word (ἀναγραφαί) that I elsewhere translate "official records", he cannot mean the same thing by it, since the records that are the main subject of the surrounding passage were completed by the time of Artaxerxes. Rather, he must be referring to the archives from which he claims to have retrieved his own genealogy (*Life* 6 – with the verb ἀναγράφω). It is not uncommon for him to play on different senses of the same word within a single passage; cf. Mason, Pharisees (1991) 285 n. 22. On the 2000 years from Moses (and Aaron) to his own time cf. *Ant.* 20.261.

of existence to consider them decrees of God, to stand by them, and for their sake, if necessary, cheerfully to die.

1.43 Thus already many of (our) prisoners of war have on many occasions been seen patiently enduring tortures and the ways of all sorts of deaths in theatres, without letting slip a single word against the laws and the related official records.

The main contribution of this section to the larger argument comes in the first sentence (37–38). Unlike the generalized Greek situation (see 1.12–18), among the Judeans only prophets could write official records: they were enabled by inspiration to learn of things beyond the limits of human knowledge; for the rest, they recorded affairs of their own times. The result is a collection of twenty-two harmonious and wholly reliable volumes of national records (plural in 1.43), which are so consistent that Josephus can also designate them all as a single record (ἀναγραφή; 1.38). The practical corollary of having such an established and carefully preserved tradition (42–43) is that Judeans know it well and are wholly committed to it.

The middle section (39–41) supports the claim that prophets wrote a unified national record by describing this material according to several criteria. In terms of *authorship*, he mentions Moses and subsequent prophets. But the authorial distinction is not paramount here. Though *Antiquities* (1.18–26) and the rest of *Against Apion* (2.173 et passim) feature Moses as the Judean legislator, the distinction between Moses and the others in this passage has mainly to do with the different periods of history they covered. Yet the *chronological* distinction is not fully developed either: Josephus does not bother to specify when the remaining four books were written, but mentions them for the sake of completeness – the record covers the history of "all time" in a trustworthy manner (1.38).

His most comprehensive criterion for distinguishing among the records here is that of *genre*. Moses' writings themselves include both laws and tradition for a period of 3000 years. The subsequent prophets continued the records up until Artaxerxes by writing about "what happened" in their days, and so also wrote history or tradition. Finally, the collection includes a small amount of hymnic and hortatory material. Of the four genres – laws, tradition/history, hymns, and advice – Josephus' argument requires his preoccupation with history.

Contrary to almost universal opinion,[9] Josephus does not offer the slightest hint that these genres correspond to 'divisions' or 'sections': he does not suggest that Moses composed two sections, though he wrote in two different genres, or that the final four books represent two (small!) sections. Still less is there anything remotely like a division called "prophets" in this passage, for all of the authors are prophets. The distinction of genres, along with the two other criteria, simply help the gentile reader understand the various kinds of material within the twenty-two volumed official Judean record.

His main point, then, seems clear. In contrast to the many Greek authors who aggressively contradict each other concerning a brief and recent period

[9] Ackroyd and Evans, History (1970) 136; Leiman, Canonization (1976) 31–34; Beckwith, Canon (1985) 125; Barton, Oracles (1986) 38, 49 (in spite of many salutary qualifications); Ellis, Old Testament (1992) 9.

of time (1.6–18), the Judeans' harmonious few records span the whole period from creation to Artaxerxes in a linear fashion. Moses had no competitors in recording the laws and the first 3000 years of history. Nor did the prophets after him, who successively took up the task of recording "what happened in their own times". And this whole process is so ancient that it was already completed by the time of the Persian Artaxerxes, successor of the famous Xerxes who had captured Athens – thus, at a time in which Greek historiography had not yet begun. Judeans do not even credit their own writings from the subsequent period, in which Greek history first appeared.

3. Key Terms

Josephus' digression on Judean traditions is highly stylized, exhibiting a marked preference for formal balance over rigorous logic.[10] His language is consciously generic: each nation is assumed to have its own *official records* (ἀναγραφαί) or *tradition* of communal lore (παράδοσις), and Josephus can impose these universal categories to the Judeans' advantage over against "the Greeks". His use of "tradition", for example, to describe what Moses taught in addition to the laws (1.39), parallels "the tradition" of the Phoenicians (1.28) and of Orientals in general (1.8; cf. also *Ant.* 20.259).[11] Similarly, Josephus takes over the "*accuracy*" (ἀκρίβεια) word group from commonplace hellenistic historiography, and applies it with vigour to all aspects of Judean culture – to the official records, to his own writings (*War* 1.9, 17; 7.454; *Ant.* 20.263), or to the failure of others to achieve precision (*AgAp.* 1.18).[12] Or again, when he says that the Judean records are rightly *trusted* (δικαίως πεπιστευμένα) he is not reflecting the Judean community's language of 'faith' or some such thing, but only providing a contrast to his earlier notice that the Greeks are loathe to trust even their oldest works (1.14; cf. 1.161). For us who wish to learn from Josephus' statement about intramural 'Jewish' phenomena, his argument is largely opaque.

The most important word in this section of the argument is ἀναγραφή, "official record(s)" – the Greeks lack ancient and stable "records" (1.7, 11, 20, 21, 23); Egyptian, Babylonian, and Judean "records" are contrasted (1.9, 28, 38, 43); and the conclusion is that non-Greeks are far superior in maintaining "records" (1.58). More than half of the 42 occurrences of this noun in his writings are in *AgAp.* 1. It is not a useage that he had just learned late in life, for his own speech in *War* 6.109, written a couple of decades earlier, already refers to "the official records of the ancient prophets". And both the introduction and conclusion to *Antiquities* designate the "holy scriptures" by

---

[10] Cf. S.J.D. Cohen, History (1988) 1–11.

[11] Josephus does use this term elsewhere to describe an internal Judean phenomenon: the special Pharisaic tradition (*Ant.* 13.297, 408). But that exception proves the rule, for he must carefully explain to his readers what the word means in that context (*Ant.* 13.297–298). Cf. Mason, Pharisees (1991) 233–235, 289–293.

[12] Cf. Mason, Pharisees (1991) 64–66, 75–79, 89–96, 108–115.

this term in the singular (1.12; 20.261). But ordinarily, when Josephus wishes to refer generically to a nation's traditional laws and customs he will use phrases like οἱ πάτριοι νόμοι, τὰ πάτρια ἔθη, τὰ πάτρια, or οἱ νόμοι (e.g., *AgAp.* 2.164; 2.237).[13] His preference for ἀναγραφαί in *AgAp.* 1 evidently reflects his desire here to stress that the Greeks, though they do have national traditions, possess only late and lacunose *written* records. He makes the point early, and later returns to an explicit contrast between Greeks and Judeans (2.155–156). Only Judeans and other Easterners have ancient official records.

Given this emphasis, it is noteworthy that Josephus uses the same term of his own major compositions (*War* 7.455; *Ant.* 1.18). Does he, then, think of his writings as an authoritative (and prophetic) continuation of the ancient records? That question brings us to Josephus's famous observation that things written after Artaxerxes are not credited by Judeans in the same way as the "records" because "the exact succession of the prophets failed" (1.41). This statement is a lynchpin in discussions of the cessation of prophecy in Israel and the closure of the 'canon'.[14] What does it mean?

Josephus' use of "*prophet*" terminology in general is a fascinating and complex subject. With reference to 'Scriptures' and 'canon', we have already noted that as early as *War* 6.109 Josephus had connected the prophets with the writing of "records". Further, in the preface to that work he proposes to begin his account in the time of Antiochus IV (1.19) because Josephus' literary predecessors, "Judean" and "Greek" – "the historians ... and our own prophets" – left off at that point (1.17–18). It seems to me that here, "our own" prophets are the Judeans, and the (by implication foreign) historians are the Greeks, who derived their information more or less accurately from the Judean records (see *AgAp.* 1.218).[15] If this interpretation is sound, then Josephus' later conception of prophets as ancient authors of the national records in *Against Apion* would also be attested early in his development (*War*), and we can conclude that his connection of the Judean ἀναγραφαί with long-gone times played a fundamental role in his long-term outlook.

This hypothesis is confirmed by Josephus' instinctive lexical choices, for it is now well known that throughout his writings he reserves the προφητ-word group for those who lived long before his own time.[16] Almost all such occurrences refer to the characters of the Hebrew Bible who play a role in *Antiquities*, where Josephus underlines his interest in the subject by even introduc-

---

[13] Cf. Mason, Pharisees (1991) 96–106.

[14] E.g., Jeremias, Theology (1971) 80 and n.6; Ackroyd and Evans, History (1970) 114–135; along with discussions in Meyer, Προφήτης, TDNT 6:817; Aune, Prophecy (1983) 103–106; Gray, Figures (1992) 7–9.

[15] Barton (Oracles [1986] 59) infers that the historians (συγγραφεῖς) wrote only until the exile, since that is the last item mentioned in Josephus' list of things already documented (1.17). But that list is representative, not exhaustive, for Josephus plainly establishes the beginning point of his narrative at the time of Antiochus (1.19); this, not the exile, must be where the "historians" finished. On the identification of the "historians" here with the "Greeks", see the close parallel in *AgAp.* 1.218, where the identical Greek phrase, "without missing much of the truth," is used of Demetrius Phalereus, Philo the Elder, and Eupolemus.

[16] Cf. Blenkinsopp, Prophecy (1974) 240–246; Feldman, Prophets (1990) 405; Gray, Figures (1992) 23–26.

ing prophetic vocabulary where it is absent in the extant biblical texts.[17] His prophets include those who wrote books, like Moses and Joshua (*Ant.* 2.327; 3.60; 4.311, 420), along with many who did not, like Jacob, Aaron, Phineas, and Nathan (*Ant.* 2.194; 3.192; 5.120; 6.57; 7.214). For the few extra-biblical applications of this terminology,[18] it may be significant that the Hasmonean John Hyrcanus (high priest and ruler, 135–104 BCE) is the last "prophet" recognized by Josephus (*War* 1.68–69; *Ant.* 13.299), and his exceptionally late date may therefore account for the phrase "exact succession of the prophets": he was a prophet long after prophecy had otherwise ceased.

This consistency of usage is the more conspicuous when we realize that Josephus refrains from using "prophet" language even of his most admired contemporaries, who nevertheless receive authentic revelations and make accurate predictions, viz.: the Essenes and himself.[19] Moreover, after discussing the roles of priests and prophets in maintaining the Judean "records", he continues our passage by offering his own writings as an example of the Judeans' concern for historical truth: "But I myself have composed a truthful record" (ἀναγραφή; 1.47). Given the context, in which "record(s)" is a key word, it is hard to avoid the conclusion that he means to insinuate himself into the company of the ancient prophets.[20] Yet he does not actually use "prophet" of himself, much less of any contemporary, and this must be significant in view of his interest in the subject of prophecy.[21] If there were prophecy in his day, he would be a prophet, but of course there is not.

As important as this chronological distinction is the ethnic one, seldom discussed.[22] Although προφήτης and cognates were well established in the

---

[17] Cf. van Unnik, Schriftsteller (1978) 52f.; Blenkinsopp, Prophecy (1974) 239–262; and especially Feldman, Prophecy (1990) 392–393.

[18] Non-biblical referents of προφητ-language in Josephus include (1) contemporary "false prophets" such as Theudas (*War* 2.261; 6.286; *Ant.* 20.97, 169); (2) an "Egyptian prophet" (sarcasm?) cited by Chaeremon (*AgAp.* 1.312, see 1.289); (3) "Cleodemus the prophet", mentioned by Alexander Polyhistor (*Ant.* 1.240). (4) the Hasmonean ruler and high priest John Hyrcanus (135–104 BCE) (*War* 1.68–69; *Ant.* 13.299) – the last prophet recognized by Josephus, whose late date may account for the phrase "exact succession of the prophets" since he was a prophet long after prophecy had otherwise ceased. (5) As REBECCA GRAY has cogently argued (Prophetic Figures [1992] 20), for Josephus the shining of the high priest's "breastplate" is a prophetic phenomenon that ceased at the time of John Hyrcanus (*Ant.* 3.218).

[19] Certainly, he is not reluctant to claim perfect accuracy for his works (*War* 1.1–16; 7.455; *Ant.* 1.17; 20.260–263); he claims to have experienced genuine divine revelations (*War* 3.350–354, 406); he explicitly and implicitly parallels his own career to Jeremiah's and Daniel's (*War* 5.391–393; *Ant.* 10.119); he everywhere stresses his priestly qualifications (*War* 1.3; 3.352; Life 1–6; *AgAp.* 1.54); and he models *Antiquities* on the much earlier Greek LXX (*Ant.* 1.10–13). But his whole point that the Judean records had been long completed, and that no one would countenance an addition would be invalidated if he seriously placed his own work on the same level. And even if he had done so, few other Judeans would have granted his records any national authority, so there is no question of his works being "trusted" in this way (cf. 1.41). It seems, rather, that he simply takes advantage of his own rhetoric about the ancient Judeans to present himself as an embodiment of the best Judean traditions.

[20] Mayer and Möller, Josephus (1974) 283–284; Blenkinsopp, Prophecy (1974) 239–262; van Unnik, Schriftsteller (1978) 42; Feldman, Prophecy (1990) 421–422; Mason, Pharisees (1991) 270; most emphatically Gray, Figures (1992) 35–79.

[21] Correctly, Feldman, Prophecy (1990) 405; contra all others mentioned in the preceding note (Mason included).

[22] Feldman (Prophecy [1990] 416–418), characteristically, discovers it.

Greek world,[23] and although Josephus elsewhere uses generic vocabulary without hesitation, he reserves prophetic language for the ancient Judean tradition; gentile and contemporary Judean phenomena are almost always designated by the μαντ-word group, along with a few other terms. Thus the gentile Balaam, the witch of Endor, and Egyptian seers are not "prophets" for Josephus.[24] Where an ancient gentile seer is called a prophet and the term is not directly traceable to Josephus's source, his (sarcastic?) emphasis is on the ineffectiveness of these "prophets" (*Ant.* 8.339; *AgAp.* 1.312). His refusal even to use the customary term "prophet" for the renowned oracle at Delphi[25] confirms his *Tendenz*. That he considers prophecy the preserve of the Judeans perhaps explains why he compares Judean prophets to Chaldeans in our passage.[26]

Also consistent with his language elsewhere is the term διαδοξή ('succession'), which he uses of kings, high priests, and prophets, despite its near absence from the LXX/OG biblical tradition.[27] The succession of prophets is not nearly as obvious in *Antiquities* as that of high priests and kings. Perhaps it would have been awkward to establish a prophetic succession in the proper sense because the office of prophet was not hereditary. Still, Josephus chooses to summarize Moses' handing on of his role to Joshua (Num 27:15–23) by saying that he appointed Joshua "his successor (διάδοξος), both in the prophetic functions and as commander" (*Ant.* 4.165; compare Sir 46.1). Deuteronomy's emphasis that there was never again a prophet like Moses (34:9–10) is also reflected by Josephus at 4.329, but he has said enough to hint at the beginnings of a prophetic "succession".

This incidental evidence tends to confirm that, although Josephus nowhere articulates for his readers a symmetrical, trilateral succession from Moses' time, he did hold such a concept in his own thought.[28] Of these three lines,

---

[23] Cf. also Krämer, Προφήτης, TDNT 6, 783–796.

[24] *Ant.* 2.241; 4.104, 112, 157; 6.330–331, 338.

[25] Cf. Feldman, Prophecy (1990) 417.

[26] Compare his remarks on exorcism as particularly prominent among the Judeans (*Ant.* 8.44–49). Barton (Oracles [1986] 48) has suggested that Josephus's concern in *AgAp.* 1 with the prophets' role as record-writers does not match his preoccupation with predictive prophecy in *Antiquities* – a contrast that has even been used to argue that Josephus regarded "only one very limited type of prophecy" as having ceased (Gray, Figures [1992] 9). But his language is consistent. While in *Antiquities* he seems genuinely impressed with various predictions (10.142, 276; 11.1–3, 331–335; 10.266), he still adheres rigorously to his goal of providing a historical account. He largely omits the major and minor prophets (Jeremiah and Daniel are his chief exemplars of predictive prophecy) except for historical material (cf. Franxman, Genesis [1979] 7). He pointedly excuses himself, as a historian, from elaborating on the predictions of Daniel (10. 210), and affirms the truth of Jonah's predictions about Nineveh without reporting them, so as not to seem "irksome" to his readers (9.242). Feldman (Prophecy [1990] 394) plausibly suggests that a focus on predictions might have inspired ridicule. Thus while insisting that the ancient Judean prophet-authors received extra-human knowledge, Josephus keeps a steady focus on Judean antiquity and does not subdivide the category "prophecy".

[27] See Sir. 46:1, 48:8; 2 Macc 4:29, 14:26; and in a different sense in 2 Chron 18:17, 26:11, 28:7. On his modification of biblical succession terminology for kings, see Mason, Pharisees (1991) 235–239.

[28] Compare the eschatological hope for a return of anointed prophet, ruler, and priest at Qumran (1QS 9:11; 4Q175). Eschatological urgency and the language of anointing are wanting in Josephus.

only the high-priestly succession has continued uninterrupted through 2000 years to the present, and this guarantees the preservation and proper exposition of the records. Royal and prophetic successions lapsed after the return from exile.[29] When Josephus writes of the failure of the prophetic succession, therefore, and of the consequent lack of recent Judean "official records", he seems to be tapping a deep and rich vein, which he only fleetingly exposes to our view. In a society in which "old is good",[30] he is quite happy to present the Judean community as thriving on the interest of the ancient deposit, as it were, and he is scandalized by newcomers who claim prophetic gifts.

4. The Integrity of Josephus' Biblical 'Record'

This broad coherence of outlook and language should not blind us to rhetorical flourishes in Josephus' programmatic statement about the national records. Most obviously: his insistence that no Judean has "dared" to alter the records (1.42) seems to conflict with his own practice in *Ant.* 1–11, which is a thoroughly tendentious interpretation of the records rather than a translation. He omits a great deal, adds significant portions, and casts the whole history into a frame that suits his literary purposes.

To be sure, his changes follow identifiable and fairly consistent criteria.[31] He sets out to prove the nobility of Judean tradition, that it is highly philosophical, and that its God is active in human affairs, always rewarding virtue and punishing vice (*Ant.* 1.6, 14, 20). Although internally consistent, his biblical paraphrase does not consistently coincide with any known version of the text or with rabbinic halakah or haggadah; he parallels all of these from time to time, but often goes his own way.

---

[29] Josephus knows that a new royal line emerged with the later Hasmoneans. John Hyrcanus was singularly privileged to revive and embody all three functions within himself (*War* 1.68; *Ant.* 13.299). Since Hyrcanus, once again, only the high-priestly succession has endured. Josephus cannot himself claim to be a king, a high priest, or a prophet. But his own διαδοχή gives him a priestly and royal heritage (*Life* 1–6), while his accurate predictions and record-writing allow him to share a bit of the old prophetic aura.

[30] Cf. Cicero *On the Laws* 2.10.27; *On the Nature of the Gods* 3.1.5–4.10; Luke 5:39 and Feldman, Jew and Gentile (1993) 177–178. It is worth stressing here that rather than regretting the absence of contemporary prophets, as the English 'lack' or 'failure' might seem to imply, Josephus apparently views the long ages since official Judean record-writing ceased as a great advantage over the Greeks, who were "born yesterday" (*AgAp.* 1.7). He conveys no sense here of prophet-deprivation, or any feeling of 'nostalgia' for the prophetic past (contra Barton, Oracles [1986] 60, 115; and Gray, Figures [1992] 8), sentiments that would run directly counter to his purpose, which is to boast that the Judean records have been so long in place.

[31] Most conveniently summarized in Attridge, Works (1984), and Feldman, Mikra (1988). Josephus omits episodes that might be used to support current anti-Judean literary slanders (e.g., about leprous origins or misanthropy); highlights and adds material that features Judean virtue; portrays Abraham, Moses, Solomon, Daniel and others as peerless philosophers; notes the rewards and punishments inevitably received by the virtuous and the impious; stresses divine providence and the fulfilment of prophecy; reflects editorially on universal philosophical issues; relentlessly moralizes; provides as much entertainment as possible; and accommodates the texts to his own times, priestly biases, and career.

In view of his pointed contrast between the unity of the official Judean records and the competing accounts of the Greeks (*AgAp.* 1.37–38), it is noteworthy that he achieves this unity in practice only with great effort, by tacitly harmonizing biblical documents that do in fact overlap and compete, e.g.: Genesis/Numbers/Deuteronomy, Isaiah/Kings, Jeremiah/Kings, and Kings/Chronicles. While failing to tell the reader about this harmonizing activity, he parades examples of apparent conflict (e.g., between Jeremiah and Ezekiel; *Ant.* 10.106–107, 141) and conspicuously resolves them, in order to reinforce the impression of harmony. He also introduces corroborating testimony from Greek and Oriental writers and quietly corrects the biblical sources (e.g., *Ant.* 10.229; 11.106, 120) to agree with the external evidence.

All of this makes it impossible to regard Josephus' Judean history as anything like a translation on the legendary model of the LXX (contra *Ant.* 1.9–13); it is a *tour de force* in the service of his literary aims. Nevertheless, even here the conflict is not between his thematic statement in *Against Apion* and his practice in *Antiquities*, but between his editorial statements and his practice in general. For his strongest assurances about his treatment of the text are those that introduce and punctuate the history itself. For example, he remarks on his carefully crafted summary of selected Mosaic laws, which we know to include non-pentateuchal items:

> All is here written as he [Moses] left it; nothing have we added for the sake of embellishment, nothing which has not been bequeathed by Moses. Our one innovation has been to classify the several subjects; for he left what he wrote in a scattered condition, just as he received each several instruction from God (*Ant.* 4.196–197, Thackeray; cf. 1.17; 10.218).

Although such statements provide ready material for those who see Josephus as an incurable liar, that facile option is excluded by the immediate juxtaposition of these statements with the product itself, and by the sheer energy that was required for him to sustain his argument over such a lengthy history. Note that he makes the preceding statement in the anticipation that Judean readers might accuse him of departing from the texts (4.197). Since he does not so excuse the major alterations that we have noted, we can only conclude that he was largely insensitive to what we post-enlightenment readers should expect in view of his promises.[32]

This insensitivity does not result from his being the "stupid copyist" of old source-critical imagination.[33] His handling of the biblical material is broadly consistent with his handling of non-biblical material in the latter part of *Antiquities* and elsewhere. Rather, for Josephus as for every other writer of the Greco-Roman period, rhetorical strategies were so instinctive that he employed them everywhere, even while repudiating rhetoric as the downfall of the "Greeks".

---

[32] S. J. D. Cohen (Galilee and Rome [1979] 27–29) suggests that this historiographical commonplace was not taken seriously (in our sense) by any of those who used it. Van Unnik (Schriftsteller [1978] 26–40) takes it to mean only that Josephus will not allow flattery or hatred to colour his work; he will recast his sources faithfully. Cf. now Feldman, Mikra (1988) 466–470.

[33] The phrase is from Laqueur, Historiker (1920), caricaturing (not excessively) the image of Josephus created by such scholars as Bloch (Quellen [1879]) and Hölscher (Josephus [1916]).

5. Scope and Arrangement of Josephus' Scripture

We turn now to consider the extent to which Josephus' use of Jewish scriptures supports and elucidates his statement about the scope and order of the Judean records. The statement in *AgAp.* 1 leads us to expect, first, that the reign of Artaxerxes (i.e. from the Esther story; see *Ant.* 11.184, 296)[34] would mark the end of his Judean history, inasmuch as that history was meant to translate the official records (*Ant.* 1.6, 17). Obviously, however, this story does not mark the end of Josephus' *Antiquities.* He does not inform the reader that he has now outrun the twenty-two volumes of *AgAp.* 1, or that he has revised his original plan and will now continue the story up until the eve of the great revolt (*Ant.* 20.223).[35]

Does the continuation of the narrative past Artaxerxes betray Josephus' underlying belief in the openendedness of Scripture? Is the "twenty-two volumes" merely a rhetorical ploy in *Against Apion*? Certainly Josephus is no more averse than any other ancient writer to creating claims about the national records to impress his readers.[36] And he does say in the preface to *Antiquities* that "the things presented in the holy writings are innumerable, seeing that they embrace the history of five thousand years" (1.13), but 5000 years would require the 3000 years from Creation to Moses (*AgAp.* 1.39), plus the 2000 years from Moses to his own time (*Ant.* 20.261; *AgAp.* 1.36). But in addition to the probability that he, like most ancient writers, was simply being careless with numbers, his treatment betrays a major editorial seam immediately after his leisurely retelling of the Esther story that alerts us to his awareness that his more or less connected sources, the "records", are exhausted.[37] In what follows, he includes material that could not be

[34] The identification of this Artaxerxes deserves comment. Many scholars assume with BARTON that the remark "is probably to be understood as meaning that it [an official document] must not postdate the age of Ezra, because it was in that period that prophets existed" (Oracles [1986] 60; see also Ackroyd and Evans, History [1970] 115–116 [who make a great deal of the connection with Ezra]; Soggin, Introduction [1989] 13). But although the biblical Ezra and 1 Esdras do name Artaxerxes as king of the Persians (e.g. Ezra 4:7, 23), Josephus systematically corrects this to "Cambyses", and replaces the Artaxerxes of Nehemiah with "Xerxes" (*Ant.* 11.21). The Artaxerxes who succeeded Xerxes appears elsewhere in Josephus only in his rendition of the Esther story.

[35] THACKERAY suggested that Josephus continued so as to imitate the twenty volumes of the Roman *Antiquities* by Dionysius of Halicarnassus (Josephus (1967 [1928]) 56–58). I would propose further that he became so engrossed in his major themes—divine providence, reward and punishment—that he thought he could fruitfully rework the period already represented by the *War* along the same lines. His plentiful and in some cases new information about the LXX/OG, the Hasmoneans, the now dastardly Herod, Gaius Caligula, and the rebels against Rome also might have invited such a fresh portrayal.

[36] Cf. perhaps *War* 6.109, 311; *Ant.* 10.210.

[37] After the Esther story (mid to late fifth century BCE; 11.296), he briefly summarizes the high-priestly succession for the following century (11.297–303), then jumps to Alexander the Great (ca. 334 BCE), who appeared "at about this time" (11.304). From now on, his account will become increasingly uneven as he tries to weave some very detailed sources (e.g., for Herod's life) together with large periods for which he lacks material, concealing the caesura from the reader. So he uses his familiar catchall bridge—κατὰ τοῦτον τὸν καιρόν (cf. *Ant* 4.226; 5.352; 6.49, 213, 271, 292; 7.21; 9.239 et passim; D.R. SCHWARTZ, "KATA TOYTON TON KAIRON: Josephus' Source on Agrippa II", *JQR* 72 (1982) 241–268)—to cover the gap, as if nothing were

thought to come from Jewish scriptural sources (e. g. the death of Gaius), and consciously makes the claim about the twenty-two volumes after the *Antiquities* was already in circulation, which suggests strongly that he perceived no conflict on this matter.[38] We conclude that, although Josephus tries to patch over the end of his biblical sources in *Antiquities*, because he has now decided to extend the narrative, he is nonetheless aware that the national records have ended with the great and beneficent king Artaxerxes.

Unfortunately, Josephus is so committed to the historian's task that he does not permit us to learn much about any internal arrangement of the Judean ἀναγραφαί. The sequence of his biblical source material in *Ant.* 1-11 is roughly as follows (*Antiquities* volume number in brackets):[39]

[1] Genesis 1-35
[2] Genesis 36-48; Exodus 1-15
[3] Exodus 16-40; Exod/Lev/Num conflated for summary of laws
[4] Numbers 14-36; Deuteronomy, conflated with Exod/Lev/Num
[5] Joshua, Judges, Ruth, 1 Samuel 1-4
[6] 1 Samuel 5-31
[7] 2 Samuel 1-24; 1 Kings 1-2 conflated with 1 Chronicles 1-29; David is a singer and musician (7.305)
[8] 1 Kings 2-22 conflated with 2 Chronicles 1-18; Solomon composed 1005 volumes of odes/songs and 3000 volumes of parables (8.44)
[9] 2 Chronicles 19-31 conflated with 2 Kings 1-17, Jonah, Zechariah 14:5, and Nahum 2
[10] 2 Kings 18-24 conflated with 2 Chronicles 32-36, Isaiah 38-39, Ezekiel 1, 12, and biographical passages (rearranged) from Jeremiah (lament also mentioned; 10.78); Daniel 1-8. Isaiah and Daniel wrote "books" (10.35, 267)
[11] 1 Esdras perhaps conflated with Ezra (generally preferring 1 Esdras); Nehemiah; Haggai and Zechariah mentioned; Esther (including "Greek additions" B-E)

By the end of his biblical paraphrase, with the period of Ezra-Nehemiah and Esther, Josephus is relying heavily on Greek biblical texts, in spite of his promise to provide a translation of the Hebrew records (1.17). The nature of his *Vorlage* is a huge and still unsettled problem: some think that he used primarily Greek texts throughout; others find more evidence of a Semitic source in the early books, and so surmise that he only later opted for the Greek – perhaps through weariness of translation.[40] We cannot tackle the source-critical problem here. We might wonder, though, how Josephus would reconcile his use of the fuller Greek texts of 1 Esdras and Esther with his

really changing. That the seam is discernible in spite of Josephus's present literary intention alerts us to his knowledge that his more or less connected sources, the "records", are exhausted. On the use of round numbers in Antiquity, see Mason, New Testament (1992) 37, 209-210.

[38] He must suppose that *Antiquities* does not overtly contradict his general statement in *AgAp.* 1. His claim to speak for all Judeans when he specifies the figure of twenty-two volumes would be vulnerable to immediate disconfirmation if it were merely an ad hoc invention, and it happens to correspond closely to other roughly contemporary means of counting; cf. Leiman, Canonization (1976) 41-50 (on the Christian evidence) and 51-56 (on the rabbinic count); also Beckwith, Canon (1985) 118-127. Granted that the number twenty-two is mainly paralleled in Christian texts, the standard rabbinic figure of twenty-four is not much different. If Josephus knew both ways of counting, as did Jerome, he would have chosen the smaller number for his present argument.

[39] Cf. also Appendix B in Schwartz, Judaean Politics (1990) 225-226.

[40] The problem is conveniently surveyed in Feldman, Mikra (1988) 455-466.

clear statement about the limited number of official records. Perhaps he knew Hebrew editions of these texts that more closely approximated the Greek than do the ones known to us. In any case, he must have seen little material difference in using the Greek. That these distinctions did not trouble him offends our sense of precision, but we can hardly hold him responsible for that.

In view of Josephus' thorough manipulation and reordering of his material, it would be unwise to make deductions about the arrangement of his sources, beyond the obvious: they start with the Pentateuch, after which he follows the best chronology he can. No clear sections or divisions are established. To be sure, Moses and his laws have an axiomatic supremacy throughout Josephus' works (e.g., *Ant.* 3.317–322). But the laws are the basis of the "constitution" by which Judean communities around the world govern themselves, and so are parallel to the national laws of other peoples.[41] Moses' laws do not appear as a peculiar feature of Judean life, much less as a section of Josephus' Bible. When he summarizes the laws (*Ant.* 3.223–286; 4.196–302), he even apologizes for digressing from the narrative, making it clear that they constitute only a small portion of what Moses wrote (3.223; 4.196). Nor can Josephus' designation of Daniel as "one of the greatest prophets" (*Ant.* 10.266) be admitted as evidence of order within Josephus' Bible.[42] Rather, this designation is consistent with his claim in *AgAp.* 1.37 that all of the recordwriters were prophets. Moses too was a prophet without equal (*Ant.* 2.327; 3.60; 4.320, 329). There is no division of "prophets" here.

The passage in *Ant.* 10.35, editorializing about a prediction by Isaiah, and mentioning "this prophet" and "also others, twelve in number," is no exception. Some commentators have linked these thirteen authors with the thirteen volumes of "the prophets after Moses" in *AgAp.* 1.40,[43] thus proposing a tripartite internal arrangement of Moses, prophets (in a narrower sense), and non-prophets.[44] Beckwith has proposed, however, that the twelve prophets in question are more likely the minor prophets,[45] which would maintain the

---

[41] Cf. Mason, Pharisees (1991) 96–106.

[42] Contra Marcus, note *d* ad loc in the LCL edition; Barton, Oracles (1986) 36–38. Curiously, Barton elsewhere recognizes that Josephus considers all biblical writers prophets (p. 19); he seems to have it both ways.

[43] That premise is often accepted as selfevident (so Leiman, Josephus [1989] 55: it "can only be understood as a reference to the (total of) thirteen historical books by the prophets"; also Feldman [Prophecy (1990) 409 n. 83] and note *c* of the LCL translator, R. Marcus, to this passage: "there seems to be no other explanation...").

[44] The narrative of *Antiquities* would suggest fifteen prophetic volumes—Joshua, Judges, Ruth, Samuel, Kings, Chronicles, Isaiah, Ezekiel, Jeremiah, Lamentations, Daniel, Ezra (or 1 Esdras), Nehemiah, Esther, and the twelve minor prophets as a group (since he mentions several of them)—but several combinations are plausible to reach the figure of thirteen—the combinations Judges-Ruth; Jeremiah-Lamentations; and Ezra-Nehemiah are all attested in later Christian and Jewish lists (cf. Leiman, Canonization [1976] 31–34; Beckwith, Canon [1985] 235–273). On the common identification of "Isaiah plus twelve" with the thirteen "prophets after Moses" of *AgAp.* 1.40, we would have in Josephus an inkling of a tripartite canon, although the second and third parts would differ in content from those of rabbinic tradition.

[45] Canon (1985) 99–100 n. 80: (1) Josephus stresses their predictive writing, whereas the prophets from Joshua onward engaged mainly in history, and (2) he is speaking of twelve authors rather than twelve books, whereas the thirteen volumes of *AgAp.* 1.40 could only include the

consistency of Josephus' language that we have noted elsewhere: he does not say simply that there were twelve prophets in addition to Isaiah, but rather that twelve prophets did the same thing as Isaiah did, namely, they wrote down their predictions. While BECKWITH's theory is not without its own logical difficulties,[46] no other solution seems more satisfactory at this time. There are simply too many variables and insufficient evidence to reconstruct Josephus' personal knowledge of any categorization of biblical materials. It is not something that he chooses to divulge. What he tell his readers, consistently, is that all of the Judean records were written by prophets long ago. What he meant by his remark about twelve prophets like Isaiah, we presently lack the resources to determine with precision.

6. The Bible in the *Judean War*

Studies of Josephus' Bible generally ignore the *War*, for obvious reasons. His first composition, which begins its story long after the biblical period (according to his exilic dating of Daniel) and deals with national history leading up to the great revolt, has little cause to mention scripture. The only sustained reference to the biblical materials comes in a part of Josephus' speech before the walls of Jerusalem, in which he adduces examples from Israel's past in favour of the pacifist option (5.379–393).

Moreover, an influential stream in Josephan scholarship has found in the *War* a work of either sheer betrayal and Roman propaganda or postwar politicking among the surviving Judean élites.[47] Scholars of this persuasion tend to argue that Josephus only becomes interested in the religious aspects of Judean culture after *War* was composed. And even this interest is sometimes regarded as a pretence to gain influence with the Yavnean Rabbis. Such views leave one hardly inclined to plumb the *War* for the possible impact of Jewish scriptures on Josephus' outlook, although SETH SCHWARTZ's recent *Josephus and Judaean Politics* extends this approach with an examination of allusions and references to biblical materials in the *War*. He concludes: "there is little evidence that [when he wrote the *War*] he knew the biblical texts at all".[48] SCHWARTZ argues that Josephus' routine contradiction of biblical details in *War*—even where this does not appear to serve his rhetorical needs—

writings of the twelve minor prophets as a single text. One might add that Josephus' introduction of these twelve near the end of the biblical paraphrase, as if they were a novelty, and his promise to discuss them in the sequel, would suit the hardly-mentioned minor prophets better than the more noted major authors.

[46] Josephus will go on to parade the fulfilled predictions of Jeremiah, Ezekiel, and Daniel (10.79, 107, 142, 269). This suggests that they should be included among the twelve who are like Isaiah. Perhaps, then, Josephus is not thinking of either the thirteen volumes of *AgAp.* 1.40 minus Isaiah or the twelve minor prophets, but is counting only the predictive prophets. Then, however, he should be left with four or fifteen, depending on whether the minor prophets were reckoned as a group or individually. In so speculating we have long since left the field of interpretation.

[47] This stream is represented by Laqueur, Josephus (1920); S.J.D.Cohen, Galilee and Rome (1979); and Schwartz, Judaean Politics (1990) among many others.

[48] Schwartz, Judaean Politics (1990) 25.

coupled with the priestly bias of his biblical interpretation, suggest that he knew only selections from the Scriptures, and that he acquired these through the oral culture of the priesthood rather than through firsthand knowledge of the texts.

Coming from another perspective altogether, HELGO LINDNER has found in *War*'s view of history clear traces of Jeremianic and Danielic influence. These influences appear not so much in direct reference as in Josephus' most basic views: that nations rise and fall under divine supervision, and that Rome is the current choice; God is also using Rome to punish Israel for its transgressions.[49] These views, which constitute the fabric of *War*, are also important themes in *Antiquities*, where they are presented as the main trend of Judean tradition, drawn from Jeremiah and Daniel.[50] As for his many and undeniable departures from the biblical text, it is worth noting: (a) one might gain a similar impression from a proportionate sampling of *Antiquities*, where Josephus has biblical texts at hand, and (b) SCHWARTZ may have underestimated the rhetorical force of some changes in *War*.[51]

The question of Josephus' use of Jewish Scriptures in *War* is far from settled in the field as a whole; my inclinations will be clear from the foregoing summary. It will doubtless remain a controversial issue for some time to come because it is closely tied to more basic issues of Josephus' literary and intellectual integrity, self understanding, and Judean identity. That Josephus publicly prides himself on the reputation that he had among his compatriots for traditional learning is not in doubt. Exactly what that might mean for a topic such as this requires further exploration.

7. Conclusions and Implications

Our conclusion may be briefly stated. Reading *AgAp.* 1.37–43 in context shows how little amenable it is to our usual questions about the first-century 'Jewish canon'. In writing to persuade Greek speakers of the nobility and antiquity of Judean culture, Josephus simply means to stress the great age, small number, harmony, and prophetic authorship of the Judean records. He uses the generic language of his implied readers, not in-house Judean terminology. His actual use of scriptural materials in *Antiquities* agrees by and large with the summary statement in *Against Apion*: he really did believe that

[49] Lindner, Geschichtsauffassung (1972) 42–48. So also Gray, Figures (1992) 70–79.

[50] Cf. Mason, Daniel (1995).

[51] See my review of SCHWARTZ in IOUDAIOS REVIEW 2.008 (April, 1992), especially 3.7. Note also that Josephus publicly prides himself on the reputation that he had among his compatriots for traditional learning; accordingly, he claims that his education between *War* and *Antiquities* consisted mainly of Greek grammar, poetry, and prose (*Ant.* 20.263). It is not clear how this claim to traditional knowledge would have helped him, in view of his many Judean antagonists (cf. *Life* 416, 424), if it did not reflect a measure of truth. Further, if, as SCHWARTZ proposes, this interim period was also devoted to acquiring a basic knowledge of the scriptures in Hebrew and Greek, along with Alexandrian and other Judean literature, then Josephus was most fortunate to discover so much in the Bible that happened to support his main emphases in *War*.

prophets wrote the records in a bygone age. Although much is omitted from his biblical paraphrase, what we have represents the heart of both traditional Hebrew and Greek canons; he seems aware, though he does not advertise it, that books like 1 and 2 Maccabees are later and separate.

This effort to engage Josephus' world of thought and language says little directly about the shape of the Jewish Bible(s) in the first century. My goal has been to clarify what exactly Josephus says that will need to be explained by any broad historical hypothesis. But rather than feign ignorance of the ways in which Josephus is used in historical reconstructions, we may spell out in a preliminary way some direct implications of this study for the historical problem.

1. Josephus boasts about the age of the Judean records and does not convey any sense of either deprivation or nostalgia. In our passage he neither pines for a closed prophetic age nor hopes for its return. Thus he provides a very poor foil for claims that Jesus or Christianity fulfilled a Jewish dream in bringing the return of the "quenched spirit". – Whether such a foil might be found in other literature is another issue.

2. He presents his positions as the common property of all Judeans – women, children, prisoners of war – and he would presumably be vulnerable to refutation if he were making this up or presenting idiosyncratic views as common. It would accordingly be hard to argue from Josephus for an open canon or for one that was recently settled – at Yavneh, for example.[52] Those who are convinced by other evidence of the fluidity of scriptural boundaries in the first century do better, perhaps, to isolate Josephus as idiosyncratic or original in spite of his claim to speak on behalf of Judeans.[53]

3. But that step, too, is hard to justify. Perhaps the most significant corollary of this study is its negative results regarding any appeal to circumstantial evidence in support of the argument for an open canon. RUDOLF MEYER, for example, argues for an open canon on the grounds that: (a) other sources such as Ben Sira's "praise of the fathers" (44.1–50.24) and the DSS make no distinction between biblical, pre-Mosaic, and post-Artaxerxian texts (e.g., 1 Enoch and Tobit); (b) even within the DSS versions of biblical texts like the Psalms, there is much rearrangement and nonbiblical material; and (c) the texts of these documents often differ from the MT. This evident freedom to interpret, add to, and subtract from biblical texts leads MEYER to isolate Josephus' fixed notion of a canon as an inner-Pharisaic view that could only have gradually come to prominence with the emergence of the rabbinic coalition after 70; it cannot reflect a common first-century Jewish view.[54]

---

[52] BARTON (Oracles [1986] 59) strains Josephus' words beyond tolerance when he suggests: "In maintaining the small compass of Jewish Scripture he does not, as a matter of fact, say that no other book could conceivably be found that would meet the criterion of prophetic authorship, only that no more than twenty-two have until now been found to do so".

[53] So Sundberg, Old Testament (1968) 143–155; and Meyer, Kanontheorie (1974) 285–299. Barton (Oracles [1986] 59): "in setting limits to the canon at all Josephus is out of step with his contemporaries".

[54] Meyer, Kanontheorie (1974) 290, 298–299.

The problem with this reasoning will now be obvious, for all of the phenomena that MEYER finds in other sources are much more clearly and fully present in Josephus' own use of the scriptures in *Antiquities*. As we have seen, he continues his narrative to the present, treating books like Pseudo-Aristeas and 1 Maccabees the same way that he treats biblical material. For the biblical period itself, he splices in all sorts of oral and written traditions. He quite thoroughly alters the texts to suit his own needs. And in numerous ways he evokes a prophetic aura for his own accounts. It is fair to say that if we lacked the *Against Apion*, Josephus himself would offer the clearest case for an open canon. But we do have the *Against Apion*, in which this same Josephus most emphatically, not to say matter-of-factly, insists that the Judean records have long since been completed in twenty-two volumes. Plainly, then, the circumstantial evidence of Josephus' own 'Bible' in *Antiquities* does not mean what it might seem to mean at first: it does not, after all, imply an open canon. Indeed, once we know *Against Apion*, we can go back to *Antiquities* and discover that Josephus really does believe that the succession of prophets has ceased, and we can discern a seam after the "records" have been exhausted. *Against Apion* was written as a deliberate sequel to *Antiquities*, so it is unlikely that Josephus is aware of any substantial conflict between the two. This means that his willingness to alter the biblical text in manifold ways proves nothing about his formal view of canon. His example removes the force from appeals to circumstantial evidence as proof that the DSS authors or Philo or Ben Sira had an open canon.

4. Josephus' remarks in *AgAp.* 1.37–43 cannot be made, no matter how long we gaze at them, to designate standard enumerations of divisions within the first-century canon. His language is on a different plane. His most consistent ordering criterion is that of genre, viz.: laws, tradition, hymns, and advice. These genres do not correlate to 'sections' of Josephus' Bible. They simply provide a means of elaborating for gentile readers on the various kinds of material to be found among the twenty-two volumes of records.

5. Because these genres confound all other categories, the phrase "the laws and the related official records" (1.43) should no longer be taken to indicate a major canonical division.[55] Josephus is working with a public world of discourse, according to which a nation's laws are self-evidently basic to its tradition. The phrase "and the related official records" would thus include everything else that Josephus has just mentioned, even Moses' non-legal writings ("tradition").

6. What we have in Josephus is not inconsistent with the most traditional views of an early and tripartite canon – or for that matter, with modified tripartite and bipartite theories. It is just that he says nothing about any of this. One cannot say either that Josephus's canon differs from traditional canons, and so supports a theory of canonical or scriptural pluralism. We presently have no way of recovering the internal shape of his Bible – if indeed

[55] Contra Barton, Oracles (1986) 48; Feldman, Mikra (1988) 470.

he even thought in such terms – from *AgAp.* 1 or from his actual use of Scripture in *Ant.* 1–11.

7. Paradoxically, the little-noticed *Ant.* 10.35 might say more about Josephus' Bible than the much discussed *AgAp.* 1.37–43 – if its twelve-plus-one prophets correspond to the thirteen prophets of the latter passage. But the meaning of that remark is unclear, and BECKWITH's connection of it with the minor prophets faces fewer obstacles than any other theory.

See further "Supplement to Chapter Five", HBOT I/2, pp. 591–617.

B.
Parting of the Ways: Jewish and Christian *Scriptural* Interpretation in Antiquity

Chapter six

Social and Institutional Conditions for Early Jewish and Christian Interpretation of the Hebrew Bible with Special Regard to Religious Groups and Sects

By Jarl Fossum, Ann Arbor

Bibliography: R. Bóid, "Use, Authority and Exegesis of Mikra in the Samaritan Tradition", *Mikra* (CRINT 2/1; Assen/Philadelphia 1988) 595–633; R. Bultmann, *Die Geschichte der Synoptischen Tradition* (Göttingen 1964); J. H. Charlesworth, "Qumran Scrolls and a Critical Consensus", *Jesus and the Dead Sea Scrolls* (ed. J. H. Charlesworth; New York 1993); D. Daube, "On Acts 23: Sadducees and Angels", *JBL* 109 (1990) 493–97; S. L. Davies, "John the Baptist and the Essene Kashruth", *NTS* 29 (1983) 569–71; F. Dexinger, "Der Ursprung der Samaritaner im Spiegel der frühen Quellen", *Die Samaritaner* (ed. F. Dexinger/R. Pummer, WdF 604; Darmstadt 1992); J. Fossum, "Sects and Movements", *The Samaritans* (ed. A. D. Crown; Tübingen 1989) 293–389; idem, "The Apostle Concept in the Qūrān and in Pre-Islamic Near Eastern Literature", *Literary Heritage of Classical Islam* (ed. M. Mir; Princeton 1993) 149–67; M. Goulder, "The Two Roots of the Christian Myth", *The Myth of God Incarnate* (ed. J. Hick; Philadelphia 1977); Z. J. Kapera (ed.), *Qumran Cave 4. Special Report on 4 Q MMT* (Kraukau 1991); H. G. Kippenberg, *Garizim und Synagoge* (RVV 30; New York 1971); J. Neusner, *The Oral Torah* (San Francisco 1986); B. A. Pearson, "Use, Authority and Exegesis of Mikra in Gnostic Literature", *Mikra* (1988) 635–52; R. Riesner, "Jesus, the Primitive Community, and the Essene Quarter of Jerusalem", *Jesus and the Dead Sea Scrolls* (ed. J. H. Charlesworth; New York 1993); P. Stenhouse (ed.), *The Kitab al Tarikh of Abu'l Fath* (University of Sydney 1980); idem, *The Kitab al Tarikh of Abu'l Fath* (Studies in Judaism 1; Sydney 1985); A. Strobel, "Die Wasseranlagen der *Ḫirbet Qumrān*", *ZDPV* 88 (1972) 55–86; J. Thomas, *Le mouvement baptiste en Palestine et Syrie* (Gembleoux 1935); R. de Vaux, *Archaeology of the Dead Sea Scrolls* (London 1973); G. Vermes, *The Religion of Jesus the Jew* (London/Minneapolis 1993); B. G. Wood, "To Dip or Sprinkle? The Qumran Cisterns in Perspective", *BASOR* 256 (1984) 45–60.

1. The Origination of Sects[1]

The existence of sects can be explained in different ways. Justin Martyr asserted that Christian heresy was the work of demons (1 *Apol.* 26.1).[2] Origen, however, would justify the existence of Christian sects. He argued

---

[1] I use much the same terminology as that established by E. Troeltsch. The term 'sect' denotes a minority group to which individuals claim adherence on the basis of conviction or experience. The demand that one has to prove one's commitment to the group would seem to be especially strong in sects. Sadduceism and main line Samaritanism would seem to have to be termed 'churches': they were religious systems which had adapted more or less to the prevalent politics and culture. The sectarians feel more or less uncomfortable in society at large.

[2] Cf. Iren., *Adv. haer.* 1.25.3.

that "heresies of different kinds have never originated from any matter in which the principle involved was not important and beneficial to human life" (*Contra Cels.* 3.12). After having pointed to the existence of "heresies" in medicine and philosophy, Origen states, "Even Judaism itself afforded a pretext for the origination of heresies, in the various acceptation accorded to the writings of Moses and those of the prophets" (ibid.). He goes on to say that the case is the same in Christianity: "... there necessarily originated heresies – not at all, however, as the result of faction and strife, but through the earnest desire of literary men to become acquainted with the doctrines of Christianity".

Few people today would subscribe to Origen's view that the Jewish and Christian sects arose simply as a result of Scriptural interpretation.[3] As for Christian sects at least, a different view was taken already by Hegesippus, a second century Jewish Christian writer who is quoted by Eusebius:

> The same writer [i.e., Hegesippus] also describes the beginning of the heresies of his time in the following way: "After James the Just had suffered martyrdom for the same reason as the Lord, Simeon, his cousin, the son of Clopas, was appointed bishop, whom they all proposed because he was another cousin of the Lord. For this cause they called the Church a virgin, for it had not yet been corrupted by vain messages. But Thebuthis, because he had not been made bishop, began its corruption by means of the seven sects existing among the people".
> (*Hist. eccl.* 4.22.4–5)

According to Hegesippus, the origin of heresy in Christianity is to be explained from psycho-sociological circumstances: a certain dissuaded person (a 'loser') allied himself with venal sects in order to get back at the group to which he formerly belonged.

Historically correct or not, Hegesippus may be taken as a witness to MAX WEBER's theory that the formation of sects may owe not a little to persons with some charismatic character. The "Legitimate Teacher" of the Qumran community, the Samaritans, Dositheus and Simon, John the Baptist, and Jesus are more well-known names which come to mind. Furthermore, Hegesippus' account illustrates the fact that persons such as these stand forth at times of political, social, cultural, or religious cruciality or discomposure.

2. The Proliferation of Jewish and Christian Sects

The seven sects are listed by Hegesippus. Eusebius reports:

> The same writer also describes the sects which once existed among the Jews as follows: "Now there were various opinions among the Circumcision, among the Children of Israel, against the Tribe of Judah and the Messiah [i.e., the Church], as follows: Essenes, Galileans, Hemerobaptists, Masbotheans, Samaritans, Sadducees, and Pharisees".
> (Ibid. 4.22.7)

The number of seven sects appears to be conventional (cf. the number of days in the week, the seven planets, etc.); it is also found in Justin Martyr

[3] Equally unconvincing is Tertullian's assertion that philosophical queries into the origin and essence of evil led people astray (*Adv. Marc.* 1.2).

and may have been the number given in the lost Syntagma of Hippolytus. Justin enumerates Sadducees, Genistae, Meristae, Galilaeans, Hellenists, Pharisees, and Baptists (*Dial.* 80.4).[4] A list of seven sects is also found in Epiphanius, a witness to the Syntagma: Sadducees, Scribes, Pharisees, Hemerobaptists, Nasareans, Ossenes, and Herodians (*Pan.* chs. 14 ff.).[5]

The other Syntagma witnesses, Philaster and Pseudo-Tertullian, are not in complete agreement with the bishop of Salamis. Philaster lists Dositheans, Sadducees, Pharisees, Samaritans, Nazoreans, Essenes, various Canaanite groups, and Herodians (*Div. her. liber* chs. 4 ff.). If we leave out the Canaanite groups, we have a list of seven sects.

Pseudo-Tertullian has only four sects: Dositheans, Sadducees, Pharisees, and Herodians (*Adv. omn. haer.* chs. 1 ff.). Every sect can be found in Epiphanius and Philaster, so Pseudo-Tertullian would seem to be a summary of Hippolytus' Syntagma.

The Dositheans were strictly speaking no Jewish sect but an important Samaritan group in the first centuries CE. This is correctly recorded by Epiphanius, who also knows three additional Samaritan sects: Essenes (*sic*!), Sebueans, and Gorothenians (*Pan.* chs. 11 ff.).[6]

The picture resulting from this quick tour of early Christian heresiography is confusing. It certainly shows that Judaism and Samaritanism at the beginning of the common era were no monolithic movements. In the Palestinian Talmud, it is even said that there were as many as twenty-four מינים, 'heresies' or 'sects', at the time of the destruction of the temple (*y. Sanh.* 10.5). Again, the number appears to be conventional (the twelve tribes multiplied by two, the number of priestly classes), but it illustrates the complexity of the situation.

It is possible to say something about the scriptural interpretation of some of these groups in the light of their social setting. This holds true for the Samaritans, the Dositheans, the Sadducees, the Pharisees, and the Essenes

---

[4] It does not seem likely that Hegesippus used Justin's Syntagma, which is lost to us. The names of the Meristae and the Genistae have been made the subject of some intelligent guesswork, but nothing plausible can be said about these sects. The Galileans may be identical with the Zealots; see below, n. 47.

[5] The Scribes are no sect; more than one group had scribes. The Nasareans (Νασαραῖοι) are said to be a pre-Christian Jewish sect; Epiphanius distinguishes them carefully from the Jewish Christian Nazoreans (Ναζωραῖοι). The Ossenes (for the name, see n. 6) are Jewish sectaries who rallied around the Jewish Christian sect-leader Elchasai. Epiphanius locates them in northern Transjordania; originally, they may have been identical with the Essenes who went to the "Land of Damascus" (CD 6:5 ff; 7–15 ff; 8–21; 19:34; 20:12; cf. 3Q 15). The Herodians, who are mentioned as a Jerusalem group in the Gospels, may also have been an Essene branch. The Essenes were favoured by Herod the Great (Joseph., *Ant.* 15.373 ff.), during whose reign Qumran was not inhabited; see de Vaux, Archaeology (1973) 21–23. For an Essene quarter in Jerusalem, see Riesner, Jesus (1993) 198–234.

[6] Removing both the Samaritans and the Dositheans from Hippolytus' list, Epiphanius substituted the Scribes and the Hemerobaptists. Since the bishop of Salamis knew the Essenes as a Samaritan sect, he invented the name form "Ossenes" for the Jewish sect. Not having heard about the Jewish sect of the Nasareans, Philaster exchanged their name for that of the Jewish Christian Nazoreans.

(granted it is possible to draw on the Qumran writings). We are left more or less in the dark when trying to probe the other groups.

What about the early Christian sects? Hegesippus says that from the seven sects, came "Simon, whence the Simonians, and Cleobius, whence the Cleobians, and Dositheus, whence the Dositheans, and Gorthaeus, whence the Gorathenians, and the Masbotheans" (Euseb., *Hist. eccl.* 4.22.5).[7] From these derivative sects, the Gnostic heresies took their rise: Menanderianists, Marcianists, Carpocratians, Valentinians, Basilidians, and Saturnilians (ibid.).

The Masbotheans appear both in the list of the "seven sects among the people" and at the end of the record of the derivative sects. Their occurrence at the latter place may be due to a gloss. The Masbotheans are the only group without an eponymous founder.[8]

3. The Samaritan Connection

Looking over the lists in Hegesippus and the witnesses to the Syntagma tradition, we are struck by the number of Samaritan components.[9] Four of the five derivative sects in Hegesippus have a Samaritan provenance, while the remaining one is associated with Samaritan sectarianism. Simon is the well-known Samaritan heresiarch of the first century CE (Acts 8). Justin and Irenaeus hold him to be the *fons e origo* of Christian heresy (Just., 1 *Apol.* 26; Iren., *Adv. haer.* 1.23.2; 27.3).[10] Some sources associate Simon and Dositheus, another Samaritan heretic (Orig., *Contra Cels.* 1.57; *Comm. in Matt.*, *Ser.* 33, *ad.* 24:4f; *Ps.-Clem. Hom.* 2.23f; *Rec.* 1.54).[11]

In the apocryphal correspondence between Paul and the Corinthians found in the *Acts of Paul*, Cleobius is a false teacher who appears in the company of the arch-heretic, Simon (ch. 8). The same pairing is found in *Didascalia Apostolorum* 6.8.[12]

Nothing is known of a sect-leader by the name of Gorthaeus, but Epiphanius lists the Gorothenians as a Samaritan sect (*Pan.* ch. 12). Moreover, he lists them after the Sebueans (Σεβουαῖοι). This name may translate צבועייא or צבואייא, from the verb צבע, 'immerse', 'baptize'. The Sebueans may thus be identical with the Masbotheans, whose name would seem to be a translation of מצבעותא, "those who baptize themselves", or are "baptized", מצבע. Apparently a Samaritan sect of baptizers, the Masbotheans were added to Hegesippus' record of the derivative sects.

---

[7] Theodoret of Cyrus lists Simon as the originator of the other sects and adds three Christian groups (*Haer. fab. comp.* 1.1).

[8] In Rufinus' Latin translation of Eusebius, the Masbotheans are derived from Masbutheus.

[9] See Goulder, Two Roots (1977) 66; Fossum, Sects (1989) 298.

[10] Irenaeus may or may not have been dependent on Justin's lost Syntagma.

[11] See further n. 12 and Photius, *Bibliotheca* 285a. See Fossum, Sects, 299–300.

[12] In *Apost. Const.* 6.8.1, Simon and Cleobius are pupils of Dositheus. Epiphanius asserts that Cleobius opposed the supranatural conception of Christ (*Pan.* 51.6). A certain Cleobulus is attacked by Pseudo-Ignatius, *Ep. ad Trall.* 11.3.

The group was significant enough to be cited alongside the Samaritans in Hegesippus' list of the seven sects among the people.[13] They are also mentioned by the Samaritan chronicler Abu'l Fatḥ.[14]

The prominence given to the Samaritans and their sects in Hegesippus is matched by the Syntagma tradition. Hippolytus apparently described Dositheus as the first heretic and the fountain-head of the church of the Sadducees.[15]

We ought to give the Samaritans careful consideration when dealing with the different sectarian positions around the turn of our era. As a matter of fact, the first breach in the Hebrew nation was the Jewish/Samaritan schism.

4. The Samaritans and Their Interpretation of Scripture

Traditionally, the origin of the Samaritans is found in 2 Kings 17. This chapter relates that the Israelites in the Northern Kingdom of Israel were deported by the Assyrian king, who turned the country into one of his provinces (Samaria, the name of the capitol, being extended to the entire land). Foreigners being brought into the country grafted a superficial Yahweh cult upon their own religion and continued the worship on the high places made by the שמרנים, an anachronistic term designating the people in the Northern Kingdom (2 Kgs 17:29).

It has now become clear that the account in 2 Kings 17, being part of the Deuteronomistic centralization program, is a strong Judaean polemic against the Israelite cult at Bethel.[16] It has been known for a long time that only a very small percentage of the population in the Northern Kingdom was carried away.[17] The Bible testifies to the existence of Israelites from the North wor-

[13] The coupling is also found in a postscript to the Armenian translation of Ephraem's commentary on the Diatessaron of Tatian: Pharisees, Sadducees, *Hasnazi* (? Essenes), Galileans, *Mazbuthazi*, Samaritans, and *Habionenses* (? Ebionites). However, the list may be a revision of that of Hegesippus.
In *Apost. Const.* 6.6, the Basmotheans (*sic*!) are reported to "deny providence, and say that the world is ruled by spontaneous motion, and take away the immortality of the soul". They occur after the Sadducees and the Pharisees, and are followed by the Hemerobaptists, the Christian sect of the Ebionites, and the Essenes. In sect. 7, Simon is described as the fountain-head of the "new heresies".
Again, we may have a revision of Hegesippus' list. In any case, the description of the Masbothean doctrine is hardly trustworthy: it is similar to Josephus' report on the Sadducees (*Ant.* 13.173; 18.17).
Equally untrustworthy is the report by Pseudo-Jerome that the Masbotheans were Jewish Christian Sabbatarians. Isidor Hispalensis asserts that the Sebueans were Christian Sabbatarians (*Etymol.* 8.4). This may be taken to corroborate the identification of the Masbotheans and the Sebueans.

[14] See below, 246.

[15] The Dosithean derivation of Sadduceism is maintained even by Epiphanius, who discusses Dositheus in his survey of the Samaritans and their sects.

[16] For the origin of Samaritanism, see now the authoritative discussion by Dexinger, Ursprung (1992) 67–140.

[17] The immigrants, who constituted the upper classes, were in minority. Moreover, they adopted the cult of Yahweh, as can be seen from their theophoric names, witnessed by the Elephantine papyri and the papyri from Wadi Daliyah.

shipping in Jerusalem after 722 (2 Chron 30; 34:9; 35:18; Jer 41:4–5, 11). However, they apparently did not regard Zion as the only legitimate place of worship.

Relations between North and South were further strained after the return of the Judaean exiles (Ezra 4:1–5).[18] The erection of the temple on Mt. Gerizim, which took place sometime between 400 and 200 BCE,[19] did nothing to diminish the tension, but the definite breach between the Israelites and the Judaeans occurred when the John Hyrcanus destroyed the Gerizim temple in 129 BCE. If this was an attempt at religious *Anschluß*,[20] it failed. From that time onwards we can talk about Samaritans and Jews.

The antagonism between Samaritans and Jews is reflected in Scriptural exegesis. The tenth commandment of the Samaritan Pentateuch (SP), which counts the Masoretic commandments as nine and adds a composition of Deut 11:29–30 and 27:2–7 to Exod 20:17 (and to Deut 5:18), is an injunction to worship on Mt. Gerizim. In Deut 11:29–30, it is charged that when the Hebrews enter the Promised Land, they should set a blessing for keeping the Law upon Mt. Gerizim and a curse for disobeying it on Mt. Ebal.[21] Deut 27 describes the rite in more detail. According to the MT text, the blessing shall be pronounced on Mt. Gerizim (27:12), but stones inscribed with the Law and an altar are to be erected on Mt. Ebal (27:4–5). In the SP, however, Mt. Gerizim is the place for the altar and the stones.

It may be discussed what was the original reading in Deut 27:4–5. Given the importance attributed to Shechem in Genesis through Judges, it is not improbable that the MT text represents an anti-Samaritan alteration of the original. As shown by the majority of LXX witnesses, the MT reading was established around the turn of our era, and the Hasmonean period would seem to be the time for the change of the original text. This would also seem true if the Samaritan text is the one having been changed. Alternatively, it may have been an earlier alteration lending legitimacy to the temple on Mt. Gerizim.

In Deuteronomy, the SP changes the MT reading "the place which the Lord your God will choose (*yibhḥar*)" to "the place which the Lord your God *has chosen* (*bāḥar*)". Deuteronomy never specifies "the place", and Jerusalem with Mt. Zion is not mentioned as a Hebrew cult place in the Torah. Shechem with Mt. Gerizim, however, was hallowed by the memory of the patriarchs and the place where Joshua sealed the inter-tribal pact. In fact, Shechem appears to have been the first sanctuary of the Hebrew tribes. When SP Deuteronomy speaks of the place which God *has chosen*, Shechem with Mt. Gerizim presents itself as a, if not *the*, prime candidate.

---

[18] Scholars distinguish two groups of opponents of the Judaeans: the ruling class in Samaria and the proto-Samaritans.

[19] Dexinger, Ursprung (1992) 102–116, accepts Josephus' account that the temple was built during Alexander's reign.

[20] This does not seem to have been considered seriously by Dexinger, Ursprung (1992).

[21] In Deut 11:30, the SP even reads, "beside the oak of Moreh in front of Shechem", while MT leaves out the reference to Shechem.

The canon of the Samaritans is the Pentateuch alone. For the Jews around the turn of our era, the Prophets and the Writings certainly did not have the same claim to authority as the Torah, so the rejection of the Prophets and the Writings on the part of the Samaritans does not have to be regarded as being bound up with the schism.[22] Like the Samaritans, the Jewish group of the Sadducees accepted the Pentateuch only.

On the other hand, the rejection of the Prophets found in the addition to Exod 20:18 (SP, v. 21 a) is clearly anti-Jewish. Here the Samaritans add Deut 5:28 b–31 and 18:18–22. The latter passage, which contains the prophecy of the advent of a Prophet like Moses and a warning against false prophets, splits the former. After God has expressed his wish that the Israelites will always keep his commandments (Deut 5:28 b–29), he promises that one day in the future he will raise up a Prophet like Moses and issues a warning against false prophets whose words will not come to pass. Thereupon God instructs Moses to bid the people to go back to their tents (Deut 5:30), and says, "As for you, stand here by me, and I shall teach you all the commandments, statutes and laws which you shall teach them" (Deut 5:31).

The false prophets against whom it is warned are of course the prophets in the Jewish Bible.[23] The Rabbis insisted that the prophets spoke only what was contained in the Law. To the Samaritans, however, their message was not in congruity with the contents of the Law; this was shown by the fact that their prophecies remained unfulfilled.

5. Samaritan Sects

The vicissitudes of the temple and its priesthood play a very decisive role in the origination of sects. The destruction of the temple on Mt. Gerizim occasioned a rupture within the Samaritan community. Abu'l Fatḥ, the fourteenth century chronicler, states that the first dissension within the community occurred when the Jews were ruled by John Hyrcanus.[24] The chronicler anachronistically refers to the sectarian movement as *Dustan* (דסתאן), which obviously suggests a connection with the name of Dositheus (דוסיס). It would seem that Dositheus in the first century CE became a central figure in an already existing Samaritan sectarian movement.[25]

A recurring trait in Abu'l Fatḥ's description of the Samaritan sects is his allegation that they altered the calendar. He offers some precise information in the case of the Dustan people. They are reported to have espoused a solar calendar and to have counted the "Fifties" from the morning of the day after

---

[22] Among the Jewish writings rejected by the Samaritans, some would actually seem to boost Samaritan ideology. Judges and Joshua readily come to mind. The Book of Hosea, the only Northern prophet, also appears as a candidate.

[23] See Kippenberg, Garizim und Synagoge (1971) 312.

[24] See P. Stenhouse (ed.), The Kitāb (1980) 80; idem (trans.), The *Kitāb Fatḥ* (1985) 109. See further Fossum, Sects, 293 n. 1.

[25] See Fossum, Sects (1989) 293 ff.

Passover, "like the Jews" (i.e., the Pharisaic Jews). The old Samaritan party had a luni-solar calendar and agreed with the Sadducees in counting from the first Sabbath which fell during Passover and the Feast of Unleavened Bread.

Epiphanius recounts that the Dositheans, together with "the Gorothenians and the others",[26] followed the same calendar as the Jews, obviously the Pharisaic Jews (*Pan.* chs. 12f.). The Essenes (who constitute a Samaritan sect in Epiphanius' book) and the Sebueans inverted the calendar and celebrated Passover in Tishri, etc. (chs. 11f.). This must be a gross exaggeration, but it stands to reason that people who broke with the temple and its priesthood would assert their rightfulness by claiming to have recovered ancient and divinely ordained practices which had been abandoned by the corrupt priests. Support for the solar calendar is of course found in the biblical story of the Flood.[27]

The sectarians were not anti-priestly *per se*. Abu'l Fatḥ says that the Dustan people had "their own priests and synagogues", and that the high priest's son, a very learned man, became their leader and composed a book in which he defamed all the high priests.

The destruction of the Gerizim temple apparently brought about the decentralization of the Samaritan community. With the dispersion of the Samaritans, the synagogue institution came into being.[28] In the synagogues, the study of the Law was the focal point of the religious life. This study would seem to have been led by priests. Abu'l Fatḥ reports that the sect of the *Sabūʿāī* had priests of their own who refused to submit to any central authority, but gave their own rulings on the text and the tradition.[29]

Although not anti-priestly *per se*, the sectaries were in opposition to the priests at Shechem. When the temple was destroyed, the cult on Mt. Gerizim did not cease. The Dustan sectarians, however, claimed that God should not be worshipped on Mt. Gerizim in this age, but that a rightful cult would be established in the age to come. According to Samaritan belief, the age of divine favour would be signalled by the recovery of the Tabernacle, which originally had been erected on the holy mount but was hidden by God when some Israelites started to worship at Shiloh. The Dustan people may have seen the destruction of the Gerizim temple as a divine punishment for having built a substitute for the Tabernacle.

It is palpable that the rejection of the Gerizim cult, however temporary, had to be justified by an authoritative text. The Dustan people claimed that the prohibition to worship on Mt. Gerizim in this age was found in a book of theirs which stemmed from the "children of the Apostle". The term for "book", *sifr*, usually means a sacred book, in particular the Bible. The title "Apostle" is frequently given to Moses. The dissidents may have claimed to

---

[26] The "others" are difficult to identify. If Epiphanius means the main line Samaritans, he is ignorant of their concurrence with Sadducean calendaric reckoning.

[27] See Fossum, Sects (1989) 310–11.

[28] For the ancient Samaritan synagogue, see Kippenberg, Garizim (1971) 145–61.

[29] See Bóid, Use, Authority and Exegesis (1988) 618–21.

possess the Bible formerly owned by Moses' family. However, we may also take "children" to mean "disciples". In the later Dositheаn movement, some groups were said to be "children" of their leaders.[30] The "children of the Apostle" may have been the seventy elders to whom Moses entrusted the Torah.

The success of Dositheus was no doubt due to the fact that his followers believed that he was the Prophet like Moses. Abu'l Fatḥ says that Dositheus "changed a lot of the Torah, like Ezra", and also composed books of his own.[31] The Dositheans obviously took his work to amount to the restoration of the genuine Law of Moses or at least the correct interpretation of it.

Abu'l Fatḥ cites one specific change of the biblical text made by Dositheus or on his authority: his followers read "marjoram" (Ar *saʿtar*) instead of "hyssop" (*'ezob*) in Exod 12:22. This was in fact an established equivalence, but while "hyssop" had a wide range of reference, "marjoram" was the plant which is known as *origanum syriacum* only. In the Passover ceremony of smearing the blood on the door frames, marjoram was actually the hyssop plant being used. Possessing a text which corresponded to the tradition, the Dositheans found their Bible to be superior to that of the priestly Samaritans.

The scribal work of Dositheus aimed at removing uncertainties and room for discussion in the understanding of the Law. This is also seen in the strict Sabbatarianism of his sect. Origen reports that Dositheus taught that people should remain in the garment and in the position in which they were overtaken on the Sabbath, until the Sabbath was over (*De princ.* 4.3.2).[32] The sect leader obviously had a very strict interpretation of Exod 16:29, "Remain every man where he is; let no man go from his place on the seventh day".

The authority of the biblical text is also seen from the fact that even Dositheus' asceticism was inferred from Num 18:17, which says that the blood of the first-born should be sprinkled on the altar. The asceticism of the Dositheans apparently was seen to be a substitute for the expiatory sacrifices which were carried out when the temple stood.[33]

Finally, it should be noted that the sectaries intensified the demand for ritual purity by their prescription of frequent water lustrations and immersion rites. The name of the sect of the Sebueans (probably identical with the Masbotheans) would seem to identify them as baptizers.[34] The Dositheans are reported by Abu'l Fatḥ to have "uttered all their prayers in water". A baptism rite would also seem to have been part of the official embracement of Dositheus' teaching.[35]

---

[30] See Fossum, Sects (1989) 352.

[31] Origen corroborates the statement that Dositheus wrote books (*Comm. in Joh.* 13.27, *ad* 4:28). Photius says that Dositheus also "adulterated the Mosaic Octateuch" [*sic*!] (*Bibliotheca* 285 a).

[32] Abu'l Fatḥ imputes strict Sabbatarianism to the Dustan group as well as the Dosithean sect; see Fossum, Sects, 314–15, 331–32.

[33] See Fossum, Sects (1989) 316–19.

[34] See above, 242.

[35] See Fossum, Sects (1989) 323–24.

The water cleansings and ritual baths of the sectarians appear to have underscored their challenge to the priests, who had to wash before beginning cultic service (*m. Yoma* 3:3 demands immersion). The sectaries were constantly in a state of purity equalling that of the officiating priest.

6. Jewish and Jewish Christian Baptismal Sects

The characteristics of the Samaritan sects recur in the Jewish and Jewish Christian sects. The Jewish sect about which we are best informed is that of the Essenes. This community originated among people being critical of the Hasmonean high priesthood. The radical branch of the group assumed an evasive attitude (to use a sociological term) and separated themselves from the temple and even the society at large (4QMMT C7; 1QS 5:1–2), which they regarded as being endangered by the unrightful priests (4QMMT B12:26–27). They founded an ascetic commune at Qumran.[36] However, they were not against the Jerusalem cult itself; they looked forward to the time when sacrifices again could be performed by a just priesthood (1QM 2:1ff; 11QTemple). Their leaders were priests, the "Sons of Ṣadoq" (1QS 5:2, 8).

While waiting for the restoration of a rightful cult, the Qumran sectaries assigned an expiatory function to their way of life. It was not primarily asceticism which was seen as a substitute for the sacrifices (as was the case in Dositheism), but strict observance of the Law and praise of God (1QS 8:4–9; 9:4–5).

The document known as 4QMMT, apparently a letter from the "Legitimate Teacher", the second (?) generation leader of the Qumran-Essenes, to the unrightful high priest in Jerusalem, deals with various cultic purity laws at some length.[37] Significantly, the letter opens with a reference to the solar calendar, which was observed by the Essenes as well as Samaritan sectarians. The Damascus Document states that God has revealed to the covenanters: "the hidden things in which all Israel has gone astray: His holy Sabbaths and His glorious feasts ..." (CD 3:14). Cultic communion with the rest of the Jewish nation was impossible for the Essenes who had a calendar of their own.

The reference to the Sabbaths in the quotation from the Damascus Document brings to mind Josephus' statement that the Essenes are stricter than all other Jews in abstaining from work on the Sabbath (*Bell.* 2.140). The Dositheans outdid the Essenes, since the latter allowed a Sabbath's day journey if the purpose was to pasture the cattle (CD 10:14ff.), but both sectarian groups were similar in that their Sabbatarianism exceeded the strictness of the priestly authorities at the cult centres.

---

[36] For the scholarly consensus that the Qumran people were Essenes, see Charlesworth, Qumran Scrolls (1993) xxxi–xxxvii.

[37] The letter was not published in a critical edition until recently, but many scholars (including the present writer) have possessed photocopies of the fragments for quite some time. On this document, see Kapera, Qumran Cave 4 (1991).

The quote from the Damascus Document also indicates that the interpretations of the Essenes were dependent upon revelations from God. This is borne out especially by the so-called Pesharim, where the Essenes take certain non-historical texts of the Bible to refer to events in their own history. The Pesher Habakkuk is a prime example of this kind of literature. But also some of the legal texts of Scripture need to be expounded by certain people (CD 5:4–5; 1QS 8:16; 1QpHab 8:2–3) whom God has given his Spirit (1QS 8:15). The "Legitimate Teacher" is a specially endowed instructor to whom God has revealed his mysteries, as is evidenced by the Thanksgiving Hymns and the Pesher Habakkuk in particular. Although the Teacher is never explicitly identified as the Mosaic-like Prophet, he certainly functioned as *a* prophet like Moses.[38]

The numerous aqueducts, cisterns and *mikveoth* found at Qumran testify to the Essene concern for constant ritual purity (cf. 1QS 5:13–14; 3:1–9; CD 10:10–13; Joseph., *Ant.* 2.128 ff.).[39] The same concern apparently is revealed by sect names such as "Morning Baptizers" (טבלי שחרית), "Hemerobaptists", and "Baptists"; they may actually denote the same general movement.[40] Epiphanius says that the Hemerobaptists insisted on the necessity of being "purified from all guilt" every day (*Pan.* 17.1.3).[41] The Morning Baptizers reproached the Pharisees for invoking God without having bathed (*t. Yad.* 2:20);[42] the former apparently held baptism to be a prerequisite for the performance of cultic acts.

The Pseudo-Clementine Homilies call John the Baptist a "Hemerobaptist" (3.23). Now John cannot be characterized as a "Daily Baptizer", but he no doubt belongs to the general Jewish baptismal movement. The once-for-all baptism of John, a priest (Luke 1:5 ff.), was probably a rite which had to be accepted by those who wanted to be members of the eschatological community. John's cultic orientation is also evidenced by his prophesy that the Coming One too would be a baptizer (Mark 1:8; Matt 3:11; Luke 3:16).

It is not implausible that John the Baptist claimed (or was claimed) to be the Prophet like Moses (cf. Luke 1:76). John baptized in the desert, and Moses was believed to have conferred a baptism upon the desert generation (1 Cor 10:1–2; cf. John 1:25).[43]

The Jewish Christian sects of the Ebionites and the Elchasaites are also said to be baptizers. The Ebionites prayed immediately upon their frequent,

---

[38] A couple of Qumran writings witness the expectation of the Prophet like Moses (1QS 9:11; 4QTest 1 ff.). Now we also hear about the future "Seeker of the Law" (4QFlor 1:11 ff; CD 7:18) and the "One Teaching Righteousness at the end of days" (CD 6:11). If the Qumran Essenes did not expect the return of the "Legitimate Teacher" himself, they apparently awaited the coming of one having a similar function.

[39] See Strobel, Die Wasseranlagen (1972) 55–86; Wood, To Dip or Sprinkle? (1984) 45–60.

[40] The monograph of Thomas, Le mouvement (1935), still awaits replacement.

[41] *Apost. Const.* 6.6 says that the Hemerobaptists do not eat if they cannot wash, and that they even cleanse their beds, tables, seats, cups, and platters. *Sib. Or.* 4.165 ff. appears to be an admonition expressing the piety of the Hemerobaptists.

[42] Cf. *Sib. Or.* 3.591 ff.

[43] John's ascetic diet (Mark 1:6) may have been that of an Essene having left the Qumran commune; see Davies, John the Baptist (1983) 569–71.

even daily purificatory baths (*Ps.-Clem. Hom.* 10.1; 11.1; 14.3; cf. Epiphan., *Pan.* 30.16). The Elchasaites prayed during their therapeutic bathings (Hipp., *Ref.* 9.15.5). Epiphanius reports that the Jewish Christians were so concerned with purity that if they met someone "upon coming up from immersion in water and washing", they returned and performed their baptism again (*Pan.* 30.2.5).

To the Jewish Christians, Jesus was the "True Prophet", in actual fact the Prophet like Moses, whose work it was to point out the false parts of the Law and establish the genuine Torah (*Ps.-Clem. Hom.* 2.38.51–2; 3.18 ff, 47 ff.). Moses had delivered the Law orally to the seventy elders, but false pericopes were worked into it when it was committed to writing (*Ps.-Clem. Hom.* 3.47).

Elchasai apparently held the same view. Epiphanius says that the Jewish Christian sect-leader "rejected the Books of Moses, like the Nasareans" (*Pan.* 19.5.1), but this "rejection" is probably to be understood in the following manner: "... he substituted some things for others" (*Pan.* 19.1.5). The Jewish sect of the Nasareans, with whom the bishop of Salamis compares Elchasai, maintained that the common version of the Pentateuch was not the one which had been given to Moses (*Pan.* ch. 18).

The Nasareans and the Jewish Christians rejected the parts of Scripture which speak of bloody sacrifices and the eating of meat (*Ps.-Clem. Hom.* 2.44; 3.52; 12.6; Epiphan., *Pan.* 30.13.5; 15.3; et passim). Different sources may be identified for this rejection on the part of the Jewish Christians. The radical anti-cultic sentiment may be derived from certain utterances in the prophetical canon, from Jesus himself (Mark 11:15–17), and from the theology of the Christian party of the "Hellenists" (Acts 6:13–14; 7:42–50). In any event, by asserting that the genuine Law did not speak of sacrifices, the Jewish Christians had a hermeneutical tool by means of which they could come to terms with the catastrophe of the year 70 CE.

The asceticism of the Jewish Christians can find a certain Israelite precedent in the way of life of the old Rechabites (Jer 35), who realized the mode of living of the desert generation (cf. Deut 29:5). But we should not discard the possibility of an influence from the general Hellenistic antithesis between the spirit and the flesh: it was a prevalent view that a mortification of the latter led to a higher spiritual state.[44]

According to Ebionite belief, Christ as the True Prophet had formerly appeared in a series of manifestations from Adam to Moses. This prophetical succession stood in opposition to that of the high priest (*Ps.-Clem. Hom.* 2.16). Again it is seen that the authority of the official priesthood is challenged by people who claim to have recovered the true meaning of the Law. Through lustration rites and asceticism, the sectaries attain to a state of purity rivalling and even superseding that of the priests.

[44] There is little evidence to the effect that the Jewish Christians regarded their asceticism as being of expiatory import. But note that James the Just, who (according to tradition) eschewed meat and wine, is said to have been found constantly in the temple, "kneeling and praying for forgiveness of the people" (Euseb., *Hist. eccl.* 2.23.6).

Carrying the prophetical succession further, Elchasai took himself to be a new manifestation of Christ. Later, Mani claimed to be the final manifestation of the eternal revealer figure. Muhammed adapted the same idea,[45] and in Shia Islam the dynamic idea of the cyclic revelation is still seen to be alive.

7. Pharisees, Sadducees, Essenes, Christians, and Gnostics

Josephus mentions the Pharisees for the first time during the reign of John Hyrcanus (134–104 BCE): the Pharisee Eleazar suggested that the king should surrender his high priestly office (*Ant.* 13.288 ff.). The Pharisees as well as the Essenes appear to have emerged from the ranks of the *Ḥasidim*, the "Pious" who supported the Maccabees (1 Macc 2:42–43). Being conservative and scrupulous observers of the Law recruited mainly from the priesthood, they turned against the Hasmonean rulers when the latter usurped the high priestly office. While some of the *Ḥasidim* isolated themselves in the wilderness at Qumran,[46] others tried to adapt to society. The latter developed into the Pharisaic sect.[47]

The Pharisees took the priestly purity rules to be incumbent upon the people at large. The linchpin for their program was Exod 19:6, which says that all Israel should be holy and priests for God. Moreover, the priests had deserted Israel and its God: therefore, penance had to be done.

The numerous and complicated priestly purity rules were extremely difficult to practise for people living in society at large. The Pharisees got together in clubs of *Ḥaberim*, where they were certain that their demands for cultic purity were met by their "associates" (cf. the name of the Pharisees, *Perushim*, which probably means the 'Separated Ones'). The *Ḥaberim* studied the Law and formulated new rules so the Torah could be made applicable to every-day situations in society (cf. the close association of "scribes and Pharisees" in the Gospels). Thus, the clubs of Pharisaic *Ḥaberim* developed into veritable schools, the most famous being Beth Hillel and Beth Shammai, named after two teachers (Rabbis) who lived at the time of Herod the Great (d. 4 BCE).

---

[45] See Fossum, The Apostle Concept (1993) 149 ff.

[46] The author of 4QMMT says that he and his associates have "separated" (*parashnu*) from the people at large (C7). *Ps.-Clem.* 1.53–54 relates a dissension in the group of the Sadducees which led some of them to "separate" themselves. Cf. also 1 Macc 2:29–38, which speaks of the retirement into the wilderness of some people who sought "righteousness and justice".

[47] There may also have been a group of Essenes sticking together in Jerusalem (see above, n. 5). Are they to be found in Luke's reference to the "priests" embracing Christianity (Acts 6:7)? The Zealots, although they too were in opposition to the official priesthood, stand by themselves in their aggressive attitude towards the ruling powers. Moreover, the Zealots, whose movement appears to have been made up of people from different social groups (the majority probably being Galilean tenants), do not seem to have been united by a religious program beyond that of a general wish to guard the honour of God and the purity of Israel. Note, however, that Josephus in one place says that the "fourth philosophy" agrees with the Pharisaic teaching (*Ant.* 18.4–10, 23–25).

The later Zealots may have fed on eschatological interpretations of Scripture, for several of their leaders are reported to have put forth "messianic" claims. In this respect, the Zealots can be seen to approach the Essenes and the Christians.

Hillel is attributed with seven rules for scriptural interpretation, so-called *middoth*. In the beginning of the second century CE, Rabbi Ishmael increased the number to thirteen. Later we hear about no less than thirty-two *middoth*.

In their interpretation of Scripture, the Pharisaic Rabbis distinguished themselves from the other sects. The Rabbis drew a clear line between biblical books, the written Law, תורה שבכתב, and their own writings, called the "oral law", תורה שבעל פה. The biblical period was regarded as a closed chapter, and the Rabbis deliberately abandoned the literary forms and language of the Bible (*b. 'Abod. Zar* 58 b; *b. Menah.* 65 a). The Holy Spirit, i. e. the prophetical inspiration, had deported from Israel (*b. Sota* 48 b; *b. Sanh.* 11 a). The expert decisions of the Rabbis, reached by means of the various *middoth*, replaced pronouncements made in the name of God.

In contrast to the Pharisees, the Essenes invoked only the written Law (4Q MMT B 77; C 10–12). 4Q MMT is no collection comparable to the rabbinic *halakoth*, which are thematically arranged rulings made by the Rabbis on the basis of tradition and majority vote. It actually would seem that the Essenes despised the *halakoth* of the Rabbis. The Pesher Nahum speaks derogatorily about the "seekers after smooth things", *doreshe halaqoth* (4QpNah 1:2, 7; 2:2, 4; 3:3, 7). These "seekers" may have been Pharisees who did not adhere to a literal interpretation of the Law, but tried to adapt the Torah to suit life in a society different from that of ancient Israel.

In rejecting the oral tradition, the Essenes were at one with the Sadducees, the predominantly priestly party (their name probably derives from that of Ṣadoq, the priest of David) which had supported the Hasmoneans and continued to make compromises with the ruling powers. Thus, the Sadducees did not believe in the resurrection of the dead (Mark 12:18–27; Acts 23:8; Joseph., *Ant.* 18.17) and predestination (Joseph., *Ant.* 13.173).[48] Now both of these beliefs are found in Essene writings (1QS 4:2 ff; 3:15–16; 4Q MMT C 32–33), but it must be kept in mind that the Essenes – in contrast to the Sadducees – did not have a closed canon. The Book of Daniel, cherished by the Qumran-Essenes,[49] teaches that the resurrection of the righteous (12:3) is part of the consummation of God's plan (12:10). The canon of the Sadducees was the Pentateuch alone.

Moreover, in contrast to the Pharisees as well as the Sadducees, the Essenes lived in the world of the Bible. Continuing the prophetical tradition, the Essenes subjected the life of their community to the guidance of men such as the "Legitimate Teacher", who possessed the divine Spirit. Being propheti-

---

[48] Josephus uses the term *heimarmenē* to denote the Essene belief that God has foreordained everything. The term, meaning 'fate', is not a happy one, but it was well known in the Hellenistic world.

According to Acts 23:8, the Sadducees also said that there is neither angel nor spirit. This is quite incomprehensible if taken to mean that they denied the belief in angels, for the Sadducees accepted the Pentateuch. Daube, On Acts 23 (1990) 493–97, has suggested that the Sadducees only denied the attested belief that a good person spent the span between death and resurrection in the mode of angel or spirit.

[49] Daniel would seem to fit the ideal of a *ḥasid:* he is a strict observer of the Law, especially the food regulations (ch. 1), a learned man possessing the Spirit of God (4:8–9; 5:11, 14), and able to interpret the mysteries for the elect (2:28).

cally inspired, the Teacher could issue decisions which were beyond questioning. This is seen in 4QMMT, where the Teacher's rulings are handed down like biblical ordinances.

In addition to the interpretation of legal texts, the Essenes produced other literary works which do not seem to have been regarded as less inspired than the biblical books. Thus, there is no indication to the effect that the Book of Jubilees was seen as less sacred than Genesis. The Temple Scroll is a kind of 'deutero-Deuteronomy', but with the significant difference that God himself, and not Moses, addresses the People of Israel. The Essenes were thus able to adapt and develop new ideas.

The Rabbis, on the other hand, distinguished carefully between the written Law and the "oral law" on the one hand, and the "extraneous books", ספרים חיצונים, on the other. Although the rabbinic writings (the "oral law") are full of arguments and discussions, the Rabbis claimed to be keepers of a tradition reaching back to the revelation given to Moses on Mt. Sinai (*m. 'Abot* 1:1). The "oral law" as well as the written Law was believed to be God's revelation. The Rabbis were the successors of Moses, and everything produced outside rabbinic circles was simply the work of fallible human minds. Working out a program of ritual and legal practice according to their conceptions of what was central in their religion, the Rabbis frowned upon other topics.[50]

In legal matters, Jesus was similar to the Essenes in that he referred directly to the Law and not to "the tradition of men" (Mark 7:7–9). In the Sermon on the Mount, Matthew portrays Jesus as the, or at least *a* prophet like Moses who gives the right interpretation of the Law at the same time as he breaks down the exposition based on oral tradition: "You have heard that it was said to the ancients ... But I say to you ..." (5:21; etc.). Although the community may be responsible for the form of the antitheses,[51] we may assume that the core of the teaching goes back to Jesus himself. This appears to be quite evident in the case of the prohibition to divorce, where Jesus' commandment supersedes even the written Law (Deut 24:1).[52]

Employing scriptural proof-texts for his activity to a rather limited extent (e.g., Mark 2:25–26), Jesus stood forth as a charismatic figure exercising authority by his own *fiat* (Mark 1:21–22, 27; 10:32; etc.). People contrasted his way of teaching with that of the "scribes", who used well-known didactic forms (e.g., pesher-type exegesis).[53]

---

[50] For the "oral law", see Neusner, The Oral Torah (1986).

[51] See Bultmann, Die Geschichte (1964) 142–44, 156–61.

[52] The most recent attempt to bring Jesus in line with other Jewish teachers on the Law is made by Vermes, The Religion (1993) 11–45, who states: "Remarriage following divorce fundamentally conflicts with" Jesus' view on marriage, which was based on Gen 1:27 and 2:24 (p. 33). It ought to be clear, however, that it is divorce itself which conflicts with Jesus' concept of marriage (Mark 10:6–9; 1 Cor 7:10). Now the Church opened up for the possibility of divorce and remarriage in the case of adultery (Matt 19:9), but the Sermon on the Mount only says that the man cannot be blamed for driving the woman to adultery by divorcing her in the case where she has already been unfaithful (5:32). However, this is also an addition to Jesus' words, as is seen from the parallel in Luke 16:18. Moreover, there is no concession to remarriage in the Sermon.

[53] It is impossible to say whether Jesus employed a method similar to that of the "itinerant

In his liberal attitude toward the ritual laws and, especially, in his association with "sinners", Jesus appears to have been very different from other Jewish teachers.[54] The corollary of this attitude was a general lack of interest in temple worship on his part; this probably made it easier for his followers to overcome the crisis created by the destruction of the temple. Very early some Christians came to see Jesus' death as the once-for-all expiatory sacrifice for the People of God (e.g., 1 Cor 15:3).[55]

Paul says that Jesus "died on behalf of our sins according to the Scriptures". The Christians had to find Jesus' words and works prophesied in the Bible; to that effect they developed an exegetical method not unlike that of the Pesharim at Qumran. The Gospel according to Matthew may even be seen to have used a source of so-called formula-quotations where all the significant events in the life of Jesus were understood as "fulfilments" of Scripture (1:22; 2:15, 17, 23; etc.). The passion narratives in the Gospels contain allusions to Psalms 22 and 69 as keys to unlock the significance of Jesus' suffering and death.

The Christians also found events in the early Church foreordained in the Bible. For instance, Luke sees the first Pentecost as having been prophesied in Joel 2:17–21 (Acts 2:14–21).

The Christians' interpretation of the Scriptures involved the concept of a new covenant with God. The term 'covenant', διαθήκη, was predominantly a juridical term; it was used of a testament, the declaration of a person's will with regard to the disposal of his or her personal property after death. In the Septuagint, however, *diathēkē* was used to render the term ברית, which denoted the covenant between God and the People of Israel (e.g., Gen 17:2, 4, 7; Exod 19:5; 24:7–8). Believing that God through Jesus had established a second covenant, the first Christians spoke of the new as well as the old covenant (Luke 22:20; Heb 8:7–13). The New Testament represents the new covenant as a fulfilment that was prophesied in the Bible (Jer 31:31). Thus, the Jewish Bible was regarded as divine revelation, but only the Christians—being members of the new covenant—had the right hermeneutical tool to unlock it.

Already Paul used the term, "old covenant", with a literary reference (2 Cor 3:14, "when they read the old covenant"), and by the end of the second century, the books of the Church were divided into the New and the Old Covenant or Testament. The way was early paved for the classic doctrine

Galilean" Bible interpreters mentioned in the Talmud (*b. Sanh.* 70a; *b. Ḥul.* 27b), for we know next to nothing about those people.

[54] Vermes, The Religion (1993) 22–23, attempts to bring Jesus' healings on the Sabbath (Mark 3:1–6; etc.) in line with the rabbinic dictum that it is permissible to save life on the Seventh Day, but there is no discussion about the likelihood that the man with a withered hand was in danger of losing his life.

[55] Pharisaic Judaism was also able to come to terms with the catastrophe of the year 70 CE. *M. 'Abot* 1:2 says that the world rests on the Law, the temple cult, and acts of mercy. Rabbi Yohanan ben Zakkai, organizing Pharisaic Judaism after the fall of the temple, said that merciful acts had assumed the expiatory function of the sacrifices. Hos 6:6, "I want mercy, not sacrifices", was the scriptural prop being used.

which Augustine was to formulate: "In the Old Testament, the New is concealed; in the New, the Old is revealed".

Finally, it must be mentioned that there were also Jews and Christians in Antiquity who had a critical view of the Bible (OT). Called Gnostics because they claimed to possess secret knowledge (Gk *gnōsis*) vouchsafed to them through special revelations, they can be seen to put forth their critical view in different shades.[56] Some documents – e. g., the *Second Treatise of the Great Seth* from the Nag Hammadi Library – contain a thorough rejection of the Jewish Bible: its heroes of faith, its salvation history, its Law, and its God. The god of the Bible is an ignorant and jealous god who is widely separated from the true and good God.

Ptolemaeus' *Letter to Flora* is more nuanced. Only some parts of the Bible were rejected by the saviour (e. g., the law of retaliation), the others were either fulfilled by him (e. g., the Decalogue) or must be subjected to an allegorical exegesis (e. g., the passages dealing with the cult). Although the Old Testament does not derive from the highest God but from the lower demiurge, it is still possible to derive *gnōsis* from it.

While the *Second Treatise of the Great Seth* and the *Letter to Flora* are Christian Gnostic texts, the *Apocryphon of John* is basically a Jewish writing which has been reworked by a Christian. The "Secret Book" of John sometimes flatly rejects "what Moses said", but may also proffer a counter interpretation by referring to another biblical passage. Thus, the Bible is not rejected, but rewritten.

The closest analogies to this kind of text are the Jewish pseudepigraphical writings, e. g. 1 Enoch and Jubilees, where parts of Genesis are rewritten. The *Apocryphon*, however, can be said to part ways with Jewish tradition in its denigration of the biblical creator, above whom there is now to be found a transcendent deity. It is one of the great puzzles in the history of religion that this split of the biblical God into two beings was made by Jews themselves. It is not much easier to explain the fact that some Christians soon followed suit, for Christians worship the same God as the Jews, even the God of the Bible.

The Gnostics would seem to have started out as disaffected intellectuals adapting dualistic views prevalent in the Hellenistic world. Meeting opposition from their more conservative co-religionists, they ended up with a pronounced dualism according to which the god of their opponents was seen as nothing but a stupid and devillish being. The political implications of the Gnostics' treatment of the biblical text are often quite evident. In the *Second Treatise of the Great Seth*, for example, the opponents of the author are ecclesiastical Christians for whom the Old Testament is still holy Scripture.

---

[56] The following survey is based on Pearson, Use, Authority and Exegesis (1988) 635–52.

Chapter Seven

From Inner-Biblical Interpretation to Early Rabbinic Exegesis

By Jay M. Harris, Cambridge, MA

Bibliography: D. Boyarin, *Intertextuality and the Reading of Midrash* (Bloomington 1990); M. Broshi (ed.), *The Damascus Document Reconsidered* (Jerusalem 1992); G. L. Bruns, *Hermeneutics Ancient and Modern* (New Haven 1992); M. Fishbane, *Biblical Interpretation in Ancient Israel* (New York 1985); D. W. Halivni, *Midrash, Mishnah and Gemarah: The Jewish Predilection for Justified Law* (Cambridge 1986); H. K. Harrington, *The Impurity Systems of Qumran and the Rabbis: Biblical Foundations* (Atlanta 1993); J. L. Kugel/R. A. Greer, *Early Biblical Interpretation* (Philadelphia 1986); J. L. Kugel, *In Potiphars House: The Interpretive Life of Biblical texts* (San Francisco 1990); J. L. Kugel, "Levi's Elevation to the Priesthood in Second Temple Writings", *HTR* 86 (1993) 1-64; S. Liebermann, *Hellenism in Jewish Palestine* (New York 1962); S. Mason, "The Problem of the Pharisees in Modern Scholarship", *Approaches to Ancient Judaism,* NS III (ed. J. Neusner; Atlanta 1993; 103-140); J. Milgrom, "The Scriptural Foundations and Deviations in the Laws of Purity of the Temple Scroll", *Archaeology and History in the Dead Sea Scrolls* (ed. L. H. Schiffman; Sheffield 1990); J. Neusner, *The Rabbinic Traditions about the Pharisees Before 70* (Leiden 1971); G. Reeg (ed.), *Die Geschichte von den zehn Märtyrern. Synoptische Edition mit Übersetzung und Einleitung* (Tübingen 1985); E. P. Sanders, *Jewish Law from Jesus to the Mishnah* (London 1990); L. H. Schiffman, *The Halakhah at Qumran* (Leiden 1975); D. Stern, "Midrash and Indeterminacy", *Critical Inquiry* 15, 3 (1988) 132-61; M. E. Stone (ed.), *Jewish Writings of the Second Temple Period* (Assen 1984); G. Vermes, *The Dead Sea Scrolls in English* (London [3]1987); S. Zeitlin, "The Legend of the Ten Martyrs and its Apocalyptic Origins", *JQR* 36 (1945) 1-11; S. Zeitlin, "Hillel and the Hermeneutic Rules", *JQR* 54 (1963).

1. Introductory

If it is true that fools rush in where angels fear to tread, the present endeavor is perhaps something only a fool would undertake. For this chapter attempts to discuss the bridge or bridges, or numerous circuitous paths from the exegesis internal to the Bible to the exegesis that characterizes rabbinic literature. However, it is not designed to focus on the Qumran library, per se, nor on the so-called apocryphal and pseudepigraphic collections, nor on the work of Philo, Josephus and other Greek writers, nor, finally, on the New Testament. All these bodies of literature are treated elsewhere in this volume. This chapter, then, is not designed to focus on the actual existing literature of the period (roughly 2nd century BCE to 2nd century CE). Rather, what is desired is some description of exegetical work that can in some way or other be considered *proto-rabbinic,* in the hope that such a discussion can help contextualize the extensive exegetical efforts of the Rabbis of the first five Christian centuries.

The problems one faces in trying to fulfill the appointed task ultimately derive from two different but related realities. The first is that we cannot definitively identify any group or groups that can be indisputably considered 'proto-rabbinic'. While no one would insist that the exegetical techniques and legal practices of the Rabbis emerged de novo in the first Christian century, devoid of deep roots in the Second Temple period, precise identification of these roots remains elusive. To be sure, many scholars point to the Pharisees particularly later ones such as Hillel and Shammai as the Rabbis' predecessors, and this claim has much to recommend it. Yet, whatever the relationship of the Pharisees and the later rabbinic sages (assuming, as I do, that there was one), it is far too simplistic to assume that there was extensive and unbroken continuity between them. And even if one wanted to assume that, one immediately confronts our second problem: the Pharisees themselves left us no literature. What we know, or think that we might know, about the Pharisees (including Hillel and Shammai) and their exegetical culture derives from other literatures, primarily rabbinic texts, the works of Josephus, and the New Testament.[1] None of these can be considered an unimpeachable source of knowledge regarding Pharisaic exegesis and learning. To compound the problem, even if we were to accept everything rabbinic literature reports regarding the Pharisees as historically accurate we would still be left with limited overt exegetical discussion; rabbinic literature attributes but few exegetical as opposed to legal traditions directly to Pharisaic masters.[2] That the Pharisees attempted to interpret and apply Scripture is beyond doubt; that, in so doing, they expanded the range of biblical laws and ideas in many ways is also beyond serious doubt. That they were convinced that their core religious values were rooted in Scripture seems likely enough. Yet precisely how they interpreted Scripture and the techniques they used to extend the field of biblical norms and ideas can be reconstructed only on the basis of conjecture and intuition. Therefore, to the extent that this chapter seeks to address a historical question it can only be written in the subjunctive mood.

There is another way of addressing the question of the bridge from inner biblical to rabbinic exegesis and that is to describe the way in which the rabbis themselves understood the link connecting their culture to that of those they considered their predecessors. Adopting this manner of dealing with the question involves abandoning all hope of teasing out historical information from the sources, and is probably the path on which the angels could most comfortably tread. Yet this would not entirely satisfy the mandate of this chapter, as such an approach would tell us only about rabbinic culture and nothing of historical value about its cultural antecedents. Nevertheless, discussion of such perceptions are critical to an understanding of rabbinic Judaism. We cannot ignore this material, however dubious its historical value. Therefore, we shall take the path of the fools in the first part and of the angels in the second

---

[1] For a recent review of the massive — and ideologically driven — scholarship on this issue, see Mason, The Problem (1993) 103–140; see also the article by Lloyd Gaston, "Pharisaic Problems" in the same volume (1993) 85–100.

[2] See Neusner, The Rabbinic Traditions (1971), vol. 3, 39–43, 62–64. This is not to say that we cannot intelligently speculate as to the exegetical foundations of other Pharisaic teachings; it is to suggest that any such speculation would inevitably be informed by rabbinic literature, and for that reason is to be avoided here, given this chapter's mandate.

part. That is, the second half of this essay will deal with rabbinic perceptions of their cultural antecedents, while the first half will address what little can be said about proto-rabbinic exegetical culture.

2. The Legal Mandates of the Torah

The need to construct a 'bridge' connecting inner-biblical and rabbinic exegesis is brought about by the fact that at a certain point most of what we know today as the Hebrew Bible was at least in substantial measure 'canonized' or granted authority as holy Scripture. This meant that new explanatory or expansive understandings of the Hebrew Bible could no longer be folded into the text. Yet groups whose cultures are guided by sacred texts can scarcely live without interpretation and media for its expression. Thus, a range of new literary forms emerged that allowed the biblical message to remain vital in the ancient Jewish communities. These include the so-called "re-written Bible", the *pesher* of Qumran, and the allegorical commentaries of Philo.[3] None of these literary forms are identical to those that give expression to rabbinic exegetical endeavors; yet each allows us to understand specific components of the Hebrew Bible that proved challenging on a broad scale, and each demonstrates techniques familiar to the student of rabbinic literature. These literatures allow us to identify a range of textual problems and concerns that were shared by many of the various 'Jewish' cultures in the ancient world. Such identification can, in turn, aid in reconstructing the links between inner biblical and rabbinic exegesis, especially in the area of *halakhah*, or Jewish legal practice.

It is a commonplace that rabbinic exegetical activity is of two types: *aggadic* and *halakhic*. The former deals primarily with the narrative sections of the Bible, while the latter addresses the legal mandates of the Pentateuch, or Torah. While both types of activity obviously represent important components of pre-rabbinic and rabbinic culture, the stakes involved in *halakhic* exegesis were far higher, as it entailed determining the right way to perform God's law, on which the prosperity and fortune of the people depended. This is made amply clear by the fact that pre-rabbinic 'sectarian' disputes revolved substantially around differing approaches to the Torah's legal materials.[4] Given the centrality of *halakhah* in these cultures and the limitations of space we will focus primarily on aspects of pre-rabbinic legal exegesis in this chapter.

The Qumran and New Testament corpora (inter alia) indicate that proper observance of the Sabbath stands out as a distinct point of contention among various Jewish groups. This is not surprising given the importance of Sabbath observance in the Pentateuch. Its violation is a capital crime, and the Book of Numbers relates the story of the wood gatherer who was actually put to

[3] See the various chapters in Stone, Jewish Writings (1984).

[4] See, e.g., the Qumran documents 4QMMT and the Damascus Document. This is not to deny that there were extensive disputes in matters we might call theological and/or political.

death for a Sabbath transgression.[5] Yet, as a rabbinic text describes the problem, "the laws of the Sabbath... are like mountains hanging from a thread, for there is little [explicit promulgation in] scripture but many laws".[6] That is, while the Torah frequently emphasizes the importance of observing the Sabbath, it provides little guidance as to *precisely* how one is to do this.[7] While a few activities are explicitly proscribed, generally the Torah is content to prohibit all manner of *mela'khah*, usually translated "work". What specifically this term forbids is almost never made clear. While other sections of the Hebrew Bible add some particulars,[8] the text as a whole does not address numerous issues that later Jews saw as critical.

Perhaps the most fundamental issue of Sabbath observance involved determining its place in the hierarchy of laws, and specifically, whether the demands of Sabbath observance superseded the exigencies of human health and life itself. While we cannot know how all of the various components of the Jewish communities dealt with this question, it is clear from the apocryphal book, I Maccabees, that at least some Jews in the second century BCE felt that one should forfeit one's life rather than violate the Sabbath. The logic of this position seems clear enough. Sabbath violation was a capital crime; thus the violator (if the act is considered a violation under these circumstances) forfeited his or her life. Better to forfeit one's life without desecrating the Sabbath, rather than committing a violation in order to preserve life, and then finding oneself subject to capital punishment. As I Maccabees describes, "the Jews" under discussion would not defend themselves on the Sabbath, arguing, "let us all die *in our innocence*; heaven and earth bear witness over us, that you condemn us unjustly".[9] The result of this reasoning, however, was "They were killed with their wives, their children, and their cattle, to the number of one thousand human beings".

To allow such a situation to continue would mean that the Torah and its laws would disappear. Thus "Mattathias and his friends" decided that the Torah's prohibition of *mela'khah* could not have been intended when life was in jeopardy. The text relates that they decided they would fight on the Sabbath day, rather than die. Those "who were fleeing the persecutions" joined them as supporters in their "defense of the Torah".[10] While we cannot really know what "Mattathias and his friends" (or whoever's ideas are actually represented here) had in mind, the formulation suggests that the thinking went along the lines of "desecrate one Sabbath so that you may observe many of them".[11] Be that as it may, in this text we find the first record of what must have been a long-standing conflict between Sabbath observance and the

[5] Num 15:32–36.

[6] *m. Ḥag* 1:8.

[7] For further discussion, see Sanders, Jewish Law (1990) 6–23.

[8] See, e.g., Is 58:13; Jer 17:19–27; Neh 10:31.

[9] I Macc 2:36–37; emphasis added.

[10] Ibid. vv. 39–43.

[11] This idea is expressed in the rabbinic text, *Mekhilta de-Rabbi Ishmael*, Horowitz-Rabin edition, p. 341.

preservation of human life, and the effort to resolve it on the part of Jews trying to live in accord with the Torah's teachings.

Whatever the thought processes that led this group of Jews (or the authors of I Maccabees) to the insistence that Sabbath observance must yield to human survival, the question of whether this was so (and, if so, why?) lived on among other Jews. In the so-called Damascus Document we find the following: "And as to any human being who falls into a place of water or into a reservoir, no one shall bring him up with a ladder, rope or instrument".[12] While scholars are divided on whether this is to be understood literally or not,[13] for our purposes the answer to this question is of little relevance. Either way, the passage indicates that the question of the conflict between Sabbath observance and the preservation of life continued to be addressed. We cannot determine the exegetical foundations of this document's treatment of the issue (if there were any) with any precision; it is, however, clear that fulfillment of Sabbath commandments in a manner consistent with the demands of the Torah was critical to this group. Proper observance involved deciding when the Torah's Sabbath laws apply, and when, if ever, they are to be superseded by other considerations. This necessarily meant that people charged with determining such issues would weigh the different systems of law against one another and look for textual clues that would provide a definitive response.

While the precise exegetical techniques the Qumran community may have used on this matter are obscure, the New Testament affords us a clearer statement of how one group of Jews (or a particular Jewish individual) resolved the Sabbath conflict. As is well known, Jesus did not merely address the question of the conflict between Sabbath and human life, but also human health. That is, he insisted that it was perfectly appropriate to heal on the Sabbath, even when the life of the individual was not at stake. The Gospel accounts all depict the Pharisees as opposed to such activity, seeing it as a violation of Sabbath law.[14] Of particular interest here is the justification provided in the Gospel of John, 7:21–24:

> Jesus gave them this answer: "I have performed just one work, and all of you are shocked. Moses has given you circumcision (really it did not originate with Moses but with the patriarchs), and so even on a Sabbath you circumcise a man. If a man can receive circumcision on a Sabbath to prevent a violation of the Mosaic law, are you angry at me because I cured the whole man on a Sabbath? Do not judge by appearances, but give an honest judgment".[15]

As Raymond Brown explains, "This is an argument *a minori ad maius* ... quite common in rabbinic logic. Circumcision affects only a part of the body; if that is permitted, an action affecting the good of the whole body should be permitted".[16] As an exegetical move, the argument *a minori ad maius* is

---

[12] *Damascus Document* 11:16. The translation is that of Lawrence H. Schiffman and is taken from his The Halakhah at Qumran (1975) 125. The text he used is consistent with that published by Elisha Qimron in Broshi ed. (1992) 31. Cp. Vermes, The Dead Sea Scrolls (1987) 95.

[13] See Schiffman, The Halakhah at Qumran (1975) 125–128.

[14] See, e.g., Matt 12:9–14; Mark 3:1–6; Luke 6:6–11, 13:10–17, 14:1–6; John 7:21–24.

[15] I have used the translation of Raymond E. Brown in his edition of the Gospel according to John (Anchor Bible, vol. 29).

[16] Ibid., vol. 1, p. 313.

grounded in the assumption that the text's legal mandates are part of a broader web of logically interlocking parts; the exegete is then free to interpret the text in accord with this basic principle of human logic. If something applies to a case that is in some way of lesser gravity, it certainly applies in (what is considered) a weightier case. However, the apparent logic of the move should not blind us to the fact that certain assumptions are at work in this particular argument. The first is that circumcision supersedes the Sabbath, itself a conclusion drawn from a consideration of the relative weight of the legal mandates of the Torah. (In rabbinic literature determining that circumcision supersedes the Sabbath occupies considerable exegetical energy.)[17] The second and more questionable assumption is that there is a comparison to be drawn here, even though what is being done to the one body part and what is being done to the entire body are quite different. The underlying assumption seems to be that each entails performance of a divine commandment; the one to circumcise, the other to heal. In any event, in rabbinic literature we find the same piece of logic; the sole and important difference is that the Rabbis limit the comparison to healing (or other actions) in the face of immediate danger, not merely discomfort.[18] Thus, in this instance we have clear evidence of the application of the argument *a minori ad maius* to the issue of *piquaḥ nefesh*, or the preservation of human life, in a pre-Mishnaic text.

The urgency of properly performing Sabbath rules demanded far more than resolving the (potential) conflict between life and text. Other potential legal conflicts inevitably emerged, among them circumcision and the Sabbath, and the paschal sacrifice and the Sabbath (among those using the solar/lunar calendar). Beyond conflict resolution, filling in the lacunae of the biblical Sabbath texts seems to have exercised exegetes of various orientations. In the pseudepigraphical book *Jubilees*, the author cites the biblical admonitions to observe the Sabbath day, and then adds a series of prohibitions not mentioned in the Torah, among them engaging in sexual relations, drawing water, discussing business matters.[19] Similarly the author(s) of the *Damascus Document* provides a form of Sabbath code, in which numerous prohibitions, among them offering sacrifices, not found in the text of the Torah are promulgated.[20] We should note that in *Jubilees* the extra-biblical prohibitions are treated exactly as if stated in the Bible, in that they are designated as capital crimes. The *Damascus Document* also seems to assume an authority equal to that of the biblical text, albeit in the opposite direction in that it seems to have no death penalty for any Sabbath violation, apparently including acts the Bible considers capital offenses.[21] Thus, while the precise exegetical techniques of

---

[17] See *b. Šabb.* 132a; Sifra ad Lev 12:3.

[18] *Mekhilta de-Rabbi Ishmael*, p. 340; *b. Šabb.* 132a.

[19] *Jub.* 50:6–13.

[20] CD 10:14–11:18.

[21] CD 12:3–6. The question of whether the sect "abolished" the death penalty (see Schiffman, 78, note 6) is beside the point. The author(s) of this text obviously assumed the authority to determine the meaning of the Sabbath laws and penalties, however he (they) would have conceptualized what he was doing.

these texts remain elusive,[22] we can see that their interpretations of Sabbath prohibitions are treated as the equivalent of laws explicitly stated in the text of the Torah, as they add or delete punishments as they see fit.

Despite its centrality, Sabbath law scarcely exhausts the legal and exegetical concerns of pre-rabbinic forms of Judaism. The various corpora of texts evince numerous concerns; among these proper application of the biblical purity laws seems to have been of paramount importance. The purity laws are certainly not like the Sabbath laws; it can hardly be said of them that there is but "limited scripture but numerous laws". Indeed, the Mishnah identifies purity laws as "the body of the Torah"; in context, this means that there is abundant Scripture to provide behavioral guidance. Yet, abundant scriptural discussion does not necessarily yield abundant clarity.

Let us consider the case of Num 19:16. The verse reads, "And in the open, anyone who touches a person who was killed or who died naturally, or human bone, or a grave, shall be unclean seven days". While the verse seems clear enough, the precise nature of the "human bone" here led to controversy. In the *Temple Scroll* the bone is explicitly identified as one that comes from a dead person.[23] In rabbinic literature, by contrast, the bone is identified as one that was detached from someone while still alive. The author(s) of the *Temple Scroll* seem to be engaging in exegetical homogenization, described by Jacob Milgrom "that a law which applies to specific objects, animals or persons is extended to other members of the same species".[24] Here that would mean that the impurity under discussion must be an extension of the categories of impurity known from elsewhere. In all other cases in which impurity results from contact with an organism, that organism is dead. Thus here, the bone in question must come from a corpse. The Rabbis, by contrast, seem to be guided by the notion that Scripture does not intend to homogenize when it specifies something that should otherwise be known by virtue of its category. If the bone in question derived from a corpse, we would know the law without a scriptural statement. The verse is then seen as coming precisely to include something new, in this case a bone severed from a living person.[25] Common to both and thus indicative of pre-rabbinic if not necessarily proto-rabbinic exegesis is the conviction that Scripture is cohesive and comprehensible, and that there is an internal logic to the nature of its mandates, even as, in this instance, the positions on how that internal logic 'works' are diametrically opposed.

Another example of these common concerns, albeit once again with different conclusions, may be seen in the area of family law, specifically in the matter of consanguinous relationships. In Leviticus 18 and 20, the Torah

---

[22] Although see the discussion in Schiffman, The Halakhah at Qumran, 22–76, 84–133.

[23] *Temple Scroll* (11QTemple) 50:4–6.

[24] Milgrom, The Scriptural Foundations and Deviations (1990) 93.

[25] I do not intend to suggest that the Rabbis never engage in homogenization, but rather that they engage in this technique under different textual circumstances. For further discussion on this issue, see now Harrington, The Impurity Systems (1993) 59–61. Her statement that when the Rabbis use the technique of homogenization they consider the result as having less than scriptural authority is for the most part unfounded.

provides extensive lists of prohibited relationships, written from the perspective of men. Among the rules is found the prohibition of relations between a man and his aunt. Nowhere does the text address the question of relations between a woman and her uncle. In the *Damascus Document* we find the following:

And each man marries the daughter of his brother or sister, whereas Moses said: You shall not approach your mother's sister; she is your mother's near kin" (Lev 18:13). But although the laws against incest were written for men, they also apply to women. When, therefore, a brother's daughter uncovers the nakedness of her father's brother, she is his near kin [and the relationship is incestuous].[26]

Again we see the predilection for homogenization; and, here as well, rabbinic law preferred to see the biblical passage as prohibiting a species rather than a genus. For our purposes, however, the more important matter is the exegetical issue itself. We see yet again the struggle to determine the exact range of the Bible's laws and the limits of acceptable analogy. Does a law prohibitng sex between a man and his aunt also preclude sexual relations between a woman and her uncle? A response to this question involves determining whether the cases are analogous, and, if so, whether that fact, by itself, allows for the extension of the law's range.

Another area of concern, in which Qumran and rabbinic documents arrive at the same conclusion, involves executing the judgment against the rapist, described in the Deut 22:28–29. The verses read, "If a man comes upon a virgin who is not engaged and he seizes her and lies with her, and they are discovered. The man who lay with her shall pay the girl's father fifty shekels of silver, and *shall be to him a wife*. Because he has violated her, he can never have the right to divorce her".[27] The ancient law thus demands that a rapist marry, and remain forever married to, his victim. With perhaps more realism than we would like, the ancient exegetes had to face the problem of a rapist who was forbidden to his victim for various reasons, most notably because he was her relative. Does the biblical demand that rapist and victim marry extend to such a case? In the *Temple Scroll* the answer is given in the negative. The understanding seems to be that when the verse states that "she shall be to him a wife" it means "eligible to him by law", thus excluding all who are not eligible by law to marry him. The same principle, in almost identical language is found in a number of rabbinic sources.[28]

Thus, pre-rabbinic literature attests to numerous exegeses in the area of Sabbath law, purities and family law that parallel rabbinic concerns and norms; sometimes the laws (and exegeses) are opposed to what is attested in rabbinic literature, sometimes they coincide. In either case, they provide a picture of the exegetical issues and techniques of late Second Temple Judaism

---

[26] CD 5:7–11 (Broshi ed., p.19); translation, Vermes, p.86. SCHECHTER and QIMRON (in Broshi) suggest emending the last clause so that it reads "he is kin" but this scarcely seems necessary.

[27] The translation is that of the the new JPS, except for the italicized portion. The new JPS properly translates "and she shall be his wife". I have opted for the more clumsy and more literal translation to highlight the textual basis of the exegesis to be discussed.

[28] For full discussion, see Halivni, Midrash (1986) 30–34.

that carry forward into rabbinic culture. The Qumran texts, inter alia, demonstrate the need of a particular Jewish community to deal with issues either not specified or ambiguously stated in Scripture. They show that textual lacunae and ambiguities were resolved by means of extension by analogy, homogenization, and typology. In general, the Qumran authors tended to be quite strict in their interpretations of the Torah's laws, indicating a preference to err on the safe side. While the Rabbis appear to have been more creative and flexible in their approach to scriptural difficulties, and while they certainly felt the need to polemicize against the results of other interpretive communities, their overall attitude obviously owes much to the exegetical cultures that preceded them.

3. Aggadic Exegesis

As in rabbinic literature, the pre-rabbinic Jewish communities display much greater creative freedom in dealing with the non-legal sections of the Pentateuch. In some cases, this meant reading their own recent history into a biblical text, as in the *Pesher Ḥabakkuk*; there are those who would be reluctant to call this exegesis at all. Yet in other places, they were motivated by a clear sense that the text was in need of supplementation. Sometimes this sense was triggered by an apparent absence of divine justice, sometimes by more local textual issues.

An example of the first type of problem and its resolution is to be found at *Jub.* 34:10–19. Genesis 37 relates the story of the sale of Joseph by his brothers. In Exod 21:16, the Torah demands the death penalty for anyone who kidnaps a person and sells him. Further, the actions of Joseph's brothers caused terrible grief to their father, Jacob, thereby violating the commandment to honor their father. Yet, Joseph's brothers were never punished either for their act of kidnapping or for the pain they caused their father. This seemed unjust to the author of *Jubilees*. The preferred method of dealing with such 'narrative' problems in this text is to relate the problematic material to some legal enactment, often by means of the calendar. Here the author connects the Joseph story with the Day of Atonement rituals, by adding actually inventing the detail that the event including the dipping of his garment in blood to make it appear that he was killed happened on the tenth day of the seventh month, the date of that was to become the Day of Atonement. After informing his readers of Jacob's inconsolable grief, the author continues,

> therefore it is decreed for the children of Israel that they mourn on the tenth day of the seventh month – on the day when that which caused him to weep for Joseph came to Jacob, his father – so that they might atone for themselves with a young kid on the tenth day of the seventh month, once a year, on account of their sin, because they caused the affection of their father to grieve for Joseph, his son. And this day is decreed so that they might mourn on it on account of their sins and on account of all their transgressions and on account of all their errors in order to purify themselves on this day, once a year.[29]

---

[29] *Jub.* 34:18–19.

In this instance, the text's intolerable silence must be broken; in the hands of this author the sins of the brothers become the prototypical sins of Israel which are addressed through detailed expiation rituals, once a year in perpetuity. It is worth noting that a medieval rabbinic text also notes the lack of punishment for Joseph's brothers, and relates it to an 'event' of more recent vintage, the legendary ten rabbinic martyrs allegedly killed in Hadrianic times.[30]

While in the above instance, the 'exegesis' is the result of narrative silence, oftentimes *aggadic* exegesis originates in textual problems or anomalies present in the text, such as the text that refers to Jacob's penultimate son as a "son of my old age" when such a phrase is seen as more readily fitting the ultimate son.[31] On the basis of examples such as this one, J. KUGEL has characterized early *aggadic* exegesis as animated by the tendency to

> view the Bible as fundamentally elliptical; it said much in a few words and often omitted essentials, leaving the full meaning to be figured out by readers alert to the tiniest irregularities in the text. The process of fully understanding a biblical text thus consisted of bringing out all possible nuances implied in the precise wording of each and every sentence. With regard to biblical narrative, this often meant "deducing" background details, conversations, or even whole incidents that were not openly stated in a narrative text, but only suggested by an unusual word, an apparently unnecessary repetition, an unusual grammatical form, and so forth.[32]

That exegetes focus on textual anomalies and irregularities is scarcely news; yet it frequently gets lost in discussion precisely because the end product seems so far from being genuine exegesis. Nevertheless, recent work has shown how exegetical irritants provide the point of departure for interpretive work that, obviously enough, is conditioned by ideology and historical circumstance.[33] We are, thus, more than justified in treating this material as illustrating the interpretive 'triggers' that led to the emergence of ancient Jewish narrative reconstruction, and in seeing it as *a bridge from inner-biblical to rabbinic exegesis*. Thus, in the area of what the Rabbis call *aggadah* we can see again that rabbinic patterns of reading and questioning the text are paralleled by the patterns of earlier Jewish communities struggling to preserve the living reality of the biblical word.

---

30 I refer to the *Ma'aseh 'Asarah Haruge Malkhut*, also known as *Midrash 'Eleh 'Ezkerah*. See the edition of Reeg, Die Geschichte (1985), 4*–7*. See also Zeitlin, The Legend (1945) 1–11. Another example of exegetes dealing with the Bible's intolerable silence is the discussion of Gen 28:20–22, in which Jacob vows to give a tenth of everything that God gives him back to God; there is no reference to Jacob fulfilling this vow, which readily engages the imagination of the exegetes. See James L. Kugel, Levi's Elevation (1993).

31 See Kugel, In Potiphar's House (1990) 68–73. Kugel's entire book addresses the issues of *aggadic* exegesis and the textual 'irritants' that elicit it.

32 Ibid., 3–4.

33 Beyond Kugel's works, see Boyarin, Intertextuality (1990); Stern, Midrash and Indeterminacy (1988) 132–61; and for broader cross-cultural discussion, see Bruns, Hermeneutics (1992) 104–123. These all address rabbinic literature, but what they argue seems to apply to pre-rabbinic exegesis as well. See also Fishbane, Biblical Interpretation (1985) 432.

4. How the Rabbis Saw All This

Before getting to the substance of this section, two disclaimers are in order. The first is that the term 'the Rabbis' is a construct that must not be taken to mean that all Rabbis saw something in a particular way. Rabbinic culture is particularly disputatious, and there is no basis for an assumption of unanimity on just about anything. What then does the section heading above mean? It means that there is a certain conception of the past that finds expression in a number of rabbinic documents, that is not explicitly challenged and that serves as the basis for other discussions in the literature. This scarcely establishes unanimity or even broad consensus; it simply shows the compatibility of certain claims and the broader culture.

The second disclaimer repeats what was noted at the outset, which is that one should not attach much historical value to the rabbinic view of the past. While it would be irresponsible to deny that something happened simply because it is found in a literature replete with myth, it would be equally irresponsible to affirm that something happened simply because it is to be found in a literature that many Jews consider sacred. What we can say is that the historical conception to be described below cannot be confirmed in any scholarly way; the most responsible position, then, is an agnostic one.

To the extent that rabbinic tradition reflects on its own emergence, it generally prefers to see itself as the culmination of many centuries of legislative and exegetical activity, whose roots extend back into the Second Temple period and beyond. A wide range of biblical figures from David to Ezra are depicted as engaging in rabbinic style discourse and behavior.[34] Similarly, post-biblical figures whose existence is, in many cases, attested only in rabbinic literature are portrayed as involved in legal discussions that characterize rabbinic literature. For the most part, these discussions involve enactment of laws and ordinances to which little overt exegetical discourse is appended. Yet, later rabbinic scholars and redactors had no compunctions about reconstructing the alleged exegetical foundations of these enactments; to them, it was apparently inconceivable that these legal teachings could be devoid of exegetical foundations, and identifying them granted the enactments greater authority.[35] Thus, in the literature of the Rabbis many pre-rabbinic sages were viewed as having interpreted the Torah in a manner similar to the methods used by the Rabbis themselves, even if little overt discourse survived. Whatever the historian may wish to say, to the Rabbis it was clear that most laws granted scriptural authority must have been derived by acceptable methods from the text of Scripture.

---

[34] When the biblical record precludes this possibility we are told *mai de-hava hava*, "what was, was" and is of no concern to us today.

[35] An example of the thought process may be found at *m. Soṭa* 5:2, where an interpretation attributed to R. Aqiba provides the scriptural foundation of a law, and R. Joshua states that this would comfort the earlier sage Rabban Yoanan ben Zakkai, who was concerned that the law would be abrogated for its scriptural foundation was, in his day, unknown.

To this perception we must contrast a famous story told, with important variations, in three different rabbinic documents. I cite what, for our purposes, is the most interesting version, the Yerushalmi's:

> The following law was unknown to the elders of Bateira.[36] Once the 14th of Nisan occurred on a Sabbath, and they did not know whether the Passover sacrifice superseded the Sabbath or not. They said that there is a Babylonian here who studied with Shemaiah and Abtalion who may know whether the Passover sacrifice supersedes the Sabbath or not. [Despite our doubts] perhaps there is hope [that the answer will come] from him ... He began to interpret before them, [deriving the answer] from a substantive analogy, from an argument *a minori ad maius*, and from a lexical analogy ... They responded, "we already said 'can there be hope from a Baylonian?' The substantive analogy can be refuted ... [and so with the other two arguments]". Even though he sat and interpreted the entire day, they did not accept the response from him, until he said "may a curse come upon me if I have not heard thus from Shemaiah and Abtalion". When they heard this they appointed him *Nasi* in their stead.[37]

Opinions differ enormously regarding what this passage and its parallels mean, and what, if anything can be learned from them. Writing in a more credulous age, the great Jewish historian, HEINRICH GRAETZ, saw in this "event" the turning point in Jewish spiritual history. He saw the story as indicating that Hillel introduced complex exegesis which rejuvenated a culture that was becoming moribund.[38] Now, as history, this reading is absurd. But did GRAETZ stumble on to a useful systemic description? That is, is this the point of the story? An affirmative answer may be provided by at least two other attempts to promote the greatness of Hillel in rabbinic literature. The first is a passage to which GRAETZ refers, found in the Tosefta (*San.* 7:11). This passage refers to Hillel expounding seven things (hermeneutic techniques) before the elders of Bateira; they are: 1. inference *a minori ad maius;* 2. inference by analogy; 3. homogenization (literally constructing a family, i.e., category) based on one biblical passage; 4. homogenization based on two biblical passages; 5. the general and the particular and the particular and the general; 6. exposition by means of a similar passage; 7. deduction from context. One certainly can read this passage as suggesting that Hillel introduced these techniques to the Palestinian leaders who were unfamiliar with them, in which case the source suggests that Hillel was the founder of the rabbinic exegetical system.

The second source comes from the Babylonian Talmud, in which it is noted that the Torah was forgotten, but Ezra ascended from Babylon and restored it; the Torah was then forgotten again, and Hillel ascended from Babylonia and restored it, presumably by introducing the hermeneutic principles.[39] Here

---

[36] Or, elsewhere, the sons of Bateira. Whoever (and whether) they were (on which see Neusner, *Rabbinic Traditions*, part 1, 242) for the purposes of this story they are to be understood as the religious leaders of the Jewish community of Judea.

[37] *y. Pesaḥ.* 6:1. I did not choose this version because I imagine it to be somehow more authentic (whatever that would mean), but because it is the version that highlights the exegetical dimension of the "event" more than the other two versions, found at *t. Pisḥa* 4:1 and *b. Pesaḥ.* 66a. The literature on these passages is enormous. For three partly overlapping, partly divergent approaches, see Lieberman, Hellenism (1962) 53–54; Neusner, Rabbinic Traditions, part 1, 231–235, 246–251, 254–257; Zeitlin, Hillel and the Hermeneutic Rules (1963).

[38] See his "Jüdisch-geschichtliche Studien", *MGWJ* 1 (1852).

[39] *b. Sūkk.* 21 a. Many traditional commentators choose to understand the passage differently.

too, one can read the story as suggesting that Hillel introduced the hermeneutic principles, although only by assuming that the Bene Bateira story is the referent. No explicit mention of this encounter is to be found in this talmudic passage.

An at least partially negative answer to our question is to be found in the passage itself, as the Bateira elders are depicted as challenging the specifics of Hillel's argument, rather than the legitimacy of the techniques he is described as using (a component of the story not found in all the variants). The Yerushalmi's story-teller (or glossator) may wish to imply that the techniques were known and used; the challenge is simply to Hillel's particular application of them regarding Passover sacrifices. This suggests that the story-teller does not wish to endow Hillel with founder status, but may rather seek to suggest that a system of law grounded in hermeneutics is inferior to one grounded in tradition.

However we reconstruct the systemically accepted message of the Hillel-Bene Bateira encounter in rabbinic literature (and we need not assume only one), it seems that there can be little doubt that the event was perceived – minimally, by a redactor of the Babylonian Talmud and a redactor of the Tosefta – as a watershed. According to this view, from the time of the encounter forward, rabbinic learning and exegesis were seen as having come under the sway of Hillel, the great scholar and exegete. If Hillel was not perceived by these redactors (and presumably others) as having introduced these techniques, he was perhaps seen as having categorized them and formalized them, such that they could now be used to reconstruct the exegetical underpinnings of the earlier law. In this way, at least some producer(s) of rabbinic culture could advance the claim that his (their) exegetical world was centuries old, while accounting for the relative youth of its overt manifestation.

In the end, then, even when we limit ourselves to efforts at inner-systemic description, we cannot state definitively what Hillel's role was in the emergence of rabbinic exegesis. What we can say is that he became a pivotal figure in rabbinic consciousness, and any attempt to draw a compelling and useful picture of the past seems to have required crafting a central place for Hillel (and his followers). Perhaps some saw fit to see him as the founder of a new system of exegesis, while others, uncomfortable with the implications of novelty, saw fit to undermine such a conception, thereby bringing forth our series of texts with their mixed messages and interpretive possibilities. In the end, the efforts to construct a portrait of Hillel came to be folded into a broader cultural vision that saw its past as deeply rooted in ancient exegetical endeavors.

Detailed knowledge of the origins of the rabbinic system of exegesis remains elusive. What we have seen here is that antecedent groups of Jews were moved by many of the same textual irritants and legal queries as were the Rabbis. They resolved their difficulties in a manner that overlaps considerably

---

It must be admitted that at least one point of the story is to insist on the greatness of Babylonian learning.

with the exegetical discourse of rabbinic documents. The latter, however, have survived more fully and manifest a much wider array of exegetical concerns and techniques than can be documented in the earlier literature. Thus, the effort to construct a bridge from the Bible to the Rabbis can achieve but modest results. All 'Jewish' cultures of Antiquity wanted to realize the message of the Bible in their actions and beliefs; this involved interpreting the Bible using analogy, homogenization and considerable imagination, inter alia. Yet each brought their own specific existential need and concerns. Thus one group added considerably to the list of capital Sabbath violations, while another seems to have done away with the category altogether.

The rabbinic documents, for the most part, seek to create an image of unbroken exegetical continuity; at the same time, one transitional figure, Hillel, is associated with some form of exegetical shift, the precise nature of which seems to have been subject to dispute.

The bridge, then, is rather narrow and shaky. There are those scholars who would comfortably add a few more support beams than I would,[40] but, I think, no one would claim that we are in a position to certify that any bridge between inner-biblical and rabbinic exegesis can be crossed without extreme caution.

---

[40] See Halivni, Midrash (1986) 18–37; Kugel/Greer, Early Biblical Interpretation (1986) 27–102.

Chapter Eight

Formative Growth of the Tradition of Rabbinic Interpretation

8.1. Local Conditions for a Developing Rabbinic Tradition

By David Kraemer, New York

Bibliography: S.J.D. Cohen, "The Significance of Yavneh: Pharisees, Rabbis, and the End of Jewish Sectarianism", HUCA 55 (1984) 36–42; D. Daube, "Rabbinic Methods of Interpretation and Hellenistic Rhetoric", HUCA 22 (1949) 239–264; R. Eisenman/M. Wise (eds.), *The Dead Sea Scrolls Uncovered* (Shaftesbury, Dorset and Rockport, MA: Element 1992); H. Fischel, "Studies in Cynicism and the Ancient Near East: The Transformation of a Chria", *Religions in Antiquity* (ed. J. Neusner), NumenSup 14 (Leiden: E.J. Brill 1968); idem, "Stories and History: Observations on Greco-Roman Rhetoric and Pharisaism", *American Oriental Society Middle West Branch Semi-Centennial Volume* (ed. D. Sinor), *Oriental Series* 3 (1969); D. Goodblatt, "The Place of the Pharisees in First Century Judaism: The State of the Debate", *JJS* 20, n. 1 (June 1989) 12–30; M. Goodman, *The Ruling Class of Judaea: The Origins of the Jewish Revolt Against Rome A.D. 66–70* (Cambridge, England: Cambridge U. Press 1987); D. Halivni, *Midrash, Mishnah and Gemara: The Jewish Predilection for Justified Law* (Cambridge, MA: Harvard U. Press 1986); idem, *Peshat and Derash: Plain and Applied Meaning in Rabbinic Exegesis* (New York: Oxford U. Press 1991); S. Lieberman, *Hellenism in Jewish Palestine* (New York: Jewish Theological Seminary [2]1962); J. Neusner, *Reading and Believing: Ancient Judaism and Contemporary Gullibility* (Atlanta: Scholars Press 1986); idem, *Judaism: The Evidence of the Mishnah* (Chicago: U. of Chicago Press 1981); A. Saldarini, *Pharisees, Scribes and Sadducees in Palestinian Society* (Wilmington, Delaware: Michael Glazier 1988), 128–132.

The history of Rabbinic Judaism proper begins following the war with Rome and the destruction of the Temple in CE 70. But there are important continuities between Rabbinic Judaism and pre-destruction Judaisms, and attention to these continuities allows for a fuller appreciation of the unique developments of this latter Judaism, including its characteristic methods of reading Scripture.

The centuries before the first Jewish war with Rome were complex and difficult. The Hasmonean dynasty, though originating as a small group of anti-Hellenistic pietists, quickly adopted Hellenistic ways. The Hasmoneans' claim on the High Priesthood – without descent from the traditional High Priestly family – and on the royal throne – without descent from the House of David – engendered not a little opposition, contributing to the overall religious turmoil which characterized this period. The political leadership of

Judea shifted from the Hasmonean kings to the Romans, to Herod and his son, then back to the Romans. Jewish leadership was, at best, imperfectly established, enjoying only limited support and subject always to competing claims. Even the narrow evidence of the Qumran scrolls shows that the Hasmoneans were blessed by some and cursed by others.[1] The High Priests, recognized leaders of the Jews for much of the Second Temple period, were, from the reign of Herod onward, virtual unknowns, making it improbable that they could claim the genuine allegience of many. Yet it is likely that the traditional authority which accrued to the High Priest served to enhance the standing of even these insignificant figures. The Pharisees may or may not have been the most popular religious party (depending upon how one reads Josephus' report),[2] but even if, now and then, they could claim this distinction, their access to official corridors of power was at best only occasional. In light of this turmoil and confusion, it is no wonder that these centuries witnessed the birth of a deeply divided Judaism.

With all of this complexity, one thing seems clear: there were no Rabbis, in the common sense of that word, before the destruction of the second Jerusalem Temple. No non-rabbinic document dating from the first century mentions the Rabbis. Gamaliel and Shimeon ben Gamliel are referred to in Acts (5:34) and Josephus (*War* 4.3.9 [159]), but both are known merely as leading Pharisees. The Rabbis' later identification of these individuals as patriarchs of the rabbinic movement may thus be understood as a rhetoric of traditional authority – "we are decended from them and we should therefore be accorded the same respect and authority". Aside from these two well-known Pharisees, no rabbinic figure who would have lived during these decades is ever spoken of; astoundingly, the great "Hillel the Elder" goes entirely unnoticed by Josephus though, if the rabbinic record were to be believed, Hillel should have been the most important religious leader of the Herodian age.[3] The title 'rabbi' is found already in the Gospel of Mark, but there it is a mere honorific term, not the appellation given to the member of an elite group of individuals ordained to serve in a particular capacity. This vast silence where there should not be allows for only two reasonable interpretations – either there were no bona fide Rabbis during this period or they were as yet so insignificant as to escape contemporary notice. Given the weight of the evidence, the emerging consensus among scholars prefers the first interpretation.

But none of this is to say that Rabbinic Judaism was a complete novelty on the Judean landscape. On the contrary, in an ancient, traditional society such

---

[1] See 1QpHab, viii:3, ix:9, and xi:4 (assuming that the common interpretation of "the wicked priest" = "one of the Hasmonean high priests" is correct), and cf. 4Q448 ("Paean for King Jonathan"), transcribed and translated in *The Dead Sea Scrolls Uncovered*, ed. and with commentary by R. Eisenman and M. Wise (Shaftesbury, Dorset and Rockport, MA: Element 1992) 280.

[2] See D. Goodblatt, The Place of the Pharisees in First Century Judaism, *JJS* 20 (1989) 12–30; A.J. Saldarini, Pharisees, Scribes and Sadducees (1988) 128–132.

[3] For other reasons, H.A. Fischel also calls "the historical Hillel" into question. See "Studies in Cynicism and the Ancient Near East", in *Religions in Antiquity* (1968) 375, and idem, Stories and History (1969) 77–78.

as that of Judea, it would be unthinkable for a group of pious individuals such as the Rabbis to offer a model of correct religious practice without promising significant continuities with well-known forms. In fact, reference to evidence from the centuries leading to the birth of Rabbinic Judaism shows that, whatever the innovations the Rabbis might have offered, there are also strong roots for their religion in late Second Temple society. Unfortunately, in the matter which concerns us here – rabbinic methods of interpreting Scripture – the evidence for such roots is lacking.

The Rabbis' own claim of important Pharisees as their own, coupled with significant parallels between positions attributed to the Pharisees (by Josephus or the authors of the Gospels) and opinions recorded explicitly in rabbinic documents, make the argument for meaningful continuities between the Pharisees and the Rabbis irrefutable. Thus, there is no doubt that the Rabbis aspired to enjoy the reputation for expertise in the law which is ascribed to the Pharisees in both Josephus and the Gospels. Naturally, they also sought the same respect and popularity which accompanied such a reputation in Jewish society. The Pharisees' support of a "tradition of the elders", described by Josephus, also obviously characterized the religion of the rabbis (see the beginning of tractate *'Abot*), and there can be no doubt that the Rabbis sought to build on the legitimacy of such a tradition in the Pharisaic context to support their own extra-biblical teachings. At the same time, the Rabbis never explicitly identify themselves with the Pharisees, and there is no evidence that the Pharisees, as a distinct group, survived the defeat to Rome. The Pharisees thus contributed significantly to the emerging rabbinic tradition, but it would be incorrect to say that the Rabbis were merely a postdestruction outgrowth of the earlier Pharisees.[4]

Neusner identifies in the Mishnah, the earliest of the rabbinic documents to come to completion, the legacy of both priests and scribes.[5] The priestly legacy may be found in the many detailed tractates which devote themselves to laws of sacrifice, purity and the Temple. Indeed, a greater proportion of the Mishnah's laws are devoted to concerns of the priesthood than to those of any other group. But the Rabbis obviously could not have hoped literally to replace the priests; without a Temple, the religion of the priests was now defunct. Nor should the Rabbis' appropriation of priestly concerns be understood as a mere claim for continuity with earlier, pre-destruction Judaism. As *Yoma* chapt. 1 and other similar texts make clear, the rabbinic authors held the priests as such in some contempt and claimed to be more expert in even the priestly law. It is the elders (= the Rabbis) who direct the High Priest in his service, and he who serves them. Thus it is once again expertise in the law which is offered to support the Rabbis' authority, and attention to priestly concerns may be understood to represent their claim to command all of

[4] S.J.D. Cohen calls the Rabbis "latterday Pharisees who had no desire to publicize the connection". See his detailed discussion of the relationship between the Pharisees and Rabbis in "The Significance of Yavneh: Pharisees, Rabbis, and the End of Jewish Sectarianism," HUCA 55 (1984) 36–42. The characterization quoted above is found on p. 41.

[5] See J. Neusner, Judaism. The Evidence of the Mishnah (1981) 241–250.

Judaism as articulated in the Torah of Moses. Or, to put it in other words, if the priests no longer have an arena in which to perform, this should be the cause of relatively little concern; the elders were more central to Judaism than the priests, and their arena – the Torah – remains intact.

Concerning Second Temple scribes whose legacy presumably informed the composition of emerging Rabbinic Judaism little may be said. Scribes were individuals who enjoyed an uncommon technical training. Their skill demanded neither elevated birth nor particular beliefs.[6] Nevertheless, their intimate involvement with scrolls of the law meant that some scribes acquired mastery of that law. As a consequence, they were much respected in the community at large, and the Rabbis undoubtedly hoped to enjoy the same respect. Moreover, the Gospel narratives commonly speak of scribes found in the company of Pharisees, and the Rabbis would comfortably have identified with such an association and its symbolism. Thus, though the Rabbis were not, as a group, scribes, the Mishnah's scribal qualities may be understood to represent their claim for continuity with the scribal tradition and values.

The Rabbis were also undoubtedly related to individuals referred to by Luke (7:30 and elsewhere) merely as 'lawyers' (νομικοὶ), meaning experts in the law of the Torah. Again, these individuals do not comprise a coherent and identifiable group in pre-destruction society, but mention of such a recognized expertise makes it clear that honor accrued to those who were masters of the Torah. The Rabbis' overriding concern with matters of law shows them as lawyers in much the same sense as those spoken of by Luke. But, again, this is only one of several qualities which informed the composition of rabbinic religion, a piece in a much more complex whole.

The Rabbis' religion represents an original synthesis of these earlier forms, a synthesis also characterized by genuine innovations. Why did this newly defined system emerge at the time that it did, and why with these particular emphases and not others?

As far as the chronology of this development is concerned, the defeats to Rome, both in the war of the destruction and the Bar Kokhba war, were the most significant factors. Had the Temple not been destroyed and Bar Kokhba, the messianic "Prince of Israel", not been defeated, it is likely that Second Temple Judaism, in the multiple expressions described above, would have continued for some time. But mere note of these events is not enough. Without considering the ways in which they irrevocably transformed Second Temple society, we will be unable to grasp fully the complex of factors which contributed to the emergence of early Rabbinic Judaism.

M. Goodman, in his *The Ruling Class of Judaea*,[7] argues that Judean society in the first half of the first century had no popularly recognized ruling class.

---

[6] A. J. Saldarini writes that, during the period at hand, "scribes do not seem to be a coherent social class with a set membership, but rather a class of literate individuals drawn from many parts of society who filled many social roles and were attached to all parts of society from the village to the palace and Temple". See Pharisees, Scribes and Sadducees, 275.

[7] The Ruling Class of Judaea, 1987.

Not long before, Herod had destroyed all viable competitors for leadership in Judea and, following his death, his house stood thoroughly discredited. As mentioned, Herod had himself assured the weakness of the high priesthood, and the Romans subsequently did nothing to restore what status had been lost. There were, during this period, no independent wealthy families of note, and besides – so GOODMAN argues[8] – little power accrued to individuals in Judean society by virtue of wealth alone. Whatever the merit of GOODMAN's precise reconstruction, one thing is clear: no earlier ruling class survived the war of the destruction unscathed. The destruction of the Temple meant that the priesthood, weakened as it was, was now entirely without a base of power. Wealthy landowners, if they escaped the actual brutalities of war, found their properties confiscated. There was no king, no council, no legislative body to provide direction in the years following the defeat.[9] Nor, as far as we can tell, did any religious party survive the defeat intact. There was thus a (near) complete vacuum of leadership in the period immediately following the destruction, and it was in the space of this vacuum that the Rabbis and their Judaism began to form.

But the picture is still incomplete. There was one sort of religious expression which remained dynamic during these centuries and emerged with particular force in the aftermath of the destruction, that is, apocalyptic prophecy, which found particular eloquence in the post-destruction apocalypses of Baruch and Ezra.[10] These pseudonymous prophecies imagine that the current age – the age following the defeat to "Babylon" and the destruction of the Temple (purportedly the first, but really the second) – heralds the imminent coming of the Messiah. Only with the immediate expectation of the redeemed world could the horrors of the recent war be tolerated. These contemporary expressions reflected a need felt by at least significant portions of the late-first century Jewish populace, and it is this same need which finally came to the fore in the revolt led by the messianic hopeful, Bar Kokhba. Perhaps, then, the most significant religious leadership following the first Roman war was the radical prophetic leadership – those who hoped to restore the Temple, the Priesthood, and the Jewish king.

The Rabbis, as we saw, advanced a distinct alternative to this vision. Borrowing the Pharisees' zealousness for the law, their concern for purity and their "tradition of the elders"; the lawyers' Torah-expertise, the scribes' technical competence, and the priests' pivitol religious position, the Rabbis' suppressed concern for the end-time and turned their attention to Torah, now in a new, larger sense. It is likely that the Rabbis' way spoke to few Jews in the decades between the wars, and had the revolt of the second century succeeded, the Rabbis may well have passed into oblivion. But there was defeat, and the ensuing vacuum was even more complete than it had been.

---

[8] Ibid. 126.

[9] GOODMAN argues cogently that the sanhedrin had not been a fixed, ongoing institution during the late second Temple period; see 113–114.

[10] As well as the book of Revelation.

The Rabbis sober synthesis now had the chance to offer direction when other Judaisms could not.

Having identified the roots of emergent Rabbinic Judaism, we now confront an insurmountable problem. While we may go some distance in reconstructing the ideologies of the Pharisees and priests, and we may describe the social positions of all the groups discussed above with some relative confidence, we are at a loss to say anything about their approaches to reading Scripture. Unfortunately, despite the wealth of the documentary record which remains to us from this period, we do not have a single work that may be assigned to any of these groups (including the priests and Pharisees!) with confidence, nor do contemporary witnesses describe their methods of reading or interpretation. Josephus, of course, attributes an extra-scriptural, ancestral tradition to the Pharisees (*Antiquities* 13.10.6 [297–298]), but what characterizes this tradition is precisely that it is *extra*-scriptural; whatever connection it might have had with the biblical text, through interpretation or otherwise, is seemingly denied. Josephus also writes that the Pharisees have a reputation for being the most accurate interpreters of the law, but he gives no hint concerning the methods by which this accuracy was presumably achieved. And the Pharisees are the best-documented of the groups which concern us here! Thus, unless we were to retroject rabbinic methods into the Pharisaic context – an unfortunately all too common scholarly practice which depends upon a complete and fatal circularity – we are forced to say that, whatever the traditions of reading of the Rabbis' more direct predecessors may have been, we have no means of recovering them. Thus, we have no way of saying what methods of scriptural interpretation the Rabbis may have learned from any of these pre-destruction groups.

If we look to those pre-destruction documents which do reveal characteristic means of reading earlier, authoritative Scripture, we also confront an absence of compelling precedents. The most common means of 'reading' earlier Scripture in the centuries between the Maccabees and the Mishnah was either to build upon and 'read into' earlier biblical stories, creating thereby new 'biblical' texts (e.g. *Jubilees, Enoch*) or to write new narratives in accepted biblical forms, generally attributing such narratives to earlier biblical heroes (Judith and I Maccabees are examples of the first sort, the apocalypses of Baruch and Ezra examples of the latter). Neither of these models was employed by the Rabbis, who insisted upon a clear distinction between canonical Hebrew Scripture and their own traditions (though this distinction was gradually muddied as the Rabbis came to call their own teachings "Torah"). Neither does the *pesher* literature, discovered at Qumran, offer a precedent for rabbinic readings. The simple "quote of Scripture – this refers to..." form of these documents is almost never paralleled in classical rabbinic works, and the methods which characterize rabbinic interpretation find no hint of a parallel in these same Qumran compositions. Even the controversial 4QMMT document, which shows affinity with early rabbinic concerns, offers us little in this context. MMT is a polemical epistle; whatever means might have been used to derive the laws for which it argues are not so much as hinted at in its lines.

D. HALIVNI argues that the Temple Scroll records a brief scriptural interpretation which is identical with that of the Rabbis, *ad locum*, and therefore evidence of the greater antiquity of their method.[11] But the Temple Scroll and parallel rabbinic midrash merely declare (using similar but not identical language) that, in order for the law requiring a rapist/seducer to marry the victimized woman to be in force, they must otherwise be fit to marry one another. On the basis of the evidence which HALIVNI offers, all we may know with confidence is that this was a commonly accepted law in late Second Temple Judaism and that the term used to express the law, a particular form of the older Hebrew root ר-א-ה (a form unprecedented in biblical literature) had already entered literary usage by the time of the composition of the Temple Scroll. Otherwise, all we see in this law of the Temple Scroll is a legal assertion which may or may not have been based upon a particular method of reading.

HALIVNI's work also offers another possible key to recovering more ancient precedents for rabbinic methods of reading Scripture. In the same context as the case just discussed, HALIVNI discusses three simple midrashim, recorded in the Mishnah, which he argues must have originated long before the destruction of the Temple. His argument is based, in each case, upon the realia assumed in the precise details of each midrash, realia which could have pertained in the two last centuries BCE but not in the more recent period, better known to the Rabbis. Suffice it to say that each of his proffered proofs has been critiqued before,[12] and none is convincing. But even if they were, we would still be left with only three 'simple' midrashim, none of which exhibits the unique methods by which even early rabbinic midrash is characterized (see chapt. 8.2 and 8.3).

In fact, the only place where reasonable (though by no means definitive) precedents for the methods of the Rabbis have been discovered are in the Hellenistic world, in contemporary readings of Homer and other Greek classics. Several of the interpretive methods attributed to Hillel find some parallel in the work of Greek rhetoricians of the first centuries CE, and rabbinic Hebrew terminology pertaining to these methods is sometimes best understood as a translation of equivalent Greek terms.[13] But LIEBERMAN argues that only two of the Rabbis' characteristic methods finds a reasonable parallel, and his conclusion is that no definitive Greek influence may be identified (that is, on the methods themselves; he agrees that the terminology is sometimes borrowed).[14] At the same time, the Hellenistic character of some rabbinic forms is undeniable, and it is thus reasonable to see at least minimal Hellenistic influence behind rabbinic conventions and even methods of reading.

Yet identifying such influence is not enough. All scholars who have noted

---

[11] See D. Halivni, Midrash, Mishnah and Gemara (1986) 30–34.

[12] See R. KALMIN's review in *Conservative Judaism* 39 (1987) 78–84.

[13] See the discussion of D. Daube, Rabbinic Methods of Interpretation, HUCA 22 (1949) 239–264. Otherwise see HBOT chapt. 4 above.

[14] S. Lieberman, Hellenism in Jewish Palestine (^{2}1962) 42–82. The judgments referred to here are found on pp. 54, 56, and 59–61.

parallels have commented on the 'hebraization' or 'judaizing' of foreign elements.[15] And the native sources of rabbinic reading can also not reasonably be denied. The problem is, simply, that we cannot identify such sources, and, for this reason, we may also not say with any confidence which of the rabbinic methods may have been the Rabbis' own innovation.

There can be no question that Jews before the Rabbis read and interpreted Scripture. But reading the ambiguities of Scripture and arriving at the same solutions for these ambiguities as would the Rabbis does not make such earlier reading proto-rabbinic (let alone rabbinic). What characterizes the Rabbis' readings is not the substance of their interpretations, which sometimes demonstrably parallels that of earlier Jewish groups, but the precise and characteristic methods of interpretation which were employed. And, despite the attribution of rabbinic methods to earlier figures like Hillel, such attributions are extremely suspect, serving, as they do, the Rabbis' self-interest by claiming greater antiquity (and therefore authority) for their methods and teachings. To be sure, it is probable that some of the Rabbis' interpretive methods predate the Rabbis themselves. But some were also surely their own innovation. The Rabbis' readings of Scripture find record in contexts where rabbinic discourse is internal and insulated, in documents where the Rabbis speak to Rabbis. Thus, the public sensibility which would demand recognition, and therefore traditionality, did not pertain here, and it is entirely conceivable that significant elements of the midrash of the rabbis were their own very unique invention. Whether the reader judges continuity, borrowing or innovation to be more likely, the precise contours of rabbinic interpretation will be described in the sections following.[16]

---

[15] See Daube, Rabbinic Methods of Interpretation, 240, and Fischel, Studies in Cynicism and the Ancient Near East, 407–411.

[16] This chapter was written with the support of the Abbell research fund of the Jewish Theological Seminary of America.

8.2. Scriptural Interpretation in the Mishnah

By DAVID KRAEMER, New York

Before discussing the Mishnah's approaches to the reading and interpretation of Hebrew Scripture, it is first necessary to explain why one would want to isolate this document in the first place. Why not speak simply of tannaitic/early rabbinic developments in scriptural hermeneutics? What justifies and/or requires that the Mishnah be dealt with on its own terms?

The answer to these questions points us to two of the most heated debates in contemporary scholarship of classical Rabbinism, those being (1) Can attributions or other apparently historical claims in early rabbinic documents be taken at face value?, and (2) What is the relationship between the scriptural interpretations recorded in the halakhic midrashim, which purport to be tannaitic, and the laws of the Mishnah which apparently relate to these interpretations? Did such interpretations actually yield the laws of the Mishnah, which would make the substance of the halakhic midrashim prior, or are these midrashim really later apologia for the Mishnah's laws?

The view of what might be called 'traditional' scholarship is that attributions are accurate and that rabbinic laws are in fact derived, by means of various accepted methods, from Scripture.[1] According to this view, it would be unnecessary to distinguish between the Mishnah's record of early rabbinic developments and the testimony of other tannaitic texts. The alternative view, propounded most vigorously by JACOB NEUSNER, rejects the historical claims of given documents and reads them as individual statements, each with its own integrity, in the unfolding canon of Rabbinic Judaism.[2] Since the halakhic midrashim (as well as the Tosefta) are acknowledged to have come to final documentary expression subsequent to the Mishnah, and because their internal claims to tannaitic provenance cannot be accepted uncritically, NEUSNER will view the Mishnah as the earliest record of rabbinic readings of Scripture. Moreover, since the claims of the halakhic midrashim to record the views of specific named sages must be viewed skeptically, we cannot supplement the evidence of the Mishnah with midrashic traditions attributed to the same sages. NEUSNER's approach, it will be clear, requires that we consider the Mishnah independently.

---

1 The assumption that attributions may be accepted at face-value is widespread. The strongest argument for the priority of Midrash to Mishnah is D. HALIVNI's *Midrash, Mishnah, and Gemara. The Jewish Predilection for Justified Law* (Cambridge, MA: Harvard U. Press 1986).

2 NEUSNER's method and its defense have been articulated repeatedly. Perhaps its most powerful (and polemical) statement is found in *Reading and Believing. Ancient Judaism and Contemporary Gullibility* (Atlanta: Scholars Press 1986).

So this section assumes, to begin with, the methodological restrictions proposed by NEUSNER. However, its conclusions will suggest that NEUSNER's position, even on its own terms, is, as often articulated, too extreme. We will find that, despite radical differences in the relationships of the Mishnah and the halakhic midrashim to Scripture, there is no question that the methods of reading typified in the latter are also attested in the former. When the Mishnah did actually read Scripture, the methods it employed were largely the same as the early midrashim. Thus, though the Mishnah may have been redacted earlier, it is clear that the sorts of readings to which the midrashim give voice were developing at the same time as the Mishnah. Therefore, whatever the agenda of the halakhic midrashim as redacted documents, it is reasonable to suppose that, in limited instances, the rabbinic methods of reading indeed yielded the laws to which they are attached.

Popular introductions to rabbinic literature have sometimes described the Mishnah as a record of rabbinic interpretations of Torah. Perhaps because the Mishnah has traditionally been approached through the lens of the Babylonian Talmud, which often seeks to find the source of mishnaic laws in Scripture, such a description generally evokes no dissent. But the simple fact is that the Mishnah quotes Scripture relatively rarely. To be precise, I count a total of approximately 265 quotations of Scripture in the Mishnah (excluding references to liturgical recitations of Scripture and excluding tractate *'Abot*). There are 517 chapters in the entire Mishnah (again, excluding *'Abot*), meaning that Scripture is quoted only slightly more than once every two chapters. If we recognize that there are certain chapters and tractates which are unusual for the quantity of Scripture they do quote, we will appreciate that, in the bulk of the Mishnah, quotation of Scripture is rather a rare occurrence (in fact, in a few tractates there are no quotations whatsoever). Therefore, not only is it incorrect to speak of the Mishnah as a commentary on the Torah, but it is only slightly hyperbolic to suggest, borrowing NEUSNER's words, that "superficially, the Mishnah is totally indifferent to Scripture".[3]

But this superficial description doesn't do justice to the actual relationship of the Mishnah to Scripture, which is far more complex than its formal independence would suggest. NEUSNER reviews the relationship of the Mishnah's laws to Scripture in some detail and suggests, in conclusion, the following three categories of relationship: (1) "there are tractates which simply repeat in their own words precisely what Scripture has to say"; (2) "there are... tractates which take up facts of Scripture but work them out in a way in which those Scriptural facts cannot have led us to predict"; and (3) "there are ... tractates which either take up problems in no way suggested by Scripture, or begin from facts at best merely relevant to the facts of Scripture".[4] It is more than a matter of coincidence that NEUSNER's categorization recreates, in large part, precisely the possibilities suggested in the Mishnah itself, at *Ḥag.* 1:8:

---

[3] J. NEUSNER, *Judaism: The Evidence of the Mishnah* (Chicago: U. of Chicago Press 1981) 217.
[4] Ibid. 221–22.

"[Laws concerning] the releasing of vows fly in the air, for they have nothing [in Scripture] on which to depend. Laws of the Sabbath, festival offerings, and the misappropriation of sacred things, they are like mountains hanging by a hair, for they have little Scripture and many laws. [And the laws of] judgments, the sacrificial service, purities and impurities, and prohibited sexual relations, they have [Scripture] on which to depend ...".

In other words, sometimes the Mishnah submits to Scripture's dictates, sometimes it reads Scripture aggressively, and sometimes it sets its own agenda, mostly ignoring what Scripture may or may not have to contribute to the subject. Behind the Mishnah, undoubtedly, lies the Torah, but how and whether it reads that Torah is, apparently, its own choice.

This complex and varied relationship suggests complex rhetorical purposes. Much of the vocabulary employed, the institutions assumed, and the occasional verse quoted, all suggest that the relationship between the Mishnah and Scripture is profound if non-specific. The less-educated reader will certainly hear the many scriptural echoes behind the Mishnah and conclude that it is a powerfully traditional document. But readers with greater erudition will quickly appreciate that, even when the Mishnah reads Scripture, its reading is sometimes not so 'traditional' (in the popular sense). They will see the Mishnah defining its own categories, even forcing Scripture into the mold which the Mishnah, alone, creates.

A superb example of the Mishnah's 'misreading' of Scripture for its own ends is found in chapter three of tractate *Baba Meṣi'a*. The Mishnah, speaking of deposits given to one's neighbor and the obligations of the bailee in such cases, obviously assumes as its background Exod 22:6–12. Verses 6 and 9 seem to make a clear and natural distinction: "If a man should give to his neighbor money or vessels to watch, and it be stolen from the man's house [there is no liability] ... If a man should give to his neighbor an ass or an ox or a sheep, or any beast, to watch ... if it be stolen from him he shall make payment to its owner". According to these verses, the law changes as a function of the nature of what is given to be watched; inanimate movables involve a lower level of liability and animals a greater level. This is clearly the simple and most natural reading of the verses at hand. But the Mishnah suggests a different category distinction, denying explicitly, in the process, the distinction offered in the Torah: "If one deposits with his fellow *an animal or vessels* to watch, and they are stolen or lost – if he paid and did not want to [instead] take an oath [eliminating his liability], for they have said, 'A gratuitous bailee may take an oath and go out [free of any liability]', if the thief is found ..." etc. (emphasis added). For the Mishnah, the important difference is whether or not the bailee is paid – a distinction utterly without precedent in the Torah's law. The Torah's distinction, at the same time, is explicitly erased, without any reason offered to justify this shift.

Now, if pressed, there is no doubt that the Rabbis behind this Mishnah could justify their proposed categorization with reference to Scripture. Some rabbinic author does just this, in fact, in the halakhic midrash to the same verses (see *Mek, Ne*z. 15; Horowitz-Rabin, 301). But the reading in the Midrash is defensive and forced, and the Mishnah, in any case, typically does not bother with such a justification. A common reader might not pick up on all this, but the rabbinic reader would surely have realized the problems posed in the present Mishnah. He would have understood, in other words, that the Mishnah's law, even when related to the Torah, is not dictated by the Torah. The Mishnah's rhetoric of Scripture allows for greater rabbinic power and independence than might at first appear.

When we turn to the Mishnah's explicit readings and interpretations of Scripture, we already discover many of the characteristic assumptions and methods which would find more widespread expression in later rabbinic documents. Before illustrating these, however, it is important to note that the majority of the Mishnah's explicit references to Scripture simply quote a verse (or part thereof) to support an opinion or assertion. They say, in effect, "the law is such-and-such because Scripture says ...". Of course, even such cases involve subtle interpretations. But these interpretations are not evident on the surface and readings of this kind tend to be quite straightforward. Far more interesting, for present purposes, are those cases which make their interpretive methods explicit.

The rabbis in the Mishnah (as later) do not insist upon literal or simple readings of Scripture, and their interpretations are sometimes quite inventive. An excellent example of the flexibility of Mishnaic reading is *Ber.* 1:3, where the Houses of Shammai and Hillel argue the proper physical position for reciting the Shema. Based upon Deut 6:7 ("when you lie down and when you rise up"), the Shammaites propose that one should actually recline in the evening and stand up in the morning. Countering with a reference to another phrase in the same verse ("when you walk on the road"), the Hillelites say that the Shema may be recited in any position, claiming that the words "when you lie down and when you rise up" may be understood to require the recitation of these words when you would ordinarily be doing these things, that is, in the evening and in the morning. The Hillelites are less bound by the literal meaning of the words, whereas the Shammaites seem to require a more literal application of what the words say.

But, in truth, even the reading of the Shammaites is not all that literal. They do, after all, require recitation at specific times of day and not at all times, as the verse might be understood to require ("when you sit in your house and when you walk on the road, and when you lie down and when you rise up"). Moreover, any application of these verses to a specific liturgy called the Shema, to be recited, in precise form, twice each day, must be understood as anything but literal. The verses at hand say merely "these words", referring, apparently, to the words of the Torah in general. Indeed, the Shema as we have it is most likely a rabbinic formulation, and this midrashic dispute may be understood, therefore, as a self-conscious and somewhat fanciful re-reading of a scriptural source.

Perhaps the most overarching principle informing rabbinic readings of Scripture, already in evidence at this stage, is the assumption that, divinely inspired as they are, all of Scripture's words, and even individual scriptural features, are meaningful. This assumption is illustrated in a homiletical reading at *Ber.* 9:5, referring again to one of the verses which comprises the Shema (Deut 6:5). Part of this midrash understands the doubling of the letter *bet* in the Hebrew word for "your heart" to imply that you should love God with *both* of your hearts, that is, with both your inclination to do good and your inclination to do evil. Behind this reading is the assumption that even individual letters of the Torah carry (potentially, at least) divine import, so if the letter is doubled, God must have intended this doubling to teach us something.

The latter part of the same mishnaic midrash shows the rabbinic willingness to read Scripture creatively and perhaps even playfully. The last phrase of this verse in Deuteronomy requires that you love God "with all your might"—בכל מאדך. In one of two interpretations, the Mishnah reads this to mean "with each and every measure by which He measures you, you should thank Him very much" (בכל מדה ומדה שהוא מודד לך הוי מודה לו במאד מאד). This is all built upon the similarity, aural and orthographic, between Scripture's "מאד" and the words מדה, מודד, מודה, and מאד (with a different meaning than Scripture's term). On one level, this interpretation shows the assumed power of even individual scriptural terms. But it also shows the inventiveness with which the early Rabbis were willing to approach these terms.

Many of the Rabbis' formal exegetical methods are already employed in the Mishnah. Relatively common is the קל וחומר (*a fortiori* reasoning), which sometimes serves as the building block for rather sophisticated disputes (see, for example, *Pesaḥ*. 6:2). The principle limiting the application of קל וחומר, insisting that the derived case be no more expansive than the case upon which the proof rests, is also already known in the Mishnah (*B.Qam.* 2:5). Similarly attested are גזרה שוה (the equation of common scriptural terms used in different contexts; see, e.g., *Sotah* 6:3), בנין אב (the construction of a general category from specified scriptural examples; see, e.g., *B.Qam.* 1:1), היקש (equation of principles or cases; *Mak.* 1:6), derivation based upon the juxtaposition of scriptural discussions (סמיכות, see *Ḥul.* 8:4), דבר שהיה בכלל ויצא מין הכלל (a lesson based upon a specific example which already would have been subsumed under a general ruling; see *B.Meṣ.* 2:5), the reconciliation of two apparently contradictory Scriptures (*Šeqal.* 6:6), and others. Many of these cases are paralleled, sometimes almost exactly, in the halakhic midrashim.

This latter fact returns us to the issue mentioned earlier, that is, the question of the relationship between the Mishnah and those early rabbinic documents which offer themselves explicitly as commentaries on the Torah. In evaluating this question, we must account for three phenomena: (1) the midrash's characteristic methods are used in the Mishnah, if only infrequently; (2) parallels between the Mishnah and these midrashim are not uncommon; and, (3) there are rare blocks of mishnaic text, such as large sections of *Soṭa* chapt. 5, 7 and 8, which are themselves clearly halakhic midrash, in both form and substance. Even if we grant, then, that the halakhic midrashim are post-mishnaic compositions which, by tying the Mishnah's laws back to Scripture, serve as apologia for the earlier document (and there are reasons to believe that this characterization is overly-neat), we must still conclude that rabbinic-midrashic reading was already alive and well in the period during which the Mishnah took shape. Nor should this conclusion be the cause for surprise. Midrashic reading, though formally confessing the superior authority of Scripture, is often, in fact, an extraordinary show of rabbinic power and even independence. In this respect, such methods of interpretation are well suited to the more general posture of the Mishnah as it relates to Scripture.

One question which has drawn considerable attention, and which is relevant already with relation to these earliest rabbinic exegeses, is whether the Rabbis were at all sensitive to what we would call "the simple sense" (the *peshat*) of Scripture.[5] This question is rendered acute by virtue of the fact that the Rabbis so often seem either to ignore or to read against the apparent simple sense. Consider, for example, *B.Meṣ.* 2:7 (with parallels at *Mek. dekaspa* 20 [pp. 324–5] and *Sifre Deut.* 223). The Mishnah offers itself as an interpretive reading of Deut 22:2: "If your brother is not near to you, or you do not know him, then you shall gather it [the lost animal which you have recovered] into your house and it shall be with you until your brother claims it, then you shall restore it to him". Allegedly based upon this verse, the Mishnah rules: "A deceiver, even though he listed its [=the lost object's] indicative characteristics, you should not give it to him, for it is said, 'עד דרש אחיך אתו: [=until your brother claims it]', [meaning] until you examine your brother [עד שתדרוש את אחיך] to see whether or not he is a deceiver". Relying upon various possibilities of meaning in the verbal root, this midrash reverses the direction of the action in the sentence, making "your brother" the object instead of the subject. This is done in complete disregard for the structure of the sentence and despite the fact that the verse, as it stands, is not ambiguous.

Now, do examples like these mean that the Rabbis did not know the simple sense of what they were reading? Mishnah *Šabb.* 8:7 makes it evident that the Rabbis behind the Mishnah did at least distinguish between different levels of proof from Scripture. There, R. Meir introduces his proof of a particular opinion (from Isa 30:14) with the phrase, "even though there is no [bona fide] proof of the matter, there is a hint for it ...". Admittedly, this does not mean that bona fide proofs relate to the simple sense of the source text, but at least these Rabbis perceived different levels of straying from the text.

A midrash at *Soṭa* 8:5 shows that rabbinic reading, at this stage, was even more appreciative (when it chose to be) of the simple sense of Scripture. There, the Mishnah records a dispute regarding the law to be derived from Deut 20:8, "And the officers shall speak further to the people and say, 'Who is the man who is afraid and fainthearted ...?'" R. Aqiba suggests that the words "afraid and fainthearted" should be taken "according to their meaning", that is, to exclude someone who is afraid of the horrors of war. R. Yose the Galilean, by contrast, suggests that the verse means to exclude someone who is "afraid of the sins which are in his hand"—presumably, if someone

[5] This question has been addressed more broadly by D. Halivni in *Peshat and Derash. Plain and Applied Meaning in Rabbinic Exegesis* (New York: Oxford U. Press 1991). Halivni's examination of the early rabbinic evidence is not sufficiently detailed, making his treatment of the Rabbis' scriptural readings during this period incomplete.

is a sinner, he cannot be assured of God's protection in war, and he will thus be afraid. This mishnaic midrash is clearly aware of the plain meaning of the verse at hand, as it indicates explicitly. This does not mean, however, that the simple reading is necessarily preferred. Whatever the value of simple reading, it has no presumed authority in questions of rabbinic halakha.

We see, then, that the first record of rabbinic reading already shows the Rabbis methods to be well developed. These are, it must be recognized, often aggressive methods, permitting the Rabbis to build significantly upon the scriptural base-texts they choose to employ. This independence of spirit which is evident already at this earliest stage of rabbinic interpretation helps to explain the considerable developments in interpretive methods to be found in the following period.[6]

[6] This chapter has been written with the support of the Abbell Research Fund of the Jewish Theological Seminary.

8.3. Patterns and Developments in Rabbinic Midrash of Late Antiquity

By Richard Kalmin, New York

Sources: Mishnah: *Šišah Sidrê Mishnah* I–VI (ed. H. Albeck; Jerusalem 1952–1958). Tosefta: *Tôsepta'* (ed. M. S. Zuckermandel; Trier 1882); *The Tosefta* I–V (ed. S. Lieberman; New York 1955–1988). Tannaitic Midrashim: *Mekhilta' de-R. Yišma'ē'l* I–III (ed. and trans. J. Z. Lauterbach; Philadelphia 1949); *Mekhîlta' de-Rabbî Yišma'ē'l* I–III (ed. H. S. Horovitz/I. A. Rabin; 2nd ed. Jerusalem 1960); *Mekhîlta'de-R. Šim'ôn bar Yôḥa'î* (ed. Y. N. Epstein/E. Z. Melamed; 1955; reprint Jerusalem 1979); *Sipra'* (ed. I. H. Weiss; 1862; reprint New York 1947); *Siprê Deuteronomy* (ed. L. Finkelstein; 1939; reprint New York 1969); *Siprê Numbers and Siprê Zûṭṭa'* (ed. H. S. Horovitz; 1917; reprint Jerusalem 1966). Palestinian Talmud (Yerushalmi), Babylonian Talmud (Bavli), Aggadic Midrashim: *Midrash Genesis Rabbah* I–III (ed. J. Theodor/H. Albeck; Jerusalem 1965); *Midrash Leviticus Rabbah* I–V (ed. M. Margaliot; Jerusalem 1953–1960); *Pesîqta' de-Rav Kahana'* (ed. B. Mandelbaum; New York 1962).

Bibliographies: H. Albeck, *Mabô' la-Talmûdîm* (Tel Aviv: Debîr 1969); H. W. Basser, *Midrashic Interpretations of the Song of Moses* (New York: Peter Lang 1984); R. Bloch, "Midrash", and "Methodological Note for the Study of Rabbinic Literature", *Approaches to Ancient Judaism. Theory and Practice* (ed. W. S. Green; Missoula, MO: Scholars Press 1978) 31, 37, and 51–75; B. M. Bokser, *Post Mishnaic Judaism in Transition* (Chico, CA: Scholars Press 1980); idem, "Wonder-Working and the Rabbinic Tradition. The case of Hanina ben Dosa", *JSJ* 16 (1985) 42–92; D. Boyarin, *Intertextuality and the Reading of Midrash* (Bloomington, IN: Indiana U. Press 1990); idem, "On the Status of the Tannaitic Midrashim", *JAOS* 112 (1992) 455–58; D. I. Brewer, *Techniques and Assumptions in Jewish Exegesis Before 70 C. E.* (Tübingen: J. C. B. Mohr 1992); M. Chernick, *Le-Ḥēqer ha-Mîdôt "Kelal û-Peraṭ û-Kelal" we-"Rîbûî û-Mî'ût" ba-Midrashîm û-ba-Talmûd* (Lod, Israel: Haberman Institute 1984); S. J. D. Cohen, *From the Maccabees to the Mishnah* (Philadelphia: Westminster Press 1987); B. de Vries, *Mabô' Kelalî le-Siprût ha-Talmûdît* (Tel Aviv: Sinai 1966); Y. N. Epstein, *Mebô'ôt le-Siprût ha-Tannaîm* (Jerusalem: Magnes Press 1957); L. Finkelstein, "The Sources of the Tannaitic Midrashim", *JQR* 31 (1940–1941) 211–43; S. D. Fraade, *From Tradition to Commentary. Torah and its Interpretation in the Midrash Sifre to Deuteronomy* (Albany, NY: State U. of New York Press, 1991); S. Friedman, "La-'Aggadah ha-Histôrît be-Talmûd ha-Bavlî", *Sēper ha-Zikarôn le-R. Saul Lieberman* (Jerusalem: Saul Lieberman Institute for Talmudic Research 1989) 44–45; D. Goodblatt, "The Babylonian Talmud", *The Study of Ancient Judaism II. The Palestinian and Babylonian Talmuds* (ed. J. Neusner; New York: Ktav 1981) 148–51 and 177–81; W. S. Green, "Palestinian Holy Men. Charismatic Leadership and Rabbinic Tradition", *ANRW* II 19/2 (1979) 628–47; idem, "Romancing the Tome: Rabbinic Hermeneutics and the Theory of Literature", *Semeia* 40 (1987) 147–68; D. Halivni, *Midrash, Mishnah, and Gemara. The Jewish Predilection for Justified Law* (Cambridge, MA: Harvard U. Press 1986); idem, *Peshat and Derash. Plain and Applied Meaning in Rabbinic Exegesis* (New York: Oxford U. Press 1991); J. Heinemann, "The Nature of the Aggadah", *Midrash and Literature* (ed. G. H. Hartman/S. Budick; New Haven: Yale U. Press 1986) 47; M. D. Herr, "Midrešê Halakhah", *EJ* (Jerusalem: Keter 1971) 1521–23; M. Hirshman, *Ha-Miqra' û-Midrashô. Bîn Ḥazal la-Abot ha-Kenesîah* (Jerusalem: Ha-Qibûṣ ha-Me'ûḥad 1992); idem, "'Al ha-Midrash ki-Yeṣîra. Yôṣrav we-Ṣûrôtav", *Mada'ê ha-Yahadût. Bamat ha-'îgûd ha-'ôlamî le-Mada'ê ha-Yahadût* 32 (1992) 83–90; M. Kahana, "Mahadûrôt ha-Mekhîlta' de-R. Yišma'ē'l li-Šemôt be-Re'î Kiṭ'ê ha-Genîzah", *Tarbîṣ* 55 (1986) 515–20; R. Kalmin, *The Redaction of the Babylonian Talmud* (Cincinnati, OH: Hebrew Union College Press 1989); idem,

"Review of Fraade's *From Tradition to Commentary. Torah and its Interpretation in the Midrash Sifre to Deuteronomy*", *Association for Jewish Studies Review* (forthcoming); idem, *Stories, Sages, Authors, and Editors in Rabbinic Babylonia* (Atlanta, GA: Scholars Press 1994); L. LEVINE, *The Rabbinic Class of Roman Palestine* (Jerusalem: Yad Yizhak ben Zvi 1989); S. LIEBERMAN, "Ḥazzanût Yannai", *Sinai* 2 (1939) 229–34; R. LOEWE, "The 'Plain' Meaning of Scripture in Early Jewish Exegesis", *Papers of the Institute of Jewish Studies* 1 (1964) 140–85; J. P. MEIER, *A Marginal Jew. Rethinking the Historical Jesus* (New York: Doubleday 1991); S. K. MIRSKY, "The Schools of Hillel, R. Ishmael and R. Akiba in Pentateuchal Interpretation", *Essays Presented to Chief Rabbi Israel Brodie on the Occasion of his Seventieth Birthday* (ed. H. J. Zimmels *et al*; London: Soncino Press 1967) 298; J. NEUSNER, *Midrash as Literature. The Primacy of Documentary Discourse* (Lanham, MD: U. Press of America 1987); idem, *Midrash in Context. Exegesis in Formative Judaism* (Atlanta, GA: Scholars Press 1988); G. G. PORTON, *The Traditions of Rabbi Ishmael* II–IV (Leiden: E. J. Brill 1977); D. ROKEAḤ, "Ben Satra' Ben Pantîra' Hû'. Le-Bērûrah Šel Baʿayah Pilôlôgît-Hisṭôrît", *Tarbîṣ* 39 (1969) 9–18; A. J. SALDARINI, "Reconstructions of Rabbinic Judaism", *Early Judaism and its Modern Interpreters* (ed. R. A. Kraft/G. W. E. Nickelsburg; Philadelphia: Fortress Press 1986) 445–46; L. SCHIFFMAN, *From Text to Tradition. A History of Second Temple and Rabbinic Judaism* (Hoboken, NJ: Ktav 1991); S. SPIEGEL, "Introduction", *Legends of the Bible* (by L. Ginzberg; Philadelphia: Jewish Publication Society 1956) xxxviii; W. S. TOWNER, *The Rabbinic "Enumeration of Scriptural Examples". A Study of a Rabbinic Pattern of Discourse with Special Reference to Mekhilta D'R. Ishmael* (Leiden: E. J. Brill 1973); G. VERMES, "Introduction. Parallel History Preview", *Christianity and Rabbinic Judaism* (ed. H. Shanks; Washington, D. C.: Biblical Archaeology Society 1992) xx.

General works: H. ALBECK, *Untersuchungen über die halakhischen Midraschim* (Berlin: Akademie 1927); Y. FRAENKEL, *Darkê ha-'Aggadah we-ha-Midrash* (Gibʿatayîm, Israel: Yad la-Talmud 1991); J. GOLDIN, *Studies in Midrash and Related Literature* (Philadelphia: Jewish Publication Society 1988); J. HEINEMANN, *Derašôt ba-Ṣibûr bi-Teqûpat ha-Talmûd* (Jerusalem: Môsad Bialik 1971); idem, *'Aggadôt we-Tôldôtêhen. ʿîyûnîm be-Hištalšelûtan Šel Mesôrôt* (Jerusalem: Keter 1974); D. Z. HOFFMAN, *Zur Einleitung in die halakhischen Midraschim* (Berlin: M. Driesner 1887); R. KASHER, "The Interpretation of Scripture in Rabbinic Literature", *Mikra. Text, Translation, Reading and Interpretation of the Hebrew Bible in Ancient Judaism and Early Christianity* (ed. M. J. Mulder; Assen/Maastricht: Van Gorcum 1988) 554, 566–71, 578, 587–89; G. G. PORTON, "Defining Midrash", *The Study of Ancient Judaism, I. Mishnah, Midrash, Siddur* (ed. J. Neusner; New York: Ktav 1981) 62, 80–81, 92, n. 214; H. L. STRACK/G. STEMBERGER, *Introduction to the Talmud and Midrash* (Minneapolis: Fortress Press 1992); G. VERMES, *Scripture and Tradition in Judaism. Haggadic Studies* (1961; reprint Leiden: E. J. Brill 1973); idem, *Post Biblical Jewish Studies* (Leiden: E. J. Brill 1975); A. G. WRIGHT, *The Literary Genre, Midrash* (Staten Island, NY: Alba House 1967).

Recent decades have witnessed an explosion of modern scholarship about rabbinic scriptural interpretation (Midrash). Contributing to this recent surge of interest are (1) the discovery of the Dead Sea Scrolls, which contain a rich corpus of exegetical materials with important similarities to rabbinic Midrash[1], and (2) possible affinities between modern literary theories and ancient rabbinic exegesis.[2]

The tremendous quantity of scholarly literature, together with the vast nature of the midrashic corpus and the lengthy period of time during which it took shape precludes any attempt to describe the subject exhaustively. In this essay, therefore, we confine ourselves to description of the most important characteristics of rabbinic Midrash, with special emphasis on historical

[1] See, for example, G. Vermes, Scripture and Tradition in Judaism (1973) 4–5.

[2] See, for example, *Midrash and Literature* (ed. G. H. Hartman/S. Budick; New Haven: Yale U. Press 1986); and Boyarin, Intertextuality and the Reading of Midrash (1990). For a critique of some of this literature, see Green, Romancing the Tome (1987) 147–68.

and literary developments and differences between the two major rabbinic centers.[3]

The term *Midrash* (plural, *Midrashim*) is used by modern scholars in a bewildering variety of ways.[4] In the following pages, we use the term only in its traditional senses, to refer either to (1) a rabbinic interpretation, virtually always of a scriptural[5] word, phrase, or verse, which searches, or ferrets out, a meaning which is not immediately obvious upon first encounter with the text; (2) a compilation of such interpretations; (3) the totality of all rabbinic compilations of such interpretations; and (4) the act of interpreting Scripture in the manner described above.[6] We rely on the context to establish clearly which meaning we intend.

As noted in section 1, above, during the pre-Tannaitic and early Tannaitic periods a wealth of non-rabbinic Jewish sources (for example, Philo and Josephus) comment on the Bible. Subsequently, however, throughout the bulk of the period under discussion, rabbinic literature is the only extant Jewish literature which interprets the Bible. Jewish and rabbinic exegesis during this period are virtually synonymous.

Midrash is preserved in several diverse rabbinic works compiled and edited over a period of more than six centuries. In addition to the Mishnah, examined in detail above, other major rabbinic works which contain Midrash include (1) the Mekhîlta' de-R. Yišmaʿēʾl, the Sipra', Siprê Numbers, and Siprê Deuteronomy, primarily halakhic (i. e., legal) commentaries on (in order) Exodus, Leviticus, Numbers, and Deuteronomy; (2) Berešit Rabbah and Wayiqra' Rabbah, primarily aggadic (i. e., non-legal) commentaries on Genesis and Leviticus; (3) the Palestinian Talmud, also known as the Yerushalmi; and (4) the Babylonian Talmud, also known as the Bavli. The Bavli and Yerushalmi, unlike the other compilations referred to above, are structured primarily as commentaries on the Mishnah, but they contain much midrashic material as well.

Several times throughout this section we distinguish between the Tannaitic and post-Tannaitic periods. The term 'Tannaitic' designates the period between the destruction of the Jerusalem Temple in 70 CE and the publication of the Mishnah in the early third century CE. The term 'post-Tannaitic' designates the post-Mishnaic period, concluding with the Arab conquests of the seventh century.

The publication of the Mishnah in the early third century CE is the conventional dividing line between the Tannaitic and post-Tannaitic periods. In

---

[3] As a result, important works such as J. Goldin, *Studies in Midrash and Related Literature* (1988); Y. Fraenkel, *Darkê ha-'Aggadah we-ha-Midrash* (1991); and S. D. Fraade, *From Tradition to Commentary: Torah and its Interpretation in the Midrash Sifre to Deuteronomy* (1991) will receive only cursory mention, or no mention at all, in the following pages. Simply to provide a bibliography of works on the subject would leave no space for analysis.

[4] See, for example, the definitions discussed in Wright, The Literary Genre, Midrash (1967) 18–25 and 33–48. See also the definition of Porton, Defining Midrash (1981) 62; and the refinement of Porton's definition by Saldarini, Reconstructions of Rabbinic Judaism, (1986) 445–46.

[5] In rare instances, ancient sources use the word *daraš* to describe interpretation of non-scriptural texts. See, for example, *b. B. Meṣ.* 104 a–b.

[6] Wright, The Literary Genre, Midrash (1967) 42.

numerous ways, the Mishnah marks a watershed in rabbinic history, with important implications for the study of Midrash as well. To briefly anticipate the discussion below, post-Mishnaic compilations quote Scripture much more frequently than does the Mishnah,[7] a difference which may indicate a major ideological or conceptual change.

Other distinctions between Rabbis with regard to Scripture, however, are geographically rather than chronologically determined. The two major rabbinic centers of late Antiquity are Palestine (Israel) and Babylonia (Persia), and Midrash, especially the aggadic (non-legal) variety, is to a large extent a Palestinian phenomenon. All of our extant midrashic compilations were edited in Palestine, and relatively few aggadic scriptural comments are attributed to Babylonian Rabbis.

How do we account for this geographical difference? It can hardly be coincidental that our sources depict Palestinian Rabbis surrounded by groups (for example, Christians) who base their claims on the Bible, but do not depict similar contacts involving Babylonian Rabbis.[8] Palestinian Rabbis use the Bible as a defense against biblically-based criticisms of Judaism, and as a polemical tool against opponents who respect scripturally-based arguments. Virtually all of the stories of *Minîm* (heretics) challenging rabbinic claims by quoting Scripture involve Palestinian rabbis. In Persia, such Scripture-reading groups were a tiny, relatively inconsequential minority, which very likely explains the Babylonian rabbinic tendency to ignore aggadic scriptural interpretation and to focus more on rabbinic texts such as the Mishnah.

Among the most important issues raised in these debates with *Minîm* are (1) the identity of the true Israel referred to in the Bible as the inheritor of God's promises, (2) the nature of God, and (3) the importance of halakhah. The following story is a typical Talmudic portrayal of an exegetical dispute between *Minîm* and a Rabbi:[9]

המינין שאלו
את ר׳ שמלאי כמה אלוהות בראו את השלם· א׳ להן ולי אתם
שואלין· לכו ושאלו את אדם הראשון שנ׳ כי שאל נא לימים
ראשונים וגומר· אשר בראו אלהים אדם על הארץ אין כתיב
כאן אלא למן היום אשר ברא אלהים אדם על הארץ: אמרו
ליה והכתיב בראשית ברא אלהים· אמר להן וכי בראו כתיב אין
כתיב אלא ברא

(A) The *Minîm* asked R. Śimla'î, "How many gods created the world?"
(B) He said to them, "You ask me? Go and ask the first man, as it is said, 'You have but to inquire about bygone ages [from the day that God created man on earth]' (Deut 4:32). It is not written 'the gods created,' but 'God created'".
(C) "But it is written, 'In the beginning *'Elohîm* [a plural form] created'" (Gen 1:1).
(D) He said to them, "It is not written '*bar'û*' [the plural form of the verb 'to create'] but '*bara*'" [the singular form]".

---

[7] The one exception is the Tôsepta', which most scholars believe was edited shortly after the Mishnah.

[8] It is unclear why virtually all of these stories are preserved only in the Babylonian Talmud.

[9] *y. Ber.* 12d–13a. See also *Gen. Rab.* 8:9 (ed. Theodor-Albeck) 62–63. For further discussion of the Jewish-Christian dialogue in late Antiquity, see, for example, M. Hirshman, *Ha-Miqra' û-Midrashô: Bên Ḥazal la-Abôt ha-Kenesîah* (1992).

One of the biblical names of God is *'Elohîm*, which is a plural form. Perhaps, the *Minîm* object, the Bible presupposes the existence of more than one God. Śimla'î responds that Deuteronomy, in describing the creative act of *'Elohîm*, uses a singular verb (*bara'*), instead of the plural (*bar'û*), thereby asserting the creator's oneness. The story continues:

אמר רבי שמלאי כל מקום שפרקו המינין :
תשובתן בצידן: חזרו ושאלו אותו· מה אהן דכתיב נעשה אדם
בצלמינו כדמתינו· אמד להן ויבראו אלהים את האדם בצלמם
אין כתיב כאן אלא ויברא אלהים את האדם בצלמו: אמרו
לו תלמידיו לאלו דחיתה בקנה לנו מה אתה משיב· אמר
להן לשעבר אדם נברא מן העפר וחוה נבראת מון האדם·
מאדם ואילך בצלמינו כדמותינו· א"א לאיש בלא אשה וא"א
לאשה בלא איש· א"א לשניהן בלא שכינה· וחזרו ושאלו
אותו מה ההן דכתיב אל אלהים ה' אל אלהים ה' הוא יודע·
אמר להן הם יודעים אין כתיב כאן אלא הוא יודע כתיב:
אמרו לו תלמידיו ר' לאלו דחית בקנה· לנו מה אתה משיב·
אמר להן שלשתן שם אחד כאינש דאמר בסיליום
קיסר אגושתום

(E) Said R. Śimla'î, "Wherever [Scripture seems to license] the *Minîm* [to] break out of control, the [text] refuting them is close by".

(F) They asked him again, "What about this verse: 'Let us make man in our image, after our likeness'" (Gen 1:26)?

(G) He said to them, "It is not written here, 'And the gods created [*wa-Yibre'û 'Elohîm*, a plural form] man in their image', but 'And God created [*wa-Yibra'*, a singular form] man in His image'" (Gen 1:27).

(H) His students said to him [R. Śimla'î], "You pushed them off with a reed. How can you answer us?"

(I) He said to them, "Originally, Adam was created from earth and Eve was created from Adam. After Adam, [it is appropriate to say] 'in our image, after our likeness'. It is impossible for a man without a woman, and it is impossible for a woman without a man, and it is impossible for both of them without the Divine Presence" [the plural refers to God, Adam, and Eve. All three help propagate the human race, and all of humanity resembles them].

(J) They asked him again, "What about this verse, 'God, the Lord God! God, the Lord God! He knows'" (Josh 22:22).

(K) He said to them, "It is not written 'they know', but 'he knows'".

(L) His students said to him, "Rabbi. You pushed them off with a reed. How can you answer us?"

(M) He said to them, "The three of them are one name, like a man who said 'Basileas, Caeser, Augustus' [addressing the Roman emperor with several titles]".[10]

According to the opinion of one Babylonian Rabbi, "there are no heretics (*Minîm*) among the idolatrous nations".[11] R. 'Abahû, for example, explains why he is well-versed in Scripture but Rav Šešet is not: "We who are frequent among you [heretics] take it upon ourselves to examine [Scripture]. They [Babylonians] do not examine [Scripture]".[12] Very likely, the absence of a significant scripturally-based challenge to Babylonian Rabbis led to the relative neglect of aggadic exegesis in rabbinic Babylonia.

The distinction drawn above between Tannaitic and post-Tannaitic literature seems straightforward, but it is actually problematic. Many rabbinic

---

[10] The dialogue continues, but the above selection will suffice to capture its flavor.

[11] *b. Ḥûl.* 13b. The anonymous editors of this passage, however, qualify the statement.

[12] *b. ʿAbod. Zar.* 4a.

statements are clearly post-Tannaitic, for example, statements in the Talmuds which interpret the Mishnah. Many other statements, however, are much more difficult to date, for example, statements attributed to Tannaim which are embedded in compilations (such as the Palestinian and Babylonian Talmuds) edited centuries after the end of the Tannaitic period. During the course of transmission many of these statements were altered, emended, and completed in subtle or not so subtle ways, such that a statement's attribution to a Tannaitic Rabbi cannot be accepted at face value.[13] How much, if anything, of the statement is Tannaitic? Has it been doctored by later generations? Is it an invention by later generations based on false assumptions about attitudes in a much earlier time? If the statement is accompanied by a scriptural proof-text, is the proof-text an addition by later generations or does it derive from the original author?

The following example[14] illustrates our difficulty:

דתני האומר לשלוחו צא הרוג את הנפש
הוא חייב ושולחיו פטור שמאי הזקן אומר
משום חגי הנביא שולהיו חייב שנא׳ אותו
הרגת בחרב בני עמון

(A) It is taught [in a Tannaitic source]:
(B) One who says to his emissary, "Go and kill someone", he [the emissary] is liable and the one who sends him is exempt.
(C) Shammai the elder says in the name of Haggai the prophet, "The one who sends him is liable, as it is said, 'You killed him by the sword of the Ammonites'" (2 Sam 12:9) [Nathan the prophet declares David guilty of Uriah's murder. David did not personally shed Uriah's blood, but only arranged for his general to send him to the front lines where the battle was fiercest. Similarly, one who instructs an emissary to kill someone is liable for murder, despite not having shed the person's blood].

The Talmud's anonymous editors, commenting on this Tannaitic source, ask, "What is Shammai the elder's proof?", and they offer two responses. The second of their responses is the biblical proof-text, 2 Sam 12:9, cited and explained immediately above. The anonymous question is peculiar, however, since Shammai explicitly supplies a biblical proof-text in support of his statement. Throughout the Talmud, biblical support is sufficient proof for any opinion, and no further explanation is necessary. Why do the anonymous editors ignore Shammai's own explicit statement?

Most likely, Shammai's statement originally lacked the proof-text, without which the anonymous question is appropriate. The proof-text was added to Shammai's statement some time after the anonymous question, most likely by a scribe convinced by the Talmud's second answer.[15] The proof-text became part of Shammai's statement centuries after the conclusion of the Tannaitic period, since anonymous discussions tend to be late[16] and the proof-text post-dates the anonymous question.

---

[13] See, for example, Goodblatt, The Babylonian Talmud (1981) 148–51.

[14] *b. Qidd.* 43 a.

[15] The scribe was unaware of, or not troubled by, the problem caused by his interpolation.

[16] See, for example, Goodblatt, The Babylonian Talmud (1981) 177–81; and Kalmin, The Redaction of the Babylonian Talmud (1989), especially 1–11 and 66–94.

Some portion of what the Talmuds designate as Tannaitic, therefore, is actually post-Tannaitic, and while it is often possible to identify later additions to early sources, it is often impossible. Any generalizations we make about the post-Tannaitic period, therefore, are based on only part of the extant material. Our goal is to trace shifts in rabbinic exegesis from the first century and beyond, but the data frequently do not allow us to do so.

The situation is not hopeless, however. While in general we cannot pinpoint the advent of a phenomenon to a particular decade or even century, we can at least draw general distinctions between early and later techniques and presuppositions, for example, between Tannaitic and post-Tannaitic exegesis. Groups of statements purporting to date from the same period often exhibit similar characteristics, and are distinguishable from statements attributed to earlier or later figures. In such cases, the texts very likely attest to genuine generational and/or geographical contrasts rather than to distortions by later editors, and it is possible to make historical generalizations with a reasonable degree of certainty.

Enunciation of the principle that "the [biblical] verse cannot depart from its *pešat* [context] completely", for example, is unique to post-Tannaitic Midrash. According to this principle, Midrash sets as its interpretive goal preservation of the context of a word or statement, and cognizance of what comes before or after in the biblical text. Some post-Tannaitic Rabbis, therefore, limit the interpreter's freedom to violate the contextual meaning of a text in unprecedented ways.[17] They do not conform to modern exegetical standards, however, since even fanciful interpretation can do justice to a statement's context.[18]

There is also evidence that a particular form of reading into the biblical text, displacing and ignoring the text's plain meaning, disappears after the Tannaitic period.[19] The Tannaitic Rabbis' understanding of the lex talionis, the biblical injunction to take "an eye for an eye", will serve as a case in point. According to the Rabbis, "an eye for an eye" means "money", i. e., monetary compensation, rather than the guilty party's loss of an actual eye. The Tannaitic interpretation displaces the biblical verse's plain meaning, asserting that it means one thing even though it explicitly says another.[20]

Such interpretations disappear after the Tannaitic period,[21] during which time Midrash uses different methods to stretch the literal meaning of Scripture. One technique found frequently in both Tannaitic and post-Tannaitic

[17] It is unclear to what extent this principle is normative. It is not attested until the fourth century CE and is presented as an innovation. See *b. Šabb.* 63 a.

[18] For more detailed discussion of the term *pešaṭ*, and in particular the rationale for translating it as "context", see Halivni, Peshat and Derash (1991) 25–26 and 52–88. See also Loewe, The 'Plain' Meaning of Scripture in Early Jewish Exegesis (1964) 140–85.

[19] See Halivni, Peshat and Derash (1991) 3–39 and 46–47. Compare Brewer, Techniques and Assumptions in Jewish Exegesis (1992), whose central thesis is that pre-70 CE sages tend to interpret in line with the plain meaning of the Bible, and preserve the context of the verse.

[20] See *Mek. de-R. Yišmaʿēʾl*, tractate *Nez.* (ed. Lauterbach 1949) III, 67–68; and *b. B. Qam.* 83 b–84 a.

[21] Or earlier.

sources adds to rather than displaces Scripture's plain meaning. A post-Tannaitic interpretation of Ps 50:23 will illustrate this point.

Ps 50:23 contains a textual anomaly which motivates several midrashic interpretations. The verb *yekabdananî*, "honors me", contains an unexpected doubling of a Hebrew letter, which the Rabbis claim refers to more than one act of honoring:[22]

אריב"ל כל הזובח את יצרו ומתודה עליו
מעלה עלין הכתוב כאילו כיבדו להקב"ה
בשני עולמים העולם הזה והעולם הבא
דכתיב זובח תודה יכבדנני

R. Yehôšûʿa ben Lewi says, "Anyone who slaughters his [evil] inclination and makes confession about it, Scripture counts it to him as if he honored God in two worlds, in this world and the world to come, as it is written, 'He who sacrifices, and confession [*Tôdah*], honor me' (Ps 50:23)".[23]

The biblical text plainly speaks about one act of honoring God. Yehôšûʿa ben Lewî, using a method found frequently throughout rabbinic literature, adds another.

As noted above, the Mishnah and post-Mishnaic compilations quote Scripture in different quantities and in different ways. The heavily scriptural component of the midrashic compilations contrasts sharply with the paucity of such material in the Mishnah.[24] Furthermore, in the rare instances when the Mishnah cites scriptural sources for its laws, it states the law first and follows with the proof-text. The midrashic compilations, in contrast, cite Scripture first. The Mishnah highlights the law; the Midrashim grant priority to the Bible.

The post-Mishnaic compilations themselves quote different quantities of Scripture. The Talmuds contain much less Midrash than do the midrashic compilations, since the primary focus of their commentary is the Mishnah rather than the Torah.

Brief selections from the various compilations will illustrate these claims. In the Mishnah,[25] for example, we read:

אַף הַשִּׂמְלָה הָיְתָה בִּכְלָל כָּל אֵלֶּה, לָמָּה יָצָאת? לְהַקִּישׁ
אֵלֶיהָ, לוֹמַר לָךְ: מַה שִּׂמְלָה מְיֻחֶדֶת, שֶׁיֶּשׁ בָּהּ סִימָנִים וְיֵשׁ
לָהּ תּוֹבְעִים – אַף כָּל דָּבָר, שֶׁיֶּשׁ בּוֹ סִימָנִים וְיֵשׁ לוֹ תוֹבְעִים,
חַיָּב לְהַכְרִיז.

Indeed, the garment is in the same category as all of the others. Why was it specified? To draw a comparison between it [and all other lost articles]. Just as a garment is distinguished by having identifiable marks and claimants, so too everything which has identifiable marks and claimants, one must announce.

---

22 *b. Sanh.* 43b. See also *Lev. Rab.* 9:1 (ed. Margaliot) 73–74.

23 This translation renders Ps 50:23 in conformity with Yehôšûʿa ben Lewî's midrashic understanding. The verse most likely means, "He who sacrifices a thank-offering (*Tôdah*) honors me", but Yehôšûʿa understands the ambiguous word *Tôdah* as 'confession' rather than 'thank-offering', in conformity with rabbinic values after the destruction of the Temple. In addition, Yehôšûʿa understands the two phrases, "he who sacrifices" and "confession", as separate elements in a list.

24 Once again, the Tôseptaʾ largely conforms to the Mishnah's patterns.

25 *Mishnah B.Meṣ* 2:5.

The Mishnah's opening line is incomprehensible unless read in connection with the following unstated scriptural passage: "If you see your fellow's ox or sheep gone astray, do not ignore it. ... If your fellow does not live near you or you do not know who he is ... it shall remain with you until your fellow claims it. ... You shall do the same with his garment ..." (Deut 22:1–3). The Mishnah asks why the Torah makes special mention of a garment, since one is obligated to return many different kinds of lost articles. The Mishnah's answer is that the garment is a paradigmatic case. A finder must announce his discovery only in the event that the lost object resembles a garment in certain specific ways. Lacking such characteristics, the lost object belongs to the finder. The Mishnah, therefore, while intimately linked to Scripture, omits the scriptural text.

As noted above, the midrashic compilations are rich in scriptural quotations. In the Mekhîlta' de-R. Šim'ôn bar Yôḥa'î,[26] for example, we find the following:

יכול יהא חייב על פחות משוה פרוטה ת"ל שלמה
מה שַׂלמה מיוחדת שיש בה שוה פרוטה וחייב להכריז כך
כל דבר שיש בו שוה פרוטה וחייב להכריז

One might think that one is obligated [to announce the discovery of lost objects worth] less than a *perûṭah* [a small coin]. Scripture [therefore] says, "garment". Just as a garment is distinguished by being worth a *perûṭah* and one is obligated to announce it, so too everything that is worth a *perûṭah* one is obligated to announce.

In contrast to the Mishnah, the Mekhîlta' explicitly cites the proof-text.

The Talmuds, as noted above, occupy a middle position between the Mishnah and the Midrashim with regard to Scripture. The Talmuds frequently specify the scriptural references presupposed, but unstated, by the Mishnah, but many Talmudic discussions proceed without the slightest connection to Scripture.

The Bavli, for example, discussing the Mishnah's requirement that criminals be executed outside of the courthouse, cites a contradictory Tannaitic source which asserts that the place of execution must be completely outside the city. The Talmud resolves the contradiction by asserting that the two sources contain different rulings because they refer to different situations. Subsequently, the Talmud tries to find the scriptural basis for the Tannaitic source's ruling. The Mishnah and closely related Tannaitic literature, therefore, provide the framework for the Talmud's discussions, but discovery of the scriptural basis of Tannaitic statements is crucial to the Talmud's interpretive agenda.

These and other differences between the various rabbinic compilations caution us not to view them as a unified corpus.[27] These compilations frequently differ and should not be artificially harmonized, but they also cannot be understood fully in total isolation from one another. Determining the proper balance between harmonization and separation of these works is a major

[26] *Mek. de-R. Šim'ôn bar Yôḥa'î* (ed. Epstein/Melamed) 203.

[27] This thesis has been pioneered by J. Neusner in a staggering number of publications. See, for example, J. Neusner, Midrash as Literature (1987) ix–xvii.

challenge facing modern scholars. When does one document genuinely elucidate another and when does it inappropriately bias our understanding? As yet, no consensus exists as to the appropriate response to this question.[28]

What is the significance of the varying quantities of Scripture in the diverse rabbinic books? One possibility is that the Mishnah and the midrashic compilations conceive of the relationship between oral and written law, rabbinic creativity and Scripture, in different ways. The exegetical compilations perhaps view the oral law as deriving from or interpreting the written law, in contrast to the Mishnah, which perhaps views the oral law as largely a supplement to the written law.[29]

Alternatively, perhaps the Mishnah and the midrashic compilations differ over the proper formulation of rabbinic law. Does law have to be learned and transmitted with an explicit connection to the Bible, or can it be formulated independently? Is there a danger that independent formulation will cause the biblical (and therefore divine) origin of rabbinic law to be forgotten or obscured, or is that not a concern?

Common to these and other comparable theories is the notion that the Mishnah and the Midrashim derive from different schools of thought and reflect fissures and tensions within the rabbinic movement. These theories need to account, however, for the fact that many of the same Rabbis are quoted in both the exegetical and non-exegetical compilations. How is it that these Rabbis are able to belong to, or at least contribute to, opposing schools of thought?[30] One can posit, of course, that late, unnamed editors systematically added to or deleted proof-texts from earlier named statements based on their conception of the proper way to formulate law. In the absence of clear proof of such editorial activity, however, the theory of diverse exegetical and non-exegetical schools remains speculative.

J. NEUSNER believes that the Mishnah and the Midrashim represent opposing schools of thought. He claims further that the midrashic compilations, qua compilations, respond to and polemicize against the Mishnah. The compilers of the Sipra', for example, react to the completed Mishnah by creating a genre, Scripture commentary, heretofore unknown in rabbinic circles.

NEUSNER claims that the midrashic compilations arose as attempts to resolve a "crisis" precipitated by the publication of the Mishnah. The Mishnah was shocking because it claimed, like the Bible, to be authoritative, holy, and revealed, despite its obvious differences from Scripture in language and style. What is the Mishnah, Jews wondered, and what is its relationship to the Torah?

All of subsequent rabbinic literature, in NEUSNER's view, responds to these questions. The Sipra' responds, for example, by polemicizing against the Mishnah, attempting to show that mere reason unaided by Scripture leads to

28 For further discussion of this issue, see R. KALMIN's review of FRAADE, *From Tradition to Commentary*, in the *Association for Jewish Studies Review* (forthcoming).

29 Cohen, From the Maccabees to the Mishnah (1987) 203–4.

30 See Vermes, Introduction. Parallel History Preview (1992).

faulty conclusions. To increase the force of its polemic, argues NEUSNER, the Sipra' chooses the Bible as the framework for its statements. Whatever is right in the Mishnah, claims the Sipra', derives from and is secondary to the Bible.[31]

NEUSNER is most likely correct that the editing of the earliest midrashic compilations post-dates that of the Mishnah, but his claim that these compilations, qua compilations, respond to and polemicize against the Mishnah is difficult to accept.[32] NEUSNER's assumption that post-Tannaitic Rabbis invented the genre of scriptural commentary is extremely unlikely, and the extant compilations are probably based on similar collections which first took shape during the Tannaitic period.[33]

True, we do not have such *Ur-texts*, and the scholarly consensus that they existed is speculative. However, NEUSNER's theory is also speculative, depending on the assumption that such collections did not exist. Given the likelihood, acknowledged by NEUSNER, that many midrashic statements derive from the Tannaitic period, and given the fact that rabbinic sources refer on several occasions to midrashic compilations dating from Tannaitic times,[34] NEUSNER's is the less likely of the two speculations. The genre of scriptural commentary most likely did not originate as a response to the completed Mishnah. Its origins are to be sought in the Tannaitic period, and not in the third century CE.

We mentioned above that post-Tannaitic Midrash attempts to adhere to the contextual meaning of biblical texts in ways not encountered earlier. Many scholars claim that already during the Tannaitic period adherence to Scripture's literal meaning was an important issue dividing two schools of exegesis. R.ʿAqîba' and R. Yišmaʿē'l, who flourished during the early second century CE, are credited with founding these schools.[35] Many view their supposedly different approaches to the biblical text as symptomatic of differing *Weltanschauungen* and religious attitudes, with Yišmaʿē'l often portrayed as a rationalist and ʿAqîba' as a non-rationalist, Yišmaʿē'l as a believer in the power of logic and ʿAqîba' as favoring revelation over logic.[36] Some exegetical compi-

---

[31] See, for example, Neusner, Midrash in Context (1988) 1–41 and 48–52.

[32] For other discussions of the dating of these sources, see, for example, Herr, Midrešê Halakhah (1971) 1521–23; and Basser, Midrashic Interpretations of the Song of Moses (1984) 1–2. For a refutation of the claim that the Mekhîlta' de-R. Yišmaʿē'l is an early medieval pseudepigraph, see Kahana, Mahadûrôt ha-Mekhîlta' de-R. Yišmaʿē'l li-Šemôt be-Re'î Qiṭʿê ha-Genîzah (1986) 515–20.

[33] Albeck, Untersuchungen über die halakhischen Midraschim (1927) 119–20, for example, who dates the editing of the midrashic compilations much later than most scholars, maintains a Tannaitic date for the bulk of the material contained in these compilations. See also H. ALBECK, *Mabô' la-Talmûdîm* (Tel Aviv: Debir 1969) 79. For more on this topic, see Strack/Stemberger, Introduction to the Talmud and Midrash (1992) 272–73; and Boyarin, On the Status of the Tannaitic Midrashim (1992) 455–58.

[34] See, for example, *b. Môʿēd Qaṭ.* 28b, *b. Qidd.* 49b, b. *Sanh.* 86a, and *b. Šebû.* 41b.

[35] The question of whether earlier schools of interpretation existed has also been discussed, although for the most part the material has not yielded clear and consistent differences. See, for example, de Vries, Mabô' Kelalî le-Siprût ha-Talmûdît (1966) 86–87.

[36] Porton, The Traditions of Rabbi Ishmael (1977) II, 2–3.

lations, for example the Mekhîlta' de-R. Yišmaʿē'l and Siprî be-Midbar, are assigned to the school of Yišmaʿē'l, and others, for example the Sipra' and the Mekhîlta' de-R. Šimʿôn bar Yôḥa'i, are assigned to the school of ʿAqîba'.[37]

Much of the evidence for Tannaitic schools of exegesis is found in post-Tannaitic sources, and also in sources which purport to be Tannaitic but which are embedded in texts edited centuries after the end of the Tannaitic period (see above). As a result, many now view the notion of Tannaitic schools as a post-Tannaitic invention, perhaps reflecting the situation in later rabbinic times, perhaps originating as an attempt to systematize conflicting tendencies and methodologies present in earlier sources.

D. Z. Hoffman claims that the schools of ʿAqîba' and Yišmaʿē'l use different technical terminology and hermeneutic principles in commenting on the biblical text. For example, Hoffman argues that the school of ʿAqîba' introduced limitations derived from a biblical verse by means of the term *peraṭ le-*, whereas the school of Yišmaʿē'l used the term *lehôṣî et*. The school of Yišmaʿē'l favored literal exegesis; the school of ʿAqîba' preferred more fanciful interpretation. Yišmaʿē'l viewed certain features of the text as present for merely stylistic reasons, whereas ʿAqîba' viewed them as sources of important laws, ethical teachings, and theological truths.

In one context, for example, ʿAqîba' and Yišmaʿē'l disagree regarding the punishment to be inflicted on an adulterous daughter of a priest. According to ʿAqîba' she is burned, while according to Yišmaʿē'l she is strangled, a less stringent form of execution. ʿAqîba' explains that "'the daughter', '*and* the daughter' I interpret", meaning that he bases his opinion on a superfluous Hebrew letter in the biblical text (Lev 21:9). Yišmaʿē'l responds sharply that the textual support used by ʿAqîba' is flimsy, especially given the weightiness of the issue: "And because you interpret 'the daughter', '*and* the daughter', we take her out to be burned?"[38] Elsewhere, Yišmaʿē'l complains that his teacher, R. 'Elîʿezer, "says to the verse, 'Be silent while I interpret'", and 'Elîʿezer responds that Yišmaʿē'l is a "mountain palm", a tree which bears no fruit.[39]

The *kelal û-peraṭ û-kelal* technique of exegesis is said to characterize the school of Yišmaʿē'l and the *rîbûî û-mîʿûṭ* technique the school of ʿAqîba'. The following Midrashim based on Lev 5:4 illustrate these different methods:

אי נפש כי תשבע
לבטא בשפתים כלל להרע או להיטיב פרט לכל אשר יבטא האדם חזר
וכלל כלל ופרט וכלל אי אתה דן אלא כעין הפרט מה הפרט מפורש
להבא אף כל להבא

או
נפש כי תשבע ריבה להרע או להיטיב מיעט לכל אשר יבטא האדם חזר
וריבה ריבה ומיעט וריבה ריבה הכל מאי ריבה ריבה כל מילי ומאי
מיעט מיעט דבר מצוה

---

37 See Hoffman, Zur Einleitung in die halakhischen Midraschim (1887) 5–12 and 20–81.

38 *b. Sanh.* 51b.

39 *Sipra' Tazrîʿa Negaʿîm* 13:1.

Kelal û-peraṭ û-kelal: "Or when a person utters an oath", [the text] generalizes; "to do evil or to do good", [the text] specifies; "whatever a man may utter in an oath", [the text] again generalizes. [When the text] generalizes, and [then] specifies, and [then] generalizes, one derives only things which resemble the specific case. Just as the specific case refers to the future, so too any [oath] regarding the future [one must bring the offerings mentioned in the Bible in the event of failure to fulfill the oath].

Ribûî û-miʿûṭ: "Or when a person utters an oath", [the text] includes; "to do evil or to do good", [the text] limits; "whatever a man may utter", [the text] again includes. [When the text] includes, and [then] limits, and [then] includes, it includes everything. What does it include? It includes everything. And what does it exlude? Oaths regarding] a commandment [In the case of oaths regarding commandments, one is not liable to bring the offerings mentioned in Scripture. Regarding all other oaths, one is liable].[40]

HOFFMAN's theory regarding diverse exegetical schools was accepted until recent decades by virtually all scholars. M. D. HERR, for example, refers to the theory as "one of the cornerstones of the research into the literature of the sages".[41]

L. FINKELSTEIN, refining HOFFMAN's theory, claims that aggadic (non-legal) scriptural interpretations by ʿAqîbaʾ and Yišmaʿēʾl often exhibit common features and therefore do not derive from diverse schools. According to FINKELSTEIN, the terminological and other distinctions noted by scholars are found only in the legal materials.[42]

R. KASHER accepts the existence of opposing schools founded by ʿAqîbaʾ and Yišmaʿēʾl, but questions whether they existed for more than a generation. S. LIEBERMAN, in contrast, claims to have found evidence of adherence to the school of Yišmaʿēʾl in the work of the fourth century CE (or later) liturgist, Yannai.[43]

H. ALBECK challenges HOFFMAN's theory, claiming that the exegetical compilations bear no clear signs of having been edited by ʿAqîbaʾ and his school or Yišmaʿēʾl and his school.[44] Each of these compilations contains more material deriving from one or the other Rabbi or his students, but this in itself is not enough to identify a book as the product of a particular school. The only criteria which ALBECK is prepared to accept as an indication of diverse origin is technical terminology. Several of the books, claims ALBECK, use distinct terminologies with total, or nearly total, consistency, and tend to use the same sets of technical terms. Technical terminology, however, says nothing about a book's connection to ʿAqîbaʾ or Yišmaʿēʾl, and ALBECK credits later editors with drawing on diverse sources and imposing terminological uniformity (or near-uniformity) on these sources.[45]

---

[40] Both selections are found on *b. Šebû.* 26 a.

[41] Herr, Midrešê Halakhah (1971) 1522. For other proponents of this view, see Epstein, Mebôʾôt le-Siprût ha-Tannaîm (1957) 521–746; de Vries, Maôʾ Kelalî (1966) 87–97; Halivni, Midrash, Mishnah, and Gemara (1986) 60–63; 69; 96–97; 124, n. 14; 128, n. 56; and 134, n. 47; and Kasher, The Interpretation of Scripture in Rabbinic Literature (1990) 566–71; 578; 587–89.

[42] See Finkelstein, The Sources of the Tannaitic Midrashim (1940–1941) 211–43; and Heinemann, ʾAggadôt we-Tôldôtêhen: ʿîyûnîm be-Hištalšelûtan Šel Mesôrôt (1974) 40.

[43] Lieberman, Ḥazzanût Yannai (1939) 229–34.

[44] Albeck, Untersuchungen (1927) 112–39; and Mabôʾ la-Talmûdîm (1969) 130–33. See also Schiffman, From Text to Tradition (1991) 198–99.

[45] Herr, Midrešê Halakhah (1971) 1521–22.

G. PORTON challenges another aspect of the older consensus. He analyzes statements attributed to Yišmaʿēʾl and claims that in Tannaitic sources no firm lines distinguish the scriptural interpretations of Yišmaʿēʾl and ʿAqîbaʾ.[46] According to PORTON, only in post-Tannaitic sources do we find the belief that Yišmaʿēʾl and ʿAqîbaʾ use different exegetical principles, but even in these sources there are no consistent differences between the scriptural comments by the two Tannaim. Two schools of exegesis may have existed, claims PORTON, but there is no proof whatsoever that they derive from ʿAqîbaʾand Yišmaʿēʾl.

In his characterization of Tannaitic sources, however, PORTON excludes from consideration statements found in compilations, such as the Talmuds, which were redacted during the post-Tannaitic period. Most likely, however, these compilations contain much material which dates from the Tannaitic period.[47] As noted above, it is often difficult to determine what is early and what is late in these heavily edited works, but it is inadmissable to ignore it all in an analysis of Tannaitic exegesis.

In addition, even if we confine ourselves to Tannaitic sources found in Tannaitic compilations, detailed study of exegetical techniques challenges PORTON's claim that there are no consistent differences between ʿAqîbaʾ and Yišmaʿēʾl. The *rîbûî û-mîʿût* technique is attributed to both Yišmaʿēʾl and ʿAqîbaʾ, but they use the technique in different ways.[48] The *kelal û-peraṭ û-kelal* technique, found several times in the name of Yišmaʿēʾl, is attributed only once in all of rabbinic literature to ʿAqîbaʾ.[49] True, the latter difference between ʿAqîbaʾ and Yišmaʿēʾl is not absolute (ʿAqîbaʾ uses the term once), but in a literature as vast and variegated as that of the ancient Rabbis virtually every pattern has a small number of exceptions. If scholarship could proceed only on the basis of complete unanimity, it would grind almost to a total halt.

PORTON's study shows, to be sure, that earlier scholars exaggerated the differences between ʿAqîbaʾ and Yišmaʿēʾl, and resorted too often to emendations and forced interpretations to conform the data to their theories.[50] PORTON correctly observes, for example, that a literal approach to interpretation is not particular to a specific group of Rabbis, and those Rabbis who

---

[46] See, for example, Porton, *Ishmael*, II, 2–7; III, 3; and IV, 55 and 204–33. Mirsky, The Schools of Hillel, R. Ishmael and R. Akiba in Pentateuchal Interpretation (1967), 298, writes, "That there were two schools of Pentateuchal interpretation of R. ISHMAEL and R. AKIBA can hardly be any doubt. ... On the other hand we find them sometimes reversing methods and changing roles".

[47] See, for example, Goodblatt, The Babylonian Talmud (1981) 148–51; and Kalmin, Stories, Sages, Authors, and Editors in Rabbinic Babylonia (1994) 61–78.

[48] Chernick, Le-Hēqer ha-Mîdôt "Kelal û-Peraṭ û-Kelal" we-"Ribûî û-Mîʿût" (1984) 80–82.

[49] See Chernick, ibid., 35; 49, n. 30. See also Halivni, Midrash, Mishnah, and Gemara (1986) 96–97, who notes that some statements attributed to R. ʿAqîbaʾ in collections identified by earlier scholars as deriving from the school of Yišmaʿēʾl use terminology found nowhere else in the purported works of the school of Yišmaʿēʾl, but which are characteristic of collections considered by scholars to derive from ʿAqîbaʾ. At the same time, HALIVNI acknowledges that many statements attributed to ʿAqîbaʾ and his students in the works ostensibly deriving from Yišmaʿēʾl use terminology ostensibly characteristic of Yišmaʿēʾl and his school, and vice versa.

[50] See, for example, Epstein, Mebôʾôt le-Siprût ha-Tannaîm (1957) 529.

advocate adherence to the plain meaning of the biblical text do not do so systematically.[51]

One can perhaps object to the theory of opposing schools founded by ʿAqîbaʾ and Yišmaʿēʾl on the grounds that attributions found in ancient rabbinic sources cannot be verified. One can argue, for example, that we lack criteria for establishing whether or not statements attributed to a particular individual actually derive from that individual. The claim that differing exegetical approaches derive from ʿAqîbaʾ and Yišmaʿēʾl is perhaps not susceptible to scholarly proof.

However, those who challenge the older consensus are asserting more than the unverifiability of attributions. They are claiming that even if we take the attributions seriously, there is no proof that ʿAqîbaʾ and Yišmaʿēʾl use different interpretive techniques. It is the latter claim which is premature, although PORTON and others have certainly shown that the older consensus made extravagant claims, and that HOFFMAN's theory, at the very least, needs to be scaled down to more modest proportions.[52] The issue demands further detailed studies like those of M. CHERNICK if it is ever to be fully resolved.

The *Sitz im Leben* of rabbinic exegesis is also an area of important concern. At one extreme, J. HEINEMANN claims that midrashic statements originated as synagogal sermons intended for a non-scholarly audience. HEINEMANN even claims that we have in our possession some of the original ancient sermons.[53] At the other extreme, Y. FRAENKEL emphasizes the sources' sophisticated, academic nature, and denies an exoteric, popular, synagogal origin for virtually all of the literature.[54] FRAENKEL points out that a popular audience would have difficulty understanding such complex compositions, and concludes that midrashic literature was created by scholars for scholars. J. PETUCHOWSKI correctly observes, however, that medieval liturgical poems are extremely abstruse and allusive, but were, and still are, read in synagogues by scholars and non-scholars alike.[55]

The possibility cannot be dismissed that some exegetical texts originated as sermons delivered in synagogues before a popular audience, although their unique stylistic features and rhetorical techniques have been editorially flattened in the texts before us.[56] Midrashic statements and compositions, at least in their present form, are the literary creation of an educated elite,[57] but what

[51] Porton, Ishmael, for example, II, 2–7. See also Kasher, The Interpretation of Scripture in Rabbinic Literature (1988) 554.

[52] The above discussion owes much to that of Strack/Stemberger, Introduction to the Talmud and Midrash (1992) 269–345. See also Brewer, Techniques and Assumptions in Jewish Exegesis (1992) 5–7.

[53] Heinemann, Derašôt ba-Ṣibûr bi-Teqûpat ha-Talmûd (1971) 1–67; and ʿAggadôt we-Tôldôtêhen (1974) 13. See also Bloch, Midrash (1978) 31 and 37 (originally published in French, DBSup 1957).

[54] Fraenkel, Darkê ha-ʾAggadah we-ha-Midrash (1991) 17–41. See also Porton, Defining Midrash (1981) 80–81. For a critique of Fraenkel, see Hirshman, ʿAl ha-Midrash ki-Yeṣîra (1992) 83–90.

[55] Cited in PORTON, Defining Midrash (1981) 92, n. 214.

[56] Wright, A Literary Genre, Midrash (1967) 52; 56–58; and Hirshman, Ha-Miqraʾ û-Midrashô (1992) 62 and 64; and ʿAl ha-Midrash ki-Yeṣîra (1992) 84–88.

[57] Spiegel, Introduction (1956) xxxviii; Bokser, Post Mishnaic Judaism in Transition (1980)

did they look like before they reached their present form? Were they originally studied by Rabbis in study houses, or delivered before a popular audience in synagogues? We must distinguish, in other words, between the *Sitz im Leben* of the original comments and the literary product presently before us. Much work needs to be done, furthermore, to develop criteria by which to determine which comments derive from which contexts.[58]

We conclude the discussion by analyzing the development of a midrashic text through comparison of different versions found in chronologically and geographically diverse rabbinic compilations. We hope the following example will show the value of such comparative analysis by demonstrating that different versions of rabbinic texts reveal interesting historical developments, or distinctions between one rabbinic center and another.[59]

The midrashic text under discussion is part of a story depicting interaction between R. ʾElîʿezer ben Hirkanûs, who flourished in the late first and early second centuries CE, and Yaʿaqôb ʾîsh Kepar Sekhanîah (Jacob of the village Sekhanîah), described in rabbinic sources as a disciple of Jesus. Comparison of two versions of this story, one early Palestinian[60] and one later Babylonian,[61] shows that a midrashic argument has been added to the latter.

The early Palestinian version of the story portrays ʾElîʿezer approving of a statement of Jesus, reported to him by the above-mentioned Yaʿaqôb. The Roman government arrests ʾElîʿezer on suspicion of being a *Mîn* [heretic], which ʾElîʿezer interprets as punishment for his improperly close contact with followers of Jesus. The early Palestinian version of the story does not specify Jesus' attractive "words" but the later Babylonian version does:

אמר לי כתוב בתורתכם לא תביא
אתגן זונה [וגו'] מהו לעשות הימגו בהכ"ס
לכ"ג ולא אמרתי לו כלום אמר לי כך
לימדני [כי] מאתנן זונה קבצה ועד אתנן
זונה ישובו ממקום הטנופת באו למקום
הטנופת ילכו והנאני הדבר על ידי זה
נתפסתי למינות

442; Basser, Midrashic Interpretations (1984) 282–84; Cohen, From the Maccabees to the Mishnah (1987) 213; Fraade, From Tradition to Commentary (1991) 69–121; and Hirshman, Ha-Miqraʾ û-Midrashô (1992) 21; 25–27; 54–64.

[58] See also Heinemann, The Nature of the Aggadah (1986) 47. Strack/Stemberger, Introduction to the Talmud and Midrash (1992) 257–58, citing no evidence, assert that the *Sitz im Leben* of Midrash is the school and the synagogue liturgy. See also ibid., p. 262, where it is argued that the collections of homiletical exegesis probably do not contain real synagogue sermons, but literary abridgements in part developed in the schools.

[59] For pioneering efforts in this area, see, for example, Bloch, Methodological Note for the Study of Rabbinic Literature (1978) 51–75 (a translation of "Note méthodologique pour l'étude de la littérature rabbinique", *RSR* 43 [1955] 194–227); Vermes, Scripture and Tradition in Judaism (1961/1973) and Post Biblical Jewish Studies (1975); and Towner, The Rabbinic "Enumeration of Scriptural Examples" (1973). For an expanded discussion of the following texts, see R. KALMIN, "Christians and Heretics in Rabbinic Literature of Late Antiquity", *HTR* 87 (1994) 155–69.

[60] *Tôseptaʾ Ḥul.* 2:24. Regarding the relative dating of the different versions, see Rokeaḥ, Ben Satraʾ Ben Pantîraʾ Hûʾ (1969) 9–18. In the version of the Tôseptaʾ, the follower of Jesus is referred to as *Yaʿaqôb ʾîsh Kepar Sikhnîn.*

[61] *b. ʿAbôd. Zar.* 16b–17a.

(A) [Said R. 'Elî'ezer ben Hirkanûs]: He [Ya'aqôb 'îsh Kepar Sekanîah] said to me: "It is written in your Torah, 'You shall not bring the fee of a whore [or the pay of a dog into the house of the Lord your God]' (Deut 23:19). Is it permissible to make from it a toilet for the high priest?"
(B) I [R. 'Elî'ezer] said nothing to him.
(C) [Said 'Elî'ezer]: He [Ya'aqôb] said to me: "[Jesus of Nazareth][62] taught me, 'For they were amassed from fees for idolatry, and they shall become harlots' fees again' (Micah 1:7), they came from a filthy place, let them go to a filthy place".
(D) [Said 'Elî'ezer]: This statement pleased me, and for this reason I was seized as a *Mîn*.

The story's message in its diverse contexts is basically the same: non-Rabbis and outsiders pose a threat to rabbinic Jews. Even (or especially) when these outsiders state opinions and offer interpretations which suit the tastes of rabbinic Jews, they are to be avoided at all costs. They are dangerous, in no small part because of the inability of many Jews and/or Rabbis to avoid contact with them.

What is the significance, however, of the midrashic statement added to Jesus' statement in the later Babylonian version? Does it affect our appreciation of the story in any significant way?

One scholar believes that it was added to the story to make Jesus look ridiculous.[63] 'Elî'ezer ben Hirkanûs, however, one of the greatest rabbinic sages who ever lived, is depicted as approving of Jesus' statement.[64] Despite the Midrash's questionable taste from a modern perspective, there is no reason to doubt the story's explicit claim that Jesus' interpretation met with rabbinic approval.

The later Babylonian version of this story, therefore, credits Jesus with the ability to derive law via scriptural interpretation, and is therefore consonant with a Babylonian Talmudic tendency to rabbinize wonder-workers, healers, and rain-makers, holy men on the periphery or outside of the rabbinic movement. This tendency is noticeable even in early Palestinian sources, but is particularly prominent in the Bavli.[65] Jesus, for example, is described in another Babylonian source as a fledgling Rabbi driven to idolatry when his teacher cruelly rejects his repeated attempts to apologize for insulting him.[66] The Palestinian parallel to the latter source shows no signs of the Bavli's attempt to rabbinize Jesus.[67]

The midrashic statement, therefore, increases the impact of the story by emphasizing the insidious quality of contact with quasi-rabbinic sages who utter pleasing words. The Bavli, by adding the Midrash, reveals its tendency

[62] Post-Talmudic censors removed Jesus' name from the text. See *Diqdûqê Sôperîm* (ed. R. RABBINOVICZ), notes מ and ס. Some versions lack the designation "of Nazareth".

[63] Meier, A Marginal Jew (1991) 97.

[64] Despite the fact that 'Elî'ezer ben Hirkanûs' excommunication is described in several stories, he was widely respected according to numerous rabbinic sources, including the story presently under discussion.

[65] See also Green, Palestinian Holy Men (1979) 628–47; Bokser, Wonder-Working and the Rabbinic Tradition (1985) 42–92; and Levine, The Rabbinic Class of Roman Palestine (1989) 108–9.

[66] *b. Sanh.* 107b and parallel.

[67] *y. Ḥag.* 2:2 and *Sanh.* 6:9.

to expand and rework earlier sources to a greater degree than Palestinian compilations,[68] as well as the natural tendency of any group to depict outsiders in terms familiar to the in-group. Why these tendencies are stronger in Babylonia than in Palestine is not clear, but perhaps better understanding of the non-Jewish milieu within which rabbinic sources took shape will yield an answer.

---

[68] See, for example, Bokser, Wonder-Working and the Rabbinic Tradition (1985) 71, and the literature cited in n. 95, there; and Friedman, La-'Aggadah ha-Hisṭorît ba-Talmûd ha-Bavlî (1989) 44–45.

8.4. The Hermeneutics of the Law in Rabbinic Judaism: Mishnah, Midrash, Talmuds

By JACOB NEUSNER, Tampa, FL
(University of South Florida)

General introductions: Three surveys of the state of studies of ancient Judaism form the background of this paper. Each presents not only bibliography but an account of the state of various questions and of the methodological issues that inhere in them and forms an introduction to the literature treated here: L. L. GRABBE, *Judaism. From Cyrus to Hadrian. The Persian and Greek Periods. The Roman Period* (Minneapolis: Fortress Press 1992); J. NEUSNER (ed.), *The Study of Ancient Judaism* (New York: Ktav 1981. Second printing: Atlanta: Scholars Press 1992). I. *The Study of Ancient Judaism: Mishnah, Midrash, Siddur.* II. *The Study of Ancient Judaism: The Palestinian and Babylonian Talmuds*; H. L. STRACK/G. STEMBERGER, *Introduction to the Talmud and Midrash.* With a foreword by Jacob Neusner (Minneapolis: Fortress Press 1992).

Hermeneutics: K. M. NEWTON, *Interpreting the Text. A Critical Introduction to the Theory and Practice of Literary Interpretation* (New York: Harvester/Wheatsheaf 1990) 40–41.

Abbreviations and special bibliography: The approach taken in this paper is particular to the author. In various monographs, as follows, points made here are expanded and spelled out in the close reading of texts.

Bavli That Might Have Been: The Tosefta's Theory of Mishnah-Commentary Compared with that of the Babylonian Talmud (Atlanta: Scholars Press 1990); *Bavli's Unique Voice. A Systematic Comparison of the Talmud of Babylonia and the Talmud of the Land of Israel* (Atlanta: Scholars Press 1993. In seven volumes, as follows: I. *Bavli and Yerushalmi Qiddushin Chapter One Compared and Contrasted.* II. *Yerushalmi's, Bavli's, and Other Canonical Documents' Treatment of the Program of Mishnah-Tractate Sukkah Chapters One, Two, and Four Compared and Contrasted. A Reprise and Revision of* The Bavli and its Sources. III. *Bavli and Yerushalmi to Selected Mishnah-Chapters in the Division of Moed. Erubin Chapter One, and Moed Qatan Chapter Three.* IV. *Bavli and Yerushalmi to Selected Mishnah-Chapters in the Division of Nashim. Gittin Chapter Five and Nedarim Chapter One. And Niddah Chapter One.* V. *Bavli and Yerushalmi to Selected Mishnah-Chapters in the Division of Neziqin. Baba Mesia Chapter One and Makkot Chapters One and Two.* VI. *Bavli and Yerushalmi to a Miscellany of Mishnah-Chapters. Gittin Chapter One, Qiddushin Chapter Two, and Hagigah Chapter Three.* VII. *What Is Unique about the Bavli in Context? An Answer Based on Inductive Description, Analysis, and Comparison*); *Canonical History of Ideas. The Place of the So-called Tannaite Midrashim, Mekhilta Attributed to R. Ishmael, Sifra, Sifré to Numbers, and Sifré to Deuteronomy* (Atlanta: Scholars Press 1990); *History of the Mishnaic Law of Purities* (Leiden: Brill 1977; XXI. *The Redaction and Formulation of the Order of Purities in the Mishnah and Tosefta*); *Judaism and Story: The Evidence of the Fathers According to Rabbi Nathan* (Chicago: U. of Chicago Press 1992); *Judaism and Zoroastrianism at the Dusk of Late Antiquity. How Two Ancient Faiths Wrote Down Their Great Traditions* (Atlanta: Scholars Press 1993); *Judaism States its Theology: The Talmudic Re-Presentation* (Atlanta Scholars Press 1993); *Judaism. The Evidence of the Mishnah* (Chicago: University of Chicago Press 1981; 2nd printing, 1985; 3rd printing, 1986; 2nd augm. edition: Atlanta: Scholars Press 1987); *Rules of Composition of the Talmud of Babylonia. The Cogency of the Bavli's Composite* (Atlanta: Scholars Press 1991); *Tosefta. An Introduction* (Atlanta: Scholars Press 1992); *Transformation of Judaism. From Philosophy to Religion* (Champaign: U. of Illinois Press 1992); *Uniting the Dual Torah: Sifra and the Problem of the Mishnah* (Cambridge and New York: Cambridge U. Press 1989); *Why No Gospels in Talmudic Judaism?* (Atlanta: Scholars Press 1988).

1. What Do We Mean by Hermeneutics?

The hermeneutics of rabbinic Judaism governs the explication of the two components of the Torah, the written ("the Old Testament") and the oral, which is written down in the Mishnah and other documents. To understand how rabbinic Judaism reads any text, we have to commence with its reading of its initial text beyond Scripture, which is the Mishnah, and follow the unfolding of the hermeneutics of the oral Torah, encompassing the Mishnah and a successor-document, of Midrash, Sifra, as well as the two principal commentaries to the Mishnah, the Talmud of the Land of Israel ("Yerushalmi"), ca. 400, and the Talmud of Babylonia ("Bavli"), ca. 600.[1] Precisely what is at stake in an account of the hermeneutics of this Judaism begins in a reliable definition of hermeneutics, that of K. M. NEWTON:

> The central concern of hermeneutics as it relates to the study of literature is the problem created by the fact that texts written in the past continue to exist and to be read while their authors and the historical context which produced them have passed away in time. Reading such texts, therefore, becomes inseparable from the question of interpretation. Before the modern period hermeneutics was concerned primarily with how scriptural texts such as the Bible should be read. Should the Bible, for example, be seen as a text which exists in its own terms and read accordingly or should any understanding of it be mediated by an acceptance of the doctrines of the church?[2]

It follows that by hermeneutics is meant "the rules of reading a text and interpreting it". Then precisely what constitutes the understanding of a text, which is what I mean by the rules for defining and reading a document – text, context, matrix of meaning? NEWTON cites W. DILTHEY's dictum, "an act of understanding constitutes what he called a 'lived experience'". DILTHEY states:

> The methodological understanding of permanently fixed life-expressions we call explication. As the life of the mind only finds its complete, exhaustive, and therefore, objectively comprehensible expression in language, explication culminates in the interpretation of the written records of human existence. This art is the basis of philology. The science of this art is hermeneutics.[3]

The hermeneutics that conveyed the rules of proper reading of the Talmud formed out of occasional rules and conceptions a single, demonstrably cogent statement, one of entire integrity. The hermeneutics of all texts of Rabbinic Judaism commences with the document, seen whole, and works backward to the components that comprise the document, downward and backward to the individual sentences. Any other approach takes sentences out of context or treats them as having no context, yielding only philology; but philology is not hermeneutics, only the basis for the initial reading of the text. We have

---

[1] I bypass the Tosefta since, strictly speaking, the document, being a mere compilation of compositions that complement or supplement the Mishnah, has no autonomous existence; it can be understood only pericope by pericope, and that is, solely in the relationship between most of its pericopes and the corresponding ones of the Mishnah. The exception is the approximately sixth part of the document of free-standing compositions, but these too are not formed into a composite that constitutes a document; not standing in relationship to the Mishnah, the Tosefta is only a scrapbook. This is spelled out in my *The Tosefta*.

[2] K. M. Newton, Interpreting the Text, 40–41.

[3] Cited by Newton, 42.

of course to distinguish between text- and literary criticism of technicalities of phrasing the writing and a hermeneutics aimed at identifying the message of a document conveyed through its recurrent inquires and usages. That distinction is feasible, in particular, in documents so uniform in their rhetoric, logic, and polemic, as the Mishnah and its successor writings.

The Mishnah, Sifra, Yerushalmi, and Bavli repeat themselves endlessly, because they say the same thing (respectively) about many things. It is that same thing – that is, the hermeneutics – that in the Mishnah sets forth one set of categories, in Sifra, an account of the right modes of taxic conceptualization, in the Yerushalmi, an altogether different set of categories, and in the Bavli, a vast re-presentation of the received categorical structure and system, now in a theological formulation. The agendum of hermeneutics encompasses the issue of the author's – in theological context, God's – original meaning in revealing the Torah and yields the secular question, what do we think the original writer or compiler of a given document meant by saying things in one way, rather than in some other, and how does a single program of thought and expression govern the document as a whole. Setting forth the explication of how the patterned language of successive, connected documents instructs us on the meaning of those documents provides the methodological understanding that comprises the hermeneutics of the writing.

2. The Hermeneutics of the Mishnah

The explication of the Mishnah, as a whole and then passage by passage, depends upon the recognition that the Mishnah is made up of lists;[4] these lists are composed of things that exhibit shared traits of an intrinsic order, e.g., they follow a common rule. They are then formed into sets of lists so as to yield the contrast with things that exhibit other traits and so follow a different rule from the one of the initial list; in the contrast between the one list and the other, we grasp the point of the lists, and the explication then takes the form of identifying lists and contrasting them; then articulating the lesson that is to be learned from the character and organization of lists. The governing hermeneutics throughout is the same: the hierarchical classification of all things, attained through showing through the comparison and contrast of lists how one thing relates to some other. That description of how the document is to be read takes account, also, of the highly formalized rhetoric of the document.[5]

---

[4] That statement is valid for all tractates, though the character of the lists is diverse. Most lists are organized by topics, but a few by names of authorities, e.g., rulings of Judah, in Mishnah-tractate *Kelim*, chap. 24; sets of rulings in the names of authorities, in the whole of Mishnah-tractate *Eduyyot*; principles that apply to diverse subject matter, represented by keywords such as "the only difference between A and B is C", or phrases such as, "because of the interest of keeping the peace". In the main, however, topical lists join diverse cases subject to a single rule, and the hermeneutics of the document is dictated by the character of those case-lists.

[5] I spell out the form-critical rules of Mishnah-hermeneutics and summarize them in *History of the Mishnaic Law of Purities* (Leiden: E.J. Brill 1980). XXI. *The Redaction and Formulation of the Order of Purities in the Mishnah and Tosefta.*

List-making places on display the data of the like and the unlike and through the consequent contrast explicitly conveys the rule governing both; the necessarily-consequent hierarchization of the lists will be implicit in the contrast between the rule governing the one and that defining the other. The Mishnah therefore is set forth as a book of lists, with the implicit order, the nomothetic traits, dictating the ordinarily unstated general and encompassing rule of hierarchization.

The inner structure set forth by the hermeneutic of a logic of classification sustains the system of ordering all things in proper place and under the proper rule. The like belongs with the like and conforms to the rule governing the like, the unlike goes over to the opposite and conforms to the opposite rule. When we make lists of the like, we also know the rule governing all the items on those lists, respectively. We know that and one other thing, namely, the opposite rule, governing all items sufficiently like to belong on those lists, but sufficiently unlike to be placed on other lists. That rigorously philosophical logic of analysis, comparison and contrast, served because it was the only logic that could serve a system that proposed to make the statement concerning order and right array that the Mishnah's authorship wished to set forth.

The hermeneutics I have described is illustrated in the following passage, drawn from Mishnah-tractate *Sanhedrin* chap. 2, in which the authorship wishes to say that Israel has two heads, one of state, the other of church (cult), the king and the high priest, respectively, and that these two offices are nearly wholly congruent with one another, with a few differences based on the particular traits of each. Broadly speaking, therefore, our exercise is one of setting forth the genus and the species. This will permit us to hierarchize the two species and tell us which is the more important. The genus is head of holy Israel. The species are king and high priest. Here are the traits in common and those not shared, and the exercise is fully exposed for what it is, an inquiry into the rules that govern, the points of regularity and order, in this minor matter, of political structure. My outline, imposed in italic type, makes the point important in this setting; I abbreviate the passage and give only the operative elements.

Mishnah-tractate Sanhedrin Chapter Two

1. *The rules of the high priest: subject to the law, marital rites, conduct in bereavement*

2:1 A. A high priest judges, and [others] judge him;
B. gives testimony, and [others] give testimony about him;
C. performs the rite of removing the shoe [Deut 25:7–9], and [others] perform the rite of removing the shoe with his wife.
D. [Others] enter levirate marriage with his wife, but he does not enter into levirate marriage,
E. because he is prohibited to marry a widow ...

2. *The rules of the king: not subject to the law, marital rites, conduct in bereavement*

2:2 A. The king does not judge, and [others] do not judge him;
B. does not give testimony, and [others] do not give testimony about him;

C. does not perform the rite of removing the shoe, and others do not perform the rite of removing the shoe with his wife;
D. does not enter into levirate marriage, nor [do his brothers] enter levirate marriage with his wife.
E. R. Judah says, "If he wanted to perform the rite of removing the shoe or to enter into levirate marriage, his memory is a blessing".
F. They said to him, "They pay no attention to him [if he expressed the wish to do so]".
G. [Others] do not marry his widow.
H. R. Judah says, "A king may marry the widow of a king.
I. "For so we find in the case of David, that he married the widow of Saul,
J. "For it is said, *'And I gave you your master's house and your master's wives into your embrace'* (2 Sam 12:8)"...

3. Special rules pertinent to the king because of his calling
2:4 A. [The king] calls out [the army to wage] a war fought by choice on the instructions of a court of seventy-one ...

This truncated abstract shows the facts of the case. The hermeneutic requires the explication of the text through recognizing the taxonomy, that is, a study of the genus, national leader, and its two species, [1] king, [2] high priest: how are they alike, how are they not alike, and what accounts for the differences.

The premise is that national leaders are alike and follow the same rule, except where they differ and follow the opposite rule from one another. But that premise also is subject to the proof effected by the survey of the data consisting of concrete rules, those systemically inert facts that here come to life for the purposes of establishing a proposition. By itself, the fact that, e.g., others may not ride on his horse, bears the burden of no systemic proposition. In the context of an argument constructed for nomothetic, taxonomic purposes, the same fact is active and weighty.

The Mishnah's hermeneutics, directing our attention to the traits of things and their classification and the hierarchical relationship between classifications of things, underscored the autonomy of the document. The original intent of its authors clearly was to set forth a statement of monotheism in the form of a demonstration through natural history: all things rise to the One, above; all things derive and descend from the One, above. When, in ca. 200 CE, the Mishnah reached closure and was received and adopted as law by the state-sanctioned Jewish governments in both the Roman empire, in the land of Israel, and Iran, in Babylonia, respectively, the function and character of the document precipitated a considerable crisis. Politically and theologically presented as the foundation for the everyday administration of the affairs of Jewry, the Mishnah ignored the politics of the sponsoring regimes. Since Jews generally accepted the authority of Moses at Sinai, failure to claim for the document a clear and explicit relationship to the Torah of Moses defined that acute issue. Why should people accept as authoritative the rulings of this piece of writing? Omitting reference to a theological, as much as to a political myth, the authorship of the Mishnah also failed to signal the relationship between their document and Scripture. Since, for all Judaisms, Hebrew Scriptures in general, and the Pentateuch, in particular, represented God's will for Israel, silence on that matter provoked considerable response. Several successor-documents, Sifra, formulated in response to the Mishnah, and the two Talmuds, set forth as commentaries to the Mishnah, then formulated their hermeneutics around the problem represented by the Mishnah's free-standing character.

But when it came forth, the character of the Mishnah itself hardly won confidence that, on the face of it, the document formed part of, or derived from Sinai. It was originally published through oral formulation and oral transmission, that is, in the medium of memorization. It is formulated in mnemonic patterns. But it had been in the medium of writing that, in the view of all of Israel until about 200 CE, God had been understood to reveal the divine word and will. The Torah was a written book. People who claimed to receive further messages from God usually wrote them down. They had three choices in securing acceptance of their account. All three involved linking the new to the old.

In claiming to hand on revelation, they could, first, sign their books with the names of biblical heroes. Second, they could imitate the style of biblical Hebrew. Third, they could present an exegesis of existing written verses, validating their ideas by supplying proof texts for them. From the closure of the Torah literature in the time of Ezra, circa 450 BCE, to the time of the Mishnah, nearly seven hundred years later, we do not have a single book alleged to be holy and at the same time standing wholly out of relationship to the Holy Scriptures of ancient Israel. The Pseudepigraphic writings fall into the first category, the Essene writings at Qumran into the second and third. We may point also to the Gospels, which take as a principal problem the demonstration of how Jesus had fulfilled the prophetic promises of the Old Testament and in other ways carried forward and even embodied Israel's Scripture.

Insofar as a piece of Jewish writing did not find a place in relationship to Scripture, its author laid no claim to present a holy book. The contrast between Jubilees and the Testaments of the Patriarchs, with their constant and close harping on biblical matters, and the books of Maccabees, shows the differences. The former claim to present God's revealed truth, the latter, history. So a book was holy because in style, in authorship, or in (alleged) origin it continued Scripture, finding a place therefore (at least in the author's mind) within the canon, or because it provided an exposition on Scripture's meaning. But the Mishnah made no such claim. It entirely ignored the style of biblical Hebrew, speaking in a quite different kind of Hebrew altogether. It is silent on its authorship through its sixty-two tractates (the claims of *'Abot*, ca. 250, of course are post facto). In any event, nowhere does the Mishnah contain the claim that God had inspired the authors of the document. These are not given biblical names and certainly are not alleged to have been biblical saints. Most of the book's named authorities flourished within the same century as its anonymous arrangers and redactors, not in remote antiquity. Above all, the Mishnah contains scarcely a handful of exegeses of Scripture. These, where they occur, play a trivial and tangential role. So here is the problem of the Mishnah: different from Scripture in language and style, indifferent to the claim of authorship by a biblical hero or divine inspiration, stunningly aloof from allusion to verses of Scripture for nearly the whole of its discourse—yet authoritative for Israel.

3. Sifra's Hermeneutics of the Mishnah

The authors of Sifra, ca. 300,[6] undertook a vast polemic against the logic of classification that forms the foundation of the system of the Mishnah. This they did two ways. The first, and less important, was to demonstrate that the Mishnah's rules required exegetical foundations. That solved the formal problem of the Mishnah's failure to link its statements in a systematic way to verses of Scripture. The second, and paramount way was to attack the very logic by which the Mishnah's authorship developed its points. The recurrent principle of the reading of the Mishnah set forth by the authors of Sifra insisted that the Mishnah's hermeneutics—systematic classification—does not work, because there is no genus, but only species. Therefore the Mishnah's *Listenwissenschaft*, its insistence that things are either like one another and therefore follow the same rule, or opposite to one another and therefore follow the opposite rule—these fundamental building blocks of Mishnaic thought prove deeply flawed. For if nothing is ever really like something else, then we cannot classify different things together, as the same thing. And, it follows, we also can make no lists of things that, whether in a polythetic or a monothetic framework, follow the same rule and therefore generate a generalization. Since, as we shall now see, the logic of the Mishnah begins with the premise that diverse species form a single genus, which can be subjected to comparison and contrast, that dogged insistence, time and again, upon the incomparability of species, forms a fundamental critique of the practical reason of the Mishnah.

The authors of Sifra mount a two-pronged polemic against the Mishnah, one a mere feint, the other the main attack.

[1] The authorship of Sifra commonly invokes the exact language of the Mishnah or the Tosefta, asks whether the position presented in that language, lacking all proof-texts drawn from Scripture, is not a matter of mere logic, and proves that it is not. That shows that what is required is law resting on scriptural proof.

[2] The authorship of Sifra systematically demonstrates the futility of the logic of *Listenwissenschaft*, classification or taxonomy, comparison and contrast, and consequent hierarchization. This it does in a very simple way. It shows that species that look as though they form a common genus do not in

[6] By "300" I mean only after the Mishnah and probably before the Talmud of the Land of Israel. We have no dates at all for rabbinic documents, but we can show how they stand in ordinal relationship to one another.

fact form such a genus. Therefore it is not possible to compare and contrast two species to find the law common to the two of them, if they compare, or the law that differentiates one from the other, if they contrast.

To see how this second principle of explicating the Mishnah accomplishes its program, we examine *Sifra* XVIII:II. 1, a handsome demonstration, with numerous counterparts throughout Sifra, of the impossibility of relying upon the intrinsic traits of things; these yield ambiguous results; only Scripture provides indubitable taxa:

XVIII:II. 1

A. "The priest shall scoop out of it a handful":

B. Is the rule that a single handful suffices not only for a single tenth ephah of the offering, but a single handful also suffices for sixty tenth ephahs?

C. Or is the rule that a single handful serves only a single tenth ephah, while there must be sixty handfuls taken up out of sixty tenth ephahs?

D. Lo, I reason as follows:

We have now to find out which classification covers our case; then the rule governing that classification obviously will pertain. The solution is to invoke the rules governing the classification of a given action, in the theory that the like follows the like, the unlike, the opposite. Hence, if we establish that a given taxon encompasses both actions, we also know the rule governing them both. Everything therefore depends on proving that both actions fall into the same classification. But if we cannot show that fact, then we have no rule at all.

E. The meal offering requires the taking up of a handful, and it also requires frankincense. Just as in the case of frankincense, a single handful serves for a single tenth ephah, and a single handful serves also for sixty tenth-ephahs, so in the case of the taking up of the handful, a single handful serves for one tenth ephah, and a single handful serves for sixty tenth ephahs.

F. Or try taking this route:

G. The meal offering requires the taking up of a handful, and it also requires oil. Just as in the case of the oil, a single log of oil serves for a single tenth ephah, while sixty logs of oil are required for sixty tenth ephahs, so in the case of a handful, the taking up of a handful serves a single tenth ephah, while for sixty tenth ephahs, there must be sixty taking ups of handfuls.

H. Let us then see to the correct analogy:

I. We should establish an analogy from something which is wholly offered up on the altar fire to something that is wholly offered up on the altar fire, but oil should not then enter the picture, since it is not wholly burned up on the altar fire.

J. Or take this route:

K. We should establish an analogy from something in which the smaller portion is indispensable to the validity of the entire portion [for instance, if any of the required fine flour or oil is lacking, the entire meal offering is null], but let us not propose proof from the example of frankincense, in which the lack of a smaller portion of the whole is not indispensable to the validity of the entire portion.

L. [Accordingly, we appeal to Scripture to settle matters, as it does when it says:] "The priest shall scoop out of it a handful":

M. It is the rule that a single handful suffices not only for a single tenth ephah of the offering, but a single handful also suffices for sixty tenth ephahs.

This elegant exercise once more proves the falsity of appealing to classification on the sole basis of the intrinsic traits of things for settling a moot point, because taxonomy, resting solely on the classification of the traits of things, and ignoring the Torah's classifications, yields contradictory results. Natural history is not possible; only the Torah's classification, brought into relationship with natural history, yields reliable philosophy. That is the power of L, which yields M; the hermeneutics of Sifra then is formed on the principle of the critique of the taxonomy of natural history, insisting on the taxonomy of the Torah as the corrective.

Conducting a sustained and brilliant polemic against the Mishnah, the authorship of Sifra presents, in a systemic and orderly way, an amazing, subtle demonstration that there is no such thing as a genus, but only species. Then, it follows for our authorship, Scripture serves as the sole source for rules governing otherwise incomprehensible, because incomparable, species. A critical corollary is that the Mishnah not only rests upon false logic, but in failing to tie its propositions to Scripture, its authorship has set the law of the Torah upon unreliable foundations. The framers of Sifra then correct the errors of logic, on the one side, and set forth solid foundations in revelation, there alone, on the other. All of this they do while working their way through what will seem, on the surface, somewhat remote facts indeed.

For its hermeneutical principle, which explains the formation of most of the document's compositions, Sifra's authorship conducts a sustained polemic against the failure of the Mishnah to cite Scripture very much or systematically to link its ideas to Scripture through the medium of formal demonstration by exegesis. Sifra's rhetorical exegesis follows a standard redactional form. Scripture will be cited. Then a statement will be made about its meaning, or a statement of law correlative to that Scripture will be given. That statement sometimes cites the Mishnah, often verbatim. Finally, the author of Sifra invariably states, "Now is that not (merely) logical?" And the point of that statement will be: can this position not be gained through the working of mere logic, based upon facts supplied (to be sure) by Scripture? If, then, we wish to understand all things all together and all at once under a single encompassing rule, we had best revert to the (written) Torah, with its account of the rightful names, positions, and order, imputed to all things. The premise of hermeneutics – explication of the document whole, then in its parts – is the priority of the written over the oral Torah.[7]

---

[7] Then the need for the myth of an oral part of the Torah is not urgent, but Sifra does contain a passage that alludes to the concept of an oral Torah; see my *The Canonical History of Ideas.*

4. The First Talmud's Hermeneutics of the Mishnah

The next stage in the unfolding of the hermeneutics of rabbinic literature is marked by the provision, for the Mishnah, of a systematic commentary. This is the contribution of the authors of the compositions and the compilers of the composites that form the Talmud of the Land of Israel.[8] What the framers of the first Talmud accomplished was not the invention of the conception of a talmud, meaning, a sustained, systemic amplification of passages of the Mishnah and other teachings accorded the status of Tannaite authority. That had already been accomplished by whoever compiled the Tosefta, which laid out the Mishnah alongside supplementary teachings that amplified or enlarged its rules.[9] The notion of a talmud as a source of information was thus established; but information was left inert. What the first Talmud contributed was the definition of a talmud in which received facts ('traditions') were treated as active and consequential, requiring analysis and deep thought.

In first Talmud's primary point of interest is the demonstration that the oral Torah, the Mishnah, rests upon the written Torah; the two components of the Torah form a single revelation, with the oral part inextricably bound to the written, and that demonstration marks the work of Mishnah-commentary as not only theological in general – defining the Torah – but doctrinal in a very particular way. That polemic will define the both Talmuds' hermeneutics: how they interpret the received text, and what they choose for the center of their own statement as well. A second hermeneutical principle concerns the perfection of the Mishnah and the laws of the Torah contained therein, both Talmuds' writers concurring that inconsistency and disharmony would flaw the Torah and must be shown not to occur therein.

Before proceeding, let me give a single example of the character of Mishnah-exegesis found in both Talmuds. In this way we see how both Talmuds frame a hermeneutics centered upon the character of the Mishnah. The intent of the hermeneutics – again formed out of a theology of the dual Torah – is to prove that the Mishnah depends upon Scripture and that it is flawless. The only narrowly-literary critical component of the Talmuds' commentary to the Mishnah concerns the correct wording of passages, but that rapidly shades over into an inquiry into principles of law. So the hermeneutics that forms the commentary-program finds its generative problematic in the myth of the dual Torah.

My illustration derives from both Talmud's reading of a brief passage of Mishnah-tractate *Makkot*. The unity of purpose – Mishnah-commentary – and the identity of proposition – the unity of the Torah, its perfection – should not obscure the simple fact that the two Talmuds do not intersect except at the Mishnah and at Scripture. The Talmuds bear each its own message, but both ask the same questions. Mishnah- and Tosefta-passages in

---

[8] For the distinction between composition and composite and how it explains the character of both Talmuds (and most Midrash-compilations, only Sifra being nearly wholly a composition), see my *The Rules of Composition of the Talmud of Babylonia*.

[9] See *The Bavli That Might Have Been*.

both Talmuds are in italics, Bavli's use of Aramaic in small caps, Hebrew in small italics. Bavli page references are in square brackets; Yerushalmi-references accord with the system of my *Talmud of the Land of Israel.*[10] We begin with the Yerushalmi:

Yerushalmi to Makkot 1:8 = Bavli to Makkot 1:10

[A] *He whose trial ended and who fled and was brought back before the same court –*

[B] *they do not reverse the judgment concerning him [and retry him].*

[C] *In any situation in which two get up and say, "We testify concerning Mr. So-and-so that his trial ended in the court of such-and-such, with Mr. So-and-so and Mr. So-and-so as the witnesses against him",*

[D] *lo, this one is put to death.*

[E] *[Trial before] a Sanhedrin applies both in the Land and abroad.*

[F] *A Sanhedrin which imposes the death penalty once in seven years is called murderous.*

[G] *R. Eleazar b. Azariah says, "Once in seventy years".*

[H] *R. Tarfon and R. Aqiba say, "If we were on a Sanhedrin, no one would ever be put to death".*

[I] *Rabban Simeon b. Gamaliel says, "So they would multiply the number of murderers in Israel".*

[I.A] *[Trial before a] Sanhedrin applies both in the Land and abroad [M. 1:8E],*

[B] *as it is written, "And these things shall be for a statute and ordinance to you throughout your generations in all your dwellings" (Num 35:29).*

[C] *And why does Scripture say, "You shall appoint judges and officers in all your towns [which the Lord your God gives you]" (Deut 16:18), in the towns of the Land of Israel.*

[D] *The meaning is that in the towns of Israel they set up judges in every town, but abroad they do so only by districts.*

[E] *It was taught: R. Dosetai b. R. Yannai says, "It is a religious requirement for each tribe to judge its own tribe, as it is said, 'You shall appoint* JUDGES *and officers in all your towns which the Lord your God gives you, according to your tribes'" (Deut 16:18).*

[II.A] *Rabban Simeon b. Gamaliel taught, "Those declared liable to the death penalty who fled from the Land abroad – they put them to death forthwith [upon recapture].*

[B] *"If they fled from abroad to the Land, they do not put them to death forthwith, but they undertake a trial* DE NOVO*".*

The Yerushalmi wants the scriptural proof for the Mishnah's allegation; it then harmonizes the implications at hand. Since the proof text, I.B, yields results contrary to the assumed implications of that at C, D must indicate otherwise. Unit II is an independent saying, generally relevant to *Mak* 1:8E. It is a simple paraphrase and clarification.

Since both Talmuds read the Mishnah in much the same way, let us first examine their common hermeneutics, and then distinguish the second Talmud from the first. The two Talmuds resemble one another, since both to begin with comment on the same prior text, the Mishnah. Both take up a few sentences of that prior text and paraphrase and analyze them. Both ask the

---

10 *A Preliminary Translation and Explanation* (Chicago 1983–1993) I–XXXV.

same questions, e.g., clarifying the language of the Mishnah, identifying the scriptural foundations of the Mishnah's rules, comparing the Mishnah's rules with those of the Tosefta or other Tannaite status. They furthermore compare because they organize their materials in the same way. They moreover take up pretty much the same topical agenda, in common selecting some divisions of the Mishnah and ignoring others, agreeing in particular to treat the Mishnah's divisions of Appointed Times, Women, and Damages. Both documents moreover are made up of already-available compositions and composites, which we may identify, in each document, by reference to the same literary traits or indications of completion prior to inclusion in the Talmuds.[11] So they exhibit traits of shared literary policy.

In both, moreover, we find not only the same received document, the Mishnah, but also citations of, and allusions to, the same supplementary collection to the Mishnah, the Tosefta, and also a further kind of saying, one bearing the marks of formalization and memorization that serve to classify it as authoritative ('Tannaite') but external to the composition of the Mishnah and the compilation of the Tosefta. The points of coincidence are more than formal, therefore, since both Talmuds cite the same Mishnah-tractates, at some points the same Tosefta-passages, and also, from time to time, the same external Tannaite formulations. When, therefore, in Chapters Five through Seven, we come to their points of difference, beginning with the fact that the second Talmud scarcely intersects with the first except at the formal points of juncture just now listed, we shall find all the more striking the fact that the second Talmud goes its own way and forms a writing that, while formally like the first Talmud, substantively differs from it, beginning, middle, and end.

What is talmudic about the two Talmuds is their unique hermeneutics, which is a critical, systematic application of applied reason and practical logic, moving from a point starting with a proposition through argument and evidence, met head-on by contrary proposition, with its argument and evidence, exchanging balanced responses, each to the position, argument, and evidence of the other, onward and for so long as it takes fully to expose every possibility of proposition, argument, and evidence – (ordinarily) ending with a firm and (occasionally even an articulated) conclusion. To develop a taxonomy of the units of discourse contained equally within either of the two Talmuds, I answer the question, what kinds of units of discourse do the documents exhibit in common and how are they arranged? Both Talmuds invariably do to the Mishnah one of these four things:

---

[11] But I hasten to add, my sustained comparison of the two Talmuds reveals remarkably little evidence that the framers of the two documents drew upon a common core of available, already-formulated compositions, that is, a counterpart to "Q"; and there is no evidence whatsoever that they shared a common core of completed composites. Where there is a corpus of shared materials, it is in the Mishnah and other sayings given Tannaite status and also in some, very few, statements of authorities who flourished in the third century; these sayings, when occurring in both Talmuds, tend to be utilized in the second Talmud in a manner unlike their use in the first. This is spelled out in *The Bavli's Unique Voice*.

(1) text criticism;
(2) exegesis of the meaning of the Mishnah, including glosses and amplifications;
(3) addition of scriptural proof texts of the Mishnah's central propositions; and
(4) harmonization of one Mishnah passage with another such passage or with a statement of Tosefta.

The first two of these four procedures remain wholly within the narrow frame of the Mishnah passage subject to discussion. Therefore, in the natural order of things, what the two Talmuds will find interesting in a given Mishnah-passage will respond to the same facts and commonly will do so in much the same way. The second pair take an essentially independent stance *vis-a-vis* the Mishnah pericope at hand. That is where the Talmuds, engaged in a theological enterprise within the definition offered here, will take, each its own path. And that is precisely the point at which theological, as distinct from literary-critical, considerations enter in. Where the Talmuds are talmudic, it is in the theological program of systematic recapitulation of cases, formulation of propositions of an abstract character, expression of theology through a prevailing hermeneutics, not merely exposition of a passage through a constant exegetical plan.

The Talmuds do not merely clarify the Mishnah; both of them in point of fact re-present the Torah — a very different thing. We understand that fact when we remember what the Mishnah looks like as it stands on its own.[12] The writers of the Mishnah created a coherent document, with a topical program formed in accord with the logical order dictated by the characteristics of a given topic, and with a set of highly distinctive formulary and formal traits as well. But these are obscured when the document is taken apart into bits and pieces and reconstituted in the way in which the Talmuds do. The re-definition of the Torah accomplished by the Talmuds therefore represented a vast revision of the initial writing down of the oral component of the Torah — a point at which the hermeneutics shaded over into a profoundly theological activity.

Both authorships take an independent stance when facing the Mishnah, making choices, reaching decisions of their own. Both Talmuds framers deal with Mishnah-tractates of their own choice, and neither provides a Talmud to the entirety of the Mishnah. What the Mishnah therefore contributed to the Talmuds was not received in a spirit of humble acceptance by the sages who produced either of the two Talmuds. Important choices were made about what to treat, hence what to ignore. The exegetical mode of reception did not have to obscure the main lines of the Mishnah's system. But it surely did so. The discrete reading of sentences, or, at most, paragraphs, denying all context, avoiding all larger generalizations except for those transcending the specific lines of tractates this approach need not have involved the utter

---

[12] My account of the Mishnah in its own terms is in my *History of the Mishnaic Law* (Leiden: Brill 1974–1986), and in *Judaism. The Evidence of the Mishnah.*

reversal of the paramount and definitive elements of the Mishnah's whole and integrated world view (its 'Judaism'). But doing these things did facilitate the revision of the whole into a quite different pattern.

The question has now to be asked, when do the Talmuds speak for themselves, not for the Mishnah? Second, what sorts of units of discourse contain such passages that bear what is 'talmudic' in the two Talmuds? These two questions produce the same answers for both Talmuds, which once more validates comparing and therefore also contrasting them.

1. Theoretical questions of law not associated with a particular passage of the Mishnah. In the first of the two Talmuds there is some tendency, and in the second, a very marked tendency, to move beyond the legal boundaries set by the Mishnah's rules themselves. More general inquiries are taken up. These of course remain within the framework of the topic of one tractate or another, although there are some larger modes of thought characteristic of more than a single tractate.

2. Exegesis of Scripture separate from the Mishnah. It is under this rubric that we find the most important instances in which the Talmuds present materials essentially independent of the Mishnah.

3. Historical statements. The Talmud contains a fair number of statements that something happened, or narratives about how something happened. While many of these are replete with biblical quotations, in general they do not provide exegesis of Scripture, which serves merely as illustration or reference point.

4. Stories about, and rules for, sages and disciples, separate from discussion of a passage of the Mishnah. The Mishnah contains a tiny number of tales about Rabbis. These serve principally as precedents for, or illustrations of, rules.

The Talmuds by contrast contain a sizable number of stories about sages and their relationships to other people. When the Talmuds present us with ideas or expressions of a world related to, but fundamentally separate from, that of the Mishnah, that is, when the Talmuds wish to say something other than what the Mishnah says and means, they will take up one of two modes of discourse. Either we find exegesis of biblical passages, with the value system of the Rabbis read into the scriptural tales; or we are told stories about holy men and paradigmatic events, once again through tales told in such a way that a didactic and paraenetic purpose is served.

The Talmuds are composites of three kinds of materials: [1] exegeses of the Mishnah (and other materials classified as authoritative, that is, Tannaite), [2] exegeses of Scripture, and [3] accounts of the men who provide both.[13] Both Talmuds then constitute elaborate reworkings of the two antecedent documents: the Mishnah, lacking much reference to Scripture, and the Scripture itself. The Talmuds bring the two together into a synthesis of their compilers' own making, both in reading Scripture into Mishnah, and in reading Scripture alongside of, and separate from, Mishnah.

---

[13] I have dwelt on the stories about sages, where and how they figure and form part of the larger canon and the medium for its systemic statement, in, among other works, *Judaism and Story* and *Why No Gospels in Talmudic Judaism?*

The hermeneutics of the two Talmuds exhibits integrity to the rules of the language of the Mishnah; that is, I cannot point to a single instance in which the talmudic exegetes in either Talmud appear to twist and turn the language and message of a passage, attempting to make the words mean something other than what they appear to say anyhow. While the Talmuds follow a coherent hermeneutics that is very much their own, there is no exegetical program revealed in the Talmuds' reading of the Mishnah other than that defined, to begin with, by the language and conceptions of one Mishnah passage or another.[14] Nonetheless, the Talmuds do follow a hermeneutics quite distinct from the Mishnah's.

5. The Second Talmud's Hermeneutics of the Mishnah

The Talmud of Babylonia speaks in one, unique voice and takes shape out of a unique singular and economical hermeneutics; there is no other like it.[15] Quite how that vast prolix (sometimes tedious) and dense writing turns out to say some few things, and to say them with such power as to impose its judgment upon an entire prior writing and also on the intellect of an entire religious world to come – that is what requires attention.[16]

The writers of the Bavli's compositions and compilers of its composites rarely made original statements of doctrine or law. Commonly, they went over the ground of received ideas in their established formulation. It was rather through the public display of right reasoning, the exposition of argument that they made an original, and governing, statement of their own; that is why the hermeneutics provides the key to the Bavli's priority in the history of Judaism. Specifically, exposing the traits of rationality again and again in concrete exercises, the framers of the document said one thing about many things, much as, we have seen, the framers of Sifra did. But what they said gained heights of abstraction, aimed at transcendent truths formed in a lofty perspective; Sifra's hermeneutics conveyed a judgment about the proper ordering of the world, the right source of taxonomy. The Bavli's hermeneutics conveyed judgments of a considerably weightier character. By showing people how to think, then, in the context of a revealed Torah, the Bavli's framers maintained, one can also guide them to what to think: by reason of right reasoning formed into right attitudes, right thoughts lead to right deeds. In

---

[14] That the second Talmud has its own hermeneutical program, as distinct from an exegetical one, of course is also the fact. But that the second Talmud has its own distinctive hermeneutics does not affect my contention that, in the ways specified here, the two Talmuds are identical.

[15] Claims of uniqueness of course can never be satisfactorily shown to be valid because we should have first to have examined all possible candidates of comparability. Having completed the comparison of the Bavli to the Yerushalmi (not to mention Scripture, the Mishnah, the Tosefta, and the prior Midrash-compilations, which required no sustained inquiry), I did compare the Talmud with counterpart writings of Zoroastrianism in my *Judaism and Zoroastrianism at the Dusk of Late Antiquity*. For the Bavli in canonical context, see *Bavli's Unique Voice*.

[16] But we have already noted how Sifra's authors say the same thing about many different things, and the same is so of the Mishnah itself. So what distinguishes the Bavli is not its capacity to impose a single program upon diverse data, but the character of that program.

the 'how' of thought, the 'what' found form and substance. Hermeneutics is what contained the rationality that translated inchoate religion – rite, belief, attitude, symbol, myth, proposition and emotion alike, even in its initial theological formation – into a cogent and compelling statement about the nature of mind itself.

The demonstration is feasible because of one characteristic of the document. The Bavli is uniform, beginning to end. Different from, much more than, a haphazard compilation of episodic traditions, upon examination this Talmud shows itself to be a cogent and purposive writing. Through a single, determinate set of rhetoric devices, which themselves signal the definition of the writing and the rules of reading that writing, a single program of inquiry is brought to bear on many and diverse passages of two inherited documents, the Mishnah and Scripture. The voice is one and single because it is a voice that everywhere expresses the same limited set of sounds. It is singular because these notes are arranged in one and the same way throughout. The words ever-changing, the music forms a singular chant. Even the very study of the Bavli for ages to come conveyed that remarkable fact: it is a sung writing, never read, always recited in its own chant and song. The hermeneutics of the Bavli is aptly compared to musical notes in more than a metaphorical sense. Their writing therefore required not reading but response. That explains, also, the reason that the form of 'reading' their document was singing: knowing the music, one could supply the right words; obviously, I identify the hermeneutics with that music. Right knowledge of how to decipher the script – musical notes, really – afforded access to the melody and its meaning, the music and the words. So the words written down form keys, signals to the modes of analysis.

The character of the writing, not only its contents, therefore, set forth the systemic statement. The Bavli's one voice, sounding through all tractates, is the voice of exegetes of the Mishnah. The document is organized around the Mishnah, and that order is not a merely formal, but substantive. At *every* point, if the framers have chosen a passage of Mishnah-exegesis, that passage will stand at the head of all further discussion. *Every* turning point in every sustained composition and even in a large composite of compositions brings the editors back to the Mishnah, *always* read in its own order and *invariably* arranged in its own sequence. So the Bavli's authors and future readers sing together in a single way about some few things. It follows that well-crafted and orderly rules governed the character of the sustained discourse that the writing in the Bavli sets forth. All framers of composites and editors of sequences of composites found guidance in the same limited repertoire of rules of analytical rhetoric: some few questions or procedures, directed always toward one and the same prior writing. Not only so, but a fixed order of discourse dictated that a composition of one sort, A, always come prior to a composite of another type, B. A simple logic instructed framers of composites, who sometimes also were authors of compositions, and who other times drew upon available compositions in the making of their cogent composites. So we have now to see the Bavli as entirely of a piece, cogent and coherent, made up of well-composed large-scale constructions.

In a probe I made,[17] I found that nearly 90% of the whole comprises Mishnah-commentary of various kinds. Not only so, but the variety of the types of Mishnah-commentary is limited. Cogent composites – a sequence of well-linked comments – are further devoted to Scripture or to topics of a moral or theological character not closely tied to the exegesis of verses of Scripture; these form in the aggregate approximately 10% of the whole number of composites. So the Bavli has one voice, and it is the voice of a person or persons who propose to speak about one document and to do so in some few ways. Let me spell out what this means.

First, we are able to classify *all* composites (among the more than three thousand that I examined for the purpose of this description of the document) in three principal categories: [1] exegesis and amplification of the law of the Mishnah; [2] exegesis and exposition of verses of, or topics in, Scripture; [3] free-standing composites devoted to topics other than those defined by the Mishnah or Scripture. These classifications were not forced or subtle; the grounds for making them were consistent; appeal throughout was to gross and merely formal characteristics, not to subjective judgments of what unstipulated consideration might underlie, or define the intention of the framer of, a passage.

Second, with that classification in place, it is a matter of simple fact that much more than four-fifths of all composites of the Bavli address the Mishnah and systematically expound that document. These composites are subject to sub-classification in two ways: Mishnah-exegesis and speculation and abstract theorizing about the implications of the Mishnah's statements. The former type of composite, further, is to be classified in a few and simple taxa, for example, composites organized around [1] clarification of the statements of the Mishnah, [2] identification of the authority behind an anonymous statement in the Mishnah, [3] scriptural foundation for the Mishnah's rules, [4] citation and not seldom systematic exposition of the Tosefta's amplification of the Mishnah. That means that most of the Bavli is a systematic exposition of the Mishnah. The abstract that you read will conform to this description in the proportion and order of its comments on the Mishnah.

Third, the other fifth (or still less) of a given tractate will comprise composites that take shape around [1] Scripture or [2] themes or topics of a generally theological or moral character. Distinguishing the latter from the former, of course, is merely formal; very often a scriptural topic will be set forth in a theological or moral framework, and very seldom does a composite on a topic omit all reference to the amplification of a verse or topic of Scripture. The proportion of a given tractate devoted to other-than-Mishnah exegesis and amplification is generally not more than 10%.

The hermeneutics, that is, voice of 'the Talmud', authoritatively defines the mode of analysis. The inquiry is consistent and predictable; one argument differs from another not in supposition but only in detail. When individuals' positions occur, it is because what they have to say serves the purposes of

[17] See my *Rules of Composition of the Talmud of Babylonia.*

'the Talmud' and its uniform inquiry. The inquiry is into the logic and the rational potentialities of a passage. To these dimensions of thought, the details of place, time, and even of an individual's philosophy, are secondary. All details are turned toward a common core of discourse. This, I maintain, is possible only because the document as whole takes shape in accord with an overriding program of inquiry and comes to expression in conformity with a single plan of rhetorical expression. Formed of compositions put together into composites, the second Talmud did not just *grow*, but rather, someone *made* it up; it is not the outcome of an incremental and agglutinative process but of a sustained hermeneutics that governed the work of composition and compilation alike.

The Bavli is a document of remarkable integrity, repeatedly insisting upon the harmony of the parts within a whole and unitary structure of belief and behavior; we ask what the Bavli says: the one thing that is repeated in regard to many things. To begin with, the answer to that question requires us to see what is special about the Bavli, which is to say, what distinguishes it from its predecessor, the Yerushalmi. Where we can identify initiatives characteristic of the Bavli and unusual in the Yerushalmi, there we describe the Bavli in particular. To state the governing hermeneutics that is unique to the second Talmud: *the task of interpretation is to uncover the integrity of the truth that God has manifested in the one and unique revelation, the Torah (oral and written).* By integrity I mean not merely the result of facile harmonization but the rigorous demonstration that the Torah, at its foundations, makes a single statement, whole, complete, cogent and coherent; harmonious; unified and beyond all division. Integrity refers to a writing that is shown to be whole, complete, cogent and coherent; harmonious; unified and beyond all division.

In the comparison with the Yerushalmi we appreciate that the Bavli's quest for unity leads to the inquiry into the named authorities behind an unassigned rule, showing that a variety of figures can concur; meaning, names that stand for a variety of distinct principles can form a single proposition of integrity. That same quest insists on the fair and balanced representation of conflicting principles behind discrete laws, not to serve the cause of academic harmony (surely a lost cause in any age!), but to set forth how, at their foundations, the complicated and diverse laws may be explained by appeal to simple and few principles; the conflict of principles then is less consequential than the demonstration that diverse cases may be reduced to only a few principles. Take for example the single stylistically-indicative trait of the Bavli, its dialectical, or moving, argument. The dialectical argument opens the possibility of reaching out from one thing to something else, not because people have lost sight of their starting point or their goal in the end, but because they want to encompass, in the analytical argument as it gets underway, as broad and comprehensive a range of cases and rules as they possibly can. The movement from point to point in reference to a single point that accurately describes the dialectical argument reaches a goal of abstraction, leaving behind the specificities of not only cases but laws, carrying us upward to the law that governs many cases, the premises that undergird many rules, and still higher to the principles that infuse diverse premises; then the principles that generate other, unrelated premises, which, in turn, come to expression in other, still-less intersecting cases. The meandering course of argument comes to an end when we have shown how things cohere.

The difference between the two Talmuds comes to the surface in hermeneutics: the Bavli's composites framers consistently treat as a question to be investigated the exegetical hypotheses that the Yerushalmi's compositions authors happily accept as conclusive. All of the secondary devices of testing an allegation – a close reading of the formulation of the Mishnah, an appeal to the false conclusion such a close reading, absent a given formulation, might have yielded, to take the examples before us – serve that primary goal. The second recurrent difference is that the Bavli's framers find themselves constantly drawn toward questions of generalization and abstraction (once more: the law behind the laws), moving from case to principle to new case to new principle, then asking whether the substrate of principles forms a single, tight fabric. The Yerushalmi's authors rarely, if ever, pursue that chimera. But what gives the Bavli its compelling, ineluctable power to persuade, the source of the Bavli's intellectual force, is that thrust for abstraction, through generalization (and in that order, generalization, toward abstraction). To spell out in very simple terms what I conceive to be at issue: *the way that the law behind the laws emerges is, first, generalization of a case into a principle, then, the recasting of the principle into an abstraction encompassing a variety of otherwise free-standing principles.*

To conclude: five hermeneutical rules which govern throughout the Bavli are as follows:

[1] *Defining the Torah and the context for meaning.* The Torah consists of free-standing statements, sentences, sometimes formed into paragraphs, more often not; and we are to read these sentences both on their own – for what they say – and also in the context created by the entirety of the Torah, oral and written. Therefore the task is to set side by side and show the compatibility of discrete sentences; documents mean nothing, the Torah being one. The entirety of the Torah defines the context of meaning. All sentences of the Torah, equally, jointly and severally, form the facts out of which meaning is to be constructed.

[2] *Specifying the rules of making sense of the Torah.* Several premises govern in our reading of the sentences of the Torah, and these dictate the rules of reading. The first is that the Torah is perfect and flawless. The second is that the wording of the Torah yields meaning. The third is that the Torah contains, and can contain, nothing contradictory, incoherent, or otherwise contrary to common sense. The fourth is that the Torah can contain no statement that is redundant, banal, silly or stupid. The fifth is that our sages of blessed memory when they state teachings of the Torah stand for these same traits of language and intellect: sound purpose, sound reasoning, sound result, in neat sentences. The task of the reader (in secular language) or the master of the Torah (in theological language, in context the two are one and the same) then is to identify the problems of the Torah, whether written or oral, and

to solve those problems. Knowing what will raise a difficulty, we also know how to resolve it.

[3] *Identifying the correct medium of discourse, which is the dialectical argument.* Since our principal affirmation is that the Torah is perfect, and the primary challenge to that affirmation derives from the named classifications of imperfection, the proper mode of analytical speech is argument. That is because if we seek flaws, we come in a combative spirit: proof and conflict, not truth and consequence. Only by challenging the Torah sentence by sentence, at every plausible point of imperfection, are we going to show in the infinity of detailed cases the governing fact of perfection. We discover right thinking by finding the flaws in wrong thinking, the logical out of the failings of illogic. Only by sustained confrontation of opposed views and interpretations will truth result.

[4] *The harmony of what is subject to dispute, the unity and integrity of truth.* Finding what is rational and coherent: the final principle of hermeneutics is to uncover the rationality of dispute. Once our commitment is to sustained conflict of intellect, it must follow that our goal can only be the demonstration of three propositions, everywhere meant to govern: [1] disputes give evidence of rationality, meaning, each party has a valid, established principle in mind; [2] disputes are subject to resolution; [3] truth wins out. The first proposition is most important. If we can demonstrate that reasonable sages can differ about equally valid propositions, for instance which principle governs in a particular case, then schism affords evidence of not imperfection but profound coherence. The principles are affirmed, their application subjected to conflict. So too, if disputes worked out in extended, moving arguments, covering much ground, can be brought to resolution, as is frequently the case in either a declared decision or an agreement to disagree, then the perfection of the Torah once more comes to detailed articulation.

[5] *Knowing God through the theology expressed in hermeneutics.* Finally, in a protracted quest for the unity of the truth, detailed demonstration that beneath the laws is law, with a few wholly coherent principles inherent in the many, diverse rules and their cases – in that sustained quest, which defines the premise and the goal of all talmudic discourse the second Talmud's writers maintain, is where humanity meets God: in mind, in intellect, where that meeting takes place in accord with rules of reason that govern God and humanity alike.

8.5. The Targums: Their Interpretative Character and Their Place in Jewish Text Tradition

By ÉTAN LEVINE, Haifa

Sources: A. DIEZ MACHO, *Neophyti 1. Targum Palestinense Ms. de la Biblioteca Vaticana* I–V (Madrid/Barcelona 1968–1978); idem, *Targum to the Prophets: Codex New York 229 from the Library of the Jewish Theological Seminary of America* (Jerusalem 1974); M. KLEIN, *The Fragment Targums of the Pentateuch According to the Extant Sources* (AnBib 76; Rome 1980); P. DE LAGARDE, *Hagiographa Chaldaice* (Osnabrück 1967); É. LEVINE, *The Targum to the Five Megillot: Codex Vatican* Urb. Ebr. 1 (Jerusalem 1979); idem, *Pentateuch, Prophets and Hagiographa: Vatican Ms. Urbinati 2* (Jerusalem 1979); A. SPERBER, *The Bible in Aramaic, Based on Old Manuscripts and Printed Texts* I–IV, I. *The Pentateuch according to Targum Onkelos* (Leiden 1959); II. *The Former Prophets according to Targum Jonathan* (Leiden 1959); III. *The Latter Prophets according to Targum Jonathan* (Leiden 1962); IV A. *The Hagiographa. Transition from Translation to Midrash* (Leiden 1968); IV B. *The Targum and the Hebrew Bible* (Leiden 1973); *Rabbinic Bible (Biblia Rabbinica)* (repr. New York 1988); A. WUENSCHE, *Bibliotheca Rabbinica* 1–12 (Leipzig 1881–5).

Bibliographies: A. DIEZ MACHO, "Bibliografía Targumica", *Neophyti 1* 4 (Madrid/Barcelona 1974) 11–29; 5 (1978) 13–40; J. T. FORESTELL, *Targumic Traditions and the New Testament* (Chico, CA 1979); M. H. GOSHEN-GOTTSTEIN, "Targum Studies: An Overview of Recent Developments", Textus 16 (1991) 1–11; B. GROSSFELD, *A Bibliography of Targum Literature* (Cincinnati/New York I. 1972; II. 1977); M. MCNAMARA, "On Englishing the Targums", *Salvacion en la Palabra: Targum, Derash, Berit* (ed. D. Múnoz Leon; Madrid/Barcelona 1986) 447–461; P. NICKELS, *Targum and New Testament: A Bibliography* (Rome 1967). See also *Newsletter for Targumic and Cognate Studies* I (1974) et seq.

General works: P. CHURGIN, *Targum Ketubim* (New York 1945; Heb); H. Z. DIMITROVSKY (ed.), *Exploring the Talmud*, I. *Education* (New York 1976); B. GERHARDSSON, *Memory and Manuscript* (Uppsala 1961); M. HIGGER, *Masseket Soferim* (New York 1936); Y. KOMLOSH, *The Bible in the Light of the Aramaic Translations* (Jerusalem 1973; Heb); R. LE DEAUT, *Introduction à la Littérature Targumique* (Rome 1966); É. LEVINE, *The Aramaic Version of the Bible* (Berlin/New York 1988); idem, *The Aramaic Version of Ruth* (Rome 1973); R. LOEWE, "Apologetic Motifs in the Targum to the Song of Songs", *Biblical Motifs* (ed. A. Altmann; Cambridge, MA 1966); S. LOWY, "Some Aspects of Normative and Sectarian Interpretation of the Scriptures", Annual of the Leeds University Oriental Society 6 (1969) 98–163; M. MCNAMARA, *Targum and Testament* (Shannon 1972); A. SHINAN, "On the Question of Beliefs and Concepts in the Targums", *Jerusalem Studies in Jewish Thought* 2 (1982) 7–32; L. SMOLAR/M. ABERBACH, *Targum Jonathan to the Prophets* (New York 1983); E. URBACH, *The Sages: Their Concepts and Beliefs* (Jerusalem 1969; Heb); G. VERMES, *Scripture and Tradition in Judaism* (Leiden 1961); A. D. YORK, "The Targum in the Synagogue and in the School", *JSJ* 10 (1979) 74–86.

1. The Background of Targum

The deepest roots of targum lie imbedded in biblical antiquity, when, following the destruction of the First Temple in 586 BCE (and even more so after the destruction of the Second Temple in 70 CE) the Jewish People evolved into a bibliocentric community. In the absence of political sovereignty, territorial commonality, functioning temple, religious or intellectual hierarchy, the traumatized fragments of Jewish civilization adopted sacred Scripture as their *'constitutio'*. The message of classical prophecy was accepted: the Sinai covenant as detailed in the 'Book of Moses' was the criterion by which Israel was judged and its destiny molded. Thus the Hebrew Bible provided commonality and unity, historical identity, juridical structure, and a religious justification for collective existence. When Ezra arrived in Palestine, polity was established on the basis of Scripture (Ezra 7:25 f.). The Bible records the ancient Jerusalem convocation wherein the populace affirmed its allegiance to the sacred text (Neh 8:1 ff.).

This historically unprecedented self-definition was maintained by 'bookmen' (Heb. *sôperîm*) who studied and interpreted the sacred text in harmony with evolving, uncodified traditions, who trained disciples, and who delivered public discourses. By the beginning of the Christian era the public reading and exposition of Scripture was the norm in all communities (cf. Josephus, *Contra Apionem* 2.17), and was regarded as a tradition harking back to biblical antiquity (Acts 15:21). The old Palestinian lectionary was divided into 154 sections and was completed in a triennial cycle (whereas the Babylonian lectionary divided the Pentateuch into 48–54 sections and was completed annually), with special readings from the Pentateuch, Prophets and Hagiographa assigned to the Festivals, New Moons and special sabbaths.[1]

This entire enterprise, the culture it transmitted and the civilization it sustained, were critically endangered by the ongoing decline of Hebrew as the language of Jewry. As a result, despite strong opposition on the part of some sages to the translation of the sacred from the 'holy language', biblical texts were translated into Aramaic, or *'targum'*, i.e. 'translation'. Qumran finds (e.g. 11QtgJob) and Mishnaic references testify to the practice. In fact, the earliest extant texts are all essentially literal translations of the Hebrew Bible and appear to be literary in origin, since targum was part of the curriculum of the Palestinian academies, placed between the Hebrew Bible and the Mishnah. Competence in the understanding of Scripture presupposed the ability to translate the text, and the recommended method of study was review of the weekly lection twice in the Hebrew original and once in Aramaic. Thus, despite widespread conjecture, there is no evidence that the extant targums originated in association with the liturgical reading of Scripture, or that, as a genre, targum derived from the synagogue and was originally oral.

2. Public Declamation of Targum

When public Bible translation became unavoidable, the declamation of the targum was governed by religious law designed both to prevent misrenderings of Scripture and to preclude conveying the conception that the targum was

[1] See J. Mann, *The Bible as Read and Preached in the Old Synagogue* 1–2 (Cincinnati 1940; 1966); cf. survey in A. Z. Idelsohn, *Jewish Liturgy and its Development* (New York 1932).

equal in sanctity and authority to the Hebrew Bible itself. The Declaimer (*metûrgeman* or *tûrgeman*) could not read his translation from a written text, nor could he be corrected by the Hebrew reader, lest either convey the impression that he was presenting canonized material. The targum was declaimed after each individual verse of the Pentateuchal reading, and after every three verses of the Prophetic lection, and the *metûrgeman* was expected to reconcile the two functions of translater and interpreter, lest the assembled populace be misled by a particular *verbum e verbo* translation or mistaught by a free *sensus de sensu* paraphrase.[2] Since the Pentateuchal reading (supplemented by a Prophetic reading chosen for its conceptual or semantic affinity) was followed by a homily, the targum frequently contains or refers to materials contained in the homiletical *midrashim*. Although the juridical as well as homiletical sources are notoriously multivocal, according to tradition this is to their credit, for "had the *Torah* been with absolute clarity (i.e. without controversy as to its meaning) there would be no room for the sage to exercise discretion in decisions (*y. San.* 4:2)". In extant targum texts there are literal translations (e.g. *Tg. Isa* 19:10) preferable to the Hebrew massoretic text itself, as well as cases (e.g. *Tg. Onq. Exod* 30:35; *Deut* 22:5, *Tg. Judg* 5:24) wherein it constitutes the *only* correct version.

In Pharisaic-rabbinic biblical exegesis, "Scripture never loses its accepted sense", hence the public reading of the Hebrew Bible could not be altered to conform to traditional exegesis. Although *additional* meaning(s) *(deraš)* may be ascribed to the text, the usual meaning *(pešat)* had to be presented. When one considers the eroticism of Song of Songs, the scepticism of Ecclesiastes, and the complications presented by other texts whose canonicity was apparently based upon their presumptive origin rather than their contents, one senses the difficulties involved in introducing them into the synagoge liturgy. These could be 'safely' used only by reinterpretation, circumlocution, alteration and even contradiction: the *midrash* genre which is so widely found in the targum. Hence the dual function of this biblical 'version': exposition as well as translation. The more elaborately paraphrastic targums became, essentially, vehicles for conveying midrash, attempting to render the biblical text more relevant, polemical, acceptable or understandable. Often midrashic allusion was interwoven into translation, forming a continuum, with the listener or casual reader unable to discern distinctions between the translations of, and the commentary upon, the Hebrew original.

---

[2] For a representative composite of targum in rabbinic law and lore cf. *m. Meg* 3:10; 4:4, 6, 9; *y. Ber.* 9c; *Bik.* 65d; *Meg* 74d; 75a; *Šabb.* 15c; 16c; *b. B. Bat.* 134a; *Ber.* 27b; 45a; Meg 3a; 8b, 9a; 17a, 21a; 23a, b; 25a, b; 32a; *Mo'ed Qat.* 3a; 21a; 28b; *Qidd.* 49a; *Šabb.* 115a b; 116a; *Sanh.* 84b; *Soṭa* 33a; 39a; 40a; 41a; *Sukk.* 28a; *Tem.* 14a, b; Yebam. 22a. See also *Sifre Deut* 161; *Tanhuma* II, 87f.; *Pesiq. R.* 14a–b; Mek. II, 17:7; *Exod Rab.* 8:3; *'Abot R. Nat* B., XII; *Sop.* 5:15; 12:6; 15:2; 18:4.

3. Exegesis in the Targum

In many respects the targum continues the earlier scribal tradition of glosses: *marginalia* later incorporated into the biblical text itself. Their functions were: a) to resolve textual difficulties by interpreting obscure words or simplifying syntax, b) to harmonize conflicting texts, c) to reconcile the biblical text with accepted tradition, d) to incorporate specifics of Pharisaic-rabbinic Judaism into the text, e) to provide specificity to historical, juridical or religious allusions, f) to either strengthen or mitigate the force of a scriptural passage. In concert these wed the original Hebrew text to the law *(halakah)* and lore (*haggadah*, var. *'aggadah*) evolving concurrently with the ongoing transmission of Scripture. Whereas the former strives for definitive, authoritative conclusions, the latter, whether deriving from populist or academic sources, does not preclude contradiction and cannot be regarded as representing authoritative beliefs or postures. The targum is *invariably* declarative rather than argumentative; it *never* cites sources, and it *never* provides exegetical logic. The wide diversity between various targums, and the fact that mutually contradictory elements may be found within the same targum testify to a dynamic conception of interpretation that resisted the dogmatic pressures to impose a single, 'official' reading and interpretation of Scripture. To force this variegated text into a dogmatic mould would be procrustean *ex definitione*, for in the Judaism(s) of late Antiquity there were neither dogmatic credal formulae nor authorities empowered to promulgate them. The targum reflects an eclectic use of sources, variant purposes to which its midrash was put, and flexibility of the genre itself.[3]

The various targums manifest the prerogative to determine which biblical verses would be translated literally and which would be expanded or explained. It also exercises the prerogative to choose from variant exegetical materials. By bringing to Scripture the plethora of law and lore that had evolved, it is perforce selective. By choosing *what* it hears within sacred Scripture and *how* it hears it, the targum becomes a statement *about* Scripture, and not simply a restatement *of* Scripture. It is a multivocal, dialectical 'conversation' with the Hebrew Bible involving a miscellany of people of various sophistication, of diverse postures and historical circumstances, widely separate in place and time, yet constituting, through *process* rather than specific *content*, a community of letters. Their creativity provided a functioning aggregate of concepts, values, metaphors, symbols and behavioral norms providing biblically-based Judaism with evolving integrity and coherence.[4]

---

[3] See J. Neusner, "Scriptures and Mishnah: Authority and Selectivity", *Scripture in the Jewish and Christian Traditions* (Philadelphia 1972) 65–84; L. Ginzberg, *On Jewish Law and Lore* (Philadelphia 1955); M. Kadushin, *The Rabbinic Mind* (New York 1952); J. Weingreen, "The Rabbinic Approach to the Study of the Old Testament", *BJRL* 34 (1961) 166–190.

[4] Biblical texts purposely *not* translated in public include the story of Reuben and Bilhah (Gen 35:22), the story of Tamar (Gen 38:13 ff.), the account of the Golden Calf (Deut 9:12–21), the story of David and Bathsheba (2 Sam 11:7–17), and the story of Amnon (2 Sam 13:1 ff.) because of their offensive nature, whereas the Priestly Blessing (Num 6:24 ff.) would not be translated

4. The Dating of Texts

Any convincing attempt at dating a given targum requires a combination of both literary (i.e. *midrashic*) considerations and philological factors. The former requires motifs and traditions that are clearly paralleled in early writings, and the latter is complicated by the fact that archaic linguistic forms frequently persist, especially in juridical and historical orthography. Thus, any question of *terminus ante quem* or *terminus post quem* must provide either irrefutable parallels in Antiquity or evidence of the targum having been rewritten in later centuries deleting early elements. The entire question of the influence of other literature on the targum, and conversely, the influence of the targum on other extant texts is so immense and complex that despite the wealth of supposed extremely close parallels or clearly attested channels of transmission (judgements which themselves involve a theoretical posture!), the difficulties involved in drawing accurate conclusions are insurmountable. Researchers generally agree that the targumim are compounds; disagreements as to dating stem largely from the relative weight accorded to the earlier and later elements these texts incorporate. For example, although Targum Pseudo-Jonathan incorporates a polemic regarding the Hasmonean High Priest Johanan (Deut 33:11) which would hardly have been composed after his day, a first century BCE dating is valid for that passage only, witness the same targum containing a polemic *at least* seven centuries later, in its reference to Mohammad's wife and daughter (Gen 21:21). Individual elements may, in fact, be historically pinpointed, as in the homily on the four kingdoms (*Tg. Hab* 3:17) where the targum predicts that "the Romans will be destroyed and they will not exact tribute from Jerusalem". Had the destruction of the Temple already occured, the targum would have related to a far greater catastrophe. Instead, it waxes indignant over the census tax imposed by the second Procurator Quirinius in 6 CE which was perceived as national servitude, and which aroused widespread hostility until the revolt of 66 CE. The targum's homily must have originated during that sixty-year period. Yet it hardly constitutes *ipso facto* justification for the dating of the targumic document as a whole.

In sum, dating techniques are of value for only a bare minimum of targumic materials, and no conclusive method exists for distinguishing between the tradition that underlies a targum text and the particular recension of that text found in the targum. It is impossible to address as varied an entity as the Aramaic targum as though it were a unitary corpus in any respect. Indeed, there is no evidence that any segment of 'The Aramaic Version of the Bible' is not itself a composite of accretions. On some of the most intriguing questions the critical scholar must enter a plea of *non liquet*: there are no reliable data as to who the authors were, how materials were compiled, how textual transmission was maintained, and for what functional purposes they were

---

because of its sacrosanct status. For a survey of targumic beliefs and values, see Levine, The Aramaic Version (1988), 45–225.

intended. And if extreme caution must be exercised in extant documents from late Antiquity where traditions *are* attributed to particular sources, *a fortiori* does this apply where the traditions are *totally* unidentified, as in the targum.

5. The 'Official' Targum

The rabbinic *Biblia Hebraica* contains targum to all of Scripture (except for those texts written in Aramaic). The most utilized of all is the so-called 'Targum Onqelos' to the Pentateuch which is invariably placed next to the Hebrew text itself in *Biblia Rabbinica.* This targum is extant in a unified, scholastic redaction which, like the Hebrew Bible, has a *massorah* for purposes of textual control. A substratum of Western Aramaic witnesses that this targum originated in Palestine, whence (along with the Mishnah and Tosefta) it was imported into Babylon where it was revised and redacted. It is the most literal of the Pentateuchal targums: despite occasionally significant exceptions for theological or juridical purposes, in diction and grammatical structure it closely follows the Hebrew original. By the third century CE it was considered the authoritative Aramaic version of the Pentateuch, and its official status is confirmed by its being cited in the Tamuld as a juridical source, with the designation "our Targum". The other 'official' targum is the so-called 'Targum Jonathan to the Prophets' which originated in Palestine and after significant revision in linguistic conformity with Babylonian Aramaic diction and morphology, by the 3rd century it was disseminated throughout the diaspora and subsequently regarded as ancient, reliable, and occasionally indispensable for the correct understanding of obscure biblical passages. Despite its somewhat more free *sensus de sensu* renderings in places, it bears a very close affinity to Targum Onqelos. These 'official targums' are also known as 'Babylonian targums', due to their a) locale of redaction, b) linguistic characteristics, c) use of supralinear punctuation in the earliest manuscripts. Their scanty historical allusions range from events as disparate as the reign of Johanan Hyrcanus (135–105 BCE) to the Sassanid regime in Babylon, with no Arabic linguistic characteristics or references to the fall of Babylon by the Arab conquest. In their largely *verbatim* renderings and the terseness of their additives they reflect their having met the criteria for synagogue, as well as academic use.

6. The 'Palestinian' Targum Texts

Palestinian targum to the Pentateuch is found, primarily, in three texts: the Pseudo-Jonathan (which tradition erroneously designates *Targûm Yônatan ben 'Uzzi'el,*) and the Fragmentary Targum (designated *Targûm Yerûšalmî*), both of which appear in the *Biblia Rabbinica*, and the recently discovered Vatican *Ms. Neophyti* 1. *Tg. Ps.-J.* is a virtually complete targum written, largely, in Galilean Jewish Aramaic, and incorporating a wealth of homiletical and juridical midrash. The datable elements encompass at least eight centuries, from the 1st century BCE through the rise of Islam in the 7th century CE. *Frg. Tg.* relates to only 850 scattered biblical verses, phrases or words. Whether or not it may once have included more material, the purpose and selection process of this targum has yet to be identified. Like *Tg. Ps.-J.* its language is Galilean Jewish Aramaic. Its additive elements are, generally speaking, older and less elaborate than those found in that text. *Tg. Neof.* is the oldest complete Pentateuchal targum. Both in its main text and in its glosses it is less paraphrastic than *Tg. Ps.-J.,* with fewer and terser additions. All of these targums contain elements that are considerably older than their final dates of compilation; the wide divergences between them clearly indicate that they are 'unofficial'. Thus, a) their texts were never fixed, b) there is no control of paraphrase, grammar or orthography, c) there is no harmonization with normative Pharisaic-rabbinic Judaism.

The targums to Hagiographa, like the Palestinian targums to the Pentateuch, never enjoyed 'official status' despite their being included in the *Biblia Rabbinica.* They too apparently originated in Palestine, witness their Western Aramaic linguistic features as well as their containing material found *only* in the Jerusalem Talmud or in midrash literature of early Palestinian origin. In time the linguistic characteristics were increasingly altered in conformity with the familiar Aramaic of the Babylonian Talmud. Similarly, lengthy addenda were incorporated, so that much of the extant texts are more midrash than they are translation. Although the various *mss. stemma* contain, by and large, the same basic text in different recensions, they do widely vary, with differences in a) degree of transition into Eastern Aramaic, b) extent of evolution from unvocalized to vocalized texts, c) syntax and morphology. The traditional attribution of the Hagiographa targum to an early date of composition is totally unfounded, witness a) the variety of translation techniques employed b) the significant differences in literary style, philological characters and exegetical methodology between (and within) the various Hagiographic targums, c) the historical allusions, loan words and morphological characteristics indicating a long process of development. The diversity of the various Hagiographic targums becomes striking when surveying their basic features:

A targum to Job in the 1st century is mentioned by the Mishnah, and a text was one of the fragments discovered among the Dead Sea scrolls (11QtgJob), yet the extant *Tg. Job* is the product of ongoing development. It contains numerous double-readings and occasional triple-readings, with the first almost invariably a literal translation and the other(s) midrashic expansion. A date of final composition prior to the establishment of the authoritative Massorah is suggested by the numerous cases where its *verbum e verbo* translation differs from the massoretic biblical text. Like *Tg. Job*, the targum to Psalms intersperses addenda, including double-readings within a literal translation. And like *Tg. Job* 4:10 it contains a midrash (ad Ps 108:10) suggesting composition prior to the fall of Constantinople in 476 CE. Whereas the targum to Ecclesiastes is paraphrastic in the extreme, attempting to reconcile the book's scepticism with the religious beliefs of post-biblical Judaism, the targum to Chronicles is basically literal translation of the Hebrew, with only occasional midrashic amplification. When citing synoptic passages from the books of Samuel and Kings it frequently follows the Targum Jonathan, and when quoting the Pentateuch it occasionally utilizes Palestinian targum, though the onomastic suggests a final composition in the 8th or 9th century. The targum to Proverbs differs from the other Hagiographic targums in that it bears Syriac linguistic characteristics. In many of the cases wherein the Peshitta differs from the Massoretic Hebrew Bible it corresponds to the former, and it includes exegesis found in the Syriac Peshitta. And these are but *some* of the reasons which militate against regarding the targum to Hagiographa as a unified corpus. This is further proven by the fact that widely differing targums to Esther are extant despite this being the only Hagiographic work with liturgical regulations (*Sop.* XII:6) governing its recitation in the Synagogue. Nevertheless, the reasons for the multifaceted latitudinarianism of these Hagiographic targum texts are: a) their not being *essential* components of worship, b) their not being utilized for establishing juridical precedent, c) their being based upon biblical texts which strongly elicited homiletic expansion.

7. The Afterlife of the Targum

Although the literary evolution of the targum genre came to a virtual halt when Aramaic ceased to be the *lingua franca* of many Jews due to the inroads of Arabic in the 7th century, it continued to flourish on three branches: a) it was cited widely by medieval and even modern commentators on the Bible and rabbinic literature, b) it was used in private preparation of the prescribed biblical sections of the liturgical calendar, c) it was maintained by isolated Jewish communities as part of the public recitation in the Synagogue, where it was also cited in sermons. The continued importance of targum is attested to also by the wealth of late manuscripts, and by the targum being maintained within the *Biblia Rabbinica* to this day.

In recent decades there has been a spectacular increase of scholarly interest in targum. In measure this is due to new archeological finds, but it also reflects the increased appreciation of the diversity that existed in Judaism, both in late Antiquity and thereafter. The various targums constitute a vast repository of both *halakah* and *haggadah* revealing 'Jewish values': human values that have a distinct concretization in the Jewish tradition. By studying these documents within the context of the history of the community and the evolution of its relationship to Scripture as expressed in law and lore, there emerges a genuine understanding of both the targum and of those people who articulated through, or assimilated, these texts. Since targum is largely a folk genre, its current renaissance in the scholarly world helps correct the longstanding tendency to attribute to The Jewish People *in toto* the ideas and values of its intellectual elite and its official institutions despite the fact that these are inadequate for understanding the life and thought of the masses. To the extent that modern scholarship moves beyond ahistorical or harmonistic methodology, or the mere classification and comparison of targum passages divorced from their contexts, the roots and branches of targum literature will provide a rich variety of academic fruit.[5]

[5] Indispensable contextual sources include J. Neusner, *The Rabbinic Traditions about the Pharisees Before 70 C.E.* 1–3 (Leiden 1971); E. P. Sanders (ed.), *Jewish and Christian Self-Definition* 2 (Philadelphia 1981). Also see I. Abrahams, *Studies in Pharisaism and the Gospels* (Cambridge 1917); C. Albeck, *Mabo la-Mishnah* (Tel Aviv 1968); S. W. Baron, *A Social and Religious History of the Jews* (New York 1952–60); B. Cohen, *Jewish and Roman Law* 1–2 (New York 1966); J. Faur, "The Character of Classical Jewish Literature", *JSS* 28 (1977) 30–45; E. R. Goodenough, *Jewish Symbols in the Greco Roman World* 1–13 (New York 1953–68); G. F. Moore, *Judaism in the First Centuries of the Christian Era* 1–3 (Cambridge, MA 1927–30). Also see relevant entries in 'General works' cited *supra*.

Chapter Nine

New Testament Interpretation of the Old Testament

By Hans Hübner, Göttingen

Selected bibliography: S. Amsler, *L'Ancien Testament dans l'Eglise* (Neuchâtel 1960); O. Betz, *Offenbarung und Schriftforschung in der Qumransekte* (WUNT 6; Tübingen 1960); M. Black, "The Christological Use of the Old Testament in the New Testament", *NTS* 18 (1971/72) 1–14; J. Blank, "Erwägungen zum Schriftverständnis des Paulus", *Rechtfertigung* (FS E. Käsemann, ed. J. Friedrich/W. Pöhlmann/P. Stuhlmacher; Tübingen/Göttingen 1976) 37–56; P. Borgen, *Logos was the True Light, and other Essays on the Gospel of John* (Trondheim 1983); H. Braun, "Das Alte Testament im Neuen Testament", *ZTK* 59 (1962) 16–31; R. Bultmann, "Weissagung und Erfüllung", idem, *Glauben und Verstehen: Gesammelte Aufsätze* II (Tübingen ^{5}1968) 162–186; B. S. Childs, *Biblical Theology of the Old and New Testaments: Theological Reflection on the Christian Bible* (Minneapolis, MN 1993); Ch. H. Dodd, *According to the Scriptures: The Sub-Structure of New Testament Theology* (London 1952); J. W. Doewe, *Jewish Hermeneutics in the Synoptic Gospels and Acts* (GTB 24; Assen 1954); E. E. Ellis, *Paul's Use of the Old Testament* (London 1957); idem, *Prophecy and Hermeneutics in Early Christianity: New Testament Essays* (WUNT 18; Tübingen 1978); J. Fekkes III, *Isaiah and Prophetic Traditions in the Book of Revelation: Visionary Antecedents and Their Development* (JSNTSup 93; Sheffield 1994); J. A. Fitzmyer, "The Use of Explicit Old Testament Quotations in Qumran Literature and in the New Testament", *NTS* 7 (1960/61) 297–333; E. Franco (ed.), *La teologia biblica: Natura e prospettive: in Dialogo con Guiseppe Segalla* (Saggi 27; Roma 1989); E. D. Freed, *Old Testament Quotations in the Gospel of John* (NovTSup 11; Leiden 1965); K. Galley, *Altes und neues Heilsgeschehen bei Paulus* (AzTh I/22; Stuttgart 1965); H. Gese, *Vom Sinai zum Zion: Alttestamentliche Beiträge zur biblischen Theologie* (BEvT 64; München 1974); idem, *Zur Biblischen Theologie: Alttestamentliche Vorträge* (BEvT 78; München 1977); L. Goppelt, *Typos: Die typologische Deutung des Alten Testaments im Neuen*, with the appendix "Apokalyptik und Typologie bei Paulus" (Darmstadt 1969); G. H. Gundry, *The Use of the Old Testament in St. Matthew's Gospel: With special Reference to the Messianic Hope* (NovTSup 18; Leiden ^{2}1975); K. Haacker et al. (eds.), *Biblische Theologie Heute: Einführung – Beispiele – Kontroversen* (BThSt 1; Neukirchen 1977); F. Hahn, "Das Problem 'Schrifttradition' im Urchristentum", *EvTh* 30 (1970) 449–68; R. Hanhart, "Das Neue Testament und die Griechische Überlieferung des Judentums", *Überlieferungsgeschichtliche Untersuchungen* (ed. F. Paschke; TU 125; Berlin 1981) 293–303; idem, "Die Bedeutung der Septuaginta in neutestamentlicher Zeit", *ZTK* 81 (1984) 395–416; A. T. Hanson, *Jesus Christ in the Old Testament* (London 1965); idem, *Studies in Paul's Technique and Theology* (London 1974); idem, *The New Testament Interpretation of Scripture* (London 1980); idem, *The Living Utterances of God: The New Testament Exegesis of the Old* (London 1983); idem, *The Prophetic Gospel: A Study of John and the Old Testament* (Edinburgh 1991, lit.); A. von Harnack, "Das Alte Testament in den Paulinischen Briefen und in den Paulinischen Gemeinden", SPAW.PH 12 (1928) 124–41; M. Hengel/H. Merkel, "Die Magier aus dem Osten und die Flucht nach Ägypten (Mt 2) im Rahmen der antiken Religionsgeschichte und der Theologie des Matthäus", *Orientierung an Jesus: Zur Theologie der Synoptiker* (FS J. Schmid, ed. P. Hoffmann/N. Brox/W. Pesch; Freiburg/Basel/Wien 1973) 139–69; F. Hesse, *Das Alte Testament als Buch der Kirche* (Gütersloh 1966); T. Holtz, "Zur Interpretation des Alten Testaments im Neuen Testament", *ThLZ* 99 (1974) 19–32; H. Hübner, *Das Gesetz in der synoptischen Tradition: Studien zur These einer progressiven Qumranisierung und Judaisierung innerhalb der synoptischen Tradition* (Göttingen ^{2}1986); idem, *Das Gesetz bei Paulus: Ein Beitrag zum Werden der paulinischen Theologie* (FRLANT 119; Göttingen [3]1982); idem, "γραφή/γράφω", EWNT 1, 628-638; idem, "πληρόω κτλ.", EWNT 3, 256-262; idem, "πλήρωμα", EWNT 3, 262-264; idem, *Gottes Ich und Israel: Zum Schriftgebrauch des Paulus in Röm 9-11* (FRLANT 136; Göttingen 1984); idem, *Biblische Theologie des Neuen Testaments:* I. *Prolegomena* (Göttingen 1990); II. *Die Theologie des Paulus und ihre neutestamentliche Wirkungsgeschichte* (Göttingen 1993); III. *Hebräerbrief, Evangelien und Offenbarung. Epilegomena* (Göttingen 1995); idem, *Biblische Theologie als Hermeneutik: Gesammelte Aufsätze* (ed. A. Labahn/M. Labahn; Göttingen 1995); idem, "New Testament, OT Quotations in the", ABD IV (1992) 1096-1104; K.-L. JÖRNS, *Das hymnische Evangelium: Untersuchungen zu Aufbau, Funktion und Herkunft der hymnischen Stücke in der Johannesoffenbarung* (SNT 5; Gütersloh 1971); P. KATZ, "The Quotations from Deuteronomy in Hebrews", *ZNW* 49 (1958) 213-223; G. KITTEL, "λέγω κτλ D. 'Wort' und 'Reden' im NT", TWNT 4, 100-140; D. A. KOCH, *Die Schrift als Zeuge des Evangeliums: Untersuchungen zur Verwendung und zum Verständnis der Schrift bei Paulus* (BHT 69; Tübingen 1986); W. G. KÜMMEL, "Jesus und der jüdische Traditionsgedanke", idem, *Heilsgeschehen und Geschichte: Gesammelte Aufsätze 1933-1964* (ed. E. Grässer/ O. Merk/A. Fritz; MThSt 3; Marburg 1965) 15-35; idem, "Jesu Antwort an Johannes den Täufer: Ein Beispiel zum Methodenproblem in der Jesusforschung", idem, *Heilsgeschehen und Geschichte* II. *Gesammelte Aufsätze 1965-1976* (ed. E. Grässer/O. Merk; MThSt 16; Marburg 1978) 177-200; B. LINDARS, *New Testament Apologetic: The Doctrinal Significance of the Old Testament Quotations* (London 1961); B. LINDARS/P. BORGEN, "The Place of the Old Testament in the Formation of New Testament Theology: Prolegomena and Response", *NTS* 23 (1976/77) 59-75; U. LUZ, *Das Geschichtsverständnis des Paulus* (BEvT 49; München 1968); idem, "Der alte und der neue Bund bei Paulus und im Hebräerbrief", *EvTh* 27 (1967) 318-336; J. MAIER, "Zur Frage des biblischen Kanons im Frühjudentum im Licht der Qumranfunde", *Zum Problem des biblischen Kanons*, JBTh 3 (Neukirchen 1988) 135-146; B. M. METZGER, "The Formulas Introducing Quotations of Scripture in the New Testament and in the Mishnah", in: idem, *Historical and Literary Studies: Pagan, Jewish, and Christian* (NTTS 8; Leiden 1968) 52-63; O. MICHEL, *Paulus und seine Bibel* (Darmstadt 1972 = Gütersloh 1929); M. P. MILLER, "Targum, Midrash and the Use of the Old Testament in the New Testament", *JSJ* 2 (1971) 29-82; H. J. VAN DER MINDE, *Schrift und Tradition bei Paulus* (Paderborn 1976); M. RESE, *Alttestamentliche Motive in der Christologie des Lukas* (SNT I; Gütersloh 1969); H. GRAF REVENTLOW, *Hauptprobleme der Biblischen Theologie im 20. Jahrhundert* (EdF 203; Darmstadt 1983); W. ROTHFUCHS, *Die Erfüllungszitate des Matthäus-Evangeliums. Eine biblische und theologische Untersuchung* (BWANT 88; Stuttgart 1969); B. SCHALLER, "Zum Textcharakter der Hiobzitate im Paulinischen Schrifttum", *ZNW* 71 (1980) 21-26; R. SCHNACKENBURG, "Joh 12,39-41. Zur Christologischen Schriftauslegung des vierten Evangelisten", idem, *Das Johannesevangelium* 4. *Ergänzende Auslegungen und Exkurse* (HThK IV/4; Freiburg/Basel/Wien 1984) 143-52; G. SCHRENK, "γράφω κτλ.", TWNT I, 742-73; F. SCHRÖGER, *Der Verfasser des Hebräerbriefes als Schriftausleger* (BU 4; Regensburg 1968); B. G. SCHUCHARD, *Scripture within Scripture: The Interrelationship of Form and Function in the Explicit Citations in the Gospel of John* (SBLDS 133; Atlanta, GA 1992); K. STENDAHL, *The School of St. Matthew and its Use of the Old Testament* (ASNU 20; Lund [2]1968); P. STUHLMACHER, *Schriftauslegung auf dem Wege zur Biblischen Theologie* (Göttingen 1975); idem, *Biblische Theologie des Neuen Testaments* I. *Grundlegung: Von Jesus zu Paulus* (Göttingen 1992); A. SUHL, *Die Funktion der alttestamentlichen Zitate und Anspielungen im Markusevangelium* (Gütersloh 1965)[1]; W. M. SWARTLEY, *Israel's Traditions and the Synoptic Gospels: Story Shaping Story* (Peabody, MS 1994); H. ULONSKA, *Die Funktion der alttestamentlichen Zitate und Anspielungen in den Paulinischen Briefen* (Diss. Theol.; Münster 1963); PH. VIELHAUER, "Paulus und das Alte Testament", idem, *Oikodome: Aufsätze zum Neuen Testament 2* (ThBü 65; München 1979) 196-228; N. WALTER, "'Hellenistische Eschatologie' im Frühjudentum – ein Beitrag zur 'Biblischen Theologie'?", *ThLZ* 110 (1985) 331-48. See also: Jahrbuch für Biblische Theologie 1 ff (1986 ff).

[1] Regarding this title and ULONSKA (1963) see M. RESE, VF 12/2 (1967) 87-97.

0. Introduction

Discussions of the reception of the holy Scripture of Israel, which was later called the Old Testament by the Christian Church, show how even central theological issues are being debated with different and opposing attitudes in a sometimes emotionally heated atmosphere. Of course this discussion touches upon principal questions. Opinions are far too easily influenced by fundamental theological convictions based on specific prior understandings or, perhaps, even on prejudices. This is, however, not surprising. Owing to the sensitive subject matter it is difficult to expect an unprejudiced approach; what is more, an unprejudiced approach to the issue is even hermeneutically impossible. A theological position which is supposed to be really *theological* implies that it is always determined by one's own existential concern.

The New Testament authors did not consider themselves as writers who provided the holy Scripture of Israel with a new conclusion that supposedly included an ultimate validity because they were proclaiming an ultimately valid message. They were firmly convinced, however, that their writings had final authority. After all, their intention was to mediate in a literal form the *final* word of God, which is the kerygma of God's final act of salvation in Jesus Christ; consequently, they intended to present the *only* correct interpretation of Israel's Scripture. It was their conviction that the christological understanding of the holy Scripture would supply it with the indisputable and indispensible eschatological-messianic meaning, which, in pointing toward the Christ event, already was the original meaning. Furthermore, the messianic interpretation of the Old Testament is reconfirmed by God through the event of Easter. Thus the identity of the God who speaks in Israel's holy Scripture with the God who accomplished salvation in Christ for all humankind, is the *theological* precondition for the *hermeneutical* basic conviction of the New Testament authors.[2]

1. Quotations – Allusions – the Language of the Septuagint

Speaking of one *single* reception of Old Testament passages in the New Testament would be an over-generalization since the New Testament contains writings of very different kinds. In particular, the Gospels must be distinguished from the Epistles. The Revelation of John has a completely original character and is, therefore, formally different from all other New Testament writings. These formal literary differences among the New Testament writings already suggest quite an individual way of referring to the Old Testament in terms of form and selection.

---

[2] Many of the arguments put forth in this essay are thoroughly presented in: H. Hübner, *Biblische Theologie des Neuen Testaments* [BThNT] I-III (1990-95) [see bibl.]. This work may serve as a reference for grounds not provided here due to the special concept and the limited space. See also H. Hübner, *Vetus Testamentum in Novo. Pars secunda: Corpus Paulinum* (Göttingen 1995. *Pars prima et tertia* forthcoming).

There are several ways in the New Testament of adopting and, thus, necessarily of interpreting the Old Testament. To put it more precisely, there are several ways of interpreting quite different passages in the Old Testament. To begin with, adoption is clear in the case of Old Testament *quotations* which are often supplied with introductory formulas, *formulae quotationis* (e.g., καθὼς γέγραπται, γέγραπται γάρ, καθώς ἐστιν γεγραμμένον, λέγει γὰρ ἡ γραφή, καθὼς προείρηκεν Ἠσαΐας). But not only quotations emphasized formally in this way show the interpretation of the Old Testament by a New Testament author. We must, furthermore, consider *allusions*. These, however, cannot be verified as easily as quotations. It is not clear in every case whether we are dealing with a conscious allusion at all, or whether the religious and theological thinking of the New Testament author has been determined by the conceptual categories and the language of the Old Testament to such a degree that he employs its language unconsciously to express his own ideas. But the border between quotation and allusion is not sharply defined either; a decision is often very difficult and can only – if at all – be determined from the character of argumentation employed by the New Testament author.[3]

The *function* of quotations is particularly clear in the *Epistles* of the New Testament. There they support *theological argumentation*. Yet in this respect, every Epistle of the New Testament has a different character. This is even true for the authentic Epistles of *Paul*. In some Epistles (e.g., 1 Thessalonians) he includes either none or only very few Old Testament quotations, but in other Epistles (especially Galatians and Romans) the whole theological reasoning is based on the line of argumentation derived from Old Testament quotations. The argumentation of the *Deutero-Pauline Epistles*, however, is based much less on the Old Testament. The observation that theological argumentation utilizes Old Testament quotations quite differently poses the question as to how their purpose within the line of argumentation can be determined more closely. Are statements from the Old Testament intended to *prove* the New Testament kerygma? Given that the kerygma had already fully received its authority regarding content from what happened to the disciples on Easter, how is it possible that God's very own action, which is the salvation he accomplished in Christ, needs further proof from the Scripture? Or are statements from the Old Testament supposed to make the kerygma more fully *understandable* for Jews? In this case, Old Testament quotations would only have an educational or didactic purpose and would be improperly devaluated. The nature of these questions shows that proceeding in such an analytical way easily creates false alternatives. What is *phenomenologically* present is a special *combination of authorities* which hardly allows, or even prohibits altogether, the division of authority according to particular preferences. Scripture is, after all, simply the authoritative word of God which was written down. Scripture, therefore, has the *full authority of God* which is *not at all dependent on its having been written*. In the Old Testament, it is God who has spoken the word which already contains its messianic fulfilment. It is the authority of one and the same God who announces messianic salvation,

---

[3] Hübner, BThNT II, 13ff.

thus principally doing it already. Because the authorities of the Old Testament word of God and of the New Testament action of God are combined, this leads to a peculiar *coincidence of authorities*. This coincidence of authorities becomes even more complicated through the addition of yet another authority: the word of Jesus spoken with divine authority. Jesus, however, does not only speak with divine authority but, being the incarnation of the messianic fulfilment, *is* himself divine authority. Bestowed with divine authority and being himself divine authority, Jesus not only preaches the interpretation and fulfilment of the word of the Old Testament, but even annuls Old Testament regulations, thus relativizing by divine authority the written word of the divine law which had been proclaimed with divine authority. Yet at this point comprehension fails when we attempt to apply Western and Aristotelian logic.

The main problem centres, however, on the theological argumentation of the New Testament itself, which has basically rational features and is normally intended as a rationally comprehensible process. Yet this argumentation points beyond itself as rational theology, i. e., theology defined in terminology; it points to an ultimate which is much more than what is terminologically comprehensible, much more than a theological system with a number of definitions. It is the encounter of the human being with God which occurs through faith.

A look at the *Gospels* proves *mutatis mutandis* what has been said about the Pauline Epistles. A strong emphasis on argumentation cannot be neglected although the type of explanation is not particularly theological deduction. But the narratives of the evangelists are, in other words, *concrete illustrations* of theological ideas, also and especially of the *theology* of the particular portion of "the Old Testament received in the New", of the *Vetus Testamentum in Novo receptum*. Theological expression is presented only partially in theological terminology but, above all, in a particular narrative which is intended to express the theological intention of the evangelist. A fundamental conviction stands behind the narrative. A most succinct example is John 1:14; καὶ ὁ λόγος σάρξ ἐγένετο may be paraphrased as follows: And the God who transcends all time has become history in time. History, however, consists of concrete events occurring in time. Superior to time, the eternal God became subject to time, which was created together with the world, and became historical reality and comprehensible reality in time and history. Yet God's history in Jesus Christ has its prehistory in the history of Israel to which the Old Testament, having developed historically, belongs. This can be part of both the sermon of Jesus and the theological concepts of the Gospels' narratives about Jesus as Christ and Son of God.

2. Jewish and Christian Hermeneutics of the Old Testament

Usually Jewish parallels are given as a reference in order to characterize the interpretive methods and the hermeneutics of the New Testament authors regarding the Old Testament. In fact these parallels are obvious. The pesher method, used at Qumran and is especially extant in 1QpHab, is pointed to as an example to make the interpretation of the Old Testament in the New understandable. Parallels are noted between the allegorical interpretation of the Pentateuch by Philo of Alexandria and the similar approach taken by New Testament authors. Jewish parallels appear also with regard to typology. All of these parallels, however, are quite *formal*. Pointing to the rules of Hillel as examples of rabbinic interpretation of Scripture, which were supposedly also used by New Testament authors, may lead to the question of how rabbinic interpretation of Scripture was practiced at the time of Jesus or Paul. Whether statements of Rabbis dated in rabbinic writings to be prior to 70 CE, really go back to this time can hardly be verified.[4]

To understand the *characteristics* of how the New Testament authors dealt with Scripture it is advisable, particularly in view of the many uncertainties mentioned above, to analyze the New Testament *phenomenologically* by describing the approaches found in the New Testament. It is fundamental that the New Testament authors read the Scripture of Israel almost unanimously as the written fixing of the word of God who used this very word to announce the act of salvation in Jesus Christ. Hence the eschatological understanding of Scripture is admittedly similar to, for example, Qumran where Scripture was interpreted as the prophetic announcement of the time of salvation initiated there.[5] But what is crucial in the New Testament eschatological interpretation is the fact that by the christological understanding of Scripture it has been given a direction clearly different from Qumran or elsewhere in Judaism.[6] Everything depends on how strongly the importance of the *content* of the New Testament Christology is emphasized. There exists an analogous problem regarding elements of Old Testament and Jewish tradition which, on the one hand, in their addition constitute New Testament theology conceptually, but thereby, on the other hand, are pulled out of their original contexts. The nearly identical number of messianic terms in the Jewish PsSal 17 and, on the other hand, in Paul's writings or in Hebrews results in a *substantially* different concept of the Messiah. The conclusion to be drawn from this is that a mere comparison of terms, motives, methods of interpretation, etc., in the field of history of religion proves little in the face of content differences, because these differences – and everything depends on this! – are *theological* differences.

That the use of a single exegetical method is traceable in Judaism as well as in the New Testament may lead to a serious misinterpretation, when, for example, 1 Corinthians is supposed to be a parallel of the Jewish method of typology.[7] Rom 5:12 ff, on the other hand, shows a clear typology, the antithetically structured Adam-Christ-typology.

---

[4] See the critical opinion of J. NEUSNER, *The Rabbinic Traditions about the Pharisees before 70* I. *The Masters;* II. *The Houses;* III. *Conclusions* (Leiden 1971).

[5] See most recently H. STEGEMANN, *Die Essener, Qumran, Johannes der Täufer und Jesus* (Freiburg/Basel/Wien [4]1994) 172 ff, especially 172 f.

[6] Similarly critical is Koch, Die Schrift als Zeuge (1986) 202. A slightly different direction (a more positive opinion of the correspondence between Jewish and New Testament exegetical method) can be found in E. E. ELLIS, *The Old Testament in Early Christianity: Canon and Interpretation in the Light of Modern Research* (WUNT 54; Tübingen 1991) 77 ff.

[7] Hübner, BThNT II, 169 ff.

3. The Septuagint as (the) Holy Scripture of the New Testament Authors

The problem of the historical and theological relation of Old Testament and New Testament is, to a large extent, understood as the relation between the *Biblia Hebraica* and the *Novum Testamentum Graece*. It is symptomatic that in academic education, the Hebrew original text of the Old Testament receives a lot of attention in contrast to the *Septuagint*, the Greek translation produced in the Egyptian Alexandria. But during the process of translation a certain shift occurred toward Hellenistic thinking. Based on this translation, a considerable *Hellenizing of the Old Testament* cannot be denied, even if the extent may be debatable. In the Septuagint the spiritual attitude of Hellenistic Judaism in the diaspora is expressed; one may refer to its greater emphasis on universalism. N. WALTER has pointed out that the Hellenistic eschatology of early Judaism can be traced in non-biblical intertestamental writings as well as in those writings of the Old Testament exclusively appearing in the Septuagint.[8] In this connection, especially the *Wisdom of Solomon* (*Sapientia*) must be mentioned. Within the inner-biblical development toward Hellenism, it may be considered one of the final stages. Jews living within the religious and theological world of ideas of the Septuagint were practicing a form of piety which G. BERTRAM rightly called Septuagint piety. Furthermore, he correctly pointed out that through the Septuagint the Old Testament religion developed toward a *religion of the book*: no longer did temple, sacrificial cult, or priesthood occupy the center of piety, but the synagogue with its services of the word.[9] The existence of a specific Alexandrian canon also containing the so-called Apocrypha as, for instance, the Wisdom of Ben Sirah, or the Wisdom of Solomon, is disputed. Attempts to deny its existence totally are too extreme an opinion to be convincing. The solution might be to follow J. MAIER's suggestion of a *graded canonicity*: the Torah understood as the Pentateuch has the highest degree of canonical authority, while the Prophets have second priority. Since the so-called Writings had the lowest degree of authority, this body of texts was probably not as well-defined.[10] If, for example, the Wisdom of Solomon was counted among the "Writings", then it might not necessarily have been considered as inspired in a strict sense. But it certainly had a weakened canonical significance, even though in this context the word 'canonical' is already anachronistic. In this point, our terminology needs to remain vague because we have no criteria to produce precise definitions within this area. At that time, there was apparently no interest in determining the problem of canonicity in precise terminology.

It was this Greek Bible with its lack of definitions just mentioned, it was this Hellenistically biased *Septuagint* which must be seen – in spite of a few,

[8] Walter, Hellenistische Eschatologie (1985) 331 ff. He uses the following topics for exemplification: 1. God's eternity (God and time); 2. heavenly world – heavenly Jerusalem; 3. judgement after death, immortality of the soul?; 4. relation of the world – relation of history.

[9] G. BERTRAM, "Septuaginta-Frömmigkeit", RGG V (1961) 1707–09.

[10] Maier, JBTh 3 (1988) 137 f; Hübner, BThNT I, 46 ff, particularly 50 f.

yet important exceptions – as the *Bible of the New Testament authors*. This remains valid even though R. HANHART rightly emphasizes that we should consider the Septuagint as being continuously reviewed in terms of correspondence with its Hebrew original, a process also reflected in the quotations of the New Testament.[11] In the Church and at theological faculties, we should hence be much more aware of the fact that the holy Scripture of the New Testament authors was not the *Biblia Hebraica*. It is clear that this insight will also have consequences for the education in Old Testament at universities, *Kirchlichen Hochschulen*, Theological Seminaries, and colleges. Of course in these institutions, the texts of the Hebrew original will need to remain the object of academic studies. Studying biblical writings without a solid command of the Hebrew language would be irresponsible. But in addition, it is essential to include also the books of the Septuagint in academic studies! Only by enhancing the awareness that the Septuagint is the *primarily* relevant Old Testament for the New Testament can we avoid creating phantasms in our efforts to interprete the New Testament.

4. Theological Treatment of the Old Testament by Individual New Testament Authors

Due to the limited scope of this study, it is impossible to present comprehensively the reception of the Old Testament by the New Testament authors – unless our intention would be merely to accumulate raw numbers. But our previous analyses have shown that the process of the Old Testament's reception by the New was a genuinely *theological* process. Hence, the presentation of its essential features requires that the most important New Testament writings be examined as to how Old Testament passages have been adopted theologically. Selected examples will be used to make the process of reception understandable. This procedure will help to illustrate the overall theological profile to the New Testament in light of the topic of this study.

For the New Testament authors the Scripture of Israel was not the *Old* Testament. The correct formulation can only be: the New Testament authors were theologically dealing with the Scripture of Israel which for them *exclusively* was holy Scripture and, thus, the literal word of God announcing Christ by divine authority. The Scripture of Israel, however, became "the Old Testament received in the New" through the process of its reception by the New Testament authors, as mentioned above. Hence, the Scripture of Israel received a *new quality* and *became* the *Old* Testament for the Church of Jesus Christ. For this theological reason and because it has become customary in the Christian Church, we will use the term Old Testament and its reception. Yet we need to be mindful of the fact that we are employing an abbreviated and not completely appropriate term. This is so because we express an *historical* process *theologically* in an anachronistic fashion, from the perspective

[11] Hanhart, Bedeutung der Septuaginta (1984) 400ff.

of later dogmatics which are, nonetheless, binding for Christians. Theologically understood, this historical process can be very complex. On the one hand, there can be no doubt about the fundamental character of the christological interpretation of the holy Scripture. On the other hand, the reception of it may vary considerably owing to particular historical circumstances and according to different theological intentions of the individual New Testament author. Paul, for example, modified his theological argumentation based on the Old Testament significantly due to different personal situations and changing congregational circumstances. Hence, it is impossible to speak about a *single* theological treatment of the Old Testament by the apostle. It is, therefore, not surprising that studies on Paul arrive at different conclusions regarding his interpretation and reception of Scripture.

4.1. Paul

Paul quotes some Old Testament passages more than once: We must therefore distinguish between how many times Paul actually *quotes* from a book of the Old Testament and how many times he simply refers to the same Old Testament passages. In his monograph *Die Schrift als Zeuge des Evangeliums*, D.-A. Koch presents the best and most solidly founded survey of Paul's quotations. His review of how quotations are distributed by individual books of the Old Testament[12] is already informative as such and can almost be regarded as a commentary on the apostle's use of Scripture.

In the following, the first number refers to the number of references, the second number refers to the number of actual passages quoted: Isaiah 28 (25); Psalms 20 (20); Deuteronomy 15 (13); Genesis 15 (12); Exodus 5 (5); Hosea 4 (3); Leviticus 4 (2); Proverbs 3 (3); 3 Kings 2 (2); Job 2 (2); Habakkuk 2 (1); Malachi 1 (1); Joel 1 (1); furthermore 4 (3) quotations which cannot be identified with certainty. Against Koch's opinion, 1 Cor 1:31 and 2 Cor 10:17 contain short quotations of Jer 9:22f.[13] If H. St. J. Thackeray were right in assuming Bar 3:9–4:4 to be a sermon on Jer 8:13–9:23 on the occasion of the ninth of Ab, the day of the destruction of the temple, then 'Baruch' and Paul would be preaching on the same text![14] In this case, however, taking the common rhetorical field of Jeremiah, Baruch and 1 Corinthians into consideration, and Baruch being adopted in 1 Cor 1:18 ff, then Paul's abbreviated version of the Jeremian text would appear in a new light. Then the abbreviated version of the quotation would be a summary of the three texts. It might be assumed that in quoting the prophet Jeremiah, Paul uses only a shortened version. Prior to this, however, he already employs the full context of the quotation, again using the phrasing of Baruch. In doing so he borrows both ideas and terms from the 'secretary' of the prophet.[15]

Clearly the *Book of Isaiah* ranks first among the books which Paul quotes. Quotations from Isaiah and the Psalms account for almost half of all scriptural quotations in the authentic Pauline writings. The theological importance of Isaiah for Romans will be discussed later.

---

[12] Koch, Die Schrift als Zeuge (1986) 33.
[13] Against Koch, ibid. 35 f.
[14] H. St. J. Thackeray, *The Septuagint and Jewish Worship* (London 1921).
[15] Hübner, "Der vergessene Baruch", *Biblische Theologie als Hermeneutik* (1995) 155–65; see in addition, idem, BThNT II, 116, n. 242.

As the earliest New Testament author, Paul is the representative of the living word, that is, of the spoken word. Therefore, confronted with the adverse circumstances that make it impossible for him to visit his congregations in person, he actually considers his letters an insufficient medium of proclamation and exhortation. In some of his Epistles, especially in Galatians and in Romans, Paul's theological line of argumentation is materially based on the Old Testament, whereas in other Epistles the Old Testament presents only the horizon of his language and thought. Facing this fact the question may be asked as to the nature of Paul's reception of the Old Testament, when he was preaching either as a missionary or to the congregations he had already established. This question, however, is difficult to answer. Opinions are divided as to whether it was Paul's missionary strategy to appear in synagogues in order to preach the gospel of the Messiah, not only to the Jews, but in particular to proselytes and so-called God-fearers. In his Acts of the Apostles, Luke portrays it this way; yet, for important reasons, it is more likely that this is his theologically motivated redaction. To Luke the continuous development from Israel toward the Church is of great import, and the way in which he depicts Paul's mission precisely fits this theological intention. But if it is more likely that Paul proclaimed the kerygma of passion and Easter to *Gentiles* then we may assume that in *this* type of sermon, the Old Testament was not too important. Yet it is probable that there were *also* so-called God-fearers among Paul's gentile audience. It is, after all, significant that Paul consulted the Old Testament only indirectly in, for example, 1 Thessalonians, an epistle to a congregation consisting mainly of gentile Christians.

This leads to an explanation of Paul's varying usage of the Old Testament in his theological argumentation in the Epistles. He especially employs the Old Testament in a conspiciously formal manner if judaizing tendencies (that Christianity is merely messianically completed Judaism) became a threat to his congregations as, for example, especially in Galatia. Following this hypothesis does not at all imply, as put forth by H. ULONSKA, that Paul quotes the Old Testament merely for opportunistic reasons against his Jewish opponents, without actually intending arguments of this kind. Paul is very serious about his theological strategy wherever he consults the Old Testament. For him, the Old Testament is the word of *God* which he, indeed, by virtue of the Holy Spirit bestowed upon him by God, understands as the word of God in messianic promises.

The problem is, however, even more complicated because Paul consults the Old Testament as the authoritative word of God especially in order to challenge the redemptive function of the Mosaic law, the *Torah*. To put it even more simply and dramatically, Scripture itself, γραφή, annuls an integral part of itself, the law, the νόμος. γραφή? Yes! νόμος? No! This must sound like a blasphemy for every Jew and for every judaistically oriented Jewish Christian since the Torah is the theological substance and, what is more, the virtual authority of Scripture. It is no exaggeration to say that for Jews, the holy Scripture derives its authority from the Torah. For the Jew, the essence of Scripture is the Torah.

More precisely, Paul supports the abrogation of the law only in a very specific sense: it is impossible to be justified through the works of the law. In *Gal 2:16*, following literally *ψ 142:2* (= Ps 143:2), he states programmatically: ἐξ ἔργων νόμου οὐ δικαιωθήσεται πᾶσα σάρξ, "no none is ever justified by doing what the law requires"; for the justification gained through the salvation of Christ occurs "through faith alone", διὰ πίστεως. ψ 142:2 does not, however, display the words ἐξ ἔργων νόμου crucial for Paul. But the entire Psalm, and thus also the context of v. 2, *lends itself to the interpretation* of the Pauline theology of justification.[16] This shows in particular how Paul could adopt Old Testament passages for central issues of his theological argumentation in such a way that the christological understanding of Old Testament passages *does not mean denying*, but *expanding* its original meaning. Thus Paul places the Old Testament passage with its genuinely literal meaning in a *larger, qualitatively different, theological grid*. The original literal meaning is not negated, but newly understood within the new situation of salvation, and thus within a newly created reality. What needs to be stressed is that in Gal 2:16, Paul consults the Old Testament in a proper fashion to express his own theological program. In terms of this important point of his theology, Paul stands in a direct line with the Old Testament tradition – *provided* the *fundamental hermeneutical principle* is taken seriously that a phrase uttered for the first time in a certain historical situation can never again be understood in exactly the same way when adopted anew in different historical situations. Understanding will always occur anew in new situations. A phrase cannot be separated from its *Wirkungsgeschichte*, its *effective history*.[17] It is the indispensible task of the theological-hermeneutical reflection to determine the *relation* of *continuity* – without which the Church would lose its identity – and *modification* – without which the church would deny its history – anew in each historical situation. History is the result of the course of historical situations and can only be understood as such.

Let us further examine the specific problem of Paul's use of Scripture, in reference to the theology of Galatians, more precisely, to yet another Old Testament quotation in this Epistle. The precondition of Gal 2:16 is that no one can actually do what is required by the law. Regarding this issue, Paul quotes in *Gal 3:10* the conclusion of the Deuteronomic Dodecalogue in *Deut 27:26*. But the quotation is no longer rendered in a sense consistent with the Old Testament literal meaning. The sentence in Deuteronomy 27 presents the conclusion of the Dodecalogue and imposes a curse on anyone failing to comply with its regulations. In the original Hebrew text of Deut 27:26, the Dodecalogue is expected to be obeyed; so the curse is intended to prevent the Israelite from infringement. Yet Paul quotes Deut 27:26 according to the slightly different version of the Septuagint, saying that *everyone*, πᾶς, is cursed who does not obey *everything* written in the book of the law, πᾶσιν τοῖς γεγραμμένοις. But particularly πᾶς and πᾶσιν have no equivalent in the Hebrew original! Paul introduces the quotation with the statement that

16 Hübner, BThNT II, 64 ff.

17 Regarding the term 'effective history', see H.-G. Gadamer, *Wahrheit und Methode* (Tübingen [5]1986) 284 ff.

whoever derives his existence from the works of the law is under the curse. For him, Deut 27:26 LXX provides the evidence. Against its original meaning, the quotation thus says that *no one* obeys the *entire* law; consequently *everyone* is under the curse and, therefore, dependent on salvation. The 'dogmatic' premise is being either *totally* obedient or being cursed. *Tertium non datur*!

Anyone who has even a limited knowledge of historical Judaism will notice at once that it is improperly portrayed by such an all-or-nothing understanding. Paul's interpretation of Deut 27:26 shows that he could not have all of the contemporaneous Judaism in mind. Does he simply characterize a Jewish minority and then project the image onto the whole of Judaism? By no means should we assume that Paul wants to present an intentionally distorted image of the religious thinking of Judaism. His understanding of Deut 27:26 was probably determined by several factors: 1. Paul comes from a rigorous branch of Judaism which demanded extremely radical obedience of the Torah. From there the theological opinion expressed in Gal 3:10 seems not too distant. 2. Paul takes the Septuagint text of Deut 27:26 with the double πᾶς very seriously. 3. Even more decisive might have been that Paul had to rethink fundamentally the function of the law after his Damascus-road experience. Rigorous about the Torah before his vocation (Gal 1:13f), he had been persecuting Jewish Christians because of their liberal views regarding the Torah; but his conversion must have taught him to see the *total* and strict obedience of the Torah, which until then he had required from himself, as a wrong track. His past understanding of the law and, thus, his past religious life were not only wrong, but even against God. These three factors together show how the interpretation of Deut 27:26 in Gal 3:10, although initially strange, is a result of biographical conditions and theological reflections. After the Damascus-road experience Paul sees himself as inspired by God's Spirit. By virtue of his pneumatic state he can now read and comprehend the *actual* contents of Scripture. For him, this new *understanding of Scripture and law* results in a radically new *self-understanding*. This is a hermeneutical circle: bestowed with the Spirit, Paul reads Scripture anew and *interpretes* it anew.[18] Bestowed with the Spirit, however, he simultaneously reads Scripture in a way which allows him to *understand* the Christ event anew. Once more the circular movement is caused by the combination of the authorities of kerygma and Scripture which has been mentioned above. The *kerygma* leads to a new understanding of Scripture – *Scripture* leads to a deeper understanding of the kerygma. In the context of this complicated hermeneutical process Scripture, being the written word of God's promise, gains theological predominance over the law. For Paul, the law is now paradoxically the word of promise and, at the same time, the realm of slavish existence. Only by remembering Paul's hermeneutics, are we prevented from understanding this paradox as a contradiction and *circulus vitiosus*.

---

[18] E. Käsemann, "Geist und Buchstabe", idem, *Paulinische Perspektiven* (Tübingen 1969) 237–85.

Due to the fact that the context of his theology of justification is so multidimensional, Paul's statements about the law can be paradoxical. Symptomatic is Paul's double way of talking about the "whole law". On the one hand, one is not allowed to be circumcised because one would be obliged to obey the *whole* law, ὅλον τὸν νόμον ποιῆσαι; thus according to Gal 5:3f, grace would be lost because being totally obedient to the law would contradict the dogma of Gal 3:10. This is a rejection of the claim that the basis of justification is the *quantitatively* complete fulfilment of the law. But on the other hand, Paul still sees the one single commandment to love one's neighbor in *Lev 19:18* as the fulfilment of the whole law, as Gal 5:14 says: ὁ γὰρ *πᾶς* νόμος. It is clear that here "the *whole* law" is simply not identical with the law fulfilled in a numerical or quantitative way. The *one* commandment as the *whole* law refers to the Christian existence in the Holy Spirit. Our moral action is the *consequence* of the fruit (singular!) of the Spirit (Gal 5:22). Paul then lists a number of "virtues" of which love, ἀγάπη, is characteristically among the first (see Lev 19:18!). These virtues are concrete expressions of the Christian existence which is understood as unity.

Though limited, our considerations on Galatians show how biographical circumstances and Christian existence have their specific self-understanding and, resulting from both, theological reflexion which takes furthermore into account the individual situation of the addressee. This leads to a complicated combination of explanations for Paul's theological treatment of the Old Testament and, thus, for his theological and existential interpretation of Scripture.

These observations may, further, be confirmed by examples from the *Epistle to the Romans*. It is no exaggeration to say that the proper understanding of the Epistle requires an intensive study of the *Septuagint*: first Genesis, Deuteronomy, and Psalms, but then in particular Deutero- and Trito-Isaiah. To a large extent, the *theology* of Romans is the result of the encounter with the Old Testament. It is not simply a continuation of Galatians' theology of justification, but a clear correction of essential issues of its theological argumentation. The path from Galatians to Romans is characterized by both continuity and discontinuity. Continuity results from the conviction maintained in both Epistles of the central significance of justification by faith alone without the works of the law. Discontinuity, on the other hand, results from a modified understanding of the Mosaic law and from a new attitude to the Israelite people. Hence, Romans presents the faith in the justification *sola gratia et sola fide* in the *framework of a new theological thinking*. It appears as though Paul himself takes seriously the reactions of Jewish Christians in Jerusalem regarding the Epistle to the Galatians which they understood antinomistically and as hostile to Israel, be this interpretation legitimate or not. Paul attempts to cope with, and answer these problems by means of newly reading in particular Deutero- and Trito-Isaiah.[19] Especially Romans 9–11 shows that by intensively studying Scripture and thus gaining a deeper com-

[19] Hübner, BThNT II, 26–346, especially 30ff and 239ff.

prehension of Isaiah, Paul arrives at a new theological answer to the problem of Israel which distinctively differs from negative statements in earlier Epistles (1 Thess 2:14–16; Gal 4:21–31). In Scripture, Paul does *not* discover anew – and this must be rigorously emphasized – the fundamental conviction of justification by faith alone. But what he *introduces* is the *theological* concept which now appears as the *framework* of his faith of justification. This new theological concept is the result of his reading the Book of Isaiah.

Indeed, in Isaiah the apostle continuously reads about God's δικαιοσύνη. There he finds statements about the δικαιωθῆναι achieved by God, about God's σωτηρία, and about Israel's πιστεύειν. There he finds all of his *theological vocabulary*. He has been stressing justification before in some of his Epistles. Therefore, reading in Isaiah about *God's* justification as saving justification, he must have understood these statements in the light of his faith in Christ. Whoever takes the effort to read Isaiah with the eyes of the apostle, constantly coming across theologically important terms also central to other Pauline Epistles, will understand how Paul must have seen this Old Testament book. Contrary to his previous understanding, the apostle now reads that God, out of justice, wants salvation for all of Israel. In part employing sophisticated rhetoric and a line of exegetical argumentation which does not need to be presented here in detail, Paul leads his readers to the insight that God will save *all* of Israel (Rom 11:26, πᾶς 'Ισραὴλ σωθήσεται). Exactly this idea he might have adopted from Isaiah (Isa 45:25, ἀπὸ κυρίου δικαιωθήσονται καὶ ἐν τῷ θεῷ ἐνδοξασθήσονται πᾶν τὸ σπέρμα τῶν υἱῶν 'Ισραήλ).

This example shows very clearly that, above all, we need to consider questions of *content* in order to understand Paul's theological treatment of the Old Testament. Our conviction mentioned above has been confirmed that parallels from the history of religion are only of secondary value with regard to exegetical methods. Indisputably they help to comprehend certain facts more precisely. But what is actually important lies beyond the perspective of these formal categories. Of course we do not intend to deny the mutual correlation of *forma* and *materia* which determine each other. But one priority must be pointed out: Paul's understanding of Scripture is determined to a large extent by the content of Scripture. Therefore, whoever talks about Paul and the Old Testament must talk about Paul's reception of the Old Testament with regard to its content. In terms of content, the difference and identity between Old Testament (*Vetus Testamentum*) and Old Testament as received by Paul (*Vetus Testamentum a Paulo receptum*) must be determined.

Rom 1:16f, the theological heading of Romans, may serve as an illustration of a further characteristic of Paul's consulting the Old Testament. The apostle says that he is not ashamed of the gospel since it is "the power of God unto salvation", δύναμις θεοῦ εἰς σωτηρίαν. Paul does not give an Old Testament reference for this statement, even though there would be sufficient instances as, for example, ψ 67:12 (Ps 68:12) κύριος δώσει ῥῆμα τοῖς εὐαγγελιζομένοις δυνάμει πολλῇ, or ψ 139:8 (Ps 140:8), κύριε κύριε, δύναμις τῆς σωτηρίας σου. But, even though the Psalms are very familiar to him and it is quite certain that he has this association in mind when making a statement like Rom 1:16, Paul does not refer to the Psalms. We may assume that this association was unnecessary for his theological argumentation to the Romans. At this point he must have seen himself in accordance with all of the Christian groups in Rome. But Rom 1:17 is different. Once more, Paul provides grounds for his argumentation: The gospel is δύναμις θεοῦ because in it the δικαιοσύνη θεοῦ is revealed – perhaps ἀποκαλύπτεται is medium: the justice of God reveals itself in the gospel – and this happens ἐκ πίστεως εἰς πίστιν. At the decisive point of argumentation which has a programmatic function for the whole Epistle, the sequence of grounds, so far characterized through repeated γάρ, is now lead on with a quotation from Scripture – the first in Romans! That the revelation of God's justice in the powerful gospel for humans occurs by faith and only by faith – it is just this Paul needs to support by grounds from Scripture in the course of his theological argumentation. This is why he now quotes *Hab 2:4* which must be translated: "The one who is just by faith – *he* will live!" The polemical emphasis cannot be overheard: against the denial of his gospel free from the law, Paul wants to point out the divine sanctioning of justification by faith alone. Right at this programmatic point which determines the topic, he presents the Old Testament basis, *Hab 2:4*, which in his opinion is decisive for the faith of justification. In Galatians, this quotation was only one among many others in the line of argumentation of the Epistle (Gal 3:11 in 3:1–5:12). It should be noticed carefully that in Rom 1:16f the law is particularly not mentioned – even though Romans deals with Paul's defence against the accusation of antinomism! Rom 3:20 and, even earlier, Gal 2:16 refer to ψ 142:2 (= Ps 143,2) to prove that the works of the law cannot justify. But Paul does not consult the Old Testament to prove that the law, according to Rom 7:12,14, is holy and spiritual, ἅγιος, πνευματικός. Again the explanation seems plausible that this issue was not disputed in Rome, at least not in the group of Roman Christians who considered themselves faithful to the law.

Still another way of Paul's dealing with Scripture must be pointed out. In the *argumentatio* of the Epistle, Paul first speaks of the *becoming* of a Christian through justification by grace and faith alone, Rom 3:21f. Chapter 8 depicts the *being* of the Christian in the Spirit. For the 'dogmatic' section Rom 3:21–26 (31), chapter 4 functions as the proof from Scripture. Interestingly enough, though, Paul does not present a proof from Scripture for the pneumatic being of the Christian. New Testament researchers have not yet paid enough attention to the observation that Romans 8, in particular Rom 8:2–17, exudes an entirely Old Testament spirit. *Ezekiel 36 and 37* stand behind this section which may be looked upon as a short summary of a theological anthropology.[20] Similarities between Paul and Ezekiel are striking: 1. God gives the Spirit to human beings who are to be saved. 2. God thus renews these human beings and liberates them from their inability to be obedient by their own efforts. 3. The bestowal of the Spirit appears in the context of the law; the purpose is to realize what is intended by the law. Regarding content, the Pauline φρόνημα/φρονεῖν also covers what Ezekiel

---

[20] Hübner, BThNT II, 301ff.

says.[21] 4. Both mention life in the context of Spirit and law. Ezek 37:5 reads πνεῦμα ζωῆς, Ezek 37:14 δώσω πνεῦμά μου εἰς ὑμᾶς, καὶ ζήσεσθε. Paul talks about the νόμος τοῦ πνεύματος τῆς ζωῆς in Rom 8:2, about ζωὴ καὶ εἰρήνη as resulting from φρόνημα τοῦ πνεύματος in Rom 8:6, and in Rom 8:13 about the actions of a Christian through the Spirit with the consequence: ζήσεσθε. 5. Ezekiel and Paul view their respective soteriological ideas in an ecclesiological framework. 6. Ezekiel and Paul view their respective community of salvation as an eschatological community. In the face of these similarities, it does not need to be mentioned in particular that there also are clear differences between the two. Above all, it must be emphasized that Ezekiel does not know the christological framework and that, furthermore, resurrection for Ezekiel is an image for the spiritual reality of this earth, occurring in the course of history, whereas for Paul, it is the event of the last day. Finally, the prophet is aiming for the spiritual restoration of Israel, but Paul for the salvation of all humankind.

Regarding the *whole Bible*, the following point is relevant: just as Ezekiel 36 and 37 is one of the theologically most significant texts of the Old Testament, so Romans 8 is the theologically most significant text of the New Testament. At the end of his theological career, Paul writes his most mature theological work, the Epistle to the Romans. At this climax he consults one of the highpoints of Old Testament prophetic proclamation. But he does this without presenting a formal quotation. This peculiar fact is open for, and calls for interpretation. Here we avoid a hypothetical explanation.

Paul's statements about his basic hermeneutic conviction – 1 Cor 9:9f; 11:11; Rom 4:23f; 15:4 – express what the individual examples have explicated.

4.2. *The Synoptic Gospels and the Acts of the Apostles*

The premise of the following remarks on how the synoptics use Scripture is the two-source hypothesis: among the three Gospels, the Gospel of Mark is the oldest, written appr. 70 CE. It is the literary *Vorlage* of Matthew and Luke who completed and reworked theologically the Gospel of Mark independently after 80 CE. Apparently both drew upon a different version of the 'sayings source' Q. Whether or not we consider these synoptic Gospels as theological writings depends on our definition of theology. At least we can say that each of the three synoptics had an individual *theological concern* which they expressed in their particular form of their Jesus narrative. In this sense, it is legitimate to talk about the *theology of each synoptic*.[22] What obtains for Paul and most of the authors of the other New Testament Epistles also holds true, *mutatis mutandis*, for the synoptics. Ignoring the meaning and significance of their Old Testament quotations and allusions would make each

---

[21] Of course in Rom 8:4, Paul's τὸ δικαίωμα τοῦ νόμου has a more precise meaning than Ezekiel's statements about the law.

[22] See most recently A. Weiser, *Theologie des Neuen Testaments,* II. *Die Theologie der Evangelien* (KStTh 8; Stuttgart 1993).

theology seem incomprehensible and without substance. Pauline theology is to a large extent kerygmatically inspired theology of the Old Testament, and the same holds true for the theology of the synoptics.

4.2.1. The Gospel of Mark

We cannot consider highly enough the fact that the Gospel of Mark starts with an Old Testament quotation which, as a fulfilment quotation, is the theological heading of the oldest Gospel. The meaning of Hab 2:4 as the theological heading of Romans (Rom 1:16f) is paralleled by the mixed quotation of *Isa 40:3 LXX / Mal 3:1 / Exod 23:20 in Mark 1:2f. Hence, the whole Gospel is oriented toward this one fulfilment quotation*. According to Mark 1:1–4 John the Baptist appeared "in the desert" (!) – actually a senseless detail regarding his activity of baptizing. This statement, however, acquires meaning if ἐν τῇ ἐρήμῳ, a literal reception of Isa 40:3, is not understood as a geographical but as a theological statement referring to the first events of the Gospel.[23] The prophet 'Isaiah' – hence for Mark, Deutero-Isaiah has an importance as theologically constitutive as for Paul in Romans! – has written the beginning of the Gospel, ἀρχὴ τοῦ εὐαγγελίου Ἰησοῦ Χριστοῦ.[24] The introductory formula καθὼς γέγραπται certainly expresses the reference to Scripture. But expressing events from the Gospel, holy Scripture has evangelical character. To say it radically: the prophet Isaiah is evangelist because he expresses the *evangelical* event. Therefore Mark's referring to the literal word is the evangelist's reference to the prophetic evangelist who wrote down his oral proclamation only because he had to preserve it for future generations. Hence, the evangelist Mark refers to God's word of evangelical promise itself. One can say that *in the word of God, past and present encounter each other; in the word of God, Old and New Testament encounter each other*. Thus for Mark, the Old Testament is less 'old' than for Paul. Recognizing a pattern of promise and fulfilment in the Gospel of Mark, the fulfilment takes priority over the promise from the perspective of the receiver of the promise, thus *from the human perspective*. Yet *from the divine perspective*, that is, from the perspective of the activity of the word of God, such an emphasis is senseless since it would mean a devaluation of the word of the promise.

It is, furthermore, εὐαγγέλιον, a considerable reduction of the term 'gospel', if we suppose that it only refers to an oral form. The beginning of the Gospel of Jesus Christ – in the perspective of the theological opinion of Mark, the genitive Ἰησοῦ Χριστοῦ can be both *objective genitive* and *subjective genitive* – is actually the *event* of the Baptist's appearance. And it would be a further reduction of the theological content of Mark 1:1 if ἀρχὴ τοῦ εὐαγγελίου would be understood 'only' as the beginning which is followed by the actual events, for the *beginning* includes the whole! After all, the first quotation includes one of the most important theological key words of Mark:

---

[23] W. Marxsen, *Der Evangelist Markus: Studien zur Redaktionsgeschichte des Evangeliums* (FRLANT 49; Göttingen [2]1959) 20ff.

[24] Despite the opinion expressed in Nestle-Aland's 26th edition, υἱοῦ θεοῦ is secondary.

ὁδὸς κυρίου. Important for Mark's *theologia crucis*, the way of the Lord is the way to Jerusalem (cf., e.g., Mark 10:32, ἐν τῇ ὁδῷ ἀναβαίνοντες εἰς Ἰεροσόλυμα).[25] The messenger of the first quotation, identical with John the Baptist, prepares the Lord's way of the cross and even walks ahead of him (Mark 1:14; 9:11–13). Therefore John's life and death are symbolic for the very events of the Gospel of Jesus Christ; he belongs to the prophetical and simultaneously to the fulfilled gospel.

Thus we cannot overestimate the theological importance of the fulfilment quotations in Mark 1:2f. In the context of Mark 1:1 and 1:4, this quotation is the gospel *in nuce* because the ἀρχή implies the whole salvation. But still, the evangelist can surpass Mark 1:1–4. In *Mark 1:9–11 God himself 'quotes' his word* written in Scripture. And on the occasion of the baptism of Jesus, God himself addresses him with the words of *ψ 2:7*, "You are my son". And God himself 'interprets' this address with words of the evangelist prophet : "the beloved (son), in whom I am (well) pleased", *Isa 42:1* (using words from Jer 38:20 LXX). If in Paul's case, we speak about a theology of the word, then the same can be said about Mark's theology.

Isa 42:1, however, addresses the *servant of the Lord* although not using the words of Isaiah 53. Also God's addressing his Son at the baptism must be understood in the context of the Markan *theologia crucis*. This is sufficiently clear from the fact that already the fulfilment quotation in Mark 1:2f alludes to the way of the cross of Jesus. Further allusions are Mark 9:7 and 15:39; both instances must be seen in the perspective of Mark 1:11. In *Mark 9:7*, God addresses the disciples directly but, once more, using words of Ps 2:7. Here the reference to the events of Good Friday and Easter as announced in Mark 8:31 is unambiguous. Peter, in particular, is asked not to resist the passion of Jesus: ἀκούετε αὐτοῦ! Here, different from Mark 1:11, the messianic verse of the Psalm quoted by God himself is clearly applied to the events of the crucifixion and Easter. And in *Mark 15:39* the centurion – a pagan speaking in a Gospel addressing pagan Christians! – confirms that Jesus was the Son of God. His words are a human resonance of faith to the words of God in Mark 1:11 and 9:7. Mark 9:7 and 15:39 do not mention the Son of Man. But in Mark 8:31, the (Markan) Jesus presents the authentic interpretation of Peter's messianic confession – Peter, of course, does not understand his own confession! – hence, the statement about the Son of Man who will suffer and rise constitutes authoritatively the connection between Christ and the Son of Man. Yet the centurion's acknowledgement of the Son of God is motivated by the crucified Jesus, although his understanding is based on the sign in the temple.

According to Mark, however, there is no *theologia crucis* without *theologia resurrectionis*, therefore not without *theologia gloriae*! Already in Mark 8:31 the Son of Man is seen as the resurrected one. So the question of the high priest in Mark 14:61 whether Jesus is the Christ, the Son of the Blessed, is answered in *Mark 14:62* by Jesus with words from *Dan 7:14* and *Ps 110:1*,

[25] See H.-J. Steichele, *Der leidende Sohn Gottes: Eine Untersuchung einiger alttestamentlicher Motive in der Christologie des Markusevangeliums* (BU 14; Regensburg 1980) 79f.

after the introductory ἐγώ εἰμι which might be an application of the Yahweh-statement "I am" (Exod 3:14). According to Daniel 7, Jesus is, as the Son of Man, the apocalyptic judge. In this connection, also *Mark 12:36* with its quotation of Ps 110:1 / *ψ 109:1* (literally LXX) must be mentioned. Thus we see that the whole of Mark's Christology is a 'compilation' of Old Testament terminology and quotations, but yet it is something totally new beyond a mere concatenation of these terms and quotations.

The basic theological concept of the *theologia crucis* which, from the perspective of the *theologia gloriae*, is introduced contrapunctually, is most closely linked to the so-called messianic secret. Even though differently interpreted in theological research, it undisputedly determines the structure of the Gospel of Mark. Interesting for this study is the fact that also the messianic secret and its constitutive motive of the misunderstanding disciples is characterized by quotations from and allusions to Scripture as, for example, Jer 5:21 in Mark 8:18 (see, however, Isa 6:9f in Mark 4:11f where, in the so-called parable theory, about the disciples the contrary of Mark 8:18 is stated).[26]

Mark 7:15 is an *authentic word of Jesus*. Exercising radical criticism of the law, Jesus here annuls the Mosaic food regulations, however conspicuously without a genuine quotation from Scripture. Also authentic is the reference of Jesus to the *fourth commandment in Exod 20:12 and Deut 5:16* opposing the inhuman regulations of the qorban.[27]

4.2.2. The Gospel of Matthew

Regarding its basic concept, the Gospel of Mark is more determined by the Old Testament than generally assumed. The Gospel of Matthew, however, is indisputably the synoptic writing whose theological concept is specifically expressed in its Old Testament quotations. But especially Matthew's reception of the Old Testament is widely debated with regard to its theological significance. An agreement is not yet in sight, not even about the question whether Matthew is a Jewish-Christian (so, e.g., G. Bornkamm, R. Hummel) or a pagan-Christian writing (so, e.g., G. Strecker). It is also under dispute whether the extensive usage of the Old Testament goes back to the evangelist or an exegetical school (K. Stendahl).

The beginning of the discussion is, however, clear. It starts with the study of the *formula quotations* (*Reflexionszitate* which more recently are rather called *fulfilment quotations* according to W. Rothfuchs). They are usually introduced by the introductory formula ἵνα πληρωθῇ τὸ ῥηθὲν ὑπὸ κυρίου διὰ τοῦ προφήτου λέγοντες (Matt 1:22f; 2:6; 2:15; 2:17; 2:23; 4:14–16; 8:17; 12:17–21; 13:35; 21:5; 26:31; 27:9f). These introductory formulae express the theological program of the evangelist. But they need further interpretation. If we assume that the Christ event with its soteriological intention (Matt

---

[26] H. Räisänen, *Die Parabeltheorie im Markusevangelium* (SESJ 26; Helsinki 1973).

[27] Regarding Mark 7 in general, see Hübner, Das Gesetz in der synoptischen Tradition (1986) 142ff.

1:21) occurred *in order to* fulfil Scripture, this might be understood as if this event only occurred *because* of its announcement in the Old Testament which, then, would have the primary theological authority. Yet such a theological program – the New Testament for the sake of the Old Testament – is not in accordance with the overall intention of Matthew. The manner of arbitrarily and violently subjecting the Old Testament wording to the Christ event already asks for a different interpretation. Obviously the Old Testament was read in view of which parts of it could be interpreted and claimed as prophecy of Jesus' activity and fate with respect to its fulfilment by Christ. In his quotations, Matthew generally pays little or no attention to the Old Testament context or the literal meaning. This has even led to the assumption that the evangelist has no interest in the overall fulfilment of Scripture in Jesus, but is rather concerned about the fulfilment of single Old Testament passages in details of the life of Jesus (PH. VIELHAUER).[28] But this hypothesis is overstated. Also the term '*allegorese*' does not appropriately describe Matthew's methodological approach. The evangelist, after all, claims to understand the Old Testament text in nothing but its literal meaning; he does not show any allegorical intention. At the most we may ask whether the evangelist's approach sometimes is *typological* as, for instance, in Matt 2:15 where he quotes Hos 11:1: as the Son of God, Jesus has typologically superceeded Israel which was the first son of God.[29] As already in our approach to Paul, however, also in view of Matthew it might be better no to use any predetermined methodological terminology. We should, instead, focus on how the theological intention is expressed in the language employed by the evangelist himself. A programmatic phrasing occurs in *Matt 26:56*: ἵνα πληρωθῶσιν αἱ γραφαὶ τῶν προφητῶν. These words, in a certain sense, sum up the specific introductory formulae of the individual fulfilment quotations in a general manner and represent the *theological motto of the Gospel of Matthew*. All of the fulfilment quotations are, after all, quotations of prophets (only Matt 13:35 quotes Ps 78:2, in part according to LXX; but characteristically the evangelist sees also this reference as a prophetical promise: διὰ τοῦ προφήτου λέγοντες!). Thus the Christ event is the *fulfilment of the prophetic promises*.

What is characteristic – and therefore widely debated – about the fulfilment quotations is the fact that, contrary to most of the other quotations in Matthew, they do *not* represent the *text of the Septuagint*, but are closer to the *Hebrew text*. A common explanation for this is the opinion that the evangelist took these quotations from a literal (e.g., G. STRECKER, W. ROTHFUCHS) or oral (G. D. KILPATRICK) source. Because of the fact of two versions of quotations in Matthew K. STENDAHL, however, developed his well-known hypothesis of "the school of St. Matthew".[30] But the assumption of such a school is

---

[28] PH. VIELHAUER, *Geschichte der urchristlichen Literatur: Einleitung in das Neue Testament, die Apokryphen und die Apostolischen Väter* (GLB; Berlin, repr. 1978) 362.

[29] See Hengel/Merkel, Die Magier des Ostens (1963) 157; a different opinion has Rothfuchs, Erfüllungszitate (1969) 62f.

[30] Stendahl, The School of St. Matthew (1968) 35: This school was "a school for teachers and church leaders, and for this reason the literary work of that school assumes the form of a manual for teaching and administration within the church". Stendahl sees the character of Scripture

just as hypothetical as the premise of an oral or literary source.[31] Also more recent attempts to cope with the problem by relativizing the discrepancy between the text form of the fulfilment quotations and of the rest of the quotations are not convincing because they are in part based on unlikely premises.[32] This short survey of scholarship shows that presently there is no really convincing solution to the problem of the quotations in Matthew. For the time being we must accept an unsatisfying *non liquet*.

Regarding the Old Testament adoption by the New Testament, the theology of Matthew is characterized by a second kind of fulfilment besides the christologically interpreted fulfilment of the prophets' promises: the *fulfilment of the law* which, in Matthew, plays a very important role. In Matt 5:17–20, the Matthean Jesus introduces the antitheses of the Sermon on the Mount with the programmatic claim that he has "come not to abolish the law and the prophets, but to fulfil them" (Matt 5:17). In this context, the emphasis is clearly on the law; the prophets are only understood as its interpreters. While in the fulfilment quotations they are theologically important because of the fulfilment of the christological promise which occurred in the meantime, they are now, compared to the Mosaic law, secondary. It is the messianic task of Christ proclaimed by the prophets to elucidate the theological priority of the law. In full accordance with the idea of the quantitatively complete law already known from Gal 5:3, Jesus explains in Matt 5:18 that until heaven and earth pass away, not an iota, and not a dot will pass from the law. In the programmatic section of Matt 5:17–20 both concepts can be found which, in Pauline writings, were still contradictory: 1. The fulfilment of the law, πληρῶσαι τὸν νόμον, Matt 5:17 (see Gal 5:14; Rom 13:8–10); 2. The call for quantitatively total obedience of the law, Matt 5:18 (see Gal 5:3). Here, however, both concepts encompass each other. It is also significant that in the pericope of the twin commandments of love, Matt 22:34–40, the evangelist changes the question about the great commandment (Mark 12:28) into: Which is the great commandment in the law (Matt 22:36)? The cathedra of Moses has absolute authority, Matt 23:2f.

---

interpretation practiced there as "the Matthean type of midrashic interpretation", "it closely approaches – the midrash pesher of the Qumransect" (ibid.). In contrast, see B. GÄRTNER, "The Habakkuk Commentary (DSH) and the Gospel of Matthew", *StTh* 8 (1954) 1–24. Questionable is a further premise of Stendahl's hypothesis which is his assumption of "an unbroken line from the School of Jesus via the 'teaching of the apostles', the 'way' of Paul – to the rather elaborate School of Matthew with its ingenious interpretation of the O.T. as the crown of its scholarship" (ibid., 34). It is very questionable whether we may consider Jesus as the teacher of a "school".

[31] Notable arguments against STENDAHL's hypothesis of the school of St. Matthew are presented by G. STRECKER, *Der Weg der Gerechtigkeit: Untersuchung zur Theologie des Matthäus* (FRLANT 82; Göttingen [3]1971) 83ff and passim.

[32] E.J. GOODSPEED, *Matthew, Apostle and Evangelist* (Philadelphia 1959) and Gundry, The Use of the Old Testament (1967) see Matthew as "note-taker during the earthly ministry of Jesus" (!). G.M. SOARES PRABHU, *The Formula Quotations in the Infancy Narrative of Matthew: An Enquiry into the Tradition History of Mt 1-2* (AnBib 63; Rom 1976) 104, talks about "free targumic translations made from the original Hebrew by Matthew, in view of the context to which he has inserted them". His study – even though quite short – of the context quotations can sensitize us against assuming too easily that the Septuagint was the Bible of Matthew. But he did not succeed in disproving the existence of Matthew's two principally different text forms of Old Testament quotations.

4.2.3. *The Lukan Writings*

Luke's interpretation of the Old Testament discloses itself only if both Lukan writings are understood as a theological whole. In his presentation of the life of Jesus and of Early Church history, Luke offers an historical and, as such, a theological continuity reflecting both Israel's national and theological significance as well as its law. It is especially Luke who explains *theology as history*. Understanding Jesus as the "centre of time" ("Mitte der Zeit", H. CONZELMANN), the history of Israel and the history of the Church are theological interrelated by virtue of this centre. Luke realizes this in his Gospel by commencing the narrative of Jesus with poetic portions (Luke 1 and 2: *Magnificat, Benedictus,* and *Nunc dimittis*) which consist almost entirely of Old Testament allusions, mostly consulting the Septuagint (also a few references to a semitic text?). These hymns, however, are probably pre-lukan. That the evangelist did recognize the text as the text of the Septuagint in the hymns can be seen in Acts. His phrasing there being naturally freer than in the Gospel, he received from the Septuagint as his holy Scripture regarding "the language material – to present the holy apostolic period, in particular in Palestine".[33]

But Luke's actual attitude to the Old Testament and, within it, especially to the Mosaic law is only partially visible in his quotations and allusions. Above all, the different perspectives from which the *law* is portrayed in both Lukan writings is characteristic for his theology which can be recognized in his presentation of history. Connected with this theme is the theme of the *Spirit* which dominates both writings. We should, therefore, pay attention to Luke's quotations, in particular those not yet appearing in the Gospel of Mark, as well as to his theological construction of history which we can only understand by studying his interpretation of the Old Testament.

4.2.3.1. The Gospel of Luke. Mark portrays Jesus at least with partial distance to the Mosaic law, escalating in the abrogation of the food regulations in Mark 7:15. But for Luke, Jesus is the law-abiding Son of God. Already the parents of the Baptist (Luke 1:6, δίκαιοι ... ἐναντίον τοῦ θεοῦ, πορευόμενοι ἐν πάσαις [!] ταῖς ἐντολαῖς καὶ δικαιώμασιν τοῦ κυρίου ἄμεμπτοι), and then also the parents of Jesus (Luke 2:23 even with a quotation from Scripture: καθὼς γέγραπται ἐν νόμῳ [not: in scripture!] κυρίου, 2:24, κατὰ τὸ εἰρημένον ἐη τῷ νόμῳ κυρίου) practice total obedience of the law. Luke smooths (similarly as, independently of him, Matthew) the Markan mixed quotation Mark 1:2f and expands in *Luke 3:4-6* – like Mark 1:2f a fulfilment quotation – the quotation introduced with the introductory formula ὡς γέγραπται ἐν βίβλῳ λόγων Ἠσαΐου τοῦ προφήτου which now introduces the passage of *Isa 40:3-5*. A clear emphasis of this prophet! *Programmatically* even *more important* is the fact that, in *Luke 4:18f*, Jesus quotes once more

[33] E. HAENCHEN, *Die Apostelgeschichte* (KEK III; Göttingen ^{7}1977) 86 ("... die sprachlichen Mittel, ... um die heilige Apostelzeit, vor allem in Palästina, darzustellen"). Critical of this opinion is T. HOLTZ, *Untersuchungen über die alttestamentlichen Zitate bei Lukas* (TU 104; Berlin 1968) 172.

from the Book of Isaiah in his inaugural sermon in Nazareth. *Isa 61:1f/58:6* is a text that he refers to himself: "The *Spirit* of the Lord is *upon me*". Reading the Isaiah text during the festive celebration of a synagogue service, Jesus proclaims his messianic honour (ἔχρισέν με!) promised by the prophet. The "*I*" *of the prophetic text* Jesus speaks as *his own messianic "I"*. With this description Luke has placed the appearance of the earthly Jesus more than any other synoptic in the light of the prophetic promise. It is theologically crucial that Jesus is introduced as *the* Spirit bearer. His actions are motivated by God's Spirit working through him. Thus Luke provides the guarantee from the Old Testament that Christology is, at the same time, pneumatology. The programmatic Markan πεπλήρωται ὁ καιρός (Mark 1:14) is now altered into the programmatic σήμερον πεπλήρωται ἡ γραφὴ αὕτη ἐν τοῖς ὠσὶν ὑμῶν (Luke 4:21). Hence for the evangelist, Isaiah 61 is a fulfilment quotation. The messianic task of Jesus is to proclaim the gospel, εὐαγγελίσασθαι πτωχοῖς.

Isa 61:1 is once more adopted in *Luke 7:22* (besides three other passages from Isaiah) when Jesus answers to the question of the imprisoned Baptist. If this answer is an authentic word of Jesus,[34] then this would not yet prove the historicity of the preaching of Jesus at Nazareth; but then we would need to consider seriously whether Isaiah 61 was constitutive for the self-understanding of Jesus, or even for his self-consciousness. But whatever our understanding might be, it is clear that for Luke, Jesus of Nazareth is *the* fulfilment of the messianic promise of the Scripture.

What in particular is theologically significant is the fact that among the evangelists, only Luke sees the passion *expressis verbis* in the light of *Isaiah 53*. In Luke 22:37 (the scene in Gethsemane) Jesus refers Isa 53:12 to himself: καὶ μετὰ ἀνόμων ἐλογίσθη (some differences from the text of the Septuagint: καὶ ἐν τοῖς ἐνόμοις ἐλογίσθη, but a certain affinity to MT). Even though already before Luke, Isaiah 53 was referred to the passion of Jesus, it is the Gospel of Luke which displays the earliest formal quotation from this chapter directly connected to the passion of Jesus (see below regarding Acts 8:32f; see also 1 Pet 2:22). Among the remaining quotations which appear as a word of Jesus, only Psalm 22 (ψ 21) may be mentioned. This Psalm is quoted twice in Mark; Luke has only ψ 21:19 (Luke 23:34). The crucified Jesus, however, no longer speaks the words of ψ 21:2 as in Mark 15:34, but ψ 30:6 (Luke 23:46), "Father, into your hands I commit my spirit", and dies while speaking these words. The passion willed by God and announced by the prophet Isaiah apparently does not allow for a word of godforsakenness by Jesus. Only a word of trust in God is appropriate.

Just as the beginning of the proclamation of Jesus is characterized in Luke by the programmatic word of Isaiah 61, so this Gospel ends with a programmatic word of Jesus which is the word of the resurrected one to the disciples at Emmaus (Luke 24:44): everything written in the law of Moses and the prophets and the Psalms must be fulfilled, δεῖ πληρωθῆναι πάντα τὰ γεγραμμένα. Jesus himself "opens" their understanding, that they might under-

[34] Kümmel, "Jesu Antwort an Johannes den Täufer", *Heilsgeschehen und Geschichte* II (1978) 177–200.

stand the Scriptures – theologically succinct: συνιέναι τὰς γραφάς – that "thus it is written" that the Christ should suffer and on the third day rise from the dead (v. 46). Even more, it is also written that repentance and forgiveness of sins should be preached in his name to all nations (v. 47). Another programmatic passage explaining the Christ event as salvation according to the Scripture is Luke 24:44–47, which formes the transition to Luke's second book, the Book of Acts. The Church and, therefore, the whole of (believing) humankind are rooted in Scripture. We can state that the *question whether something is in accordance with Scripture is an essential and central element of the theology of the Gospel of Luke*. It finds its clear expression in the quotations from Scripture and in the programmatic, redactional statements of the evangelist mentioned above.

4.2.3.2. The Acts of the Apostles. Acts displays a peculiar distribution of scriptural quotations. Of the somewhat over twenty quotations – depending on how one counts – most are in Peter's speeches and sermons in Acts 1–3, in the speech by Stephen in Acts 7, and in the first speech of Paul, delivered at Antioch in Pisidia, in Acts 13; furthermore, another quotation appears in the same chapter after the uproar caused by his second sermon there. At the synode on the Gentile mission, the so-called Apostles' Council at Jerusalem, also James refers to a quotation from Scripture. We can state that most Old Testament quotations occur in speeches and sermons. According to *Acts 8:26–40*, the eunuch and minister of the Ethiopian queen Candace receives an exegetical lesson on *Isa 53:7f LXX* upon asking Philip for "guidance" (ὁδηγήσει, v. 31) on the prophet Isaiah. Once more programmatically formulated, the way from this Scripture passage to Jesus becomes clear in Acts 8:35, ἀρξάμενος ἀπὸ τῆς γραφῆς ταύτης εὐηγγελίσατο αὐτῷ τὸν Ἰησοῦν. *Scripture and Scripture interpretation necessarily belong together*. Only with Christian interpretation is Scripture understandable Scripture. Also Luke points out that *preaching* and *Scripture interpretation* are specific to the adoption of the Old Testament in the New. *Only comprehended Scripture is God's holy Scripture!* The meaning of James quoting Amos (Acts 15:16f) during the synode on the Gentile mission will be pointed out below, just as Paul's quoting Isa 6:9f in Acts 28:26f.

We will now examine the beginning of this Lukan writing. It is Luke's ecclesiological construction that the probable pre-Easter circle of the twelve becomes the institution of the twelve apostles which is the constitutive structural element of the Early Church. This corresponds to the providing of scriptural grounds for the betrayal and replacement of Judas, *ψ 68:26* and *ψ 108:8* in *Acts 1:20*. For Luke only the twelve are apostles in the actual sense (despite Acts 14:4,14).[35] We should not fail to notice that in Acts 9, Luke can do without grounds from Scripture for the vocation of Paul.

So according to Acts 1:15–26, Matthias has received the apostleship, ἀποστολή (v. 25), by virtue of the divine promise in the Psalter and by virtue of the divine lot. The new apostle's vocation is seen in the light of the ἔδει

[35] Haenchen, Apostelgeschichte, 123.

πληρωθῆναι τὴν γραφήν (γραφή here means again "scriptural passage") in Acts 1:16. At the same time the *Holy Spirit* is claimed to be the one who already made David point toward Jesus. Just as the Gospel of Luke ends with δεῖ πληρωθῆναι πάντα τὰ γεγραμμένα (Luke 24:44) in a *soteriological* perspective, so Acts starts with the previously mentioned ἔδει πληρωθῆναι in an *ecclesiological* perspective. It is, however, the Spirit who is, as it were, the main actor in Acts. Yet besides this pneumatological aspect, one is to see the law-abiding behavior of Jesus according to Luke in correspondence to the statements about the *law* in Acts in order to comprehend Luke's concept of *historical theology*. That the evangelist omits Mark 7:15 is not, as widely assumed, due to the fact that the *Vorlage* of Mark he had available did not contain this chapter. Consciously omitting this passage, he postpones the abrogation of the law – more precisely, the partial abrogation of the law – into the "time of the church" (H. CONZELMANN).[36] Understanding ecclesiology, pneumatology, and the theology of the law as a whole, in fact understanding the three components under the aspect of their accordance with Scripture, allows for the Lukan theology to be comprehended in its overall structure.

According to Jesus' promise of the Spirit in *Acts 1:8*, Peter's *Pentecost sermon* in *Acts 2:14ff* consists to a large extent of Scripture quotations which, however, do not deal with the law but with the Spirit. So in Acts 2:17–21 Peter quotes in detail *Joel 2:28–32 LXX* (= 3:1–5 MT) which is an eschatological text. Luke, however, inserts ἐν ταῖς ἐσχάταις ἡμέραις, thus qualifying the "time of the church" as eschatological time in spite of his concept of the delay of the parousia. In Acts 2:25–28 he then quotes the passage of *ψ 15:8–11* which he interprets christologically, calls in 2:30 the psalmist David a prophet, and interprets the Psalm by reference to ψ 131:11, thus returning to ψ 15. In Acts 2:34f Peter finally quotes *ψ 109* which is also interpreted christologically elsewhere in the New Testament. Peter's Pentecost sermon is, therefore, intended as proclamation of a prophetic promise. It exclusively addresses Jews, however those Jews who, for Pentecost, came to Jerusalem as pilgrims from all over the world (Acts 2:7ff). The resemblance to the inaugural sermon of Jesus in Luke 4 is striking: in the Gospel, Luke depicts Jesus as the sole Spirit bearer; in Acts it is again Jesus who promises the Spirit for Pentecost (Acts 1:8) so that then the Church becomes the bearer of the Spirit. At first it was the messianic task of Jesus who was gifted with the Spirit to proclaim the gospel, then at Pentecost the Church was bestowed with the Spirit in order to carry the gospel into the world. In *this* respect the Church continues the task of Jesus. The resurrected Christ explicitly told his disciples in Acts 1:8, ἕως ἐσχάτου τῆς γῆς. Acts 2 does not indicate yet that the worldwide proclamation is supposed to address *Gentiles*. The address of Peter in Acts 2:14, ἄνδρες Ἰουδαῖοι καὶ οἱ κατοικοῦντες Ἰερουσαλὴμ πάντες leaves the reader who knows about the mission to the Gentiles expecting a special act of God to make the apostles understand that Gentiles are to be included in the task of mission. This finally happens in *Acts 10* – yet according to

[36] H. CONZELMANN, *Die Mitte der Zeit: Studien zur Theologie des Lukas* (BHT 17; Tübingen [7]1993) passim.

Luke's understanding of apostleship, characteristically not through Paul (who, however, was called to be a proclaimer already in Acts 9), but through Peter who is first among the apostles (see Acts 1:13). The whole intention of the narrative in Acts 10 is to emphasize that it is God who declared all food clean through the vision which has happened to Peter – contrary to *Leviticus 11*! Even though this passage is not quoted it is beyond doubt that Luke had this passage and its religious tradition in mind. In Acts 10:15 ἃ ὁ θεὸς ἐκαθάρισεν (Aorist: in this moment God has declared as clean) σὺ μὴ κοίνου it is God who annuls the Mosaic food regulations which were valid for Luke as divine law until Acts 10. The abrogation of Leviticus 11 and, thus, the partial abrogation of the Torah which, according to Mark 7:15, was already initiated by the pre-Easter Jesus is postponed by Luke to this "time of the church".[37] In this connection it is important that God's declaration of the total cleanness of all foods declares also all human beings clean. It is, therefore, God who legitimates the mission to the Gentiles. *Thus regarding theology, Acts 10:15 is one of the most important programmatic statements in the book of Acts*. Later in Peter's sermon to Cornelius and his house, it is once more a word of God which provides grounds for the abrogation of the idea of cultic cleanness; Acts 10:35 probably refers to Esdras A' 4:39, καὶ οὐκ ἔστιν παρ' αὐτῇ λαμβάνειν πρόσωπα οὐδὲ διαφορά. God's acceptance of all human beings is within the context of the proclamation of the gospel, Acts 10:36 (allusion to Isa 52:7 and ψ 106:20) and in the context of the pneumatically phrased proclamation of Christ, Acts 10:38 ff (allusion to Luke 4:18 and thus simultaneously to Isa 61:1). Peter's defending his behaviour as a missionary to the Gentiles in Jerusalem (Acts 11:1 ff) demonstrates how much Luke wants to emphasize this event through the fact that he considered a second report as necessary.

In *Acts 15* the next step in the direction of the partial abrogation of the Mosaic law occurs. At the synode on the Gentile mission, the Gentile Christians are liberated from the duty of *circumcision*. And it is James of all the disciples who, as a reference, quotes the Old Testament, namely the eschatological text *Amos 9:11f* (influenced by Jer 12:15). Here, once more the soteriological difference between the Old Testament and the Old Testament received in the New is obvious: now the restoration of the destroyed house of David does no longer refer to the eschatological return of the Davidic line, but to the establishment of the reign of Jesus. Luke's retrojection of the so-called Apostles' *decretum* which actually is to be dated into an earlier time is a redactional concept of his with the intention to save a portion of the Mosaic law for the sake of harmony between Jewish Christians and Gentile Christians.

At the end of Acts, we find the decisive reflexion on the theology of mission by Paul – and thus the one of Luke – in Acts 28:25–28. The apostle acknow-

---

[37] Conzelmann, Mitte der Zeit, 137: "The preservation of the law is assigned to a particular time of church development during which, however, it is rigorously exercised" (*"Das Bewahren des Gesetzes ist einer bestimmten Entwicklungsphase der Kirche zugeordnet, in dieser allerdings mit Konsequenz durchgeführt"*).

ledges that the Holy Spirit has already announced the blindness of the Jews to the patriarchs through the prophet Isaiah in Isa 6:9f. Now "this (!) salvation" is sent to the Gentiles, that is former the salvation for the Jews. Acts thus ends with the emphatic statement that the Scripture of the Jews denies these Jews the salvation and now grants it to the Gentiles. Interestingly Isa 6:9f repeatedly appears in the course of the New Testament tradition. This means in Acts that the group to whose favour the law is gradually annulled is now almost the only group in the Church.

4.3. The Gospel of John

In modern scholarship, probably no other New Testament writing is so widely disputed regarding its development and its evaluation in the light of literary criticism as the Gospel of John. This fact also influences opinions about whether the Old Testament was adopted by the evangelist or already by the sources he was consulting. Where does the evangelist adopt the Old Testament, and where does he take over references to the Old Testament already found in his sources? Even without regarding the puzzle presented by literary criticism, the image of Scripture quotations in the Gospel of John appears confusing at first glance because any search for a clear direction is in vain. An easily understandable scheme which fits into the overall structure of John does not seem to exist.

At second glance, however, several structural elements appear quite clearly. First, there is a formal matter of fact. Five quotations are introduced with the introductory formula γεγραμμένον ἐστιν or the like (John 2:17; 6:31,45; 10:34; 12:14; see also 8:17 where the peculiar introductory formula ἐν τῷ νόμῳ δὲ τῷ ὑμετέρῳ γέγραπται apparently introduces Deut 17:6 or Deut 19:15); but especially here significant differences from the Old Testament text appear (regarding John 7:42 see below). Clearly reminiscent of Matthew, the *fulfilment quotations* are a special group. Apparently important for the structure of John, they only occur in John 12:38 and afterwards; their specific introductory formula is ἵνα ἡ γραφὴ πληρωθῇ or the like (John 19:28: ἵνα τελειωθῇ ἡ γραφή). In John 12:38 and 19:24,36 they can be identified as remarks of the evangelist, in John 13:18 and 15:25 it is Jesus who quotes Scripture, and in John 18:9,32 they do not introduce an Old Testament passage but refer to the word of Jesus.[38]

Particularly in the context of quotations an affinity with the *synoptic tradition* can be recognized. But we should not necessarily conclude that the evangelist knew the synoptic Gospels as sometimes assumed. Parallels can be sufficiently explained by the widespread reference to certain Old Testament texts in the Early Church. The comparision between John and the synoptics shows in particular the following similarities: the quotation of Isa 40:3 which, in the synoptics, is spoken about the Baptist is now spoken by the Baptist himself with the preceding "I" and the following introductory formula καθὼς εἶπεν Ἠσαΐας ὁ προφήτης (John 1:23). Also Isa 6:10, known already from Mark 4:12, appears in John, but only toward the end of Jesus' public appearance (John 12:40). Although introduced with the formula πάλιν εἶπεη Ἠσαΐας (John 12:39) it is yet placed immediately behind the fulfilment quotation of Isa 53:1 in John 12:38, thus obviously participating in its fulfilment character. At the end of the Book of Acts (Acts 28:26f) also Isa 6:9f is formally not a fulfilment quotation, but it clearly functions as such. This parallel is conspicuous. Zech 9:9, known from Matt 21:4f, appears as fulfilment quotation in John 12:14f, introduced

---

[38] Regarding the fulfilment quotations in the Gospel of John see especially Rothfuchs, Erfüllungszitate (1969) 151ff. Generally, regarding John's theological treatment of the Old Testament see the excursus "John's Use of Scripture" in Hanson, The Prophetic Gospel (1991) 234–53, but also the remaining chapters of this monograph.

by καθώς ἐστιν γεγραμμένον. Like in Matthew it is a mixed quotation, although of a different kind.

Asking for the different *speakers of the quotations* does not clarify the issue either. There is the Baptist, repeatedly also the people, Isaiah, or the evangelist. The question of the underlying text is even more complicated. We encounter literal correspondence to the text of the Septuagint (however only four exact quotations from the Septuagint). Yet modifications of this text are clear. Sometimes the evangelist possibly referred to the Hebrew original, but at other instances neither the Septuagint nor the Hebrew Bible can be identified as the main influence. It is not always clear which passage of the Old Testament was consulted as, for example, in the case of John 7:42 οὐχ ἡ γραφὴ εἶπεν ὅτι ἐκ τοῦ σπέρματος Δαυὶδ καὶ ἀπὸ Βηθλέεμ τῆς κώμης ὅπου ἦν Δαυὶδ ἔρχεται ὁ χριστός. The particular problem of John 7:38 will be discussed later.

It is once more ROTHFUCHS who helps substantially to clarify the issue at stake. He brings to our attention that the evangelist says ὁ λόγος always when the fulfilment quotation is more closely determined regarding its source.[39] But when the introductory formulae of the fulfilment quotations do not define the origin, they employ ἡ γραφή. It is, furthermore, characteristic that the introductory formulae of the remaining quotations mention neither ὁ λόγος nor ἡ γραφή. They present only forms of the verbs λέγω and γράφω; here the origin is partially indicated. ROTHFUCHS also noticed correctly that with ἡ γραφή, the evangelist refers to a *Scripture passage*, while he employs the plural αἱ γραφαί to refer to the whole body of Old Testament Scripture (see John 5:39).[40] The situation becomes more complicated, however, through the fact that the four introductory formulae with ὁ λόγος introduce an *Old Testament* quotation only twice: Isa 53:1 in John 12:38, and ψ 34:19 (or ψ 68:5?) in John 15:25. Yet in the other two instances a word of *Jesus* is qualified as fulfilled (John 18:9,32); however the word of Jesus is not identified. ROTHFUCHS recognizes that apart from John 12:38ff all fulfilment quotations deal with Jesus' opponents and their actions.[41] Yet this clarifies also the two Isaiah quotations in John 12:38 f with respect to their intention: the failure by human beings described in the remaining fulfilment quotations is ultimately caused by no one else but God. It is God who blinds their eyes and hardens their hearts. This helps us to understand the theological concept of the Gospel even more clearly: for this concept, *Isa 53:1* and *Isa 6:10* are of central importance. They help to make the theological function of the fulfilment quotations transparent because both quotations reflect the differing image of each of the remaining fulfilment quotations, if not of all of John's quotations. R. SCHNACKENBURG[42] has proven that the evangelist changed the passage Isa 6:10 very consciously: he deleted the "listening" and established the order "eyes-heart" to show that God's oppressive action starts at the exterior of the human being and proceeds into the interior as documented by the Pharisees' "blindness" to see in John 9. With the change to ἐπώρωσεν he consciously consults a well-known concept of his tradition which was spread in the Early Church (e.g., Mark 3:5; 6:52; 8:17; 2 Cor 3:14; Rom 11:7,25;

---

[39] Ibid. 153.

[40] Ibid. 153.

[41] Ibid. 170.

[42] Schnackenburg, HThK IV/4 (1984) 147ff; see also Hanson, Jesus Christ in the Old Testament (1965) 104–108, and idem, The Prophetic Gospel (1991) 166–170.

Eph 4:18). The evangelist quotes Isa 53:1 exactly according to the Septuagint, but in his reference to Isa 6:10 he deviates from the text of the Septuagint. Therefore we are to conclude that he *adopted the text of the Septuagint where it fit his theological concept*, but that *he considerably changed the text at his own discretion where, for the sake of the theological statement, he considered it as appropriate*, if not *as inevitable*.[43]

Therefore by modification of the Old Testament text, the evangelist expresses his theological or, more precisely, his *christological* concept. His modification of the Old Testament text is not clearly revealed until his comment on the quotation in John 12:41, which is where he consults Isa 6:1 and, thus, the *immediate context of the quotation: Isaiah did not see the glory of God, but of Christ*. This is in accordance with John 1:18. Theologically relevant is that it is the *preexistent Christ* who appeared to the prophet.

At the beginning of this section on the Gospel of John we pointed out that the problem of tradition and redaction remains unsolved, and how this effects any study of how the Old Testament is utilized in the Gospel of John. Based on the above considerations, however, we are on the way to relativizing this problem. It is of course possible that at certain passages of his writing, the evangelist referred to the Old Testament based on traditions or sources available to him. But despite our initial impressions of a lack of concept, it became clear that the evangelist pursues the interesting strategy of stating theological positions with the help of the Old Testament. In his theological concept he not only considers the individual Scripture passage which he refers or alludes to, but also its *context*. This proves that he not only utilizes Old Testament terms and concepts possibly handed down to him, but that his reference to the Old Testament developed to a considerable extent out of his independent studies of the text. John 12:41 proves this for Isaiah 6, and several exegetes have provided convincing evidence that the same holds true also for different passages of the Gospel of John.[44]

The theological intention of the evangelist can be recognized in particular at his description of the *death of Jesus*. Certainly, among his key theological statements belongs *John 19:28–30* where Jesus' death is depicted as the triumphant completion of his work. This death is ultimately God's act of glorification, hence through an *understanding* way of reading the reader of the Gospel of John is introduced to the theological depth dimension of an event which, at first glance, seems terrible. Yet especially from there the divine paradox that the death of Jesus is his glorification is to be understood: this shows that the Gospel of John – no less than the letters of Paul – is a highly *hermeneutical writing*. It is only the believer who sees the death as an histori-

---

[43] A different opinion regarding John 12:39 f has G. Reim, *Studien zum alttestamentlichen Hintergrund des Johannesevangeliums* (MSSNTS 22; Cambridge 1974) 38.

[44] Hanson, The Living Utterances of God (1983) 113 ff; A. H. Francke, *Das Alte Testament bei Johannes: Ein Beitrag zur Erklärung und Beurtheilung der johanneischen Schriften* (Göttingen 1885) 267; C. K. Barrett, "The Old Testament in the Fourth Gospel", *JTS 48* (1947) 155–69, 168; Freed, Old Testament Quotations (1965) 129 f. A different opinion has Reim, Studien (1974) 96: The evangelist has only ψ 68 as written source, otherwise he knows only whole narratives with integrated testimonies.

cal event of the divine δόξα. *John 12:32* is eloquent evidence of this: "And I, when I am lifted up from the earth, ὑψωθῶ ἐκ τῆς γῆς, will draw all people to myself". Characteristically, shortly after this passage the inability to believe is mentioned and, especially in this context, *Isa 6:10* is quoted. In addition, the evangelist consults Isa 53:1 and thus says with Scripture reference (John 12:39): "*Therefore* – hence because Scripture, because actually God says so – they could not believe, οὐκ ἠδύναντο πιστεύειν". The hermeneutical Gospel of John is at the same time simultaneously a terrible reference to the hermeneutic prevented by God! It goes without saying that also John 17 must be mentioned in this connection. The hour has come, meaning the moment of Jesus' death has come, and thus the glorification of the Son through the Father and of the Father through the Son. The Old Testament כבוד יהוה remains what it is, but it is now hidden behind the cruel and repulsive image of the crucifixion. And this is exactly the perspective of John 19:28–30: Jesus, knowing, εἰδώς – he, too, is participating in the hermeneutical process – that all was now finished, τετέλεσται, says to "fulfil" the Scripture, ἵνα τελειωθῇ ἡ γραφή: "I thirst", alluding to Ps 69:22. These words are not simply a quotation of the Old Testament spoken by Jesus. Their being spoken is the *process* of the fulfilment of the passage from the Psalm. Therefore the centre of the Johannine *theologia crucis* is the death of Jesus as *theologically interpreted* from his elevation and, thus, the death of Jesus as *theological interpreted* from his elevation through the faith of the reader of John. Hence it is theologically relevant that exactly this glorified death is fulfilment and completion of Scripture. *In the Gospel of John the theology of the cross and the theology of Scripture are inseparably connected with each other*. But such a theology of Scripture does not postulate an absolute priority of Scripture over God's revelation in Jesus. This is contradicted by the above-mentioned fact that, with the introductory formula of the Johannine *fulfilment quotations*, Jesus twice characterized also *his own words* as being fulfilled (John 18:9 refers to John 6:39, etc., and John 18:32 refers to John 3:14). Very appropriately, Rothfuchs therefore talks about the "unity between the Old Testament word of Scripture and the words of Jesus".[45] Yet it hardly means relativizing Scripture if Jesus says "your law" (John 8:17; 10:34) when referring to Scripture. Here, much more, an accusation of the Pharisees or "the Jews" is intended. Against Jesus they claim scriptural grounds, but it is Scripture which is the ground of their failure (John 7:40–44). They are, after all, blind because God has blinded their eyes (John 12:40). Yet at the same time their misfortune is their inexcusable sin (John 9:41). Once more we face the fact that John also is the Gospel of prevented hermeneutics.

This leads to another characteristic which is theologically very important. At its core a struggle about Scripture, the peculiar correlation between hermeneutic and anti-hermeneutic is, at the same time, a struggle between the old and the new people of God. In the exegetical literature the opinion is widely held that the Jews are merely the representatives of the unbelieving

[45] Rothfuchs, Erfüllungszitate (1969) 154: "... Einheit zwischen dem alttestamentlichen Schriftwort und den Worten Jesu".

world. The discussion between Jesus and the Jews is, however, so specifically related to the struggle between Christians and Jews that this opinion remains unsatisfactory. There is, for instance, a struggle about the origin of the Christ (John 7:25 ff) or, continuing this passage, a struggle about the testimony, μαρτυρία, for Jesus (John 8:12 ff) addressing also the specifically Jewish problem of the descent from Abraham (John 8:37 ff). All of these passages do not allow for an understanding assigning only symbolic meaning to the Jews in the Gospel of John. Again, in this Gospel we encounter a feature which was already significant for other New Testament writings. It is the observation that the effort to understand the relationship between New Testament and Old Testament is less a discussion about how *written material* as such is received, and more about whether Scripture is genuinely the Jewish or Christian word of God. This is, finally, the question whether God's word allows Jews to have their traditionally national and religious identity, or whether it constitutes the identity of Christians as non-Jews.

Written toward the end of the New Testament era, the Gospel of John is a theological document in which the interpretation of the Old Testament is a fundamental part of its theology. Even if we do not agree with E. D. FREED that in his use of Scripture, the evangelist was literally dependent on the synoptics,[46] still his hypothesis should be considered seriously when he states: "But in no other writer are the O. T. quotations so carefully woven into the context and the whole plan of composition as in John".[47] In any case his following position should be supported:

> ... when John was quoting a passage of O. T. scripture, he was bound by no roule or fixed text, testimony or other. In every instance his quoted text appears to be adopted to its immediate context, to his literary style, and to the whole plan of the composition of his gospel.[48]

Further, A. T. HANSON rightly says:

> As we review John's technique in using scriptures, we must concede that he is as much a master as is Paul, and perhaps more of a master than Matthew ... Above all we must admire his christological use of scripture ... John represents the *ne plus ultra* of the New Testament interpretation of scripture.[49]

Interestingly the Epistles of John do not contain any quotations.

4.4. The Epistle to the Hebrews

Regarding the scriptural quotations of the Epistle to the Hebrews, two basic questions are important: 1. Which *Old Testament* text was available to the author of the Epistle? 2. How do the quotations structure the *theology of the Epistle to the Hebrews*? Of course the second question is clearly more impor-

---

[46] Freed, Old Testament Quotations (1965) pass.

[47] Ibid. 129.

[48] Ibid. 129.

[49] Hanson, The Living Utterances of God (1983) 130–32. Until today, no convincing solution has been presented to the difficult problem of verifying the quotation of John 7:38; see, for example, Freed, ibid. 21 ff; Reim, ibid. 56 ff. The suggestions of these exegets remain either too hypothetical or are little, or not at all, convincing.

tant. But given the complicated problems of historical research and isagogical knowledge regarding this Epistle, we will also reflect on the first question.

Already in 1828, F. BLEEK called attention to the textual tradition of the quotations. He discovered that many of the quotations correspond to the text of the Septuagint as found in Codex Alexandrinus, although some of these quotations are based on the text of Codex Vaticanus.[50] He concluded that the *Vorlage* of the author of Hebrews was a recension with an affinity to Codex Alexandrinus.[51] A. SPERBER supported the hypothesis that LXX^A and LXX^B represent two independent translations of the Hebrew original.[52] This opinion was contradicted by K.J. THOMAS who assumed that LXX^A and LXX^B present two traditions of a single translation which could be called Septuagint; yet the author of Hebrews also had a text of the translation's original form. "Through the process of editing, the text of LXX^A and LXX ^{B} eventually became a mixture of primitive and edited readings, as they are in their present forms".[53] Regarding our problem, one of the most important monographs is a dissertation written in Munich by F. SCHRÖGER, *Der Verfasser des Hebräerbriefes als Schriftausleger* (1968). He assumes that it was the author of Hebrews who changed the Septuagint text. Referring to BLEEK, THOMAS, KATZ,[54] KAHLE, and SPERBER, he maintains the opinion that the research of the events of the formation of the Septuagint is still in its initial stage; the quotations of Hebrews, however, could "certainly provide a valuable contribution to the solution of this problem".[55] Also the dissertation written in Göttingen by E. AHLBORN, *Die Septuaginta-Vorlage des Hebräerbriefes* (1966), should be mentioned here. According to AHLBORN, the usual question whether the quotations are from the tradition of Codex A, B, or even of a different codex is not only irrelevant but also misleading because the manuscripts in the individual books belong to different recensions.[56] He concludes that an Alexandrian recension could not have been the *Vorlage* of Hebrews. A text tradition with this title is questionable in any case. "Also the Alexandrinus by itself can be ruled out as *Vorlage* of the quotations. Instead we should rather assume that A knew Hebrews and consulted it".[57] The survey shows that gradually the questions have become more appropriate to the subject matter insofar as more recent scholarship on the Septuagint has paid more attention to the subtly differentiated results of other scholars. But a generally convincing solution of the problem has not yet been found. A solution which may be possible within the course of the next few years might be located between the opinions of THOMAS and AHLBORN.

As mentioned above, more important than the question of the textual *Vorlage* of the author of Hebrews is his *theological treatment of Scripture*. Already when dealing with other New Testament authors, this question was at the centre of attention. The way in which the author of Hebrews treats Scripture is reflected very clearly and distinctively in the introductory formulae, which

---

[50] F. BLEEK, *Der Brief an die Hebräer erläutert durch Einleitung, Uebersetzung und fortlaufendem Commentar* I (Berlin 1828) 371 f.

[51] Ibid. 374.

[52] A. SPERBER, "New Testament and Septuagint", *JBL* 59 (1940) 193–293, 248.

[53] K. J. THOMAS, "The Old Testament Citations in Hebrews", *NTS* 11 (1965) 303–65, 325.

[54] P. Katz, Quotations from Deuteronomy (1958) 221.

[55] F. Schröger, Schriftausleger (1968) 30 f: "... zur Lösung dieser Aufgabe zweifellos einen guten Beitrag liefern ...". (AHLBORN's dissertation was published in the year in which SCHRÖGER handed in his dissertation; therefore both scholars could not pay attention to the work of each other.)

[56] E. AHLBORN, *Die Septuaginta-Vorlage des Hebräerbriefes* (Diss. Göttingen 1966) 10.

[57] Ibid. 141: "Auch der Alexandrinus allein scheidet als Zitatvorlage aus; vielmehr ist umgekehrt damit zu rechnen, daß A den Hebr kannte und mitbenutzte". Furthermore the dissertation *Hebrew and the Old Testament*, written by J. C. MCCULLOUGH (Belfast 1971), must be mentioned; like AHLBORN the author approaches the question of the *Vorlage* of the author of Hebrews fundamentally. He concludes that the *Vorlage* can be found neither in a single codex nor in the archetype of several known codices, but in the recensions as described in the Göttinger Septuagint. The same author wrote the essay "The Old Testament Quotations in Hebrews", *NTS* 26 (1980) 363–79, concluding that the quotations are modified by the author of Hebrews.

differ remarkably from those of the other New Testament authors. Interestingly enough, formulae such as καθὼς γέραπται or the like do not occur in the entire letter. There is no instance of an introductory formula emphasizing that the quotations have been written. For the author of Hebrews this might be relevant because he continuously presents introductory formulae containing forms of λέγειν, especially λέγει, λέγων, εἶπεν and εἴρηκεν. It is crucial for him that the quotations to which he refers were *said*. In this connection, however, it is theologically highly relevant *who* the individual speaker of the quotations is. In most cases it is *God*. But the other New Testament writings show that, for the proof from Scripture, only sometimes is the word of the speaking God important. In numerous quotations in Romans 9–11, for example, it is actually God who speaks in the 1st person singular. This phenomenon dominates in Hebrews. *In the quotations of the Epistle to the Hebrews the speaking God is quoted*. But also the *Son of God* speaks (Heb 2:12–14; 10:5–7), and so does the *Holy Spirit* (Heb 3:7–11; 10:15–17). One could almost talk about God as revealing in the Trinity. It is remarkable that hardly any human being from the Old Testament is introduced as speaking (exceptions are, for instance, Moses in Heb 9:19, with Exod 24:8 in Heb 9:20; of course we may ask whether this is a real quotation or whether Moses is called a speaker in the context of an argumentative story).

The author of Hebrews, first of all, has a *christological* intention when he quotes God speaking. In the context of an argumentation of this kind, the function of these quotations is to provide proof from Scripture. In the other New Testament writings we encounter the *proof from Scripture* as the *written word of God*; yet in Hebrews, even though quotations are – of course! – written down, we find the *proof of the spoken word of God*. For the author it is beyond question that what God *says* is theologically indisputable and, therefore, cannot be questioned. In such christological contexts God speaks *to his Son*, especially in the accumulation of Psalm quotations in Heb 1:5–13; then the Son speaks again to *the Father* (Heb 10:5–7, characteristically once more with a Psalm quotation from ψ 39:7–9). But in case of parenetic quotations, the Holy Spirit is mentioned as speaking (Heb 3:7 with the introductory formula διό, καθὼς λέγει τὸ πνεῦμα τὸ ἅγιον with ψ 94:7–11 in Heb 3:7–11; Heb 10:15 with the curious introductory formula μαρτυρεῖ δὲ ἡμῖν καὶ τὸ πνεῦμα τὸ ἅγιον with Jer 38:33f LXX in Heb 10:16f). Hence God as the Father speaks to the Son (and the Son speaks to the Father), and God as the Holy Spirit speaks to the congregation. To put it in the terminology of later History of dogma, the introductory formulae of Hebrews express a *trinitarian* event as an inner-trinitarian activity, as well as an activity to the outside. Furthermore, God, ὁ θεός, is also speaking to human beings as, for example, in Heb 6:13f which refers to God's addressing Abraham in Gen 22:17.

Particularly the words of the Father to the Son and of the Son to the Father are often quotations from the Psalter. This reflects the fact characteristic for Hebrews that in particular especially the *Psalms* play a dominant role in scriptural references. Among appr. 30 scriptural quotations (the number may vary slightly depending on how one counts) there are 15 Psalm quotations. But contrary to most of the New Testament writings studied so far, the Book of Isaiah is hardly relevant. Only in Heb 2:13 is the double quotation Isa 8:17f quoted.[58] Among the Psalms especially ψ 2 and ψ 109 are of particular theological, or christological importance for Hebrews. In Heb 1:5, ψ 2:7 is already presented as the Epistle's first quotation with the polemic introductory formula τίνι γὰρ εἶπέν ποτε τῶν ἀγγέλων. It recurs in Heb 5:5 with, once again, a special introductory formula: ὁ λαλήσας πρὸς αὐτόν. Hebrews' Christology is also characterized by the fact that both Psalms occur in a sequence of quotations in Heb 1:5–13 (first and last quotation!) as well as in Heb 5:5f as a double quotation (in Heb 5:6 with a special introductory formula: καθὼς καὶ ἐν ἑτέρῳ λέγει). In Heb 1:13, however, ψ 109:1 (Christology of exaltation) is quoted, but in Heb 5:6 ψ 109:4 (priest after the order of Melchizedek). This quotation recurs furthermore in Heb 7:17 and 7:21 after the chapter started with the paraphrasing of Gen 14:17–20 (Melchizedek as ἱερεὺς τοῦ θεοῦ τοῦ ὑψίστου).

Hebrews thus emphasizes the theological importance of Christ in a double manner: he is *Son of God* and *high priest*, although priest of a special type. An Old Testament testimony of Jesus' divine reign, ψ 2:7 is, however, not specific to Hebrews, as became clear already in the examination of other New Testament writings. Mark 1:11 and parallels, Mark 12:36f and parallels, and Acts 2:34f show that also elsewhere this Psalm passage has been used as inner-trinitarian word of God, as the Father's word to the Son.

In the remarks regarding *Jesus' high priesthood*, it is, furthermore, theologically relevant that Hebrews continuously alludes to the *Old Testament cultic law* but hardly honours this cult with a quotation (only Exod 25:40 in Heb 8:5 as a cultic instruction of God to Moses, and Exod 24:8 in Heb 9:20 which, however, is a word of Moses). The Old Testament cult was only a temporary cult for the author of Hebrews. Thus in Heb 9:23, he speaks about τὰ ὑποδείγματα τῶν ἐν τοῖς οὐρανοῖς τούτοις, and in Heb 10:1 about σκιά. In his position as the new high priest, Jesus himself speaks against the Old Testament cult with the words of ψ 39:7–9 where he says that the Father no longer desires Old Testament sacrifices. Especially as high priest he does the Father's will: he dies at the cross. The author of Hebrews describes Jesus' office as high priest in cultic categories; but the manner in which he employs cultic terminology aims at the *negation of these cultic categories*. *Surpassing* and *abrogating* the cult result in a peculiar dialectic. A certain imbalance exists between the two facts that according to Hebrews, the Old Testament law is indisputably God's law, and that, simultaneously, it leads to the negation in principle of the high priesthood. But one may conclude that it is this inequality which accounts for the letter's theological characteristic. H. Braun says rightly:

---

[58] In the reference to Hab 2:3f which is quoted in Heb 10:37f, the few words μικρὸν ὅσον ὅσον from Isa 26:20 LXX can hardly be understood as component of a mixed quotation. Merely for the sake of underscoring the passage of Habakkuk, the author added words from Isa 26:20 like a proverb; this is also suggested by further addition of ἔτι γάρ. A different opinion has, for example, Schröger, Schriftausleger (1968) 185f.

Instances dealing with the imperfectness of the Levitic priesthood, 7:11, the Old Testament law, 7:19.28, and the Old Testament order, 8:7, the need to change the priesthood and the law, 7:12, even with the annulment of the Old Testament commandment, 7:18; 9:9, and of the old order, 8:13, are never phrased in a way that God devaluates or abrogates *his* old regulations. Then the incriminated Old Testament characteristics appear separate from God who criticizes or annuls. This is a further indication of the – problem: *God* spoke in the Old Testament, and he himself criticizes his revelation and abrogates it.[59]

Another peculiarity of Hebrews is the placement of the promise of the new covenant, *Jer 38:31–34 LXX*: it occurs as an announcement of God's act of salvation placed in the middle of a dogmatic passage about Jesus' high priesthood in a parenetic sense. This is not surprising regarding the Epistle's characteristics mentioned above that combines continuously dogmatic and parenetic passages. But we must also bear in mind that the term *new covenant* provides "the decisive category" for the annulment of the old covenant.[60]

Further remarks on the last chapters of the Epistle: the eschatological outlook on the parousia of Christ which is parenetically motivated and employs the quotation Isa 26:20 from the Apocalypse of Isaiah in Heb 10:37f, is followed by the so-called testimony of the patriarchs in *Heb 11:1–40*. In Heb 11:1, faith, πίστις, defined as ἐλπιζομένων ὑπόστασις, πραγμάτων ἔλεγχος οὐ βλεπομένων, is illustrated through the testimony of the πρεσβύτεροι. Beginning with Abel and continuing with Rahab the harlot, the individuals are more or less briefly characterized with respect to their faith. After this Gideon, Barak, Samson, Jephthah, David, and Samuel are mentioned, then also the prophets; and, finally, there is an exhortation to look to Jesus as the pioneer and perfecter of faith, *Heb 12:1–3*. Once more, it is alluded to *ψ 109:1*.

In the remaining parenetic portion Heb 12:4–13:25 there are only three formal quotations (Prov 3:11f LXX in Heb 12:5f, Hag 2:6.21 in Heb 12:26, and ψ 117:6 in Heb 13:6) but a number of allusions to Scripture. Regarding the latter ones however, a clear line of connection cannot be found; it may at least be said that Old Testament texts dealing with cult and sacrifice have somehow been employed typologically. It is certainly noticeable that in *Heb 13:15*, the theologically characteristic word *ψ 49:14* of the "sacrifice of praise", θῦσον τῷ θεῷ θυσίαν αἰνέσεως, is quoted; it was also popular during the Reformation (Confessio Augustana XXIV: "*Idem docet epistola ad Ebraeos*

---

[59] H. Braun, *An die Hebräer* (HNT 14; Tübingen 1984) 21: "Wo die Unvollkommenheit des levitischen Priestertums 7,11, des alttestamentlichen Gesetzes 7,19.28 und der alttestamentlichen Ordnungen 8,7, wo die Veränderungsbedürftigkeit des Priestertums und des Gesetzes 7,12, ja die Aufhebung von alttestamentlichem Gebot, 7,18; 9,9 und alte Ordnungen 8,13 zur Sprache kommt, da wird nie so formuliert, daß Gott *seine* alten Satzungen für minder erklärt oder aufhebt. Die inkriminierten alttestamentlichen Gegebenheiten figurieren dann sozusagen gelöst von Gott, der sie tadelt oder abschafft; ein weiterer Hinweis auf die – Aporie: *Gott* hat im AT geredet; und: Er selbst tadelt seine Offenbarung und hebt sie auf".

[60] E. Grässer, *Der Glaube im Hebräerbrief* (MThSt 2; Marburg 1965) 112: "die entscheidende Kategorie". See also ibid. 113f: Hebrews hardly contain any positive statements on the old covenant without the context of the new covenant. The replacement in principle of the old covenant through the covenant in Christ means that the old covenant is the negative counterpart of the new.

cap. 13.: Per ipsum offeramus hostiam laudis semper Deo, et addit interpretationem id est, fructum labiorum confitentium nomini eius").

Noticeable is also the way in which the author of Hebrews treats quotations when employing them in his exegesis. As can be clearly seen in Heb 3:7ff, he repeats small portions of a considerably long quotation. Each portion is introduced with a certain introductory formula, whereby expressions with the perfect εἴρηκεν are preferred (for example, Heb 4:3, καθὼς εἴρηκεν, 4:4, εἴρηκεν γάρ που περὶ τῆς ἑβδόμης οὕτως) – and then individually commented upon (see also Heb 10:5ff).[61]

4.5. *The Remaining Epistles of the New Testament*

In the *Epistle of James*, 3 out of 4 quotations occur in James 2 in connection with the general topic of law (love commandment Lev 19:18 with the introductory formula κατὰ τὴν γραφήν in Jas 2:8, and two commandments of the decalogue with ὁ γὰρ εἰπών … εἶπεν καί in Jas 2:11). In Jas 2:23, the quotation of Gen 15:6, which was central for Paul, is used with the introductory formula καὶ ἐπληρώθη ἡ γραφὴ ἡ λέγουσα against Paul himself or against a misunderstood Paulinism. In Jas 4:6 Prov 3:34 is quoted with διὸ λέγει.

In the only 5 chapters of the *First Epistle of Peter*, there is a comparatively large number of 8 scriptural quotations. Interestingly, the first 3 quotations (Lev 11:44f in 1 Pet 1:16; Isa 40:6–9 in 1 Pet 1:24f; Isa 28:16 in 1 Pet 2:6) are introduced with introductory formulae starting with διότι (διότι γέγραπται, διότι, διότι περιέχει ἐν γραφῇ). The next 4 quotations (ψ 117:22 in 1 Pet 2:7; ψ 33:13–17 in 1 Pet 3:10–12 [longest quotation in 1 Pet]; Isa 11:2 in 1 Pet 4:14 [if this is a quotation and not an allusion]; Prov 11:31 in 1 Pet 4:18) are presented without introductory formulae. In 1 Pet 5:5, Prov 3:34 is only introduced with ὅτι. This Epistle, then, includes 3 quotations from Isaiah as well as 3 quotations from the Psalms.

4.6. *The Revelation of John*

The Revelation of John does not have a single formal quotation from the Old Testament, but yet like no other book of the New Testament it is influenced by the Old Testament in terms of language and content. The last book of the New Testament can only be fully comprehended in its spiritual, religious, and theological structure if its content is understood in the language of the Old Testament and its intentions. In the New Testament, no other book is influenced so thoroughly by the Old Testament as Revelation, not even the

[61] Some authors like to see parallels to the pesher interpretation at Qumran, or to the midrashim (regarding Hebrews 7, for example, J. W. THOMPSON, "The Conceptual Background and Purpose of the Midrash in Hebrews vii", *NovT* 19 (1977) 209–23, 209ff). As for the interpretive methods employed in Hebrews, and the background of the exegetical method see, above all, Schröger, Schriftausleger (1968) pass.; he mentions also parallels of Philo; see, furthermore, O. MICHEL, *Der Brief an die Hebräer* (KEK XIII; Göttingen [12]1966) 151–58; H. FELD, *Der Hebräerbrief* (EdF 228; Darmstadt 1985) 33f. G. W. BUCHANAN, *To the Hebrews: Translation, Comment and Conclusions* (AB 36; New York 1972 xix–xxiii), understands Hebrews as "homiletic midrash", "which is based on Ps 110" (ibid. xxi–xxvii).

Epistles to the Romans or to the Galatians. In this Epistle, *Paul* presents Old Testament quotations with the theological intention of providing grounds for his evangelical kerygma in a "New Testament" style. Even though the problem of time and, therefore, the problem of the fulfilment of the promise, ἐπαγγελία (Gal 3:14ff), in the πλήρωμα τοῦ χρόνου (Gal 4:4), is quite complicated, Paul understands fulfilment and promise ultimately in a *system of temporal coordinates*: *first* the ἐπαγγελία, *then* the coming of the πίστις (Gal 4:23) – although Abraham who received the ἐπαγγελία(ι) *was* already a man of πίστις (Gal 3:6).

The author of Revelation, however, does not know a system of coordinates of an Old Testament promise and its later New Testament fulfilment. Using the language of the Old Testament as *the* language of a heavenly world and a heavenly worship (Rev 4 and 5) according to which all earthly reality, simultaneously, *is* heavenly reality – even the war of the evil forces against God, respectively against his Son and the Church, is a continuation of the fight which has begun already in heaven (Rev 12:7ff) – the seer of Patmos describes what happens between heaven and earth, and thus on earth. Not in the least do we find the idea that what is said in the Old Testament might be fulfilled in Christ. If we want to maintain the scheme of promise and fulfilment in Revelation – although this is not totally adequate – then it is not the scheme of a promise contained in Scripture, and of the fulfilment of this written word of God; for the problem of the correlation of Old and New Testament is completely beyond the perspective of the author of Revelation. This holds true also for the modified opinion mentioned above that the word *spoken* by God, which was eventually written down for the sake of its preservation, was historically fulfilled in the Christ *event*. In Revelation, the *time frame* rather contains *present* and *future*. Above all, passages from Scripture are employed to express what is to happen in the immediate future, ἃ δεῖ γενέσθαι (ἐν τάχει), Rev 1:1; 4:1 (beginning of the heavenly liturgy); 22:6 (see also 1:19). The present, even though it will be terrible, and even though this terribleness will be willed by God (according to Rev 6 and 8, it is the Lamb in its divinity which solves the seal), is still the prelude of the time of salvation. After all, the worship described in Revelation 4 has its goal in the worship of the new Jerusalem (Revelation 21). Only a short time will pass from the first to the second worship which will be eternal (Rev 22:7): "And behold, I am coming soon, ἔρχομαι ταχύ". Hidden under the history of damnation, the history of salvation will eventually lead to the reality beyond history; therefore, time and history are 'sublated' into God's eternity ('sublated' in the double meaning of Hegel!). This is why also biblical language is 'sublated' from the dilemma of time. Because of these imaginative premises, the seer of Patmos can fit in the words of Scripture wherever they suit his concept. And since it is *he* who sees "what must take place", *he knows more than the prophets and the other authors of Scripture*. Because of what he sees and, thus, comprehends as final reality, he can combine the ideas and pictures of the Old Testament, which for him is even less *Old* Testament than for all other New Testament authors, and create a mosaic full of new pictures. This procedure might seem, of course, arbitrary; it might seem like a puzzle. But

John would not understand such a complaint. For him, what he sees and, therefore, writes is the reality of Christ, of the Church, and of the world, and all of this is in *accordance with Scripture*.

The question of which of the Old Testament writings are favoured by John may best be answered by quoting R. H. CHARLES:

> Our author makes most use of the prophetical books. He constantly uses Isaiah, Jeremiah, Ezekiel, and Daniel; also, but in a less degree, Zechariah, Joel, Amos, and Hosea; and in a very minor degree Zephaniah and Habakkuk. Next to the prophetical books he is most indebted to the Psalms, slightly to Proverbs, and still less Canticles. He possessed the Pentateuch and makes occasional use of all its books, particularly of Exodus. Amongst others, that he and his sources probably drew upon, are Joshua, 1 and 2 Samuel, 1 and 2 Kings.[62]

The survey presented above already suggests that the way in which the author of Revelation treats the Old Testament is very multi-faceted, and that he covers topics most diverse. It is therefore impossible in the limited scope of this study to depict how the theological content depends on the Old Testament, as has been done in the discussion of the other New Testament writings. So, two examples may be sufficient: first Rev 1:12–18 will be examined according to A. T. HANSON,[63] and then Revelation 12 and 13, since in both chapters the transition from heavenly to earthly events is illustrated vividly.

Regarding *Rev 1:12–18*, HANSON states: "Fourteen allusions to scripture in seven verses!"[64] Among others, he names Dan 7:13 "one like a Son of Man", Dan 10:5 the "golden girdle", Zech 4:2f the "golden lampstands", and Ezek 9:2 the "long robe".[65] And in fact, the character of the Son of Man known from the synoptic tradition has its scriptural foundation in *Daniel 7*. In addition to Daniel, it is evident that also the throne chariot *vision* in *Ezekiel 1* strongly influenced John's theological conception. Daniel presents himself as an apocalyptic in the book of Daniel, and he is understood as such by the apocalyptic John; Ezekiel 1 has, after all, apocalyptic features, so that the prophet can be understood in an apocalyptic perspective. Regarding the theological overall view of Scripture passages which form the substance of John's christological intention, it is crucial that the passage characterizing the Ancient of Days in Daniel 7:9 as having hair like pure (probably white!) wool is now applied to the one who resembles the Son of Man: the Christ who is like the Son of Man is God![66] This is not an arbitrary application, but the *relecture* of Scripture from the viewpoint of a Christian conviction. Once more, HANSON is worthy of being quoted in great length because of his striking characterization of the approach of the author of Revelation:

---

[62] R. H. CHARLES, *The Revelation to St. John* I (ICC; Edinburgh [1920] 1975) lxv. Still one of the best synoptic surveys on the text of Revelation and its Old Testament allusions is Charles, ibid. lxviii–lxxxvi.

[63] Hanson, The Living Utterances of God (1983) 167ff.

[64] Ibid. 168.

[65] Ibid. 167f.

[66] See, e.g., E. LOHMEYER, *Die Offenbarung des Johannes* (HNT 16; Tübingen [3]1970) 17: "The image of the 'ancient' is here transfered to Christ; 14ab = Dan 7:9 (see Enoch 46:1), v. 14c = Dan 10:6 (see Slavonic apocalypse of Enoch 1:5)". ("Das Bild vom 'Alten' wird hier auf Christus übertragen; 14ab = Dan 7,9 [cf. Hen 46,1], 14c = Dan 10,6 [s. sl. Hen 1,5]").

John the Divine is clearly master of scripture: he is like an artist laying on his paints in order to bring about the effect he requires. But we cannot on the other hand dismiss the use of scripture as if it was purely illustrative with no theological implications. When John uses of Christ language used in scripture of an angel, he means that Christ represents the activity of God, as does the angelic ministry in scripture. When he calls him 'one like a son of man' he means to claim for Christ everything that Jewish tradition believed of the mysterious figure in the Book of Daniel. And certainly when the uses of Christ language which in scripture is applied to God, he means that Christ has divine status; he belongs to the dimension of God and not of creatures.[67]

We now turn to *Revelation 12 and 13*! H. KRAFT has rightly pointed out that, after the sounding of the seventh trumpet announcing the climax of the final events, the seer of Patmos goes all the way back and starts with the mythical pre-history. In the events described in the following portion of Revelation, political history and church history are indissolubly intermingled as final history. The fall of Satan is the decisive event introducing the part of the final history which occurs on earth. "It starts as an event of divine history, of myth, hence its beginning lies beyond time".[68] This fall of Satan, however, continues on earth. When the Messiah and the anti-Christ enter history as the representatives of God and Satan, then "political history becomes the continuation of divine history. What has begun in heaven beyond time and could be seen as a timeless sign in the heaven now continues rapidly on earth as final history".[69] Regarding this transition from myth to history, it is clear that the reception of Scripture by the author of Revelation is of special interest for us.[70] Again we find imagery of Daniel 7 and 8. In Rev 12:3f the fourth beast with the ten horns of the vision in Dan 7:7ff is adopted and equated with the he-goat in Dan 8:5ff which "cast down to the ground" a third "of the host of the stars". In Daniel 7, the coming of the one like the Son of Man brings about the immediate end of the fourth beast, while Rev 12:7ff first reports the fight between Michael and the dragon during the course of which the dragon, explicitly called devil and Satan, is thrown down to earth. The triumphant chorus in *Rev 12:10–12* employing terms like ἡ σωτηρία, ἡ δύναμις, ἡ βασιλεία τοῦ θεοῦ ἡμῶν and ἡ ἐξουσία τοῦ χριστοῦ αὐτοῦ is certainly inspired from Daniel 7, because Dan 7:14ϑ'—immediately after Dan 7:13!—says καὶ αὐτῷ ἐδόθη ἡ ἀρχὴ καὶ ἡ τιμὴ καὶ ἡ βασιλεία … ἡ ἐξουσία αὐτοῦ ἐξουσία αἰώνιος, ἥτις οὐ παρελεύσεται, καὶ ἡ βασιλεία αὐτοῦ οὐ διαφθαρήσεται see also Dan 7:20).[71]

In Revelation 12 the description of the transition from heaven to earth, or from myth to history, is clearly a reception of Daniel 7. The same occurs in

[67] Hanson, The Living Utterances of God (1983) 168.

[68] H. KRAFT, *Die Offenbarung des Johannes* (HNT 16a; Tübingen 1974) 162: "Er beginnt als ein Ereignis der Gottesgeschichte, des Mythos, und so liegt sein Beginn außerhalb der Zeit".

[69] Ibid. 163: "… wird die politische Geschichte Fortsetzung der Gottesgeschichte. Was im Himmel außerhalb der Zeit begonnen hatte und am Himmel als zeitloses Zeichen zu sehen war, das setzt sich nun auf Erden in schneller Folge als Endgeschichte fort".

[70] Unfortunately neither in the NTG[26] nor in the *Greek New Testament* the frequent allusions to the Old Testament are emphasized visually. This is particularly deplorable since today, when often even theologians have an only limited knowledge of biblical contents. (The editorial principle depraves to support the lack of knowledge!)

[71] Regarding Rev 12:10–12 see especially Jörns, Das himmlische Evangelium (1971) 110ff.

Revelation 13 where the number of the four beasts of Daniel 7, however, is reduced to only two. Rev 13:1 refers to Rev 12:3. While in Dan 7:6 dominion is given to the third beast (ϑ': καὶ ἐξουσία ἐδόθη [*passivum divinum*!] αὐτῇ[72]), Rev 13:2 says καὶ ἔδωκεν αὐτῷ ὁ δράκων (!) τὴν δύναμιν αὐτοῦ καὶ τόν θρόνον αὐτοῦ καὶ ἐξουσίαν μεγάλην. Rev. 13:5 says καὶ ἐδόθη αὐτῷ στόμα λαλοῦν μεγάλα καὶ βλασφημίας, καὶ ἐδόθη αὐτῷ ἐξουσία ποιῆσαι μῆνας τεσσεράκοντα καὶ δύο corresponds to the description of the fourth beast in Dan 7:8 καὶ στόμα λαλοῦν μεγάλα.[73] So far we have exercised restraint with regard to the suggestion that Jewish exegetical concepts and methods were adopted by New Testament authors. Here, however, it is certainly justified to call Revelation 12 and 13 a *midrash* on Daniel 7 (and also on some other passages of the Book of Daniel which continue the same pattern of thought) – a midrash, of course, which uses Daniel with tremendous freedom. Once more A. T. HANSON should be heard here. Regarding the book of Revelation in general, he says, drawing on SWEET, that its author was normally dealing more with the Hebrew text of the Old Testament than with the Septuagint. But he was also familiar with the text of the Targum. HANSON then concludes:

> As we might expect, there is more evidence in Revelation of a knowledge of Jewish exegetical tradition than in any other book of the New Testament. Indeed, one is tempted to say that Revelation shows more signs of the influence of Jewish exegetical tradition than do all the rest of the books of the New Testament put together![74]
>
> John the Divine is so free and creative in his use of scripture that we are driven occasionally to wonder whether he really regarded scripture as inspired. We have noted ... Sweet's admirable phrase for the way John the Divine uses scripture: 'creative freedom'. Does this mean that he could do anything he liked with scripture, make it serve any purpose which he chose, regardless of what it 'really meant'? This is the sort of question which we could relevantly ask in connection with almost any method of interpreting scripture. We could certainly put it to Philo: when we see how he allegorizes the Pentateuch we cannot be blamed for concluding that Philo could use his allegorical method to make his text say absolutely anything he liked. One could make very much the same judgement about a great deal of rabbinic exegesis. ... But we would be mistaken if we made such a judgement about either Philo or the rabbis or John the Divine.[75]

5. Final Remarks

Regarding the theology of the New Testament, or to put it more precisely, regarding the theologies of the New Testament writings, it became clear that a full understanding is impossible if the reception of the Old Testament by the New Testament authors is not seen as constitutive. To a large extent, theological thinking in the New Testament comprises the christological understanding of the Old Testament. If this understanding determines our theological interpretation, then it would imply that the *Vetus Testamentum in*

---

[72] But Dan 7:6 LXX: καί γλῶσσα ἐδόθη αὐτῷ.

[73] The juxtaposition of the New Testament text and of the ϑ' text is not intended to suggest that the author of Revelation was influenced by the text of the Septuagint.

[74] Hanson, The Living Utterances of God (1983) 171.

[75] Ibid. 175.

Novo receptum is *substantially* different from the *Vetus Testamentum per se*. To put it simply, this substantial difference consists of the fact that, according to the literal meaning of the Old Testament, eschatological salvation is available primarily to the people of Israel while Gentiles, if at all, only participate in Israel's salvation. According to the Old Testament as it is adopted by the New, however, God has accomplished salvation through Christ for the Church worldwide and, thus, for all of humankind, while Israel *as* the people of Israel has no more soteriological priority. Differently nuanced, the individual New Testament authors each put forth constitutively the so-called theory of substitution which refers to Israel's replacement through the Church in a soteriological perspective.

Time and again, this theory has been criticized as hostile to Israel. But the opposite is true – provided the historical and theological differences of Old Testament *per se* and Old Testament adopted by the New are respected! As for its original literal sense, the Old Testament is open for Christian interpretation only to a limited extent. The largest part of the *Biblia Hebraica* is, according to its original sense, thoroughly Jewish. If, therefore, the Christian biblical scholar admits – and this is what must be admitted – that the Old Testament *per se* remains in Jewish possession, then the Church did not snatch the Old Testament *per se* away from Judaism! Then the Christian Church must also admit that, wherever the Old Testament *per se* was declared as belonging to Christians, grievous injustice has been caused to Judaism. But in this case the Christian understanding of the Old Testament is its interpretation from a christological viewpoint. The fact that extremely important Old Testament passages are open for the Christian kerygma as demonstrated in, for example, the reception of ψ 142:2 in Gal 2:16, must be respected at the same time.

A crucial issue is, furthermore, the observation that the relation between Old and New Testament is not the relation between two books, and it is not at all the relation between *Biblia Hebraica* and *Novum Testamentum Graece*. The New Testament authors mainly considered the Septuagint as holy Scripture relevant for them. To evaluate the relation of both testaments appropriately we must pay attention to the fact that the early Church, separating from Israel, reflected on its *oral* sermons *also* with regards to Israel's Scripture and, thus, to Israel's credo. The relation between the two books of Old and New Testament must thus be understood as the relation between Israel and the Church with respect to continuity and discontinuity. It is a question of the historicity of Israel and of the historicity of the Church. The issue at stake here is not just a literary problem, but the problem of the historicity of the Christian faith and, therefore, of our own Christian historicity. Finally the question of Scripture is the question of *ecclesiology* which has its fundament in *Christology* and *soteriology*.

After what has been said about the core of the problem it should be evident that, in view of questions which touch upon Christian dogmatics substantially, the problem of differences and agreement between Jewish and Christian exegetical methods is secondary.

Chapter Ten

The Development of Scriptural Interpretation in the Second and Third Centuries – except Clement and Origen

By Oskar Skarsaune, Oslo

Works of reference: *Biblia Patristica. Index des citations et allusions bibliques dans la littérature patristique* (ed. Centre d'analyse et de documentation patristiques, Strasbourg; A. Benoit et al.), 1. *Des origines à Clément d'Alexandrie et Tertullien* (Paris 1975), 2. *Le troisième siècle (Origène excepté)* (Paris 1977); M. Geerard, *Clavis Patrum Graecorum*, I. *Patres antenicaeni* (CC; Turnhout 1983).

General works: P. R. Ackroyd / C. F. Evans (eds.), *The Cambridge History of the Bible*, I. *From the Beginnings to Jerome* (Cambridge 1970); J. N. S. Alexander, "The Interpretation of Scripture in the Ante-Nicene Period", *Int* 12 (1958) 272–280; *La Bible et les Pères. Colloque de Strasbourg (1–3 octobre 1969)* (ed. A. Benoît / P. Prigent; Paris 1971); W. J. Burghardt, "On Early Christian Exegesis", *TS* 11 (1950) 78–116; P. T. Camelot, "L'exégèse de l'Ancien Testament par les Pères", *L'Ancien Testament et les Chrétiens* (Paris 1951) 149–167; H. Freiherr von Campenhausen, "Das Alte Testament als Bibel der Kirche", (in idem:) *Aus der Frühzeit des Christentums* (Tübingen 1963) 152–196; idem, *Die Entstehung der christlichen Bibel* (BHT 39; Tübingen 1968); J. Daniélou, *Sacramentum Futuri: Études sur les origines de la typologie biblique* (Études de Théologie Historique; Paris 1950); idem, *Théologie du Judéo-Christianisme* (Tournai 1958), ET: *The Theology of Jewish Christianity* (London 1964); idem, *Message évangelique et culture hellenistique aux IIe et IIIe siècles* (Paris/Tournai 1961), ET: *Gospel Message and Hellenistic Culture* (London/Philadelphia 1973); idem, *Études d'exégèse judéo-chrétienne (Les Testimonia)* (Théologie historique 5; Paris 1966); idem, *Les origines du christianisme latin* (Paris 1978), ET: *The Origins of Latin Christianity* (London/Philadelphia 1977); L. Diestel, *Geschichte des Alten Testaments in der christlichen Kirche* (Jena 1869); C. H. Dodd, *According to the Scriptures. The sub-structure of New Testament Theology* (London 1952; paperback ed. 1965); H. Dörrie, "Zur Methodik antiker Exegese", *ZNW* 65 (1974) 121–138; E. Flessemann-van Leer, *Tradition and Scripture in the Early Church* (Assen 1953); K. Froehlich, *Biblical Interpretation in the Early Church* (Sources of Early Christian Thought; Philadelphia 1984); R. M. Grant / D. Tracy, *A Short History of the Interpretation of the Bible* (rev. ed.; Philadelphia 1984); P. Grelot, *Sens chrétien de l'Ancien Testament* (Tournai 1962); W.-D. Hauschild, "Der Ertrag der neueren auslegungsgeschichtlichen Forschung für die Patristik", *VF* 16 (1971) 5–25; W. Horbury, "Old Testament Interpretation in the Writings of the Church Fathers", *Mikra* (ed. J. Mulder / H. Sysling; Assen/Philadelphia 1988) 727–787; G. Jouassard, "Les Pères devant la Bible, leurs perspectives particulières", *Etudes de critique et d'histoire religieuses* (Bibliothèque de la Faculté catholique de théologie de Lyon 2; Lyon 1948); D. Juel, *Messianic Exegesis: Christological Interpretation of the Old Testament in Early Christianity* (Philadelphia 1988); J. L. Kugel / R. A. Greer, *Early Biblical Interpretation* (Philadelphia 1986); H. de Lubac, "'Typologie' et 'Allégorisme'", *RSR* 34 (1947) 180–226; B. de Margerie, *Introduction à l'histoire de l'exégèse*, I. *Les Pères grecs et orientaux* (Paris 1980), Ital. transl.: *Introduzione alla storia dell' esegesi*, I. *Padri greci i orientali* (Roma 1983); idem, *Introduction à l'histoire de l'exégèse*, II. *Les premiers grands Exégètes latins. De Tertullien à Jérome* (Paris 1983), Ital. transl.: *Introduzione alla storia dell' esegesi*, II. *Padri Latini* (Rome 1984); *Le monde grec ancien et la Bible* (BTT I, ed. C. Mondésert; Paris 1984); G. Pelland, "Que faut il attendre de l'histoire de l'exégèse ancienne?", *Greg* 69 (1988) 617–628; H. Graf Reventlow, *Epochen der*

Bibelauslegung, 1. *Vom Alten Testament bis Origenes* (München 1990); M. Simonetti, "L'interpretazione patristica del Vecchio Testamento fra II e III secolo", *Aug* 22 (1982) 7–33; idem, *Biblical interpretation in the Early Church. An historical introduction to patristic exegesis* (Edinburgh 1994); O. Skarsaune, *Da Skriften ble åpnet. Den første kristne tolkning av Det gamle testamente*, (Oslo 1987); idem, "Schriftbeweis und christologisches Kerygma in der ältesten kirchlichen Schriftauslegung", *Schrift und Auslegung* (Veröffentlichungen der Luther-Akademie e.V. Ratzeburg 10, ed. H. Kraft; Erlangen 1987) 45–54; H. F. D. Sparks, *The Old Testament in the Christian Church* (London 1944); A. Freiherr von Ungern-Sternberg, *Der traditionelle alttestamentliche Schriftbeweis "de Christo" und "de Evangelio" in der Alten Kirche bis zur Zeit Eusebs von Caesarea* (Halle a. S. 1913); R. McL. Wilson, "The Gnostics and the Old Testament", *Proceedings of the International Colloquium on Gnosticism Stockholm August 20–25, 1973* (ed. G. Widengren, Kungliga Vitterhetsakademiet, hist. och antikvitetsakad. Handlingar, filol.-filos. serie 17; Stockholm 1977) 164–168.

Jewish and Christian exegesis: E. L. Abel, "Jewish-Christian controversy in the second and third centuries A.D.", *Judaica* 29 (1973) 112–125; I. H. Dalmais, "L'heritage juif chez les premiers auteurs chrétiens", *Bible et Terre Sainte* 161 (1974) 6–7; R. le Deaut, "Un phénomène spontané de l'herméneutique juive ancienne: le 'targumisme'", *Bib*. 52 (1971) 505–525; idem, "La tradition juive ancienne et l'exégèse chrétienne primitive", *RHPR* 51 (1971) 31–50; L. Ginzberg, "Die Haggada bei den Kirchenvätern und in der apokryphischen Litteratur (Genesis)", *MGWJ* 42 (1898) 537–550; 43 (1899) 17–22. 61–75. 117–125. 149–159. 217–231. 293–303. 409–416. 461–470. 485–504. 529–547; idem, "Die Haggada bei den Kirchenvätern (Exodus)", *Livre d'hommage à la memoire du Dr. Samuel Poznánski* (Warsaw 1927) 199–216; idem, "Die Haggada bei den Kirchenvätern (Numeri-Deuteronomium)", *Studies in Jewish Bibliography in Memory of A. S. Freidus* (New York 1929) 503–514; W. Horbury, "Messianism among Jews and Christians in the Second Century", *Aug* 28 (1988) 71–88; K. Hruby, "Exégèse rabbinique et exégèse patristique", *RSR* 47 (1973) 341–372; R. Loewe, "The Jewish midrashim and patristic and scholastic exegesis of the Bible", StPatr 1 (TU 63; Leipzig 1957) 492–514; J. J. Petuchowski, "Halakhah in the Church Fathers", *Essays in Honor of S.B. Freehof* (ed. W. Jacob et al.; Pittsburg 1964) 257–274; M. Simon, "La Bible dans les premières controverses entre Juifs et Chrétiens", *Le monde grec ancien et la Bible* (BTT I, ed. C. Mondésert; Paris 1984) 107–125; O. Skarsaune, "Oldkirkens kristologi og de jødiske frelsesforventningene", *Judendom och kristendom under de första århundradena* 2 (ed. S. Hidal et al.; Stavanger 1986) 201–219; idem, "'Hva intet øye så...'. Litt om strukturen i tidlig kristen og jødisk eskatologi", *Florilegium patristicum* (FS Per Beskow; ed. G. Hallonsten / S. Hidal / S. Rubenson; Delsbo 1991) 201–213; G. N. Stanton, "Aspects of Early Christian-Jewish Polemic and Apologetic", *NTS* 31 (1985) 377–92; H. Villadsen, "Philon og den oldkirkelige skriftfortolkning", *Judendom och kristendom under de första århundradena* 2 (ed. S. Hidal et al.; Stavanger 1986) 93–112; B. L. Visotzky, "Jots and Tittles: On Scriptural Interpretation in Rabbinic and Patristic Literatures", *Prooftexts* 8 (1988) 257–269.

Special themes: G. T. Armstrong, *Die Genesis in der Alten Kirche. Die drei Kirchenväter, Justinus, Irenäus, Tertullian* (BGBH 4; Tübingen 1962); C. G. Bellido, "Simbolismo del vestido. Interpretación patrística de Gen. 49,11", *Estudios Ecclesiásticos* 59 (1984) 313–357; R. Bodenmann, *Naissance d'une Exégèse. Daniel dans l'Eglise ancienne des trois premiers siècles* (BGBE 28; Tübingen 1986); B. Dehandschutter, "'Le Messie est déjà venu': à propos du thème de la double venue du Messie chez les pères de l'église", *Bijdragen. Tijdschrift voor filosofie en theologie* 50 (1989) 314–321; A. von Harnack, *Über den privaten Gebrauch der heiligen Schriften in der alten Kirche* (Beiträge zur Einleitung in das Neue Testament V; Leipzig 1912); D. M. Hay, *Glory at the Right Hand: Psalm 110 in Early Christianity* (SBL Mon. Ser. 18; Nashville/New York 1973); *In Principio. Interprétations des premiers versets de la Genèse* (Paris: École pratique des hautes études 1973); E. Kähler, *Studien zum Te Deum und zur Geschichte des 24. Psalms in der Alten Kirche* (Veröffentlichungen der Evangelischen Gesellschaft für Liturgieforschung 10; Göttingen 1958); D. Lerch, *Isaaks Opferung christlich gedeutet. Eine auslegungsgeschichtliche Untersuchung* (BHT 12; Tübingen 1950); O. Linton, "Interpretation of the Psalms in the Early Church", StPatr 4,2 (TU 79; Berlin 1961) 143–156; F. Nikolasch, *Das Lamm als Christussymbol in den Schriften der Väter* (Wien 1963); P. Prigent, "Quelques testimonia messianiques. Leurs histoire littéraire de Qoumrân aux Pères de l'église", *TZ* 15 (1959) 419–430; G. Q. Reijners, *The Terminology of the Holy Cross in Early Christian Literature as based upon Old Testament Typology* (Graecitas Christianorum Primaeva 2; Nijmegen 1965); K. Schlütz, *Isaias 11,2 (die sieben Gaben des Hl.*

Geistes) in den ersten vier christlichen Jahrhunderten (ATA 11,4; Münster/Westf. 1932); R. McL. Wilson, "The Early History of the Exegesis of Gen 1.26", StPatr, 1 (TU 63; Berlin 1957) 420–437; C. Wolff, *Jeremia im Frühjudentum und Urchristentum* (TU 118; Berlin 1976); H. W. Wolff, *Jesaja 53 im Urchristentum. Die Geschichte der Prophetie "Siehe, es siegt mein Knecht" bis zu Justin* (Giessen [4]1984).

In many respects, Christian literature of the period 30–250 CE may be said to be one single large commentary on the Scriptures, the Hebrew Bible. Judaism was a religion of the holy Scriptures. In the attempt to define itself, first within, then with regard to, Judaism, the early Church could not avoid a direct or indirect *Auseinandersetzung* with the Jewish Bible. This runs through all extant early Christian literature – in varying degrees, though – and presents us with an overwhelming wealth of material for the survey of this chapter. Not only is the literature extensive in quantity. The different writings also represent a baffling variety of literary genres. In part, this reflects the many different settings in which the Old Testament was applied and interpreted.[1] It would seem that any attempt to discern a clear and simple pattern in all of this material is futile.

In order to limit the material and make the scope of this essay manageable, only such early Christian writings are selected for comment, which are explicitly *interpretative* with regard to the Old Testament. This does not mean that we are looking only for formal *commentaries*. If such were the case, the material would shrink drastically, and hardly be more than the two commentaries by Hippolytus on Daniel and Song of Songs. By interpretative texts is meant texts in which the Old Testament is (1) explicitly quoted, and (2) commented upon, either by direct commentary of an exegetical nature, or, more indirectly, by making the Old Testament quotation the basis for a certain argument.

In the group of Christian writings from the first half of the second century, somewhat arbitrarily grouped together under the name "Apostolic Fathers", only *1. Clement* and *Barnabas* qualify as interpretative texts with regard to the Old Testament. Among the Apologists, Justin's *Apology* chs. 31ff and his *Dialogue* are clearly interpretative, as are Theophilus of Antioch's *Ad Autolycum*. Melito of Sardis' *Paschal Homily* is an obviously interpretative work; Irenaeus' *Proof of the Apostolic Preaching* likewise. In Irenaeus' *Adversus Haereses* books 4 and 5 are mainly devoted to Old Testament interpretation, book 3 partly. In Tertullian it is more difficult to single out the most relevant works in our context; we shall concentrate on *Adversus Iudaeos*, *Contra Marcionem*, and *Adversus Praxean*. In Hippolytus, the two commentaries on Daniel and Song of Songs claim our interest; the preserved fragments of his other exegetical works are also relevant. Novatian's *De Trinitate* contains a substantial amount of proof-texts from the Old Testament. Cyprian's '*Testimonies*' (*Ad Quirinum*) may be said to be the final compendium of the Old Testament proof-texts used in this tradition.

This list of relevant source material is rather restrictive, but even so one encounters a great variety of exegetical methods. Looking, however, at the aim and purpose of the Old Testament interpretation within these works, it

[1] In his comprehensive essay on early Christian interpretation of the Old Testament, W. Horbury, Old Testament Interpretation (1988) 731–758, distinguishes 8 different "settings in literature and life": homily, commentary, catechesis, apologetic, ecclesiastical law, liturgy, poetry, and art.

seems one can single out three basic types of exegesis, and group the material accordingly.

1. The "proof from prophecy". The largest proportion of the material is concerned with *proving* from Old Testament "proof-texts" that Jesus is the Messiah, that the ritual commandments in the Law are no longer obligatory,[2] and that the Church, not the Jews, is now the people of God.[3] In short, one may say that this material represents the "prophecy – fulfilment" pattern, and that this pattern contains two basic types of prophecy: (1) prophetic oracles, and (2) prophetic events, persons or institutions: the *typoi*.[4]

The classic study of this material is that of A. VON UNGERN-STERNBERG. He shows that a rather stable selection of Old Testament proof-texts recur from one author to another, right from the New Testament to Eusebius. The main representatives of this tradition are found to be Barnabas, Justin, Irenaeus, Tertullian, Hippolytus, Novatian, and Cyprian (Melito's *Peri Pascha* was not known to VON UNGERN-STERNBERG, but should now be added). VON UNGERN-STERNBERG's last and concluding chapter is properly given the title "The stability of the tradition of the Scriptural Proof". The present survey will confirm our right to speak of such a tradition. At the same time a diachronic perspective reveals developments and modifications not sufficiently noticed by VON UNGERN-STERNBERG.

2. The paraenetic homily. The earliest one of the sources mentioned above stands apart as not belonging to the "proof from prophecy" tradition: *1 Clement*. Among the so-called Apostolic Fathers, this document is second only to *Barnabas* in the vast amount of Old Testament texts that are quoted or alluded to. But VON UNGERN-STERNBERG is certainly correct when he states that "*1 Clement* has very little to offer concerning our theme" (the Scriptural Proof).[5] *1 Clement* is a homily-like document in which a vast amount of Old Testament '*exempla*' (not *typoi*) and *paraenetic* texts are adduced as hortatory admonitions to Christians. The "prophecy-fulfilment" scheme is not prominent in this document. On the other hand, a striking sense of immediate *continuity* with the Old Testament people of God permeates the epistle.

3. "Biblical antiquities". Theophilus' *Ad Autolycum* also falls outside the "prophecy-fulfilment" scheme, but in another way. The second book to Autolycus contains the first example of a Christian exposition of Gen 1–11; the third book contains an extensive proof of the greater antiquity of the Old Testament prophets compared to the Greek poets and philosophers.

Generally speaking, the "proof-text" tradition of the first group of writings has Judaism as its polemic counterpart, as in Justin's *Dialogue* and the *Ad-*

---

[2] Cp. esp. K. HOHEISEL, "Die Auslegung alttestamentlicher Opferzeugnisse im Neuen Testament und in der frühen Kirche", *Frühmittelalterliche Studien* 18 (1984) 421–436; P. G. VERWEIJS, *Evangelium und neues Gesetz in der ältesten Christenheit bis auf Marcion* (Utrecht 1960); D. WENDEBOURG, "Die alttestamentlichen Reinheitsgesetze in der frühen Kirche", *ZKG* 95 (1984) 149–170.

[3] Cp. esp. N. BONWETSCH, "Der Schriftbeweis für die Kirche aus den Heiden als das wahre Israel", *Theologische Studien, Festschrift Th. Zahn* (Leipzig 1908) 1–22; P. RICHARDSON, *Israel in the Apostolic Church* (Soc. for NT Stud., Monogr. Ser. 10; Cambridge 1969).

[4] Cp. H. CLAVIER, "Esquisse de Typologie comparée, dans le Nouveau Testament et chez quelques écrivains patristiques", StPatr 4,2 (TU 79; Berlin 1961) 28–49; J. Daniélou, Gospel Message (1973) 197–300; K. J. WOOLCOMBE, "The Biblical Origins and Patristic Development of Typology", *Essays on Typology* (ed. G. W. H. Lampe / K. J. Woolcombe; London 1957) 39–75.

[5] Schriftbeweis (1913) 274.

versus Ioudaeos texts. But the scriptural proof which originally was developed in intense debates with Jews, proved to be useful in other debates, too.

When addressing Gentiles, a Christian author could use the traditional "proof from prophecy" in order to show the *antiquity* of Christianity, and he could exploit the apologetic argument implied in the "prophecy – fulfilment" scheme: events predicted hundreds of years earlier proved the truth of the predictions, and vice versa. This use of the "proof from prophecy" is to be observed i.a. in Justin's *Apology* and Irenaeus' *Proof of the Apostolic Preaching*. But even in the debate with Marcion and Gnostics one finds an extensive use of the same proof-text tradition. Marcion agreed with Judaism on a crucial point: Jesus was not the Messiah promised in the Old Testament. Therefore, the traditional Christian "proof from prophecy" had to be repeated and strengthened in debate with Marcion. One observes this most vividly in Tertullian: Large portions of his *Adversus Ioudaeos* recur almost *verbatim* in *Adversus Marcionem*. A similar mechanism is at work in Irenaeus in his debate with the Gnostics. Gnostics generally showed little or no interest in Messianic prophecies, and – like Marcion – denied the father-son relationship between Christ and the creator God of the Old Testament. In order to combat this, Irenaeus once again marshals the proof-text tradition. But the "direction" of the proof has been reversed. While discussing with Jews, one could take the authority of the Old Testament for granted, while the fulfilment of the Old Testament prophecies in Jesus and the Church were the objects of proof. In debate with Gnostics, it was the other way round: the authority of Jesus as the revealer of truth was uncontested. The very possibility, however, of proving that Jesus had been predicted by the prophets, and that therefore the Old Testament was a revelation given by His Father, was the best possible vindication of the authority and the divine origin of the Old Testament.

In this way the proof-text tradition is developed and modified in different settings, and also becomes a cherished piece of supporting argument in internal Christian instruction, as in Novatian's *De trinitate*. This development will be studied a little more in detail below.

1 Clement is also a polemical document, but the polemic counterpart is inner-Christian. Therefore the anti-Jewish proof-texts of the "proof from prophecy" tradition recede almost completely in this author. The same is true, but for different reasons, of Theophilus. His opponent is a Gentile, who brings the same arguments against Christianity as he would do against Judaism. Therefore, Theophilus' answer is very much the same as the Jewish answer would be. In other words, Theophilus is a strikingly "Jewish" author, and there is a strong a priori assumption that he relies heavily on Jewish apologetics.

After this rough outline of the material in question, we shall proceed in a mainly chronological sequence, paying closer attention to details, but at the same time keeping in mind the overarching categories of aim and purpose we have seen so far.

1. The Apostolic Fathers and Their Time

Sources: O. de Gebhardt / A. von Harnack / T. Zahn, *Patrum Apostolicorum Opera* I–III (in 4 vols.; Lipsiae 1876–78); J. B. Lightfoot, *The Apostolic Fathers* I–II (in 5 vols.; 2nd ed. London 1889–90; repr. Hildesheim/New York 1973); K. Lake, *The Apostolic Fathers, with an English Translation* I–II (LCL; London/Cambridge, MA 1965 [orig. publ. 1912]); *Schriften des Urchristentums*, I. *Die Apostolischen Väter* (ed. J. A. Fischer; Darmstadt 1956; 7th. ed. 1976); *Schriften des Urchristentums*, II. *Didache (Apostellehre), Barnabasbrief, Zweiter Klemensbrief, Schrift an Diognet* (ed. K. Wengst; München/Darmstadt 1984); A. Lindemann / H. Paulsen, *Die Apostolischen Väter. Griechisch-deutsche Parallelausgabe auf der Grundlage der Ausgaben von Franz Xaver Funk/Karl Bihlmeyer und Molly Whittaker* (Tübingen 1992).

Works of reference: E. J. Goodspeed, *Index patristicus sive clavis patrum apostolicorum* (Leipzig 1907; repr. 1960); H. Kraft, *Clavis Patrum apostolicorum* (Darmstadt 1963).

General works: L. W. Barnard, *Studies in the Apostolic Fathers and their Background* (Oxford 1963); J. D. M. Derrett, "Scripture and Norms in the Apostolic Fathers", ANRW II:27,1 (ed. W. Haase; Berlin/New York 1993) 649–699. E. Flesseman-van Leer, "Het Oude Testament bij de Apostolische Vaders en de Apologeten", *NedTT* 5 (1954/55) 230ff; L. Goppelt, *Christentum und Judentum im ersten und zweiten Jahrhundert. Ein Aufriss der Urgeschichte der Kirche* (BFChrT 2. Reihe 55; Gütersloh 1954); N. Hyldahl, "Kampen om skriftforståelsen i det andet århundrede", *Judendom och kristendom under de första århundradena* 2 (ed. S. Hidal et al.; Stavanger 1986) 65–76; O. Knoch, "Die Stellung der apostolischen Väter zu Israel und zum Judentum. Eine Übersicht", *Begegnung mit dem Wort* (FS H. Zimmermann; ed. J. Zmijewski / E. Nellessen, BBB 53; Bonn 1980) 347–378; R. Knopf et al., *Die Apostolischen Väter* (HNT, Ergänzungsband; Tübingen 1923); J. Klevinghaus, *Die theologische Stellung der Apostolischen Väter zur alttestamentlichen Offenbarung* (BFChrT 44,1; Gütersloh 1948); G. N. Stanton, "Aspects of Early Christian-Jewish Polemic and Apologetic", *NTS* 31 (1985) 377–92; A. Freiherr von Ungern-Sternberg, Schriftbeweis (1913) 268–275.

> "For the most part, the interpretation of the Old Testament in the Apostolic Fathers is uninteresting, and apart from some far-fetched allegorizing in Barnabas, receives very little space in discussions of the history of interpretation".[6]

The latter part of this statement is no doubt true, but the first part is open to discussion.

Except for *1 Clement*, the Apostolic Fathers may be said to belong generally to the "proof from prophecy" tradition in their use of the Old Testament. The only document, however, which displays this tradition in any detail is *Barnabas*. But before treating these two, we shall begin with a brief survey of the relationship to the Old Testament in some of the other writings in this group.

Ignatius[7] never quotes or uses this tradition directly in his own argument;

---

[6] D. A. Hagner, *The Use of the Old and New Testaments in Clement of Rome* (NovTSup 34; Leiden 1973) 125.

[7] *Literature*: E. F. von der Goltz, *Ignatius von Antiochien als Christ und Theologe. Eine dogmengeschichtliche Untersuchung* (TU 12,3; Leipzig 1894) 80–86, 124–127; S. Reinach, "Ignatius, Bishop of Antiochia and the Archeia", *Anatolian Studies presented to W. M. Ramsey* (ed. W. H. Buckler / W. M. Calder; Manchester/London 1923) 339–340; D. van den Eynde, *Les Normes de l'Enseignement Chrétien dans la littérature patristique des trois premiers siècles* (Dissertationes ad gradum magistri in facultate theologica 2,25; Gembloux-Paris 1933) 30–38; J. Klevinghaus, Die theologische Stellung (1948), 78–112; E. Flessemann-van Leer, Tradition and Scripture (1953) 31–35; H. Freiherr von Campenhausen, Das Alte Testament als Bibel der Kirche (1963) 163–166; R. M. Grant, "Scripture and tradition in St. Ignatius of Antioch", *CBQ* 25 (1963) 322–335; idem, "Hermeneutics and Tradition in Ignatius of Antioch. A methodological Investigation", *Ermeneutica* (ed. E. Castelli; Rome 1963) 183–201; D. Daube, "TRIA MYSTERIA KRAUGÆS, Ignatius Ephesians 19,1", *JTS* NS 16 (1965) 128–129; H. Freiherr von Campenhausen, Die Entstehung (1968) 86–88; P. Meinhold, "Die geschichtstheologischen Konzeptionen des Ignatius von Antiochien", *Kyriakon* (FS J. Quasten), I (ed. P. Granfield / J.A. Jungmann; Münster/Westf. 1970) 182–191; R. M. Grant, "Jewish Christianity at Antioch in the second century", *RSR* 60 (1972) 97–108; K. Bommes, *Weizen Gottes. Untersuchungen zur Theologie des Martyriums bei Ignatius von Antiochien* (Theophaneia 27; Bonn/Köln 1976) 114–118; H. Paulsen, *Studien zur Theologie des Ignatius von Antiochien* (FKDG 29; Göttingen 1978); W. R. Schoedel, "Ignatius and the Archives", *HTR* 71 (1978) 97–106; P. J. Donahue, "Jewish Christianity in the Letters of Ignatius of Antioch", *VC* 32 (1978) 81–93; P. Meinhold, *Studien zu Ignatius von Antiochien* (Veröffentlichungen des Instituts für Europäische Geschichte in Mainz 97; Wiesbaden 1979) 26–29. 37–47; W. R. Schoedel, *Ignatius of Antioch. A Commentary on the Letters of Ignatius of Antioch* (Hermeneia, ed. H. Koester; Philadelphia 1985); H. Paulsen, *Die Briefe des Ignatius von Antiochia und der Brief des Polykarp von Smyrna* (HNT 18, Die Apost.

in fact, he only quotes the Old Testament three times, and only for paraenetic purposes.[8] At the same time, he clearly knows and alludes to the "proof from prophecy" more than once.

In *Smyrn.* 5.1 he hints that the prophecies and the law of Moses witness to the same truth as "the gospel"; and in 7.2 he indicates that the passion and resurrection of Jesus is the "gospel" predicted by the prophets. In *Philad.* 8.2 he reports a discussion on the validity of the "proof from prophecy". When Ignatius says here that to him the Scriptures "are" Jesus Christ, his passion and resurrection, this should probably not be taken to mean that the passion and resurrection of Christ *replace* the Old Testament as a new "Scripture", but rather that, for Ignatius, the passion and resurrection are the central contents of the Old Testament. This would agree not only with *Smyrn.* 5 and 7 (cp. above), but also with *Philad.* 5.2 (the prophets "have announced the gospel") and 9.2.

This would indicate that in the famous "creeds" of Ignatius,[9] there is an implied "*kata tas grafas*", since these creeds have the same three-fold structure: (1) the coming (= birth) of the Saviour; (2) his passion, and (3) resurrection:

Be deaf when anyone speaks to you apart from Jesus Christ,
(1) Who was of the stock of David,
Who was from Mary, Who was truly born, ate and drank,
(2) was truly persecuted under Pontius Pilate,
was truly crucified and died in the sight of beings heavenly, earthly and under the earth,
(3) Who also was truly raised from the dead... (*Trallians* 9).

This "creed" is clearly anti-docetic (cp. the repeated "truly"), and it agrees with this tendency when the coming of Jesus is described in Messianic, Old Testament categories: *ek genous Daveid.*[10]

This creed-like formula has important New Testament precursors, first and foremost the passion-resurrection formula in 1 Cor 15:3b-4 (with explicit *kata tas grafas*).[11] In combining the passion-resurrection motif with the coming/birth motif, Ignatius' credal formulas have the same structure as the scriptural "proof" in Matthew's "fulfilment quotations".[12]

It is interesting to compare Ignatius' three-fold structure with the roughly contemporary credal formula in the fragments of the *Kerygma Petrou* (in Clement of Alexandria) – usually dated to ca. 125 CE:

We, *unrolling the books of the prophets* which we possess, who name Jesus Christ, partly in parables, partly in enigmas, but also unmistakably and in so many words, found
(1) His coming and
(2) death, and cross ... and
(3) His resurrection and assumption to heaven ...
As it is written, these are the things that he was to suffer ... (Fragm. 6 = Clem. Alex. *Strom.* 6.15.128).

In this text, the *kata tas grafas* is again quite explicit, and this strengthens our interpretation of Ignatius' formulas along the same lines.

Väter II; Tübingen 1985); C. Munier, "Où en est la question d'Ignace d'Antioche? Bilan d'un siècle de recherches 1870–1988", ANRW II:27,1 (ed. W. Haase; Berlin/New York 1993, 359–484) 388–91.

[8] *Eph.* 5.3 = Prov 3:24 "God resisteth the proud"; *Magn.* 12 = Prov 18:17 "The righteous man is his own accuser"; *Trall.* 8.2 = Isa 52:5 (freely rendered) "Woe unto him through whom my name is vainly blasphemed among any".

[9] Cp. J. N. D. Kelly, *Early Christian Creeds* (London [3]1972) 68–70.

[10] Ignatius very likely presupposes the premiss that Mary was of David's stock, as is spelled out in full in the *Protevangelium Iakobi*.

[11] For the Davidic descent motif, cp. in Paul the old formula in Rom 1:3f.

[12] Cp. esp. W. Rotfuchs, *Die Erfüllungszitate des Matthäus-Evangeliums. Eine biblisch-theologische Untersuchung* (BWANT 88; Stuttgart 1969). P. Borgen has argued that Ignatius' formulas on the Virgin Birth are similar to, but independent of Matthew's: "En tradisjonshistorisk analyse av materialet om Jesu fødsel hos Ignatius", *TTK* 42 (1971) 37–44.

It should also be added that this Davidic Christology of a Messiah who suffers and rises is not the only Christological model present in Ignatius. He also knows another Christological scheme, orientated around the focal points of (1) divine pre-existence and (2) incarnation in humility. Also in this case, there is an Old Testament basis, an implicit Christological interpretation of an important Old Testament motif: God's Wisdom.

The divine prophets ... convinced the disobedient that
(a) there is one God, who manifested himself
(b) through Jesus Christ his son,
who is His Word proceeding from silence (*sigee*),
who in all respects was well-pleasing to him that sent him (*Magn*. 8.2).

This reads like a Christological version of Wis 18:14f:[13]

For while gentle silence (*sigee*) enveloped all things, ... Thy all-powerful Word leaped from heaven, from the royal throne.

This Old Testament Wisdom background is probably also to be seen behind the well-known hymn on the incarnation in *Ephesians* 19, with its central Christological statement: "God became manifest as man" (*theou anthroopinoos faneroumenou*).

It thus seems that Ignatius knows two Christological models, both based on the Old Testament: a "Messianic-Davidic" type and a "Wisdom" Christology.[14] We shall see the significance of this shortly.

In the *Didache*[15] one also gets glimpses of a prophecy-fulfilment scheme in Christology and also with regard to the eucharist.[16] The "vine of David" motif in the eucharistic (?) prayer *Did*. 9.2 is certainly a reference to the Davidic-Messianic promises of the Old Testament, although the exact reference or meaning is difficult to determine.[17] In the one and only scriptural quotation in the section on the eucharist, *Did*. 14, the (polemic) fulfilment motif is present by implication (and is spelled out more fully in Justin's comments on the same text): Mal 1:11–14 (in *Did*. 14.3 a conflated and shortened quotation). The sacrifice of the eucharist is the *pure* sacrifice which the prophet predicted would be brought to the Lord by the Gentiles in the end-time, whereas the sacrifices of Israel cause God's name to be blasphemed (cp. the full statement to this effect in Justin's comment in *Dial*. 117.) In the *Didache*, this polemic contrast motif is toned down, and the "pure sacrifice" motif is instead given an inner-Christian paraenetic twist: see to it that *your* sacrifice really *is* pure – therefore be reconciled to your brother (14.1f)! The fact that Mal 1:11–14 should become such an important testimony concerning the eucharist – one should probably say: *the* testimony – clearly shows the dominance of the prophecy-fulfilment scheme in early Christian hermeneutics with regard to the Old Testament.

---

[13] Cp. A. CABANISS: "Wisdom 18,14f: An Early Christmas Text", *VC* 19 (1956) 97–102; B. L. MACK: *Logos und Sophia. Untersuchungen zur Weisheitstheologie im hellenistischen Judentum* (WUNT 10; Göttingen 1973) 102–105.

[14] On these two Christological schemes, see O. Skarsaune, Oldkirkens kristologi (1986); idem, Schriftbeweis und christologisches Kerygma (1987); idem, *Incarnation: Myth or Fact?* (St. Louis 1991).

[15] For a general bibliography, see K. NIEDERWIMMER, *Die Didache* (Kommentar zu den Apostolischen Vätern, 1; Göttingen 1989) 280–294.

[16] Select bibliography: J. Klevinghaus, Die theologische Stellung (1948), 130–146; J.-P. AUDET, *La Didaché. Instruction des Apôtres* (Ebib; Paris 1958) 372ff; J. BETZ, "Die Eucharistie in der Didache", *ALW* 11 (1969) 10–39; B. SANDVIK, *Das Kommen des Herrn beim Abendmahl im Neuen Testament* (ATANT 58; Zürich 1970); K. Niederwimmer, Die Didache (1989) 173–209. 234–241.

[17] Cp. esp. Klevinghaus, 132f, and Niederwimmer, 183–185.

Second Clement[18] also clearly belongs to the "proof" tradition, although the polemic setting is inner-Christian and mainly paraenetic. The great theme of this document, as far as scriptural exposition is concerned, is ecclesiology.

In 2.1-3 the polemic Pauline testimony on Gentiles versus Jews, Isa 54:1 (cp. Gal 4:27), is quoted and expounded, but the application is strikingly non-polemical and instead strongly paraenetic. The same is true of other testimonies which are quoted as anti-Jewish by other authors within the "proof" tradition. The grand theme of ecclesiology is highlighted in ch. 14. Here the Church is portrayed as the pre-existent female counterpart of the likewise pre-existent but male Christ (Gen 1:27). The pre-existent Church was "created before the sun and moon" (Ps 72:5/17)—a Christological testimony in other writers. It seems that *2 Clement* envisages Christ and his Church in such intimate unity that Christological statements can be extended to include the Church. In 1.4–8 there is an important Christological passage in which Christ is portrayed in the role of God's Wisdom, and the Wisdom concept seems to linger in the background of the sayings about the Church in 14, too. In giving the Wisdom concept a double reference, to Christ and his Church, *2 Clement* to a certain extent anticipates later writers who identified Wisdom with the Son *and* the Spirit, cp. below on Theophilus and Irenaeus.

1.1. First Clement

Sources: Gebhardt/Harnack/Zahn I:1 2–110; Lightfoot I:2 5–188; Lake I 8–121; Fischer 1–107; A. Jaubert, *Clement de Rome* (SC 167; Paris 1971).

General works: O. Andrén, *Rättfärdighet och frid. En studie i det första Clemensbrevet* (Stockholm 1960) 81–97; L. W. Barnard, "The Early Roman Church, Judaism, and Jewish-Christianity", *ATR* 49 (1967) 371-384; K. Beyschlag, *Clemens Romanus und der Frühkatholizismus. Untersuchungen zu I Clemens 1–7* (BHT 35; Tübingen 1966) 48–134; G. Brunner, *Die theologische Mitte des ersten Klemensbriefes* (FTS 11; Frankfurt 1972) 76–83; C. Eggenberger, *Die Quellen der politischen Ethik des 1. Klemensbriefes* (Zürich 1951) 45ff; D. A. Hagner, *The use of the Old and New Testaments in Clement of Rome* (NovTSup 34; Leiden 1973); A. Jaubert, "Thèmes Lévitiques dans la Prima Clementis", *VC* 18 (1964) 193–203; O. Knoch, *Eigenart und Bedeutung der Eschatologie im theologischen Aufriss des ersten Clemensbriefes* (Theophaneia, Beiträge zur Religions- und Kirchengeschichte des Altertums 17; Bonn 1964); H. T. Mayer, "Clement of Rome and His Use of Scripture", *CTM* 42 (1971) 536–540; M. Mees, "Die Hohepriester-Theologie des Hebräerbriefes im Vergleich mit dem Ersten Clemensbrief", *BZ* NF 22 (1978) 115–124; P. Meinhold, "Geschehen und Deutung im Ersten Clemensbrief", *ZKG* 58 (1939) 82–129; A. W. Ziegler, *Neue Studien zum ersten Klemensbrief* (München 1958).

One feature of *1 Clement*[19] has leapt to the eye of every commentator and has been stated over and over again: the strong feeling of *immediate continuity* with the Old Testament, its people and institutions, displayed by the author.

For him, the Old Testament is the one and only Scripture. In the Old Testament, God speaks directly to his people, which for the author is the Christian community. The Old Testament patriarchs are the ancestors of the Christian community; Old Testament injunctions are applied directly to the Christian Church, or—more specifically—to the Corinthian community. So directly is the Old Testament applied to the Church, that the author betrays no awareness of a

[18] Cp. esp. E. Baasland, "Der 2. Klemensbrief und frühchristliche Rhetorik: 'Die erste christliche Predigt' im Lichte der neueren Forschung", ANRW II:27.1 (Berlin/New York 1993, 78–157) 122–124; K. P. Donfried, *The Setting of Second Clement in Early Christianity* (NovTSup 38; Leiden 1974); A. Frank, *Studien zur Ekklesiologie des Hirten, II. Klemens, der Didache und der Ignatiusbriefe unter besonderer Berücksichtigung der Idee einer präexistenten Kirche* (theol. diss., München 1975) 186–252; R. Knopf, "Die Anagnose zum zweiten Clemensbrief", *ZNW* 3 (1902) 266–279; A. Lindemann, *Die Clemensbriefe* (HNT 17, Die Apostolischen Väter 1; Tübingen 1992) 185–261, esp. 192f.

[19] Commonly dated—since von Harnack—to ca. 96 CE.

radical new beginning, a new covenant established by Christ; no awareness of the deep disruption between the Christian community and the Jewish people. He seems to be completely silent about the Jewish people, at the same time he regards the Church as the immediate continuation of Old Testament Israel.

It would probably be rash to conclude from this that *1 Clement* is an *Einzelgänger* in early Christianity, with a non-typical attitude towards Judaism and the Old Testament. One should rather consider the possibility that the features mentioned above have to do with the literary *genre* of this document. The occasion was obviously a purely *inner-Christian* conflict in Corinth. The author of *1 Clement* argues against the schismatics, not with doctrinal arguments, but with an enormous arsenal of *paraenetic* traditions. As far as the Old Testament is concerned, the largest bulk of Old Testament quotations derive from the Psalms, Isaiah, and the Wisdom books, especially Job. Most of these quotations are paraenetic in character, as are the many enumerations of Biblical "exempla". In fact, one gets the impression that some of the texts and traditions employed by the author are less polemical than the use to which Clement puts them, and that much material in this homily-like document simply reflects the basic *genre* of the Hellenistic Jewish homily: *logos parakleeseoos* (Acts 13:15).[20]

The "normal" Christian homily during Sunday morning worship seems to have been a rather direct appropriation of this synagogal *logos parakleeseoos*, as is witnessed in Justin's famous description:

When the reader has finished, the president in a discourse *urges and invites us to the imitation of these noble things* (1. *Apol*. 67.4).

This could be called a very precise description of the use of the Old Testament in *1 Clement*:[21] The great majority of scriptural quotations and all the scriptural *exempla* are *paraenetic* in character – this explains the high frequency of quotations from Job, the other wisdom books, and paraenetic passages from the Psalms and Prophets. It also explains the very direct and seemingly unreflecting application of the scriptural texts to the situation of the writer's audience. He picks and chooses scriptural injunctions that seem to him directly applicable to the situation in Corinth. He therefore feels no need for extended exegetical argument as to the *meaning* of the scriptural quotations, nor is there any need for hermeneutical reflection on the applicability of Old Testament texts to the present Christian community. This is simply taken for granted, and therefore the modern scholar finds this use of the Old Testament "uninteresting" from a hermeneutical point of view.

As a homilist, the author of *1 Clement* has the Old Testament at his fingertips. Many of his short quotations seem to be quotations from memory, which explains some "free" renderings of the LXX text, and also some composite quotations. On the other hand, he is the first Christian writer to insert rather long quotations which obviously are copied *verbatim* directly from LXX manuscripts. This is interesting, because it is non-typical in comparable Jewish documents.

The typical Jewish practice is the one we find in the NT: the short, often free, quotation. It presupposes *great familiarity* with the biblical text, in author as well as readers. Very likely

[20] Cp. esp. H. Thyen, *Der Stil der jüdisch-hellenistischen Homilie* (FRLANT 65; Göttingen 1955); L. Wills, "The Form of the Sermon in Hellenistic Judaism and Early Christianity", *HTR* 77 (1984) 277–299; C. C. Black, "The Rhetorical Form of the Hellenistic Jewish and Early Christian Sermon: A Response to Lawrence Wills", *HTR* 81 (1988) 1–18.

[21] Cp. the programmatic saying in 13.1: *poieesoomen to gegrammenon*!

Clement is writing to addressees in some of whom he could not presuppose this degree of familiarity with the Bible. His long excerpts allow his readers to familiarize themselves with the text in question; he so to speak involves his readers in a Bible study. Somewhat later, the author of *Barnabas*, and even more so Justin, did the same.

If we take it that Clement for the most part chose freely the paraenetic texts he quotes, we should not overlook the possibility that he sometimes used quotations which were already grouped together in written sources he had at his disposal, Jewish or Christian. All surmises about such sources must remain hypothetical, but seem plausible or even highly probable in some cases.

In ch. 15 there is a sequence of quotations about the people of God being deceitful and unfaithful: Isa 29:13; Ps 62:5; Pss 78:36f/31:19; Ps 12:4–6. Isa 29:13 is quoted as an anti-pharisaic testimony in Matt 15:8f, and recurs as an anti-Jewish testimony in Justin, *Dial.* 27.4; 48.2; 80.4; 140.2. Looking at the whole sequence in *1 Clem.* 15, the thematic unity of the quotations has suggested to several scholars the use of some sort of anthology, and one could add that the purpose of these quotations could be anti-Jewish in Clement's source. Other examples of quotation sequences that could derive from anthologies include chs. 23 (against those who doubt the second parousia); 26 (on the resurrection of the faithful); 52 (right sacrifices). There are also Christological testimonies which somehow seem added, almost as an afterthought, to the main flow of the paraenesis, as in 12.7: the scarlet thread of Rahab was a prophecy "that all who believe and hope on God shall have redemption through the blood of the Lord". This, by the way, is the only instance of explicit typology in *1 Clement*, accompanied by the comment that Rahab was "an instance not only of faith but also of prophecy" (12.8). In 16.3–14 the whole of Isa 53 is quoted, and to this Ps 22:7–9 is added as a word spoken by Christ. Neither of the two Old Testament passages are quoted as prophecies fulfilled by Christ, but quite simply as pertinent descriptions of Christ's *humility*, which should be paradigmatic for believers. Prophecy is turned into paraenesis (as already in 1 Pet 2:21–24).

The loftiest Christological passage in *1 Clement* is ch. 36. This chapter has many points of interest. First, it proves practically beyond doubt that Clement sometimes took his Old Testament quotations from sources in which they were already collected for him – in this case the source is Heb 1. Second, it proves that even when Clement took his quotations from sources other than the LXX, his familiarity with the Old Testament was such that he could go beyond his source and refer directly to the Old Testament background. The most interesting instance of this in ch. 36 is contained in the introduction to the quotation of Heb 1:3:

> Through Christ we fix our gaze on the hights of heaven, through him we see the reflection of his faultless and lofty countenance, through him the eyes of our hearts were opened, through him our foolish and darkened understanding blossoms towards the light, through him the Master willed that we should taste the immortal knowledge.

This rather "gnostic" sounding passage should probably be seen as a slightly Christianized version of the Jewish sayings about enlightenment through the Torah/Wisdom of God. Most often one encounters such sayings in contexts that deal with conversion from idolatry to faith in the God of Israel and a life according to his Torah (= Wisdom). The Christological quotation from Heb 1:3 is – in the context of Hebrews – itself a quotation of Wisd 7:26. The preexistent Christ, the mediator of creation, is thus cast in the role of God's Wisdom in Heb 1:3, and Clement seems to be aware of this Jewish background. He stylizes his introductory passage accordingly: Christ fulfils the role of Wisdom, granting enlightenment and knowledge.

To conclude, the main bulk of Old Testament quotations and interpretations in *1 Clement* is *paraenetic* and has for its typical setting the paraenetic homily in which Old Testament paraenesis is applied directly to the audience of the homilist, without much explicit hermeneutical reflection, and without polemics against outside or inside opponents (Jews, Gentiles or heretics). Some material, however, is included from the more polemical Scripture-proof tradition. In any case, the author of *1 Clement* displays a remarkable familiarity with the Septuagint Bible, and with Jewish traditions of scriptural interpretation.

1.2. Barnabas

Sources: Gebhardt/Harnack/Zahn I:2 2-83; Lightfoot/Harmer 243-265; Lake I 340-409; Wengst 103-202; R. A. Kraft/P. Prigent, *Épître de Barnabé* (SC 172; Paris 1971).

General works: L. W. Barnard, "The Epistle of Barnabas and the Tannaitic Catechism", *ATR* 41 (1959) 177-190; idem, "The Epistle of Barnabas and the Dead Sea Scrolls", *SJT* 13 (1960) 45-59; J. Carleton Paget, *The Epistle of Barnabas: Outlook and Background* (WUNT 2. Reihe 64; Tübingen 1994); A. Hermans, "Le Pseudo-Barnabé est-il millénariste?" *ETL* 35 (1959) 849-876; W. Horbury, "Jewish-Christian Relations in Barnabas and Justin Martyr", *Jews and Christians. The Parting of the Ways A.D. 70 to 135* (ed. J. D. G. Dunn; WUNT 66; Tübingen 1992) 315-345; R. Hvalvik, *The Struggle for Scripture and Covenant. The Purpose of the Epistle of Barnabas and Jewish-Christian Competition in the Second Century* (Theol. diss. Oslo 1994; WUNT 82; Tübingen 1996); A. E. Johnson, "Interpretative Hierarchies in Barnabas I-XVII", StPatr 17.2 (ed. E. A. Livingstone; Oxford 1982) 702-706; R. A. Kraft, *The epistle of Barnabas, its quotations and their sources* (Harvard diss. on microfilm; Harvard 1961); idem, "Barnabas' Isaiah Text and Melito's *Paschal Homily*", *JBL* 80 (1961) 371-373; S. Lowy, "The Confutation of Judaism in the Epistle of Barnabas", *JJS* 11 (1960) 1-33; A. Marmorstein, "L'Épitre de Barnabé et la polémique juive", *REJ* 60 (1910) 213-220; J. P. Martin, "L'Interpretazione allegorica nella lettera di Barnaba e nel giudaismo alessandrino", *Studi storico-religiosi* 6 (1982) 173-183; P. Meinhold, "Geschichte und Exegese im Barnabasbrief", *ZKG* 64 (1940) 255-303; P. Prigent, *Les Testimonia dans le Christianisme Primitif. L'Épître de Barnabé I-XVI et ses sources* (Ebib, Paris 1961); F. Scorza Barcellona, *Epistola di Barnaba* (Corona Patrum 1; Turin 1975); O. Skarsaune, "Tidlig kristen dåpsteologi i Barnabas' brev", *TTK* 47 (1976) 81-105; K. Thieme, *Kirche und Synagoge. Die ersten nachbiblischen Zeugnisse ihres Gegensatzes im Offenbarungsverständnis: Der Barnabasbrief und der Dialog Justins des Märtyrers* (Olten 1945); K. Wengst, *Tradition und Theologie des Barnabasbriefes* (AKG 42; Berlin 1971); H. Windisch, *Der Barnabasbrief* (HNT, Ergänzungsband III; Tübingen 1920) 299-413.

Research on *Barnabas* (ca. 130 CE?) has changed quite markedly in this century. Until H. Windisch's commentary in 1920, it was commonly taken for granted that *Barnabas* was an epistle occasioned by a specific situation in a specific community, and written by an author with a distinct theology and for a distinct purpose. H. Windisch, however, raised the question of *sources* employed in the epistle, and gave this point of view such a prominent position that *Barnabas* dissolved into a badly connected patchwork of different sources with different tendencies. The author almost totally disappeared behind his sources, and came out as little more than a collector of fragments. In the more recent studies of P. Prigent and R. A. Kraft, the same tendency is prevalent.

One should not overlook, however, that 'Barnabas' is propounding some distinct *theologoumena* that seem to be his own, and that the considerable amount of traditional material incorporated in his treatise, is made to serve and illustrate these *theologoumena*.[22] This often creates a certain tension between the tendency inherent in the material, and the purposes to which 'Barnabas' uses it.

---

[22] R. Hvalvik in his study on Barnabas (cp. the bibliography above) rightly emphasizes that Barnabas is a profiled author writing with a stated purpose and addressing a specific historic situation. In what follows, I am generally indebted to Hvalvik for ideas and observations.

It seems that the best way to sort out *Barnabas*' exegetical material is first to state the crucial *theologoumena* that directs his over-all approach to the Old Testament – his hermeneutical programme – and then to analyse the exegetical material he uses to carry out this programme.

In the opening statement of his epistle, 'Barnabas' sums up the contents of God's revelation as "God's ordinances", *ta tou theou dikaioomata* (1.2). The most urgent task of a Christian is "to seek out the ordinances of the Lord" (2.1). In 21.1 and 21.5 there is an *inclusio* corresponding to these initial statements: "It is good therefore that he who has learned the ordinances of the Lord as many as have been written should walk in them." To the author of *Barnabas*, the Scriptures primarily contain ordinances, commandments (*entolai*). One could say that *Barnabas* has a *halakhic* approach to Scripture: One should *walk* in the ordinances of the Lord; they describe the *way* of light.

These ordinances of the Lord are summed up in the concept of covenant. The ordinances of the Lord were not different ones at different epochs; they have always been the same. Therefore there is only one covenant of the Lord, not two. The Jews never received the covenant of the Lord. It was offered to them by Moses, but they were not worthy to receive it: "They turned to idols and lost it" (4.7–8, referring to Exod 32). Moses threw away the tablets of the covenant; the covenant did not enter history at that point. But now, in Christ, the *same* covenant, the same ordinances of the Lord, are realized, are received. (Cp. also the fuller statement of this point in ch. 14).

'Barnabas' is therefore not a two-covenant, but a one-covenant theologian, and to him there is no question of the Jews having any part in this one covenant: the covenant does not belong to "them" and "us"; it only belongs to "us".

This means that Jewish observance of the commandments never had any legitimacy; it was never right. In order to substantiate this fundamental discrediting of Jewish *halakhah*, 'Barnabas' once resorts to the idea – singular to him – that *literal* observance of God's ordinance (the commandment of circumcision) was due to the deception of an evil angel: "(The Lord) declared that circumcision was not of the flesh, but they erred because an evil angel was misleading them" (9.4).[23]

In all of this one may observe the contours of a hermeneutical programme: the true meaning of the ordinances offered through Moses, and now received in Christ, has always been the same. The ordinances were never meant to be taken literally, but in a spiritual sense – roughly speaking: allegorically ('Barnabas' never uses the term).

Some of 'Barnabas'' exegetical excercises seem to be very straightforward executions of this programme. In ch. 9 he adduces several Old Testament sayings on circumcision, proving that inward circumcision, not fleshly, was meant by God.[24] In ch. 10 he goes on to present the purest example of allegorical interpretation in the entire epistle: different animals declared unclean by Moses were only metaphors for different human vices and sinful acts. *Barnabas* is close to Philo's type of allegory here, and especially to Aristeas'. In chs. 2f 'Barnabas' marshals an impressive

---

[23] Cp. J. Carleton Paget, "Barnabas 9:4: A peculiar verse on circumcision", *VC* 45 (1991) 242–254.

[24] In 9:7–9 he adds the famous and intriguing midrash on Abraham circumcising his 318 men, cp. R. Hvalvik, "Barnabas 9.7–9 and the author's supposed use of *gematria*", *NTS* 33 (1987) 276–282.

arsenal of Old Testament testimonies on the futility of Jewish observance of the commandments on sacrifices, festivals, and fasts. In *Barnabas'* train of thought, it can easily be understood as a condemnation of Jewish *literal* and outward (only) observance of these commandments. In ch. 16 (the climax of the exegetical part), an outward, literal temple (of the Jews formerly, the Romans now) is contrasted with the spiritual temple that was all along the only one intended by God.

Surveying this material, the allegorical expositions of ch. 10 stand out as peculiar to *Barnabas* and without parallel in other Christian writers of the second century. The anti-cultic or anti-ceremonial testimonies of chs. 2f, 9, and 16, on the other hand, are frequent in other early authors (Justin, Tertullian, Cyprian et al.). The special imprint of 'Barnabas' is the idea that the flaw of Jewish cult and ceremony is the *literal* observance of commandments that were only meant to be observed spiritually. There is no hint in *Barnabas* of the idea found in later writers, viz. that Jewish observance was right *until Christ*, and only became illegitimate after Christ's coming.

In the Old Testament material treated in the two remaining blocks of *Barnabas*, chs. 5–8 and 11–15, one is transposed into a different world of thought. The commandments of the law are not treated here as timeless spiritual ordinances, but as *prophecies* and *types* which are fulfilled or realized in the story of Jesus and the institutions of the Christian community (baptism, eucharist), or in the endtime events. Here there is no emphasis on Jewish observance of the law being a mistake; on the contrary, it is the actual *practice* prescribed in the law which is seen as typologically significant (see esp. chs. 7f). One suspects that this prophecy/fulfilment scheme was so fundamental to the Old Testament material 'Barnabas' is using here, that it spilled over into his own exposition. In *Barnabas* there is a strong eschatological awareness of living in the last days (esp. chs. 4; 15), and he sometimes applies a past-present-future scheme as a kind of hermeneutical key to the teaching of Scripture (without harmonizing it with the other hermeneutical programme outlined above):

> The Lord made known to us through the prophets things past and things present and has given us the firstfruits of the taste of things to come; and when we see these things coming to pass one by one, as he said, we ought to make a richer and deeper offering for fear of him (1.7; cp. 5.3).

In fact, 'Barnabas' himself often emphasizes that the main points of the Jesus story, or Christian sacraments or ethos, were *predicted* by the prophets (5.6f; 6.7; 8.1; 11.1 etc.), and that some of the prophets' predictions are to be fulfilled only in the eschaton (6.18f; 15.6f). In other words: 'Barnabas' is here employing material from the "mainstream" proof-from-prophecy tradition, focusing on Christology and sacraments rather than ethics and commandments.

Reviewing the material in chs. 5–8 and 11–15, one is struck by its diversified nature, formally as well as in content. *Barn.* 5.1–6.7 is mainly a collection of Christological proof-texts, most of which can be traced in Christian writers earlier than *Barnabas*, and which recur in later writers. In other words: 'Barnabas' is here working with Christological "mainstream" testimonies.[25] *Barn.*

[25] The most ambitious analysis of this material as traditional in Barnabas is Prigent, '*Barn.* 5–6,7: Les *Testimonia*', in idem, Les Testimonia (1961) 157–182.

6.8–19, on the other hand, is a midrash-like exposition of Exod 33:1.3, having no close parallel in other contemporary writers.[26] It is not tuned to the prophecy/fulfilment scheme, but rather to a typological reading of Gen 1f according to a *Urzeit/Endzeit* scheme (6.13: "I make the last things as the first"). It looks very much like an independent piece of exegesis incorporated at this point in *Barnabas'* exposition because of its theme: baptism.

Chs. 7 and 8 seem to belong closely together, and represent a rather unique type of typological *midrashim*, rich in extrabiblical halakhic details (verified by the *Mishnah*). This seems to indicate close contact with rabbinic halakhah; one suspects that this is due to 'Barnabas" sources rather than himself.[27]

Barn. 11.1 – 12.1 is again a midrash-like exposition focusing on baptism and the cross; in method not unlike the baptismal midrash in 6.8–19. *Barn.* 12.2–11 is a strongly typological exposition of the Amalek battle in Exod 17 (again with extrabiblical details like chs. 7f). Ch. 13 takes Jacob's blessing of Ephraim and Manasseh to be a type of the Jewish people and the Christians; ch. 14 repeats ch. 4 on the covenant theme; ch. 15 takes the meaning of the Sabbath commandment to be: the perfect Sabbath is the millennium.

In all of this, *Barnabas* has much original material and comment, not recurring in this peculiar form in later writers. It seems that *Barnabas* is depending on sources that stem from an early Christian milieu still in close contact with Jewish scholarship, possibly a Jewish-Christian milieu. Much of it recurs in later writers, first and foremost Justin, but Justin seems to get his material from sources very similar to *Barnabas*, not directly from him.

2. The Apologists

Sources: I. C. Th. Otto, *Corpus Apologetarum christianorum saeculi secundi* I-IX (1st-3rd ed.; Jena 1857–1880; repr. Wiesbaden 1969); E. J. Goodspeed, *Die ältesten Apologeten* (Göttingen 1914; repr. New York 1950; repr. Göttingen 1984). ET: A. Roberts / J. Donaldson / A. C. Coxe, *The Ante-Nicene Fathers* [=ANF] I-II (Grand Rapids, MI 1976ff).

Works of reference: E. J. Goodspeed, *Index apologeticus sive clavis Iustini Martyris operum aliorumque Apologetarum pristinorum* (Leipzig 1912; repr. Leipzig 1969).

General works: E. Flesseman-van Leer, "Het Oude Testament bij de Apostolische Vaders en de Apologeten", *NedTT* 5 (1954/55) 230ff; W. H. C. Frend, "The Old Testament in the Age of the Greek Apologists A.D. 130–180", *SJT* 26 (1973) 129–150; R. M. Grant, *Greek Apologists of the Second Century* (Philadelphia 1988); A. von Harnack, *Die Überlieferung der griechischen Apologeten des zweiten Jahrhunderts in der alten Kirche und im Mittelalter* (TU I.1–2; Leipzig 1883); M. Pellegrino, *Gli apologeti Greci del II secolo* (Roma 1947); P. Pilhofer, *Presbyteron Kreitton. Der Altersbeweis der jüdischen und christlichen Apologeten und seine Vorgeschichte* (WUNT 2. Reihe 39; Tübingen 1990); A. Puech, *Les Apologistes Grecs du IIe siècle de notre ère* (Paris 1912).

What has come down to us from the age of the Apologists (roughly 140–180 CE) is a narrow selection of a rich literature; we know the titles of many lost works. Some of these titles make us expect works wholly or mainly devoted

---

[26] Cp. esp. N. A. Dahl, "La terre où coulent le lait et le miel selon Barnabé 6,8–19", *Aux sources de la tradition chrétienne* (Mélanges M. Goguel; Neuchâtel-Paris 1950) 62–70.

[27] For details, see Windisch's commentary and the extensive analysis in Prigent, Les Testimonia (1961) 99–115. Cp. also A. Jaubert, "Echo du livre de la Sagesse en Barnabé 7.9", *RSR* 60 (1972) 193–198; O. Skarsaune, "Baptismal typology in *Barnabas* 8 and the Jewish background", StPatr 18.3 (ed. E. Livingstone; Kalamazoo/Leuven 1989) 221–228.

to biblical exegesis. Among the extant works, many contain direct as well as implicit interpretation of the Old Testament.

In this chapter, therefore, the selection of works is stricter than in the previous one, otherwise the material would be too extensive. Three authors and four works are singled out for more detailed comment.

One theme, however, is common to all the authors traditionally gathered under the heading "Apologists". In the literary genre which has given them their name, the *Apologies*, there is always an apologetic argument concerning biblical monotheism and God as the world's creator. In this context, when the Apologists make paraphrases of Gen 1:1ff, they always include some comment on the Logos as the mediator of creation:

> Yet another testimony (Prov 8:22–36) from the Scriptures will I give you, my friends, ... namely that God has begotten as a Beginning before all his creatures a kind of Reasonable Power *(dynamis logikee)* from himself, which is also called ... the Glory of the Lord, and sometimes Son, and sometimes Wisdom ... and sometimes Lord and Logos. ...But do we not see that this is much the same as takes place within ourselves? For when we put forth any word, we beget a word, not putting it forth by scission, as though the word within us was diminished. And as we see in the case of fire another fire comes into being, without that one from which the kindling was made being diminished, but remaining the same, while that which is kindled from it appears as itself existing, without diminishing that from which it was kindled (Justin, *Dial.* 61.1–2).
>
> God 'was in the beginning', and we have received (the tradition) that 'the Beginning' was the Power of the Logos (*logou dynamis*). ... In so far as all power over things visible and invisible was with God, he with himself and the Logos which was in him established all things through the power of the Logos. By his mere will the Logos sprang forth and did not come in vain, but became the 'firstborn' work of the Father. Him we know as the 'Beginning' of the universe. He came into being by partition, not by section, for what is severed is separated from its origin, but what has been partitioned takes on a distinctive function and does not diminish the source from which it has been taken. Just as many fires may be kindled from one torch, but the light of the first torch is not diminished because of the kindling of the many, so also the Word coming forth from the power of the Father does not deprive the begetter of the power of rational speech. ... Surely when I address you I am not myself deprived of speech ... (Tatian, *Oratio ad Graecos* 5).[28]
>
> We have brought before you a God who ... created, adorned, and now rules the universe through the Logos that issues from him. ... The Son of God is the Logos of the Father in Ideal Form and Energy; for in his likeness and through him all things came into existence. ... The Son of God is the mind and reason of the Father, ... he is the Firstbegotten of the Father. The term is used not because he came into existence – for God, who is eternal mind, had in himself his Logos from the beginning, since he was eternally rational – but because he came forth to serve as Ideal Form and Energy for everything... The prophetic Spirit also agrees with this account. 'For the Lord,' it says,'made me the Beginning of his ways for his works' (Prov 8:22) (Athenagoras, *Legatio* 10.1.4).[29]

---

[28] The current edition of Tatian (ca. 178 CE) is M. WHITTAKER, *Tatian: Oratio ad Graecos and Fragments* (Oxford Early Christian Texts; Oxford 1982). Relevant literature: E. SCHWARTZ, *Tatiani Oratio ad Graecos* (TU 4,1; Leipzig 1888); R. C. KUKULA, *Tatians sogenannte Apologie. Exegetisch-chronologische Studie* (Leipzig 1900); A. PUECH, *Recherches sur le Discours aux Grecs de Tatien* (Paris 1903); R. M. GRANT, "Tatian and the Bible", StPatr 1 (TU 63; Berlin 1957) 297–306; M. ELZE, *Tatian und seine Theologie* (Göttingen 1960); G. F. HAWTHORNE, "Tatian and His Discourse to the Greeks", *HTR* 57 (1964) 161–188; A. E. OSBORNE, *Tatian: A literary analysis and essay in interpretation* (diss.; Cincinnati: Univ. of Cincinnati 1969); R. M. GRANT, Greek Apologists (1988) 112–132.

[29] The current edition of Athenagoras (176–180 CE) is W. R. SCHOEDEL, *Athenagoras: Legatio and De Resurrectione* (Oxford Early Christian Texts; Oxford 1972). Relevant literature:

There is a striking identity of ideas in these passages: The 'Beginning' of Gen 1:1 is none other than the Logos of God, who also is the Wisdom speaking in Prov 8:22 and calling herself 'Beginning'. As we shall see when we study the fullest and most explicit statement of this idea in Theophilus (*Ad Autolycum* II.10, 18, 22), this combination of Prov 8:22 (Wisdom calling herself 'Beginning') and Gen 1:1 (God creating *en archee* = by Wisdom) is entirely Jewish. So is the identification of Wisdom with Logos. In other words, what has often been called the Hellenistic Logos-Christology of the Apologists is really a piece of Jewish-biblical tradition. Logos Christology is Wisdom Christology, and as such runs through the main *apologias* as a grand main theme.

After this preliminary discussion, we turn to the four works providing the richest material for our purpose: Justin's *First Apology* and his *Dialogue with Trypho*; Melito's *Peri Pascha*, and Theophilus' three books *Ad Autolycum*.

2.1. *Justin Martyr*

Sources: Otto I-II; Goodspeed 24–265; L. Pautigny, *Justin: Apologies. Texte grec, traduction française* (Textes et Documents; Paris 1904); G. Archambault, *Justin, Dialogue avec Tryphon. Texte grec, traduction française... I-II* (Textes et Documents; Paris 1909). Translations: *ANF* I 163–306; G. Rauschen, *Des heiligen Justinus des Philosophen und Märtyrers Zwei Apologien aus dem Griechischen übersetzt* (BKV 13; München 1913); P. Häuser, *Des heiligen Philosophen und Märtyrers Justins Dialog mit dem Juden Tryphon aus dem Griechischen übersetzt und mit einer Einleitung versehen* (BKV 33; München 1917); A. L. Williams, *Justin Martyr: The Dialogue with Trypho. Translation, Introduction, and Notes* (London 1930; quoted in HBOT); T. B. Falls, *Writings of Saint Justin Martyr* (FC 6; Washington 1948; repr. 1965); E. R. Hardy, "The First Apology of Justin, the Martyr", LCC I (ed. C. C. Richardson; London 1953) 242–289 (quoted in HBOT).

Bibliography: E. R. Goodenough, *The Theology of Justin Martyr. An Investigation into the Conceptions of Early Christian Literature and Its Hellenistic and Judaistic Influences* (Jena 1923; repr. Amsterdam 1968) 294–320; A. Davids, *Iustinus Philosophus et Martyr. Bibliographie 1923–1973* (Nijmegen 1983).

General works: D. E. Aune, "Justin Martyr's use of the Old Testament", *Bulletin of the Evangelical Theological Society* 9 (1966) 179–197; H. Bacht, "Die Lehre des heiligen Justinus Martyr von der prophetischen Inspiration", *Scholastik* 26 (1951) 481–495; 27 (1952) 12–33; L. W. Barnard, "The Old Testament and Judaism in the Writings of Justin Martyr", *VT* 14 (1964) 395–406; idem, *Justin Martyr. His Life and Thought* (Cambridge 1967); B. Z. Bokser, "Justin Martyr and the Jews", *JQR* NS 64 (1973/74) 97–122. 204–211; W. Bousset, *Die Evangeliencitate Justins des Märtyrers in ihrem Wert für die Evangelienkritik von neuem untersucht* (Göttingen 1891) 18–32; idem, *Jüdisch-Christlicher Schulbetrieb in Alexandria und Rom. Literarische Untersuchungen zu Philo und Clemens von Alexandria, Justin und Irenäus* (FRLANT, NF 6; Göttingen 1915); F. C. Burkitt, "Justin Martyr and Jeremiah XI,19", *JTS* 33 (1932) 371–373; H. Chadwick, "Justin Martyr's Defence of Christianity", *BJRL* 47 (1965) 275–297; K. A. Credner, *Beiträge zur Einleitung in die biblischen Schriften*, II. *Das alttestamentliche Urevangelium* (Halle 1838); J. D. M. Derrett, "HO KYRIOS EBASILEUSEN APO TOU XYLOU", *VC* 43 (1989) 378–392; P. J. Donahue, *Jewish-Christian Controversy in the Second Century: A Study in the Dialogue of Justin Martyr* (Yale diss. on microfilm, Yale 1973); M. von Engelhardt, *Das Christentum Justins des Märtyrers. Eine Untersuchung über die Anfänge der katholischen Glaubenslehre* (Erlangen 1878); C. L. Franklin, *Justin's concept of deliberate concealment in the Old Testament* (Harvard diss. on

---

A. J. Malherbe, "The Structure of Athenagoras, 'Supplicatio pro Christianis'", *VC* 23 (1969) 1–20; L. W. Barnard, *Athenagoras* (Paris 1972); idem, "Athenagoras and the Biblical Tradition", *Studia Evangelica 6* (TU 112; Berlin 1973) 1–7; R. M. Grant, Greek Apologists (1988) 100–111; T. D. Barnes, "The Embassy of Athenagoras", *JTS* NS 26 (1975) 111–114.

microfilm, Harvard 1961); M. Friedländer, *Patristische und talmudische Studien* (Wien 1878 [repr. Westmead 1972]); J. Gervais, "L'argument apologetique des propheties messianiques selon saint Justin", *Revue de l'Université d'Ottawa* 13 (1943) 129–146. 193–208; A. H. Goldfahn, "Justinus Martyr und die Agada", *MGWJ* 22 (1873) 49–60. 104–115. 145–153. 193–202. 257–269; E. R. Goodenough, *The Theology of Justin Martyr. An Investigation into the Conceptions of Early Christian Literature and Its Hellenistic and Judaistic Influences* (Jena 1923; repr. Amsterdam 1968); J. C. Gregory, *The Chiliastic Hermeneutic of Papias of Hierapolis and Justin Martyr compared with Later Patristic Chiliasts* (diss.; Baylor University 1983); A. von Harnack, *Judentum und Judenchristentum in Justins Dialog mit Trypho* (TU 39,1; Leipzig 1913, 47–98); P. Heinisch, *Der Einfluss Philos auf die älteste christliche Exegese (Barnabas, Justin und Clemens von Alexandria). Ein Beitrag zur Geschichte der allegorisch-mystischen Schriftauslegung im christlichen Altertum* (ATA 1/2, Münster/Westf. 1908); M. Hengel, "Die Septuaginta als von den Christen beanspruchte Schriftensammlung bei Justin und den Vätern vor Origenes", *Jews and Christians. The Parting of the Ways A.D. 70 to 135* (ed. J. D. G. Dunn; WUNT 66; Tübingen 1992) 39–84; A. J. B. Higgins, "Jewish messianic belief in Justin Martyr's *Dialogue with Trypho*", *NovT* 9 (1967) 298–305; A. Hilgenfeld, "Die alttestamentlichen Citate Justins in ihrer Bedeutung für die Untersuchung über seine Evangelien", *Theologische Jahrbücher* 9 (1850) 385–439. 567–578; M. Hirschman, "Polemic literary units in the classical midrashim and Justin Martyr's *Dialogue with Trypho*", *JQR* 83 (1992–93) 369–384; W. Horbury, "Jewish-Christian Relations in Barnabas and Justin Martyr", *Jews and Christians. The Parting of the Ways A.D. 70 to 135* (ed. J. D. G. Dunn; WUNT 66; Tübingen 1992) 315–345; A. B. Hulen, "The 'Dialogues with the Jews' as sources for the early Jewish argument against Christianity", *JBL* 51 (1932) 58–70; M. de Jonge, "The Pre-Mosaic Servants of God in the Testaments of the Twelve Patriarchs and in the Writings of Justin and Irenaeus", *VC* 39 (1985) 157–170; H. Koester, *Septuaginta und Synoptischer Erzählungsstoff im Schriftbeweis Justins des Märtyrers* (Habilitationsschrift; Heidelberg 1956); W. S. Kurz, *The function of Christological proof from prophecy for Luke and Justin* (Yale diss. on microfilm; Yale 1976); F. Manns, "L'exégèse de Justin dans le Dialogue avec Tryphon, témoin de l'exégèse juive ancienne", idem, *Essais sur le Judéo-Christianisme* (Studii Biblici Fransiscani Analecta 12; Jerusalem 1977); J. L. Marshall, "Melchizedek in Hebrews, Philo and Justin Martyr", *Studia Evangelica* VII (TU 126; ed. E. A. Livingstone; Berlin 1982) 339–342; J. P. Martin, "Hermeneútica en el cristianismo y en el judaismo según el "Dialogo" de Justino Mártir", *Revista Bíblica* 39 (1977) 327–44; J. Nilson, "To whom is Justin's *Dialogue with Trypho* addressed?", *TS* 38 (1977) 538–546; E. F. Osborn, *Justin Martyr* (BHT 47; Tübingen 1973) 87–119; G. Otranto, "La tipologia di Giosué nel Dialogo con Trifone ebreo di Giustino", *Aug* 15 (1975) 29–48; idem, *Esegesi biblica e storia in Giustino (Dial. 63–84)* (Quaderni de "Vetera Christianorum" 14; Bari 1979); I. Posnoff, *Les Prophètes dans la synthèse chrétienne de saint Justin* (Louvain 1948); P. Prigent, *Justin et l'Ancient Testament* (Ebib, Paris 1964); J. S. Sibinga, *The Old Testament Text of Justin Martyr*, I. *The Pentateuch* (Leiden: Brill 1963); W. A. Shotwell, *The Biblical Exegesis of Justin Martyr* (London 1965); E. Sjöberg, "Justin als Zeuge vom Glauben an dem verborgenen und den leidenden Messias im Judentum", *Interpretationes ad Vetus Testamentum pertinentes Sigmundo Mowinckel septuagenario missae* (Oslo 1955) 173–83; O. Skarsaune, *The Proof from Prophecy. A Study in Justin Martyr's Proof-Text Tradition: Text-Type, Provenance, Theological Profile* (NovTSup 56; Leiden 1987); T. Stylianopoulos, *Justin Martyr and the Mosaic Law* (SBLDS 20; Missoula 1975); K. Thieme, *Kirche und Synagoge. Die ersten nachbiblischen Zeugnisse ihres Gegensatzes im Offenbarungsverständnis: Der Barnabasbrief und der Dialog Justins des Märtyrers* (Olten 1945); D. C. Trakatellis, *The Pre-Existence of Christ in the Writings of Justin Martyr* (Harvard Dissertations in Religion 6; Missoula 1976); W. C. van Unnik, "Der Fluch der Gekreuzigten. Deuteronomium 21,23 in der Deutung Justins des Märtyrers", *Theologia crucis – signum crucis* (FS E. Dinkler; Tübingen 1979) 483–499; G. Visonà, *S. Giustino, Dialogo con Trifone* (Milan 1988).

In the Apostolic Fathers we have seen glimpses – and in *Barnabas* some larger fragments – of a polemical interpretation of the Old Testament which is primarily directed against Judaism. The point is to *prove from the Scriptures* that (1) Jesus is the Messiah, Son of God; (2) the Law has a different position after Christ; (3) the community of believers in Jesus rather than the Jewish people is now the people of God. The scriptural proof can be said to have three foci: *de Christo, de lege, de ecclesia*.

In Justin we encounter, for the first time, this "proof from the Scriptures" in a full-scale presentation. "Der Schriftbeweis, den Justin ... führt, ist in dieser Form hinfort ein nahezu unveränderliches und in der Fülle der Belege auch später kaum übertroffenes Hauptstück der apologetisch-didaktischen Literatur geblieben".[30]

It is true that the number of Old Testament quotations in Justin is cverwhelming. Yet, if one compares his quotations with those in other Christian writers before him (or contemporaneous, but independent of him), it is surprising to observe how extremely seldom Justin picks out "new" quotations that were not already used by his precursors.[31] In other words, Justin is seen to be the transmitter of a *tradition* in his Old Testament quotations and his Old Testament exegesis. This can be seen in another way, too. Very frequently, Justin quotes rather long excerpts from the LXX text, sometimes exceeding a whole chapter. But in most cases, the occasion for these long quotations, and the only point which really matters in Justin's argument, is a traditional proof-text of one or two verses included in the long quotation. In *commenting* on his long excerpts, Justin always focuses on this traditional "nucleus" within the long quotation. He almost never dares to exploit that part of the text which is added to the traditional testimony.[32]

The fact that Justin to such an extent turns out to be a traditionalist in his exegesis corresponds to his own self-understanding. He speaks about his exegesis of the Scriptures as a tradition he has *received* – ultimately from the Apostles, who were taught by the risen Christ himself (1. *Apol.* 49.5; 50.12; *Dial.* 53.5; 76.6).[33] Precisely how the exegetical tradition was handed to him – through oral teaching, homiletic discourses or written sources – is a question to which we shall return shortly.

One fascinating aspect of Justin's scriptural proof from prophecy is that he has presented it *twice*, in two different literary formats. In the so-called *First Apology* (ca. 150 CE) it is contained in chs. 31–64. The second presentation comes in his *Dialogue with Trypho* (ca. 160 CE) chs. 10–142. Concerning the relationship between these two works, the parallels between them should probably not be explained by assuming that Justin is using his own *Apology* as the one and only *Vorlage* when writing his *Dialogue*. As i.a. Bousset, Köster, Prigent, and Skarsaune have argued, it seems rather that Justin is *twice* depending on *Vorlagen* not his own. The same source or sources seems to be at play in the *Apology* and the *Dialogue*.[34] Besides, when writing the *Dialogue* Justin seems to use additional sources that were not used much in

---

[30] Von Campenhausen, Die Entstehung der christlichen Bibel (1968) 109.

[31] The evidence is displayed in some detail in the analytic tables of Justin's entire allusion and quotation material in Skarsaune, The Proof (1987) 454–471. The only biblical book in which Justin seems to be "on his own", is Genesis, especially the stories about the Patriarchs.

[32] Concerning the few exceptions to this, see below on his treatment of the Genesis theophanies and Psalm 22.

[33] On this basically Lukan concept in Justin, see Aune (1966) 179–182, and Skarsaune, Proof (1987) 11–13.

[34] Prigent, though, posits the use of Justin's own *Syntagma against all heresies*.

the *Apology*. In other words: by comparing parallels in the two works, there is much material for redactional criticism in Justin.

Let us take a closer look first at the short version of the scriptural proof in the *Apology*, comparing it with relevant parallels in the *Dialogue*. Writing for a Gentile Roman audience not familiar with the Greek Bible nor the biblical history and characters, Justin begins with an interesting introduction of the scriptural proof in ch. 31. This contains the following elements:

(1) The Old Testament contains the words of *prophets* who spoke under the direction of the Prophetic Spirit. Their words were written down in Hebrew and arranged in books by the prophets themselves, and afterwards carefully preserved from one generation to the other by "the rulers of the Jews". In the time of Ptolemy the prophetic books were translated into Greek by Jewish experts; this Greek translation of the prophetic books is still extant in Egypt and "the Jews everywhere have them too".

(2) The Jews do not understand their own Scriptures, wherefore they deny the Messiahship of Jesus and persecute Christians – proof: Bar Kokhba's persecution of Christians during the recent war in Palestine.

(3) In the prophetic books the following points are predicted:

(A) "that Jesus our Messiah would come,
born of a virgin,
grown to manhood,
healing every sickness and every disease and raising the dead,
hated and unacknowledged and crucified,
dying and rising again
and ascending into heaven,
both really being and being called Son of God ...

(B) and that men sent by him would proclaim these things to every race of mankind, and that men of the Gentiles especially would believe in him".

All this was prophecied 5000, 3000, 2000, 1000, and 800 years in advance.

Element 1 is the first known instance of the "Septuagint legend" in a Christian author, and it seems to be literarily independent of the two known Jewish versions in Ps. Aristeas and Philo.[35] The most obvious 'Christianization' of the legend consists in the new concept of what was translated. In Ps. Aristeas and Philo it was the *Torah*, the five books of Moses. In Justin, it is "the prophetic books". This includes the whole Hebrew Bible; Moses is always called "the first of the prophets". This general understanding of the Hebrew Bible as the prophetical books corresponds to element 3 above: this summary of what the prophets foretold is, for Justin, a succinct summary of what the Old Testament is all about. Compared with contemporary Jewish (including Qumranic) understanding of the Scriptures – which almost without exception took the Law to be the center of the Bible – this signals a drastic hermeneutical reorientation with regard to the Old Testament.

It should be noted that in element 1 there is no anti-Jewish twist; on the contrary: Justin is here out to show the *reliability* of the transmission and translation of the prophetic oracles. Accordingly, the Jews are cast in the role as *faithful transmitters* of the Biblical text, right up to the present. This is in marked contrast to the portrayal of the Jewish scribes in the *Dialogue*, where they are branded as corruptors of the Biblical text (see below). One could soften this contrast by saying that in 1. *Apol.* 31 Justin has in mind the Jewish handling of the text until and

[35] Cp. esp. the very extensive discussion of Justin's (non)dependence in Hengel, Septuaginta (1992) 41–46.

including the LXX translators, whereas in the *Dialogue* he is speaking about Jewish scribal activity after Christ. This may be so, but one should not overlook the different *apologetic* purposes that guide Justin in each case: vis a vis a Gentile audience he needs to assure his readers that the prophetic oracles they are going to read, really correspond to what the prophets actually said. In the *Dialogue*, on the other hand, he has to defend a Christian version of the LXX text over against the "Jewish" text of the LXX manuscripts.

Element 2, on the other hand, is strikingly anti-Jewish. When one considers that Justin is writing this in Rome between 150–160, the specific reference to the Bar Kokhbah war in Palestine some 20 years earlier is rather surprising. But here the *Dialogue* comes to our help. More than once, Justin's interlocutors in the *Dialogue* are portrayed as being intensely occupied with the "recent war in Judaea" (*Dial.* 1.3; 9.3; cp. also 16.2; 108.3); in fact, Trypho himself is a refugee from the war (*Dial.* 1.3). Thus, in the *Dialogue* the Bar Kokhbah war and its consequences is a constant backdrop to the exegetical discussion, and as we shall see, this background is also present *in some of the modified Old Testament quotations*. It is therefore hardly by accident that the Bar Kokhbah war crops up in 1. *Apol.* 31.5, and once more in 1. *Apol.* 47 (Hadrianic decree following the war). This makes one ask whether Justin's sources in the *Apology* and the *Dialogue* set their exegetical discourse in the context of the Bar Kokhbah war and its aftermath.

Element 3 contains the first intimation of the contents of the scriptural proof. It is clearly a proof based on the prophecy-fulfilment pattern, and the summary in 1. *Apol.* 31.7 contains the elements (a) *de Christo* and (b) *de ecclesia*. Apparently, the element *de lege* is lacking from the summary, and it is, as a matter of fact, not a very prominent part of the scriptural proof itself. But the anti-cultic testimonies in 1. *Apol.* 37 clearly belong to the Law complex.

The passage in 1. *Apol.* 31.7 is not only a summary of the scriptural prophecies, it is also an anticipatory summary of the scriptural proof actually carried out in the subsequent chapters of the *Apology*, viz. 32–35, 48 and 50–53. The summary itself has in its element A the structure of a *historia Iesu*, and the same structure recurs in the scriptural proof:

(1) The coming of the Messiah: 1. *Apol.* 32 (Gen 49:10f; Num 24:17/Isa 11:1/Isa 51:5).
(2) The virgin birth: 1. *Apol.* 33f (Isa 7:14; Mic 5:1).
(3) The hidden growing up: 1. *Apol.* 35.1f (Isa 9:5).
(4) The passion and death: 1. *Apol.* 35.3ff (Isa 65:2/58:2; Ps 22:17/19; Zech 9:9). (Great insertion: 1. *Apol.* 36–49)
(5) The healings: 1. *Apol.* 48.1–3 (Isa 35:5f etc.).
(6) The passion and death: 1. *Apol.* 50f (Isa 52:13–53:12).
(7) The ascension: 1. *Apol.* 51.7 (Ps 24:7ff).
(8) The glorious return: 1. *Apol.* 51.8f (Dan 7:13).
(9) The resurrection of the dead to be judged: 1. *Apol.* 52 (Ezek 37:7f; Isa 66:24; Zech 12:10–12).

One may call this sequence of texts and exegesis "the creed sequence".

Element B in the scriptural proof comes in 1. *Apol.* 53 (Gentiles believing rather than Jews: Isa 54:1; Isa 1:9; Jer 9:25).

This leaves us with the great insertion in chs. 36–49 as unaccounted for by Justin's introductory summary in 1. *Apol.* 31.7. In fact, at the beginning of the insertion Justin makes it clear that he is side-tracked from his main line of argument because he has to insert a necessary instruction on prophetic modes of speech. Formally, chs. 36–49 are thus a small tractate on "prophetical hermeneutics".

The disposition is given in 1. *Apol.* 36.1f: Examples will be given in which (A) the prophecy is a formal prediction; (B) the Father is speaking; (C) the Son; (D) the people responding to one of them. This classification contains two kinds of criteria which may cross each other: the tense of the prophetic saying; past, present or future? (A); and the speaking subject (BCD). The disposition is carried out in the sequence BCADC: Utterances by the Father, 1. *Apol.* 37; utterances by the Son, 1. *Apol.* 38; future and past tense in the prophecies, 1. *Apol.* 39–45; utterances by the people, 1. *Apol.* 47; a prophecy in which the Son speaks, 1. *Apol.* 49.1–4.

Even a superficial reading of chapters 36–49 is sufficient to observe that many of the quotations adduced are inappropriate as examples of the hermeneutical principles they are said to exemplify. A closer analysis confirms that the quotations are not grouped together ad hoc but seem to derive from quotation sequences which were composed for other purposes. Especially from 1. *Apol.* 40 onwards the theme inherent in the quotation material frequently breaks through Justin's intended line of thought.

(1) Some of the material in the insertion seems to belong together with the "creed sequence" testimonies:
The passion and crucifixion of the Messiah: 1. *Apol.* 38 (Isa 65:2/58:2; Ps 22:19/17/Ps 3:6; Ps 22:8f; Isa 50:6–8).[36]
The present reign of the Messiah: 1. *Apol.* 39–46 (Isa 2:3f; Ps 19:3–6; Ps 1f; Ps 96/1 Chr 16; Ps 110:1–3).[37]

(2) The anti-cultic testimonies in 1. *Apol.* 37 (Isa 1:3f; Isa 66:1; Isa 1:11–15/Isa 58:6f) and the baptismal testimonies in 1. *Apol.* 44 (Deut 30:15/19; Isa 1:16–20) may belong together (see below).

(3) In 1. *Apol.* 47 and 49 we have quotation material that seems to belong together as one group, cp. the parallel in *Dial.* 15–17 and 28 (also 108/119): Because the Jews slew the Just One, their land is devastated, and the Gentiles are to take their place (Isa 64:9–11; Isa 1:7/Jer 50:3; Isa 57:1f; Isa 65:1–3; Isa 5:20).

After this survey of the quotation material in 1. *Apol.* 32–53, we turn to a summary analysis of some of its characteristics.

A. Testimonies de Christo („creed sequence")

One may easily recognize a core of testimonies that are already frequently used in the New Testament as scriptural proof of the cross, resurrection, ascension, enthronement and return of the Messiah. The Virgin birth in Bethlehem is also part of the scriptural proof in Matthew (expressly) and Luke (indirectly). In these early proof-texts, the focus is on those aspects of Jesus' career which were new and unforeseen from the standpoint of traditional Jewish Messianism – especially the cross and the ascension complex. Therefore, most of these Old Testament proof-texts are "new" as such. We have no Jewish evidence showing that these texts were used as Messianic testimonies in Judaism prior to their New Testament use.

But in Justin this core of proof-texts has received some important additions. In general, these additions have a solid Jewish tradition as Messianic testimonies. In other words, we observe an amplification of the Christian proof-text dossier to include more of the traditional Jewish Messianism.

---

[36] Cp. the parallel in *1. Apol.* 35, and the detailed analysis in Skarsaune, Proof (1987) 80–82. 146f. 158.

[37] Cp. the detailed analysis ibid. 158–160.

First, Justin's dossier has an important preamble added to it: the rather extensive exposition of Gen 49:10f, and the added quotation of a combined text based on Num 24:17 (Num 24:17/Isa 11:1/Isa 51:5) in 1. *Apol.* 32. Gen 49:10f has a well documented history as a crucial Messianic testimony within Jewish exegesis right from the Qumran document *4QPatr.*[38] The same is true of Num 24:17; in *4QTestim.* (9–13) Num 24:15–17 is quoted as a Messianic testimony, and recurs as such in the Targums.[39] The special interest attached to this proof-text is of course the role it played as the slogan of Bar Kokhbah (y.Ta^can 4.5).[40] The fact that Justin's "creed sequence" is introduced by exactly these two testimonies is probably significant: they are *Torah* testimonies on the coming of the Messiah; they are the only two Torah texts taken as Messianic by the official Targum Onqelos; Justin's reading and exegesis of the famous Shiloh oracle in Gen 49:10 agrees exactly with *Tg.Onq*; Justin's combined text of Num 17:24 reads like an anti Bar Kokhbah polemic.[41] All of this speaks for rather close contact with Jewish exegetical traditions.

This can be further substantiated when we look at *the exegetical technique* of Justin, and his way of presenting it. In 1. *Apol.* 32.4–8, the exposition of Gen 49:10f, we find a typical example:

(A) The (saying) "He shall be the expectation of the nations"
(B) shows that (*meenytikon een*) men of every nation will look forward to his coming again,
(C) as you can clearly see and be convinced by the facts...
(A) The (saying) "Binding his foal to the vine ..."
(B) is a symbolic exhibition (*symbolon deelootiokon een*) of the things that would happen to Christ ...
(C) For an ass's foal was standing at the entrance of a village ...
(A) The (saying) "washing his robe in the blood of the grape"
(B-C) was predictive (*proangeltikon een*) of the passion which he was to suffer, cleansing by his blood those who believe on him. For the men who believe on him are what the divine Spirit through the prophet calls a garment...

This lemma-by-lemma (= A) exposition is structured by a rather fixed scheme of (B) an explanation of the *meaning* of the lemma, and (C) a report on the historic realisation of the prophecy. Formally, this is very close to the Qumran *pesher* commentaries, in which short lemmas (sometimes introduced by "and that which was said" (*waasher amar*)—cp. Justin's *to de (rethen)*) are regularly followed by the comment: "The interpretation of this (these words) is... (*pishro* or *pesher had-dabar hazeh*)", and then a concrete historical reference is given as the one intended by the prophecy.[42] This frequently implies that words in the prophecy are taken as metaphors describing concrete realities or persons in the time of fulfilment, as in *4QpNah* on Nah 2:12:

---

[38] See the survey in Skarsaune, Proof (1987) 262–264, including Josephus *Bell. Jud.* VI.312f; the Targums ad loc; *bSanh.* 5a; *Gen Rab* 98.8.

[39] Cp. the survey in Skarsaune, Proof (1987) 264f, and M. Aberbach / B. Grossfeld, *Targum Onquelos on Genesis 49* (SBL Aramaic Studies 1; Missoula, MT 1976) 12–27.

[40] The failure of Bar Kokhbah may be the reason why this testimony disappears in the Babylonian Talmud and the Rabbinic midrashim.

[41] The "star from Jacob" is *Davidic* (Isa 11:1)—which apparently Bar Kokhbah was not—and shall be a Messiah in whom *the Gentiles* put their trust (Isa 51:5).

[42] As in *1QpHab*, *4QFlor*, *4QpNah*, *4QpPs37* etc.

(A) "The lion went there, and the lioness, and the cubs, and there is no one who frightens them".
(B-C) The interpretation of this concerns king Demetrius, King of Jawan, who craved to come to Jerusalem …

The same type of exegesis is present in *4QPatr* on Gen 49:10, in which f.ex. MT *mehoqeq*, "ruler's staff", is interpreted as "the covenant of kingship", while MT "feet" of Judah are said to be "the thousands of Israel". Basically the same metaphorical reading of Gen 49 is still practised in the Targums, with many ideas strikingly close to Justin's. If one calls this an allegorical interpretation of the biblical text, one should remember that in this case concrete biblical words are *not* taken to mean abstract virtues or spiritual realities of a higher level (as in Philo and Origen). The point is rather that the biblical text is taken to refer to quite specific historic events in the present or recent past, and the allegorical interpretation of the text is only introduced to make the text match the events perfectly and in all details. This is a far way from the lofty allegorisations of Philo, and equally far from the philonic allegories of Origen. It is quite simply an interpretation which reads words in the prophetic text as metaphors for the events that the interpretor is convinced are the fulfilment of the prophetic oracle. Events in the present or recent past are taken to be the rule of interpretation for the prophetic oracles predicting these events.[43]

To conclude: a basic core of testimonies introduced in the New Testament writings to substantiate, on the one hand, the cross and resurrection/ascension/return of the Messiah, on the other hand, his virgin birth, is enriched in Justin with traditional Jewish Messianic testimonies, creating a comprehensive "proof from prophecy" with a strikingly Jewish profile. This holds true as well with regard to the selection of proof-texts, as with regard to the exegetical technique applied to the texts, and the basic hermeneutical approach: the prophecy-fulfilment scheme.

It remains to be added that in a polemic riposte to the Jewish objection (raised in the *Dialogue* by Trypho, *Dial.* 32.1) that Jesus did not bring the Messianic kingdom, Justin introduces the important hermeneutical concept of the two parousias:

> The prophets foretold two comings of Christ—one, which has already happened, as that of a dishonored and passible man, and the second, when as has been foretold he will come from heaven in glory with his angelic host, when he will raise the bodies of all the men who have ever lived, and will clothe the worthy with incorruption … (1. *Apol.* 52.3)[44]

The main catchword characterizing Christ in his first parousia is *pathetos*, Isa 53 being the crucial biblical foundation. The second parousia is to be *with glory*, bringing the Messianic kingdom in power and fullness. The Old Testament prophecies about the Messiah refer partly to the first, partly to the

[43] Cp. the emphatic defense of this exegetical point of view in R. L. WILKEN, "'In novissimis diebus': Biblical Promises, Jewish Hopes, and Early Christian Exegesis", *Journal of Early Christian Studies* 1 (1993) 1–19.

[44] In the *Dialogue* the idea of the two parousias is stated over and over again, always in the context of and with reference to the creed sequence testimonies: 14.8; 31.1; 32.2; 34.2; 36.1; 49.2; 49.7; 52.1.4; 110.2; 120.4; 121.3. Cp. the analysis of this concept in Skarsaune, Proof (1987) 154–156 and 285–287.

second coming. Although Justin never says in so many words that the prophecies referring to the first parousia are more cryptic than the ones referring to the second advent, he may tacitly recognize this. It was stated plainly by Tertullian against Marcion:

> Since, therefore, the first advent was prophetically declared both as *most obscure in its types*, and as deformed with every kind of indignity, but the second as glorious and altogether worthy of God, they [the Jews] would on this very account, while confining their regards to that which they were easily able both to understand and to believe, even the second advent, be not undeservedly deceived respecting *the more obscure*, and, at any rate, the more lowly first coming (*Adv. Marc.* III.7.8).

It is time to place Justin's arsenal of creed sequence testimonies within the wider setting of other second century writers. In the fragments of the "Preaching of Peter" (ca. 125 CE) preserved in Clement of Alexandria, Peter says the following:

> We looked up the books of the prophets which we had. They mention Christ Jesus, partly in parables, but also straightforward and in plain words. There we found mentioned
> his coming,
> his death and his cross ...
> likewise his resurrection and ascension to heaven...
> all of this *as it is written*: that he had to suffer and what afterwards should happen (*Strom.* VI.15.128).

The two parousias scheme may be implied here; in any case we have a clear indication of the creed sequence testimonies, since Peter adds: "We realised that God had ordained the prophecies, and without Scripture we say nothing" (ibid.). *Which* dossier of proof-texts the Preaching of Peter worked with, is impossible to say, due to the sparseness of the fragments, but one point of contact with Justin's material should not be overlooked: Peter called Christ Law and Word, *nomos kai logos* (*Strom.* I.29.182; II.15.68; *Ecl. Proph.* 58), and as Clement indicates, this no doubt echoes Isa 2:3 – the main testimony on Christ's Messianic reign in Justin's material. There are other points of contact between the "Preaching" and Justin (see below), so we should probably conclude that the Preaching belongs to the trajectory of tradition leading up to Justin's creed sequence testimonies.

The next parallel is much closer and more explicit: the passage I.33–71 in the Pseudoclementine *Recognitions*. G. STRECKER[45] has analysed this and concluded that *Rec.* I.33–71 represents a separate source, not used elsewhere in the Recognitions, which is very close to a writing mentioned by Epiphanius, the *Anabathmoi Iakobou*. STRECKER therefore calls *Rec.* I.33–71 "AJ II", and dates it to the middle of the second century, i.e. roughly contemporary with Justin, but clearly independent of him.[46]

In *Rec.* I.49 there is a full statement on the doctrine of the two parousias, with reference primarily to the prophets Jacob and Moses. Gen 49:10 is given a primary position, and the point is made that "the prophets ... said that Christ should be the expectation *of the Gentiles* (Gen 49:10b), and not of the Jews" (I.50).

There are more parallels between *AJ II* and Justin's testimony material (see below). It thus seems that the *AJ II* provides corroborating evidence for the Jewish-Christian provenance of Justin's proof-text material.

---

[45] *Das Judenchristentum in den Pseudoklementinen* (TU 70; Berlin 1958).

[46] STRECKER's conclusions with regard to the literary criticism of the Pseudoclementines as a whole are of course not uncontested, but his reconstruction of *Rec.* I:33–71 as a separate unit with a theology markedly different from the rest of Ps.Clem. is convincing on its own merit, and was anticipated independently of his analysis by. i.a. H.-J. SCHOEPS, *Theologie und Geschichte des Judenchristentums* (Tübingen 1949) 381–417. 435 ff. Cp. also J. L. MARTYN, "Clementine Recognitions 1,33–71, Jewish Christianity, and the Fourth Gospel", *God's Christ and His People. Studies in Honor of N.A. Dahl* (ed. J. Jervell / W.A. Meeks; Oslo 1977) 265–295; and Skarsaune, Proof (1987) 252 f.

The third interesting parallel, pointing in the same direction, is the Christological passages in the *Testaments of the Twelve Patriarchs*, especially *T. Levi* 18 and *T. Judah* 24. Gen 49:10 and Num 24:17 are already alluded to in the Jewish *Grundschrift* more than once (*T. Reub.* 6.11; *T. Simon* 7.1; *T. Judah* 21:1f; *T. Iss.* 5:7; *T. Dan* 5:4; *T. Napht.* 8:2f). In *T. Judah* 24 a Christian redactor capitalizes on this in the following way:

> After these things shall a star arise to you from Jacob (Num 24:17) in peace and a man shall arise from my seed like a sun of righteousness (Mal 3:20) walking with the sons of men in meekness and righteousness ... And you shall be unto him sons in truth, and you shall walk in his commandments first and last. This is the branch (Isa 11:1; Jer 23:5 etc.) of the most high God, and this is the fountain giving life unto all. Then shall the sceptre of my kingdom (Gen 49:10) shine forth, and from your root shall arise a stem and from it shall grow a rod (Isa 11:1) of righteousness to the nations, to judge and to save all that call upon the Lord (Isa 11:10/Joel 3:5).

The parallels to 1. *Apol.* 32 are obvious, as is the idea of Christ as mediator of a new Law. Christ fulfilling the function of the Law (giving enlightenment) is even more pronounced in *T. Levi* 18. Like the proof-texts in Justin's creed sequence, the interpolator of the *Testaments* seems to reckon with a final conversion and salvation of the Jewish people.

Thus the Jewish-Christian interpolator(s)[47] of the *Testaments* is seen to draw on the same dossier of Messianic proof-texts as is present in Justin's material, and to exhibit the same Christological and soteriological ideas.

B. Testimonies de lege[48]

If we hold together the related passages in 1. *Apol.* 37 and *Dial.* 13–15, the following ideas emerge: God has no pleasure in the Jewish festivals because he cannot stand the sacrifices brought him (Isa 1:11ff); instead, Israel should turn to true fasting, which consists in doing good to the needy (Isa 58:6f); atonement for sin is now provided by the sacrificial death of Christ, the lamb of God (Isa 53:5–7; Ps Ezra); this is applied to the individual man through Christian baptism (Isa 1:16–20). – The whole has a preamble in *Dial.* 11f: new covenant theme.

Again we seem to encounter a first parallel to this in the *Preaching of Peter*. In the long fragment in *Strom.* VI.5.39–41 Peter dissuades his audience from worshipping God in the Jewish way, because the Jews really worship angels and archangels, the month and the moon – i.e. probably: the spirits of the celestial bodies. Then he continues: "If the moon be not visible, they do not hold the Sabbath, which is called the first; nor do they hold the new moon, nor the feast of unleavened bread, nor the Feast [of Tabernacles], nor the great Day [of Atonement]." The reason why Jewish worship is criticised here, is different from the one in Justin. But the sequence of practices singled out for criticism shows a striking coincidence with the non-LXX sequence in Justin's version of Isa 1:11ff in 1.*Apol.* 37.5–8. And for his "new covenant" theme Peter in the *Preaching* quotes Jer 31:31 in a non-LXX version that recurs in an allusion in *Dial.* 67.9. One should probably not exclude the possibility of direct dependence of Justin upon the *Preaching* here.[49]

The most important antecedent to Justin's material is contained in *Barn.* 2–5: God has no pleasure in sacrifices (Isa 1:11ff etc.); what he wants is true fasting (Isa 58:4ff); covenant theme; remission of sins now given (in baptism) through Christ's blood (Isa 53:5/7).

---

[47] On the interpolator and his theology in general, and on the possibility of Christian interpolations in several stages, see esp. J. Jervell, "Ein Interpolator interpretiert. Zu der christlichen Bearbeitung der Testamente der zwölf Patriarchen", *Studien zu den Testamenten der Zwölf Patriarchen* (BZNW 36; ed. W. Eltester; Berlin 1969) 30–61.

[48] The most extensive treatment of the Law question in Justin is Stylianopoulos, Mosaic Law (1975), cp. also Skarsaune, Proof (1987) 295–326.

[49] Cp. the detailed analysis in Skarsaune, Proof (1987) 72f.

In *Barnabas* as well as in Justin, we discern in the testimony material an idea that baptism now substitutes all sacrifices as the only means conferring forgiveness of sins – although neither author states this explicitly (Justin comes close in *Dial.* 13.1).

The explicit statement, however, comes in the *AJ II*:

> Lest they might suppose that on the cessation of sacrifice there was no remission of sins for them, he instituted baptism by water amongst them, in which they might be absolved from all their sins on the invocation of His name, and for the future, following a perfect life, might abide in immortality, being purified not by the blood of beasts, but by the purification of the Wisdom of God (*Rec.* I.39).

Here we see, once more, that the *AJ II* express most clearly what seems to be the organizing principle and idea behind Justin's proof-text dossier.

This proximity between Justin and the *AJ II* is also seen when we compare the *reason* given by both authors for the giving of the Law. If Justin regarded Isa 1:11ff and other anti-cultic saying of the prophets as statements to the fact that God *after the coming of Christ* would have no pleasure in Jewish observance of the ritual Laws, he was left with the question: Then why did God give all these ritual commandments in the first place?

The answer is often given in the *Dialogue*, e.g. like this:

> When Israel made the calf in the wilderness ... God accommodated himself to that people, and commanded them to bring sacrifices, as unto his name, in order that you should not commit idolatry (*Dial.* 19.5f).

The idea of this is perfectly clear: since the episode with the golden calf proved that Israel had an ineradicable propensity for bringing sacrifices (to idols), God allowed them to sacrifice to himself instead. The people suffered from *sklerokardia*, that made the ritual laws necessary, but only as a temporal remedy.

The reference to the golden calf incident, and the exegetical premiss that the main bulk of the Law on sacrifices was given after this event, clearly shows that this argument originally must have been constructed with primary reference not to the whole of the ritual laws, but only to the laws on sacrifices. However, to Justin and his Jewish counterpart, debating long after the cessation of the temple service, other ritual commandments are far more important. And Justin "stretches" the golden calf argument to somehow cover all ritual commandments, including some given long before the exodus: sabbath and circumcision (*Dial.* 18.2; 19.5f; 20.4; 22.1; 27.2; 43.1; 67.8 et al.).

Turning to the *AJ II*, we find, once more, the idea in Justin's testimony material expressed in its simple, original form:

> When Moses had gone up to the mount ... the people ... made and worshipped a golden calf's head, after the fashion of Apis, whom they had seen worshipped in Egypt; and (even) after so many and so great marvels which they had seen, were unable to cleanse and wash out from themselves the defilements of old habit. ... When Moses, that faithful and wise steward, perceived that the vice of sacrificing to idols had been deeply ingrained into the people from their association with the Egyptians, and the root of this evil could not be extracted from them, he allowed them indeed to sacrifice, but permitted it to be done only to God, that by any means he might cut off one half of the deeply ingrained evil, leaving the other half to be corrected by another, at a future time (*Rec.* I.35f).

There is no polemic against sabbath or circumcision here (or elsewhere in the *AJ II*), nor any general theory of all ritual commandments being necessitated by the *sklerokardia* evidenced by the golden calf incident. The *AJ II* seems to present the argument in the simple, original form that is discernible *behind* Justin's presentation.

It is interesting to encounter this same original version in a rabbinic midrash ascribed to a Rabbi of the 3rd century, Levi – probably the argument originated in rabbinical circles struggling with the why-question of the cultic temple service after its cessation in 70 CE: "Because Israel were passionate followers after idolatry in Egypt and used to bring their sacrifices to the satyrs, as it is written, 'And they shall no more sacrifice their sacrifices to the satyrs' (Lev 17:7) ... the Holy One, blessed be he, said: 'Let them offer their sacrifices to me at all times in the Tent of Meeting, and thus they will be separated from idolatry and saved from punishment'" (*Lev. Rab.* 22.8).

The saying in *AJ II* that Moses left "the other half" of the ingrained evil to be corrected "by another, at a future time", links up with the idea we have encountered in *AJ II* already, viz. that baptism now replaces all sacrifices. Since the testimony material in Justin which embodies the same idea occurs close to the sections dealing with the *sklerokardia* argument concerning the giving of the law, it seems a reasonable surmise that all of this material in Justin derives from the same source – a tradition very close to the one represented by the *AJ II*.

In order to complete the picture of Justin's handling of the Law complex, two facets must be added.

(1) The one is the idea that the Law has two components. One is the ritual commandments (and we have seen Justin handling this complex already). The other is what Justin calls "that which is righteous at all times and in all places", *ta aei kai di' holou dikaia* (*Dial.* 93.1 – cp. similar terms in *Dial.* 23.1.5; 28.4; 30.1; 45.3;), i.e. the timeless and always valid ethical commandments of the Law. With regard to this component of the Law, the coming of Christ makes no basic difference. But Christ authorises this part of the Law and expounds it with unsurpassed clarity. Justin's summary in *Dial.* 93 reads like a paraphrase of an ethical cathechism structured according to the two tablets of the Decalogue (love of God and neighbour), very much like the one in *Did.* 1.3–6. In *AJ II*, we find the same idea: the eternal part of the Law is the Decalogue, while the cultic Law is a temporary admission (*Rec.* I.35).

(2) The ritual precepts of the Law were given because of Israel's *sklerokardia*, but at the same time some (or even all! *Dial.* 42.4) of them have significance as *types* of Christ, sacraments, or the Church.[50] Again there seems to be a connexion between this "typological" Law material and the anti-cultic testimonies.[51] The basic idea seems to be that precisely because the cultic precepts are types pointing to Christ as their realization (*Dial.* 40–42 etc.), it is futile and sinful to continue with these practices after Christ (1. *Apol.* 37; *Dial.* 12.3; 13.1 etc., esp. *Dial.* 40.1).[52]

[50] Stylianopoulos, Mosaic Law (1975) 51–68 has mistakenly argued for the view that Justin distinguished between two groups of commandments, one given because of *sklerokardia*, and one given as Christological types. But it can hardly be denied that Justin speaks of the *same* commandments from two points of view, cp. Skarsaune, Proof (1987) 323 f.

[51] The ritual precepts singled out for criticism in the anti-cultic passages (*1. Apol.* 37; *Dial.* 12.3; 13.1ff etc.) are largely *the same* as the ritual commandments given a typological interpretation (*Dial.* 13f; 40–42; 111.3f). Cp. the detailed analysis in Skarsaune, Proof (1987) 168–173. 295–313.

[52] According to Justin, nobody is hurt if Jewish Christians continue to observe some of the Mosaic ritual precepts, provided they do not try to impose these precepts on others, *Dial.* 47.1. As the context makes plain, however, the basic question is whether one regards the observance of these precepts as necessary *for salvation* (*Dial.* 46; 47.2ff). If one does, it amounts to a denial that Christ has come, i.e. a denial that Jesus is the Messiah, *Dial.* 47.4.

Taking *Dial.* 12.3; 13f; 40–42; 72, and 111.3f together, one gets the following list of *typoi* contained in the Law:

Sabbath (Christians live free of the slave's work: sin)
Circumcision (Christians receive the true, spiritual circumcision through baptism)
Ritual baths (Chritians are cleansed by the blood of Christ through baptism)
Passover lamb (type of Christ; Christians apply his blood to their "houses", i.e. their bodies = baptismal anointing)
Unleavened bread (Christians lead a new life)
The two goats of the Day of Atonement (type of Christ and his two parousias)
Offering of fine flour (Exod 14) (type of the eucharist)
Twelve bells on the High Priest's robe (gospel preached in all the world by the twelve Apostles)

As one can easily see, this list does not reflect a learned attempt to read a typological significance out of all and every precept in the Law. It rather looks like an attempt to deal with those aspects of Jewish observance that were (1) most conspicuous in everyday encounters between Jews and their neighbours, or (2) central in the Law, but now made obsolete through the disappearance of the Temple and its service (*Dial.* 40.1). As to what is signified by these types, Justin focuses on Christ's death and resurrection, on baptism, and on the eucharist. The centrality of baptism is striking.

C. Testimonies de ecclesia

In the *Apology*, this theme is rather hinted at than fully developed. In the "creed" summary in 1. *Apol.* 31.7 the bottom line is: "and that men from among the Gentiles rather should believe in him (than the Jews)". Though brief, this statement is a good summary of what Justin has to say on this theme. The full development of his argument comes in the *Dialogue*.

There can hardly be any doubt that Jewish rejection of the Messianic claims of Jesus was a great and permanent embarrasment to the early Church, not least in its missionary address to Gentiles. If Jesus had fulfilled the Messianic prophecies of Scripture in a clear and unmistakable way—why did not his own people, steeped in the very same Scriptures, recognize him?

The only effective rebuttal was to show that exactly this was predicted in the Scriptures: his own people, expecting the Messiah, would reject him; the Gentiles, not expecting him, would believe in him. Did not f. ex. Isa 65:1f say this as clearly as anyone could demand? On the one hand: "I became manifest to those who asked not after me, I was found by those who sought me not ..." (Isa 65:1). On the other hand: "I stretched out my hands over a disobedient and contradicting people ..." (Isa 65:2). Again and again Justin adduces this prophecy (1. *Apol.* 35.3; 38.1; 49.2–4; *Dial.* 24.3f; 97.2; 114.2; 119.4), and he has a multitude of other prophetic utterances and even prophetic types in biblical history and Law proving the same point. The final touch to this argument is his observation that the main Messianic prophecy of the Law, Gen 49:10 itself, clearly indicates that the Messiah would find faith *among the Gentiles*: he is to be the *prosdokia ethnoon*. As we have seen already, Justin read the other Messianic prophecy in the Law, Num 24:17, in an expanded version containing the same point: "... upon his arm shall *Gentiles* put their hope" (1. *Apol.* 32.12).

But even if Jewish unbelief in this way could be turned into an argument in favour of Jesus being the Messiah, there still was no answer to the why-question: Why did the Jews reject him? Again the answer was found in Scripture, this time in the sayings focusing on the golden calf incident: Scripture branded the Jews as always being a stiffnecked people, hard of heart (*sklerokardia* – cp. on this catchword above) and slow to believe (*Dial.* 27.4 etc.). Again the searching in the Scriptures is not directed by any abstract scholarly interest in biblical teaching about the people of God. The Scriptures are believed to contain the clue to every old and new element in the dramatic and eventful history of the Jewish-Christian relation:

(1) The introduction of the *Birkat-haminim* into the main prayer of the synagogue service was found to be predicted and condemned in Scripture: "Woe to those who call sweet bitter and bitter sweet" (Isa 5:20, 1. *Apol.* 49.6; cp. the fuller excerpts from Isa 5:18ff in *Dial.* 17.2 and 133.4, with explicit references in the context to cursing of Christians). In Justin's testimony material, this theme seems to have been inserted into a larger complex of testimonies which express the idea of Jewish guilt for having murdered the "Righteous One". This is a Christian adaption of the Jewish and Biblical tradition about the "murder of the prophets";[53] the typical feature is that the killing of Jesus here is seen as the climax within a *sequence* of persecutions: the prophets and other righteous men in Israel before Jesus, his followers after him. We encounter this tradition in 1. *Apol.* 47–49; *Dial.* 16f; 108.2f; 133; 136f, and its three main testimonies are Isa 57:1f; Isa 3:10; and Isa 5:20, which we have quoted already. In the biblical texts, and especially in some early Jewish examples of the "killing of the prophets" motif, this motif is set within the so-called sin-exile-return pattern: God's punishment for Israel's rejection of his messengers is that he sends them into exile. This leads us to the second historic event that is mirrored in Justin's quotation material:

(2) The Hadrianic decree barring Jews from entering Jerusalem after 135 CE, is expressly mentioned several times by Justin, and he has some strikingly modified Old Testament quotations which almost certainly refer to it:

Dial. 114.5	*Barn.* 11.2
Woe to you, because you have left a living spring, and have dug for yourselves cisterns that are broken, which will not be able to hold water (Jer 2:13).	... this people ... have deserted me, the spring of life, and they have dug for themselves a cistern of death.
Is there to be a desert where the mountain of Sion is? (Isa 16:1)	Is my holy mountain Sinai a desert rock? For ye shall be as the fledgling birds, fluttering about when they are taken away from the nest.
For I have given Jerusalem a bill of divorce in front of you (Jer 3:8).	

In Justin as well as in *Barnabas*, Jer 2:13 and Isa 16:1(f) are woven together to form one quotation, Justin's text also comprising Jer 3:8. Both versions exhibit several non-LXX features, but not in a single instance do they agree with each other against the LXX text. In other words, there is certainly some kind of relationship between Justin's and *Barnabas'* deviant quotations, but the one is not directly dependent upon the other. In both authors the context suggests that the quotations played a role in polemics concerning Jewish ritual baths – maybe including proselyte baptism – and Christian baptism.[54]

---

[53] The standard monograph on the theme is O. H. Steck, *Israel und das gewaltsame Geschick der Propheten. Untersuchungen zur Überlieferung des deuteronomistischen Geschichtsbildes im Alten Testament, Spätjudentum und Urchristentum* (WMANT 23; Neukirchen-Vluyn 1967).

[54] In Justin one should add the context in *Dial.* 19.2. Cp. the analysis in Kraft, Barnabas'

The decisive element in Justin's composite quotation is the italicized part, Jer 3:8. In the Septuagint one reads that the Lord has dismissed Israel and given her "a bill of divorce into her hand". Israel here means the Northern kingdom; "her sister Judah" did not learn from Israel's calamity. In Justin's composite text, *Jerusalem* is introduced as the recipient of the bill of divorce, and it is given *emprosthen hymin*! It is as if Jerusalem is cut off from her "husband", the Jewish people. We are hardly wrong to see in this strangely modified text an obvious reference to the Hadrianic decree.

With the next text, we are not left with guesswork.

> That Jerusalem would be laid waste, and *no one permitted to dwell there*, was said through Isaiah the prophet:
> "Their land is a desert,
> their enemies eat it up in front of them (Isa 1:7)
> *and none of them will dwell in it*" (Jer 50[LXX: 27]:3).
> You [Romans] certainly know that under your guard there is no one in it, and that death has been decreed against any Jew caught entering it (1. *Apol.* 47.5f).[55]

In this composite, non-LXX quotation, the added element from Jer 50:3 may seem strange, since in the context of Jeremiah its reference is the deserted *Babylon*. However, if verse 3 is read as belonging with the subsequent verses, we get a rather moving description fitting the post-135-situation perfectly:

> In those days ... the sons of Israel and the sons of Judah will come together, walking slowly and crying will they seek the Lord their God; they will ask for the way to Zion, and turn their faces towards it ... (Jer 50[27]:4f LXX).

Thus, in Justin's testimony material, we see Christians reading the Scriptures, searching for clues and confirmation of contemporary events, interpreting the Bar Kokhbah uprising and its consequences in the light of Scripture, or vice versa. This is a Scripture interpretation based on the consciousness of living in the time of fulfilment, the end-time the prophets were talking about. It is basically the same type of direct application of prophetic texts as we find in the Qumran *pesharim* and the New Testament.

We find the same in Justin's positive counterpart to these condemning sayings about the Jews being excluded from Jerusalem. According to Justin God has now made Jerusalem ready to receive its *new* inhabitants – the new people of God, the Christians!

> Come with me all who fear God, who wish to see the good things of Jerusalem. Come, let us go in the light of the Lord, for he has dismissed his people, the house of Jacob. Come, all ye nations, let us be gathered together at Jerusalem, which is no longer attacked because of the iniquities of the peoples (*Dial.* 24.3).

There is hardly any doubt that Justin meant this quite literally. His eschatology comprises a millennium located in a rebuilt Jerusalem (*Dial.* 80f), and it seems he expected this in the very near future.[56]

In geographical terms, this means that Justin envisaged a *replacement* of the Jewish people by the Church: he expects the Church to occupy the deserted Jerusalem in the wake of Hadrian's expulsion of the Jews from the city. And this has more than symbolic significance for Justin. In all his thinking on the people of God concept, he is a "substitution" theologian. There has come about a complete reversal of roles between Israel and the Gentiles. Israel has turned out to be

---

Isaiah text (1961) 346–348; Prigent, Les Testimonia (1961) 91–93; Skarsaune, Proof (1987) 170. 183; idem, Dåpsteologi (1976) 84–86 (cp. bibliography to Barnabas).

[55] Cp. the close allusive parallels in *Dial.* 16.2; 52.4, and 108.3. Analysis in Skarsaune, Proof (1987) 53–54. 160–162.

[56] Cp. the time perspective in *Dial.* 32.3f, and the pertinent comment by Osborn, Justin Martyr (1973) 190f.

idolaters (*Dial.* 19.5f; 20.4; 34.8; 46.6; 67.8; 93.4 etc.), while the Gentiles, who used to worship idols, have become truly devout and fearing God alone, in Christ (*Dial.* 11.4; 30.2f; 34.8; 52.4; 83.4; 91.3; 110.2–4 etc.). "For in the same way that you [Jews] provoked him by committing idolatry, so also has he deemed them [the Gentiles], though [formerly] idolaters, worthy to know his will, and to inherit the inheritance that is with him" (*Dial.* 130.4).

In this way, Justin set a precedent for Christian hermeneutics with regard to the Jews and the Church that was to dominate for centuries to come: every negative and critical remark about Israel in the Bible was taken to describe in a timeless, almost ontological way, the very *nature* of the Jewish people. On the other hand, every positive saying about Israel was transferred to the Church, and the Gentiles were found to be believers almost by *nature* as well. The ingrained unbelief of Israel was seen primarily in the golden calf incident *and* in the killing of the Righteous One (and his predecessors and followers).

It may be worthwile to reflect a little on the genesis of this strongly anti-Jewish trait in early (and later) Christian hermeneutics.[57] We have noticed already the importance of the deuteronomistic scheme of preaching repentance (sin-exile-conversion-return scheme) in early Christian use of the "slaying of the prophets" theme. As long as this tradition is used in an inner-Jewish setting, there can be no question of anti-Jewish (far less 'anti-semitic') tendencies, but rather of extreme Jewish self-criticism. This holds true even for the earliest Christian adaptions of this tradition; they are still inner-Jewish. It goes without saying that within this framework, the only relevant *guilt* to be addressed is the guilt of the addressees, i.e, Jewish guilt for the slaying of the Righteous (or in the Jewish version: the prophets). "Israel selbst ist es, das die Vorstellung ausgebildet und überliefert hat, es ist darin in einer Tiefe mit sich zu Gericht gegangen".[58] – Something very fateful happened to this tradition when it was appropriated by Gentile Christians with no basic feeling of solidarity with the Jewish people. Very soon it deteriorated into a slogan about Jews being unbelievers by nature and Christ-killers by habit. In Justin, we can see this transformation of the tradition nearly completed.

D. The recapitulation motif

In *1. Apol.* 33 Justin treats the virgin birth of Jesus on the basis of Isa 7:14, quoted in a non-LXX version very close to Matt 1:23. In his comments Justin takes issue with the accusation that the virgin birth seems to be just another myth like the ones told about Zeus having intercourse with women on earth. Justin answers this by pointing out that the prophecy is explicit about the mother of the Messiah still being a *virgin* at the time of birth, i.e. no intercourse has taken place. Besides, the very fact that the virgin birth had been *predicted* in this unambiguous manner by the prophet, makes the otherwise incredible miracle believable. – In his rendering of the New Testament fulfilment report, Justin has material that combines Luke 1:31f and Matt 1:21: the angel said to Mary that she would conceive by the Holy Spirit and that she would call his name Jesus.

The treatment of the virgin birth of Jesus in *Dial.* 48ff is completely different. The whole is structured to meet two Jewish objections: (1) The text of Isa 7:14 does not read *parthenos* but *neanis* (young woman), hence no extraordinary birth is meant (*Dial.* 43.8; 67.1; 71.3; 84.3). (2) Isa 7:14 concerns the birth of Hezekiah, not a future Messiah (*Dial.* 43.8; 67.1; 71.3). Against these objections, the simple prophecy-fulfilment material from 1. *Apol.* 33 would no longer be sufficient, and in the *Dialogue* one can observe how Justin introduces a new textual basis for his discussion, and develops an argument that actually circumvents the textually disputed Isa 7:14.

---

[57] Cp. i.a. F. Blanchetière, "Aux sources de l'antijudaïsme chrétien", *RHPR* 53 (1973) 354–398.

[58] Steck, Das gewaltsame Geschick (1967) 321.

First, concerning the disputed reading *parthenos*, Justin develops one general and one specific argument. The general argument is that Jewish scribes are known to have altered the readings of the Seventy in more places than this (*Dial.* 71–73, cp. also 120.4f; 124.3–4; 131.1; 137.3). The specific argument is that the prophet said that God would give a *sign*, i.e. something miraculous, and only the reading *virgin* makes sense of this (*Dial.* 84.1f).

The Hezekiah argument is answered in several rounds, but mainly in *Dial.* 77f; 83; 85. As far as Isa 7:14 is concerned, Justin quotes the whole of Isa 7:10–17 in *Dial.* 43.5f and 66.2f. In both cases the verse Isa 8:4 is interpolated into Isa 7:16, *and it is precisely on this interpolated verse (not 7:14) that the whole argument against Hezekiah hinges*: The Isaiah prophecy speaks about a child who "takes the power of Damascus and the spoil of Samaria" *before* the child "knows how to call father and mother", i. e. while still a little baby (*Dial.* 77.3). Taking the power of Damascus and the spoil of Samaria means setting men free from the power of Satan, the Wise Men (Matt 2) coming to worship the baby Jesus demonstrated that he had already liberated them from demons (*Dial.* 78.9f).

Justin's main point is this: the Isaiah prophecy speaks about a new-born child doing a divine, super-human work: liberating men from demons, from Satan's power. This shows that the prophecy not only is "too big" for Hezekiah, it is too big for any king in Israel's history, as is the case with other Messianic prophecies, too:

> It is not possible to prove that it (Ps 24:7) has been spoken either of Hezekiah or of Solomon, or in fact any who was called your king, but only of our Christ ... For when exorcised by the name of this very One who is the Son of God and the first-born of every creature, and was born by a virgin ... every demon is overcome and subdued (*Dial.* 85.2f).

For example, Justin says, Ps 110:1 cannot possibly be said about Hezekiah. Verse 2 in the same Psalm speaks about a king liberating Jerusalem with his own "rod of power"; Hezekiah did not do this,

> but our Jesus, though He has not come in glory, sent forth a rod of power into Jerusalem, the word of calling and repentance unto all the nations, where the demons used to bear rule over them, as David says: The gods of the heathen are demons. And with might has his word persuaded many to forsake the demons whom they were serving, and by him to believe on God the All-ruler ... (*Dial.* 83.4).

One may in these passages observe how the anti-Hezekiah polemic centered upon Isa 7:10–17 (interpolated) is set into a quite distinct framework: Christ is the conqueror of Satan and his host (the demons).

Interspersed in *Dial.* 48ff we find several more passages expressing the same idea, and it is interesting to notice that two of them contain the only two "etymological" references to Hebrew/Aramaic in Justin: (1) *Dial.* 103.5f (Jesus after his baptism overcoming Satan, "*sata* in the language of Jews and Syrians is 'apostate', and *nas* is a name from which the interpretation of 'serpent' is taken"; hence: the tempter of Jesus was the same as the tempter in Paradise); (2) *Dial.* 124.3 – 125.4: Jesus overcoming Satan was prefigured by Jacob wrestling with a "power" (Gen 32). („The name *Israel* means this: 'a man overcoming power'. For *Isra* is 'a man overcoming', and *el* is 'power'".) It seems clear that these passages belong together and express the idea of Christ the second Adam who conquered where Adam was conquered, in other words the "recapitulation" idea. The Hebrew-Aramaic etymology for the Greek word *Satanas* expresses the same idea: the Satan of the Gospel temptation story is none other than the Serpent of the temptation story in Gen 2f, since *Satanas* means 'apostate serpent'.

In *Dial.* 77–85 as well as the passages just quoted, the ideas of divine pre-existence and the virgin birth implying an *incarnation* of the divine, pre-existent Son, are clearly expressed. Christ, the pre-existent Son of God, could do superhuman, divine deeds already from the moment of his birth precisely because of his divine nature.

Justin treats this explicitly in his discussion of Christ's baptism. Trypho quotes Isa 11:1–3 and refers this text to Christ's baptism. He asks: How could Jesus be endowed with the Spirit at this point, if he pre-existed as fully divine prior to his birth? Justin admits that this is a tricky question (*Dial.* 87.2f). Justin's solution to this problem is again to give the "recapitulation" motif precedence, and harmonize the pre-existence idea with the account of Jesus' baptism – it did *not* imply that Christ at his baptism was endowed with powers he previously did not have (*Dial.* 87.3; 88.4).

There is thus a consistent framework for the interpretation of Jesus' virgin birth, baptism, and temptation throughout this material in Justin: Jesus, the incarnated divine Son of God, the second Adam, conquers Satan and the demons. Because he is divine, he has this power from his birth. This framework is also dominant in Justin's treatment of *the passion and death of Jesus* in *Dial.* 90–94:

(1) Israel won the battle against Amalek (Exod 17) while Moses made the sign of the cross and Joshua carried the name of Jesus (*Dial.* 90.4f). Cp. the parallels in *Dial.* 49 and 131:

> The Lord is said to "fight with hidden hand against Amalek" (Exod 17:16). ... You can perceive that some hidden power of God belonged to Christ in his crucifixion, at whom even the demons tremble, and, in fact, all the powers and authorities of the earth (*Dial.* 49.8). [„Joshua" (= Jesus) should wipe out the remembrance of Amalek, this cannot mean Joshua son of Nun, since the memory of Amalek survived him]. But that by Jesus who was crucified – of whom even those figures were predictions of all the evil that should be done to him – the demons were to be utterly destroyed, and were to fear his name, and that all the principalities and kingdoms were likewise to cower before him ... God makes plain (*Dial.* 131.5).

(2) In Moses' words about Joseph, Deut 33:13–17, there is a symbol of Christ's cross: the horn of the unicorn. "Men of all nations have by means of this mystery turned to the worship of God from their vain idols and demons, while to unbelievers the same sign is made known for their destruction and condemnation" (*Dial.* 91.1–3).

(3) The brazen serpent (Num 21:1–9) was also a sign of salvation.

> It was intended to proclaim that by him who was to be crucified death was to come to the serpent, but salvation to them that are bitten by it, and flee for refuge to him who sent his crucified Son into the world (*Dial.* 91.4). He proclaimed that he would destroy the power of the serpent, who caused the transgression to be made by Adam, but bring salvation to them that believe on him who was by this sign ... to be put to death, from the bites of the serpent, namely, evil deeds, idolatries, and other iniquities (*Dial.* 94.1; cp. 112.1f; 131.4).

All the material surveyed here lacks parallels in the "creed sequence" in 1. *Apol.* 31ff and has a distinctly different orientation than the testimonies in the *Apology*. Basic to the *Dialogue* material is the demonological framework, the recapitulation idea (Christ = second Adam), the polemic against historizing and humanizing the prophecies of a divine, super-human Messiah by applying them to Hezekiah, Solomon, or any human Jewish king.

To round off the review of this material in Justin, we have to take a closer look at the pre-existence idea itself. How does Justin argue this point? In *Dial.* 61 he says that Scripture clearly testifies

> that God has begotten as a Beginning before all his creatures a kind of *dynamin logikeen* from himself, which is also called ... the Glory of the Lord, and sometimes Son, and sometimes Wisdom, and sometimes Angel, and sometimes God, and sometimes Lord and Word ... (*Dial.* 61.1).

The sequence of designations here mostly refers back to Justin's treatment of the Old Testament theophanies in *Dial.* 56–60 (on which see below), but the implicit paraphrase of Gen 1:1 and the name Wisdom points forward to the quotation of Prov 8:22-36 in *Dial.* 61.3-5, and Gen 1:26-28 in *Dial.* 62.1.[59] Christ is identified with personified Wisdom.[60] This identification is nothing new in Justin; it is present in the New Testament and in the Apostolic Fathers. What is new in Justin, is the enormous widening of the testimony dossier on Christ's preexistence and divinity. We shall take a look at this in two steps.

(1) In Justin and – interestingly – in the Babylonian Talmud we find quotation sequences in which the point is to prove that Scripture knows of *two* who are both called God or Lord.[61] The following stand out: Gen 19:24; Ps 45:7; Ps 110:1 (*Dial.* 56.12-15; 68.3).[62] The two last mentioned are to be found in a similar function prior to Justin; but he is the first Christian writer known to us who makes much out of Gen 19:24, paraphrased in this way in *Dial.* 60.5: "In the judgement of Sodom the Lord (on earth, speaking with Abraham) inflicted the judgement from the Lord who was in the heavens". The point is: Gen 19:24 speaks of two Lords, one on earth talking with Abraham, one in heaven, raining fire and brimstone upon Sodom.

It is interesting to notice that Justin's testimony on two Lords, Gen 19:24, is mentioned as well as refuted in *bSanhedrin* 38b: "A *Min* once said to R. Ishmael b. Jose [ca. 180 CE]: It is written, 'Then the Lord caused to rain upon Sodom and Gomorrah brimstone and fire from the Lord', but 'from him' should have been written! A certain fuller said, Leave him to me, I will answer him. It is written, 'And Lamech said to his wives, Ada and Zilla, Hear my voice, ye wives of Lamech'; but he should have said, 'my wives'. But such is the Scriptural idiom – so here too, it is the Scriptural idiom. – Whence do you know that? asked he (R. Ishmael). I heard it in a public discourse of R. Meir, (he answered)".

If the attribution of the argument to R. Meir – Justin's contemporary – can be trusted, we have here evidence of a debate on the "two Lords" question between Jewish Christians and a Rabbi in Justin's days, or possibly a little prior to him. Actually, the rabbinic counter-argument that the two *terms* Lord in Gen 19:24 do not imply two "Lords" in reality, is not a very strong one. It would not apply easily to Ps 45:7f and Ps 110:1, and as Justin takes great pains to point out, the first "Lord" in Gen 19:24 seems to be the man talking with Abraham.

(2) Justin has not felt satisfied with these simple "two Lords/two Gods" testimonies. In *Dial.* 56-62; 75 (parallelled in *Dial.* 126-129) he has constructed a closely reasoned argument, based on detailed observations within

---

[59] Justin's idea that the "us" in Gen 1:26 implies a conversation between the Father and the Son is a Christianization of the Jewish concept that God conversed with his Wisdom, Wis 9:1ff; 10:2; *2 Enoch* 30.8. The Christian version is already present in *Barn.* 5.5 and 6.12, and recurs in a form very close to the Jewish "Vorlage" in Theophilus of Antioch, *Ad Autol.* II.18. On the whole complex, cp. Ginzberg, Haggada (*MGWJ* 43) 61-63; J. Jervell, *Imago Dei. Gen 1,26f im Spätjudentum, in der Gnosis und in den paulinischen Briefen* (FRLANT 70; Göttingen 1960) 48-51.

[60] On Wisdom Christology in the NT, see in particular G. Schimanowski, *Weisheit und Messias* (WUNT 2. Reihe, 17; Tübingen 1985) with further literature, and on Wisdom Christology in early Christian literature in general, O. Skarsaune, *The Incarnation: Myth or Fact?* (St. Louis 1991).

[61] In the Talmud, of course, this is quoted in order to be refuted.

[62] On this cluster of testimonies, cp. esp. Trakatellis, Pre-existence (1976) 65f. The Talmudic parallel is to be found in *b Sanhedrin* 38b, where we meet the following sequence said by the *minim* (heretics) to prove a duality of Gods or Lords: Gen 1:26; 11:7; 35:7; Deut 4:7; 2 Sam 7:23; Dan 7:9; Exod 24:1; Gen 19:24. Cp. Skarsaune, Proof (1987) 413.

large passages of biblical text, for the view that in general the Old Testament theophanies were appearances of the Son, not the Father.[63]

Briefly summarised his argument runs like this: (a) One of the three men appearing to Abraham at Mamre (Gen 18) was not an angel (as first claimed by Trypho), but God, as Gen 18:10 taken together with Gen 21:12 proves. But this God was not identical with the Father, as Gen 19:24 proves. (b) In the Jacob theophanies the God appearing to Jacob cannot be God the Father, since the appearing God also is called Angel of God – that is, he carries out the Father's will and must be numerically distinct from the Father. (c) In the thornbush theophany the God who appeared to Moses was not the Father, since the appearing God calls himself the God of Abraham, Isaac, and Jacob, which means the God *who appeared* to Abraham etc. It has already been proved that this God was not the Father. Besides, this God is identical with the appearing Angel of the thornbush theophany, because the sliding from "Angel of the Lord" to "God" in Exod 3 has striking parallels in the Jacob theophanies (*Dial.* 56–60). (d) The *name* of the second God who appeared to Abraham etc. was not made known to them (Exod 6:3), but was made known to Moses as *Jesus*, Exod 23:20 (*Dial.* 75).

As has been shown, this could be a counter-attack against Jewish refutations of the "two Lords" testimonies. The pivotal role of Gen 19:24 speaks for this. On the other hand, the carefully constructed theory that all theophanies are appearances of the Son (*Dial.* 60.2) seems to be more than the Jewish/Christian debate on the issue of the "two Lords/two Gods" called for. And in this part of the *Dialogue*, Justin has made Trypho much more cooperative and consenting than in any other part. This could indicate that a third party is the primary target of this argument. It could well be Marcion and his disciples.

(1) Marcion complained that the allegorical exegesis of ecclesiastical writers was unsound; Jewish literalism was much to be preferred.[64] In *Dial.* 56–60 Justin is almost pedantic in his insistence upon the exact wording of the texts, and has Trypho praise this and commend him for faithfulness towards the words of Scripture (*Dial.* 56.16; 58.2; 63.1 et al.).

(2) There are some anti-Marcion remarks not provoked by Trypho or Justin. Justin: "There both exists and is mentioned in Scripture a God and Lord other than, and less than, the Maker of the universe ... *above whom there is no other God*... (*Dial.* 56.4; cp. 56.11; 60.5). Trypho: "You are anxious to draw your proofs from the Scriptures, and you declare that *there is no God above the Maker of the universe*" (*Dial.* 56.18). In the whole of *Dial.* 56–60 it seems Justin is eager to make Trypho his exegetical ally against an unnamed opponent: Marcion.

(3) While a general statement that the divine agent upon earth in Old Testament salvation history was the Son, bearing the name Jesus, might be useful in the Jewish/Christian debate, it would be a triumphant clinchpin against Marcion, who did his utmost to dissociate Jesus (and his heavenly Father) from any involvement with Old Testament history and the Old Testament God.[65]

---

[63] General bibliography on the OT theophanies in the early Fathers: G. Aeby, "Les missions divines de Saint Justin a Origène", *Paradosis* 12 (1958) 7–15; A. d'Alès, "La Théophanie de Mambré devant la tradition des Pères", *RSR* 20 (1930) 150–160; E. Evans, "Verbum sive Sermonem Dei in Veteris Testamenti theophaniis semper visum fuisse", StPatr 11,2 (TU 108; Berlin 1972) 152–157; L. Thunberg, "Early Christian interpretations of the three angels in Gen 18", StPatr 7 (TU 92; Berlin 1966) 560–570. Fundamental on Justin is B. Kominiak, *The Theophanies of the Old Testament in the Writings of St. Justin* (The Catholic University of America, Studies in Sacred Theology, Sec. Ser. 14; Washington 1948). Cp. also Trakatellis, Pre-existence (1976) 53–92; Skarsaune, Proof (1987) 409–24.

[64] References in A. von Harnack, *Marcion. Das Evangelium vom fremden Gott* (2. ed. = TU 45; Leipzig 1924; repr. Darmstadt 1985) 62–63. 84–85.

[65] According to Marcion, the Old Testament God was *visible* and *known* (cp. the theophanies), whereas the true God was invisible and unknown, cp. esp. Harnack, Marcion (1924/1985)

(4) The only occurrence of the theophany motif in the Apology, in 1. *Apol.* 63, can be seen to have an anti-Marcion twist.[66]

P. Prigent (Justin, 1964) has argued for the general theory that Justin in the *Apology* as well as the *Dialogue* re-used his own *Syntagma against all heresies* (1. *Apol.* 26.8). While not accepting the theory in this general form, I believe there is much to be said for it with regard to 1. *Apol.* 63 and *Dial.* 56–60/75 (with parallels).

Be this as it may, what is clear in any case is that Justin in his argument on the theophanies makes a decisive move beyond the quotation of selected testimonies which dominates most of his exegesis. In this case, he works directly with the full LXX text of Genesis and Exodus, often combining detailed observations gleaned from verses chapters apart. There is nothing of the figurative, allegorical interpretation of (supposed) metaphors in the text which otherwise abound in his comments. I would suggest that Justin in his handling of the theophanies is doing original exegetical work, provoked by a new challenge – possibly coming from Marcion.

It should be added that the theophany argument in *Dial.* 56ff and parallels without any difficulty could be combined with the older Wisdom Christology of *Dial.* 61 f. In the book of Wisdom we find the idea of *Wisdom* being the divine agent on earth throughout the Genesis and Exodus events, chs. 10 f. The argument on the theophanies in *Dial.* 56–60 can on this Jewish background be seen as an extension of the Wisdom Christology, but it does not seem that Justin was very aware of this Jewish "wisdom" background.

E. The commentary on Psalm 22

The other point where Justin definitely breaks through his "testimony" approach is in *Dial.* 98–106. Here he quotes the whole of Psalm 22 and goes on to give a lemma by lemma commentary on the whole Psalm.

One can easily observe, however, that the traditional testimonies within this Psalm (vv. 2; 8f; 17–19) were his clue to the whole Psalm. They told him to see Ps 22 as a text predicting details of the passion story. To some extent, Justin succeeds in extending this point of view to the whole Psalm. The traditional testimonies have been enriched by the following:

2b.3:	Prayer in Gethsemane (*Dial.* 99.2f).
7:	Christ despised at his passion (*Dial.* 101.2)
12–14:	Christ surrounded and without help at his arrest (*Dial.* 103.1–4).
16:	Christ silent before Pilate (*Dial.* 102.5, repeated in 103.9).
16b.17a:	Death of Jesus (*Dial.* 104.1f).
21:	Death on a cross (*Dial.* 105.2, with excursus on the fate of souls after death, *Dial.* 105.4–6).
21f:	Jesus' prayer in death (*Dial.* 105.3).
23:	Christ resurrected (*Dial.* 106.1f).

But Justin has not been able to carry through this constant reference to the passion story. Some lemmas are referred to Christ's humility without specific reference to the passion:

265*–268*. Justin identifies the visible and known God with the Son, whereas the Father, the creator-God of the Old Testament, is said to be incapable of appearing visible upon earth. Tertullian states the same argument explicitly against Marcion (*Adv. Marc.* II.27.6), Irenaeus against the heretics in general (*A. H.* IV.20.10f).

[66] Detailed argument in Prigent, Justin (1964) 122f; Skarsaune, Proof (1987) 211 f.

5f: Jesus recognized the fathers as his fathers and set his hope on God alone (*Dial.* 101.1f).
11b.12a: Jesus puts his hope on God alone, not on his own wisdom etc. (*Dial.* 102.6).

One lemma is referred to Christ's birth:

10b: Christ was saved from Herod's murder of the children (*Dial.* 102.1f, with excursus on free will in 102:3f).

Finally, three "recapitulation" passages (*Dial.* 100.1–6 ad v. 4; *Dial.* 103.5f ad v. 14b; *Dial.* 106.3f ad v. 23) have been included in the commentary, only superficially attached to the verses they are supposed to comment upon, but clearly related to each other and the other "recapitulation" passages in the *Dialogue* (cp. above).

One gets the impression that the commentary on Psalm 22 in *Dial.* 98–106 is a pioneering attempt at writing a new kind of *continouous* comment on a biblical text by an author who is still very much depending on the testimony tradition. It is the hermeneutics of this tradition which directs his efforts; his primary objective is to discover what event in the passion story the Psalmist could have in mind. But when this does not work, he looks at other parts of the Jesus story to find the "fulfilment" that fits the Psalm. A hermeneutic that worked well with selected testimonies is here put to a new task which seems beyond its capacity. Later, we shall see Hippolytus attempt the same approach, with greater success.

The *Nachwirkung* of Justin was most formidable in his immediate successors Irenaeus and Tertullian. They exploit his works liberally, as well for Old Testament quotations as for exegetical comment. This massive take-over of Justin's work in Irenaeus and Tertullian makes it difficult to assess to what extent Justin is directly used by later writers, and/or via his successors. By Eusebius he is first and foremost presented as an apologist and an anti-heretical polemicist, not as an interpreter of Scripture.

2.2. *Melito of Sardis*

Sources: C. Bonner, *The homily on the passion by Melito bishop of Sardis and some fragments of the apocryphal Ezekiel* (Studies and documents 12; London/Philadelphia 1940); M. Testuz, *Papyrus Bodmer XIII, Méliton de Sardes Homélie sur la Pâque* (Genève 1960); O. Perler, *Méliton de Sardes: Sur la Pâque et fragments* (SC 123; Paris 1966); S. G. Hall, *Melito of Sardis: On Pascha, and fragments* (Oxford Early Christian Texts; Oxford 1979). Translation and commentary: J. Blank, *Meliton von Sardes. Vom Passa, die älteste christliche Osterpredigt* (Sophia. Quellen östlicher Theologie 3; Freiburg/Br. 1963).

Bibliography: R. M. Mainka, "Meliton von Sardes. Eine bibliographische Übersicht", *Claretianum* 5 (1965) 225–255.

General works: I. Angerstorfer, *Melito und das Judentum* (diss.; Regensburg 1986); C. Bonner, "The homily on the passion by Melito bishop of Sardis", *Mélanges F. Cumont* (Annuaire de l'Institut de philologie et d'histoire orientale et slave 4; Bruxelles 1936) 107–119; idem, "The new homily of Melito and its place in Christian literature", *Actes du Ve Congrès International de Papyrologie, Oxford 1937* (Bruxelles 1938) 94–97; idem, "A supplementary Note on the Opening of Melito's Homily", *HTR* 36 (1943) 317–319; R. Cantalamessa, "Méliton de Sardes. Une christologie antignostique du IIe siècle", *RSR* 37 (1963) 1–26; idem, "Questioni melitoniane. Melitone e i latini; Melitone e i quartodecimani", *Rivista di storia e letteratura religiosa* 6 (1970) 245–267; idem, "Les homélies pascales de Méliton de Sardes et du Pseudo-Hippolyte et les extraits de Théodote", *Epektasis. Mélanges J. Daniélou* (Paris 1972) 263–271; J. Daniélou, "Figure et événement chez Méliton", *Neotestamentica et Patristica* (FS O. Cullmann, ed. H. Baltensweiler

/ B. Reicke; Zürich 1962) 282–292; A. GRILLMEIER, "'Das Erbe der Söhne Adams' in der Paschahomilie Melitons", *Scholastik* 20–24 (1949) 481–502 (rev. and repr. in idem, *Mit ihm und in ihm. Christologische Forschungen und Perspektiven* [Freiburg/Basel/Wien 1975] 175–197); S. G. HALL, "Melito, Peri Pascha 1 and 2. Text and interpretation", *Kyriakon* (FS J. Quasten I; Münster/Westf. 1970) 236–248; idem, "Melito in the Light of the Passover Haggadah", *JTS* NS 22 (1971) 29–46; T. HALTON, "Stylistic device in Melito, Peri Pascha", *Kyriakon* (FS J. Quasten I; Münster/Westf. 1970) 249–255; W. HUBER, *Passa und Ostern. Untersuchungen zur Osterfeier der alten Kirche* (BZNW 35; Berlin 1969); A. T. KRAABEL, "Melito the bishop and the synagogue at Sardis: text and context", *Studies presented to G.M.A. Hanfmann* (ed. D.G. Mitten et al.; Mainz 1971); R. A. KRAFT, "Barnabas' Isaiah Text and Melito's *Paschal Homily*", *JBL* 80 (1961) 371–373; G. KRETSCHMAR, "Christliches Passa im 2. Jahrhundert und die Ausbildung der christlichen Theologie", *RSR* 60 (1972) 287–323; B. LOHSE, *Das Passafest der Quartadezimaner* (BFChrT 2. Reihe 54; Gütersloh 1953); idem, *Die Passah-Homilie des Bischofs Meliton von Sardes* (Leiden 1958); P. NAUTIN, "L'homélie de "Meliton" sur la passion", *RHE* 44 (1949) 429–438; idem, *Le dossier d'Hippolyte et de Méliton* (Paris 1953); O. PERLER, *Ein Hymnus zur Ostervigil von Meliton?* (Paradosis 15; Fribourg/CH 1960); idem, "Typologie der Leiden des Herrn in Melitons Peri Pascha", *Kyriakon* (FS J. Quasten I; Münster/Westf. 1970) 256–265; E. PETERSON, "Ps.-Cyprian, Adversus Iudaeos und Meliton von Sardes", *VC* 6 (1952) 33–34 (repr. in idem, *Frühkirche, Judentum und Gnosis* [Rom/Freiburg/Wien 1959; repr. Darmstadt 1982] 137–145); J. SMIT SIBINGA, "Melito of Sardis. The Artist and His Text", *VC* 24 (1970) 81–104; E. J. WELLESZ, "Melito's homily on the passion, an investigation into the sources of Byzantine hymnography", *JTS* 44 (1943) 41–52; G. ZUNTZ, "On the opening Sentence of Melito's Paschal Homily", *HTR* 36 (1943) 299–315.

Since the identification of the text of Melito's *Peri Pascha* (henceforward *PP*) by C. BONNER in 1936, this work has occupied the center of interest among scholars who focus on the biblical exegesis of Melito. It should not be forgotten, however, that even though Melito prior to this discovery was mainly seen as the *apologist* of the Eusebian fragments,[67] there were also sufficient fragments of his works left to accord him a place in the history of typological OT exposition even without the evidence of the *PP*.

Melito is strikingly different from Justin: he is not primarily quoting and interpreting prophetic *oracles*; he is the great poet of biblical *types*.

In the *Peri Pascha* this could be explained by the fact that the basic text, Exod 12, contained only types (the paschal lamb and the exodus events) and no prophetic oracles. But it seems that Melito excelled in typological poetry in other works also, if the preserved fragments are representative.[68] And vice versa: in the *Peri Pascha* he has included several catenas of biblical types with no immediate relationship to Exod 12.

And he carried the wood on his shoulders
 as he was led up to be slain like Isaac by his Father.
But Christ suffered, whereas Isaac did not suffer;
 for he was a model (*typos*) of the Christ who was going to suffer.
But by being merely the model of Christ
 he caused astonishment and fear among men.
For it was a strange mystery to behold,
 a son led by his father to a mountain for slaughter, whose feet he bound and whom he put on the wood of the offering,
 preparing with zeal the things for his slaughter.
But Isaac was silent, bound like a ram,
 not opening his mouth nor uttering a sound.

[67] Cp. fragment 1 in Hall's edition (62–65), contained in Eusebius *H. E.* IV.26.4–11.
[68] Cp. esp. fragments 9–11, 14–15, and Hall's "New Fragments I-III" (Hall 74–96).

For not frightened by the sword
nor alarmed at the fire
nor sorrowful at the suffering
he carried with fortitude the model of the Lord.[69]

This fragment from another work than the *PP* is very characteristic for the style of large portions of the *PP*.

The *PP* itself begins with a summary statement on the "mystery of the pascha" in 1–10: the Old Testament model was temporary, the reality in Christ eternal, "perishable the sheep, imperishable the Lord" (4). In 11–33 there follows a *narratio*, a paraphrase of the exodus story replete with allusions to the New Testament realization. Then Melito adds one of the most interesting passages of the homily, a reflection on the nature of biblical typology as such, 34–45.

What is said and done is nothing, beloved,
without a comparison and preliminary sketch ...
This is just what happens in the case of a preliminary structure:
it does not arise as a finished work,
but because of what is going to be visible through its image acting as a model.
For this reason a preliminary sketch is made
of the future thing out of wax or clay or of wood,
in order that what will soon arise
taller in height, and stronger in power,
and beautiful in form, and rich in its construction,
may be seen through a small and perishable sketch.
But when that of which it is the model arises,
that which once bore the image of the future thing
is itself destroyed as growing useless
having yielded to what is truly real the image of it ...
As then with the perishable examples,
so also with the imperishable things;
as with the earthly things,
so also with the heavenly.
For the very salvation and reality of the Lord
were prefigured in the people,
and the decrees of the gospel
were proclaimed in advance by the law (36–39).

After this excursus on the rationale and nature of types, Melito goes on to set the passion of the true paschal lamb, Christ, in its proper framework. This requires a new *narratio*, this time of the first man, Paradise, the fall, and its consequences (slavery to Satan and sin, 47–56). Slavery to Satan and sin is the significant typological framework for the interpretation of the exodus events: "He ransomed us from the world's service as from the land of Egypt, and freed us from the devil's slavery as from the hand of Pharao" (67).

But before this continued *narratio* about the saving work of Christ, Melito inserts an interesting passage on OT types and predictions (57–60), giving substance and content to his earlier excursus on the principle of biblical types:

If you look carefully at the model,
you will perceive him through the final outcome.

---

[69] From fragm. 9, Hall 74f. On the "binding of Isaac" (*aqedath Jizchaq*) in early Jewish and Christian tradition, cp. G. Vermes, *Scripture and Tradition in Judaism* (Leiden 1961) 193–227; R. le Deaut, *La nuit pascale* (AnBib 22; Rome 1963) 133–208. This type is not mentioned in Justin, but is briefly hinted at in *Barn.* 7.3. It may form the background of NT passages like Rom 8:32, cp. N.A. Dahl, "The atonement – an adequate reward for the akedah?", in idem, *The Crucified Messiah and Other Essays* (Minneapolis 1974) 146–160/184–189. On the Isaac typology in Melito, cp. D. Lerch, Isaaks Opferung (1950) 27–43; F. Nikolash, Lamm als Christussymbol (1963) 24–60; R.L. Wilken, "Melito and the sacrifice of Isaac", *TS* 37 (1976) 53–69.

Therefore if you wish to see the mystery of the Lord,
look at Abel who is similarly murdered,
at Isaac who is similarly bound,
at Joseph who is similarly sold,
at Moses who is similarly exposed,
at David who is similarly persecuted,
at the prophets who similarly suffer for the sake of Christ.[70]
Look also at the sheep which is slain in the land of Egypt,
which struck Egypt and saved Israel by its blood (58–60).

To this Melito adds a passage which demonstrates that although he does not often quote traditional "proof from prophecy" testimonies, he knows this tradition well:

But the mystery of the Lord is proclaimed by the prophetic voice.
For Moses says to the people:
'And you shall see your life hanging before your eyes night and day; and you will not believe on your life'.[71]
And David/Jeremiah/Isaiah said: ... (follows quotations of Ps 2:1f; Jer 11:19; Isa 53:7f).
Many other things have been proclaimed by many prophets
about the mystery of the Pascha, which is Christ ... (61–65).

This is the only explicit statement of the proof from prophecy in Melito, but scattered allusions prove that it is only a selection of a rich dossier known to him. This is especially true of the "blaming Israel" section that follows in 72–99.[72]

The parallelism between fallen man's condition and the slavery of Israel in Egypt implies that behind the paschal lamb/Christ typology there lurks another: Adam/Christ.[73] As in other writers, there is a connection between the idea of Christ the second Adam, new Man, and Christ as God's Wisdom incarnate. But rather than stating explicitly the identification of Christ with God's Wisdom, Melito elaborates on two concepts implied in this idea: (1) Christ is – together with the Father – the Creator; and (2) he is the real agent of salvation history (as Wisdom is in Wis 10f).

(1) You did not know, Israel,
that he is the firstborn of God,
who was begotten before the morning star,
who tinted the light,
who lit up the day,
who divided off the darknes ...
who formed man upon earth (82)
(2) It was he who chose you and guided you
from Adam to Noah ...
from Abraham to Isaac and Jacob and the twelve patriarchs.
...
It was he who guided you into Egypt,
and watched over you and there sustained you.
It was he who lit your way with a pillar
and sheltered you with a cloud ... (83f).

---

[70] Similar catenas are frequent in Melito, cp. *PP* 69; fragm. 15; New fragm. II.

[71] On this non-LXX version of Deut 28:66, which was to become a favourite testimony on "the crucified creator" in later writers, see esp. J. Daniélou, "La vie suspendue au bois (*Deut.*, 28,66)", in idem, Études d'exégèse (1978) 53–75.

[72] It contains the infamous deicide charge, 96. Cp. esp. E. Werner, "Melito of Sardes, the first poet of deicide", *HUCA* 37 (1966) 191–210.

[73] It becomes explicit i.a. in 66 and 100–102.

Christ being the pre-existent creator together with his Father, Melito describes the crucifixion in the starkest contrasts, echoing his favourite testimony Deut 28:66:

He who hung the earth is hanging;
he who fixed the heavens has been fixed;
he who fastened the universe has been fastened to a tree ...(96).

Thus, while there are great differences between Justin and Melito in literary genre, style, and emphasis on types rather than prophecies, there are many parallels in basic ideas and also in hermeneutical approach. For Melito as for Justin the Old Testament is first and foremost a *prophetic* book, as a whole as well as in its different parts.

2.3. *Theophilus of Antioch*

Sources: Otto VIII; R. M. Grant, *Theophilus of Antioch: Ad Autolycum* (Oxford Early Christian Texts; Oxford 1970). Translations: *ANF* II 85–121; G. Bardy / J. Sender, *Théophile d'Antioche: Trois livres à Autolycus* (SC 20; Paris 1948).

General works: A. Davids, "Hésiode et les prophètes chez Théophile d'Antioche (Ad Autol. II,8–9)", *Fides sacramenti, sacramentum fidei* (FS P. Smulders; ed. H. J. Auf der Maur et al.; Assen 1981) 205–211; R. M. Grant, "The Bible of Theophilus of Antioch", *JBL* 66 (1947) 173–196; idem, "The problem of Theophilus", *HTR* 43 (1950) 179–196; K. E. McVey, "The Use of Stoic Cosmogony in Theophilus of Antioch's *Hexaemeron*", *Biblical Hermeneutics in Historical Perspective* (FS K. Froehlich; ed. M. S. Burrows / P. Rorem; Grand Rapids, MI 1991) 32–58; M. Simonetti, "La sacra scrittura in Teofilo d'Antiochia", *Epektasis* (FS J. Daniélou, ed. J. Fontaine / C. Kannengiesser; Paris 1972) 197–207; N. Zeegers-Vander Voorst, "La Création de l'Homme (Gen 1,26) chez Théophile d'Antioche", *VC* 30 (1976) 258–267; idem, "Satan, Eve et le serpent chez Théophile d'Antioche", *VC* 35 (1981) 152–169.

With Theophilus of Antioch we are entering a somewhat different exegetical universe, compared with Justin and Melito. Theophilus is more of an apologist than Justin, and in the three books against Autolycus he most of all casts himself in the role of the *historian* of universal and biblical history. "I think that I have now accurately set forth, as well as possible, the complete accounting of the antiquity of our religion and of the periods of time" (concluding remark in III.29). Josephus' *Contra Apionem* was his apologetic model, and Josephus one of his main sources outside the Bible (= Old Testament). His readership being Gentile, Theophilus is not concerned with the relationship between the Church and the Jewish people, nor with anti-Jewish polemic. He rather presupposes without any discussion that the Law and Prophets are "our writings" (III.29), that Abraham is "our Patriarch" (III.24) and "our forefather" (III.28), as is David (III.25, 28). The Hebrews of the exodus story also are "our forefathers" (III.20). Theophilus' dependence on Jewish apologetics, and his own emphasis on biblical history and monotheism, makes his writing strikingly "Jewish". Were it not for some New Testament quotations and allusions, and the inclusion of the Logos Christology in his account of creation, Theophilus could be taken for a Jewish author. Even considering his readership and his apologetic aim, the absolute lack of any hint of the Christological *proof from prophecy* and the prophecy-fulfilment scheme is remarkable. In Theophilus the prophets do not prophesy about the coming Messiah; they teach monotheism (I.6; II.9f, 34f etc.).

(A) Theophilus and the Old Testament.

There is of course a lot of implicit interpretation of Old Testament texts and stories in this treatise so obsessively concerned with Old Testament history and chronology. But to our purpose it is most relevant to concentrate on the *hexaemeron* treatise found in II.11 ff.[74]

In II.12–18 there is a more or less continuous exposition of the works of the six days of creation, after the quotation of Gen 1:3 – 2:3 in II.11. The works of the three first days are treated more or less as a unity in II.13–14, thereafter the works of days four through six are treated separately in II.15–18. Apart from some polemics against the faulty cosmology of Hesiod (II.12f), Theophilus at once begins the type of allegorical exposition which he afterwards continues until he comes to the creation of man in II.18.

Briefly summarized, it goes like this: (1) Small seeds become big trees: a sign of the resurrection of all men. (2) The ocean is kept fresh through the water from springs and rivers: a similitude of how the world is kept alive through the words of the law and the prophets. (3) In the sea there are habitable and fertile islands, as well as inhabitable and sterile ones: symbols of the Churches of the Lord on the one hand, and the assemblies of the heretics on the other. (4) The sun and the moon are symbols of God and man. (5) "The three days prior to the luminaries are types of the triad of God and his Logos and his Wisdom". (6) The animals created in water were blessed: men reborn in baptism are blessed. (7) Some sea animals and some birds kill and eat the ones smaller than themselves; others do not: models of destructive men and peaceful men. (8) Quadrupeds and wild animals represent earth-bound souls of sinners, while the birds represent human souls turning towards God in heaven. (9) The wild animals became wild because of man's fall.

One can hardly escape the impression of a somewhat improvised and haphazard collection of allegorical expositions; but two overriding principles may be discerned, which are characteristic of Theophilus elsewhere, too. (1) One is the tendency always to extract *moral lessons* from all biblical texts and stories, especially evident here in examples 7 and 8 above, which reminds one of the moral lessons 'Barnabas' extracts from the laws on unclean animals in *Barn.* 10. (2) The other is the *anti-heretical* polemic that is evident in other parts of Theophilus' work as well. He seems to combat Marcion and Apelles in II.25–27[75], and it would be no surprise if he became an apologist for the Creator, the goodness of creation etc. precisely in a commentary of Gen 1. Thus, he singles out *resurrection* (1), the *law and prophets* as salutary (2), the heretical churches as destructive (3), the positive symbolical correspondence between the first creation of life and new creation in baptism (6), the original complete goodness of creation (9).

---

[74] Strictly speaking, the treatise comprises more than the exposition of the six days of creation, Gen 1; it adds a "history" of the world through the flood and the re-settling of the world afterwards. But it is mainly in the hexaemeron part (11–28) that Theophilus becomes an exegete. R. M. GRANT observes that the whole treatise on Gen 1–11 in II.11–32 probably existed separately prior to its inclusion in *Adv. Autol.* (Introd. x).

[75] Cp. GRANT's notes ad locc. in his text edition.

In fact, it is among Gnostic writers that allegorical exegesis of the six days of creation may have originated. The *Great Revelation* fragments (attributed to Simon Magus) in Hippolytus' *Refutation* VI.2–15 (7–20) contain a hexaemeron allegory that seems very close to something Theophilus could be arguing against in his allegories. F. ex., in the *Great Revelation* the three days before the luminaries are said to be Mind and Intelligence and The Seventh, Indefinite Power (= the Logos? *Ref.* VI.9). This could explain Theophilus' 'orthodox' rebuttal in his allegorization of the three first days. There are other detailed correspondences, too, that could indicate that Theophilus' hexaemeron allegories are provoked by Gnostic precursors.

Before the treatment of the six-days scheme, Theophilus has an interesting passage on God's creating activity as such in II.10, this is resumed in what he has to say on man's creation in II.18 ff.

> God, having his own Logos innate in his own bowels, generated him together with his own Wisdom, vomiting him forth (Ps 45:2) before everything else. He used this Logos as his servant in the things created by him, and through him he made all things (John 1:3). He is called 'Beginning' because he leads and dominates everything fashioned through him. It was he, 'Spirit of God' (Gen 1:2) and 'Beginning' (Gen 1:1) and 'Wisdom' (Prov 8:22) and 'Power of the Most High' (Luke 1:35) who came down into the prophets and spoke through them about the creation of the world and all the rest. For the prophets did not exist when the world came into existence; there were the Wisdom of God which is in him and his holy Logos who is always present with him. For this reason he speaks thus through Solomon the prophet: "When he prepared the heaven I was with him, and when he made strong the foundations of the earth I was with him, binding them fast" (Prov 8:27–29) (II.10).

In his exegesis of Gen 1:1f Theophilus is clearly dependent upon the Jewish concept of God creating the world by means of *reshit* (Gen 1:1) = Wisdom (Prov 8:22: God begot me (Wisdom) as *reshit* ...). In rabbinic sources this idea is explicit in the Targums from Neofiti onwards, and in midrash *Genesis Rabba* ad loc. It is probably implied already in Sirach 24, where Wisdom is further identified with the Torah, as in the rabbinic sources.[76]

Theophilus' Jewish *Vorlage* is thus binitarian: God creating through the mediatorship of his Wisdom. But Theophilus himself is thinking in trinitarian terms:

> The three days prior to the luminaries are types of the triad of God and his Logos and his Wisdom ... (II.15).
>
> After making everything else by a word ... he regarded the making of man as the only work worthy of his own hands. Furthermore, God is found saying "Let us make man after the image and likeness" (Gen 1:26) as if he needed assistance; but he said "Let us make" to none other than his own Logos and his own Wisdom (II.18).

This makes for a certain vacillation in Theophilus' identification of Wisdom. He so to speak duplicates it: the Logos as well as the Spirit is identified with Wisdom. This results in the idea of a double mediatorship in creation – the Logos and the Spirit = Wisdom – and Theophilus is the first to quote

[76] In early Christian literature the typical combination of Gen 1:1 and Prov 8:22 is probably presupposed in John 1:1ff and esp. Col 1:15ff: *prootototokos pasees ktiseoos* (Prov 8:22), *en autoo ektisthee ta panta* (Gen 1:1). Cp. the fascinating study by C. F. Burney, "Christ as the APXH of Creation (Prov VIII 22, Col I 15–18, Rev III 14)", *JTS* 27 (1926) 160–177.

the later classic testimony on this double mediatorship: "By his Logos the heavens were made firm and by his Spirit all their power" (Ps 33:6; I.7). Theophilus is also the first to reflect on the 'how' of the Logos' being begotten by the Father. He does so employing stoic terminology, while his exegetical intention is to state plainly the meaning of the biblical testimony on the begetting of the Logos: Ps 45:2 ("My heart has emitted a good Logos", II.10):

> What is 'the voice' [Gen 3:8] but the Logos of God, who is also his Son?—not as the poets and mythographers describe son of gods begotten of sexual union, but as the truth describes the Logos, always innate [*endiathetos*] in the heart of God. For before anything came into existence he had this as his Counsellor [Isa 9:5 Hebr.], his own Mind and Intelligence. When God wished to make what he had planned to make, he generated this Logos, making him external [*proforikos*], as "the firstborn of all creation" [Col 1:15]. He did not deprive himself of the Logos but generated the Logos and constantly converses with his Logos. Hence the holy Scriptures and all those inspired by the Spirit teach us, and one of them, John, says, "In the beginning was the Logos, and the Logos was with God" [John 1:1]. (II.22).

The context of this passage is a discussion of who walked in Paradise: the Father or his Logos? Theophilus is not in doubt:

> The Father's Logos, through whom he made all things, who is his 'Power and Wisdom' [1 Cor 1:24], assuming the role of the Father and Lord of the universe, was present in Paradise in the role of God and conversed with Adam. ... Since the Logos is God and derived his nature from God, whenever the Father of the universe wills to do so he sends him into some place where he is present and is heard and seen (II.22).

In this way Theophilus arrives at the same conclusion with regard to the theophanies as Justin:

> No person whatever, even though he be of slight intelligence, will dare to say that the Maker and Father of the universe left all that is above heaven and appeared on a little section of earth (*Dial.* 60.2).
>
> The God and Father of the universe is unconfined and is not present in a place, for "there is no place of his rest" (Isa 66:1—Theophilus II.22).

As for the rest of Theophilus' exposition on Gen 2ff, we only mention (1) his idea that Adam and Eve were infants (II.25); and (2) his idea that man was created neither mortal nor immortal, but his fate in this regard depended on his own choice with regard to God's commandment (II.27).

(B) Theophilus and his successors.

Theophilus' allegorical exposition of the works of the six days of creation seems to have found little echo in his immediate successors. Tertullian may depend on him for the idea that the creation of the sea animals (Tertullian: the fishes) on the fifth day was a type of new creation in baptism: Christians are *pisciculi* because born in water (*De baptismo* 1). Irenaeus very likely took his idea that Adam and Eve were created as small children directly from Theophilus (*Proof of the Apostolic Preaching* 12; 14; *Adv. Haer.* III.22.4; IV.38.1–4; 39.1). He also repeats the idea of God = Logos walking in Paradise and conversing with Adam, in terms very close to Theophilus (*Adv. Haer.* V.17.1).

In his exposition on creation through Wisdom's mediatorship, on the other hand, Theophilus is clearly in touch with 'mainline' exegetical and Christological tradition. His idea of *double* mediation through the Logos and the Wisdom (= Spirit) is developed further by Irenaeus (*Adv. Haer.* IV.20.4), who transfers some of the traditional Christological Wisdom testimonies to the Spirit, first and foremost Prov 8:22ff (*Adv. Haer.* IV.20.3; *Proof* 5 – cp. below, sect. 4.1).

Tertullian, on the other hand, does not adopt this Wisdom = Spirit identification, but sticks to the older identification of Wisdom with Christ, like Justin. So do Cyprian[77] and Origen[78] (!), too.

3. The *testimonia* Tradition

Literature: J.-P. Audet, "L'Hypothèse des testimonia: remarques autour d'un livre récent", *RB* 70 (1963) 381–405; A. Benoît, "Irénée *Adversus haereses* IV 17,1–5 et les Testimonia", StPatr 4,2 (TU 79; Berlin 1961) 20–27; H. Chadwick, "Florilegium", RAC 7 (1969) 1131–1160; J. Daniélou, *Études d'exégèse judéo-chrétienne (Les Testimonia)* (Théologie historique 5; Paris 1966); J. R. Harris, *Testimonies* I-II (Cambridge 1916/20); E. Hatch, *Essays in Biblical Greek* (Oxford 1889; repr. Amsterdam 1970) 131–214; R. Hogdson, "The Testimony Hypothesis", *JBL* 98 (1979) 361–378; N. J. Hommes, *Het Testimoniaboek. Studiën over O.T. citaten in het N.T. en bij de Patres, met critische beschouwingen over de theorieën van J. Rendel Harris en D. Plooy* (Amsterdam 1935); R. A. Kraft, "Barnabas' Isaiah Text and the "Testimony Book" Hypothesis", *JBL* 79 (1960) 336–350; idem, Review of P. Prigent, *Les Testimonia dans le christianisme primitif*, *JTS* NS 13 (1962) 401–408; D. Plooij, *Studies in the Testimony Book* (Verhandelingen der koninklijke Akademie van Wetenschappen te Amsterdam. Afdeeling letterkunde Nieuwe Reeks, 32,2; Amsterdam 1932); P. Prigent, "Quelques testimonia messianiques. Leurs histoire littéraire de Qoumrân aux Pères de l'église", *TZ* 15 (1959) 419–430; idem, *Les Testimonia dans le christianisme primitif. L'Épître de Barnabé I-XVI et ses sources* (Ebib, Paris 1961); O. Skarsaune, "From Books to Testimonies. Remarks on the Transmission of the Old Testament in the Early Church", *The New Testament and Christian-Jewish Dialogue* (FS D. Flusser, ed. M. Lowe; Immanuel Nr. 24/25; Jerusalem 1990) 207–219; H. Stegemann, Review of P. Prigent, *Les Testimonia dans le christianisme primitif*, *ZKG* 73 (1962) 142–153; A.-C. Sundberg, "On Testimonies", *NovT* 3 (1959) 268–281; L. Wallach, "The Origin of Testimonia Biblica in Early Christian Literature", *Review of Religion* 8 (1943/1944) 130–136.

Before tracing the development of the Apologists' Old Testament exegesis in later Christian writers of the 2nd and 3rd centuries, it may be relevant to insert a short discussion on the vexed question of "testimonies" or *testimonia*. Ever since the publication of J. Rendel Harris' two slight volumes on "Testimonies", this term has been associated with the concept of a "testimony book" or "testimony collections". The basic idea is that very early, within the NT period, a standard collection or anthology of selected Old Testament proof-texts was produced, carrying great authority, and being used as a source of Old Testament quotations by the whole sequence of early Christian expositors of the Old Testament, surfacing as a literary work (in a personally edited version) in Cyprian's *"Testimonia"*.

After the severe and well founded criticism of this concept by J. Hommes, it has survived only in the modified version of "testimony collections". The

[77] *Test.* II.1.
[78] *De Principiis* I.2.1 (= Koetschau 28.5ff); I.4.4 (= 67.8ff).

discovery of one (or more) such collection at Qumran has been seen as new support for this modified version of the "testimony hypothesis".

The following criteria have been said to indicate the use of a testimony collection: (1) Text-type very deviant from the standard LXX, (2) composite quotations, (3) wrong attributions, (4) no awareness of the biblical context of the quotation, (5) one or more of the above characteristics recurring in several authors, (6) the same quotation sequences recurring in more than one author, (7) quotation sequences containing quotations not appropriate to the stated purpose of the author.

Taken one by one, none of these criteria provides undisputable proof for the existence and use of testimony collections (as these are portrayed in the hypothesis). (1) Non-LXX readings could derive from biblical manuscripts containing text-types now lost, or quite simply be free quotations from memory. (2) Composite quotations could be made *ad hoc* by the author in question, and later recurrences of the same composite quotation in later authors could be loans from the earlier ones. (3) False attributions could be sufficiently explained by the faulty memory of the first author making the attribution, later authors repeating the mistake. (4) Early biblical exegesis seems to pay little attention to the biblical context in any case. (5) If the above characteristics recur in a series of writers, they may only be dependent upon each other, not a common source. (6) Identical quotation sequences in several writers may have the same explanation. (7) If an author includes quotations which apparently do not fit his stated purpose, this may indicate the use of a source which had a different purpose, but there is also the possibility that we fail to see the relevance of a quotation that was obvious to the author.

With these arguments pro et contra the existence of testimony collections, let us make some observations on an interesting test-case: Justin Martyr's Old Testament quotations. Roughly speaking, Justin's quotations belong to one of two categories: (1) short quotations with markedly non-LXX readings, often composite, often with Christian interpolations or modifications of the biblical text, as a rule quoted with no awareness of the biblical context; (2) long quotations with standard LXX text-type, always correctly attributed, sometimes with comments that betray an intimate knowledge of the quotation's context (especially true of the passage on theophanies in *Dial*. 56–60/75 and parallels). The most interesting aspect of this is that some biblical texts occur in both categories in Justin, and that he himself in some cases has noticed this *and has made comments about it*. He says that the short, non-LXX quotations represent the true LXX, whereas the long (LXX) quotations represent a "Jewish" version of the biblical text.[79] This adds up to the inevitable conclusion that Justin's "short" quotations are taken from written sources that were (1) Christian, and (2) *not* biblical manuscripts. In other words: "testimony collections"? Here one should exert great care. The very term "testimony collection" suggests the idea of a very definite literary format, viz. a mere *anthology* of Old Testament proof-texts. But it is very difficult to find arguments in favour of Justin's sources having this format. The indications we have rather point in another direction: Justin's sources also contained *exposition* of the Old Testament quotations, and – in some cases – Gospel story reports on the fulfilment of the prophecy in the quotation.

It is often overlooked that some of Justin's "testimony" sources are in fact well known to us. In *Dial*. 78, f. ex., there is a non-LXX quotation of Mic 5:1 in 78.1 and a non-LXX version of Jer 31:15 in 78.8. The context in *Dial*. 78 leaves us in no doubt about the "testimony source" in this case: it is

---

[79] On his comments, see further details in ch. 11 below.

Matthew (2:6 and 2:18).[80] Likewise, in *Dial.* 17–47 and 114–119 there is a remarkably large number of Old Testament quotations taken from Romans.[81] In *Dial.* 131.1 the source of the "testimony" version of Deut 32:8 could well be *1 Clem.* 29.2.[82]

It should be noticed that *all* the arguments or criteria that have been adduced in support of the use of "testimony collections" (points 1–7 enumerated above) are equally, if not more, valid with regard to the use of sources like Matthew, Romans, or *1 Clement*. In other words, when we talk about "testimony sources" we may talk quite simply about a lost part of early Christian literature – probably comprising more than one literary format,[83] but certainly containing a high frequency of Old Testament quotations and interpretations.

This means that the "testimony tradition", i.e. the transmission of an expanding dossier of selected Old Testament proof-texts, should not be located exclusively to a separate literary channel of (now lost) quotation anthologies, "testimony collections". Very likely one should rather think of the "testimony tradition" as part and parcel of the growing theological heritage within early Christianity, which was transmitted within the 'mainstream' of early Christian literature, in varying literary formats. Each author within this traditions borrowed Old Testament quotations from his predecessors, but only some of these predecessors are known to us.

The early creators of the many variant, harmonizing, combined, interpolated versions of central Old Testament proof-texts no doubt had an intimate familiarity with the Old Testament as a whole. They probably had no intention of creating a 'mini-Old Testament' reduced to isolated quotations, being read and quoted again and again with no sense of the biblical context. But it can hardly be denied that this was to a considerable extent what happened to this tradition.

In Justin one can easily observe to what extent his exegesis, his hermeneutics, his whole approach to the Old Testament is determined by the traditional testimonies, the "proof-text" approach. Even with regard to biblical books he seems to be well read in, as Isaiah and Psalms, he seldom ventures into original exegesis of passages that did not contain a traditional testimony. We have seen his insecure approach when writing a commentary on those verses of Ps 22 that were not part of the traditional testimony dossier. The only significant exception to this almost complete dependence on the testimony approach is Justin's original treatment of the Genesis theophanies. But *after* him, the rather complicated theophany argument in *Dial.* 56–60 etc. soon was simplified and taken for granted and included in the testimony dossier.

One final question: What do the *Eclogae* of Melito and the *Testimonia ad Quirinum* of Cyprian say about the question of "testimony sources"? If they

[80] Generally on Justin's use of Matthew, cp. É. Massaux, *Influence de l'Évangile de saint Matthieu sur la littérature chrétienne avant saint Irénée* (Universitas catholica Lovaniensis Dissertationes Series II, 42; Louvain/Gembloux 1950) 466–555; especially on the Old Testament quotations common to the two authors, Skarsaune, Proof (1987) 100–103, 119–122.

[81] Cp. the detailed study in Skarsaune, Proof 92–98.

[82] Cp. the argument in favour of this in Skarsaune, Proof 30.

[83] Although there is much to be said for W. Bousset's and H. Koester's proposal of "Schriftbeweistraktate" – provided one keeps in mind that on their formal criteria, *Barnabas* would no doubt qualify as a "Schriftbeweistraktat".

say much at all, it is that prior to Melito, *he* and Onesimus (the one who asked him to make the excerpts from the prophets) did not know of the existence of any "testimony book" or "testimony collection".[84] Melito travelled all the way to Palestine to get reliable information on the Old Testament canon (and, presumably, text), and "from these [books] I have also made the extracts, dividing them into six books" (fragm. 3).[85] One gets the impression that Melito is proud of having done a pioneering piece of work. What his extracts looked like, and how far they were read and used by others, we cannot know.

The situation is much the same with Cyprian's "Testimonies".

> Indeed, as you [Quirinus] have asked, so has this discourse been arranged by me; and this treatise has been ordered in an abridged compendium, so that I should not scatter what was written in too diffuse an abundance, but, *as far as my poor memory suggested*, might collect all that was necessary in selected and connected heads, under which I may seem, not so much to have treated the subject, as to have afforded material for others to treat it. ... And these things may be of advantage to you meanwhile, as you read, for forming the first lineaments of your faith. More strength will be given to you, and the intelligence of the heart will be effected more and more, as you examine more fully the Scriptures, old and new, and read through the complete volumes of the spiritual books.[86]

Quite clearly, Cyprian is here speaking as the author of a handy *anthology* that was to serve as (first) a substitute for the whole of Scripture, then as an introduction to the continuous reading of the full text of Scripture. He acts like a good teacher introducing his pupil to a literature that at first seems overwhelming.[87]

There are no indications at all that a pre-existent "testimony book" is so to speak 'published' by Melito or Cyprian. On the contrary, their works look more like the mature summing up of the testimony tradition, not the presupposition for it.

4. Irenaeus, Tertullian, Hippolytus, Novatian, Cyprian: A Tradition Come of Age

While relying heavily on the traditional testimonies, Justin sometimes ventured into fresh exegesis of Old Testament texts outside the testimony dossier contained in his sources. In such cases, he was still devoted to the hermeneuti-

[84] Cp. the section from Melito's preface quoted in ch. 11 below.

[85] Hall, 64–67.

[86] From the preface to books I–II; the separate preface to book III says very much the same, and contains the famous phrase "I have laboured for once, that you might not always labour": *laboravi semel ne tu semper laborares.*

[87] In practice, of course, anthologies like that would often become permanent substitutes for the original works; this happened all the time with anthologies, "school textbooks" of classical literature, cp. esp. Chadwick, Anthologien. It seems, however, not to have been widespread in the case of biblical anthologies, possibly because the Christian Bible format, the codex, was a handy format and allowed the complete Bible to be used as a handbook and book of reference much more than the ordinary book format: the cumbersome scroll, cp. O. Skarsaune, "Den første kristne bibel. Et blad av kodeksens historie", *Det levende Ordet* (FS Å. Holter, ed. I. Asheim et al.; Oslo 1989) 29–43.

cal approach of the proof-text tradition, except in his treatise on the theophanies.

It is this tendency to expand the textual basis of the testimony approach we can follow further in the writers treated in this section. In different settings and vis à vis different polemical counterparts, they claim new scriptural 'territories' as their own, even to the point of making the "testimony" hermeneutics the basis of full-fledged commentaries on whole Old Testament books, as in Hippolytus. At the same time, their use of important precursors like *Barnabas*, Justin, and Theophilus, is everywhere to be seen.

4.1. Irenaeus

Sources: W.W. Harvey, *Sancti Irenaei Episcopi Lugdunensis Libros quinque adversus Haereses I-II* (Cantabrigiae 1857); A. Rousseau / L. Doutreleau, *Irénée de Lyon. Contre les hérésies. Livre I*: tom. I. Introduction, notes justificatives, tables (SC 263; Paris 1979); tom. II. Texte et traduction (SC 264; 1979). Iid., *Livre II*: tom. I. Introduction, notes justificatives, tables (SC 293; 1982); tom. II. Texte et traduction (SC 294; 1982). Iid., *Livre III*: tom. I. Introduction, notes justificatives, tables (SC 210; 1974); tom. II. Texte et traduction (SC 211; 1974). A. Rousseau / B. Hemmerdinger / L. Doutreleau / Ch. Mercier, *Livre IV* (SC 100*-100**; 1965). A. Rousseau / L. Doutreleau / Ch. Mercier, *Livre V*: tom I. Introduction, notes justificatives, tables (SC 152; 1969); tom. II. Texte et traduction (SC 153; 1969).

Translations: ANF I 309-578. – *The Proof*: K. Ter-Mekerttschian / E. Ter-Minassiantz, *Des hl. Irenäus Schrift zum Erweise der apostolischen Verkündigung in armenischer Version, entdeckt, herausgegeben und ins Deutsche übersetzt. Mit einem Nachwort und Anmerkungen von A. Harnack* (TU 31,1; Leipzig 1907); K. Ter-Mekerttschian / S. G. Wilson, *The Proof of the Apostolic Preaching with seven Fragments. Armenian Version edited and translated* (PO 12,5; Paris 1919) 651-804. Latin transl.: S. Weber, *Sancti Irenaei Demonstratio Apostolicae Praedicationis* (Friburgi Brisgoviae 1917); ET: J. P. Smith, *St. Irenaeus: Proof of the Apostolic Preaching* (ACW 16; Westminster, MD/London 1952); French transl.: L. M. Froidevaux, *Irénée de Lyon: Démonstration de la prédication apostolique* (SC 62; Paris 1959).

Reference work: B. Reynders, *Lexique comparé du texte grec et des versions latine, arménienne et syriaque de l'"Adversus Haereses" de Saint Irénée I-II* (Subsidia 5f; Louvain 1954).

General works: A. d'Alès, "La doctrine de la récapitulation en saint Irénée", *RSR* 6-7 (1916) 185-211; idem, "Le mot "oikonomia" dans la langue théologique de saint Irénée", *REG* 32 (1919) 1-9; P. Bacq, *De l'ancienne à la nouvelle alliance selon S. Irénée: Unité du livre IV de l'Adversus Haereses* (Paris 1978); A. Bengsch, *Heilsgeschichte und Heilswissen. Eine Untersuchung zur Struktur und Entfaltung des theologischen Denkens im Werk "Adversus haereses" des heiligen Irenäus von Lyon* (ETS 3; Leipzig 1957); A. Benoît, *Saint Irénée, introduction à l'étude de sa théologie* (Paris 1960) 74-102; idem, "Irénée *Adversus haereses* IV 17,1-5 et les Testimonia", StPatr 4,2 (TU 79; Berlin 1961) 20-27; E. C. Blackman, *Marcion and his influence* (London 1948); A. Le Boulluec, "Exégèse et polémique antignostique chez Irénée et Clément d'Alexandrie: l'exemple du centon", StPatr 17,2 (ed. E. A. Livingstone; Oxford 1982) 707-713; W. Bousset, *Jüdischer und christlicher Schulbetrieb in Alexandrien und Rom. Literarische Untersuchungen zu Philo, Clemens von Alexandria, Justin und Irenäus* (Göttingen 1915); N. Brox, "Zum literarischen Verhältnis zwischen Justin und Irenäus", *ZNW* 58 (1967) 121-128; J. Daniélou, "Saint Irénée et les origines de la théologie de l'histoire", *RSR* 34 (1947) 227-231; D. Farkasfalvy, "Theology of Scripture in St. Irenaeus", *RBén* 78 (1968) 319-333; B. Hägglund, "Die Bedeutung der 'regula fidei' als Grundlage theologischer Aussagen", *StTh* 12 (1958) 1-44; esp. 7-19; P. Hefner, "Theological Methodology in St. Irenaeus", *JR* 44 (1964) 249-309; S. Herrera, *Saint Irénée de Lyon, exégète. Étude historique* (Paris 1920); A. Houssiau, *La christoligie de saint Irénée* (Louvain/Gembloux 1955); M. de Jonge, "The PreMosaic Servants of God in the Testaments of the Twelve Patriarchs and in the Writings of Justin and Irenaeus", *VC* 39 (1985) 157-170; M. Jourjon, "Saint Irénée lit la Bible", *Le monde grec ancien et la Bible* (BTT I, ed. C. Mondésert; Paris 1984) 145-151; J. Kunze, *Glaubensregel, Heilige Schrift und Taufbekenntnis* (Leipzig 1899) 100-127; J. Lawson, *The Biblical Theology of Saint Irenaeus* (London 1948), J. T. Nielsen, *Adam and Christ in the Theology of Irenaeus of Lyons*

(Van Gorcum's theologische bibliotheek 40; Assen 1968); A. ORBE, "Cinco exégesis ireneanas de Gen 2,17b. Adv. haer. V 23,1-3", *Greg* 62 (1981) 75-113; idem, "San Ireneo y el régimen del milenio", *Studia missionalia* 32 (1983) 345-372; idem, *Theologia de San Ireneu*, I. *Commentario al Libro V del "Adversus haereses"* (Biblioteca de autores cristianos 25; Madrid 1985); W.-S. REILLY, "L'inspiration de l'A.T. chez saint Irénée", *RB* 16 (1919) 216-219; W. R. SCHOEDEL, "Theological Method in Irenaeus", *JTS* NS 35 (1984) 31-49; D. R. SCHULTZ, "The Origin of Sin in Irenaeus and Jewish Pseudepigraphical Literature", *VC* 32 (1978) 161-194; J. P. SMITH, "Hebrew Christian Midrash in Iren. Epid. 43", *Bib.* 38 (1957) 24-34; H.-J. VOGT, "Die Geltung des AT bei Irenäus von Lyon", *TQ* 60 (1980) 17-28; idem, "Schöpfung und Erlösung: Recapitulatio. Zur Geschichtstheologie des Irenäeus von Lyon", *Saeculum* 35 (1984) 222-224; G. WINGREN, *Man and the Incarnation: A Study in the Biblical Theology of Irenaeus* (Philadelphia 1959).

As an interpreter of the Old Testament Irenaeus is very much a disciple of Justin, but one can also recognize some links to Theophilus of Antioch, especially with regard to the Wisdom pneumatology in Theophilus. For his own part, Irenaeus often refers to "the elders" as sources for specific exegeses of Old Testament texts. It seems this term may sometimes refer to written sources now lost, e.g. Papias' *Interpretation of the Lord's sayings*.

Of the two works preserved complete, the *Proof of the Apostolic Preaching* and the *Refutation and Subversion of Knowledge falsely so called (= Against Heresies)*, the first is almost completely devoted to an Old Testament proof of the main points in the Rule of Faith, mainly its Christological part. In *Against Heresies* books 4 and 5 are predominantly occupied with Old Testament exegesis, but also book 3 contains important material. In the following survey of Irenaeus' exegetical material I shall roughly follow the disposition of the *Proof*, adding some comments on parallel or supplementary material in *Against Heresies*.

The Rule of Faith is summarised like this in *Proof* ch. 6:

(A) God, the Father, uncreated, beyond grasp, invisible, one God the Maker of all; this is the first and foremost article of our faith.
(B) But the second article is the Word of God, the Son of God, Christ Jesus our Lord,
(B') who was shown forth by the prophets according to the design of their prophecy and according to the manner in which the Father disposed;
and through him were made all things whatsoever.
He also, in the end of times, for the recapitulation of all things, is become man among men, visible and tangible, in order to abolish death and bring to light life, and bring about the communion of God and man,
(C) And the third article is the Holy Spirit, through whom the prophets prophesied and the patriarchs were taught about God and the just were led in the path of justice, and who in the end of time has been poured forth in a new manner upon humanity over all the earth renewing man to God.

Very much like Justin's 1. *Apol.* 31 this summary functions like a disposition of the Old Testament proof which follows:

ABC: Ch. 5: The triune God of the Rule of Faith (Ps 33:6).
A: Chs. 8-10: God the Father and the heavenly world; a prelude to:
ABC: Chs. 11-42a: the *summary of biblical history* (from creation to incarnation and Church).
B': Chs. 42b-85: the scriptural proof *de Christo*.
C: Chs. 86-97: the scriptural proof *de evangelio et de lege*.

The extensive summary of biblical history in chs. 11-42a clearly demonstrates the *cathechetical* nature of Irenaeus' treatise; in later cathechetical practice this was called the *narratio*. The function, however, of this part is not merely to introduce ignorant readers to the biblical history. For Irenaeus, this biblical history is the very *content* of the apostolic preaching and the Rule of Faith (or: the Rule of Truth). It is, so to speak, a fleshing out of the three articles of the "creed" comprised in short format in the Rule of Faith.

In his introductory passages on the Trinity, creation, and Paradise, Irenaeus is clearly dependent upon Theophilus of Antioch:

(1) God's Wisdom is primarily identified with the Spirit, resulting in the idea of double mediatorship in creation:

God is *logikos*, and therefore produced creatures by his *Logos*,
and God is a spirit, and so fashioned everything by his Spirit,
as the prophet also says,
"by the word of the Lord the heavens were established,
and all the power of them by his Spirit" [Ps 33:6].
Hence, since the Word "establishes", that is, works bodily and consolidates being,
while the Spirit disposes and shapes the various "powers",
so the Word is fitly and properly called the Son,
but the Spirit the Wisdom of God (ch. 5).

In ch. 10 this concept of the Trinity is combined with Isa 6 in a way that is not met with before Irenaeus:

This God, then, is glorified by his Word, who is his Son forever, and by the Holy Spirit, who is the Wisdom of the Father of all. *And their powers*[88] (those of the Word and Wisdom), *which are called Cherubim and Seraphim,*[89] with unfailing voice glorify God, and the entire establishment of heaven gives glory to God, the Father of all.

(2) Man was fashioned by God's two hands, which are identical with the Son and the Spirit (Iren. *Proof* 11; *Adv. Haer.* IV. 20. 1; cp. Theophilus *Ad Autol.* II. 18).

(3) Man was created as a child (Iren. *Proof* 12 and 14;[90] cp. *Ad Autol.* II. 25).

(4) The God walking in the Garden of Eden was the Logos (Iren. *Proof* 12; cp. *Ad Autol.* II. 22).

The *narratio*, chs. 11–42a, is of course interspersed with scriptural quotations, and sometimes interrupted by interpretative excurses on the – mostly typological – meaning of some of the words or events, e.g. the curse and blessings of Noah (Gen 9:25–27), chs. 20f;[91] the Adam-Christ typology, chs. 31f; Eve and Mary, ch. 33;[92] the tree of knowledge and the tree of the cross, ch. 34; promise to Abraham, ch. 35; promise to David, ch. 36; etc. Through

---

[88] The MS has singular, probably due to a misreading in the Greek: *dynamis* for *dynameis*. Probably angelic powers are meant, transferring to the Word and the Spirit the concept of "the heavenly Hosts" of God. Cp. Melito, Fragm. 15: "Christ the charioteer of the cherubim, the chief of the army of angels" (Hall, Melito 84). Cp. note 62 in Smith 148.

[89] In Philo the two *seraphim* of Isa 6:2 are identified with the *cherubim* covering the Ark of the Covenant, Exod 25:22, and are called the two highest *dynameis* of God, the creative and the royal, indicated by the the two names *theos* and *kyrios*; cp. references and instructive comment in G. Kretschmar, *Studien zur frühchristlichen Trinitätstheologie* (BHT 21; Tübingen 1956) 82ff. It should be noted that Irenaeus does not *identify* the Son and the Spirit with the seraphim. In the context to the passage quoted here, he is careful to point out the difference between the mediator(s) of creation and the created beings: "He has established with the Word the whole world; and angels too are included in the world". Cp. also E. Lanne, "Cherubim et Seraphim. Essai d'interpretation du chapitre 10 de la Dém. de saint Irénée", *RSR* 43 (1955) 524–535.

[90] Cp. also *A.H.* III.22.4.

[91] Very close to Justin, *Dial.* 139; maybe more original than Justin's version, cp. Skarsaune, Proof (1987) 341–344.

[92] Cp. *A.H.* III.22.3f; V.19.

all of this the *recapitulation* idea is the basic concept (the *anakefalaioosasthai* of Eph 1:10 – the seminal New Testament basis – being quoted in *Proof* 30).

In the *scriptural proof de Christo*, chs. 42a-85, the dependence upon Justin is everywhere evident. The very beginning, however, seems to depend on a source other than Justin, but maybe related to – or even identical with – the "recapitulation" source in Justin:

> That there was born a Son of God, that is, not only before his appearance in the world, but also before the world was made, Moses, who was the first to prophesy, says in Hebrew:
> *BARESITh BARA ELOVIM BASAN BENUAM SAMENThARES*,
> of which the translation is,
> *A Son in the beginning God established then heaven and earth.*[93]
> As Irenaeus probably knew no Hebrew, it seems evident that he is exerpting some kind of testimony source here, which probably also contained the two supplementary testimonies on pre-existence quoted immediately afterwards: Ps 110:3/72:17 ("Before the daystar I begot thee, thy name is before the sun") and Ps. Jer. ("Blessed is he who existed before he was made man").[94]

In chs. 45f Irenaeus has a masterly short summary of Justin's complicated argument on the Genesis theophanies in *Dial.* 56–60, followed in ch. 46 by a short statement on the theophany in the bush (Exod 3). If Justin made an original contribution by his theophany argument, Irenaeus shows us how this was soon included in the dossier of Christological proof-texts.

Irenaeus also seems to know the "two Gods, two Lords" testimonies we surmised behind Justin's treatment: "Therefore the Father is Lord, and the Son is Lord, and the Father is God and the Son is God; for he who is born of God is God", introducing Ps 45:7f (non-LXX, two Gods); Ps 110 (v. 1, two Lords, is the testimony "nucleus" prompting the quotation of the whole Psalm in ch. 48, cp. the repetition of v. 1 in ch. 49); Isa 45:1 (non-LXX reading *Kyrioo*: two Lords); and Ps 2:7 (Son born from the Father).[95] This section on the divine pre-existence of the Son is concluded in ch. 50 with a nice *inclusio* linking back to ch. 43: "And now thus saith the Lord, who formed me as his servant *from the womb* ..." (Isa 49:5f).[96]

> For here, in the first place, we have that the Son of God was pre-existent, from the fact that the Father spoke with him, and caused him to be revealed to men before his birth ...

With this, Irenaeus has concluded his proof on the pre-existence and nature and incarnation of the Logos, Son of God, and turns to his "historical" career, beginning with the virgin birth. He is here (chs. 53–85) very close to the "creed sequence" testimonies in Justin:

---

93 In an ingenious deciphering of Irenaeus' somewhat distorted Hebrew (probably also corrupted during transmission by Greek and Armenian scribes), J. P. SMITH has proposed the following restoration, in basic agreement with Irenaeus' translation: BERESITh BARA ELOHIM, BARUCH SHEMO, BEN, WEAHAR (?) ETh HASHAMAIM WEHAARETZ. Cp. Smith, Hebrew-Christian midrash (1957).

94 Both quotations given as "Jeremiah". Perhaps Ps 110:3/Ps 72:17 *and Jer 1:5* ("Before I formed you *in the womb*, I knew you") were combined in Irenaeus' source, introduced or followed by a paraphrase which Irenaeus mistook for a quotation. Cp. Smith, Proof 181f (notes 206f). It seems Justin had access to the same source, cp. his casual allusions to a combined text of Ps 110:3 and Ps 72:5.17 in *Dial.* 45.5 and 76.7; analysis in Skarsaune, Proof (1987) 235.

95 Cp. the parallel to this section in *A.H.* III.6.1.

96 Cp. the "womb" motif in the two testimonies in *Proof* 43, above.

Isa 7:14–16 (virgin birth);[97] Isa 61:1a (the title Christ = Anointed);[98] Isa 66:7 (virgin birth); Isa 9:5 (non-LXX text, but = MT; Messiah's name: Wonderful Counsellor – the Father took counsel from him before the creation of man, Gen 1:26); Isa 9:5–7 (LXX text! – prophecy of kingdom and cross); Gen 49:10f (exegesis partly *verbatim* according to Justin); Num 24:17; Isa 11:1–10 (Jesus a descendant of David through Mary);[99] Am 9:11 (Christ's resurrection; his body of David's seed); Mic 5:1 (born in David's city); Ps 132:10–12 (of David's seed).

Zech 9:9 (entry on an ass); Isa 53:4, Isa 29:18, Isa 35:3–6, Isa 26:19 (healings, raisings of dead); Isa 52:13–53:5, Ps 38:9 (?), Isa 50:6, Lam 3:30, Isa 53:5f.7.8, Lam 4:20; Isa 57:1f (passion and death of Christ); Ps 21:5, Ps 3:6 (death and resurrection); Ps 2:1f, Ps 89:39–46, Zech 13:7, Hos 10:6, Ps. Jer (= Justin, *Dial.* 72:4), Isa 65:2, Ps 22:17, Ps 22:15b, Ps 22:21/119:120/22:17 (= *Barn.* 5:13),[100] Deut 28:66, Ps 22:18f, Ps. Jer (= Matt 27:9f), Ps 69:22 (passion and death of Christ).

Ps 68:18f, Ps 24:7 (ascension), Ps 110:1 (enthronement), Ps 19:7 (judgement).

In all of this Irenaeus is safely within the "testimony" approach in his hermeneutics, just like Justin in the *Apology*.

When he comes to the third main part of his proof in chs. 86ff, Irenaeus is still relying heavily on Justin, but adds new testimonies, i.a. from Romans:

Chs. 86–90: New Law, new covenant: Isa 52:7 (= Rom 10:15 – apostles' preaching); Isa 2:3 (apostolic kerygma = new law); Isa 10:23 (= Rom 13:10); Isa 50:8f/2:11.17 (= *Barn.* 6.1f)[101] (Christ's superiority); Isa 65:15f, Isa 63:9 (salvation in Christ); Isa 43:18–21 (salvation through faith in Christ, not the old Law); Jer 31:31–34 (new covenant).

Chs. 91–97: The new people: Isa 17:7f (Gentiles forsaking idols and believing in God); Isa 65:1 (cp. Rom 10:2), Hos 2:23f/1:10 (= Rom 9:25f), Ezek 11:19f (Gentiles believing, cp. *Barn.* 6.14); Isa 54:1 (more children to the Gentile Church than to the old synagogue); Deut 28:44, Deut 32:21 (Gentiles more pious than Jews); Decalogue commandments fulfilled in double commandment of love; Hos 6:6 (cp. Matt 9:13), Isa 66:3, Joel 3:5 (salvation through faith, not sacrifices); Bar 3:29–4:1 (salvation in Christ, cp. Rom 10:6–8).

If one compares Irenaeus' scriptural proof in the *Proof* as a whole with Justin's, the basic similarity in hermeneutical approach is evident. Like Justin, Irenaeus is convinced that the endtime and the endtime events envisaged by the prophets have now arrived; therefore the New Testament events are the key to the true meaning of the prophetic oracles (and also to the events or prescriptions having a typological significance).[102]

> The treasure hid in the Scriptures is Christ, since he was pointed out by means of types and parables which, humanly speaking, could not be understood prior to the consummation of those things which had been predicted, that is, (before) the coming of Christ. And therefore it was said to Daniel the prophet, "Shut up the words, and seal the book even to the time of consummation, until many learn, and knowledge be completed. For at that time, when the

---

[97] The interpolation of Isa 8:4 and the whole discussion on the reading *parthenos/neanis* in Justin's *Dialogue* is lacking in the *Proof* of Irenaeus, but the application of Isa 8:4 to the Magi recurs in *A. H.* III.16.4 – obviously dependent upon Justin, *Dial.* 78 – and the discussion on *parthenos* comes in *A. H.* III.21.1, again partly *verbatim* quoting Justin, but with additional information on the sources of the *neanis* reading which seems to be first-hand.

[98] Cp. the parallel in *A. H.* III.18.3.

[99] It is interesting to notice that in Justin Gen 49:10f is followed by a combined quotation of Num 24:17a/Isa 11:1/51:5. Irenaeus, following Justin closely, seems to have recognised the combined quotation, and has "untied" it: Num 24:17 and Isa 11:1–10.

[100] On this quotation, cp. L.-M. Froidevaux, "Sur trois textes cités par saint Irénée", *RSR* 44 (1956) 408–421; esp. 408–414.

[101] On this quotation cp. Froidevaux, Trois textes (1956) 414ff.

[102] Irenaeus does not delve much into *typoi* in the *Proof*, but in the *A. H.* he repeats some of Justin's rich material, and adds a few more, cp. IV.5.4; 14.3; 16.1; 17.4; 21; 25; 30f; V.8.4.

> dispersion ends, they shall know all these things" (Dan 12:4.7) ... For every prophecy, before its fulfilment, is to men enigmas and ambiguities. But when the time has arrived, and the prediction has come to pass, then the prophecies have a clear and certain exposition (*A. H.* IV.26.1).

As in Justin, the whole of the Old Testament is here subsumed in the category of prophecy, prediction; what is sought in the Old Testament is mainly prophetic oracles. This corresponds to the "testimony" approach; Irenaeus never embarks on anything like a continuous commentary on an Old Testament book.

Nevertheless Irenaeus is working more independently within the "testimony" framework than Justin. He seems more often to find new testimonies of his own; he normally quotes the full LXX text (in many cases where Justin exhibits shortened or combined "testimony" versions), although occasionally he has recourse to non-LXX testimony sources of a similar nature – perhaps the same – as in Justin.[103]

The traditional dossier of testimonies *de Christo*, *de evangelio*, and *de lege*, originally had its setting in a debate with Jewish understanding of Scripture. In Irenaeus – as in Justin[104] – it is the debate with Marcion and the Gnostics that often prompts Irenaeus to do fresh and innovative Old Testament exegesis of his own. But this mainly comes in the *Adversus Haereses*, to which we now turn briefly.

In books 3–5 of *Adversus Haereses* Irenaeus is out to prove the harmony between the apostolic writers and the Old Testament (book 3), between Jesus and the Old Testament (book 4); between Jesus, Paul, Revelation and the Old Testament prophecies (book 5). He repeats much of the traditional proof from prophecy (notice especially the summary statement in *A. H.* IV.33). But against the Gnostics and Marcion the *function* of this proof changes. Against Jews, the Old Testament prophecies are the *demonstrantes*, and the New Testament events are the *demonstranda*. Against the Gnostics and Marcion, this is reversed: the Old Testament prophecies, and with them the Old Testament as a whole, become the *demonstrandum*. The *harmony*, the *correspondence* between prophecy and fulfilment is still decisive, but for the opposite reason: it now proves that the Old Testament is the Bible of Jesus and the New Testament writers, that the prophets were true messengers of Christ, and that the God of the Old Testament is the Father of Jesus Christ. Having re-stated the traditional proof from prophecy in IV. 33, Irenaeus says this quite explicitly in IV.34.

> Whence could the prophets have had power to predict the advent of the King, and to preach beforehand that liberty which was bestowed by him, and previously to announce all things which were done by Christ, ... if they had received prophetical inspiration from another God, they being ignorant, as ye allege, of the ineffable Father ... and his dispensation, which the Son of God fulfilled when he came upon earth in these last times (IV. 34. 3)? ... Such are the arguments ... in opposition to those who maintain that the prophets were inspired by a different God, and that our Lord came from another Father ... *This is my earnest object in adducing these*

---

103 No complete study of this is known to me, but cp. the pilot study in Skarsaune, Proof (1987) 435–453.

104 Cp. our comments on the theophany argument in Justin above.

Scriptural proofs, that by confuting the heretics by these very passages, I may restrain them from such great blasphemy, and from insanely fabricating a multitude of gods (IV.34.5).

Irenaeus is not, however, satisfied with this plain repetition of the scriptural proof developed by his predecessors in the debate with Judaism. On specific points he takes the Gnostic position as a challenge to fresh exegetical argument from Old Testament texts that were not part of the traditional dossier. A few examples:

(1) The Old Testament states explicitly that there is only one, not two Gods, and that the God bestowing eternal life through the Son is the same as the Demiurge, the creator-God (Isa 43:10–12; Isa 41:4 – *A. H.* IV.5.1).[105] As one can see, this argument would hardly be relevant in debate with Jews, and seems to be developed *ad hoc* in its present setting in the *Adversus Haereses*.

(2) Not only is the New Testament fulfilment of Old Testament prophecies a great proof of the *recapitulation* principle, but the Old Testament itself announces the salvation in recapitulation terms, e.g. in its message of the bodily resurrection (Isa 26:19; 66:13f; Ezek 37:1–10.12–14 – *A. H.* V.15.1).

(3) The most extensive argument comes in the concluding section on eschatology in V.25ff. Irenaeus here i.a. argues that the concreteness of the Old Testament prophecies is not meaningless nor impossible, since the millennium proclaimed by John (and Jesus!) will be the scene of the literal fulfilment of a lot of Old Testament promises (Isa 11:6–9; 65:25; 26:19; Ezek 37:12–14; 28:25–26; Jer 16:14f/23:7f; Isa 30:25f; 58:14; 6:11f; Dan 7:27; 12:13; Jer 31:10–14; Isa 31:9–32:1; 54:11–14; 65:18–22; 6:11; 13:9; 26:10; 6:12; 65:21; Bar 4:36–5:9; Isa 49:16 – *A. H.* V.33.4–35.2). Any attempt to allegorize these prophecies ends in contradiction and confusion.

If, however, any shall endeavour to allegorize prophecies of this kind, they shall not be found consistent with themselves in all points, and shall be confuted by the teaching of the very expressions (of the prophecies) (*A. H.* V.34.1).

In fact, Irenaeus is so eager to refer the prophetic oracles about eschatological peace and blessing to the millennium ("the Kingdom"), that he has little to say about any Old Testament prophecies being fulfilled in the "New Jerusalem" (= eternal life) following after the Kingdom. Isaiah envisaged the New Jerusalem in his words about the new heaven and the new earth – Isa 65:17f; 66:22 – and that is all Irenaeus has to say on the subject, as far as the Old Testament prophecies are concerned (*A. H.* V.35.2; 36.1). In the concluding passage on eschatology, Irenaeus hints that the prophets in general only spoke about the Kingdom (the millennium), but that the New Jerusalem, the new heaven and earth, was beyond the range of their prophetical view. The prophets foresaw the Kingdom which was distinctly described by John (in Rev 20:1ff) and indicated by Jesus in his words about drinking the cup new with his disciples.

In all these things ... the same God the Father is manifested, who fashioned man,
(A) and gave promise of the inheritance of the earth to the fathers (Gen 12:7 etc.),
(B) and who will realize[106] it in the resurrection of the just and fulfil the promises in his Son's kingdom (the millennium),
(C) and afterwards in fatherly fashion will provide "those things which neither eye has seen, nor the ear has heard, nor has arisen within the heart of man" (Isa 64:3 in the non-LXX version of 1 Cor 2:9). (*A. H.* V.36.3).

Whether accidental or not, this is structurally exactly parallel to one of two conflicting views among contemporary Rabbis. The Rabbis discussed whether the prophets spoke about the Days of the Messiah (the Messianic *Zwischenreich* between this world and the coming world), or the *haolam-habah*, the world-to-come.[107] Rabbi Akiba held that the prophets only spoke about the

---

105 Isa 43:10a is part of a combined testimony in Justin *Dial.* 122.1, but the point there is totally different from Irenaeus', and it seems unlikely that Irenaeus took his clue from Justin's quotation. For Irenaeus the point lies in that part of Isa 43:10ff not quoted by Justin.

106 On this reading, emending the Latin *eduxit*, cp. the note in SC 153:2 351.

107 Cp. the excellent review of the Jewish source material by P. Billerbeck, "Diese Welt, die Tage des Messias und die Zukünftige Welt", Str-B IV:2, 799–976.

Days of the Messiah,[108] and in the third century CE Rabbi Jochanan formulated this view in the following way:

All the prophets prophesied with regard to the Days of the Messiah, but with regard to the Coming World it is said: No eye (even of a prophet) has seen, O God, except you, what he has made ready to those that wait for him (Isa 64:3; *bSanh* 99A).

The similarity between the rabbinic idea and Irenaeus', and the lack of any known Christian precursor, points to the conclusion that Irenaeus' point of view may be due to cross-contacts between himself (or maybe his "presbyters") and Jewish exegesis.

The resultant picture in Irenaeus is strikingly different from the one in Revelation. In Revelation, the New Jerusalem (chs. 21f) is no doubt the scene of the fulfilment of Old Testament eschatology in general, whereas the passage on the millennium proper in 20:1-6 is rather poor in Old Testament allusions. For Revelation the prophets no doubt *saw* the New Jerusalem, and primarily this. In Irenaeus, the New Jerusalem (and the new heaven and earth) was beyond their vision, they only saw the Kingdom of Rev 20:1 ff.[109]

Irenaeus influenced Tertullian and Hippolytus in many respects, but in the 'classic' period of the Greek Fathers from the 4th century onwards, he was eclipsed by Origen and seems to have been largely forgotten.[110] It was the Latin and the Armenian Churches which preserved his heritage.

4.2. Tertullian

Sources: CCL I:1-2; E. Evans, *Tertullian's Treatise Against Praxeas* (London 1948; ²1956 – text and engl. transl.); idem, *Tertullian: Adversus Marcionem* (Oxford Early Christian Texts; Oxford 1972); H. Tränkle, *Q.S.F. Tertulliani Adversus Iudaeos mit Einleitung und kritischem Kommentar* (Wiesbaden 1964). ET: ANF III; IV.

General works: C. Aziza, *Tertullien et le Judaisme*, (Publications de la Faculté des Lettres et des Sciences Humaines de Nice 16; Paris 1977); G. T. Armstrong, *Die Genesis in der Alten Kirche. Die drei Kirchenväter* (BGBH 4; Tübingen 1962); H. Freiherr von Campenhausen, *Die Entstehung der christlichen Bibel* (BHT 39; Tübingen 1968) 318-337; J. E. L. van der Geest, *Le Christ et l'Ancient Testament chez Tertullien. Recherche terminologique* (Latinitas Christianorum primaeva 22; Assen 1972); A. von Harnack, "Tertullians Bibliothek christlicher Schriften", SPAW 1914 (Berlin 1914) 303-334 (repr. in idem, *Kleine Schriften zur Alten Kirche* II, ed. W. Peek, Opuscula IX,2; Leipzig 1980, 227-258); H. Karpp, *Schrift und Geist bei Tertullian* (Gütersloh 1955); O. Kuss, "Zur Hermeneutik Tertullians", *Neutestamentliche Aufsätze* (FS J. Schmid; Regensburg 1963) 128-160; P. de Labriolle, "Tertullien a-t-il connu une version latine de la Bible", *Balac* 4 (1914) 210-213; T. P. O'Malley, *Tertullian and the Bible: Language – Imagery – Exegesis* (Latinitas Christianorum primaeva 21; Nijmegen/Utrecht 1967); D. Satran, "Fingernails and Hair: Anatomy and Exegesis in Tertullian", *JTS* NS 40 (1989) 116-120; C. Tibiletti, "Il cristiano e la Sacra Scrittura in un passo di Tertulliano (*De testimonio animae* 1,4)", *Giornale italiano di filologia* 15 (1962) 254-256; J. H. Waszink, "Tertullian's principles and methods of exegesis", *Early Christian Literature and the Classical Intellectual Tradition* (FS R. M. Grant, ed. W. R. Schoedel / R. L. Wilken; Théologie Historique 53; Paris 1979) 17-31; G. Zimmermann, *Die hermeneutischen Prinzipien Tertullians* (diss., Leipzig 1937).

In most of his writings Tertullian underpins his brilliant argument with scriptural quotations. Making a complete survey of all Old Testament texts and themes he has touched upon in his many works would be an immense task,

---

[108] References to primary sources in Billerbeck 816 ff.

[109] The development of early Christian chiliasm is analysed in some detail in O. Skarsaune, "'Hva intet øye så…'. Litt om strukturen i tidlig kristen og jødisk eskatologi", *Florilegium patristicum* (FS P. Beskow, ed. G. Hallonsten / S. Hidal / S. Rubenson; Delsbo 1991) 201-213.

[110] Except by the learned Eusebius, who devotes considerable space to Irenaeus in his Church History (*H. E.* V.4.1 – 8.15).

by far exceeding the scope of the present presentation. Instead, we shall concentrate on those aspects of his use and exegesis of the Old Testament which are most relevant as we try to assess his place within the *exegetical tradition* we have traced through *Barnabas*, Justin and Irenaeus. In so doing, we shall restrict the comments to the three works most extensively devoted to biblical exegesis: *Adversus Iudaeos*, *Adversus Marcionem*,[111] and *Adversus Praxean*.

With regard to the three predecessors mentioned above, it seems certain that Tertullian made direct and extensive use of all three of them. His use of *Barnabas* is especially evident in *A.I.* 14.9f (par. *A.M.* III.7.7f), where the argument of *Barn.* 7.4–10 on the two goats (Lev 16) is restated with so many details peculiar to *Barnabas* that there is no reason to deny direct dependence.[112] His use of Justin's *Apology* and *Dialogue* is everywhere evident in all three works, and will be dealt with in chosen examples below. His use of Irenaeus' anti-Gnostic polemic is perspicuous in *A.M.*, as well in details as with regard to the over-all structure of this work. J. Daniélou has argued that Tertullian also made use of Melito.[113]

A special problem in Tertullian is the question of his Latin quotations from the Old Testament: Were they translated ad hoc by him from the Greek Old Testament, or did he have access to an already existing Latin Bible? It seems to the present writer that neither of these alternatives should be excluded.[114] Sometimes Tertullian quotes the same text in three or more cases, often in different works of his. There are minor differences in wording between all the texts, following no consistent principle. They look very much like translation variants, pointing to fresh translations ad hoc in each case.[115] In other cases, Tertullian seems to rely on readings typical of the Old Latin Bible. Being bilingual, there is no reason why he should not use the Greek as well as the Latin Bible.[116]

In Justin and Irenaeus we have repeatedly come upon the question of how the anti-Jewish and anti-Gnostic/anti-Marcion setting influenced and shaped the Old Testament exegesis of the early Fathers. We have surmised that since Marcion to a considerable extent aligned himself with Jewish exegesis of the contested Messianic prophecies of the Old Testament, and therefore made

---

111 On the vexed question of the literary relationship between *Adversus Iudaeos* and *Adversus Marcionem*, and the literary unity and authorship of the former, I follow the position argued in great detail, and to my mind convincingly, by H. Tränkle in the introduction to his edition of *Adv. Iud.*, xi–lxxxviii: *Adv. Iud.* is a loosely sketched, early tractate by Tertullian himself, probably slightly edited and published against the author's will by an admirer. It was written some time before the *Adv. Marc.*, and the parallels between the two works show that Tertullian restated the arguments of *Adv. Iud.* more succinctly and well-organised in *Adv. Marc.* Short bibliography on the question: P. Corssen, *Die altercatio Simonis et Theophili Christiani auf ihre Quellen geprüft* (Berlin 1890); A. Noeldechen, *Tertullians Schrift gegen die Juden auf Einheit, Echtheit, Entstehung geprüft* (TU 12.2; Leipzig 1894); M. Akerman, *Über die Echtheit der letzteren Hälfte von Tertullians Adversus Iudaeos* (Lund 1918); G. Quispel, *De bronnen van Tertullianus, Adversus Marcionem* (Diss. Utrecht 1943); P. Prigent, Justin (1964) 138–140; H. Tränkle, loc. cit.

112 Cp. esp. the detailed analysis of Tränkle lxxvi–lxxix.

113 Cp. J. Daniélou, "Bulletin d'histoire des origines chrétiennes", *RSR* 49 (1961) 593f; idem, Latin Christianity (1977) 266f.

114 Cp. the same verdict in Daniélou, Latin Christianity (1977) 5f. 140f.

115 For two examples of this, cp. the variants in the apparatus *ad* Mal 1:10f in Skarsaune Proof (1987) 440; and *ad* Dan 7:13f ibid. 444.

116 The latter may not yet have comprised all the OT books.

the same objections against 'mainstream' Christian exegesis as the Jews did, it was natural that the Fathers – to a very great extent – repeated and defended against Marcion the scriptural proof which had originally been shaped in the Jewish/Christian debate. In the same way, the harmony between Old Testament prophecies and New Testament fulfilment was an important point in vindicating the Old Testament against the Gnostics.

But from Justin we only have preserved his anti-Jewish treatise, not his anti-heretic one. From Irenaeus we have only his *Adversus Haereses*, no anti-Jewish treatise. We therefore have no possibility of studying directly the relationship between anti-Jewish and anti-heretical arguments in these two authors. It is this which makes Tertullian especially interesting in our context, because here we can compare both settings in the same author. How does the same material look in the *Adversus Iudaeos* and the *Adversus Marcionem*? And which material is different in the two cases? The evidence may be displayed in a table like this:

AI 1-6:	old and new law, no direct correspondence in *AM*.
AI 7-8:	at which date should the Messiah come? answered from Dan 9:24-27, no parallel in *AM*.
AI 9.1-20	= *AM* III.13.1-14.7: the Messiah born of a virgin and fulfilling the name Immanuel, Isa 7:14/8:4.
AI 9.21-25	= *AM* III.16.3-6: the Messiah should be called Jesus, Exod 23:20f.
AI 9.27-10.16	= *AM* III.17.4-19.9: the Messiah of David's seed (Isa 11:1ff) should suffer (Isa 53:3ff; Ps 22; Ps 69 etc.).
AI 10.17-11.11:	the Jews punished for the slaying of Christ by devastation of their land, no parallel in *AM*.
AI 11.11-12.2	= *AM* III.20.1-3: calling of the Gentiles.
AI 13.1-23:	Jews barred from Bethlehem, and Jerusalem destroyed: the Messiah must have come. Further oracles and types on the passion, no parallel in *AM*.
AI 13.24-29	= *AM* III.23.1-7: punishment of Jews foretold in Scripture.
AI 14.1-10	= *AM* III.7.1-8: the two parousias.
AI 14.11-14	= *AM* III.20.1-4: Christ's universal reign proof of his Messiahship.

Some general conclusions seem to emerge from this: (1) The critique of the Jewish cultic practices in *AI* is left out in *AM* because Tertullian is not interested in supporting Marcion in any way in *his* criticism of Old Testament law. (2) From *AI* 7-14 those passages are left out in *AM* which either are very complicated and technical (*AI* 7f), or concern the Jews most directly (*AI* 10.17 – 11.11; 13.1-23). (3) The scriptural material in *AI* 7-14 is for a great part borrowed from Justin, and is in many places a mixture of the "creed sequence" testimonies and the "recapitulation" texts in Justin. But the latter seem to dominate, and sometimes seem to derive from Justin's source. This raises the question whether *AI* chs. 7f (no parallel in the extant writings of Justin) might also derive from the "recapitulation" source used by Justin. (4) It is interesting to notice that Justin's theophany argument (*Dial.* 56-60 and parr.) is lacking in *AI*, while it is present in *AM* (II.27; III.9 et al.). In Justin we surmised that this argument was not primarily anti-Jewish but anti-Marcion; Tertullian's use of it seems to corroborate this.

In this way Tertullian uses and expands on the traditional proof from prophecy in *AI* and *AM* III. Exactly as in Irenaeus, there is a reversal of function when the same proof is applied against Marcion as against the Jews:

It is sufficient for my purpose to have traced thus far the course of Christ's dispensation in these particulars. This has proved him to be such a one as prophecy announced he should be. ... And the result of this agreement between the facts of his course and the Scriptures of the Creator *should be the restoration of belief in them* ... (*AM* III.20.1).

One characteristic of the traditional proof from prophecy which Marcion made the target of his attacks was the allegorical expositions of details in the prophetical oracles. Marcion insisted that the literal reading of these texts – as practised by the Jews – was the only one corresponding to the meaning of the prophets themselves. Tertullian therefore has to justify that in some cases the prophet's words *must* be taken figuratively, in others quite literally.

In discussing the combined testimony of Isa 7:14/8:4 this becomes crucial: according to Tertullian, the saying about the virgin giving birth (while yet a virgin) is to be taken quite literally, whereas the new-born baby taking the riches of Damascus and the spoils of Samaria in front of the king of Assyria must be taken figuratively. The latter is shown by the sheer impossibility of a baby conducting a war. "To be sure, he might be about to call to arms by his cry as an infant; to sound the alarm of war not with a trumpet but with a little rattle, to seek his foe not on horseback ... but from the nursemaid's back, and so be destined to subjugate Damascus and Samaria from his mother's breasts!" But is not a virgin giving birth also impossible? True, but this announcement is introduced as *a sign*, i.e. something miraculous, whereas the saying about the baby conquering Damascus etc. is not (*AM* III.13).[117] – Principal statements on allegory and literalism occur in III.5 and III.14.

Marcion had not only raised objections against the traditional proof from prophecy, however. He had, in his *Antitheses*, argued for a lot of detailed contradictions within the Old Testament and between the genuine Jesus and Paul and the Old Testament. In *AM* IV and V Tertullian comes to grips with these new objections, and while there are many scattered fragments of the traditional proof in these books, too, Tertullian often seems very original and creative in this part. Very often the Old Testament texts he chooses in such instances have not been quoted before him, and often are not quoted after him.[118] We have thus every reason to believe that Tertullian found these references himself, in an argumentation created ad hoc against Marcion. Basically, Tertullians' project is to demonstrate the unity and harmony of the Testaments. One example:

(Christ in his beatitudes and woes (Luke 6) blesses the poor and curses the rich – is this consistent with the Creator's acts in the Old Testament?). "I shall have to show that the Creator is also a despiser of the rich, as I have shown him to be a defender of the poor, in order that I may prove Christ to be on the Creator's side in this matter ... Accordingly, in Deuteronomy, Moses says, 'Lest, when you have eaten and are full ...' (Deut 8:12–14). In similar terms, when king Hezekiah became proud of his treasures ... the Creator breaks forth against him by the mouth of Isaiah, 'Behold, the days come when all that is in your house ... shall be carried to Babylon'" (Isa 39:6).

---

[117] One observes here the tendency in Tertullian emphasised by J.H. Waszink, Principles (1979): to work out an interpretation that can be shown to be compelling according to the text itself.

[118] In *AM* IV.15.8–12 Tertullian quotes Deut 8:12–14; Isa 39:6; *Jer 9:22f*; *Isa 3:16ff*; Isa 5:14f; *Isa 10:33f*; *Ps 49:17f*; Ps 62:11; *Am 6:4–6*. In vols. I and II of the Biblia Patristica, that is, in all writers of the 2nd and 3rd centuries except Origen, only the italicized testimonies have parallels. (One notices that most of Tertullian's "new" material is taken from Isaiah and Psalms – the two books with which he was most familiar.)

In this way Tertullian creates a kind of harmonious biblical theology in *AM*. Whereas against the Jews he often insists on contrasts between e.g. the ceremonial laws and God's eternal will, in *AM* he becomes an apologist even for these laws. In II.21 he defends the sabbath commandment, in II.22 the prohibition of images. In IV.34 he even succeeds in showing that Jesus and Moses were in agreement on divorce!

There is one part of the traditional scriptural proof that is not presented at all in *AI* and only briefly intimated in *AM*: The Christological exegesis of Gen 1:1 and 1:26, and a full statement of the theophany argument. In Tertullian this comes in *Adversus Praxean*, in an inner-Christian debate on how the "monarchy" of God is to be understood. *AP* 5–8 contains the fullest statement yet on the Son being the pre-existent Wisdom of the Father (Prov 8:22ff), creating the world as the Father's mediator, emanating from the Father as the river from the spring, the tree from the root and the ray from the sun.[119] Tertullian follows this up with the old Justinian series of testimonies on *two* Lords and Gods, adding more Old Testament testimonies on God's Son (*AP* 11–13). He then adds the theophany argument in his own re-stated version: since Scripture clearly teaches that the Father is invisible, the God seen in the Old Testament theophanies could not be the Father, but must of necessity be the Son (14–16). The Wisdom Christology is once more brought in to explain how the distinction between God the Father and his Wisdom/Son in no way precludes their unity of will and substance (*AP* 19).[120]

Tertullian's brilliant treatises were to become quite influential in the Latin Church, in spite of the stigma of heresy (Montanism) attached to their author.[121] Hippolytus, Novatian, and Cyprian – they all use him, sometimes almost *verbatim*, but without mentioning his name or giving any reference. Only Lactantius refers to him explicitly. He was the only Latin author we know of who was translated into Greek (the *Apologeticum*), thus he came to the attention of the learned Eusebius.[122] Ambrose did not know him, Augustine often referred to him, but put him among the heretics. Even so, his works continued to be transmitted and read – the Latin Church simply

---

[119] In *AP* 8.5 Tertullian says: "Protulit enim Deus sermonem, *quemadmodum etiam Paracletus docet*, sicut radix fruticem et fons fluvium et sol radium". The implication must be that he found these mataphors *in Scripture*. All three are used of Wisdom in the Old Testament and the Apocrypha: Wisdom is a tree (the tree of life), Prov 3:18; God is Wisdom's source, Bar 3:12; it is an effluence (*apaugasma*) of God the eternal light, Wis 7:26. In Sir 24 all three metaphors occur in one Wisdom text: Wisdom is light, v. 32; it is a tree of Paradise, vv. 12ff; it is a Paradise river, vv. 25ff.

[120] The basic structure of the argument in *AP* is binitarian, following the tradition from Justin. Even when Tertullian quotes Irenaeus' classic testimony on creation through the Logos and the Spirit, Ps 33:6 (*AP* 19.3), he gives it a purely Christological interpretation and completely ignores the saying about the Spirit. But Tertullian sometimes patches on references to the Holy Spirit in contexts where this seems almost like an after-thought, or an attempt to adjust binitarian material to a trinitarian *regula fidei* (esp. *AP* 8.7 and 25.1ff).

[121] Cp. esp. A. von Harnack, "Tertullian in der Literatur der alten Kirche", SPAW (Berlin 1895) 545–579; repr. in idem, *Kleine Schriften zur alten Kirche* I (Leipzig 1980) 247–281.

[122] *H.E.* II.2.4 – the only mention of Tertullian in Eusebius. But Eusebius uses the *Apologeticum* in several places – see Harnack, op. cit., 266.

could not discard him. This means that his Old Testament exegesis, too, continued to impress and influence theologians who otherwise took their clues from the tradition originating in Origen.

4.3. *Hippolytus*

Sources: PG 10; 16,3; N. Bonwetsch, *Hippolytus Werke* I,1 (Daniel commentary) (GCS I; Leipzig 1897); H. Achelis, *Hippolytus Werke* I,2 (On Christ and Antichrist) (GCS I; Leipzig 1897); M. Lefèvre, *Hippolyte. Commentaire sur Daniel* (SC 14; Paris 1947); M. Brière / B. C. Mercier, *Hippolyte de Rome. Sur les bénédictions d'Isaac, de Jacob et de Moïse* (PO XXVII,1-2; Paris 1954); G. Garitte, *Traités d'Hippolyte sur David et Goliath, sur le Cantique des cantiques et sur l'Antéchrist* (CSCO 263 (texts), 264 (translations); Louvain 1965); M. Richard, "Les fragments du Commentaire de S. Hippolyte sur les Prouerbes de Salomon. Édition provisoire", *Muséon* 78 (1965) 257-290; 79 (1966) 61-94; 80 (1967) 327-364; M. Marcovich, *Hippolytus: Refutatio omnium haeresium* (PTS 25; Berlin/New York 1986). – ET: ANF 3-259. German transl., N. Bonwetsch, *Die altslavische Übersetzung der Schrift Hippolyts "Vom Antichristen"* (AGWG 40; Göttingen 1895); idem, *Hippolyts Kommentar zum Hohenlied auf Grund von N. Marrs Ausgabe des grusinischen Textes* (TU 23,2c; Leipzig 1902).

General works: A. d'Alès, *La théologie de saint Hippolyte* (IIe ed. Paris 1929); L. Bertsch, *Die Botschaft von Christus und unsere Erlösung bei Hippolyt von Rom* (Trier 1966); R. Cantalamessa, *L'omelia in S. Pascha dello pseudo-Ippolito di Roma* (Milano 1967); G. Chappuzeau, "Die Exegese von Hohelied 1,2a.b und 7 bei den Kirchenvätern von Hippolyt bis Bernhard. Ein Beitrag zum Verständnis von Allegorie und Analogie", *JAC* 18 (1975) 90-143; idem, "Auslegung des Hohenliedes durch Hippolyt von Rom", *JAC* 19 (1976) 45-81; E. Dassmann, "Ecclesia vel anima. Die Kirche und ihre Glieder in der Hohenliederklärung bei Hippolyt, Origenes und Ambrosius", *RQ* 61 (1966) 121-144; D. G. Dunbar, *The eschatology of Hippolytus of Rome* (diss., Madison/NJ 1979); idem, "Hippolytus of Rome and the Eschatological Exegesis of the Early Church", *WTJ* 45 (1983) 322-339; V. Loi, "L'omelia in sanctum Pascha di Ippolito di Roma", *Aug.* 17 (1977) 461-484; L. Mariès, "Le Messie issu de Levi chez saint Hippolyte", *RSR* 39 (1951-1952) 381-396; P. Nautin, *Hippolyte et Josipe. Contribution à l'histoire de la littérature chrétienne du troisième siècle* (Paris 1947); idem, "Une homélie inspirée du traité sur la Pâque d'Hippolyte", in idem, *Homélies pascales* I (SC 27; Paris 1950); idem, *Le dossier d'Hippolyte et de Méliton* (Patristica I; Paris 1953); idem, "L'homélie d'Hippolyte sur le psautier et les oeuvres de Josipe", *RHR* 179 (1971) 137-179; M. Richard, "Pour une nouvelle édition du commentaire de S. Hippolyte sur Daniel", *Kyriakon* (FS J. Quasten I; Münster 1970) 68-78; idem, "Les difficultés d'une édition du commentaire de s. Hippolyte sur Daniel", *Revue d'histoire des textes* 2 (1972) 1-10; idem, "Les difficultés d'une édition des oeuvres de s. Hippolyte", StPatr 12,1 (TU 115; Berlin 1975) 51-70; M.-J. Rondeau, "Les polémiques d'Hippolyte de Roma et de Filastre de Brescia concernant le psautier", *RHR* 171 (1967) 1-51; R. Schmidt, "Aetates mundi", *ZKG* 57 (1956) 288-317; D. Trakatellis, "LOGOS AGONISTIKOS: Hippolytus' Commentary on Daniel", *Religious Propaganda and Missionary Competition in the New Testament World* (FS D. Georgi, ed. L. Bormann et al.; Leiden/New York/Köln 1994) 527-550.

Hippolytus of Rome (died 235 CE) seems to have been the most prolific author of the Roman Church in the 2nd and 3rd centuries, and the last to write in Greek. The literary transmission of his works, however, is so scattered, fragmentary and incomplete, and raises so many questions of attribution, that even the identity of the author has been disputed.[123] In our context, these questions of authorship and indentity may not be decisive, since there is great consensus that most of the material attributed to Hippolytus origi-

[123] Two Hippolytus'es? (V. Loi, "L'identità letteraria di Ippolito di Roma", *Richerche su Ippolito* [Studia Ephemeridis "Augustinianum" 13; Roma 1977] 67-88). One Josephus and one Hippolytus? (Nautin). Cp. the survey of positions and literature in Geerard, Clavis (1983) 256f.

nated in his time, i.e. the first third of the third century. Whoever wrote these works, they certainly are important material for the history of exegesis. As a matter of convenience, I shall call the author of the works and fragments treated in this chapter "Hippolytus", also because I incline to the traditional position on the question, like M. Markovich in his recent TRE article on Hippolytus.

The startling fact about Hippolytus, if the majority of "genuine" fragments from his exegetical works are to be trusted, is that he wrote *commentaries* on a great number of biblical books and passages: on 1 and 2 Samuel (LXX Kings), on Psalms, on Proverbs – according to preserved fragments; and maybe also on the Octateuch (Gen-Ruth), Ecclesiastes, Isaiah, and Ezekiel, if the preserved fragments belong to complete commentaries. But this is far from certain; the only commentary one can posit with certainty from the mentioned fragments is the one on *Proverbs*, and very likely one on (some?) *Psalms*.

Still extant (partly in the original Greek, partly in Armenian, Georgian, and Old Slavonic versions) are the following treatises: commentaries on the *Blessings of Isaac and Jacob* (Gen 27 and 49), the *Blessing of Moses* (Deut 33), on *David and Goliath*; and on *Canticles* and *Daniel*.

Gen 49 and Deut 33 comprise texts that are important testimonies in Justin and his successors, and Hippolytus' attempt to write continuous commentaries on the entire blessings of Jacob and Moses can be seen as analogies to Justin's commentary on Psalm 22: the "testimony" approach and hermeneutics is extended to the whole literary unit from which important testimonies had long been taken. The whole unit is seen as a catena of prophetic predictions. The following exposition of the blessings of Joseph and Naphtali from an *On Genesis* fragment is typical:

"Against him the archers took counsel together, and reviled him" (Gen 49:23). For the "archers", that is, the leaders of the people, did convene their assemblies, and take bitter counsel. "But their bows were broken, and the sinews of their arms were relaxed, by the hand of the Mighty One of Jacob" (Gen 49:24), that is to say, by God the Father, who is the Lord of power, who also made his Son blessed in heaven and on earth. And Naphtali is adopted as a figure of things pertaining to us, as the Gospel shows: "the land of Zabulun, and the land of Naphtali ... to them the light has arisen (Matt 4:15/17 = Isa 8:23–9:1)". And what other light was this but the calling of the Gentiles, which is 'the trunk' (Gen 49:22), i.e. the tree of the Lord, in whom engrafted it bears fruit? And the word "giving increase in beauty in the case of the shoot" (ibid.), expresses the excellency of our calling. And if the words, "giving increase ..." are understood, *as perhaps they may* (!), with reference to us, the clause is still quite intelligible. For, by progressing in virtue, and attaining to better things ... we rise to ever higher beauty.

By far the most ambitious extension of this "testimony" approach comes in the commentary on Daniel, in which the first six "historical" chapters (including the LXX "additions") are read as full of types.

„At noon Susannah went into (her husband's garden)". Susannah prefigured the Church; and Joacim, her husband, Christ; and the garden, the calling of the saints, who are planted like fruitful trees in the Church. And Babylon is the world; and the two elders are set forth as a figure of the two peoples that plot against the Church, the one, namely, of the circumcision, the other of the Gentiles.

This is exactly the same typological reading of biblical stories as we find concerning the sons of Isaac, Joseph blessing his two sons, etc., from *Barnabas* and Justin onwards.[124] We find the same in the other comments on the historical Old Testament texts in Hippolytus:

> The patriarchs not only prophesied by word on the subject of what was to come to pass; they also carried out in action that which was fulfilled in Christ. ... How is it that men do not understand that spiritually these things were prefigured by blessed David, and later fulfilled by the Redeemer (*David and Goliath* 3).[125]

In Dan 7ff Hippolytus finds, of course, prophetic oracles that not only predict several aspects of Christ's career, but also the exact time of his coming: Dan 9:25 ff. Here Hippolytus is able to develop further the complicated chronological computations of Tertullian in *AJ* 7 f, arriving at a simpler and somewhat more elegant scheme.[126]

After this – which basically shows us an exegete depending on the previous tradition of testimonies, even in his verse-by-verse commentaries – one is curious about his *Canticles* commentary. What will he make of this book, from which hardly any traditional testimony had been taken,[127] and which is so different in character compared to the other books providing types and testimonies?

It almost goes without saying that he takes the bride and the bridegroom to be the Church and Christ (not the individual soul and Christ, as sometimes in Origen). But often he discards this scheme and reads Canticles as a collection of prophecies on specific episodes in the career of Christ or the Church. One of his favourite episodes is the morning of resurrection in the Garden of Joseph, with Mary Magdalen searching for Jesus. On Cant 3:4 ("I held him and would not let him go") Hippolytus comments:

> O happy woman, who threw herself at the feet of Christ in order to be carried with him to heaven! ... "Ascend to the Father, and present the new offering! Offer Eve, who is no longer going astray, but with her hands has laid hold passionately upon the tree of life! Leave me no longer upon the earth to wander out of the way, but carry me to heaven!" O holy woman, who desired nevermore to be separated from Christ!

---

124 But cp. the comment by J. Daniélou, Gospel Message (1973) 265: "This ... example (the typology of Susannah etc.) highlights a particular consequence which inevitably followed, once whole sections of Scripture were given continuous typological commentary, and that is the tendency to multiply detailed parallels where the primitive types had been concerned with just one special feature or incident, seen as pregnant with vital significance".

125 J. Daniélou, Gospel Message (1973) 262–65, observes that the three biblical types of Joseph, David, and Susannah, seems to be favourites of Hippolytus, and developed much more by him than by any of his predecessors.

126 See the detailed and excellent analysis in Bodenmann, Naissance (1986) 358 ff.

127 In the Biblia Patristica 1 (roughly covering the 2nd cent.), only four (!) references to *Song of Songs* are recorded; two in Tertullian (4:8 in *AM* IV.11.8 and 8:6 in a fragment), two in *Odes of Solomon* – not surprisingly (one is perhaps surprised there are no more, in this "bridal" poetry!). In *BP* vol. 2 (roughly 3rd cent. except Origen) 7 more are added from that part of the *Song* on which Hippolytus commented (1:1–3:8), 3 in Methodius Olympius' *Symposion*; two in dubious fragments of Dionysius Alexandrinus; two in Ps. Cyprian *De montibus Sina et Sion* – all of these probably after Hippolytus and after Origen.

The bride in Canticles is here made a type of Mary Magdalen, who is cast as the anti-type of Eve: Eve lost life through the tree of knowledge, Mary gains life through the tree of life = Christ.[128]

In this way, Canticles is interpreted along the lines of the old "testimony" approach,[129] but this only makes the question more urgent: Why did Hippolytus all at once write a full-fledged commentary on precisely this book, on which the earlier Christian tradition had been almost completely silent? Could it be that some Jewish allegoric exposition was published or otherwise made known at this time, so that Hippolytus felt the need to develop a Christological alternative? The Jewish sources, regrettably, are very scanty for this period, but there seem to be some detailed correspondences between rabbinic allegorical exegesis and that of Hippolytus.[130]

To conclude: it seems that J. Daniélou has chosen a very apposite title for his chapter on Hippolytus in Gospel Message: "the extension of typology". In a way, Hippolytus can be said to represent the culmination and the fullest realization of the potential of the old "testimony" tradition: the hermeneutics and the interpretational techniques of the proof-text approach is extended to a continuous commentary on whole passages or books. The assumption is that the implicit premiss of the testimony approach – that the Old Testament is a book of prophetic oracles and types – is valid for each and every passage and lemma, and accordingly for the Old Testament text in its entirety.

Hippolytus' gigantic effort was soon to be eclipsed, however, by another somewhat younger exegete, who approached the biblical text from a new angle: Origen. In Origen, the approach of an old pioneer in the art of continuous allegorical commentary was appropriated and developed further: the approach of Philo. Apart from some scattered quotations and adaptions in some of the Western Fathers (foremost Ambrose), and in catenae, Hippolytus' exegetical works seem to have been almost completely forgotten in the Greek Church, and are preserved mostly in translations.

4.4. *Novatian*

Sources: PL 3; CSEL 3,2; 3,3; H. Weyer, *Novatianus: De Trinitate. Über den dreifaltigen Gott. Text und Übersetzung mit Einleitung und Kommentar* (Darmstadt 1962); G. Landgraf / C. Weymann, *Archiv für lateinische Lexicographie* 11 (1898/1900) 221–249 (*De cibis iudaicis*). Translations only: ANF V 645–650; H. Moore, *The Treatise of Novatian on the Trinity* (Translations of Christian Literature, Series II; London 1919); I. Hector, *Novatianus' skrift om Treenigheten. Översättning med inledning och förklaringar* (Uppsala 1981).

General works: A. d'Alès, *Novatien. Étude sur la Théologie Romaine au Milieu du IIIe Siècle* (Paris 1924); V. Ammundsen, *Novatianus og Novatianismen* (København 1901); J. O. Andersen, *Novatian* (København 1901); J. Barbel, *Christos Angelos* (Bonn 1941) 80–94; idem, "Zur 'Engelchristologie' bei Novatian", *TTZ* 67 (1958) 96–105; T. Hermann, *Das Verhältnis von Novatians De trinitate zu Tertullians Adv. Prax.* (Diss. Marburg 1918); H. Koch, "Zum novatianischen Schrifttum", *ZKG* 38 (1920) 86–95; E. Lupieri, "Novatien et les Testimonia d'Isaïe", StPatr 17,2 (ed. E. A. Livingstone; Oxford 1982) 803–807; F. Scheidweiler, "Novatian und die Engelchristo-

---

[128] On this topic in Hippolytus' commentary, cp. Chappuzeau, Auslegung (1976) 56 f.

[129] On "das Hohelied als Weissagungsbeweis" in Hippolytus, cp. Chappuzeau, Auslegung (1976) 51 f. 56 ff. 69 ff.

[130] Cp. Chappuzeau, 49 f. 58.

logie", *ZKG* 66 (1957) 126–139; R.J. Simone, *The Treatise of Novatian the Roman Presbyter. A Study of Text and Doctrine* (Rome 1970); F. Torm, *En kritisk Fremstilling af Novatianus' Liv og Forfattervirksomhed* (København 1901).

Jerome enumerates 9 works by Novatian, which he says are often ascribed to Cyprian or Tertullian.[131] Among these, *De trinitate* and *De cibis Iudaicis* have come down to us, and are most relevant to our purpose. Besides, Novatian himself in *De cibis* 1 mentions two more works of the same category: *De sabbato* and *De circumcisione*, but these are no longer extant.

The comprehensive tractate *De trinitate* can be said to belong to roughly the same *genre* as Irenaeus' *Proof of the Apostolic Preaching*. It is, and to a greater extent than Irenaeus' treatise, an attempt to expound the *trinitarian regula veritatis* with constant reference to Scripture. No work prior to Novatian's has such a high frequency of scriptural quotations as his; in many ways this medium-size tractate is the comprehensive summing-up of the "proof-text" tradition we have been tracing. At the same time, the polemical setting and – with it – the function of the biblical proof-texts have changed in a significant way. The debate with Judaism is not a live issue in Novatian. For him, different Christian heresies are the burning issue. H. Weyer has an instructive analysis of this, showing how Novatian's polemic setting has determined the very structure of his treatise:

1. On God the Father, Creator of the world, above whom there is no other god (against Marcion), chs. 1–8.
2. On the Son of God, chs. 9–28. He is:
   a) the Son of the Creator (against Marcion), ch. 9.
   b) true man (against Docetists), ch. 10.
   c) true God (against Adoptionists), chs. 11–25.
   d) different from the Father (against Modalists), chs. 26–28.
3. On the Holy Spirit, ch. 29.
4. On the unity of God, chs. 30 f.

To what extent this treatise presents itself as an exposition of the Rule of Truth, is made very clear by the introductory clauses to each main part:

> The rule of truth requires that we should first of all things believe on God the Father and the Lord Almighty, that is: the perfect Creator of all things … (1)
>
> The same rule of truth teaches us to believe, after the Father, also on the Son of God, Christ Jesus, the Lord our God, the Son of God – of *that* God who is … the Creator of all things … This Jesus Christ … we read of as having been promised in the Old Testament … fulfilling the shadows and figures of the mysteries by the bodily presence of truth (9).
>
> Moreover, … the authority of the faith in the disposition of the words and in the Scriptures of the Lord admonish us after these things to believe also on the Holy Spirit … (29).[132]

In chs. 1–8 on God the Father, Novatian is concerned to ward off misunderstandings of the anthropomorphisms in Scripture's picture of God.

> The prophet was still speaking about God in parables according to the period of the faith, not as God was, but as the people was able to receive him (6).

[131] *De vir. ill.* 70; cp. also *Ep.* 10.3; *Apologia adv. libros Rufini* II.19.

[132] It has been observed by many commentators that the section on the Spirit is very rudimentary in Novatian, and that the tract as a whole is binitarian rather than trinitarian in its structure (like so many others in the pre-Nicene period).

In the section on the Son, one notices with interest that ch. 9 on Christ as the Creator's Son is replete with the traditional Old Testament Messianic prophecies, while ch. 10 (anti-docetic) is without a single one, and only quotes John 1:14. The section on Christ's divinity opens with a few Old Testament proofs (Isa 7:14; 35:3ff; Hab 3:3) in ch. 12, but then continues with proof-texts mainly drawn from John (chs. 13–16). In ch. 17 Novatian demonstrates that John 1:1–3 is in harmony with Gen 1 by stating the traditional Christological reading of Gen 1:26 ff. This is followed by the "theophany argument" very much along the lines of Tertullian's *Adv. Prax.* This, of course, leads naturally into the argument against the Sabellians in chs. 26–28, which is drawing heavily on Tertullian's similar argument against Praxeas. Here Old Testament and New Testament testimonies are quoted and discussed quite indiscriminately, Scripture being the two testaments.

WEYER is probably right to regard the concluding two chapters on the unity and diversity of God the Father and God the Son as the climax and the burning issue of the whole treatise, which explains that Tertullian's book against Praxeas is the one predecessor most often called to mind.

The change of setting and function of the scriptural proof in Novatian is also evident in the one preserved "anti-Jewish" tractate of his. In *De cibis Iudaicis* Novatian poses the problem: If God created all animals clean – and according to Gen 1 he did – why did he subsequently in the Law declare some of them unclean? The heretics turn this contradiction against the creator-God of the Old Testament, and the Jews are not able to give any spiritual reasons for these laws, accordingly the heretics are strengthened in their error by the Jews (ch. 2).

The spiritual reasons, however, for the precepts concerning unclean animals are these:

(1) Some animals symbolise characteristics that are natural and not blameworthy in those animals, but highly blameworthy in men; therefore, to teach men moral lessons, God declared those animals unclean (ch. 3).[133]

(2) Restrictions on meat had the pedagogical function of restraining the bad habit of luxury in foods (ch. 4).

With the advent of Christ, his teaching on temperance and abstinence makes the ritual commandments on food superfluous, and all meat is restored to its inherent cleanness (chs. 5f). Meat offered to idols, however, is polluted and has become a medium of contact with demons (ch. 7).

It is evident that the purpose of Novatian is no longer, as e. g. in Justin, to provide justification for Christian non-observance of the ritual commandments. Jews blaming Christians for their failure to observe God's commandments are no longer in view, nor other opponents blaming Christians for lack of consequence in this regard. The opponents Novatian has in view blame the *God of the Old Testament* for giving these laws at all. Novatian is not defending his own non-observance of the ritual commandments (as was Justin), he is defending God, the originator of these commandments. Unlike Trypho in Justin's *Dialogue*, Novatian's opponents find the ritual commandments irrational, arbitrary, maybe even ridiculous. Therefore Novatian cannot content

[133] Novatian is very close to *Barn.* 10 here, but he refrains from blaming the Jews for having observed these commandments literally before Christ. The commandments were meant as a temporary remedy, to be made superflous at the advent of Christ.

himself, as did Justin, with finding a general reason for all the ritual commandments in the *sklerokardia* of Israel. He has to find a rational principle that works as an explanation for each and every commandment on uncleanness of animals. He finds his clue in the kind of reasoning that is present already in *Barnabas* (ch. 10).

4.5. *Cyprian*

Sources: CSEL III,1-3 (ed. G. Hartel; Wien 1868-1871); CCL 3 (ed. R. Weber / M. Bevenot; 1972); 3a (ed. M. Simonetti; 1976). ET: ANF V 267-596. German transl., J. BAER, *Des heiligen Kirchenvaters Caecilius Cyprianus Traktate I* (BKV 60; München 1928).

General works: A. D'ALÈS, *La théologie de Saint Cyprien* (Bibliothèque de théologie historique 6; Paris 1922); P. ANTIN, "Saint Cyprien et Jonas", *RB* 68 (1961) 412-414; J.-P. AUDET, "L'hypothèse des Testimonia", *RB* 70 (1963) 381-405; P. CAPELLE, *Le texte du psautier latin en Afrique* (Collectanea Biblica Latina 4; Rome 1913); J. DANIÉLOU, "Christos Kyrios. Une citation des *Lamentations* de Jéremie dans les *Testimonia*", *RSR* 39 (1951) 338-352; idem, *The Origins of Latin Christianity* (ET by D. Smith / J. A. Baker; London/Philadelphia 1977) 251-258. 273-295; C. DUMONT, "La lecture de la Parole de Dieu d'après S. Cyprien", *Bible et vie chrétienne* 22 (1958) 23-33; M. A. FAHEY, *Cyprian and the Bible. A Study in Third Century Exegesis* (BGBH 9; Tübingen 1971); P. GLAUE, "Zur Echtheit von Cyprians drittem Buch der Testimonia", *ZNW* 8 (1907) 274-289; idem, "Die Vorlesung heiliger Schriften bei Cyprian", *ZNW* 23 (1924) 201-213; S. L. GREENSLADE, "Scripture and Other Norms in Early Theories of the Ministry", *JTS* 44 (1943) 162-176; R. P. C. HANSON, "Cyprian's *Testimonia*, Appendix A", in idem, *Tradition in the Early Church* (London 1962) 261-264; J. N. D. KELLY, "The Bible and the Latin Fathers", *The Church's Use of the Bible Past and Present* (ed. D.E. Nineham; London 1963) 41-56; A. LUNEAU, "Moise et les Pères latins", *Cahiers Sioniens* 8 (1954) 401-421; J. MICHL, "Der Weibessame (Gen 3,15) in spätjüdischer und frühchristlicher Auffassung", *Bib.* 33 (1952) 371-401. 476-505; P. MONAT, "Les *testimonia* bibliques, de Cyprien à Lactance", *Le monde latin antique et la Bible* (BTT 2; ed. J. Fontaine / C. Pietri; Paris 1985) 499-507; G. NICOTRA: "Interpretazione di Cipriano al cap. IV, Vers. 12, della Cantica", *Scuola Cattolica* 68 (1940) 380-387; H. L. RAMSEY, "On Early Insertions in the Third Book of St. Cyprian's *Testimonia*", *JTS* 2 (1901) 276-288; A. SOUTER, "The Interpolations in St. Cyprian's *Ad Quirinum*", *JTS* 34 (1933) 45-46; C. H. TURNER, "Prolegomena to the Testimonia of St. Cyprian", *JTS* 6 (1905) 246-270; 9 (1908) 62-87; 29 (1928) 113-136; 31 (1930) 225-246; L. WOHLEB, "Cyprians Spruchsammlung ad Quirinum", *RQ* 33 (1925) 22-38.

If Hippolytus makes the crowning achievement within the testimony tradition by extending it into full-fledged commentaries on biblical books, Cyprian (died 258) can be said to summarize and collect the testimony tradition in a format more suited to its character: the three books of testimonies *Ad Quirinum*.

The disposition of this work is simple: Book I contains testimonies *de ecclesia* (1-7; 19-24) and *de lege* (8-18); book II testimonies *de Christo*; book III moral precepts. Book III has a separate preface and may have been written somewhat later than the first two. All books contain New Testament testimonies added to the Old Testament ones, but in book III the New Testament testimonies dominate. It reads like a moral cathechism; the placing side by side of New Testament and Old Testament testimonies may reflect the earlier attempts by Irenaeus and especially Tertullian – in many respects Cyprian's '*magister*'[134] – to document a harmony in ethical questions between the testa-

[134] So, quite correctly, Jerome in *De vir. illustr.* 53.

ments. But as H. Koch and J. Daniélou have shown,[135] Cyprian seems very original in book III, most of the texts assembled are his own choices, and often reflect his own particular ethical, sacramental and ecclesiological interests.

In books I-II the dependence upon Tertullian's *Adversus Iudaeos*, *Adversus Marcionem III*, and *Adversus Praxean* is everywhere evident, but on many points Cyprian adds new testimonies, apparently found by himself, especially in the historical books of the Old Testament,[136] and also some eschatological testimonies in II.28–30.[137] It also seems that the *arrangement* is Cyprian's own. Within each chapter he follows the order of the Old Testament books, and eventually adds New Testament testimonies on the fulfilment. The most striking feature, however, compared with the testimony tradition of his predecessors, is that Cyprian almost consistently substitutes the deviant (non-LXX) and composite quotations of his sources (Tertullian's treatises, reproducing the non-LXX versions of his sources Barnabas, Justin etc.) with "correct" quotations directly from his Latin bible.[138] We observed a tendency in this direction already in Irenaeus and Tertullian, compared with the high frequency of non-LXX "testimony" readings in Justin. In Cyprian this development comes to its logical conclusion: the deviant "testimony" readings disappear almost completely, the text of the (now Latin) biblical manuscripts is consistently quoted. Even the famous "from the tree" in Ps 96:10 – so dear to Christian expositors – is left out in Cyprian's quotation of this verse (II.29).

In terms of hermeneutics, Cyprian is not innovative; he continues the approach of testimonies and types we have seen in his predecessors.[139]

In general terms, Cyprian remained an influential 'magister' of later African writers (Augustine names and quotes him frequently) and even of other Latin authors (like Jerome). Augustine and Jerome have explicit quotations from *Ad Quirinum*, but always from the third book, which *may* have been the only book known to them under this title.[140] Books I–II seem to have left few traces, except in Lactantius' *Institutions* (book IV) and some African *Altercationes*,[141] but here a direct recourse to a common source behind Tertullian

---

135 H. Koch, "Das dritte Buch der cyprianischen Testimonia in seinem zeitlichen Verhältnis zum ersten und zweiten", *ZKG* 45 (1926) 1–9; Daniélou, Latin Christianity (1977) 293–295.

136 E.g. 1 Sam 1 and 2:5 (Hannah and Penninah as types) in I.20; 1 Sam 6:15 (Christ = the stone on which the ark was placed) and 1 Sam 7:12 (Christ = the stone raised by Samuel) in II.16.

137 Cp. Daniélou, Latin Christianity (1977) 291f.

138 This is documented in great detail by Daniélou, op. cit. 274–288.

139 On his hermeneutics and exegetical terminology, cp. Fahey (1971) 46–56 and 612–622.

140 Cp. esp. Monat (1985) 504.

141 (1) *Evagrii altercatio legis inter Simonem et Theophilum christianum* (CSEL 45, ed. E. Bratke; Wien 1904; ca. 430 CE). Studies: A. von Harnack, *Die Altercatio Simonis Judaei et Theophili Christiani, nebst Untersuchungen über die antijüdische Polemik in der alten Kirche* (TU I,1–3; Leipzig 1883); P. Corssen, *Die Altercatio Simonis Judaei et Theophili Christiani auf ihre Quellen geprüft* (Berlin 1890); A. L. Williams, *Adversus Judaeos: A bird's-eye view of Christian* apologiae *until the Renaissance* (Cambridge 1935) 298–305; B. Blumenkranz, *Les auteurs chrétiens latins du moyen âge sur les Juifs* (Paris 1963) 27–31; H. Schreckenberg, *Die christlichen Adversus-Judaeos-Texte und ihr literarisches und historisches Umfeld (1.–11. Jh.)* (Europäische Hochschulschriften, Reihe XXIII Theologie 172; Frankfurt/M./Bern 1982) 367f.

and Cyprian seems probable.[142] Cyprian the exegete, like Hippolytus the exegete, has been eclipsed by Origen and his followers when we come to the most influential Latin writers like Ambrose[143] and Augustine. Even the learned Jerome seems to neglect Cyprian, even though he had read him.[144] In Hilary, however, the "founder of Latin exegesis", there are still important traces left of the Tertullianic-Cyprianic testimony tradition,[145] side by side with spiritualistic Origenistic allegory.

(2) *De altercatione ecclesiae et synagogae dialogus* (Ps. Augustine, PL 42 1131–1140; 5th cent.?). Studies: A. L. Williams (1935) 326–338; Schreckenberg (1982) 354.

(3) *Consultationes Zacchaei et Apollonii* (Ps. Firmilian, PL 20 1071–1182; ca 420?). Studies: B. Blumenkranz, *Die Judenpredigt Augustins* (Basel 1946) 30–33; A. L. Williams (1935) 295–97; P. Courcelle, "Date, source et genèse des Consultationes Zacchaei et Apollonii", *RHR* 146 (1954) 74–93; Schreckenberg (1982) 331.

[142] Cp. esp. P. Monat, *Lactance et la Bible* I–II (Paris 1982) *passim*, summarized in idem, Les *testimonia* (1985) 504–507. Monat suggests that the common source behind the "African" dossier of testimonies could be the lost Disputation between Jason and Papiscus by Aristo of Pella. It was soon translated into Latin and seems to have been widely spread in North Africa.

[143] Ambrose never quotes him and seems to be ignorant of him as well as of Tertullian, cp. A. von Harnack, "Tertullian in der Literatur der alten Kirche", SAPW (Berlin 1895) 545–579; repr. in idem, *Kleine Schriften zur alten Kirche* I (Leipzig 1980; 247–281) 255.

[144] Cp. J. N. D. Kelly, *Jerome: His Life, Writings, and Controversies* (London 1975) 64; 292.

[145] Esp. in *De trinitate* books 4–7. Cp. J. Doignon, "Les premiers commentateurs latins de l'Écriture et l'oeuvre exégétique d'Hilaire de Poitiers", *Le monde latin antique et la Bible* (BTT 2, ed. J. Fontaine / C. Pietri; Paris 1985; 509–521) esp. 515.

Chapter Eleven

The Question of Old Testament Canon and Text in the Early Greek Church

By Oskar Skarsaune, Oslo

General works: J.-P. Audet, "A Hebrew-Aramaic List of Books of the Old Testament in Greek Transcription", *JTS* NS 1 (1950) 135–154; D. Barthélemy, "Redécouverte d'un chaînon manquant de l'histoire de la Septante", *RB* 60 (1953) 18–29; idem, *Les Devanciers d'Aquila. Première publication intégrale du texte des fragments du Dodécapropheton* (VTSup 10; Leiden 1963); idem, *Études d'histoire du texte de l'Ancient Testament* (OBO 21; Fribourg/Göttingen 1978); idem, "L'État de la Bible juive depuis le début de notre ère jusqu'à la deuxième révolte contre Rome (131–135)", *Le Canon de L'Ancien Testament: Sa formation et son histoire* (ed. J.-D. Kaestli / O. Wermelinger; Le monde de la Bible; Genève 1984) 9–45; R. Beckwith, *The Old Testament Canon of the New Testament Church and its Background in Early Judaism* (London 1985); H. Freiherr von Campenhausen, *Die Entstehung der christlichen Bibel* (BHT 39; Tübingen 1968); E. Flesseman-van Leer, "Prinzipien der Sammlung und Ausscheidung bei der Bildung des Kanons", *ZTK* 61 (1964) 404–420; M. Harl / G. Dorival / O. Munnich, *La Bible Grecque des Septante* (Paris 1988); M. Hengel, "Die Septuaginta als von den Christen beanspruchte Schriftensammlung bei Justin und den Vätern vor Origenes", *Jews and Christians. The Parting of the Ways A.D. 70 to 135* (ed. J. D. G. Dunn; WUNT 66; Tübingen 1992) 39–84; idem, "Die Septuaginta als "christliche Schriftensammlung" und das Problem ihres Kanons", *Verbindliches Zeugnis* I (ed. W. Pannenberg/Th. Schneider; Freiburg/Br./Göttingen 1992) 34–127; G. Howard, "Lucianic Readings in a Greek Twelve Prophets Scroll from the Judaean Desert", *JQR* NS 62 (1971/72) 51–60; S. Jellicoe, "Some Reflections on the *kaige* Recension", *VT* 23 (1973) 15–24; É. Junod, "La formation et la composition de l'Ancien Testament dans l'Église grecque des quatre premiers siècles", *Le Canon de l'Ancient Testament* (1984), 105–134; H. Karpp, "'Prophet' oder 'Dolmetscher'? Die Geltung der Septuaginta in der Alten Kirche", in idem, *Vom Umgang der Kirche mit der Heiligen Schrift. Gesammelte Aufsätze* (Kölner Veröffentlichungen zur Religionsgeschichte 3; Köln/Wien 1983) 128–150; idem, *Schrift, Geist und Wort Gottes. Geltung und Wirkung der Bibel in der Geschichte der Kirche – von der Alten Kirche bis zum Ausgang der Reformationszeit* (Darmstadt 1992) 11–60; P. Katz, "The Early Christians' Use of Codices instead of Rolls", *JTS* 46 (1945) 63–65; idem, "The Old Testament Canon in Palestine and Alexandria", *ZNW* 47 (1956) 191–217; idem, "Justin's Old Testament Quotations and the Greek Dodekapropheton Scroll", StPatr 1 (TU 63; Berlin 1957) 343–353; J. C. H. Lebram, "Aspekte der alttestamentlichen Kanonbildung", *VT* 18 (1968) 173–189; S. Z. Leiman, *The Canonization of Hebrew Scripture: The Talmudic and Midrashic Evidence* (Transactions of the Connecticut Academy of Arts and Sciences 47; Hamden 1976); M. Müller, *Kirkens første bibel. Hebraica sive Graeca veritas?* (Fredriksberg 1994); A. Rahlfs, "Über Theodotion-Lesarten im Neuen Testament und Aquila-Lesarten bei Justin", *ZNW* 20 (1921) 182–199; H.-P. Rüger, "Das Werden des christlichen Alten Testaments", *JBTh* 3 (1988) 175–189; J. S. Sibinga, *The Old Testament Text of Justin Martyr I. The Pentateuch* (Leiden 1963); O. Skarsaune, "Den første kristne bibel. Et blad av kodeksens historie", *Det levende Ordet* (FS Å. Holter, ed. I. Asheim et al.; Oslo 1989) 29–43; O. H. Steck, *Der Abschluss der Prophetie im Alten Testament. Ein Versuch zur Frage der Vorgeschichte des Kanons* (BThSt 17; Neukirchen 1991); A. C. Sundberg, *The Old Testament of the Early Church* (HTS 20; Cambridge, MA 1964); E. Tov, "Lucian and Proto-Lucian: Toward a new solution of the problem", *RB* 79 (1972) 101–113; idem, "Die griechischen Bibelübersetzungen", ANRW II:20,1

(Berlin/New York 1987) 121–189; idem, "The Greek Minor Prophets Scroll from Nahal Hever (8HevXIIgr)", DJD 8 (1990); B. F. Westcott, *The Bible in the Church. A Popular Account of the Collection and Reception of the Holy Scriptures in the Christian Churches* (London 1875); J. Ziegler, "Der Bibeltext im Daniel-Kommentar des Hippolyt von Rom", NGWG.PH 8 (Göttingen 1952) 163–199.

The purpose of this chapter is not to trace in a comprehensive way the history of Old Testament canon and text within the early Greek Church (from New Testament times to Irenaeus). Our sole concern here is to consider the significance of questions of canon and text insofar as they relate to the history of interpretation of the Old Testament.

In chapter 10.3 above, it was suggested that two phases may be recognized in early Christian attitudes to textual questions. During the first phase – prior to Justin – great 'freedom' prevailed with regard to the biblical text. It seems that Christian authors felt free to pick and choose among variant readings, Hebrew or Greek, and to combine, modify and expand biblical quotations. It was also suggested that this should probably be seen as stemming from accepted Jewish ways of handling the text of Scripture. To choose alternative readings when these brought home the point of the exegete, was standard procedure among the Rabbis of Talmudic and Midrashic literature. Examples of the formula "read not... (standard reading); but read... (alternative reading)" are legion in the whole of rabbinic literature. The rabbinic authors of the Targums apparently saw no objection to making explicit (by way of additions) the meaning they found to be implicit in the biblical text. They did not, however, interpolate these additions in the Hebrew text itself. Their more 'liberal' attitude in the Targums probably had to do with their awareness that the Targums were translations or interpretations of the biblical text, they were not the text itself. The early Christian 'freedom' with regard to the Greek Bible could have a similar background: the text of the Greek Bible was considered a (Greek) Targum, elucidating and making plain the meaning of the biblical (Hebrew) text.

It seems to be a reasonable surmise that this way of allowing for different readings and interpretations of the same text had to do with the *ketib/qere* phenomenon. Jewish exegetes had as their authoritative text a consonant text which could be read in more than one way, and *was* read in more than one way. This must have fostered the idea that the biblical text was a text with a fullness of meanings, to be spelled out through a plethora of readings.

To early Christian interpreters, this provided a welcome opportunity to read and interpret the old texts in ways which made them more applicable to the events which were held to be the fulfilment prophesied in the Old Testament. Contemporary Jewish exegetes would probably object fiercely to the concrete conclusions of Christian exegesis, but they would hardly object to the exegetical *technique* as such; they used the same techniques themselves.

But would Jewish exegetes object that Christians employed a greater range of books as 'Scripture' than they did themselves? Was the Christian Bible wider or more loosely defined than the Jewish?

Perhaps this is what one would expect, for *a priori* reasons. The "closing" of the Jewish canon had very much to do with the idea that the epoch of prophecy (= inspiration) had come to an end, f.ex. in the days of Ezra or Nehemiah. Books written after that time may be good history, but are not regarded equal to the inspired books of the canon, "because of the cessation of the exact succession of prophets" (Josephus, *Contra Apionem* I.41).

Christians were convinced that a new chapter of sacred history had been opened in their own days; that the prophets had prophecied until John (the Baptist), and that the crowning message had been delivered in these latter days by the Son. One would expect this conviction to result in a loosening up of the upper canon limit: prophecy, inspiration, had not ceased hundreds of years ago; on the contrary, it had recently reached its climax.

On this background, it is all the more striking to observe that early Christian authors do not deviate in any significant way with regard to which books they treat as Scripture and quote as such. Regardless of whether one takes Nestle's or Aland's lists of Old Testament quotations[1] in the New Testament, the picture is basically the same: the formal quotations of the Old Testament in the New Testament are strikingly limited to the "Hebrew Canon", with only one *formal* quotation falling outside the canonical books: 1. *En.* 1:9 in Jude 14f.

There has been much scholarly debate on the question of whether "circumstantial evidence" (i.e. the actual *use* of authoritative books) in the first century CE supports or contradicts the notion of a "closed" canon in that period. If quotation frequency[2] is regarded as significant circumstantial evidence, the New Testament seems to indicate that its authors (with the one exception mentioned) quoted the Hebrew canon, *and its books only*, as Scripture.

The picture is strikingly the same when we turn to the Greek Church of the second century. If we disregard Clement of Alexandria (on whom see below), there is an almost complete lack of quotations from the "apocrypha" of the later LXX codices. There are, of course, several allusions and some non-formal quotations,[3] but the frequency of these is markedly lower than with comparable canonical books.[4] In the Christian Greek authors of the second century (Apostolic Fathers included, Clement of Alexandria excluded), only *two* formal quotations are to be found in which one of the Old Testament Apocrypha is quoted as Scripture: Baruch 3:29–4:1 in Irenaeus *Proof of the Apostolic Preaching* 97; and Baruch 4:36–5:9 in Irenaeus *Adv. Haer.* V.55.1. In both cases, however, Irenaeus quotes the texts as "Jeremiah", which indicates that Baruch, like Lamentations,[5] was added to the edition of

[1] In the 25th edition of Nestle's Greek New Testament, K. Aland has compiled a new list of quotations and allusions, with many differences compared with the previous editions.

[2] By 'quotation' meaning a *formal* quotation, introduced by a citation formula indicating that the quotation is taken from Scripture, God's word, or similar. There are in early Christian literature – as in any literature – many non-formal quotations and allusions to a wide range of books, but these do not allow conclusions concerning the extent of the canon of the authors.

[3] See the lists in BP I, 217–223.

[4] A comparison between Proverbs and Sirach gives the following result: in the *BP* I, 334 references to Proverbs are recorded, only 112 to Sirach. Considering that Sirach is almost twice the size of Proverbs (94 pages in Rahlfs over against 55 for Proverbs), one gets the following ratio of "references per Rahlfs page": Proverbs 6,1; Sirach 1,2. There are 97 references to Sapientia, giving the ratio 3,0.

[5] In *Proof* 71 he quotes Lam 4:20 as "Jeremiah" (in *A.H.* III.19.3 anonymously, as in Justin 1. *Apol.* 55.5).

Jeremiah which Irenaeus used. For him, Lamentations as well as Baruch were part of Jeremiah's book.[6]

This seems to indicate that as far as the first and second century CE are concerned, Christian authors seem to have restricted themselves rather rigorously to the Hebrew canon (listed by the roughly contemporary Josephus) when they (formally) quoted Scripture. There seems to be no trace of a debate with the Jews about which books belong in the Bible. The only indication that is to be found for a *concern* about the question of canon, is Melito's story in the preface to his prophetical *Extracts*:

> Melito to Onesimus his brother, greeting. Inasmuch as you have often made request, in the zeal which you show for the word, to be made possessor of extracts from both the law and the prophets concerning the Saviour and all our faith, and further have desired also to be precisely informed about the ancient books, both as to their number and as to their arrangement, I was zealous to do such a thing .... So, going back to the east and reaching the place where it was proclaimed and done, I got precise information about the books of the Old Covenant, of which I now send you a list ... [= Hebrew canon without Esther]. (Fragm. 3 = Eus. *H.E.* IV. 26.13 f).[7]

This is hardly to be taken as a sign of Jewish/Christian controversy, but rather as an indication of inner-Christian uncertainty about the exact limits of the canon.

There is, however, a debate about which *texts* belong in the Bible, and which *readings* are correct. Most of the material for this comes in Justin's *Dialogue*. And some of his material also seems to reopen the question of canon, because he insists that some Old Testament *agrapha* should be regarded as canonical. Does this mean that the ones responsible for Justin's "testimony sources" had a wider or looser concept of canon?

We shall treat this material in Justin in some detail, first with regard to the canonical problem related to the *agrapha*, then with regard to his discussion of readings.

(1) In *Dial.* 72 Justin quotes an apocryphal "Esdras" text and an apocryphal "Jeremiah" text, and claims that the Jews have removed these texts from (canonical) Esdras and Jeremiah. The passage on Ps. Esdras runs like this:

> From the interpretations which Esdras interpreted of the Law about the passover, they have removed this: "And Esdras said to the people: This passover is our Saviour and our refuge. And if ye understand, and it come up into your heart, that we are about to humble him on a cross, and afterwards put our hope in him, then this place will never be laid desolate, saith the Lord of Hosts. But if ye do not believe him, nor listen to his proclamation, ye shall be a laughing stock to the Gentiles" (*Dial.* 72.1).

Scholars have often assumed the existence of an Esdras apocryphon to account for a quotation like this. The Ps. Jeremiah quotation would, according to the same principle, derive from a Jeremiah apocryphon. In this way, non-canonical *agrapha* in the early Christian authors give rise to the idea of a whole library of Christian Old Testament apocrypha now lost – and considered by the composers of Justin's testimony sources to be canonical.

---

[6] R. Beckwith (1985) 339–342 rightly emphasizes that with regard to the "additions" to the canonical books in the LXX (Esther, Daniel, Baruch, etc.); this is not primarily a question of canon at all, but of different versions of the same books.

[7] Quoted here according to Hall's translation of Melito, Hall 67.

It should be obvious in any case that Justin did *not* take his spurious quotations directly from such apocrypha, since the problem for him is that he does not find these texts in the *canonical* books. Whatever his sources looked like, they made him expect to find these quotations in canonical Esdras and Jeremiah.

Suppose Justin's source was a Christian writing containing quotations from canonical Esdras, and then also comments in the form of *interpretative paraphrases*, targumlike paraphrases of the biblical text. We find this phenomenon frequently in a work like *Barnabas*. In *Barn*. 7.4f, e.g., an uninformed reader could find the following "quotations" from the Law (Lev 16):

What then does he say in the Prophet (Moses)? "And let them eat of the goat which is offered in the fast for all their sins". Attend carefully: "and let all the priests alone eat the entrails unwashed with vinegar". Why? "Because you are going to give me gall and vinegar to drink when I am on the point of giving my flesh for my new people, therefore you alone shall eat, while the people fast and mourn in sackcloth and ashes". To show that he must suffer for them.

If Justin had read this and turned to Lev 16 to verify the quotations, he would probably conclude that the Jewish scribes had cut these passages out of Leviticus because they proclaimed Christ too clearly!

The way Justin introduces his Ps.Esdras quotation is interesting and claims our attention: "From the *exegeseis* which Esdras interpreted concerning the Law of Passover, they have removed ...". As J. Daniélou has well observed, the passage Justin quotes as "Esdras" reads like an *interpretative paraphrase* of LXX Esdras II 6:19–21. In Justin's source, this could be added to a quotation of, or an allusion to, Esdras II 6:19–21, and Justin mistook it for a new quotation from the same book.

In this way one can account for non-canonical "quotations" without positing a whole library of otherwise unknown Christian apocryphal Old Testament books.

(2) As we have seen (in chap. 10.3 above), Justin often quotes the same texts in two versions; one (short) non-LXX (most often in the *Apology*); one (long) Septuagint version. In some cases he has discovered the discrepancy in readings. This makes him comment on the difference in readings in a most interesting way:

(A) In *Dial*. 71.1f he says that he only quotes texts and passages *reckognized by the Jews*, although he could have quoted others, which the Jews claim are not in the text produced by the Seventy.

(B) "From the ninety-fifth Psalm of the words spoken by David they (the Jewish scribes) have removed this short saying 'from the tree'. For although the word says, 'Tell it among the Gentiles: the Lord reigned from the tree' (Ps 96:10 with Christian interpolation), they left only 'Tell it among the Gentiles, the Lord reigned'" (*Dial*. 73.1).

(C) "I could contend with you about the passage which you interpret by affirming that it runs 'until those things that are laid up for him come' (= Gen 49:10b LXX). For this is not *the interpretation of the Seventy*, but, 'until he come for whom it is laid up' (= Gen 49:10b as quoted in the *Apology*). But since the words that follow indicate that this is said of Christ (in any case) ... I do not enter into a discussion of the exact phrase. (I only argue from texts *'which you acknowledge still'*)" (*Dial*. 120.4f).

(D) "'... he set the bounds of nations according to the numbers of the sons of Israel ...' (= Deut 32:8 Hebrew). On saying this I added that *the Seventy* interpreted thus: 'He set the bounds of the nations according to the number of the angels of God' (= Deut 32:8 LXX). But since, once more, my argument is not at all weakened by this, *I used your interpretation*" (*Dial.* 131.1).

(E) "I will now, my friends, also adduce the Scriptures *as the Seventy interpreted them*. For when I stated them before (i.e. in *Dial.* 133.2) *as you yourselves have them*, I was making trial of you ... For in adducing (in *Dial.* 136.2) the Scripture which says, 'Woe to them ...' (Isa 3:9f) I added, *as the Seventy interpreted it*, 'Let us *take away* the Righteous ...'. Though at the beginning of our discourse (i.e. in *Dial.* 17.2) I also stated it *as you wish it to be said*, 'Let us *bind* the Righteous ...'" (*Dial.* 137.3).

(F) "The following are the words of David, *as you yourselves interpret them*, '... But ye die as *a man* ...' (Ps 82:7 within a LXX text of Ps 82). Now *in the translation of the Seventy* it is said, '... ye die as *men* ...', that he may declare also the disobedience of men, I mean Adam and Eve ... I have not however cited this passage with this object, but in order to prove ..., let the interpretation of the Psalm be as you will" (*Dial.* 124.2–4).

A rather consistent pattern emerges from these remarks. In the *Dialogue* Justin is quoting long excerpts from the LXX, obviously copying them from complete LXX scrolls. He says that this is the text *recognized by the Jews*, therefore he will argue his case on the basis of this text. He himself, however, does not in all cases recognize this text as the original LXX. He claims that this text (of the long LXX quotations) is a text with some Jewish distortions.

The readings claimed by Justin to be the true LXX, coincide with the non-LXX texts of the short quotations in the *Apology* (examples B and C). Some conclusions seem inevitable: (1) *Both* textforms in Justin must be original – he comments on the difference between them. (2) The short, non-LXX quotations cannot be explained as *his* free quotations from memory, since Justin insists that these, not the text of the LXX manuscripts, are the true LXX. In fact, a closer study of his short quotations seems to prove that they are not anybody's free quotations from memory, but rather carefully constructed (if composite) or modified or interpolated texts, representing a deliberate Christian 'targumizing' of the standard LXX text. (3) The short, non-LXX quotations are not Justin's own products, since the discrepancies between these texts and the LXX text of his long quotations is a problem to him. He solves the problem by blaming the Jews for having tampered with the text of the biblical manuscripts (from which he took his long quotations). (4) Justin must have obtained his biblical manuscripts from Jewish sources, since he characterizes their text as "Jewish".

The last point has in recent years been surprisingly substantiated by the discovery of a Jewish LXX scroll of the Twelve Prophets in the Cave of Horror by the Dead Sea. The text of this scroll is clearly LXX in character, but a *revised* version of the LXX text. D. Barthélémy in his pioneering studies of this text has called it the *kaige* recension. The revision seems to have been carried out between the two Jewish wars with Rome, the purpose being to adjust the Greek Bible into closer correspondence with the emerging standard Hebrew text. The interesting fact about this is that Justin's quotations from the Twelve Prophets represent this *kaige* recension of the LXX. In some of his other long LXX quotations one may also observe signs of 'hebraizing' recensional activity. Justin may have had some elementary knowledge of these revisions of the LXX text among Jewish scribes, and this may have prompted him to think that all discrepancies between his short quotations and the text of the biblical scrolls were due to Jewish scribal activity.

Let me add a remark on the many non-LXX readings, combined quotations and interpolated texts in the early "testimony" tradition. It is clear that for a writer like Justin, this 'free' way of handling the biblical text was no longer an option. To him, even minute differences in wording between different recensions of the same biblical text could represent a problem, and it is obvious that he took great pride in quoting Scripture with absolute exactness. In the sources of his short quotations, however, we encounter a completely different attitude with regard to the text of Scripture. As often in the Jewish Targums, interpretative modifications or interpolations are incorporated into the rendering of the biblical text itself. The Targumists certainly did not think of this as changing or modifying the text, but only as a bringing out or making clear the deeper meaning of the text. *Mutatis mutandis* one could probably think of the 'free', 'interpolated' Old Testament quotations within the 'testimony sources' of early Christian writers as Christian – possibly Jewish-Christian – 'targumizing' of the text of the Greek Bible.

If we compare the many non-LXX "testimony" quotations in 'Barnabas' and Justin with the recurrence of the same quotations in Irenaeus and Tertullian, one tendency is unmistakable: very often a non-LXX quotation in the first two writers recur as a perfect LXX text in the two latter. Combined quotations are dissolved into their different components, and each component quoted separately according to the LXX. In Cyprian, this process reaches its logical conclusion: in him, the deviant "testimony" readings disappear almost completely, to be replaced by "correct" quotations from the text of his Latin Bible.

This means: from Justin on, there is a gradual wearing down of the distinct characteristics of the testimony tradition (its deviant, combined, interpolated etc. quotations). This holds true for the Greek Fathers, and for the Latin Fathers treated below. But in the early Latin Church of the 2nd and early 3rd centuries there seems to be a kind of backwater in which the testimony tradition is kept much more intact, and where we can find other relics of the early testimony sources than in *Barnabas* and Justin. Especially four Pseudo-Cyprianic treatises[8] – all of them apparently prior to him, and representing a genre of 'low', vulgar literature (unliterary, sometimes crudely hebraizing or "Greek" Latin!) – are rich in non-LXX "testimony" quotations. Here the techniques and hermeneutics of Justin's testimony sources are continued. These tracts may be said to be "more of the same", compared to the testimony material in Justin.

---

[8] They are:

(1) *Adversus Judaeos*, text: CCL 4 (ed. G.F.Diercks; 1972) 265–278; and D. VAN DAMME, *Pseudo-Cyprians Adversus Judaeos. Gegen die Judenchristen, die älteste lateinische Predigt – Text, Übersetzung, Kommentar* (Paradosis 22; Freiburg/CH 1969). Cp. also E. PETERSON, "Ps.-Cyprian, Adversus Iudaeos, und Melito von Sardes", idem, *Frühkirche, Judentum und Gnosis. Studien und Untersuchungen* (Darmstadt 1982) 137–145; J. Daniélou, Latin Christianity (1977) 31–39.

(2) *De montibus Sina et Sion*, text: CSEL III,3 (ed. G. Hartel; Wien 1871) 104–119. Cp. P. CORSSEN, "Eine Theologie aus der Werdezeit der kirchlichen Literatur des Abendlandes", *ZNW* 12 (1911) 1–36; H. KOCH, *Cyprianische Untersuchungen* (Bonn 1926) 421–425; A. STUIBER, "Die Wachthütte im Weingarten", *JAC* 2 (1959) 86–89; J. Daniélou, Latin Christianity (1977) 39–57.

(3) *De centesima, sexagesima, tricesima*, text: R. REITZENSTEIN, "Eine frühchristliche Schrift von den dreierlei Früchten des christlichen Lebens", *ZNW* 15 (1914) 74–88. Cp. E. SEEBERG, "Eine neugefundene lateinische Predigt aus dem 3. Jahrhundert", *NKZ* 25 (1914) 472–494; H. KOCH, "Die pseudocyprianische Schrift *De centesima, sexagesima et tricesima* in ihrer Abhängigkeit von Cyprian" *ZNW* 31 (1932) 248–272; J. Daniélou, Latin Christianity (1977) 63–92.

In this way, early Christian interpretation of the Old Testament may be said to rest on a Jewish foundation with regard to canon and with regard to the way of handling the biblical text. But during the second century, the 'targumic' freedom in handling and interpreting the Greek Old Testament gradually gave way to a different attitude. The Greek text was now increasingly regarded as the *Grundtext*, to be quoted *verbatim*. Interpolated or modified or expanded quotations of the Greek Old Testament that had entered the "testimony tradition" during the early period, gradually gave way to a strict adherence to the standard Septuagint text of the biblical manuscripts (of the canonical books).

This means: during the second century and afterwards, the old "testimony approach" which from the beginning characterized Christian hermeneutics, was applied to an increasingly 'standard' and rigidly understood LXX text. This went parallel with the attempt to expand the testimony approach to cover complete biblical books. The inherent discrepancy in this approach indirectly paved the way for a completely new hermeneutical approach: that of Origen. With him, the questions of text and canon were also brought to a new level of scholarly treatment, as is evident from his *Hexapla* and his debate with Julius Africanus on Susannah.

Chapter Twelve

Greek Philosophy, Hermeneutics and Alexandrian Understanding of the Old Testament

By J. F. Procopé †
(University of Cambridge)

Sources: Alcinous: *Alcinoos, Enseignement des doctrines de Platon* (ed./trans. J. Whittaker; Paris 1990); *Alcinous: The Handbook of Platonism* (trans. J. Dillon; Oxford 1993). Atticus: *Atticus fragments* (ed./trans. E. des Places; Paris 1977). Chaeremon: *Chaeremon: Egyptian Priest and Stoic Philosopher* (ed./trans. P. W. van der Horst; Leiden 1987). Cornutus: *Cornuti theologiae graecae compendium* (ed. C. Lang; Leipzig 1881). Heraclitus: *Héraclite: Allégories d'Homère* (ed. F. Buffière; Paris 1962). Numenius: *Numénius fragments* (ed./trans. E. des Places; Paris 1973). Presocratic Philosophers: *Die Fragmente der Vorsokratiker* (ed. H. Diels/W. Kranz; [10]Berlin 1960–61). stobaeus: *Ionnis Stobaei Anthologium* (ed. C. Wachsmuth/O. Hense; Berlin 1884–1909). *Stoicorum Veterum Fragmenta* I–IV (ed. J. von Armin; Leipzig 1903–24).

General works: C. Andresen, *Logos und Nomos: Die Polemik des Kelsos wider das Christentum* (Berlin 1955); R. Arnou, "Platonisme des pères", DTC XII 2, 2258–2392; J. A. Coulter, *The Literary Microcosm. Theories of Interpretation of the late Neoplatonists* (CSCT II; Leiden 1976); P. de Lacy, "Stoic Views of Poetry", *AJP* 69 (1948) 241–271; D. Dawson, *Allegorical Readers and Cultural Revision in Ancient Alexandria* (Berkeley 1992); J. Dillon, *The Middle Platonists* (London 1977); H. Dörrie, "Zur Methodik antiker Exegese", *ZNW* 65 (1974) 121–138; A. J. Festugiere, *La révélation d'Hermés Trismegiste*, IV. *Le dieu inconnu et la gnose* (Paris 1983); M. Frede, "Chaeremon der Stoiker", ANRW II/36, 3 (1989) 2067–2103; idem, "Numenius", ANRW II/36, 2 (1987) 1034–75; idem, "Celsus philosophus Platonicus", ANRW II/36, 7 (1994) 5183–5213; R. Frye, "Allegory", The Princeton Encyclopedia of Poetry and Poetics (ed. A. Preminger; Princeton 1974) 5–8; P. Hadot, "Les divisions des parties de la philosophie dans l'Antiquité", *Museum Helveticum* 36 (1979) 201–23; idem, "Théologie, exégèse, révélation, écriture dans la philosophie grecque", *Les règles de l'interprétation* (ed. M. Tardieu; Paris 1987) 13–34; W. R. Inge, "Alexandrian Theology", ERE (ed. J. Hastings; Edinburgh 1908) 309–319; J. N. D. Kelly, *Early Christian Doctrine* (London 1977); R. Lamberton, "The Neoplatonists and the Spiritualization of Homer", *Homer's Ancient Readers* (ed. R. Lamberton/J. Keaney; Princeton 1992) 115–33; S. R. C. Lilla, *Clement of Alexandria: a Study in Christian Platonism and Gnosticism* (Oxford 1971); A. A. Long, "Stoic Readings of Homer", *Homer's Ancient Readers* (ed. R. Lamberton/J. Keaney; Princeton 1992) 41–66; B. Neuschäfer, *Origenes als Philologe* (SBA 18/1, 2; Basel 1987); M. Pohlenz, *Die Stoa* (Göttingen 1964); J. Pépin, *Mythe et Allégorie* (2nd ed.; Paris 1976); R. Pfeiffer, *History of Classical Scholarship* (Oxford 1968); J. I. Porter, "Hermeneutic Lines and Circles: Aristarchus and Crates on the Interpretation of Homer", *Homer's Ancient Readers* (ed. R. Lamberton/J. Keaney; Princeton 1992) 67–114; N. J. Richardson, "Homeric Professors in the Age of the Sophists", PCPS 21 (1975) 65–81; "Aristotle's Reading of Homer and its Background", *Homer's Ancient Readers* (ed. R Lamberton/J. Keaney; Princeton 1992) 30–40; D. A. Russell, *Criticism in Antiquity* (London 1981); H. Schreckenberg, "Exegese I (heidnisch, Griechen u Römer)", RAC 6 (1966) 1174–94; H. P. Steinmetz, "Allegorische Deutung und allegorische Dichtung in der Alten Stoa", *Rheinisches Museum* 129 (1986) 18–30; J. Whitman, *Allegory: The Dynamics of an Ancient and Medieval Technique* (Harvard 1987); J. Whittaker, "Platonic Philosophy in the Early Centuries of the Empire", ANRW II/36, 2 (1987) 81–123.

1. Introduction

Jewish and Christian expositors of the Bible in the first three centuries CE made remarkable efforts to understand and expound its teachings in the language and concepts of Greek philosophy. Many of them in fact saw themselves as engaged in 'philosophy'. Philo (ca. 20 BCE–ca. 50 CE) speaks of "philosophizing according to Moses", Clement (ca. 150–215 CE) of "philosophy according to Christ",[1] while Origen (ca. 185–ca. 254 CE) was described by a grateful pupil as his "guide to philosophy, this divine man".[2] Philo, Clement and Origen all believed that the Bible could be mined for answers to the very questions about God, the universe and the purpose of human existence, which had exercised pagan thinkers, and that their answers would accord with what these thinkers really believed. But the texts of revealed Hebrew religion and the reasoning of Greek philosophers were products of very different cultures. To find the accepted truths of Greek philosophy in the Old Testament required considerable powers of assimilation and creative exegesis. We shall see, however, that a pagan tradition of hermeneutics provided Philo, Clement and Origen with techniques for extracting philosophical truths from the most unpromising material.

The fullest fusion of Greek and Jewish thought was achieved at Alexandria, home of Philo, Clement and (for much of his life) of Origen. Capital of Egypt under the Ptolemies and then the Romans, it was a cosmopolitan city with a large and long-established Jewish community. Under royal patronage, Alexandria had soon become pre-eminent in science, scholarship and literature. As a centre for philosophy, however, it had been rather less important – at least, for its first three centuries.[3] The four great Hellenistic schools of philosophy – the Academy founded by Plato (429–347 BCE), the Lyceum or Peripatos of Aristotle (384–322 BCE) and his followers, the Stoa of Zeno (335–263 BCE) and the garden of Epicurus (341–270 BCE) – were all in Athens. Only in the first century BCE, some time after the capture of Athens by the Romans under Sulla in 87 BCE (an event with considerable impact, in several ways, on the course of Greek philosophy), were philosophers of any eminence settled in Alexandria. These included Aenesidemus (ca. 50 BCE), a reviver of Scepticism, who formulated the celebrated 'ten modes' for suspending belief (our earliest source for these, incidentally, is Philo[4]), and Eudorus (ca. 35 BCE), who seems to have given its distinctive religious orientation to what is now known as 'Middle Platonism', the philosophy to which in their different ways Philo, Clement and Origen all subscribed.

---

[1] Philo, *Mut.* 223, *Q. Div. Her.* 291; Clement, *Str.* VI. 67.1.
[2] Gregory Thaumaturgus, *in Origenem oratio panegyrica* 11.133.
[3] See P. M. Fraser, *Ptolemaic Alexandria* (Oxford 1972) 480–94.
[4] *Ebr.* 154–205.

2. Middle Platonism

2.1. *Eclecticism*

By the time of Clement in fact most philosophers were Platonists of one sort or another,[5] expounding, along with doctrines from various other sources, a view of God, the universe and the purpose of human existence which went back to Plato. In the Hellenistic period there had been no such consensus. The rival schools of philosophy at Athens – Academy, Peripatetos, Epicureans and the Stoic followers of Zeno and Chrysippus (ca. 280–207 BCE) – had all offered their own versions of the truth. From this Hellenistic perspective, the traces of Greek philosophy in Philo and Clement are a mixture of Platonist, Stoic and other doctrines. In an oft-cited passage, Clement himself adopts an eclectic attitude:

> By 'philosophy' I mean not the Stoic nor the Platonic or the Epicurean or Aristotelian. No, whatever has been well said by any of these, teaching righteousness together with an informed piety (δικαιοσύνην μετὰ εὐσεβοῦς ἐπιστήμης) – this eclectic entirety I call philosophy.[6]

Clement's own mixture of Stoic and Platonist theory is not, however, any more 'eclectic' than that of contemporary pagan philosophers. Stoics and Platonists in the first two centuries CE were much more open than they had earlier been to one another's doctrines. The truth is not that Clement had thumbed through the works of Plato, Aristotle, Epicurus and the Stoics, picking out whatever he fancied, but rather that the dominant philosophy of his time, generally known now as 'Middle Platonism',[7] was itself a compound of Platonist, Stoic, Aristotelian and Pythagorean ingredients, however much its more eminent exponents – Eudorus of Alexandria, Plutarch of Chaeroneia (ca. 50–ca. 120 CE), Atticus (ca. 176 CE) , Alcinous,[8] Apuleius of Madaura (mid 2nd century CE), Moderatus of Gades (ca. 90 CE), Numenius of Apamaea (ca. 150 CE) – might differ in the relative importance which they attached to these ingredients.

2.2. *Origins and Development*

The explanation for this composite character of Middle Platonism goes back to Plato himself. His written works offer almost every obstacle to any attempt at constructing a 'system', a tidy arrangement of interconnecting logical, physical and ethical doctrine, of the kind required in the Hellenistic schools. Many

---

[5] Apart from the Peripatos which remained vigorous for another hundred and fifty years. By 200 CE Stoics and Epicureans were a spent force.

[6] *Str.* I.37.6. On the idea of righteousness and piety as the supreme virtues, see A. Dihle, *Der Kanon der zwei Tugenden* (Köln/Opladen 1968).

[7] In the eighteenth century, it used to be called 'eclectic'. Even Plotinus was given that label (Frede, Numenius, 1040) – perhaps with some justification. Porphyry noted that "his writings are full of concealed Stoic and Peripatetic doctrines" (*Life of Plotinus* 14).

[8] 1st or 2nd cent. CE, author of a *Handbook of Platonism*, transmitted under this name in the MSS, but ascribed by J. Freudenthal in 1879 to his contemporary Albinus, to whom the work has regularly been attributed till very recently.

of his dialogues are openly inconclusive, designed to set the reader thinking rather than to provide firm answers.[9] This had two consequences. It led some of his successors to see him as an undogmatic, and not just an unsystematic, thinker. For two hundred years, starting with Arcesilaus (316/5–241/0 BCE), the Academy maintained a sceptical position on philosophical questions, principally against the Stoics.[10] A second consequence was that when, at the start of the first century BCE a leading member of the school, Antiochus of Ascalon (ca. 120–ca. 68 BCE),[11] did return to dogmatism, his system of positive doctrine was heavily laced with Stoic and Peripatetic theory.[12] His epistemology was a somewhat nondescript mixture of the two, while his answer to the prime ethical question of what our supreme goal in life should be was couched in the language of Stoic controversy: "to live virtuously while enjoying the primary blessings of nature"[13] such as health. Antiochus' successors disagreed, sometimes fiercely, about the amount of Stoic or Aristotelian doctrine to take on board.[14] But he at least ensured that they rejected two other schools of thought. He had turned his back on Scepticism, maintaining as he did that definite answers *are* possible to philosophical questions, and also on Epicureanism with its hedonistic ethic and mechanistic account of the world.[15] All his successors were firmly committed to a teleological view of the universe.[16]

A generation or so after Antiochus came the decisive development in Middle Platonism. Plato had believed in the existence of an intelligible world, transcending yet somehow reflected in that of the senses:

> What is that which is always real and has no becoming? And what is that which is always becoming and is never real? That which is apprehensible by thought with a rational account is what is always unchangeably real; that which is the object of belief along with unreasoning sensation is what comes to be and passes away, but never has real being.[17]

---

[9] So much so that texts of Plato were later produced with a special diacritical sign, the *diple* ('>'), to show where Plato's own doctrines and opinions were to be found (Diogenes Laertius, *Vitae philosophorum* III. 66).

[10] See A. A. Long, *Hellenistic Philosophy* (London 1974) 88–106.

[11] On whom see Long (1974) 222–229, Dillon (1977) 52–105, and J. Barnes, "Antiochus of Ascalon", in *Philosophia Togata* (ed. M. Griffin/J. Barnes; Oxford 1989) 51–96.

[12] He claimed in fact that he was simply resurrecting the doctrines of the 'Old Academy' to which Aristotle had belonged and from which Zeno had dissented only in words, not in matters of substance. See Cicero, *De Natura Deorum* I. 16, *De Finibus* V. 74, etc..

[13] Cicero, *Lucullus* 131; "honeste vivere fruentem rebus in quas primas homini natura conciliet".

[14] See Whittaker (1987) 110–117. To cite one example, Antiochus maintained with the Peripatos that bodily and external goods are necessary to the happy life (Cicero, *Ac. Pr.* I. 4), followed in this by Plutarch and others. Eudorus (to judge from Stobaeus II. 57.22 f.). Atticus (Fr. 2; des Places) and Alcinous (*Handbook* 27.2) took the opposite, Stoic view and denied this.

[15] See, further, Barnes (1989) 81: "in logic, the struggle of the time was between scepticism and science; in physics, the tussle concerned a mechanistic atomism on the one side and teleology and a material continuum on the other; in ethics, there was a duel between virtue and pleasure. In each of these great battles, the Old Academics and the Peripatetics stood shoulder to shoulder with the Stoics against the barbarian attacks of sceptics and voluptuaries".

[16] From this point of view, even Aristotle was to be found wanting (e.g. by Atticus Fr. 3; des Places) since he denied that providence operates in the sublunary sphere. See Lilla (1971) 47 f.

[17] Plato, *Timaeus* 27 d–28 a (Cornford tr. adapted). Cf. Celsus ap. Origen, *Contra Celsum* VII. 45.

This metaphysical dualism was now reinstated, perhaps by Eudorus of Alexandria,[18] as the pillar of the whole system. With it came a belief in a transcendent, non-material deity and an interest – commonly seen as Pythagorean, though also a preoccupation of Plato's old age[19] – in finding a mathematical model for reality. Platonists now could distance themselves sharply from the materialism of the Stoics[20] who had defined even God as simply a kind, albeit a very special kind, of fire.[21]

With its renewed commitment to a transcendent world, Platonism took on an increasingly otherworldly character. Where Antiochus had seen the end of human existence in terms of "living virtuously according to nature", Platonists from Eudorus[22] onwards identified it, in Plato's own words, with "assimilation to God", "becoming as like God as possible".[23] The idea of philosophy itself underwent a gradual change. Having been advertised by its Hellenistic practitioners as the vital means to living a good and happy life, it could now be defined, in thoroughly Platonic language, as a "freeing and turning round of the soul towards the intelligible and truly existent".[24] The ideal philosopher was no longer a 'wise man', a moral paragon like Socrates or Diogenes, so much as a *'divine* man', a man in touch with the deity.[25] As we saw, that was how Origen was described by his grateful pupil.

2.3. *The Parts of Philosophy*

In time, too, the subject-matter of philosophy was reorganized. Hellenistic philosophy had normally come in three parts: logic, physics or natural science (which included theology, since the gods were seen as part of the natural order), and ethics. The Stoa could treat these as the same rational endeavour, only directed towards different objects – towards one's own thinking, towards the outside world or towards other people.[26] Logic, physics, ethics – on those

---

[18] On whom see Dillon (1977) 114–35.

[19] No attempt need be made here to disentangle Platonist from Pythagorean doctrines. The two were thorougly intertwined from the start, since (1) Plato's metaphysics owed much to Pythagorean teaching (Aristotle, *Metaphysics* 187a. 30ff.), while (2) much of what was later passed off as Pythagorean theory (e.g. at Diogenes Laertius, VIII 24–33) seems to have begun life in the 'Old Academy' of Plato and his immediate successors. (3) In the period of the sceptical 'Middle' and 'New Academy' (3rd and 2nd centuries BCE), reworkings of Platonic texts appeared ascribed to Pythagorean worthies such as Timaeus of Locri and Ocellus of Lucania (see Frede, Numenius, 1043f.). Thus (4) by the 2nd century CE, it was possible to see Plato as simply a disciple of Pythagoras.

[20] See Plutarch 426bc, 1051f–2a; Lilla (1971) 48–50.

[21] *Stoicorum Veterum Fragmenta* II 1027.

[22] Stobaeus, II. 49.8–5.10; Wachsmuth (Stobaeus is quoting a summary of Eudorus' work by Areius Didymus); Philo, *Fug.* 63, *Virt.* 168; Alcinous, 28. 181.19–182.14 H.

[23] Plato, *Theaetetus* 176b: ὁμοίωσις τῷ θεῷ κατὰ τὸ δυνατόν. On this theme see H. Merki, Ὁμοίωσις θεῷ (Fribourg/CH 1951) and 'Ebenbildlichkeit', RAC 4 (1959) 459–79.

[24] Alcinous, *Handbook* 1.1 (152.2f.), recalling Plato, *Republic* 521c, and *Phaedo* 67d.

[25] See, generally, L. Bieler, Θεῖος ἀνήρ (Wien 1935).

[26] Hadot (1979) 210: "la sagesse est indissolublement éthique, physique et logique, les distinctions entre les trois parties ne provenant que des relations du sage avec le cosmos, les autres hommes et propre pensée".

lines Andronicus had arranged the rediscovered works of Aristotle,[27] and that was still the order in which Alcinous' *Handbook of Platonism* discussed its subject-matter. Gradually, however, this division gave way to one based on the stages of the philosopher's own ideal progress: ethics, physics, and theology. Ethics provide the soul with initial purification, physics turn the mind from the material world to its transcendent causes, while *epopteia* or mystical theology culminates in contemplation of God.[28] It was on those lines that Porphyry arranged the treatises of Plotinus[29] and Origen discussed the three books of Solomon, describing Proverbs as a book of ethics, Ecclesiastes as a work of physics and the Canticle as a text of mystical theology.[30]

2.4. *Theology*

Where Platonist thought had its most striking development, and its most significant cross-fertilization with Stoic and Aristotelian ideas, was in metaphysics and theology. At the centre of Plato's philosophy stood the theory of 'Forms' or 'Ideas', eternal, transcendent realities apprehended by thought, in contrast to the transient, contingent phenomena of the world as we experience it. In Plato's writings, these Forms serve a variety of barely compatible functions,[31] working sometimes as universals, sometimes as ideal standards, sometimes as models or blueprints of things in our perceptible world. That is how they make their appearance in the *Timaeus*, perhaps the most influential of Plato's works, which describes the formation of the world by a divine craftsman or Demiurge. At some time, this concept of the Forms as models was combined with Aristotle's doctrine[32] that the making of any artefact requires the presence of its 'form' in the mind of whoever is making it (i. e. that he must have some idea of what he is producing), and the result was the very common doctrine – we find it first in Philo – that the Forms are simply "thoughts in the mind of God".[33] But it was also possible to read the *Timaeus* treating the Forms, or at least their source as coexistent or even prior to the Demiurge. For Plato's dialogues offer more than one concept of God. The Demiurge of the *Timaeus*, even if the account there of the world's formation is not taken literally,[34] is at the very least an organizing force at work on chaotic matter to produce an orderly, purposeful cosmos. As such he operates to the same effect as the Stoic *Logos*, the divine 'reason' or 'plan' which

[27] This arrangement is still with us. It was retained by A. I. Bekker in the Berlin edition of Aristotle's works (1831–70), which are still cited by his pagination (works on logic : 1–184, on natural philosophy and metaphysic: 184–1092, on ethics and politics: 1094–1342).

[28] See Hadot (1979) 219–221 and Hadot (1987) 17.

[29] Porphyry, *Life of Plotinus* 24–26.

[30] Origen, *In Cant.* prol, p. 75.2–23.

[31] With what follows compare Alcinous, *Handbook* 9.1 (163.14–7): "Form, considered in relation to God, is his thinking; in relation to us, the primary object of thought; in relation to Matter, measure; in relation to the sensible world, its paradigm; in relation to itself, essence".

[32] Aristotle, *Metaphysics* 1032a. 322–b2.

[33] Philo, *Op.* 17.20; *Cher.* 49; *Conf.* 114; *Spec. Lg.* I. 47 f. Here, as so often, Philo is our earliest source for an important philosophical doctrine. See also Seneca, *Ep.* 58.18 f; 65.7.

[34] Among Platonists, in fact only Plutarch and Atticus (Fr. 19; des Places) understood it literally as a narrative of creation in time.

permeates and is coextensive with matter. (Quite possibly, Zeno derived his idea of it from the Academy.)[35] Elsewhere, however, Plato appeared to be thinking of a higher, altogether transcendent principle with a still better claim to be called 'God'.[36] He had written in the *Parmenides* of a 'One' about whom, on the first hypothesis, nothing whatever can be said, in the *Symposium* about the "Beautiful itself" which can only be described in negative language, and in the *Republic* of the Good which is "even beyond being".[37] The difference between this sort of supreme principle and the Demiurge led some Platonists to conclude that there must be at least two gods,[38] a transcendent god conceivable only by abstraction, analogy or reflections on his pre-eminence,[39] and, secondly, a divine intellect comprising the world of Forms, and responsible for generating and controlling the cosmos.[40]

Committed to monotheism, Jewish and Christian theologians could hardly go that far with their pagan counterparts. They could, however, assign the functions of the secondary Platonist deity to God's *Logos*. Intermediary between God and the universe, this acts, so Philo maintained, both as God's agent in creation[41] and as the means by which created minds can apprehend God.[42] It comprises not only the ideas in God's mind but also their utterance, their expression in creation at large. For the Greek noun λόγος meant 'word' as well as 'reason', and Philo here could invoke a Stoic distinction between 'internal' (ἐνδιάθετος) and 'uttered' (προφορικός) *logos*.[43] Moreover he could justify his use of terms by recalling the biblical accounts of creation: God spake and it was done. Christian writers—Justin, Athenagoras, Theophilus and Clement—had still more uses for the concept of the *Logos* as God's mind at work in creation and revelation. It showed them a way to account for the second person of the Trinity and the 'Word made flesh'.[44]

---

[35] See F. H. Sandbach, *The Stoics* (London 1975) 74 f.

[36] On what follows see Festugière, Le dieu inconnu et la gnose (1983) 79–140.

[37] Plato, *Parmenides* (141 e–2 a), *Symposium* (210 e–1 b), *Republic* (509 e).

[38] Alcinous (*Handbook* 181.43–182.1) distinguishes between a "god in the heavens", whose virtues we should attempt to imitate, and a "god above the heavens", who is also "above virtue". Not all Platonists made this distinction. Atticus (Fr. 12; des Places) stood out against it.

[39] See Alcinous, *Handbook* 10.5 f. (165.14–34; Hermann), Celsus ap. Origen, *contra Celsum* VII. 42. Cf. Clement, *Str.* V.81.5. See Frede, Celsus 5206 f.

[40] This double role, intellectual and creative, of the second deity led Numenius and others to claim that there were in fact *three* gods in the Platonic system, the proof-text being Plato, *Epistle* 2.112de with its avowedly 'enigmatic' talk of "three kings". For Numenius, however, the Third god was little more than a transformation of the Second, being simply the divine intellect at work in the world. "The god, however, who is the second and the third is one" (F. 11.13 ; des Places). See Frede, Numenius, 1056–70.

[41] *Cher.* 125–27.

[42] *Confus.* 97; *Migr.* 174. See Kelly (1977) 10.

[43] *Stoicorum Veterum Fragmenta* II. 175 (= Sextus Empiricus *M.* VIII. 275).

[44] See Kelly (1977) 95–101. Traces of current Platonism—in particular, Numenius' idea of the Third God as essentially the Second God (see above)—can also be found in the trinitarian theology of Christian Alexandria with the decidedly subordinate role that it assigns to the Holy Spirit as "the light issuing from the Word .. to illuminate the faithful" (Kelly, 1977, 127).

2.5. *Ethics*

Platonist writers – pagan, Jewish and Christian alike – went on for centuries using terms and concepts of Hellenistic and earlier philosophy, such as the scheme of the four cardinal virtues – courage, temperance, justice and wisdom[45] – or the definitions, Stoic and Aristotelian, of virtue itself,[46] to deal with problems first raised by earlier philosophers: "How far can virtue be taught?",[47] "Is virtue enough for the happy life?",[48] "Must one virtue entail all the others?".[49] Understandably, their writings have served as sources for Hellenistic philosophy, particularly Stoicism, for which we have little earlier evidence. But the change in metaphysical outlook from the first century BCE onwards was often enough to transform their treatment of the concepts and questions which they had inherited.

A striking example of such a transformation can be seen in how writers of the period discuss the emotions or 'passions'. These had been the subject of prolonged and lively debate between the Stoics and the followers of Aristotle.[50] The latter had claimed, in line with ordinary common sense, that the emotions are natural and positively useful, provided that they are not excessive. Their ideal went by the name of μετριοπάθεια or "moderation in emotion".[51] Against that, the Stoics advocated a total "freedom from emotion", ἀπάθεια, and taught that the wise man will have attained this freedom. But that could imply one of two things.[52] Either the wise man is some sort of yogi impervious to feeling – or else the 'emotion' from which he has freed himself must be redefined and the connotations of the term heightened to the point where most of what would normally count as emotion is excluded. Which is what the Stoics did. They defined 'passion' as a perversely irrational misjudgment, a vicious, exaggerated and voluntary response to things wrongly perceived as good or bad,[53] thereby leaving the wise man free to have a variety of involuntary reactions,[54] reasonable impulses (εὐπάθειαι)[55] and so forth. Needless to say, this refinement was regularly overlooked or misunderstood by their opponents, in whose eyes the Stoic wise man remained a stony-hearted monster. Some Middle Platonists, however, gave the debate a new turn, taking μετριοπάθεια and ἀπάθεια as complementary, not as contraries. Moderated emotion is appropriate for ordinary mortals in ordinary life; a total freedom from emotion is the mark of the sage. This double ideal first

---

45 See Lilla (1971) 72–80.

46 Lilla, 61–66.

47 Lilla, 66–69.

48 Lilla, 69–72.

49 Lilla, 83 f.

50 See Cicero, *Tusculan Disputations* IV. 38–57, Seneca, *de ira* I. 5–19.

51 The idea, if not the term itself, goes back to Aristotle (*Nicomachean Ethics* 1109 a 26–9 and elsewhere).

52 See J. Dillon "*Metriopatheia* and *Apatheia*. Some Reflections on a Controversy, in Later Greek Ethics", *Essays in Ancient Greek Philosophy* (ed. J. Anton/A. Preuss; Albany, NY 1983, 508–17) 509.

53 *Stoicorum Veterum Fragmenta* I. 203, 207; III. 377–85, 391, 476 etc.

54 See Seneca, *de ira* I. 16.7; II. 2–4.

55 *Stoicorum Veterum Fragmenta* III. 431–442.

appears in Philo, when he sees Aaron as the man who simply governs his passions in contrast to Moses who has eradicated them altogether.[56] We find it again in Clement.[57] Reappearing in Plotinus and Porphyry,[58] it was extensively elaborated by later Neoplatonists. The idea that there may be more than one level of moral aspiration goes well enough with the fundamental idea of Platonist metaphysics, that there is more than one level of reality. At the same time, the concept of "freedom from passion" is now notably different from what it had been for the Stoa. The Platonist sage has achieved something more than the unimpeded rationality of his Stoic counterpart. He really *is* something of a yogi. The pursuit of ἀπάθεια could be linked, indeed identified, with "assimilation to God";[59] and God is a being on an altogether different plane from that of the bodily world around us. But the passions are a function of life in the body – the idea goes back to Plato.[60] Liberation from passion, for pagan and Christian ascetics alike, is thus an aspect of liberation from the body, of "living in the flesh ... as one free of the flesh".[61]

2.6. *Philosophy and Exegesis*

A further development, this time in the *form* of contemporary Greek philosophy, was to be of considerable importance to Jewish and Christian theologians. From the first century BCE, philosophy came increasingly to be an exercise in expounding canonical texts.[62] Thus even Plotinus claims that he is simply interpreting Plato and the ancients.[63] This development followed the capture of Athens by Sulla in 86 BC. Hellenistic philosophy had been dominated by the four great schools there, permanent institutions with a succession of scholarchs going back to their founders, Plato, Aristotle, Epicurus and Zeno. Leading philosophers in these schools continued, or claimed to be continuing, in their own way the work of their predecessors, addressing problems as they arose, defending or expanding their inherited positions, and so forth. Students would learn from them in lectures and discussion how to deal with the problems of philosophy. With the fall of Athens, this institutional continuity was destroyed or badly disrupted.[64] Academy and Stoa were no longer schools so much as persuasions or 'schools of thought' with exponents in numerous parts of the Greco-Roman world. But these exponents could no longer claim the authority of inherited institutional position or rely as they had formerly relied on oral traditions of their schools. Their only way to show that they were true successors of Plato or Aristotle was to expound the *writings* of Plato or Aristotle. Courses of philosophy consisted more and

[56] *Leg. all.* III. 129–44.
[57] *Str.* VI. 105.1.
[58] Plotinus, *Enn.* I. 2; Porphyry, *Sent.* 32 (25.6–9; Lamberz).
[59] Plotinus, *Enn.* I. 2.3.19–21; Porphyry, *Sent.* 32 (25.6–9; Lamberz).
[60] *Phaedo* 66bd, *Republic* 611bd, *Timaeus* 42a.
[61] Clement, *Str.* VII. 79.2
[62] What follows is heavily indebted to Hadot (1987) 14–23.
[63] Though not slavishly. He still needs to ask which of them have come closest to the truth. See *Enneads* III. 7.1.15.
[64] See J. Glucker, *Antiochus and the Late Academy* (Göttingen 1978) 330–79.

more of reading and commenting on such works,[65] focusing less on philosophical problems themselves than on what the founding fathers of the school had said about them,[66] and on the interpretation of the relevant texts. Commentary came to be the vehicle, in pagan circles no less than in the catechetical school at Alexandria, of theological reflection and spiritual instruction.[67] Commentaries on Plato and Aristotle appeared, each fuller than its predecessor. Seneca might well have complained here, as he did elsewhere, that "what was philosophy has become philology".[68]

Philosophers of the first three centuries CE and later had remarkable philological acumen. They knew their texts well and had thorough rules for interpreting them. A snippet in Diogenes Laertius, for instance, tells us that the interpretation of Plato's dialogues needs to do "three things: (i) to examine the meaning of each statement; (ii) its purpose – as a primary utterance or just an illustration, to establish a teaching or to refute an interlocutor – and (iii) its correctness".[69] The last of these was the most important. The prime interest of philosophers in late antiquity was not, as that of a modern philologist would be, in what Plato or Aristotle had meant or thought he was saying, but rather in the *truth* of what he had said, and its bearing on questions of current concern to themselves but which he might not have dreamed of asking. Moreover, they were working in a tradition, and what they saw to be the truth would have rested as much on the authority of that tradition as on the texts themselves. Thus it is hardly surprising to find Porphyry, for instance, accommodating Plato's text to fit his own Neoplatonic doctrine,[70] in much the same way that Christian commentators, proceeding the best traditions of legal reasoning "*ex eo quod scriptum est ad id quod non sit scriptum*", [71] have been able to find teachings of the Church in every phrase of the Bible.

2.7. *Primal Wisdom*

To find in Plato traces of Neoplatonism might, however, seem less hazardous than to discern, as commentators of the Old Testament from Philo onwards were to discern, the cosmogony of the *Timaeus*, or something like it, in the first chapter of Genesis. Such interpretation, however, was less outlandish than it might now seem to be. "Barbarian philosophy in its turn", wrote

[65] On the technical vocabulary of such reading (ἀναγιγνώσκειν 'reading and commenting on a text with a master', ἐπαναγιγνώσκειν 'reviewing a pupils commentary', συναναγιγνώσκειν 'listening to a master's commentary', etc.) see Hadot (1987) 15 ff.

[66] "La réflexion ne porte pas directement sur les problèmes eux-mêmes, mais sur les problèmes tels qu'ils sont traités par Aristotle ou Platon" (Hadot, 1987, 18). To use Hadot's example, the interest would be less in the abstract conditions of motion than in what Aristotle had said about them in *Metaphysics* XII.

[67] Hadot (1987) 18.

[68] *Epistle* 108.23. Cf. Plotinus comment on Longinus "a philologist .. but certainly not a philosopher" (Porphyry, *Vita Plotini* 14.19). See Whittaker (1987) 120.

[69] Diogenes Laertius, *Vitae philosophorum* III. 65.

[70] See Hadot (1987) 19 f, on Porphyry's treatments (*In Parmenidem* XII. 25–8) of Plato, *Parmenides* 142 b.

[71] Cicero, *de inventione* II. 152.

Clement, "knows about the intelligible world and the perceptible, the archetype and the image of what they call the paradigm".[72] This was the principle on which Plutarch could read Platonism into Egyptian mythology. In the legend of Isis and Osiris[73] he found documentation for his own dualism, his belief which he shared with Atticus and Numenius (it goes back to Plato's *Laws*) that there is an evil as well as a good World Soul.[74] He could also find it in Greek Presocratic philosophy and the teachings of the Mages.[75] For "this primeval belief has come down to us from theologians and lawgivers to poets and philosophers, anonymous in origin, but strongly – indeed indelibly – convincing, circulating widely not only in words and reports but in rituals and sacrifices, barbarian and Greek".[76] Plutarch here is appealing to a concept of ancient wisdom (Celsus called it the "true account"),[77] a *philosophia perennis* which had been given its clearest articulation by Plato and Pythagoras, but which was also present, as Numenius put it, in "the rites, beliefs and institutions of Brahmins, Jews, Mages and Egyptians".[78] This concept[79] provided a useful springboard for cultural synthesis between pagans, Jews and Christians. Numenius himself, in a famous phrase, described Plato as "Moses speaking in Attic",[80] and he recalled the words of Exod 3:14 "I am that I am" in his own account of the First God as "He that is" and "Absolute Being".[81] Philo, Justin, Clement and others repaid the compliment, allowing that Greek philosophy had attained to some truth, either through derivation from the work of Moses, having been 'stolen' by the Greeks, or independently through natural revelation by the *Logos*.[82] (Needless to say, there were Christian writers[83] who firmly denied this, as well as pagans like Chaeremon the Stoic and Celsus who no less firmly denied that Jews and Christians had anything but a corrupt account of the primal truth.)[84] Ancient wisdom, Plutarch adds, can only be discovered in ancient myths and rites if these are taken symboli-

---

[72] *Str*. V. 9.3.4.

[73] Plutarch, *de iside* 369a-d. See Andresen (1955) 265f.

[74] Plutarch, *de an. procr*. 1014b; Atticus, Fr. 23 (des Places); Numenius, Fr. 52. 37, 63–70 (des Places); Plato, *Laws* 897ab. See Frede, Numenius, 1053.

[75] Plutarch, *de iside* 369e–71a.

[76] Plutarch, *de iside* 369b.

[77] "The True Account" was in fact the title of Celsus' polemic against Christianity (Origen, *Contra Celsum* III. 1, IV. 50, etc.), though he also spoke of ancient account (I 14, III. 16), an account true by reason of its antiquity. See Frede, Celsus, 5192, and Andresen (1955) 129f.

[78] Fr. 1 (des Places). See, further, Frede, Celsus, 5194.

[79] Not every one accepted it. See Diogenes Laertius, *Vitae philosophorum Praef*. 3.

[80] Fr. 8 (des Places): ἀττικίζων 'speaking pure, elegant Attic', in contrast to the cruder, less pure Greek of the Septuagint.

[81] As Professor M. Burnyeat argues in a paper as yet unpublished, Numenius seems to be recalling Exod 3:14: 'Εγω εἰμὶ ὁ ὤν when he writes of the first God as ὁ μέν γε ὤν (Fr. 13; des Places) and αὐτοόν (Fr. 17; des Places).

[82] See Lilla (1971) 12–31.

[83] E.g. Ps-Justin, *Cohort*. 1 (PG 6.241), 5 (PG 6.249).

[84] Chaeremon (Fr. 1; van der Horst) maintained that the Jews had been runaway slaves. Celsus maintained, further, that Moses had been no more than a half-educated sorcerer (I. 21; V. 47). Jews and Christians had thus no right to claim that doctrines derived from him were inspired (I. 20). Even if they were, their beliefs were too poorly argued to count as philosophical (I. 9, VI. 7,10f. See Frede, Celsus 5197f.). Worse still, their intransigent monotheism had effectively cut them off from the common religious heritage of mankind (Frede, 5212f.).

cally. Interpreted in the light of true philosophical insight, they can be seen as reflections of physical and metaphysical truth. But the interpretation has to be allegorical. Stories like that of Isis and Osiris cannot be understood literally – attempts to do so must be rejected out of hand.[85] In short, they need the same sort of treatment that Philo, Clement and Origen gave to much of the Old Testament.

3. Hermeneutics

3.1. Homer and Homeric Problems

Christian theologians at Alexandria expounding the Old Testament to an educated Greek public could in fact draw on a venerale hermeneutical tradition which had first served to expound the poems of Homer.[86] Depicting a long since vanished society of warrior chieftains, the *Iliad* and the *Odyssey* reflected the outlook and values of that society, but had retained their pre-eminence and cultural authority long after its disappearance. Far from becoming texts of merely antiquarian interest, they remained the foundation of Greek literary culture, of παιδεία, and they were to go on doing so for centuries after Clement and Origen. "Our infant children", wrote a commentator on Homer in the first century CE, "in their first moments of learning are suckled on him; we are wrapped in his poems as babies, and nourish our minds on their milk".[87] Studied by every school-boy (children used the *Odyssey* as a reading primer), they could be quoted at length by any literate adult and cited as authority on all manner of questions to do with ethics, philosophy, even (in later antiquity) with theology.

Homer's poems in fact have been described as 'the Bible' of ancient Greece.[88] The description is, admittedly, an exaggeration. Unlike the Torah, the *Iliad* and the *Odyssey* were never law books, though it was possible to invoke their authority in political disputes.[89] Nor were they held to be divinely inspired in the same rigorously veracious way as the Christian Scriptures. The Muses were quite capable of "speaking many falsehoods that resemble the truth".[90] Poets, it was thought, can contaminate the truth with mere opinion;[91] they can lie. Even Homer has his bad moments; *bonus dormitat Homerus*.[92] None the less, the poems of Homer provided the Greeks, as the Torah provided the Jews, with the foundation of their cultural identity. Any difficulties that arose from them had to be addressed with the utmost seriousness.

---

[85] Plutarch, *de iside* 359a, 363d.
[86] On what follows, see, further, Dörrie (1974) 121f., and above Siegert, ch. 4.1.
[87] Heraclitus, 1.3 (Russell tr.).
[88] Dörrie (1974) 122; Long (1992) 44.
[89] See Richardson (1992) 31.
[90] Hesiod, *Theogony* 27f.
[91] See Strabo I.2.7, Plutarch, *de audiendis poetis* 16a; Dio Chrysostom 53.4 (= SVF I 274).
[92] Horace, *de arte poetica* 359.

The poems of Homer contained two main kinds of difficulty; and these generated two distinguishable disciplines. From very early on, there were problems in understanding what was being said in parts of the *Iliad* and the *Odyssey*. Their language was an artifical mixture of dialects. It contained numerous archaic words that were no longer readily understood and which needed to be explained. Explanations of them – Homer himself in places offers one or two[93] – were the first step towards *philology*, towards a scholarship concerned with understanding and explaining, and later with restoring or emending, the text of such works, its prime aim being to clarify the author's meaning, his διάνοια. But a further set of problems remained. For what the poet 'meant', what he was apparently saying, might well be found unacceptable – that is, immoral or patently untrue. The values, beliefs and attitudes of Classical and Hellenistic Greece were different in many respects from those of Homer's society. Already by 500 BCE, his exuberant polytheism had come under attack. Homer and Hesiod, claimed Xenophanes, had credited the gods with "all that is shame and blame for men – stealing, adultery and deceiving each other".[94] But what right, in that case, had Homer and Hesiod to enjoy the authority that they did? Only if they were interpreted as really saying something rather more acceptable, something more in line with current cultural expectations, than what they appeared to be saying. What was needed, in short, were techniques of creative *hermeneutics*.

The following pages are principally about such 'hermeneutics'. They are concerned with the quest for the 'real' meaning of texts, as against such 'philological' activities as textual criticism, discussions of style, explanations of vocabulary, mythical details or historical *Realien*. It should, however, be noted that nearly every one of any importance who interpreted works of literature, from Theagenes of Rhegium (sixth cent. BCE) onwards, went in for both kinds of activity. As well as allegorizing the gods Theagenes is also said to have begun the study of correct usage (Ἑλληνισμῶς) and to have proposed a variant reading for *Iliad* 1.381.[95] The Stoics Zeno and Chrysippus, for all their later notoriety as interpreters of myths, did a great deal of straighforward philology.[96] Centuries later, Porphyry could produce a scholarly work on Homeric Questions as well as allegorical speculations in his treatise "On the cave of the nymphs in the *Odyssey*". When the Christian Origen combined his highly allegorical interpretations of Scripture with detailed and wide ranging philology,[97] he was following procedures long established by his pagan predecessors.

---

93 See Pfeiffer (1968) 4f.

94 Fr. 11 (Diels/Kranz). Philosophers and moralists were to go on shaking their heads over episodes like the binding of Hera, the ejection of Hephaestus from heaven (*Iliad* 1. 586–94), the battle of the gods (*Iliad* 21. 385–513), the wounding of Aphrodite and Ares by a mortal (*Iliad* 5. 330–51, 711–901). See Plato, *Republic* 378e, and Plutarch, *de audiendis poetis* 20e.

95 See Richardson (1975) 67f.

96 See Long (1992) 44.

97 On which see the excellent monograph by B. Neuschäfer, *Origenes als Philologe* (1987). See also Carleton Paget, sect. 3.5 below.

3.2. *Lines of Interpretation*

If a work of literature appeared to contain untruths or improprieties, there were broadly three ways of dealing with them.[98] It was possible, firstly, to *allegorize* the passages in which they occurred; or, secondly, to *relativize* them, by setting them in the broader, more wholesome context of the work as a whole; or, thirdly, to *marginalize* them – that is, to claim that a work of literature is its own domain, to be judged on its own terms, and that truth or morality are secondary considerations, external to it. All three lines of interpretation were pressed into service by exegetes of the Bible.

Of the three, far the most prominent in Philo, Clement and Origen – and far the most useful to anyone out to extract philosophical truth from literature – was allegory. Indeed it can seem, albeit wrongly, as though their hermeneutics consisted of little else. An obvious way to deal with an offensive passage was to discover a hidden sense to it, to imply that underneath the author's ostensible meaning, his διάνοια, lay a hidden and far more acceptable 'sub-meaning', a ὑπόνοια,[99] which it was the business of the interpreter to decipher. These 'sub-meanings' came to be known as 'allegories' – the two terms appear alongside each other when Plutarch speaks of invoking "what used to be called ὑπόνοιαι and are now called ἀλληγορίαι",[100] to salvage one of Homer's more disreputable stories.

The story, recited to Odysseus at the Phaeacian court, is that of Aphrodite's adultery with Ares. Plutarch rejects the attempt to allegorize it into a piece of astrology. What the passage shows, he asserts, is rather that if you pay attention to such coarse tales you will end by being as decadent as the Phaeacians themselves![101] Plutarch, in other words, is neutralizing the painful passage by putting it in context and distancing the poet from it. We shall see how interpreters of the Bible could use this kind of hermeneutic procedure.

A third line of interpretation goes back to Aristotle. In response to Plato's attack on the untruths and indecencies of poetry he argued that poetry has its own function, which is not primarily to teach truth or sound morals, and that it must be judged by how well it carries out this function. Literature has its own internal criteria. It must be understood on its own terms. This provided a broad philosophical basis for the exegetic principle known as "elucidating Homer by Homer" which, in its turn, was taken over by Christian interpreters of the Bible, Scripture, under the formula *scriptura ... sui ipsius interpres*.[102]

---

[98] I owe this very serviceable distinction to Coulter (1976) 5–31 (ch. 1 "The Three Streams").
[99] We find the term first in Plato (*Republic* 378d) and Xenophon (*Symposium* 3.5f.).
[100] *de audiendis poetis* 19e.
[101] Plutarch 19e–20a, on *Odyssey* 8.266–369. See Coulter (1976) 10f.
[102] See Neuschäfer (1987) 279.

3.3. *Allegory*

3.3.1. *General Principles*

Compounded of the words ἄλλο 'other' and ἀγορεύειν 'speak in public', the term ἀλληγορία had connotations of 'saying something other (than what you really mean) for public consumption'.[103] Allegory, 'which says one thing but signifies something else',[104] was a vital hermeneutic concept where the *truth* of a text was at issue. It was also and it is earlier attested as a 'figure' in rhetoric,[105] a standard departure from the straightforward and obvious way of saying things. (Needless to say, the tricks of saying one thing while signifying another, which exegetes and rhetoricians classed as 'allegorical', were a good deal older than either exegetical or rhetorical theory. Devices of figurative discourse had been employed long before rhetoricians discusssed their proper use in oratory or interpreters pondered the various ways in which meanings might be disguised.) As a rhetorical device, allegory had its associations with other devices for implying something without explicitly saying it—with *catachresis,*[106] with *emphasis* or 'hinting',[107] with the *aenigma* or 'riddle'.[108] Its principal connection, however, was with metaphor, "the transferred use of a term which properly belongs to something else",[109] primarily on the basis of analogy, as when we talk of 'ploughing through' paperwork.[110] Allegory in fact was ranked as an extension of metaphor: *allegoriam facit continua metaphora.*[111] To speak of the state as a 'ship' is to use metaphor; to speak further, as Horace does, of its being swept out to sea is to produce an allegory.[112] The extension might vary. The term 'allegoria' could be applied to anything from some gnomic utterance like "Dionysius is in Corinth"[113] to what we would now think of as 'allegory', a full-blown narrative signifying some analogous structure of events or ideas—as when the slaying of the

---

[103] See Whitman (1987) 262-68 (Appendix I "On the History of the Term 'Allegoria'").

[104] Heraclitus 5.2. Cf. Ps.Plutarch, *de Homero* II. 70.

[105] Demetrius, *de elocutione* 99, 100, 101, 102, 151; Cicero, *de oratore* III. 166, *Orator* 94.

[106] *catachresis* (Latin *abusio*) meant applying the nearest available term to something else that strictly has no name of its own (Quintilian, VIII. 6.34: "catachresis .. quae non habentibus nomen suum accommodat quod in proximo est"), e.g. when we use the word 'box' for containers not made of boxwood.

[107] Glossed by Quintilian (IX. 2.3) as "illam plus quam dixeris significationem", "signifying more than you are in fact saying".

[108] Glossed by Quintilian (VIII. 6.52) as "allegoria, quae est obscurior".

[109] Aristotle's definition (*Poetics* 1457b6f.).

[110] Aristotle's concept of metaphor was somewhat broader than ours. What we now think of as 'metaphor', he specifically called "metaphor κατ' ἀναλογίαν", regarding it as the most effective kind of metaphor (see the discussion at *Rhetoric* 1411a1-b21). Our modern concept of 'metaphor' is roughly that of Quintilian (VIII. 6.8) who describes it as *brevior similitudo*, "a briefer form of simile", with the added difference that a simile compares, whereas a metaphor actually replaces one thing with another.

[111] Quintilian, IX. 2.46, echoing Cicero, *De oratore* III. 166, *Orator* 94.

[112] Quintilian, VIII. 6.44, citing Horace, *Odes* I. 14.1.

[113] Demetrius, *de elocutione* 102. Dionysius, formerly tyrant of Syracuse, lived as an exile in Corinth. The point of the utterance, addressed by the Spartans to Philip of Macedon, was that he too might come to a bad end. Aristotle notes the effectiveness of such menacing hints (*Rhetoric* 1412a22).

many-headed Hydra by Hercules symbolizes the conquest by the philosopher of his passions.[114]

Allegory was regularly used in tandem with the *personification* of abstract ideas.[115] As a hermeneutic procedure too, it went with a further technique in the orator's repertory, the 'argument from the meaning of names' or, as we might put it, the use of *etymology*, the analysis of words into their elements in such a way as to bring out their real and original, if not always expected, meaning.[116] But the hermeneutical application of allegory grew steadily wider. Whole episodes in a work, indeed whole works of literature, could be given allegorical treatment, interpreted in terms of some hidden doctrine or story – historical, moral, physical or religious – connected with the text either by one-to-one correspondences between individual elements in both (e.g. between the many-headed hydra and the multifarious passions of the soul) or by structural similarities between the two. By now, though, allegory is something vastly grander than a mere figure of rhetoric, a *temporary* departure for purposes of beauty or persuasiveness from the normal way of saying things. It has been noted that Origen speaks rather seldom of metaphor or allegory.[117] The concept, which we learn in grammar lessons as small children, of *sometimes* saying one thing while meaning another[118] is hardly appropriate to Scripture which, on Origen's view, is charged *throughout* with hidden, 'spiritual' meaning.

If allegorical interpretation, rests upon the idea of a meaning to be found underneath the surface of a text, this meaning itself could be seen in two ways.[119] Either it had been deliberately veiled by an author intending his text to be taken allegorically – in which case it would be allegorical in a rather strong sense. Or else the text could be taken as allegorical in the weaker sense of inviting, whatever its author's conscious intentions may have been, some interpretation that went beyond his surface meaning. In that case any allegorization would just be the work of the reader. If most allegorical interpretations of Homer assumed that he had allegorized on purpose (he would have

[114] de Lacy (1948) 257. Here again, in contrast to modern concepts of 'allegory' which insist that it must have a "narrative base" (Frye, 1974, 5) or 'narrative' character (Dawson, 1992, 5; cf. Long, 1992, 54) and make this its distinguishing mark, ancient definitions were much broader. Indeed, 'allegory' could cover virtually any form of figurative language (cf. Russell, 96), even irony (Quintilian, VIII. 6.54) and euphemism (Quintilian, VIII. 6.57), though Quintilian promptly (VII. 6.58) notes the objection that these are too transparent to be classed as forms of allegory which needs to have something problematic – *obscurior* – about it in order to work.

[115] See Quintilian, IX. 2.29–37. The technique goes back to Homer himself with his personified account of supplications as "daughters of Zeus, lame, wrinkled, with downcast eyes" (*Iliad* 9.502f.). See Whitman (1987) 269–72 (Appendix II: "On the History of the Term 'Personification'") and Pfeiffer (1968) 4.

[116] See Aristotle, *Rhetoric* 1400b19–25. This device, too, goes back to Homer who speculates on the melancholy implications of the name Odysseus, connecting it with ὀδύρομαι, ὀδύσσομαι 'bewail' (*Odyssey* 1.55, 62). See Pfeiffer (1968) 4.

[117] See Neuschäfer (1987) 233–235.

[118] See Jerome's definition (*Comm. in ep. ad Gal.* 2.4), almost certainly derived from Origen (Neuschäfer, 1987, 233): "Allegoria proprie de arte grammatica est et quo a metaphora vel ceteris tropis differat, in scholis parvi discimus; aliud praetendit in verbis, aliud significat in sensu".

[119] On the distinction between 'strong' and 'weak' allegory, see Long (1992) 43.

been guilty of total impiety had he not done so, as one critic[120] put it), it was also possible to mine his stories, as the Stoics did, for truths of which he need never have been aware.[121] On either assumption, the aim of allegorical interpretation was not confined to defending its author. As well as showing that the poem came up to current cultural expectations, that the poet had not been guilty of impiety or outright falsehood, the interpreter could also invoke its authority to support his own personal and perhaps novel views, arguing that it had really said or intimated, however obscurely, what he himself was now saying[122] – in much the same way that modern exegetes have found support in the unlikeliest literature for their own psychoanalytical, anthropological or Marxist theories.[123]

3.3.2. Early Allegorical Interpretation

Allegorical interpretation was soon in full swing. Already in the sixth century BCE, Theogenes of Rhegium was explaining the warring gods of the *Iliad* as personifications of conflicting cosmic forces – fire, water, moon, air and the like, or moral qualities (Athena standing for wisdom, Ares for folly, Aphrodite for lust and so forth). In the next century, Metrodorus of Lampsacus, a pupil of the philosopher Anaxagoras, is reported to have interpreted them as parts of the human body and the heroes of the *Iliad* as parts of the universe. We know very little about these early interpreters. Our evidence for them is mostly late.[124] Their views and theories were overtaken by those of later critics.

We have, however, an extended and remarkable specimen of early exegesis in a papyrus from the early fourth century BCE, found at Derveni in Northern Greece and first unrolled in 1952.[125] The greater part of the surviving text is a line-by-line commentary on a cosmogonical poem ascribed to the legendary Orpheus, a mythical narrative which it expounds in the terms of current 'Presocratic' natural philosophy. The commentator combines some careful, if inaccurate, philology – he tries to determine the meaning of a word by reference to Homeric usage (XXII), with strongly allegorical interpretation – indeed, he tells us, "we must state that Orpheus turns the poem into a riddle about things at every word" (IX. 5 f.). The poet may use the language of ordinary mortals, but this can be 'misleading' (XIX παραγωγόν). The realities of which he speaks are quite different, known only to a few. Thus the air,

---

[120] Heraclitus, I. 1.

[121] See Cicero, *de natura deorum* I. 41, and Long, 49, 53. The Stoics seem in fact to have been more interested in demythologizing Hesiod than Homer (see Long, 62–64).

[122] See J. Tate, "The Beginnings of Greek Allegory", *Classical Review* 41 (1927) 214–15; idem, "Plato and Allegorical Interpretation", *CQ* 23 (1929) 142–54 and 24 (1930) 1–10; idem, "On the History of Allegorism", *CQ* 24 (1934) 105–14.

[123] Cf. Frye (1974) 8.

[124] See Diels-Kranz § 8 for the scanty fragments of Theagenes and § 61 for Metrodorus. The work of these and other early interpreters of Homer, such as Stesimbrotus of Thasos and Glaucon of Rhegium, are usefully discussed by Richardson (1975) 69–77.

[125] On which see particularly W. Burkert, "Orpheus und die Vorsokratiker: Bemerkungen zum Derveni-Papyrus und zur pythagoräischen Zahlenlehre", AuA 14 (1968) 93–114. A text of the papyrus can be found in *ZPE* 47 (1982) 301–12.

which masters all things, is really divine reason. The knowledge which the author possesses, and which he ascribed to Orpheus, turns out to be an astonishing mixture of ideas derived from Diogenes of Apollonia, from Anaxagoras and from the Atomists, Democritus and Leucippus. His eclecticism is significant. We find it again in later exegesis, when Heraclitus credits Homer with doctrines from more than one school of philosophy,[126] or when Philo, forsaking his usual mixture of Stoicism and dogmatic Platonism, resorts to sceptical theory – Anesidemus' 'modes' – to expound the drunkenness of Noah.[127] In such cases, the expositor is less concerned with staking out a philosophical position of his own than with 'translating' a received text into a recognizably contemporary intellectual idiom.[128]

3.3.3. Plato

The validity of such exposition, and the value of the literature which it expounded, was radically challenged by Plato. An expert on Homer like Ion, he argued,[129] may certainly be an interpreter of the poet's meaning, but he will need much more than a knowledge of Homer to judge whether what the poet says is right.[130] Plato notoriously condemned the work of Homer and other poets on various grounds, moral, psychological and metaphysical. Their disgusting tales – the binding of Hera, the casting out of Hephaestus, the battle of the gods – cannot be allowed in the ideal republic – with or without ὑπόνοιαι.[131] But poetry is not only immoral in its contents. Worse still, it attracts and strengthens the lower, emotional parts of the soul[132] at the expense of its rational element, the reason which enables it to grasp the true intellectual realities, the world of 'forms' or 'ideas'. Nor can poetry depict that true world. It can only mimic the sensible world around us, which itself is a mere reflection of the true intellectual world. Art and poetry can only deliver an "imitation of an image".[133]

But Plato himself, on occasion, had to follow the poets and resort to myth, thereby generating his own share of hermeneutical difficulties. It was hardly possible, for instance, to treat the fate of the soul after death – a theme of the *Gorgias*, the *Phaedo* , and the *Phaedrus* as well as the *Republic* – in any other manner. Again, his most influential dialogue, the *Timaeus*, describes its account of the world's creation as no more than an εἰκὼς μῦθος, a 'likely tale'.[134] True knowledge, as Plato saw it, can only be about the eternal truths in the world of ideas, of which our constantly changing perceptible world is

---

126 See F. Buffière, Introduction to *Héraclite: Allégories d'Homère* (1962) xxxi–xxxix.

127 Philo, *Ebr.* 169–205.

128 Another remarkable, albeit fictitious and even satirical, piece of extended exegesis comes in Plato's *Protagoras* (338e–348b), when the speakers turn their attention to a poem by Simonides. See Schreckenberg (1966) 1176f.

129 Plato, *Ion* 530c.

130 Plato, *Ion* 536e.

131 Plato, *Republic* 378d. These 'sub-meanings' would simply not be understood by the school children whose education Plato is discussing at this point.

132 Plato, *Republic* 602c–605c.

133 Plato, *Republic* 598b.

134 Plato, *Timaeus* 29d.

simply a 'likeness', an εἰκών. Hence no account of our world can be more than 'likely'. Nor was it clear to his successors whether the narrative of creation in the *Timaeus* was to be understood literally or, as most Neoplatonists saw it, allegorically, i.e. as an extended metaphor illustrating, like the diagrams which mathematicians draw 'for the sake of instruction',[135] the continuous ordering of an uncreated universe.

Hostile as he was to allegory, the thrust of Plato's own philosophy was in a sense allegorical:[136] beyond the world of the senses, concealed yet intimated by it, lies the world of reality waiting to be discovered – in rather the same way that, for Origen, there are 'spiritual' senses of Scripture awaiting discovery beyond its literal sense. Moreover, on Plato's view, what 'drags' the mind to seek out the intelligible world are the oddities presented to it by the senses, the fact, for instance, that the same object may look both large and small.[137] On similar lines, Origen was to argue that the 'scandals', 'stumbling blocks' and 'impossibilities' of Scripture in its literal sense arouse us to find its 'diviner' content.[138]

3.3.4. Hellenistic and Stoic Approaches

Plato could hardly stop people from believing that there is truth in poetry or from using allegory to extract it. The centuries after his death saw a variety of views on the subject. Eratosthenes, the great Alexandrian scholar and scientist, argued that poets aim to entertain, not to instruct, and that it would be wrong to look for factual information (ἱστορία) in poetry.[139] But most people clung, like Strabo, to the traditional view of Homer as a source of wisdom and factual knowledge.[140] They had to admit, however, that he and the other poets had provided this knowledge in somewhat diluted form, adding fable to real events, like gold plating on silver.[141] Their attempts to penetrate the plating of fable ranged from relatively casual rationalizations, like the claim that the myth of the golden fleece had grown from accounts of how mountain torrents in the Caucasus were once panned for gold with fleecy sheepskins,[142] to the extravagant allegorizations with which Crates of Mallos interpreted the *Iliad* in terms of his own eclectic cosmology.[143] We

---

[135] Aristotle, *de caelo* 280a1 f.

[136] Coulter (1976) 26f.

[137] See Plato, *Republic* 523a–524c.

[138] Origen, *de principiis* IV. 2.9.

[139] See Strabo, I.2.3. See D.M. Schenkevelt, "Strabo on Homer", *Mnemosyne* 39 (1976) 52–64.

[140] Strabo went so far as to call Homer "the founder of empirical geography" (I. 1.2).

[141] Strabo, I. 2.9. Cf. Ps.-Plutarch, *de Homero* II. 6.

[142] Strabo, XI. 2.19.

[143] On Crates, see Porter (1992) 85–114. The fragments of Crates have been collected by H.J. Mette in *Sphairopoiia: Untersuchungen zur Kosmologie des Krates von Pergamon* (München 1935), and *Parateresis: Untersuchungen zur Sprachtheorie des Krates von Pergamon* (Halle 1952). The first head of the library at Pergamum, Crates (2nd century BCE) was notorious for applying his σφαιροποιΐα, his spherical model of the universe, to passages of Homer. The shields of Achilles and Agamemnon were images of the circular cosmos in the making (*Iliad* 18.481–9, 11.32–40; Porter, 1992, 91–94); the theomachy was a picture of the cosmos at strife with itself (*Iliad* 21.385–20; Porter, 99f.), while the casting of Hephaestus down from heaven turned out to be

also know of attempts to defend Homer by running through the problematic episodes of the Iliad and the Odyssey and showing that they can all be given a respectable philosophical interpretaton, the procedure of pseudo-Heraclitus' *Quaestiones Homericae*, or to argue, like the *De Homero* attributed to Plutarch, by allegory and selective quotation, that he had possessed up-to-date knowledge of all the disciplines and had indeed been a philosopher[144] – even if his allegiance, Stoic, Epicurean, Peripatetic or Academic, was uncertain and unimportant.[145] (Both these works come from the first two centuries CE.)

The most serious and successful Hellenistic attempt to get philosophical truth out of poetic fable was made by the Stoics. To do so, they were quite prepared to use allegory, believing as they did that divine *Logos* was at work everywhere,[146] not least in ancient religion and primitive poetry. On the surface, these might have little to do with Stoic doctrine; they might also, if deeply investigated, reveal a pure pristine truth. Our natural ideas, the 'common notions' with which all human beings are born about what is good and what the gods are like,[147] were clearest at the beginning of history. Since then they have been obscured, in the same way that human language, through centuries of careless usage, has lost its original clarity.[148] In language and literature alike, the primal rationality has to be sought under the surface.

The Stoics looked on early Greek poetry as a source for this primal rationality. Recognising that much of Homer's or Hesiod's poetry was merely 'in line with opinion',[149] Zeno and Chrysippus were not concerned with the poet's intention or literary merits, but just with the truths which, known or unbeknown to him, his poetry might contain. The myths which it related might themselves be shocking. They could still offer intimations of natural principles – *physica ratio non inelegans inclusa est in impias fabulas* – and of primitive insights into nature. Underlying the stupid story about the castration of Ouranos, for instance, lay the quite correct observation that ether, the highest principle, does not need genitals in order to procreate.[150] Nor was it only literature which contained such intimations. The Stoics could find them in

---

part of a somewhat bizarre attempt by Zeus to measure the universe (Crates, Fr. 22a; Mette [= Heraclitus 27.2] on *Iliad* 1.589–93; see Porter 95–97). What Homer said in his archaic and personal manner Crates translates into truths of σφαιροποιΐα (Fr. 34A (238.9–11); Mette). His interpretations were frequently far fetched; and he was prepared to do violence to Homer's text, in order to establish them (Fr. 33 = Plutarch 938 d). His aim, however, was not to support his cosmology by interpretations of Homer, so much as to illuminate Homer by means of that cosmology, to bring out the cosmic resonances and hence the sublimity of Homer's narrative (see Porter, 1992, 101–103). Crates, in short, was a literary critic.

144 On these works see, further, Siegert 4.1, above.

145 Seneca, *Epistle* 88.5.

146 Cp. Pfeiffer (1968) 237.

147 See Plutarch, 1041 e, 1051 e; and Frede, Chaeremon, 2088 f.

148 Language is now, with its glaring discrepancies between grammatical form and semantic content (e.g. the fact that we speak of single cities like 'Thebes' or 'Athens' in the plural), in a state of 'anomaly'. (Chrysippus wrote volumes on the subject.) See Pohlenz (1964) 42 f; and M. Frede, "Principles of Stoic grammar", *The Stoics* (ed. J. Rist; Berkeley 1978; 27–76) 69–74.

149 Long (1992) 61.

150 Cicero, *De natura Deorum* II. 64.

ritual and even in works of art.[151] Their principal route to the original beliefs of mankind, however, seems to have been etymology, the enquiry into the true original meaning of words. Analysis of what the names and epithets of a god such as 'earthshaking Posidon', had first meant would reveal, they thought, the beliefs of those who had first given him them,[152] and these beliefs could contain a kernel of truth. (The idea goes back to Plato.)[153] Stoic etymology was less an exercise in historical linguistics than in theology. Our fullest document for it, a manual by a certain Cornutus from the reign of Nero, is in fact entitled "Compendium of the Traditions of Greek Theology".[154] Discussing not only the names and epithets of gods, but also the symbolism of their attributes,[155] the work aims to reconstruct those traditions and instil an enlightened piety.

But the primitivism of the Stoa, or at least of the 'Old' Stoa, was limited. The Stoics were certainly interested in primitive religion, not only of the Greeks but of Mages, Egyptians, Phrygians, Libyans and Celts;[156] in reading the poets, they were eager to distinguish original material from later invention, and to reveal what insights it might contain.[157] But natural insight into moral or theological truth is not the same thing as wisdom, the 'understanding of things divine and human', though it can certainly provide a basis for philosophical theory. Such insight can fade, as history has shown. It needs to be reinforced and articulated by philosophy, the active pursuit of wisdom, if men are to become truly good and wise. "Virtue is not a gift of nature", as Seneca put it, "to become good takes art".[158]

Stoic interpretations of ancient poetry are commonly seen as the model for Jewish and Christian interpretations of the Old Testament.[159] But the contrast between their premises and those of the Stoa is striking. Jews and Christians believed that their Scriptures were divinely inspired and true throughout, even if their truth is sometimes – deliberately – veiled in obscurity. The Stoics made no such claim for Homer or any other ancient poet, maintaining simply that men of old had seen things a bit more clearly than we do, though their insights may have been obscured by the passing of time. Nor was the ancient material that authoritative. It served, at most, as a support for Stoic teachings and was to be evaluated accordingly. The work of the ancient theologians could never be more than a handmaid of Stoic philosophy. In Jewish and

[151] Chrysippus notoriously allegorized the fellation of Zeus by Hera, depicted in a mural at Argos, as the ingestion by matter of seminal principles to form the cosmos (*Stoicorum Veterum Fragmenta* II. 1071–5).

[152] Compare Long (1992) 54.

[153] *Cratylus* 397 d, etc.

[154] See A. D. Nock, "Kornutos", PWSup 5 (Stuttgart 1931) 995–1005; G. Most, "Cornutus and Stoic Allegoresis", ANRW II/36.3, 2014–65.

[155] E. g. the fact that Aphrodite likes the dove more than any other bird (46.9–12) or that Rhea is shown rejoicing in drums, cymbals, horn-blowing and torch-light processions (5.11–15).

[156] See Cornutus, ch. 17, 26.9–11 (Lang).

[157] There was nothing unprecedented in this. Aristotle too (*Metaphysics* XII. 1074 c1–14) had believed that there might be some truth in the oldest theological traditions.

[158] *Epistle* 90.44: "Non enim dat natura virtutem; ars est bonum fieri".

[159] E. g. by Dörrie (1974) 130 f.

Christian theology, the order was reversed. Philosophy, like any other product of mere human reason, was accepted only as a servant of revealed religion. *Ancilla theologiae philosophia*.

3.3.5. Later Antiquity

In the first two centuries CE, the restrained approach of the Stoa to ancient poetry and myth gave way to something rather more ambitious. By Seneca's time there was a tendency, already a century old (it goes back to Posidonius), to play down the distinction between natural insight and philosophical theory.[160] According to "some of the younger Stoics", "the first, earth-born men ... possessed, as it were, an extra organ of sense in the sharpness of thought with which they apprehended the divine nature".[161] On this view, shared by – amongst others – Seneca's contemporary the Egyptian Stoic Chaeremon,[162] what counts is simply awareness of the major moral and theological truths, an awareness which the first, as yet uncorrupted mortals possessed in abundance, and which may, it was hoped, be regained; in comparison, philosophical reflection is at most a secondary activity.

This idea of 'ancient wisdom', awaiting discovery in the poetry and literature of ancient peoples, set the stage for the hermeneutic extravagances of late antiquity. Where the Stoa had sought a basis, not a substitute, for its own philosophy, later Stoics and Neoplatonists increasingly held the idea that the wisdom of ancient peoples contained in fragments a primal revelation of the truths which they themselves were expounding. The ancients had said it all, but not 'explicitly'.[163] They were now credited with a much fuller philosophical picture of the universe than the Stoics had allowed them – and also with much greater guile in concealing it. The ancient Egyptians in fact had invented allegory for that purpose, Chaeremon maintained;[164] and it was to be the standard belief that Homer had been a 'strong' allegorist, deliberately employing allegory and riddles.[165]

Allegorical interpretation was correspondingly extended and systematized. Where the Stoics had sought information piecemeal through etymologies of words and epithets, whole episodes and even whole poems were now taken as allegories. Neoplatonists came to interpret the *Iliad* in its entirety as a story about souls drawn by transient beauty, symbolized by Helen, into a world of incessant strife. They saw the *Odyssey* as the tale of one soul's escape from the perilous sea of generation. This platonizing account of the *Odyssey* goes back at least to Numenius, who attempted to harmonize, amongst other things, its lines on the cave of the nymphs[166] with details from the myth of Er in Plato's *Republic*. The two gates which Homer mentions correspond, he

---

[160] See Frede, Chaeremon, 2089; Celsus, 5193.

[161] Sextus Empiricus, *Adversos mathematicos* IX. 28.

[162] Frede, Chaeremon, 2091.

[163] Plotinus, *Enn.* V. 1.8.11 f.

[164] Test. 12 (van der Horst). Cf. Fr. 12 (van der Horst).

[165] Porphyry at Stobaeus, II. 14 f. Compare Origen, *De principiis* IV. 2.9.

[166] *Odyssey* 13.102–12 See F. Buffière, *Les Mythes d'Homère et la pensée grecque* (Paris 1956) 444–66.

claimed, to the two chasms seen by Er as well as to the tropics of Cancer and Capricorn.[167] These in their turn correspond to the 'gates of the sun' mentioned at *Odyssey* 24.12 along with the 'people of dreams' who themselves are to be identified, according to Pythagoras, with souls gathered into the Milky Way, so called from the milk with which they are nourished when they fall into genesis.[168] Numenius' conflation was readily justified. Homer and Plato were both of them mouthpieces of the same *philosophia perennis*; and fragments of the primeval text should be brought into harmony. Nor had this philosophy been confined to the Greek world. Numenius boldly drew the consequences, cheerfully bringing Parmenides into the discussion along with information about the Roman *saturnalia* and the Egyptian New Year.[169] In the same way, he supported his interpretation of the Naiads as souls settling on the waters with references to Egyptian mythology and Gen 1:2, "the spirit of God hovered on the water".[170] Christian attempts to harmonize the Old and the New Testaments look tame in comparison.

3.4. *'Impersonation'*

If allegory was the supreme device for squeezing truth out of ancient texts, it was not the only hermeneutical principle that Jews and Christians derived from classical culture. There were other, less drastic ways of rescuing the literary classics from at least charges of self-contradiction or immorality. It might be enough to show, by setting an offensive passage in its broader context that the author did not himself subscribe to what he was saying, as Plutarch does with the story of Aphrodite and Ares.[171] Offensive utterances in a work may be by speakers from whom the author can be seen to dissociate himself: he need not be speaking *in propria persona*. In the same way, if a poem says one thing in one place and another elsewhere, if Homer appears to be recommending wine in one line and rejecting the recommendation a few lines later,[172] the reason may simply be that the speakers are different; the poet need not be contradicting himself.

This solution of asking which person was speaking in any given passage, the λύσις ἐκ προσώπου as it was called, was one which interpreters of the Bible were happy to use. It brought with it a further consideration. If a character was meant to be vile, it was quite proper, indeed a mark of literary excellence, for his utterances too to be vile,[173] since that would show the author's mastery of προσωποποιΐα. This rhetorical technique of 'personification' or 'impersonation',[174] of putting words into the mouth of some person

[167] *Odyssey* 13.109–111; Plato, *Republic* 614cd, 615de, Numenius, Fr. 31 (des Places).
[168] Numenius, Fr. 32 (des Places).
[169] Parmenides, Fr.1. 1 (Diels-Kranz). Numenius, Fr. 31 (des Places).
[170] Numenius, Fr. 30 (des Places).
[171] Plutarch, 19e–20a, on *Odyssey* 8.266–369. See Coulter (1976) 10f.
[172] *Iliad* 6.261 and 265. See Neuschäfer (1987) 263f.
[173] Cf. Plutarch, 18d: "to imitate something fine is not the same thing as to imitate something finely".
[174] See, above, 3.2. Here, as in the case of allegory, hermeneutic and rhetorical theory went hand in hand.

other than oneself, or even of some abstraction like the city of Rome or the laws of Athens, could only work if the words were in character with their purported speaker. The trick was to match the two.

Origen was familiar enough with the principles of προσωποποιΐα. He knew that Euripides had been ridiculed for giving barbarian women and slave girls verses containing ideas which could only have come from a philosopher like Anaxagoras.[175] He could also exploit the difference between the author's own views and the utterances of his speakers. It was Christian belief, anyway, that the true author of Scripture was the Holy Ghost. In a highly original way, Origen combined this with his own belief in the double sense of Scripture.[176] A verse like Ps 3:6, "I lie down and sleep; I wake again, for the Lord sustains me", is literally a historical utterance by King David and mystically an intimation by Christ of his future death and resurrection; the Holy Ghost has put the same words into the mouths of both speakers. Conversely, Ps 29:4, "O Lord thou hast brought up my soul from Hell", is literally the utterance of Christ and only in a more figurative way of David.[177]

Even here, however, Origen may have found a certain precedent in pagan literary criticism. The *Art of Rhetoric*, ascribed to Dionysius of Halicarnassus, takes a passage from Euripides' *Melanippe* as an example of doubly 'figured' or veiled speaking (λόγος ἐσχηματισμένος): when the heroine begins: "It is not my story – it comes from my mother – that earth and sky were once one",[178] the Anaxagorean discourse which follows serves not only to further her own ulterior motives (she has exposed her children who have just been discovered in the care of a bull, and is now attemping to dissuade her father from burning them as ominous monstrosities); it is also introduced with the hint that Euripides himself is no longer committed to the doctrines in it.[179]

3.5. *'Elucidating Homer from Homer'*

An entirely different approach[180] to poetry and literature goes back to Aristotle, the greatest of Plato's pupils. He was as aware as his master of the charges that could be levelled against poetry.[181] But his response,[182] unlike Plato's, was not to judge and condemn poetry by external standard of truth or morality; it was rather to claim that poetry is its own proper domain with its own function and its own rules, to be judged accordingly.[183] Thus the aim of a tragedy is to arouse and purge the emotions of pity and fear[184] (so much for Plato's complaint about poets' pandering to the passions!); and the ques-

175 Origen, *Contra Celsum* VII. 36.
176 See Neuschäfer (1987) 272f.
177 Neuschäfer, 275.
178 Euripides, Fr. 884 (Nauck).
179 [Dionys. Hal.] *Rhet*. 8.10, 9.11. See Russell (1981) 124f.
180 See above, 3.2, and Coulter (1976) 7–9.
181 It says things which are impossible, irrational, morally dangerous, self-contradictory or simply incorrect when it comes to arts like medicine or warfare (1461b22–5).
182 See, above all, *Poetics* c. 25 1460b1–1461b25.
183 See Porter (1992) 75f.
184 Aristotle, *Poetics* 1449b24–8.

tion to ask of a tragedy is how far it achieves that end, not whether its plot is morally acceptable or reflects an external reality.[185] Correctness in poetry is not the same thing as correctness in morals[186] – in the same way, incidentally, that one cannot demand of an orator the intellectal rigour that one requires of a mathematician.[187] For poetry has its own internal standards. The truth of a poem is at most a contingent part of it. The poet portrays not only what is the case, but also what was, or what people say is, or what ought to be the case; and he can take all manner of liberties with language – by way of metaphor, unusual vocabulary, and so forth – in order to express himself.[188] On this basis, Aristotle could counter a good many of the objections raised against poetry, without resorting to allegorical interpretation.[189] His strictly literary approach could only be of limited use to exegetes expounding the truth in Scripture, and his claim that "Homer taught other poets the right way to tell lies"[190] would hardly have recommended him or Homer to them! But the principle that poetry, indeed the works of any one poet, is its own domain had an enduring hermeneutic importance. It underpinned the principle associated with the great Alexandrian scholar Aristarchus and formulated as "clarifying Homer by Homer".

The formulation "clarifying Homer from Homer"[191] is not attested before Porphyry: "seeing fit to clarify Homer by Homer, I showed him expounding himself, sometimes from the immediate context, sometimes in other passages".[192] Whether or not the formulation goes back to Aristarchus himself,[193] it does summarize his philological method, though what he himself is reported to have said is somewhat broader; "interpreters should take what Homer said more in the manner of myth (μυθικώτερον), not fussing about with anything that the poet did not say", that is, with allegorical interpretations.[194]

As a philological device for explaining the meaning of words, the principle of "clarifying Homer by Homer", i.e. by the use of parallels, was obvious and time honoured.[195] Nor was it confined to the interpretation of poetry. Galen writes of using Hippocrates himself to expound Hippocratean terminology.[196]

---

185 It may indeed suit the poet's purpose to choose a plausible impossibility in preference to a possibility that is implausible (1461b11).

186 *Poetics* 1460b13f.

187 *Nicomachean Ethics* 1094b26f.

188 Aristotle, *Poetics* 1460b8–13.

189 In his six books of *Homeric Questions*, on which *Poetics* 25 is based, Aristotle in fact used a variety of methods to deal with problems in Homer – appeals to poetic usage, historical research, textual emendation, even the occasional allegorical interpretation. See Lamberton, Introduction to *Homer's Ancient Readers* (1992) xiii–xv.

190 Aristotle, *Poetics* 1460a18f.

191 See Neuschäfer (1987) 276–85; cf. also, above, Siegert, chap. 4, sect. 1.4.

192 Porphyry, *Quaestiones Homericae* (297.16; Schräder) on *Iliad* 6.201.

193 Contrast Neuschäfer (1987) 277 with Porter (1992) 73–77.

194 D-scholium on *Iliad* 5.385. See Porter, 70f.

195 It would have been suggested by the way in which Homer himself can elucidate one word by a phrase immediately following it. See Pfeiffer (1968) 4.

196 Galen, *De comate secundum Hippocratem* 1.5 (Corpus Medicorum Graecorum V. 92, 182.23f). See Schreckenberg (1966) 1192, Neuschäfer (1987) 277, Porter (1992) 74f.

In the context of legal interpretation and forensic rhetoric, it made sense to deal with cases of obscurity or ambiguity by looking at what the lawgiver or testator had said elsewhere; as an indication of his intentions, these would certainly be better than one's own guesswork.[197] Later on, the principle was to be extended by commentators on Plato and Aristotle.[198] Where a hard or ambiguous passage invited capricious, far-fetched interpretations, parallel passages in the author provided a welcome check.[199] What the exegete needs is a feeling for the consonance (τὸ σύμφωνον) of his oeuvre as a whole.[200]

Christian commentators cultivated a similar attitude towards the consonance of the Bible, particularly that between Old and New Testaments. Origen was as assiduous as any pagan commentator in explaining difficult words with the aid of *loci paralleli*. Where he went far beyond mere philology was in using such parallels to give a spiritual meaning to texts that were literally obscure, "to trace out from similar words that meaning that is strewn all over Scripture for whatever is impossible if taken literally".[201] Even here, though, Origen's practice may have been more in line with the Aristarchan principle than one might have supposed. The 'Homer' invoked to 'clarify Homer' could mean either the poems of Homer, or it could mean something like the genre, the narrative framework and inner logic, of Homeric poetry.[202] On that principle Aristarchus could interpret a passage from the *Iliad* with a passage from Hesiod![203] 'According to Homer' could mean simply 'in line with Homer's way of thinking', with allowance for 'poetic license'. Aristarchus had pleaded for an interpretation of Homer that respected the conventions of myth, without importing allegories from outside. But if you believe, as Origen believed, that Scripture is intrinsically full of allegorical, spiritual meaning and you seek in some other part of the Bible a spiritual meaning for a passage that is literally obscure, you are not going outside Scripture at all. You are still elucidating Scripture from Scripture.

4. Epilogue: Pagan and Biblical Exegesis

In his work *Against the Christians*, Porphyry wrote that Origen, "a Greek with a Greek education" had "foisted Greek conceptions on foreign myths".

> For he always had Plato with him. He was familiar with the works of Numenius and Cronius, Allophanes, Longinus and Moderatus, Nicomachus and the well-known Pythagoreans. He also made use of books by Chaeremon the Stoic and Cornutus from whom he learned the transpositional mode (μεταληπτικὸς τρόπος) of explaining Greek mysteries, which he applied to Jewish texts.[204]

197 Cicero, *De inventione* II. 128.
198 Neuschäfer (1987) 276.
199 Proclus, *Theologia platonica* I. 2.
200 Elias, *In Aristotelis categorias*, CAG 18.1 (1900) 122.25–123.11.
201 *De principiis* IV. 3.5.
202 Porter (1992) 79, 84.
203 He explained *Iliad* 23.632 by invoking Hesiod Fr. 18 (Merkelbach-West).
204 Porphyry ap. Eusebius, *HE* VI. 19.7f.

Origen's way of thinking was indeed highly Platonist, as was that of his predecessors. But the philosophy that he read into the Bible was no more incongruous than the Platonism which Porphyry himself and Numenius before him extracted from Homer or "foisted on foreign myths". He certainly made use of hermeneutic methods associated with Cornutus, Chaeremon and others. But his debt to Greek hermeneutics went way beyond mere allegorical interpretations of ritual.

The hermeneutic theory which Origen expounds in *De principiis* IV. 1–3, with its account of providential inspiration running all through the Bible (though of course, like Providence itself, more discernible in some places than in others), of literal and spiritual meanings, and of the relations between them, is remarkable for its systematic thoroughness. It owes much to Stoic theories of cosmic providence.[205] Where Origen goes beyond the Stoa is in treating his Scriptures as no less providential, no less permeated by God's *Logos*, than the cosmos itself. "All scripture is divinely inspired" (2 Tim 3:16). The divine inspiration which its expositors, Jewish and Christian alike, claimed for it, however they envisaged the process,[206] was vastly more thorough and serious than anything understood as such by their pagan counterparts, for whom inspiration, most of the time, was as much a guarantee of literary excellence as of truth.[207] Moreover, Philo, Clement and Origen were working on a canon of writings rather more restricted and unified than the materials available to a pagan in search of ancient wisdom. They could examine it, and trace the workings of divine Providence in it, with correspondingly greater thoroughness.

Origen's work on the Bible anticipates – in part it provoked – the still more systematic attempts by pagans in the following centuries to arrange the canonical texts of late Neoplatonism – the works of Orpheus, Pythagoras, Plato and the Chaldaean oracles – in a hierarchy, as expressions at different levels – mythical, mathematical, dialectical and categorical – of divinely revealed truth.[208] In the same way, the Prologue to Origen's *Commentary on the Canticle*, with its schema of topics to be discussed, looks forward to the elaborate introductions of commentaries by later Neoplatonists on Plato and Aristotle.[209] In both cases, Origen appears to be way ahead of his time. The appearance may be deceptive, due simply to the fact that his works are better preserved than those of Numenius and his other pagan competitors. What is clear is that he and they were using very similar methods for very similar purposes, and that he was in no way lagging behind.

---

205 See, particularly, M. Harl, *Origène Philocalie 1–20: Sur les écritures et la lettre sur L'histoire de Suzanne* (ed. M. Harl/N. de Lange; SC 303; Paris 1983) 59–74.

206 On Philo's 'mediumistic' concept of inspiration, see above, Siegert 4.4. For Origen's rather more differentiated ideas, see E. Nardoni, "Origen's concept of Biblical Inspiration", *SCent* 4 (1984) 9–23.

207 Russell (1981) 69–83.

208 See Hadot (1987) 30–33.

209 See Neuschäfer (1987) 57–84 ('Die Topik des Kommentarprologs'); I. Hadot, "Les introductions aux commentaires exégétiques chez les auteurs néoplatoniciens et les auteurs chrétiens", *Les règles de l'interpréation* (ed. M. Tardieu; Paris 1987) 99–122.

CHAPTER THIRTEEN

The Christian Exegesis of the Old Testament in the Alexandrian Tradition

By J. N. B. CARLETON PAGET, Cambridge

General bibliography: H. FRHR. VON CAMPENHAUSEN, *The Formation of the Christian Bible* (ET London 1972); H. CHADWICK and J. E. L. OULTON, *Alexandrian Christianity: Selected translations of Clement and Origen with introduction and notes* (LCC 2; London 1954); B. DE MARGERIE, *Introduction à l'histoire de l'exégèse. 1. Les Pères grecs et orientaux* (Paris 1980); R. M. GRANT, *The Letter and the Spirit* (London 1957); R. P. C. HANSON, *Allegory and Event: A Study of the Sources and Significance of Origen's Interpretation of Scripture* (London 1959); W. HORBURY, "Old Testament Interpretation in the Works of the Church Fathers", Mikra (1988) 727–787; C. MONDÉSERT (ed.), *Le Monde grec ancien et la Bible* (BTT 1; Paris 1984); J. PÉPIN, *Mythe et Allégorie: Les origines grecques et les contestations judéo-chrétiennes* (Revised edition, Paris 1976); M. SIMONETTI, *Lettera e/o allegoria. Un contributo alla Storia dell'esegesi patristica* (Roma 1985; ET: *Biblical Interpretation in the Early Church*, Edinburgh 1994); T. F. TORRANCE, *Divine Meaning: Studies in Patristic Hermeneutics* (Edinburgh 1995).

1. The Context of Alexandrian Exegesis of the Old Testament

General books: Y. AMIR, "Authority and Interpretation of Scripture in the Writings of Philo", Mikra (1988) 421–453; G. BARDY, "Aux Origines de l'Ecole d'Alexandrie", *RSR* 27 (1937) 65–90; W. BAUER, *Orthodoxy and Heresy in Earliest Christianity* (ET New York 1971) 44–53; P. BORGEN and L. SKARSTEN, "Quaestiones et Solutiones: Some Observations on the Form of Philonic Exegesis", StudPhil 4 (1976–77) 1–15; W. BOUSSET, *Jüdisch-christlicher Schulbetrieb in Alexandria und Rom; literarische Untersuchungen zu Philo und Clemens von Alexandria, Justin und Irenäus* (Göttingen 1915); R. VAN DEN BROEK, "Juden und Christen in Alexandrien im 2. und 3. Jahrhundert", *Juden und Christen in der Antike* (ed. J. van Amersfoort/J. van Oort; Kampen 1990) 101–115; D. DAWSON, *Allegorical Readers and Cultural Revision in Ancient Alexandria* (Berkeley 1992); N. R. M. DE LANGE, *Origen and the Jews* (Cambridge 1975); C. W. GRIGGS, *Early Egyptian Christianity from its origins to 451 c. e.* (Leiden 1990); A. VAN DEN HOEK, *Clement of Alexandria and his use of Philo in the Stromateis* (Leiden 1988); idem, "How Alexandrian was Clement of Alexandria? Reflections on Clement and his Alexandrian Background", *HeyJ* 31 (1990) 179–194; A. F. J. KLIJN, "Jewish Christianity in Egypt", *The Roots of Egyptian Christianity* (ed. J. Goehring/B. A. Pearson; Philadelphia 1986) 161–175; S. LILLA, "Pantaenus", *The Encyclopedia of the Early Church*, 2 (ed. A. di Beradino; ET Cambridge 1992) 639; B. A. PEARSON, "Christians and Jews in First Century Alexandria", *HTR* 79 (1986) 206–216; idem, "Earliest Christianity in Egypt: Some Observations", *The Roots of Egyptian Christianity* (1986) 132–156; C. H. ROBERTS, *Manuscript, Society and Belief in Early Christian Egypt* (The Schweich Lectures of the British Academy, Oxford 1977); D. T. RUNIA, *Philo of Alexandria and the Timaeus of Plato* (Leiden 1986); idem, "The Structure of Philo's allegorical treatises; a review of two recent studies and some additional comments", *VC* 38 (1984) 209–256; idem, *Philo in Early Christian Literature: A Survey* (Assen 1993); R. WILDE, *The Treatment of Jews in the Greek Christian Fathers of the First Three Centuries* (Catholic University of America, Patristic Studies, vol. LXXXI; Washington 1949).

1.1. *The Jewish Context*

While we possess a relatively rich vein of Alexandrian Jewish sources for the period up to the death of Philo, for the period after that until the fourth century we have very little information. Some have explained this strange silence by reference to the Jewish revolt of 115–117 in the principate of Trajan. The results of this revolt, the argument goes, were so severe for the Jewish community in Alexandria and Egypt that it almost ceased to exist.[1] While this argument is sometimes exaggerated,[2] the thesis that the Jewish community in Alexandria was in a depleted state, at least towards the end of the second century, is confirmed by the lack of papyrological and inscriptional evidence and perhaps by the relative paucity of references to Jews in Clement's writings.[3] The evidence from Origen is much more difficult to assess in this respect. For while in his writings there is frequent reference to Jews, the majority of these come from the latter part of his life when he was resident in Caesarea.[4]

Hence, for whatever reason, we cannot say very much about the late second century Jewish community in Alexandria. But we can state with certainty that Christian exegesis owed much to Jewish writers of an earlier period, above all to Philo. From an early stage his writings seem to have been preserved by Christians and not Jews,[5] and Clement and Origen probably had access to the works via a library.[6] Philo's philosophical exegesis of the Pentateuch,[7] which no doubt followed in and developed earlier traditions,[8] provided Christian exegetes in Alexandria with a hermeneutical model, which could be adapted and modified to suit their own sometimes different needs. In this context it is important to note that the majority of borrowings from Philo are exegetical in character.

Before we describe the major tendencies in Jewish-Hellenistic exegesis, it is important to make two observations. First, the Jewish community in Alex-

---

[1] For the most recent endorsement of this thesis see Runia, Survey (1993) 120.

[2] See in this respect *CPJ* II no. 158 a where we have a papyrus indicating Hadrian's favoritism for the Jews; and also *Sib. Or.* 5:48–50, possibly of Egyptian origin, where the Jewish writer praises Hadrian. For the evidence relating to the Egyptian Jewish community in the second and third centuries see de Lange, Jews (1975) 8–9, though he describes this as "flimsy".

[3] For Clement's contacts with Jews see *Strom.* 1.11.2 where he speaks about learning from a Hebrew in Palestine, and also *Strom.* 2.2.1 for his desire to convert Jews. We should probably not place much store by Jerome's claim (*C. Ruf.* I.13, recorded in GCS III 225) that whenever Clement (he also mentions Origen and Eusebius) had a dispute about the Scriptures he would say that a Jew was the source of his opinion. Wilde, Treatment (1949) 171 and 180, who has brought together the other references to Jews in Clement's works, plays down the significance of their relative absence by arguing that his works are mainly directed to a pagan audience.

[4] See de Lange, Jews (1975), who lists Alexandrian references to Jews in Origen's Alexandrian works, and van den Broek, Juden (1990) 112–115.

[5] See Runia, Survey (1993) 22–23, who argues for Christian preservation after 117.

[6] For this view see Van den Hoek, Clement (1990) 190. There is no need to present the evidence for Clement's and Origen's knowledge of the text of Philo. See the studies by Van den Hoek (for Clement); and Runia, Survey (1993) 132–183 (for both).

[7] A term used by Runia in conscious opposition to those scholars like Wolfson who argue that Philo is a philosopher first and an exegete second (i.e. an exegetical philosopher).

[8] See the comments by Siegert above.

andria was diverse, consisting of groups with different interests to those represented by Philo. This is worth bearing in mind when we discuss the Alexandrian Christian community.[9] Secondly, Clement's and Origen's knowledge of Jewish exegetical traditions was not restricted to the works of Philo and his ilk. We should reckon also with a knowledge of some rabbinical traditions (in Origen's case vastly supplemented during his time in Caesarea),[10] a knowledge of versions other than the LXX, of apocryphal traditions such as *The Assumption of Moses* and the *Sibylline Oracles*, and, in the case of Clement, of a large number of other Jewish writers.[11]

1.2. Some Assumptions of Jewish-Hellenistic Exegesis of Scripture

1.2.1. The Greek Bible

Alexandrian Jewish exegetes were primarily interested in the interpretation of the Greek OT, especially the LXX. In the *Letter of Aristeas* the need is felt, implicitly at least, to defend this version (here referring exclusively to the translation of the Pentateuch), while Philo at one point implies that the translation was so perfect that it constituted a sister text to that of the Hebrew (*VM* 2.26–44).[12] In the time of Philo rival translations to the LXX probably existed, as suggested by New Testament biblical quotations following a version like that of Theodotion, the Greek Minor Prophets scroll from the Judean desert, and the defence of the LXX in the *Letter of Aristeas*.

1.2.2. The Priority of the Pentateuch

Philo, and his forerunner Aristobulus,[13] wrote almost exclusively on the Pentateuch.[14] Of course, other books traditionally placed amongst the Jewish scriptures were also regarded as sacred – Philo quotes from these as if they were part of a privileged canon. But they were evidently not accorded a position of similar authority to the Pentateuch. Why this should be the case is difficult to determine. Liturgical practice may have been a significant factor,[15] as also may have been the wider context in which exegesis took place: an emphasis upon the laws and the decisive events of early Israelite history would have seemed appropriate in the mixed cultural environment of Alexandria.

---

9 See Pearson, Earliest Christianity (1986) 145f.

10 Clement (*Strom.* 1.11.2) explicitly mentions a Jewish teacher he had in Palestine, who may well have provided him with rabbinic material.

11 On these see Van den Hoek, Clement (1990).

12 At 2.26 Philo states that in ancient times the laws were written in the Chaldean tongue, and remained in that form for many years. This could be taken to mean that the text was originally written in Hebrew, but is in Hebrew no longer, implying that its primary location is now in the Greek. For a discussion of the reference see Amir, Philo (1988) 442f. For the importance of the translation to Philo see his claim at *Mos.* 2.41–44 that every year there was a festival in which Jews commemorated the day on which the translation was presented to Ptolemy.

13 See Siegert, chap. 4.3 above.

14 In the LCC vol. 10 of the works of Philo, references to the Pentateuch take up 65 pages, and those to other OT writings a mere 5.

15 See Amir, Philo (1988) 423.

1.2.3. *Greek Paideia and the Scriptures*

Our fragments of Aristobulus make it clear that early on in the history of the Alexandrian Jewish community a need was felt to defend the Bible from intellectual attack by showing that its wisdom was not at odds with the Greek philosophy with which many educated Jews were becoming familiar. In this apologetic endeavour Moses, the assumed author of the Pentateuch, came to be regarded as the "fons et origo" of Greek thought and the utterer of superior teachings.[16] On this view, one was meant to study Greek philosophy, but only as a stage to the greater biblical truths.[17]

1.2.4. *Allegorical Exegesis*

A synthesis between Greek paideia and biblical theology was achieved by the use of the allegorical method. The text had a body consisting of the literal meaning, which was sometimes unworthy of the God who had inspired its writing, and a soul, which contained its deeper truths. All exegesis was a quest for this soul.[18] In this form of interpretation the Bible became a guide to the virtuous life, and the means by which one attained the ultimate vision of truth.

1.2.5. *The Lexical Character of Exegesis*

All exegesis consisted of the interpretation of the words of Scripture. What was written had to be taken seriously in the form in which it was found, however opaque that might appear. Much of Philo's exegesis consists of the interpretation of individual lemmata of Scripture in which grammatical, historical or other peculiarities act as the initial stimuli for interpretation. This feature of Philonic exegesis has led some scholars to conclude that in origin Hellenistic-Jewish exegesis began in the 'Questions and Answers' form, most obviously represented in Philo's *Quaestiones in Genesim et Exodum*, partially preserved in an Armenian translation.[19]

1.2.6. *Scripture Interpreting Scripture*

Because all Scripture was inspired, the use of one or several passages to interpret another was a quite legitimate means of interpretation. A particular feature of Philonic exegesis is the constant reference to other passages of Scripture to illuminate the initial passage under discussion.[20]

---

[16] Moses was regarded as the true sage, great teacher, and steward of the mysteries (*Gig.* 48; *Spec.* 1.59; *Plant.* 26). He also had attained the summit of philosophy (*Opif.* 8). For a concise dismissal of the view that he was regarded as in some sense divine see Runia, Timaeus (1986) 535 n.35. For the idea that the Greeks acquired their ideas from Moses see *Leg. alleg.* 1.108; *Spec.* 4.61. For the thesis that it was the preeminence accorded to Moses which led to an emphasis on the Pentateuch see Amir, ibid. 423.

[17] See *De Cong.* for this theme.

[18] For a classic description of the text in terms of body and soul, and the role of the exegete, see *De Vit. Cont.* 78

[19] See Borgen and Skarsten, Quaestiones (1976-77), for the view that Philo's commentaries are heavily influenced by the "Quaestiones" form, and see Runia, Structure (1984), for a measured endorsement of this view.

[20] On this aspect of Philo's exegesis see Runia, "Observations".

Many of the tendencies of this exegetical tradition were to be reflected in the writings of Clement and Origen, especially in terms of the actual methods of exegesis. However, their presupposition that Christ was the centre of revelation and not the Law understood as the Pentateuch, was to lead to the creation of an essentially Christian application of the allegorical method, in which the Mosaic revelation was to be seen in the shadow of another more significant revelation.

1.3. *The Christian Community*

A strange silence surrounds the origins of the Alexandrian Christian community.[21] In recent times, and in opposition to the radical thesis of heterodox/gnostic origins,[22] scholars have seen the Jewish community as the matrix out of which Christianity emerged.[23] In this context early Alexandrian Christianity is thought to have reflected the varieties of Alexandrian Judaism.[24] If the *Epistle of Barnabas* is an Alexandrian document, and this seems the most convincing theory,[25] then its contents would seem to confirm this thesis, for here sitting side by side we have material coming from a variety of theological provenances, all of which are of a palpably Jewish character.[26]

Again we can only speculate about the precise nature of the Alexandrian Christian community when Clement came to the city in c. 180. Much emphasis has been placed upon the somewhat elusive figure of Pantaenus, and the school, which Eusebius associates with him.[27] The evidence itself is difficult to assess,[28] and certainly does not allow us to create anything more than a skeletal reconstruction. We may venture to assert a number of things:

(1) Pantaenus, who seems to have been a Stoic philosopher from Sicily (Eusebius, *HE* 5.10.1), did not found the school at Alexandria, but he appears to have been its most distinguished "leader" before the arrival of Clement.[29] Clement held him "in higher esteem than all his other teachers ... to whose oral teaching Clement claims to have listened" (*Strom.* 1.11.1 and 3).[30]

(2) The term 'school' is probably too strong a term for the loose body which gathered around Pantaenus.

---

21 See Griggs, Alexandrian (1990) 28.

22 See Bauer, Orthodoxy (1971).

23 See Roberts, Manuscript (1977); Pearson, Earliest Christianity (1986); Klijn, Jewish (1986).

24 Pearson, Alexandrian (1986).

25 See Pearson, ibid. 212; and Dawson, Readers (1992) 174f.

26 Dawson, Readers (1992) 174f. In the epistle we have rabbinic (chs. 7 and 8), apocalyptic (4.3f. and 15.1f.) and allegorical (10) traditions nestling side by side.

27 Eusebius states that Pantaenus was the head of a school which had existed for some time (*HE* 5.10.1), that Clement joined the school as his own pupil, and that Clement became the head of the school and was succeeded by Origen (6.6.1).

28 For a sceptical assessment see Bardy, Origines (1937); and Dawson, Readers (1992) 219f. (echoing Bardy). For a more affirmative assessment and a critique of Bardy see Méhat (1966) 62–70. For a recent bibliography see Runia, Survey (1993) 133 n. 3. For the most thorough discussion of the matter see Lilla, Pantaenus (1992) 639.

29 As Runia, Survey (1993) 133, points out, it is strange that Eusebius, who was a pupil of Pamphilus, who himself knew two previous leaders of the school, gives us no information about leaders of the school before Pantaenus.

30 Lilla, ibid. 239.

(3) Its relationship with the Bishop of the city was equally loose and probably only reached official status under the leadership of Origen in the aftermath of the Severan persecution.[31]

(4) Its principle concern was the exegesis of Scripture. This is confirmed not only by Eusebius,[32] but Clement himself. If Pantaenus is the Sicilian Bee referred to in *Strom.* 1.11.2,[33] he is a bee who culls his teaching from the Scriptures. The only explicit reference to him in the Clement's work occurs at *Ecl. Proph.* 56 (Πάνταινος δὲ ἡμῶν) where we find a reference to Pantaenus' conviction that the prophets often use the present tense instead of the future or past.

(5) It is probable that the exegesis which was characteristic of the group attempted to draw together biblical revelation and philosophy, and that in the pursuit of this they made extensive use of Philo's works. This group may well have been responsible for the preservation of Philo's works.[34] It is also probable that the group engaged in debate with Gnostic Christians, and that their own Christianity laid a heavy emphasis on the attainment of revelation or gnosis through exegesis. The 'gnostic' character of their theology may have led other members of the Alexandrian community to treat them with suspicion.[35]

(6) There is no support for the view, first espoused by Bousset,[36] that *Strom.* 8, the *Excerpta ex Theodoto, Ecl. Proph.* and *Strom.* 6 and 7 are notes taken from lectures delivered by Pantaenus.

But the group around Pantaenus, to which Clement, and indirectly Origen, owed a good deal, was not the only group to expound Christianity.

The Alexandrian community no doubt contained Jews who had become Christians. These may have contributed their expertise to the exegesis of the OT. Daniélou has identified Judaeo-Christian traditions especially in the exegetical sections of the *Ecl. Proph.* Origen himself mentions the interpetations of converted Jews, though it is difficult to know whether such people formed an important element of his life in Alexandria. The presence in the community of Christians who advocated the adoption of Jewish practices is supported by the fact that we know Clement wrote a now almost completely lost work κατὰ Ἰουδαϊζόντων.[37]

Clement's need to defend his application of philosophy to the exegesis of the Bible witnesses to the presence in his community of those who suspected the whole "allegorical" enterprise. In their opinion philosophy was the prostitute, mentioned in Proverbs, whose lips dripped with honey (*Strom.* 1.29.6).

---

[31] See Dawson, ibid. 220–221.

[32] At *HE* 5.10.4 Eusebius describes Pantaenus as τοὺς θείων δογμάτων θησαυρὸς ὑπομνηματιζόμενος.

[33] This is the view of Eusebius (*HE* 5.11.1), most recently endorsed by Lilla, ibid. 639.

[34] Runia, Survey (1993) 22–23.

[35] See Lilla, ibid. 239 for a discussion of the synthetic nature of the theological system developed by the group.

[36] Schulbetrieb (1915) 156 f.

[37] Jewish-Christians, however, hardly feature at all in his works; and Eusebius states that he wrote the work for Alexander, the Bishop of Jerusalem (*HE* 6.13.3).

Origen in his *De Princ.* criticises these literalists because their interpretation of the OT forces them to adopt absurd opinions (*De Princ.* 4.2.2). Anti-philosophical/literalist positions were no doubt common amongst Christians from a variety of backgrounds. The Christian chiliasts with whom Bishop Dionysius had to deal were no doubt representatives of such a group.[38]

Gnostic exegetes also existed. Indeed there were probably two types of groups. The first group rejected the OT as an inspired text, pointing to the inferiority of its God, and the inadequate nature of its laws. These could be followers of Marcion, who was probably not, strictly speaking, a Gnostic, and of other individuals unrelated to Marcion. A second type of group regarded the OT as inspired, though perhaps with some reservations. Their exegesis could range in sophistication from the more philosophical type of exegesis of a Valentinus or a Basilides (especially focusing on the early chapters of Genesis),[39] where their theories of creation etc. were read into the text of Moses,[40] to a more literalist interpretation which used OT texts to support various idiosyncratic practices, such as encratism.[41]

Thus within the Alexandrian Christian community there was a wide range of approaches to the exegesis of the OT.[42] Its interpretation could be a polemical exercise. Not only was the interpreter bound to justify his own method of interpretation, and its results which often had a broadly revisionary character, but he was sometimes forced to defend the OT against the attack of those who deemed it a document unworthy of a place in the Christian canon. When we talk about the Alexandrian tradition of interpretation we invariably refer to Clement and Origen. We should be aware that their interpretative tradition, which had its origin in Jewish Hellenistic circles, did not have a monopoly on the hearts and the minds of the communities for which they wrote.

2. Clement and the Old Testament

Texts: O. Staehlin, *Clemens Alexandrinus erster Band: Protrepticus und Paedagogus* (GCS 12; Leipzig 1905; 3rd ed. U. Treu; Berlin 1972); O. Staehlin, *Clemens Alexandrinus zweiter Band: Stromata Buch I–VI* (GCS 15; Leipzig 1906; 4th ed. U. Treu; Berlin 1985); O. Staehlin, *Clemens Alexandrinus dritter Band: Stromata Buch VII–VIII; Excerpta ex Theodoto; Eclogae Propheticae; Quis dives salvetur; Fragmente* (GCS 17; Leipzig 1909; 2nd ed. L. Früchtel/U. Treu; Berlin 1970); O. Staehlin, *Clemens Alexandrinus vierter Band: Register* (GCS 39; Leipzig 1936; partial 2nd ed. U. Treu; Berlin 1980). Also see the following with commentaries: C. Mondésert/A. Plassart, *Le Protreptique* (SC 2; Paris 1949; repr. Paris 1976); C. Mondésert/P. Caster, *Les Stromates. Stromate I* (SC 30; Paris 1951); C. Mondésert/P. Camelot, *Les Stromates. Stromate II* (SC 38; Paris

[38] For this see Eusebius *HE* 7.24, who records Dionysius' reply to a certain chiliast called Nepos who had written a book entitled "The Allegorists Refuted".

[39] See *Excerpta ex Theodoto* in SC 23 241 f. where in a list of the biblical passages cited by Valentinus, the OT passages come exclusively from the Pentateuch and especially Genesis.

[40] On Valentinus' exegesis see Dawson, ibid. 126 f.

[41] See expecially *Strom.* 3.38.1 where Clement accuses one group of cobbling together passages to support particular positions.

[42] For a more nuanced typology see Runia, Survey (1986) 120.

1954); H. I. Marrou/M. Harl, *Le Pédagogue I* (SC 70; Paris 1960); C. Mondésert/H. I. Marrou, *Le Pédagogue II* (SC 108; Paris 1965); C. Mondésert/H. I. Marrou, *Le Pédagogue III* (SC 158; Paris 1970); A. le Boulluec/P. Voulet, *Les Stromates V* (SC 278 and 279; Paris 1981); C. Nardi, *Clemente Alessandrino, Estratti prophetici – Eclogae propheticae* (Bibl. Patristica IV; Firenze 1985).

Bibliography: A. van den Hoek, *Clement of Alexandria and his use of Philo in the Stromateis* (Leiden 1988) 232–247.

General books: W. den Boer, "Hermeneutic Problems in Early Christian Literature", *VC* 1 (1947) 150–167; P. Th. Camelot, "Clément d'Alexandrie et l'Écriture", *RB* 53 (1946) 242–248; H. Frhr. von Campenhausen, *The Formation of the Christian Bible* (ET London 1972) 293f; D. Dawson, *Allegorical Readers and Cultural Revision in Ancient Alexandra* (Berkeley 1992); H. Chadwick, *Early Christian Thought and the Classical Tradition: Studies in Justin, Clement and Origen* (Oxford 1966) 31–65; J. Daniélou, *Sacramentum Futuri* (ET Paris 1950); idem, "Typologie et allégorie chez Clément d'Alexandrie", StPatr 4 (1961) 50–57; idem, *Gospel Message and Hellenistic Culture* (ET London 1973); R. M. Grant, *The Letter and the Spirit* (London 1957) 85–89; R. P. C. Hanson, *Allegory and Event: a study of the sources and significance of Origen's Interpretation of Scripture* (London 1959); A. van den Hoek, *Clement of Alexandria and his use of Philo in the Stromateis: An Early Christian reshaping of a Jewish Model* (Leiden 1988); idem, "The concept of σῶμα τῶν γραφῶν in Alexandrian Christianity", StPatr 19 (Leuven 1989) 250–254; H. J. Horn, "Zur Motivation der allegorischen Schriftexegese bei Clemens Alexandrinus", *Hermes* 97 (1969) 436–496; S. R. C. Lilla, *Clement of Alexandria: a study in Christian Platonism and Gnosticism* (Oxford 1971); A. Méhat, *Étude sur les "Stromates" de Clément d'Alexandrie* (Pat. Sorb. 7; Paris 1966); idem, "L'hypothèse des "Testimonia" à l'épreuve des *Stromates*: remarques sur les citations de l'Ancien Testament chez Clément d'Alexandrie" (*La Bible et les Pères*, Coll. de Strasbourg 1–3 Oct. 1969; Paris 1971); idem, "Clément d'Alexandrie et les sens de l'Ecriture", *Epektasis* (Mélange J. Daniélou; Paris 1972) 355–365; H. Mondésert, "Le Symbolisme chez Clément d'Alexandrie", *RSR* 26 (1936) 158–180; idem, *Clément d'Alexandrie; introduction à l'étude de sa pensée religieuse à partir de l'Écriture* (Paris 1944); R. Mortley, *Connaissance religieuse et herméneutique chez Clément d'Alexandrie* (Leiden 1972); E. F. Osborn, "La Bible inspiratrice d'une morale chrétienne d'après Clément d'Alexandrie", *Le monde grec ancien et la Bible* (BTT 1; 1984) 127–144; idem, "Logique et exégèse chez Clément d'Alexandrie", *Lectures anciennes de la Bible* (Cahiers de Bibl. Patr.; Strasbourg 1987) 169–190; J. Pépin, *Mythe et Allégorie: les origines grecques et les contestations judéo-chrétiennes* (Paris 1976) 265–275; M. Simonetti, *Allegoria e/o Lettera* (Roma 1982); O. Staehlin, *Clemens Alexandrinus und die Septuaginta* (Nürnberg 1901); R. B. Tollinton, *Clement of Alexandria: a study in Christian Liberalism* 2 vols. (London 1914); T. F. Torrance, *Divine Meaning: Studies in Patristic Hermeneutics* (Edinburgh 1995) 130–178; U. Treu, "Etymologie und Allegorie bei Klemens von Alexandrien", StPatr 4 (1961) 191–211; W. Völker, "Die Verwertung der Weisheits-Literatur bei den christlichen Alexandrinern", *ZKG* 64 (1952–53) 1–33.

2.1. Introductory Observations

Clement bases himself on the Christian Bible. While he quotes the NT more frequently than the OT, the OT is still a significant presence in his writings.[43] He is the first Christian writer known to us to use the term παλαιὰ διαθήκη not only in reference to the former covenant which belonged to the Jews,[44] but also to a *body of writings* distinguished from the collection of writings known as the New Testament.[45] Ironically, given this fact, he makes no attempt in his extant writings to list the members of that collection, as a little

---

[43] Of his approximately 8200 scriptural quotations or allusions, 3200 of these come from the OT.

[44] See *Paid.* 1.56.3. Elsewhere he refers to four covenants (*Strom.* 5.34.4).

[45] For this see amongst other references *Strom.* 3.54.4; 71.3; 5.61.1; 85.1. He is also the first writer known to us to refer to the New Testament as the νέα διαθήκη (*Strom.* 1.28.2; 3.71.3).

earlier Melito had done (*HE* 4.26), or to give any indication that he in fact knew of a list.[46] He refers to all the books in the Jewish Scriptures except Ruth, Obadiah, Nehemiah and the Song of Songs.[47] He quotes from or alludes to a number of deutero-canonical books including Maccabees, Tobit, Judith, Wisdom and Ecclesiasticus, the last two of these quite frequently. He also cites the Sibylline Oracles, as though they too were inspired (*Prot.* 6.71.4).[48]

Clement uses the LXX, though some of his citations, above all those taken from the prophets, agree with the versions, especially Theodotion.[49] Despite this apparent knowledge of different translations of the Hebrew Bible, he shows no interest in textual problems, though he castigates his opponents for their tendency to corrupt the OT text.[50] His uncritical repetition of the legend of the miraculous translation of the Hebrew Bible into Greek by 70 Hebrew scholars shows that at least in theory he accepts the ultimate authority of the LXX (*Strom.* 1.148.1f.). Clement refers to the LXX as a kind of Greek prophecy (τὴν ἑρμηνείαν οἱονεὶ Ἑλληνικὴν προφητείαν (1.149.3)), and its translation as the translation of individual prophecies (*Strom.* 1.149.2). For him the OT is primarily prophecy, and virtually all its writers are prophets, Moses included (*Paid.* 1.96.3). By this description Clement wants to emphasise the inspired nature of the OT text, and the predictive qualities of its oracles, especially as these relate to Christ. But we should not attempt to narrow down what is a very general term in Clement's writings. Prophecy can contain philosophy, and mystical truths unrelated to prediction. It is often linked with Law in the description of the OT as "the law and the prophets" (*Paid.* 1.96.1; *Strom.* 3.76.1). In general, though, the Law refers to the Pentateuch, and the legislation in it, written by Moses.

Of the OT books which he quotes Clement shows the customary Christian penchant for the Pentateuch (especially Genesis), the Psalms, Isaiah, and more singularly for the Wisdom literature, especially Proverbs, a book from which he quotes more than from either Isaiah and the Psalms,[51] and Ecclesiasticus. It is in his use of the Pentateuch that he shows his greatest debt to Philo, who provides him with allegorical interpretations with a philosophical orientation, and with useful apologetic material. Adapted by Clement, this, amongst other things, bolsters his view that the study of philosophy provides a necessary training for the study of wisdom (*Strom.* 1.28–32), that Hebrew

---

[46] On Clement and the OT canon see Staehlin, Clemens (1901); Tollinton, Clement II (1914) 168–171; Campenhausen, Formation (1963) 292f.

[47] Tollinton, Clement II (1914), argues that a failure to quote Obadiah, Ruth or Nehemiah is of no consequence because one is one of the twelve prophets, the other a part of the book of Judges, and the third linked with Ezra, all three of which are mentioned by Clement.

[48] "His rule or canon is something other than a list of authoritative writings, and to a very large extent his strong preference and affinities determine his use of the church's literature, rather than any decision of authority from without." (Tollinton, Clement II (1914) 175).

[49] On this see Staehlin, Clemens (1901). For the view that any attempt to establish the Greek text of Clement's OT is a hopeless exercise see Méhat, Testimonia (1969) 240.

[50] On this see especially *Strom.* 3.38–39.

[51] According to Staehlin's Sachregister (1936) Clement quotes from the Psalms 300 times, Isaiah 240, and from Proverbs 320.

is older than Greek philosophy (*Strom.* 1.150–182), and that Marcionite disparagement of OT law was unfounded (*Strom.* 2.78–100).[52]

Clement's mode of quotation varies. He often cites a text directly, mentioning in varying forms of particularity its provenance.[53] Sometimes he gives no provenance, and here Scripture merges into the general flow of his theologising. Quotations may be long[54] or short; isolated, or part of a string, which may contain quotations from the NT and/or pagan literature.[55] Often times it appears that Clement had a Bible open in front of him when he was working,[56] but it seems probable that sometimes he derived quotations from testimony sources,[57] or other types of secondary material.[58] Sometimes he paraphrases citations,[59] or summarises stories or events taken from the OT.[60]

Clement can cite the OT to refute an assertion or practice,[61] exhort his readers,[62] give a teaching,[63] confirm a claim/thesis,[64] or illustrate a point.[65] But the OT is not his principal subject, nor is the NT. Both testaments are the authoritative material which provide him with the foundational support for his theological system, but Clement is not a biblicist in the way Philo and later Origen were, that is, he is not principally a commentator on specific

---

[52] On this see Van den Hoek, Clement (1988) 206f. For a summary of her findings and some suggestions see Runia, Survey (1993) 137f.

[53] See in this respect the various ways in which he cites books from the Pentateuch: ἐν τῇ Γενέσει; ἐν τῷ Λευιτικῷ; ἡ λέξις ἡ προφητική; ἡ προφητεία; δόκει διὰ Μωϋσέως etc.

[54] See *Paid.* 1.95.1f. (Ezek 18:4–9); *Strom.* 2.7.1f. (Prov 1:2–6); *Strom.* 2.46.1 (Lev 18:1–5). See also those places where he does not quote a long text in full, but simply refers to its opening and closing line (*Strom.* 2.5.1 and 2.69.3).

[55] See *Strom.* 2.59.1 where quoted together we have Psalm 103:13; 126:5; 128:1; 49:16–17; 5:7–8; and 2.20.1f. for a mixture of quotations from OT, NT and pagan literature.

[56] For the evidence in favour of this thesis see Mondésert, Clément (1944) 66–69.

[57] See Mondésert, Clément (1944) 75: "L'oeuvre de Clément ... ferait bien supposer l'existence de collections de ce genre (testimonia)". For a good example of such a string see *Paid.* 1.61.1–3 where a variety of OT quotations from various books cluster around the messianic title of ῥάβδος (Isa 11:1). See Méhat, Testimonia (1969), who compiles the evidence in favour of seeing sources other than the OT as lying behind some of Clement's OT citations.

[58] Méhat, Testimonia (1969), argues that Clement is often reliant for his OT citations on secondary material. In support of this he notes how frequently Clement quotes OT citations from sources such as Philo, 1 Clement, and Barnabas, or from his opponents (*Strom.* 3). For Philonic OT citations see Van den Hoek, Clement.

[59] See *Strom.* 2.88.4 where Clement paraphrases Deut 24:10–14.

[60] See especially in this respect his account of the life of Moses in *Strom.* 1.151f.

[61] See *Strom.* 1.47.1f. where a series of citations are presented to attack the "sophistic and disputatious" methods of the sophists.

[62] An excellent example of such usage occurs in *Prot.* 8.77.1f. where a series of citations taken from the Psalms, Isaiah, Deuteronomy and Proverbs serve to exhort Clement's supposedly gentile audience to convert.

[63] *Strom.* 2.4.4 where Prov 8:13 is said to teach us clearly that the fear of God is a movement away from evil.

[64] This is probably the most common usage Clement makes of the OT. So at *Strom.* 1.29.1f. Clement backs up his assertion that there is not one way to the truth, but many with a quotation from Prov 4:10–11, 21; and at *Strom.* 1.30.3, before his exposition of the story of Hagar and Sarah, he explicitly states: τῶν εἰρημένων μαρτυρίαν παρέξει ἡ γραφὴ διὰ τῶνδε. See also the series of citations at *Strom.* 5.64.1, which confirm the mysterious quality of biblical language.

[65] See *Strom.* 6.115.4f. where a series of OT citations act as insights into the nature of the true Gnostic; and *Paid.* 1.78f. where OT citations serve to illustrate different types of disapproval. For all the categories mentioned above see Mondésert, Clément (1944) 83.

texts of the OT.[66] Texts are ripped from their original context, and placed within the wider context of his discussion. They are *rarely* a starting point for discussion, and the focus is *rarely* upon individual words or other peculiarities, as with Philo and Origen. This may, of course, partly be due to the nature of his surviving works. In his *Protreptikos*, *Paidagogos*, and *Stromateis*, which constitute the great bulk of his extant opera, Clement is concerned to argue a theological case. These are not commentaries, though Scripture is the principle material out of which Clement constructs his argument. In the fragments of his *Hypotyposeis*, which consisted supposedly of expositions of New Testament books only,[67] and in his *Prophetic Eclogues*, which includes an extended interpretation of Psalm 19 (51 f.), we are nearer to commentary, but still, as far as we can gauge, some distance from the way Philo and Origen understood that word.[68]

2.2. *The Authority and Inspiration of the Old Testament*

Clement assumes rather than argues for the authority of the OT.[69] For him, along with the NT, it is the primary material for all demonstration, exceeding the testimony of Greek philosophy in its importance, and the foundation of the higher γνῶσις. As he writes: "The higher demonstration, which we have alluded to as scientific, instils faith by presenting the Scriptures and opening them up to the souls who are eager to learn, and this could hardly be other than knowledge" (*Strom.* 2. 49. 3).[70] It was precisely from the Bible that the Sicilian Bee (probably Pantaenus) culled "a pure substance of true knowledge for the souls of his hearers".[71]

This strong belief in the authority of the Bible stems from a conviction about its divine origin. "If a person has faith in the divine Scriptures (ταῖς γραφαῖς ταῖς θείαις) and a firm judgment, then he receives as an irrefutable proof the voice of God who has granted him those Scriptures" (*Strom.* 2. 9. 6).[72] Hence Clement often speaks of God as the inspirer of the biblical words (*Prot.* 1. 79. 1). The spirit, too, is a source of inspiration;[73] but much more frequently, and for Clement's theology, much more significantly, it is God's word or λόγος that is the source of inspiration. It is the Logos

[66] Dawson notes that "in all of these writings (referring to the *Prot.*, *Paid.*, and *Strom.*) Clement does not put scriptural quotations on display as specific lemmata that will be commented on" (Exegesis 218).

[67] At *HE* 6. 14. 1 Eusebius states that in his *Hypotyposeis* Clement commented on all canonical Scripture. But all the preserved fragments relate to the NT.

[68] For confirmation of this judgment see Mondésert, Exégèse (1936); and Osborn, Bible (1984) 128, who denies that Clement is an exegete, but affirms that he is very interested in the Bible.

[69] The authority of Scripture, "C'est pour lui un caractère si incontestable, qu'il ne se soucie jamais d'en faire la preuve ou d'expliquer ..." (Mondésert, Clément (1944) 82–83).

[70] See Lilla, Clement (1971) 138, who argues from a postulated connection between *Strom.* 7. 96. 1 and 96. 5 that Scripture in Clement is the ἀρχὴ of demonstration.

[71] See *Strom.* 1. 11. 2 Σικελικὴ τῷ ὄντι ἦν μέλιττα προφητικοῦ τε καὶ ἀποστολικοῦ λειμῶνος τὰ ἄνθη δρεπόμενος ἀκήρατόν τι γνώσεως χρῆμα ταῖς τῶν ἀκροωμένων ἐνεγέννησε ψυχαῖς.

[72] For other references to the OT as θειάι γραφαί see *Strom.* 2. 144. 4; 3. 42. 5; 6. 149. 2.

[73] *Ecl. Proph.* 5 where the spirit speaks by the prophet Hosea.

who has revealed himself by the burning bush, in the cloud, by Moses, and by the choir of the prophets (*Prot.* 1.8.1–3). And it is the Word who has given the law through Moses (*Paid.* 1.60.1). In fact the Logos is both the subject of OT revelation and its creator. So convinced is Clement of the Logos' intimate involvement in the writing of the OT that he appears to endorse the idea of a double incarnation, one in the writings of the prophets, and one in Christ.[74] This conviction allows him to read the OT text as a kind of autobiography on the facts of the Logos in which he reveals his threefold character (as Protrepticos, Paidagogos and Didaskalos). Furthermore, as with Justin before him, it allows Clement to argue that all truth in the OT is Christian truth.

The authority which Clement attaches to the OT is due not simply to the provenance of its inspiration, and its role in the writings of early Christians.[75] It is authoritative precisely because it is old. In his debate with conservative Christians and sceptical pagans about the admissability of using Greek philosophy in the interpretation of the Christian gospel, Clement is keen to show that the former is in fact derivative of the latter.[76] Clement can justify this claim by showing that the writings of Moses and the prophets predate those of the Greeks,[77] and that the Greeks have in fact stolen their ethical and philosophical ideas from Moses and the prophets. Large chunks of the *Stromateis* go to proving this.[78] In this schema the OT becomes the foundational text for the oldest and most respectable aspects of pagan culture,[79] and Moses is given the place of honour. Without blushing, Clement can quote the words of Numenius: "What is Plato but Moses speaking in Attic (ἀττικίζων)?" (*Strom.* 1.150.4).[80]

---

[74] See *Exc. ex Theod.* 19.2 where Clement writes: καὶ πάλιν σὰρξ ἐγένετο (a clear reference to John 1:14) διὰ προφητῶν ἐνεργήσας; and *Paid.* 1.88.2–3. For this latter passage see Mondésert, Clément (1944) 99–100.

[75] At *Strom.* 4.134.2–4 Clement states that Paul is entirely reliant upon it.

[76] It is precisely because Clement sees Greek philosophy as deriving from the Hebrew scriptures that we should not see his claim that they both have the function of preparing for Christ (*Strom.* 1.28.3; 6.42.1–3; 44.1 and elsewhere) as indicating equality of status. Equally his claim of the dependence of one on the other is an attempt to attribute a divine origin to pagan philosophy.

[77] See *Strom.* 1.101–150. In this he follows Philo and his Hellenistic Jewish predecessors, as well as the chronological calculations of Justin's pupil Tatian.

[78] See *Strom.* 2.1.1; 5.10.1–2; 5.89–141 and elsewhere for philosophical reliance; and 1.170.4 for the claim that Greek legislation is dependent upon Mosaic prophecy. For a discussion of these references see Lilla, Clement (1971) 31–33; Le Boulluec, SC 278 13f.; and Dawson, Readers (1992) 203–204. It would be wrong to assert that Clement's sole explanation for the perceived conjunction between biblical revelation and Greek philosophy lay in the argument from theft. As Lilla has shown, at least two other arguments were used: that from natural endowment or divine inspiration, and that from fallen angels who stole philosophy from God. For the conjuction of these arguments in Clement's mind see Lilla, Clement 12f.

[79] See especially *Strom.* 1.101.2f. Clement's claim, unique to him, that there was a translation of the Pentateuch before the time of Plato, to which Plato had access, is another example of his desire to link philosophy and the biblical testimony (*Strom.* 1.150.1).

[80] For the high position Moses holds in Clement's writings see his encomiastic account in *Strom.* 1.150.1–182. Here Moses is described as prophet, legislator, general, statesman and philosopher (1.158.1), the law incarnate insofar as he was governed by the word (1.167.1), and a better dialectician than Plato (1.176.1). Elsewhere he is seen as living with the angels (*Strom.*

Something of the general authority with which Clement regards the OT is brought out in a passage from the *Protreptikos*: "Now that we have dealt with the other matters in due order, it is time to turn to the writings of the prophets (τὰς προφητικὰς γραφάς). For these are the oracles which, by exhibiting to us in the clearest light the grounds of piety, lay a firm foundation for the truth. The sacred writings are also models of virtuous living, and short roads to salvation. They are bare of embellishment of outward beauty of language, of idle talk and flattery, yet they raise up man when fast bound in the grip of evil. Despising the snare of this life, with one and the same voice, they provide a cure for many ills, turning us aside from delusion that works harm and urging us onward with clear guidance to salvation set before our eyes" (*Prot.* 8.77.1).[81]

Clement's conviction that the Logos is the subject and author of the OT and NT alike makes him keen to emphasise their unity.[82] It is in fact a κανὼν ὁ ἐκκλησιαστικός that the two are in accord with each other (*Strom.* 6.125.2–3; 7.94.5); and he will have no truck with Marcionite dismissal of the OT revelation.[83] While there may be two covenants in name there is one in power (*Strom.* 2.29.1). All decent exegesis must assume such harmony. But does Clement in fact accord the same importance to both testaments?

Clement believes in the progressive nature of revelation. What the Logos taught through Moses he has now revealed in his own person face to face (*Paid.* 1.59).[84] The incarnation of the Logos reveals the obscure truths contained within the OT, because the Logos is himself the fulfillment of those truths, and expounds them.[85] Here belief in Christ and his incarnation, as narrated in the NT, becomes the means through which the OT is understood.[86] Furthermore, the NT constitutes in places an advance on the teaching

---

5.90.5), and coming as close as any man to approaching the deity. He is, however, subordinate to Christ (see *Strom.* 2.21.1), a point that is made clear if we examine the way Clement edits his Philonic material. For this see Van den Hoek's discussion of Clement's use of Philo's *Vita Mosis* in *Strom.* 1.150.1–182, Clement (1988) 48–68.

[81] See Campenhausen's claim that "although … he (Clement) strongly prefers the NT, the solemn emphasis of the sacral concept of scripture for him falls time after time on the OT", Formation (1972) 293.

[82] Εἰ δὲ ὁ αὐτὸς νομοθέτης ἅμα καὶ εὐαγγελιστής, οὐ μαχεταί ποτε ἑαυτῷ (*Strom.* 3.88.4). For other passages emphasising the harmony of the Scriptures see *Strom.* 6.88.5 and 7.95.3.

[83] For criticisms of Marcion see *Strom.* 2.32.1; 34.4; 39.1. For a good insight into his awareness of Marcionite criticism of OT law see the additions he makes to Philo's *De Virt.* in his *Strom.* 2.78–100. On a number of occasions he stresses that the Law is just and good (*Strom.* 2.78.3f; 86.1; 91.1; 95.1). For a discussion of these references see Van den Hoek, Clement (1988) 112. See also Dawson, Readers (1992) 211–212.

[84] See also *Prot.* 1.8.1–3 where revelation progresses from portents (the burning bush, the cloud etc.), through words mediated by Moses and the prophets (Isaiah is particularly mentioned), to unmediated words in the incarnation.

[85] See *Strom.* 5.90.3: "The sense (δήλωσις) of the mysterious scriptures was not revealed until the coming of Christ"; and for a similar sentiment *Strom.* 5.55.1f. where Jesus' advent allows John the Baptist to unveil the meaning of the oracles in the OT.

[86] Clement expresses this conviction most clearly at *Strom.* 4.134.4 where he states that faith in Christ and the knowledge of the gospel are the explanation and fulfillment of the Law. After quoting Isa 7:9 ("If you do not believe, neither will you understand"), he continues: "Unless you believe what is prophesied in the Law and what is oracularly delivered by the Law (ὑπὸ νόμου θεσπισθέντι) … you will not understand the Old Testament, which by his advent (παρουσίαν) he expounded (ἐξηγήσατο)".

contained within the OT.[87] Fear has now been replaced by love – the Law, after all, was only a paidagogos to Christ.

But does this mean that the NT is accorded a greater position of authority than the OT? First, to say that the NT is the correct exposition of the OT is only a half truth. Certainly the centre of salvation history lies in Christ's incarnation, and Clement's conviction that the Logos is the inspiration behind both testaments allows him to subordinate Hebraic truth to Christian revelation (the NT) in his interpretation of the OT.[88] But it does not mean that the NT is the ultimate reference point for this truth. Both testaments have been expounded by the Logos, and those expositions have been concealed in a secret tradition handed down by the apostles.[89] Their truth has been hidden and this fact serves to blur the distinctions between them. Secondly, there is little in Clement's actual exposition of these two testaments to indicate that he saw a difference in the quality of their content. When Christ arrives what he reveals is the truth within the OT. Both testaments merge into the one truth, and both must be read in relation to each other.

2.3. Interpretative Assumptions

At no point in his extant writings does Clement attempt a systematic exposition of his hermeneutical assumptions. But, scattered through his *Stromateis*, appropriately one might say, we find allusions to these assumptions.

The OT, like the NT, is the word of God. Nothing can be said directly of God, and so language about him is necessarily symbolic.[90] Symbolism is a form of concealment and only the enlightened are allowed access to the truths beneath the symbols.[91] Nor is the concealment restricted to the Christian Bible. It is evidenced in Greek and Egyptian writings. Hence Clement can confidently exclaim: "All then, in a word, who have spoken of divine things, both Barbarians and Greeks, have veiled the first principle of things, and delivered the truth in enigmas and symbols and allegories and metaphors and such like tropes" (*Strom.* 5. 21. 4).

Clement's conviction that all of the OT is written in this enigmatic, symbolic way is clear. "It would be tedious (μακρόν) to go over all the prophets and the law specifying what is spoken in enigmas; for almost the whole of Scripture gives its utterance in this way" (*Strom.* 5. 32. 1). He applies the opening words of Psalm 77, where the Logos says he will open his mouth in

---

[87] See *Strom.* 3. 82. 4; 7. 86. 3; 84. 7; 85. 4.

[88] See *Q.D.S.* 8. 2 where Clement explicitly states that if all truth was found in the Law of Moses there was no point in Jesus' life and death.

[89] For this see *Strom.* 1. 11. 3; 5. 61. 1; 6. 61. 1; 6. 61. 3. For a discussion of the secret tradition in Clement see Lilla, Clement 155.

[90] "L'Ecriture, parce qu'elle nous apporte la parole de Dieu, est mystérieuse" (Mondésert, Clément (1944) 89). See *Strom.* 2. 72. 4 where Clement states that it is not possible to speak directly of the divine, but is is possible to hear the Lord accommodating himself to human weakness for our salvation.

[91] This method of concealment (ἐπίκρυψις) is, according to Clement, hinted at by the Egyptians by means of inner shrines called *adyta*, and by the Hebrews by the veil through which only the enlightened can pass (*Strom.* 5. 19. 3–20. 1).

parables, to the whole of Scripture (*Strom.* 5. 25. 1), emphasising in particular the obscure nature of prophecy (*Strom.* 6. 127. 3 and 126. 4).[92] This obscurity is entirely appropriate for the pursuit of truth should not be an easy matter, nor should its contents be available to all and sundry (*Strom.* 6. 126. 1).

What people must pursue in their exegesis is that which is concealed (τὸ ἐπικρυμμένον). Hence Clement describes his method of interpretation in words with a strong emphasis on the enigmatic, mysterious quality of the subject of interpretation (αἴνιγμα; αἰνίττομαι; ἀλληγορία, ἀλληγορεῖν; παραβολή; σύμβολον, συμβολικός, συμβολικῶς).[93] He summarises his understanding of scriptural interpretation at *Q. D. S.* 5. 2: "We are clearly aware that the saviour teaches his people nothing in a merely human way (ἀνθρωπινῶς), but everything by a divine and mystical wisdom. Accordingly, we must not understand his words literally (σαρκίνως), but with inquiry and intelligence we must search out (ἐρευνᾶν) and master (καταμανθάνειν) their hidden meaning (κεκρυμμένον νοῦν)". To use another image employed by Clement, and probably inherited from Philo,[94] it is the aim of the interpreter to advance from the body of Scripture to the soul (*Strom.* 5. 90. 3). It is only by doing this that the interpreter will become a true gnostic, that he will begin to embrace Christ the διδάσκαλος.[95] He can contrast those faithful people who only take a taste of Scripture (οἱ μὲν ἀπογευσάμενοι μόνον τῶν γραφῶν πιστοί)[96] with those who progress to the truth. These he describes as Gnostics (*Strom.* 7. 95. 9).

At the end of *Stromateis* 1, Clement analyses the content of the Torah (what he calls Μωυσέα φιλοσοφία). He divides it up into three parts on a Platonist model. First there is history and law (τὸ ἱστορικὸν καὶ τὸ κυρίως λεγόμενον νομοθετικὸν), both of which come under the title of ethics. Then there is liturgy (ἱερουγικὸν), which appears to be related to physics and the study of nature; and finally there is τὸ θεολογικὸν εἶδὸς, which is described as ἐποπτεία, a word from the vocabulary of classical mysticism, and related to the ultimate vision of the initiate. It is this vision (the equivalent of the higher gnosis) that all exegesis of Scripture aims to attain.[97]

---

[92] See *Strom.* 6. 115. 1–2, where after citing Psalm 17:12–13, Clement states that the Scriptures are mysterious and obscure like coal. One has to light them.

[93] Mondésert, Clément (1944) 87 f, rightly notes that Clement makes very little distinction between these words. For other references to the hidden nature of Scripture's truths see *Strom.* 5. 35. 5; 80. 3; 6. 70. 2; 116. 1; 124. 5; 126. 1–2.

[94] See Philo, *De Vita Cont.* 78. For probable dependence on Philo see Van den Hoek, "Concept".

[95] See *Paid* 1. 3. 1 where the Logos' function as διδάσκαλος is contrasted with his function as persuader and pedagogue. For other relevant passages see see *Paid.* 1. 1. 4; 1. 3. 1; 1. 8. 3; 1. 92. 3; 2. 76. 1.

[96] For attacks on literalists see *Strom.* 3. 38 and 5. 53. 2.

[97] For discussions of this complex passage see Den Boer, Problems (1948); and Méhat, Clément (1972). For the former the passage contains a purely formal definition of the contents of the Pentateuch, while for the latter the definitions relate to different stages in the progression of the interpreter, from literal interpretation to spiritual. For a summary of the positions see Van den Hoek, Clement (1988) 61.

2.4. Method

To understand Scripture one requires a rigorous method. Clement's idea of such a method can be discerned from the way in which he characterises the "false" interpretation of those Christian writers he opposes. They fail to make use of all Scripture, they are selective, and in their selections they wrest ambiguous phrases from their contexts. Furthermore, they do not look to the sense of words, preferring to base their interpretations on the change of a tone of voice, the relocation of an accent, or marks of punctuation. Good interpretation should avoid this type of sophistry, take account of context, and demonstrate the validity of individual interpretations by comparing them with other parts of Scripture, OT and NT, accepting the ultimate harmony of the two.[98] In all this it is necessary to apply the rules of logic.[99] This need for a nuanced logical interpretation should manifest itself in an awareness of the different ways in which the OT might be read. Scripture is not, to use an image of Clement, a single bald-headed inhabitant of Mykonos. "There are four ways", he writes, "in which we can receive the meaning of the Law: it may present a type; it may show a symbol; it may lay down a precept for right conduct; it may pronounce a prophecy" (*Strom.* 1. 179. 4).[100]

2.5. Senses and Use of the Old Testament

The quotation above implies that Clement had an almost technical understanding of the different senses of the OT, and indeed a technical and methodical approach to exegesis. The reality is quite different. As MONDÉSERT wrote: "S'il y a une terminologie compliquée et anarchique (in Clement's writings), c'est bien celle qui concerne les diverses sens possibles de l'écriture".[101]

In what I write below I shall take a lead from MONDÉSERT's five categories. The essential distinction made will be between historical/literal exegesis, and symbolical interpretation. In the latter I will include a discussion of typological exegesis. This does not mean that I make no distinction between this, or the other categories of exegesis I place under the title symbolical. It merely indicates that I do not believe that Clement made such a distinction.[102]

---

[98] See especially *Strom.* 7.96.1–3 and *Ecl. Proph.* 32: "We must, then, search the scriptures accurately, since they are admitted to be uttered in parables, and from the names hunt out the thoughts, which the Holy Spirit ... teaches by imprinting his mind, so to speak, upon the expressions; that the names used with various meanings, being made the subject of accurate investigation, may be explained, and that which is hidden under many integuments may, being handled and learned, come to light and gleam forth".

[99] For the importance of logic as a tool of interpretation see especially *Strom.* 1.45.1; and Osborn, Logique (1987).

[100] For the textual problems encountered here see Den Boer, Problems (1948) 158, who argues that the words ὡς τύπον τινὰ δηλοῦσαν are not part of the original text. The words are in fact an addition from a Psalm scholion, added in order to make sense of the reading τετραχῶς.

[101] Clément (1944) 153. This judgment is largely confirmed by Den Boer's detailed study.

[102] This point is endorsed by Den Boer, ibid. 147 f.

2.5.1. The Literal Sense

What matters most for Clement is the symbolic or hidden meaning of the OT. He is not interested in the literal sense of the OT as a technical problem (except in the case of antropomorphisms), and does not feel compelled, as Origen did later, to discuss it as of principle. However, the occasions in his writing when the literal/historical understanding of a text is taken seriously are surprisingly frequent.

First, we have already seen that Clement, in his claim that Israelite wisdom lies at the root of all pagan culture and in his belief that the founder of the nation was an exemplary figure, had an interest in the chronology of OT history and in the life of Moses (*Strom.* 1.100f.). While having more of an apologetic than an exegetical character the relevant passages show an interest in the OT as a faithful record of past events. Clement himself states that the Pentateuch contains material that is τὸ ἱστορικόν.

Clement turns to historical exegesis when he has to confront what he takes to be a false interpretation of an OT text. In *Strom.* 3.38.1f, for instance, he refutes in detail a Gnostic interpretation of Mal 3:15 ("They opposed God, and found salvation").[103] Against the view that the verse supports a rejection of the creator God, he shows (1) how the addition of the word "shameless" to "God" is false, and even if correct, would mean that the verse referred to the devil, and (2) that the words uttered by Malachi are not the words of God – not all prophetic words are a recording of the words of God – but of Jews who complain that the other nations are not punished even though they sin. In support of this interpretation Clement cites Jer 12:1. That he himself describes this form of interpretation as allegorical should not detract from an appreciation of its strongly historical character.[104]

In other areas apart from history Clement is reliant upon a non-symbolical interpretation. This manifests itself in a variety of ways. At times he simply cites OT passages with barely any interpretation, allowing the texts to speak for themselves. So at *Protreptikos* 8.77.3f. we find a string of citations from Isaiah, Proverbs, Deuteronomy, Amos and Jeremiah praising the greatness of God and denouncing pagan practices. Simple citation without any allegorical embellishment can accompany ethical instruction. Clement can praise the literal import of Mosaic laws, holding them to contain all the necessary virtues (courage, self-control, practical wisdom, justice, endurance, patience, propriety, continence, and above all, piety).[105] Of course, he joins his Christian predecessors in a willingness to allegorise Torah,[106] and dispense with its ritual prescriptions. He can also describe it as a *paidagogos* to Christ. But he

---

103 It is interesting to note that many OT passages in *Strom.* 3 are in fact citations from Clement's opponents.

104 For another example of such exegesis see *Strom.* 3.100.1f.

105 *Strom.* 2.78.1f.

106 In her analysis of *Strom.* 2.78.1f. Van den Hoek shows how Clement, unlike Philo in his *De Virt.*, a text on which Clement is heavily reliant at this point in his *Stromateis*, allegorises Jewish laws where Philo does not (see *Strom.* 2.81.2; 93.1; 98.2). For her interesting conclusion see Clement (1988) 114–115.

nowhere subjects it to brutal criticism, or regards it as in any way defective.[107] He wholeheartedly endorses a literal understanding of the Ten Commandments (*Strom.* 3. 89. 1), even though elsewhere he presents a detailed exegesis of them (*Strom.* 6. 133.1 f.).

But the Christian does not learn ethics exclusively from Torah. In *Paid.* 2 and 3 he peppers his discussion of the correct ethical existence with admonitions taken especially from Wisdom literature. In speaking against gluttony, he quotes the declaration of Prov 23:3, which declares that a desire for the meats of the rich belongs to a shameful life. At *Paid.* 2. 34 he summarises his teaching on drunkenness with a reference to Ecclus. 31:22 ("Wine is sufficient for a man well taught, and upon his bed he shall rest"). This exploitation of the ethical content of Wisdom books, with their summary, admonitory tone is a persistent feature of *Paid.* 2 and 3.[108]

The literal meaning of the text is significant in another form of ethical teaching – the use of OT exempla. At *Paid.* 1. 90, Clement discusses possible methods of backing up advice. The first of these is to give examples from times gone by, such as the punishment the Jews experienced after they had worshipped the golden calf, for fornicating, or committing similar misdeeds. In this context OT stories act as a literature of warning. The punishments inflicted upon Israel and others act as exhortations to contemporary Christians not to act in a similar way. Nor is it examples of what should be avoided that Clement finds in the OT. Some of the characters there – Job, Moses, Abraham and Sarah – are ideals to be followed (*Paid.* 3. 12).

2.5.2. *Symbolic Exegesis*

Prophecy and Typology

Clement, like the majority of Christians, believed that the OT contained intimations of Christ's coming (*Strom.* 6.166–167). He could express this belief in at least two ways: by citing a passage from the OT which he believed to speak prophetically of Jesus' coming (*Paid.* 1. 24. 1 (Isa 9:6, 7); 61. 1 (Isa 11:1); *Strom.* 5. 105. 3); or by means of typological exegesis, which treats events and stories as anticipatory impressions of later Christian realities. This form of interpretation finds its clearest theoretical expression in Melito's *Homily on the Pascha.* There are many examples in Clement's work of typology. Isaac is a type of the suffering Christ would experience, and, insofar as Isaac did not suffer, of Christ's divinity (*Paid.* 1. 23. 1f).[109] Abel's blood crying out from the ground (Gen 4:10) becomes a prediction of Christ's suffering (*Paid.* 1. 47. 4). The story of the Burning Bush (Exod 3:2) provides Clement with a typology which brings to the surface his major assumption about the continuity of the

[107] At *Strom.* 3. 46. 1 he can write: "The design of the Law is to divert us from extravagance and all forms of disorderly behaviour; this is its object to draw us from unrighteousness to righteousness ...". He then proceeds to quote Matt 5:17 (The Lord comes to fulfil, not destroy the Law), and comments: "Fulfillment does not mean that it (the Law) was defective".

[108] See Völker, Verwertung (1953) 6: "Wieviel konkretes Material geben ihm allein bei der Bekämpfung der Unsittlichkeit Prov und Sir. an der Hand".

[109] On the special status afforded Isaac in Clement's writings see Daniélou, Gospel (1973) 241 f.

old and the new covenant. "He sent Moses", Clement writes, "a divine vision with the appearance of light in the burning bush. Now, a bramble bush is full of thorns. So, too when the word was concluding the legislation and his stay among men, again he permitted himself to be crowned with thorns as a mystical symbol (μυστικῶς)" (*Paid.* 2.75.1–2). Clement is capable of more involved typologies in which a variety of OT verses and images are brought together and centred upon the figure of Christ (*Strom.* 5.72.2–4).[110] Some typologies incorporate Philonic material. So Isaac represents the self taught, and that is precisely why he is a type of Christ (*Strom.* 1.31.3).[111] But not all typologies in Clement are exclusively christological in orientation. Some can refer to aspects of the life of the church. Abraham's three day journey before catching sight of Mount Moriah can, at one level, be interpreted in terms of Christian baptism (*Strom.* 5.73.2),[112] or Melchizedek's offerings of bread and wine can become a type of the eucharist (*Strom.* 4.161.3).[113]

Philosophical Interpretation

By philosophical interpretation I mean interpretation based on philosophical assumptions. This may be said to apply to much of Clement's exegesis. But it is particularly the case in passages like *Strom.* 5.94.5 where the reference in Gen 1:6 to the creation of heaven, earth and light becomes a reference to the creation of the intelligible world of Platonic philosophy; or *Strom.* 2.131.5 where Plato's understanding of ὁμοίωσις θεῷ in *Theaeteus* 176b is used to interpret Gen 1:26. This exegesis has a strongly Philonic base.[114]

Cosmological Interpretation

This type of exegesis, for which Clement is heavily reliant upon Philo, apprehends physical features or characteristics of the universe behind the words/events etc. of the OT. Typical in this respect is Clement's exegesis of the furnishings of the Temple and the High Priest's clothing in *Strom.* 5.32.1f. Here the altar of incense between the curtain and veil becomes a symbol of the world (5.33.1); the seven-sticked candelabra indicates the orbits of the seven bright heavenly bodies which complete their course in the sky (37.1); the five stones and the two carbuncles represent the seven planets (37.3).[115]

Psychological Interpretation

In this type of exegesis individuals/places in the OT become representatives of what MONDÉSERT called "le monde psychologique".[116] Enoch becomes a representative of the person who repents and elicites repentance

---

[110] See Daniélou's discussion of this passage ibid. 238.

[111] For a more complex example of this transposition of Philonic allegorical material into Christian typology see *Paid* 1.21.1–3 (discussed by Daniélou, ibid. 240; and Simonetti, Lettera (1985) 71f).

[112] For another typology of Christian baptism see *Ecl. Proph.* 7.

[113] Daniélou argues that such passages as *Strom.* 5.55.1–3 indicate that since the coming of Christ the passages which looked forward to his arrival have now been fulfilled. But there still remain other secrets. These he associates with the secrets of the endtime.

[114] For these passages see Lilla, Clement (1971) 191–192 and 109 respectively.

[115] See also Clement's interpretation of the Decalogue at 6.134.1–4 where the two tables of laws represent the physical world, and the Decalogue is viewed as an image of Heaven, embracing sun and moon, stars, cloud, light, wind etc.

[116] Clément (1944) 158f.

(*Strom.* 2.70.3); Egypt represents the world (*Strom.* 5.30:3–4), as does Canaan (*Strom.* 2.47.1); the eunuch of Isa 56:3–5 represents the man sterile to truth (*Strom.* 3.99.1); Gen 4:16 ("Cain left God's presence and went to live in the land of Naid opposite Eden") is interpreted by Clement with the aid of etymology ("Naid" means disturbance and "Eden" the good life) to mean that the good life consists in faith, knowledge and peace, and those who live in disturbance are the self-taught who do not listen even to the first commandment of God (*Strom.* 2.56.1). In this example psychological exegesis comes close to a form of moral exegesis.[117]

Mystical Interpretation

This relates to the purpose of the soul's journey, namely a form of divine revelation. Abraham's three day journey to Mt. Moriah becomes a type of this journey. Clement quotes Gen 22:3–4 ("Abraham when he came to the place which God told him of on the third day, saw the place afar off"), and goes on to state how the first day is that which is constituted by the sight of good things, the second is the soul's best desire, and the third the apprehension of spiritual things. The entrance of the High Priest into the Holy of Holies becomes a type of the movement of the true Gnostic from the world of sense to the world of forms (*Strom.* 5.39.4), and an indication of the advance through the Heavens to the ultimate vision.[118] Here mystical exegesis takes on an eschatological colouring.

2.5.3. Some Observations on Clement's Symbolic Exegesis

(1) In eliciting symbolic interpretations from a particular text Clement is keen to make use of etymologies and number symbolism, many of which are borrowed from Philo.

(2) Often Clement will give more than one interpretation of a single text. For instance, in his interpretation of the High Priest's entrance into the temple, the 5 columns are connected with the five loaves of the feeding of the five thousand and with the five senses (*Strom.* 5.33.4f.). The candlestick is both a symbol of the seven light bearing stars, which perform their revolutions to the south, and of the cross (34.8). The five stones together with the two carbuncles represent the seven planets (37.1), but the five stones can also represent the various phases of salvation (37.3). The logion represents the Logos and is a symbol of heaven (38.1), and also signifies the judgment which is to come (39.1). The high-priestly robe is a symbol of the world of sense (37.2) and of the incarnation (39.1). The harp of the psalmist is given four possible meanings. It may symbolise the Lord, the angels, the saved people of God (*Strom.* 6.88.3), or the man saved by means of the Logos.[119]

---

[117] See also Clement's interpretation of Gen 37:23–24 (the story of Joseph being thrown into the pit and stripped of his multi-coloured coat) at *Strom.* 5.52.5–53.4.

[118] See *Strom.* 5.40.1: πρόσωπον ἤδη πρὸς πρόσωπον ἐμπίπλαται τῆς ἀκορέστου θεωρίας. For a similarly mystical interpretation see *Exc. ex Theod.* 27; and *Ecl. Proph.* 51–62. Méhat argues that allegory is principally used by Clement to explore the interior life.

[119] For another passage which is interpreted in a variety of ways by Clement see *Paid.* 1.21–23 and his interpretation of Gen 26:8.

(3) The mode of Clement's interpretation varies. Sometimes it can take on the character of a Pesher-like piece of exegesis with an individual passage being divided up, and its separate verses expounded consecutively. This is most clearly the case in the interpretation of Psalm 19 in *Proph. Ecl.* 51 f,[120] though there are many other less elaborate but equally good examples in Clement's work.[121] Sometimes, however, one verse, or series of verses is used to interpret another verse – commentary is conducted on an intra-textual basis (*Strom.* 1. 95. 1 f.). Sometimes actual citation will play a small part, though comment will be extensive (*Strom.* 5. 32–40).

(4) Clement's interpretations are not highly lexical, that is they do not pay much attention to the wording of the OT. In one of the passages cited above we see an example of this (*Strom.* 5. 73. 1). In his interpretation of Gen 22:34, Clement does not comment on the strange repetition of the word "place". Yet it was precisely this aspect of the text which caught Philo's attention.[122] Again at *Strom.* 5. 52. 3–53. 4 Clement links: Ex 15:1, 21, a passage from Plato's Phaedrus, and Gen 37:23–24. The three passages are linked by three terms all of which refer to falling.[123] But rather than concentrate on the meaning of these three terms, as Philo would have done, Clement prefers to draw attention to the general image of falling.[124]

2.6. Conclusion

For Clement the Bible is the central focus of his theological meditation. While the OT is quoted less frequently than the NT, Clement still accords it great authority.[125] Inspired by the Logos, it is the most ancient and sacred of literature.

Like Philo before him, Clement is primarily an allegorist of the OT, and sees no disjunction between philosophy and biblical revelation. Plato and Pythagoras have borrowed many of their ideas from it, and they can therefore help the interpreter in his quest for gnosis. Above we have delineated the assumptions lying beneath Clement's hermeneutical method. His primary aim was to penetrate beneath the outer skin of the text to its hidden meaning.

But it would be wrong to see Clement's interpretation of the OT as exclusively allegorical/symbolic. At times he was forced into a piece of literal exegesis in defence of a particular position, and often he cites the OT without allegorical embellishment, allowing it to speak with its own authority. This observation especially applies to parts of his ethical exegesis found in the *Paidagogos.*[126]

---

[120] See Nardi, Clemente (1985) 16 f.

[121] See also *Strom.* 1. 29. 6 and the interpretation of a number of verses from Proverbs 5.

[122] See *Post.* 17–20; *Mig.* 139 f, 154; *Somn.* 1. 64–67. For further support of this thesis see Dawson, Readers (1992) 213 f.

[123] The words used are ἀποβαλλεῖν; καταπιπτειν and ἐκπιπτεῖν.

[124] For this point see Dawson, Readers 213, who argues that the reason for this difference is simple: in Clement the interest is in the voice (the Logos) of Scripture, but in Philo in the actual text (Moses is a scribe).

[125] Campenhausen, Formation 293.

[126] It would be tempting to see a link between Clement's understanding of the Logos as

Clement did not interpret the OT in the same way as Philo, or Origen. For Clement individual lemmata of the OT are rarely the subject of exegesis in the way they were for the other two. The wording of Scripture is rarely afforded the same significance, and his interpretation does not proceed as of principle from literal to spiritual. Clement may espouse rules of interpretation, but his exegesis is not a technical affair. In the end he sees the OT, not as material for commentary, but for meditation.

3. Origen as Exegete of the Old Testament

Texts: For a list of editions of texts by title of work see B. NEUSCHÄFER, *Origines* (1987) 301–305. Listed below are other editions from the *Sources Chrétiennes* series which do not appear in NEUSCHÄFER's list, or are referred to directly in my own text: M. BORRET, *Homélies sur le Lévitique* (Tomes 1 and 2, SC 286 and 287; Paris 1981); idem, *Homélies sur l'Exode* (SC 321; Paris 1985); H. CROUZEL, *Grégoire le Thaumaturge: Remerciement à Origène suivi de la Lettre d'Origène à Grégoire* (SC 148; Paris 1969); idem, and M. SIMONETTI, *Traité des Principes* (Tomes 3 and 4, SC 268 and 269; Paris 1980); L. DOUTRELEAU/P. H. DE LUBAC, *Homélies sur la Genèse* (SC 7; Paris 1943); M. HARL, *La chaîne palestinienne sur le Psaume* 118 (SC 189 and 190; Paris 1972); M. HARL/N. R. M. DE LANGE, *Philocalie 1–20: Sur les écritures et la lettre sur l'histoire de Suzanne* (SC 302; Paris 1983); A. JAUBERT, *Homélies sur Josué* (SC 71; Paris 1960); P. NAUTIN/P. HUSSON, *Homélies sur Jérémie* (SC 232 and 238; Paris 1976–7); P. and M. T. NAUTIN, *Homélies sur Samuel* (SC 328; Paris 1986); DOM. O. ROUSSEAU, *Homélies sur le Cantique des Cantiques* (SC 37; Paris 1953).

Bibliography: H. CROUZEL, *Bibliographie critique d'Origène* (Instrumenta Patristica 8; Den Haag/Steenbrugge 1971; Supplément 1, Instrumenta Patristica 8 A; 1982).

General works: C. P. BAMMEL, "Die Hexapla des Origenes: Die Hebraica Veritas im Streit der Meinungen", *Aug* 28 (1988) 125–149; idem, "Origen's Definitions of Prophecy and Gnosis", *JTS* 40 (1989) 489–493; G. BARDY, "Commentaires patristiques de la Bible", DBSup 2 (Paris 1934) 73–103; D. BARTHÉLEMY, "Origène et le texte de l'Ancien Testament", *Epektasis:* Mélanges patristiques offerts au Cardinal Danièlou (Paris 1972) 247–261; W. A. BIENERT, *Allegoria und Anagoge bei Didymos dem Blinden von Alexandria* (PTS 13; Berlin/New York 1972); S. P. BROCK, "Origen's aims as a textual critic of the Old Testament", StPatr 10 (TU 107; 1970) 215–218; H. FRHR. VON CAMPENHAUSEN, *The Formation of the Christian Bible* (ET London 1972) 307 f; H. CHADWICK, *Origen. Contra Celsum. Translated with an Introduction and Notes* (2nd ed. Cambridge 1965); idem, *Early Christianity and the Classical tradition* (Oxford 1966) 67–94; H. CROUZEL, *Origène et la Connaissance mystique* (Paris 1961); idem, "Le sens littéral dans ses homélies sur l'Hexateuque", *BLE* 70 (1969) 241–263; idem, *Origen* (ET San Francisco 1989); J. DANIÉLOU, "L'unité des deux Testaments dans l'œuvre d'Origène", *RSR* 22 (1948) 27–56; idem, *Origen* (London 1955); idem, "Origène comme exégète de la Bible", StPatr 1 (TU 63; 1957) 280–290; idem, *From Shadow to Reality: Studies in the Biblical Typology of the Fathers* (ET London 1960); idem, *Gospel Message and Hellenistic Culture. A History of early Christian Doctrine before the Council of Nicea* (ET London 1973); J. A. EMERTON, "The Purpose of the Second Column of the Hexapla", *JTS* 7 (1956) 79–87; idem, "A Further Consideration of the Second Column of the Hexapla", *JTS* 22 (1971) 15–28; R. GOEGLER, *Zur Theologie des biblischen Wortes bei Origenes* (Düsseldorf 1963); R. M. GRANT, *Letter and Spirit* (London 1957); R. P. C. HANSON, *Allegory and Event: A Study of the Sources and Significance of Origen's Interpretation of Scripture* (London 1959); M. HARL, *Origène et la fonction révélatrice du Verbe incarné* (Patristica Sorbonensia 2; Paris 1958); idem, "Origène et les interprétations patristiques grecques et l'obscurité biblique", *VC* 36 (1982) 324–371; idem, "Le langage de l'expérience religieuse chez les Pères

---

Protreptikos, Paidagogos and Didaskalos, and the modes in which he exegetes Scripture. As the first two the Logos speaks clearly, but as the last he speaks obscurely and can only be understood through allegorical exegesis.

Grecs", *RSLR* 13 (1977) 5–34; A. von Harnack, *Der kirchengeschichtliche Ertrag der exegetischen Arbeiten des Origenes*, 2 parts (TU xlii, 3 and 4; Leipzig 1918–1919); M. Hornschuh, "Das Leben des Origenes und die Entstehung der alexandrinischen Schule", *ZKG* 71 (1960) 1–25, 193–214; S. Jellicoe, *The Septuagint and Modern Study* (Oxford 1968); A. Kamesar, *Jerome, Scholarship and the Greek Bible: A Study of the Quaestiones Hebraicae in Genesim* (Oxford 1993) 4–28; E. Klostermann, "Formen der exegetischen Arbeiten des Origenes", *ThLZ* 72 (1947) 203–208; N. R. M. de Lange, "Jewish Influence on Origen", *Origeniana*: Premier colloque des études origéniennes (ed. H. Crouzel/G. Lomiento/J. Rius Camps; Paris 1975); idem, *Origen and the Jews. Studies in Jewish Christian Relations in third century Palestine* (Cambridge 1976); idem, "The *Letter of Africanus*: Origen's recantation?", StPatr 16 (1985) 242–247; W. J. Lienhardt, "Origen as Homilist", *Preaching in the Patristic Age*: Essays in honour of W. J. Burghardt (ed. D. G. Hunter; New York 1989) 36–52; A. Louth, *The Origins of the Christian Mystical Tradition* (Oxford 1981); H. de Lubac, *Histoire et Esprit. L'intelligence de l'Ecriture d'après d'Origène* (Paris 1950); P. C. Miller, "Poetic Words and Abysmal Words: Reflections on Origen's Hermeneutics", *Origen of Alexandria: His World and His Legacy* (ed. C. Kannengiesser/W. L. Petersen; Notre Dame 1988) 165–178; W. Mizugaki, "'Spirit' and 'Search': The Basis of Biblical Hermeneutics in Origen's On First Principles 4. 1–3", *Eusebius, Christianity and Judaism* (ed. H. W. Attridge/G. Hata; Wayne State University and Leiden 1992); E. Molland, *The Conception of the Gospel in the Alexandrian Theology* (Oslo 1938); E. Nardoni, "Origen's Concept of Biblical Inspiration", *SCent* 4 (1984) 9–23; P. Nautin, *Origène: Sa vie et son œuvre* (Christianisme antique I; Paris 1977); B. Neuschäfer, *Origenes als Philologe* (Basel 1987); J. Pépin, *Mythe et Allégorie* (Paris 1958); L. Perrone, "Argumentazione di Origene nel tratto di ermeneutica Biblica: Note di lettura su Περὶ ἀρχῶν IV. 1–3", SCO 40 (1990) 161–203; M. J. Rondeau, *Les commentaires patristiques du Psautier (IIIe–Ve siècles)*, vol. 1, Les travaux des Pères grecs et latins sur le Psautier, Recherches et bilan (OCA 219; Rome 1982); vol. 2, Exégèse prosopologique et théologie (OCA 220; Rome 1985); D. T. Runia, *Philo in early Christian Literature: a Survey* (Assen 1993); C. J. Scalise, "Origen and the Sensus Literalis", *Origen and his Legacy* (ed. C. Kannengiesser; Notre Dame 1988) 117–129; J. L. P. Schaper, "The Origin and Purpose of the Fifth Column of the Hexapla (a paper delivered at the Rich Seminar on the Hexapla; forthcoming 1995; ed. A. Salvesen); G. Sgherri, "Sulla valutazione origeniana dei LXX", *Bib.* 58 (1977); idem, *Chiesa e Sinagoga nelle opere di Origene* (Studia patristica Mediolanensia 13; Milan 1982); idem, "A proposito di Origene e la lingua ebraica", *Aug* 14 (1974) 220–257; M. Simonetti, *Lettera e/o Allegoria. Un contributo alla storia dell'esegesi patristica*, 73–98; H. B. Swete, *An Introduction to the Old Testament in Greek* (London 1900; second edition revised by R. R. Ottley, London 1914); K. J. Torjesen, *Hermeneutical Procedure and Theological Method in Origen's Exegesis* (New York/Berlin 1986); J. W. Trigg, *Origen: The Bible and Philosophy in the Third Century Church* (London 1985); E. Ulrich, "Origen's Old Testament Text: The Transmission History of the Septuagint to the Third Century CE, *Origen of Alexandria, His World and His Legacy* (ed. C. Kannengiesser; Notre Dame 1988) 3–33; W. Voelker, *Das Vollkommenheitsideal bei Origenes* (Tübingen 1931); M. Wiles, "Origen as Biblical Scholar", CHB 1, *From the Beginnings to Jerome* (ed. P. Ackroyd/C. F. Evans; Cambridge 1970) 454–489; J. Wright, "Origen in the Scholar's Den: A Rationale for the Hexapla", *Origen of Alexandria* (1988) 48–62; A. Zoellig, *Die Inspirationslehre des Origenes* (Strassburg 1902).

3.1. Introduction

Δῶρον τὸ μέγιστον οὗτος τοῦτο θεόθεν ἔχει λαβὼν καὶ μοῖραν παγκάλην οὐρανόθεν, ἑρμηνεὺς εἶναι τῶν τοῦ θεοῦ λόγων πρὸς ἀνθρώπους, συνιέναι τὰ θεοῦ ὡς θεοῦ λαλοῦντος, καὶ διηγεῖσθαι ἀνθρώποις ὡς ἀκούουσιν ἄθρωποι (Gregory on Origen, *Orat.* 181).[127]

[127] "This man received from God the greatest gift and from Heaven the happiest lot, namely to be an interpreter of the words of God to men, to understand the things of God as if God was speaking them to him, and to explain these words to men so that men might understand them".

"There has never been a theologian in the church who was so exclusively a Biblical exegete" (HARNACK, Ertrag 221).

Origen's contribution to the Christian interpretation of the Old Testament was immense.[128] He was the first Christian as far as we know to attempt to establish an accurate text of the LXX by reference to the external criterion of the Hebrew original. His production of the Hexapla is testimony to the importance he attached to his textual endeavours, and indirectly to the importance he attached to the OT itself. He was the first Christian to attempt to construct a systematic theory of hermeneutics. When interpreting the OT, more than any Christian writer before him, he saw it as appropriate to *consult* Jewish exegetes whose influence on him stems principally from his period in Caesarea.[129] These, after all, were Jewish scriptures (*c. Cels.* 6. 23). His central hermeneutical conviction that *all* Scripture was divinely inspired (θεόπνευστος) and was therefore a harmonious, self-interpreting whole, which formed the foundational text for all theologising, led him to write on almost all the books of the OT,[130] and in a diversity of forms (scholia, commentary and homily). As a trained grammarian (Eusebius, *H. E.* 6. 2 f.)[131] he applied to his exegesis of the OT many of the rules and practices which had long been applied to the exegesis of Homer and other texts by pagans (the production of the Hexapla being just one manifestation of this). He gave to the Christian interpretation of the OT a precision and clear-sightedness which had previously been lacking.[132]

Unfortunately his writings reach us in a much reduced state, and mainly in translations into Latin which are not entirely trustworthy.[133] But what we do possess is sufficient to indicate the sheer extent of Origen's biblical knowledge and the all pervading nature of his biblical interest.[134]

Like Clement before him, Origen wrote at a time when the OT's position in the Christian canon was being questioned by a number of groups, either directly by the Marcionites who simply dismissed it as the revelation of a

---

[128] "Origen's exegetical writings represent a stage of primary importance in the history of the Christian interpretation of scripture in general and of the Old Testament in particular" (Daniélou, Message 273).

[129] On this important subject see de Lange, Jews (1975).

[130] Simonetti, Lettera (1985) 74, notes that Origen was the first Christian exegete to draw attention in any systematic way to the books of Ecclesiastes and Job, and that his interest in the books of Joshua and Judges remains almost unique in the history of the ancient church.

[131] For a positive assessment of the relevant evidence in Eusebius see Neuschäfer, Origenes (1987) 32 f., and the same author's introduction, where he shows how in recent scholarship the philological side of Origen's exegesis has been neglected.

[132] "Insomma, Origene ha fatto dell'ermeneutica biblica una vera e propria scienza, e in tal senso ha condizionato in modo decisivo tutta l'esegisi patristica ..." (Simonetti, ibid. 73). For similar sentiments see Wiles, Origen (1970) 454.

[133] For a discussion of the transmission history of Origen's works see Neuschäfer, ibid. 42 f. He identifies four different types of transmission: quotation, catenae, translations into Latin, and allusions. He discusses the difficulty associated with each form. For his discussion of the Latin translations of Rufinus and Jerome see 46 f. For a discussion of recent debate about the accuracy of Rufinus' translations see Torjesen, Procedure (1986) 14 f. The general consensus seems to be that he was accurate in rendering the spirit of a passage, but not its exact wording.

[134] On Origen's knowledge of the Scriptures and his ability to interpret, in addition to the statement of Origen's pupil Gregory (referred to above), see also Jerome in *Ep.* 84. 8.

lesser deity, or indirectly by Christians who could not see the relevance or usefulness of many of its writings.[135] Behind much of Origen's exegesis of the OT lies an apologetic strain. All Scripture was inspired (θεόπνευστος) and useful (ὠφέλιμος), St. Paul had written (2 Tim 3:16). Origen was keen to emphasise the truth of this assertion, even in the case of books like Leviticus, which appeared at first sight to have no edificatory content for Christians.[136] Origen did much, whether in his scholarly commentaries and scholia, or his more popular homilies, to convince Christians of the doctrinal and edificatory significance of the OT.[137]

Origen's defence of the OT's significance for doctrine and edification was not only aimed at an internal audience. Jews who strongly objected to many aspects of its Christian exegesis and who could influence Christian audiences particularly in their practices,[138] and pagans who made use of Jewish criticisms and added their own (which accorded more with Marcionite objections), also constituted significant opponents.[139]

At the most general level it is the aim of this discussion to examine the presuppositions which underpinned Origen's interpretation of the OT, and to observe how these manifested themselves in his surviving works. Against the background of this wider aim we will examine a number of significant questions. What precisely was the position of the OT in Origen's understanding? What was the purpose of the Hexapla? What was its relevance to Origen's wider hermeneutical interests? How were Origen's technical/exegetical interests, inherited from his early grounding in the rules of ancient grammar, related to his image as *allegoricus semper interpres*? It is the aim of this essay to see the many facets of Origen's exegetical enterprise as an integrated whole.

3.2. Canon and Text

Origen is amongst the first Christians to take an interest in the question of the OT canon (Melito of Sardis before him appears to have been interested in the subject), and the first to concern himself with the complex question of the text of the OT.

3.2.1. Canon

In the context of a discussion of Origen's biblical canon, Eusebius quotes from a passage in Origen's commentary on Psalm 1 (*HE* 6.25.1–2) which

[135] For places where Origen refers to such Christians see *HNum.* 7.2 and *HJos* 8.2.

[136] For such a reference to Leviticus see *HNum.* 28.2.

[137] Origen's emphasis in his exegetical works is forever on the ὠφέλεια of Scripture, namely the relevance of the passage under discussion to his Christian readers. On this concept see below, and especially Neuschäfer, ibid. 259 f.

[138] In the context of Origen's work in Caesarea we should not underestimate the significance of the Jewish influence. This has been particularly emphasised by de Lange, Jews (1975) 86–87. He argues that on many occasions in his extant homilies Origen attacks a Jewish literal understanding of the Law. These polemics should not be regarded as hot air. Many of his congregation may have gone to the synagogue on Saturday and the church on Sunday. The temptation to observe Jewish laws must have been tempting. See *HLev.* 5.8 where Origen objects to Christians who expound in church what they have heard from Jews the day before.

[139] See Origen's *c. Cels.* 1.20; 4.39, 42.

begins by stating that in the Hebrew Tradition there are 22 canonical (ἐνδιαθήκους) books and outside of these (ἔξω δὲ τούτων) the book of the Maccabees. The list is not, however, as Eusebius seems to think, Origen's OT canon. Not only is this indicated by the fact that in the quotation Origen states that the number 22 is ὡς Ἑβραῖοι παραδιδόασιν, but also by the fact that elsewhere he quotes from other books as if they were scriptural. These are Judith, Tobit, Wisdom, Ecclesiasticus, Baruch and the parts of Esther and Daniel (the story of Susannah) none of which are found in the Hebrew Bible. In his letter to Africanus, he defends the canonical status of the book of Susannah against Africanus' claim that it should not be in the Bible because it is not in the Hebrew canon,[140] by arguing from ecclesiastical practice (*Africanus* 3 (2)).[141] He affirms the divine origin of Tobit, Esther, Judith and Wisdom at *HNum.* 27.1.

But we should balance these statements with those found elsewhere. In *On Prayer* 14.4, after quoting from Tobit, Origen says that he will quote from another text because Tobit is not received in the canon of the Jews; and in the prologue to his commentary on the Song of Songs, he does not list Wisdom as a book of Solomon,[142] and discounts the use of apocryphal works in the church.[143]

What the above indicates is:

(1) Origen is interested in the question of the OT canon in a way Clement never was.

(2) He treated with seriousness Jewish testimony on this subject.[144]

(3) He also took seriously, and may have regarded as canonical, books that were used in the Christian community, but were not in the Jewish canon.

(4) Opinions 2 and 3 caused a tension to exist in his mind on this matter. He was a churchman (his apparent endorsement of books read in the Christian Church, which were not in the Jewish canon), and a scholar (his obvious interest in Jewish opinion on this matter). This tension may also be reflected in his attitude to the text of Scripture.

3.2.2. *Text*

Educated in the rules of ancient grammar, Origen knew that the establishment of a correct text (διορθωτικόν) was the necessary preliminary to exegesis

---

[140] Africanus states the rule simply: Ἐξ Ἑβραίων τοῖς Ἕλλησι μετεβλήθη πανθ'ὅσα τῆς παλαιᾶς διαθήκης φέρεται.

[141] de Lange, Africanus (1985) 246–247, argues that Origen's attitude to the OT canon as expressed in his *Epistle to Africanus* is disingenuous. According to Jerome (In Dan. xiii, CC LXXVA. 948f.) Origen had stated in his lost *Stromateis* that if it could not be shown that the book of Susannah was originally written in Hebrew then it could not be accepted as Scripture. As de Lange notes, "This argument concedes precisely the point which was made by Africanus and vigorously rebutted by Origen in his reply: that the existence of a Hebrew original is the criterion for accepting a work as scriptural".

[142] He only lists three books of Solomon (Proverbs, Ecclesiastes and the Song of Songs), arguing that only three books are accepted by the church and only three are in the Jewish canon.

[143] On apocryphal works see de Lange, Influence (1975) 232–233.

[144] See de Lange, ibid. 232–233.

(ἐξηγητικόν).[145] Furthermore, if Scripture was inspired to the very last word (as we will see, an assumption of his hermeneutical system), then the establishment of an accurate text constituted an important preliminary to exegesis.

The LXX or Septuagint, which was the text of the OT used by the Christian church, contained many variant readings within its manuscript tradition. The problem of establishing the right reading was complicated by two additional factors. First, the LXX was a translation from the original Hebrew; and secondly, there existed rival Greek translations to the LXX, the most important of which were those of Aquila, Theodotion and Symmachus. These complications led Origen to construct his famous Hexapla, which he himself never referred to by that name, probably because it was for his own private use,[146] a suggestion made more likely by the sheer bulk of the work.[147]

The Hexapla[148] seems to have consisted of 6 separate columns.[149] The first column was probably occupied by the Hebrew text.[150] Then followed a Greek transliteration of the Hebrew text,[151] the Greek translation of Aquila and Symmachus, then the LXX itself with its obeli and asterices (for these see below),[152] the translation of Theodotion and two other versions discovered by Origen himself, and perhaps only used in his commentaries on the Psalms.[153] The columns were arranged in such a way that at a glance a reader could see how individual words were rendered in the different translations.[154]

But was the purpose of the Hexapla purely textual? We can only establish this if we look at Origen's own statements on the subject, and more importantly the way he conducts his textual criticism in his extant works.

At *Comm. in Matt.* 15. 14, Origen gives his readers a succinct insight into his textual methods when dealing with the LXX. He notes that where there existed variants amongst copies of the LXX, he adopted the reading which agreed with that found in the Greek versions (ἐκδόσεις). He goes on to state that he has obelised passages in the LXX which did not appear in the Hebrew,

---

[145] For ancient text critical methods see Neuschäfer, Origenes (1987) 122f, and Procopé in the previous essay in this volume.

[146] de Lange, Philocalie (1985) 493 n. 1.

[147] Swete, Introduction (1914) 74, estimates its size at 6500 pages, but Wright, Origen (1988) 52, regards this as a conservative figure.

[148] For an easily accessible discussion of the Hexapla see Trigg, Origen (1985) 82–86.

[149] For the most significant reference to the Hexapla see Eusebius, *HE* 6. 16. 1 f. For a critique of Eusebius' description of the Hexapla, and other descriptions see Nautin, Origène (1977) 301 f.

[150] For a sustained and detailed argument against the presence of a column in Hebrew script see Nautin, ibid. 301 f. His argument is based upon the fact that (a) the Mercati fragments of the Hexapla, the Ambrosian palimpsest O 39 supp. and the Hexaplaric remains have no Hebrew column, and (b) that the description of the Hexapla found in Eusebius can be interpreted to imply that there was no Hebrew column. For the most recent refutation of these arguments see Ulrich, Text (1988) 24 f.

[151] On the purpose of the transliterated text see Emerton, Purpose (1956), and Consideration (1971). He contends that it was designed for the use of readers with some knowledge of Hebrew as a guide to the vocalisation of the text in Hebrew characters in the first column. For a refutation of this view see Jellicoe, Septuagint (1968) 110–111, who argues that originally it was intended for the use of Jews in Palestinian synagogues who did not know Hebrew but wanted to read the Scriptures in Hebrew. Nautin, ibid. 337 f, also argues for its provenance in Jewish synagogues.

[152] See Nautin, ibid. 455–8, for the difficulties of arguing that this column (the so-called Hexaplaric column), was part of the Hexapla.

[153] On these see Nautin, ibid. 312 f.

[154] See Wright, ibid. 51.

for he did not dare to drop them, and that he has asterised passages which appeared in the Hebrew, but not in the LXX.[155]

This passage gives us the impression of a relatively rigorous method of text criticism, in which the Hebrew text, seemingly mediated to Origen through the consciously 'accurate' Greek versions,[156] for it seems clear that he knew very little Hebrew,[157] became the final court of appeal in the cases of LXX variants, and could also be used as a means of determining where the LXX had omitted or added something to its translation. This would confirm the view that Origen's primary motive in constructing his Hexapla was the construction of a 'pure' text of the LXX.[158] But does Origen's actual practice of text criticism, witnessed in his commentaries and homilies, confirm this seemingly straightforward picture? Furthermore, how are we to square the comments made in this passage with those found in *Ep. ad Afric.* 9 (5) where Origen states that the primary motivation for the construction of the Hexapla was to enable Christians to be well informed in their debates with Jews, and 8 (4) where, in his assertion that the book of Susannah is part of Scripture, he appears to ascribe priority to the witness of the LXX?[159]

Before we proceed a note of caution should be sounded. Because we possess Origen's OT commentaries in such a damaged state, and it is clear that there was more textual comment in these than in his homilies which survive in greater profusion, the attainment of a full understanding of Origen's text critical method is beyond us.[160]

In his exegetical works Origen invariably regards the reading witnessed in the Hebrew and/or the versions as the more accurate.[161] This applies both in instances where there is disagreement amongst the copies of the LXX,[162] or where the LXX reading disagrees with the reading in the Hebrew/versions.[163] He corrects proper names to accord with the Hebrew;[164] and as Sgherri

[155] For another passage which speaks of the 'obelising' and 'asterising' of passages see *Ep. ad Afric.* 7. For the difficulties in associating the LXX discussed here with that found in the Hexapla see Neuschäfer, Origenes 96 f.

[156] In *Comm. in Rom.* 6.41 Origen admits that the greater age of the LXX in relation to the other editions meant that it was more likely to suffer from corruptions. Origen regarded Aquila as the most accurate translation (*Ep. ad Afric.* 2 and *Philoc.* 14-1).

[157] For the view that Origen had a good knowledge of Hebrew see Eusebius *HE* 6.16 and Jerome *Vir. ill.* 54, and for a recent and partial endorsement of their assertion see Sgherri, Proposito (1974); but see now also Schaper, Purpose (1995) 3. For the view that he only had a rudimentary knowledge of Hebrew, which seems now to be the standard view, see de Lange, Jews (1975) 22–23, who argues that Origen probably required the help of friendly Jews in the construction of the Hexapla. For specific examples of places where Origen has dismissed the literal meaning of an OT passage when an understanding of Hebrew would have brought sense to the text see Crouzel, Origène (1969) 255. For a discussion of the relationship between the role of the Hebrew text and the ἐκδόσεις in Origen's text critical endeavour see Neuschäfer 89 f. Brock, Aims (1970), indirectly addressing the question of Origen's knowledge of Hebrew, notes that Origen is not interested in the Hebrew text as such, but rather in Jewish versions current at the time, precisely because his textual endeavours have as their primary motive debate with contemporary Jews. In support of this thesis he shows how quite often Origen will not mention the Hebrew at all, but just the editions (see *HNum.* 18.3; *HGen.* 3.5).

[158] The sense of διαφωνίαν … εὕρομεν ἰάσθαι. In addition see Schaper, Purpose (1995) 3 and 10.

[159] In support of a polemical purpose for the Hexapla see Brock, Aims (1970). For a refutation of the view see de Lange, Philocalie (1985) 496 f, and Africanus (1985).

[160] Jerome, in the Prologue to his translation of Origen's *Homilies* on the Song of Songs, indicates that in his *Commentary* Origen interpreted the Song in relation to the LXX and a number of other Greek versions. Yet in the *Commentary*, as translated by Rufinus, there are very few references to the versions.

[161] See *HJer.* 14.3 ἐν δὲ τοῖς ἀκριβεστάτοις καὶ συμφουνοῦσι τοῖς Ἑβραϊκοῖς.

[162] See *HJer.* 15.4.

[163] *HEz* 6.4; also see his comment on Psalm 118 (119):28 in Devresse, p. 31. For a discussion of this latter reference see Neuschäfer, Origenes (1987) 105.

[164] See Kamesar, Jerome (1993) 10–11.

has pointod out,[165] he invariably interprets asterised passages, that is, he interprets passages which appear in the versions/Hebrew, but not in the LXX.[166]

But there also exists evidence which complicates this picture. First, it should be noted that Origen exhibits what one scholar has called an exegetical maximalism in his treatment of the text of the LXX.[167] Even at points where he agrees that the reading found in the Hebrew/versions is the correct reading, he will often interpret the text in relation to both readings.[168] Consonant with this is the observation that Origen interprets obelised passages.[169] On the basis of his comments in *Comm. in Matt.* 15.14 he was not obliged to this.[170] But most interesting in this respect is Origen's conviction that the majority of 'additions' to or 'omissions' from the Hebrew in the LXX are themselves intentional and the result of the work of providence, a theory which appears quite compatible with Origen's claim, found in *Ep. ad Afric.* 8, that providence (πρόνοια) has given the LXX to the church.[171] So commenting on the Hebrew reading of Ps 2:12 which reads ("lest ye perish from the way"), and the LXX ("lest ye perish from the right (δικαίας) way"), Origen states that the word 'right' is there as a result of a divine device (κατ' οἰκονομίαν προσέθηκαν). Similarly at *HJer.* 16. 5 Origen agrees that the LXX reading of Jer 16:18 without πρῶτον is not the original reading. However, he states that it is not an oversight but divine intention which has lead the translator to omit these words.[172] Similarly Origen attributes the workings of providence to non-literal but accurate translations of the Hebrew original.[173]

The above observations should go some way to rebutting the argument that when Origen expresses confidence in the LXX in *Ep. ad Afric.* 8 (4), he simply repeats the arguments of his opponents who were critical of his textual studies.[174]

---

[165] Valutazione (1977) 28.

[166] See *HJer.* 16.10. Here Origen notes that the editions of Jer 17:1, which he assumes reflect the Hebrew, have a longer text. He goes on to interpret the text noting that πεπλήρωται πραγμάτων ἀναγκαιοτάτων, δύναμενων ἐὰν προσέγωμεν ἐπιστρέψαι τὴν ψυξὴν ἡμῶν.

[167] Kamesar, Jerome (1993) 17.

[168] A classic example, often quoted by scholars, is *HJer.* 14.3. Here Origen cites two variant readings of Jer 15:10 represented in most of the manuscripts. He states that the more numerous manuscripts read: οὐκ ὠφέλησα, οὐδὲ ὠφέλησέ με οὐδείς, while the most exact concur with the Hebrew, reading οὐκ ὠφείλησα, οὐδὲ ὠφείλησέ με οὐδείς, and that he will expound both passages, that prevalent in the churches and that prevalent in the Hebrew scriptures. At *HJer.* 15.5 he clearly states a preference for the Hebrew reading (the second of the two mentioned above), claiming that the one found in the many of LXX manuscripts is a scribal error (ἁμάρτημα γραφικὸν). But in spite of this judgment he still maintains that it is possible to expound both passages. For the presence of tension between the two judgments and an explanation see Nautin, *Jérémie* I 46–49. See also *HJer.* 16.5.

[169] See *In Ps.* 2.12 (PG 12, 1116 C 14–1117 A 4). See also his comments on the final words of the book of Job, which appear to make reference to the resurrection, and are only found in the LXX. For a reluctance to make use of obelised passages see *On Prayer* 14.4 where Origen quotes a passage from an obelised section of Daniel, but states that he will make use of another passage precisely because the passage in question was obelised.

[170] "Die adäquate textkritische Operation bezüglich der Interpolationen wäre, seiner eigenen Aussage nach, ihre radikale Verwerfung gewesen", Neuschäfer, ibid. 102.

[171] For a discussion of this concept in Origen see Hanson, Allegory (1959) 163f; Neuschäfer, ibid. 111–113; and Kamesar, ibid. 14f. For an exception to the rule of intentional/inspired change see Origen's comments on the additional words αὕτη ἡ βίβλος γενέσεως to Gen 2:4 (*PG* 12, 97 C 7–14). He attributes this to a scribal error on the part of a copyist of the *Hebrew* which found its way into the LXX. This reference is discussed by Neuschäfer, ibid. 110–11.

[172] Neuschäfer, ibid. 112, argues that Origen's theory of οἰκονομία accounts for his text critical conservatism.

[173] For examples of this see *HJer.* 2.4 (Latin); *HJer.* 18.6. For a similar use of the concept of πρόνοια amongst pagan grammarians see Neuschäfer, Origenes 136f.

[174] "He expresses complete confidence in the Greek text with regard to both the deviations from the original and the attempts to reflect it accurately. Indeed his admonition to pay attention to the smallest details of [Greek] biblical language which he uses in the *Philocalia* would

What might we conclude from the above:

(1) Origen entertains a much more critical attitude to the text of the LXX than all his known Christian predecessors, and many Christian writers who followed him.[175] In his extant works there is no account of the translation of the Hebrew Bible with the legendary accretions present in writers like Philo and Clement.[176] He clearly found the presence of διαφωνία amongst the LXX manuscripts a difficulty which had to be confronted. In confronting this problem he was the first Christian scholar to realise the importance of the Hebrew (albeit mediated through the editions) for the text critic of the LXX. The significance which he attached to his text-critical task is proven by the sheer size of the Hexapla.

(2) Whether dealing with disagreements between LXX manuscripts, or between the LXX and the Hebrew/editions, Origen often favours the readings found in the Hebrew/editions. His text critical judgments are made almost entirely on the basis of this external criterion.

(3) This does not, however, mean that Origen dispensed with the readings found in the LXX. Even where he clearly states that the Hebrew/editions reading is right, he will attach an interpretation of the passage/verse according to a number of readings (LXX and Editions/Hebrew). He often interprets obelised passages.

(4) While not regarding the LXX as inspired in the same way as his predecessors and many of his successors, Origen espied the work of providence in its translation, whether this related to the question of translation, or to the additions to and omissions from the Hebrew.

(5) Origen had been brought up to regard the LXX as the OT of the Christian church. In a number of his writings, some of which are preserved in the *Philocalia*, he expressed the view that each word of the Bible was inspired (see below), and by this he meant the Greek Bible. Yet he knew that the LXX contained variant readings in its own manuscript tradition and that it was a sometimes not very literal translation of the original Hebrew text.[177] As a trained grammarian and a respecter of Hebrew wisdom, he could not overlook these matters. Origen's complex attitude towards the text of the LXX emerged from the tension which existed between these convictions. Or stated in another way, ecclesiastical and hermeneutical assumptions clashed with the acknowledged difficulty associated with the textual witness.[178]

(6) A purely polemical use for the Hexapla seems unlikely. Its size and the fact that many of Origen's text-critical discussions are not polemical support such a conclusion.[179]

---

hardly make sense if this were not the case." (Kamesar, ibid. 17). See also Harl, Philocalie (1985) 127.

175 For this see Bammel, Hexapla. She is particularly keen to point out the differences between Origen's attitude to the LXX, and the more conservative attitudes of Eusebius, Epiphanius, Rufinus and Augustine. She also discusses Jerome's attitude.

176 On this see Hanson, Allegory (1959) 165: "We find no childish accusations in Origen, and no credulous wonder at the thaumaturgy accompanying the making of the LXX translation".

177 For explicit statements on this matter see *Ep. ad Afric.* 6 and 7. Origen notes specifically the cases of the books of Job, Jeremiah and Genesis.

178 On this see Neuschäfer, ibid. 135f.

179 See de Lange, Africanus (1985) 246.

(7) It should be noted that Origen's exegetical maximalism (his tendency to interpret a passage in relation to a number of readings) may well have arisen from his hermeneutical conviction that Scripture has a multitude of meanings. By expanding the size of the Bible Origen is able to expand the possibilities of meanings.[180]

3.3. Hermeneutical Presuppositions and the Place of the Old Testament

3.3.1. Hermeneutical Presuppositions

Περὶ τοῦ θεοπνεύστου τῆς θείας γραφῆς, καὶ πῶς ταύτην ἀναγνωστέον καὶ νοητέον (part of the opening heading of ch. 1 of the *Philocalia*).[181]

Origen's most extended utterance on biblical hermeneutics occurs in his *De Princ.* 4.[182] This forms part of the last chapter of an early work, dating from about 229, before Origen left Alexandria for Caesarea.[183] Fortunately, the majority of this section of the work is preserved in the original Greek in the *Philocalia*, a collection of Origen's exegetical comments compiled by Basil and Gregory Nazianzen in the second half of the fourth century.[184] Origen probably wrote *De Princ.* in response to those in Alexandria who were criticising his theological opinions. As a relatively early work it should not be taken as Origen's last will and testament on the subject of biblical interpretation, and as theory it should not be taken as the precise reflection of praxis. But with the exception of various digressions found in his surviving commentaries and homilies, it constitutes his only extended utterance on the subject which survives. My analysis of Origen's hermeneutical presuppositions will use *De Princ.* 4 as the basic framework for discussion, amplifying it with statements found in Origen's other works, especially as these appear in the *Philocalia*.[185] I shall attempt to draw out the significance of these comments for Origen's understanding of the OT.[186]

---

[180] Wright, ibid., has argued that the Hexapla itself indicates this desire to expand the possibilities of exegesis. While admitting that the LXX takes centre stage in its construction, both physically and in terms of grammatical emphasis, he argues that the other texts were not simply there to correct it. If this had been the case it would not have been necessary for Origen and his assistants to write down all the versions, and he would have dispensed with the obelised passages. Rather the structure of the Hexapla reflects Origen's desire to extend his exegetical options. This conclusion might seem to be supported by Jerome's prologue to his translation of Origen's Homilies on the Song of Songs where, as we mentioned above, he states that in his commentary Origen expounded the text from the versions of the LXX, Aquila, Symmachus and Theodotion, and finally a fifth found at Actium.

[181] The heading should not be regarded as an imposition, for at *De Princ.* 4.2.1 talks about τῷ τρόπῳ τῆς ἀναγνώσεως καὶ νοήσεως αὐτῶν (Scriptures understood).

[182] For the full Greek text see Simonetti/Crouzel, SC 268 259 f. For discussions of the passage see the same authors' commentary, SC 269 151 f, and Mizugaki, Search (1992). For an excellent and detailed discussion of Origen's biblical hermeneutics see Harl, SC 302 19 f; and, with less detail, Simonetti, Lettera (1985) 78 f, and Trigg, Origen (1985) 120–128.

[183] I adopt Nautin's dating of the work. For his arguments and alternative positions see Origène (1977) 368 f.

[184] For a discussion of the historical background and form of the same work see Harl, Philocalie (1985) 19 f, and also our discussion below.

[185] For the view that the quotations in the *Philocalia* are accurate see Neuschäfer, ibid. 43.

[186] See de Lubac, Esprit (1950) 33, who judged *De Princ* 4.1–3 as an inadequate introduction

The central tenet of Origen's biblical hermeneutics lies in his conviction that all Scripture is divinely inspired. He often attributes this inspiration to the Holy Spirit (*Praef. Princ.* 8), but more importantly to the Logos. Scripture is the permanent incarnation of God, and exegesis constitutes encounter with the Logos.[187] At the beginning of *De Princ.* 4 Origen defends the view that Scripture is inspired. This is necessary because in the previous three chapters he has presented his readers with a lengthy discussion of the most significant Christian doctrines, basing his arguments almost exclusively on scriptural testimony. His argument is based upon two observations. The first relates to history. The writings of Moses (described as the legislator of the Jews) and Jesus (the introducer of the saving doctrines of Christianity) have proven their divine origin by the fact that in contrast to other legislators and philosophers, and in the face of great opposition they have persuaded people to abandon their ancestral laws, and follow new ones. This was predicted by the prophets who stated long before Christ's arrival that he would convert the nations. The second is an argument from prophecy, namely the accurate prediction of Christ's life by the prophets. As if to emphasise the connection between Christ and the inspiration of the OT Origen continues: "And we must add that it was after the advent of Jesus (ἐπιδημήσαντος Ἰησοῦ) that the inspiration of the prophetic words and the spirit of Moses' law (τὸ τῶν προφητῶν λόγων ἔνθεον καὶ τὸ πνευματικὸν τοῦ Μωσέως) came to light. For before the arrival of Christ it was not at all possible to bring forward clear proofs of the divine inspiration of the old scripture (τὰς παλαιὰς γραφὰς)" (4.1.6). One grasps the inspired nature of the OT as a result of the incarnation, an assertion which is very important if one wishes to understand Origen's approach to the OT. For Origen the arrival of Christ constitutes a hermeneutical event in which the obscurity of one revelation is illuminated by the light of another, or to express it in the Pauline language Origen uses, the veil of the Law of Moses is removed (2 Cor 3:6), and the good things which the letter of the Law had concealed are revealed (Heb 10:1). Christ's coming reveals the spiritual nature of the texts which have looked to him, and in so doing reveals his own personality, for he is the content of scriptural revelation. In all exegesis one must turn to him (*HEx.* 12.2; *HNum.* 27.1 f).

Origen is aware, however, that it is not always obvious that Scripture is inspired (4.1.7). Drawing an analogy between its inspiration and the presence of providence in the world, he writes: "For just as providence is not abolished because of our ignorance, at least not for those who have rightly believed in it, so neither is the divine character of scripture, which extends through all of it (διατείνουσα εἰς πᾶσαν αὐτὴν), abolished because our weakness cannot discern in every sentence the hidden splendour of its teachings, concealed

---

to Origen's hermeneutics. This seems only to be half true – chronologically it is placed between one of his commentaries on the Psalms and the commentary on John; and though an early work, it was still regarded by the Cappadocians as an adequate introduction to Origen's hermeneutics. For a defence of the importance of the passage see Mizugaki, Search (1992) 564–565.

187 ἀεὶ γὰρ ἐν ταῖς γραφαῖς ὁ λόγος σὰρξ ἐγένετο ἵνα κατασκηνώσῃ ἐν ἡμῖν (*Philoc.* 15.19 = *c. Cels.* 6.77).

under a poor and humble style (τῇ κεκρυμμένῃ λαμπρότητι τῶν δογμάτων ἐν εὐτελεῖ καὶ εὐκαταφρονήτῳ λέξει)". There are at least two important observations arising from this statement. First, the obscure and difficult character of Scripture forms a persistent topos in Origen's exegetical works. It is not easy to interpret Scripture, but this is entirely appropriate, for these are the words of God which cannot be understood by any undiscriminating individual.[188] To overcome its obscurity, the exegete must penetrate beneath the 'earthenware vessel', the poverty of its style in the literal reading, to its hidden truths. The poverty of the biblical style belies the power of its words, which conceal beneath them divine doctrines. The second relates to the absolute nature of Scripture's inspiration. In *Philoc.* 2.4 Origen writes: "... if the Holy Spirit has dictated (ἐξητασμένως) them (τὰ λογία τοῦ κυρίου) with a scrupulous accuracy (μετὰ πάσης ἀκριβείας) by the mediation of the servants of the word ... then the wisdom of God reaches the whole of scripture to the very last word (μέχρι τοῦ τυχόντος γράμματος)".[189] This has the consequence that there is nothing superfluous in Scripture,[190] and even the most minor detail, as with the most minor detail in God's providential creation,[191] can carry a resonant theological meaning.[192] Exegetes must labour hard at their task. Just as botanists and doctors are able to understand plants and bodies down to the smallest detail, so must the exegete be able to explain Scripture. An admission of defeat in the face of a difficult text is an admission of personal failing.[193] For Origen, then, the difficulty in the interpretative enterprise lies in discovering a method of exegesis, which will overcome the tension between, on the one hand,

[188] On the obscurity of biblical language as understood by Origen see Harl, Obscurité (1982), who discusses Origen's contribution to this idea. For a clear expression of Origen's conviction that Scripture is obscure see *Philoc.* 2.2 (a passage taken from the introduction to Origen's commentary on Psalm 1): ἀλλὰ καὶ περὶ πάσης θείας γραφῆς, ὁμολογουμένως παρὰ τοῖς κἂν μετρίως ἐπαΐειν λόγων θείων δυναμένοις πεπληρωμένης αἰνιγμάτων καὶ παραβολῶν σκοτεινῶν τε λόγων καὶ ἄλλων ποικίλιων εἰδῶν ἀσαφείας, δύσπλήτων τῇ ἀνθρωπίνῃ φύσει; and numerous places in his extant writings. Interestingly, when describing Origen as an exegete, Gregory chooses to begin by stating that: αὐτὸς ὑποφητεύων καὶ σαφηνίζων ὅ τί ποτε σκοτεινὸν καὶ αἰνιγματῶδες ᾖ, οἷα πολλὰ ἐν ταῖς ἱεραῖς ἐστι φωναῖς (174). Gregory muses as to why so much in Scripture is obscure, stating that either it is because if Scripture was clear unworthy souls would apprehend its truths, or because divine language, though in itself clear, is obscure to man who is distant from God.

[189] See also *Philoc.* 1.28, para B: πρέπει δὲ τὰ ἅγια γράμματα πιστεύειν μηδεμίαν κεραίαν ἔχειν κενὴν σοφίας Θεοῦ; and the call in *Comm. in Jo.* 32.68 μέχρι τῶν ἐλαχίστων εἶναι νομιζομένων ἐρευνᾶν τὴν γραφήν.

[190] We cannot change the wording of Scripture, even in the face of a grammatical solecism (*Philoc.* 8).

[191] Harl, Philocalie (1985) 60f, has shown how Origen describes the inspiration of Scripture with the vocabulary (see the verbs διοικεῖν, φθανεῖν, διατείνειν) and themes he employs to describe the presence and action of God in creation. Harl goes on to show how these themes are in fact borrowed from Stoic writers who argued that the action of providence was discernible in the minutest aspect of creation. For another comparison of Providence's working in the world, and the divine working in Scripture see the fragment of Origen's commentary on Psalm 2 preserved in *Philoc.* 2.5.

[192] de Lange, ibid. 110f, has argued that for this particular opinion Origen is directly reliant upon R. Akiba. He cites the argument between Akiba and Ishmael, found at *BSanh* 4ab. Over against Ishmael, Akiba argued that every letter, every particle of Scripture had to be explained in relation to some deeper meaning.

[193] ἀλλὰ σαυτὸν μᾶλλον ἢ τὰ ἱερὰ γράμματα αἰτιῶ, ὅτε μὴ εὑρίσκεις τὸν λόγον τῶν γεγραμμένων (*Philoc.* 10.2).

Scripture's obscurity associated with its literal text, and, on the other, his belief in its absolute inspiration.

It is therefore appropriate that Origen moves on to discuss the method by which Scripture should be interpreted. How should we read and understand such a work (4.2.1 f.)? This discussion is necessary because of the presence of numerous incorrect interpretations, which themselves arise from a faulty method.[194] As examples of the purveyors of such false exegesis, Origen mentions Jews, Gnostics and simple believers. All come to incorrect conclusions because they attribute an exclusively literal understanding to the texts – Jewish literalism leads to a failure to see that the prophecies of the OT point forward to Jesus; Gnostic literalism leads to a dismissal of the OT as the revelation of a lesser deity; and the literalism of the simple believers leads to the holding of absurd opinions, which are not worthy of God, and therefore have no place in the interpretation of his Scriptures.[195] For Origen the appropriate method of interpretation is indicated by the divine origin of the texts concerned. People admit that there are divine revelations (οἰκονομίαι τινὲς μυστικαί) in Scripture, but they are often unable to understand what these are (4.2.2). Indeed, the many faults of interpretation arise from the fact that the understanding of these texts is difficult. Here obscurity becomes the reason for error.

Because of Scripture's obscurity, because it is easy to make a mistake in its interpretation, it is necessary for the interpreter to possess the key of knowledge (κλεῖς τῆς γνώσεως) (*De Princ.* 4.2.4). Origen famously finds this key in Prov 22:20, which he interprets to mean that Scripture has a threefold meaning, which itself corresponds to the threefold structure of man, namely body, soul and spirit. This threefold meaning is not itself related to the salvation of the three parts of man, but rather to three different types of readings, where the movement from literal to spiritual interpretation is construed in terms of three stages of progress.

We enter here into a controversial area of Origenist interpretation. First, while Origen is quite specific about the point that Scripture has three meanings, depending upon the admissability or inadmissability of the literal meaning (on this see below), he does not make it clear what the precise content of the second meaning is. Many scholars hold it to be the moral meaning, and this on the basis of such passages as *HNum.* 9.7, and the implication of the example Origen gives of such interpretation in the passage under discussion (see 4.2.6 where Origen cites Paul's interpretation of Deut 25:4 in 1 Cor 9:9–10), but this is nowhere stated in *De Princ.* As Torjesen observes, at the two points at which Origen comes closest to doing such a thing (4.2.4 and 4.2.6), he simply indicates that it is the level of meaning before the spiritual, a type of interpretation fitting for those who cannot understand the

---

[194] The word he uses for method is τὴν ὁδὸν.

[195] "Now the reason why all those we have mentioned hold false opinions and make impious or ignorant assertions about God appears to be nothing else but this, that scripture is not understood in its spiritual sense, but they interpret it according to the letter alone (ἀλλ' ὡς πρὸς τὸ ψιλὸν γράμμα ἐξειλημμένη)" (*De Princ.* 4.2.2).

more elevated teachings contained within a spiritual reading (τοὺς ὑψηλοτέρων ἀκούειν μὴ δυναμένους).[196] Secondly, it seems clear from the extant homilies and commentaries that Origen does not often divide his interpretation of a passage into three separate sections. Sometimes he exceeds three, but the majority of times he gives only two, the literal and the spiritual.[197] In this passage therefore, it seems, that Origen is more interested in indicating that the understanding of Scripture is progressive than he is to assert the precise content of each stage in the progress.[198]

In this schema it is therefore the third level, the spiritual level, which is the most important, and to which Origen believes Paul refers in a number of passages (4.2.6).[199] Origen states that the aim (σκοπός), of the spirit is primarily concerned with "the unspeakable mysteries" related to the affairs of men. When the attentive reader apprehends these (implicitly with the aid of the spirit),[200] by searching them out, he becomes a partaker of the spirit's doctrines (4.2.7). These doctrines concern the relationship of the son to the father Trinity, the fate of rational creatures, and the problem of evil (4.2.8). While at least one of these is the subject of the exegesis Origen gives his readers in 4.3.6f, they do not in fact correspond with the spiritual meaning as we find it expounded in his exegetical works where Christ and the salvation he brings are the central focus. But as Harl has pointed out, we need not see these two descriptions of the central content of spiritual exegesis as contradictory: "Le sens des Écritures est le 'dessein' de Dieu qui se réalise par l'incarnation de son verbe dans le monde. Le sens des textes est le vouloir salutaire de Dieu, le plan du Salut".[201] The spirit has a secondary aim, namely the concealment of these truths beneath stories and laws, which at their literal level are not unedifying (ἀνωφέλες) for the simpler believers.[202] The term ἀνωφέλες constitutes the negative expression of a vital presupposition of Origen's exegesis, namely that all Scripture must bring benefit (ὠφέλεια) to the believer. Often this concept (ὠφέλεια) is used precisely to move the reader beyond the literal meaning.[203]

---

196 Harl, Philocalie (1983) 119f, is keener than some to argue that Origen sees the second interpretation as moral in character. For her detailed discussion of the intellectual background to this passage see Philocalie 110f.

197 de Lubac, ibid. 143, argues that in the places where Origen does in fact posit a threefold meaning for a text, it is often in the order literal, spiritual, moral (*HGen.* 2.6; *HEx.* 1.4; 3.3, and *Sel. in Psalm* 3.4), an interpretation which he regards as more Christian than the other way round, for the spiritual/Christian interpretation has preceded the moral and not noticeably Christian.

198 For the idea of progress see 4.2.4 where we move from the ἁπλούστερος to ὁ ἐπὶ ποσὸν ἀναβεβηκῶς to ὁ τέλειος.

199 Origen often makes use of Pauline passages to justify his allegorical exegesis. Particularly popular in this respect are Gal 4:22–6; 1 Cor 9:9–10; 1 Cor 10:1–4; and Col 2:17.

200 For the idea that all interpretation of the spiritual sense of Scripture is aided by the spirit see Gregory *Orat.* 179.

201 Ibid. 79.

202 At 4.2.6 Origen has noted that the large number of simple believers in the church witnesses to the efficacious character of the literal meaning. The literal level of Scripture, with its simple style, exists as a concession of God to simpler believers, an example of his willingness to accommodate himself to different types of people (*c. Cels.* 4.71 and 6.2).

203 On the concept of ὠφέλεια in Origen's hermeneutics see Neuschäfer, ibid. 258f.

The Bible, then, for Origen, contains a double discourse, one which is obvious and open to everybody to understand and another which is concealed, and available only to an elect who have 'searched'. This corresponds to an essentially Platonic distinction between things seen and things unseen, between the sensible and the intelligible.[204] As with Plato, however, there is implicit within this schema the idea that a relationship exists between the sensible and the intelligible discourse. In his discussion of Scripture's threefold meaning Origen had spoken of a *progression* from literal to spiritual via the psychical. And at *Philoc.* 1.30 he is explicit on this point: the visible parts of the law and the prophets have a relationship (συγγένειαν ἔχει) with that part of the Law which is not seen but understood.[205]

But a minority of events/laws recorded in the Bible have no literal meaning.[206] These are the so-called ἀδύνατα or σκάνδαλα.[207] Origen justifies their presence by stating that had everything in Scripture been clear at the literal level, the reader would never have been forced to move beyond that level (παρὰ τὸ πρόχειρον) to the spiritual. That is precisely why Scripture contains within it "stumbling blocks, as it were, hindrances and impossibilities to be inserted in the midst of the law and history" (4.2.9).[208] These ἀδύνατα correspond to spiritual realities which could not be clothed in the outward husk of the narrative of actual events. Hence his statement at 4.3.5 that all Scripture has a spiritual meaning, but not all Scripture has a bodily meaning.

We need to make three further observations. The first relates to what Origen calls the εἱρμὸς τῶν πνευματικῶν (the interconnectedness of spiritual things – 4.2.9),[209] the idea that all Scripture at its deepest level is related to itself, and is hence self-illuminating. One word, one phrase, one sentence can be illuminated by reference to another word, phrase, sentence. Such a method assumes the Bible to be a harmonious whole, a single organ, free of division or contradiction,[210] thus allowing the reader to interpret one part of it by another.[211] This is made particularly clear at *Philoc.* 2.3, in a fragment from the commentary on Psalm 1, where Origen quotes the parable of a Jewish

---

[204] For other images conveying this idea see the opened and the closed book (*Phil.* 5.5); the treasure in the field (*Phil.* 1.27); and the image of the incarnate Christ who is both visible and invisible (*Comm. in Matt.* 10.6).

[205] For this see *Comm. Cant.* 3.12 where the visible and the invisible, the corporeal and the incorporeal are closely linked.

[206] Origen affirms that the majority of texts in the Bible are in fact historically true (4.3.4), though at *De Princ.* 4.3.10, in a passage only preserved in the Latin, he appears to contradict this view.

[207] For a discussion of these see Harl, ibid. 90f.

[208] See *Philoc.* 2 and 10 for further discussions of ἀδύνατα.

[209] For this term and its use in Stoicism to describe the organic unity of the world where each feature is explained by reference to another see Harl, ibid. 72f.

[210] See the heading of *Philoc.* 6: ὅτι ἓν ὄργανον Θεοῦ τέλειον καὶ ἡρμοσμένον πᾶσα ἡ θεία γραφή. In the passage which follows the heading (taken from the second book of the commentary on Matthew) Origen describes one type of peacemaker as the exegete who is able to show up the harmony which exists within the Bible: γίνεται δὲ καὶ τρίτος εἰρηνοποιὸς ὁ τὴν ἄλλοις φαινομένην μάχην τῶν γραφῶν ἀποδεικνὺς εἶναι οὐ μάχην.

[211] "La méthode d'Origène consiste en un va-e-vient incessant entre le detail et l'ensemble, entre le mot isolé et la Bible dans sa totalité" (Harl, ibid. 126. For her discussion of the passage see ibid. 97–101).

exegete who likened Scripture to a house with many flats in it. In each door is placed a key, which does not in fact open the door. Each key has signs on it, and it is the aim of the exegete to find the right key for the right door. Comparison affords illumination especially in the face of obscurity.[212]

The second observation relates to Origen's emphasis on the absolute nature of Scripture's inspiration. If Scripture is inspired in such a way it is necessary to pay attention to the most minute details contained within it.[213] Hence for Origen, it is an axiom that the rules of language should be closely attended to in the interpretation of scripture. As readers of the text we should be alive to its grammatical features ranging from the presence of homonyms to punctuation. Exactitude is called for in the interpretative enterprise, and in attaining that exactitude it is entirely appropriate to use the profane tools of philology.[214]

But however scrupulous, however careful we may be in our examination of Scripture a perfect understanding of Scripture is not possible (*De Princ.* 4.3.15), for God's word is filled with infinite meaning and complexity (*HEx.* 1.1). In *HEz* 14.2 Origen notes that some things in Scripture cannot be understood, and that is why the Temple of God is closed; and at *De Princ.* 2.11.5, he remarks that it is only in Heaven that certain scriptural passages will be understood.[215]

Conclusion

For Origen all Scripture is inspired, and because it is inspired it contains within it the truths necessary for salvation.[216] These are concerned with all the most significant questions of theology, and ultimately with the person of Christ, who, as in Clement, is the cause of inspiration and its subject. But an understanding of these truths, of this person, is difficult for they are appropriately concealed beneath an often obscure literal husk. The only way therefore to apprehend them is to move beyond the literal sense, a sense which is usually not without some value for the simpler believer, to the spiritual sense. All interpretation therefore is a progression from visible to the invisible, from the word to the spirit, from the flesh of Christ to his soul (*HLev.* 1.1). Read at the spiritual level the Scriptures form a coherent chain of interconnecting truths, and one text, one word, may illuminate another text, another word. But because Scripture is difficult, obscure, precisely because it is the word of God, it must be interpreted with care and exactitude, and hence it is entirely appropriate to use the profane tools of philology in its interpretation. As Scripture is inspired to the last word the interpreter must account for each detail contained within it. But the interpretative exercise, likened at one point

---

212 On this method see Harl, ibid. 135f.

213 See our discussion of 4.1.7.

214 On this see *Philoc.* 14.1f. See also *De Princ.* 4.1.6, where an apprehension of Scripture's inspired nature is connected with a reading μετ' ἐπιμελείας καὶ προσοχῆς; and 4.3.1 where he attacks those who read the text carelessly.

215 On this see Miller, Poetic Words (1988).

216 As Harl has written: "Dieu a infusé en elle son esprit, sa 'puissance', la 'parole', sa 'volonté', un ensemble de vérités (νοήματα, θεωρήματα, μυστήρια etc.), un 'enseignement' dont le but c'est 'le salut des hommes'" (ibid. 144).

by Origen to the smashing of brass gates (*De Princ.* 4.3.11), requires faith and the help of God, and is a task which is never completed.[217]

It is important to see Origen's hermeneutics as prescriptive as well as creative. It is in the nature of difficult texts to elicit mistakes from their readers (*De Princ.* 4.2.1), and Origen wishes to prevent such mistakes. In the *De Princ.* and elsewhere he is keen to present rules for interpretation, which go beyond a simple cry for allegory. His creation of the Hexapla, his advocacy of the thesis that Scripture must interpret itself, and his commitment to philology, all stem in part from a desire to take seriously the linguistic and semantic constraints of the biblical text.

3.3.2. *The Place of the OT in Origen's Thinking*

In the *De Princ.* Origen makes no attempt to differentiate qualitatively between the OT and the NT,[218] though he distinguishes between them by name,[219] and he regards Jesus as revealing the inspired quality of the OT revelation. For Origen the OT is a text full of power, whose law, has changed the mores of many nations. The creator of the Law, Moses, is the OT character for whom Origen, like Clement, has the highest praise.[220] At *c. Cels.* 1.19 Origen describes Moses as above all that is created and a man completely united to the creator. In him dwelt the divine spirit which showed a truth much clearer than that found in Plato and the wise men of the Greeks. Indeed, following the apologetic topos, present in Philo and Clement, Origen can state that Moses' writings are of the greatest antiquity (*c. Cels.* 4.21; 6.7), and that the Greek philosophers are reliant for their thinking upon them (*c. Cels.* 4.11). Moses possessed great compassion (*HNum.* 9.3), and a purity of mind that allowed him to see that behind the visibilia of the world dwell the "mysteria et occulta intelligentiae". Importantly, Origen is keen to stress that he understood the intention (βούλημα) of what he wrote (*HNum.* 5.1f.). The prophets, though distinguished from Moses who is "maximus et eximius prophetarum", are also praised. Like him, they predate Homer and the Greek philosophers (*c. Cels.* 6.7), and are hence sources of great wisdom.[221] Their teaching, while clear in its presentation of information relevant to the moral reform of people's characters, is obscure and full of riddles when expounding mysteries and esoteric truths.[222] Like Moses the prophets point forward to Christ.[223]

---

[217] See Gregory's *Thanksgiving* 179.

[218] A similar point is made by Harl, Fonction (1958) 148–149.

[219] Perhaps reluctantly. At *De Princ.* 4.1.1 he speaks of τῆς λεγομένης παλαιᾶς διαθήκης καὶ τῆς καλουμένης (the so-called) καινῆς.

[220] See Sgherri, Chiesa (1982) 154f.

[221] For other characters in the OT whom Origen calls prophets see Adam (*Comm. in Cant.* II); Abraham (*HJer.* 1.5); Isaac (*c. Cels.* 7.7); and Jacob (*c. Cels.* 7.7).

[222] On the obscurity of the prophetic writings see *c. Cels.* 1.12; 4.49; 7.10 and *De Princ.* 4.2.3. See also *c. Cels.* 3.58; 6.17; and *HJud.* 5.3 where the prophets are described as excelling high above the ordinary people and exhorting them to begin their glorious ascent to the spiritual heights they have already attained. Origen comes close to giving us some sense of this understanding of prophecy in a preserved fragment from his commentary on 1 Cor: προφητεία ἐστὶν ἡ διὰ λόγου τῶν ἀφανῶν σημαντική. I follow Bammel's reading of this text, Definitions (1989) 498.

[223] For the importance of prophecy as prediction see *De Princ.* 4.1.3 and many other places.

Origen's praise for the principal writers of the OT is in part linked to his desire to distinguish the inspiration they received from that associated with the pagan oracles as his comparison of the prophets with the Pythian priestess shows. In contrast to the priestess they did not speak in a state of ecstasy, were not under the influence of an impure spirit (*c. Cels.* 7.3), nor were they corrupt (*c. Cels.* 8.46).[224] Furthermore, as we indicated above, they were not the unconscious spouters of oracles, the intended meaning of which they did not understand (see *HGen.* 8.1; *Comm. in Jo.* 6.4.24).[225] But his high opinion of them is principally linked to his strongly held belief that their source of inspiration came from the Logos.[226] So he can state that when we talk about Jesus' coming into the world, we should not restrict ourselves to the incarnation for χρὴ μέντοι γε εἰδέναι, ὅτι καὶ πρότερον ἐπεδήμει. Who else could the word have been which came to Jeremiah, Isaiah and Ezekiel (*HJer.* 9.1)? Indeed Origen has such a high opinion of their inspiration that he is sometimes even wary of claiming that the apostles are wiser than the prophets.[227]

These comments, while obviously indicating that Origen held the OT in the highest regard, are also aimed at those who criticised its contents. These people could be outside the Christian community like Celsus, or within it like the Marcionites, who with their claim for the complete disjunction of OT from NT, are a significant presence in Origen's work.[228] But at what point did Origen himself distinguish between the OT and the NT? Or did his belief in the former's inspiration and his sensitivity to Marcionite and others' criticism of its content preclude him from articulating fully his understanding of their relationship?

Some might argue that Origen appears to make a distinction between the literal level of the OT and the literal level of the NT. There is some truth behind this assertion. When Origen discussed false exegesis in *De Princ.* 4.2.1 he gave as examples three groups' literal interpretation of the OT, not the NT. An exclusively literal interpretation of the OT is dangerous because it can lead to the unbelief of the Jews, Marcionite rejection of the OT, or, in the case of the Christian literalists, absurd opinions unworthy of God. But the contrast here is only implicit, not explicit. Elsewhere it is not. At *Series in Matt.* 27, Origen states that if the spirit of the gospel vivifies, its letter does not kill (an allusion to 2 Cor 3:6).[229] But those who follow the letter of the

---

224 Origen often praises their characters (*HJer.* 12.1; 20.8).

225 For a defence of Origen's theory of inspiration see de Lubac, *Ésprit*, 120, and most recently, Nardoni, Inspiration (1984). While it is true that one might understand Origen's theory of the inspiration of the spirit as totalitarian, that is, it does not take into account the individual nature of the inspired person, Nardoni shows how Origen's theological presuppositions, especially those related to human freedom, are contrary to this totalitarian view.

226 For a classic statement of this belief see *Praef. 1 Princ.* 1.

227 The claim in Matt 13:17 that many prophets and righteous men desired to see these things does not imply that the prophets are somehow inferior. The greater of them did not desire to see such things for they had already seen them (in *Jo.* 6.3.16). For further examples see Molland, Gospel (1938) 109f; and Hanson, Allegory (1959) 200f.

228 See *De Princ.* 2.5 for Origen's extended arguments against the Marcionites.

229 This is a text which appears with regularity in Origen's writings on the OT. For the bitterness of the letter of the OT see *HLev.* 7.1 and *HNum.* 9.7.

OT can fall into vain superstitions. At its literal level the text of the OT is more difficult (the constant emphasis on the obscurity of its writings),[230] less clearly relevant, and often offensive. Unlike the NT, the OT's literal meaning is not obviously Christian. Indeed, if it is read literally it is often nothing more than Jewish fable (*HGen.* 6.1; *HEx.* 2.3). Its relevance for the Church is preserved precisely because it can be allegorised, and that mode of interpretation is what Christ has endorsed at his incarnation by unveiling its truths.

However, the assertion that the literal level of the OT is more problematic, or even more pernicious than that of the NT needs some qualification. First, as we will see below, Origen is by no means always intent upon attacking the literal meaning of the OT, and where he is, this is invariably associated with the ritual law (as in the passage quoted above), interpretations he deems unworthy of God, or in situations where individuals will not proceed to a spiritual interpretation. Secondly, though admittedly less frequently, there are places in the gospels where the letter kills,[231] and where texts understood at a literal level are also impossible.[232] Interestingly, in *De Princ.* 4 Origen makes no *explicit* distinction between the literal level of the NT and the OT, nor at the level of hermeneutical theory. In both we proceed from literal to spiritual interpretation.[233]

There are other more conscious attempts to differentiate between the two. In the opening chapter of his commentary on John, Origen discusses the position of the gospels in the church. He states that they are the first fruits (ἀπαρχή) of all the Scriptures. This does not imply, however, that they are written before the other works of Scripture. It is necessary to discriminate between πρωτογέννημα (the OT) and ἀπαρχή (NT), "For the perfect word has blossomed forth after all the fruits of the prophets up to the time of the Lord Jesus". He goes on to state that in a certain sense the whole of the NT is the Gospel (that is, the gospel message) and differs from the OT which could not point to him who cometh as present, but only preached him beforehand. Here the difference betweeen the OT and the NT lies in the fact that one proclaims the advent of Christ, while the other witnesses *directly* to it. The NT (and especially the gospels) differs from the OT in that Christ proclaims himself without intermediaries in one, but through intermediaries in another. This, as TORJESEN has pointed out, obviously affects the exegetical procedures used in the interpretation of the two testaments. In one it is progress through an intermediary, in another through the Logos himself.[234] This idea is well conveyed in Origen's comments on the Song of Songs 1:2. Here he states that

---

230 In *De Princ.* 4.2.2 Origen cites four OT passages (Gen 19:30f; Gen 16; Gen 29:21f; Gen 30:1–13) as examples of texts which caused Christians difficulties. See also the numerous refrains, especially in his homilies, where Origen calls for divine help in the face of a difficult passage in the OT.

231 For an example see *HLev.* 7.5 on John 6:53 and the eating of flesh.

232 See the end of *De Princ.* 4.2.9 where Origen affirms that the Spirit has arranged the material in the NT in the same way as that in the OT. Not everything in it makes sense at a literal level.

233 Harl, Fonction (1958) 149.

234 See Procedure (1986) 66–67.

up to his arrival, Christ had sent his kisses via the prophets. But with his advent the bride will receive these kisses directly.

There are also passages in Origen's surviving works which indicate that he explicitly thought in terms of degrees of revelation. Moses and Elijah had not before seen Jesus' face as illuminated as they saw it at the Transfiguration (*Comm. in Jo.* 13. 47 f.). They had up till then been awaiting the unique advent of Jesus when the most unique things would be revealed.[235] Origen can state that the grace of perfection was not given to the Patriarchs and the prophets before the Incarnation (*Comm. in Cant.* 1. 11 f.), and that the Law was a *paidagogos* to Christ (*De Princ.* 3. 6. 8). He interprets Isaac's spiritual growth as a procession through the Law to Prophecy and the Gospel (*HGen.* 12. 5). We seem therefore to be getting close to a prophecy/fulfillment relationship between OT and NT. Moses and the prophets announce Christ, and his arrival fulfills that announcement. But a final passage is worth citing. In *Ser. in Matt.* 54 (GCS 11, p. 123, 1. 25 and 31) Origen can state that the words of Moses and the prophets have passed away, but those of Christ will not, for while each day they are being fulfilled, they are never entirely fulfilled. But as if checking himself, he can go on: "Perhaps it is necessary to say that neither the words of Moses, nor those of the prophets are perfectly fulfilled, for they themselves are properly speaking the words of the Son of God and they are always being fulfilled".[236]

These words in fact bring us close to the problem we face in dealing with Origen's understanding of the relationship between OT and the NT. Origen often states that the incarnation is the event which reveals the inspired nature of the OT, that the OT can only be understood in the light of the arrival of Christ – the watery OT has become wine (*Comm. Jo.* 13. 60), the bitter waters of the law have been sweetened (*HEx.* 7. 1), the veil over the law has been removed (*De Princ.* 4. 1. 6), the previously filled in wells of Scripture have been opened up (*HGen.* 13. 2).[237] But he rarely attempts, *in a post incarnational context*, to differentiate between the *truths* contained within the OT (now revealed) and the NT. Stated otherwise we might say that at a hermeneutical level Origen blurs the distinction between the two Testaments. As he at one point writes: "I do not call the law the Old Testament if I understand it spiritually. The law only becomes the Old Testament to those who understand

---

[235] Sgherri, Chiesa (1982) 169–170, argues that Moses requires the coming of Christ fully to understand the meaning of that event.

[236] See *Comm in Jo.* 10. 18 for an explicit rejection of a purely prophecy/fulfillment conception of the relationship of the OT to the NT. For a rejection of the view that Origen consistently holds the OT to be a shadow in relation to the image of the NT (language found in Heb 8:5 and 10:1), a view advanced by de Lubac (Esprit (1950) 219–220), see Harl, Fonction (1958) 151 f. She argues that Origen does not differentiate between the terms and often uses them together to contrast what we know now with the truths we will know in the future. See also Sgherri, Chiesa (1982) 204 f, for further discussion of the Origenist interpretation of Heb 8:5 and 10:1.

[237] See *HJos* 9.7 where Joshua's reading the law of Moses to the people becomes a type of Jesus interpreting the mysteries of the law to the people. See also *HLev.* 6. 1 where the more complete our conversion to Christ the more complete our understanding of the law.

it carnally. But to us who understand and expound it spiritually and with its gospel meaning, it is always new" (*HNum.* 9.4).[238]

Conclusion

Origen did have some sense of the superiority of the NT over the OT. What the OT proclaimed, the NT declared as present. The NT constituted in some respect the fulfillment of the OT, and the OT was to be interpreted through the prism of the NT.[239] Indeed, so dependent was the OT on the NT that Origen could state that it was only since the arrival of Christ that the inspired nature of the OT had become apparent. But at the level of its inspired meaning it is unclear how Origen distinguishes between it and the NT. This lack of clarity can be explained on two grounds. First, Origen's emphasis in his exegesis lies always on the harmony of the two Testaments, in a form of exegetical monism where the Bible is a single ὄργανον in complete harmony with itself (*Philoc.* 6). Secondly, Origen is only too aware of the lurking presence of Marcion. Any attempt to explicate in detail the difference between the two Testaments may have played into Marcionite hands.[240]

3.4. Origen's Exegetical Approach to the Old Testament

3.4.1. Introduction: Types of Evidence

We possess two types of evidence for Origen's exegesis of the OT. The first consists of letters and theological tracts which, while sometimes making substantial use of the OT, are not specifically concerned with its exegesis. The second type of evidence, which is by far the most significant and most representative of the surviving Origenist corpus, consists of specifically exegetical works. Traditionally scholars, following Jerome,[241] have divided this second type of evidence into 3 different groups: scholia (σχολία), commentaries (τόμοι), and homilies (ὁμιλίαι). The first two, for which we have less evidence

---

[238] For an endorsement of this view with special reference to the Platonic character of Origen's hermeneutics see Wiles, Origen (1970) 483. For a passage which does perhaps make such a distinction see Origen's commentary on Psalm 1 found in *Philoc.* 3 where Origen notes that there is a coincidence between the number of books in the OT and the number of letters in the Hebrew alphabet. He continues: "Thus the 22 books are an elementary instruction (στοιχείωσις) in (εἰς) the wisdom of God, and an introduction (εἰσαγωγὴ) into the knowledge of beings". But he does not explicitly state that it is an introduction to the NT. *Comm. in Matt.* 10.10 comes closer to indicating such a view. "Here it is stated that the law and the prophets perfectly conceived act as a στοιχείωσις to the gospel perfectly conceived." On this text see Harl, Philocalie (1985) 268. For other passages which seem to make a distinction at the deepest level of understanding between OT and NT see Crouzel, Connaissance (1961) 292f. These include *HNum.* 12.2; and *Comm. in Cant.* 1.10. These passages are certainly suggestive, but even Crouzel is willing to admit that there is a certain inconsistency in Origen's understanding (309).

[239] See *HEx* 7.3: "It is therefore not sufficient for the people of God to drink the waters of Mara even though it has been made sweet, even though the bitterness of the letter has been cast out by the tree of life and the mysteries of the cross. The old document alone is not sufficient for drinking. They must come to the NT from which they are given a drink without hesitation and without any difficulty".

[240] For this argument see Simonetti, Lettera (1985) 89.

[241] *Hier. Ez. Orig. Prolog.*, (GCS 33, p. 318, 13–19).

than the homilies,[242] seem to have been similar in their emphasis.[243] The former consisted of comments on obscure or difficult biblical verses,[244] along the lines of Philo's Quaestiones, while the latter consisted of similarly scholarly comment conducted over a whole book or Psalm, on occasions being very long,[245] and certainly more digressive. Both were written for private consumption by educated readers.

The OT Homily, in contrast to the scholia or commentary, arose out of the public and liturgical context of a sermon delivered upon a particular text of the OT, and consisting of comments on the individual passages read.[246] Origen appears to have allowed these sermons to have been written down in about 239, and all our OT homilies date from this period or a little later. While Origen was no doubt constrained in what he could say by time (each homily lasted an hour),[247] the oral character of the homily, and the extent of the knowledge/educational level of the audience he was addressing – NAUTIN argues that all our OT homilies come from daily liturgies (without a eucharist) which catechumens were allowed to attend[248] – it would be wrong to exaggerate the difference between a homily and the commentary/scholia. Certainly a homily, with its emphasis on the edification of the hearer, tended to eschew some of the more scholarly characteristics of the commentary/scholia (philological and textual comment) and to be less elaborate and digressive in

[242] Apart from *Philoc.* 27, which contains comments on the hardening of Pharaoh's heart, we have no complete scholia on the OT, and have to rely on catena fragments, which we can never be sure were in fact taken from a scholion. In the case of commentaries on the OT we only fare a little better. We possess Rufinus' translation of the first four books of Origen's later commentary on the Song of Songs, and fragments of a number of different commentaries in the *Philocalia*. Otherwise, as with the scholia, we are heavily reliant upon catena fragments whose authenticity it is often difficult to assess.

[243] In support of the thesis that the two forms were similar in their orientation see Neuschäfer, ibid. 41: "Die kurz gefassten Texterklärungen unterscheiden sich von den ausführlichen Kommentarbänden lediglich in Hinsicht auf ihren quantitativen Aspekt. In beiden Gattungen trifft man auf eine Textauslegung, in der philologische Beobachtungen mit theologischen Sachaussagen verbunden sind" (Neuschäfer, ibid. 41).

[244] See Jerome's definition in the passage cited above: "Primum eius opus excerpta sunt, quae Graece σχόλια noncupantur, in quibus ea, quae sibi videbantur obscura aut habere aliquid etam difficultatis, summatim breviterque perstrinxit". With the exception of the citation from Jerome, the only other evidence for the genre title σχολία comes from Codex Lawra 184 B 64 for. 93r to Heb 11:5. In *Philoc.* 27.10 (a series of discussions on the subject of the hardening of Pharaoh's heart) the title heading mentions σημειώσεις (καὶ πάλιν ἐν ἄλλῳ τόπῳ ἐν ταῖς αὐταῖς εἰς τὴν ἔξοδον σημειώσεσιν). For a discussion of the terms σχολία and σημειώσεις see Neuschäfer, ibid. 40–41, who argues for the essential similarity between the meanings of both terms.

[245] Origen needed 12 chapters for Gen 1–4, and thirty chapters for the first part of Isaiah.

[246] On the form of Origen's OT homilies see Nautin, Jérémie (1977) 123f.

[247] See *HJud* 6.1 where he refers to the love of brevity on the part of his hearers; and *HSam.* 5.1 where he states that in order to expound the text he needs more than one sitting.

[248] Nautin argues that catechumens could only hear sermons on the NT a few weeks before their baptism. The homilies followed the LXX order of texts, and it probably took three years to read and preach on the whole of the OT. Nautin believes that Origen did not preach on the historical books after 1 Samuel, and that he may have been forced to stop because of his method of interpretation, doctrine etc. (see *HGen.* 12.4 where he appears to be conscious of opposition to his type of preaching). For Nautin's discussion of the homilies see ibid. 389f. See also Lienhardt, Homilist (1989), who usefully summarises many of Nautin's observations.

its exegesis,[249] a point upon which Origen is explicit.[250] But it should also be noted that in his homilies Origen was not afraid to indulge in philological or scholarly discussion.[251] Furthermore, as with his commentaries and his scholia, Origen's main focus lay in expounding the spiritual meaning of the text, though this is carried out with a greater emphasis on the personal application of the text in question.[252]

From the surviving lists of Origen's works[253] it is clear that in one form or another he commented on almost all the books of the OT,[254] and that he ascribed particular importance to the Psalms on which he seems to have written three series of commentaries,[255] to the Pentateuch (especially Genesis), to the prophets Isaiah and Jeremiah, and to the Song of Songs on which he wrote two commentaries, one in his youth and one later.[256]

3.4.2. Origen and the Sensus Literalis of the Old Testament

When Origen discusses the literal meaning of a biblical text, he is not referring in any way to the intention of the author whose work he is interpreting. As we saw above, the principal intention or βούλημα/σκοπός of any text is bound up with its spiritual meaning, of which, according to Origen, the OT author was conscious (*HGen.* 4.2; *HLev.* 6.3; *HNum.* 5.1). Rather, as Crouzel has put it: "... chez Origène le sens littéral désigne l'expression dans sa materialité

[249] Homilies did not contain extended prologues, as we find, for instance, in the commentary on the Song of Songs, or in the Commentary on the Psalms. For a discussion of function of the prologue in Origen's writings and its relationship to the same genre in pagan exegetical works see Neuschäfer, ibid. 57f. In essence it consisted of a type of introduction to the commentary in which questions of form and interpretation were addressed. So, for instance, in his prologue to the Commentary on the Song of Songs Origen discusses the form of the book as an epithalamium (a nuptial song), the type of love to which it refers, and its place amongst Solomon's works, and its title.

[250] See *HNum.* 14.1; *HLev.* 1.1; *HJud.* 8.3 for the avoidance of comment on smaller details; and *HGen.* 10.5; *HEx.* 1.1 and *HLev.* 7.1 for the stress on the edificatory nature of the homily.

[251] On this see Klostermann, Formen (1947) 205. His conclusion about the relationship between the homily and commentary is balanced: "Die in Origenes Homilien getriebene Exegese ist von der der Kommentare nicht grundsätzlich, sondern nur dem Masse nach verschieden. Doch wenn auch die Auslegung hier gemeindengemässiger erscheint, so stellt Origenes auch als Prediger keine geringen Anforderung an die Fassungskraft der Hörer".

[252] For the similarity in hermeneutical procedure between a commentary and a homily see Torjesen, Procedure. The same author does, however, argue that the difference in audience assumed by the two types of exposition led to a difference in character. From an examination of Origen's surviving sections of commentary and homilies on the Song of Songs she concludes: "They are composed with different audiences in mind. The commentary presupposes the more advanced Christians ... The homily, on the other hand, is more concerned with the beginner who requires purification before he can approach the mysteries" (ibid., 54).

[253] In Eusebius' lost *Life of Pamphilus* 3 there was a full list of Origen's works which Jerome appears to have used in a rather arbitrary way in *Epistle* 33. For a reconstruction of the list see Nautin, ibid. 245f, who helpfully notes what survives, if anything, of the individual works named. For other discussions see Bardy, Commentaire (1934); and Crouzel, Origen (1989) 37f, who is largely in agreement with Nautin.

[254] In the surviving lists we have no reference to a work on Esther.

[255] For an introduction to the complex evidence relating to Origen's writings on the Psalms see Nautin, Origène (1977) 261f; and Rondeau, Psautier I (1985) 45f, who discusses Nautin's ideas.

[256] For a useful description of the concerns of these works see Simonetti, Lettera (1985) 88f.

brute",[257] that is the meaning of the words as they stand on the page. He can describe the literal meaning with different expressions: κατὰ τὸ γράμμα· κατὰ λέξιν· κατὰ τὸ ῥητον τῆς λέξεως· κατὰ τὴν πρόχειρον ἐκδόχην· κατὰ ἱστορίαν· κατὰ τὴν αἴσθησιν· κατὰ τὸ ἁπλοῦν· κατὰ τὴν σάρκα· τὸ βλεπόμενον. Of these τὸ ῥητον is the most frequently used.

Origen's understanding of the literal interpretation of the OT is complex. For him it is clear that with the arrival of Christ the veil has been lifted from the OT, and its intended meaning revealed. If the veil is not lifted, if the OT is simply understood at its literal level, as a history book, or a legal text, it ceases to appear inspired, and can simply become an irrelevance.[258] Hence Origen can be both critical and dismissive of those who are only willing to understand the document literally. This, as we will see, is partucularly noticeable in his interpretation of the Jewish ritual laws. However, in his *De Princ.* 4. 2. 8 Origen states that a literal understanding can be beneficial to those who are not capable of progressing beyond that level; and he perceives there to exist a direct relationship between the spiritual and literal levels of interpretation (4. 2. 9). It was precisely this conviction which led Origen to show more concern for the literal level of interpretation than, for instance, Clement.

The OT as an Historical Book

Origen is often keen to criticise a literal understanding of OT history. If one reads the book of Joshua at a literal level it is no more than an account of cruel wars (*HJos* 13. 1). Indeed, if the book possessed an exclusively literal meaning, it would never have been transmitted by the apostles (15. 1). What is the use of knowing about the weaning of Isaac (*HGen.* 7. 1), or about the games Isaac played with Ishmael (*HGen.* 7. 2)? Of what interest to the reader are the stories which open the book of Numbers (*HNum.* 1. 1)? Is it not unworthy of the word of God that it should describe Him as jealous (*HEx.* 8. 6), or Joshua destroying Ai (*HJos* 8. 7)? But, as we have noted above, Origen can go beyond declaring passages literally understood as irrelevant or unworthy, and declare them to be impossible. This may arise from the fact they are figurative expressions which when read literally, make no sense. Typical in this respect is the statement found in Prov 26 : 9 that thorns give birth in the hand of a drunkard (*HGen.* 2. 6). It may be that they make no sense within the flow of an individual passage. At *De Princ.* 4. 3. 1 Origen asks what intelligent man could believe that the first and the second and the third day could exist without the sun, the moon, or the stars. It may be that they contradict statements made elsewhere in the OT (*HLev.* 8. 11), or that they are anthropomorphisms unworthy of God. For *De Princ.* he dismisses the idea that God could have been walking in the garden of Eden, and in a fragment of his commentary on Psalm 50 he notes how unworthy the tale of David and Uriah is.

But Origen shows his interest in the literal sense in a number of ways. First, he is sometimes keen to *defend* the literal understanding of a text. Two significant examples of this apologetic

[257] Origène (1969) 249.

[258] See *HGen.* 10. 2; *HEx.* 1. 5; 12. 2; *HLev.* 1. 4.

exegesis occur in *HGen.* In the first example Origen defends the dimensions of Noah's ark against the criticisms of the Marcionite Apelles, who argued that they were insufficient to accommodate the number of animals recorded in the Bible. Origen argues at some length that Moses, the writer of Genesis, reckoned the size according to the art of geometry, and concludes: "Let these things be said as much as pertains to the historical account against those who endeavour to describe the scriptures of the OT as containing certain things that are impossible or irrational" (*HGen.* 2.2). The second occurs in the fifth homily on the same book and concerns the rape of the sleeping Lot by his daughters. Origen, rather than dismissing the story as unworthy of its divine author, proceeds, in midrashic vein, to excuse the behaviour of the major protagonists. The daughters were forced to be incestuous because they knew that along with their father they were the only survivors left on earth. There are other examples of places where Origen defends the historicity/morality of apparently unconvincing or unworthy tales.[259]

But Origen was not interested in simply defending the literal sense. Sometimes the stories possessed an immediately useful meaning. This usefulness, in accord with Origen's hermeneutical principles, was always connected with some perceived link with the spiritual sense.

In the passage from *HNum.*, mentioned above, Origen states that the difficulties associated with the literal interpretation of the episode are related to the difficulties associated with the spiritual interpretation. Most interesting in this respect is Origen's interpretation of the story of the witch of Endor (1 Sam 28) in his fifth Homily on the Book of Samuel, the relevant portion of which survives in Greek. Origen begins by stating that there are some stories which only possess a useful meaning at the spiritual level, but there are some which possess a useful meaning at the literal level too (τῶν οὖν τῆς ἱστορίας τινὰ μὲν χρήσιμα πᾶσιν, τινὰ δὲ οὐ πᾶσιν). For Origen's own theology of the resurrection, it is very important that over against those who argue that in the story the witch calls up a spirit which only pretends to be Samuel, he can prove that in fact it is the spirit of Samuel himself.[260] He subjects the literal text to careful examination. Its author, he notes, is the Holy Spirit. When the narrative text reads: "And the woman (the witch of Endor) saw Samuel", there can be no doubt that it was Samuel she saw and not a spirit simulating Samuel (*HSam.* 5.4). The homily is important precisely because so much space is devoted to such careful scrutiny of the literal text. Of similar relevance in respect of linking literal and allegorical exegesis are Origen's Commentary on the Song of Songs and his nine surviving Homilies on the Psalms. In the former the first step in the interpretative process is a systematic exegesis of the literal setting, in part linked to the identification of the characters (on this see below), and in the latter, exegesis consists of a transposition of the Psalmist's situation into the situation of the reader.[261] Other connections between literal and spiritual interpretation are equally striking. So, when Origen wants to expound the spiritual meaning of Jer 1:1-3, there is no need for allegory – the spiritual meaning here arises from a historical generalisation.[262]

We should note that Origen is aware of the simple narrative excellence of certain OT stories. An example of this occurs in *HGen.* 8 where Origen spends much time relishing the remarkable qualities of the father Abraham who was willing to sacrifice his son at the behest of God.[263]

Origen and the Law

Origen inherited from his predecessors the view that since the coming of Christ the Jewish law was redundant. This had the consequence that he was more caustic in his criticism of literal interpretations of OT/Jewish law. Those

---

[259] See *c. Cels.* 4.45 where Origen defends the story of Lot's daughters, and states that Celsus should have approved of the honesty of the biblical writers who did not conceal even discreditable events. He goes on to argue that Celsus should have been won over to regard even the more remarkable stories as not fictitious. These comments should, however, be interpreted with caution. In *c. Cels.* Origen is keen to defend the OT against the slanderous attacks of the pagan Celsus. See also his extended defence of the story of Balaam (Num 22-24) at *HNum.* 13.3-8. Here much time is spent explaining those aspects of the tale which appear improbable.

[260] On the theological issues see Nautin, Samuel 81 f.

[261] For the exegetical procedure here see Torjesen, Procedure (1986) 23 f.

[262] On this see Torjesen, ibid. 142 f.

[263] See also *HNum.* 22.3 where Origen praises the account of Moses' death.

who continued to observe the Law, be they Jews or Ebionites, were often attacked by him.[264] When Celsus questions him on Christian failure to obey Jewish legal prescriptions,[265] Origen replies that the law has a twofold interpretation, the one spiritual and the other literal.[266] The literal interpretation is redundant, and is shown to be so by Ezekiel who describes the ritual laws when he speaks of God giving Israel laws that were not good (Ezek 20:25). This concurs with Paul's statement that it is the letter that kills (2 Cor 3:6). The redundancy of Jewish cultic laws is proven by the destruction of the temple and the conquest of the land (*HLev.* 4.10).[267] However, Origen is quite prepared to endorse the literal understanding of certain laws when they do not serve to blur the distinction between Jew and Christian. In *De Princ.* 4.3.3 f. he mentions the Ten Commandments, and in *HNum.* 11:1 f, distinguishing between a law, and a commandment, precept, or testimony,[268] he notes that the commandment to give the first fruits to the priests is a good commandment and should be observed. But in the same passage he notes that the acceptance of the literal understanding of a commandment does not preclude the need for a spiritual understanding.[269] The movement in all Origen's exegesis is towards the spiritual away from the literal.

A Reading κατὰ λέξιν and the Philological Side of Origen's Interpretation

As we have seen from our discussion of his hermeneutics, Origen insisted that readers of the text of Scripture pay close attention to its wording. This can be described as a reading κατὰ λέξιν, but it is not strictly speaking always related to an interpretation of the *sensus literalis*, for Origen invariably attends to philological details of the text with a view to illuminating its allegorical meaning. However, the philological side of Origen's exegesis arises precisely from a close observation of the wording of the OT, and so finds an appropriate place in this section.

Origen's interest in the philological aspect of the OT text extends widely. It shows itself in his desire to establish the meaning of words (γλωσσηματικόν),[270] in his close attention to grammatical details,[271] and the figures of speech employed in the OT (τεχνικόν);[272] and in what the ancients described as ἱστορικόν, that is the illumination of specific historical, geo-

[264] See *HLev.* 4.10; 10.12; *HNum.* 28.1; 23.1; 23.5.

[265] *c. Cels.* 7.20.

[266] See *HLev.* 16.7: "We cast out the law according to the literal sense so that we may establish the law according to the spiritual sense".

[267] For a good example of Origen's dismissal of the literal interpretation of a ritual law see *HGen.* 3 on circumcision. For a discussion of Origen's interpretation of the ritual laws see de Lange, Jews (1975) 89f.

[268] For the same argument see *Sel. in Psalm* 118 (119); *HEx.* 10.1 and *Sel. in Ex.* 21.1–2.

[269] In support of this argument Origen cites NT evidence. At Matt 19:5–6 Gen 2:24 is interpreted literally, but at Eph 5:32 the same passage is interpreted spiritually.

[270] For this see *in Psalm* 51 (52).3; *HJer.* 17.6 and *HJer.* 18.6. And for a discussion of the various methods Origen employs to establish these meanings and the question relating to his possession of lexica see Neuschäfer, Origenes 140f.

[271] *Philoc.* 8 and 14 and in *In Gen.* 1.28, ibid.

[272] See Neuschäfer's discussion of both of these aspects of Origen's interpretation, ibid. 202f.

graphical, topographical and scientific references in the OT.[273] This in broad terms implies an interest in the application of the ἐγκύκλιος παιδεία to the scriptures, something which Origen, like Philo before him, deemed perfectly legitimate as long as it did not become the object of discussion in itself.[274] At Lam 4:10 the reference to women cooking and eating their children is with the help of Josephus' description of the seige of Jerusalem seen as a prophecy of the events of that siege. At *HJer.* 8.4 the metorological words in Jer 10:19 (καὶ ἀστραπὰς εἰς ὑετον ἐποιήσεν) cause Origen to discuss the lightening theory of scientific specialists which in turn leads to an allegorical explanation of the verse; and commenting on the words in Ps 118:127 (ἠγάπησα τὰς ἐντολάς σου ὑπέρ χρυσίον καὶ τοπάζιον), Origen discusses in detail the qualities of topaz.[275]

Also relevant to this discussion is Origen's interest in identifying the spokesman or προσώπα of individual verses,[276] which in the interpretation of the OT can cause the exegete particular difficulty.[277] This is manifestly the case in a drama like the Song of Songs which consists entirely of dialogues between the bride and the bridegroom, and where verses are sometimes written in the plural and have to be attributed to other personalities (the friends of the bride and friends of the groom). It is important for Origen to determine the identity of the speaker at the literal level, for each speaker corresponds to personality/ies in the allegorical exegesis.[278] The same problem constantly occupies him in his exegesis of the Psalms, where the identification of the speaker of the Psalm is never easy to determine.[279]

Conclusion

In *HGen.* 10.4 Origen stated that he had often said that in the OT he is not interested in history, but the mysteries concealed beneath history. This conviction often manifests itself in an over-hasty dismissal of the literal meaning of the OT,[280] or in a lack of appreciation for the literary quality of the text.[281] Origen wanted to tease out of some of the most unpromising texts a meaning

[273] Neuschäfer, ibid. 290, notes Origen's great interest in the ἱστορικόν of the Bible: "Die Mühe, die es sich Origenes kosten lässt, die historischen und naturwissenschaftlichen Probleme zu lösen, die der biblische Text noch und noch aufgibt, ist beträchtlich".

[274] For a discussion of the role of the ἐγκύκλιος παιδεία in Origen see Neuschäfer, ibid. 155f.

[275] For more historically orientated discussions see *HJer.* 4.1; 13.2.

[276] See *HNum.* 26.3 for the importance of identifying characters in the biblical text.

[277] Harl, Philocalie (1985) 332f, notes that for Origen the unannounced changes of characters appear as a problem particular to the Bible. It constitutes one of the συνήθεια of Scripture adding still further to its obscurity and strongly contrasting with the beautiful ἀκολουθία of classical texts.

[278] See also *Philoc.* 7.1 where in a section from his first commentary on the Song of Songs, written when he was still very young, he discusses the confusing nature of the πρόσωπα in the Song.

[279] On the πρόσωπα in the Psalms see *Philoc.* 7.2; and Rondeau's discussion of the whole matter, Psautier II 44f.

[280] For a number of good examples taken from the homilies on the Hexateuch see Crouzel, Sens littéral (1969).

[281] See his treatment of figurative language. See Crouzel, Origène (1969), who in an examination of Origen's homilies on the Hexateuch, shows that Origen is often blind to certain obvious features of the literal text.

that was useful to his readers, that was applicable to the situation of his hearers, and that was worthy of God. Some will forgive him his exegetical gymnastics when they understand his motive.

But Origen is not consistently dismissive of the literal meaning of the OT. At times he defends it, at times he sees it as useful to his readers, at times he sees it as intimately linked to the spiritual meaning. Moreover, like Philo before him, he is rigidly bound to the words of Scripture, deeming them to be the basic material of his allegorical exegesis.

We should not, however, overlook the fact that Origen's theological assumptions led him to treat the literal level in a sometimes dismissive manner. It is by no means always clear how the spiritual interpretation is linked to the literal, and at times Origen is too swift in dismissing or passing over the literal interpretation.[282]

3.4.3. Beyond the Literal

Language

Origen uses a variety of terms to describe the spiritual interpretation of Scripture, and it is difficult to make clear distinctions between them. The first observation to make is that all spiritual interpretation involves an ascent from one sense to another, from the literal sense to the spiritual. This idea is best conveyed by the expression πρὸς ἀναγωγήν, of which Origen is the first to make use in an exegetical context.[283] But ἀναγωγή does not describe the procedure by which this spiritual meaning is attained, but rather, as Torjesen puts it, "the meaning of the text which leads toward the higher realities".[284] For the procedure/technique Origen uses such words as τροπολογεῖν, or more generally μεταλαμβάνειν,[285] both conveying the idea of a transposition of meaning, invariably by the use of allegory.[286] By transposing the meaning of the text to the higher or spiritual level, one at once confronts the intention or βούλημα of Scripture. In *HJer.* 4.2 Origen gives voice to this idea: εἰ νενόηται τὸ ῥητόν, ἴδωμεν τί βούληται ἐν τούτοις δηλοῦσθαι.[287]

Themes:

The Logos

As we have noted above, a central tenet of Origenist theology is the idea that the Logos is the chief inspiration behind the writing of the OT. In his *De*

---

282 For divergent opinions on Origen's treatment of the literal sense see on the negative side Hanson, Allegory (1959), and Scalise, Sensus Literalis (1988); and on the positive, de Lubac, Esprit (1950).

283 For a discussion of this term see Bienert, Allegoria (1972) 59–62; Simonetti, Lettera (1985) 80 n. 46; and Torjesen, Procedure (1986) 144, especially n. 107: "The term (ἀναγωγή) is not used to describe an exegetical procedure before Origen. This implies that Origen developed and introduced a term to express the theological character of exegesis because the available Hellenistic terms were inadequate".

284 Ibid. 144.

285 On this term see Harl, ibid. 133.

286 The actual term ἀλληγορία is not used so frequently in Origen. For a discussion of its use see Simonetti as above.

287 Other words used to convey the meaning of a text are θεωρία, νοεῖν, νόησις, νοῆμα. For a discussion of these see Crouzel, Connaissance (1961) 382 f.

Princ. he writes: "For at first Christ was the word of God in Moses and the prophets. For without the word of God how would they have been able to prophesy Christ?"[288] Hence exegesis of the OT is exegesis of Christ's word, and is a form of contemporary encounter with that word.[289] Scripture is ultimately christocentric.

While Christ is evidently the central testimony of Moses and the prophets, he is also prefigured in individual characters and actions in the OT. He is prefigured in Noah who gave rest to mankind (*HGen.* 2.3), in the sacrifice of Isaac which prefigures his own sacrifice (*HGen.* 8. 8–9). He is the true Joseph who opens the eyes of the blind (*HGen.* 15.7), and the true Joshua who leads the people into the promised land. Various sacrifices in the OT act as types of his sacrifice (*HLev.* 2.6; 4.8). At *HGen.* 14.1 Origen states that though Christ is a unity he is represented in a variety of ways in Scripture. These examples place Origen in a tradition of typological exegesis which stretched back as far as Paul.[290] But while Origen was keen to endorse a form of christocentric typology, it has a more spiritual character in his hands than an historical one. That is, he is not principally interested in giving his readers types in the OT which conform to historical events in the NT, or the practices in the church.[291] For him the exegesis of the OT is useful in the sense that it is contemporary, that is, the OT reveals things about Christ for the reader in his present situation, and exegesis therefore becomes a means of meditation upon the nature of the relationship between the Christian and Christ/Logos. This follows because Christ is the inspiration of the OT, and so the OT contains his teaching. In his introduction to his homilies on the Song of Songs this becomes especially clear. Origen tells the reader to listen to the text and make haste to understand it and to join with the bride in saying what she says, so that he may hear also what she has heard. What she has heard are the mysteries concerning Christ.

The Conduct of the Soul

When we talk about the moral theme in Origen's exegesis we enter into a complex area of debate. We have already discussed this in relation to Origen's so-called threefold theory of scriptural interpretation. There is no need to repeat these arguments here. Such a schema is not consistently represented in the extant works.

[288] *De Princ.* Praef. 1.

[289] On this see Torjesen, ibid. 116f, who argues that there are three forms in which the Logos has appeared and taught. The first is at his incarnation, the second in his encounter with the prophets, and the third in his Scriptures.

[290] The term τύπος is used with relative frequency in Origen, invariably to describe the sensible reality of the OT when compared with the truth of the OT. For the view that a distinction between typology and allegory in Origen has been overplayed see Wiles, Origen (1970) 482. For a broader understanding of typology in Origen and a discussion of a range of passages see Daniélou, Origen (1955).

[291] See in this respect *Comm. in Jo.* 10.18; and *HGen.* 12.3 where Origen, interpreting the story of Jacob and Esau (Gen 25:23), appears uninterested in the traditional interpretation in terms of the two peoples (Jews and Gentiles), and prefers to linger on the spiritual interpretation in which the two figures represent the presence of vice and virtue within us.

But what do scholars mean when they refer to Origen's moral exposition of Scripture? In *HEx.* 2.3 Origen writes: "Do not think, therefore, O people of God who hear this that stories of the forefathers are read to you. Think rather that you are being taught through these stories that you may learn the right order of life, moral teaching, the struggles of faith and virtue". Here the individual experiences of personalities in the Pentateuch become stories relevant to the conduct of individual souls. An example of this form of exegesis occurs in *HGen.* 6.2. Having described the story of the death of Lot's wife Origen asks why she died when she looked back? The answer lies in the spiritual nature of the law and the fact that the things which happened to the ancients "happened figuratively". In this example Lot is the rational understanding and the manly soul, and his wife represents the flesh, "for it is the flesh which always looks to vices, which when the soul is proceeding to salvation looks behind and seeks after pleasure". This form of moral/allegorical exegesis, whereby individuals mentioned in the OT stand for aspects of the soul, occurs much more frequently in the homilies, and is very close in character to the type of allegorical exegesis witnessed in Philo.[292] Similarly moralistic in its tone, but reliant upon a different type of allegorical exegesis, are Origen's homilies on Numbers and Joshua. Here the journeys and struggles of the Israelites through the wilderness and subsequently in the promised land, are seen as reflections of the journies and struggles of the individual soul as it moves from paganism to baptism and from baptism to citizenship of the heavenly realms. A form of moral allegory leads into a form of eschatological allegory. So Origen, previewing his interpretation of the 42 stations of Israelites, writes: "Thus, employing a double line of interpretation, we must examine the entire order of stages as it is narrated, so that our soul may make progress by both interpretations, when we learn from them how we ought to live the life that turns from error and follow the law of God; and how great an expectation we have which is promised in the coming of the Resurrection" (*H.Num.* 27).

Mystical Union

All interpretation of the OT is encounter with the Logos, for all the OT is written under his inspiration. By engaging in the very act of spiritual exegesis one is engaging with the Logos. Nowhere is this clearer than in Origen's interpretation of the Song of Songs. He places this book at the end of a progressive stage of spiritual advancement, which he sees in terms of a reading of the three sapiental books (Proverbs, Ecclesiastes and the Song of Songs itself). In this essentially Platonic schema Proverbs represents ethics, Ecclesiastes physics, and the Song of Songs enoptics or the contemplation of divine things.[293] Origen sees the last of these three stages, the ultimate stage, in ecclesiastical and individual terms, in terms of the church's relationship to the Logos, and in terms of the soul's relationship to the latter. While these two

292 See also *HGen.* 4.4; 16.2; *HJos* 10.4–6. For an extended discussion of the significance of Philo for Origen see Runia, Survey (1993) 157–183.

293 For a discussion of the meaning of these successive stages see Louth, Origins (1981) 59f.

relationships are linked, the latter is the ultimate relationship, whereby, through allegorical exegesis, the soul is afforded an intimate encounter with the Logos. Origen's interpretation of the Song of Songs in terms of the union of the soul with Christ represents in a pungent from the σκοπός of all interpretation, and the inevitable result of God's gift of Christ in the text of the OT.[294] It is in this text more than anywhere else that we can see the truth of LOUTH's and others' assertion that the ultimate vision of the divine is afforded by exegesis.[295]

3.4.4. Characteristics of Origen's Exegesis of the Old Testament

In our discussion of Origen's hermeneutical principles we noted that a consequence of his view that the Holy Spirit inspires all Scripture is that all of Scripture is in total harmony with itself. This view is succinctly summarised in the title appended to the sixth chapter of the *Philocalia*: ὅτι ἓν ὄργανον τέλειον καὶ ἡρμοσμένον πᾶσα ἡ θεία γραφή. For Origen there arises from this assumption a fundamental hermeneutical rule, namely that the interpreter can illuminate one biblical text, word, phrase, by other biblical texts, words or phrases. In pagan grammatical practices this rule had come to be known as Ὅμηρον ἐξ Ὁμήρου σαφήνιζειν.[296] For Origen the word σαφήνιζειν had a particular resonance because it implied the illumination of a text that was obscure, and for Origen the obscurity of the Bible, and perhaps particularly the OT, was, as we have noted, a constant topos in his hermeneutics. While in the works of pagan grammarians the rule was generally used to illuminate the literal meaning of a text, for Origen it was almost exclusively used as a means of unveiling the spiritual meaning. It is not an exaggeration to say that Origen's interpretation of the Old Testament could be summarised as one extended application of this rule, a rule which took on a particular coloring in a Christian context because of the conviction that OT and NT were two witnesses to one revelation.

Examples of this type of exegesis can vary from the simple to the complex. So, for instance, in his Homilies on Leviticus Origen wishes to know what the meaning of the word 'oven' is in Lev 7:9 where it is stated that every sacrifice of the priest will be made in an oven. By referring to Hosea 7:4 ("All adulterers are as an oven ignited for burning") and 7:6 ("Their hearts glowed as an oven"), he is able to conclude that the human heart is an oven. Often, however, Origen's comparative exegesis is more complex, involving a number of passages from both the OT and NT. A brief example of this occurs in *HJer.* 10.1. Here Origen seeks to interpret the Jer 11:18: "Make me to

---

294 See especially a passage like *Comm. in Cant.* III.11: "And when he has begun more and more to draw near to her senses and illuminate the things that are obscure" (within the text), then she sees him "leaping upon the mountain and the hills": that is to say, he then suggests to her interpretations of a high and lofty sort, so that this soul can rightly say: "Behold, he cometh leaping upon the mountain, skipping over the hills".

295 "In this engagement with scripture, Origen enters more and more deeply into communion with God" (Louth, ibid. 64).

296 On the application of the principle in Origen see Neuschäfer, ibid. 276–285; in general on this see F. SIEGERT, chap. 4.1, and J. F. PROCOPÉ, chap. 12.3, above.

know (γνώρισόν), Lord, and I will know". In order to illuminate the word "to know" Origen cites the next verse (Jer 11 :19) where it is written: "Like a blameless young lamb which one leads to slaughter I did not not known the schemes they were plotting against me". Via Isa 53 :7 he identifies Christ with the lamb, and wonders what it is that Christ has not known. A third passage, this time from the NT, furnishes him with an answer: "He who has not known sin, he has made sin for us" (2 Cor 5 :21).[297] At *HJos.* 23 Origen is faced with the problem of the mention of 'lots'. Are we to assume that these are open to chance? To solve this Origen methodically cites a number of texts from OT and NT and concludes that we are not. In his homilies on 1 Samuel (*HSam.* 1.9) he notes that in 1 Sam 2 :1 Anna's words are described as a prayer, and yet Anna only prays two half verses to God. How therefore can this be a prayer? To solve the problem Origen quotes 1 Thess 5:17 which speaks about praying without ceasing. But how can one pray without ceasing? A redefinition of prayer in this context must be found. The redefinition aligns prayer with action, and Origen's exegesis can continue. In a fragment of his commentary on Hosea, preserved in *Philoc.* 8, Origen notes that in Hosea 12 :5 there is an inconsistent use of number (plural and singular of a verb – the sentence reads: ἔκλαυσαν καὶ ἐδεήθησάν μου. ἐν τῷ οἴκῳ ῎Ων εὕρωσάν με καὶ ἐκεῖ ἐλαλήθη πρὸς αὐτὸν). Chiding those who would try to correct the solecism, he states that he will resolve the issue by comparing the sentence with biblical sentences which contain the same feature.[298] By such a method he is able to extract a theological interpretation from an unpromising verse.

While such comparative exegesis serves chiefly to illuminate the obscurities in Scripture, it also serves to prove its coherence. Discussing the appearance of the words 'going up' and 'coming down', Origen notes how in Scripture one nearly always goes up to a holy place and down to a base one. "These observations", he writes, "show that the divine scripture was not composed, as it seems to most, in an illiterate and uncultivated language, but was adapted in accord with the discipline of divine instruction" (*HGen.* 15. 1). Furthermore, it serves to lead the reader into ever new interpretations of the same word or phrase. Origen appears to make this point at the beginning of his homilies on Exodus (*HEx.* 1. 1). Here he compares the word of Scripture to a seed whose nature is to multiply diffusely when reborn into an ear of corn. Its increase is porportionate to the diligent labour of the skillful farmer or the fertility of the earth. While the passage is speaking about the irreducibility of the word of God, the polyvalent quality of Scripture's meaning,[299] by extension it also bears upon Origen's desire to open up the interpretative possibilities of individual words, a thesis that is proven by the fact that what follows is a piece of comparative exegesis.

---

[297] It is important to note the number of times Origen uses a passage from the NT to justify a movement from a literal interpretation to a spiritual one. This is not, strictly speaking, a comparative form of exegesis, but it nevertheless constitutes an example of the use of a New Testament passage to dictate the direction in which the exegesis of an OT passage will go.

[298] The relevant sentence reads: ῎Εκ παρατηρήσεως δὲ ὁμοιῶν ῥητῶν καὶ τοῦτο ἀκολούθως εἰρῆσθαι δείξομεν.

[299] See Miller, Poetic Words (1988).

Origen is keen to make it clear that in the application of this rule the question of the context in which the individual word appears must be taken into consideration. So at *HJer.* 17.1 he writes that it is necessary to make sure that in instances where we want to interpret the word 'adversary', we give an interpretation that is entirely coherent (ἀκολουθεῖ). This carries with it the implication that in different contexts a word can have different meanings, a point that Origen is keen to emphasise elsewhere.[300]

While it is clear that the principal method of exegesis Origen employs for the interpretation of the OT could be termed comparative exegesis, he also employs a variety of other methods.

Often he will base a spiritual interpretation on an unusual or minor detail in the text, that is the LXX, or perhaps the versions, but not the Hebrew. At *HLev.* 1.2 Origen notes that Lev 1:2 reads: "When any person (ἄνθρωπος) bring any offering of livestock". But at 2:1 the text reads: "When any soul (ψυχή) presents a grace offering to the Lord". This becomes a springboard for a spiritual interpretation in the second homily. The peculiar description of Elkanah as one man ('unus vir' in the Latin translation) (a reading witnessed in both the Hebrew and Aquila) at 1 Sam 1:1 leads Origen to a moral discussion of oneness (*HSam.* 1.4). The man who is one becomes an imitator of God because he does not change. The appearance in Exod 17:3 of the superfluity, "They thirsted for water", leads Origen to discuss the variety of thirsts. He demands that his audience take seriously the minor detail that Abraham was standing under a tree when he met God. (*HGen.* 4.3).

Origen is keen to make use of symbols. Sometimes this symbolism can manifest itself in simple correspondences, one thing stands for another – on one level the most accurate understanding of allegorical exegesis. Many things connected with water can stand for law,[301] the mountain for Christ (*HJer.* 13.3), or for the prophets (*HJer.* 16.1); winds can stand for spirits (*HJer.* 5.8), and the wells can symbolise the Scriptures. Animals also play a role in this symbolism. At *HJer.* 17.1–3 Origen wishes to comment on the word 'partridge'. By making use of information he possessed concerning the behaviour of the partridge, he is able to state that the bird stands for the devil.

Like Philo, Origen is quick to emphasise the importance of numbers as symbols. In the fragment of the commentary on Psalm 1, preserved in Philocalia 3, Origen states that one should pay close attention to the value of the meaning of numbers (προσέχειν δεῖ καὶ ἐξικνεύειν ἀπὸ τῶν γραφῶν τὰ περὶ αὐτῶν καὶ ἑνὸς ἑκάστου αὐτῶν). In *HNum.* 5.2, commenting on Num 4:47 which states that the ages between which a Levite should work are 25 and 50, he notes that 25 signifies the perfect number of the five senses because it is 5x5. This proves that the man called on to accomplish the work of all works (referred to in the verse) is he who is perfect in every way.[302]

---

300 For a discussion of the presence of homonyms in the Scriptures see *Philoc.* 9.

301 See de Lange, Jews (1975) 116, and esp. p. 198 n. 80.

302 For other examples of the use of number symbolism see *HGen.* 2.2; *HEx.* 9.3; *HNum.* 22.1.

Origen also attaches great significance to the symbolic value of names, believing that names convey the essence of the things or persons named. In this context he nearly always makes use of etymologies derived from Hebrew names, which he probably read in a manual,[303] or in Philo, or gleaned from contemporary Jewish tradition.[304] The use of such etymologies is significant for Origen because the OT proliferates with geographical and personal names. For instance, all Origen's homilies on the Pentateuch makes extensive use of the interpretation of names. A good example of such a passage is one we have already mentioned, namely *HNum.* 27, where the names of the 42 stations of the Israelites become the starting point of Origen's interpretation of the passage in terms of the advance of the individual soul.[305]

3.5. Concluding Remarks

In Origen's interpretation of the OT we are in an exegetical world both similar to and yet sharply different from that of Clement.[306] At the level of general hermeneutical theory they coincide. Like Clement, Origen believed wholeheartedly in the twofold meaning of Scripture and in the supremacy of the spiritual over the literal meaning of a text. Like Clement, Origen endorses an essentially philosophical hermeneutic with Plato playing a prominent role, though Clement is much more intent than Origen upon emphasising the compatibility of philosophy and Christian philosophy.[307] Like Clement, Origen thought it entirely appropriate that the spiritual meaning was obscure by dint of its concealment beneath a sometimes unattractive literal husk. Like Clement, he affirmed the harmony of the OT and the NT, and defended it against Marcionite and other criticism. Like Clement, he believed the Logos to be the inspiration behind the OT and at his incarnation the revealer of its truths.

But in Origen these assumptions are allied to a technical commitment to the OT and its exegesis not found in Clement. He was interested in bringing order to the discipline of OT exegesis, of establishing criteria by which to distinguish a good interpretation from a bad one. Unlike Clement, he took an interest in the question of the canon of the OT, and attributed value to Jewish opinion on the matter. While Clement possessed a hermeneutical theory, he provided his reader with no detailed statement on the subject; Origen did. He is the first Christian exegete seriously to consider the problem of how one should read and understand the Bible. Origen was a biblicist and

---

[303] On this see *HNum.* 20.3, and *c. Cels.* 4.34, where he notes that he has learnt the interpretation of names from Hebrews who take pride in them and explain them in their ancestral script. For a general discussion of Origen's etymologies and Jewish etymologies see de Lange, ibid. 117f.

[304] de Lange, ibid. 199f.

[305] See *Philoc.* 12 (*HJosh.* 20) for the idea that the names in the OT possess a power of their own which can be conveyed irrespective of understanding.

[306] Origen never mentions Clement in his extant works, though it is generally agreed that he was familiar with his works as his association with Pantaenus indicates.

[307] For the role of philosophy in Origen's teaching see Gregory's farewell speech to Origen (Harl, Remerciement); and Neuschäfer's discussion.

an exegete whereas Clement was not.[308] For him the writing of commentaries, scholia and homilies on OT and NT texts constituted his most significant work. All show a strong interest in the wording of Scripture, either in establishing what that wording was (his creation of the Hexapla, which was eventually to lead to Jerome's affirmation of the *Hebraica Veritas*), or in a minute attention to the meaning, function etc. of words. The obviously scholarly character of Origen's exegesis, his commitment to matters philological, historical etc., his willingness to consult Jewish exegetes on these and related matters, stemmed from his early training as a *Grammatikos*. But we should not seek an explanation of the scholarly character of Origen's Scripture in his intellectual background alone. If the OT was inspired to its very last word, it was necessary to know what that word was, and how to establish what it meant. To wonder aloud whether we should separate Origen the philologist from Origen the allegorist[309] is perhaps to fail to see Origen's hermeneutics in an integrated light. Admittedly, there exist, especially in his commentaries, examples of interpretation of an exclusively scholarly character; and there is less scholarship and more allegory in the edificatory homilies where the concept of the application/usefulness (ὠφέλεια) of Scripture looms large. But all Scripture is inspired and useful, and so all study of it is a promotion of that presupposition.

Origen saw the OT as much more than the foreshadowing of events in the NT. While it was a shadow of the good things to come, not all those good things had in fact come. The OT, when interpreted through the prism of Christ, not only confirmed the truth that Christianity was the rightful inheritor of God's promises, but it had a moral, ecclesiological and eschatological content. Moreover, through careful exegesis of its text, Christ would come springing forth from its pages.

Origen wrote much more on the OT than the NT, and together with the evidence of the Hexapla this implies that he probably spent more time studying it. The reason for this lay partly in the fact that the OT was a much larger body of literature. Furthermore, it was a more difficult set of texts containing in it much that appeared strange and irrelevant. But in assessing why Origen wrote so much on the OT, we should not lose sight of the context out of which much of his extant exegesis emerged. Caesarea was a city with a large Jewish population, some of whom were Rabbis skilled in the interpretation of Scripture. Much of Origen's interpretation of the OT can be seen as the result of interaction with Jews whose interpretations many Christians must have found appealing.[310]

Origen did much to set in motion the forms in which later Christians would write about the OT and the methods they would use in its exposition. The criticisms which were to be and still are directed at the arbitrary nature of his exegesis have some validity. Many of these more arbitrary features had

---

[308] In many respects Origen is probably closer in his exegesis to Philo than to Clement. But there are important differences here, too.

[309] See Neuschäfer, ibid. 292.

[310] See de Lange, Jews (1975) 7f. and 86–87.

their source in Origen's desire to defend the usefulness of the OT for the Christian community. There is in Origen's interpretation a strongly pastoral interest. As he stated it was impious that things in Scripture should be considered irrelevant for salvation (*HNum.* 27.2). Porphyry had good reason to complain that Origen owed his success as an exegete of the OT to the allegories which enabled him to soften the repulsiveness of Jewish scripture (Eusebius, *HE* 6.14.8).

4. Origenism in Some Later Writers

4.1. Introductory Remarks: What do we mean by Origenism?

Bibliography: H. Crouzel, "Origenism" (EEC, ed. A. De Beradino; ET Cambridge 1992) 623.

Origenism in its broadest sense refers to that body of theological thought associated with Origen. From the end of the fourth century certain views associated with Origen began to be deemed heretical. In the context of this essay the term is used to refer to exegesis which appears to show Origenist influence. This influence may express itself in a technical way (a concern with the Hexapla etc.), or in a looser, more general way (a penchant for allegorical exegesis as expounded by Origen).

4.2. Eusebius of Caesarea

Texts: Commentaria in Psalmos (PG 23); *Der Jesajakommentar* (GCS Eusebius Werke 9, ed. J. Ziegler)

Bibliography: T. D. Barnes, *Constantine and Eusebius* (Cambridge, MA: Harvard University Press 1980) 106–125; E. des Places, *Eusèbe de Césarée commentateur: Platonisme et Écriture Sainte*; M. J. Hollerich, "Eusebius as a Polemical Interpreter of Scripture" (*Eusebius, Christianity and Judaism*, ed. H. W. Attridge/W. Hata; Leiden 1992) 585–615; C. Sant, "Interpretatio Veteris Testamenti in Eusebio Caesarensi", *VD* 45 (1967) 79–90; M. Simonetti, "Esegesi e ideologia nel commento in Isaia", *RSRL* 19 (1983) 3–44; idem, *Allegoria e/o lettera*, 113–124; idem, "Eusebio e Origene per una storia dell'Origenesimo", *Aug* 26 (1986) 323–334; D. S. Wallace-Hadrill, *Eusebius of Caesarea* (London 1961).

Eusebius was a student of Pamphilus, a great enthusiast for the works of Origen. Throughout his career Eusebius was to show a persistent admiration for the Alexandrian,[311] and an intimacy with his works made possible by their presence in the library at Caesarea.[312] But Eusebius' wider concerns, affected by his own personal interests and the context in which he wrote, led him to produce exegetical writings on the OT with different emphases to those found in Origen.

---

[311] For confirmation of this see the fact that he collaborated with Pamphilus in the writing of an apology for Origen; and his own account of Origen's life in *HE* 6.1f.

[312] Eusebius never refers to Origen explicitly in his exegetical writings, but as Ziegler has shown for his Commentary on Isaiah, there are plenty of places where Origen appears to be the source of his ideas. See Ziegler, Kommentar xxiiif.

4.1.1. The Text of the Old Testament

Eusebius was originally trained to copy and correct biblical manuscripts of the LXX by reference to Origen's Hexapla.[313] This early training impressed upon him the interpretative importance of textual variants, and he made regular use of the Hexapla in his exegetical writings.[314] While these writings are normally based on the LXX, they often adopt other readings to illuminate an obscurity,[315] or bring out more clearly the messianic implications of a verse.[316] Indeed scholars have often noted that the criteria used by Eusebius to favour one reading over another are invariably apologetic rather than scholarly/scientific.[317] This conclusion seems to be supported by Eusebius' own statement concerning his text critical procedure in the prologue to the *Demonstration*. After affirming the central position of the LXX, he continues: "But whenever necessary, I shall call in the help of the editions of the later translators, which the Jews are accustomed to use today, so that my proof may have stronger support from all sources".

4.2.2. Interpretation of Scripture

Eusebius' interest in the OT was not in the main speculative or moral in the sense we find this in Origen's works, but rather historical and, as with his text critical work, apologetic. The OT was primarily a history book in which there were to be found numerous prophecies relating to events within the OT itself, in the NT and in the period subsequent to the NT, especially the Constantinian era. This interest in the prophetic dimension of the OT is reflected in all his works but especially the *Proph. Ecl.*, the *Demonstration* and his two surviving commentaries on Isaiah and the Psalms, texts specifically chosen because they contained so much traditional prophetic material.

The above implies a movement away from Origen's concern with allegory. At the beginning of ch. 3 of his Commentary on Isaiah Eusebius seems to abandon Origen's two level approach, claiming that sometimes the prophetic sense is found in the literal meaning of Scripture and sometimes in the allegorical. So, for instance, at 90.12, the 'branch' and 'flower' of Isa 11:1 are interpreted allegorically, while Jesse is interpreted literally; and a large number of prophecies are thought to have an exclusively literal reference.[318] Furthermore, in his commentaries Eusebius shows a greater interest than we find in Origen for the actual historical reference of the texts under discussion

---

[313] For a list of manuscript colophons corrected by Eusebius see Harnack, *Geschichte der altchristlichen Literatur* Pt. 2 573 f.

[314] "Questo testo egli ha costamente sotto gli occhi quando si occupa di interpretazione biblica", Simonetti, Lettera (1985) 113. See also Ziegler, 443 f. for the over 700 references in the Comm. in Isaiah.

[315] *Comm. in Isaiah* 110.12–112.33 (all references are to page numbers in Ziegler)

[316] When commenting on Isa 53:2 he prefers the reading of Aquila which has "from untrodden ground" to the reading of the other versions which has "in the thorny ground", because the first reading appears to be a clear reference to the virgin birth (335.2 f.).

[317] Of recent writers on this subject Wallace-Hadrill is most assertive: "His canon of textual criticism was this: the version which is most plainly messianic, with the least obscure additional material, is the best text" (Eusebius 62).

[318] See Hollerich, Eusebius 591.

within the OT.[319] But it would be wrong to think of Eusebius as abandoning Origenist allegory, or Origenist procedure in his exegesis. There are still allegorical interpretations to be found in the major commentaries, and there are still references to two levels of meaning, the literal and the spiritual. Commenting on Isa 19:1, Eusebius can still write of an interpretation πρὸς ἱστορίαν and one κατὰ δὲ βαθύτερον νοῦν (124. 15).[320] In order to proceed to an allegorical meaning, like Origen, he often points to the impossibility of a literal/historical exegesis;[321] and in his exegesis he makes use of symbol[322] and etymology. It is perhaps not for nothing that the mature Jerome noted that in the *Commentary on Isaiah*: "Historicam expositionem repromittens interdum obliviscitur propositi et in Origenis scita concedit" (*Is Comm.* 1. 5).[323]

But even if we may talk about an Origenist substratum evident in Eusebius' exegesis, we should still note that the emphasis has shifted considerably from an Origenist interest in theological and moral speculation to one in history and prophecy.[324] This shift can be explained in a number of ways. Eusebius' interest in history reflects his own tendencies and mental framework. Here, after all, was the author of the *Chronicon* and the *Onomasticon*, works which show a massive erudition. Equally we may point to the attacks on Origen's allegorical exegesis made by Porphyry, which Eusebius himself records (*HE* 6. 19. 4–8). This sensitivity to the claim that Christian arguments relied heavily upon an exclusively allegorical exegesis is at least implicit in Jerome's assertion that Eusebius wished to write an historical commentary on Isaiah.[325]

4.3. *Athanasius*

Bibliography: B. De Margerie, *Introduction à l'histoire de l'exégèse. 1. Les pères grecs et orientaux* (Paris 1980) 137–64; M. Rondeau, "L'épître à Marcellinum sur les Psaumes", *VC* 22 (1968) 176–197; T. E. Pollard, "The Exegesis of Scripture and the Arian Controversy", *BJRL* 41 (1958–59) 414–429; H. J. Sieben, "Athanasius über den Psalter: Analyse seines Briefes an Marcellinum", *ThPh* 48 (1973) 157–173; idem, "Herméneutique de l'exégèse dogmatique d'Athanase", *Politique et théologie chez Athanase d'Alexandre* (ed. C. Kannengiesser; Paris 1974) 195–214; G. C. Stead,

[319] See for instance Eusebius' comments on Isaiah 13–23 and 36–39; and the strong interest we find in the Psalmic commentaries in the historical context of the titles. Barnes contrasts the strongly moralistic/allegorical nature of Origen's two surviving homilies on Psalm 37, and the much more historically orientated commentary of Eusebius on the same Psalm (Constantine, (1980) 95 f.).

[320] See also contrasts between the σωματικός meaning and the spiritual meaning at 16. 12; 369. 14 and 405. 32. These contrasts are also visible in his commentary on the Psalms and his *Demonstration.* For the Alexandrian terminology of the Isaianic commentary see Simonetti, Esegesi (1983) 17 n. 8.

[321] See *Comm. in Is.* 89. 25–92. 5 and *Ps.* 80. 14–15.

[322] For a discussion of symbol see Wallace-Hadrill, Eusebius (1961) 84–86.

[323] Simonetti, Eusebio (1986) 328, notes that the tendency to abandon allegory and the Origenist method is only incipient in the works of Eusebius.

[324] Wallace-Hadrill say Eusebius' position in Caesarea, half way between Antioch and Alexandria, is, metaphorically at least, indicative of the character of his exegesis.

[325] Simonetti, Esegesi (1983) 6, talks about Eusebius wanting to mitigate the more radical aspects of Origen's allegory; and Wallace-Hadrill notes a shift from the more allegorically oriented *Prophetic Eclogues* to the Commentaries on Isaiah and the Psalms.

"Athanasius on the Psalms", *VC* 39 (1985) 65–78; idem, "Athanasius als Exeget", *Christliche Exegesis zwischen Niceae und Chalcedon* (ed. J. van Oort/U. Wickert; Kampen 1992) 174–184; T. F. Torrance, *Divine Meaning: Studies in Patristic Hermeneutics* (Edinburgh 1995) 179–288.

Any analysis of Athanasius' exegesis is obviously dogged by the fact that we posses no exclusively exegetical work written by him.[326] When we wish to talk of his Origenism we are in yet more uncertain terrain.[327] Below are some preliminary comments, which set out the main areas of debate.

In recent times some scholars have sought to illuminate some of the assumptions which underpinned Athanasius' exegesis: his belief in the sufficiency of Scripture,[328] his occasional specific staements on the rules of exegesis,[329] and perhaps most interestingly in the context of this study, his claim that Scripture has a σκοπός. At *C. Ar.* 3.28–29 he writes: "Now the σκοπός and character of scripture is this: it contains a double account of the saviour, that he was ever God and is the son, being the Father's logos, radiance and wisdom, and that afterwards for us he took flesh from a virgin … and was made man. And this is the purpose (σκοπός) to be found throughout scripture". When we compare this obviously anti-Arian statement with Origen we note that the σκοπός is more restricted, and furthermore that whereas in Origen the primary σκοπός is bound up with the secret or spiritual meaning, this is not so in Athanasius.[330] This, of course, should not be taken to imply that Athanasius was uninterested in allegory. Sieben, for instance, implies that when he exhorts his readers in the face of obscure passages in Scripture (*C. Ar.* 2.2), we come close to a call to allegorisation;[331] and there are examples of allegorical exegesis in his writings. But this is not the predominant form of exegesis,[332] where typology appears to play a greater role.[333]

One writing of Athanasius where we do perhaps gain an insight into an exegetical perspective which might be described as Origenist is the *Letter to*

[326] See Stead, Exeget (1992) 174: "Im technischen Sinn kommt Athanasius als Exeget kaum in Betracht". Also Simonetti, Lettera (1985) 201: "L'esegesi fu attività del tutto marginale". But such observations do not seem to accord with Gregory Nazianzen's comment in his funeral oration for Athanasius. See his Oratio XXI, *In laudem Athanasii*, 6 (PG XXXV, 1088).

[327] Athanasius refers directly to Origen once. This is in the context of a discussion of the everlasting coexistence of the Father with the son. The reference to the work of φιλοπόνου 'Ωριγένους (*Decr.* 27.1) is certainly not negative.

[328] "The sacred and divine scriptures are sufficient to declare the truth" (*C. Gen.* 1).

[329] See *C. Ar.* 1.54 where Athanasius states that the time in which a verse was uttered, the person who uttered it and the circumstances in which it was uttered should be taken into account. For an application of this rule see *Decr.* 14 and the interpretation of Prov 8:22.

[330] See Sieben, Exégèse (1974) 213.

[331] Ibid. 213.

[332] Athanasius' claim that many of the Psalms have Christ as their subject (*Ep. ad Marc.* 27) has prompted some (Simonetti, Allegoria (1983) 204) to assume an allegorical dimension to his exegesis. Stead, Psalms (1985) 78, is sceptical here, especially when he compares the few examples of Psalmic exegesis in the *Ep. ad Marc.* (6–8) with the exegesis of the Psalms in the Pseudo-Athanasian *Expositions in the Psalms.* Such a comparison leads him to argue that Athanasius, under the influence of Bishop Peter, may be reacting against the allegory of Origen. Pollard, Exegesis (1959), argues that Athanasius moves away from allegorism.

[333] In this respect see especially the *Festal Letters* 4.3, 4; 5.4; 14.3, 5.

Marcellinus on the Psalms.[334] This constitutes an explanation of the unique qualities of the Psalter for the individual Christian. The Psalter, Athanasius states, like a paradise, contains within it the vegetation of all the books of the OT – Pentateuch, history books and prophets (*Epist.* 2–8), and conversely is itself echoed in all these books. The quality which distinguishes it from the other books lies in its capacity to mirror and reflect the different movements of the soul (*Epist.* 10–12), and thus provide the reader with the ultimate means to gain spiritual and moral harmony, which is itself encouraged and reflected by the melody of the Psalms (28). Different Psalms can be used in different life settings (see 15–26 where he gives a detailed list of these), and their construction in the first person allows the reader to appropriate more easily the teachings within them (11). Their wording is entirely appropriate, and there is no need to improve upon it (31). Athanasius' interpretation is not exclusively sapiential and he divides the Psalms into two categories, those which reflect the movements of the soul and the more numerous Psalms, which announce the coming of Christ (27). The sense in which this interpretation of the Psalter might be described as Origenist, lies not so much in its method of exegesis, but rather in its endorsement of what one commentator has called Psalmotherapy, the capacity of the Psalms to cure spiritual ills. Such a view of the function of the Psalms is not so far from the spirit of Origen's 9 surviving homilies on the Psalms.

4.4. The Cappadocian Fathers

4.4.1. The Philocalia

Text: J. A. Robinson, *The Philocalia of Origen* (Cambridge 1893).

Bibliography: M. Harl/N. R. M. de Lange, *Philocalie* (1983) 19–41; E. Junod, "Remarques sur la composition de la 'Philocalie' d'Origène par Basil de Césarée et Grégoire de Nazianze", *RHPR* 52 (1972) 149–156; idem, "Particularités de la Philocalie", *Origeniana* (Quaderni di *Vetera Christianorum* 12, Bari 1975) 181–197.

It has usually been thought that the collection of writings known as the *Philocalia* was compiled by Gregory Nazianzen and Basil of Caesarea, probably between 360 and 378.[335] This would seem, *prima facie*, to be the implication of the letter Gregory writes to Bishop Theodore in 383, which along with a later prologue, we find attached to the collection. The letter states that Gregory is sending the Bishop a copy (πυκτίον) of the Philocalia of Origen (Ὠριγένους φιλοκαλίας) as a memento (ὑπόμνημα) of himself and the late Basil.[336]

---

[334] For the text see PG 27 (1857) 12–45, and its interpretation see Sieben, Psalter (1973); and Stead, Psalms (1985).

[335] On the difficulties see Junod, Remarques (1972) 155f, who dates the collection between 364 and 378; and Harl, Philocalie (1985) 21–22, who is more sceptical.

[336] For the text Harl, ibid. 170. For the view that the collection was not compiled by Gregory and Basil see Harl, ibid. 24. She notes that even if we agree that the two Cappadocians had studied Origen's works thoroughly in their youth (the implication of a statement in Sozomen (6. 17. 2–3) which explicitly mentions the study of the interpretation of τῶν ἐκκλησιαστικῶν βιβλίων), there is no explicit statement in the letter to Theodore that Basil and his friend are

The *Philocalia* indicates the compilers' intimate knowledge of Origen's works (they have borrowed from 21 works, 12 of which are either homilies, commentaries or scholia from the OT), and, above all, the respect in which they held him as an interpreter of the Bible.[337] What the compilers sought to emphasise in their presentation of Origen's hermeneutics was his central conviction that all Scripture was inspired, and this in spite of its unseemly style and the presence within it of passages of great difficulty. In order to adhere to this conviction it was necessary to know how to read and understand Scripture, and this involved a movement beyond scripture's literal meaning, and a close attendance to the wording and grammar of the text. Furthermore, and within reason, the application of philosophy to the reading of the Bible was perfectly legitimate.

In his letter to Theodore, Gregory states that he hopes that the collection will prove useful (χρήσιμος) to the philologians (τοῖς φιλολόγοις), a term that is quite general in its application, and probably simply refers to the cultivated reader. The *Philocalia* constitutes a guide to the correct reading of the Bible, and an affirmation of its central position in the Christian's life.[338] What is interesting is that as late as the 360s theologians could appeal to Origen as the expositor par excellence of its contents.

4.4.2. Basil of Caesarea

Texts: *Homiliae in Psalmos* (PG 29) 208–494; S. Giet, *Homélies sur L'Hexaéméron* (SC 26; Paris, 1948).

Bibliography: J. Gribomont, "L'Origénisme de Saint Basile", *L'Homme devant Dieu* (Mélanges H. de Lubac; Paris 1963); M. Simonetti, *Lettera* (1985) 140–144.

Basil, as one of the probable compilers of the *Philocalia*, would be expected to reflect a strongly Origenist tendency in his exegesis. But often scholars note a strange disjunction between the endorsement of Origen implied in the *Philocalia* and the exegesis witnessed in the *Hexaemeron*. In this work, consisting of nine devotional homilies on the first six days of creation delivered in Holy Week, Basil is strongly literalist in his exegesis,[339] and rejects allegorical approaches, at one point explicitly attacking an interpretation associated with Origen.[340]

---

responsible for the collection. Furthermore, Basil in his extant writings, makes no reference to it. Harl concludes: "Nous nous contenterons donc de parler désormais, sans plus de précisions, des 'Philocalistes'" (24). It seems to us that Harl is being too astringent in her use of evidence, and that the view that the two Cappadocians are responsible for the collection is still the best view (Junod, Remarques (1972) 150, argues that Gregory wrote it and Basil gave his approval).

[337] It is possible to see the whole collection as centred on the Bible and its interpretation. For this view see Harl, ibid. 29. She argues that chs. 15–20, which consists of quotations from *c. Cels.*, and is sometimes described as apologetics, is strongly concerned with the Bible; and that chs. 21–27, though connected with the question of free will, presents its solution to the problem from the Bible (see the title to ch. 21).

[338] Harl, ibid. 38, argues that the composition may have its *Sitz im Leben* in the theological debates of the second half of the fourth century in which the Bible played a prominent part.

[339] Gribomont, L'Origénisme (1963) 292, refers to his exaggerated literalism.

[340] *Hex.* 31B. Here he rejects the allegorical interpretation which sees the separation of the waters in terms of separation into corporeal and incorporeal powers, (an interpretation endorsed by Origen at *HGen.* 1.2: "Let us reject these dreams and old wives' tales, and understand that

To explain this disjunction scholars assume a development in Basil's attitude to Origen's exegesis. In the early 360s, at the time of the writing of the *Philocalia*, Basil was an enthusiastic Origenist; in the 370s, when he wrote the *Hexaemeron*, possibly influenced by Diodore of Tarsus, he had moved away from this initial enthusiasm and was now much more critical of the allegorical method. We should, however, be wary of adopting such a simple thesis. Though difficult to date with certainty, the thirteen homilies on the Psalms probably date from a similar time to the *Hexaemeron*. They present a counterpoint to the literalism of that work. While not predominantly allegorical in their method, allegory is still an important feature, along with the terminology sometimes associated with that method. So in his interpretation of Ps 28[29]:2–4, "the voice of the Lord over the waters", is understood literally as the dominance of God over creation, and symbolically as the baptism of Christ. The rubric of Psalm 29 ("For the dedication of the House of David") is referred literally to the house of Solomon, and spiritually to the incarnation of Christ.[341]

The above observations have led some, not to deny that there was a movement away from Origen in Basil, but to argue that the movement was not absolute. In this interpretation the literalism of Basil's *Hexaemeron* is accounted for partly by Basil's interest in the scientific culture of his time,[342] by the homiletic nature of what he is writing, the humble audience he is addressing (at *Hom.* 3:1 he refers to labourers and artisans),[343] and the nature of the text, which of all the opening chapters of Genesis, appears to sit most easily with a literal interpretation. In this interpretation of the *Hexaemeron* Basil's literalism is seen as compatible with his aims in these nine homilies, and his own understanding of the first chapter of Genesis, and not necessarily as a general riposte to Origenist hermeneutics.

4.4.3. *Gregory of Nyssa*

Texts: *In inscriptiones Psalmorum: in sextum Psalmum: in Ecclesiasten homiliae* (*Gregorii Nysseni Opera* [*GNO*] V, ed. J. McDonough/P. Alexander; Leiden 1962); *In Cantico Canticorum* (*GNO* VI, ed. H. Langerbeck; Leiden 1960); *De Vita Mosis* (*GNO* VII, pt. 1, ed. H. Musurillo; Leiden 1964).

Bibliography: M. Canévet, *Grégoire Nysse et l'herméneutique biblique* (Paris 1983); J. Daniélou, *L'Être et le Temps chez Grégoire de Nyssa* (Leiden 1970), esp. chs. I and II; H. Dörries, "Griechentum und Christentum bei Gregor von Nyssa. Zu H. Langerbeck's Edition des Hohelied-Kommentars in der Leidner Gregor Ausgabe", *ThLZ* 88 (1963) 569–585; R. E. Heine, "Gregory of Nyssa's Apology for Allegory", *VC* 38 (1984) 360–370; C. W. Macleod, "Allegory and System in Origen and Gregory of Nyssa" (*Collected Essays*, Oxford 1983) 309–326; M. J. Rondeau, "Exégèse du Psautier et Anabase spirituelle chez Grégoire de Nyssa", *Epektasis* (Mélanges patristiques offerts au Cardinal Jean Daniélou; Paris 1972) 517–531; idem; "D'où vient la technique

by water water is meant"). See also the words at 80C, which have an almost Antiochene ring to them: Ἐγὼ δὲ χόρτον ἀκούσας, χόρτον νοῶ, καὶ φυτὸν, καὶ ἰχθὺν, καὶ θηρίον, καὶ κτῆνος, πάντα ὡς εἴρηται οὕτως ἐκδάχομαι.

[341] The terminology here is κατὰ μὲν τὸ σωματικὸν and κατὰ δὲ τὸ νοητόν.

[342] See Simonetti, Letera (1985) 144.

[343] A point made by his brother, Gregory of Nyssa, in his own continuation of the *Hexaemeron* (see *PG* 44, 65A–B).

utilisée par Grégoire de Nysse dans son traité 'Sur les Titres de Psaumes'" (*Mélanges des Religions* offerts à H. Ch. Puech; Paris 1975) 263 f; M. Simonetti, *Lettera* (1985) 145 f; idem, "La tecnica esegetica di Gregorio di Nissa nella Vita di Mosé", SSR (1982) 401 f.

With Gregory of Nyssa we are in the presence of an exegete who is much more obviously Origenist in his assumptions than his brother Basil. Admittedly, this description is not true for his earlier works (the *Hexaemeron* and the *De Opif.*), both consciously defences of his brother, but it does apply to his most significant later works, on the Psalm titles (*GNO* V:3–175), Ecclesiastes (*GNO* V:277–442), the Song of Songs (*GNO* VI), and the Life of Moses (*GNO* VII. 1), and particularly to the last of these. But to call these works Origenist is to overlook their strongly individual character.

Hermeneutical Assumptions and the Aim of Exegesis

It is well known that for whatever reason, Gregory's preface to his commentary on the Song of Songs consists of a justification of the allegorical method.[344] As Langerbeck's edition (pp. 3 f.) indicates the vocabulary is very much that of Origen, and so are a number of the arguments. What is interesting is that it lacks the intensity of Origen's theory of inspiration, or an exclusive association of the aim of a text with its spiritual meaning. When we delineate some of the principals underpinning Gregory's interpretation of the OT, it will become clear why this is the case.

σκοπός

For Gregory, individual books of Scripture have a unitary purpose. This unitary purpose is invariably bound up with the idea of spiritual advance, an idea we find in some of Origen's works (particularly his Homilies on Numbers and Joshua), but an idea which does not dominate the whole course of his exegesis in the way it does in Gregory's work.[345]

ἀκολουθία

The σκοπός of a text is intimately linked to the sequence or ἀκολουθία of the same text, that is, the sequence of historical events recorded, but more importantly to the order by which the beatitude of the soul is attained. In the case of his Commentary on the Psalm titles this order expresses itself in a progression through the five sections into which the Psalms were traditionally divided, or in the case of the Life of Moses, through the progression of Moses' life, in which Moses becomes a symbol of the Christian soul, and the highest it can achieve.[346] If this order does not correspond to the chronologi-

---

344 Heine, Gregory (1984).

345 For the view that Gregory's application of this idea to the Psalms in unique see Rondeau, Technique (1975).

346 See Daniélou's translation of *Ps.* 1.1, which expresses very clearly the idea of ἀκολουθία: "La divine Psalmodie présente selon un ordre (ἀκολουθία) savant et naturel la route qui conduit à la béatitude sous forme d'un enseignement apparement simple et sans apprêt, traitant sous des formes variés de la méthode à prendre pour l'acquisition de la béatitude".

cal order, as it does not in the case of the Psalms, this does not matter, for the Holy Spirit is not interested in historical but spiritual progress.[347]

θεωρία

θεωρία refers to the means by which the ἀκολουθία of a text is established. Often this will lie in an allegorical interpretation of the text, in a movement beyond the historical events, to their spiritual meaning.[348]

The interplay of these three principals of exegesis explain the difference between the style and tone of Gregory's and Origen's exegesis of the OT. First, Gregory's exegesis of an OT book, being dominated by a particular σκοπός, can appear more ordered and less digressive. Individual details of the text are not examined in the way they are in Origen's writings, and philology plays an only minor role.[349] Gregory's failure to emphasise the inspiration of the text in an absolutist way is in this context understandable. Secondly, in Gregory's interpretative model allegory, the means by which he often unravels the concealed ἀκολουθία of a text, is more a method than it is in Origen where it is bound up with the mystical experience itself.[350] Thirdly, the central pivot of exegesis shifts from a description or explanation of the Logos to an establishment of the stages of spiritual progress indicated in the text.[351] Christological exegesis is, of course, present, but it is invariably subservient to the demands of the text's perceived σκοπός.

---

[347] For the possible link between Gregory's idea of the ἀκολουθία of a text and the same idea in rhetoric see Rondeau op.cit.

[348] This is most obviously the case in the Life of Moses where the history of Moses' life literally understood precedes that of his life spiritually understood. The Commentary on the Song of Songs in also unremittingly allegorical in its concern, but here the literal level, which receives a good deal of attention from Origen, receives no attention from Gregory. For places where θεωρία is used in an allegorical sense see *Cant. Prol.* 6.13; 12.3; 12.12.

[349] This is not to say that Gregory is not digressive. He has a tendency on occasions to move from a concrete concept to an abstract concept to a moral idea. For examples of this see *GNO* VI, 396, 4f. and his comment on the Words 'eyes like doves' (Song of Songs 5:12).

[350] "What sets apart Gregory's treatment of allegory is the attempt to find a structure and a sequence in the texts that he deals with. Allegory becomes a literary form then in so far as Gregory seeks to create a scheme in his allegorical work", Macleod, Mysticism (1983) 372.

[351] This quest in Gregory's thought is an eternal one. See *Life of Moses* 113.2–114.1 where everything achieved by Moses is simply a quest; and 114.5–116.23 where to find God is never to cease searching for him.

Chapter Fourteen

Exegesis of the Old Testament in the Antiochene School with its Prevalent Literal and Historical Method

By Sten Hidal, Lund

Sources: Diodore of Tarsus: CPG 2 (1974) 3815-3822; PG 33, 1561-1628; *Diodori Tarsensis Commentarii in Psalmos I. Commentarii in Psalmos I-L* (ed. J.-M. Olivier; CCG 6; Brepols-Turnhout 1980); J. Deconinck, *Essai sur la chaîne de l'Octateuque* (Bibliothèque de l'école des hautes études, sciences historiques et philologiques, fasc. 195; Paris 1912); L. Mariès, "Extraits de commentaires de Diodore de Tarse sur les Psaumes. Préface du commentaire. Prologue du Ps CXVIII", *RSR* 10 (1919) 79-101. – Eusebius of Emesa: CPG 2 (1974) 3525-3543; PG 86, 509-562; R. Devreesse, *Les anciens commentateurs grecs de l'Octateuque et des Rois* (Studi e Testi 201; Vatican City 1959; 55-103); E. M. Buytaert, *L'héritage littéraire d'Eusèbe d'Emèse* (Louvain 1949). – John Chrysostom: PG 53-56; *Homélies sur Ozias* (ed. J. Dumortier; SC 277; Paris 1981); *Commentaire sur Isaïe* (ed. J. Dumortier; SC 304; Paris 1983); Commentaire sur Job (ed. I. H. Sorlin; SC 343; Paris 1988); *Kommentare zu Hiob* (ed. U. & D. Hagedorn; PTS 35; Berlin 1990). – Julian of Eclanum: CPL 2 (1961) 773-774; PL 21, 959-1104; *Iuliani Aeclanensis expositio Libri Iob. Tractatus prophetarum Osee Joel et Amos* (ed. M. J. d'Hont/L. de Coninck; CCL 88; Brepols-Turnhout 1977); *Bedae in Cantica Canticorum allegorica expositio*, PL 91, 1065-1236. – Polychronius: CPG 2, 3878-3880; PG 93, 13-470; PG 64, 739-1038 (a disputed commentary on Jeremiah). - Severian of Gabala: GPG 2, 4185-4295; PG 56, 429-500. – Theodore of Mopsuestia: GPG 2, 3827-3873; PG 66, 124-700; R. Devreesse, *Le commentaire de Théodore de Mopsueste sur les Psaumes* (Studi e Testi 93; Vatican City 1933); *Commentarius in XII prophetas* (ed. H. N. Sprenger; Göttingen 1977); R. Devreesse, *Les anciens commentateurs grecs de l'Octateuque et des Rois* (Studi e Testi 201; Vatican City 1959); *Theodori Mopsuesteni expositionis in Psalmos Iuliano Aeclanensi interprete in Latinum versae quae supersunt* (ed. M. J. d'Hont/L. de Coninck; CCL 88 A; Brepols-Turnhout 1977); L. Van Rompay, *Théodore de Mopsueste. Fragments syriaques du Commentaire des Psaumes (Psaume 118 et Psaumes 138-148)* (CSCO 435-436/Syr. 189-190; Louvain 1982; Syriac and French transl.). – Theodoret of Cyrrhus: CPG 3, 6200-6288; PG 80-81; *Commentaire sur Isaïe* (ed. J.-N. Guinot; SC 279 [1980], 295 [1982], 315 [1984]; F. Petit, "La tradition de Théodoret de Cyr dans les chaînes sur la Genèse", *Le Muséon* 92 (1979) 281-286.

Bibliographies: L. Abramowski, "Diodore de Tarse", DHGE 14 (1957) 496-504; J. S. Alexander, "Julian von Aeclanum", TRE 17 (1988) 441-443; B. Altaner/A. Stuiber, Patrologie. Leben, Schriften und Lehre der Kirchenväter (Basel/Wien 1978); Y. Azéma, "Théodoret de Cyr", DictS XV (1991) 418-435; G. Bardy, "Diodore", DictS III (1955) 986-993; *Encyclopedia of Early Christianity* (ed. E. Ferguson; New York/London 1990); *Encyclopedia of the Early Church* (Produced by the Institutum Patristicum Augustinianum and ed. by A. di Beradino. Translated from the Italian by A. Walford, with a Foreword and Bibliographic Amendments by W. H. C. Frend [= EEC]; Cambridge 1992); A. Harnack/W. Möller, "Antiochenische Schule", RE 1 (1896) 592-596; J. M. Lera, "Théodore de Mopsueste", DictS XV (1991) 385-400; J.-M. Leroux, "Johannes Chrysostomus", TRE 17 (1988) 118-127; J. Quasten, *Patrology III* (Westminster Maryland 1960); C. Schäublin, "Diodor von Tarsus", TRE 8 (1981) 763-767; H.-J. Sieben, *Voces. Eine Bibliographie zu Wörtern und Begriffen aus der Patristik (1918-1978)* (Bibliographia Patristica Suppl. 1; Berlin/New York 1980); S. J. Voicu, "Sévérien de Gabale", DictS XIV (1988) 752-763; A. Wenger, "Jean Chrysostome", DictS VIII (1972) 332-355.

General works: L. ABRAMOWSKI, "Der Streit um Diodor und Theodor zwischen den beiden ephesinischen Konzilien", *ZKG* 67 (1955/56) 252–287; idem, "Zur Theologie Theodors von Mopsuestia", *ZKG* 72 (1961) 263–293; R. ABRAMOWSKI, "Der theologische Nachlass des Diodor von Tarsus", *ZNW* 42 (1949) 19–69; G. W. ASHBY, *Theodoret of Cyrrhus as exegete of the Old Testament* (Grahamstown 1972); O. BARDENHEWER, *Geschichte der altkirchlichen Literatur* III (Freiburg/Br. 1924); G. BARDY, *Recherches sur Saint Lucien d'Antioche et son école* (Paris 1936); idem, "Interpretation. Chez les pères IV", DBSup 4 (1949) 579–582; E. DASSMANN, "Hiob", RAC 15 (1989) 366–442; L. DENNEFELD, *Der alttestamentliche Kanon der antiochenischen Schule* (Biblische Studien 14:4; Freiburg/Br. 1909); R. DEVREESSE, *Essai sur Théodore de Mopsueste* (Vatican City 1949); B. DREWERY, "Exegese III", RAC 6 (1966) 1211–1229; R. A. GREER, *Theodore of Mopsuestia. Exegete and Theologian* (London 1961); J.-N. GUINOT, "Un évêque exégète: Théodoret de Cyr", *Le monde grec ancien et la Bible* (BTT 1; Paris 1984) 335–360; A. KAMESAR, *Jerome, Greek Scholarship, and the Hebrew Bible* (Oxford 1993); H. KIHN, *Theodor von Mopsuestia und Junilius als Exegeten* (Freiburg/Br. 1880); M. L. W. LAISTNER, "Antiochene exegesis in Western Europe during the Middle Ages", *HTR* 40 (1947) 19–35; J. PÉPIN, "Hermeneutik", RAC 14 (1987) 751–771; L. PIROT, *L'oeuvre exégètique de Théodore de Mopsueste* (Rome 1913); A. M. RITTER, "Die antiochenische und die alexandrinische Christologie", HDTG 1 (1982) 236–244; C. SCHÄUBLIN, *Untersuchungen zu Methode und Herkunft der antiochenischen Exegese* (Theophaneia 23; Köln/Bonn 1974); E. SCHWEIZER, "Diodor von Tarsus als Exeget", *ZNW* 40 (1941) 33–75; P. TERNANT, "La theoria d'Antioche dans le cadre des sens de l'Ecriture", *Bib.* 34 (1953) 135–158, 354–383, 456–486; D. S. WALLACE-HADRILL, *Christian Antioch* (Cambridge 1982); M. F. WILES, "Theodore of Mopsuestia as Representative of the Antiochene School", CHB 1 (ed. P. R. Ackroyd/C. F. Evans; Cambridge 1970) 489–510; D. Z. ZAHAROPOULOS, *Theodore of Mopsuestia on the Bible. A study of his Old Testament Exegesis* (New York 1989); A. ZIEGENAUS, *Kanon. Von der Väterzeit bis zur Gegenwart* (HDG I, Fasz. 3 a; Freiburg/Basel/Wien 1990).

In this essay the scriptural references are according to the Septuagint (with possible deviations in comparison to MT references).

1. The Elder Antiochene School

In contrast to the catechetical school in Alexandria, there never existed a school in the strict sense of the word at Antioch. Rather, we can observe a marked tendency in the theological work, a development and strengthening of certain characteristics. In the following short survey we focus on biblical commentaries and leave out the problems related to the Trinitarian and Christological debate.[1]

Theophilus, bishop of Antioch 169–188, is the first tangible upholder of Antiochene theological principles – apart from, of course, Ignace of Antioch, who does not belong to the school. Of his writings only the three books of *Ad Autolycum* remain. They are apologetic and display a peculiar combination of Jewish and Greek influence. Theophilus' exposition of the OT aims at the *sensus litteralis* and has only a few typologies. *Paul of Samosata*, bishop around 260, is an enigmatic person in the history of the Early Church, difficult to evaluate. He seems to have taken up and developed the position of Theophilus, including a stress on Deut 6:4, which gave him the – probably unfair – reputation of denying Christ's divinity. We cannot pass any judgement on Paul's exegesis, since nearly all his writings have been lost.[2]

---

[1] B. DREWERY, "Antiochien II", TRE 3 (1978) 104–106.

[2] R. P. C. HANSON, *The Search for the Christian Doctrine of God. The Arian Controversy 318–381* (Edinburgh 1988) 70–72.

Lucian, presbyter of Antioch, around whom many theories have been created, is another vague figure. A. VON HARNACK made Lucian the real founder of Arianism, which modern scholarship now largely dismisses. As a matter of fact, there were two Lucians at Antioch in the beginning of the fourth century, and it is uncertain whether they are one and the same person. The conclusions of H. C. BRENNECKE are discouraging for any attempt to use Lucian in the history of biblical interpretation: "Historisch lassen sich über Lucian von Antiochien so gut wie keine Aussagen machen".[3] If there exists at all a Lucianic version of the LXX, the evidence for Lucian's part in it is very meagre. So much can be said, that the LXX always had a very strong position at Antioch, where otherwise the Hebrew text could have been expected to prevail or at least be held in great esteem.

Eusebius of Emesa is somewhat older than both Diodore and Theodor of Mopsuestia (he lived 300–359), but does not belong in the proper meaning to the elder Antiochene school. His writings have only recently been published in critical editions, and that is the reason why research into his biblical scholarship has been delayed. Now we have access to a commentary on the books from Genesis to 2 Kings in an Armenian translation.[4] The commentary belongs to the genre *quaestiones et solutiones* and is very occupied with different versions of the biblical text. The repeated quotations in the Antiochene commentaries from 'the Hebrew' and 'the Syrian' have one of their principal sources in Eusebius of Emesa.[5] Eusebius was born at Edessa and mastered the Syriac language. In his commentary there is a marked tendency towards the historical sense of the text. There seem to be connexions between Eusebius and the Antiochene school, particularly Diodore, but the whole issue has to be investigated further.

2. Diodore of Tarsus

The sources of our knowledge of Diodore's life are very limited and almost entirely dependent on the Antiochene schism in the fourth century. Emperor Julian (in ep. 55) says that Diodore studied in Athens and already then attacked paganism. He was later to become the chief obstacle in Antioch of Julian's attempt to restore paganism. We know that he was raised to the see of Tarsus in 378 and that he must have died before 394, when a new bishop

[3] H.-C. BRENNECKE, "Lukian von Antiochien", TRE 21 (1991) 474. Regarding Lucian's supposed importance in the Antiochene School, Brennecke says: "Es gibt in den Quellen keinen Anhaltspunkt für diese Hypothese", 475. For a consistent summary of the Lucianic problem, see Hanson, The Search (1988) 79–83, esp. 83: "No less futile is the suggestion made by some scholars that Lucian represents one link in the chain of teachers of the Antiochene School".

[4] Eusèbe d'Emèse, *Commentaire de l'Octateuque* (prep. par V. Hovhanessian; Paris 1980). The Greek fragments are edited by R. Devreesse in *Les anciens commentateurs grecs* (1959). Generally on Eusebius, see H. LEHMANN, *Per piscatores. Studies in the Armenian Version of a Collection of Homilies by Eusebius of Emesa and Severian of Gabala* (Århus 1975); idem, "Den jødiske hellige skrift og jødiske traditioner hos en kristen syrisk forfatter i 4. årh.", *Judendom och kristendom under de första århundradena* II (ed. S. Hidal et al.; Oslo 1986) 220–228.

[5] Lehmann, Den jødiske hellige skrift (1986) 221.

held the office.[6] Almost nothing is known of him before he was consecrated bishop. During his lifetime he was regarded a pillar of orthodoxy of the Nicene type; this reputation, however, rapidly diminished and he was seen as a forerunner of Nestorius together with his disciple Theodore of Mopsuestia. The fact of his orthodoxy may be seen in his participation as one of the leading bishops at the council of Constantinople in 381, and also in Basil the Great's endorsement of his theology (the epp. 135 and 150 are directed to Diodore, and he is mentioned in 244). His writings were anathematized at a synod in Constantinople in 499; therefore, today only small remains have survived. Diodore was a famous interpreter of the Bible and is justly regarded as founder of Antiochene exegesis in its classical form.

The paucity of the remaining works make the assessment of Diodore as exegete very difficult. This is a quality he shares with his pupil Theodore of Mopsuestia, while the literary heritage from Theodoret of Cyrrhus and – above all – from John Chrysostom is enormous. The article in the Suidas gives the impression of Diodore's wide-ranging activity and manifold interests. He seems to have devoted considerable energy to refuting the various forms of astrological fatalism en vogue in Late Antiquity. As for his exegetical writings, no complete work of undoubted authenticity has come down to us. MARIÈS has adduced good although perhaps not entirely convincing arguments for accepting a commentary on the Psalms in the important ms Coisl. 275 as a genuine work of Diodore. The commentary on the first fifty Psalms is edited by J.-M. OLIVIER.[7] Although the problem with the attribution still has not been satisfactorily solved, the commentary clearly exhibits all the main features of Antiochene exegesis and thus confidently can be taken to illustrate Diodore's biblical scholarship.

Apart from the commentary there exist some small fragments, among which the prologue to Ps 118 is of particular interest. These fragments contain comments on the Pentateuch and are abstracted from the Octateuch chain.[8] The authenticity of these fragments cannot seriously be questioned. They exhibit all the typical features of Theodore's commentaries. After all it must be said, that the textual basis for an evaluation of Diodore's exegesis is very small, indeed. This is to be deplored, since Diodore was the very founder of the Antiochene school. Enough material remains, however, to enable us to make a fairly good picture of Diodore's attitude to the Bible. Antiochene exegesis was first of all marked by a strong tendency to uphold the *sensus litteralis* of the text. This has repeatedly been stressed in the handbooks and

---

[6] For a putting together of the meagre biographical details, see C. Schäublin, Diodor von Tarsus (1981) 763, and R. GREER, "Diodore of Tarsus", Encyclopedia of Early Christianity (1990).

[7] C. Schäublin (1981) 764, doubts the Diodoran authorship, but it is accepted by others. See M.-J. RONDEAU, "Le commentaire des Psaumes de Diodore de Tarse", *RHR* 176 (1969) 5–33, 153–185; 177 (1970) 5–33.

[8] According to Schäublin, Untersuchungen (1974) 43, the Octateuch commentary is not typical for Antiochene exegesis. He does not substantiate this claim, and if Diodore's commentary belongs to the genre of *quaestiones et solutiones* – as Schäublin here (49) thinks – it is very similar in form as well as in content to Theodoret's work on the historical books of the OT.

deserves to be iterated. Often quoted is the Antiochene principle in fragm. 93: "we much prefer the historical sense to the allegory". Suidas mentions a now lost work by Diodore dealing with the difference between the *theōria* and the allegory. In his prologue to Ps 118 (119) he carefully distinguishes between *historia*, *theōria* and *allēgoria*. These terms stand in the focus of not only Antiochene but also Alexandrian exegesis in the fourth century and need to be elucidated.[9] *Historia* is, of course, the historical sense of the biblical text. The expositor's duty is first of all to uncover the historical sense. This means to place the text firmly in the historical context and to point out its goal or *skopos*. It was important for the Antiochenes to decide which period of Israel's history is intended in a certain Psalm. This has nothing to do with historian – antiquarian curiosity; rather, it is an expression of a fundamental will to "incarnate" the text in creation and history.

An important instrument in these efforts was the *hypothesis*. The term was borrowed from the pagan exegesis, as has been thoroughly discussed by C. Schäublin.[10] In the *hypothesis* the *skopos* of the text was set forth and the historical situation discussed.[11] This could sometimes lead to a censure on the inscriptions of the LXX Psalter. These are considerably expanded in comparison with the MT and may indeed be seen as a sort of preliminary *hypothesis*.[12] Theodore of Mopsuestia became known for more or less completely ignoring the inscriptions in the Psalter. This is not the case with Diodore. He, nevertheless, sometimes criticizes obscure expressions in the inscriptions, e.g. Ps 8 (ὑπὲϱ τῶν ληνῶν), 33 (34) (rather Hezekiah than David) and 50 (51) (too narrow). In the epilogue to Ps 29 (30) Diodore even says that many of the inscriptions of the Psalms are "ridiculous".

In his prologue of the commentary on the Psalms Diodore (or perhaps another expositor in the Antiochene tradition) enumerates several genres or – with a modern exegetical term – Gattungen. A Psalm might be *ethikos, dogmatikos*, even *katholikos* (so Ps 1). The historical situation might be David's reign (as is clearly indicated in many cases), Hezekiah's reign, the exile or the period of the Maccabees. Diodore in his commentary has an obvious tendency to assigne a rather large number of Psalms to Hezekiah's reign. Pss 13 (14), 14 (15), 19 (20), 20 (21), 26–29 (27–30), 31–33 (32–34), 40 (41) and 47 (48) are said to reflect conditions during his reign. All these Psalms, however, with the exception of 47 (48) are said to derive from David. How is this to be explained? Another borrowing from the pagan exegetical terminology shows a way out of the dilemma.[13] David speaks ἐκ πϱοσώπου Hezekiah's,

---

[9] As for the Alexandrian exegesis, see i.a. A. Kerrigan, *St Cyril of Alexandria. Interpreter of the Old Testament* (Rome 1952).

[10] Schäublin, Untersuchungen (1974) 92–94.

[11] Sometimes a Psalm is divided as to the *hypothesis*, e.g., Ps 9 with a dividing line after v. 21. The first part is a psalm of thanksgiving, the second part an accusation of the rich people. Diodore was well aware of the difference between Hebrew and Greek traditions in the numbering of the Psalms.

[12] S. Hidal, "Den antiokenska exegetikskolan och judisk skriftlärdom", *Judendom och kristendom under de första århundradena* II (ed. S. Hidal et al.; Oslo 1986) 190–200.

[13] For the background of the expression ἐκ πϱοσώπου see Schäublin, Untersuchungen (1974) 85, n. 7: "Dies ist ein gängiger Terminus der Scholiensprache, mit dem zumal ausgedrückt wird,

he visionarily places himself in the historical context of which he intends to write and, as it were, anticipates a part of Israel's history. Thus both the Psalm's title and its *skopos*, as detected by the *hypothesis*, can be defended at the same time.

Diodore seems to have had a certain predilection for Hezekiah, no doubt related to the vivid description of this king's reign in 2 Kings 18–20 with a parallel in Isaiah 36–39. Especially Hezekiah's lamentation in Isa 38:10–20 with its many and obvious similarities to the psalmodic language might have served as a point of departure. The following Psalms belong to the Babylonian exile: 5, 30 (31), 41 (42), 42 (43) and 50 (51). Ps 30 constitutes a special problem because it breaks off the series of Hezekian Psalms. Diodore is concerned with the arrangement of the Psalms and deplores the lack of *akolouthia* and *taxis* in the book.[14] The other Antiochenes as well are concerned with the right order of the Psalms and are anxious to establish the correct *akolouthia*. Theodoret of Cyrrhus assumes that the absence of an inscription in the Psalter suggests that the psalm in question is closely related to the preceding one.[15]

We now move on from *historia* to *theōria*. It should first be noted, that the Antiochene terminology regarding the historical sense is rather complex. Other expressions are *kata lexin, kata tēn alēthē ennoian* and *kata to rhēton*.[16] When we advance beyond this *sensus*, the terminology is still rather varied, but centers in the word *theōria*. This is the typical Antiochene way of expressing the "higher" sense of the Bible. As is known, the Alexandrian tradition made no distinction between *theōria, allēgoria* and *anagōgē* and this usage extends into the Cappadocian Fathers.[17] For the Antiochenes *allēgoria* and *theōria* were two very different things. Diodore dwells upon this theme in the prologue to the Psalms. He says that the primary aim of the commentary is to explain the text "according to the history and the letter". He then goes on to say: "we shall not prevent the *anagōgē* and the higher *theōria*".[18] The *theōria*, however, must not be an overthrow of the obvious sense of the text, in which case it turns into an allegory. To say *something else* than is intended in the text (or its *theōria*), that is an allegory. The apostle has not used allegories – although he employs the verb in an imprecise meaning in Gal 4:24 – but only the *theōria*. The innovators and those who believe themselves to be wise have introduced allegories, "but not according to the apostolic mind".[19] Such allegories Diodore altogether dismisses, but he is not

daß gewisse Worte nicht aus der Absicht des Dichters, sondern aus den Umständen der sprechenden Person (oder umgekehrt) zu verstehen seien".

14 See Schäublin, Untersuchungen (1974) 71, 143, and for the exegetical term *akolouthia*, see J. Daniélou, "*Akolouthia* chez Grégoire de Nysse", *RevScRel* 27 (1953) 219–249.

15 Thus Ps 42 (43) is interpreted as having the same *hypothesis* as Ps 41 (42), i.e. the exile in Babylonia; PG 80, 1176 A.

16 Diod. *Prol. in Is 36*, Theod. Mops. *Comm.* in Ps 15:10, Theodoret of Cyrrhus in Isa 40:4; PG 81, 404 B.

17 J. Pépin, Hermeneutik (1987) 763. Eusebius of Caesarea can speak of *allegorikē theōria*.

18 Diod. *Prol. in Ps.*, 125 f.

19 Diod. *Prol. in Ps.*, 141.

opposed to the higher *anagōgē* (ἀναγωγὴν ὑψηλοτέραν), seeing, e.g., the Jewish synagogue and the Church in Abel and Cain.

In this connexion it is important to note, that according to the Antiochenes the *theōria* under no circumstances can make away with the historical sense of the text. It takes its starting point in the *sensus litteralis* and never leaves it.[20] The historical sense of the text is transcended by the higher sense, the *theōria*, but it is not abolished. The *theōria* makes it possible to see *typoi* in the OT and to proclaim Christ as prefigurated in the ancient dispensation. In this exegetical device the Antiochenes had one of the things binding the two testaments together. They showed a tendency to regard the OT as a closed salvation economy, a tendency strengthened by their rhetorical skill. As Christians, nevertheless, they were obliged to see the New Testament in the Old and this 'Antiochene dilemma' could be solved by means of the *theōria*.[21] This means is but sparingly used. In Diodore's view only the following Psalms are Messianic: 2, 8, 44 (45) and 109 (110). It is to be noted that we, so far, possess commentaries only on 1–50 and 109 (110). Ps 21 (22), interestingly enough, takes up an intermediate position. In its totality this Psalm cannot be accomodated to Christ, who was not far from salvation and had not committed any crime (as the LXX seems to indicate in v. 2 b). Diodore admits that v. 17 c fits well into the evangelic story of the Passion, but v. 18 a does not when compared with Ps 33:21. The entire Psalm is thus distributed between David and Christ, but its primary *skopos* is David. Because of the similarities between the sufferings of David (especially when he was persecuted by Absalom) and those of Christ, it is possible to regard the Psalm as Messianic to a certain degree.

Ps 44 (45), on the other hand, is said to be about Christ and not, as the Jews will have it, about Solomon. A close reading of the Psalm makes this evident, for Solomon was certainly not called "god" and did not reign in eternity (v. 7 a). This Psalm ends with mentioning the Lord's funeral; and the second part is interpreted ecclesiologically. It would seem that Diodore got himself into a rather awkward position, when a Psalm is quoted with a Messianic interpretation in the NT and the Antiochene interpreter did not see any such features in it. Ps 21 (22) is a good example of this, and so is Ps 15 (16), partially quoted by Peter in Acts 2:25–28, where the apostle explicitly says that David uttered these words "with regard to Christ". Diodore's comment is that nothing prevents us from both rescuing (σώζεσθαι) the historical sense of these words and at the same time referring them to the Lord, for their strongest fulfilment (ἡ ἔκβασις κυριωτέρα) lies in the New Testament's dispensation.[22]

---

[20] G. Bardy, Interpretation (1949) 580: "La *theōria* ou considération se superimpose à l'histoire; elle ne la détruit pas: c'est ainsi qu'un sens historique d'un psaume peut s'appliquer à l'époque de l'exil ou à celle des Machabées, tandis que, du point de vue de la considération, il se rapporte aux temps du Messie". Cf. idem, Diodore (1955) 991 f.

[21] For the Antiochene dilemma, see Schäublin, Untersuchungen (1974) 170.

[22] Diod. *in Ps 15*, CCG 84.

It has already been noted that Diodore places quite a number of Psalms in connection with king Hezekiah. Ps 26–33 (27–34) are regarded as being composed by David ἐκ προσώπου Hezekiah's, with the exception of Ps 30 (31). Otherwise Diodore is clearly bound by the *akolouthia* in this series of Psalms and he uses a number of exegetical devices in order to vindicate the place of Ps 28 (29) in this connection. For the modern exegete this Psalm is a good example of ancient cultic poetry, strongly influenced by a Canaanite prototype. Diodore and his contemporaries had no recourse to explanations of that kind.[23] The OT according to its own words is definitely opposed to Canaanite religion, and the context in the Psalter made it plausible that it was about the political crisis in the reign of Hezekiah. For Diodore then, the Psalm is a thanksgiving, in which the king exhorts his subjects to sacrifice to Him, who has protected the city and its temple. "Sons of God" are those called who have been protected. The various poetical features in the Psalm are all expounded as being poetical expressions for the Assyrians having besieged the holy city: the waters (3), the cedars (5 a), the hinds (9). Kades in 9 is said to mean "holy" in the Syriac language and so refers to the temple. The whole exposition is a bold piece of work and shows the ingenuity of an Antiochene exegete when compelled by his own principles. The commentary also displays a certain degree of insensitivity towards the poetic language. Theodoret of Cyrrhus in a similar way connects the Psalm with Hezekiah, but immediately adds that it also has a bearing on Christ, since the OT is a type for the NT. In the commentary this aspect is dominant, and Theodoret says that the "sons of God" are the apostles, and so on.[24]

It is to be noted, that Diodore does not comment upon the interesting rubric of the psalm in the LXX, which Theodoret does. Wo have no commentary of Theodore of Mopsuestia on this Psalm.

It is deeply to be regretted, that we cannot form an overall picture of Diodore's biblical scholership. However, enough material remains to give the impression of a thorough acquaintance with the Scriptures, a resolute intention to set forth the *historia* or literal sense of the text without giving up what was regarded as central in all ancient exegesis: to expound the usefulness of the Bible in the Christian life.

3. Theodore of Mopsuestia

Theodore of Mopsuestia is commonly regarded as the foremost representative of the younger Antiochene school. He was not the founder, but it was he who developed and refined the exegetical tools inherited from his teacher, Diodore. The Nestorians venerate him as "the blessed interpreter", second to none.

---

[23] The *veto* on all form of Canaanite religion in the OT excluded this effectively.

[24] PG 80, 1061–1064.

Theodore was born at Antioch[25], where he studied under Libanius. For a while he considered a secular career; two letters from his good friend John Chrysostom may belong to this period (*ad Theodorum lapsum;* it is, however, not certain that these two texts were addressed to Theodore of Mopsuestia). But he returned to monastic life, was ordained priest about 383 and consecrated bishop of Mopsuestia in Cilicia in 392. He died in 428, highly venerated by his orthodox contemporaries. Theodore shared the same fate as Diodore. He came under suspicion of Nestorianism and his writings were suppressed. Migne offers only a small collection of fragments, apart from the extensive commentary on the Minor Prophets, but some works have been preserved in Syriac and Latin translations. The commentary on Genesis has been partially restored and we now possess Theodore's explanation of Genesis 1–3. The commentary on the Psalms evidently was Theodore's first work and large parts of it have been rediscovered. The acts of the Fifth Council mention other works, now lost. However, since we know that Julian of Eclanum was a pupil of Theodore's during his exile in the East, there is the possibility of tracing Theodorian influence in his exegetic writings.[26] Theodore's commentary on the Minor Prophets must, after all, remain our primary source of knowledge, since we possess it in the original Greek.

Theodore was a pupil of Diodore's, and all the important features of Diodore's art of biblical exposition are to be found in Theodore as well. Each prophetical book is introduced by a *hypothesis*, which endeavours to fix the *kairos*, the *topos* and the *ēthos* of the prophet's message. Of these *hypotheseis* only that of Jonah differs from the rest in a significant way. This very long prologue displays a consequent christological perspective.[27] No doubt Matt 12:40f. has been the decisive factor in regarding Jonah's life as a type for Christ's death and resurrection. This fact established, the commentary does not mention it again but moves on in the ordinary Antiochene way.[28]

Theodore's commentary on the Minor Prophets is a good example of how a biblical text can be elucidated. The author is at pains to explain the text, and even the obscure passages in the LXX are not seldom rendered intelligible. An example from his commentary on Hos 13:15:

> Having said this he (the prophet) goes on to show the violence and the cruelty used towards them by the Assyrians. "The Lord will bring a burning wind from the desert on them and he will dry up his veins and make his fonts desolate and all his coveted vessels". He will bring the enemy against him; he thinks of the Babylonian king, who coming from a far distant region like a burning wind suddenly will come over him and totally destroy Israel. The enemy will turn Israel's prosperity and affluence of good things into a desert, and everything considered to be of value he will destroy. For the words "Where is your victory, o death, where is your

---

[25] On Theodore's life, see J. Quasten, Patrology III, 401, and M. Simonetti, "Theodore of Mopsuestia", EEC 824. See also Ritter, Die antiochenische und alexandrinische Christologie (1982) 236–245, esp. 237f.

[26] On Julian of Eclanum, see p. 567.

[27] PG 66, 317C–327D. Schäublin, Untersuchungen (1974) 168, n. 47: "Der Prolog zum Jonaskommentar ist die Hauptstelle für die Beurteilung der Typologie Theodors".

[28] It should be noted that nearly all typological interpretations in Theodore also are found in the NT. The exceptions are Ps 88 (89):37f. and Ps 88 (89):30 – in this order mentioned in PG 66, 557A.

sting, o Hades" are followed by the words "Therefore he will divide between the brothers" and the rest, and in the middle the following words stand: "Consolation is put out of your sight". With these words the prophet hints at that which will happen but so far is obscure to them. After having mentioned their conversion to a better state of things, he again talks of the punishment which will come over them.[29]

A large part of Theodore's commentary is taken up by more or less paraphrasing the text. The interpreter is always observant on the *akolouthia* of the text but has unfortunately no means of rearranging it. Theodore is well versed in Israel's history as is evident in the prologues to the Minor Prophets. If the reign of Hezekiah was the favourite period for Diodore, the short and enigmatic period of Zerubbabel holds a spell on Theodore. In at least two of the traditional Messianic passages, i.e. Mic 5:1 and Zech 9:9–10 Theodore introduces Zerubbabel. The passage in Micah aims primarily at Zerubbabel, but "the truth in what is said" is related to Christ.[30] This aspect of the text is not independent of the primary, historical sense, since Christ was of David's lineage and the line of succession within David's house was very important, Ps 88:31 f. Also in the case of Zechariah 9, one can observe how Theodore by no means is opposed to a Messianic interpretation, provided that the *sensus historicus* first is duly recognized. Some interpreters, he says, will have the first part of the passage apply to Zerubbabel and the second part to Christ, but this is utmost folly, *anoia*. The Scripture, however, often speaks hyperbolically of such things as will be fulfilled in Christ, who is the truth in his person.[31] Also the following part of the commentary is relevant for this issue.

On the other hand, Zech 12:10 receives no Messianic interpretation. Indeed, "the spirit of grace and compassion" is said to refer to the Maccabean period. The last chapters of Zechariah are in a number of places expounded as referring to the Maccabees, an interesting anticipation of a tendency in modern scholarship.[32] Sometimes Theodore is directly opposed to a Messianic interpretation but a few lines later such a statement usually is weakened.

Joel 3:1 f. (LXX) cannot possibly refer to what is described in Acts 2, for the Holy Spirit as the Third Person in the Holy Trinity was not known in the old dispensation, where "spirit" stands for "protection", not a person.[33] But since Theodore cannot deny the obvious fact that St. Peter quoted the passage in question in his sermon on the Pentecost day, a lenghty discussion on the theme prophecy – fulfilment is introduced, in which Theodore admits that "the truth of the incident" is in Christ.[34] Likewise Mal 3:3 f. does not apply to Christ who cleansed not only the sons of Levi but all men – 1 Cor 5:7 is quoted – and the sacrifices in Jerusalem were actually abolished. On the

---

[29] PG 66, 205 D–207 A.

[30] PG 66, 371 C.

[31] PG 66, 555 C–557 B. Also the following part of the commentary, 557 D–560 D is highly relevant for this issue.

[32] See R. Albertz, *Religionsgeschichte Israels in alttestamentlicher Zeit* (Göttingen 1992) 637–643, who himself does not favour a dating in the Maccabean period.

[33] PG 66, 229.

[34] PG 66, 232 B.

other hand, it is quite possible to see an allusion to the Maccabean restoration of the temple cult in Jerusalem in Malachi's words.[35] The Antiochene knowledge of Israel's history as well as their predilection for it sometimes lead them astray, but as a whole they had a far better apprehension of the Bible as being a time related document than most of their predecessors and contemporaries. Theodore is particularly eager to show that the numbers in the biblical text have no symbolical meaning whatsoever. They are only used to indicate the quantity, nothing else. Commenting upon Mic 5:5 Theodore mentions that some have seen a deeper significance of the numbers seven and eight, but it is a scriptural *idiōma* to express fulness with "seven".[36]

Like all the Antiochenes Theodore had no knowledge of Hebrew. This of course was a serious obstacle in his efforts to investigate the historical sense of the text, but the interpreter does not seem to be aware of this fact. On the contrary, he is filled with a glowing passion for the LXX, which indefatigably is defended against other translations, the Hebrew text being regarded almost as another 'translation'. Commenting upon Zeph 1:5 Theodore makes a lenghty digression on Bible translation, the content of which is that the LXX widely surpasses all other versions of the OT.[37] It is foolish to believe that such excellent translators as the men behind the LXX could have erred. The Hebrew text was translated into the Syriac language but this translation is not to be preferred against the LXX. Once the Syriac translations (in the plural) are even called *mythologoi* and a mistranslation in the LXX vehemently upheld.[38] It is uncertain whether the Syriac translation means an Aramaic targum or the Old Syriac translation.[39] This stubborn holding to a Greek translation does not prevent Theodore from mentioning certain Hebrew *idiōmata* in his commentaries. This applies first of all to the tenses in the text; due to a more or less dogmatic view of the Hebrew perfect as expressing past time the prophetic character of the text has not seldom been obscured. The past tense ἐζήλωσεν in Joel 2:18 (the context clearly indicating the future) is due to a Hebrew *idiōma*.[40] This *idiōma* is sometimes called the ἐναλλαγὴ χρόνων, *mutatio temporum*.[41] According to Theodore, the imperative in the Scriptures often denotes the future.[42]

Observations like these ought to be seen against the background of the lack of knowledge of Hebrew. As far as can be established from the preserved writings, the Antiochenes have virtually no knowledge of Hebrew and therefore no real instrument for evaluating a Hebrew *idiōma*. On this issue there

---

[35] PG 66, 631 C–623 B. John the Baptist is clearly intended (in Mal 3:1) 619 C.

[36] PG 66, 377 C; cf. *Comm.* in Am 1:3; PG 66, 249 A.

[37] PG 66, 452 C–453 C.

[38] *Comm.* in Zeph 3:1; PG 66, 467 A.

[39] In fact, the Antiochenes quotations from the 'Syriac' translation often seem to derive from Eusebius of Emesa, see p. 545.

[40] PG 66, 225 C. This is even the case in other passages in the prophets and the Psalms. Also the other Antiochenes make observations of this kind, e. g. when Diodore wishes to read the future instead of the aorist in Ps 21 (22):30.

[41] So Comm. in Ps 15:6 (CCL 88 A), translated by Julian of Eclanum.

[42] So Zech 11:4; PG 66, 569 D, 587 A.

is complete scholarly agreement.[43] As a matter of fact, the Antiochenes often quote Hebrew words in a transliterated form, but this in no way proves a working knowledge of Hebrew. Such words are often found in John Chrysostom's commentary on the Psalms.[44] Occasionally Diodore and Theodore do the same thing. A recurring theme in the commentaries on Genesis is the observation that the Hebrew (or Syriac) word for 'forgiveness' is the same as the unusual word denoting the thicket in the Hebrew text of Gen 22:13.[45] Theodore's very high regard for the LXX makes it less imperative to have access to the Hebrew text. It will be noted, that the Greeks in contrast to the Romans had no long tradition of translations into their own language. Many of the difficulties connected with translation were hardly discussed in the Greek tradition.[46] Nevertheless, Theodore's way of recognizing *idiomata* merits our attention and places him in the context of pagan Greek exegesis. One example: in his commentary on Ps 32(33):7b Theodore says that it is a Hebrew *idiōma* to omit the particle ὡς in a comparison. In the scholion on Pindar's Olympic Ode 10,13a the same feature is said to be a Pindaric *idiōma*. "Was bei Pindar als Eigentümlichkeit des Stils gewertet wird, hat also in der Septuaginta als Hebraismus zu gelten".[47] In ancient Greek philology two kinds of *idiōmata* were recognized: those belonging to the style of the author and those depending on his dialect. Theodore, on the other hand, does not see the intention of the author (in the last instance for him the Holy Spirit) in the LXX, but thinks that the peculiarities of the Hebrew language survive in the translation.[48] The most frequent *idiōma* is according to him the *mutatio temporum*, which means the inconsistent and sometimes perplexing use of tenses in the Hebrew text with its results in the LXX. Observations like these were common in the Hellenistic exegesis on Homer, where deviations from the customary syntax were duly annotated, e.g. in Aristarchos.[49]

Another stylistic feature in the biblical text deserves mentioning: the assumption that the Scripture not seldom deliberately uses the exaggeration as a stylistic device. The Greek word for this is *hyperbolē*. In his commentary on Joel 2:10 Theodore says, that the prophet speaks "exaggeratedly *(hyperbolikōs)* ... so that the listeners will be more astonished".[50] Sometimes this observation is connected with a typological discussion. Theodore notes in connection with Zech 9:9–10 that the Scripture often speaks *hyperbolikōs* of things having their *alētheia*, 'truth', in Christ.[51] The interpreter often uses the

[43] Schäublin, Untersuchungen (1974) 29, 124, 127.

[44] See p. 562.

[45] See S. Hidal, *Interpretatio Syriaca. Die Kommentare des heiligen Ephräm des Syrers zu Genesis und Exodus mit besonderer Berücksichtigung ihrer auslegungsgeschichtlichen Stellung* (ConBOT 6; Lund 1974) 47–49 (with other references).

[46] W. Hommel, "Übersetzungen", LAW, 3155 f.

[47] Schäublin, Untersuchungen (1974) 128.

[48] Schäublin, Untersuchungen (1974) 130.

[49] "So konnte er feststellen, es seien Personen, Numeri, Tempora, Modi, Genera der Verben vertauscht oder sämtliche Casus miteinander ausgewechselt", Schäublin, Untersuchungen (1974) 131.

[50] See R. Devreesse, Essai (1949) 60.

[51] PG 66, 575 B.

verb *ainittesthai* when he encounters a daring, sometimes unintelligible expression. Due to a certain lack of sensitivity towards the nature of poetic language, this occasionally leads them astray.[52] When Theodore comments on the grasshoppers in Joel 1:4–5 he thinks that the prophet *tropikōs* alludes to Assyrian and Babylonian kings.[53] This exegesis is part of the Antiochene programme: "tropische Redeweise in den Schriften aufzuspüren und in eigentliche umzusetzen".[54] The hyperbolic language of Scripture thus opens a small gate leading to a Messianic understanding. The *sensus litteralis* is regarded as too strange; hence the truth of the text must be searched elsewhere. On a deeper level, we have the two main presuppositions of all ancient Christian exposition of the Bible: the content of the Scripture must conform to the norms inherent in the words *ōpheleia* and *to prepon*, usefulness and decency. Theodore as well as other Antiochene exegetes are all in line with the Early Church when they vigorously defend the biblical heroes against all accusations of immorality. The apologetic tendency is in no way abolished by their more or less 'scientific' approach to the text. Theodore defends Hosea's marriages as being justified as an expression of God's *paidagōgia*.[55] Diodore excuses Noah for his behaviour in Gen 9:20–27, and Theodoret states that Moses was a *typus ecclesiae* when he married a foreign woman.[56] In the Philonian and Origenistic exegesis passages like these often were allegorized, but the allegory was not a way out of difficulties for the Antiochenes. The allegory was no real *lysis* or solution of an exegetical problem. Indeed, the Antiochene aversion to allegories has been explained as partially proceeding from their background in the commentary genre *problēmata kai lyseis*.[57]

At the same time it is obvious, that the Antiochenes have had the same problem as their predecessors with seemingly absurd passages in the Bible. The difference was that they resisted to the very last all solutions detached from history. Another urgent problem was the extent of the biblical canon. This problem in relation to the Antiochenes has been investigated by L. Dennefeld.[58] The result is, that the Antiochene canon included the deuterocanonical books. Theodore, however, rejected 1–2 Maccabees, Tobit, Judith and Wisdom. What is more conspicuous, he also had severe doubts regarding some of the books in the commonly recognized canon. He declared that the Song of Songs deals with Solomon's marriage to a Egyptian princess. In a letter preserved in Latin translation Theodore says that this book was read neither among the Jews nor among the Christians and that it does not fit into the Holy Scripture. "If the book had earned the prophetic grace, it would

---

[52] Cf. p. 550.

[53] PG 66, 213 B. Likewise in Am 7:1–3; PG 66, 287 A. Cf. the interpretation of Ps 28 (29) by Diodore, see p. 550.

[54] Schäublin, Untersuchungen (1974) 111.

[55] PG 66, 129 A – God provided the prophet with an opportunity to tell the people what they needed to hear.

[56] PG 66, 228 C.

[57] Schäublin, Untersuchungen (1974) 59. See also Lera, Théodore de Mopsueste (1991) 385–400, esp. 389–393.

[58] Dennefeld, Der alttestamentliche Kanon (1909). See also Ziegenaus, Kanon (1990) 109–121.

have mentioned God somewhere ... it is an emulation of a wedding poem, like Plato afterwards wrote the Symposion about love".[59] Theodoret of Cyrrhus took an altogether other view of the book, and in his prologue to the Song of Songs he actually criticizes Theodore without mentioning his name.[60]

Theodore takes up a still more emphatic view on the book of Job.[61] In this case no compromise was possible: *per omnia reprobans scripturam Iob*, "in everything he rejected the book of Job".[62] Theodore seems to have regarded the book as utterly unsuitable in the Christian Bible. The authenticity of this statement has been questioned, since, after all, Theodore did write a commentary on the book, but it is nevertheless evident that Theodore did not regard the book as fitting in the canon.[63] Already the fact that Job curses the day of his birth is inproper in a saint's mouth. The book is also replete with unfitting mythological allusions, hardly to be expected in a book ascribed to "a barbarian from Edom". According to Theodore, the author of the book is entirely dependent on Greek tragedies as pattern. The attitude towards Job amply illustrates the difference between the Alexandrian and Antiochene schools. In the Origenistic monasticism, which developed out of the Alexandrian tradition, the book of Job was held in high esteem. Job became a monastic paradigm. He suffered and was severely tempted, but out of his tribulations he emerged a victor. The Antiochenes, however, did not find much of interest in the book – although they occasionally commented upon it.[64]

In spite of great scholarly effort in this century, Theodore still remains a rather enigmatic figure in the interpretation history of the OT. Like his teacher Diodore, he was seen in his lifetime as a warrant of Nicene orthodoxy and his dogmatic writings confirm this picture. The impact of Hellenistic hermeneutics is heavy on Theodore, perhaps due to the fact that a larger bulk of his works is preserved than in the case of Diodore. It is true that predictive prophecy is severely reduced, but Theodore's use of *theōria* is, as far as can be judged, rather expanded when compared with his predecessor.

Theodore's overall view of the OT is impressive. He regards the OT as a unified evidence of God's planning and linking of Israel's history. The principle *Scriptura sui ipsius interpres*, Scripture is its own interpreter, is firmly adhered to, and the historical sense is never disregarded but at times complemented by a spiritual one. The use of allegories is rejected, but a limited use of typologies is granted, the typology being explained on the basis of *theōria*. Theodore is at his best when he expounds a historical text from the prophets, where his commentary – largely paraphrasing – helps to elucidate a number of problems. He is less fortunate in the poetical parts of the OT.

---

59 PG 66,700. See Dennefeld, Der alttestamentliche Kanon (1909) 47.

60 Dennefeld, Der alttestamentliche Kanon (1909) 67 f.

61 See Ziegenaus, Kanon (1990) 112. Theodore's own brother Polychronius of Apamea (see p. 566 f.) defended the book of Job against his brother, Ziegenaus, ibid. 113 f.

62 PG 66, 697 C.

63 Devreesse, Essai (1949) 33 f.

64 For the following, see Dassmann, Hiob (1989) 419 f.

Are there any grounds for assuming a Jewish influence on Theodore and the Antiochene school as a whole? The question has often been raised and not infrequently answered in an affirmative way. A certain amount of Jewish influence on the elder Antiochene school can hardly be denied, but when we come to the classical period with Diodore and Theodore, there is good reason for not postulating such an influence. Already in their own days, it is true to say, they were charged of being Judaizers, but these accusations were never substantiated and were, in fact, an example of 'stock charges' in the Early Church.[65] Already the fact that the Antiochenes were ignorant of Hebrew makes it less than probable that they would have been influenced by Jewish exegesis. As has been showed primarily by Schäublin, they were instead heavily indebted to contemporary Greek hermeneutics. This applies not least to Theodore, who almost paradigmatically exposes the characteristics of the younger Antiochene school.

4. John Chrysostom

John (ca. 347–407), with the byname Chrysostom, is justly seen as one of the leading exponents of the younger Antiochene school. His life is well known, even in details, and consequently only a brief summary will be given here.[66]

Born at Antioch he studied with Libanius, the outstanding rhetorician of the day. In 381 he was ordained deacon and in 386 priest. The next decade was filled with an immense pastoral activity in his home town. From this period come his sermons on Genesis, and a number of books in the NT. John was primarily devoted to explaining the NT and above all he admired St Paul. At Antioch he also gave his sermons *Adversus Iudaeos*, which amply illustrate the fascination still emerging from the synagogue by the Christians. Raised to the see of Constantinople in 398 John soon found himself facing great problems. This is not the place for describing his troubles with the empress Eudoxia and bishop Theophilos of Alexandria. His preaching continued on a lesser scale. Twice exiled from the imperial capital he died on September 14th 407, in Pontus.

Among the Greek fathers none has left so extensive a literary heritage as has John Chrysostom. He is the only one of the Antiochenes whose writings are almost entirely preserved – the contrast to Diodore and Theodore is striking. The manuscript situation is unusually good; the host of manuscripts outnumbers any other Greek Father. In addition, there are translations of many of his works.

The *Old Testament homilies* fall into four groups:

1) Homilies on Genesis. Two series, both delivered at Antioch, exist. The first one consists of nine homilies on Genesis, all – with the exception of the last one – dealing with the first three chapters. These are dated in 386. The second series is much larger, *Homiliae 67 in Genesin*, and forms a complete commentary on the book. The dating of these homilies is disputed, perhaps 388. Some of the homilies of the two series have identical passages.[67]

---

[65] On stock charges, see G. C. Stead, "Rhetorical method in Athanasius", *VC* 30 (1976) 121–137.

[66] See Leroux, Johannes Chrysostomus (1988) 118–127 [lit.], and A. Wenger, Jean Chrysostome (1972) 332, 355 [lit.].

[67] The first series is found in PG 54, 581–630, the second one in PG 55, 23–580. Several

2) Homilies on the Psalms. Homilies on 58 selected Psalms have been preserved. It is uncertain whether John explained the entire Psalter; indeed, it is not beyond doubt that we possess even the extant homilies in their original form. The exegetical method employed here is partly different from that in the Genesis homilies.[68]

3) Homilies on Isaiah and some other homilies. Six homilies on Isaiah 6 have survived.[69] Some were delivered at Antioch, others in Constantinople. They are important mainly because of some declarations of principle regarding the exegetical method. – To this group we also adduce a number of homilies on Anne and David and Saul.[70] They comment on some chapters in the Books of Kings and were delivered in 387. The two homilies *De prophetiarum obscuritate* were held at Antioch in 386.

A great number of catenae fragments bearing John's name exist on Jeremiah, Daniel, Proverbs and Job. Their authenticity is not sufficiently established.

4) Homilies on Job. Discovered in the 18th century this commentary was not edited until 1975 and published in 1988.[71] The text is called *hypomnēma* in the Greek manuscripts and carries all the characteristics of a commentary of John Chrysostom. Fragments of the commentary are extant in the Syro-hexapla as well as in numerous catenae.

The exegetical work of John Chrysostom is thus, to a great extent, delivered in a homiletical context. However, the distinction between a 'scholarly' commentary and a sermon on a biblical text is not rigidly upheld in the Early Church, and many a sermon was re-edited to form a commentary on the text. The stylistic beauty of John's homilies is commonly regarded as unsurpassed in antiquity. U. von Wilamowitz-Moellendorff declared his style to be "the harmonious expression of an Attic soul".[72] His apostolic zeal and his courageous attitude towards the imperial court deserve attention in all times. Among his writings only the homilies *Adversus Iudaeos* have been severely criticized for having fostered antisemitic feelings.[73]

---

translations are extant, one recently in English by R. Hill (FC 24; 1985). This translation covers the first seventeen homilies in the second series. Homilies 16–45 appear in the same collection. Concerning the relations between the series, see the discussion in Hill's introduction.

[68] PG 55, 35–498.

[69] PG 56, 97–142. These homilies are sometimes called *In Oziam*, and under that title they were the first exegetical work of John Chrysostom to appear in a modern critical edition, *Homélies sur Ozias* (ed. J. Dumortier; SC 277; 1981). See also *Commentaire sur Ozias* (ed. J. Dumortier; SC 394; 1983), which, if authentic, is a "dehomiliticized" (R. Hill) form of the homilies *In Oziam*.

[70] PG 54, 631–708.

[71] H. Sorlin, *Un commentaire grec inédit sur le livre de Job attribué à Saint Jean Chrysostome. Introduction, texte, traduction* (Lyon 1975) and *Jean Chrysostome, Commentaire sur Job I–II* (ed. H. Sorlin, avec la collaboration de L. Neyrand; SC 346, 348; 1988). The text with a translation into German is independently edited by U. and D. Hagedorn, *Johannes Chrysostomus. Kommentar zu Hiob* (1990).

[72] Quoted by J. Quasten, Patrology III (1960) 429. A great amount of philological work has been done on John's language, see i. a. C. Fabricius, *Studien zu den Jugendschriften des Johannes Chrysostomus* (Lund 1962).

[73] On this complicated matter, see R. L. Wilken, *John Chrysostom and the Jews. Rhetoric and Reality in the Late 4th Century* (*The Transformation of the Classical Heritage*, ed. P. Brown, IV;

Diodore of Tarsus was John's teacher, and he delivered a panegyric on his master in 392 in the latter's presence, *Laus Diodori episcopi.* John is influenced by his teacher in many ways, but not in the same degree as Theodore was. He is devoted to the *sensus litteralis* and uses allegories very rarely. Above all, he wished to develop a sort of Biblical Hermeneutics, which has no parallel in the Early Church, except in Augustine's writings. This is not done in any coherent treatises, but throughout the homilies there are scattered notes on the nature of the Holy Scripture. These put together form an impressive sketch on Biblical Hermeneutics.[74] John Chrysostom sees the Bible as God's inspired word, a clear expression of his lovingkindness towards men and an infinitely diversified medium of divine revelation.[75] To a certain degree his doctrine on biblical inspiration can be extracted from a number of technical terms in Greek, the most important of which will be discussed in the following. John's doctrine of the *synkatabasis* deserves attention.[76] In this context the word should not be translated 'condescension' but rather 'considerateness'. As in the historical incarnation the eternal Word became flesh, so in the Bible God's glory veils itself in the fleshly garments of human thought and human language.[77] God accomodates himself to the human weakness or *astheneia.* This fact – observed by many Fathers of the Church before John – in no way diminishes the reliability of the divine Word. On the contrary, John never ceases to praise the *akribeia* of the Scripture, another of his key terms. This 'accuracy' or, perhaps better, 'precision' of the Scripture leads the interpreter into a painstaking work with the *minutiae* of the biblical text.

John Chrysostom is extremely careful when he expounds the biblical text. He never satisfies himself with simply paraphrasing the text – as Theodore of Mopsuestia often does – but always searches for the *skopos.* The message of difficult verses is carefully scrutinized, and the evidence of other translations not infrequently adduced. This is particularly common in his homilies on the

---

Berkeley/Los Angeles/London 1983). It is not possible to enter into a discussion of the genre *Adversus Iudaeos* in the Early Church, but the opinion that it at least in some cases may have been a controversy *within* the Church is not to be lightly dismissed. "John's sermons, usually entitled *Against the Jews,* were preached against these Judaizers, not against the Jews", Wilken, John Chrysostom and the Jews (1983) 67. See also F. A. Grisson, *Chrysostom and the Jews. Studies in the Jewish-Christian Relations in Fourth Century Antioch* (Louisville, KY 1978). The homilies are translated in *Saint John Chrysostom's Discourses against Judaizing Christians* (by P.-W. Harkins, 1979).

[74] The literature is vast; see Leroux, Johannes Chrysostomus (1988) 118–127 [lit.], and R. Hill, *St John Chrysostom's teaching on the inspiration in his Old Testament Homilies* (Sydney 1981).

[75] "... die Schrift als eine Art Kontaktmedium, das dem Menschen erlaubt, mit dem Unaussprechbaren in ein Gespräch zu treten, und beiden wie Freunden eine wechselseitige Teilnahme an ihren jeweiligen Anliegen und gegenseitiges Helfen ermöglicht", Leroux, Johannes Chrysostomus (1988) 121.

[76] See the literature listed s.v. in H.J. Sieben, Voces. Eine Bibliographie (1980). The first technical use of the word appears to have been made by Origen, *Hom. 4 in Lucam,* PG 17, 317 A. In the pagan literature the word is used of "condescension", e.g. to the level of an audience. In the longer series of homilies on Genesis, the idea of *synkatabasis* is quite frequent, cf. i.a. PG 53, 29 A, 34 B, 44 A, 103 A, 108 C, 109 B, 138 A.

[77] F. H. Chase, *Chrysostom. A study of Biblical interpretation* (1887) 42, quoted by R. Hill, St John Chrysostom's Homilies on Genesis 1–17 (1985) 17.

Psalms, where Aquila, Symmachus and Theodotion are quoted (often without being expressly mentioned).

Closely associated with divine *synkatabasis* is scriptural *pachytēs*. This word means 'grossness', 'materiality', but also 'earthliness', 'concreteness'.[78] Due to our *astheneia* God must use 'earthly' words to convey his message. "Our weakness is the reason for the concreteness of the text".[79]

This carefulness is joined with another feature in the Bible, its *akribeia*. Nothing is said by random by Moses, as is often repeated in the homilies on Genesis. Even the smallest detail can be of great significance.[80] As John himself says: "Who could adequately extol the precision of Holy Scripture?"[81] The *akribeia* of Scripture is, however, balanced by another principle: the *oikonomia*. The word had already then a long background in the trinitarian and christological doctrinal debate, but here it has retained more of its original meaning: 'housekeeping', 'economizing', 'thrift'. "Notice here the economy of the blessed author, how he does not describe all created things one by one, but teaches which of them were produced together by mentioning heaven and earth and passing over the rest".[82]

In John Chrysostom's writings we also find the other exegetical tools in the Antiochene armoury, e.g. the principle of *akolouthia* and the recognition of Hebrew *idiōmata*. The transition from the first account of creation to the second in Gen 2:4 is a classical example of the problems supposed to be solved by the principle of the *akolouthia*. John's discussion of the problem in homily 12, 5 is a masterly attempt of solving a source critical problem without having access to modern scholarly instruments.[83] In this connection, however, he does not use the actual word *akolouthia*. Likewise, in a comment on the plural of "heavens" he says that it is idiomatic in Hebrew to use the plural instead of the singular: "If there were several heavens, the Holy Spirit would not have neglected to teach us through the words of the blessed author about the creation of the other ones".[84]

It goes without saying in an Antiochene context that John Chrysostom firmly adheres to the principle of *Scriptura sui ipsius interpres*. There are in his writings an almost incredible host of quotations from and allusions to passages in the Bible, many of them intended to elucidate other passages.[85] Hence his reluctance to employ the method of allegorization. In his fifth homily on Isaiah 5 John says that *allegory is allowed only when the Scripture clearly states that an allegory is intended*. There is no need to explain this

---

78 LPGL s.v., 1054.

79 PG 53, 107A. See J.-M. Leroux, "Relativité et transcendence du texte biblique d'après Jean Chrysostome", *La Bible et les Pères: Colloque Strasbourg 1969* (1971) 72.

80 The word *akribeia* with its equivalents is very frequent in the longer series of homilies on Genesis. Here are a few selected passages: PG 53, 29A, 52C, 85B, 87A.

81 PG 53, 87A.

82 PG 53, 33B, although the actual word is not used here. John uses *oikonomia* in the meaning 'thrift' elsewhere.

83 PG 53, 100A.

84 PG 53, 43B.

85 Only in his homilies 80000 explicit references to the Bible have been found, Leroux (1988) 111f.

otherwise than by his Antiochene background. The fact that pagan myths commonly were allegorized and that John feared a confusion with this custom, is hardly plausible.[86] Typologies, on the other hand, are accepted as a matter of fact. Since the large bulk of John's homilies deal with the NT, there is not much evidence for this in the OT.

The Alexandrian allegorism is dismissed. In connection with Isa 1:22 John says that he does not wish to reject the *anagogē* altogether, but the historical sense is more true.[87] Isa 5:7 makes him declare that the Holy Scripture itself explains an allegory, if such a thing is intended, and in Isa 6:6f he quotes an allegorical interpretation only to continue: "But we stick to the historical sense".[88] Instructive is the note on the Behemoth in Job 40: "We are not ignorant that many take these verses in a figurative way (*kata anagōgēn*) and understand them to be said about the devil. However, we must strive after the historical sense, and then, if the listeners will profit from a figurative interpretation, use also that. For he says: All of these must aim at one thing: to build up the Church".[89]

The relation between the two testaments is often discussed by John. He does not share the tendency observed in Diodore and Theodore to see the OT as a sort of finished collection of books. His thoughts are often developed in opposition to a Jewish understanding of the Scripture, as, e.g., in his homily on Ps 109(110):

> If you tell about what is said of Christ in the OT and show that the truth in the events bear witness of the fulfilment of the prophecy, he (the Jew) will not be able to resist. If you attack that which is ours, o Jew, how can you defend the OT? Suppose someone says to you: How can that which Moses has written be true? What do you answer? "Because we believe in him". Does this not go for us as well? We also believe. You are one people, I admit, but we embrace the whole world. Moses has not convinced you to such a degree as Christ has convinced us ... This is what I wish to prove, that the Jew, having eliminated the prophecies about Christ, uses violence against most prophecies and cannot clearly reproduce the nobleness of the OT unless he recognizes the NT.[90]

In the beginning of his commentary the interpreter discusses the identification of the *dramatis personae* in Ps 109(110). Some, he says, have even wanted to see Zerubbabel here (one of the Antiochenes' favourites!) or the Jewish people (an interesting evidence for a collective understanding of the Psalm).

John does not share "the Antiochene dilemma" to the same extent as do his masters in scriptural interpretation, Diodore and Theodore.[91] He stands

[86] Against Leroux (1988) 122.

[87] PG 56,73.

[88] PG 56,72. Bardenhewer, Geschichte III (1924) 355, says rightly: "Der Typus ist ihm eine vom Heiligen Geist intendierte Prophetie nur dadurch unterscheidet, daß sie nicht in Worte, sondern in Sachen gekleidet ist". This is the usual Antiochene distinction between 'words' and 'events'.

[89] See the note in Hagedorn's edition, p. 277, about the interpretation of these animals in the Early Church. Generally on the book of Job in this period, see Dassmann, Hiob (1989) 366–442; on John Chrysostom, see 415–417.

[90] PG 53, 266D–267A.

[91] About this, see p. 549.

closer to Theodoret of Cyrrhus and so represents a more traditional Christian approach to the problem. It seems as if his intense admiration for St Paul's letters has increased his Messianic understanding of the OT. John's predilection for the typological interpretation of the OT falls in line with this approach. Particularly noteworthy in this respect are his homilies on the Psalms. Whereas his homilies on Genesis are very much coloured by their *Sitz im Leben*, the presence of a listening congregation being felt on almost every line, his homilies on the Psalms belong more to the commentary type. However, the address is evident in some cases, e.g., when he says: "Be silent and listen attentively".[92] They are far more exhaustive than the commentaries by Diodore and Theodore. In all are 58 Psalms commentated: 4–12 (13), 49 (50), 108 (109)–117 (118), 119 (120)–150. They have reached us under the title Explanations, *hermeneiai*, rather than homilies. The Antiochene tradition with a *hypothesis* is upheld, but John does not always place the Psalm in a historical context. He is not so fascinated by Israel's history as his predecessors are; his main interest is a pastoral one. There are some excursions containing attacks on his dogmatic opponents, e.g., the Anhomoeans.

An outstanding feature in this commentary is the recurring quotations of the Hebrew text in transliterations. We have already established that the Antiochenes had no Hebrew, but does this apply to John as well? A few examples may be warranted. In his commentary on Ps 8:7 John quotes the original Hebrew in the following form: οθαρηοῦ μὰτ μὴ ἐλωείμ. The Hebrew text behind shines through, but that is no proof of a *working* knowledge of Hebrew. In fact, John nowhere makes the claim of mastering Hebrew and isolated instances like these might well be based on hearsay or – which may be the most probable – from the second column of the Hexapla.

By far most common is the quotation of a single Hebrew word, like *sason* 'joy' in Ps 44 (45):8, and *ra* 'evil' in Ps 48 (49):6 a. In the textually very problematic Ps 48 (49), several Hebrew words are introduced, but nowhere does the commentator discuss the meaning of these words. They are introduced as an argument in favour of one of the Greek translations but only as one of many 'versions'.

John Chrysostom represents the Antiochene school of exegesis in a clarified and moderate way. This makes him in many respects the most readable of the Antiochene Fathers. He has no wish of seeing Zerubbabel or the Maccabees in so many contexts. Above all, he is interested in keeping the two testaments together as a coherent testimony of God's salvific action with his people. This coherence is achieved not by introducing allegories but by a moderate use of typology and a stressing on God's action in history. There is no question of his immense erudition in the Bible but, first of all, John Chrysostom was a preacher with a glowing apostolic zeal. His first question to text from the OT was not: which is the *sensus litteralis*? but: how can God's people be edified from these words? And he found the usefulness of Holy Scripture primarily in the historical sense of the text.

---

92 *Comm.* in Ps 8, PG 55, 106 C.

5. Theodoret of Cyrrhus

The last of the famous theologians of the Antiochene school was born at Antioch about 393. Not older than thirty years Theodoret was elected bishop of Cyrrhus, a small neighbouring town, where he exercised his office until his death in 466. He was deeply involved in the christological debates of the fifth century and was suspected of Nestorianism. At the *Latrocinium* synod of Ephesus in 499 Theodoret was deposed by Dioscurus, the successor of Cyril of Alexandria, and forced into exile. At the council of Chalcedon in 451 he was reinstated after having pronounced – reluctantly – an anathema to Nestorius and was recognized as an orthodox teacher.[93]

Theodoret is one of the most prolific writers of the Eastern Church. Nowadays he is chiefly known for his *Historia ecclesiastica*, taking up from Eusebius but extending only to 428 (it ends with the death of Theodore of Mopsuestia). But the large bulk of his writings is exegetical and consists of commentaries. Preserved are commentaries on the following books of the OT: the Octateuch, the Books of Kings and the Chronicles, the Psalms, the Song of Songs, Daniel, Ezekiel, the Minor Prophets, Isaiah and Jeremiah. Of these commentaries, those of the Octateuch and the Books of Kings and the Chronicles belong to the genre of *quaestiones et solutiones* and form a separate unit. As to the others, most of them are evidently not created for homiletic purposes but are 'scholarly' commentaries intended for reading. It is to be noted that of the commentaries coming down to us only one deals with the NT. Theodoret's exegetical skill was almost exclusively devoted to the OT.

Our knowledge of Theodoret's life is rather limited and we do not know who his teachers in Holy Scripture were. Once (in his commentary on the Song of Songs) he vehemently criticizes Theodore's view of the book without expressly mentioning him. It is, of course, quite possible that he nevertheless profited from Theodore's teaching and writings. "Though Theodoret does not pretend to originality, his exegetical writings are among the finest specimens of the Antiochene School and remarkable for their combination of terseness and lucidity".[94] Theodoret is an eclectic writer and often brilliant in his capacity of holding a middle course between the radicalism of Diodore and Theodore on the one hand and the excessive symbolical interpretations of the Alexandrian School on the other hand. He resembles John Chrysostom in his eagerness for the practical application of the text, but he is closer to Diodore and Theodore in his wish to find the historical context and in his painstaking *hypotheseis*.[95]

Theodoret's exegetical method has been dealt with by G. W. Ashby and the results need not to be repeated here.[96] Suffices it to say, that Theodoret in

---

[93] On the life and work of Theodoret, see Quasten, Patrology III (1960) 536, and Azéma, Theodoret de Cyr (1991) 418–435 [lit.].

[94] Quasten, Patrology III (1960) 539.

[95] "Theodoret gehört zum rechten Flügel der Antiochener und steht einem Chrysostomus ungleich näher als einem Theodor", Bardenhewer, Geschichte IV (1925) 239.

[96] Ashby, Theodoret of Cyrrhus as exegete (1972). See also Azéma, Théodoret de Cyr (1991) 427–429, and the introduction by J.-N. Guinot in SC 276 (1980) 57–74.

all essential aspects adheres to the principles of the Antiochene School. In a lost work he defended Diodore and Theodore against the accusations in Cyrill's *Contra Diodorum et Theodorum.* At the *Latrocinium* parts of it were publicly read. Theodoret himself mentions the writing in one of his letters.[97] Theodoret gives a good outline of his exegetical principles in the prologue to the commentary on the Psalms, in which following words are found:

> I hope that nobody will regard my work as superfluous, since other writers before me have undertaken the same task. I have got hold of several commentaries, of which some indulge too much in allegories, while others adapt the prophecy to the history to such a degree, that the interpretation pleads the case of the Jews rather than that of the children of Faith. I have deemed it my duty to avoid the extreme on both sides. Whatever refers to history, I shall explain as referring to history, but the prophecies about Christ our Lord, about the Church gathered from the gentiles, about the life according to the gospel and the preaching of the apostles shall not be explained as referring to certain other things, as is customary with the malevolent Jews.[98]

This does not mean that Theodoret totally rejects the use of allegory. In his commentaries on the Psalms and on the prophetical books no unequivocal allegory is found, but quite a number of Messianic and typological interpretations. In the *Quaestiones in Octateuchum* there are some, e.g. when the two birds in Lev 14:51 ff. are explained.[99] The red cow in Numbers 19 is a type of the saving passion.[100] When Moses married a foreign woman he was a type of the Church, composed of Jews and Gentiles.[101] Expositions of this kind, however, are mainly confined to the *Quaestiones.* In the commentary on the Minor Prophets there are a number of Messianic interpretations not to be found in the commentary of Theodore of Mopsuestia. Christ (and not Zerubbabel) has fulfilled the promise in Am 9:11 f, Jonah typified Christ, Mic 5:2 is a prophecy about Christ, the stone in Zech 3:8 is on a deeper level Christ, Zech 9:9 f is interpreted as referring to Christ.[102] Theodoret says in connection with Zechariah 9 that he wonders over the stubbornness of the Jews, who take this passage as aiming at Zerubbabel. So does Theodore of Mopsuestia, although he admits that the *alētheia* of the verses is in Christ. The temple in Mal 3:1, finally, stands for Christ's human nature.[103]

In his prologue to Isaiah Theodoret states that all prophets have spoken about what will happen with Israel, the salvation of the Gentiles and Christ's

---

[97] *Ep. 16,* PG 83, 1193. See Quasten, Patrology III (1960) 549.

[98] PG 80, 860 C. See *In Ezech.* PG 81, 1232 B, and Azéma (1991) 429. See also the interesting account by Guinot, Un évêque exégète (1984) 335–360. GUINOT states that Theodoret distinguished three levels in the biblical text: the literal sense, the figurative sense and the typological sense; 343 f.

[99] PG 80, 324. The description of the tabernacle and the various prescriptions about ritual purity in Leviticus are often heavily allegorized in the Early Church, and Theodoret is no exception.

[100] PG 80, 385 A – also a commonplace in patristic literature.

[101] PG 80, 228 C.

[102] PG 80, 1705 C, 1768 B, 1896 A, 1921 B–1924. As for Mic 5:2 Theodoret says, that the Jews see Zerubbabel in this passage. But in ancient times, he goes on, they also have read the verse in a Messianic light, as is shown in Matt 2:4. Regarding this, see J.-N. GUINOT, "La cristallisation d'un différence. Zerubbabel dans l'exégèse de Théodore de Mopsueste et de Théodoret de Cyr", *Aug* 24 (1984) 527–547.

[103] PG 80, 1977 A – with a reference to John 2:19.

coming, but this is especially true of Isaiah. But Theodoret's commentary is also a reliable source of information as to the historical setting of the book. An interesting feature is that some passages in the first part of the book are said to predict the Jewish war in 70 CE and the siege of Jerusalem. This is said of 2:13, 3:1, 5:26, 6:13 and 8:14.[104] Theodoret once refers to Josephus and his *Bellum Judaicum*, which was widely read in the Early Church. The author is not content merely to paraphrase the text, he also endeavours to explain it and does not avoid the difficult issues. Theodoret, like the other Antiochenes, bases his understanding of the Bible on the text of the LXX. Not seldom does he quote the other Greek versions and, incidentally, the Hebrew text. In connection with Isa 8:21 he mentions that some manuscripts have the word πάταχρα which is the Syriac word for 'idols'. In Hebrew the word is βελοαῦ i.e. באלהיו.[105]

Sometimes a note on the realia is given. Commenting upon Am 7:14 Theodoret says that he has heard someone telling him that the fruits of the sycamore do not mature unless they are insized, which explains the verb in the LXX.[106] Theodoret is interested in the chronology of the biblical events. Am 1:1 brings up a lenghty discussion about the dating of the prophet's appearance. The earthquake must not be identified with the one mentioned in Isa 6:4.[107]

Part of the biblical imagery is wrongly taken to stand for historical realities; thus the grasshoppers in Joel 1 and Amos 7 are said to be the Assyrians and the Babylonians.[108] The reason for this is that the passages in question are seen as rhetorical allegories and, according to the Antiochenes, there are many of this kind where we find only the historical sense.[109]

Theodoret is anxious to place the Psalms in their historical context and like Diodore he thinks that some of them describe conditions under Hezekiah's reign, e.g., Ps 28 (29), 29 (30) and 32 (33). Ps 43 (44) is Maccabean and some are said by David ἐκ προσώπου the exulants, so Ps 41 (42). At times different *hypotheseis* are discussed, and the fact that a Psalm is assigned Hezekiah does not exclude its being Messianic as well. As a rule the rubrics in the Greek text are respected, and there is no example of an outright denial of the information given in a rubric (as is the case with both Diodore and Theodore). Rubrics not extant in the Hebrew text are, nevertheless, criticized, e.g. Ps 64 (65). All the Psalms traditionally regarded as Messianic in the Antiochene tradition (Ps 2, 8, 44 [45] and 109 [110]) retain their status in Theodoret's commentary. Ps 21 (22) is also Messianic without any restriction. Certain other Psalms are with limitations recognized as Messianic, e.g. Ps 66 (67) and 71 (72). In the case of the latter Psalm the rubric ("for Solo-

---

104 PG 80, 241 B, 244 C, 261 A, 272 A, 287 B. Theodoret once refers to Josephus and his *Bellum Judaicum*, which was widely read in the Early Church.

105 PG 80, 289 C. Theodoret's text has πατριά but both Rahlfs and the Göttingen Septuaginta prefer πάταχρα which obviously is a better reading.

106 PG 81, 1700 B.

107 PG 81, 1665 A–C.

108 PG 81, 1636 B, 1697 B.

109 Schäublin, Untersuchungen (1974) 120 f.

mon") is called into question, which is admitted even by the Jews according to Theodoret. The Psalm does not at all suit Solomon, but Christ is the true bringer of peace (with a wordplay on Solomon).[110] Ps 68 (69) is primarily aimed for the exulants, but contains also a prophecy of Christ's passion. Many Psalms ascribed to David may be seen as prophecies of Christ, because Christ *secundum carnem* is of David's lineage.[111]

Theodoret's exegetical terminology corresponds largely to the established Antiochene one. We find the distinction *kata to rhēton* and *kata tēn dianoian*, e.g. in Isa 40:4, where the valleys and roads on a deeper level are spiritual conditions and demons defeated by Christ.[112]

The enigmatic verse Hab 2:11 attracted great attention in the Early Church. According to Theodoret both the stone and the scarab might be taken *hyperbolikōs* to stand for Christ, cf. Luke 19:40.[113] The exegete is constantly loyal to the interpretation found in the NT. The apostle has given the *anagōgē* of Deut 25:4 (the ox treading out the corn), but also the *sensus historicus* of the verse is edifying.[114] Interestingly enough the pericope Ex 12:35 f. (the Israelites plundered the Egyptians when leaving their country) is interpreted only as referring to how the people at last got their wages.[115] Theodoret is neither an exegetical innovator like Diodore nor an inspired preacher like John Chrysostom. He is rather the one who tersely and effectively summarizes the Antiochene tradition. What he lacks in originality, he abundantly compensates for in learning and assiduity.

6. The Development and Influence of the Antiochene School

The Antiochene School has a rather wide-ranging impact on biblical scholarship in the fifth century. Unfortunately, it is difficult to estimate this influence, since most texts have perished or have been suppressed. The following is only a brief sketch.

Polychronius, bishop of Apamea in Syria, was a brother of Theodore of Mopsuestia.[116] He seems to have died just before the council of Ephesus in 431. Of his many commentaries on the books of the OT enough remains to confirm the impression that he shared his brother's exegetical methods in all essentials. He was strongly opposed to allegories and displayed the same rationalizing tendency as far as passages, traditionally regarded as Messianic, were concerned.

---

110 PG 80, 1429 A–C.

111 Thus, e.g. Ps 131 (132), see PG 80, 1904 C.

112 PG 81, 404 B.

113 He notes that Symmachus omits the word for 'scarab', PG 81, 1821 B. Theodore merely says that the Greek word stands for a small insect and refrains from all further speculations, PG 66, 437 C.

114 PG 80, 432 C.

115 PG 80, 411 A.

116 See Quasten, Patrology III (1960) 423 f, and O. Bardenhewer, *Polychronius, Bruder Theodors von Mopsuestia und Bischof von Apamea* (Freiburg/Br. 1879).

More important as exegete was *Severian*, bishop of Gabala in Syria, near Laodicea.[117] The dates of his life are uncertain, but he must have died between 408–431. He was deeply involved in the turmoil of Constantinople during the episcopacy of John Chrysostom. Although opposed to John, he nevertheless shared his exegetical allegiance and might be seen as belonging to the strict Antiochene school. His writings have to a large extent been confused with those of John Chrysostom. Those of undoubted authenticity show all the features of the Antiochene tradition, including an almost complete incapacity for understanding biblical poetic imagery. Typically Antiochene are his cosmology and his urge to find the litteral sense.[118]

Julian of Eclanum (385–450) is in the history of the Church mostly known for his controversy with Augustine regarding Pelagianism. However, he was an outstanding biblical scholar, who due to his knowledge of Greek was capable of transferring part of the Antiochene exegetical heritage to the West. Julian was elected bishop of Eclanum (near Benevento), but was exiled to Asia, where he studied under the auspices of Theodore of Mopsuestia.[119]

Julian's biblical commentaries are mostly translations and as such are of great value, since they have rescued Antiochene writings, which otherwise would have been lost. He translated Theodore's *Expositio in Psalmos*. His commentaries on Job and on Hosea, Joel and Amos seem to be original. A commentary on the Song of Songs is occasionally quoted by Bede.[120]

In all, Julian probably gives a good impression of average Antiochene exegesis. His exegetical terminology is in Latin, which sometimes makes it difficult to detect the underlying Greek term. With the Antiochenes he shares a predilection for finding the *skopos* of the text in Israel's history. In his commentary on Amos he sometimes introduces Hezekiah's reign as the prophecy's goal.[121] Of special interest in regard to his exegetical method is the commentary on Job. He distinguishes two senses in the book. The deeper one he calls the *sensus subtilis*, which makes a typological interpretation possible. As a rule he prefers the literal sense, faithful to his Antiochene principles.[122]

The Antiochene tradition in biblical study did not continue for long. Gregory the Great's commentary on Job, the *Moralia*, e.g., is very different from those of Chrysostom and Julian and indulges in allegories and moral interpretations. The Middle Ages certainly did not lack theologians who upheld

---

[117] See Quasten, Patrology III (1960) 484–486, and Voicu, Sévérien de Gabale (1988) 752–763 [lit.].

[118] "Occasionally he reveals a high level of philological knowledge, but often his "Hebrew" etymologies are explicable only as from the Aramaic", S.J. Voicu, "Severian of Gabal" (EEC; 1992) 772. About Severian, see also Lehmann, Per Piscatores (1975).

[119] On Julian's life, see Alexander, Julian von Aeclanum (1988) 441–443.

[120] *Theodori Mopsuesteni expositionis in Psalmos* (1977); Bedae in Canticum Canticorum allegorica expositio (PL 91, 1065–1236); *Iuliani Aeclanensis expositio libri Iob; Tractatus prophetarum Osee, Ioel et Amos* (CCL 88; ed. M.J. d'Hont/L. de Coninck; Turnhout-Brepols 1977). See G. Bouwman, *Des Julian von Aeclanum Kommentar zu den Propheten Osee, Joel und Amos* (AnBib 9; Roma 1958).

[121] See E. Dassmann, "Amos" (RAC, Suppl 3) 342.

[122] See Dassmann, Hiob (1989) 403 f.

the literal sense of the Bible, but that does not prove their indebtedness to the Antiochene tradition.[123] The Victorine School in Paris often gives the impression of being influenced by Antioch.[124]

In later times the Antiochene school has been noticed as a sort of forerunner of critical biblical scholarship. It has been said, nevertheless, that they in all essentials share the common Christian (and Jewish) views on the Bible. Their tools of interpretation are, as we have seen, borrowed from contemporary pagan exegesis and not necessarily leading to a critical understanding of the text. Their concentration on the historical sense is, of course, something which they have in common with modern scholarship. It is significant that R. BULTMANN wrote a study on Theodore of Mopsuestia, which has been published posthumously.[125]

---

[123] See Laistner, Antiochene exegesis (1947) 19–35.

[124] See J. VAN ZWIETEN, *The Place and Significance of Literal Exegesis in Hugh of St Victor* (Amsterdam 1992).

[125] R. BULTMANN, *Die Exegese des Theodor von Mopsuestia* (ed. H. Feld/K. H. Schelke; Stuttgart 1984).

Chapter Fifteen

Exegetical Contacts between Christians and Jews in the Roman Empire

By Günter Stemberger, Vienna

Bibliographies: J. R. Baskin, "Rabbinic-Patristic Exegetical Contacts in Late Antiquity: A Bibliographical Reappraisal", *Approaches to Ancient Judaism* V (ed. W. S. Green; Brown Judaic Studies 32; Atlanta GA: Scholars Press 1985) 53–80; E. Lamirande, "Etude bibliographique sur les Pères de l'Eglise et l'Aggadah", *VC* 21 (1967) 1–11.

General works: S. Brock, "Jewish Traditions in Syriac Sources", *JJS* 30 (1979) 212–232; N. R. M. de Lange, *Origen and the Jews. Studies in Jewish-Christian Relations in Third-Century Palestine* (Cambridge: University Press 1976); S. Krauss, "The Jews in the Works of the Church Fathers", *JQR* 5 (1893) 122–157; 6 (1894) 82–99, 225–261; idem, "Church Fathers", *Jewish Encyclopedia* 4 (New York: KTAV 1903) 80–86; J. Maier, *Jüdische Auseinandersetzung mit dem Christentum in der Antike* (EdF 177; Darmstadt: Wissenschaftliche Buchgesellschaft 1982); J. Neusner, *Aphrahat and Judaism. The Christian-Jewish Argument in Fourth-Century Iran* (SPB 19; Leiden: Brill 1971); G. Sgherri, *Chiesa e Sinagoga nelle opere di Origene* (Studia Patristica Mediolanensia 13; Milano: Vita e Pensiero 1982); O. Skarsaune, *The Proof from Prophecy. A Study on Justin Martyr's Proof-Text Tradition: Text-Type, Provenance, Theological Profile* (NovTSup 56; Leiden: E. J. Brill 1987).

1. Delimitation of the Topic

This chapter deals with contacts between Christian and Jewish exegesis after the NT. It thus leaves apart the question of Jewish exegetical traditions in the NT itself. It does not deal, neither, with the continuing influence of Jewish exegetical traditions which were part of the common heritage of Judaism and Christianity, in Christian texts. There are hardly any Jewish texts in this period which were not part of the rabbinic corpus: exceptions are later Sibylline Oracles which do not contain, however, any exegetical traditions, and the most probably Jewish *Collatio legum Mosaicarum et Romanarum*; the *Liber Antiquitatum Biblicarum* of Pseudo-Philo would be of highest interest if it could really be dated to the late second or early third century, but practically all authors opt for the first century.[1] The problem is, therefore, reduced to that of *contacts between early Christian interpreters of the Bible and the exegesis of the Rabbis*. This does not automatically reduce the discussion to the geographic orbit of the rabbinic world, i. e. Palestine and Babylonia and, to some

[1] For a late date see J. Maier, *Zwischen den Testamenten. Geschichte und Religion in der Zeit des Zweiten Tempels* (NEchtB Erg.band/AT 3; Würzburg: Echter 1990) 113.

degree, Syria which had a large Jewish population and close contacts with the rabbinic centers of Palestine and Babylonia. But for all parallels between Jewish and Christian exegesis outside this area one has to find an explanation of how the contacts could have come about.

2. History and Problems of Earlier Research

The study of exegetical contacts between Christian and Jews in late Antiquity started in the middle of the nineteenth century and remained for decades an almost exclusive domain of Jewish scholars. At that time, Jews had only recently been admitted to university. Many of them came from yeshivot and had a traditional Talmudic education; for admission to university, those who had not studied in a classical gymnasium had to pass examinations in Latin and Greek. Those desiring to make use of their double expertise found the comparison of the Church Fathers with the rabbinic sources a congenial field of study.[2] It also served the apologetic slant of the early *Wissenschaft des Judentums* that they were able to demonstrate how much early Christian scholars had learned from the Jews.[3] At the same time, these studies could serve apologetic purposes directed toward traditional Jewish scholars critical of their having forsaken the yeshiva for the university: "Many sentences of Talmud and Midrash can be brought into the right perspective only by the light of the exegesis and the polemics of these Christian writers. Therefore modern Jewish learning turns, although not yet with sufficient eagerness, to the investigation of the works of the Church Fathers".[4]

The pioneer in this field of study was the historian H. GRAETZ who in 1854/55 published a long article on Haggadic Elements in the Church Fathers, insisting on the value of such studies for the dating of haggadot and certain aspects of Jewish history. M. RAHMER followed with a long series of studies, starting in 1861, on Jerome and the *Quaestiones* attributed to him. D. GERSON studied the relationship between Ephrem's commentaries and Jewish exegesis in 1868, to be followed by S. FUNK's study of Aphrahat in 1891. The results of this first period of studies were drawn together and supplemented by S. KRAUSS in 1893/94 and in his article on the Church Fathers of 1904, and culminated in several studies of L. GINZBERG and the rich harvest of parallels to be found in his monumental *The Legends of the Jews*.[5]

As may easily be understood, the enthusiasm of discovery and the double apologetic of the early period of research led to highly excessive claims regarding the dependence of the Church Fathers on the Rabbis. The main defect of early research was to see dependence wherever there were parallels

---

[2] See Neusner, Aphrahat (1971) 192 n. 4; Baskin, Exegetical Contacts (1985) 53 f.

[3] A similar approach may be seen in the dissertation of A. GEIGER, *Was hat Mohammed aus dem Judenthume aufgenommen?* (Wiesbaden 1833).

[4] Krauss, Church Fathers (1893) 86.

[5] For bibliographical details see the bibliography of J. BASKIN.

of any kind without sufficiently considering the historical circumstances in which these Church Fathers lived and worked. Many of the parallels between rabbinic and Christian exegesis may be traced back to the common heritage. Wherever a certain interpretation may be found already in the writings of Philo or Josephus or in the Apocrypha and Pseudepigrapha, its occurrence in rabbinic and patristic texts cannot be taken to prove exegetical contacts between Jews and Christians in late Antiquity. Many other parallels may be explained as the result of similar methods and presuppositions in the interpretation of the same biblical text. One has to be cautious even in cases where a Church Father explicity refers to a Jewish source: too frequently such references are copied from earlier Christian texts, as is well known in the case of Jerome, but also elsewhere; in other cases, the *Hebraeus* referred to in a text may simply be Philo, Josephus, or another Jewish text. Taking into consideration only such parallels which cannot be explained by pre-Christian Jewish texts or common exegetical methods certainly excludes also cases which actually reflect direct contacts between Christians and Jews, but, for methodical reasons, we have to take a minimalist approach.

3. The Disproportion of Jewish and Christian Exegesis

Before entering into the discussion of possible Jewish influence on certain Christian authors and eventual Jewish reactions to Christian exegesis, it is necessary to point out the essential disproportion of Jewish and Christian exegesis. Jews and Christians had, at least to a large extent, the same Bible, and confessed its divine origin. In reality, however, their centers of interest were quite different, as may immediately be seen when comparing the biblical books which were commented upon.

On the Christian side, the *prophetic books* attracted the special interest of the interpreters already before the earliest full-scale commentaries were written. One just has to look up the index of biblical references in the editions of Justin Martyr or other Christian authors of the second century to see the prominence of the biblical prophets. Starting with Origen, a long series of commentaries on Isaiah, Jeremiah, Ezekiel, Daniel and the Minor Prophets were written, whereas in Jewish tradition, none of these books received a Midrash.

In Christian tradition, the *Pentateuch* fared considerably better than the Prophets did in the rabbinic interpretation. Origen composed a series of sermons on Numbers, John Chrysostom on Genesis, Basilius the Great on the Hexaemeron; Victorinus of Pettau is known to have written commentaries on Genesis, Exodus and Leviticus (all of them lost) etc. This cannot, however, be compared with the centrality of the Pentateuch in Jewish tradition. For Judaism, the Torah is the center of the Bible and of highest authority as the most direct revelation of God's will. As such, its reading always formed the center of the liturgy in the synagogue and was surrounded by special reverence.

The Torah was read as *lectio continua*, interrupted only for special occasions. The origin of the lectionary cycles is unknown. We can only guess how the early diaspora synagogues arranged their liturgy and do not know anything about the Palestinian liturgy of the synagogue before 70 CE (if there was any regulated liturgy at all); all our information derives from rabbinic sources and may not antedate the destruction of the Temple. Two systems of reading the Torah are known: A 'triennial' Palestinian cycle (in reality ranging between three and nearly four years) and an annual cycle, called 'Babylonian', but probably also of Palestinian origin. The selection of a prophetic text (including the 'historical' books from Joshua to Kings) was left to the discretion of the community except for special days for which the prophetic reading was already fixed in the Mishnah. It was only expected that the prophetic reading could be related to that of the Torah. As a consequence, the interpretation of the biblical reading also centered on the Torah text.

A natural outcome of this Torah-centered theology and liturgy is the predominance of the Torah in the midrashic activity of the Rabbis. It is closely related to the overall importance of religious practice, the fulfilment of the *miṣvot*, in Jewish tradition, whereas questions of *dogma* were not without importance but not so central as in Christianity. These remarks are not intended to contrast Judaism and Christianity in oversimplistic terms: they only point to quite different centers of interest in the interpretation of the common Bible which should be kept in mind when evaluating parallels between rabbinic and Christian exegesis.

4. A Different Biblical Text

Another difference between Jewish and Christian tradition should also be pointed out: the different *text of the Bible*. Since the Christians depended on the *Septuagint*, they certainly found the exegetical tradition of Hellenistic Judaism, mainly Philo, more congenial than the living rabbinic tradition of their own time. Jewish communities in the diaspora and even in Palestine (e.g. Caesarea) did not immediately and completely give up the use of the Septuagint because of its Christian usurpation.[6] But the revision of the Greek text which had begun already before the rise of Christianity, was now continued with greater urgency because of the Christian usurpation of the Septuagint. Since Origen, Christian exegetes became aware of the importance of the revised texts and used them in different degree for their interpretation. *Aquila*'s translation is frequently regarded as depending on the exegetical methods of R. Aqiva;[7] as to *Symmachus*, many authors follow Epiphanius and consider him as a Samaritan who converted to Judaism and stood under the

[6] For the continued Jewish use of the Septuagint see K. Treu, "Die Bedeutung des Griechischen für die Juden im römischen Reich", *Kairos* 15 (1973) 123–144, esp. 138–143.

[7] See D. Barthélemy, *Les devanciers d'Aquila* (VTSup 10; Leiden: Brill 1963) 3–30; against a close relationship of Aquila and the Rabbis: L. L. Grabbe, "Aquila's Translation and Rabbinic Exegesis", *JJS* 33 (1982) 527–536.

influence of some Rabbis: "Symmachus' revision of the Pentateuch displays a thorough knowledge of rabbinic exegesis of that time. Some of his interpretations are paralleled by the haggadists of third and fourth century Caesarea".[8] The arguments in favour of these theses or against them cannot be discussed in this context; that 'Jewish' traditions are derived from these revisions of the Septuagint is, however, a serious possibility always to be checked before claiming direct dependence of a certain Christian exegesis on the Rabbis. The same is true for the *Peshitta*; its (partly) Jewish origin is still controversial but it is also frequently regarded as reflecting Jewish exegetical traditions.[9] Similar claims have been made, with weaker arguments, for the *Vetus Latina*, especially as used in Africa (*Vetus Afra*): G. Quispel and others have surmised that it possibly was translated directly from the Hebrew or, at least, influenced by a Hebrew source, possibly through the synagogue service in African communities.[10] As to Jerome's *Vulgate*, its direct dependence not only on the Hebrew text, but also on Jewish exegetical traditions is generally conceded; but even in his case it can sometimes be shown that he used another Hebrew text and not directly a contemporary Jewish tradition.[11]

5. Jews Influenced by Christian Exegesis?

As a result of the Jewish dominance in this field of research and also because of certain preconceptions regarding Jewish history, Christian influences on Jewish exegesis in late Antiquity have never been explored systematically. It is only natural that the main direction of influence was from the mother religion to its daughter and not vice versa. It would, however, be strange, if there had been no reaction whatsoever on the Jewish side. Certain shifts in Jewish exegesis, changes in comparison with Jewish interpretations of the Second Temple period, may frequently be explained with good reason as reactions against the theological use of a biblical text in the Christian tradi-

[8] A. Salvesen, *Symmachus in the Pentateuch* (JSSMon 15; Manchester: University 1991) 297. For earlier literature see E. Tov, *Textual Criticism of the Hebrew Bible* (Minneapolis: Fortress 1992) 146.

[9] Tov, Textual Criticism (1992) 152; P. B. Dirksen, "The Old Testament Peshitta", *Mikra* (ed. M. J. Mulder; CRINT II/1; Assen/Maastricht: Van Gorcum 1988) 255–297; H. Drijvers, "Syrian Christianity and Judaism", *The Jews among Pagans and Christians* (ed. J. Lieu/J. North/T. Rajak; London: Routledge 1992) 124–146; M. Weitzman, "The Syriac Version of the Hebrew Bible", ibid. 147–173. The strongest claim for the dependence of the Peshitta on a Jewish Targum has been made by A. Vööbus, *Peschitta und Targumim des Pentateuchs* (Papers of the Estonian Theological Society in Exile 9; Stockholm 1958).

[10] See G. Quispel, "The Discussion of Judaic Christianity. Additional Note", *VC* 22 (1968) 81–93; J. Trebolle Barrera, "Lo Cristiano y lo Judío en la Vetus Latina", *El Olivo* 15 (1991) 123–141; Tov, Textual Criticism (1992) 139. Very cautious B. Kedar, "The Latin Translations", *Mikra* (1988) 299–338, esp. 308–311: Hebrew-influenced patches of the Old Latin may be the result of later corrections by a half-learned person.

[11] G. Miletto, "Die 'Hebraica Veritas' in S. Hieronymus", *Bibel in jüdischer und christlicher Tradition* (FS J. Maier, ed. H. Merklein/K. Müller/G. Stemberger; BBB 88; Frankfurt/M.: Anton Hain 1993) 56–65; idem, *L'Antico Testamento ebraico nella tradizione babilonese. I frammenti della Genizah* (Torino 1992).

tion. But in most cases this remains at the level of educated guesses; too much has changed in Judaism after 70 CE to attribute every break of continuity directly and exclusively to rabbinic reaction against Christianity.

We must not overestimate the concern of Judaism with Christianity. It probably was a greater problem for Jewish communities in the Diaspora where, however, no Jewish writings from this period survived. In Palestine, on the other hand, direct contacts between Jews and Christians would have been possible mainly in the coastal cities like Caesarea. Christians in the Jerusalem area could live without ever seeing a Jew; many Christian pilgrims to the Holy Land also seem to have been hardly aware of the existence of contemporary Jews, as may be seen from the surviving accounts. On the other hand, the north-eastern part of Galilee remained nearly exclusively Jewish until the fifth century.

Another point to be considered is what kind of Jews came into contact with Christians. It may be suggested that the Rabbis for religious reasons (*ʿAvoda Zara*) tried to avoid contact with non-Jews wherever possible and found this easier than the less educated Jewish people in areas of mixed population, where they might have to mingle with all kinds of people in their daily work. This is not to suggest a splendid isolation of the rabbinic establishment; but high-level interreligious contacts and direct disputations with Christians about dogmatic questions and the interpretation of certain biblical texts were certainly not the norm. It is questionable whether Rabbis ever had the chance to read a Christian book; they certainly would never have entered a Christian church to hear a sermon.[12] Information about Christian issues and beliefs was in general more indirect and casual.

There are, nevertheless, Jewish developments which may be considered as reactions to Christianity. The revision of the Greek text of the Bible, continued with renewed vigour in the second century, has already been mentioned. Another frequently adduced example is the exclusion of the Ten Commandments from the phylacteries and their removal from the daily prayer "on account of the claims of the *minim* so that they may not say: Only these were given to Moses on Sinai" (*y.Ber.* I:5:3c). For most of rabbinic exegesis, the Ten Commandments have no pre-eminence over against the rest of the commandments in the Torah. We may consider this development as reaction against tendencies to reduce the Torah to its 'essence' which alone is to be kept for all time and under all circumstances. Such tendencies may be found already in Hellenistic Judaism and are not exclusively Christian; but they certainly received a renewed urgency in the confrontation with Christianity.[13]

Of greatest interest in this context is the development of the Jewish interpretation of Genesis 22. In pre-rabbinic Jewish texts, the emphasis is on the

---

[12] For the case of a Jewish girl from Tyre who converted to Christianity after hearing a sermon of Peter the Iberian see B. Rosen, "An Apostate Jewess from Tyre: The Abbess of a Monophysite Monastery south of Caesarea" (in Hebrew), *Cathedra* 61 (1991) 54–66.

[13] G. Stemberger, "Der Dekalog im frühen Judentum", JBTh 4 (1989) 91–103; J. Maier, Jüdische Auseinandersetzung (1982) 150 ff.

willingness of Isaac to be offered as a sacrifice; in these texts, Isaac is always at least thirteen years old, fully grown up and responsible for his actions. Rabbinic interpreters tend to see him as a small child; the main actor of the scene is Abraham, Isaac's offering becomes one of the ten temptations of Abraham. It is tempting to understand this shift of emphasis as a reaction against the Christian use of this scene as a model of Christ's voluntary self-sacrifice on the cross. It has been suggested that the depiction of Genesis 22 on the mosaic floor of the synagogue of Bet Alfa (6th century) with the ram hanging from the branches of the tree is influenced by Christian models.[14] Only in the Middle Ages, as a consequence of Jewish martyrdom in the period of the crusades, did Isaac once again become the central person of this text, a proto-type of the Jewish martyrs.[15]

It would be worthwhile to study systematically how biblical texts important in the NT and later Christian argumentation fared in rabbinic exegesis, especially where a comparison can be made to earlier Jewish treatments of the same texts (to give just a few examples: Isa 7:14 is not even mentioned in rabbinic texts; Gen 15:6 is of no importance; Psalm 22 is related to the Esther story). Such comparative studies cannot strictly prove polemic against Christian exegesis or conscious avoidance of biblical texts important to Christians; but they certainly demonstrate the very different agenda of rabbinic and Christian interpretation.[16] After a (wide-ranging, if not very detailed) comparison of Jewish and Christian exegesis in the fourth century, J. Neusner rightly concludes:

> the confrontation with Scripture did not provoke for Judaic sages and Christian theologians, a confrontation *over* Scripture, in the way in which the confrontation with the categories of history, Messiah, and Israel clearly produced a confrontation over those categories ...
> The twin issues of exegesis and canon hardly brought the two sides together into an equivalent confluence, a genuine debate. I do not believe that the one side meant by exegesis what the other did, nor do the processes that led to the canonization of "the Bible" for Christianity in any way correspond to those that yielded "the one whole Torah of Moses, our rabbi, oral and written" for Judaism.[17]

Possible reactions of rabbinic exegesis to Christian exegesis still need further exploration, but it is already very clear that it was mainly, if not exclusively, the Christian side which learned from and reacted to the Jewish one.

---

[14] M. Bregman, "The Depiction of the Ram in the Aqedah Mosaic at Beit Alpha" (in Hebrew), *Tarbiz* 51 (1981–2) 306–309; for more examples of possible Christian influence see G. Foerster, "Allegorical and Symbolic Motifs with Christian Significance from Mosaic Pavements of Sixth-Century Palestinian Synagogues", *Christian Archaeology in the Holy Land. New Discoveries. Essays in Honour of V. C. Corbo* (ed. G. C. Bottini et al.; Jerusalem: Franciscan Printing Press 1990) 545–552.

[15] G. Stemberger, "Die Patriarchenbilder der Katakombe in der Via Latina im Lichte der jüdischen Tradition", *Kairos* 16 (1974) 19–78, esp. 50–76.

[16] For further examples and literature see Baskin, Exegetical contacts (1985) 69–71; B. L. Visotzky, "Anti-Christian Polemic in Leviticus Rabbah", *PAAJR* 56 (1989) 83–100.

[17] J. Neusner, *Judaism and Christianity in the Age of Constantine. History, Messiah, Israel, and the Initial Confrontation* (Chicago Studies in the History of Judaism; Chicago: University Press 1987) 142,144.

6. Christian-Jewish Contacts in Alexandria?

S. Krauss says correctly about *Clement of Alexandria* that "His information about Judaism he seems to have derived exclusively from Greek writings, particularly from Philo and Josephus"; but then he proceeds: "he possessed a certain acquaintance with Hebrew", and claims that "Agadic elements are more plentiful in Clement's writings than the course of his studies would naturally lead us to expect".[18]

These statements confront us immediately with methodological problems. As is well known, the important Jewish community of Alexandria was nearly extinguished in the Diaspora uprisings of the years 115–117. After this revolts, there are hardly any archaeological traces of Jews in Alexandria (and other parts of Egypt) or literary references to them until the fourth century. This does not prove that Alexandria had no Jewish community or even individual Jews in this period; but if there was one, it was certainly without any importance. As to Clement's alleged rudimentary knowledge of Hebrew, where should he have learned it? Among Alexandrian Jews, such knowledge was uncommon even in more prosperous times (even Philo probably knew no Hebrew). Parallels with Jewish traditions have to be examined in each case. The parallel regarding the sixty years of Elisha's activity relies on an emendation of Clement's text; as to the names of Moses, Krauss himself later discovered a parallel in Pseudo-Philo.[19] Clement's historical situation makes it advisable to consider parallels with rabbinic texts as part of the common exegetical tradition and not as proof of personal contacts with Jews.[20]

Based on a misunderstanding of Jerome's *Ep.* 39.1, S. Krauss also claimed that *Origen*'s mother was Jewish and knew Hebrew.[21] This would be a most interesting detail about Jews in Alexandria, but the text does not speak of Origen's mother. Did Origen have other Jewish contacts when still in Alexandria? G. Sgherri thinks that this was the case:

> Origene ha indubbiamente avuto contatti con Ebrei già ad Alessandria. Non possiamo dire se egli fosse in rapporto personale con due o tre persone soltanto, o se invece avesse stabilito relazione con tutta la Sinagoga. Dei Giudei ad ogni modo vengono nominati in opere di sicura origine alessandrina.[22]

This is not quite impossible. But our information is so scanty, that it is safer to leave this question open. Origen had spent some time in Palestine in his early thirties, and while there he could have acquired a considerable amount of knowledge about

---

[18] Krauss, The Jews (1893) 134,136.

[19] S. Krauss, "The Names of Moses", *JQR* 10 (1898) 726. A.-M. Denis, *Fragmenta pseudepigraphorum quae supersunt Graeca* (PVTG 3; Leiden: Brill 1970) 64, rightly includes in his collection this and another text of Clement referred to by Krauss.

[20] R. van den Broek, "Juden und Christen in Alexandrien im 2. und 3. Jahrhundert", *Juden und Christen in der Antike* (ed. J. van Amersfort / J. van Oort; Kampen: Kok 1990) 101–115, is rightly cautious: "In den Werken des Klemens findet sich kein einziger Hinweis auf direkte Kontakte mit Juden" (111).

[21] Krauss, The Jews (1893) 139. Against this error see de Lange, Origen (1976) 23.

[22] Sgherri, Chiesa (1982) 44.

Judaism. Such knowledge as he displays of non-rabbinic Judaism he may have acquired in Alexandria, or on his travels in Rome, Achaea and Asia, or in Palestine.[23]

Even in a later period when the Jewish presence at Alexandria was again much stronger, there seems to be hardly any exegetical contact with living Jews. Hellenistic-Jewish traditions, mainly Philo, still dominate, as may be seen clearly when comparing the commentary of Didymus the Blind on Zechariah with that of Jerome who used it so extensively, or even in the writings of Cyril of Alexandria.[24]

7. Palestine

Palestine is, of course, the country where contacts and confrontation with the living Judaism (and not just with Jewish traditions of an earlier period) are to be expected. *Justin Martyr*, born in Samaria (Flavia Neapolis) in ca. 100 CE, displays in his writings personal knowledge of contemporary Judaism.[25] In spite of his Palestinian origins, this is not the early rabbinic Judaism, but the Hellenistic tradition. His Bible is the Septuagint and (Jewish) revisions of the Greek text; to assume "that Justin had access to the Targumim, or Aramaic translations, and the Hebrew texts in Neapolis",[26] goes beyond our evidence. He does not seem to have known Hebrew or Aramaic. Interpretations of biblical texts attributed to Trypho are sometimes clearly non-rabbinic (e.g. Deut 21:23: "one who hangs is cursed by God", in *Dial.* 89.1);[27] in other cases, as in the messianic interpretation of Gen 49:10f and Num 24:17, there are rabbinic parallels, but also pre-Christian Jewish parallels from Qumran.[28] O. Skarsaune concludes: "all the main texts were familiar Messianic testimonies within Jewish exegesis prior to, contemporary with, and later than Justin ... This would seem to indicate that Justin's material evolved in a milieu being in close contact with Jewish exegesis".[29] He probably refers correctly to a Judaeo-Christian exegetical tradition taken over by Justin; it is, however, very doubtful to regard "Justin himself, or his immediate predecessors, – in debate with *rabbinic* exegesis"[30]: Contacts with the world of nascent rabbinism cannot be shown. The frequent references to "targumizing texts" or "targumic tradition" are too general and do not really specify which kind of Judaism Justin or his sources know. Justin himself says (*Dial.* 112.4; cf. 38.1)

---

[23] de Lange, Origen (1976) 9.

[24] R. L. Wilken, *Judaism and the Early Christian Mind. A Study of Cyril of Alexandria's Exegesis and Theology* (New Haven: Yale University Press 1971).

[25] See most recently W. Horbury, "Jewish-Christian Relations in Barnabas and Justin Martyr", *Jews and Christians. The Parting of the Ways A. D. 70 to 135* (WUNT 66; ed. J. D. G. Dunn; Tübingen: J. C. B. Mohr 1992) 315–345, esp. 317ff.

[26] R. S. Maclennan, *Early Christian Texts on Jews and Judaism* (Brown Judaic Studies 194; Atlanta GA: Scholars Press 1990) 63.

[27] B. Z. Bokser, "Justin Martyr and the Jews", *JQR* 64 (1973–74) 97–122, 204–211, p. 108.

[28] Correctly emphasized by Skarsaune, The Proof (1987) 263–65.

[29] Skarsaune, The Proof 269; cf. 287.

[30] Skarsaune, The Proof 429. My emphasis.

that Jewish teachers warned their fellow Jews not to enter into debate with Christians. If Justin could debate with Jews, they were more probably Diaspora Jews not too well versed in the most recent developments of rabbinic exegesis; the proposal to identify Trypho with R. Tarfon, is completely unlikely.

Origen moved to Caesarea in about 230 and remained there for most of the rest of his life (+ 254). Interested in Judaism, especially in the Hebrew Bible and Jewish exegesis, already before, he now had the chance to learn much first-hand by personal observation, participation in disputes and through contacts with Jewish acquaintances. Since Greek was widely used among Jews as *lingua franca*, the active *knowledge of Hebrew* was not necessary for this purpose. It seems that, in spite of the testimonies of Eusebius and Jerome, Origen could not read or speak Hebrew.[31] The exact degree of his personal knowledge of Jews and contacts with them remains open to dispute. The only Jew he mentions by name is "Ioullos the patriarch" (PG 12, 1056 B). No Jewish patriarch or other member of the patriarchal family of this name (probably Hillel) is known for this period; Origen, moreover, always calls the patriarch *ethnarches*, not *patriarches*. DE LANGE may, therefore, be right that Origen here refers to "the head of a local community".[32] Together with Ioullos, Origen mentions "one with the title of Sage among the Jews" (cf. *Ep. ad Afr.* 7.11; SC 302,538: "a learned Hebrew with the title of Son of a Sage"). Attempts to identify Origen's rabbinic contacts with known talmudic Rabbis have not been successful, although it is quite possible that Origen was acquainted with R. Hoshaya who taught in Caesarea at the same time as Origen. Some of his Jewish informants were converts to Christianity, as Origen himself sometimes explicitly says.[33] In many places where Origen refers to "the Hebrew", this is not an informant, but the Hebrew text of the Bible. But even where "the Hebrew" is certainly a concrete person, he is credited with interpretations found in rabbinic texts as well as with clearly non-rabbinic or Jewish-Christian views: "The problem of the identity of 'the Hebrew' must remain one of the great enigmas connected with the name of Origen".[34]

For his great text-critical enterprise of the *Hexapla*, Origen certainly needed help from Jews or converts from Judaism. Some have doubted that the Hexapla ever contained a first column with the Hebrew text of the Bible, but the contrary is certainly much more probable.[35] "It is quite conceivable that Origen borrowed a Jewish source which already had in parallel columns the

[31] See e.g. G. BARDY, "Les traditions juives dans l'oeuvre d'Origène", *RB* 34 (1925) 217–252, p. 219 f. E. ULRICH, "The Old Testament Text of Eusebius: The Heritage of Origen", *Eusebius, Christianity, and Judaism* (ed. by H.W. Attridge/G. Hata; SPB 42; Leiden: Brill 1992) 543–562, defines as the minimalist position beyond which one is hardpressed to move: "Perhaps Origen knew no Hebrew or very little Hebrew, so little that it was virtually nonfunctioning" (551).

[32] de Lange, Origen (1976) 24.

[33] See the references in Bardy, Les traditions (1925) 221 f.

[34] de Lange, Origen (1976) 132.

[35] See the discussion by Ulrich, The Old Testament Text (1992) 551–56; P. NAUTIN, *Origène: Sa vie et son oeuvre* (Christianisme antique 1; Paris: Beauchesne 1977) 303–309, argues against the existence of a Hebrew column.

Hebrew, a Greek transliteration, and Aquila's corresponding version – and possibly even Symmachus's version as well".[36] But even if Origen could make use of pre-existing compilations, he still needed copyists competent enough in Hebrew to correctly transcribe the texts. For his own comparison of the Septuagint with the Hebrew text of the Bible, he could, on the other hand, rely on the text of Aquila.[37]

As to Origen's interpretation of concrete Old Testament texts, G. Bardy has listed 69 texts which he considered to be a fairly complete list (excluding the interpretation of names and the discussion of variants of the biblical text). Many of the interpretations quoted are to be found already in Philo or Hellenistic Jewish literature, and may have been taken from there even where Origen refers to Jews from whom he has heard them. Thus, for example, Origen justifies the biblical measurements of the ark as sufficient for the number of animals to be transported. The numbers signify proportions and not absolute dimensions, as Moses was used to from Egyptian geometry; Origen says that he learned this "a prudentibus viris et Hebraicarum traditionum gnaris atque a veteribus magistris" (*In Gen. hom.* II.2, GCS Origen 6, 29). The first part is paralleled in Philo (*Quaest. in Gen.* II. 5); that Moses was trained in all sciences, is a commonplace in Hellenistic Judaism; Origen may have taken the argument from Philo's books. Another text which Bardy regards as "interprétation grossièrement littérale qu'Origène devait sans doute aux rabbins", is *In Gen.* I.8 (PG 12, 100A).[38] But the etymology of Eden as *hedy* may be due to contacts with Philo;[39] the etymology of *Pheison* as *stoma kores* in the same context has no direct parallel, but the idea that the paradise was located in the center of the world, was known in pre-rabbinic Judaism (see *Jub.* 8:12.19). Many contacts between Origen's exegesis and Jewish interpretation listed by Bardy can be accounted for by Origen's acquaintance with earlier (pre-Christian) Jewish literature. But there remains quite a number of instances which are best explained by direct exchange with Jews known to Origen.[40]

Of special interest is Origen's remark (*In Cant., prol.*, GCS 8,62f) that Jews may not study the Song of Songs before having reached the age of thirty. For this we have no explicit rabbinic testimony, but it corresponds well with the esoteric use of some texts of this book in Jewish mystical traditions (*shiᶜur qomah*: "the measurements of [God's] body") and the limitations imposed on it. E. E. Urbach tried to demonstrate that the rabbinic interpretation of Canticles directly reacts against Origen's commentary which had attacked certain rabbinic positions. Studying synoptically the two interpretations one could

---

36 Ulrich, The Old Testament Text (1992) 556. On transliterated Hebrew texts among Jews see de Lange, Origen (1976) 57f.

37 Cf. D. Barthélemy, "Origène et le texte de l'Ancien Testament", *Epektasis. Mélanges patristiques offerts au Cardinal Jean Daniélou* (Paris: Beauchesne 1972) 247–261 (= *Etudes d'Histoire du Texte*; OBO 21; Fribourg/Göttingen 1978, 203–217) 258 (214).

38 Bardy, Les traditions (1925) 229.

39 See L. L. Grabbe, *Etymology in Early Jewish Interpretation. The Hebrew Names in Philo* (Brown Judaic Studies 115; Atlanta, GA: Scholars Press 1988) 151f.

40 See the cautious discussion by de Lange, Origen (1976) 123–132.

reconstruct the 'Jewish-Christian dialogue' of this period.[41] As a matter of fact, one can easily understand a number of interpretations as reactions against positions of the other side, but in concrete details one can hardly prove direct dependence of one text on the other.[42] The basic idea shared by both sides that Canticles is to be understood as a dialogue between God and his chosen people, may explain certain (possibly polemical) emphases in the commentaries without having to postulate a direct disputation.

Following W. Bacher's suggestion that Origen may have stirred the interest of Jews at Caesarea like R. Hoshaya in Philo's work, D. Barthélemy went so far as to propose that it was R. Hoshaya who censured Philo's Allegorical Commentary.[43] Such evidence for a Jewish reaction to Origen's work would be most welcome, but remains very doubtful. Nor is there any other uncontestable evidence for a reaction of this kind. It is always easier to prove Christian dependence on Jewish exegesis than the other way round.

N. R. M. de Lange states about Origen: "In general it may be assumed that the Tannaitic literature as a whole was available to him, and in a fuller form than that in which it has come down to us". This statement goes beyond the limits of what can be demonstrated, but one can fully agree with de Lange "that, even granted a good deal of scepticism, there is enough evidence to prove that Origen does preserve aggadic material not found in earlier Greek sources".[44] No Christian exegete before Origen has made so much use of Jewish exegetical methods and tradition.

Although in the time of *Eusebius* the rabbinic school of Caesarea still continued to thrive, and Eusebius considered Origen as his teacher, his contacts with Jews seem to have been much more limited, something which may be due to the changed position of the Christian Church. S. Krauss thinks: "Though there is no clear statement to that effect, we may confidently assume that Eusebius enjoyed direct intercourse with Jews ... It will also clearly appear ... that Eusebius had a Jewish teacher".[45] M. J. Hollerich is equally confident that Eusebius "may have been influenced by discussion with Jewish exegetes ... whom elsewhere in the commentary [on Isaiah] he admits to have consulted":[46]

---

[41] E. E. Urbach, "Rabbinic Exegesis and Origenes. Commentaries on the Song of Songs and Jewish-Christian Polemics", *Studia Hierosolymitana* 22 (1971) 247–275. R. Kimelman, "Rabbi Yoḥanan and Origen on the Song of Songs: A Third-Century Jewish-Christian Disputation", *HTR* 73 (1980), 567–595, took up this argument and identified R. Yoḥanan bar Nappaha as the man who answered Origen. See also F. Manns, "Une tradition juive dans les commentaires du Cantique des Cantiques d'Origène", *Anton.* 65 (1990) 3–22.

[42] See Maier, Jüdische Auseinandersetzung (1982) 193.

[43] D. Barthélemy, "Est-ce Hoshaya Rabba qui censura le 'Commentaire Allégorique'?", *Philon d'Alexandrie*. Lyon 11–15 septembre 1966 (Editions du CNRS; Paris 1967, 45–78) 69f (= Etudes [1978] 140–173, 164f); but see also the cautious formulation at the end of the essay: "Ces quelques coïncidences ... ne nous permettent pas de donner au retoucheur le nom de R. Hoshaya Rabba, mais du moins elle nous confirment que le milieu juif de Césarée offrait à l' époque d'Origène un 'Sitz im Leben' idéal pour le travail de ce retoucheur de l'édition du Commentaire Allégorique" (76 = 171).

[44] de Lange, Origen (1976) 8,131f.

[45] Krauss, The Jews (1894) 83.

[46] M. J. Hollerich, "Eusebius as a Polemical Interpreter of Scripture", Eusebius, Christianity, and Judaism (1992) 585–615, 605 f.

Eusebius was quite willing to use Jewish exegetical expertise when other resources were lacking. His chief sources for this were probably the works of Josephus and personal contacts in the flourishing Jewish community of Caesarea. On a couple of occasions he mentions a Hebrew teacher who examined passages with him. Origen may also have been a mediator of Jewish lore, but none of the interpretations in the Commentary on Isaiah which appeal to Jewish authorities can be shown to have come from him.[47]

The examples given by the two scholars are not as clear as one might wish. According to the Commentary on Isa 39:1–2 (GCS 9,245) ὁ τῶν Ἰουδαίων διδάσκαλος ἔλεγεν that Hezekiah's illness was a punishment for not having chanted a song of praise to God for Sanherib's fall (Josephus, *Ant.* 20.24 adds to the biblical text that Hezekiah *did* offer sacrifices of thanksgiving to God after his deliverance; this shows that he, too, expected Hezekiah to thank God at this point of the account). This interpretation is certainly Jewish although the precise version is to be found only in a late text.[48] But Eusebius does not say that this Jew was *his* teacher nor that he himself had heard him giving this interpretation.

Another text which Hollerich considers an excellent example of Eusebius' use of Jewish exegesis, is his interpretation of Isa 7:8 (GCS 9, 46 f):[49] Ephraim will be destroyed in 65 years; if the prophecy was uttered during the reign of Ahaz, this would be chronologically impossible. "The children of Israel say" (φάσιν Ἑβραίων παῖδες) that one arrives at exactly this number when starting the count in the 25th year of the reign of Uzziah. In this year, two years before the earthquake (Amos 1:1), the prophecy was uttered (Amos 7:11,17). Sixty-Five years later, in the sixth year of Hezekiah's reign (2 Kgs 18:10), Samaria fell. Eusebius had already dealt with the problem before (*Dem.* 6.18.36, GCS 6, 281) where he attributed his solution to Josephus with his precise knowledge of δευτερώσεις (*Ant.* 9.222–7), but only now could he offer a detailed solution. Hollerich sees the same chronological scheme in *S. ʿOlam* 20, but has to concede that Eusebius did not use this source uncritically. As a matter of fact, the text does not really correspond to Eusebius' solution; there is no question of the 65 years; *S. ʿOlam* 28, end, would be more relevant, but again does not offer the same count as Eusebius. Does Eusebius with his distinction between Jews and Hebrews really refer to contemporary Jewish informants as Ἑβραίων παῖδες (quoted also in the Commentary on Isa 30:1–5, GCS 9, 194; 30:30–31, p. 202; 36:1–10, p. 232)? The case of Isa 7:8 is not convincing. There certainly are points of contact between Eusebius' exegesis and rabbinic literature; but they are comparatively few and not clear evidence of his personal contacts with contemporary Jews.

In the case of *Jerome* who from 386 until his death in 420 lived in the Holy Land, our documentation is much better. He himself writes extensively about his efforts to master the Hebrew language and to gather all Jewish information which might be of use in the translation and interpretation of the Bible; he also frequently refers to his Jewish teachers and even gets into a contro-

[47] Hollerich, Eusebius 607.
[48] See the sources in Krauss, The Jews (1894) 84 f.
[49] Hollerich, Eusebius (1992) 607f.

versy with his former friend Rufinus who accused him of relying too much on Jews, "enumerans doctores suos, quos se de synagoga esset mercatum ... Barabban eius de synagoga magistrum" (*Apol. c. Hier.* 2.15, CChr 20, 94f). Jerome in his answer complains that Rufinus changed the name of his teacher Baranina to Barabbas, and refers to his predecessors:

> Ipse Origenes et Eusebius et Clemens aliique conplures, quando de Scriptura aliqua disputant et uolunt approbare quod dicunt, sic solent scribere: 'Referebat mihi Hebraeus'; et: 'Audiui ab Hebraeo'; et: 'Hebraeorum ista sententia est'. Certe Origenes ... nec dedignatur, hebraeam Scripturam interpretans, per singula loca quid de Hebraeis uideatur, inserere (*Apol. c. Rufinum* I.13, CChr 79, 12f).

In many details Jerome's translation of the OT reflects Jewish exegetical traditions.[50] In his biblical commentaries, Jerome frequently quotes Jewish interpretations, many of which have parallels in rabbinic writings. M. Rahmer and others collected Jerome's Jewish exegeses without examining Jerome's exact sources. A closer analysis, however, shows that Jerome's claims are not always to be taken literally. G. Bardy has already demonstrated that many of the interpretations which Jerome claims to have heard from his Jewish teachers, in reality were copied from Origen, Eusebius and other authors.[51] Others have doubted the extent of Jerome's knowledge of Hebrew.[52] P. Nautin even goes so far as to state that Jerome

> diese Sprache praktisch kaum kannte. Wenn immer er in seinen Kommentaren oder anderen Werken den transkribierten hebräischen Text zitiert – und das tut er oft – oder Anmerkungen zur hebräischen Sprache macht, verdankt er die jeweilige Information seinen Quellen ...; sobald er sich jedoch von seinen Quellen entfernt, ist alles reine Erfindung.[53]

This scepticism is certainly exaggerated;[54] Jerome's knowledge of Hebrew was considerable, although not as solid as he sometimes claimed. He himself once confessed: "Hebraeam linguam ... multo labore ac sudore ex parte didici et infatigabili meditatione non desero, ne ipse ab ea deserar" (*Ep.* 108.26, CSEL 55, 344f). He probably could not speak Hebrew and used Greek when discussing with his Jewish informants. In the prologue to the book of Tobit 6 (PL 29,25f) he claims that somebody, a very experienced speaker of both Hebrew and Chaldaic (Aramaic or Syriac?) translated for him the Chaldaic text into Hebrew: "et quidquid ille mihi Hebraicis verbis expressit, hoc ego, accito notario, sermonibus Latinis exposui". Why should the translator have made the detour via Hebrew? We may certainly doubt whether Jerome could directly translate the Hebrew text he heard.[55]

---

50 Kedar, The Latin Translations (1988) 331–34.

51 G. Bardy, "Saint Jérôme et ses maîtres hébreux", *RBén* 46 (1934) 145–164. For a recent summary (with bibliography) see S. Rebenich, "Jerome: The 'Vir Trilinguis' and the 'Hebraica Veritas'", *VC* 47 (1993) 50–77, who speaks of "Jerome's carefully disguised plagiarism" (55).

52 J. Barr, "St. Jerome's Appreciation of Hebrew", *BJRL* 49 (1966/67) 281–302; idem, "Jerome and the Sounds of Hebrew", *JSS* 12 (1967) 1–36.

53 P. Nautin, "Hieronymus", TRE 15 (1986) 304–315, 309.

54 See the very positive evaluation of Jerome's expertise in Hebrew by Kedar, The Latin Translations (1988) 315–318.

55 But see Kedar, ibid. 318, who regards mistakes based on a confusion of gutturals in Hebrew as a proof that Jerome translated directly what was read to him; "this kind of error, paradoxically, constitutes additional proof of Jerome's expertise".

During his decades in Palestine, Jerome hardly ever left the region of Bethlehem/Jerusalem where—officially at least—Jews were not allowed to reside. The occasions where Jerome could contact Jews (not Jewish Christians) were thus severely limited. Members of the rabbinic establishment were principally opposed to teaching non-Jews the oral Torah. Jerome gives no names of his Jewish teachers except the already mentioned Baranina who for fear of the Jews taught him in the night and thus became for him another Nicodemus (*Ep.* 84.3, CSEL 55,123). The comparison with Nicodemus might indicate that he was a convert to Christianity. In other cases, too, the Jewish teachers to whom Jerome refers, may have been baptized Jews; even the teacher from Tiberias whom Jerome mentions in the preface to Chronicles, "legis quondam doctorem, qui apud Hebraeos admirationi habebatur" (PL 29,423), may have been a former Jew. Another source of information may have been Judaizing Christians who frequented the synagogues.

As to Hebrew or Aramaic books which Jerome claims to have read, one has again to be very cautious. In *Ep.* 36.1 (CSEL 54,268) Jerome describes how a Jew in Rome brought him "non pauca uolumina quae de synagoga quasi lecturus acceperat". J. Braverman, following S. Krauss, thinks that these books "certainly were not books of the Hebrew Bible, for these he already had. They were most probably certain midrashim".[56] One may doubt whether a Roman synagogue in the late fourth century possessed Hebrew books (Hebrew was hardly known in the Western Diaspora) and whether Jerome in those years (382–85) knew already enough Hebrew to use such manuscripts; there is no evidence that midrashim were known in the Diaspora. Jerome himself does not claim that the books were Hebrew. During his long stay in Palestine he certainly had more possibilities to acquire or to copy Hebrew manuscripts; he explicitly mentions a Hebrew gospel of the Nazareans (PL 23,643); if he had access to Jewish non-biblical manuscripts, we do not know.[57]

There is no doubt that Jerome was very well acquainted with Jewish exegetical traditions; we know much less about the exact sources of his knowledge. The role of Jewish or Judaizing Christians may have been greater than that of educated Jews, not to speak of Rabbis with whom Jerome probably had no contacts at all. In spite of a vast literature on Jerome and the Jews, an in-depth analysis of Jerome's Jewish traditions still remains a desideratum.

8. Syria

It is sometimes suggested that the Antiochene school of exegesis with its insistence on the literal meaning of the biblical text is particularly indebted to Jewish exegetical tradition. The co-existence of an important Jewish com-

[56] J. Braverman, *Jerome's Commentary on Daniel: A Study of Comparative Jewish and Christian Interpretations of the Hebrew Bible* (CBQMS 7; Washington DC 1978) 8.

[57] See G. Stemberger, "Hieronymus und die Juden seiner Zeit", *Begegnungen zwischen Christentum und Judentum in Antike und Mittelalter* (FS H. Schreckenberg, ed. D.-A. Koch / H. Lichtenberger; Göttingen: Vandenhoeck & Ruprecht 1993) 347–364, 351 f, 358 f.

munity at Antioch with an ancient Christian Church seems to favour this possibility. But it oversimplifies a much more complex situation: rabbinic exegesis is not exclusively 'literal', as the Church Fathers frequently claimed (the dead letter against the vivifying spirit of Christian understanding); nor are the Antiochenes with their fondness of typology exclusively literalists. B. L. VISOTZKY rightly observes:

> It is tempting to simply identify the Akiban method with the Alexandrian and then to group Yishmael with the literalist Antiochenes. This is much too simple, however. In real, physical terms, rabbinic tradition records Akiba visiting Antioch and Yishmael in dialogue with the Alexandrians ... the Antiochenes and Alexandrians agreed on more matters than they disagreed regarding scriptural interpretation. And the rabbis weren't so tidily divided into isolated schools.[58]

Theodore of Mopsuestia, John Chrysostom and above all Theodoret of Cyrrhus do know Jewish exegetical traditions, but not as many as their possible contacts with Jews might lead us to expect. A much richer harvest of common traditions can be gathered from Syriac texts where, however, the biblical text of the Peshitta already offers many points of contact with Jewish tradition. It is often very difficult to ascertain whether such contacts are due to an exchange with Jewish teachers of the period, or are caused by the biblical text, similar mentality and comparable modes of interpretation.

The recent discussion about Jewish influences on *Aphrahat*'s exegesis is typical in this regard. Since S. FUNK it has been a commonplace how much Aphrahat depended on Jewish exegesis.[59] J. NEUSNER, on the other side, completely denied Aphrahat's contacts with contemporary rabbinic Judaism:

> When we find instances in which Aphrahat and rabbis held in common certain views of religion and ethics, we had best look for common exegetical traditions, on the one hand, or a common cultural and conceptual framework of reference, on the other ... Indeed, if we compare the parallel comments on Scriptures with the substantially larger numbers of comments which are not parallel at all, and which stand in no polemical or exegetical relationship ... we can conclude only one thing. Aphrahat and the rabbis had practically nothing in common, other than they lived in a single cultural continuum and believed in the same revelation.[60]

M.-J. PIERRE reacted against NEUSNER, stating apodictically: "L'influence juive sur Aphraate n'est plus à demontrer".[61] P. BRUNS steers a middle course: "Die Konvergenzen in der Exegese zwischen den Rabbinen und den syrischen Kirchenvätern resultieren aus dem breiten Strom mündlicher Überlieferung, der in die Peschitta und in die aramäischen Targume eingeflossen ist".[62] These basic differences of opinion demonstrate how difficult it is to evaluate exegetical contacts, and what in a common cultural and linguistic milieu constitutes meaningful parallels.

---

[58] B. L. VISOTZKY, "Jots and Tittles: On Scriptural Interpretation in Rabbinic and Patristic Literatures", *Prooftexts* 8 (1988) 257–269, 262.

[59] S. FUNK, *Die haggadischen Elemente in den Homilien des persischen Weisen* (Wien 1891).

[60] Neusner, Aphrahat (1971) 187 f.

[61] M.-J. PIERRE, *Aphrahat le Sage Persan. Les Exposés* (SC 349; Paris 1988) 112. Even if Aphrahat never mentions halakhic details beyond what is known from Scripture, his terminology and hermeneutics show his knowledge of traditional Jewish procedures in textual analysis (119 f).

[62] P. BRUNS, *Aphrahat. Unterweisungen* (FontC 5/1; Freiburg: Herder 1991) 56.

In the case of Aphrahat's younger contemporary, *Ephrem*, we are confronted with similar problems. Since D. GERSON's initial studies, many scholars have pointed out parallels between Ephrem and rabbinic exegesis.[63] T. KRONHOLM summarizes the scholarly consensus:

> the exegetical influence of fundamental significance to Ephrem was that of Jewish tradition, ironically, as it seems, in view of his fierce anti-Jewish bias ... the question of whether the contact between Ephrem and the Rabbis was immediate or indirect seems to be impossible to answer. Nonetheless, parallels to Jewish Midrashic approach, hermeneutical practice, and above all Haggadic features are discernible in almost every phase of Ephrem's works dealing with OT themes.[64]

As KRONHOLM himself points out, "the influence of Jewish Haggadah on the exegesis of Ephrem's hymns in no case can be called a literary one". Ephrem's haggadah is closest to that embedded in *Pirqe R. Eliezer* and, among the Targumim, Pseudo-Jonathan, although both are much younger than Ephrem's work.[65] The same could be said of other Christian works in Syriac, like the Cave of Treasures (6th c., but earlier sources), certainly the richest source for Jewish traditions. It is extremely difficult to offer concrete evidence for direct dependence on Jewish sources or personal Jewish contacts (with what kind of Jews?) as a source of exegetical information. We still lack methodological criteria for how to evaluate 'parallels'. It may not be very satisfactory, but is certainly on the safer side, to explain most details in common between Jewish tradition and Christian exegesis by an appeal to the common heritage and cultural environment.

9. The Latin West

Here we may be very brief since a priori there are not many exegetical contacts to be expected; the Christian exegetical tradition in the West started rather late, and the Jewish communities of the West seem not to have known very much about the rabbinic developments.

There have been claims that *Tertullian* was acquainted with the rabbinic exegesis of some Psalms and with halakhic and haggadic material in general;[66] others have rightly been much more reticent.[67] In *Cyprian*'s writings, too, we do not find any real evidence of a dialogue between Christians and Jews in Carthage.[68] *Augustine*'s exegetical writings also do not offer points of contacts with Jewish exegetical traditions.

---

[63] D. GERSON, "Die Commentarien des Ephraem Syrus im Verhältnis zur jüdischen Exegese", *MGWJ* 17 (1868) 15–33, 64–72, 98–109, 141–152.

[64] T. KRONHOLM, *Motifs from Genesis 1–11 in the Genuine Hymns of Ephrem the Syrian with particular reference to the influence of Jewish exegetical tradition* (ConBOT 11; Lund: Gleerup 1978) 27.

[65] Kronholm, Motifs (1978) 222, 224.

[66] See C. AZIZA, *Tertullien et le Judaïsme* (Publications de la Faculté des Lettres et des Sciences Humaines de Nice 16; Nice: les belles lettres 1977) 195–224, who certainly exaggerates Tertullian's knowledge of Judaism.

[67] See the good summary by MacLennan, Early Christian Texts (1990) 117–144.

[68] C. A. BOBERTZ, "'For the Vineyard of the Lord of Hosts was the House of Israel'. Cyprian of Carthage and the Jews", *JQR* 82 (1991/92) 1–15, p. 15.

More interesting is the case of the so-called *Ambrosiaster* in the late 4th century. His identification with the former Jew Isaac, the accuser of Pope Damasus, is no longer maintained. He seems to know contemporary Judaism very well;[69] but his discussion of biblical texts in Quaestio 44 (*Adv. Judaeos*) of his *Quaestiones Veteris et Novi Testamenti* CXXVII (CSEL 50, 71–81) does not betray any knowledge of Jewish exegetical traditions. *Apponius*, author of a commentary on the Song of Songs in the 5th century, has been thought to be a former Jew;[70] but there is no real evidence and the interpretation does not reveal any contacts with Jewish exegesis of the period.

Later Christian writers who reveal some knowledge of Jewish interpretation, as Gregory the Great or Isidore of Sevilla, normally depend on Jerome. "The Church Fathers who lived after Jerome knew less and less about Judaism, so that the history of the later periods is no longer of any interest in this connection".[71]

---

[69] A. Stuiber, "Ambrosiaster", TRE 2 (1978) 356–62.
[70] G. Gerleman, *Ruth. Das Hohelied* (BKAT 18; Neukirchen-Vluyn: Neukirchener 1965) 44f.
[71] Krauss, Church Fathers (1893) 83.

Chapter sixteen

The Interpretative Character of the Syriac Old Testament

By Michael Weitzman, London
(University College)

Sources: A new edition reporting the manuscript evidence is *Vetus Testamentum Syriace: The Old Testament in Syriac* (ed. by the Peshitta Institute; Leiden 1972–). For the moment the most accessible complete edition is *Vetus Testamentum Syriace* (ed. S. Lee; London 1823; often reprinted).

Bibliography: P. B. Dirksen, *An Annotated Bibliography of the Peshiṭta Old Testament* (Leiden 1989).

General works: J. Perles, *Meletemata Peschitthoniana* (Breslau 1859); L. Haefeli, *Die Peschitta des Alten Testamentes* (Munich 1927); Cl. van Puyvelde, "Versions syriaques", DBSup 6 (1960) 835–855; S.P. Brock, "Bibelübersetzungen, I. 4. Die Uebersetzungen ins Syrische, 4.1.1. Peschitta", TRE 6 (1980) 182–189; P.B. Dirksen, "The Old Testament Peshitta", *Mikra* (ed. M.J. Mulder; CRINT II/1; Assen 1988) 255–297; idem, *La Peshitta dell' Antico Testamento* (Padua 1993).

Special abbreviations: Gelston = A. Gelston, *The Peshiṭta of the Twelve Prophets* (Oxford 1987). *Symp.* = P.B. Dirksen/M.J. Mulder (eds.), *The Peshiṭta: Its Early Text and History* (Leiden 1988).

1. Introduction

Syriac is the Aramaic dialect of Edessa (modern Urfa, in south-east Turkey) and its province Osrhoene. Edessa was, at least from the late second century, a centre of Christianity, from which the new faith spread, through the medium of the Syriac language, over Mesopotamia and the Iranian plateau. The Syriac version of the Hebrew Bible – known since the ninth century as the Peshitta (here: P) – became the Bible of the Syriac-speaking church, which was divided by the controversies of the fifth century. It has been preserved by the Church of the East ('Nestorian') in Iraq and further east, by the Syrian Orthodox ('Jacobite') Church in Turkey and Syria, and (from the seventh century) by the Maronite Church in Lebanon. Until the late Middle Ages P was also the Bible of the Byzantine Syrian ('Malkite') Church in Syria and Palestine, long after Arabic had begun to encroach as the sacred language of that church.

While transmitted by the Church exclusively,[1] P was made from a Hebrew

[1] There was some Jewish scholarly interest during the Middle Ages. In the 13th century,

original, and its religious context has long been debated (see sect. 5 below). Edessa is the likeliest place of origin,[2] and references to neighbouring places are occasionally introduced (see sect. 9). One clue to the date of P is that it is quoted widely by the fourth century fathers Afrahat (who even quotes Dan 9:1–27 in full)[3] and Ephrem (who found it necessary to explain some words already obsolete). On the other hand, P uses future forms of the type *nqbr*, rather than the usual Semitic *yqbr*, which survives in Edessene inscriptions until the late second century.[4] Hence a date in the second or third centuries is usually supposed.[5] Native traditions, however, hold that this version was made for Solomon by Hiram of Tyre, or alternatively for the first Samaritans by a priest called Asa, or for Abgar king of Edessa (supposedly a contemporary of Christ) by the apostle Addai.[6]

The name Peshitta (Syriac: *pšiṭtā*) means 'simple'. According to Barhebraeus, the name indicates P's "rejection of ornate language" (*tark al-balāġat*).[7] The name is first attested in the Hexaemeron of Moses bar Kepha (ca. 813–903), to distinguish this from the more literal and hence cumbersome Syrohexaplar version (based on LXX) produced in 615–617 CE. The same name is applied to the standard Syriac version of the New Testament, in contrast with the more literal Harklean version likewise produced in the seventh century.[8] The etymological sequence /ṭt/ in the name is not tolerated in pronunciation, which would be Pshittā in the east and Pshito in the west.[9]

2. Construal and Interpretation

Not all translation is interpretation. In principle, to put a simple biblical passage from Hebrew into Syriac could be a straightforward linguistic exercise. Interpretation will therefore be defined here as the difference between the plain sense which the translator perceived in his Hebrew *Vorlage* and the

---

Joseph b. Nissim Masnut of Aleppo cites P as an "Aramaic targum" in his extant biblical commentaries, and Nachmanides cites P on Wisdom and Judith in his comments on Gen 1:1 and Deut 21:14 respectively. On these see M. P. WEITZMAN, "Peshitta, Septuagint and Targum", OCA 247 (1994) 51–84.

[2] A. VAN DER KOOIJ, *Die alten Textzeugen des Jesajabuches* (Göttingen 1981) 292. The influential theory of an origin in Adiabene, argued by P. E. KAHLE, *The Cairo Geniza* (Oxford ²1959) 272–73, involves the suspect assumption that P derives from the Palestinian targum tradition.

[3] J. PARISOT (ed.), *Aphraatis Sapientis Persae Demonstrationes*, PS (Paris 1894–1907) I/1, 872–882.

[4] H. J. W. DRIJVERS, *Old-Syriac (Edessean) Inscriptions* (Leiden 1972) 18.

[5] Dirksen, Peshitta (1988) 259, 295.

[6] Barhebraeus (1226–1286) cites all three traditions; see M. SPRENGLING/W. C. GRAHAM (eds.), *Barhebraeus' Scholia on the Old Testament* (Chicago 1931) 26. Išoʿdad (ca. 850), who appreciated that some books of the Hebrew Bible were later than Solomon, ascribed these to Abgar's day and the rest to Solomon's. See J. M. VOSTÉ/C. VAN DEN EYNDE (eds.), *Commentaire d'Išoʿdad de Merv sur l'Ancien Testament* I. *Genèse* (CSCO 126 [text] and 156 [French transl.]; Louvain 1950 and 1955), text p. 3 and translation p. 4 (with n. 1).

[7] Arabic text cited in N. WISEMAN, *Horae Syriacae* (Rome 1828) 92.

[8] Syriac text with French translation cited in J. P. P. MARTIN, *Introduction à la Critique Textuelle du Nouveau Testament: Partie Théorique* (Paris [1883]) 100.

[9] See the exchange between E. NESTLE and E. KÖNIG in *ZDMG* 47 (1893) 156–59, 316–19.

sense of what he wrote down in Syriac. The concept of plain sense is intuitively valid, if not easily defined.

The process of deriving the plain sense may be called construal. At any point in the text, the first step was to locate in the *Vorlage* the phrase to be translated and physically to perceive it. The constant need to switch between the *Vorlage* and the translation being made may have caused errors here. The conscious stages which followed sometimes required considerable mental effort. The *Vorlage* was unpointed, and unlikely to have been accompanied by a reading tradition; for example at Deut 1:44, where MT rightly vocalises the consonants תעשינה as *taʿăśenā* ('do'), P instead vocalised as *tĕʿušannā* ('are smoked'). Most words in the consonantal text were thus patient of more than one meaning. The translator had to consider the overall sense of a phrase and at the same time the meaning of each constituent word. When he arrived at the plain sense, he had construed the phrase but not yet begun to interpret it.

The translator's idea of the plain sense will usually coincide with that of modern scholars, but not always. The construal of the plain sense involves identifying the Hebrew lexical item(s) present in the sequence of consonants read, and the basic meanings of those lexical items. There are passages where modern scholarship would not accept those identifications, but the translators may still have been following what for them was the plain sense (see sect. 7 below).

The need for the translator to consider whole phrases means that cases of interpretation fall under two headings. The first case is where the translator was satisfied that he understood the plain sense of the whole phrase but went beyond that plain sense. The motive may be, for example, to convey explicitly something left implicit in the Hebrew, or to accomodate some external constraint (sect. 3 below). The second case of interpretation is where the translator could find no satisfactory plain sense for the whole phrase. The impediment may have been ignorance of Hebrew (or even of biblical Aramaic) or textual corruption or physical damage in the *Vorlage*. Here interpretation can still be defined as the gap between whatever plain sense the translator recognised and his final translation. That plain sense, however, will be incomplete or unsatisfactory, so that interpretation will involve guesswork or recourse to alternative sources (sect. 4). Passages of particular theological significance, whether or not the translator had identified a satisfactory plain sense, are discussed separately (in the sections 5–6), given the importance of the question of theological context.

In all this there is the fundamental problem that we cannot be certain either of the starting-point or of the end-point of the interpretation stage. The starting-point, namely the plain sense perceived by the translator, depends on the text of his *Vorlage*, his knowledge of the Hebrew language, and his skill in applying the latter to the former, none of which is known to us *a priori*. Likewise the end-point, namely the original sense of the translation, depends on the original text of P. This needs to be reconstructed from the extant manuscripts, which sometimes disagree;[10] moreover, even unanimous readings

---

[10] In particular, the truth sometimes survives in one manuscript only; see M.P. Weitzman, "The Originality of Unique Readings in Peshiṭta Ms 9a1" in *Symp.* 225–258.

may be affected by inner-Syriac corruption or deliberate revision. Differences between P and the plain sense found by modern scholarship in MT that are due to such factors, which are anterior or subsequent to interpretation, are examined in sections 7–8. Any discussion of the interpretative character of P has to acknowledge that we do not possess with accuracy either the Hebrew text translated or the original work of the translators.

3. Text Believed to have been Understood

The drive for clarity

P often selects a more specific word than MT, albeit on the basis of information implied by the Hebrew. Thus Balak's servants (Num 22:18) become 'messengers'. The threat הדמין תתעבדון (Dan 2:5) is spelt out: "you will be cut limb from limb". The translators often replace the colourless verb היה, e. g. at Gen 13:13 (*nqš*), Isa 7:24 (*etmlī*). This striving for precision means that a Hebrew word may be differently rendered in different passages according to nuance. Thus in Gen 22:5, where MT uses נער both of the Abraham's servants and of Isaac, P has *ʿlaymā* and *ṭalyā* respectively. More generally, דבר tends to be rendered by *petgāmā* to indicate 'thing, matter' or a divine word (especially law or prophecy), but by *meltā* for human utterances.

P's word selection may be dictated by the wish to avoid ambiguity. Thus in Josh 2, the translator renders רדף not by its Syriac cognate (which could also mean 'persecute') but by *npq bātar* (though from Josh 7:5 he becomes resigned to using Syr. *rdp*). Many books avoid Syr. *gli* 'go into exile' (since the root may also mean 'reveal') and substitute *eštbi* 'be captured' (even at Ezek 12:3).

Where the Hebrew is elliptic, P makes insertions based on the context to obtain acceptable syntax. Examples are 1 Sam 20:12 "may the Lord God of Israel *testify*", 1 Kgs 6:6 "*and he made* the arcade", Prov 31:1 "*who received* prophecy". Other additions are required for understanding, e. g. at Gen 36:6 "to the land of *Seir*", Exod 4:24 "and *Moses* was on the way". Tantamount to addition is the explication of pronouns, which is very frequent, e. g. Isa 44:9 "the craftsmen who make them" (MT המה), Job 3:1 "the day that he was born" (MT יומו). More subtly, P inserts the Syriac enclitic particles to indicate emphasis. Thus at Deut 32:27 P highlights the phrases "our hand" [*īdan (h)ū*] and "not the Lord" [*w-lā (h)wā māryā*]. In particular, P makes additions to identify speakers or addressees (e. g. Exod 3:12 'the Lord to him') or the onset of direct speech (e. g. 2 Sam 18:23; Job 27:10 c). Some expansions, however, seem almost superfluous, e. g. Lev 24:23 "and they stoned him *and he died*". Here we may also note the tendency to provide names with their standard epithets, e. g. Eleazar *the priest* (Josh 24:33), Ezra *the scribe* (Ezra 7:25), and indeed the Lord *thy God* (Deut 6:18).

Again for clarity's sake the translators often resolve metaphors. Thus at Gen 44:31 קשורה בנפשו becomes "beloved as himself". At Ezra 9:8 יתד is explained as *duktā* 'place'. Less often a metaphor is replaced by a commoner alternative; thus at Job 40:11 wrath is poured out rather than scattered.

The drive for logic

Sometimes the translator makes radical changes to improve the perceived logic within the verse. At Ps 1:1, for example, P inverts the nouns and so blesses the man who "has not walked in the *way* of the wicked nor stood in the *counsel* of sinners", to accord better with the verbs. At Isa 44:16–17, the Hebrew states that the idolator uses half his wood for warmth, half for cooking and the rest to make an idol; P corrects the arithmetic by substituting "its coals" for the second "half".

On other occasions the translators strove for a logical relationship with outside passages. Thus the name of Ishmael's daughter who married Esau is changed at Gen 28:9 from Maḥalat to Bāsmat to agree with Gen 36:3. Whereas Deuteronomy speaks of priests and Levites in apposition, P names them separately with a suitable conjunction ('and', 'or'), e.g. at Deut 17:9; 18:1. At 1 Sam 16:19, P removes אשר בצאן in Saul's reference to David, as Saul did not yet know this detail, and instead makes Saul say that David is "useful to me".

For the sake of the perceived logic the translators might even add a negative (e.g. Gen 41:54; Lev 25:35; Deut 29:11; 33:29; Josh 10:20; 1 Sam 17:39; Mal 2:16; Ps 68:19) or omit it (Deut 20:19; Josh 11:13; 17:17; 22:20; 2 Sam 23:5; Ps 37:33; Ruth 2:13; Dan 11:18). This technique of converse translation has been noted in the Targums by KLEIN.[11]

More generally, the translators often felt free to improve on the Hebrew. At Num 10:33 P decided that the ark would better guide the Israelites if placed one day's journey ahead, rather than three as in MT. P also levels the wording between passages, e.g. at Lev 23:26 inserting "speak to the children of Israel" as in the other section of that chapter. Sometimes P dramatises the text, e.g. at Ruth 3:3 rendering ושמת שמלתיך as: "*adorn thyself in* thy garments" or at Dan 2:24 כל קבל דנה as: "at that very hour". The omission of Psalm titles seems due to the same radical attitude.[12]

In some passages it is limited linguistic knowledge that has made the translator feel the need to improve the text. At 1 Sam 2:13 the Hebrew uses the definite article of an object not previously mentioned, where the priest's servant held המזלג שלש השנים. P did not know this biblical Hebrew usage, and, considering that the fork needed an earlier reference, prefaced the verse: "now they [the sons of Eli] had made themselves a three-pronged fork". At 1 Kgs 11:18 the translator missed the sense 'allocate' for אמר and so supplied direct speech: "Dwell with me!" In some other passages the translator made a slip and proceeded to correct the text accordingly. Thus at Josh 18:21–24 he sub-divided in error two of the twelve city-names, and so changed the total in v. 24 to fourteen. Such passages illustrate the radical treatment of

[11] M.L. KLEIN, "Converse Translation: A Targumic Technique", *Bibl.* 57 (1976) 515–537.

[12] W. BLOEMENDAAL, *The Headings of the Psalms in the East Syrian Church* (Leiden 1960).

which P was capable, and so support the view that the renderings noted in this section (3) indeed result from translation technique.

Factors external to the text

The translators may adjust the text to conditions in their own day. So Joshua dismisses the people to their cities rather than their tents (Josh 22:4–8). Burnished or yellowed bronze is called Corinthian, the most precious bronze of the age (1 Kgs 7:45; Ezra 8:27; 1 Chr 29:7).[13] The term שקל is sometimes modernised to *sal'ā* or *estērā* (stater), while גרה becomes *zūz*. "Mother's son" at Deut 13:7 is becoming "father's son" (cf. Lev 19:3; 21:2), as also in LXX. Other external factors are the translators' theology (see sect. 5), their Jewish exegetical heritage (sect. 6) and the political situation (sect. 9).

The linguistic fit between Hebrew and Syriac

Where the Hebrew seems redundant, the translators condense the text.[14] Parallelism caused particular problems, both because of redundance and because of the lack of Syriac equivalents for the synonyms utilised. Sometimes the translator omitted one of the parallel words or clauses – a tendency particularly noticeable in Ezekiel, where 33:5 is reduced to four words.

In some fields Hebrew is richer than Syriac in synonyms. Where the Hebrew uses two words, P may be content to repeat one, e.g. *ṭm'* for both שקץ and טמא at Lev 11:43. Where two synonyms are available in Syriac, the translators may eke them out by treating one as the 'A-word' and the other as the 'B-word'. If any of the Hebrew synonyms occurs alone, P tends to use the 'A-word'; if two Hebrew synonyms occur in a single verse, P tends to use the 'A-word' for the first and the 'B-word' for the second. Thus the Hebrew synonyms for 'anger' (e.g. אף זעם חמה קצף) are covered by *rugzā* ('A') and *ḥemtā* ('B'). Similarly the many Hebrew terms for 'lion' are rendered by *aryā* ('A') and *guryā d-aryā* ('B').

Some linguistic features in Hebrew have no Syriac counterpart. For example, Syriac until the late fourth century possessed no passive causative for strong verbs, so that Hophal forms in Hebrew and biblical Aramaic are regularly rendered by the simple stem (e.g. Job 7:3; Dan 5:13).[15] Adjectives tend to replace abstract nouns (e.g. for מטמני מסתרים at Isa 45:3) and verbs to replace other parts of speech (e.g. Isa 4:5; Am 3:11). Often the Hebrew infinitive absolute is ignored, as are various particles (e.g. אך, גם, נא). Sentences are linked with *waw*, notably in Lamentations.[16]

Hebrew interrogatives are seldom reproduced in P. The word הלוא introducing questions is often rendered by *hā* 'behold', or omitted, so that a

[13] D. M. Jacobson/M. P. Weitzman, "What was Corinthian Bronze?", *American Journal of Archaeology* 96 (1992) 237–247.

[14] Gelston, 133.

[15] C. Meehan, "*Qal/Pe'al* as the Passive of *Hif'il/Af'el* in Mishnaic Hebrew and Middle Aramaic", K. Jongeling/H. L. Murre-van den Berg/L. Van Rompay (eds.), *Studies in Hebrew and Aramaic Syntax* (FS J. Hoftijzer; Leiden 1991) 112–131.

[16] B. Albrektson, *Studies in the Text and Theology of the Book of Lamentations* (Lund 1963) 210–213.

positive statement results; sometimes the rendering is *lā*, but presumably intended as interrogative.[17] Positive sentences in question form are often rendered by negative statements, e.g. at Deut 20:19. The distinction between positive and negative questions is not always clear, so that the desired and undesired fasts of Isa 58:6 and 5 respectively are indistinguishable in P.

4. Text not Believed to have been Understood

Inferences from the existing Hebrew text

Where the translator knew the meaning of the words individually but made no satisfactory sense of them together, he might stretch the known meaning. For example at 2 Sam 23:7 ימלא ברזל is rendered "with iron one *gathers them*". At Jer 20:3, Pashhur's new name מגור מסביב becomes "sojourner and vagrant" (Syr. *ḥādōrā* 'one who goes about').

In the above cases, some semantic path between the Hebrew and the translation can be discerned. Some renderings, however, seem to have had no basis apart from fitting the immediate context. Thus at Num 4:13 *prq* 'dismantle' gave fair (but incorrect) sense for דשן; and at Am 6:11, the obscure nouns רסיסים ... בקיעים become the verbs *w-nar'li(ywhy)* ... *w-naṣde(ywhy)*, apparently through sheer guesswork.

In poetry, guesswork might be based on parallelism within the verse. Thus at Job 31:10 the translator missed the sexual reference in תטחן לאחר אשתי, rendering: "my wife milled for others"; hence the second clause ועליה יכרעון אחרין was guessed: "and she baked in another place". Less often the translator looked beyond the verse; thus at Gen 49:14 P renders משפתים as *šbile* after ארח in V. 17. In the wise woman's plea at 2 Sam 20:19, P did not find עיר ואם (להמית) satisfactory as it stood, and instead rendered *ṭalyā w-emeh* with a glance at the other wise woman of 2 Sam 14:6.[18]

Sometimes the translation arises from association with a similar sounding word in Syriac. Examples are:

Exod 13:4, MT האביב, P *habābe* 'flowers'
Deut 29:20, MT יעשן, P *ne'šan*
2 Kgs 11:6, MT מסח, P *men surḥānā*
Jer 23:19, MT סער, P *su'rānā* (but *'al'ālā* in the parallel 30:23)
Mi 2:8, MT אתמול, P *etmalli*
Job 6:9, MT וידכאני, P *wa-ndakkēn(y)* 'and cleanse me'

Even in the Aramaic portions of Ezra, P renders טעם by *ṭegmā* or *diyaṭegmā*, from Greek τάγμα. In some such cases it might conceivably be argued that P has not erred but recovered a forgotten Hebrew word by comparing the cognate Syriac language, but certainly not in all.

---

17 Gelston, 137.

18 R.P. Gordon, "The Variable Wisdom of Abel: the MT and Versions at 2 Samuel XX 18–19", *VT* 43 (1993) 215–226; 222.

Sometimes the translator did not catch any definite meaning, and uses a word of very general sense. At Deut 33:3 אשדת becomes *y(h)ab* "he gave". At Isa 10:18 כמסס נסס becomes: "as if he had never been". At Hab 1:4 מכתיר is rendered *dābar bīš bīš* "treats very badly".

Vague guesses often involve the use of a 'drudge word'. Probably the commonest root so used is *ʿšn*, including *ʿušnā* 'strength' and *ʿašīnā* 'strong', which renders not only the usual words denoting strength but also many words which the translators found difficult (at least in context), such as תועפות (Num 23:22), גור (Deut 32:27), עקב (Jer 17:9), חגוי (Obad 3), קדימה (Hab 1:9), הזכיר (Ps 20:8) and אפיק (Job 40:18). In some such cases in the Pentateuch Onkelos has the equivalent root *tqp*, as for דבא (Deut 33:25) and even the name זוזים (Gen 14:5). Another drudge word is *eṭṭarap* 'be buffetted, exhausted', representing מזי (Deut 32:24) and especially common in Jeremiah and Psalms. A drudge word over a limited stretch is *ettnīḥ*, serving within Psalms 35–39 for האח (35:25), רפה and עזב (37:8), שכן (37:27), נחת (38:3) and בלג (hi. 39:4). A variant of the drudge word technique appears in technical contexts. Thus the same sequence of three words (*qadsā*, *īrā*, *qardlā*) is used in lists of pots at Exod 27:3 = 38:3, 1 Sam 2:14; 1 Kgs 7:40, 45; 2 Kgs 25:14 = Jer 52:18, 2 Chr 35:13, whatever the specific Hebrew terms used.[19]

Use of alternative sources

There are numerous parallels with LXX in the Prophets (including Daniel), Psalms and the Solomonic books, and some in the Pentateuch. Of all the reasons suggested, the likeliest is that the translators themselves utilised LXX.[20] Jerome in the Vulgate likewise consulted LXX on occasion, as he states in his prologue to Qohelet: "sed de Hebraeo transferens, magis me Septuaginta Interpretum consuetudini coaptavi".[21] Job and the historical books, however, offer no convincing cases of LXX influence upon P.

The Prayer of Azariah and the Song of the Three have been incorporated from LXX into the P version of Daniel 3, as have various couplets in Proverbs (after 9:12, 18; 11:16a; 13:13; 14:22; 18:22; 22:10; 25:20; 27:21). At Jer 48:34, for MT עגלת שלישיה, P adds: "and up to the city of 'LS", an attempt to interpret the (corrupt) Lucianic variant αγγελ(ε)ιαν εις ελισαν. Sometimes, instead, Hebrew and Greek elements have been amalgamated. Thus at Mic 7:3–4 MT reads ויעבתוה טובם כחדק ישר ממסוכה, which P renders: "and they rejected their good like a patch which a moth devoured". P has adopted the first word (as if from תועבה), the second and the last (as 'covering'), but the devouring moth is due to LXX σῆς ἐκτρώγων.

---

[19] M.A. Zipor, "A Striking Translation Technique of the Peshiṭta", *JSS* 26 (1981) 11–20.

[20] A. Vogel, "Studien zum Pešiṭta-Psalter besonders im Hinblick auf sein Verhältnis zu Septuaginta", *Bibl.* 32 (1951) 32–56, 198–231, 336–363, 481–502, inclines cautiously towards positing LXX influence on copyists rather than the translator (p. 501). J. Lund, *The Influence of the Septuagint on the Peshitta: A Re-evaluation in light of Comparative Study of the Versions in Genesis and Psalms* (diss. Jerusalem 1988), argues against LXX influence altogether. See, however, the article cited in n. 1.

[21] PL xxiii, 1011–12.

Meanings apparently derived from LXX in one passage may be used in other passages also, even where LXX disagrees. For example, the rendering *zawgā* 'pair' (of garments) for חליפה originates at Gen 45:22a, where LXX has δισσὰς (στολάς), but re-appears in later passages where LXX renders otherwise (e.g. Gen 45:22b; Judg 14:12).

Other scriptural passages could also serve as alternative sources. At Job 36:20, עמים תחתם led the translator to adduce Isa 43:4a: "and he will give nations for thee and peoples for thyself". At Cant 8:11, המון 'multitude' in the context of a vineyard reminded the translator of Dan 4:9, so that בבעל המון becomes: "and its fruit was plentiful". Appeal to outside passages is especially common in Chronicles, where the *Vorlage* seems to have been damaged. Thus at 2 Chr 21:11 MT says that Jehoram made the Jerusalemites commit whoredom, while P instead says he made the Nazirites drink wine. This is sometimes explained as a euphemistic Midrash, but more probably the translator misread ויזן as ויין and drew on Am 2:12. On a larger scale, one long gap at 2 Chr 11:5–12:12 was filled by parallel material in 1 Kgs 12–14. Occasionally the translators seem to have thought of the Syriac rather than the Hebrew text of the outside passage. Thus at Jer 15:9, where MT has נפחה נפשה, P writes *nepḥat kersāh* "her belly has swollen", citing P's version of the law in Num 5:27.

Tacit change of the Hebrew text

Grammatical elements may be ignored or changed in order to yield sense. Thus at 2 Sam 7:23 גוים ואלהיו is rendered "the people whose God thou art". At Zeph 3:1, for MT העיר היונה, P ignores the definite articles and renders: "the city of Jonah" (referring to Nineveh). The word order may also be varied, e.g. Ps 16:11 בימינך נצח becoming "by the victory of thy right hand".

Sometimes the translator's wilful misreading of the *Vorlage* changes the lexical items. At Lev 26:16 and Deut 28:22, MT שחפת was treated as if it were ספחת 'scab', and so rendered (together with the following word קדחת) with terms from the leprosy laws *garbā w-qalpitā*. At Ezra 4:14, for MT מנדה בלו והלך, P renders: "There is no tribute for thee" (מנדה לא לך). Such instances are too numerous to be explained on the basis of a different *Vorlage*.[22]

Ch. Heller compared this technique to the rabbinic principle of Al-Tiqre, noting that some of P's 'misreadings' were paralleled in rabbinic sources, e.g. 1 Sam 9:23 והאליה for והעליה, Ps 49:10 קברם for קרבם. Again, the use of one passage to illuminate another is an established rabbinic principle. Heller adds that the Rabbis were aware that grammatical particles could be interchangeable or redundant, though this was first stated formally by Ibn Janāḥ (ca. 1000 CE). Hence Heller supposes that the translators of P were directly influenced by rabbinic exegetical methods.[23] This is a needless hypothesis,

[22] Some two hundred instances in the Psalter alone were collected by Vogel, Studien (1951) 208–213.

[23] Ch. Heller, *Untersuchungen über die Peschittâ zur gesamten hebräischen Bibel* (Berlin 1911).

however, since all these adjustments are natural for any interpreter of an obscure text.

Abdication of the translator's function

In some obscure passages the translators abdicate their function. They may translate literally and so pass on the obscurity of the original, as inevitably sometimes happens in Job. There are also instances elsewhere, e.g. at Jer 6:11: "and thou (f.) art filled with the wrath of the Lord, and weary. Measure and pour over children ...".[24] Alternatively, difficult words or phrases might simply be omitted, e.g. at Exod 34:19 תזכר, 1 Sam 9:24 לאמר העם קראתי, 1 Kgs 7:28 ומסגרת בין השלבים and Prov 19:7c. In Job a few particularly difficult lines or verses are omitted (29:6; 30:3–4; 38:25a; 41:21a, 22–24a) or compressed (39:3–4).[25] In Chronicles, several passages are omitted, presumably because they were illegible in the *Vorlage*, viz. 1 Chr 2:23, 47–49, 53–55; 4:7–8; 7:34–38; 8:17–23; 24:27–30; 25:5–6; 28:13–14; 2 Chr 3:9; 4:11–17, 19–22; 29:10–19.

Another device in Chronicles is free composition, when the translator had to construct the meaning of a passage on the basis of a few legible letters. At 1 Chr 12:23 we may reconstruct:

MT :	לעזרו עד למחנה גדול כמחנה אלהים
legible letters:	ל למח כ לה ם

Taking למח as לחם and filling the gaps, P rendered: "to (eat) bread (before them) f(or he loved) them (greatly)". Again, at 1 Chr 29:7 MT has ואדרכנים רבו. The translator, recognising the context of building the Temple, thought that he could discern the letters אנך as well as the numeral, and so renders: "and 200,000 measures of good lead (Syr. *ankā*) for the pipes".

Combination of devices

The translators were particularly taxed by long lists of unfamiliar words. In Daniel 3, the translator exhausts his general terms with the first three offices (*rabbay ḥaylā, mārawātā, šallīṭāne*) and transliterates the remaining four. In Isa 3:18–23 P has to render 21 items of ladies' finery. After two vague renderings ('clothes', 'ornament'), P attempts a logical progression, from four hairstyles (cf. LXX ἐμπλόκια for no. 2), through decorations of the temples and face, and a nose-ring, to four types of chain (cf. שירות earlier in the sequence) and eight types of robe. The robes are distinguished partly by colour, as in LXX but with differences in the order and the colours.

P sometimes shows a doublet, where the translator hesitated between two alternatives. Thus at Ruth 1:13 מר ... מכם is first rendered "bitter concerning you" and then "more bitter than you". Such cases are common in Job. Thus Job 24:10 is rendered twice, with עמר becoming first 'bread' and then 'measure' (*sa'tā w-kaylā*). Again, the description at 1 Chr 12:1 of David with his

---

[24] The construal is unusual (ואת as *wĕ-'at*, suffixes תי as 2sf and הכיל as imperative), but the translation is literal.

[25] See also Gelston, 147.

men as being עצור מפני שאול occasioned two translations: first, that he was fleeing from Saul (a guess from the general context); second, that he restrained his men from killing Saul (using the verb עצר and appealing to 1 Sam 24:8).

5. Theological Attitudes of the Translators

The translators seldom express their own theological concerns. For the most part they felt bound by the plain sense. In addition, they incorporate some rabbinic exegesis and many Aramaic renderings common to the Targums, so that attitudes and interpretations inherited from the broader Jewish milieu can be traced (see sect. 6). In this section, however, we shall discuss those passages where the translators expressed a different set of attitudes which characterise their own circle.

Prayer rather than sacrifice

Terms relating to Temple service are sometimes carelessly rendered in P. Thus the אשם is vaguely rendered *qurbānā*, as if identical with אשה. The three different types of sacrifice at Josh 22:23 are reduced to "sacrifice and other worship". At 2 Chr 31:18–19, by misreading בשדה as בשר and stretching the sense of מגרש ('expulsion, divorce, celibacy'), P says of the priests, quite inaccurately: "holy was their flesh and to women they did not draw near". Actual hostility to the cult surfaces at Jer 7:5–6, where P changes the pronoun 'they' to 'you', rendering: "You are the temple of the Lord ... if you treat one another justly" (cf. 4QFlor6; 1 Cor 3:16–17).

By contrast, reference is introduced to prayer. Thus *ṣallī* replaces התחולל (Ps 37:7) and יחל (Ps 71:14). The 'fixed times' of Ezra 10:14 become the time of prayer. To 'seek the Lord' becomes to 'pray before the Lord' at Ezra 6:21 and frequently in Chronicles. At 1 Chr 16:29, the command to bow down before God is amplified in P: "with the prayer of your mouth". References in the Hebrew to musical instruments in worship are replaced in P by 'praise', 'voice' and 'mouth' (1 Chr 15:28; 2 Chr 29:25; 30:21). At 1 Chr 16:42, where MT states that the Levites worshipped with musical instruments, P insists that "righteous men offered praise not with instruments of song (five are listed) but with a goodly mouth and pure and perfect prayer and uprightness and integrity".[26] The musical term שמינית in the Hebrew at 1 Chr 15:21 is transformed in P, which instead states that prayer was offered at the third, sixth and ninth hours. David's prayer in 1 Chr 29:10–19 was supplied largely by free composition (apparently the *Vorlage* was hardly legible), and concluded with a citation of the Jewish Qaddish prayer: *d-netqaddaš šmāk rabbā w-neštabbaḥ b-ʿālmā da-brayt qdām dāḥlayk.*[27] Overall, prayer is viewed as superior to sacrifice, rather than a mere substitute (cf. also 1QS 9:4–5).

---

[26] Evidently music was banned in worship in the translator's community, conceivably as a token of mourning for Jewish statehood (cf. *m. Soṭa* 9:11, forbidding music at secular feasts).

[27] M.P. Weitzman, "The Qaddish Prayer and the Peshitta of Chronicles" (Hebrew) in

Faith and eternal life rather than external observance

Indifference to other external observances appears in some of the translator's guessed renderings. At Exod 23:11, P (guessing for Heb. תשמטנה) permits ploughing (*tekrbeh*) in the sabbatical year, against MT and *m. Šeb.* 1:4. Deut 25:6 is taken to mean that the first son of a levirate marriage is to be named after the deceased brother, against Sifre ad loc. At 2 Chr 8:13, MT has "Feast of Weeks" (between the Feasts of Unleavened Bread and Tabernacles), while P writes: "feast of the fast", apparently confusing it with the Day of Atonement.

Instead we find emphasis on faith and (eschatological) hope. The Syriac term for faith (*haymānutā*, itself a loan-word from Hebrew) is introduced at Prov 19:8 to replace תבונה: "he who maintains faith finds what is good". It also replaces the faithfulness (אמת) shown by God to man at Jer 33:6 ("I shall reveal to them the paths [for עתרת] of peace and faith") and Ps 26:3 ("I have walked in faith"). At Ruth 4:6 Boaz's rival cannot redeem "because of my lack of faith". Though this may be due to a misreading of LXX (ΑΓΧΙΣΤΕΙΑΝ as ΑΠΙΣΤ(Ε)ΙΑΝ), it nevertheless betokens a preoccupation with faith. In Chronicles too, P replaces rectitude (מישרים, ישר) by faith (1 Chr 29:17) and writes that "in faith (for האמנם) the Lord caused his presence to dwell upon his people Israel" (2 Chr 6:18) and that "all Israel were sanctified in faith" (2 Chr 31:18).

References to the hereafter are introduced at Ps 88:11 ("behold for the dead thou wilt perform wonders") through converse translation and at Ps 49:9–10 by adapting LXX (ἐκόπασεν): "Labour continually that thou mayest live for ever and not see destruction". Using the Syriac meaning of נחם, P renders Job's closing words: "I shall be resurrected upon the dust" (42:6; cf. 42:17 a in LXX). More commonly we find references to 'hope', at least some of which seem eschatological. At Ps 34:6, נהרו is guessed: "Hope in [God]!" In Proverbs 'hope' is introduced at 2:7; 8:21 (cf. *m. ʿUq.* 3:12); 10:24; 11:3 and 13:12 ("the tree of life brings hope"). In some passages where Hebrew בטח means physical security, P instead has 'hope' (*sabrā*), viz. Deut 12:10; Isa 30:15; 32:17; Ezek 28:26; 34:27 f*; Hos 2:20*; Mi 2:8*; Ps 78:53*; Prov 1:33; 3:23; 10:9. This rendering seems to have come in from LXX, which has ἐλπίς in those passages marked by an asterisk. A consequence is that wealth is qualified as being merely "of (this) world" (1 Chr 29:28), and Prov 22:7 is inverted: "the poor will rule the rich".

Israel and the nations

There are a number of unfavourable references to the Israelite people, who regard the divine word as "dung and vomit" (Isa 28:13) and "were filled with force and delighted in sin" (Isa 40:2), and whom God "despised" (*bsēt*) at Jer 31:32. They are dropped from passages which in MT look forward to their joy (Ps 106:5) or resurrection (Ezek 37:12).

H. Ben-Shammai (ed.), *Hebrew and Arabic Studies in honour of Joshua Blau* (Tel Aviv/Jerusalem 1993) 261–290.

The other nations, however, are viewed positively. The "nation" amongst whom the psalmists pray becomes "nations" in P (Ps 35:18; 107:32). According to Gen 27:40 in MT, Esau will shake off Jacob's yoke when he "grows restive" (Heb. תריד, lit. "wander"), but P instead envisages that Esau will repent. At Deut 33:3 P declares that God "loved the nations, and blessed (MT בידך) all his saints", while the Targums and even LXX are particularistic. In some books גר is rendered: "he who turns to me", an interpretation of προσήλυτος, which means "one who comes unto", with the object unstated; he comes not to the Israelite people but directly to God.

The translators seem to belong to a specific community. In the Psalms, where the Hebrew has (or was misread) חסיד, P renders *gbayā* "the elect" (30:5; 31:22; 32:6; 50:5). In rabbinic literature the potentially divisive term 'elect' is avoided, even in the translation of biblical references to the election of Israel.[28] The translator's community may also be intended by the "congregation" (*knušyā*) that will belong to God at the end-time (Mal 3:17 for סגלה) and in the "men from Judah [who] are a new and beloved plant" at Isa 5:7. The same introspection appears in Dan 3:45 (LXX), where God is praised ἐφ' ὅλην τὴν οἰκουμένην in the Greek but only "among all thy servants" in P.

Apart from such hostility we can trace in other passages a different attitude, where the translator identifies himself with the Jews and feels guilty and endangered. At Ezra 9:14 P pleads: "we have transgressed thy commandments ... leave for us remnants in the world". In 1 Chr 29:15–16 P acknowledges: "thou didst rule over our fathers and command them by which way they should go ... save us from all the nations that harm and revile us". Exile was an especially sensitive issue. At 2 Chr 15:3–7 P confesses: "we were scattered in every nation for we had forsaken the Lord". Where Dan 3:37 (LXX) describes Israel as ταπεινοὶ (ἐν πάσῃ τῇ γῇ), P renders *mbaddre* "scattered". At Dan 9:16 the cry that "thy people has become a reproach" becomes: "thy people have been scattered to every place".

A few passages, it is true, suggest proud self-identification with the Jews. These renderings in P, however, all agree with the Jewish Targums, and seem to have been inherited from the broader Jewish movement of biblical translation into Aramaic (see sect. 6).

Possible Christological references

In some passages reference to a 'son' is introduced:

(a) Isa 16:1 "send the son (Syr. *bar*, Heb. כר) of the ruler of the earth".
(b) Ps 2:12 "kiss the son" (for בר).
(c) Ps 110:3 "I have begotten thee, O child" (*ṭalyā* for טל).

References to the crucifixion have also been detected:

(d) Isa 25:7 "the sacrifice slaughtered for all the peoples" (מסכה, rendered by the like-sounding Syr. root *nks*).

[28] M.P. Weitzman, "Usage and avoidance of the Term 'Chosen People'" (Hebrew with English summary), *Language Studies* (Jerusalem 1990) 101–128.

(e) Zech 12:10 "they shall look to me through him that they pierced", cf. John 19:37. Here a preposition is varied (Heb. את, Syr. *b-*).
(f) Dan 9:26 "the Messiah shall be slain", for יכרת משיח, cf. Aquila ἐξολοθρευθήσεται ἠλειμμένος.

All these, however, are obscure passages, where the rendering is predominantly literal. The translator may have been too preoccupied with rendering the individual words to consider the overall meaning produced. A further Christian reference is claimed at Isa 7:14, where עלמה is rendered *btultā*, but this may merely reflect the influence of LXX παρθένος.

The absence of explicit Christian reference (in contrast, say, to Jerome's *Psalterium iuxta Hebraeos*)[29] suggests that the community responsible for P in the canonical books was only later absorbed into the Church. Prolonged exile may have convinced them finally of the rejection of the Jewish people. The P version of the Apocryphal books of Sirach and Wisdom, however, offers some convincing Christian references. The commendation of poverty, and the glorification of prayer over sacrifice and of the Gentiles over Israel, also receive greater emphasis there than in the canonical books.[30]

Other theological concerns

Angels and mankind are sharply differentiated at Dan 10:5–6. The 'man' who speaks to Daniel is according to P clothed in "glory" (MT בדים), and girt in "glory of praise" (MT כתם אופז). Moreover, "his appearance was different with none like him" (MT וגויתו כתרשיש).

To the term משכילים ("those who understand"), who in Dan 12:3 will shine at the eschaton, P adds *ʿābday ṭābātā* "doers of good". The משכילים are wholly replaced by the "righteous" at Dan 11:33 and by the "doers of good" at 12:10. These renderings may be anti-gnostic.

The elevation of David in the Hebrew of Chronicles is carried even further in P, which denies that David killed any Ammonites (1 Chr 20:3) and comments that "David did right before the Lord, departing not from all that he commanded him, all the days of his life" (1 Chr 29:30).[31] The motive may have been the hope for a Messiah of David's line. In a lengthy piece of free composition at 1 Chr 23:5, P changes the role of David's appointees from the use of musical instruments in worship to the upkeep of the Temple building and the support of the poor through alms (*zedqātā*).

Conclusion

If P emanates from the Jews of Edessa, it was no doubt indebted to Jewish traditional exegesis (see sect. 6). However, it may be that this community, far

---

[29] There the name Jesus is introduced where the Hebrew has root *yšʿ*, at Pss 51:14; 79:9; 85:9; 95:1; 149:4.

[30] M. Winter, "The Origins of Ben Sira in Syriac", *VT* 27 (1977) 237–253, 494–507, on which see R.J. Owens, "The Early Syriac Text of Ben Sira in the Demonstrations of Aphrahat", *JSS* 34 (1989) 39–75; H.J.W. Drijvers, "The Peshitta of the Wisdom of Solomon", in H.L. Vanstiphout et al. (eds.), *Scripta Signa Vocis* (FS J.H. Hospers; Groningen 1986) 15–30.

[31] P.B. Dirksen, "Some Aspects of the Translation Technique in Peshitta Chronicles", in P.B. Dirksen/A. van der Kooij (eds.), *The Peshitta as a Translation* (Leiden 1995) 17–24.

from the Temple site, had long been disaffected with external observance generally. Its varying attitudes to the Jews may represent alternative reactions to Jewish political eclipse. Some continued to identify with the Jewish people, in guilt and shame, and to long for an end to exile. Others turned to seek salvation for the individual and their own group, which Gentiles might enter as proselytes. Later, this community might have embraced the Church, which shared their dearest values – prayer and faith – while providing a rationale for the neglect of ritual.[32]

6. Elements Inherited from a Jewish Background

Other elements in P recall the rabbinic sources, especially the Targums, in content or in attitude, and may have been inherited from a common Jewish milieu.

Emphasis on the gulf between God and man

The translators tolerate anthropomorphisms for the most part, retaining references to the hand or voice of God. However, certain expressions are altered regularly. Notably, the nouns מגן and צור become *msayʿānā* 'helper' and *taqqīpā* 'strong'; 'walk with God' is usually changed to 'be pleasing (*špr*) to God'; and passages where God is said to 'repent' (נחם are changed in various ways.[33] Divine omniscience is affirmed, e.g. at Gen 22:12 ("I have made known" (for ידעתי) and Deut 1:33 (*l-matqānu* [as Targums] 'to establish' for לתור). At Dan 3:18 P omits והן לא, not even admitting the possibility of God failing to save. God is occasionally replaced by an angel (e.g. Gen 32:31, as Targums; Ps 8:6; 1 Chr 14:11) or, in Chronicles, by the divine presence (*škintā*).[34] A foreign deity is not called a god but a thing feared (*deḥltā*).

Israel and the nations

In contrast to both attitudes in sect. 5, we also find traces of rabbinic attitudes towards Israel and the nations. Given the early rabbinic dislike for terms suggesting an exclusive group, the Targums to the Pentateuch render סגלה as חביב 'beloved' (Exod 19:5; Deut 7:6; 14:2; 26:18), and P agrees. Like LXX and the Targums, P baulked at the universalism of Isa 19:25 and confined the blessing to Israel. Here in P Egypt and Assyria are merely the location of the contemporary diaspora (so also LXX; in the Targum they were rather the scene of earlier exile). This inherited nationalistic element sits uncomfortably with the hostile references to Israel in the same book.

---

[32] M.P. Weitzman, "From Judaism to Christianity: the Syriac Version of the Hebrew Bible", in J. Lieu/J. North/T. Rajak (eds.), *The Jews among Pagans and Christians* (London 1992) 147–173, esp. 166–168.

[33] R. Loewe, "Jerome's Treatment of an Anthropopathism", *VT* 2 (1952) 261–272.

[34] Gelston, 153; N. Séd, "La Shekhinta et ses amis 'Araméens'", *Mélanges Antoine Guillaumont* (Geneva 1988) 233–242.

Rabbinic exegesis

Most of the rabbinic exegesis incorporated by the translators appears in the Targums also. In this paragraph, however, some instances of rabbinic exegesis which entered P but not the Targums are noted. P on Exod 40:17 states that the tabernacle was dedicated on a Sunday, as in *b. Šabb.* 80b. The "strange fire" in Lev 10:1 is explained as "not in its [right] time" as in *Sifra* ad loc. At 2 Sam 24:15 עת מועד is explained as "midday" (*šet šāʿyān*), as in *b. Ber.* 62b. The image made by Manasseh at 2 Chr 33:7 is called four-faced, as at *b. Sanh.* 103b.[35] This rabbinic knowledge may be overworked. For example, *m. Roš. Haš.* 3:3–4 mentions two types of horn (for which one term is חצוצרה), namely straight or curved. The translator of Chronicles parades the phrase "straight and curved horns" to render not only חצוצרה (six times) but also the derivative verb (2 Chr 7:6) and even חצר 'courtyard' at 1 Chr 23:28.

Rabbinic influence can only be posited, however, if P exhibits a parallel, too specific to be accidental, with a known rabbinic source. For example at Gen 4:8, where Cain speaks to Abel, no words are quoted in MT, while P has *nerde la-pqaʿtā* "let us proceed to the plain/valley". It has been suggested that P reflects a rabbinic legend: Cain and Abel agreed to divide the world and parted company, but Cain then treacherously pursued Abel "from mountain to valley".[36] However, the parallel is so incomplete that rabbinic influence cannot be inferred. More probably P has consulted LXX διέλθωμεν εἰς τὸ πέδιον, in which case the original meaning of *pqaʿtā* was 'plain' – even though Ephrem, who located Paradise on a mountain (cf. Ezek 28:14), understood it as 'valley'.[37]

Parallels with Targums

P shows numerous parallels with the Targums in the Pentateuch. Some have concluded that here the translator of P consulted from time to time a copy of one of the extant Targums,[38] or that P is a transcription into Syriac of an earlier Targum in Jewish Aramaic.[39] However, many of the parallels between P and the Targums may be coincidental, since translators of the same Hebrew text into dialects of the same language may agree independently. Thus both fill out breviloquences from the context (e.g. "*a place of* serpents" at Deut 8:18), add precision (e.g. "be slain" rather than "die" at Deut 17:12), explain obscurities (e.g. "the stores" rather than "what was in them" at Gen 41:56), avoid inner-biblical contradictions (e.g. "had gone" rather than "had fled" at Exod 14:5) and resolve metaphors (e.g. "acquire property" for כשית at Deut 32:15). Other parallels may be ascribed to common tradition, relating

[35] These were all pointed out by Perles, Meletemata (1859) 16, 37.

[36] Lund, Influence (1988) 30, quoting *Tanh. Bereshit* 9.

[37] Thus Ephrem writes *wa-nḥet* (and later *aḥteh*) *la-pqaʿtā*, see R.-M. Tonneau (ed.), *Sancti Ephraem Syri in Genesim et in Exodum Commentarii* (Louvain 1955) 49 (sect. III.5).

[38] A. E. Silverstone, *Aquila and Onkelos* (Manchester 1931) 145.

[39] C. Peters, "Peschittha and Targumim des Pentateuchs", *Muséon* 48 (1935) 1–54; Kahle, Geniza (1959) 272–73.

to lexical items (e.g. the unclean birds in Lev 11 and Deut 14)[40] or to obscure passages (e.g. "late-born ... early-born" at Gen 30:42).

Common traditions also occur in the later books but less frequently. Examples are "archers and slingers" for כרתי ופלתי (1 Kgs 1:38 etc.), or the derivation of תאנתה from תן 'jackal' (Aramaic: *yārōrā*) at Jer 2:24. At Judg 9:27, where MT has טבור (הארץ), P has an obscure form *tuqnāh*, which seems a corruption of *tuqpāh* as in the Targum.[41]

Literary dependence of P upon a given Targum would be indicated if P could be shown to have misread or mistaken that Targum, but no convincing cases have been adduced.[42] On the contrary, the many cases where P stands alone in its treatment of the Hebrew testify to its independence. Indeed, P includes Daniel, Ezra and Nehemiah, where no Targum is known ever to have existed. The parallels between P and the Targum in Proverbs are particularly close, but here it is the Targum which has drawn from P.[43] Such borrowing from the church is not inconceivable in the age of Hai Gaon (939–1038), who consulted the Nestorian Catholicos on the meaning of Ps 141:5b and also makes the first extant reference to rabbinic Targums on the Writings.[44]

Non-rabbinic exegesis

Some of the exegesis in P appears to reflect earlier tradition that differed from rabbinic norms. At Exod 13:13, P extends the law of redemption of asses to all unclean beasts (cf. Josephus *Antiq.* 4.4.4, Philo *De spec. leg.* I.135), against *m. Bek.* 1:2. P's rendering at Lev 18:21 and 20:2–4 ("to impregnate a foreign woman") is condemned in *m. Meg* 4:9, though upheld by R. Ishmael (*y. Meg* 4:10) and paralleled by Pseudo-Jonathan. *m. Ber.* 9:5 prescribes the use of the Tetragrammaton in greetings, citing Ruth 2:4 "the Lord be with thee". Yet P on that verse replaces the Tetragrammaton, substituting "peace". The Rabbis were apparently protesting against the excessive avoidance of the Tetragrammaton by sectarians (cf. its removal from some biblical citations at Qumran, e.g. at 1QS 2:16; CD 20:19).

7. Factors Anterior to Interpretation

Not every difference between P and the plain sense of MT is due to interpretation. In this and the next section we must consider how to identify differences which arise either before or after the interpretation stage.

[40] J.A. Emerton, "Unclean Birds and the Origin of the Peshitta", *JSS* 7 (1962) 204–211.

[41] J.M. Wilkie, "The Peshiṭta Translation of Ṭabbur Ha'areṣ in Judges ix 37", *VT* 1 (1951) 144 prefers to emend to *twwn'*.

[42] F. Rosenthal, *Die aramaistische Forschung* (Leiden 1939) 202–3.

[43] T. Nöldeke, "Das Targum zu den Sprüchen von der Peschita abhängig", *Archiv für Wissenschaftliche Beforschung des Alten Testamentes* 2/2 (1872) 246–249.

[44] A.S. Halkin (ed.), *Joseph b. Judah b. Jacob ibn Aknin: Hitgallut ha-sodot w-hofa'at ha-m'orot* (Arabic text with notes and translation in Hebrew; Jerusalem 1964) 494; L. Ginzberg, *Genizah Studies* 3 (New York 1929) 85–87.

Differences in the actual Vorlage

The *Vorlage* of P was not everywhere identical with MT. A different *Vorlage*, however, can hardly be the explanation for most of the discrepancies between MT and a retroversion of P into Hebrew. These discrepancies are far more numerous than those between MT and the Qumran manuscripts, which offer a direct indication in Hebrew of the extent of variety among biblical manuscripts in Antiquity.

In order for a different *Vorlage* to be posited in a given passage, there must be a credible palaeographic relationship between the alleged variant and MT. For example, the alleged variant may be supported by another witness, without any question of P having been influenced thereby. A well-known example is 1 Sam 20:19, where MT has תרד but both LXX ἐπισκέψῃ and P *metbʿē a*[*n*]*t* imply a consonantal text תפקד. The difference in meaning shows that P has not borrowed from LXX. Alternatively, even without outside support, the alleged variant may lay claim to being the original text. For example, at Ezra 6:3 MT states that the ark in the Temple was 60 cubits square (the third dimension is not given), while P gives these dimensions as 20 cubits and 60 cubits. P's figures agree with 1 Kgs 6:2 (60×20×30), but not so closely as to suggest assimilation to that passage.[45]

Differences in the perceived Vorlage

It may happen that the *Vorlage* was identical with MT but was perceived differently by the translator owing to fatigue. Eye-skip between similar expressions in the Hebrew has caused some omissions, e.g. Lev 11:40a; Num 13:19b–20a. The six-word omission (ושב ... תהיה) at Dan 11:28–29 also appears accidental.

The supposed error of perception can sometimes be related to the external appearance of the text. An instructive example is 1 Chr 9:35; where the *Vorlage* seems to have been set out thus:

... אבי גבעון
יעואל ושם אשתו מעכה
ובנו הבכור עבדון ...

P renders: "(At Gibeon dwelt) the father of Gibeon, and the name of his first-born son (was) JWʾYL, and the name of his wife (was) MʿKH, and his second son was ʿBRWN". Evidently the translator jumped prematurely to the third line, and processed its opening words ובנו הבכור, before resuming at the beginning of the second line. On reaching the words ובנו הבכור again, he avoided contradiction by radically changing the phrase to "second son" (see sect. 3).

Differences in identification of lexical items

The next stage in construing the Hebrew is to identify the lexical items and their grammatical forms. In this the translator may disagree with the conventional construal. Thus at Exod 18:18 the verb תבל, which most derive from root נבל 'wither', is translated by P as *meṣtaʿar a*(*n*)*t* "you will be disgraced" and so connected rather with the noun נבלה. An instance where P agrees with

---

[45] C. Hawley, *A Critical Examination of the Peshitta Version of the Book of Ezra* (New York 1922) 15.

LXX against the usual construal is the derivation of הסתיר, with God's face as object, from סור 'turn away'.[46] Often these construals will contradict the vocalisation of MT, which of course was not available to the translator. For example, at 2 Sam 23:1 MT has *huqam ʿal* "was raised above", while P renders *d-aqīm nīrā* "who raised the yoke", vocalising *hēqīm ʿōl.*

It is sometimes arguable that P is superior to the conventional construal. Thus NEB follows P in relating חציו (Num 24:8) to Syriac *ḥaṣṣe* "loins" and יראה at Ezek 1:18 to ראה (P: *w-ḥāzyān [h]way*, NEB: "the power of sight").

Differences in meaning attached to lexical items

Here we are concerned with the translator's pre-existing lexical knowledge, rather than interpretations reached in the course of the translation. Even where P agrees with modern scholarship which lexical item is present, they may not agree on the basic meaning of that item. For example, תירוש is conventionally understood as 'wine', but P renders *ādšā* (Judg 9:13; 2 Kgs 18:32) or *ṭoṭitā* (Isa 65:8), both meaning 'berry' or 'grape'. The meaning 'grape' is in fact supported in rabbinic sources and fits the majority of biblical occurrences better than the conventional 'wine'.[47]

The meanings attached by P are not always so valuable. For example, סוללה 'siege-works' is everywhere understood by P to mean 'ambush' (root *kmn*) — at 2 Sam 20:15; 2 Kgs 19:32; Dan 11:15, twice in Jeremiah and four times in Ezekiel. The only exception is Jer 33:4, where we find the similar rendering 'marauders'. This may stem from prior familiarity with Jer 32:24, which seemed to state that the סוללות were about to enter the city. We may recall here the meanings attached in P to חליפה (sect. 4) and בטח (sect. 5), apparently under the influence of LXX.

8. Factors Subsequent to Interpretation

Variation within the Syriac manuscript tradition

The textual evidence within the Syriac tradition must be considered before a different *Vorlage* is posited. Thus, according to BHS, P prefaces Exod 14:15 with the words: "and Moses cried out before the Lord". This phrase does not appear in the oldest manuscript (5b1), which often uniquely preserves the true reading.[48] Apparently it was added later to explain God's question: "Why do you cry to me?" Again, at Ezra 4:2 BHS cites P as reading "Sennacherib"; the earliest manuscripts, however, have "Esarhaddon" like MT.[49]

---

[46] S.E. BALANTINE, *The Hidden God* (Oxford 1983) 80–114. Gelston, 143, provides further examples of unexpected lexical identification.

[47] S. NAEH/M. WEITZMAN, "Tirosh — Wine or Grape?", *VT* 44 (1994) 115–120.

[48] M.D. KOSTER, *The Peshiṭta of Exodus* (Assen 1977) 528.

[49] C. MOSS, "The Peshiṭta Version of Ezra", *Muséon* 46 (1933) 55–110; 104. The older reading is SRḤDWM.

Inner-Syriac change in all extant witnesses

Differences between P and the plain sense of MT can arise through inner-Syriac change, whether accidental corruption or deliberate revision. Any conjectural emendation must be credible in palaeographic terms, and must also bear a more satisfactory relation to MT than does the existing Syriac text. Possible cases include the following:

	MT	mss	emendation
Gen 49:13	חוף	*šuprā*	*spārā*
Lev 24:8	השבת	*da-štā*	*d-šabtā*[50]
Josh 15:12	הימה הגדול	*la-mrībā*	*l-yammā rabbā*
2 Kgs 11:6 (read סיר 'pot')	סור	*qrs'*	*qds'*
Isa 24:23	זקניו	*qadišaw(hy)*	*qašišaw(hy)*
Hab 3:4	חביון	*bṭušyā*	*b-laqḥā*[51]
Zeph 2:14	בחלון	*b-gawwāh*	*b-kawwāh*[52]
2 Chr 21:19	שרפה	*īqārā*	*yaqdā*

Again in eight passages in Leviticus where MT has the hi. of סור, the reading *ʿbd* in the P manuscripts may result from corruption of the afel of *ʿbr*.

Even a corrupt text may inspire interpretation. Thus at Isa 9:17, for MT ויתאבכו גאות עשן, the current P text is *metʿarqlin gbayā ba-tnānā*. Apparently *gbayā* is a corruption of *g'ayā*, but Afrahat learns from the existing text ("the chosen are enveloped in the smoke") that where evil dominates even the righteous suffer.[53]

Conscious revision rather than corruption may explain certain changes of names (sect. 9). It may also be the reason for assimilations to parallel passages (e.g. at Deut 16:20, where MT has צדק צדק תרדף, while the current P text has "in righteousness judge thy fellow" as at Lev 19:15) and for insertions from these (e.g. at Num 35:6 "who killed his neighbour without wishing" as at Deut 19:4).

Scholarly activity led to the insertion of titles and colophons, of books and their constituent sections. Some books include a note of their midpoint, based apparently on the space taken up rather than the number of verses as in Jewish tradition. Thus the midpoints of Isaiah and Chronicles are noted immediately before Isa 35:3 and 2 Chr 6:1 respectively, unlike Isa 33:21 and 1 Chr 27:25 in MT.[54] The note introducing the second half of Isaiah is *zuhārā w-lubābā*

---

[50] In defence of the current text Perles (1859) 43, pointed to the statement in Sifra ad loc. (and *b. Men.* 97a) that the staves to hold the loaves were set out on Friday. However, it is the loaves themselves that are in point, and the rabbinic sources fully support the biblical commandment that these were to be presented on the Sabbath.

[51] R.P. Gordon, "Inner-Syriac Corruptions", *JTS* 22 (1971) 502–504.

[52] G. Gerleman, *Zephanja, textkritisch und literarisch untersucht* (Lund 1942) 88.

[53] See J. Parisot, PS I/2, 12.

[54] This division takes no account of the section 1 Chr 26:13–27:34, transmitted by 7a1 and 8a1 only, which may be among the many passages omitted by the original translators. Unlike P elsewhere in Chronicles it presents many obscurely literal renderings, actually transliterating דברי הימים (27:24), and prefers gentilic adjectives (e.g. *Rublāyā* rather than *d-bēt Rubēl* for 'Reubenite').

da-mḥile d-āte pāroqā w-pāreq lhon, which has become incorporated in the text.

Daniel 7–11 has been provided with historical notes maintaining the identification of the four kingdoms as Babylon, Media, Persia and Greece, the final enemy being named Antiochus.[55] In the west, by contrast, Rome became the fourth kingdom, in both Jewish and Christian tradition (Josephus *Antiq.* 10.11.7 § 276; *Mek. Baḥodesh* 9; Matt 24:15).

This discussion has aimed to examine the different possible reasons why the extant text of P might not agree with the plain sense of MT. It is not claimed, of course, that the correct possibility can be identified in every case. Where doubt exists, it is prudent to err on the side of attributing P to those processes that lay in the translator's mind, namely construal and interpretation. There is one essential proviso, namely that the overall picture of the translation technique must be coherent.[56] Subject to that, one should not lightly posit either a variant Hebrew reading or an inner-Syriac corruption.

9. Names

The great majority of names are simply transcribed. Geographical names and adjectives, however, are sometimes modernised according to traditions paralleled in the Targums, e.g. Matnin for Bashan, Arab for Ishmaelite, Indian for Ethiopian,[57] MPS ('Memphis') for Moph or Noph, Spain for Sepharad (Obad 20). At Josh 13:11, 13, Maʿachah becomes Kuros, which name appears in the Targum as Apekeros, i.e. Ἐπίκαιρος mentioned as one of the five cities east of the Jordan by Ptolemy V.16.9. Hamath becomes Antioch at 1 Chr 13:5; 18:9 and 2 Chr 8:4. Apparently the translator thought of it as the northern boundary of the Holy Land, which in turn was identified as the nearby Taurus Mountains (Gen. Apocr. 21:16).[58]

The translators claimed other places for their own vicinity. The Aramean district of Soba is thus equated with Nisibis in 1 Chr 18–19.[59] Harran was substituted for Aram Maʿachah at 1 Chr 19:6 and Mabbug (i.e. Hierapolis) for Carchemish (which is in fact 25 miles further north) at 2 Chr 35:20.

The translators also introduce the great powers of their own day. Thus ששך at Jer 25:26 becomes *Aršakyā* 'Arsaces' and at 51:41 *Aršakitā* 'the Arsacid city'. In this way the biblical antecedents of Parthia are identified with the Babylonians rather than the benign Persians. A reference to Rome may have

[55] Afrahat (see n.3) instead places the climax in 70 CE, treating Rome as a continuation of Greece.

[56] Thus in Jeremiah LXX tends to be literal, so that the shorter text of LXX cannot be ascribed to radical translation technique. See E. Tov, *The Text-Critical Use of the Septuagint in Biblical Research* (Jerusalem 1981) 52.

[57] This identification reappears in *b. Meg* 11 a, but has classical antecedents in the "Ethiopians of Asia" described by Herodotus 7.70 as straight-haired and serving with the Indians in the Persian army.

[58] N. Avigad/Y. Yadin, *A Genesis Apocryphon* (Jerusalem 1956) 25*–26*.

[59] This equation also appears in Saadia's version of Ps 60:2.

been introduced by the rendering 'Edom' (MT *'ādām*) at Ps 12:9.[60] The name Aram is usually replaced by Edom, so that we even read of "the king of Edom who dwelt in Damascus" (1 Kgs 15:18). In such cases Edom may again allude to Rome,[61] unless the motive is rather to avoid the terms Aram and Aramean, which latter had come to mean 'pagan'.[62]

We find further evidence of speculation about toponyms. Five times in Josh 12-13, Geshur becomes Endor, apparently because both were mentioned as unconquered spots which lay (Josh 17:11-12) or could have lain (Josh 13:7, 13) in Manasseh's territory. Again, Jaffa becomes Eilat at Josh 19:46, and the sea of Jaffa becomes the Red Sea at 2 Chr 2:15. Apparently the translators identified the ports of Jaffa and Eilat as the point of departure for Tarshish, on comparing Jonah 1:3 with 2 Chr 20:36. In 2 Sam 23, the mention of more than one "Shamma the Hararite" (vv. 11, 33) led the translator to distinguish them as hailing from different mountains, namely 'of Olives' and 'of the King'.[63]

The translators might occasionally take a common noun as a name, e.g. אשדת (Deut 3:17) as Ashdod, or מלצר at Dan 1:11. At 2 Chr 1:16, where MT has ומקוא "and from Que" (in Cilicia). P rightly detects a toponym, though the form ('PLY') seems corrupt, perhaps for nearby Apamaea or Pamphylia. Conversely, sometimes the translator did not acknowledge the presence of a name, and so translated פתורה (Num 22:5) as *pāšōrā* 'interpreter', or מרתים (Jer 50:21) as *mmarmrānītā* 'rebellious'. Intermediate between such translations and the usual system of transliteration is the etymologising of ציון as *ṣehyon* (cf. *ṣahyā* 'thirst' as from ציה 'dryness') and of רות as *r'ūt* 'favour'. While suggesting meanings, these forms remain names.

Divine names are usually translated. The Tetragrammaton, as well as Yah and Adonay, regularly becomes *māryā* (cf. LXX κύριος), in contrast with the transliterations in the Targums. The names El and Elohim normally become *'ălāhā*, though *māryā* is substituted in Qohelet[64] and sometimes elsewhere, and the phrase בני אלהים is usually transliterated. The combination Adonay YHWH is normally *māryā alāhā*, after the Qere, but P in Ezekiel and the Twelve Prophets instead has *māre mārawātā* after the Kethib. Seba'ot is transliterated between 1 Sam 1:3 and 2 Sam 6:2 but elsewhere usually rendered *ḥayyeltānā* (cf. LXX παντοκράτωρ). El Shaddai (in Genesis and Exodus) is transliterated, but Shaddai alone usually becomes *alāhā* or *ḥassinā*. At Exod 3:14, אהיה אשר אהיה is transliterated as a divine name.

In many cases, names have been disfigured by textual corruption, examples being especially plentiful in the opening chapters of Chronicles. Thus the names of three of the kingdoms in Gen 14:1 are transliterated, but for the fourth, viz. גוים, P has GLY'. Rather than search for an obscure nation of Gelians, we may suppose that P is a corruption of GYY', a virtual transliteration of the Hebrew (cf. the spelling גיים at Gen 25:23). Corruption from Yodh to Lamedh occurs at Num 13:13 (MT מיכאל, P MLKY'YL) and in the Old Syriac Gospels at Mark 7:26, where *armaltā* is corrupt from *armāytā* ('Aramean', rendering Συροφοινίκισσα τῷ γένει).[65]

---

60 R. Duval, "Notes sur la Peschitto, I. Edom et Rome", *REJ* 14 (1887) 49-51.

61 van der Kooij, Die alten Textzeugen (1981) 293-94.

62 Compare the preference for 'Syriac' to indicate the language. For a different view see N. Walker, "The Peshitta puzzle and its implications", *VT* 18 (1968) 268-270.

63 The term הר המלך in rabbinic Hebrew indicates an extensive area north of Jerusalem; see S. Applebaum, *Judea in Hellenistic and Roman Times* (Leiden 1989) 24-28.

64 R.B. Salters, "The word for 'God' in the Peshiṭta of Koheleth", *VT* 21 (1971) 251-254.

65 Compare P. Borbone, "'Comprensione' o 'speranza'? Osea 2,17 nella Pešitta", *Henoch* 10 (1988) 277-281. Barhebraeus may likewise have stated originally (in the name of Eusebius) that Origen found a text of P in the house of an Aramean woman; the manuscripts in fact divide between *'rmt'* and *'rmlt'* (see n. 6 above).

The disfigured form may be used repeatedly, e.g. ḤMNWN for אמנון, MḤNYM for מנחם, NDB for מרב, suggesting later revision to impose uniformity. The same is suggested by forms in P which differ palaeographically from MT too far to be mere corruptions, and yet agree with names found in P elsewhere. Apparently a reviser recognised that certain names were corrupt, and tried to match them with known names within the closed field of P. Hence the extant text of P shows Sepharwaim for Aqbrabim (Num 34:4), and even Ono (Syr: *'ynw*) for Lšm (Josh 19:47).

10. Conclusion

P can fairly be described as an idiomatic, though faithful, translation. The translators aim primarily to convey the plain sense, despite the attention given here to departures from it. They broadly follow the classical ideal of expressing the sense rather than the words[66] – provided that they believed that the sense could be recovered. In the Holy Land, where continued access to the Hebrew could be assumed, some translators could afford to depart from the classical ideal, either towards literalism (as in the Greek fragments from Qumran and ultimately in Aquila)[67] or towards periphrasis (as in most Targums). Neither tendency is characteristic of P.

There is thus a common philosophy of translation in P. The books are further linked by some idiosyncratic but widespread features mentioned above, such as the rendering 'ambush' for סוללה or the use of *guryā d-aryā* as the 'B-word' for 'lion', and by the quotations of the Syriac text of one book in another. It seems that the translators sometimes consulted one another and in that sense belonged to a single school, i.e. a team collaborating in the translation of the whole Hebrew Bible into Syriac.

A single translator is unlikely, however, because the books also display differences, in three principal ways. First, a spectrum from 'conservative' to 'modern' – where 'modern' means later lexical usage, such as *mdi(n)tā* for 'city' rather than the older *qritā*, and readiness to consult LXX – can be detected, with Judges-Kings at the former end and Ezekiel, the Twelve Prophets and the Solomonic books at the latter.[68] Secondly, there is a spectrum from literalism to freedom, with Song of Songs and Qohelet at one end and Ruth and Chronicles at the other.[69] The question is in fact more subtle, since one can point to 'free' elements in the former group and 'literal' elements in the latter.[70] Though the breadth of this spectrum has been exag-

[66] S.P. Brock, "Aspects of Translation Technique in Antiquity", *Greek Roman and Byzantine Studies* 20 (1979) 69–87.

[67] D. Barthélemy, *Les devanciers d'Aquila* (VTSup 10; Leiden 1963) 266–269.

[68] M.P. Weitzman, "Lexical Clues to the Composition of the Old Testament Peshitta"; M.J. Geller/J.C. Greenfield/M.P. Weitzman (eds.), *Studia Aramaica. New Sources and New Approaches* (Oxford 1995) 217–246.

[69] For example, at Ruth 1:22 the seemingly superfluous השבה is interpreted: "who desired to return with a full heart". As to literalism in Song of Songs and Qohelet, note the use of *yāt* to indicate the object.

[70] Cf. the change from 'companions' (חבריך) to 'sheep' at Cant 1:7 or from פתגם to *tba'tā* 'retribution' at Qoh 8:11. As to Chronicles, this translator's version of 1 Kings 14 (with which he filled a gap after 2 Chr 11:5) is in some respects freer than the P version of Kings but in others more literal, e.g. in retaining נא (v. 2) and ויהי (v. 6) and rendering נתן (v. 7) by *yhb* rather than *'bd*.

gerated,[71] a degree of variation certainly exists. Thirdly, Jewish traditional exegesis has left more traces in the Pentateuch (always the particular object of Jewish exegesis) and in Chronicles (perhaps because despair of recovering the plain sense left the translator receptive to any tradition available) than in the other books. Nevertheless, all these differences could be accommodated within a single school.

It may be noted that differences of translation policy also appear within a single book, though they need not betoken different translators. In Gen 1:1 the first word is transliterated, and את rendered *yāt*; thereafter the translator abandons such attempts to reproduce the Hebrew form. In Exod 8:26, where תועבת מצרים occurs twice, the translator rendered the first mechanically *ṭanputā d-meṣrāye* and the second as required by the context *deḥlātā d-meṣrāye*. At Cant 1:13 דודי is rendered *d-rāḥem lī* but thereafter the translator settles for the neater *dād(y)* despite its ambiguity. A translator could thus vary his practice, without going back to impose consistency.

Hence, and also out of consideration for context (see sect. 3), P does not render a given Hebrew word mechanically by the same Syriac word on each occurrence.[72] Failure to appreciate this may lead to precarious inferences from P's particular choice of words. Thus the Hebrew at Gen 4:5 states that Cain's face fell, while P has *etkamar* "was darkened". Levine infers that P here represents Cain's face as dark and satanic.[73] In fact, however, 'dark' is a stock epithet for a sad face, and is likewise substituted by P at Gen 40:6–7.

At least until the seventh century, P was the only continuous version of the Hebrew Bible in Syriac. On the basis of textual divergences within citations in patristic literature and in Arabic translations from Syriac, it has been suggested that P arose out of a supposed Vetus Syra, i.e. a welter of older Syriac versions originating within the Jewish Targum tradition.[74] In fact, however, these divergences can readily be explained otherwise. Church fathers may quote from memory or intend merely to paraphrase;[75] in verse, the metre may force textual adjustment; and translators from Syriac into Arabic may quote the Old Testament freely, just as they sometimes quote the New.[76]

Occasionally, the Syriac fathers cite a different version, as opposed to an older form of P. Scripture is sometimes cited after LXX, even once by Afrahat, at Ps 37:35 ("I saw the wicked man raised up and exalted like a

---

[71] E.g. in B.J. Roberts, *The Old Testament Text and Versions* (Cardiff 1951) 221; O. Eissfeldt, *Einleitung in das alte Testament* (Tübingen 1934) 711. In Chronicles insufficient allowance has been made for the state of the *Vorlage*.

[72] On this aspect of literalism see J. Barr, *The Typology of Literalism* (Göttingen 1979) 305–314.

[73] E. Levine, "The Syriac version of Genesis iv 1–16", *VT* 26 (1976) 70–78.

[74] A. Vööbus, *Peschitta und Targumim des Pentateuchs. Neues Licht zur Frage der Herkunft der Peschitta aus dem altpalästinischen Targum* (Stockholm 1956); L.G. Running, "An Investigation of the Syriac Version of Isaiah", *Andrews University Seminary Studies* 3 (1965) 138–157; 4 (1966) 37–64, 135–148.

[75] R.J. Owens, *The Genesis and Exodus Citations of Aphrahat the Persian Sage* (Leiden 1983) 241.

[76] On the whole question see M.P. Weitzman, "The Origin of the Peshitta Psalter", J.A. Emerton/S.C. Reif (eds.), *Interpreting the Hebrew Bible* (FS E.I.J. Rosenthal; Cambridge 1982) 277–298.

cedar of Lebanon"), where the biblical manuscripts agree with MT.[77] Again, phrases known from the Jewish Targums, and not from P, appear in Ephrem's commentaries, some being ascribed to the "Hebrew" (*ʿEbrāyā*). Apparently a fund had grown up of Aramaic renderings of particular biblical words and phrases, independently of P, and Ephrem still had access thereto.[78] The very few literal translations that depart both from the Targums and from P, such as *ba-ṣlem alōhīm* in Bar-Daisan,[79] may be due to occasional Jewish contacts.

By the seventh century, the literal ideal had become dominant in Syriac translation from the Bible, through the conviction that the form of the biblical original needed to be conveyed no less than the content.[80] This, together with exaggerated regard for the accuracy of LXX, led Paul of Tella in 615–617 CE to make the Syrohexapla, a literal Syriac translation of the fifth column of Origen's Hexapla. P was not displaced by this version, however, nor by the version made by Jacob of Edessa in ca. 705 CE, which attempted to combine the clear wording of P with the perceived accuracy of the Syrohexapla.[81] Thus P remained the principal version of the Old Testament for the Syriac-speaking church, and a mainspring of its rich and imaginative literature.

---

[77] F.C. Burkitt, *JTS* 6 (1905) 289, suggests that Afrahat had been reading some Greek patristic work which quoted the verse according to LXX.

[78] S.P. Brock, "Jewish Traditions in Syriac Sources", *JJS* 30 (1979) 212–232; 218–223.

[79] PS I/2, 547.

[80] S.P. Brock, "Towards a history of Syriac translation technique", OCA 221 (1983) 12.

[81] M.H. [Goshen-]Gottstein, "Neue Syrohexaplafragmente", *Bibl.* 37 (1956) 162–183; 165.

CHAPTER SEVENTEEN

The Christian Syriac Tradition of Interpretation

By LUCAS VAN ROMPAY, Leiden

General works: A. BAUMSTARK, *Geschichte der syrischen Literatur* (Bonn 1922); P. BETTIOLO, "Lineamenti di patrologia siriaca", *Complementi interdisciplinari di patrologia* (ed. A. Quacquarelli; Rome 1989) 503–603; S. BROCK, "Jewish Traditions in Syriac Sources", *JJS* 30 (1979) 212–232; idem, "Genesis 22 in Syriac Tradition", *Mélanges Dominique Barthélemy* (ed. P. Casetti / O. Keel / A. Schenker; OBO 38; Fribourg / Göttingen 1981) 2–30; idem, "Syriac Tradition", DBI (1990) 664–665; A. GUILLAUMONT, "Genèse 1,1–2 selon les commentateurs syriaques", *In Principio. Interprétations des premiers versets de la Genèse* (Études augustiniennes; Paris 1973) 115–132; R. MACINA, "L'homme à l'école de Dieu. D'Antioche à Nisibe, Profil herméneutique, théologique et kérygmatique du mouvement scoliaste nestorien. Monographie programmatique", *Proche-Orient Chrétien* 32 (1982) 86–124 and 263–301; 33 (1983) 39–103; R. MURRAY, *Symbols of Church and Kingdom. A Study in Early Syriac Tradition* (Cambridge 1975); I. ORTIZ DE URBINA, *Patrologia syriaca* (Rome [2]1965); W. STROTHMANN, "Das Buch Kohelet und seine syrische Ausleger", *Erkenntnisse und Meinungen* I (ed. G. Wiessner; GOF I,3; Wiesbaden 1973) 189–238; E. TEN NAPEL, "Some Remarks on the Hexaemeral Literature in Syriac", *IV Symposium Syriacum 1984* (ed. H. J. W. Drijvers / R. Lavenant / C. Molenberg / G. J. Reinink; OCA 229; Rome 1987) 57–69; J. W. TRIGG, *Biblical Interpretation* (Message of the Fathers of the Church 9; Wilmington, DE 1988) 31–38 and 161–220 ("The Antiochene and Syriac Tradition"); J. C. M. VAN WINDEN, "Hexaemeron", RAC 14 (1988) 1264–1266 ("Die syr. Exegese"); A. VÖÖBUS, *History of the School of Nisibis* (CSCO 266/Subs. 26; Louvain 1965); D. S. WALLACE-HADRILL, *Christian Antioch. A Study of Early Christian Thought in the East* (Cambridge etc. 1982) 27–51 ("The interpretation of the biblical record").

Bibliography: (publications until 1960:) C. MOSS, *Catalogue of Syriac Printed Books and Related Literature in the British Museum* (London 1962); (publications after 1960:) S. BROCK, "Syriac Studies 1960–1970. A Classified Bibliography", *Parole de l'Orient* 4 (1973) 393–465; idem, "Syriac Studies 1971–1980. A Classified Bibliography", *Parole de l'Orient* 10 (1981–1982) 291–412; idem, "Syriac Studies 1981–1985. A Classified Bibliography", *Parole de l'Orient* 14 (1987) 289–360; idem, "Syriac Studies 1986–1990. A Classified Bibliography", *Parole de l'Orient* 17 (1992) 211–301.

1. Introduction

1.1. The Place of Syriac Christianity

Although very little is known about the beginnings of Syriac Christianity, the Aramaic preaching of the Gospel in the course of the first centuries reached a wide area, from the region of Antioch and the Mediterranean coasts in the West to Mesopotamia and the Arab-Persian Gulf in the East. These parts of the Near East were populated mainly by Semitic groups and various Aramaic language forms were used both for literary purposes and for daily communication. The presence of the Aramaic language, in a number of distinct though mutually understandable dialects, contributed to the rapid expansion of Aramaic forms of Christianity and remained for a long time one of the main unifying factors of Syriac Christianity. On the other hand, this same region was always characterized by great political and cultural diversity.

In the formative period of Syriac Christianity, the city of Edessa, in Northern Mesopotamia, played a role of prominence. As an heir to the Aramaic culture and at the same time open to both the Graeco-Roman culture in the West and the Persian civilization in the East, this town of tradesmen, travellers and thinkers reflects the complexity of Syriac Christianity. Further east in Mesopotamia, Christian communities arose which in many respects occupied an independent position *vis-à-vis* Edessene Christianity. The fact that the greater part of Mesopotamia belonged to the Persian Empire (from 226 CE onwards the Persian-Sassanid Empire) meant that relations between Mesopotamian Christians of this region and their co-religionists in the Roman (subsequently Byzantine) Empire were delicate. The Christological discussions of the 5th and 6th centuries, therefore, completed rather than created the split between East- and West-Syrian Christians, the former mainly choosing the Dyophysite Antiochene dogma, the latter opting for the Monophysite (anti-Chalcedonian) Creed. Contacts between the various Syrian communities continued to exist and were even intensified under Arab and Muslim rule, although the latter led to the gradual decline of Christian culture in the Near East.

Whereas for the first period of Syriac literature (2nd to 4th centuries) some – largely anonymous – works have been preserved, which all have their own characteristics, the 4th century is dominated by the works of Aphrahaṭ and Ephrem. From the 6th century onwards most writings are attributed to either the East- or West-Syrian literature, according to the dogmatic position of their authors, without however making the partition between the two communities watertight. When in the 8th century creative Syriac literature waned, the need was felt to collect and to consolidate the achievements of the former periods, resulting in some important works of an encyclopaedic nature. The figure of Barhebraeus, the greatest of all Syriac polymaths (d. 1286), stands at the close of the creative period of Syriac literature. In the subsequent period the classical Syriac language continued to be used, right up to the present day, without however regaining the prestige which Aramaic and Syriac had enjoyed in former periods.

The Syriac language, vehicle of Syriac literature, is a literary form of Aramaic which on the one hand emerged from the older Aramaic literary tradition, known to us in Biblical Aramaic, Qumran Aramaic, and the language of the earliest Targum, and on the other hand reflected the local Aramaic dialect of Edessa. This new literary dialect underwent a process of standardization resulting in what is known as the classical Syriac language, the common heritage of all Syrian Christians, irrespective of their church or denomination.

The fact that the Syrian Christians shared with the Palestinian and Mesopotamian Jews the same literary Aramaic tradition and that, particularly in

Mesopotamia, the adherents of both religions used language forms that must have been close to each other, is not without significance for the study of the sources of Syriac literature. Moreover, both in the Roman and the Persian Empire, Jewish communities played an important role in the expansion of Syriac Christianity. Jews and Syrian Christians were neighbours who, when it came to defending their own identities, turned enemies.

Apart from their obvious links with Judaism, Syrian Christians felt themselves part of Christianity as it developed in the Graeco-Roman world. The spread of the Greek language in Syria and Mesopotamia, as well as the presence of bilingual centres of learning, opened the way to intensive translation activities, both from Syriac into Greek and from Greek into Syriac. It is no wonder, therefore, that Syriac literature, though maintaining its own distinctive features, has been deeply influenced by Greek literary culture.

1.2. The Sources of Syriac Biblical Interpretation

1.2.1. The Biblical Text

The Syriac Peshitta of the OT is a translation of the Hebrew Bible.[1] The oldest manuscripts go back to the 5th century, but it appears that the 4th-century writers Aphrahaṭ and Ephrem already knew a form of the text almost identical to the Peshitta. There is reason, therefore, to suppose that the OT Peshitta antedates the whole of Syriac literature and had been created in the 1st or 2nd century.

There is an ongoing debate among scholars with regard to the question whether the OT Peshitta is the work of Jews, Christians or Judaeo-Christians (a group which has been variously defined).[2] Irrespective of the answer that has been given, or will be given, to this question, Jewish influence on the Peshitta cannot be denied. This influence, stronger in the Pentateuch, Chronicles and Proverbs than in other biblical books, is reflected in the incorporation of Jewish exegetical traditions by the translators and their use of phraseology and terminology similar to that found in the Targum.[3]

Although the position of the Peshitta has remained basically unchallenged, Syrian exegetes were always aware of the existence of alternative readings, if not of other biblical versions, which might have an equal claim to authority. This awareness, which is already attested in the earliest biblical commentaries[4] and further developed in later writings, is evidence for the idea of the

---

[1] The apocryphal or deuterocanonical books, which are generally regarded as parts of the Peshitta tradition, were translated from Greek (with the exception of Sirach). The history of the canon in the Syrian churches has not yet satisfactorily been described; for a first attempt, see E. B. Eising, *Zur Geschichte des Kanons der Heiligen Schrift in der Ostsyrischen Kirche im ersten Jahrtausend* (Ph.D. thesis; Würzburg 1972).

[2] P. B. Dirksen, "The Old Testament Peshitta", *Mikra. Text, Translation, Reading, and Interpretation of the Hebrew Bible in Ancient Judaism and Early Christianity* (CRINT II/1, ed. M. J. Mulder; Assen / Maastricht / Philadelphia 1988) 255–297. See also the preceding ch. 16 by M. Weitzmann.

[3] S. P. Brock, "Bibelübersetzungen I", TRE 6 (1980) 182–183.

[4] In his *Commentary on Genesis,* Ephrem [see sect. 3] first quotes Gen 49:23 according to the Peshitta ("the lords of the troops", as a rendering of MT "the lords of the arrows", i.e. the

'textual plurality' of the Bible.[5] It may be considered a characteristic of the whole of Syriac exegesis.

With the increasing translation activity in the 5th century, a number of LXX elements found their way into Syriac exegetical literature, the more so since the Greek works that were being translated were based on the LXX. This process can be studied in some detail in the Syriac translations of the biblical commentaries of Theodore of Mopsuestia, the translation of which commenced in the first half of the 5th century [see 5.2]. Whereas the first translators tried to substitute Peshitta quotations (occasionally slightly adapted) for LXX verses in Theodore's work, in some cases the discrepancies between Peshitta and LXX were such that more drastic solutions were necessary in order to make the commentary understandable in Syriac circles. The translators then proceeded either to provide a more or less literal translation of the Greek verse, or to first quote the verse in its Peshitta form, followed by a literal translation of the Greek text, explicitly presented as "Greek" (*Yawnāyā*), and serving as the basis for the comments to follow. This procedure has left its traces upon later East-Syrian exegetical literature, where quotations from "the Greek" are common practice whenever Peshitta and LXX are substantially different. In most West-Syrian biblical commentaries, too, quotations from "the Greek" or "the Seventy" regularly occur, having been derived by the commentators either from Greek works consulted or directly from the LXX.

Despite the acquaintance of Syrian scholars with the LXX, it was not until the years 613–617 that a full Syriac translation of the Greek Bible was produced under the direction of the West-Syrian bishop Paul of Tella.[6] It was based on Origen's Hexaplaric recension of the LXX. This translation, known as the Syro-Hexapla and preserved in fragmentary form, has occasionally been used by West-Syrian scholars. A letter written by the East-Syrian Patriarch Timothy I (780–823) shows that in any case from the end of the 8th century onwards the Syro-Hexapla was also available in East-Syrian circles.[7]

In commentaries where Syro-Hexaplaric quotations occur, the latter are generally included for their exegetical value or with the intention of adding to the commentary's learned character. In West-Syrian literature, however, especially in two *Catenae* of the Islamic period [see HBOT I/2, ch. 36, 2.3], the Syro-Hexaplaric version of some biblical books occasionally serves as the

archers), and then gives an alternative reading ("the lords of division"), which is found in *Tg. Onq.*. When speaking about Gen 3:22, Eusebius of Emesa [see sect. 3.3] notes that some Syrians read the words "Behold, Adam has become like one of us (in order to know good and evil)" as it is in the LXX (which holds true for the Peshitta), whereas others read: "Behold, Adam has become as one, in order to have from himself the knowledge of good and evil", which closely agrees with *Tg. Onq.* (Heb *mimmennû* understood not as "from us" but as "from him(self)").

[5] This expression is taken from M. Harl, "La Septante et la pluralité textuelle des Écritures", *La langue de Japhet. Quinze études sur la Septante et le grec des chrétiens* (Paris 1992) 253–266.

[6] Some sources point to the East-Syrian Patriarch Mar Aba (who died in 552) or to the West-Syrian author Polycarpus (early 6th c.) as translators of (parts of) the LXX. These assumptions, however, cannot be substantiated.

[7] O. Braun, "Ein Brief des Katholikos Timotheos I über biblische Studien des 9 Jahrhunderts", *OrChr* 1 (1901) 299–313.

basis for the commentary. A special use of the Syro-Hexapla has been made by Dionysius bar Ṣalibi (d. 1171), in that for some biblical books this version was the basis for his 'spiritual' commentary, which he juxtaposed to his 'factual' commentary, based on the Peshitta [see HBOT I/2, ch. 36, 4].

Apart from quotations from the Greek Bible, most Syriac commentaries also present references to, or quotations from, "the Hebrew (Bible)" (*'Ebrāyā*). The origin of these quotations cannot easily be determined. In a few cases it cannot be excluded that Syrian exegetes either directly or indirectly had access to the Hebrew Bible. However, it is unlikely that Syrian scholars had a more than superficial knowledge of the Hebrew language. Moreover, many of the *'Ebrāyā* quotations and references do not agree with the Hebrew Bible, but rather reflect Targum readings or Midrashic traditions. It is plausible, therefore, that they reached the Syrians through oral transmission or through consultation with contemporary Jews.[8] Whereas the practice of quoting "the Hebrew" has early patristic precedents (e.g. Origen, Eusebius of Caesarea, Eusebius of Emesa), in Syriac exegetical literature this practice has been further developed and slightly expanded. References to "the Hebrew" (less frequently to "the Hebrews") form part of the traditional pattern of Syriac biblical commentaries and prove that the transmission of the Hebrew biblical text and Jewish interpretations by contemporary Jews fell within the intellectual horizon of Syrian biblical scholars.

1.2.2. Jewish Sources

The proximity of Jews and Christians in Northern Syria and Mesopotamia, already referred to in the preceding sections, will also account for the presence of Jewish elements in Syriac literature.[9] It is mostly impossible to establish a direct relationship between extant Jewish and Christian texts, but the presence of the same motifs, approaches and identifications in Syriac and Jewish sources points to some degree of interdependence.

Syriac works which are particularly rich from this point of view, are Aphrahaṭ's *Demonstrations,* Ephrem's *Commentaries on Genesis and Exodus,* and the anonymous *Cave of Treasures.* The authors of these works show a keen interest in reconstructing the historical events related in the Bible as well as in questions of chronology, the identity of biblical persons, and the motives behind human actions or divine interventions. In order to solve questions to which the biblical text did not provide immediate or sufficient answers, they developed certain techniques – ways of reasoning as well as the combination of different biblical passages – which could produce the required information. Not only this approach itself but also many of its results are reminiscent of rabbinic exegesis. Uncertainty about how Cain came to his end is solved by supposing that Lamech killed him (cf. Gen 4:23); the mystery of Melchizedek's ancestry and priestly status (cf. Gen 14:18–20) is disclosed by

[8] Cf. L. Van Rompay, *Le commentaire sur Genèse-Exode 9,32 du manuscrit (olim) Diyarbakir 22* (CSCO 484/Syr. 206; Louvain 1986) XXXVIII–XL.

[9] Cf. Brock, Jewish Traditions (1979); H. J. W. Drijvers, "Jews and Christians at Edessa", *JJS* 36 (1985) 88–102.

identifying him with Shem, Noah's son, or with Shem's great-grandson; an explanation as to why the Lord would have sought to kill Moses (Exod 4:24) is found in assuming that Zipporah had prevented Moses's son (or one of his two sons) from being circumcised.

While it is certainly useful to investigate further the parallels between Jewish and Syriac exegetical literature, the juxtaposition of passages will not suffice to explain the nature of the interrelationship between the texts. If Syriac authors have borrowed from written Jewish sources, the latter are no longer extant. No doubt oral tradition may account for part of the parallels. In addition, however, one may suppose that the corpus of Jewish literature available in the first centuries was different from the rabbinic literature presently known to us. One may think here of the vast field of Jewish literature of the Second Temple Period, anterior to classical rabbinic literature. The genre of the 'Rewritten Bible' in particular may have inspired early Syrian exegetes. The *Genesis Apocryphon* is an example; it presents a more elaborate and more personal picture of Abraham than the one found in the biblical text, giving more attention to Abraham's feelings, fears and prayers. It is not presumptuous to see in it a precedent for Ephrem's portrayal of the patriarch in his *Commentary on Genesis*. The chronological preoccupation of the author of *Jubilees* has its parallel in the Syriac *Cave of Treasures*. More important perhaps are the traditions related to Adam, Paradise, and the ante-diluvian history. Although Syriac literature has not preserved independent witnesses of any of the primary Adam books, parts of the complex Adam traditions were incorporated into the *Cave of Treasures* as well as the *Testament of Adam*.[10] In addition, some motifs and themes originating from the Adam literature were embedded in Syriac literature. An interesting example is the theme of the paradisaic "robe of glory", prominently present in various early Syriac exegetic and theological works.[11]

1.2.3. Greek Literature

Whereas Aramaic literary culture as well as Jewish traditions had prepared the ground from which Syriac exegetical literature sprang, the same area had for centuries been exposed to the pervasive influence of Graeco-Roman civilization. Although this influence may have been weaker in those regions that were part of the Parthian, and later of the Sassanid Empire, familiarity with Hellenistic material and intellectual culture must have been widespread. Despite its genuine Semitic character, Syriac literature was never isolated from the Graeco-Roman world.

With the increasing translation activity from Greek into Syriac in the early 5th century, Greek exegetical works became known in the Syrian area. In the first place, the work of Antiochene exegetes enjoyed great popularity among the Syrians, especially the writings of Theodore of Mopsuestia [see 5.2]. In

---

[10] Cf. M. E. Stone, *A History of the Literature of Adam and Eve* (SBL, Early Judaism and Its Literature 3; Atlanta 1992) esp. 90–98.

[11] Kowalski, Rivestíti di gloria (1982) [see sect. 3 below].

addition, Basil of Caesarea's *Homilies on the Hexaemeron*[12] and other writings of the Cappadocians, especially Gregory of Nazianzus, may have been part of school curricula from the 5th century onwards.

In the School of Edessa, the foundation was laid for the exegetical activity of the East-Syrian Christians, for whom Theodore of Mopsuestia became the main authority. However, in the years following the Council of Ephesus (431), the controversy over Antiochene Christology aroused opposition to Theodore's works and the Antiochene orientation of exegesis at Edessa. Those who opted for Ephesan orthodoxy turned away from Theodore. Syrian authors like Jacob of Serug [see 6.1], when rejecting Theodore, preferred Ephrem's interpretation of the biblical text. Alternatively, the writings of the Alexandrian theologians, like Cyril and Athanasius of Alexandria, rapidly won popularity in Edessa and were first translated into Syriac in the 5th century. These developments contributed to the establishment of an independent West-Syrian branch of exegesis.

In later centuries, especially in the Muslim period, knowledge of Greek among the Syrians decreased and became limited to certain schools and monasteries. However, since so many Syriac translations of Greek works were available, the process of the hellenization of Syriac literature did to some extent continue. Existing translations were revised, adapted and reshaped, or became the subject of commentaries. Syriac works were modelled on Greek examples or drew largely on Greek sources. Syriac literary culture remained hybrid, capable of incorporating and harmoniously uniting Greek and Syriac traditions, without completely assimilating the one into the other and without giving up the distinctive features of authentic Syriac tradition.

1.3. *The Earliest Period of Syriac Literature*

A number of Syriac texts have come down to us from the period between the 2nd and 4th centuries, all of which pose their own problems of interpretation. In most cases it is extremely difficult to ascertain how, and to what extent, they are related to each other and to the mainstream of later Syriac literature. As a matter of fact, prior to the 4th century, Syriac Christianity was characterized by great diversity. Various Christian groups created their own literature, reflecting the complexity of cultural patterns in Syria and Mesopotamia. Some of them inherited ideas of the Semitic or Greek Hellenistic world, others were closer to Judaism or underwent the influence of Persian dualistic doctrines. Since the works of this period often did not comply with the standards of later orthodoxy, many of them have disappeared, whereas others were only very imperfectly transmitted, sometimes in expurgated versions.[13]

---

[12] A Syriac fragment of this work (ms. British Library, Add. 17.143) probably dates from the 5th century. See most recently R. W. Thomson, "The Syriac and Armenian Versions of the *Hexaemeron* by Basil of Caesarea", StPatr 27 (ed. E. A. Livingstone; Leuven 1993) 113–117.

[13] For a survey of the literature of this period, see Murray, Symbols (1975) 4–37; idem, "The Characteristics of the Earliest Syriac Christianity", *East of Byzantium. Syria and Armenia in the Formative Period* (ed. N. G. Garsoïan / T. F. Mathews / R. W. Thomson; Washington 1982) 3–16;

The line between heterodoxy and orthodoxy cannot easily be drawn with regard to early Syriac literature, and indeed these terms are rather meaningless prior to the establishment of Nicene orthodoxy in the 4th century. In addition, language boundaries hardly imposed themselves. Many works are known to have circulated in both a Syriac and a Greek version (e.g. the *Odes of Solomon* and the works of Bardaisan) and some works of Syriac origin occasionally turn up in a Coptic version (e.g. some of the *Odes of Solomon* as well as the *Gospel of Thomas* and the *Gospel of Philip*), into which language they may have been translated either directly or through a Greek intermediary. On the other hand, works written in Greek in a bilingual Syrian context may shed some light on Syriac Christianity (e.g. the *Pseudo-Clementine* writings and the *Didascalia of the Apostles*).

None of the works of this period deals explicitly with the interpretation of the OT. Only isolated elements can be detected. Bardaisan, in the *Book of the Laws of the Countries,* has a note on man as the image of God, explained by him as man's ability to act according to free will (an idea that was later adopted and elaborated by Ephrem). He differs, however, from later Syriac tradition, when – in line with the *Book of Enoch* – he identifies the "sons of God" or "sons of (the) gods" (Gen 6:2 and 4) as angels, whose fall was provoked by their intercourse with the "daughters of men".[14] The biblical story of Paradise and of the original state of human happiness may have contributed to the imagery found in the *Odes of Solomon* as well as in the *Hymn of the Pearl.*[15] In the *Didascalia* OT verses are sometimes quoted to illustrate or to support prescriptions concerning liturgy, and ecclesiastical organization and discipline. However, for a fuller and more coherent treatment of the OT we must turn to the main representatives of 4th-century Syriac Christianity, Aphrahaṭ and Ephrem.

2. Aphrahaṭ

Editions and translations: I. Parisot, *Aphraatis Sapientis Persae Demonstrationes* (PS I,1–2; Paris 1894–1907; Syriac and Latin transl.); M.-J. Pierre, *Aphraate le sage persan. Les exposés* (SC 349 and 359; Paris 1988–1989; French transl.); P. Bruns, *Aphrahat. Unterweisungen* 1–2 (FontC 5; Freiburg etc. 1991; German transl.)

Studies: J. Neusner, *Aphrahat and Judaism. The Christian-Jewish Argument in Fourth-Century Iran* (SPB 19; Leiden 1971); G. G. Blum, "Afrahaṭ", TRE 1 (1977) 625–635; R. J. Owens, *The Genesis and Exodus Citations of Aphrahat the Persian Sage* (Monographs of the Peshiṭta Institute 3; Leiden 1983); P. Bruns, *Das Christusbild Aphrahats des Persischen Weisen* (Hereditas. Studien zur Alten Kirchengeschichte 4; Bonn 1990), with further references.

H. J. W. Drijvers, "East of Antioch. Forces and Structures in the Development of Early Syriac Theology", *East of Antioch. Studies in Early Syriac Christianity* (Variorum Reprints; London 1984) 1–27.

[14] Ed. F. Nau, *Bardesanes. Liber legum regionum* (PS I,2; Paris 1907) 547–548 and 560. The same idea is reflected in the *Acts of Judas Thomas* III. 32: H. J. W. Drijvers, "Thomasakten", *Neutestamentliche Apokryphen,* II. *Apostolisches, Apokalypsen und Verwandtes,* 5. Auflage (ed. W. Schneemelcher; Tübingen 1989) 316. It is, however, strongly rejected by Ephrem, cf. Kronholm, Motifs from Genesis (1978) 166–168 [see sect. 3].

[15] Cf. Drijvers, Thomasakten (1989) 297.

2.1. General Remarks

The twenty-three homilies (or *Demonstrations, taḥwyātā*) which in Syriac tradition are attributed to Aphrahaṭ, "the Persian Sage", can be dated to the years 337–345. Their author lived in the Persian Empire, where he must have occupied an important position in the Christian community, in that period prey to both internal crises and persecution by the Persian authorities.

While the *Demonstrations* are based mainly on the Bible and are replete with quotations and biblical arguments, Aphrahaṭ's approach to the biblical text cannot be divorced from the general tendency of the work, which is not primarily exegetic. Rather Aphrahaṭ concentrates on essential aspects of Christian life, e.g. in the *Demonstrations* on faith, love, fasting, prayer, the members of the "Covenant", or on themes on which Mesopotamian Christians had to defend their identity against the Jews (or Judaizing groups within Christianity), e.g. in the *Demonstrations* on circumcision, the Paschal Sacrifice, the Sabbath, the distinctions made among foods, the peoples substituted for the (chosen) people, virginity and sanctity, and the Jews' expectation that they are destined to be gathered together.

Among the many Christians who wrote against the Jews, Aphrahaṭ is one of the very few who did not use fictitious arguments, but gave serious attention to the Jews' actual objections against Christianity. As to the practical commandments of the OT, he did not regard them as futile or explain them symbolically or allegorically, but placed them in their historical context. Moreover, "he met the opposition mostly on the neutral grounds provided by Hebrew Scriptures and Israelite history".[16] Rather than reading the OT from the viewpoint of the NT, he read the NT from the viewpoint of the OT. This distinction may be subtle; it has, however, considerable consequences. The NT does not simply take the place of the OT, rather Christianity is given a place within the framework of the OT. Even Christ's divinity, the fact that he is called "God", is justified on the grounds of the OT practice that men can be called "God", as happened to Moses, according to Exod 4:16 and 7:1.

2.2. Historical and Typological Interpretation

It is no wonder, therefore, that in Aphrahaṭ's reading of the OT many features of his Jewish context can be detected. In his historical interpretation he included traditions of Jewish origin [see 1.2.2], e.g. concerning Paradise, the acceptance of Abel's sacrifice through fire from heaven, which did not touch Cain's sacrifice (cf. Gen 4:4–5), and God's nocturnal encounter with Moses (Exod 4:24–26).[17]

In his typological interpretation,[18] which is based on the continuity of God's work of salvation in the OT and the NT, Aphrahaṭ uses the terms *rāzā*

---

[16] Neusner, Aphrahat and Judaism (1971) 244.

[17] Cf. A. Guillaumont, "Un midrash d'Exode 4,24–26 chez Aphraate et Ephrem de Nisibe", *A Tribute to Arthur Vööbus. Studies in Early Christian Literature and Its Environment, Primarily in the Syrian East* (ed. R. H. Fischer; Chicago 1977) 89–95.

[18] Bruns, Das Christusbild (1990) 100–121.

'mystery, symbol' and *ṭupsā* 'type'. Jacob's vision (Gen 28:12–15) is a symbol of our Redeemer; the gate of heaven is Christ; the ladder itself is a symbol of our Redeemer as well as a symbol of the Cross. The stone on which Jacob poured oil (Gen 28:18 and 22) is a type of the peoples. The most prominent symbol is the Paschal Sacrifice of the OT (Exod 12:3–28), which points directly to Christ: "it was given as a symbol to the first people, and its truth (*šrārā*) is today heard among the peoples" (*Dem.* 12.5).

In order to demonstrate the continuation of the OT in the NT, Aphrahaṭ juxtaposes Christ with OT figures. Along with the common Adam/Christ parallel, Aphrahaṭ establishes extensive comparisons of Moses and Elijah with Christ. Not only through their divine election, but also through their virtuous and ascetic life, they prefigure Christ. Moreover, in lists of OT examples, especially in those formulated in the literary form which MURRAY called "comparison-series",[19] Christ appears as the one who shares much with OT figures (Joseph, Moses, Joshua, Jephthah, David, Elijah, Elisha, Hezekiah, Josiah, Daniel, the Three Children, Mordecai), and yet surpasses them. Aphrahaṭ shows little interest in speculative theology or dogma; the prominence of the NT over the OT is expressed by him in terms of the former's outweighing the OT with respect to salvation, because it raises the events of the OT to a more spiritual level, and gives them a wider scope.

Aphrahaṭ's view on history comes to the fore in *Dem.* 5 ("On Wars").[20] In Daniel's vision (Daniel 7), Aphrahaṭ interprets the first beast as the kingdom of Babel, the second as the kingdom of Media and Persia. The third beast is Alexander, and the fourth the kingdom of the sons of Esau, i.e. the kingdom of the Greeks. Among the latter, he first counts seventeen kings of the Greeks, who reigned during 269 years, from Seleucus Nicanor (*sic*) to Ptolemaeus, and then twenty-seven "Caesars", from Augustus to Philippus Caesar, a period of 293 years, to which eighteen years of Severus (Septimius Severus, 193–211?) should be added. Furthermore, the ram of Daniel's second vision (Dan 8:4–8) is seen as Darius, the king of Media and Persia, while the he-goat is Alexander. Although its two horns (i.e. Media and Persia) were broken (Dan 8:7), the ram – which now becomes Shapur, the Sassanid king, although the latter is not explicitly named – wages war against the fourth beast, which is now the Roman Empire. Since the latter is Christian, however, it will not be defeated until the coming of Christ. This interpretation gives us some inkling of the delicate position of the Christians of the Sassanid Empire in a period when their rulers were almost continuously at war with the Christian Roman Empire.

2.3. *Aphrahaṭ's Place in Tradition*

Writing in the Sassanid Empire, Aphrahaṭ must have been quite isolated from Christianity as it developed in the Roman Empire. The Council of Nicaea (325) did not touch his theology and he probably knew no Greek. However,

---

[19] R. MURRAY, "Some Rhetorical Patterns in Early Syriac Literature", *A Tribute to Arthur Vööbus* (1977) 109–131 [see note 17].

[20] Cf. P.F. BEATRICE, "Pagans and Christians on the Book of Daniel", StPatr 25 (ed. E.A. Livingstone; Leuven 1993) 27–45, esp. 34.

he himself emphasizes that what he writes is "according to the understanding of the entire Church" (*Dem.* 22.26). His interpretation of Daniel's vision likewise shows that he identified himself with a Christianity not restricted by political frontiers. Moreover, the artistic style of his work attests to his full participation in the literary culture of his day, which was highly complex, and moulded by both Semitic and Hellenistic traditions.

Although Aphrahaṭ is occasionally quoted in later works, his impact on the development of Syriac exegesis was limited. Apparently his theological and exegetical concepts did not meet the requirements of later exegetes. The *Demonstrations* did, however, find their way into Armenian, and – to a lesser extent – Georgian, Christian-Arabic and Ethiopic literature.

3. Ephrem

Editions and translations: R.-M. Tonneau, *Sancti Ephraem Syri in Genesim et in Exodum Commentarii* (CSCO 152–153/Syr. 71–72; Louvain 1955; Syriac and Latin transl.); E. Beck, *Des Heiligen Ephraem des Syrers Hymnen De Paradiso und Contra Julianum* (CSCO 174–175/Syr. 78–79; Louvain 1957; Syriac and German transl.); P. Féghali, "Note sur l'exégèse de Saint Ephrem. Commentaire sur le déluge (Gn 6,1–9,17)", *Parole de l'Orient* 8 (1977–1978) 67–86 (French transl.); idem, "Les premiers jours de la création. Commentaire de Gn 1,1–2,4 par Saint Ephrem", *Parole de l'Orient* 13 (1986) 3–30 (French transl.); K. E. McVey, *Ephrem the Syrian. Hymns* (CWS; New York 1989; English transl.); S. Brock, *Saint Ephrem. Hymns on Paradise* (Crestwood, New York 1990; English transl.), with a survey of Ephrem's works (230–233); A. G. P. Janson / L. Van Rompay, *Efrem de Syriër. Uitleg van het boek Genesis* (Christelijke Bronnen 5; Kampen 1993; Dutch transl.); E. G. Mathews/J. P. Amar, *St. Ephrem the Syrian. Selected Prose Works* (FC 91; Washington 1994; English transl.).

Studies: T. Jansma, "Ephraems Beschreibung des ersten Tages der Schöpfung. Bemerkungen über den Charakter seines Kommentars zur Genesis", *OCP* 37 (1971) 295–316; S. Hidal, *Interpretatio Syriaca. Die Kommentare des Heiligen Ephräm des Syrers zu Genesis und Exodus mit besonderer Berücksichtigung ihrer auslegungsgeschichtlichen Stellung* (ConBOT 6; Lund 1974); Murray, Symbols (1975); idem, "The Theory of Symbolism in St. Ephrem's Theology", *Mélanges offerts au R. P. François Graffin, S. J.* (*Parole de l'Orient* 6–7; 1975–1976) 1–20; T. Kronholm, *Motifs from Genesis 1–11 in the Genuine Hymns of Ephrem the Syrian. With Particular Reference to the Influence of Jewish Exegetical Tradition* (ConBOT 11; Lund 1978); B. de Margerie, *Introduction à l'histoire de l'exégèse,* I. *Les Pères grecs et orientaux* (Paris 1980) 165–187 ("La poésie biblique de Saint Ephrem exégète syrien [306–373]"); A. Kowalski, "Rivestíti di gloria. Adamo ed Eva nel commento di sant'Efrem a Gen 2,25. Ricerca sulle fonti dell'esegesi siriaca", *Cristianesimo nella storia* 3 (1982) 41–60; T. Bou Mansour, *La pensée symbolique de Saint Éphrem le Syrien* (Bibliothèque de l'Université Saint-Esprit 16; Kaslik 1988); A. Salvesen, "The Exodus Commentary of St. Ephrem", StPatr 25 (ed. E. A. Livingstone; Leuven 1993) 332–338.

3.1. General Remarks

Ephrem, born at the beginning of the 4th century, spent part of his life in Nisibis and moved to Edessa in 363 when, after Julian the Apostate's death, the Romans had to surrender Nisibis to the Persians. He died in Edessa in 373. He is the most outspoken representative of Syriac Christianity prior to the Christological discussions of the 5th century and was held in high esteem by all later Syrian Christians.

His œuvre is of an amazing complexity. Whereas his hymns (*madrāšē*) and metrical homilies (*mēmrē*) attest to the poet's artistry, some of these, as well as certain of his prose works, contain ardent refutations of heretical doctrines or bitter attacks on the Jews' unwillingness to accept Christ. From his specifically exegetical works, a *Commentary on the Diatessaron* has been preserved, as well as a *Commentary (puššāqā) on Genesis* and a more succinct *Explanation (turgāmā) of Exodus.*[21] These works are the first Syriac representatives of the specific genre of exegetical commentaries.

3.2. The Various Levels of Exegesis

3.2.1. Historical Exegesis and Christian Message

Ephrem holds the view that the earlier generations had a natural knowledge of the Creator. Only when Abraham's descendants settled in Egypt did they abandon themselves to idolatry and forget God's commandments. This is why God entrusted Moses with the task of leading the people out of Egypt and subsequently restoring the true knowledge about the Creator and his creatures by means of Scripture. As Ephrem explicitly states in the preface to his *Commentary,* Moses also wrote about the "symbols (*rāzē*) of the Son", "the types (*ṭupsē*) of the latter in the just", and "the prefigurations (*pel(')ātā*) indicated by Moses's staff".[22]

In the *Commentary* itself the reader will find above all a historical explanation of the biblical text. From the first moment of creation onwards, Ephrem tries to ascertain what really happened and why it happened. The first two chapters of Genesis are explained in great detail by Ephrem, whose reconstruction of creation is based primarily on a scrupulous pondering of the biblical text, supported at times by passages taken from elsewhere in the Bible. Ephrem is anxious that the reader should understand that everything did happen exactly as it is reported in the Bible. At the same time he is preoccupied with disproving heretical doctrines, especially those of Mani and Bardaisan. The same can be said with regard to his treatment of the history of sin and expulsion from Paradise (Genesis 3). Although no opponents are named, he is refuting here Marcion's ideas about the imperfect and punishing God of the OT. As opposed to Marcion, Ephrem insists on human free will[23] on the one hand and God's grace on the other.

---

[21] In later Syriac compilations (e.g. the *Catena* of the monk Severus, see HBOT I/2, ch. 36, 2.3) as well as in Armenian translations and reworkings, Ephrem's name is also mentioned in connection with other OT books. However, in the present state of research, no clear picture of these secondary materials can be provided. As for the *Commentaries on Genesis and Exodus,* some scholars have voiced doubts concerning their authenticity, most recently Kowalski, Perfezione (1989) 45, note 22 [see sect. 4.1]. However, the arguments adduced against the authenticity (of the entire works or some passages of them) carry little weight and lack conviction. Cf. J. Melki, "Saint Ephrem le Syrien. Un bilan de l'édition critique", *Parole de l'Orient* 11 (1983) 49-50.

[22] For a parallel statement in the *Acts of Judas Thomas,* see Hidal, Interpretatio Syriaca (1974) 44.

[23] According to Ephrem, God created man in an intermediary state, neither mortal nor immortal. If he obeyed the commandment, he would be rewarded with the fruit of the Tree of Life; if he disobeyed, he would be reduced to the state of mortality. The same idea is found in Theophilus of Antioch, *To Autolycus* II. 27; in Nemesius of Emesa, *On the nature of man* 46, it is ascribed to "the Hebrews", cf. D.T. Runia, *Philo in Early Christian Literature* (CRINT III/3; Assen / Minneapolis 1993) 263-264. See also below, 6.1 (Jacob of Serug).

It will be clear from this that Ephrem's historical exegesis is not restricted to reporting and analysing biblical events. Although strictly adhering to the biblical text, he sagaciously fills the gaps in the biblical narrative and thereby succeeds in unfolding his own concept of God and man in early human history. Biblical interpretation becomes a way of expressing theological views and refuting heterodox doctrines. The term 'historical exegesis' (Ephrem rather uses the term 'factual', *su'rānāyā)* is justified, in that the historical framework of the Bible constitutes the starting-point of the interpretation. The interpretation itself, however, is more than once the work of a defender of orthodox theological schemes and an opponent of unorthodox views, rather than that of an unbiased exegete.

While in the commentary on the first chapters of Genesis the origin of evil is Ephrem's prime concern, in the following chapters man's ability to behave righteously and to please God gradually comes to the fore. This becomes clear in the case of Enoch, who was translated by God (Gen 5:24), as well as in that of Noah (Gen 6:8), who for five hundred years lived celibate and chaste. Abraham's righteousness is extensively discussed. His faith, right from the first moment of his election, is strongly defended and he is depicted as a model of virtuous and ascetic life. Ephrem's portrayals of Jacob and Joseph equally extol the virtue of these patriarchs. Apart from their uprightness, Ephrem also points to God's guidance in their lives. As a matter of fact, their excellence or splendour (for which Ephrem uses the term *ziwā* 'shining') has to do both with divine election and the human response to it, i.e. virtuous behaviour.

Throughout his *Commentary* Ephrem explains OT history largely within its own framework. This approach, far from being self-evident, must rest on a deliberate choice on the part of the author. One of the reasons may be that, since Ephrem as well as many of his readers must have been acquainted with Jewish traditional material, he may have opted for a genre and an approach which allowed him to select and incorporate into his own perspective certain traditions current in his day. At first sight, Ephrem's *Commentary* does indeed look very Jewish, both in its hermeneutical approach and in its many haggadic features. The use of *a fortiori* arguments, the motif of the interplay between Divine Justice and Divine Grace, traditions about Paradise, the antediluvian generations, Cain being killed by Lamech, the provenance of Hagar, as well as certain identifications (e.g. Iscah/Sarah, Melchizedek/Shem) and many minor elements must have been familiar to Ephrem's readers. Ephrem may even have wished to create a Christian counterpart to Jewish exegesis, using some of the same ingredients and developing them according to his own needs. It should also be noted that the *Commentary* is one of the very few of Ephrem's works which do not contain overt polemics against the Jews.

3.2.2. Limited Use of New Testament Typology

Notwithstanding his leaning on Jewish tradition, Ephrem occasionally advances his own Christian position. Sometimes he does so by briefly pointing to a verse or an event in the NT for support or comparison. More important are those cases where OT events are seen as representations or prefigurations of the NT (both the roots *ṣwr* ʿdepict, representʾ and *ršm* ʿmark, expressʾ are used): the sound which preceded God's coming to Paradise (Gen 3:8) represents John's voice preceding the coming of the Son; in Seth, who was begotten in Adam's likeness (Gen 5:3), the image of the Son is represented; Abraham's walking through the length and the breadth of the land (Gen 13:17) is an expression of the Cross; in the ram "hung" in the tree (Gen 22:13 – Ephrem uses *tlē* instead of the common Peshitta reading *'aḥid* "caught") the Day (cf. John 8:56) of Christ's crucifixion is represented; Jacob's oil (Gen 28:18) represents a symbol of Christ, whereas a symbol of the Church is expressed by the stone (Gen 28:22); Jacob was able to roll the stone from the mouth of the well (Gen 29:10) through the Son hidden in him; Tamar's three pledges (Gen 38:18) are witnesses to the Son; the crossing of Jacob's hands while blessing Joseph's sons (Gen 48:14) expresses the Cross.

Thus far the list is limited and the typologies are not elaborated, but only briefly indicated, so that they scarcely interrupt the historical reconstruction of the biblical events. Ephrem's explanation of Jacob's blessings (Genesis 49) offers a somewhat different picture. In the historical explanation of this chapter – where most of the blessings and prophecies are interpreted within the historical context of the OT – he makes an exception for the second part of Judah's blessing (Gen 49:10–12), which according to him no longer points to David, but to Jesus, David's offspring. Rather than a typology, we have here a straightforward messianic prediction, fulfilled in Christ. Unlike the succinct use of typologies in the preceding chapters of Genesis, Ephrem devotes a lengthy section to the verses concerning Judah.[24]

After having finished the commentary on Jacob's blessings, Ephrem embarks on a second commentary on the same verses. The approaches of the two commentaries are different: the first is said to have been "according to the facts" (*suʿrānā'it*), the second "according to the spirit" (*ruḥānā'it*). The spiritual explanation focuses on the triumph of Christ and the Church, of which the events related in the OT are images (*dmutā*). Zebulon (Gen 49:13) is a type (*ṭupsā*) of "the peoples living close to the prophets", whereas in Benjamin (Gen 49:27) the apostle Paul is seen. The blessing of Judah, which already received a messianic interpretation in the factual commentary, is omitted here.

Again, in the *Explanation of Exodus,* there are on the one hand cursory references to Christ and the Church: the staffs of Moses and Aaron are seen as a sign (*nišā*) or a symbol (*rāzā*) of the Cross (Exod 8:1–2 (5–6); Exod 14:16; Exod 17:9; Exod 17:11); wood is a symbol of the Cross (Exod 15:25); blood is a symbol of the Gospel which through Christ's death was given to all nations (Exod 24:6); the tabernacle (in Syriac: "Tent of time") will finally make way for the Church, which will remain forever (Exod 25:9). On the

[24] After Judah's blessing, Ephrem returns to the historical interpretation of the remaining blessings (Gen 49:13–27). Only for the word "redemption" in Gen 49:18 (in Dan's blessing) does he juxtapose the historical interpretation and the alternative of seeing all historical liberators as representing the great Redemption which would come about in Jesus.

other hand, a longer typological explanation is found for the biblical prescriptions concerning the paschal lamb (Exod 12:3–28), which are interpreted as related to the NT.

The Christological interpretation of Gen 49:10–12, as well as the spiritual explanation of the whole chapter 49 and the elaborate typology of Exod 12:3–28, are integral parts of Ephrem's exegesis. His search for types in the OT could be restrained in most narrative sections, but was unavoidable in the passages under discussion. The importance attached to them in Jewish exegesis may also have contributed to these typological elaborations. Ephrem may have wished to oppose his own Christian understanding to the Jewish interpretation.

3.2.3. A Different Approach: A Wealth of Symbols

In his *mēmrē* and *madrāšē* and, to a certain extent, in his *Commentary on the Diatessaron,* Ephrem deals with the OT much more freely than he does in his *Commentaries on Genesis and Exodus.* The scope of these works is quite different. They concentrate on the messages of Christianity and on Christ's work of salvation brought about in the Church. Now Ephrem's theological vision spans the whole of human history, from the first moment of creation until the *eschaton.* As an interpreter, therefore, he strives to point out the correlations between the various phases of history, as well as between visible historical events and the underlying scheme of God's dealings with man. Analogies, references, links between events, types, and symbols express the unity of history and God's solicitude for man. This symbolic vision is not restricted to the Bible, but holds true for the whole world, in which the believing eye will discover everywhere revelatory symbols of Christ.[25]

Exemplary for the way Ephrem handles biblical material is his understanding of the story of Paradise, both in his *Hymns on Paradise* and in his other poetic works. Ephrem insists that the terms in which Scripture describes Paradise are only "pale colours" or "metaphors", in themselves unsuitable to express God's majesty, but deliberately chosen by God to adapt to man's weak understanding. It is therefore incorrect, he argues, to concentrate solely on the literal meaning of Scripture, without being aware of its inner meaning (or "hidden power").[26] By locating biblical Paradise outside time and space, Ephrem is able to view it simultaneously as the primordial and eschatological Paradise. It is replete with references to later OT themes and events (Noah's ark, Mount Sinai, the tabernacle, the promised land, the temple) as well as to the *eschaton* which will be reached through Christ's work of salvation. The two trees in Paradise, the fence and the sword (cf. Gen 3:24) and the robe of glory, in which Adam and Eve were wrapped while in Paradise but which

---

[25] Cf. Murray, The Theory of Symbolism (1975–1976); Bou Mansour, La pensée symbolique (1988); S. H. Griffith, "The Image of the Image Maker in the Poetry of St. Ephraem the Syrian", StPatr 25 (ed. E. A. Livingstone; Leuven 1993) 258–269.

[26] See esp. *Hymns on Paradise* XI. 6–7 and the discussion in Brock, Hymns on Paradise (1990) 47–49.

they lost through sin, give further room for reflections on man's original state, his deliberate sin and the possibility of regaining Paradise through Christ.[27]

If we compare Ephrem's understanding of Paradise in his hymns and in his *Commentary on Genesis,* the differences between the two approaches are obvious. The treatment of Paradise in the *Commentary* is much more restricted to the immediate biblical and historical context than in the hymns. Since, however, the interpretations in the hymns are also based on the plain meaning of Scripture, there is a common layer of exegetical and theological themes and motifs, so that both branches of Ephrem's œuvre should be studied together.

3.3. *The Sources and Historical Context of Ephrem's Exegesis*

It may be due in part to the genius of Ephrem as a poet and theologian that so far very few satisfactory conclusions have been reached as to the question of his sources. The affinity between Jewish biblical interpretation and Ephrem's exegesis, especially in his *Commentary on Genesis,* has long puzzled scholars. Since it can nowhere be proved that Ephrem used written Jewish sources, it has been suggested that the traditions which he incorporated into his work, although they may have been of Jewish origin, were in Ephrem's day common property ('Allgemeinbesitz') in the Near East.[28] While this may be true to a certain extent, it is hard to believe that Ephrem, who must have had direct contact with Jews both in Nisibis and in Edessa, was unaware of the fact that (some of) the same traditions were part of contemporary Jewish interpretation. It is more likely, therefore, that he deliberately adopted certain traditions known to him as Jewish and re-used them in the context of his own Christian *Commentary.*

With regard to Ephrem's place in the Christian exegetical tradition, various scholars have pointed to the similarity which exists between Ephrem's approach to the biblical text in his *Commentaries on Genesis and Exodus* and that of the Antiochene exegetes.[29] To the extent that his interpretation is mainly non-allegorical (except in some sections of the 'spiritual' interpretation of Genesis 49) and has its basis in the plain meaning of the text, this similarity does indeed exist. Furthermore, the limited use of types and symbols in the *Commentaries on Genesis and Exodus* establishes a further parallel between these works and the exegetical methods of the Antiochenes. However, although in the *Commentaries* types are indeed found there where according to the Antiochenes they are to be expected, Ephrem does not clearly distinguish between types and symbols.[30] Moreover, elements which may be regarded as

---

[27] Brock, Hymns on Paradise (1990) esp. 49–74; Bou Mansour, La pensée symbolique (1988) esp. 491–526.

[28] Hidal, Interpretatio Syriaca (1974) 137.

[29] Hidal, Interpretatio Syriaca (1974) 139; Murray, The Theory of Symbolism (1975–1976) 5; Kronholm, Motifs from Genesis (1978) 26; Wallace-Hadrill, Christian Antioch (1982) 39–43. Wallace-Hadrill also notes a certain similarity to Theophilus of Antioch: op. cit. 43. See also above, note 23.

[30] A similar fluctuation in terminology may be found in Greek 4th c. Fathers, cf. G. Dorival,

symbols are identified by him quite arbitrarily. In this respect there certainly is a great difference between the author of the *Commentaries* and the much more systematic approach employed by the later Antiochene exegetes.

It seems legitimate to explore possible connections between Ephrem's exegesis and that of the Cappadocian Fathers. There is no evidence, however, that Ephrem used any of their works. In his interpretation of "the spirit (or wind) of God" (Gen 1:2) Ephrem seems to refute ideas that are expressed by Basil of Caesarea,[31] but no literary dependence can be established. Whereas Ephrem's double interpretation of Genesis 49 may have a parallel in Gregory of Nyssa's *Life of Moses,* which also consists of two sections (the second of which contains a *theoria* of Moses's life),[32] and some analogies exist between Ephrem's and Gregory's understanding of Paradise,[33] here again a lack of evidence precludes any conclusions.

A more promising field of research may perhaps be found in the *Commentary on the Octateuch* of Eusebius of Emesa, Ephrem's (slightly older) contemporary, who was born ca. 300 in Edessa. Unlike Ephrem, he received a Greek education and wrote his works in Greek. In the *Commentary on Genesis,*[34] his general approach to the biblical text is similar to Ephrem's in that he, too, is interested in carefully reconstructing biblical history.[35] Though explaining the LXX text, he has incorporated into his commentary Jewish and Syrian traditions, some of which also occur in Ephrem's *Commentary.* A further parallel between the commentaries of the two Syrians may be seen in their limited use of typology and symbolism and the apparent lack of strict criteria for their application.[36] Notwithstanding the distinctive features of each of the two commentaries, these works interestingly show the proximity of early Syriac and Antiochene exegesis in the bilingual context of 4th-century Syria.[37]

"Sens de l'Écriture, I. Le sens de l'Écriture chez les Pères, I. Les Pères grecs", DBSup, fasc. 67 (Paris 1992) 429.

[31] Guillaumont, Genèse 1,1–2 (1973) 127–128.

[32] Hidal, Interpretatio Syriaca (1974) 59–60.

[33] Brock, Hymns on Paradise (1990) 51 and 54–55.

[34] Ed. V. Hovhannessian, *Eusèbe d'Émèse,* I. *Commentaire de l'Octateuque* (Venice 1980; Armenian). For the complicated textual tradition of the work, see F. Petit, "Les fragments grecs d'Eusèbe d'Émèse et de Théodore de Mopsueste: L'apport de Procope de Gaza", *Le Muséon* 104 (1991) 349–354.

[35] On the basis of a study of the Greek fragments of Eusebius's *Commentary,* Hidal was one of the first to draw attention to the similarity between the two men's works. Cf. Hidal, Interpretatio syriaca (1974) esp. 49, 100, 127.

[36] For some general remarks on Eusebius's exegesis, see J. A. Novotny, "Les fragments exégétiques sur les livres de l'Ancien Testament d'Eusèbe d'Émèse", *OCP* 57 (1991) 30–34; A. Kamesar, *Jerome, Greek Scholarship, and the Hebrew Bible. A Study of the* Quaestiones Hebraicae in Genesim (Oxford Classical Monographs; Oxford 1993) 126–175.

[37] In addition to the Armenian branch of the textual tradition, there are some traces of Eusebius's works in Syriac literature: Jacob of Edessa [see HBOT I/2, ch. 36, 2.1] explicitly quotes Eusebius's name in one of his letters and Išoʿdad of Merv [see HBOT I/2, ch. 36, 3.5] borrows passages from his *Commentary,* without, however, mentioning his name.

4. Other Writings Prior to the Dogmatic Split

4.1. *The Book of Steps*

Edition and translation: M. Kmosko, *Liber Graduum* (PS I,3; Paris 1926; Syriac and Latin transl.).

Study: A. Kowalski, *Perfezione e Giustizia di Adamo nel Liber Graduum* (OCA 232; Rome 1989).

A quite different approach to the biblical text is found in the "Book of Steps" (*Ktābā d-massqātā,* "Liber Graduum"), an anonymous work consisting of thirty discourses, which takes a somewhat singular position in Syriac literature. It may be dated to the end of the 4th or the beginning of the 5th century and is probably the product of what has been called "an enthusiastic charismatic movement". In his description of the various steps of ascetic life, the author has a practical goal, namely, to present the reader with the perfect way of life, which consists of radical ascetism.

Paradise and the history of sin play an important role in this work. As a matter of fact, man in his original state of perfection (*gmirutā*) represents the ascetic ideal. Through sin, which was a conscious act of human free will provoked by man's desire to become like God, this original state was lost. God, in his mercy, then established the laws of justice (*kēnutā*), protecting man against further losses and offering him the possibility of eventually regaining his original state.

It is not so much biblical history in its own right which interests the author, but rather its significance for the theological and ascetic system of his work. Though basing himself on the plain meaning of Scripture, he applies a 'metaphoric' or 'symbolic' interpretation (the term *rāzā* 'mystery, symbol' is sometimes used). Yet, apart from the Paradise story, the use of symbols is less developed than in Aphrahaṭ or Ephrem. The author of the *Book of Steps* also differs from these writers in that he gives very little attention to traditions of Jewish origin.

The author shares with Aphrahaṭ and Ephrem the idea of the original androgynous creation of man, the representation of Paradise as a mountain, the insistence on ascetism and sexual abstinence, and the theology of clothing (both for man in Paradise and for the divine incarnation). But no clear links with any of the other 4th-century Syriac writers can be established.

4.2. *The Cave of Treasures*

Edition and translation: Su-Min Ri, *La Caverne des Trésors. Les deux recensions syriaques* (CSCO 486–487/Syr. 207–208; Louvain 1987; Syriac and French transl.).

The anonymous work known as the "Cave of Treasures" (*M'arrat gazzē*) retells the biblical history from the creation to the Christian Pentecost. Detailed accounts are provided for the period up until Melchizedek, but the subsequent events are dealt with in much less detail.[38] The present forms of

[38] For a general presentation of the work, see Stone, A History (1992) 90–95 [see note 10].

the work (an East- and a West-Syrian recension) are probably no older than the 6th century, but most scholars suppose that an older form ('Urschatzhöhle') once existed, going back to the 4th or even to the 3rd century.

The "cave of treasures" is the place, just outside Paradise, where Adam had put gold, incense and myrrh, taken from Paradise upon his expulsion. This became the antediluvian forefathers' place of prayer and cult as well as their burial-place. At the time of the deluge, when the generation of Noah had to leave the area around Paradise, Adam's body was taken into the ark and subsequently deposited by Shem on Golgotha, the centre of the earth and the place where Christ would be crucified. Melchizedek was entrusted with the custody of that site.

The author exhibits a special interest in OT genealogies and chronology. He wants to stress the continuity between the OT and the NT and to smooth away discrepancies and gaps in the biblical narrative which were apparently used by opponents to disprove Christian claims to the OT. The ancestries of Christ, the Virgin Mary, and Melchizedek play an important role in this regard.

According to the author, NT realities are not only prefigured in the OT, but sometimes actually present.[39] This is the case for the Church and Christian liturgy, which are traced back to Eden and to Noah's ark. However, notwithstanding the symbolic structure of the whole work (the first Adam and the second Adam, brought together at Golgotha, the centre of the earth), the number of symbols and types is limited. The text leaves plenty of room for historical interpretation and was apparently written for an audience that was accustomed to a haggadic approach to the biblical text. Apart from the passages where symbolic or typological interpretation is to be expected (e. g. Genesis 22), it seems to occur rather arbitrarily: e. g. Noah, after having drunk wine, is a symbol for Christ's crucifixion, an interpretation explicitly based on the words of Ps 78:65 ("The Lord awoke as one who sleeps and as a man who has shaken off his wine", according to the Peshitta).

The text consists of various sections, all of which have their own characteristics. The re-telling of sections of Genesis, which occupies more than half of the Syriac text, has many features in common with Ephrem's exegesis. The descriptions of Paradise found in Ephrem's works and in the *Cave of Treasures* are clearly interrelated.[40] Ephrem's evocation of the libidinous behaviour of Seth's descendants on the eve of the Flood has an extensive counterpart in the *Cave*. Lamech's killing of Cain, mentioned briefly by Ephrem, is reported in great detail in the *Cave*. Ascetic features in the description of the lives of the patriarchs are common to Ephrem and the author of the *Cave*. On other occasions, however, the author of the *Cave* seems to deliberately take an

---

[39] Cf. M. SIMON, "Melchisédech dans la polémique entre juifs et chrétiens et dans la légende", *RHPR* 17 (1937) 85: "Le christianisme n'est pas seulement préfiguré dans l'Ancien Testament, il y est avec toute la réalité de ses institutions et de ses rites." It should be noted, however, that in this regard the West-Syrian recension is sometimes more outspoken than the East-Syrian, cf. III. 17: "Eden is the type of the real Church" (East) – "Eden is the Holy Church" (West).

[40] G. ANDERSON, "The Cosmic Mountain. Eden and its Early Interpreters in Syriac Christianity", *Genesis 1-3 in the History of Exegesis. Intrigue in the Garden* (ed. G. A. Robbins; Studies in Women and Religion 27; Lewiston / Queenston 1988) 187–224.

independent position. He does not identify Melchizedek as Shem, as Ephrem does, but as Shem's great-grandson.[41] Whether in such cases the author is drawing on existing haggadic traditions or presenting personal inventions cannot always be ascertained. The same uncertainty exists with regard to some rather fanciful elaborations, e.g. the story about Eve's looking at the serpent and seeing in it, as in a mirror, her own likeness.

The *Cave* incorporates a number of traditions which originally belonged to the Jewish Adam literature. Reflections and repentance of the protoplasts following their expulsion, their living in the still somewhat holy area around Paradise and their longing to fully regain the life of Paradise, their concern to transmit to their descendants (often in the form of 'testaments') the secrets of Paradise, are constituent elements of this genre, which in the *Cave* are adapted to a Christian context. Together with the *Testament of Adam,* the *Cave* attests to the connections that exist between the Jewish literary traditions of the Second Temple period and early Syriac exegesis.[42]

The *Cave* exists in a large number of Syriac manuscripts, many of them exhibiting their own characteristics. Parts of it have been included in other Syriac works, the most important being the *Apocalypse of Pseudo-Methodius.*[43] The Syriac text has also been translated into various languages: Arabic, Ethiopic, Coptic, Georgian and Armenian.[44]

4.3. *John the Solitary's Commentary on Qohelet*

Edition: W. STROTHMANN, *Kohelet-Kommentar des Johannes von Apamea* (GOF I,30; Wiesbaden 1988; Syriac).

Study: Strothmann, Das Buch Kohelet (1973) 209–215.

"John the Solitary" or "John of Apamea" is known as an important writer of treatises, dialogues and letters of an ascetic and spiritual nature. He must have lived in the first half of the 5th century,[45] in a monastery near Apamea on the Orontes. In the present state of research it is difficult to ascertain whether he should also be regarded as the author of a *Commentary on Qohelet,* which in the oldest manuscripts bears the name of "John the Solitary" and which in later times was consulted by both East and West Syrians.[46]

---

[41] Cf. Simon, Melchisédech (1937) 88–91.

[42] In addition to the Adam Books, J.-P. Mahé has pointed to parallels with other Jewish Hellenistic writings, esp. the *Book of Enoch* and the *Martyrdom of Isaiah,* as well as with gnostic hermetic literature. Cf. J.-P. MAHÉ, *La Caverne des Trésors. Version géorgienne* (CSCO 527/Iber. 24; Louvain 1992) VIII–XV.

[43] Cf. G.J. REININK, "Der Verfassername "Modios" der syrischen Schatzhöhle und die Apokalypse des Pseudo-Methodios", *OrChr* 67 (1983) 46–64; idem, *Die syrische Apokalypse des Pseudo-Methodius* (CSCO 541/Syr. 221; Louvain 1993) esp. XXIX–XLI.

[44] See the survey in Su-Min Ri, La Caverne (1987) transl. XXIV–XXVI, as well as the recent edition and translation of the Georgian version, C. KOURCIKIDZÉ / J.-P. MAHÉ, *La Caverne des Trésors. Version géorgienne* (CSCO 526–527/Iber. 23–24; Louvain 1992; Georgian and French transl.).

[45] Cf. A. DE HALLEUX, "Le milieu historique de Jean le Solitaire", *III Symposium Syriacum 1980* (ed. R. Lavenant; OCA 221; Rome 1983) 299–305. R. LAVENANT, *Jean d'Apamée. Dialogues et Traités* (SC 311; Paris 1984) distinguishes three authors of this name, without mentioning the author of the *Commentary on Qohelet.*

[46] The recent editor of the text accepts this identification, despite his earlier rejection of it.

In his introduction the author defends the Book of Qohelet against those who despise it because of its lack of good style. Solomon, he argues, only aimed at bringing profit to his readers and instructing them. After having explained the name (*Qohelet* = 'the one who gathers', a name which applies to Solomon both because of the many peoples that came to listen to his wisdom and because of the many products, coming from many different places, which were needed for the building of the temple and the royal palace), the author presents the historical circumstances and the considerations that led Solomon to compose this book.

The commentary itself provides a paraphrase of the text, in which biblical expressions and words are illuminated and the paraenetic character of the book is broadened. To achieve this, the author sometimes makes use of allegoric interpretation. The two "lands" of Qoh 10:16–17 ("cities" according to Peshitta) are a likeness (*dmutā*) of a foolish and a wise soul respectively. In Qohelet 12 a description is seen of the weakening human body approaching death: "the sun", "the moon", and "the stars" (Qoh 12:2) are used as a type (*ṭupsā*) of the brain, the heart, and the thoughts.

While commenting on the Peshitta, in his introduction the author shows that he is aware of differences between the Hebrew, Greek, and Syriac languages. For Qoh 4:17 (5:1) he first quotes the Peshitta: "they (i.e. the fools) do not know to do good", and then states that "another copy" has: "they do not know to do evil" (which is similar to both MT and LXX: "they do not know that they are doing evil"). Although he expresses a clear preference for the first reading "because it agrees better with the purpose (*nišā*) of the book", the second reading is acceptable to him as well, but only after he has introduced a different subject: "the dispositions of God do not know to do evil".

Whereas the attention paid to the historical setting and purpose of the Book of Qohelet as well as the author's use of paraphrase betray proximity to Antiochene exegesis, John apparently felt much more free than the Antiochene exegetes to depart from the plain meaning of the text and to apply non-literal exegesis.

5. The School of Edessa and the Creation of the East-Syrian Exegetical Tradition

5.1. *Exegesis in the School of Edessa*

We have very little information about the history of the School of Edessa prior to Ephrem's arrival in the city (363). Later sources tend to allot an important role to Ephrem in the formation of the School, if not as its founder, then as an important transmitter of venerable old traditions to later genera-

Unpublished fragments of a *Commentary on Job* (on Job 2:8–13; 3:1–3; 3:11–12; 3:13; 29:13), attributed to "John the Solitary" and preserved in ms. British Library, Add. 18.814, are based on the LXX and are most probably not by the author of the *Commentary on Qohelet.* They provide an allegorical interpretation, which betrays some affinities with Didymus of Alexandria's *Commentary on Job.*

tions. A telling testimony is found in a work which surveys the history of the schools in Syria and Mesopotamia and is ascribed to Barḥadbšabba, writing ca. 600.[47] Looking back at the period of Qiyore, director of the School of Edessa somewhere in the first half of the 5th century, the author notes the following:

However, the only thing that grieved him was that the commentaries of the Interpreter had not yet been translated into the Syriac language. But at that moment he was commenting (on the Bible) according to the traditions of Mar Ephrem, those that, as they say, were transmitted from Addai the Apostle onwards, who originally had been the founder of that assembly of Edessa, since he himself and his disciple came to Edessa and sowed there this good seed. For as to that which we call the tradition of the School, we do not mean (by it) the commentary of the Interpreter, but those other (traditions) that from mouth to ear were transmitted from the beginning. Afterwards, the blessed Mar Narsai incorporated them in his homilies and in the rest of his compositions.

Whereas this passage focuses on the Syriac translation of the exegetical works of Theodore of Mopsuestia ("the Interpreter"), it also provides an interesting insight into the early history of Syriac biblical interpretation. With regard to the tools of the exegetical teaching, Barḥadbšabba draws a clear distinction between "traditions" (*mašlmānwātā*, pl. of *mašlmānutā*) and "commentaries" (*puššāqē*, pl. of *puššāqā*). Whereas the latter term refers to compositions written by individual authors, the former seems to refer to an oral transmission of teachings and ideas that passed anonymously from generation to generation. The "traditions of Mar Ephrem", mentioned by Barḥadbšabba, are not Ephrem's written works, but the exegetical heritage which was created and moulded before him, to which he may have contributed, and which he passed to the next generation. As a dynamic reservoir of interpretations of various origins, the oral tradition may indeed have played an important role in the activities of the School, during its early history as well as in the later period.

5.2. The Syriac Translation of the Works of Theodore of Mopsuestia

Editions and translations: E. Sachau, *Theodori Mopsuesteni Fragmenta Syriaca* (Leipzig 1869; Syriac and Latin transl.); R. M. Tonneau, "Théodore de Mopsueste. Interprétation (du Livre) de la Genèse", *Le Muséon* 66 (1953) 45-64 (Syriac and French transl.); T. Jansma, "Théodore de Mopsueste, Interprétation du Livre de la Genèse. Fragments de la version syriaque (B. M. Add. 17,189, fol. 17-21)", *Le Muséon* 75 (1962) 63-92 (Syriac and French transl.); H. N. Sprenger, *Theodori Mopsuesteni Commentarius in XII Prophetas. Einleitung und Ausgabe* (GOF V,1; Wiesbaden 1977) 431-453 (Syriac); L. Van Rompay, *Théodore de Mopsueste. Fragments syriaques du Commentaire des Psaumes (Psaume 118 et Psaumes 138-148)* (CSCO 435-436/Syr. 189-190; Louvain 1982; Syriac and French transl.); W. Strothmann, *Das syrische Fragment des Ecclesiastes-Kommentars von Theodor von Mopsuestia* (GOF I,28; Wiesbaden 1988; Syriac).

Studies: I.-M. Vosté, "De versione syriaca operum Theodori Mopsuesteni", *OCP* 8 (1942) 477-481; Macina, L'homme à l'école de Dieu (1982-1983); L. Van Rompay, "Quelques remarques sur la tradition syriaque de l'œuvre exégétique de Théodore de Mopsueste", *IV Symposium Syriacum 1984* (ed. H. J. W. Drijvers / R. Lavenant / C. Molenberg / G. J. Reinink; OCA 229; Rome 1987) 33-43.

---

[47] A. Scher, *Barḥadbšabba ʿArbaya, Évêque de Ḥalwan (VIe siècle). Cause de la Fondation des Écoles* (PO 4,4; Paris 1907) esp. 382-383.

Perhaps even during his lifetime there were the beginnings of a Syriac translation of the writings of Theodore of Mopsuestia (d. 428). The work was carried out in or around the School of Edessa and the names associated with it are those of Hiba (Greek: Ibas), teacher of the School prior to his consecration as bishop of Edessa in 435, Qiyore, director of the School somewhere in the first half of the 5th century, Kumi, and Maᶜna of Rewardašir.

Little is known about the earliest phase of Theodore's writings in Syriac. The manuscripts in which small portions of his Syriac commentaries have survived are in general very old and thus may tell us something about the original rendering of these works in Syriac. Fragments from the *Commentary on Genesis* (preface and interpretations of Genesis 1, 2, 3, 4, 6 and 8), as well as on the *Twelve Prophets* (extracts concerning Hosea 8, Joel 1–2, the preface to Amos, as well as Amos 2) are preserved in 6th-century manuscripts. The manuscript which contained a long fragment of the *Commentary on Qohelet* (preface and interpretation of Qohelet 1–7) may be ascribed to the 6th or 7th century. The fragments from the *Commentary on Psalms,* preserved in a 19th-century transcript of an old manuscript, may also date back to the earliest phase of the Syriac translation.

The Syriac translation of Theodore's exegetical works is a most interesting example of how, after a period of frequent contacts and mutual influence between the Greek Antiochene and early Syriac world, the Antiochene approach to the Bible, embodied in a broad theological and anthropological system and nourished by Greek philosophy, was able to impose itself on Syrian scholars. For one branch of the Syrian tradition Theodore's works would decisively determine the orientation of the exegesis. The conceptual framework underlying Theodore's commentaries and their hermeneutic principles and terminology were adopted, imitated and expanded in the Syrian schools.

Theodore regarded biblical history as a manifestation of God's paedagogic dealing with man. Examples of virtuous life recorded in the Bible, revelations, prophecies and types aimed at instructing man and guiding him along the ascending line of history up to Christ's Epiphany and eventually to man's introduction into the second *catastasis.* Within this broad anthropological concept, Theodore always wanted to give full credit to the biblical text as it stood and to disclose the historical sense of the text, i.e. the sense which the writer of the text intended and which is largely restricted to the framework of the OT itself.[48] Allegorical interpretation, connected with the names of Origen and Philo of Alexandria, is categorically rejected.[49] Most OT prophecies apply primarily to Israelite history. Only in exceptional cases does the text point to Christ. Typologies are accepted only under strict conditions and the acceptance of most of them is supported by NT precedents (e.g. Jonah in the whale, the brazen serpent, and Hagar and Sarah). Of the Psalms only four (Psalms 2, 8, 45[44] and 110[109]) are regarded as messianic.

---

[48] Cf. Wallace-Hadrill, Christian Antioch (1982) 32–33 [see note 29].

[49] Cf. Theodore's *Treatise against the Allegorists,* preserved among the Syriac fragments of the *Commentary on the Psalms:* Van Rompay, Théodore (1982) 1–14 (text) and 1–18 (transl.), and the discussion of this text in Runia, Philo (1993) 265–270 [see note 23].

5.3. Narsai and East-Syrian Exegesis of the Sixth Century

Editions and translations: A. Mingana, *Narsai doctoris syri Homiliae et Carmina* 1–2 (Mosul 1905; Syriac); Ph. Gignoux, *Homélies de Narsaï sur la Création* (PO 34,3–4; Turnhout 1968; Syriac and French transl.); Trigg, Biblical Interpretation (1988) 203–220 ("Narsai of Nisibis, *On the Expression 'In the Beginning', and Concerning the Existence of God*"), (English transl.); J. Frishman, *The Ways and Means of the Divine Economy. An Edition, Translation and Study of Six Biblical Homilies by Narsai* (Ph.D. thesis Leiden 1992; Syriac and English transl.).

Studies: J. Frishman, "Type and Reality in the Exegetical Homilies of Mar Narsai", StPatr 20 (ed. E. A. Livingstone; Leuven 1989) 169–175; eadem, The Ways and Means (1992).

Narsai, having arrived at the School of Edessa somewhere in the second quarter of the 5th century, belonged to the first generation of those who studied Theodore's works, which were then in the process of being translated into Syriac. He became the head of the School, probably after 449, but some time later, perhaps around 471, he had to leave Edessa as a result of the Christological discussions. He fled to Nisibis, in Persian territory, where a new school was established which he headed until his death in 502/503. The school of Edessa was finally closed in 489.

As head of the school, first in Edessa and subsequently in Nisibis, Narsai must have been responsible for the teaching of biblical exegesis. His preserved works, however, do not include biblical commentaries, but consist mainly of metrical homilies (written in dodecasyllabic or heptasyllabic metre), a popular genre in Syriac literature. Many of these deal explicitly with OT themes or characters, e.g. the creation, Enoch and Elijah, the Flood, Noah's blessings, the Tower of Babel, Abraham, Joseph,[50] Moses, the tabernacle, the brazen serpent, Samson, David and Saul, Solomon, Elijah, Job, the Three Children, and Jonah.

Narsai's general approach to the biblical text is quite similar to Theodore's. Like Theodore, he sees human history as the unfolding of God's predetermined plan, from mortal man's creation and inexperience towards his progressive maturity and the fulfilment of God's plan in Christ and in the second *catastasis*. Following Theodore, he attaches great historical value to the OT. Throughout history God instructs man and guides him by means of revelations, prophecies and types. In addition to a number of hints which were not directly understood by man or by the angels (e.g. the plural forms in Gen 1:26 pointing to the Trinity), other things or events in the OT were so unusual that they must be seen as a purposeful foreshadowing of Christ and/or the future world. Direct references to Christ are seen in the sacrifice of Isaac, the tabernacle, Isaiah's vision, the story of Jonah, Micah, Malachi and Daniel. Not only in these general characteristics, but in many specific interpretations as well, Narsai's treatment of the OT is fully consonant with what we know of Theodore's exegesis. Moreover, though generally basing his interpretation on the Peshitta, whenever the Peshitta differs from LXX, Narsai is inclined to follow the Greek biblical text underlying Theodore's commentary.

Narsai's homilies betray a profound acquaintance with Theodore's theo-

[50] Other metrical homilies dealing with Joseph have sometimes been ascribed to Narsai, cf. A. S. Rodrigues Pereira, "Two Syriac Verse Homilies on Joseph", JEOL 31 (1989–1990) 95–120.

logical and exegetical ideas. This proves that as early as in the 5th century – and perhaps prior to the completion of the Syriac translation of the whole Theodorean corpus – the latter's works had acquired a firm position in the East-Syrian schools. From Barḥadbšabba's note on the exegetical teaching in the School of Edessa [see 5.1] we may deduce that the growing influence of Theodore's works implied a drifting of attention from the works of Ephrem. This shift can indeed be witnessed in Narsai's homilies. In fact, in the elaborate theological scheme borrowed from Theodore there was little room left for Ephrem's theology and exegesis. In many respects, however, Narsai still stood in the indigenous Syriac tradition represented by Ephrem. Not only the genre of Narsai's works and his use of literary techniques and rhetorical figures have their counterpart in Ephrem's œuvre. The expressions used by him when speaking about God and the way he represents God in history are also reminiscent of Ephrem. Further traces of Ephrem's influence may occasionally be found, e.g. in Narsai's homily on the Flood, where the interplay of Divine Justice and Divine Grace is introduced, a motif which plays an important role in Ephrem's exegesis.

Not only the School of Nisibis, but other institutions as well helped to propagate the works and ideas of Theodore. A collection of lectures delivered and written down either in Nisibis or in Seleucia (where a school was founded ca. 540) by Thomas of Edessa, Posi, Cyrus of Edessa, Išai, and Ḥenana of Adiabene, show how faithfully East-Syrian teachers reproduced Theodore's ideas, slightly simplified and adapted to the level of a general audience.[51] Moreover, some of Theodore's ideas are echoed in the *Christian Topography* of Cosmas Indicopleustes, whose informant was Mar Aba, a fellow student of Thomas and Cyrus at Nisibis.

The 6th century was clearly a period of a great exegetical activity. The names of a number of exegetes are known, to whom exegetical works are attributed, which were presented either as running commentaries or as "Questions and Answers". Among these are Elišaʿ bar Quzbaye, Abraham and John of Bet-Rabban, Mar Aba, Ḥenana of Adiabene and Michael Badoqa. These authors' exegetical works, however, have not been preserved. Apart from their names, we have only fragments of their writings, incorporated in later biblical commentaries.

5.4. *Further Developments of East-Syrian Exegesis*

Alongside the commentaries of Theodore of Mopsuestia, an ongoing oral transmission of exegesis undoubtedly existed in the East-Syrian schools. Following Barḥadbšabba's remark quoted above [5.1], one may suppose that the "tradition of the School" included old interpretations and themes which were handed down anonymously and to some extent integrated into later exegetical compilations. In the course of time, however, the "tradition of the School"

[51] For a partial edition of this collection, see W. F. Macomber, *Six Explanations of the Liturgical Feasts by Cyrus of Edessa. An East Syrian Theologian of the Mid Sixth Century* (CSCO 355–356/Syr. 155–156; Louvain 1974).

also dealt with Theodore's exegesis and with the continuous process of elaborating and clarifying the latter's interpretations and adapting them to the Syriac milieu. When in later compilations the "tradition of the School" (or "the common tradition" or "the tradition of all the teachers") is quoted, the reference is often to questions provoked, or not satisfactorily settled, by Theodore's commentaries, so that the Syrian teachers felt the need to make some adjustments to their Interpreter's views.[52]

Whereas in a number of Synods the East-Syrian Church pronounced its full and exclusive adherence to Theodore's exegesis, teachers and students have not always displayed the same strictness. Towards the end of the 6th century the School of Nisibis entered a deep crisis due to the controversial positions taken by its head, Ḥenana of Adiabene. Not only did he hold Origenist views and unorthodox Christological ideas, he is also said to have replaced Theodore of Mopsuestia by John Chrysostom as the highest authority in the field of exegesis. Since very little of Ḥenana's work has been preserved, it is difficult to ascertain what his position really was. The choice of Chrysostom, an Antiochene like Theodore though less rigid in applying historical exegesis, may have been some kind of compromise.[53] Ḥenana was not able, however, to gain sufficient support for his innovative ideas. The protest manifested itself in a massive exodus, which took place ca. 600 and involved hundreds of students and teachers. After this dramatic event the School of Nisibis never regained its former prestigious and influential status in the East-Syrian Church and had to bequeath its legacy of teaching and scholarship to other schools, like those of Seleucia and Balad.

The episode concerning Ḥenana shows that despite outward appearances the East-Syrian exegetical tradition was not monolithic. Although Chrysostom's exegetical works have left no traces in early East-Syrian literature, in all probability it was not Ḥenana who first introduced him in East-Syrian circles. His name and some of his works may have already been known in the Schools of Edessa and Nisibis.

6. The Creation of the West-Syrian Exegetical Tradition

6.1. *Jacob of Serug*

Editions and translations: P. Bedjan, *Homiliae Selectae Mar-Jacobi Sarugensis* 1–5 (Paris-Leipzig 1905–1910; Syriac); Trigg, Biblical Interpretation (1988) 184–202 ("Jacob of Serug, *On the Establishment of Creation, Memra One, The First Day*"), (English transl.); Kh. Alwan, *Jacques de Saroug. Quatre homélies métriques sur la Création* (CSCO 508–509/Syr. 214–215; Louvain 1989; Syriac and French transl.).

Studies: T. Jansma, "L'Hexaméron de Jacques de Sarug", *L'Orient Syrien* 4 (1959) 3–42, 129–162, 253–284; B. M. B. Sony, "La méthode exégétique de Jacques de Saroug", *Parole de l'Orient* 9 (1979–1980) 67–103; W. Hage, "Jakob von Sarug", TRE 16 (1987) 470–474, with further references.

---

[52] Cf. Frishman, The Ways and Means (1992) 39–41.

[53] Baumstark, Geschichte (1922) 127; Vööbus, History (1965) 244.

As has been shown, the foundations of the Antiochene and Theodorean orientation of East-Syrian exegesis were laid at the School of Edessa, where in the second and third quarters of the 5th century Theodore's works were studied and absorbed by Narsai and his contemporaries. The School at that time, however, was far from unanimous and a number of its members resisted the introduction of Antiochene exegesis and Christology. Among them was Jacob of Serug.

Born in a village on the river Euphrates, Jacob went to study in the School of Edessa, where he arrived ca. 470. Apart from letters and a limited number of prose homilies, his œuvre, like Narsai's (whom he probably knew in Edessa), mainly consists of metrical homilies (mostly of the dodecasyllabic metre), many of which deal with biblical exegesis. Jacob died in 520 or 521.

Right from the beginning, Jacob's comments on the creation and the story of Paradise differ strikingly from Narsai's. Unlike Narsai, Jacob does not adopt Theodore's scheme of human history [see 5.2], but remains much closer to Ephrem's views. He maintains that man was created neither mortal nor immortal and was at liberty to choose for himself either life or death. The idea that sin and expulsion from Paradise occurred according to God's predetermined plan is strongly rejected. Following Ephrem, Jacob holds man fully responsible for both his transgression and the consequences. However, after the fall, God treats man with grace, which mitigates the necessary measures of justice and creates new chances for repentance and restoration. Like Ephrem, Jacob places great emphasis on chastity and the ascetic life as the ideal of righteous behaviour.

In addition to certain interpretations which Jacob borrows from Ephrem and which have no parallel in Narsai, Jacob and Narsai basically differ in their use of typology and their views on the relationship between the OT and the NT. Narsai, following Theodore, admitted in his understanding of the OT only a limited number of types, which were always placed in their historical context first, and were then additionally seen as the foreshadowing of Christ. Jacob sees Christ much more frequently and openly present in the OT. There is no question here of the limitations formulated by Theodore and adopted by Narsai. Jacob may even have deliberately opposed the narrow application of typology as defended by Theodore and Narsai.

The biblical homilies of Narsai and Jacob have much in common. The literary form and techniques of their works, the similarity of some of their theological terminology and a number of identical motifs, some of which are of Antiochene origin, reflect common Edessene tradition. However, when it came to the basic points of Christology and exegesis, Jacob felt at home with Ephrem and to a certain extent with the Alexandrian theologians,[54] whereas Narsai deliberately and radically followed in Theodore's footsteps.[55] Thus the

---

[54] Cf. R.C. Chesnut, *Three Monophysite Christologies. Severus of Antioch, Philoxenus of Mabbug, and Jacob of Sarug* (Oxford 1976) 113–141.

[55] For further comparison of Narsai's and Jacob's exegetical approaches, see Frishman, The Ways and Means (1992) 59–65, 102–114 and 171–179 [see sect. 5.3].

works of these two gifted poets, each of whom must have had his own audience in Edessa, represent two sides of a complex situation, one in which Syrian Christians had to make choices which had far-reaching consequences.

6.2. *Daniel of Ṣalaḥ's Commentary on the Psalms*

Edition and translation: G. Diettrich, *Eine jakobitische Einleitung in den Psalter in Verbindung mit zwei Homilien aus dem grossen Psalmenkommentar des Daniel von Ṣalaḥ* (BZAW 5; Giessen 1901) 129–167, (Syriac and German transl.).

Study: P. Cowe, "Daniel of Ṣalaḥ as Commentator on the Psalter", StPatr 20 (ed. E. A. Livingstone; Leuven 1989) 152–159.

From the middle of the 6th century we have a genuine piece of West-Syrian exegesis in Daniel of Ṣalaḥ's *Commentary on the Psalms.* The author, about whom little is known, dedicated his *Commentary* to an abbot in the region of Apamea, a region which in this very period was divided between defenders and opponents of the Council of Chalcedon (Daniel himself belonged to the anti-Chalcedonians). The textual tradition is complicated and a long and a shorter version are extant, as well as translations into Armenian and Arabic. Up to now only an extract of the longer version has been published, containing the explanation of the first two Psalms.

When in the introduction to the first Psalm Daniel explains the occasion on which David sang this Psalm, one is reminded of the practice of the Antiochene exegetes of determining the historical setting of the Psalm before embarking on a detailed explanation. It soon appears, however, that for Daniel this is only the first step towards understanding the full meaning, which is not the historical meaning. On the authority of "those who know the Hebrew language" Daniel accepts that this Psalm was pronounced by David concerning Saul, when he was walking the path of the wicked at the time of his necromancy at Endor (1 Samuel 28). However, "when ascending (*metᶜallēn*) the height of contemplation (*theoria*)", we discover that David, in his prophetic view, also had Adam in mind, who likewise had abandoned the enlightened path of Paradise. After these "two *theoriae*", Daniel takes yet a further step, which leads him to an allegorical interpretation concerning the soul, which should refrain from walking the dark path of evildoers. It is this interpretation on which Daniel concentrates most of his attention, developing this Psalm into "an instruction and admonition and a revelation concerning the Economy of God the Word".

For the second Psalm as well Daniel quotes "the Hebrews", who maintain that this Psalm had been said by David after he was anointed king. This time, however, the historical approach is rejected and the Psalm receives an exclusively messianic interpretation. A further point of interest is that Ps 2:6–7 is first quoted and explained according to "the Syriac language" ("I have set my king on Zion, the mountain of my holiness, that he may tell about my covenant"), "as if the Father spoke this word about the Son". However, Daniel goes on to mention that "in other languages" these words are read as "I have been set by him as king on Zion his holy mountain, I will tell about his covenant" and that "it is likely that this other tradition is correct", expressing thus his preference for the LXX reading.

Daniel's *Commentary* yields a most interesting insight into the exegetical activity of 6th-century Syrian Monophysites. On the one hand they made use of some of the methods of Antiochene exegesis, but on the other hand, while having access to both Hebrew and Greek traditions, they developed their own ideas concerning the various meanings of the biblical text.

7. Epilogue

The literature surveyed in this chapter originated in the heyday of Syriac literature, the period from the 4th to the 6th century. In Syria and Mesopotamia, the conjunction of traditions of Semitic origin and Graeco-Roman culture has given Syriac Christianity its own distinctive characteristics. Throughout their history Syrian Christians have been aware of the complexity of their literary culture and its interrelationship with surrounding cultures. When they read the OT, they were defining the place of their Bible, the Peshitta, in relation to the Hebrew Bible and the Greek translation of the LXX. In their interpretation, they not only adopted and reshaped ideas and concepts of Jewish origin, but also assimilated the products of Greek literature. At the same time, and with the help of the various streams of tradition, they developed their own ideas and expressed their own interests.

For most Syrian exegetes, biblical interpretation had to start with historical exegesis. This approach, which has its precedents in certain branches of Jewish exegesis of the Hellenistic and later periods, is consonant with the ideas prevailing among Greek Antiochene exegetes. Christian typology was, of course, admitted by all Syrian exegetes and the same is true of some forms of symbolic exegesis (often regarded as an extension of typological exegesis). However, the extent to which these types of non-literal exegesis were found and the conditions which were set to them differed greatly among the various authors. While Ephrem, the greatest of all Syrian authors, was able to integrate various types of exegesis into his œuvre, most of his successors gave predominance to either historical or symbolic exegesis. The Syrian followers of the Antiochene exegetes were guided mainly by the works of Theodore of Mopsuestia. The emphasis which Theodore placed on historical exegesis, his complex of hermeneutic principles, and his theology and anthropology, had considerable influence on the East-Syrian theologians working at the School of Nisibis and, later on, at the other schools in Persian territory.

The opponents of Antiochene exegesis, in Syria representing the West-Syrian branch of the tradition, strongly criticized Theodore's categorical insistence on historical interpretation. They did not, however, take refuge in the camp of Theodore's enemies, i.e. Origen and the allegorists. They were not rejecting the historical approach, but rather superimposing typological and spiritual exegesis on the first level of exegesis – which they, too, saw as the historical one – much more freely and abundantly than would have been acceptable to Theodore's followers. In this moderate and balanced approach, Syrian scholars were led by Ephrem, as well as by such Greek authors as Chrysostom, Athanasius and Cyril of Alexandria, and the Cappadocians. Since most of these authors were also read and studied among the East Syrians, and gradually left their mark on the latters' exegesis as well, the distance between the two branches of Syriac exegesis tended to narrow. This development becomes even more clearly visible in the literature of the Islamic period.

In this regard it should be noted that—as far as we know—neither Philo's nor Origen's exegetical works have been translated into Syriac. Origen's influence only entered into the Syrian world through the Syriac translations of the works of Evagrius of Pontus, which became very popular among both East and West Syrians and would have a great impact on the exegetical literature of the later period.

The present survey deals with the main Syrian authors of the pre-Islamic period as well as with a number of important anonymous works. Other categories of texts are deserving of much more attention than is possible within the scope of this study. A great deal of exegetical material was transmitted in homilies in either prose or verse form. Unlike exegetical commentaries, which were used by scholars and students, homilies reached a much wider audience and were often used in liturgy; they tended to give more weight to the paraenetic aspect of exegesis. In the vast field of—mainly anonymous—homilies much work still remains to be done.[56] A wider description of the exegetical activity and its literary expression should also take into account other literary genres, such as various sorts of prayers,[57] dispute poems[58] etc. As Syriac literature is, above all, of a religious nature, no literary genre can be excluded from a study of the Syriac interpretation of the Bible.[59]

---

[56] For some recent editions, see e.g. T. Jansma, "Une homélie anonyme sur la chute d'Adam", *L'Orient Syrien* 5 (1960) 159–182, 253–292; idem, "Une homélie anonyme sur la création du monde", *L'Orient Syrien* 5 (1960) 385–400; idem, "Une homélie anonyme sur les plaies d'Égypte", *L'Orient Syrien* 6 (1961) 3–24; S. Brock, "An Anonymous Syriac Homily on Abraham", *Orientalia Lovaniensia Periodica* 12 (1981) 225–260; idem, "Two Syriac Verse Homilies on the Binding of Isaac", *Le Muséon* 99 (1986) 61–129; idem, "A Syriac Verse Homily on Elijah and the Widow of Sarepta", *Le Muséon* 102 (1989) 93–113; S. P. Brock / S. Hopkins, "A Verse Homily on Abraham and Sarah in Egypt: Syriac Original with Early Arabic Translation", *Le Muséon* 105 (1992) 87–146. For anonymous homilies on Joseph, see above note 50.

[57] See e.g. the prayers attributed to Balai, which have been published and translated by K. V. Zetterstéen, *Beiträge zur Kenntnis der religiösen Dichtung Balai's* (Leipzig 1902). These prayers, as well as other early compositions, should be studied in connection with Ephrem's œuvre.

[58] A number of dispute poems deal with biblical themes. For a general survey, see S. P. Brock, "Syriac Dialogue Poems: Marginalia to a Recent Edition", *Le Muséon* 97 (1984) 29–58; idem, "Syriac Dispute Poems: The Various Types", *Dispute Poems and Dialogues in the Ancient and Mediaeval Near East. Forms and Types of Literary Debates in Semitic and Related Literatures* (ed. G. J. Reinink / H. L. J. Vanstiphout; Orientalia Lovaniensia Analecta 42; Leuven 1992) 109–119.

[59] For the Syriac exegetical literature of the Islamic period, see HBOT I/2, ch. 36 ("Development of Biblical Interpretation in the Syrian Churches of the Middle Ages").

Chapter Eighteen

The Latin Old Testament Tradition

By Eva Schulz-Flügel, Beuron

Sources: P. Sabatier, *Bibliorum Sacrorum Latinae versiones antiquae seu Vetus Italica* 1–3 (Reims 1743–1751); *Vetus Latina, die Reste der altlateinischen Bibel, nach Petrus Sabatier neu gesammelt und in Verbindung mit der Heidelberger Akademie der Wissenschaften herausgegeben von der Erzabtei Beuron* (Freiburg 1949–); *Biblia Sacra iuxta Latinam Vulgatam versionem ad codicum fidem iussu Pii PP XII cura et studio monachorum Abbatiae Pontificiae Sancti Hieronymi in Urbe Ordinis Sancti Benedicti edita* (Roma 1926–1987); *Biblia Sacra iuxta Vulgatam versionem*, Editio tertia emendata quam paravit Bonifatius Fischer OSB cum sociis H. I. Frede, Iohanne Gribomont OSB, H. F. D. Sparks, W. Thiele (Stuttgart 1983); Augustinus, *De civitate Dei libri 22* (CCL 47–48; 1955); idem, *Confessionum libri* 13 (ed. M. Skutella; Leipzig 1934); idem, *Epistulae* (CSEL 34, 1; 1895; 34, 2; 1898; ed. A. Goldbacher); idem, *Quaestionum in Heptateuchum liber* 1 (CCL 33; 1958, 1–69); Hieronymus, *Commentarius in Ecclesiasten* (CCL 72; 1959, 247–361); idem, *Commentariorum in Esaiam libri* 18 (CCL 73–73A; 1963); idem, *Commentariorum in Hiezechielem libri* 14 (CCL 75; 1964); idem, *Commentarii in Prophetas minores* (CCL 76; 1969; 76A; 1970); idem, *Commentarius in epistulam ad Titum* (PL 26; 1845, 555–600); idem, *Epistulae* (CSEL 54; 1910; 55; 1912; 56; 1918; ed. I. Hilberg); idem, *Hebraicae quaestiones in libro Geneseos* (CCL 72; 1959, 1–56); R. Gryson/P.-A. Deproost, *Commentaires de Jérôme sur le prophète Isaie*. Introduction (par R. Gryson). Livres I–IV, Vetus Latina (Aus der Geschichte der lateinischen Bibel 23; Freiburg 1993); R. Gryson/J. Coulie, *Commentaires de Jérôme sur le prophète Isaie*. Livres V–VII, Vetus Latina (Aus der Geschichte der lateinischen Bibel 27; Freiburg 1994).

General works: F. Allgeier, *Die altlateinischen Psalterien. Prolegomena zu einer Textgeschichte der hieronymianischen Psalmenübersetzung* (Freiburg 1928); idem, *Die Psalmen der Vulgata. Ihre Eigenart, sprachliche Grundlage und geschichtliche Stellung* (Paderborn 1940); C. Bammel, "Die Hexapla des Origenes: Die *Hebraica Ueritas* im Streit der Meinungen", *Aug* 28 (1988) 125–149; G. Bardy, *La question des langues dans l'Église ancienne* 1 (Paris 1948); A. V. Billen, *The Old Latin Texts of the Heptateuch* (Cambridge 1927); B. Botte, "Latines (versions) antérieurs à s. Jérôme", DBSup 5 (1952) 334–347; S. Brock, "Bibelübersetzungen 2", TRE 6 (1980) 163–172; D. Brown, *Vir Trilinguis. A Study in the Biblical Exegesis of Saint Jerome* (Kampen 1992); P. Capelle, *Le texte du psautier latin en Afrique* (Roma 1913); L. Diestel, *Geschichte des Alten Testamentes in der christlichen Kirche* (Jena 1869) 68–176; H.-G. Gadamer, *Wahrheit und Methode. Grundzüge einer philosophischen Hermeneutik* (Tübingen 1960; [2]1965); H. Marti, *Übersetzer der Augustin-Zeit* (Studia et Testimonia antiqua 14; München 1974); H. Ruef, *Augustin über Semiotik und Sprache* (Bern 1981); W. Sanday, *Old Latin Biblical Texts* II (Oxford 1886); J. Schildenberger, *Die altlateinischen Texte des Proverbien-Buches, untersucht und textgeschichtlich eingegliedert, erster Teil: Die alte afrikanische Textgestalt* (Beuron 1941); A. Schoepf, "Wahrheit und Wissen. Die Begründung der Erkenntnis bei Augustin" (Epimeleia 2; München 1965); F. Stummer, *Einführung in die lateinische Bibel. Ein Handbuch für Vorlesungen und Selbstunterricht* (Paderborn 1928).

0. A Survey

The very premises and problems which characterized the use of the Old Testament in the Christian East, were adopted together with the text by the Latin West. Since the text had to be translated, however, problems increased and new ones arose. Those problems finally led to a completely new translation, no longer based on the Septuagint but on the Hebrew original.

The theological premise which made Old Testament texts acceptable in Eastern as in Western Christianity, was their being understood as prophecy announcing Christ. It is for this reason, that there were – until Jerome's time – only a few commentaries on complete Old Testament books, except on the Psalms and the Song of Songs. The first was most important in Christian theology, the second was extremely hard to explain in a Christian context. Usually, only single Old Testament quotations were given and interpreted in connection with Christological matters. Allegorical interpretation, modelled on Origen's works, was supported to a great extent by this mainly Christological understanding of Old Testament texts.

Western Christianity met with the Old Testament in its Greek form of the Septuagint, which for a long time remained an undisputed authority. As the complicated history and tradition of the Greek text was completely unknown, Greek texts available for Latin Christians were considered to be the very translation made by the Seventy, inspired by the Holy Spirit and legitimized by Apostles and Evangelists. Even later on, when Jerome increasingly criticized that authority, the majority, and in particular Augustine, insisted on its legendary origin and indisputable value. While Origen's balanced review of the Septuagint in the East had made possible an appropriate criticism, hard discussions arose in the West, based on Jerome's preference for the Hebrew text and Augustine's opposition against it.

Special Western problems resulted from the fact that the Old Testament – and the New of course, too – was available only in a translated form, or, more precisely, in several different versions. Their different and sometimes contradictory forms not only confused the Latin audience, but drew attention to the problems of the Greek original. Inasmuch as the current Latin versions were felt to be insufficient and unreliable, especially in discussions with the Jews, demands for a proven and reliable Latin text gradually emerged.

Offence to the Latin Old Testament was also caused by the linguistic form of the various versions. Their stylistic and translational quality was markedly inferior to that of the Greek translation, presumably because the first Latin translations developed from oral rendering *ad hoc* during the worship service. Mistakes and errors and a certain liberty in rendering, which characterized the first versions, soon led to corrections. In spite of these corrections, the intellectual and learned were repelled by the colloquial and even clumsy style.

On the other hand, the large variety of Latin versions, produced by different corrections, supported an interpretative technique: by comparing and adding disparate versions, different aspects of exegesis could be pointed out and connected to each other. This realization of the varieties of the biblical text stimulated an interest in textual criticism. We must, however, take into consideration that this interest was motivated not so much by philological reasons as by apologetic problems, in peculiar those arising in debates with the Jews about the christological character of the Old Testament. Heretical arguments, too, based on a certain wording, stimulated efforts to find and to fix the 'correct' rendering.

Corrections, up to Jerome's time, were exclusively aligned with the standard of the Septuagint. Jerome's biblical activities finally drew attention to Origen's Hexapla and to the later Greek translators, as well. In this way, then, Jerome's interest was led to a new standard underlying the Old Testament text, the Hebrew original.

Claiming a completely new standard marked the beginning of quite another situation. Authors before Jerome, like Ambrosius, who used Greek texts and even the readings of Aquila, Symmachos and Theodotion, had never called into question the authority of the Septuagint and had never mentioned that a new Latin translation was necessary. Jerome's contemporaries, too, did not share his growing criticism of the Greek form of the Old Testament, but kept hold on the Septuagint. The main reasons for their refusal were to keep in use the familiar wording of the old versions, to avoid the splitting of Western from Eastern Christian communities, to eliminate Jewish influences and, last but not least, to preserve the sacrosanct authority of the Septuagint. Most of the theologians of that time, in fact, were not enough acquainted with textual criticism and its problems concerning the biblical text tradition.

We must not forget that the discussion about the translation from the Hebrew was principally the matter between Jerome and Augustine and Rufinus and their supporters. Of course these discussions caused a split between the interests of theologians whose main concern was with pastoral work, and of those whose most important pursuit was research and translation. Even Origen himself had made the distinction between the *Hebraica veritas*, used among his learned friends, and the familiar Septuagint text, used in liturgy.[1]

The discussion about the authority of the Septuagint and the *Hebraica veritas* stimulated new developments in interpreting Old Testament texts. The awareness of problems arising from translation in general and the *proprietates* of each language opened new horizons for onomasiology and for etymological questions. On the one hand Christian explanation of biblical proper names greatly enriched exegetic work; on the other hand, the care for the precise meaning of words and idioms led to a keener interest in the reality and historical background of the Old Testament, and to an 'historical' or 'literal' interpretation as well. This is especially true of Jerome who stressed the importance of this kind of interpretation in his later writings.[2] As the under-

[1] Jerome, *Hebraicae quaestiones in Genesim*, Prol. 2: "de Adamantio autem sileo ... quod cum in homiliis suis, quas ad vulgum loquitur, communem editionem sequatur, in tomis, id est in disputatione maiori, hebraica veritate superatus et suorum circumdatus agminibus, interdum linguae peregrinae quaerit auxilia". Cf. also *Ep.* 106. 46, where Jerome mentions his own similar practice.

[2] Cf. especially Jerome, *Commentariorum in Abdiam Prophetam prologus*: "mereri debeo

standing of the Old Testament as Christian prophecy remained, however, allegorical interpretation was by no means given up; and a purely historical explanation did never succeed. Even those commentators who deliberately used Jerome's new translation from the Hebrew did not accept the method of interpretation Jerome had recommended. Justus of Urgel, for instance, describes his work about the Song of Songs as an *explanatio mystica*, the sense of which has to be revealed by the Holy Spirit himself.

The first Latin translations of the Old Testament developed to the new standard text following the Hebrew by four stages:

1. In the second century the first fixed Latin translations of the New and Old Testament are known in Africa and Southern Gallia. Different 'types' of the text developed by corrections after the Greek.
2. Jerome tried to get rid of the disadvantages caused by the variety of versions by revising the text on the base of Origen's *Hexapla* (about 387). He realized the uncertain character of the Greek text tradition, and its authority became more and more dubious to him.
3. Jerome postulated the recourse *ad fontes*, that is to the *Hebraica veritas*. In about 390 he started to translate the Old Testament from the Hebrew. The new translation met with vehement disapproval by the majority, the most prominent opponent being Augustine.
4. The translation from the Hebrew succeeded step by step. Finally, in the eighth century, it was accepted as the standard text and incorporated in Alcuin's Bible (except the Psalter and those non-canonical parts not translated by Jerome).

1.1. Old Latin Translations

The beginnings of translating biblical texts into Latin still are not quite clear; the first traces of Latin Old Testament versions are to be found in Tertullian's works.[3] They are apparently already defined in a written form, but there is no information about their former history and tradition.

In all probability the first translations were made in a manner according to synagogal custom: biblical text passages were translated orally *ad hoc* during worship for those who did not understand the original language.[4] We may presume that those oral translations were soon written down and spread to other Christian communities in the neighbourhood as well. In Cyprian's work and those of his contemporaries an already established text is evident.[5] According to the region in which that text is used, it is called the 'African', but it has not been proven that its origin has to be presumed to be African.[6]

---

veniam, quod in adolescentia mea provocatus ardore et studio scripturarum allegorice interpretatus sum Abdiam prophetam, cuius historiam nesciebam".

[3] Stummer, Einführung (1928) 12–15.

[4] B. Fischer, "Die Bibel im Abendland", Vortrag in der Württembergischen Landesbibliothek in Stuttgart 25.3.1955 (Vetus Latina, 4. Arbeitsbericht; Beuron 1955) 12–14.

[5] Stummer, Einführung (1928) 15.

[6] B. Fischer (ed.), *Genesis* (Vetus Latina 11; Freiburg 1951) 15*f.

Though it cannot be excluded definitely that different translations were made at the same time at different places and that the variety of Latin versions or types of text are based on those different translations, it seems probable according to results of the latest research that there was one basic translation of each biblical book or group of books.[7] These texts soon were revised and corrected in several ways: by these corrections of the Greek and by bringing the vocabulary into line with actual and regional linguistic necessities, versions grew apart from each other and got a special *Übersetzungsfarbe*[8] of their own.

While the Greek translators and revisors were held in high regard and their names were known by the learned, no names of Latin translators are handed down to us. Perhaps, this is due to the genesis of the first versions: the oral renderings *ad hoc* might have been made by bilinguistic slaves or other persons of lower social rank, whose proper names were never mentioned. In any case, the Latin text was not regarded as an inspired one, and therefore the proper names of its authors, too, were not worth remembering.

The character of the earliest Latin versions corresponds to their genesis: the main endeavour was to render the Greek text as faithfully as possible. Those first versions, however, seem to be rather more 'free'[9] than the following corrected ones, but this term may be misleading. They are 'free', inasmuch as they do not imitate the structure of the original, but use the syntactical and grammatical characteristics of the target language, which may be due to the oral form of their genesis.

Though the governing principle of translation was fidelity, the choice of the vocabulary was influenced by Christian pre-understanding as well,[10] especially in those parts which could be interpreted in a christological manner. The second factor shaping the vocabulary, was the colloquial language of the time. Being integrated into the language of the Holy Scripture, the potential of colloquial language significantly influenced Christian literature.

The fact that the earliest versions soon were corrected and adapted to the standard of the authorized Septuagint, makes evident the fact that the principle of standardizing was very important, a tendency parallel to the fixing of the Canon. Unfortunately, the different attempts to bring the Latin versions into line with the Greek authority, achieved the opposite effect, namely, the often-lamented variety.[11]

---

[7] Fischer, Genesis (1951) 15*; W. Thiele (ed.), *Sapientia Salomonis* (Vetus Latina 11/1; Freiburg 1977–1985) 11; *Sirach (Ecclesiasticus)* (Vetus Latina 11/2; Freiburg 1987–) 100; E. Schulz-Flügel (ed.), *Canticum Canticorum* (Vetus Latina 10/3; Freiburg 1992–) 12f; R. Gryson (ed.), *Esaias* (Vetus Latina 12; Freiburg 1987–) 16.

[8] H. J. Vogels, "Übersetzungsfarbe als Hilfsmittel zur Erforschung der neutestamentlichen Textgeschichte", *RBén* 40 (1928) 122–129.

[9] Even the first translators intended to render the text as correct as possible; when their translations seem to be more or less 'free', this fact is due to a certain incapability.

[10] Some examples concerning the translation of the Song of Songs are given in E. Schulz-Flügel, "Interpretatio. Zur Wechselwirkung von Übersetzung und Auslegung im lateinischen Canticum canticorum", *Philologia Sacra. Biblische und patristische Studien für H.J. Frede und W. Thiele zu ihrem siebzigsten Geburtstag* (Vetus Latina. Aus der Geschichte der lateinischen Bibel 24/1, ed. R. Gryson; Freiburg 1993) 131–149.

[11] For instance Jerome, *Praefatio in libro Iosue*; "... maxime cum apud Latinos tot sint exemplaria quot codices, et unusquisque pro arbitrio suo vel addiderit vel subtraxerit quod ei visum

The character of the corrections often aimed at an extreme literalness, even at a phonetic imitation,[12] a method contradictory to the usual theory of translation of the time, which preferred the rendering *sensum de sensu.*[13] By treating the biblical text in an exceptional manner, a special theory of language became evident, by which form and content of the sacred text were thought to be an undivisible unity. Corrections were made in order to reestablish this unity and the 'magic' powers of the original text.

Two important consequences resulting from the variety of Latin versions may be mentioned. On the one hand, the clumsy and partly even erroneous renderings caused theological and dogmatic disputes. Tertullian, for instance, mentions the misleading rendering of Gen 2:7 ἀναπνοὴν ζωῆς by *spiritus (vitae)* instead of *adflatus*, which causes serious theological misinterpretations.[14] So corrections were necessary by apologetical arguments. On the other hand, the breadth of variety supported an exegesis using different renderings for explaining one and the same biblical text according to different views. Differences in rendering were understood not so much as inconsistencies but as parts of one and the same divine truth complementing each other. Augustine and many of his contemporaries liked to use this kind of exegesis to bring into accord the historical facts of the Old Testament writings with Christian interpretation.

Whether the variety of versions was considered either an opportunity or an obstacle, depended on the special interest a Christian author pursued and on his knowledge of languages and translational problems as well. Tertullian, a bilingual author, whose main concern was with apology, has already been mentioned. Cyprian for his part was mainly interested in pastoral work; therefore, problems concerning the biblical text as a translation were not very important to him,[15] apart from the fact that in his time the Latin text was still relatively uniform and his knowledge of the Greek was not sufficient for a careful comparison of the two texts. Hilary and Ambrose, however, were aware of the questionable character of any a translation, both of them being familiar with the Greek language. Whereas Hilary was led to a certain caution in exegesis by those problems,[16] Ambrose not only made use of the different Latin versions known to him, but also of Greek manuscripts and the readings of the later translators. Though he himself seems to have sometimes corrected

est, et utique non possit verum esse quod dissonet". Surely this opinion, often repeated by Jerome, is not without exaggeration. Augustine, though he considers the variety a chance, repeats Jerome's verdict in *De doctrina Christiana* 2.16 and *Ep.* 71.6.

[12] Stummer, Einführung (1928) 65f.; Thiele, Sapientia (1977–1985) 216–220.

[13] Marti, Übersetzer der Augustin-Zeit (1974) 61–79.

[14] Tertullian, *Adversus Marcionem* 2.9.1–9.

[15] Even in Cyprian's work about the meaning of certain biblical sentences (*Testimoniorum libri tres ad Quirinum*), he does not mention the difficulties arising from the Latin text as a translation at all.

[16] Hilary, *De synodis* 9: "ex graeco in latinum ad verbum expressa translatio affert plerumque obscuritatem, dum custodita verborum collatio eamdem absolutionem non potest ad intelligentiae simplicitatem conservare". This is said not specially concerning biblical translations, but surely encloses them.

the biblical text,[17] he neither complained about the variety of Latin versions nor demanded a new standard text.

Augustine was for some time considered to have been one of the most important revisors of the Latin Bible, but this hypothesis could not be maintained.[18] It is true that he was earnestly interested in the problems of the biblical text, and of the Latin versions in particular. In different periods of his life and work he preferred different versions according to their value and treated textual problems by a critical method.[19] Though he was aware of errors and mistakes caused by an imperfect text tradition and the necessities of emendation, he principally regarded the variety of versions to be useful for understanding the Old Testament text and its exegesis.[20] His statements in his letters to Jerome about the difficulties arising from this variety seem to be rather a reaction to Jerome's textual activities than to express his real annoyance.[21] Augustine's main concern was with the one divine spirit influencing the different forms of the biblical text and unifying their various renderings. So he uses the different Latin versions as an emendational instrument and as a means for understanding the *obscuritates* the Holy Spirit has worked into the biblical text. A new and standardized text, however, is not his avowed object, and struggling about a special wording becomes irrelevant to him, because all statements found in the Bible are according to the truth.[22] Nevertheless, Augustine does not regard as arbitrary the differing details of the versions; inasmuch as they might be caused by human errors and even by intentional adulteration, they have to be emended before using. Augustine has given his instructions for an adequate understanding of the Holy Scripture, including the establishing of a correct text, in his *de doctrina Christiana*.[23] By the following brief survey Augustine's method and intentions become evident:

The first step in understanding the divine word is to become acquainted with the canonical books, the authority of which is determined by their use in apostolic communities. By the second step, the *obscura*, especially the *signa ignota*[24] (that is, uncertainties arising from translation and from difficulties

17 The biblical text containing Ambrose's corrections is called type M in the Vetus Latina edition, cf. Fischer, Genesis (1951) 18*.

18 D. De Bruyne, "Augustin, reviseur de la bible", Miscellanea Agostiniana 2 (1931) 521–656. Against this theory cf. A. Vaccari, *I Salteri di S. Girolamo e di S. Agostino*, Scritti di erudizione e di filologia 1 (Roma 1952) 207–255, and H.J. Frede *Altlateinische Paulushandschriften* (Freiburg 1964) 106–117.

19 The different using of biblical texts by Augustine is described by W. Thiele, "Probleme des augustinischen Bibeltextes", *Deutsches Pfarrerblatt* 68 (1968) 406–408.

20 Augustine, *De doctrina Christiana* 2.17: "quae quidem res (scil. varietas interpretationum) plus adiuvit intellegentiam quam impedivit, si modo legentes non sint neglegentes".

21 The chronology of the correspondance between Jerome and Augustine makes evident that the bishop of Hippo echoes to the problems, which Jerome had brought up. The letters concerning biblical textforms and translations date from the years 395–405, that is after Jerome's hexaplaric revision at all. The passage concerning those problems in *De doctrina Christiana* 2 is written in 396/7, when Jerome already had translated some parts from the "Hebraica veritas".

22 Augustine, *Confessiones* 11.3.5; 12.16.23–26.36; 12.30.41–32.43.

23 Augustine, *De doctrina Christiana* 2, especially 2.14–22.

24 'Signa' has to be understood within the context of the theory concerning *res et signa*; cf. Augustine, *De doctrina Christiana* 1.2–5; cf. also sect. 18.3, note 86, below.

which result from the native language as well), have to be elucidated. The best *remedium* against these *obscura* is the knowledge of the original languages, Hebrew and Greek. That knowledge is necessary not so much for a better understanding of the words or idioms which are not translated or which are untranslatable (they may be identified by asking an expert), but in order to discern the value of the different Latin versions. If, however, it is not possible to learn the original language, the variety of Latin versions is useful for the sense as well, because they cannot diverge so much that they do not clarify the sense by comparing one version to another. The *signa ignota* arising from the native language, too, can be elucidated by comparison of the different Latin renderings. But before interpreting the sense of a text, it has to be emended. Emendation would be done best by comparison with the original, that is in case of the Old Testament the Septuagint text. The Holy Spirit destined this form of the text to be used by Christians arising from paganism; and this form is authorized by the Apostles and Evangelists. Even if the Septuagint differs from the Hebrew text, is must be preferred by reasons of that authority. If, however, there is a lack of knowledge of the Greek, then by comparison between the different Latin versions, it is possible to distinguish between right or wrong renderings. Suitable for this task are those translations in particular which keep extremely close to their *Vorlage*.[25] They may be insufficient concerning style and elegance, but they best preserve the literal sense of the original.

It is evident that Augustine thought it possible that both textual criticism and understanding of the sense might be successful by means of Latin versions on their own. Surely Augustine here takes into consideration practical reasons and the abilities which the exegetes in his environment possessed. But when he emphasized that the authority of the Septuagint must absolutely be preferred to the Hebrew original, he made its use superfluous for Christian interpretation and so separated the Christian Old Testament from its Jewish roots. Admittedly, in his later works he conceded a certain value to the Hebrew text, but only by reason of the argument that the Apostles and Evangelists sometimes used this text as well.[26] It has to be mentioned that Augustine, in spite of his negative view of the Hebrew text, partly quotes Jerome's translation *ex Hebraica veritate* and sometimes concedes that it gives a better rendering.[27] He also recommended using the *Onomastica* concerning Hebrew proper names[28] (without mentioning the author's – Jerome's – name) and in his later work *de quaestionibus in Heptateuchum* he says that behind

[25] Augustine, *De doctrina Christiana* 2. 19: "... habendae interpretationes eorum, qui se verbis nimis obstrinxerunt". By those "interpretationes" Augustine does *not* mean the translation of Aquila into the Greek. The context proves that Augustine – like in 2. 22 – thinks of Latin translations only.

[26] Augustine, *De civitate Dei* 18. 44.

[27] Especially in his work *Quaestiones in Heptateuchum* (anno 419) he partly uses and prefers the translation from the Hebrew, but he never demands the correction of the common biblical text.

[28] Augustine, *De doctrina Christiana* 2. 23: "sic etiam multa ... nomina hebraea non est dubitandum habere non parvam vim atque adiutorium ad solvenda aenigmata scripturarum, si quis ea possit interpretari".

the *proprietates* of the Hebrew language a special sense which is important for Christians may be hidden as well.[29]

In spite of these concessions, Augustine in principle regarded the Old Testament to be a Christian book: its special Christian form had originated by the Holy Spirit who inspired the translation of the Seventy. For Latin Christians it was possible to use and understand it independently of its original form by means of their native language.

1.2. Jerome's Hexaplaric Recension

In 387 Jerome still agreed with common opinion concerning the divine authority of the Septuagint text for all Christians.[30] He had a quite different judgement about the value of the Latin versions, however. He criticized their variation resulting from errors, negligent copying and malicious adulteration.[31] Therefore, it seems to him impossible to reestablish the real text used by Apostles and Evangelists by punctual emendation only. So Jerome started to revise the biblical text based on the best copies of the Greek original. Concerning the Gospels, he based his work on the best manuscripts authorized by apostolic communities (*anno* 383).[32] The revision of Old Testament texts, however, he did not establish by means of those 'apostolic' manuscripts, but by means of Origen's *Hexapla*. Through this he showed that he not only wanted to emulate his master Origen and his treating the biblical text in an academic and philological manner, but also that he no longer accepted the authority of the Septuagint text exclusively. The store Jerome set by the importance of the critical signs, marking missing or additional passages in comparison with the Hebrew,[33] proves that he was becoming more and more interested in the relationship between the Greek and the Hebrew original. Another evidence of that interest is given by Jerome in his Commentary *in Titum*, written in 387: the distortion of Hebrew proper names in the Septuagint version had encouraged the Jews to heap scorn and derision on the Christians. For that reason Jerome now examined the form of these proper names by means of the second column of the *Hexapla*, which was the transcription of the Hebrew.[34] During that time he also took up again his Hebrew studies. In 383 Jerome was already instructed about the complicated state of the Greek text tradition. He was still convinced, however, that he would find

---

[29] Cf. Augustine, *Retractationes* 2.54 (concerning the *Quaestiones*): "multa autem in litteris sacris obscura cognito locutionis genere dilucescunt".

[30] Jerome, *Praefatio de translatione Graeca* (scil. Prov, Qoh, Cant) (Biblia sacra iuxta Latinam Vulgatam versionem ad codicum fidem … XI [Roma 1957] 6–7): "… tres libros Salomonis … veteri Septuaginta *auctoritati* reddidi". In 383 (*Praefatio in Evangelio*) he had condemned Lukian and Hesychius, because they had dared to "emend" the text of the Seventy: "… quibus nec … post septuaginta interpretes emendare quid licuit".

[31] For instance *Praefatio in Evangelio*: "quae vel a vitiosis interpretibus male edita vel a praesumptoribus imperitis emendata perversius vel a librariis dormitantibus addita sunt aut mutata".

[32] Jerome, *Praefatio in Evangelio*: "sit illa vera interpretatio, quam Apostoli probaverunt …" and: "quattuor … evangelia … codicum graecorum emendata conlatione sed veterum".

[33] Cf. Jerome's *Praefationes* of his hexaplaric recension in the Psalms, in Job and Paralipomenon.

[34] Jerome, *Commentarius in epistolam ad Titum* 3.9 (PL 26,594B–596C).

in the fifth column of the *Hexapla* the Seventy's real translation.[35] Of course he was acquainted with the readings of Aquila, Symmachos and Theodotion and used them, though he had condemned others in strong terms, because they had dared to "correct" the Seventy's translation.[36]

So on the one hand, it is due to Jerome's loyalty to the Septuagint as the 'apostolic text', that he based his revision in 387 on the fifth column of the *Hexapla*. On the other hand, he was already convinced that the Old Testament text cannot be absolutely detached from its Hebrew origin.

It is not quite clear how many books of the Old Testament Jerome revised by the *Hexapla*.[37] He started treating the Psalter, which is preserved under the name of the "Psalterium Gallicanum" in the Vulgate. The texts of Job and the Song of Songs, too, and traces of the Proverbs and Ecclesiastes have come down to us, together with their prefaces and that of Chronicles as well.[38] There is no reliable information about the other parts of the Old Testament. Jerome's remark in one of his letters to Augustine that somebody had defrauded him of the rest of his work,[39] does not prove that there existed a complete revised edition of the Old Testament.

The remaining parts of the revision give an impression of its character: Jerome did not establish a completely new translation, but used current Latin versions and corrected single words or passages according to the Greek text. Sometimes he followed readings of the 'three'. In the manner of Origen's *Hexapla* he marked out missing or additional parts in comparison with the Hebrew text.

In correcting the text, Jerome's main concern was with an alignment with the Greek text more than with an improvement of Latin style and syntax. Replacement of the vocabulary is neither motivated by theological means nor by reasons of elegance, even if Jerome emphasizes that a good style must be employed, provided that the original sense is not disturbed.[40]

Jerome's hexaplaric recension enriched Latin Old Testament interpretation, inasmuch as those passages missing in the Septuagint[41] now became available to Latin readers too. In addition, attention was drawn to the fact that other translations, which partly preserved the Hebrew original much better existed apart from the Septuagint. In this way the Hebrew original itself gradually came out of its shadowy existence.

---

[35] Jerome, *Epistula* 106.2.

[36] In his preface to the Gospels he condemns Lukian's and Hesychius' recensions; cf. above note 30.

[37] Stummer, Einführung (1928) 80–90.

[38] C. P. Caspari, *Das Buch Hiob in Hieronymus's Übersetzung aus der alexandrinischen Version nach einer St. Gallener Handschrift saec. VIII* (Christiania 1893); A. Vaccari, *Cantici canticorum translatio a S. Hieronymo ad graecum textum hexaplarem emendata* (Roma 1959) and idem, "Un testo dommatico e una versione biblica", La Civiltà Cattolica 64 (1913) 190–205. The prologue to the Chronicles is to be found in: Stummer, Einführung (1928) 241–242.

[39] Jerome, *Epistula* 134.2: "pleraque enim prioris laboris fraude cuiusdam amisimus".

[40] Cf. Jerome, *Epistula* 106.30.54.55.

[41] Jerome especially mentions Isa 11:1; 64:4; Hos 11:1; Zech 12:10; Prov 18:4 (cf. his prologues to the Pentateuch and to Ezra).

Jerome in peculiar takes the credit for his work that Jewish scorn now is excluded by the new corrected text,[42] an important fact in apologetic disputes.

It is difficult to know how Jerome's contemporaries – apart from Augustine – reacted to the new version. Probably there was too short a time up to the following translation from the Hebrew, for a wider acceptance and exegetic or even liturgical application. Intellectual circles seem to have accepted the new text more willingly. Epiphanius Scholasticus, for instance, later used the recensed text as lemma for his translation of Philo's of Carpasia commentary in the Song of Songs, which was initiated by Cassiodorus. But there are other traces of use as well.

Augustine was enthusiastic about Jerome's work and asked him for the complete Old Testament text revised in this manner.[43] He praised Jerome, because he "gave back" the text (*scil.* of the Septuagint) to the *veritas Latina.*[44] Once more Augustine's opinion concerning Old Testament versions became evident: the Septuagint is the authorized form for Christian use; its outstanding authority, however, can be transmitted to a Latin translation, if sense and wording of the *Vorlage* is preserved at its best.

2. The Vulgate, Its Translational and Interpretative Character

A few years after the hexaplaric recension, Jerome started his new translation of the Old Testament from the Hebrew. While the hexaplaric prefaces to Job, the Psalms and the Books of Wisdom presumably had been written in 387, the first translations from the Hebrew date from about 390. It has already been pointed out that Jerome in his work with the hexaplaric recension became more and more interested in the Hebrew original. He had descovered that there were problems and difficulties with the Greek tradition quite similar to those of the Latin. His suspicions about the Septuagint, in particular about the legend of its genesis, had increased; in several steps Jerome became reserved about its authority.[45] He quoted Josephus as his source for the fact that it was the Pentateuch only, which had been translated by the Seventy who deliberately withheld prophecies announcing Christ from the public, in order to avoid the suspicion of polytheism.[46] Then he had become convinced

---

[42] Jerome, *Prologus in Isaia propheta*: "... qui scit me ob hoc in peregrinae linguae eruditione sudasse, ne Iudaei de falsitate scripturarum ecclesiis eius diutius insultarent".

[43] Augustine, *Epistula* 28.2 and 82.34.

[44] Augustine, *Epistula* 71.4: "ac per hoc plurimum profueris, si eam scripturam Graecam, quam septuaginta operati sunt, Latinae *veritati* reddideris". 'Reddere' in this context is not to be rendered by 'translate', but – like in Jerome's letters too – by 'to give back, to restitute'. When Augustine here uses 'veritas', he alludes to Jerome's usage of the "veritas Hebraica", that means: Augustine is convinced that the original sense of biblical texts may be expressed by the Latin versions as well.

[45] Cf. J. Forget, "Jérôme (Saint)", DTC 8 (1924) 939–943.

[46] Jerome, *Hebraicae quaestiones in Genesim* (prologue): "accedit ad hoc quoque Iosephus, qui LXX interpretum proponit historiam, quinque tantum ab eis libros Moysi translatos refert, quos nos quoque confitemur plus quam ceteros cum hebraicis consonare". Some lines above Jerome writes: "cum illi (scil. septuaginta interpretes) Ptolomaeo regi Alexandriae mystica quaeque in

that the Evangelists and Apostles, too, had partly used the Hebrew Bible,[47] and therefore the apostolic legimitation was not exclusively limited to the Septuagint.

Jerome says that he was forced to start the new translation by the differences between the Old Testament text of the Jews on the one hand and the Septuagint on the other,[48] and so once more emphasized the apologetical background of his biblical activities. But it is evident, especially from Jerome's later works, that the new translation was intended not only to be an apologetical instrument, but to replace Origen's *Hexapla* in the West.[49] Though Jerome often recommended that those who refuse the translation from the Hebrew, should carry on using the translation from the Greek,[50] he seemed to be convinced of the outstanding value of his new version, especially because his opinion about the inspired character of the Septuagint had changed. In the preface to the Pentateuch he describes the story of its origin as a lie and sharply distinguishes between *interpres* and *vates*, that is between the Seventy, who merely were translators, and the authors of the Old Testament text themselves, who were prophets.[51] Jerome no longer believed that the current Greek text represents the Septuagint used by Apostles and Evangelists, but a version revised and adulterated by Lukian.[52] Dealing with onomastic and etymological problems, Jerome more and more became aware of the *proprietates* causing difficulties in translating and understanding. In view of the extant differing Greek and Latin versions he concluded that "that which is

scripturis sanctis prodere noluerint et maxime ea, quae Christi adventum pollicebantur, ne viderentur Iudaei et alterum deum colere: quos ille Platonis sectator magni idcirco faciebat, quia unum deum colere dicerentur". Cf. also *Prologus in Pentateucho* and *Prologus in Isaia propheta.*

[47] For instance in the same prologue to the *Hebraicae quaestiones*: "sed et Evangelistae et Dominus noster atque salvator nec non et Paulus apostolus multa quasi de veteri testamento proferunt, quae in nostris codicibus non habentur".

[48] In his *Praefatio in libro Psalmorum* (iuxta Hebraicum) Jerome mentions his apologetical intention: "quia igitur nuper cum Hebraeo disputans quaedam pro Domino Salvatore de Psalmis testimonia protulisti volensque ille te eludere, per sermones paene singulos adserebat non ita haberi in hebraeo ut tu de septuaginta interpretibus opponebas, ... postulasti ut ... novam editionem latino sermone transferrem". Often he points out that important quotations from the Old Testament used in the New are missing in the Septuagint; so, for instance, in the prefaces to the Pentateuch, Paralipomenon and to Ezra.

[49] Jerome, *Praefatio in libro Iosue*: "... ut pro Graecorum ἐξαπλοῖς quae et sumptu et labore maximo indigent, editionem nostram habeant et, sicubi in antiquorum voluminum lectione dubitarint, haec illis conferentes inveniant quod requirunt, maxime cum apud Latinos tot sint exemplaria quot codices".

[50] For instance *Epistula* 112.19 and in most of his prologues to his translations from the Hebrew.

[51] Jerome, *Praefatio in Pentateuchum*: "aliud est enim vatem, aliud esse interpretem: ibi spiritus ventura praedicit, hic eruditio et verborum copia ea quae intellegit transfert". Augustine, however, held to his opinion that both, the authors of the biblical books and the so called "Seventy" where prophets (*De civitate Dei* 18.43).

[52] Jerome, *Epistula* 106.2: "ut sciatis aliam esse editionem quam ... omnesque Graeciae traditores κοινά id est communem appellant atque vulgatam et a plerisque nunc Λουκιάνειος dicitur, aliam septuaginta interpretum, quae et in ἐξαπλοῖς codicibus repperitur et a nobis in Latinum fideliter versa est. ... κοινή pro locis et temporibus et pro voluntate scriptorum vetus corrupta editio est".

contradictory and dissimilar cannot be true".[53] Therefore, the very truth can only be found by recourse *ad fontes.*

In the preface to Ezra Jerome also mentions practical reasons for his new translation: even if one would be able to gather all existing Greek versions in order to obtain the exact text by comparison, evidence would be impossible without knowledge of the Hebrew. As for himself a lot of the Greek texts were available to him and he knew the Hebrew language; his Latin contemporaries should therefore be grateful to him, who had undertaken this great task for them.[54]

Jerome has not handed down to us a coherent description of the method he prefers in translating from the *Hebraica veritas*. Several points, however, can be noted from the prefaces to the Old Testament books and to his commentaries, as well as from his letters. They may be summarized as follows: Jerome is aiming in particular for fidelity in regard to the extent of the text, according to the principle: "I neither took away nor added anything".[55] To obtain a better understanding of the sense, he enlists the help of Jewish friends.[56] Sometimes Jerome uses one of the current Latin versions as a basic text for his translation, sometimes he renders an Old Testament text completely new word by word (*verbum e verbo*). This is necessary, if both the Greek and the Latin versions are "totally corrupted".[57] In some cases the new translation may seem to be only slightly different from old versions, but Jerome hopes that a diligent reader will notice that it is coming *statim de praelo* and that it is not *in tertium vas transfusa.*[58]

Regarding the question of whether the biblical text has to be rendered *verbum de verbo* or *sensum de sensu,* Jerome's statements seem to be inconsequent. Dealing with his translation from the hexaplaric text, he had emphasized that in the Bible even the order of the single words conceals a mystery, and often he repeats that behind proper names and single words of the Old Testament there is hidden a secret sense.[59] Nevertheless, Jerome in his letter to Augustine describes his method of translation from the Hebrew as follows: *Hic de ipso Hebraico, quod intellegebamus, expressimus sensuum potius veritatem quam verborum interdum ordinem conservantes.*[60]

---

[53] For instance *Epistula* 27.1 and in the prefaces to the Gospels, Iosue, Judges, Paralipomenon and Ezra.

[54] Jerome, *Prologus in libro Ezrae*: "quanto magis Latini grati esse deberent, quod exultantem cernerent Graeciam a se aliquid mutuari. Primum enim magnorum sumptuum est et infinitae difficultatis exemplaria posse habere omnia, deinde etiam qui habuerint et hebraei sermonis ignari sunt, magis errabunt ignorantes quis e multis verius dixerit".

[55] Jerome points to this principle in the prefaces to the Psalms (iuxta Hebraeum), to the Kings and to Esther. For the ancient tradition of this principle, cf. W.C. Van Unnik, "De la règle Μήτε προσθεῖναι μήτε ἀφελεῖν dans l'histoire du canon", *VC* 3 (1949) 1–36.

[56] Cf. Epistula 84.3.2 and the prefaces to Job, Tobia and the hexaplaric prefaces to Job and Paralipomenon. Cf. also Marti, Übersetzer der Augustin-Zeit (1974) 31–33.

[57] Jerome, *Prologus Hester.*

[58] Jerome, *Prologus in libros Salomonis*: "neque enim sic nova condimus ut vetera destruamus. Et tamen, cum diligentissime legerit, sciat magis nostra intellegi, quae non in tertium vas transfusa coacuerint, sed statim de prelo purissimae commendata testae suum saporem servaverint".

[59] Cf. G.J.M. Bartelink, *Hieronymus, Liber de optimo genere interpretandi (Epistula 57), ein Kommentar* (Leiden 1980) 45 f.

[60] Jerome, *Epistula* 112.19.

Jerome's inconsistency regarding these problems often has been mentioned, but presumably the slogan *verbum de verbo* in connection with biblical translations has to be understood in such a manner that no single word of the holy text might be neglected to preserve the divine mystery, whereas in a secular text a paraphrastic translation is possible and sometimes to be preferred, if required by sense and linguistic elegance. Jerome himself, in one of his letters,[61] demands a translation of biblical texts which preserves each single word and their order as well. In his letter concerning the translation of the Psalms from the Greek, however, he calls for a rendering by which εὐφωνία, *proprietas et elegantia* of the target language is not neglected, if only the sense is not destroyed. To preserve those *proprietates* as well as a good sense, even the addition of single words may be necessary and useful.[62] Though Jerome often states that the two principles *sensum de sensu* and *verbum de verbo* contradict each other, in practice he tried to combine them. There is still another point, which had to be taken into consideration by Jerome, namely, not to confuse the feelings of the Christian audience, who was used to the wording of the old versions.

A summary of his principles is given by Jerome in the preface to the commentary *In Ecclesiasten*:

> *nunc in Bethlehem positus, augustiori videlicet civitate, et illius memoriae et vobis reddo, quod debeo, hoc breviter admonens, quod nullius auctoritatem secutus sum; sed de hebraeo transferens, magis me septuaginta interpretum consuetudini coaptavi, in his dumtaxat, quae non multum ab Hebraicis discrepabant. Interdum Aquilae quoque et Symmachi et Theodotionis recordatus sum, ut nec novitate nimia lectoris studium deterrerem, nec rursum contra conscientiam meam, fonte veritatis omisso, opinionum rivulos consectarer.*

According to Jerome's different principles and intentions, the new translation is not very homogeneous.[63] In spite of his negative view of the Septuagint, he takes over parts of it in his new version. When he says that he has translated directly from the Hebrew, this assertion is not without exaggeration.[64] His knowledge of this language surely was noteworthy in his time, but not sufficient enough for translating quite independently. Therefore, many corrections "from the Hebrew" result from the readings of Aquila, Symmachus and Theodotion. But there are also traces which point to the possibility that Jerome made use of the assistance of his Jewish friends.[65]

Concerning the method *verbum de verbo* or *sensum de sensu*, passages are found which are translated word by word, side by side with rather free formulations. According to his intention not to confuse his audience by too serious innovations,[66] he preserves many old Latin passages. In particular he

---

[61] Jerome, *Epistula* 57.5.

[62] Jerome, *Epistula* 106.54.55.

[63] Stummer, Einführung (1928) 97–123; Marti, Übersetzer der Augustin-Zeit (1974) 73–76.

[64] E. Burstein, "La compétence de Jérôme en hébreu. Explication de certaines erreurs", *RE Aug* 21 (1975) 3–12; R. Gryson, "Saint Jérôme traducteur d'Isaïe. Reflexions sur le text d'Isaïe 14, 18–21 dans la Vulgate et dans l'*In Esaiam*", *Le Muséon* 104 (1991) 57–72.

[65] Cf. Stummer, Einführung (1928) 105–110.

[66] For instance Jerome, *Praefatio in Evangelio*: ... quae ne multum a lectionis Latinae consuetudine discreparent, ita calamo temperavimus, ut his tantum, quae sensum videbantur mutare, correctis, reliqua manere pateremur ut fuerant.

did not encroach upon the sphere of text passages used in liturgy and those connected with christological themes.

The characteristics mentioned above are all due to the necessities and insufficiencies Jerome was confronted with, whereas the following results came from his own deliberate intentions to adapt Old Testament texts to Christian interpretation. The Christian pre-understanding unconsciously influenced the choice of the vocabulary to some degree. At the same time, however, Jerome deliberately decided on genuine Christian terms.[67] Jerome, interested in onomastic problems, put the stress on rendering and explaining Hebrew proper names within the context of the Hebrew language itself and so avoided inappropriate allegories.[68] In contrast to this practice, Jerome in some cases transferred into a Hellenistic sphere special terms and proper names,[69] a method already practised in the translation of the Septuagint. Most of these terms and names belonged to a pagan aerea, and Jerome put them in opposition to the Christian field intentionally. Since he did not want his audience to be confronted with matters absolutely strange and incomprehensible, he transplanted them into a hellenistic context well known to Christian readers.

Another important means of accommodating the Old Testament to Latin readers, was to raise the style and linguistic form of old Latin versions to a higher level, so that even intellectuals might be willing to accept the form of the text. Jerome, however, did not consequently treat the entire text in this manner, but here, too, left unchanged many parts frequently quoted and familiar to the audience.

Because of the variety of principles, the character of Jerome's work is not very homogeneous, but he did not apply arbitrarily the different views of method: all of them were used as means to make the text acceptable for Latin Christians within their own cultural context.

Though the Old Testament by this translation in every respect becomes a Latin Christian text, its Jewish origin is not denied and the historical background of Christendom is preserved, whereas by a restriction to the Greek text and by the emphasis laid on its inspired character, the connection between Jews and Christians was blurred.

Jerome's translation at first was refused by the majority of his contemporaries for various reasons: in spite of Jerome's endeavours the Christian audiences were troubled by the novelties of wording,[70] exegetes did not want to do without certain *topoi* connected with old versions (Jerome himself partly continued to use those versions); the unity of Greek and Latin Christians seemed to be in danger; Jewish influence was feared and, most important of all, the authority of the Septuagint was to be defended by all means.

---

67 Stummer, Einführung (1928) 119–120. In general.

68 Jerome, *Hebraicae quaestiones in libro Geneseos*, in Gen 27: "non Graecam, sed Hebraeam debeat habere rationem, cum ipsum nomen Hebraicum sit, nemo autem in altera lingua quempiam vocans ἐτυμολογίαν vocabuli sumit ex altera".

69 Stummer, Einführung (1928) 110–114; Marti, Übersetzer der Augustin-Zeit (1974) 113.

70 The best known example is the replacing of Jona's "cucurbita" by "hedera", cf. Augustine, *Epistula* 71.5; 82.35 and Jerome, *Epistula* 112.22.

Gradually, however, the new text gained acceptance. Cassiodorus, for instance, provided his library with three complete biblical texts,[71] the *Codex grandior*, the Old Testament text of which was that of Jerome's hexaplaric recension, a pandect *minutiore manu ... conscribendum*, following Jerome's translation from the Hebrew, and – still as the standard text – the old Latin text. The versions from the Hebrew and the hexaplaric Greek, however, should be used only as emendation instruments, quite in the manner Augustine had recommended.[72] It has already been mentioned that Augustine himself partly quoted the new translation, but never in order to replace all other current versions.

Gregory the Great used the translation from the Hebrew simultaneously with the old versions, Isidor of Sevilla and Bede in their own works applied the modern text, but quoting their predecessors preserved the old biblical versions uncorrected.

Finally, Carolingian tendencies of centralization supported Jerome's translation to become the authorized standard text, when Alcuin decided to incorporate it into his Bible.[73]

3. The Problem of *Hebraica veritas* in Jerome and Augustine

The success of Jerome's translation did not result from the fact Jerome himself stressed, that is, the necessity to go back *ad fontes* in order to get nearer to the real truth, the *Hebraica veritas*. Rather, it was the tendency to obtain a standard text which caused its final victory. Those tendencies more or less existed from the beginnings of the Latin Bible. We have already mentioned that corrections were made in order to bring into line the Latin versions with the Greek authority representing the biblical standard text.

Augustine, too, stressed the Septuagint version as being the obligatory standard for Latin Christianity. When he asked Jerome for the complete translation of the Old Testament according to the *Hexapla*,[74] he perhaps hoped to get a Latin standard text.

Recommending the *Itala*, because he considered this version to be more precise and more intelligible than others,[75] he wanted to point out that there

---

[71] B. Fischer, "Codex Amiatinus und Cassiodor", *BZ* NF 6 (1962) 57–79 (= Lateinische Bibelhandschriften im frühen Mittelalter, Vetus Latina. Aus der Geschichte der lateinischen Bibel 11 [Freiburg 1985] 9-34).

[72] Augustine, *De doctrina Christiana* 2.16–22.

[73] B. Fischer, "Bibeltext und Bibelreform unter Karl dem Großen", *Karl der Große, Lebenswerk und Nachleben* (ed. Wolfgang Braunfels; II: *Das geistige Leben*, ed. Bernhard Bischoff; Düsseldorf 1965) 156–216.

[74] Augustine, *Epistula* 82.4.6: "ac per hoc plurimum profueris, si eam scripturam Graecam, quam septuaginta operati sunt, Latinae veritati reddideris, quae in diversis codicibus ita varia est, ut tolerari vix possit".

[75] Augustine, *De doctrina Christiana* 2.21/22: "tantum absit falsitas, nam codicibus emendandis primitus debet invigilare sollertia eorum qui scripturas divinas nosse desiderant, ut emendatis non emendati cedant ex uno dumtaxat interpretationis genere venientes. 22. In ipsis autem interpretationibus Itala ceteris praeferatur, nam est verborum tenacior cum perspicuitate sententiae".

is a Latin version close to the Greek standard. But he never stressed that one version should supersede oll other current versions. Though he in principle closely held to the maxim that only unity and consensus gives evidence to the truth, while contradiction and variety indicates the opposite,[76] he did not apply this demand to the variety of Latin biblical versions. Complaining, on the one hand, about the unbearable variation,[77] he used the different renderings, on the other hand, as an opportunity, and finally he quoted even Jerome's translation from the Hebrew, if he was convinced that – in single cases – it represented the best text.

Nevertheless, Augustine is known to have been the most important opponent of Jerome's *veritas Hebraica*, and his arguments stand for the majority of the opposition against the new version.

The central point of this opposition was not to refuse the Hebrew original as a standard as such, but to defend the obligatory authority of the Septuagint against that of the Hebrew claimed by Jerome.

Even to his final works Augustine remained convinced that the Septuagint was the Biblical version specially destined for Christian use.[78] He knows about the differences between the Hebrew Bible and the Greek version, but he does not prefer the Hebrew reading on account of being original, but stresses the value of the translated wording, being originated by the Holy Spirit and, by this fact, being part of the Christian *Heilsgeschichte* and its progress.

To prove the 'truth' of the Septuagint version, Augustine made use of the mentioned maxim that "what is true, has to be uniform and may not be contradictory". The Seventy's miraculous agreement in translating guarantees the true value of this version, while the later translators Aquila, Symmachus and Theodotion did not succeed in establishing a corresponding translation and left a lot of questions unsolved. Much less can Jerome, a single translator, be able to discover something new and something which is nearer to the truth than the overwhelming agreement of the Seventy.[79]

Another important argument of Augustine's proving the authority of the Septuagint is its use by Evangelists and Apostles and its use by the apostolic Eastern communities as well.[80]

As a result of these arguments Augustine rejected the Hebrew text, because, by abandoning the Greek authority, the unity of the Church and its apostolic tradition would be in danger.[81] Moreover the *consuetudo* would be disregard-

The meaning of 'Itala' has been discussed very often, but today it seems sure that Augustine here speaks of the biblical text he had found in use in Italian regions.

[76] By the argument of the unity as a prove for the truth Augustine postulates the absolute pre-eminence of the Christian faith in opposite to pagan philosophy and religion (*De civitate Dei* 18.40–44).

[77] Cf. Augustine, *De doctrina Christiana* 2.16: "ut enim cuique primis fidei temporibus in manus venit codex graecus et aliquantum facultatis sibi utriusque linguae habere videbatur, ausus est interpretari", and *Epistula* 71.4.6.

[78] Augustine, *De civitate Dei* 15.14 and 18.43.

[79] Augustine, *Epistula* 28.2 and *De civitate Dei* 18.43.

[80] For instance *Epistula* 82.35; *De civitate Dei* 18.44.

[81] Augustine, *Epistula* 71.2.4: "perdurum erit enim, si tua interpretatio per multas ecclesias frequentius coeperit lectitari, quod a Graecis ecclesiis Latinae ecclesiae dissonabunt".

ed, if the Latin audience would be confused by new and unusual biblical formulations.[82]

An additional reason prejudicing Augustine, like many of his contemporaries, against the Hebrew text, was an anti-Jewish position in general,[83] by which any Jewish influence on Christian affairs should be avoided.[84] Augustine also mentioned that a new biblical text would give the heretics an opportunity to mock the uncertain text of the Catholic Bible.

Concerning philological problems, Augustine – as it is said before – did not consider the Hebrew original to be necessary for textual criticism and emendation of the Latin versions.[85]

So Augustine thought a new translation from the Hebrew to be unnecessary and dangerous for Christian peace and unity. His opposition, however, against Jerome's version from the *Hebraica veritas* was based not only on the arguments mentioned above, which he shared with many of his contemporaries. It was Jerome's slogan of the *Hebraica veritas* itself, which inevitably provoked Augustine's opposition, using philosophical and theological reasons. Connecting the Hebrew text with the term of the *veritas*, Jerome postulates that 'truth' can be identified with linguistic phenomenons in general and with the Hebrew biblical text in particular. Augustine's theory of language as well as his theological understanding of *veritas* contrast sharply with Jerome's opinion.

Augustine's theory of language is embedded in the Stoic doctrine of the *res et signa*,[86] and in his shaping of that doctrine the only real *res* is God himself, and therefore the term of *veritas* is a synonym and appellative of God. Language, however, belongs to the *signa*, and written language is no more than "a sign for a sign",[87] because it means only an attempt to overcome the fleetingness of the spoken sound. So language can never be identified with the truth itself. But language is not only characterized by its nature as a mere sign, but by human sinfulness, too: the variety and diversity of human languages result from human presumption to build up the Babylonian tower.[88]

---

[82] Augustine, *Epistula* 82.35: "... intellegant propterea me nolle tuam ex Hebraeo interpretationem in ecclesiis legi, ne contra septuaginta auctoritatem tamquam novum aliquid proferentes magno scandalo perturbemus plebes Christi, quarum aures et corda illam interpretationem audire consuerunt, quae etiam ab apostolis adprobata est".

[83] Cf. B. Blumenkranz, "Augustin et les juifs; Augustin et le judaisme", *REAug* 4 (1958 = Suppl. des Recherches augustiniennes 1; Paris 1958) 225–241.

[84] Cf. Augustine, *Epistula* 71.4.5, where he points out that it would be impossible, if Christian problems only could be decided by Jews knowing the original language of the Old Testament texts.

[85] Augustine, *De doctrina Christiana* 2.14–22.

[86] Ibid. 1.2–5 and 2.1–8.

[87] Ibid. 2.5: "sed quia verberato aere statim transeunt nec diutius manent quam sonant, instituta sunt per litteras signa verborum. Ita voces oculis ostenduntur non per se ipsas, sed per signa quaedam sua".

[88] Ibid. 2.5.6: "ista signa igitur non potuerunt communia esse omnibus gentibus peccato quodam dissensionis humanae, cum ad se quisque principatum rapit. Cuius superbiae signum est erecta illa turris in caelum, ubi homines impii non solum animos, sed etiam voces dissonas habere meruerunt. 6. ex quo factum est, ut etiam scriptura divina, qua tantis morbis humanarum voluntatium subvenitur, ab una lingua profecta, qua opportune potuit per orbem terrarum disseminari, per varias interpretum linguas longe lateque diffusa innotesceret gentibus ...".

Therefore difficulties in understanding are inevitable by the nature of language and by its corrupted form as well. Moreover, divine providence interspersed the Holy Scripture with *obscuritates* in order to prevent mankind from becoming arrogant by a too easy understanding and to give rise to reader's delight.[89] So it is impossible to obtain knowledge of the truth by the text of the Holy Scripture exclusively and directly, and it is still more impossible to identify the *veritas* with a special wording, even if it is that of the original language.

Augustine logically distinguishes between the divine *veritas* being the origin of the Holy Scripture, and its human authors, whose intentions cannot be defined by later readers unambigiously.[90] Discussions about these questions are useless on the grounds that in fact nothing untrue can be found in the divine text at all and nothing of it is contradictory to the two commandments of love.[91] The cognition of this *veritas*, which is the central idea of Christian faith and the premise to understand the Scriptures, is caused by God himself beyond all words and sensual means altogether.[92] So Augustine with good reason evolves his method of the right understanding of the biblical text and of its emendation on the background of his theory about *res et signa*. Within this context a recourse *ad fontes* becomes irrelevant: a Latin version – on the condition that errors and mistakes are eliminated – is as more or less a suitable instrument for understanding as the Hebrew, which is a human text as well, corrupted by human sin.

Jerome's insisting on the value of the *Hebraica veritas*, too, was not motivated by philological reasons, first of all, nor by his experiences concerning the bad state of text tradition of both, the Latin and Greek versions. His reverting to the Hebrew original is based on a certain theory of language as well, which, however, is contradictory to the view of Augustine. Probably influenced by Origen, Jerome followed the principles of pre-Aristotelian philosophy and – in peculiar – the biblical understanding of language, by

---

[89] Ibid. 2.7: "quod totum provisum esse divinitus non dubito ad edomandam labore superbiam et intellectum a fastidio revocandum, cui facile investigata plerumque vilescunt". Cf. also: B. Studer, "'Delectare et prodesse' ein exegetisch- homiletisches Prinzip bei Augustinus", *Signum Pietatis* (FS C. P. Mayer, ed. A. Zumkeller; Würzburg 1989) 497–513.

[90] Augustine, *Confessiones* 12.14.17–25.35 (especially 12.18.27); 12.23.32: "duo video dissensionum genera oboriri posse, cum aliquid a nuntiis veracibus per signa enuntiantur, unum, si de veritate rerum, alterum, si de ipsius qui enuntiat voluntate dissensio est. Aliter enim quaerimus de creaturae conditione, quid verum sit, aliter autem quid in his verbis Moyses, egregius domesticus fidei tuae, intellegere lectorem voluerit". Cf. also ibid. 12.30.41–31.42.

[91] Augustine, *Confessiones* 12.25.35: "propter quae duo praecepta caritatis sensisse Moysen quidquid in illis libris sensit, nisi crediderimus, mendacem faciemus dominum, cum de animo conservi aliter quam ille docuit opinamur. Iam vide, quam stultum sit tanta copia verissimarum sententiarum, quae de illis verbis erui possunt, temere adfirmare, quam earum Moyses potissimum senserit, et perniciosis contentionibus ipsam offendere caritatem, propter quam dixit omnia, cuius dicta conamur exponere".

[92] Augustine, *Confessiones* 11.3.5: "... intus utique mihi, intus in domicilio cogitationis, nec hebraea nec graeca nec latina nec barbara, veritas sine oris et linguae organis, sine strepitu syllabarum diceret: verum dicit et ego statim certus confidenter illi homini tuo (scil. Moysi) dicerem: verum dicis".

which the undivisible nature contained in both, ὄν and ὄνομα, is emphasized, and a noetic and dynamic power is ascribed to the spoken and written word.[93]

Though Jerome did not hand down to us a summary of his theory of language, his principles can be deduced from several statements and by the manner in which he treated biblical texts. When he stressed that a translation of biblical texts had to be done by the method *verbum de verbo* – in contradiction to his own practice in general – and when even the order of the words had to be preserved, he accounted for this method, because there is a mystery (*mysterium/sacramentum*) behind every word and their composition too.[94] By Jerome's special interest in etymological problems and the original meaning of Hebrew proper names it is proved as well that the correct wording is indispensible to understand the sense. For instance the meaning of the Hebrew proper names of those stations in the desert visited by the Israelitic people, served as a basis for the Christian interpretation of that Old Testament passage.[95] But not only did the original shape of Hebrew words contain a concealed sense, even the number of letters of the Hebrew alphabet is not without importance.[96]

Once Jerome calls the Hebrew language the *matrix omnium linguarum*,[97] without explaining this theory in more detail, but we may conclude that Jerome was convinced that the Hebrew language was the very first to be spoken by mankind, and from it all other languages derived. Therefore the connection between ὄν and ὄνομα in the Hebrew language must be the closest one possible, that is to say the *veritas* is expressed and preserved best by that *matrix*. Jerome did not deny the possibility of translations completely, but he was aware that every transformation into another language means a removal from the *veritas* to some extent.[98] It is within this context, Jerome's often repeated slogan of the *Hebraica veritas* has to be understood.

The philosophical background by which Jerome's and Augustine's opposite views were determined, also influenced their understanding of *history* and of their own historical position. This understanding, however, influenced their attitude concerning a new biblical translation as well.

Jerome was still remaining in the traditional ancient decadence theory of history, when he equated origin (that is the Hebrew text) with the truth as

---

[93] Cf. E. Schick, Art. 'Wort', LTK 10 (1965) 1229–1231, und F. Mayr, Art. 'Sprache', LTK 9 (1964) 981–986. The theory of the identity between ὄν and ὄνομα is pointed out especially in Plato's Kratylos.

[94] Jerome, *Epistula* 57.5.2: "... absque scripturis sanctis, ubi et verborum ordo mysterium est". Jerome often mentions the "mysteria" or "sacramenta" hidden in the biblical text; cf. also Bartelink, Hieronymus (1980) 46.

[95] Jerome, *Epistula* 78 (ad Fabiolam).

[96] Jerome, *Praefatio in libro Psalmorum (iuxta Hebraicum)*: "... sed et numerus viginti duorum hebraicorum librorum et mysterium eiusdem numeri commutabitur". Cf. also the prologue to Kings, where Jerome mentions the importance of the number of the Hebrew letters.

[97] Jerome, *Commentariorum in Sophoniam prophetam liber* 3.14/18: "id quod diximus 'nugas', sciamus in Hebraeo ipsum Latinum esse sermonem (נוּגֵי), et propterea a nobis ita ut in Hebraeo erat positum, ut nosse possimus linguam Hebraicam omnium linguarum esse matricem, quod non est huius temporis disserere". (Of course Jerome here did not understand the meaning of the Hebrew text).

[98] Cf. Jerome's expression: "in tertium vas transfusa" (*Prologus in libros Salomonis*).

such, while all further steps in the development of the biblical text were to be considered a diminution of the original truth. But it was according to the Christian theory of history which presumes progress to a positive destination, that he was convinced that he himself, living after Christ's epiphany, was able to translate and to explain the Old Testament texts much better than the Seventy.[99]

Augustine, on the other hand, who principally believed in the progress of history in a Christian sense, assented that a progress in biblical exegesis is possible, but he denied the possibility of a better translation after the inspired Septuagint.[100]

In summary, the positions of both of them could not respond completely and consequently to the historical situation they lived in. Both Augustine and Jerome insisted on their own view, but neither of them could hold on to it without compromise.

Augustine in a long process of learning, finally accepted the new translation from the Hebrew as one of the various aspects of the universal divine truth in addition to the Septuagint. Jerome, though he was convinced that he could come nearest to that truth be means of the Hebrew original, never dared to condemn the Septuagint as a totally out-dated text, but he himself continued to use it in his later works.

The new translation did not succeed because of decisions about Jerome's and Augustine's problems concerning the *veritas*, but because it turned out that it was a modern version, suitable for acceptance as a new obligatory standard, due to its stylistic and linguistic qualities.

---

[99] Jerome, *Prologus in Pentateucho*: "illi (scil. Septuaginta interpretes) interpretati sunt ante adventum Christi et quod nesciebant dubiis protulere sententiis, nos post passionem et resurrectionem eius non tam prophetiam quam historiam scribimus; aliter enim audita, aliter visa narrantur: quod melius intellegimus, melius et proferimus".

[100] Augustine, *Epistula* 28.2: "satis autem nequeo mirari, si aliquid adhuc in hebraeis exemplaribus invenitur, quod tot interpretes illius linguae peritissimos fugerit".

Chapter Nineteen

Jerome: His Exegesis and Hermeneutics

By René Kieffer, Uppsala

Sources: Complete editions: Editio princeps, the incunabula from Rome, 1468 ff; D. Erasmus, *Opera omnia divi Eusebii Hieronymi Stridonensis* I–IX (Basel 1516–1520); M. Victorius, *Opera D. Hieronymi Stridonensis Ecclesiae Doctoris* I–II (Rome 1566–1572); J. Martianay, *S. Eusebii Hieronymi Stridonensis Presbyteri opera* I–V (Paris 1693–1706); D. Vallarsi, *S. Eusebii Hieronymi Stridonensis Presbyteri opera* I–XI (Verona 1734–1742; ²1766–1772), reproduced by J. P. Migne, PL XXII–XXX (Paris 1845–1846), and partially in PLSup 2 (1960) 17–328.

Partial editions: *Bibliographia; Hebraicae Quaestiones in Libro Geneseos; Liber Interpretationis Hebraicorum Nominum; Commentarioli in Psalmos; Commentarius in Ecclesiasten*, CCL 72; *Commentariorum in Esaiam libri I–XI*, CCL 73; *Commentariorum in Esaiam libri XII–XVIII*, CCL 73 A; *In Hieremiam libri VI*, CCL 74; *Commentariorum in Hiezechielem libri XIV*, CCL 75; *Commentariorum in Danielem libri III (IV)*, CCL 75 A; *Commentarii in Prophetas Minores* (in Osee ... in Michaeam), CCL 76; *Commentarii in Prophetas Minores* (in Naum ... in Malachiam), CCL 76 A; *Tractatus sive homiliae in Psalmos*, CCL 78; *Contra Rufinum*, CCL 79; *Corpus scriptorum ecclesiasticorum latinorum* (= CSEL), 54–56 (= *Epistulae*); 59 (= *in Jeremiam*); P. Antin, *Sur Jonas*, SC 43 (Paris 1956).

English translation quoted: P. Schaff/H. Wace, *A Select Library of Nicene and Post-Nicene Fathers of the Christian Church*, II/6: *The Principal Works of St. Jerome*, translated by W. H. Fremantle, with the assistance of G. Lewis and W. G. Martley (Grand Rapids: Eerdmans 1892; repr. 1979).

Bibliographies: U. Chevallier, *Répertoire des sources historiques du Moyen Âge* II (Paris ²1907) 2563–2569; O. Bardenhewer, *Geschichte der altkirchlichen Literatur* 3 (Freiburg i. Br. 1912) 605–654; A. Vaccari, "Bolletino geronimiano", *Bib.* 1 (1920) 379–396; 533–562; R. Klussmann, *Bibliotheca Scriptorum Classicorum* II/I (Leipzig 1912) 394–400; S. Salaville, "Littérature hiéronymienne", *Echos d'Orient* 24 (1921) 320–329; J. Forget, "Jérôme (Saint)", DTC 8 (1924) 894–983; N. I. Herrescu, *Bibliographie de la littérature latine* (Paris 1943) 392–395; P. Antin, "Bibliographia selecta", CCL 72 (Brepols 1959) IX–LIX; F. X. Murphy, "Jerome (St.)", New Catholic Encyclopedia 7 (1967) 872–874; J. Buckler, "Jerome", EncRel 8 (1987) 7–10; D. Brown, *Vir trilinguis. A Study in the Biblical Exegesis of Saint Jerome* (Kampen 1992).

General works: S. L. de Tillemont, *Mémoires pour servir à l'histoire ecclésiastique* XII (Paris 1707); F. Z. Collombet, *Histoire de S. Jérôme* I–II (Paris 1844); O. Zöckler, *Hieronymus, sein Leben und Wirken aus seinen Schriften dargestellt* (Gotha 1865); A. Thierry, *S. Jérôme, la société chrétienne à Rome et l'émigration romaine en Terre Sainte* I–II (Paris 1867; ²1875); G. Grützmacher, *Hieronymus. Eine biographische Studie zur alten Kirchengeschichte* 1 (Leipzig 1901); 2–3 (Berlin 1906–1908); J. Brochet, *Saint Jérôme et ses ennemis* (Paris 1905); L. Schade, *Die Inspirationslehre des heiligen Hieronymus* (Freiburg/Br. 1910); F. Cavallera, *Saint Jérôme. Sa vie et son œuvre* 1/I–II (Spicilegium sacrum Lovaniense, 1–2; Louvain/Paris 1922); F. Stummer, *Einführung in die lateinische Bibel* (Paderborn 1928); A. Penna, *S. Gerolamo* (Turin 1949); P. Antin, *Essai sur Saint Jérôme* (Paris 1951); *A Monument to Saint Jerome: Essays on Some Aspects of His Life, Works, and Influence* (ed. F. X. Murphy; New York 1952); H. Hagendahl, *Latin Fathers and the Classics. A Study on the Apologists, Jerome and Other Christian Writers* (Göteborg 1958) 89–328; H. Frhr. von Campenhausen, *Lateinische Kirchenväter* (Urban-Bücher 50; Stuttgart 1960) 109–150; D. S. Wiesen, *Saint Jerome as a Satirist* (Ithaka, NY 1964); E. F. Sutcliffe, "Jerome", CHB 2 (1969) 80–101; H. F. D. Sparks, "Jerome as Biblical Scholar", CHB 1 (1970)

510–541; I. Opelt, *Hieronymus' Streitschriften* (Heidelberg 1973); J. N. D. Kelly, *Jerome. His Life, Writings, and Controversies* (London 1975); Ph. Rousseau, *Ascetics, Authority, and the Church in the Age of Jerome and Cassian* (Oxford 1978); R. Kieffer, *Foi et justification à Antioche. Interprétation d'un conflit (Ga 2,14–21)* (Paris 1982) 82–103; B. Albrektson, "Om Hieronymus och Vulgata", Religion och Bibel 41 (1982) 3–12; P. Jay, "Jérôme et la pratique de l'exégèse", BTT 2 (1985) 523–542; P. Nautin, "Hieronymus", TRE 15 (1986) 304–315; B. Kedar, "Jerome and the Vulgate", *Mikra* (CRINT II/1; ed. M. J. Mulder; Assen/Maastricht/Philadelphia 1988) 313–334; D. Brown, *Vir trilinguis* (see above).

1. Biographical Elements

Hieronymus Sophronius Eusebius was born at Stridon "on the confines of Dalmatia and Pannonia",[1] probably near Emona (Laibach), about the year 347.[2] His wealthy parents, who were Christians,[3] sent him early to Rome, where he studied grammar under the famed grammarian Donatus and rhetoric under other masters. He formed a friendship with a pupil from his native country, Rufinus of Aquileia, and was finally baptized, probably in the year 366. The Latin authors which he studied then had a strong impact on him; that is confirmed by a famous dream at Antioch in 374–375, in which he heard himself condemned by the sentence: "You are a Ciceronian, not a Christian".[4] A journey through Gaul led him to Treves, the town of imperial residence, where he probably intended to work in the administration.[5] But he changed his mind when he came in contact with monastic life. His knowledge of the Christian doctrine increased when his friend Rufinus asked him to copy Hilary's commentary on the Psalms and his treatise *De Synodis.* He finally visited a group of ascetics in Aquileia, together with Rufinus and Chromatius.

A "sudden disturbance",[6] which caused the displeasure of the bishop, forced Jerome to leave for Jerusalem in order to live an ascetic life there.[7] The journey in 374 through Thrace, Pontus, Bithynia, Galatia, Capadocia and Cilicia was so exhausting that he fell ill in Antioch, where his friend Evagrius took care of him.[8] He stayed for a while in the city and after his recovery he wanted to become an anchorite in the nearby desert of Chalcis. But whether he really practised much of that way of life is unclear, as the letters from the desert in Chalcis were first published in 387 and perhaps partly rewritten.[9] He devoted seven or eight years at Antioch and its environs

---

[1] Cf. *De vir. ill.* 135: "patre Eusebio oppido Stridonis quod a Gothis eversum Dalmatiae quondam Pannoniaeque confinium fuit" (PL 23, 715–717).

[2] The date 331 which we have from Prosper of Aquitaine is difficult to accept, because it would make the life of Jerome excessively long, despite the arguments which Kelly, Jerome (1975) 337–339, adduces in its favour.

[3] Cf. *In Hiob*, prol. and *Epist.* 82.2.

[4] *Epist.* 22.30: "Ciceronianus es, non Christianus".

[5] Nautin, Hieronymus (1986) 304.

[6] *Epist.* 3.3 uses the expression *subitus turbo.*

[7] *Epist.* 22.30 uses the word *militare* for the ascetic life he wants to live.

[8] See *Epist.* 3.3.

[9] These letters are probably not entirely new, contrary to Nautin, Hieronymus (1986) 304, who writes: "Zwar stammen diese Briefe mit größter Sicherheit von Hieronymus selbst, doch

to a serious study of the Bible. He learned the Greek language and consulted the library left by bishop Eustathius. As this bishop had come into conflict with Origen, the library probably contained many books of this writer. His teacher in biblical exegesis was Apollinaris, the bishop of the neighbouring city of Laodicea, but Jerome did not accept Apollinaris' heretical doctrine on Christ's incarnate humanity.[10] He also learned some Hebrew in order to be able to check the Septuagint's accuracy in the original version.[11]

Jerome was ordained a priest at Antioch by bishop Paulinus, but on the condition that he could remain a monk and would not be obliged to exercise pastoral duties. As violent dogmatic discussions arose in the city he fled to Constantinople around the year 381, where he could fulfil his exegetical studies under the guidance of Gregory of Nazianzus,[12] and gained the friendship of both Gregory of Nyssa and Amphilochius of Iconium. His enlarged knowledge of the Greek tradition enabled him to translate exegetical homilies of Origen and the Chronicle of Eusebius. The study of Origen gave him a strong desire to write his own exegetical works, but later on he had to defend himself against accusations of having adopted heretical views from him.

In 382 Jerome accompanied bishop Paulinus of Antioch and bishop Epiphanius of Salamis in Cyprus to Rome. Pope Damasus soon recognized Jerome's broad literary culture, made him his secretary[13] and asked him to revise the Old Latin versions of the Gospels. In a letter to Lucinius Jerome

---

einige störende Momente legen die Vermutung nahe, daß er sie erst 387 nachträglich geschrieben hat, um seinen Verleumdern zu beweisen, daß er wirklich unter Mönchen gelebt hatte. Fest steht lediglich, daß er sich im Jahre 378 und zu Beginn des Jahres 379 am Rande der Wüste in Maronia, einem Evagrius gehörenden Dorf fünfzig Kilometer östlich von Antiochien, aufhielt, in dessen Nähe sich eine Mönchskolonie befand".

[10] Cf. *Epist.* 84.2.

[11] He writes himself in *Epist.* 125.12 (Schaff/Wace, Select Library II/6): "I betook myself to a brother who before his conversion had been a Jew and asked him to teach me Hebrew. Thus, after having familiarised myself with the pointedness of Quintillian, the fluency of Cicero, the seriousness of Fronto and the gentleness of Pliny, I began to learn my letters anew and to study to pronounce words both harsh and guttural. What labour I spent upon this task, what difficulties I went through, how often I despaired, how often I gave over and then in my eagerness to learn commenced again, can be attested both by myself, the subject of this misery and by those who then lived with me". One definitely gets the impression, that the pupil Jerome was not very gifted at learning Hebrew. There is a suspicion in recent litterature, that his knowledge of that language remained rather poor. Most often he seems to be dependent on others, when he claims to translate from the Hebrew. Nautin, Hieronymus (1986) 309, writes: "Allerdings läßt es sich beweisen, daß er diese Sprache (= Hebräisch) praktisch kaum kannte. Wenn immer er in seinen Kommentaren oder anderen Werken den transkribierten hebräischen Text zitiert – und das tut er oft – oder Anmerkungen zur hebräischen Sprache macht, verdankt er die jeweilige Information seinen Quellen (Origenes, Eusebius, vielleicht auch Acacius v. Caesarea); sobald er sich jedoch von den Quellen entfernt, ist alles reine Erfindung". Brown, Vir trilinguis (1992) *passim*, has a more positive appreciation of Jerome's knowledge of Hebrew.

[12] In *Epist.* 52.8 he calls Gregory of Nazianzus his teacher, of whom he on one occasion could ask an explanation of a difficult expression in Luke.

[13] In *Epist.* 123.10 Jerome writes: "A great many years ago when I was helping Damasus bishop of Rome with his ecclesiastical correspondence, and writing his answers to the questions referred to him by the councils of the east and west ...". Nautin, Hieronymus (1986) 305, is sceptical about this notice, as it figures in the context of an incredible story (about a marriage between a man who had buried twenty wives and a woman who had had twenty-two husbands). One could argue, on the contrary, that the incredible story makes the casual remark more credible.

writes, that he has "restored the New Testament to the authoritative form of the Greek original",[14] which seems to imply that he also worked on other texts than the Gospels. H. F. D. Sparks has shown that Jerome's translation of the Gospels was rather conservative and contains many inconsistencies.[15] Jerome also corrected the Latin Psalter through a closer examination of the Septuagint, of which it was a translation. His interest in Origen was still very strong, as is shown by his translation of two homilies on the Song of Songs.

He became a kind of spiritual adviser to a group of noble women on the Aventine, among whom were Marcella, her mother Albina and sister Asella, Paula and her two daughters Blesilla and Eustochium. His zeal for an austere life and his daring changes in the traditional text of the Gospels caused him enmity in Rome.[16] When Damasus died in 384, Jerome had too many adversaries to be elected bishop, though, as he himself underlines, his friends considered him worthy of that office.[17] His relationship with Paula and Melanium was suspected, because their love of ascetic life had made them despise their wealth and leave their children. The death of Blesilla was attributed to his harsh words of advice.[18] Jerome decided therefore, as he writes to Asella, "to return from Babylon to Jerusalem".[19]

In August 385 he left Rome from Ostia, with his young brother Paulinianus and some monks. Paula and her daughter Eustochium joined them at Reggio di Calabria. On their arrival at Cyprus they were received by bishop Epiphanius and at Antioch by bishop Paulinus. During the cold winter they visited different places in Palestine,[20] journeyed on to Egypt and visited the monks of the desert of Nitria. In Alexandria Jerome listened to the lectures of the blind exegete Didymus, who gave him a copy of his commentary on Isaiah. During the Spring of 386 the group came back to Palestine to settle at Bethlehem, the women in a convent near the church of Nativity, the men in a monastery outside the town.

At Bethlehem, Jerome could finally live the ascetic life of a monk he had yearned for, without the distractions he had had in Rome. He could also whole-heartedly devote his time to the study of the Bible. He delivered instructions to his monks and, in order to attract new recruits, he wrote lives of the monk Malchus and Hilarion, as he had already done at Antioch for Paul the hermit. For this purpose he also translated the rule of Pachomius which then was extant in Coptic and Greek, and he wrote two books against Jovinian in praise of virginity. In his *De viris illustribus* he describes 135 Jewish and Christian authors, including himself.

He had a vast correspondence with men and women in various countries, in which he wrote positively about ascetic life and fought as a champion of orthodoxy. He defended himself against accusations of having indulged in

[14] *Epist.* 71.5.

[15] Sparks, Jerome (1970) 520–524. Sparks is very hesitant on the question if Jerome also revised other parts of the New Testament, contrary to Sutcliffe, Jerome (1969) 84.

[16] See *Epist.* 27.1 to Marcella: "... a report suddenly reached me that certain contemptible creatures were deliberately assailing me with the charge that I had endeavoured to correct passages in the gospels, against the authority of the ancients and the opinion of the whole world". Jerome considers his opponents as "asses" and "ignorant" people, a language which must have exasperated them.

[17] *Epist.* 45.3: "Almost every one concurred in judging me worthy of the episcopate. Damasus, of blessed memory, spoke no words but mine. Men called me holy, humble, eloquent".

[18] *Epist.* 45.3f.

[19] *Epist.* 45.6: "de Babylone Ierosolyman regredi".

[20] See the description of these places in *Epist.* 108.8–13, a letter sent in the year 404, after the death of Paula, to her daughter Eustochium, in order to console her by a description of the mother's character, her long journey to the East, and her life at Bethlehem.

the heretical views of Origen or other authors. He wrote also in defence of his own biblical exegesis, e.g. in the famous correspondence with Augustine. The bishop of Hippo was upset by Jerome's and Origen's interpretation of the conflict at Antioch (Gal 2:11 ff.) as a kind of faked arrangement between Peter and Paul. In his reply Jerome is very ironic about Augustine's passion for the truth of the Gospel.[21] Generally one may say that the composite nature of Jerome's temperament is best illustrated in his correspondence. We meet there a rhetorician who also is a sensitive and irascible man, at times very tender and affectionate, at other times sarcastic, vindictive and aggressive. His polemics against his former friend Rufinus, who had remained faithful to Origen, shows how merciless he could be, attacking his opponent even after his death.[22]

Jerome's main work at Bethlehem consisted of commentaries on the Bible and the revision of the existing Latin versions of the Hebrew Bible, with the help of Origen's Hexapla. In his commentaries Jerome relies much on his predecessors, especially the Greek exegetes from the schools of Alexandria, Antioch and Cappadocia, who were not as well known by Latin exegetes. Some commentaries are almost simple translations of Origen's Greek originals. Jerome often seems impatient to finish his works quickly, without caring too much about making a fresh analysis of the structure of the biblical text. But he frequently has interesting philological remarks on some details in the original language.

The long disease of Paula who had accompanied him for twenty years and died in 404, was a hard blow to Jerome. He wrote one of his longest letters in memory of her (*epist.* 108), but could not produce any major work from 403–405. In 410 another good friend died, Marcella, on whom he writes in his *epist.* 127. Finally, in the 72nd or 73rd year of his life, Jerome died on the 30. 9. 420. His bones were first deposited in the grotto at Bethlehem, and later transferred to the crypt of Santa Maria Maggiore in Rome.

2. Jerome's Exegesis and Hermeneutics

Among Jerome's voluminous writings five groups may be distinguished: his translations of the Bible, his different studies of Holy Scripture, his letters, his polemic works, and his historical books. As our study is devoted to Jerome's exegesis of the Old Testament, we shall deal at most length with the three first groups; also, we shall occasionally quote his studies on the New Testament.

---

[21] See Kieffer, Foi et justification à Antioche (1982) 82–103.

[22] In the *In Hiez.*, prol. he alludes to Rufinus' death in Sicily in 410 by the words: "Now that the scorpion lies buried in Tinacria ..." ("Scorpiusque inter Enceladum et Prophyrionem Trinacriae humo premitur"; CCL 75, 3).

2.1. *The Translations of the Old Testament*

At Bethlehem, during the years from 386 to 390, Jerome reworked the text of the Vetus Latina of the Psalms, Job, Proverbs, the Song of Songs, Ecclesiastes and Chronicles, with the help of Origen's Hexapla. He seems to have used a manuscript which reproduced the text of the Septuagint, where *obeli* (daggers) indicated the sentences which were lacking in the Hebrew text, and asterisks pointed out (with a Greek translation) passages which were only extant in the Hebrew text. Thus Jerome could make the Old Latin version closer to the text of the Septuagint.[23] In the preface to the translation of the Psalms "according to the Septuagint", Jerome indicates that the work began already in Rome. But that work was only a very incomplete and hasty revision of the text, which penetrated into the Roman liturgy and was called *psalterium romanum*, in contrast to the *psalterium vetus* of the Itala-text. The thorough revision at Bethlehem is preserved in the *psalterium gallicanum*, and later became the Vulgata-text of the Roman office. Much of the early work of Jerome disappeared, but the text of Job 1:1–38:16 is still extant.

Jerome's commentary on Ecclesiastes (Qoh) in 389 was the first Latin work also to take into account the Hebrew text. From 391 onwards Jerome worked intensively on a new Latin translation of the Old Testament, which was meant to be much closer to the Hebrew text. He started with the books of Samuel and Kings, the sixteen prophets, the Psalms, Job, Ezra, Nehemiah and the Chronicles. After an illness in 398 he translated the book of Proverbs, Ecclesiastes, the Song of Songs and finally the Pentateuch, Josuah, Judges, Ruth, Esther, Tobias and Judith. He did not translate Baruch, 1 and 2 Maccabees, Sirach and Wisdom, probably because he was hesitating about their canonicity. From 393 to 406 he could publish an almost complete new version of the Bible. In this case also he probably used especially the Hexapla, together with other works of Origen, Eusebius and different Greek writers.[24] Of the deutero-canonical writings only Tobias and Judith were translated from the Aramaic text, whereas the deutero-canonical parts of Daniel remained close to Theodotion and the Septuagint. In his translation Jerome tried to maintain a good quality in the Latin style and, generally, he took into account the traditional text of the Septuagint and the Itala. One can also find influences from rabbinic traditions and from Jerome's broad cultural background.

The quality of the translation is uneven, as Jerome sometimes wrote in haste. He confesses himself in his prefaces to Tobias and Judith, that he respectively spent only one day and one night on the translation. The new version was no doubt his *opus magnum*, which caused him much trouble and demanded energy, but found its way rather late into the liturgy. Since the 7th century it was generally accepted in the Latin Church and was from the 13th century onwards designated under the name of "Vulgata". The second revision of the psalter by Jerome (= *psalterium gallicanum)* had been so successful, that the new translation was not adopted. The texts which Jerome had not translated were taken from the Itala.

---

[23] See Nautin, Hieronymus (1986) 309.

[24] See Nautin, Hieronymus (1986) 309 f.

2.2. *The Commentaries and Other Works on the Old Testament*

As mentioned above, Jerome translated two Homilies of Origen on the Song of Songs about 382. In 381–382 he completed his translation of Origen's Homilies on Jeremiah and Ezekiel. Around the year 389 he wrote, under the title *Hebraicae Quaestiones*, a critical commentary on some difficult passages of Genesis. The work was probably meant as justification for a new translation, which would be closer to the Hebrew text. It forms a kind of trilogy with two other treatises, the *Liber de nominibus hebraicis* and the *Liber de situ et nominibus locorum hebraicorum*, which were written at about the same time.

Around the year 389 he also wrote a commentary on Ecclesiastes (Qoh), which took into account the Hebrew text. Jerome uses here much of Origen's work, but also some oral teachings from his Jewish teachers. With the help of Origen's important commentary, he wrote in 402 explanatory notes on the Psalms (*commentarioli*). This work was meant to elucidate selected problems and thus complete the too short *scholia* of Origen. A more highly elaborated commentary, the *Tractatus in librum Psalmorum*, has been vindicated by G. Morin as an authentic work written at Bethlehem.[25]

During the last fifteen years of his life Jerome produced his most interesting commentaries: those on the twelve prophets were finished in 406,[26] that on Daniel in 407; the commentary on Isaiah was written from 404 to 410 and that on Ezekiel from 410 to 414. The commentary on Jeremiah unfortunately remained unfinished.

For the commentaries on the twelve prophets Jerome used Origen's detailed commentaries,[27] other Christian works he mentions in his prologues, and information he got from Jews. The quality of the commentaries is very uneven. The work on Obadiah was dictated in two nights, as Jerome himself confesses in his conclusion. The first commentaries on Nahum, Micah, Zephaniah and Haggai were adressed to women, Paula and Eustochium, who wanted to be guided in their spiritual life. The commentary on Habakkuk, adressed to the bishop Chromatius, is much more learned, with many variant readings from the Greek translations Jerome found in the Hexapla.

In his commentary on Daniel, Jerome did not analyse the whole text any more, but picked up difficult and important passages which he wanted to elucidate, especially the prophecy on the seventy weeks of years.

---

[25] The arguments of Morin are reproduced in CCL 78, VII–XXI; the text he has reconstructed is printed in the same volume, 1–447.

[26] In the year 393 he writes: "Scripsi in Michaeam explanationum libros duos, in Nahum librum unum, in Abacuc libros duos, in Sophoniam librum unum, in Aggaeum librum unum", *De vir. ill.* 135 (PL 23, 715–717). The same order is given in *In Ion.*, prol.: "Triennium circiter fluxit, postquam quinque prophetas interpretatus sum: Michaeam, Nahum, Abacuc, Sophoniam, Aggaeum" (CCL 76, 377). In *In Am.* 3, prol. he gives the following order for his commentaries: Nahum, Micah, Zephaniah, Haggai, Habakkuk, Obadiah, Jonah, Zechariah, Malachi, Hosea, Joel, Amos. He admits that in his writings he did not follow the order in which they are read in the manuscripts: "Non enim a primo usque ad novissimum, iuxta ordinem quo leguntur, sed ut potuimus, et ut rogati sumus, ita eos disseruimus" (CCL 76, 300).

[27] See *De vir. ill.* 75.

The commentary on Isaiah was prepared for by a first short study, *De Seraphim et calculo*, which Jerome wrote at Constantinople in 381, and sent to pope Damasus.[28] In 397 he had dedicated to bishop Amabilis a study on the ten visions in Isaiah 13–23, which is now integrated in the commentary.[29] Each of the eighteen books of the final commentary is introduced by a prologue as they were sent to Eustochium as soon as they were finished. These prologues, far from indicating the structure of the text of Isaiah, are mainly concerned with how Jerome's work is getting on. In the commentary itself Jerome comments on his own new translation, and concerns himself with both the historical and the spiritual or allegorical sense of the text.

The commentary on Ezekiel is addressed to the same Eustochium and also has similar prologues to each of the fourteen books. The historical meaning of the text is elaborated on here much more than in the commentary on Isaiah. Finally the commentary on Jeremiah in six books, dedicated to Eusebius of Cremona, would have been the finest, but it had only reached chapter 32 when Jerome died.

2.3. *Jerome's Principles of Interpretation and Translation*

Unlike Augustine Jerome did not write a systematic treatise on hermeneutics, but from his works we can gather occasional remarks, which show how he conceived the interpretation of the Bible. He believed that the Scriptures were inspired by the Holy Spirit, according to the *dictum* in 2 Tim 3:16. Therefore he saw him at work in every part of the Bible. In his commentary on Isaiah he cites Rev 5:2,5 and writes: "The lion of the tribe of Judah, the Lord Jesus Christ, (who) broke the seals of the book, not only of one, the psalms of David, as many think, but of all the scriptures, which are written by one and the same Holy Spirit and therefore are called one book".[30] The different authors in the Bible are considered as God's instruments, as is underlined in a note on Ps 45 (44):2: "I must prepare my tongue as a pen, so that by it the Holy Spirit may write in the heart and the ears of the audience. My work it is to present my tongue as a kind of organ, his it is to let sound his own sounds through this organ".[31] One can therefore say that the Scriptures are the work of the Holy Spirit: "They are written and edited by the Holy Spirit".[32] In one of his letters he underlines an important principle for his own

---

[28] This treatise is now integrated in the *Epist.* 18. In *In Es.* ad 6.1 he calls it "brevem subitumque tractatum" (CCL 73, 83).

[29] See *In Es.* 5, prol.

[30] "Leo autem de tribu Iuda Dominus Jesus Christus est, qui solvit signacula libri, non proprie unius, ut multi putant, psalmorum David, sed omnium scripturarum, quae uno scriptae sunt Spiritu sancto; et propterea unus liber appellantur", *In Es.* 9.29 (CCL 73, 374).

[31] "Debeo et linguam meam quasi stilum et calamum praeparare, ut per illam in corde et auribus audientium scribat Spiritus Sanctus. Meum est quasi organum praebere linguam, illius quasi per organum sonare quae sua sunt", *Epist.* 65. One can compare with what he says in his commentary on the Psalms: "Vides quoniam Deus non in auribus sed in corde loquitur; sicut et Zacharias dicit: 'Et angelus qui loquebatur in me dixit mihi'. Ibi angelus Dominus noster intelligitur, qui Patris annuntiat voluntatem, qui in Esaia angelus magni consilii appellatur", *Tract. de Ps.* 84 (CCL 78, 396).

[32] "A spiritu Sancto conscriptae sunt et editae", *In Mich.* 7.5–7 (CCL 76, 513).

exegesis: "Whatever we read in the Old Testament we find also in the Gospel; and whatever we read in the Gospel is deduced from the Old Testament. There is no discord between them, no disagreement. In both Testaments the Trinity is preached".[33]

But this does not mean, that the holy writers were, like the pagan sibyls, unconscious of what they were saying: "It is not true what Montanus has dreamed, and crazy women with him, that the prophets spoke in such a state of ecstasy, that, whilst they gave instructions to others, they were unconscious of what they were saying".[34] For Jerome to be in a state of ecstasy is to have lost all control over one's possibility to speak or to be silent.[35] The prophets keep their individual features. The aristocrat Isaiah is quite different from the rustic Amos, and Jeremiah writes a simpler language than Isaiah, Hosea and others.[36]

Jerome often underlines the divine or sacred character of the Bible. He uses therefore a multitude of expressions to denominate the Holy Scriptures: *scriptura sancta, scriptura sacra, libri sancti, volumina sancta, historia sacra, litterae sacrae, volumina sacra, scriptura divina, scriptura Dei, scripturae dominicae, sermo Dei, sermo divinus, sermo Domini, sermo dominicus, verbum Dei, verba divina, codices divini, libri divini, volumina divina, volumina divinarum litterarum, scripturae caelestes, caelestis scripturarum panis.*[37]

The enthusiasm with which Jerome embraces Holy Scripture makes him recommend to all the priests a zealous reading of it: "Read the divine Scriptures constantly; never, indeed, let the sacred volume be out of your hand. Learn what you have to teach".[38] He is sceptical about people who have a very vague knowledge of the Bible: "The art of interpreting the Scriptures is the only one of which all men everywhere claim to be masters ... The chatting old woman, the doting old man, and the wordy sophist, one and all take in hand the Scriptures, rend them in pieces and teach them before they have learned them".[39] He himself has so high an esteem of the Bible, that he does not want to correct anything in it, unless the manuscripts are faulty: "I am not so dull-witted nor so coarsely ignorant ... as to suppose that any of the Lord's words is either in need of correction or is not divinely inspired; but the Latin manuscripts of the Scriptures are proved to be faulty by the variations which all of them exhibit, and my ambition has been to restore them

---

33 *Epist.* 18, which integrates the short study on *De Seraphim et calculo* from 381.

34 "Neque vero, ut Montanus cum insanis feminis somniat, prophetae in ecstasi sunt locuti, ut nescirent quid loquerentur et cum alios erudirent, ipsi ignorarent quid dicerent", *In Es.*, Prol. (CCL 73, 2); cf. *In Eph.* 3.5 and *In Naum*, prol.

35 He writes: "Qui autem in ecstasi, id est invitus loquitur, nec tacere nec loqui in sua potestate habet", *In Abac.*, prol. (CCL 76A, 580).

36 See *Praef. in Is.* (PL 28, 771) and *Prol. in Jerem.* (PL 28, 847).

37 See the detailed study of Schade, Inspirationslehre (1910), and cf. Forget, Jérôme (1924) 928.

38 *Epist.* 52.7. Jerome quotes Tit 1:9; 2 Tim 3:14; and 1 Pet 3:15 to confirm his exhortation to Nepotian; in *Epist.* 53 he similarly adduces 2 Tim 3:14f. and Tit 1:9 in order to encourage Paulinus to study the Scriptures.

39 *Epist.* 53.7.

to the form of the Greek original, from which my detractors do not deny that they were translated".[40] What he says here of the New Testament is also true of his ambition to make a Latin version of the Old Testament closer to the Hebrew original.

In translating the Chronicle of Eusebius into Latin, Jerome made prefatory remarks which are interesting for his own work on the Bible: "It is difficult in following lines laid down by others not sometimes to diverge from them, and it is hard to preserve in a translation the charm of expressions which in another language are most felicitous. Each particular word conveys a meaning of its own, and possibly I have no equivalent by which to render it, and if I make a circuit to reach my goal, I have to go many miles to cover a short distance. To these difficulties must be added the windings of hyperbata, differences in the use of cases, divergencies of metaphor; and last of all the peculiar and if I may so call it, inbred character of the language. If I render word for word, the result will sound uncouth, and if compelled by necessity I alter anything in the order of wording, I shall seem to have departed from the function of a translator ... In quoting my own writings my only object has been to prove that from my youth up I at least have always aimed at rendering sense not words".[41]

This statement is important, if one wishes to understand the mind with which Jerome translated the Scriptures. Here probably he was more bound by the sacred character of the original and the traditional renderings of words, but still he tried to be faithful to the insights he had obtained from his long practice as a translator. He was a stylist conscious of the different genius of every language and could therefore criticize Aquila's all too literal version: "We do right to reject Aquila, the proselyte and controversal translator, who has striven to translate not words only but their etymologies as well ...; because Hebrew has in addition to the article other prefixes as well, he must with an unhappy pedantry translate syllable by syllable and letter by letter ... How many are the phrases charming in Greek which, if rendered word by word, do not sound well in Latin".[42]

Jerome's principles for a good translation make him also adhere to the theory that Holy Scripture is inspired in the meaning it conveys, and not in its single words. Commenting on Paul's letter to the Galatians, he writes: "We must not think that the Gospel is found in the words of the Scripture, but in its meaning".[43] He stresses, that even Jesus, the apostles and the evangelists did not always follow the letter of the Septuagint or of the Hebrew text, because they cared less for the words than for the meaning of the sentences.[44]

---

[40] *Epist.* 27.1.

[41] The prefatory remarks are quoted and commented on in *Epist.* 57.5f. The whole letter, addressed to Pammachius in 395, is a kind of treatise on the best method of translation.

[42] *Epist.* 57.11.

[43] "Nec putemus in verbis Scripturarum esse Evangelium, sed in sensu", *In Gal.* 1.11 (PL 26, 322).

[44] In *In Mal.* 3.1 he underlines the differences between the Hebrew and the Greek text of Mal 3:1, which Mark and Luke on one side, and John on the other side, formulated with even other words: "Ex quo perspicuum est, apostolos et evangelistas et ipsum Dominum Salvatorem non

Even if one can say that Jerome is no adherent of a verbal inspiration of the Bible, he sometimes, especially in his earlier works under the influence of Origen, expresses himself as if every word of the Bible contained a mystery. Thus he can write in his commentary on the Psalms: "The different words of the Scripture are as many mysteries".[45] But that does not reflect Jerome's mature conception on the Bible's inspiration.

Concerning the inspiration of the *Septuagint*, one can accept J. FORGET's subtle presentation of the documentation.[46] As a young scholar Jerome had come into contact with St. Hilary's and Origen's opinions on the question and followed their respectful attitude towards the inspired Septuagint version. In the Preface to the text of the *Paralipomenôn* according to the Septuagint (between 389 and 391), he still affirms that the inspired version of the Septuagint is correct, but that the copyists have added mistakes to mistakes.[47] A closer comparison between the Greek version and the Hebrew text obliged him to reconsider the question. Progressively he abandoned the high esteem in which he held this version. Already in the Preface to the *Paralipomenôn* according to the Hebrew text (from 396), he questions the legend about the cells where different translators were gathered,[48] but he is even more explicit in his preface to the Pentateuch (from 398–404), where he considers the Greek translators as men of erudition, but not as prophets.[49] From now onwards he dares to criticize more openly the reliability of the Septuagint.[50] In his last commentary he even gets so weary of that translation, that he finds it superfluous to mention the places where it differs from the Hebrew text.[51] In his letter to Pammachius, he sums up his objections against the Septuagint in the following way: "It would be tedious to enumerate what great additions

---

LXX interpretum auctoritatem sequi, qua Hebraeae linguae habentes scientiam, non indigent, sed ex Hebraeo transferre quod legerint, non curantes de syllabis punctisque verborum; dum modo sententiarum veritas transferatur" (CCL 76 A, 928).

[45] "Singula verba scripturarum singula sacramenta sunt", *Tract. de Ps.* 90 (CCL 78, 130); see also *Epist.* 53.7: "Single words occuring in the book are full of meaning".

[46] Forget, Jérôme (1924) 939–943.

[47] "Nec hoc LXX interpretibus, qui Spiritu Sancto pleni, ea quae vera fuerant, transtulerunt, sed scriptorum culpae adscribendum, dum de inemendatis inemendata scriptitant", *Praef. in Par. juxta LXX* (PL 29, 402).

[48] "Post septuaginta cellulas, quae vulgo sine auctore jactantur", *Praef. in Par.* (PL 28, 1325).

[49] "Nescio quis primus auctor septuaginta cellulas Alexandriae mendacio suo exstruxerit, quibus divisi eadem scriptitarent, cum Aristeas, ejusdem Ptolemaei ὁ ὑπερασπιστής et multo post tempore Josephus, nihil tale retulerint, sed in una basilica congregatos contulisse scribant, non prophetasse. Aliud est enim vatem, aliud esse interpretem. Ibi Spiritus ventura praedicit, hic eruditio et verborum copia ea quae intelligit transfert", *Praef. in Pent.* (PL 28, 150 f.).

[50] See e.g. *In Os.* 13.1–2 (CCL 76, 141): "nescio quid volentes, δικαιώματα id est iustificationes, LXX transtulerunt"; *In Os.* 14. 2–4 (CCL 76, 154): "Pro vitulis qui Hebraice appellantur pharim, fructum Septuaginta transtulerunt, qui dicitur pheri, falsi sermonis similitudine"; *In Es.* 5.17 (CCL 73, 75): "nescio quid volentes LXX transtulerunt : *Pascentur direpti quasi tauri*, pro agnis tauros intelligentes, et rursum pro advenis interpretantes agnos"; *In Es.* 14.21 f. (CCL 73, 248): "Et hoc putant loco convenire iuxta LXX interpretes, qui dixerunt : *Pro peccatis patris tui*; cum perspicue in Hebraeo abotham non patris tui, sed patrum suorum significet"; *In Es.* 21.6 f. (CCL 73, 292): "nescio quid volentes LXX Οὐρίαν posuerunt ".

[51] "Hucusque in LXX non habetur, quae asteriscis praenotavi; cetera enim, in quibus vel singuli versus vel pauca ab eis praetermissa sunt verba, victus taedio annotare nolui, ne fastidium legenti facerem", *In Hier.* 29. 14–20 (CCL 74, 281).

and omissions the Septuagint has made, and all the passages which in church-copies are marked with daggers and asterisks".[52] He even admits that "the Jews generally laugh when they hear our version of this passage of Isaiah, 'Blessed is he that hath seed in Zion and servants in Jerusalem' (Isa 31:9 LXX)".[53] But he can find a good excuse for the churches' use of the Septuagint: "either because it is the first of all versions in time, made before the coming of Christ, or else because it has been used by the apostles".[54]

But what is to be said about the *truth* of Holy Scripture itself? When one goes back to the original text, one may get the impression that there are real contradictions in the Bible. Jerome is much concerned about that problem, especially since he does not agree with the pagans' objections to the reliability of the Bible: "I refer to these passages (apparent contradictions between Matthew and the Old Testament), not to convict the evangelists of falsification – a charge worthy only of impious men like Celsus, Porphyr, and Julian – but to bring home to my critics their own want of knowledge".[55] Jerome maintains the important principle of the Bible's infallibility, whilst he is at a loss to explain the apparent contradictions in it. He underlines the different perspectives of time and space from which the texts were written, the different meanings a word or a sentence can have. But at times he does not find any solution to his problem: "No man save Him who for our salvation has deigned to put on flesh has full knowledge and a complete grasp of the truth".[56] In his commentary on Galatians, he enunciates the principle, that the gospel is necessarily true, and that to adhere exclusively to its letter, may lead to the destruction of its special purpose.[57] In other words, one has to take account of the mysteries contained in Holy Scripture: "There are many things in Scripture which sound incredible and yet are true".[58] (A modern scholar who is a Christian believer admits more frankly than Jerome, that there are historical and other errors in the Bible, due to the hagiographers' own limitations).

Under the influence of Origen, Jerome was in the beginning of his scholarly work fascinated by the spiritual or mystical meaning of the Holy Scriptures, a meaning which was quite in keeping with his own monastic ideals. But his hard labour with philological aspects of the Bible made him more and more interested in the literal or historical meaning of the texts. He admits himself that the spiritual commentary he had written in his youth on the prophet Obadiah was immature.[59] At times he distinguishes between *three meanings*: the historical or literal, the tropological or allegorical, and the spiritual or

[52] *Epist.* 57.11.

[53] Ibid.

[54] Ibid.

[55] *Epist.* 57.9.

[56] *Epist.* 36.

[57] *In Gal.* 1.6: "hujus naturae est, ut non possit aliud esse quam verum est ... Si quis tantum litteram sequitur, posteriora ponit in faciem" (PL 26, 319).

[58] *Epist.* 72.2: "Multa (et alia) dicuntur in Scripturis, quae videntur incredibilia, et tamen vera sunt". This principle is even more explicit in the commentary on Philemon (PL 26, 608 f.).

[59] He regrets that: "in adolescentia mea provocatus ardore et studio scripturarum, allegorice interpretatus sum Abdiam prophetam, cuius historiam nesciebam", *In Abd.*, prol. (CCL 76, 349).

mystical.[60] But more often he simply opposes the literal or historical sense to what he calls with the following different names: the spiritual, the allegorical, the tropological or tropic, the anagogical, the typical, the mystical, the figurated, and even the moral, the parabolic, or the metaphorical signification.[61]

2.4. *Jerome's Concrete Work as an Interpreter of Holy Scripture*

It is instructive to see which kind of questions Jerome is asking as regards the biblical texts and what the problems are that he discusses in his commentaries.

In his first major work on the Bible, the *Hebraicae quaestiones in Libro Geneseos*, Jerome defends himself against those who have no knowledge of the Hebrew text. In order to do this he picks up details in the book of Genesis, where the Greek and the Latin texts and manuscripts are faulty. He also tries to explain the etymology of objects and of personal or topographic names. He thus underlines that in contrast to what Hilary says, the Hebrew text does not read: "In the Son God created heaven and earth" (Gen 1:1). He critizises the translation: "The spirit of God was borne (*ferebatur*) over the waters"; it would be more accurate to say that it "hovered over the waters or warmed them" (*incubabat sive confovebat*) like a bird (Gen 1:2). Concerning Gen 2:23, Jerome rightly emphasizes that the Greek and the Latin translations generally have not rendered the etymological proximity between "woman" (אִשָּׁה) and "man" (אִישׁ). Symmachus had tried to do it, when he used the word ἀνδρίς, and Jerome proposes *virago* in Latin.

Generally it may be stated, that Jerome is well informed about the Hebrew text and the Greek and Latin translations, information he can have obtained by a close study of the Hexapla. This work is one of Jerome's best and most scholarly achievements.

The *Liber Interpretationis Hebraicorum Nominum* is a less satisfying study. Jerome uses the works of Philo and Origen, but as the manuscripts of Philo's books were faulty and contradictory, he had to rework much of the material himself. This systematic review of Hebrew names in the whole Bible is still readable, but modern scholarship questions many of the etymologies that are proposed. The science of etymology was still not born.

The *Liber de situ et nominibus locorum hebraicorum*,[62] which sometimes is cited as *De distancia locorum* and *De locis hebraicis*, is a Latin translation of Eusebius' famous Onomasticon, but Jerome has tried to improve it. It still has a historical and archaeological value.

When we come to the *Commentaries* of Jerome, we have to distinguish between those that present only short philological notices, such as the *Commentarioli* on the Psalms or the commentary on Obadiah; those that pick up

---

[60] See e.g. *Epist.* 120.12 and especially *In Hiez.* 16.30f. (CCL 75, 194f.): "Legimus in Proverbiis: *Tu autem describe ea tripliciter, ut respondeas sermones veritatis qui proponuntur tibi*, et iubetur nobis ut eloquia veritatis, id est scripturas sanctas, intellegamus tripliciter: primum, iuxta litteram; secundo, medie, per tropologiam; tertio, sublimius, ut mystica quaeque cognoscamus".

[61] See Forget, Jérôme (1924) 958–965 (especially 960).

[62] See PL 23, 859–928.

only some main problems, like the commentary on Daniel; and, finally, the bulk of commentaries which cover the whole text.

Jerome himself has defined the purpose of a commentary in the following way: "To explain what has been said by others and make clear in plain language what has been written obscurely".[63] At times he may be modest and write: "while I lay no claim to be a master, I readily pledge myself to be a fellow-student".[64] He also indicates a detailed programme for a good commentary: "(It should always) repeat the opinions of the many, and say, 'Some explain this passage in this way, others interpret it in that: these try to support their sense and understanding of it by these proofs and by this reasoning'; so that the judicious reader, when he has perused the different explanations and familiarised himself with many that he can either approve or disapprove, may judge which is the best, and, like a good banker, reject the money from a spurious mint".[65]

Unfortunately Jerome does not always follow his own good recommendations. He borrows much from his predecessors, which he generally mentions in his prologues, but he does not systematically analyse their various arguments in his commentaries. He is normally in a hurry and picks up some argument for the interpretation he chooses and quickly refutes one or other opinion. He may give different interpretations and let the reader choose between them. He is always very concerned about the orthodoxy of the previous commentators.

In his *Commentarioli* on the Psalms Jerome intentionally chooses not to be an interpreter, but only a philologist who raises some questions he finds interesting.[66] In the first Psalm he discusses the absence of a title, the way of enumerating the Psalms, the use of the psalm in Jewish and Christian literature, and finally some differences in the Hebrew and the Greek text. The notes on several psalms are very short, indicating e. g. only their main content, which for Jerome is often a spiritual one.[67]

In contrast to the *Commentarioli*, the *Tractatus in Psalmos* contain very extensive explanations of a spiritual kind. Here Jerome insists less on his knowledge of Hebrew. The introduction to the first Psalm gives a good idea of what Jerome intends to do. He compares the whole psalter to a big house with one key for the outside door, but with many special keys inside to different rooms. The Holy Spirit is the key to the great door, but you need

---

[63] *Apol.* 1.16.

[64] *Epist.* 53.10.

[65] *Apol.* 1.16; I quote the translation of Sparks, Jerome (1970) 536.

[66] Jerome writes in his prologue: "Igitur pro familiaritate, quae inter nos est, studiose et sedule postulasti, ut quaecumque mihi digna memoria videbantur, signis quibusdam potius quam interpretationibus adnotarem" (CCL 72, 177).

[67] In Psalm 38, Jerome underlines only the words: "Obmutui, et non aperui os meum, quia tu fecisti". He writes: "Ideo patienter fero, quia te scio ad probationem me temptationibus reliquisse" (CCL 72, 207). Of Psalm 41, he comments only on v. 11 in the following way: "Cum ergo te per paenitentiam et adflictionem corporis animaeque placare desiderarem, inimici mei, quasi in cassum haec facerem, dicebant: Ubi est Deus tuus?" (CCL 72, 208). One guesses in both cases Jerome's interest for an ascetic life.

also special keys for the many rooms. The first Psalm is in its turn called the great door to the whole building.[68]

Jerome does not accept the christological interpretation of the first verse: "happy the man who does not follow the example of sinners", even if it is a pious one. He thinks that it is rather the portrait of a just man in general. The malediction which was pronounced on Adam is now replaced by a benediction over the just man, who does not sin, or at least, is willing to repent when he has sinned. His will is entirely determined by God's law (v. 2). The tree that grows beside a stream (v. 3 a) makes Jerome draw associations with the tree of life and with wisdom, which is found in Christ. A just man will therefore be similar to Christ. "The leaves that do not dry up" (v. 3 b) make Jerome think of "the leaves for the healing of the nations" (Rev 22:2). As a biblical scholar he adds here a short remark on the canonicity of the book of Revelation.

In opposition to the just man we have the portrait of the sinners. Here Jerome refers to Adam's sin and shows how God finally chose the just man Abraham.

The conclusion sums up the spiritual message of the psalm: "God may help us, to avoid three things and to do two things: we may be compared to the tree of life, and not be evil men who are compared with dust; we ought not to be sinners who will not rise up in the counsel of the righteous, because the evil way must perish; we ought to bless God, to whom belongs the glory for ever, Amen".[69] We have here a kind of homiletic exegesis, where associations with biblical texts are used in order to make a religious impression on the reader. This is not the learned exegete who discusses philological problems in the original text.

In the preface to his *Commentary on Ecclesiastes*, Jerome mentions that he read Qohelet's book to Blesilla, in order to make her despise this world. Blesilla asked him to write a commentary on it, but this was postponed, as the result of the young girl's death.[70] As we mentioned above, her death was partly attributed to Jerome's austere advice. Fifteen years later, at Bethlehem, he finally wrote his commentary, addressed to Eustochium and Paula, Blesillas mother.

It may be said that Qohelet's reflexions on how short and contradictory human life is, admirably fits Jerome's austere world-view. He has no difficulty in embracing Qohelet's saying on the vanity of this world: "If a living man is vanity, then a dead man is a vanity of vanity". By a kind of contrast, Jerome comes to think about the glory of Moses which the sons of Israel could not

---

[68] *Tract. in librum Ps.*, Ps. 1: "Psalterium ita est quasi magna domus, quae unam quidem habet exteriorem clavem in porta, in diversis vero intrinsecus cubiculis proprias claves habet. Licet amplior una clavis sit grandis portae Spiritus sanctus, tamen unumquodque cubiculum habet proprias claviculas suas ... Grandis itaque porta istius domus primus psalmus est" (CCL 78, 3).

[69] Ibid. 11 f: "Deus ergo hoc nobis praestet, ut tria non faciamus, duo faciamus: ligno vitae conparemur, non simus peccatores, quoniam peccatores non resurgunt in consilio iustorum, ut via mala pereat: et benedicamus Deum, cui sit gloria in saecula saeculorum. Amen".

[70] See *In Eccl.* praef. (CCL 72, 249).

look at. But the glory of Moses was, according to Paul, nothing in comparison with the glory of the gospel. Similarly Jerome says, that the heaven, the earth, the sea and everything in it, are good things, but compared to God, they are nothing.[71] In contrast to the servants which Qohelet mentions, the Christians are in principle free in Christ, but still many have not really been liberated by the knowledge of the Scriptures.[72]

The *Commentary on Daniel* is devoted to chronological and prophetic aspects of the book. As Porphyr had written on Daniel, claiming that it was the work of a contemporary of Antiochus Epiphanes, Jerome, without trying to refute Porphyr in every detail, shows how prophetic Daniel really was about Jesus Christ.[73] In order to achieve this purpose, Jerome keeps to the Hebrew text, as Origenes, Eusebius, Apollinaris and many other ecclesiastical writers had done before him. He therefore needs not answer the objections of Porphyr due to the Greek text.[74] In his prologue Jerome claims to use all information he can get from Greek and Latin historians whom he mentions by name, but he is far from quoting all of them in his commentary.[75]

His main purpose is to show that the description of the Antichrist does not fit Epiphanes, as Porphyrius claims, but one who coming from Babylon will defeat Egypt. He will be a figure of the Antichrist who later on will persecute the Christian people, Domitian or Nero.[76]

---

[71] "Si vivens homo vanitas est, ergo mortuus vanitas vanitatum. Legimus in Exodo glorificatum vultum Moysi intantum, ut filii Israel eum aspicere non possent. Quam gloriam Paulus apostolus ad comparationem evangelicae gloriae, dicit esse non gloriam ... Possumus igitur et nos in hunc modum, caelum, terram, maria et omnia quae hoc circulo continentur, bona quidem per se dicere, sed ad Deum comparata, esse pro nihilo", *In Eccl.* 1.2 (CCL 72, 252).

[72] Cf. *In Eccl.* 2.7 (CCL 72, 265).

[73] "Contra prophetam Danielem duodecimum librum scribit Porphyrius, nolens eum ab ipso cuius inscriptus est nomine esse compositum sed a quodam qui temporibus Antiochi, qui appellatus est Epiphanes, fuerit in Iudaea, et non tam Danielem ventura dixisse quam illum narrasse praeterita; denique quidquid usque ad Antiochum dixerit, veram historiam continere, siquid autem ultra opinatus sit, quae futura nescierit esse mentitum ... Verum quia nobis propositum est non adversarii calumniis respondere, quae longo sermone indigent, sed ea quae a propheta dicta sunt nostris disserere, id est Christianis, illud in praefatione commoneo, nullum prophetarum tam aperte dixisse de Christo", *In Dan.*, prol. (CCL 75A, 771 f.).

[74] "Unde et nos ante annos plurimos cum verteremus Danielem, has visiones obelo praenotavimus, significantes eas in hebraico non haberi; et miror quosdam μεμψιμοίρος indignari mihi, quasi ego decurtaverim librum, cum et Origenes et Eusebios et Apollinaris aliique ecclesiastici viri et doctores Graeciae has, ut dixi, visiones non haberi apud Hebraeos fateantur, nec se debere respondere Porphyrio pro his quae nullam scripturae sanctae auctoritatem praebeant", ibid. (CCL 75A, 774).

[75] "Ad intelligendas autem extremas partes Danielis, multiplex Graecorum historia necessaria est: Sutori videlicet Callinici, Diodori, Hieronymi, Polybii, Posidonii, Claudii Theonis et Andronyci cognomento Alipi, quos et Porphyrius secutum esse se dicit, Iosephi quoque et eorum quos ponit Iosephus, praecipueque nostri Livii, et Pompei Trogi, atque Iustini, qui omnem extremae visionis narrant historiam et, post Alexandrum usque ad Caesarem Augustum, Syriae et Aegypti id est Seleuci et Antiochi et Ptolemaeorum bella describunt", ibid. (CCL 75A, 775).

[76] See especially *In Dan.* IV: "Nostri autem secundum superiorem sensum interpretantur omnia de Antichristo, qui nasciturus est de populo Iudaeorum et, de Babylone venturus, primum superaturus est regem Aegypti qui est unus de tribus cornibus de quibus antea iam diximus"; and p. 920: "ut rex sceleratissimus qui persecutus est populum Dei, praefiguret Antichristum qui Christi populum persecuturus est -unde multi nostrorum putant, ob saevitiae et turpitudinis magnitudinem, Domitianum, Neronem, Antichristum fore" (CCL 75A, 918).

Of the *Commentaries on the twelve prophets*, the one on *Habakkuk* is especially learned, with its discussion of variant readings in the Greek versions. But we find in it also personal spiritual considerations on prayer. Commenting Hab 1:2f, Jerome states that God's judgements are profound and full of wisdom and knowledge. God does not see things as man sees them; man looks only at present things, whereas God knows future and eternal things. Therefore God sometimes does not fulfil our prayers, in order to purify our demands, as through fire.[77]. The commentaries on *Amos* and *Jonah* are likewise generally considered to be of good quality, whereas those on *Hosea, Joel* and *Zechariah* are judged as rather weak.[78]

The three major commentaries are those on *Isaiah*, *Ezekiel* and *Jeremiah.* Unlike a modern exegete, Jerome does not give any survey of these extensive books. He does not bother about problems of structure or redaction. He starts as it were *in medias res* by quoting one or several verses, which he generally comments on according to their historical or literal truth, but sometimes also according to their spiritual contents.

As an example we can take the commentary on Isa 1:1,[79] where Jerome first underlines the fact that his own translation (*super Iudam et Hierusalem*) is closer to the Hebrew than that of the LXX and Theodotion (*contra Iudaeam et Hierusalem*). This later translation seems to suggest that the book contains hostile prophecies against the whole country of the twelve tribes. With Symmachus Jerome thinks, on the contrary, that the prophecies are both positive and negative, and that they are addressed only to the two tribes of Judah and Benjamin. He then affirms that Isaiah, Hosea, Amos and Joel have prophesied during about the same period.

Jerome reminds his readers that the prophets were called "those who see" (*videntes*). This leads him to make associations with different texts in the Bible where the 'spiritual' look is mentioned, as in Ps 123:1 ("I look up to you, up to heaven"), John 4:35 ("take a good look at the fields"), Cant 4:9 ("the look in your eyes, my sweetheart and bride, has stolen my heart"), and Matt 6:22 ("the eyes are like a lamp for the body"). As the Bible also says that "they saw his voice" (cf. Exod 20:18), the Montanists wrongly thought, that the prophets had ecstatic visions and could not understand their own utterings. What some commentators say about the heavenly Jerusalem, Jerome prefers to interpret as being about Christ's Church, which some people leave because of their sins, and others come back to, when they do penitence. Jerome refers here to Isa 60:2–7.

Finally, the commentator emphasizes that the prophecies in the book of Isaiah took place successively under four kings of Judah: Uzziah, Jotham, Ahaz, and Hezekiah. He reminds the reader that the latter one began to reign

---

[77] *In Abac.* 1.2–3: "Haec autem loquuntur nescientes iudicia Dei investigabilia, et profundum divitiarum sapentiae et scientiae eius, quod non ita videat Deus ut videt homo. Homo tantum praesentia respicit Deus futura et aeterna cognoscit ... Ita et Dominus Deus noster sciens clementiae suae pondera atque mensuras, interdum non exaudit clamantem, ut eum probet, et magis provocet ad rogandum, et quasi igne excoctum iustiorem et puriorem faciat" (CCL 76A, 581f.).

[78] See Forget, Jérôme (1924) 911, and Antin, Sur Jonas (SC 43, Paris 1956) 17.

[79] See *In Es.* 1.1 (CCL 73, 5ff.).

in Jerusalem in the twelfth year of Romulus, a proof that the biblical history is older than that of other peoples. After having rendered the meaning of the Hebrew names Isaiah, Judah, Jerusalem, Uzziah, Jotham, Ahaz and Hezekiah, Jerome combines their signification in order to sum up the spiritual meaning of the text, concluding with a quotation of Luke 17:10: "We are ordinary servants; we have only done our duty".[80]

Jerome shows in this typical passage his special interest in Hebrew words and in historical or geographical details, which he combines in such a way as to give the reader spiritual guidance. The Hebrew words are used in a rather arbitrary way in order to sum up Isaiah's message with the help of the gospels.

The same kind of procedure is found in most of Jerome's commentaries, and especially in that on *Ezekiel.* One could perhaps add, that the details here are sometimes analysed with even more prolixity. For instance in Ezek 1:5 ff. Jerome picks up every word in the description of the four living creatures, with their four faces, four wings, and straight legs. He mentions the traditional interpretation of the four creatures as symbols of the four evangelists, but he is keen to add to it philosophical and moral interpretations with the help of Plato, Hippocrates, Cicero, and Virgil. He seems to be fond of showing how learned he is, but fails to make a real analysis of the text according to the Hebrew background. One must, nevertheless, admire much of the historical exegesis in this extensive commentary, e. g. the interpretation of Ezek 37:1–14 as Israel's national resurrection.

The commentary on *Jeremiah* is in many respects the most satisfactory of all commentaries, as it keeps close to the text and has less 'wild' associations to different cultural backgrounds. Jerome wants to be deliberately short but convey as much information as possible.[81] His style is still very vivid, especially in the famous prologue to the first book, where he attacks Pelagius as a "dolt of dolts, with his wits dulled by a surfeit of his native Scotch porridge".[82] In the sixth book, he wants to deal also with the mystical interpretations of Jer 30 (= LXX 37) ff. He does not accept Jewish explanations according to which the prophecies will be realized at the end of the world. Jerome keeps to the apostolic tradition, especially to Paul, according to which what has been promised to Israel in a 'carnal' way is already fulfilled among the Christians in a 'spiritual' way. Christ has come and the Christians are now the real children of Abraham.[83] But Jerome unfortunately could not finish this part of his commentary.

---

[80] Ibid. 6 f: "Interpretatur autem Esaias: salvatus Domini. Iuda: confessio. Hierusalem: visio pacis. Ozias: fortitudo Domini. Ioatham: Domini perfectio. Achaz: tenens sive robustus. Ezechias: imperium Domini. Qui igitur Domino praesidente salvatur et est filius Amos, id est fortis atque robusti, cernit spiritaliter visionem confessionis, dum antiqua peccata deplangit; et pacis, dum post paenitentiam transit ad lucem, et aeterna pace requiescit; cunctaque illius tempora transeunt sub fortitudine Domini et perfectione eius ac robore. Cumque omnia fecerit, dicet illud evangelicum: *Servi inutiles sumus; quod enim debuimus facere, fecimus*".

[81] See *In Hier.* VI. 1: "Prolixitas voluminis Hieremiae prophetae vincit nostrum propositum, ut qamvis breviter, tamen multa dicamus" (CCL 74, 289).

[82] *In Hier.* prol.: "stolidissimus et Scottorum pultibus praegravatus" (CCL 74, 2). I quote the expressive translation of Sparks, Jerome (1970) 516.

[83] *In Hier.* VI. 1: "Unde et praesens sextus liber commentariorum in Hieremiam repromissiones

3. Conclusion

Summing up Jerome's way of commenting on biblical texts, it may be said that in his later works he is fond of displaying his knowledge of the Hebrew language and of Greek and Latin culture; he picks up such details in the texts which show his information about geographical and historical facts; he is keen to underline ascetic and mystical aspects in the texts, but is always concerned about an 'orthodox' Christian interpretation. He seems to have no interest at all in the composition and the overall structure of biblical texts. But one ought not to forget that the commentaries generally were dictated, which automatically made them rhetorical rather than technical in the modern sense of the word.

It may be added that, with the exception of Augustine, there is no Latin Church Father who has left so many different kinds of writings as Jerome. But unlike Augustine, he was truly a trained scholar and seems to have precise information about the original languages. His observations very often are correct, but a modern scholar will notice his lack of comprehensive analysis of the structural composition of biblical literature. Nevertheless, exegetes even today must admire Jerome, one of the four Latin doctors, for his immense learning and his exceptional knowledge of the whole Bible.

---

mysticas continebit, quas Iudaei putant et nostri iudaizantes in consummatione mundi esse conplendas; necdum enim sub Zorobabel possunt expletas convincere. Nos autem sequentes auctoritatem apostolorum et evangelistarum, et maxime apostoli Pauli, quidquid populo carnaliter repromittitur, in nobis spiritaliter conpletum esse monstramus hodieque impleri ...". "Qui igitur Christum venisse iam credimus, necesse est, ut ea, quae sub Christo futura dicuntur, expleta doceamus nosque esse filios Abraham ..." (CCL 74, 289 f.).

Chapter Twenty

The Reception of the Origenist Tradition in Latin Exegesis

By Christoph Jacob, Münster

Sources: CPL 123–165; 427–472. PL 9–10; 14–17. CSEL 22; 32, 1–4; 62; 64; 72; 73; 82, 1–3. CCL 14; 62; 62 A. SC 19bis; 25bis; 45; 52; 179; 239; 254; 258; 334; 344; 347. Several translations in BKV; BKV²; FC; FontC; NPNF; SC.

Critical editions: Ambrose: *Exameron, De paradiso, De Cain et Abel, De Noe et arca, De Abraham, De Isaac vel anima, De bono mortis* (ed. C. Schenkl; CSEL 32, 1; Wien 1897); *De Iacob et vita beata, De Ioseph, De patriarchis, De fuga saeculi, De interpellatione Iob et David, Apologia prophetae David, Apologia prophetae David altera, De Helia et ieiunio, De Nabuthae, De Tobia* (ed. C. Schenkl; CSEL 32, 2; Wien 1897); *Explanatio psalmorum XII* (ed. M. Petschenig; CSEL 64; Wien 1913); *Expositio psalmi CXVIII* (ed. M. Petschenig; CSEL 62; Wien 1913); *De excessu fratris, Explanatio Symboli, De obitu Valentiniani, De paenitentia, De mysteriis, De sacramentis* (ed. O. Faller; CSEL 73; Wien 1955); *De spiritu sancto* (ed. O. Faller; CSEL 79; Wien 1964); *Epistulae* (ed. O. Faller; CSEL 82, 1–3; Wien 1968 ff.); *Expositio evangelii secundum Lucam* (ed. M. Adriæn; CCL 14; Turnhout 1957).

Hilary: *Tractatus super psalmos* (ed. A. Zingerle; CSEL 22; Wien 1891); *Tractatus super psalmum 118* (ed. M. Milhau; SC 344; 347; Paris 1988); *Commentarius in Matthaeum* (ed. J. Doignon; SC 254; 258; Paris 1978 f); *Libri II ad Constantium, Collecta antiariana Parisiana, Fragmenta minora, Hymni* (ed. K. Federer; CSEL 65; Wien 1916); *Liber ad Constantium* (ed. A. Rochier; SC 334; Paris 1987); *De trinitate* (ed. P. Smulders; CCL 62; 62 A; Turnhout 1979 f); *Tractatus mysteriorum* (ed. J.-P. Brisson; SC 19bis; Paris 1967).

General works: Ambroise de Milan. XIVe centenaire de son éléction episcopale (ed. Y. M. Duval; Paris 1974); *Ambrosius Episcopus. Atti del congresso internazionale di studi ambrosiani* I–II (ed. G. Lazzati; Milano 1976); H. C. Brenneke, *Hilarius von Poitiers und die Bischofsopposition gegen Konstantius II* (Berlin/New York 1984); E. Dassmann, *Die Frömmigkeit des Kirchenvaters Ambrosius von Mailand. Quellen und Entfaltung* (Münster 1965); J. Doignon, *Hilaire de Poitiers avant l'exil* (Paris 1971); M. Durst, *Die Eschatologie des Hilarius von Poitiers. Ein Beitrag zur Dogmengeschichte des vierten Jahrhunderts* (Bonn 1987); *Hilaire et son temps. Actes du colloque de Poitiers* (ed. E.-R. Labande; Paris 1969); J. Daniélou/H.-I. Marrou/B. Le Gaffier et al., *Hilaire de Poitiers. Evêque et docteur* (Paris 1968); C. Jacob, *"Arkandisziplin", Allegorese, Mystagogie. Ein neuer Zugang zur Theologie des Ambrosius von Mailand* (Frankfurt 1990); G. Madec, *S. Ambroise et la philosophie* (Paris 1974); L. F. Pizzolato, *La dottrina esegetica di Ambrogio di Milano* (Milano 1978); H. Savon, *S. Ambroise devant l'exégèse de Philon juif* (Paris 1977); J. Schmitz, *Der Gottesdienst im altchristlichen Mailand. Eine liturgiewissenschaftliche Untersuchung über Initiation und Meßfeier während des Kirchenjahres zur Zeit des Bischofs Ambrosius von Mailand (†397)* (Köln/Bonn 1975).

1. Allegory and the Text of the Bible

Hilary of Poitiers and Ambrose of Milan are considered to be the two theologians in the Latin West who by their personal fate or by the thoroughness of their education learned to know the Origenist interpretation of Scripture, assumed it wholeheartedly and paved the way for subsequent Latin exegesis. From Origen they learned how to get away from a literal understanding of the Old Testament, but they did not inherit his speculative ability. Their allegorical interpretation is said to be centred on parenetics, which fits well with the common understanding of the Latins as being more practically oriented. This general judgement is widespread in modern Christian theology. Ambrose and Hilary did rely on Origen; they may indeed have profited from their study of his writings and they may have adapted several of his exegetical interpretations. But there is a basic assumption of this view that can be put into question today.

Why did Hilary and Ambrose adopt the allegorical interpretation of the Bible? A modern European will point to the difficulties which arise from a purely historical reading of the OT and he may even refer to Origen who declares that the Holy Spirit has inserted stories in Scripture that cannot have happened or which are not logical (*De principiis* IV. 2. 9) in order to safeguard it against a literal understanding. But is it really possible to take this defensive statement – Origen is arguing against those who oppose his allegory – as a positive explanation for his interpretation of Scripture?[1] To put it otherwise: Can there be an explanation of allegory that does not start from the shortcomings of a purely historical reading of the Bible?

A closer look at the interpretation of Ambrose's *relecture* of Philo's exegesis will allow for a different evaluation of the allegorical interpretation. In his *De sacrificiis*, Philo has transposed the Hellenic parable of Heracles' decision between the broad way of 'Vice' and the steep path of 'Virtue' (cf. Xenophon, *Memorabilia* II. 1. 21–34) into a biblical environment (cf. §§ 19–44). Ambrose does not simply repeat this Alexandrian allegory; he reshapes it in an ecclesiastical context: The rather ephemeral remark of 'Virtue' – in Philo's version she has become lady 'Wisdom' – who invites to her table (Prov 9:5), receives a key position in the reinterpretation of the story by Ambrose. Modern interpreters agree that in *De Cain et Abel* I. 5. 19 he is alluding to the "meal of the Church", to the Eucharist.[2] What does this mean? Further investigation shows that this reference is not a chance remark, but that he in fact reinterprets the Philonic adaptation of the Hellenic diatribe according to the way this decision between good and bad, virtue and vice takes place in an actual ecclesiastical setting:[3] the invitation of Wisdom to her table is in fact an invitation to the Eucharist within Christian Initiation.[4] Heracles' decision is

---

[1] L. Diestel, *Geschichte des Alten Testaments in der christlichen Kirche* (Jena 1869; repr. Leipzig 1981) 28 f, as well as most modern interpretations start from this assumption. For a more recent version of this prejudice, cf. J. Pepin, "A propos de l'histoire de l'exégèse allégorique: l'absurdité, signe de l'allégorie", StPatr 1 (TU 63) 395–406. Concerning Ambrose cf. H. Frhr. von Campenhausen, *Lateinische Kirchenväter* (Stuttgart ^{5}1983) 82.

[2] (CSEL 32, 1; 355 f; Schenkl). Cf. e. g. F. H. Dudden, *The Life and Times of St. Ambrose*, II (Oxford 1935) 431, n. 1; Dassmann, Die Frömmigkeit des Kirchenvaters Ambrosius (1965) 163 f; Savon, L'exégèse (1977) 302–305.

[3] Cf. especially the thorough study of this passage showing the different sources Ambrose is alluding to by Savon, L'exégèse (1977) 243–325.

[4] Cf. C. Jacob, "Allegorese: Rhetorik, Ästhetik, Theologie", *Neue Formen der Schriftauslegung* (ed. T. Sternberg; QD 140; Freiburg 1992; 131–163) 137–139.

not only the decision of the believer for a life following the precepts of Wisdom (as Philo puts it), but also – and more concretely – the decision of the catechumen to join the Christian Church in baptism. This does not only show Ambrose's sovereign handling of the Alexandrian method of interpretation. It is of key importance for an understanding of his approach to Scripture in general.[5] From this passage it becomes evident that Ambrose does not use allegory because he feels compelled to give some passages of the Bible an acceptable meaning.[6] He rather makes use of allegorical techniques in order to reshape the biblical imagery which Philo had used in order to rewrite the Proclian story; Ambrose has adapted it to an ecclesiastical horizon.

With this example of allegorical interpretation in mind, it is not possible to follow the common explanations starting from the difficulties provoked by the holy text itself. They might in fact exist, but they cannot be considered as the true reason for this quest of a more spiritual interpretation. Is it by accident that Ambrose's transposition of the Hellenic parable ends up in an ecclesiastical vision? Is there no purpose behind his reinterpreting the famous decision of Heracles? Does not the situation of the catechumen who becomes a member of the Church through the sacraments of Christian Initiation provide the pattern which discretely directs this new interpretation? The Ambrosian rendering of the story might in fact be rather practical, but its mystagogical dimension reinforcing its sacramental dynamic shows that his intention is not only to moralize.

The general approach to allegorical interpretation has to be different. There has to be a shift in the perspective that does not only focus on the situation of the production of the text. Its later reception and reinterpretation is to be regarded as a key to the construction of its meaning as well. It is the possibility of an ecclesiastical *mise-en-scène* that makes this interpretative method so attractive in the Ancient Church. This indicates the possibility of a new approach to allegory in general. Is it not this reversal of the perspective – in the 70s H. R. Jauss thought it to be a provocation of contemporary literary science[7] – which could open a new understanding of ancient allegory? From the very outset Christian allegorical interpretation has to be considered as an ever new, reshaping, rereading, mirrowing of biblical narratives in the horizon of the Christian Church.

---

[5] Cf. Jacob, "Arkandisziplin" (1990) 139–150; Jacob, Allegorese (1992) 135–144.

[6] In the discourse of Lady Wisdom in Proverbs (Prov 7–9), there are for instance no 'moral' problems that would put the authority of Scripture into question and call for an allegorical rendering.

[7] Cf. H. R. Jauss, "Paradigmawechsel in der Literaturwissenschaft", *Linguistische Berichte* 3 (1959) 54–56; Jauss, *Literaturgeschichte als Provokation* (Frankfurt 1970).

2. Hilary of Poitiers

2.1. *The Fullness of His Exegetical Work*[8]

Towards the end of his *Tractatus mysteriorum*, Hilary remarks that all these mysteries were appropriately written down so that "posterity ... should contemplate the present also in the past and venerate the past in the present as well".[9] This can be considered as a rough sketch outlining the principles of his hermeneutics. A Christian who can understand the deeper meaning of the Bible will find the present described in it and he will appreciate the past just because of its prophetic dimension. At the same time, there is a quite functional definition of prophecy: 'prophetic' is what can be seen as an announcement of the future from an ecclesiastical perspective. To put it in other words: there is no true understanding of the past that would abstract from its fulfilment in Christianity. Hilary's treatise about the mysteries e.g. illustrates the possibility of a christological or ecclesiological understanding of Scripture. Different moments of the salvation history receive a spiritual, typological dimension in so far as they can be interpreted as prefiguring some aspects of the reality of the Church and in so far as they can be regarded as a response to (contemporary) issues of Christology. This possibility of receptive interpretation should be considered as the real cause for the allegorical understanding of OT passages.

As an example, Hilary's spiritual interpretation of the life of Noah as prefiguring Christ and the Church may be mentioned.[10] The notes of J.-P. Brisson referring to the writings of Origen and Cyprian as well as to Augustine show, that Hilary moves in the tradition of Christian interpretation. The prophecy of Lamech about the name 'Noah' points to the rest Christ is going to serve (give) those who take up his burden and follow him (Matt 11:28f.). Different events in Noah's life—his order to build an ark, his entering of the ark, the missions of the dove, the exit from the ark, the plantation of the vine and his drunkenness[11]—are to be seen as figures of the true Noah, Christ. The ark corresponds to the Church and Noah's wine-drinking foreshadows the passion of Christ since it is an announcement of the cup Christ is going to drink (Matt 20:22). The three sons of Noah, Ham, Shem and Japhet are to be understood as symbolizing the pagans, the Jews (*lex*) and the Christians (*gratia*): Noah blesses the latter two who covered their father's nakedness and curses Ham who looked at it and telling his

---

[8] In this way J. Doignon, "Les premiers commentateurs latins de l'Ecriture et l'œuvre exégétique d'Hilaire de Poitiers", *Le monde latin antique et la Bible* (BTT 2, ed. J. Fontaine/Ch. Pietri; Paris 1985; 509–521) 517, characterizes Hilary's later exegetical writings on the Psalms and the Mysteries.

[9] *Tractatus mysteriorum* II.14 (SC 19bis; 160; Brisson): "Haec ergo ab omnibus significata in uno illo cognita et expleta reservari in memoriam scriptis et consignatis voluminibus conuenit, ut posteritas successionum gestis temporis anterioris instructa et praesenta etiam in praeteritis contemplaretur et praeterita nunc quoque in praesentibus veneraretur".

[10] Cf. loc. cit. I.12–15 (SC 19bis; 96–104; Brisson).

[11] Loc. cit. I.12 (SC 19bis; 98; Brisson).

brothers about it made fun of it – being a figure of the pagans who are pouring scorn on the death of Christ and the naked body of God.[12]

Hilary's interpretation of the order Noah receives to enter and leave the ark (Gen 6:18; 8:16) as figuring the sanctification of the Church were less successful in the later exegetical tradition. Hilary highlights the fact that in the first order men and women are listed as two separate groups and interprets it as a sign for the continence required of those who want to enter the Church; afterwards, he says, everyone receives the faculty to marry.[13] Towards the end of the fourth century, this statement would hardly be accepted as the result of a spiritual reading of the Bible. The attention given to these – in the prospective – not so very important biblical verses suggests that it is the reality of the Church, Hilary's concrete experience of Christian Initiation, which lets him comment upon them. There are definitively no moral or logical problems that would arise from a historical reading of these orders.

The allegorical explanation of the first two verses of Psalm 137 ("By the waters of Babylon, there we sat down and wept, when we remembered Zion. On the willows, there we hang out lyres") is adduced by J. Doignon as an example illustrating Hilary's conception of the spiritual sense of the Bible.[14] According to Hilary, a purely historical understanding of this passage would give rise to questions like the following: Which rivers are flowing through Babylon? Had Israel been lead into captivity serving there with an orchestra of musical instruments? Which willows would be planted in the middle of a city so that the Israelites could hang their instruments on them? Since an historical reading of these verses would be inane, Hilary says, one has to adopt the method under the authority of the prophets of finding a spiritual meaning.[15] This goes well with the modern idea that allegory has to be used whenever the historical lecture of a text would be impossible.

It would be wrong, however, to consider this remark as the starting point of Hilary's allegory.[16] Before speaking about the difficulties arising from a matter-of-fact conception of the rivers and the willows, he has already given a spiritual interpretation of the captivity of Israel. According to Hilary, this interpretation is justified by the testimony of Ps 78:1 f. showing that God is speaking in parables and by Heb 10:1 and 1 Cor 1:11, saying that all these things were written down in order to be a doctrine for later generations; the

---

[12] Loc. cit. I. 15 (SC 19bis; 102–104; Brisson). One problem arising from Hilary's identification of the Jews with Shem could be the question whether he really thinks that they did accept the idea of Christ's Incarnation. Do they in this point really differ from the pagans who are making fun of the "nakedness of God"? Augustine seems more consequent; for him Shem and Japhet represent the Church from the Jews and from the Gentiles: Cf. *Contra Faust.* XII. 23 (CSEL 25, 351; Zycha).

[13] *Tractatus mysteriorum* I.13 (SC 19bis; 100–102; Brisson); cf. the attention given to these orders by Origen, *Com. in Gen.* (PG 12; 106 B).

[14] Cf. Doignon, Les premiers commentateurs latins (1985) 518.

[15] Cf. *Tractatus super psalmum CXXXVI*, 6 (CSEL 22; 727; Zingerle): "quae si omnia gestis negotiorum corporalium inania sunt, sequenda ea ratio est, quae ex propheticis auctoritatibus ad spiritalem nos scientiam cohortatur".

[16] 'Allegoresis' is supposed to indicate the process of interpretation whereas 'allegory' may be regarded as the result of this process.

acts of ancient times are to be seen as a *forma futuri*.[17] The spiritual understanding of Israel's captivity shows that Ps 137:1 f. refers to the human mind dominated by bodily and worldly desires.[18] Hilary's remark about the difficulty of a literal understanding of these verses follows only after his comments upon the grief experienced in Babylon and upon the opposition of "our heavenly mother Jerusalem" and this city troubled by confusion and irrational powers, Babylon.[19] The so-called difficulties of a historical reading are definitively not forcing Hilary to engage in an allegorical interpretation.

It is possible already from here to see the plan behind his *relecture* of the situation of Israel in Babylon: Hilary interprets it as describing different aspects of the spiritual life as it is experienced at present in the Christian Church. It is the saints and the faithful who are really meant by the 'willows' of Psalm 137, just as Isaiah says "They shall spring up like grass amid waters, like willows by flowing streams" (Isa 44:4): *oritur enim ex mortuo, quisquis antea peccatis aridus et ab anterioris vitae radice decisus nunc eloquio dei et sacramento baptismi aquis vitalibus revivescit*.[20] These branches vivified by the sacrament of baptism allow at the same time for a new understanding of the feast of the tabernacles; the Jews were told to use these branches as well (Lev 23:40), showing by this the heavenly joy of the saints in the future.

Doignon has stressed the institutional frame of Hilary's commentary.[21] Should not this interpretative option be considered as the true reason for his allegorical reception of the longing for and the possibility of new life as expressed in Psalm 137 and Isaiah 44? What the prophetical authority foretells, what—for Hilary—cannot receive a true meaning in a historical perspective, is the spiritual life as it is revealed in his present, in the experience of the Christian Church. The true cause for his allegory, the principle directing his individual interpretations is not the dissatisfaction with the historical sense of a certain passage of the OT. This discontent itself is prompted by the possibility of an ecclesiastical *mise-en-scène*. It may be more appropriate to consider Hilary's comment on the impossibility of a historical interpretation of the rivers of Babylon and of the willows in Psalm 137 as a pretext supporting an interpretation in which he is already involved and which he prefers because of its aptitude for an institutional reception.

There might in fact be a certain dependance on Origen; it seems quite possible that Hilary has read his allegorical interpretations of the opening lines of Psalm 137 and that it paved the way for his own explanation drawing the attention to these verses and demonstrating a possible spiritual interpretation. In Origen's homilies on the prophets, for example, there is a metaphorical interpretation of Babylon and Zion, Babylon being the area of the unsteady passions and the remembrance of Zion expressing the longing for new life and indicating the way to be followed by observing the commandments

---

[17] Loc. cit. 2 (CSEL 22; 724 f; Zingerle).
[18] Loc. cit. 3 (CSEL 22; 725; Zingerle).
[19] Cf. loc. cit. 4 f (CSEL 22; 726 f; Zingerle).
[20] Loc. cit. 7 (CSEL 22; 728; Zingerle).
[21] Doignon, Les premiers commentateurs latins (1985) 518.

of the Lord and engaging into spiritual life.[22] Origen's interpretation *de anima* is, as he says in a homily on Ezechiel, meant for those who can perceive the Scriptures spiritually whereas the historical sense may satisfy the *simplices.*[23] This view may well have inspired the general frame Hilary gives to these words of Psalm 137; but it is not his reliance on Origen which should be considered as the true cause for his adaptation of these ideas. The spiritual interpretation of the captivity in Babylon and of the souls longing for their true home receives its meaning from an ecclesiastical perspective: Humanity imprisoned in this world through the sin of Adam is shown the concrete steps on the way towards the heavenly Jerusalem.[24]

In the conclusion to the treatise on the mysteries, Hilary speaks about the difficulties of allegorical interpretation in general: it is not easy to discern whether a certain passage of Scripture is to be understood as a simple historical narrative or in the typical sense; the knowledge of the simple event is corrupted if treated vainly as a prophecy and its prefigurative dynamic is destroyed if it is considered as a historical fact only.[25] This is said to be one of the wisest statements of Christian antiquity.[26] This may be correct; it would be wrong, however, to trust J. Daniélou's introductory remark: he believes he has discovered here a distinction between allegory and 'typology'. But Hilary does not oppose a "true exegesis", i.e. an ecclesiastical typology, to an allegorical or literal understanding of Scripture.[27] This is the distinction Daniélou is trying to promote. Hilary rather speaks of the general difficulty arising from the decision about the suitability of an historical or a spiritual reading of the Bible. One may in fact approve of the question raised by Hilary, but it is not possible to claim him to be an adherent of a 'typological exegesis' as opposed to allegorical interpretations. His question is more fundamental, asking about the meaning of 'holy' Scripture as such.

2.2. The Bible in the Christological Debates

In the fourth century different conceptions of orthodox Christology correspond to the different ways of reading the Bible in Christianity itself. The knowledge and the intensive study of Holy Scripture is characteristic of the

---

22 Cf. Origen, *In Ezech. hom.* I.5 (GCS 33; 330f; Baehrens); *In Ierem. hom.* L (II).1 (SC 238; 336–338; Nautin); *In Num. hom.* XV.1 (GCS 30; 130,15–25; Baehrens). In the first homily on Ezechiel, Origen points to Isa 44:4 as well and gives a spiritual interpretation of the Feast of Tabernacles Lev 23:40.

23 Origen, *In Ezech. hom.* I.5 (GCS 33; 330,11–14; Baehrens).

24 Cf. Doignon, Les premiers commentateurs latins (1985) 518. One may disagree with his statement that it is not until Hilary that there was a liberation from the Philonic impact; did Origen really just repeat Philo's interpretation without being aware of a possible ecclesiastical staging of the scene described in the beginning of Psalm 137?

25 Cf. *Tractatus mysteriorum* I.13 (SC 19bis; 156–158; Brisson): "Admonuimus frequenter eam lectioni divinarum scripturarum diligentiam adhiberi oportere. quae sollicito examine et iudicio non inani posset discernere, quando rerum gestarum commemoratio vel simpliciter esset intellegenda vel typice, ne intemperanter atque imperite ureoque abusi utrumque inutile audientibus redderemus, si aut simplicium cognitio inani praefigurationum assertione corrumperetur aut virtus praefigurationum sub simplicium opinione ignoraretur".

26 J. Daniélou, Saint Hilaire évêque et docteur (1968) 9–18; 12.

27 Ibid. 12.

'Arian' party in general as well as of Hilary's opponents in the Latin West.[28] Scripture is claimed to be the prominent source of authority by the partisans of the Nicean creed as well as by those considered today as adherents of 'Arian' ideas.

One of the most important quotes from Scripture interpreted by the 'Arians' as an argument supporting their Christology is Prov 8:22 ("God created me at the beginning of his ways"). In his work on the Trinity, Hilary does not question the reference of this verse to Christ, but he says that it would be wrong to understand it as a proof that Christ is submitted to temporality.[29] Against any 'Arian' conception, Hilary underscores the human nature of Christ. The words of Ps 54:5, for instance, are spoken by Christ himself: the Only-begotten Son of God, the Word of God and God the Word – Hilary quotes John 5:19 in order to stress the identity of the actions of the Father and the Son – prayed for and suffered all that is human.[30] This extends as well to assuming the idea of a descent of Christ's soul into Hades which was thought to belong to a consequent understanding of Incarnation.[31] Ps 139:8 ("If I ascend to heaven, you art there! If I make my bed in Sheol, thou art there!") is understood as referring to the divine and human nature in Christ respectively and John 3:13 ("No one has ascended into heaven but he who descended from heaven, the Son of man") is quoted as a proof of the first statement; the descent into the underworld shows that Christ fulfills the law of humankind, that he is to be considered as a true man.[32]

Many more examples could be added. They all can illustrate that it would be impossible to understand Hilary's treaties without knowing the Christological controversies of his time and without regarding his interpretations as a contribution to these debates. Hilary is not an exegete inspired only by the text of the OT: he knows that his explanation of Scripture will be seen and evaluated against the background of the contemporary Christological dispute, and his way of thinking is deeply influenced by the positions forwarded in a conflict which has not only been intellectual. Hilary's personal fate – his exile because of his disturbance of the imperially decreted harmony – points to the existential dimension of this controversy.

From this perspective it is possible to understand that in his letter against Constantius Hilary refers to 2 Maccabees 7 as an example that his accusation

---

[28] Cf. for instance R. GRYSON's outline of the 'Arian' theology and the importance of Scripture in their education and argumentation: "Scolies ariennes sur le concile d'Aquilée" (SC 261; Paris 1980; 173–200) 175–177.

[29] *De Trinitate* XII.36 (CCL 62A; 606f; Smulders); cf. also loc. cit. I.35 (CCL 62; 34f; Smulders); loc. cit. IV.11 (111f); loc. cit. XII.1 (CCL 62A; 579; Smulders); loc. cit. 35 (605f); loc. cit. 42 (612); loc. cit. 43–45 (612–616); loc. cit. 47 (617f); loc. cit. 49 (619f).

[30] *Tractatus super psalmum LIII.7* (CSEL 22; 140; Zingerle). Cf. loc. cit. (CSEL 22; 140; Zingerle): "omnis ergo eius in psalmis ex naturae nostrae affectu querella est. Nec mirum, si ita nos intellegimus dicta psalmorum, cum ipse dominus secundum evangelicam fidem passionis suae sacramenta scripta esse fuerit testatus in psalmis".

[31] *Tractatus super psalmum CXXXVIII*, 22 (CSEL 22; 759; Zingerle); cf. Durst, Die Eschatologie des Hilarius von Poitiers (1987) 178f.

[32] *Tractatus super psalmum CXXXVIII*, 22 (CSEL 22; 759; Zingerle).

of the emperor as an Antichrist is no sign of impertinence.[33] He draws a parallel between his own courage judged to be an insane enterprise by some of his contemporaries and that of the Maccabees who denounced unjust exercise of authority at their time and are nowadays venerated because of that. These biblical charades, as H.-I. Marrou calls these applications of Scripture to concrete situations in the life of individuals, have been quite common in the fourth century; they are of no exegetical value, but they are – as he pointed out – playing the same game as the allegorical interpretations adapting biblical texts to new ideas and situations.[34] Many of these parallels may truly be considered as rather artificial approximations: do these examples of a lower value, however, not show that there may be something that could be called the artistry of allegory?

3. Ambrose of Milan

3.1. Towards the Principles of His Exegesis

There has been a considerable shift in the study of Ambrose in recent times: for too long he has been regarded as a man of very little own intellectual capacity being only able to adopt and translate his different sources. His debt especially to Origen and Philo of Alexandria has been treated as a key to understand his work, consisting of little other than a clumsy repetition of their thoughts.[35] The picture drawn in more recent investigations is quite different.[36] In a very fundamental way this change affects the basic judgement about his approach to Scripture. G. Nauroy speaks of Ambrose "ruminating" the Bible and of the difficulty of any modern attempt to decipher this language permeated with constant allusions to Scripture illustrating his incredible familiarity with these books.[37] Nevertheless, the role Scripture plays in Ambrosian thought is not yet sufficiently outlined by these observations. They may indicate his procedure but there remains the question about his source of inspiration. Is the principle directing Ambrose's teaching, selection and interpretation of different events reported in the holy writings of the Bible alone?

The outer form of his publications which are in fact saturated with quotes from the Bible does not necessarily indicate the principle behind Ambrose's orchestration of certain verses of Scripture. As H. Savon rightly has pointed

---

[33] *Liber contra Constantium Imperatorem* 6 (SC 334; 178; Rocher).

[34] H.-I. Marrou, *Augustinus und das Ende der antiken Bildung* (Paderborn 1982) 417, 420, n. 119.

[35] See for example the basic assumption of H. Lewy, *Sobria ebrietas. Untersuchungen zur Geschichte der antiken Mystik* (BZNW 9; Gießen 1929), but also the more recent remarks of S. Sagot, "La triple sagesse dans le *De Isaac vel anima:* Essai sur les procédés de composition de saint Ambroise", *Ambroise de Milan* (1974; 67–114) 112f.

[36] See e.g. G. Nauroy, "L'Ecriture dans la pastorale d'Ambroise de Milan", *Le monde latin antique et la Bible* (BTT 2, ed. J. Fontaine/Ch. Pietri; Paris 1985; 371–408) 372–374.

[37] Loc. cit. 371.

out, Ambrose does not simply adopt Philo but he christianizes him; this correction of Philonic allegory does not only pertain to the range of scriptural reminiscences. The Christian 'retractatio' replaces Philo's spiritualism by an 'evangelical' realism.[38] It is for instance not the reference to the Last Supper which subtly directs Ambrose's rendering of Heracles decision, but the process of Christian Initiation: his 'realism' is not only evangelical but also ecclesiastical.[39] It is the concrete life of his Church that guides his scripturally erudite eclecticism.

Recent research has pointed to the philosophical writings Ambrose knew and took as a source of inspiration for his publications. The different opinions about the importance of Scripture and philosophy in the thought of the Bishop of Milan however can be substituted by a rather simple alternative. There are not two poles of the Ambrosian *Weltanschauung* centred on the Bible as well as on philosophy as it has been presupposed in several recent investigations;[40] there is *one* centre of gravity directing his thought. It is the pattern provided by the Church to any spiritual progress, the different stages of Christian Initiation. Verses and stories of Scripture are highlighted in so far as they can mirror this experience, and philosophical convictions are adduced in so far as they support this general approach.[41] So, Ambrose's prime interest is neither the Bible nor philosophy as such: *the culture promoted by him is biblical in its very outlook but deeply ecclesiastical in its essence.* Certain ideas are taken from contemporary philosophy but no professional philosopher would agree with his reasoning just as no exegete would subscribe to his use of Scripture. However, whoever accepts the ecclesiastical reality as the starting-point and pattern that structures Ambrosian thinking will be able to follow its logic. So, it would be wrong to speak of the arbitrariness of his exegetical or philosophical endeavours, because they are to be read and understood as arrangements which draw their logic from their relatedness to the life of the Church.

3.2. *Allegorica dissimulatio: the Ambrosian Rhetoric*

A major difficulty for modern approaches to Ambrose is the allusive character of his language. This trait of his homilies has been pointed out several times as for example in the above mentioned Ambrosian redaction of the famous scene reenacting the decision between Virtue and Vice. Ambrose is only alluding to the Eucharist; the sacramental frame seems to be atomized by his moralizing allegory, but it is his specific way of speaking, and not only in this context.[42] This shows that his literary aesthetics is very different from

---

[38] H. SAVON, "Ambroise et Jerôme lecteurs de Philon", ANRW II/21.1 (Berlin/New York 1984; 731–759) 740f.

[39] Cf. Savon, L'exégèse (1977) 302–307; 325.

[40] Cf. e.g. G. NAUROY, "Méthode de composition et la structure du *'De Iacob et vita beata'*", *Ambroise de Milan* (1974) 115–153, and the critical remarks by G. MADEC, "Les embarras de la citation", *FZPhTh* 29 (1985) 361–372; 368f.

[41] Cf. Jacob, "Arkandisziplin" (1990) 199–204.

[42] Cf. Dudden, Life and times II (1935) 453, n. 1; Dassmann, Frömmigkeit (1965) 163f; Savon, L'exégèse (1977) 302–305.

the one embraced in modern times which was wrongly supposed to be the only one possible.[43] NAUROY characterizes the Ambrosian language as "allusif, 'labyrinthique', de charactère initiatique, qui invite le lecteur, en fonction de son degré d'initiation aux mystères chrétiens, à tirer de cet enseignement 'mystérique' la nourriture ... qui lui convient le mieux".[44] Since Ambrosian language as a whole is to be regarded in this way, since there has to be a process of decoding which will only reveal the real meaning of certain passages, it becomes obvious why he has been misunderstood for such a long time. The centre that his thought is revolving around will only be disclosed by a step which deciphers his allegory.

This is especially true for the sacramental dimension of his writings. Ambrose could for instance publish one series of mystagogical catecheses, for even there, he never speaks of the sacraments explicitly, for his references to their liturgical dimension has to be inferred from an analysis particularly of his quotes from Scripture.[45] Ambrose is using these quotes as a modus loquendi about the sacraments.[46] Why did he avoid direct references? The allusive character of his language is normally attributed to his observance of the so-called arcane discipline.[47] There may indeed be some remnants of a certain discipline of the secret in the fourth century, but they alone cannot explain the rhetorical allegory of Ambrose. It is an overall mode of communication that was very familiar in the principate, especially amongst the educated, and Ambrose used it not only because he felt compelled to do so. His literary heritage contributed to creating and shaping the Medieval world which was biblical in its outlook and ecclesiastical in its core.

Ambrose was not always forced to use this language for fear of divulging certain secrets; this labyrinthine way of expression, this preference for the detour is not only a caprice of his oratory style.[48] It can lead to discovering the pattern of his way of thinking: the *excessus* of Abraham before his encounter with God (this is how Ambrose interprets the dread and great darkness reported in Gen 15:12) shows that the mind of the prophet has to go beyond (excedere) the limits of human understanding, and that he has to get rid of the cogitations and deceptions of this world in order to get ready for

---

[43] Literary obscurity is quite common in antiquity; cf. M. FUHRMANN, "Obscuritas. Das Problem der Dunkelheit in der rhetorischen und literarästhetischen Theorie der Antike", *Immanente Ästhetik – Ästhetische Reflexion* (ed. W. Iser; Poetik und Hermeneutik 2; München 1966) 47–72.

[44] G. NAUROY, "La structure du '*De Isaac vel anima*' et la cohérence de l'allégorèse d'Ambroise de Milan", *REL* 63 (1985) 210–236; 219.

[45] C. JACOB, "Zur Krise der Mystagogie in der Alten Kirche", *ThPh* 66 (1991) 75–89; 85f.

[46] P. JACKSON, "Ambrose of Milan as Mystagogue", *Augustinian Studies* 20 (1989) 93–107; 96–103, focuses on his use of Scripture in the postbaptismal catechesis. This mystagogical dimension is present in other writings as well; the scriptural verses can only in so far be employed as a "proof by argument" (loc. cit. 103) as these catecheses introduce the neophyte into a world of scriptural images which unfolds its own logic; see Jacob, "Arkandisziplin" (1990) 121–146; cf. also the remarks about the different theories of this 'discipline of the secret' and the necessity of a completely new approach, loc. cit. 97–117.

[47] Among the more recent authors cf. Savon, L'exégèse (1977) 305f; Nauroy, La structure du '*De Isaac vel anima*' (1985) 235.

[48] Cf. H. SAVON, "Maniérisme et allégorie dans Ambroise de Milan", *REL* 55 (1977) 203–21.

the arriving spiritual grace.[49] This necessity of emptying oneself of worldly thought before the infusion of the Holy Spirit is neither the main point of the biblical narrative nor is it really suggested by it. It does, however, play an important role in the contemporary Christian conception of progress. The absence of worldly corruption is the main goal of the process of Christian Initiation; it is to be achieved as a prerequisite of receiving the sacrament of baptism.[50] From this point of view, the Ambrosian version of this story displays its logic: Abraham is a prophet because his life foreshadows this step which the *competentes* have to realize in their process of conversion in the Church of Milan.

This is what Ambrose uses the allegorical techniques for, in the first place. His orchestration of the OT narrative is directed by principles that become visible after decoding his allegorical mode of expression. His writings demonstrate a real virtuosity within this paradigm.[51] Whoever grasps this pattern providing the plan for an essential part of the Ambrosian allegory will admire his artistry. In this context it is not necessary to discuss whether or not it was appropriate to make Scripture describe the experience of Christian Initiation. The reference to this dimension of his allegory can show a main concern of his homiletics and this has to be acknowledged by anyone who wants to understand Ambrose.

3.3. The Song of Songs in Ambrosian Allegory

Ambrose himself has several times 'explained' the Canticum which may be considered one of his favorite books of the Bible.[52] In his homilies on Psalm 119, he continuously refers to it, pointing out its ecclesiastical dimension; in *De Isaac vel anima* he focuses on the more individual aspect of the mystery of the soul's unification with God – as it is seen in the Christian Church.[53] There are more specific interpretations as well: the bride of the Song of Solomon is taken as a description of different aspects of the life of the virgins, for instance, and in a consolatory oration, some verses of the Canticle are applied to emperor Valentinian II.[54] Ambrose's orchestration of this book of Scripture differs according to the general frame which conditions and guides his allegorical interpretation. There has been a quite famous attempt to draw a continuous commentary of the Canticle from the writings of Ambrose[55] and

---

[49] *De Abraham* II. 9.61 (CSEL 32, 1; 614; Schenkl).

[50] Cf. *De mysteriis* 3.10 (CSEL 73; 92f; Faller).

[51] For more examples cf. Jacob, "Arkandisziplin" (1990) 180–254.

[52] Cf. esp. Dassmann, Frömmigkeit (1965) 135–200; he speaks of a discovery of the Canticle by Ambrose coinciding with his discovery of Origen (loc. cit. 137f); see also E. DASSMANN, "Ecclesia vel anima. Die Kirche und ihre Glieder in der Hoheliederklärung bei Hippolyt, Origenes und Ambrosius von Mailand", *RQ* 61 (1966) 121–144.

[53] Cf. *De Isaac vel anima* 4.17 (CSEL 32, 1; 654, 16–20; Schenkl) and the summary statement in *Epistula XXXIV* (*Maur. 45*), 4 (CSEL 82,1; 233; Faller): "Denique Solomon in spiritu paradisum in hominem esse evidenter declaravit. Et quia mysteria exprimit anima et verbi vel Christi et ecclesiae, ideo ait de virgine anima vel ecclesia, quam volebat virginem castam adsignare Christo (II Cor 11:2): Paradisus clusus mea sponsa, paradisus clusus, fons signatus (Cant 4:12)".

[54] Cf. *De obitu Valentiniani* 58–77 (CSEL 73; 357–365; Faller).

[55] Cf. *Commentarius in Cantica cantic. e scriptis S. Ambrosii collectus* (PL 15; 1948–2060).

it was followed by others. These endeavours start from the assumption that it is the text of the Bible alone that directs its reception. However, this cannot be sustained for the Ambrosian approach. The topic which his allegory revolves around will mould its results as well.

As an example, one might look at one particular verse of the Song of Songs and its use by Ambrose. Cant 4:12 ("A garden locked is my sister, my bride, a garden locked, a fountain sealed") is cited in order to support different arguments. In his considerations of the progress of the individual soul, the comparison of the bride being a garden which is sealed and closed gives rise to the following explanations:[56] the garden is equated with the plentiful field whose fragrance is praised by Isaac (Gen 27:27), and the soul is a fountain sealed, because she may wash away her sins by the integrity of the seal and by perseverance in faith. She is a fountain sealed, because the image of the invisible God (Col 1:15) is represented in her, and the gifts, with which a pious soul comes endowed by the bridegroom are good fragrances, myrrh and aloe and saffron, which beautiful gardens exhale and with which the stench of sins is destroyed. There are several implicit references to Baptism in this text[57] and they in fact indicate that Ambrose regards Christian Initiation to be of crucial importance in the life of an individual.

In his exposition of Psalm 119, the Pastor of Milan interprets Cant 4:12 together with Cant 4:15 and 4:8 (LXX).[58] *Fons, puteus* and *impetus* are equaled as it is written in Cant 4:15. These sources of water may differ as to their appearance – according to the individual ability to grasp the *gratia spiritalis* – but their effect is the same: the sins are washed away. The *hortorum fons* is a dowry of the Church and the *impetus*, which will not dry up (Jer 18:13), makes the bride come from Lebanon and pass through (Cant 4:8 LXX) to the kingdom. Even if Ambrose does not say it explicitly, it is not difficult to guess where this fountain can be found. The main difference between *De Isaac vel anima* and the *Expositio psalmi CXVIII* is the attention Ambrose gives to the fountain, its effect and its place in the latter explanation, whereas he stresses the process required of the individual soul in the other treatise.[59]

A certain concept of the process of the soul is the pattern directing his exegesis of this verse of the Canticle in the *Expositio evangelii secundum Lucam* as well.[60] The itinerary of Christ is to be followed, because it indicates the way from the desert back to paradise. Christ dwells in the desert, where he teaches and anoints man with spiritual oil; as he sees him grow stronger,

[56] *De Isaac vel anima* 5.48 (CSEL 32, 1; 672 f; Schenkl); cf. the translation of M. P. McHugh in: Ambrose, *Seven Exegetical Works* (FC 65; Washington 1972) 38 f.

[57] Cf. loc. cit. 39; McHugh interprets the reference to the seal as a reference to the seal of baptism. This *signaculum* and the *imago Dei* (Col 1:15) are also referred to in the mystagogical catechesis at the description of the confirmation: Cf. *De mysteriis* 7.41 (CSEL 73; 106; Faller); the point of reference here is Cant 8:6, that also speaks of the *signaculum.* Cf. further *Expositio psalmi CXVIII* 19.28 (CSEL 62; 436; Petschenig).

[58] *Expositio psalmi CVIII* 17.32 (CSEL 62; 393; Petschenig).

[59] Cf. *De Isaac vel anima* 5.47 f (CSEL 32,1; 671–673; Schenkl).

[60] *Expositio evangelii secundum Lucam* IV.12 f (CCL 14; 110 f; Adriaen).

he goes with him through the fields and he transfers him into paradise at the time of his passion. The garden of Cant 4:12 is equated with the garden Jesus entered with his disciples (John 18:1), and this garden is said to bring forth a paradise (Cant 4:12b). The reason for these connections is to be found on the spiritual level; it is not very explicit but it is from this perspective that the different associations make sense. The pure and stainless soul who has returned to paradise (cf. Luke 23:43), cannot be troubled by any threat of punishment or worldly desire. The itinerary back to paradise reveals the deeper meaning of the itinerary Jesus Christ has undertaken for our sake: it represents the progress of Christian Initiation. This becomes completely evident in the following paragraph: Jesus' fight with Satan mystically signifies the liberation of every Adam from banishment and it is a warning illustrating the envy of the devil towards those who tend to higher things and shows the necessity of remaining strong in order to keep the grace of Baptism.[61]

An ecclesiastical dimension is also present in his reference to Cant 4:12 in the exegesis of Cant 8:13 ("O, you who dwell in the gardens, my companions are listening for your voice; let me hear it"). It is Christ whose voice can be heard in the garden and the Church could not hear it as she wanted, because of the disobedience of mankind expelled from paradise. Whoever wants to have Christ sit inside and hear the Lord Jesus talk with the angels has to be a closed and fortified garden (cf. Cant 4:12).[62] This identification of the garden mentioned in Cant 8:10–13 and Cant 4:12 is at the basis of his comparison of the ecclesiastical soul to a locked garden and a sealed fountain in *De bono mortis* as well:[63] the garden entered by the soul on her flight from the world is described in the Song of Songs and this idea is taken over by Plato in the Symposion (203B). By a subtle transformation Ambrose switches to the image of the soul herself as a garden bearing the flowers of virtue and inviting the bridegroom to come (Cant 4:16) so that she may be bedewed by him and be saturated by his wealth. The Church can also be described as a garden locked and a fountain sealed:[64] wherever there is purity, chastity, devotion, faithful discretion of the mysteries (cf. Virgil, *Aeneis* III.112) and the bright glare of the angels, there are the violets of the confessors, the lilies of the virgins and the roses of the martyrs.

A rather chance remark justified only by the word 'closed' stressed in the context is to be found at the beginning of the treatise of Isaac,[65] and in his explanation of the sacraments. In *De mysteriis*, Cant 4:10–12 is quoted in order to illustrate the necessity of keeping the mystery of the Eucharist sealed by a life of virtue and by avoiding its divulgence among those who should not hear it nor disperse it among unbelievers.[66] This rather prima facie reading of Cant 4:12 can also be found in his book on the virgins: the gate that Christ

[61] Loc. cit. 14 (CCL 14; 111; Adriaen).
[62] *Expositio psalmi CXVIII* 22.43 (CSEL 62; 509; Petschenig).
[63] *De bono mortis* 5.18f (CSEL 32,1; 719f; Schenkl).
[64] *Expositio evangelii secundum Lucam* VII.128 (CCL 14; 257f; Adriaen).
[65] *De Isaac vel anima* 1.2 (CSEL 32,1; 643; Schenkl).
[66] *De mysteriis* 9.55 (CSEL 73; 112; Faller).

wants to be closed is our mouth and since women should not talk in the Church (this is how he interprets 1 Cor 14:34) a virgin should keep her mouth sealed all the more.[67] When talking about the institution of a virgin Ambrose refers to Cant 4:12 in order to stress that nobody should be allowed to take the fence of her chastity away; she is a fountain sealed so that nobody may pollute her water and her door is closed by Christ who holds its key (Rev 3:7).[68] The garden of the virgin is also compared to the place where Susanna walked about and preferred death to being raped (cf. Sus 7). The fragrance of this garden is again equated with the perfume of Jacob (Gen 27:27) but its scent is different from the one mentioned in *De Isaac vel anima*. This garden is fragrant of the grape, the olivetree and the rose: the vine pointing to religious observance, the olivetree to the peace and the rose to the chastity of virginity.[69]

It would be impossible to trace these different treatments of Cant 4:12 back to an elaborate theory of a double, threefold or fourfold sense of Scripture. It would be wrong to start from this verse of the Bible and then come up with these different meanings. It is in fact the other way round: in the first place, there is the concrete situation Cant 4:12 is said to refer to, and different parts or words of it are adduced because they fit in this context. This reversal of the perspective[70] is of course not without danger. Is there any protection against arbitrariness in this approach? Ambrose used the same verse of the Bible in very different contexts. Do these orchestrations of Cant 4:12 not demonstrate the pitfalls of allegorical interpretation? There can be made a difference between Ambrose's explanations of this verse and his short allusions. Whoever asks for their meaning according to the Bishop of Milan will focus on *De Isaac vel anima* or on the *Expositio psalmi CXVIII*. The different references to Cant 4:12 on the basis of the word 'closed' contained in this verse cannot really be taken as explanations. But it is obvious that Cant 4:12 as such does not prevent these applications. This interpretative 'arbitrariness', however, will not allow for making the Bible say just anything. It is possible to name a horizon which can receive these different interpretations: the Christian Church of Milan in the fourth century. The diverse staging of Cant 4:12 does not question this general frame. Ambrosian allegory then may be described as a technique which adapts Scripture to situations not intended by its historical sense, to situations that are related to the contemporary experience of the Christian Church. Is this ecclesiastical retrospective a viable access to the spiritual sense of Scripture as it was perceived by Ambrose of Milan?

The examples of the Ambrosian allegory of Cant 4:12 have also shown that he often uses the Canticle as a mode of expression. The sacramental dimension of his explanations must not always be made explicit, it can be only

---

[67] *De virginitate* I.80 (PL 16; 286).
[68] *De institutione virginis* I.9.60–62 (PL 16; 321).
[69] *De virginibus* I.45 (PL 16; 201).
[70] Cf. C. Jacob, "Der Antitypos als Prinzip ambrosianischer Allegorese. Zum hermeneutischen Horizont der Typlogie", StPatr 25 (Leuven 1994) 107–114.

alluded to.[71] This is to say that the real meaning of his allegorical interpretation has to be disclosed by a step decoding his literary allegory. This again shows that the starting-point of his allegorical exegesis is not the Bible alone – nor the Bible in the first place. When Ambrose reshapes the parable of Heracles within an ecclesiastical horizon, it is by a verse of the Canticum canticorum (Cant 5:1) that he alludes to the Eucharistic meal of the Church as the climax of Christian Initiation. His ecclesiastical conception of the process of the soul not only moulds his commentaries on the Song of Solomon in *De Isaac vel anima* and in the *Expositio psalmi CXVIII*. The above quoted paragraph of his explanation of the Gospel of Luke interpreting the itinerary of Jesus as a model for human progress in the Church displays the same structure. These interpretations point to an ecclesiastical and to a liturgical appropriation of the Bible. This differs from a "purely exegetical" reading. Ambrose would hardly disagree with this evaluation of spiritual interpretation. Whoever does not possess the *gratia spiritalis*, whoever is not illuminated by the Holy Spirit, will not be able to follow his interpretation of Scripture nor be able to decipher his rhetoric allegory.

4. Allegory and Interpretative Pluralism

Allegory is no emergency solution that has to keep up the faith in the divine nature of the biblical writings. From the very outset, it has to be regarded as a possibility of creative and innovative application of texts to a new situation, i.e. texts which draw their holiness just from this reception into a religious community. The biblical stories can be staged in front of an ever new background, they can receive a special significance in the horizon of the Christian Church. In this sense, Ambrose and Hilary are dependent upon the Origenist tradition.

This thesis permits a new approach to allegorical interpretation: the true reason for interpreting a text in disregard of its historical meaning is its applicability to different historical situations. These new situations – which are historical as well – explain and legitimize the allegorical exegesis. In a Christian tradition, Christ and his Church set the parameters for such a reception of the Bible. This hermeneutics reveals a certain circularity – like any hermeneutics. Whoever wants to understand Hilary of Poitiers or Ambrose of Milan must be able to appreciate their approach on the grounds of their own hermeneutics. The results of their exegesis must not immediately be evaluated and confronted with those of contemporary approaches; it would even be misleading to read them in this perspective. There has to be a suspension of judgement at least until the intentions of this way of looking at

---

[71] For the sacramental dimension of the interpretation of the Song of Songs in general cf. Dassmann, Frömmigkeit (1965) 161–180; his ideas have been taken up and elaborated on by Nauroy, La structure du '*De Isaac vel anima*' (1985) 210–236; Jacob, "Arkandisziplin" (1990) 234–254.

Scripture can be understood – and it will never be understood, if it is regarded only from within the hermeneutics of an historic-critical exegesis.

One basic characteristic of the allegorical approach is its openness to interpretative plurality. Several christological or ecclesiological conceptions of the same story or of the same biblical verse may stand side by side – if there are no dogmatic problems – and they do not force the interpreter to make up his mind nor oblige him to accept only one of them.[72] This has to be taken into account by any theory about the different 'senses of Scripture'. In retrospect, various applications of the Bible can be said to correspond to its moral, mystical etc. sense, but it would be wrong to start from a certain verse of Scripture and then come up with different explanations.[73] It is not the theory which is first. There are different ways to approach the Bible, and it is here that the distinction between an historical or spiritual, between a moral or mystical access has to be situated. The two levels of the text – a literal understanding or a metaphorical (spiritual) reading – do not coincide with the different categories – natural, moral, or mystical – which direct its reception; in this sense, even a literally conceived passage of Scripture can be part of its mystical or moral reception.[74]

The interpretative pluralism of this scriptural hermeneutics can be a challenge to its contemporary understanding. It is not only a matter of historical justice to appreciate the hermeneutics of Hilary and Ambrose even if it differs essentially from the position of modern exegesis. These approaches start from perspectives which do not exclude each other. Whereas contemporary exegesis focuses on the situation of the production of the text, allegory demonstrates the possibilities of its reception in later contexts. Both conceptions of looking at the Bible would be wrong if they regarded their own approach as the only one possible. In recent times, allegory especially has been misunderstood because it was read too often under the presuppositions of contemporary exegesis.[75]

In a multicultural world it is – fortunately – no longer possible for one religious group to enforce its own perspective. In Christian theology there has been a widespread attempt to trace a tradition of a typological understanding

---

[72] Ambrose, for instance, offers not only different explanations of the same biblical verse as has been demonstrated concerning Cant 4:12. Various translations of the Bible do not give rise to the question which one would have to be regarded as the correct one, but it can serve as another starting-point of an allegorical interpretation; cf. *De Isaac vel anima* 7.63 (CSEL 32,1; 686f; Schenkl).

[73] The importance of the ecclesiastical retrospective for the Bishop of Milan can also be seen in the fact that he subtly changes the text of the Bible, e.g. by introducing a negation, in order to make it fit to his ecclesiastical conception of human progress. Cf. Savon, L'exégèse (1977) 202–204; 210f; and Jacob, Allegorese (1992) 157f, with reference to *De Cain et Abel I* 8.31 (CSEL 32, 1; 366; Schenkl); a similar conclusion is suggested by an analysis of his quote of Cant 1:6 in *De Isaac vel anima* 4.13 (CSEL 32, 1; 652).

[74] Cf. Savon, L'exégèse (1977) 55–81.

[75] A.J.H. Gunneweg, "Hermeneutische Grundsätze der Exegese biblischer Texte", *Standort und Bedeutung der Hermeneutik in der gegenwärtigen Theologie* (Bonner Akademische Reden 61; Bonn 1986; 43–62) 43, says the fundamental question to the Church Fathers would be whether or not they did justice to the "true sense of Scripture", whether they acknowledged the fundamental hermeneutic principle that a text has to be read as it wants to be understood.

of Scripture. The monography of L. GOPPELT about such a reading of the OT from a NT perspective has become quite famous in Western thought.[76] But this attempt to control the results of biblical exegesis from its NT reception has failed; it is no longer sustained in OT exegesis nor in Patristics.[77]

Opposition to allegorical interpretation has always pretended to know "the true, real" meaning of a certain text. The remarks of Plutarch about physical allegory or the evaluation of biblical allegory by Celsus or Porphyry have judged other approaches to be "false", because they preferred a different reading of the same story (Plutarch) or wanted to enforce their conviction that the Bible is of no value at all (Celsus and Porphyry).[78] Such a criticism of allegory is based on their own *Weltanschauung* which they want to suggest as an alternative. This can be seen and questioned today. Nevertheless, the control of interpretations seems to be an intriguing idea. Hilary's remarks about the legitimacy and the necessity of an allegorical conception of the beginning of Psalm 137, for instance, could show that he was rather apologetic about his approach. Towards the end of his treatise on the mysteries there are again reflections about the legitimacy of a spiritual reading of the Bible which could point into the same direction. Do these deliberations indicate a certain dispute with opponents of the allegorical approach?[79] The spiritual interpretations of the Bishop of Milan seem to be untouched by a general questioning. However, the Ambrosian writings of this kind are particularly susceptible to misunderstanding, because Ambrose is using a literary aesthetics which needs to be deciphered before it discloses its true meaning. This applies especially to the sacramental dimension of his allegory which is often latent in apparently moralizing expositions.

Ambrose and Hilary use allegorical techniques in order to get away from a semantical reading of the Bible. They regard Scripture as a crystal being able to reflect contemporary christological or ecclesiastical issues. These different interpretations do no harm to this crystal and at the same time its transparency is not complete: it scatters the light shining through it and gives rise to its many different colours. Is not this exactly the objective of allegorical expositions of the Bible?

---

[76] Cf. L. GOPPELT, *Typos. Die typologische Deutung des AT im NT* (Güthersloh 1939; repr. Darmstadt 1969) 4–7: he considers such an understanding of the Bible as the real one and calls other interpretations to be caught in the literal meaning ("jüdische Buchstäblichkeit") or to be a result of wild associations ("alexandrinische Fabelei"). In Patristics, these ideas were developed and taken as a key to the interpretation of patristic exegesis by J. DANIÉLOU; cf. for instance his *Sacramentum futuri. Etudes sur les origines de la typologie biblique* (ETH 25; Paris 1950).

[77] For a contemporary evaluation of the typological approach, see for instance: J. SCHREINER, "Das Verhältnis des Alten Testaments zum Neuen", *Segen für die Völker. Gesammelte Schriften zur Entstehung und Theologie des Alten Testaments* (ed. E. Zenger, Würzburg 1987; 392–407) 402 f, and C. KANNENGIESSER, "Fifty Years of Patristics", *TS* 50 (1989) 633–666; 655: "The controversy of the 50s about typology and allegory now seems like a baroque entertainment for oldfashioned clergymen; the real problems that remain unsolved call for more elementary answers about what faith in a written revelation of God means in our postmodern culture".

[78] Cf. Jacob, Allegorese (1992) 154–159; 154 f.

[79] It would be interesting to confront his exegesis for instance with the principles of interpretation underlying the publications of the anonymous author named Ambrosiaster who was not an adherent of "Alexandrian allegory".

A new look at allegory in the Latin West has become necessary in order to understand the principles behind the Ambrosian and Hilarian interpretations. This is not without repercussions for the general approach to Origen of Alexandria. His allegory can also be regarded in the perspective of receptive interpretation and it may very well disclose its ecclesiastical meaning only after a step deciphering its literary aesthetics.[80] This approach can pave a way to the liturgical dimension of Origen's interpretation of the Bible – but this is not the place to demonstrate its possibilities.

[80] For an understanding of Origen's allegory without the interpretative model "typology" cf. C. Jacob, "Möglichkeiten und Grenzen der patristischen Allegorese veranschaulicht am Beispiel Gen 22", *Die Bibel Jesu im Gottesdienst der Kirche* (ed. A. Franz, Pietas Liturgica 8) (in print).

Chapter Twenty-one

Augustine: His Exegesis and Hermeneutics

By David F. Wright, Edinburgh

Sources: nearly all Augustine's works are in PL and PLSup, very many in CSEL and CCL. Texts with French transl. and ample introductions etc. are in BAug (Paris: Desclée 1949–); English translations in NPNF, ACW, FC, LCC and other smaller series and sets, including *The Works of St Augustine* (ed. J. E. Rotelle; New York: New City Press 1990–).

Indexes: Works, editions, translations etc. are *listed* in CPL 250–359; TRE 4 (1979) 690–92; A. Di Berardino (ed.), *Patrology* IV (Westminster, MD: Christian Classics 1986) 342–462 (A. Trapè); C. Mayer (ed.), *Augustinus-Lexikon* (Basel/Stuttgart: Schwabe 1986) 1, xxvi–xl.

Bibliographies: Fichier Augustinien I–IV (Boston, MA: G. K. Hall 1972), and *Suppl.* (1981)— exhaustive, from Institut des Études Augustiniennes, Paris; T. van Bavel, *Répertoire bibliographique de Saint Augustin, 1950–1960* (Instr. Patr. 3; Steenbrugge: St Peter's Abbey 1963); C. Andresen, *Bibliographia Augustiniana* (Darmstadt: Wiss. Buchgesellschaft [2]1973); listings in Di Berardino (ed.), *Patrology* IV, in Augustinus-Lexikon, and in TRE 4 (1979) 646–98 (A. Schindler); H. J. Sieben, *Exegesis Patrum. Saggio bibliografico sull' esegesi biblica dei Padri della Chiesa* (Sussidi Patristici 2; Rome: Istituto Patristico Augustinianum 1983); comprehensive annual review in *REAug.*

General works: in addition to those noted above, P. Brown, *Augustine of Hippo. A Biography* (London: Faber 1967); A. Mandouze, *S. Augustin. L'aventure de la raison et de la grâce* (Paris: Études Augustiniennes 1968); E. Gilson, *The Christian Philosophy of St Augustine* (1943; tr. L. E. M. Lynch; New York: Random House 1960); E. TeSelle, *Augustine the Theologian* (New York: Herder and Herder 1970); K. Flasch, *Augustin. Einführung in sein Denken* (Stuttgart: Philipp Reclam jun. 1980); H.-I. Marrou, *S. Augustin et la fin de la culture antique* (Paris: E. de Boccard [4]1958); F. Van der Meer, *S. Augustin pasteur d'âmes* I–II (Colmar and Paris: Éditions Alsatia 1959); O. Perler/J.-L. Maier, *Les voyages de S. Augustin* (Paris: Études Augustiniennes 1969); R. A. Markus, *Saeculum: History and Society in the Theology of St Augustine* (Cambridge: Cambridge UP [2]1988).

0. Introduction

Sources: Augustine's *Confessions* I–III (ed. and commentary by J. J. O'Donnell; Oxford: Oxford UP 1992); tr. H. Chadwick (Oxford: Oxford UP 1991).

Studies: J. J. O'Meara, *The Young Augustine* (London: Longmans, Green 1954); P. Courcelle, *Recherches sur les* Confessions *de S. Augustin* (Paris: E. de Boccard [2]1968).

Augustine's first encounters with the Bible revealed no promise of the enormous and massively influential efforts he would later devote to explaining and inculcating its mysteries, as first presbyter and then bishop (395–430) of the Catholic Church of Hippo in Roman North Africa (modern Annaba in Algeria). His reading of Cicero's *Hortensius* at Carthage in 372/3 when he was probably eighteen enthused him for "the immortality of wisdom" (*Con-*

fessions 3.4.7). But when, in pursuit of his goal, he turned to the Holy Scriptures (in the VL, of course), their uncultured style repelled him as unworthy of comparison with Cicero's elegance (*Confs.* 3.5.9).

On the rebound, as it were, he was fair game for Manichaeism, which retained his allegiance, albeit with diminishing relish, for the next nine years. Among its attractions to the young Augustine was its rejection of the Old Testament (which subsequently evoked from him an extensive programme of apologia).[1] Books 3–5 of his *Confessions* depict him as sharing fully in the Manichees' scorn for the absurdities, immoralities and crass materialism of the OT, which they insisted on reading literalistically. Only occasionally, it seems, did he hear any defence of the Scriptures (*Confs.* 5.11.21).

It was the preaching of Ambrose, bishop of Milan, to which Augustine moved in 384, that opened his eyes to a better way of treating the OT.

> Above all, I heard first one, then another, then many difficult passages in the Old Testament scriptures figuratively interpreted, where I, by taking them literally, had found them to kill. So after several passages in the Old Testament had been expounded spiritually, I now found fault with that despair of mine, caused by my belief that the law and the prophets could not be defended at all against the mockery of hostile critics.[2]

Augustine was delighted to hear Ambrose repeating, as though explicating a principle (*regulam*) of exegesis, "The letter kills, the spirit gives life" (2 Cor 3:6).[3]

Attempts to identify Ambrose's OT expositions during Augustine's sojourn in Milan (384–86) have not yet issued in consensus. PIERRE COURCELLE made claims for *On Isaac or the Soul, On Jacob and the Blessed Life* and particularly the nine homilies on the Hexaemeron preached one Holy Week, but none of these works can be dated with the required precision.[4] Yet this uncertainty in no way qualifies the importance of Ambrose's spiritualizing exegesis in rehabilitating the OT in Augustine's eyes.

The first book of the OT that Augustine truly enjoyed was the Psalter. After his conversion in July 386, he retired with family, friends and pupils to Cassiciacum (most probably Cassago Brianza, about 35 km north-west of Milan), where according to the *Confessions* he revelled in the Psalms.

> My God, how I cried to you when I read the Psalms of David, songs of faith, utterances of devotion which allow no pride of spirit to enter in! .. how they kindled my love for you! I was fired by an enthusiasm to recite them, were it possible, to the entire world in protest against the pride of the human race. Yet they are being sung in all the world.[5]

---

[1] In *On the Advantage of Believing* 6.13 (PL 42,74) Augustine attributes his rejection of the OT to youthful impetuosity. On Manichaeism and Augustine's engagement with it see S.N.C. LIEU, *Manichaeism in the Later Roman Empire and Medieval China* (Manchester: UP 1985; 2nd ed. WUNT 63; Tübingen: J.C.B. Mohr 1992).

[2] *Confs.* 5.14.24, tr. Chadwick 88.

[3] *Confs.* 6.4.6, where CHADWICK 94 n.8, refers to Ambrose, *Sermon* 19 (i.e. 19.5; PL 17,641); but this sermon is by Maximus of Turin, *Sermon* 67.4 (CCL 23, 282): see CPL 180.

[4] Recherches (1968) 93–138. The lists of Ambrose's uses of 2 Cor 3:6 given by Courcelle (98 n.4) and O'Donnell, Confessions II (1992) 325, are neither complete nor restricted to the sense given by Augustine. Close is *On Flight from the World* 2.13 (PL 14, 603–04), on Josh 20:6. See L.F. PIZZOLATO, *La dottrina esegetica di sant'Ambrogio* (Scripta Patristica Mediolanensia 9; Milan: Vita e Pensiero 1978) 194–201, and on the chronology of Ambrose's works, R. GRYSON, *Le prêtre selon saint Ambroise* (Louvain: Imprimerie Orientaliste 1968) 35–42.

[5] *Confs.* 9.4.8, tr. Chadwick 160.

Augustine particularly emphasized Psalm 4,[6] and Psalm 80 is also attested.[7] In addition, the Psalter would have been used in his private or communal devotions.

The Psalms would become the special love of the African father. He produced expositions of them all, informed by his distinctive, Christological and ecclesiological exegesis. When, in the late 390s, he recorded God's mercy in his own wayward life, the *Confessions* were shot through with quotations, allusions and echoes of the Psalter from their opening words.[8] Thus the language of the Psalms was woven deeply into the warp and woof of Augustine's piety.[9] His second most famous work, *City of God*, opens with an echo of Ps 87:3. During his final illness, according to his biographer Possidius, he had the "very few" penitential Psalms posted up on the walls of his sick-room for daily meditation.[10]

Yet in the autumn of 386, when Ambrose recommended Augustine to read Isaiah in preparation for baptism, he stumbled at the first obscure chapter, and laid it aside until he was better versed *in dominico eloquio*.[11] Ambrose may well have expounded Isaiah in Milan in 386 or early 387, and perhaps intended Augustine to be prepared for pre-baptismal catechesis from Isaiah.[12]

In the years that followed, prior to his ordination to the presbyterate at Hippo in 391, it is not easy to trace his coming to terms with the OT, except in controversial engagement with Manichaeism (see below). The demands of this campaign were uncompromising, as he writes in perhaps his first post-ordination treatise:

> I call my conscience to witness, Honoratus, I call God who dwells in pure souls to witness, that I am convinced there is nothing more wise, more chaste, more religious than those Scriptures which the Catholic Church accepts under the name of the Old Testament.[13]

After his ordination, he requested from bishop Valerius a couple of months' leave to familiarize himself with the Bible.[14] From now on, his ever-deepening immersion in the Scriptures was driven not only by apologetic exigencies but increasingly by the expectations laid on one *qui populo ministrat sacramentum et verbum Dei*.[15]

---

[6] *Confs.* 9.4.8–11. For a comparison with his *Enarr. in Ps* 4 (produced ca. 394) see O'Donnell, Confessions III (1992) 91–94.

[7] *On Order* 1.8.22–3 (PL 32,987–88).

[8] O'Donnell, Confessions II (1992) 9, *ad loc.* Cf. S. Poque, "Les Psaumes dans les *Confessions*", *Saint Augustin et la Bible* (BTT 3, ed. A.-M. La Bonnardière; Paris: Beauchesne 1986) 155–66; G. N. Knauer, *Psalmenzitate in Augustins Konfessionen* (Göttingen: Vandenhoeck & Ruprecht 1955); P. Burns, "Augustine's Distinctive Use of the Psalms in the Confessions: the Role of Music and Recitation", *Augustinian Studies* 24 (1993) 133–46.

[9] On Ps 67:7 (68:6) in his monastic ideal see G. Lawless, *Augustine of Hippo and his Monastic Rule* (Oxford: Clarendon Press 1987) 43–44.

[10] *Life of Augustine* 31 (PL 32,63).

[11] *Confs.* 9.5.13.

[12] Gryson, Le prêtre (1968) 37; Courcelle, Recherches (1968) 215–16.

[13] *On the Advantage of Believing* 6.13 (PL 42,74); tr. J. H. S. Burleigh, *Augustine: Earlier Writings* (LCC 6; London: SCM Press 1953) 301.

[14] *Letter* 21.3 (PL 33,88–89).

[15] Ibid.

1. The Exegetical Work of Augustine

Studies: M. Pontet, *L'exégèse de S. Augustin prédicateur* (Théologie 7; Paris: Aubier 1945); G. Bonner, CHB I (1970) 541–63; H. Chadwick, DBI (1990) 65–69; *S. Augustin et la Bible* (BTT 3, ed. A.-M. La Bonnardière; Paris: Beauchesne 1986); A. D. R. Polman, *The Word of God according to St. Augustine* (1955; tr. A. J. Pomerans; London: Hodder and Stoughton 1961); G. Strauss, *Schriftgebrauch, Schriftauslegung und Schriftbeweis bei Augustin* (BGBH 1; Tübingen: J. C. B. Mohr 1959); M. Simonetti, *Biblical Interpretation in the Early Church: An Historical Introduction to Patristic Exegesis* (1981; tr. J. A. Hughes; Edinburgh: T&T Clark 1994); G. Pelland, *Cinq études de S. Augustin sur le début de la Génèse* (Recherches. Théologie 8; Tournai: Desclée 1972); M.-J. Rondeau, *Les commentaires patristiques du Psautier (IIIe–Ve siècles)* I–II (Orientalia Christiana Analecta 219–20; Rome: Pontifico Istituto Orientale 1982–85); La Bonnardière, *Biblia Augustiniana* (Paris: Etudes Augustiniennes 1960-)—details given below; H. Rondet et al., *Études augustiniennes* (Théologie 28; Paris: Aubier 1953); B. De Margerie, *Introduction à l'histoire de l'exégèse* III. *Saint Augustin* (Paris: Éditions du Cerf 1983); P.- P. Verbraken, *Études critiques sur les Sermons authentiques de S. Augustin* (Instr. Patr. 12; Steenbrugge: St Peter's Abbey/The Hague: Martin Nijhoff 1976), with revisions in "Mise à jour ...", *Aevum inter utrumque: Mélanges offerts à Gabriel Sanders* (Instr. Patr. 23, ed. M. van Uytfanghe/R. Demeulenaere; 1991) 483–90.

The first three chapters of Genesis preoccupied Augustine's earliest exegetical labours on the OT. Their motivation was explicitly anti-Manichaean.

i. *De Genesi contra Manichaeos* (CPL 265; PL 34, 173–220)
This was Augustine's first writing after returning from Italy to Africa, to his home town Tagaste. Written ca. 388–89, its two books cover Genesis 1–3, "very manifestly published against the Manichaeans in defence of the old law".[16] Augustine later explained that here he followed the allegorical meaning, not daring to expound such great mysteries *ad litteram*, that is, *secundum historicam proprietatem.*[17] But in his most expansive exposition of Genesis, he gave a more differentiated account of his first attempt:

> At that time I did not see how all of Genesis could be taken in the proper sense (*proprie*), and it seemed to me more and more impossible, or at least scarcely possible or very difficult, for all of it to be so understood.
> But not willing to be deterred from my purpose, whenever I was unable to discover the literal meaning of a passage, I explained its figurative meaning as briefly and as clearly as I was able, so that the Manichees might not be discouraged by the length of the work or the obscurity of its contents ... I was mindful, however, of the purpose which I had set before me and which I was unable to achieve, that is, to show how everything in Genesis is to be understood first of all not in the figurative but in the proper sense (*non figurate sed proprie*); and since I did not completely despair of the possibility of understanding it all in this sense, I made the following statement ...[18]

Augustine then quoted what he had written in *De Genesi contra Manichaeos* as he embarked on the exposition of Gen 2:4–3:24:

---

[16] *Retractationes* 1.10(9).1 (PL 32, 599). There is a good translation with introduction by R. J. Teske, *Saint Augustine on Genesis. Two Books on Genesis against the Manichees and On the Literal Interpretation of Genesis: An Unfinished Book* (FC 84; Washington, DC: Catholic University of America Press 1991).

[17] Ibid. 1.18(17) (PL 32, 613).

[18] *De Genesi ad litteram* 8.2.5 (PL 34, 373–74), tr. J. H. Taylor, *St Augustine. The Literal Meaning of Genesis* II (ACW 42; New York/Ramsey, NJ: Newman Press 1982) 35.

> Anyone who wants to interpret in a literal sense (*secundum litteram*) everything said here, that is, to understand it only as the letter reads (*littera sonat*), and if he avoids blasphemy and explains everything in harmony with the catholic faith, not only is he not to be dissuaded but to be considered a distinguished interpreter worthy of high praise. But if there is no way to understand what is written in a devout manner worthy of God without believing it to be set forth figuratively and enigmatically (*figurate atque in aenigmatibus*), we have the authority of the apostles, who resolved so many enigmas in the books of the Old Testament, and should hold to our intended method ... to explain all these figures of things in accord with the catholic faith, whether they belong to history or prophecy, without prejudice to an improved and more attentive exposition.[19]

In Book 1 of this work, as he engages closely with Manichaean attacks on Genesis 1, Augustine rarely resorts to allegory. But "have dominion over fish" (1:28) is given both a straightforward and a spiritual sense (subduing the passions), and when God's resting on the seventh day is made to speak of *our* resting from all *our* works, we observe how the spiritual and prophetic senses almost coincide. This also prompts Augustine to a similar treatment of the seven days of creation as a *praedicatio* of the seven ages of the world from creation to consummation, and a "prophetic" spiritualization in terms of seven phases of spiritual progress.[20]

But in Book 2, after the manifesto quoted at length above, Augustine resorts to allegory almost routinely. As he asserts at the outset, "The whole of this account is explained not self-evidently (*aperte*) but figuratively".[21] So the plant of the field (Gen 2:5) is the soul, the garden of paradise (2:8) is blessedness, the four rivers (2:10) the four virtues, and so forth.[22]

ii. *De Genesi ad litteram, imperfectus liber* (CPL 268; PL 34, 219–46; CSEL 28:1, 459–503)

This second attempt at Genesis composed ca. 393 at Hippo, reached only Gen 1:26 before the author abandoned it. Augustine here undertook "the most taxing and difficult task" of an exposition *secundum historicam proprietatem*, but "my inexperience (*tirocinium*) in expounding the Scriptures collapsed under the weight of such a burden". It remained unpublished, and when he unearthed it while compiling his *Retractationes* ca. 427 he at first thought to destroy it. On further reflection he retained it (adding two final sections, 16:61–2), as "a not wholly useless measure of my rudimentary efforts in unravelling and searching the divine oracles".[23]

Augustine presents four ways of interpreting the OT which "certain expositors" have transmitted, in terms of *historia, allegoria, analogia* (demonstrating the agreement of OT and NT) and *aetiologia* (giving the causes of things said and done).[24] Since he is proceeding *secundum historiam*, beasts are beasts, plants are plants, and thirty "days" make a month.

---

[19] *De Genesi contra Manichaeos* 2.2.3 (PL 34, 197), cited at *De Genesi ad litteram* 8.2.5 (PL 34, 374).

[20] *De Genesi contra Manichaeos* 1.20.31; 1.22.34; 1.23.35–24.42; 1.25.43 (PL 34, 187–88, 189–90, 190–93, 193–94).

[21] Ibid. 2.1.1 (PL 34, 195).

[22] Ibid. 2.3.4; 2.9.12; 2.10.13 (PL 34, 198, 202–03, 203).

[23] *Retractationes* 1.18 (17) (PL 32, 613). For the translation by R. J. Teske in FC 84 see n. 16 above.

[24] *De Genesi ad litteram imperf.* 2.5 (PL 34, 222). On the four senses, see further below.

iii. *Confessions* 11–13

These merit inclusion as Augustine's third exposition of the beginning of Genesis. Written in the last years of the fourth century, these books have taxed the ingenuity of scholars seeking an overall design for the *Confessions.* Chadwick suggests that in Bks. 11 (or 10)–13 we see writ large throughout the created order what in Bks. 1–9 is an individual human story of exile and return.[25]

Augustine appears to embark on an account of the whole of Scripture: "Let me confess to you what I find in your books ... – from the beginning in which you made heaven and earth until the perpetual reign with you in your heavenly city".[26] What follows is unsystematic musing – in Bk. 11 especially on time, Bk. 12 chiefly creation, and Bk. 13 ranging over most of Gen 1–2:3, applying it allegorically to the community of faith.

Here we encounter Augustine the Platonic Christian at work: "What wonderful profundity there is in your utterances! The surface meaning lies open before us and charms beginners. Yet the depth is amazing, my God, the depth is amazing".[27] A multiplicity of interpretations is consistent with the many and varied embodiments in the physical realm of the unvarying realities of the intelligible world, such as wisdom and knowledge (*Confs.* 13.20.27).

In Bk. 12 Augustine addresses critics – not Manichees but presumably catholic Christians – of his earlier interpretation of Genesis, in *De Genesi contra Manichaeos,* no doubt (*Confs.* 12.14.17, 12.15.19, 22–23, etc). His response holds to "a diversity of true views" (*Confs.* 12.30.41), even if it conflicts with the author's (Moses') intended meaning.

> In Bible study all of us are trying to find and grasp the meaning of the author we are reading, and when we believe him to be revealing truth, we do not dare to think he said anything which we either know or think to be incorrect. As long as each interpreter is endeavouring to find in the holy scriptures the meaning of the author who wrote it, what evil is it if an exegesis he gives is one shown to be true by you, light of all sincere souls, even if the author he is reading did not have that idea and, though he had grasped a truth, had not discerned that seen by the interpreter.[28]

iv. *De Genesi ad litteram* (CPL 266–67; PL 34, 245–486; CSEL 28:1, 3–435)[29]

These twelve books on Genesis 1–3 were started in 401 and completed in 415, with at least nine written near to 401. They constitute Augustine's most substantial work of biblical exegesis (apart from series of preached expositions – see below), which deserves to be ranked with other better-known *magna opera* of the African church father.

It is called *ad litteram,* he commented later, because Genesis is explained *non secundum allegoricas significationes, sed secundum rerum gestarum proprie-*

---

[25] Chadwick xxiv. See the discussions in O'Donnell, Confessions I (1992) xxxii–xli; III (1992) 150–54, 250–52.

[26] *Confs.* 11.2.3, tr. Chadwick 222.

[27] Ibid. 12.14.17, Chadwick 254.

[28] Ibid. 12.18.27, Chadwick 259–60. See the whole section, *Confs.* 12.16.23–32.43.

[29] There is an English translation by J. H. Taylor in ACW 41–42 (see n. 18 above), and an excellent Latin-French edition by A. Agaësse and A. Solignac in BAug 48–49 (1972).

tatem, although he added that it raises more questions than it resolves – and resolves often provisionally rather than definitively.[30]

Since Augustine's insistence that this is a literal commentary must puzzle modern readers, we must look more closely. He certainly leaves no dubiety on the point. The *narratio* of Gen 2:8, he asserts, is not in a figurative genre (*genere locutionis figuratarum rerum*) like the Song of Songs, but historical like Kings.[31] It is the unfamiliarity of the subject-matter that induces some people to treat Genesis 1–3 (rather than 4 ff) *figurate*. Augustine disputes both the claim that happenings in Genesis 4 ff, such as Enoch's translation and Sarah's child-bearing, fall within the compass of natural human experience, and the supposition that the unparalleled uniqueness of Genesis 1–3 is a bar to its character as event. Are we to believe that God never made a world because he does not do so every day?[32] Why should the historical creation of paradise be more incredible than that of the first human being? Both lie wholly beyond our experience, but if Adam is understood only figuratively, who begot Cain and Abel?[33]

So Augustine commits himself to defending the *proprietatem litterae* of what the scriptural writer reports historically (*gestum narrat*).[34] This approach has no difficult in recognizing anthropomorphic or anthropopathic expressions,[35] or the metaphorical figurativeness of "your eyes will be opened" (Gen 3:4), but such usages do not justify the allegorical treatment of the whole passage. The serpent's warning and its subsequent fulfilment (Gen 3:7) are written just like the rest of the narrative.[36]

Sometimes, however, the literal sense (*corporaliter*) is absurd, or prejudicial to the analogy of faith (*fide veritatis; regulam fidei*). In such cases a figurative reading is obviously preferable.[37] For example, whenever God is said to know anything in time, we cannot take this literally; in accordance with a common scriptural practice, the outcome is signified by the cause, and hence God makes humans or angels know in time.[38]

The greatest profit comes from both ascertaining the original meaning and preserving the *regula pietatis*. When what the author intended is uncertain or altogether elusive, the interpreter's criterion must be the *circumstantia Scripturae* or *sana fide*. In unclear cases, we may properly believe that the author intended two different meanings if both have the support of the context.[39] Thus the "light" of Gen 1:3 may rightly be spiritual or physical, although Augustine's preference is clearly for the former: it is the illumination of intelligent creatures.[40]

---

30 *Retractationes* 2.24(50).1 (PL 32, 640).
31 *De Genesi ad litteram* 8.1.2 (PL 34, 372).
32 Ibid. 8.1.3 (PL 34, 372–73).
33 Ibid. 8.1.4 (PL 34, 373).
34 Ibid. 11.1.2 (PL 34, 430).
35 E.g. ibid. 6.12.20 (PL 34, 347).
36 Ibid. 11.31.41 (PL 34, 446).
37 Ibid. 8.1.4; 11.1.2 (PL 34, 373, 430).
38 Ibid. 5.19.39 (PL 34, 335).
39 Ibid. 1.21.41; cf. 1.18.37 – 19.38 (PL 34, 262, 260–61).
40 Ibid. 1.17.32 (PL 34, 258).

The obscurity of a text may even be deliberate, in order to stimulate reflection. In such instances Augustine refrains from insisting on one explanation to the exclusion of a possibly better one, leaving each reader to choose the version that he can cope with.[41] In general, Augustine accepts that "paradise" is sometimes to be taken materially and sometimes spiritually, but in Gen 2:8 he stipulates that it is simply a place on earth.[42] (But Book 12 is an appendix devoted to Paul's vision of paradise in the "third heaven" of 2 Cor 12:2–4.) Nevertheless, when he comes to "the tree of life" (Gen 2:9), he cannot resist viewing it also as a sacrament, a mystery of spiritual reality.[43]

Yet however explicitly and lucidly Augustine clarifies his approach to exegesis, the reader is scarcely prepared for the complexities of his grappling with the early verses of Genesis, where he has to struggle to expose the *ad litteram* meaning. Finding a non-allegorical sense for "In the beginning God created heaven and earth" lands him in an endless series of questions. How can we understand God's *saying* "Let there be light"? As for the "days" of creation, "morning" is the beginning of each creature's nature and "evening" the limit of its making.[44] Similarly "day" itself might denote the form of the created being and "night" the privation of its form.[45]

Thus in this rambling and frequently inconclusive discussion, the bishop of Hippo only too readily inclines towards a "literal" meaning located in an immaterial order of being. He is well aware of the diversity of Christian interpretations of Genesis, and is anxious that they should not pronounce ignorantly on matters belonging to the physical scientists. On the other hand, he is mindful of vulnerable Christians whose faith fails when they hear unbelieving experts expatiating on cosmology or astronomy.[46]

For all these reasons, Augustine's "literal" exposition is highly sensitive to the apologetic challenges raised by Genesis 1 (e.g., the relation between the "heaven" of 1:1 and 1:8; how could there be time, i.e. literal day and night, before earth existed?). But he normally resists the temptation of an allegorical or prophetic significance until he has determined the sense in which what is recorded took place. Adam's naming of the animals cries out for a prophetic meaning: "once the historical happening is established (*re gesta confirmata*), we are left free to seek its figurative significance".[47]

v. *Locutiones in Heptateuchum* (CPL 269; PL 34, 485–546; CCL 33, 370–465) These seven books on *Expressions in the Heptateuch*, compiled ca. 419, aim to clarify the obscurities of the Latin of the Vetus Latina, especially when its reproduction of Hebraisms or, more often, Grecisms might misrepresent the author's intended meaning. The interest of the work is largely linguistic,

41 Ibid. 1.20.40 (PL 34, 261).
42 Ibid. 8.1.1 (PL 34, 371).
43 Ibid. 8.4.8 (PL 34, 375).
44 Ibid. 1.17.35; 4.1.1; 4.18.32 (PL 34, 259–60, 295–96, 308).
45 Ibid. 2.14.28 (PL 34, 274–75).
46 Ibid. 1.19.39; 2.1.3–4: 2.9.20–22 (PL 34, 261, 263–64, 270–71).
47 Ibid. 9.12.20 (PL 34, 400). On *ad litteram* see Agaësse and Solignac in BAug 48, 32–50.

bearing on Augustine's knowledge of Greek (see below) and use of the Vetus Latina (see below).

vi. *Quaestiones in Heptateuchum* (CPL 270; PL 34, 547–824; CCL 33, 1–377)
These seven books were composed at the same time as the *Locutiones.* (Augustine reports that he had made a start on 1 Samuel also, but other urgent demands frustrated further progress.[48]) They are more strictly exegetical. Augustine does himself less than justice when he explains the title as issues presented for investigation rather than resolution.[49] With a reference to his earlier exposition of Genesis 1–3, he begins with Gen 4:17. Most *quaestiones* deal with a single phrase or verse, but longer passages are also covered, e.g. Num 15:24–29; Deut 10:1–4; 22:13–21. In default of a continuous exposition of the bulk of the Pentateuch, the *Quaestiones* was heavily used in later centuries.

This work belongs to a recognized if flexible genre of biblical *quaestiones*.[50] A comparison with Jerome discloses not only their deeply differing attachments to the LXX and the *veritas hebraica* respectively, but also Augustine's preoccupation with more taxing apologetic and doctrinal questions over against Jerome's dominant linguistic, geographical and historical interests.[51]

vii. *De octo quaestionibus ex Veteri Testamento* (CPL 277; CCL 33, 469–72; PLSup II, 386–89)
This is included for completeness' sake.

viii. *Adnotationes in Iob* (CPL 271; PL 34, 825–86, CSEL 28:2, 509–628)
Written, it seems, ca. 400, Augustine hesitates in his *Retractationes* to call it his own. Augustine's marginal notes to a text of Job had been collected and issued by others. These notes' brevity and obscurity were compounded by the incorrigible defectiveness of the MSS available to Augustine. Only regard for his brethren's attachment to them dissuaded him from disowning them.[52]

The above comprise Augustine's writings devoted specifically to exegeting parts of the OT. But they by no means exhaust the efforts he expended on elucidating its wisdom for the people of God – and its enemies and critics.

ix. *Sermones* (CPL 284, 287–88; Verbraken, Études critiques)
About 565 individual *sermones* of Augustine survive (i.e. excluding his major series of expositions on the Psalms and on John's Gospel and First Epistle). Verbraken (p. 18) listed 544, to which must be added some twenty new ones

---

[48] *Retractationes* 2.55 (81).1 (PL 32, 652).

[49] Ibid. (PL 32, 651).

[50] G. Bardy, "La littérature patristique des Quaestiones et Responsiones sur L'Écriture sainte", *RB* 41 (1932) 515–37.

[51] F. Cavallera, "Les 'Quaestiones hebraicae in Genesim' de saint Jérome et les 'Quaestiones in Genesim' de saint Augustin", in *Miscellanea Agostiniana* II. *Studi Agostiniani* (Rome: Tipografia Poliglotta Vaticana 1931) 359–72. (Jerome had sent his *Hebrew Questions on Genesis* to Aurelius of Carthage ca. 392–93, [Augustine] *Letter* 27*:2, ed. Divjak et al., BAug 46B, 396–98.) It is in this work that Augustine uttered his celebrated dictum, "The New Testament lies hidden in the Old, and the Old is laid open in the New" (2.73; PL 34, 623).

[52] *Retractationes* 2.13 (39) (PL 32, 635).

(and several supplements) recently discovered in a Mainz MS by F. Dolbeau and in course of publication.[53] Of this number the classification *Sermones de Vetere Testamento* established by the seventeenth-century Maurist editors embraced fifty sermons,[54] increased to over sixty by post-Maurist discoveries, including three of Dolbeau's new pieces (6, 8, 9 = *Sermones* 23 B, 29 B, 28 A). Most were expertly edited in 1961 by Cyrille Lambot in CCL 41.[55] Almost half take their text from the Psalter (including all three new Dolbeau ones).

But many other sermons are inspired in part by OT verses and passages, especially among the liturgical readings. A patchy first attempt to establish Augustine's "lectionary" was made by G. G. Willis,[56] but in reality Augustine as bishop had almost total freedom of choice. By far the largest number of references to OT lections are to Psalms.

x. *Enarrationes in Psalmos* (CPL 283; PL 36–37; CCL 38–40)
This collection – the only exposition of the whole Psalter surviving from any of the Fathers – may be viewed as the largest of Augustine's works, but it is far from constituting a unitary production. These expositions were given in different forms over some three decades. First treated were Psalms 1–32 early in Augustine's years in Hippo, ca. 394–96, and last was the longest, Psalm 118 (119). His preface to the thirtytwo sermons on this Psalm explains that its strange profundity – which was not its obscurity so much as its elusive clarity – had long deterred him, despite persistent entreaties from his brethren, from expounding it and thereby completing his exposition of the Psalter. When he finally yielded, he did so by dictating *sermones* "to be delivered to the people" (presumably by other preachers) – "what the Greeks call *homiliai*".[57] These thirty-two sermons have been most reliably dated in or soon after 422.[58]

But the problems of dating the *Enarrationes* are in general far from resolution.[59] Those on "the songs of degrees" (*Cantica graduum*), Psalms 119–133 (MT 120–134), have attracted much attention, partly because they are known to have been intercalated with the early *Tractatus* on John's Gospel. They can

---

[53] Progress is surveyed by G. Madec in *REAug* 38 (1992) 389–91.

[54] PL 38, 23–332.

[55] For details of the rest see Verbraken and Madec (n. 53 above). All the post-Maurist sermons to date were edited by G. Morin in *Miscellanea Agostiniana* I (1930 – see n. 51 above), and reprinted with later discoveries in PLSup II, 405–1360.

[56] *St Augustine's Lectionary* (Alcuin Club Collections 44; London: SPCK 1962). Cf. A.-M. La Bonnardière, "La Bible 'liturgique' de saint Augustin", C. Kannengiesser (ed.), *Jean Chrysostome et Augustin. Actes du Colloque de Chantilly 22–24 septembre 1974* (Théologie Historique 35; Paris: Editions Beauchesne 1975) 147–60.

[57] *Enarr. in Ps* 118, prooem. (PL 37, 1501).

[58] A.-M. La Bonnardière, *Recherches de chronologie augustinienne* (Paris: Études Augustiniennes 1965) 119–41. A closely similar dating, ca. 420–22, was reached by C. Kannengiesser, "Enarratio in psalmum CXVIII: Science de la révélation et progrès spirituel", *RAug* 2 (1962) 359–81.

[59] Perler/Maier, Les Voyages (1969) 247 n. 1. The dates arrived at earlier by S. Zarb, and reproduced in tabular form in CCL 38, xv–xviii, are unreliable, not least because they fail to distinguish between widely ranging degrees of probability. They have been overtaken in important respects by later studies.

be fairly confidently dated to the winter, December to April, of 406–7.[60] LA BONNARDIÈRE has studied another recognizable group, those on Psalms 110–17 (111–18), and argued that their singular qualities, e.g. in the use of other verses of Scripture, are best explained if they are dated ca. 400.[61] But for the rest, although clusters of three or more *Enarrationes*, often without regard to numerical sequence, can sometimes be shown to belong together, there is no alternative to painstaking investigation to date each one separately.[62]

The listing of the *Enarrationes* in Possidius' *Elenchus* of Augustine's works distinguishes between two categories – those dictated (*dictati*) and the rest preached (*tractati/disputati/habiti in populo*).[63] Augustine drew the same distinction himself in the preface to his expositions on Psalm 118 (119).[64] Quite apart from the textual uncertainties of this entry in Possidius' inventory, scholars are not all persuaded that Possidius got it right in every case.[65] In fact, a bare division between dictation and preaching is unsatisfactory. Possidius himself may hint at different categories of *dictati*, and there is certainly a considerable gulf between the *Enarrationes* on Psalms 1–32, which are little more than concise glosses, and even the short *sermones* on Psalm 118 (119), let alone the extended exposition of some of the others known to have been dictated, such as Psalms 67 (68), 71 (72) and 77 (78). Some of those not first of all preached before the congregation may have been delivered by Augustine, in a manner not too different from dictation to a class of pupils, in the monastery or to a weekday assembly limited *de facto* to the religious, clergy and members of the episcopal household. Augustine informs

---

[60] La Bonnardière, Recherches (1965) 19–62 (building on the work of M. LE LANDAIS), endorsed with additional evidence by M.-F. BERROUARD, "La date des *Tractatus I-LIV in Iohannis Evangelium* de saint Augustin", *RAug* 7 (1971) 105–68 at 105–19, and more briefly in the first volume of his Latin-French edition of the *Tractatus* (BAug 71, 1969).

[61] La Bonnardière, Recherches (1965) 143–64. ZARB had dated them in 414. Cf. S. POQUE "L'énigme des Enarrationes in Psalmos 110–117 de saint Augustin", *BLE* 77 (1976) 241–64 (and La Bonnardière's critique, *REAug* 23 [1977] 356–58).

[62] See H. RONDET, "Essais sur la chronologie des 'Enarrationes in Psalmos' de saint Augustin", *BLE* 61 (1960) 111–27, 258–86; 65 (1964) 110–36; 68 (1967) 180–202; 71 (1970) 174–200; 75 (1974) 161–88; 77 (1976) 99–118. LA BONNARDIÈRE, "Les *Enarrationes in Psalmos* prêchées par saint Augustin à l'occasion de fêtes de martyrs", *RAug* 7 (1971) 73–104; eadem, "Les 'Enarrationes in psalmos' prêchées par saint Augustin à Carthage en décembre 409", *RAug* 11 (1976) 52–90. Detailed indications relating to many *Enarrationes* will be found via the index to Perler/Maier, Les Voyages (1969).

[63] X^4.1–4 (ed. A Wilmart in *Miscellanea Agostiniana* II (1931) 181–82). Cf. F. GLORIE, "Das 'zweite Aenigma' in Augustins Opusculorum Indiculus cap. X^4, 1–4: 'Tractatus Psalmorum'", in *Corona Gratiarum ... Eligio Dekkers O.S.B ... Oblata* (Steenbrugge: St. Peter's Abbey/The Hague: Martin Nijhoff 1975) I, 289–309.

[64] See n. 57 above: he had expounded all the other Psalms *partim sermocinando in populis, partim dictando.*

[65] E.g., La Bonnardière, Recherches (1965) 155–56, claims that *Enarr. in Pss.* 110–17 were preached and not dictated, as Possidius asserts. On Possidius' text see A. WILMART, "La tradition des grands ouvrages de saint Augustin", in *Miscellanea Agostiniana* II (1931) 257–315 at 295–300. For a reconsideration of the "dictated or preached?" question in the light of the newly discovered *Letter* 23*A, see BERROUARD, "L'activité littéraire de saint Augustin du 11 septembre au 1er décembre 419 d'après la Lettre 23*A à Possidius de Calama", *Les lettres de saint Augustin découvertes par Johannes Divjak. Communications présentées au colloque des 20 et 21 septembre 1982* (Paris: Études Augustiniennes 1983) 301–26 at 314–18.

us that the *sermones* on Psalm 118 (119) were intended for popular delivery – which *Enarr. in Pss. 1–32* could not have sustained.[66] Thus the unity of the *Enarrationes in Psalmos* is deceptive, at least in respect of genre.

The chronological spread of these Psalms' expositions means that they inevitably encompass a wide range of themes, emphases and applications. "Toute la carrière d'Augustin y est en quelque sorte résumée".[67] Thus the sermons on Psalm 118 (119), dictated after a decisive phase in the Pelagian controversy, interpret the Psalmist's insistent prayers, in his zeal for the righteousness of God's law, in terms of the continued dependence of the regenerate on divine grace, which alone enables us not only to know but even to accomplish God's will. Augustine interiorizes the piety of the Psalmist in what is almost a synthesis of Paul and the Psalm.[68]

Elsewhere the expositor's treatment of the bleaker features of David's experiences – persecution, the prosperity of the wicked, the faithlessness of the people of God – makes the *Enarrationes* comparable to the *City of God*. It has been pointed out that many of them were preached at Carthage, in a metropolitan pulpit, as it were, where it was particularly fitting for Augustine to address the grand fortunes and misfortunes of the church in the world.[69] The Psalms give him ready-made opportunities to speak of the two cities, Jerusalem and Babylon, their contrasting origins and destinies and yet inseparable intermingling in this life.[70]

Yet if there is one distinctive hermeneutical thread running through the *Enarrationes*, it is the unity of the body of Christ with Christ its head. Thus the provocation, "Kill the man, all of you" (Ps 61 (62):3) evokes the following clarification from Augustine:

> How huge is the size of the body of one man that he can be killed by all? We should rather recognize here our person, the person of our church, the person of the body of Christ. For Jesus Christ with his head and his body is a single man, the saviour of the body and the limbs of the body, two in one flesh and in one voice and in one passion, and when iniquity has passed away, in one rest. Therefore the sufferings of Christ are not in Christ alone – though the sufferings of Christ are not other than in Christ. If you understand Christ to be head and body, the sufferings of Christ are not other than in Christ; but if you understand Christ to be head alone, the sufferings of Christ are not in Christ alone.[71]

In his early glossed explanation of Psalm 21 (22) such an exegesis is barely hinted at, but in his later more expansive treatment of this Psalm it comes to the fore. Why did the Lord cry "God, my God ... why have you abandoned me?" (v. 2; Matt 27:46), for God did not abandon him since he was himself God?

[66] Berrouard contrasts the *Enarr. in Ps* 118 (119) with the *Tractatus in Iohannem* 55–124: both sets were dictated and are similar in other respects, but whereas the former were dictated to be preached, the latter were dictated solely to complete the series in John's Gospel; *Homélies sur l'Évangile de saint Jean LV–LXXIX* (BAug 74 A, 1993) 39–44.

[67] Wilmart, La tradition (1931) 295.

[68] De Margerie, S. Augustin (1983) 130–34; Kannengiesser, Enarratio in Ps. CXVIII (1962); La Bonnardière, Recherches (1965) 126–32.

[69] Pontet, L'exégèse (1945) 388.

[70] E.g., *En. in Ps.* 61 (62). 6–8; 74 (75) (PL 36, 733–36, 772–85). Pontet (1945) 387, speaks of Augustine portraying in the *Enarr.* "une histoire spirituelle de l'humanité".

[71] *En. in Ps.* 61 (62). 4 (PL 36, 730).

Why is it said unless because we were there, unless because Christ's body is the church? Why did he say "God, my God ..." unless in some way to catch our attention and say "This Psalm was written about me"? "Far from my salvation are the words of my offences" (v. 2). Which offences, since it was said of him, "He did no sin ..."? How then can he say "my offences" unless because he himself prays for our offences and makes our offences his own ...?[72]

When Christ complained "Day and night I have cried and you will not hear me" (v. 3), "that voice was the voice of his members, not of the head".[73] Yet much of the rest of the Psalm is without difficulty set in the mouth of Christ himself.

Repeatedly in the *Enarrationes* Augustine reminds his hearers that sometimes Christ speaks in the Psalms in the person of his members, at other times in his own person as our head.[74] One cannot but admire Augustine's versatility in applying a profound theological theme that here becomes an interpretative device serving highly diverse ends. Often it enables him to resolve an apparent contradiction, or even a harmless inconsistency between a plural, "We will confess to you, O God" (Ps 74 (75):2), and a singular, "I will tell of all your wonders" (*ibid.*, VL).

The discourse begins in the person of the head. Whether the head speaks or the limbs speak, Christ is speaking: he speaks in the person of the head, he speaks in the person of the body. What is it that was said? "The two will be in one flesh. This is a great sacrament: I am speaking in Christ and in the church." And he himself in the Gospel, "Therefore they are now not two, but one flesh". So that you may realize that these are in some sense two persons, and yet again are one by the union of marriage, he speaks as one in Isaiah and says, "He has bound a headband on me like a bridegroom, and clothed me with ornament like a bride" (Isa 61:10). He called himself a bridegroom as the head (*ex capite*), the bride as the body (*ex corpore*). So he speaks as one; let us hear him, and let us also speak in him: may we be his members, so that this voice can be ours also.[75]

Augustine can ring all the possible changes: Christ speaks alone, of his own special role, as we have seen in much of Psalm 21 (22); or his members speak alone, when complaint or confession of sins makes attribution to the head inappropriate; or sometimes different companies of the members may be identified, some at ease and others in distress;[76] or the emphasis is on head and members speaking in perfect unison, as "the whole Christ". Yet in all cases Augustine is clear that it is Christ that is speaking. It is an exercise in exegesis that calls for wonderful suppleness, not to say ingenuity, on

---

[72] *En. in Ps.* 21 (22). II. 3 (PL 36, 172).

[73] Ibid. 4 (PL 36, 172–73).

[74] Pontet, L'exégèse (1945) 400–411.

[75] *En. in Ps.* 74 (75). 4 (PL 36, 948–49).

[76] So *En. in Ps.* 30 (31). II/2. 1 (PL 36, 239–40). Cf. 85 (86). 5 (PL 37, 1085), on "to you have I cried all the day long": "the body of Christ cries all the day long, its members departing and succeeding one another. A single person is extended to the end of the world. The same members of Christ cry, and some members are already at rest in him, some are crying now, some will cry when we ourselves have passed to our rest, and after them yet others will cry". The beginning of this *Enarr.* is a particularly fine statement of the "one Christ, head and body" theme: "when the body of the Son prays, it does not separate its head from itself ... he both prays for us and prays in us and is prayed to by us. He prays for us as our priest, he prays in us as our head, he is prayed to by us as our God. So let us recognize both our voices in him and his voices in us" (85 (86). 1; PL 37, 1081).

Augustine's part.[77] Yet its fruitful suggestiveness is not in doubt as Augustine copes with the contrasting tones and moods of the Psalter. The variations he plays on the theme of the identification of Christ with his people, especially in their tribulations – even if, as he commonly puts it, the head is above in heaven, the body below on earth – promote a spirituality that can glimpse "transfiguration" in that identity. In another comment on Ps 21 (22):2, "My God ... why have you abandoned me?", he says: "Transfiguring (*transfigurans*) us into what he was saying, and into his body (for we are his body and he our head), he uttered from the cross not his own voice but ours".[78]

In addition to the writings listed above, which, with the partial exception of *Confessions* 11–13, are all devoted wholly to the OT, a number of other works deal with it directly to a significant extent.

xi. *Contra Adimantum Manichaei discipulum* (CPL 319; PL 42, 129–72; CSEL 25:1, 115–90)[79]

Written ca. 393–94 in refutation of a demonstration by one Adimantus, a follower of Mani, that the law and the prophets conflicted with the NT, it deals point by point with twenty-eight alleged disagreements. In the by-going Augustine touches repeatedly on the unity of the two Testaments. One general statement to this effect he subsequently wished slightly to revise:

> That people who had received the Old Testament were held fast before the coming of the Lord by certain shadows and figures of realities, in accord with a wonderful and excellently ordered dispensation of the times; yet in it there is such strong prediction and pre-announcement of the New Testament that nothing is found in the teaching of the Evangelists and the apostles, however exalted and divine the precepts and promises, that is lacking in those ancient books.[80]

On reviewing this book for his *Retractationes*, Augustine added "almost" before "nothing is found", since although in figures "everything is found prophesied (in the OT) which was realized or is expected to be realized through Christ", not all of the precepts of the NT are prefigured in the OT. In illustration Augustine cites "You have heard that it was said ... but I say to you" (Matt 5:21).[81]

---

[77] "une lecture moins grammaticale que divinatrice", Pontet, L'exégèse (1945) 391.

[78] *En. in Ps.* 43 (44). 2 (PL 36, 483). Cf., on the same biblical verse, *personam in se transfiguraverat primi hominis, En. in Ps.* 37 (38). 27 (PL 36, 411). See Rondeau, Les commentaires patristiques II (1985) 365–88 at 380. This exegesis is by no means restricted to the *Enarr.* Thus in *Letter* 140, this verse is repeatedly to the fore: Christ says these words "in the person (*ex persona*) of the weakness of the flesh of sin, which he transfigured (*transfiguravit*) into the flesh which he took from the Virgin, the likeness of the flesh of sin"; by this utterance Christ "transfigured his martyrs into himself, who, although unwilling to die ... and for that reason apparently abandoned by their God for a time, ... voiced that cry from the heart and displayed that spirit of devotion which the Lord expressed from his own mouth as the passion was imminent, transfiguring them into himself at the same time, 'But not what I will, but what you will, Father'" (140. 6. 18; 10. 27; PL 33, 545, 550).

[79] Note also the Latin-French edition by R. Jolivet in BAug 17 (1961), and the excellent brief notice, with further literature, by F. Decret in Mayer, Augustinus-Lexikon I (1986) 90–94.

[80] *Contra Adimantum* 3. 4 (PL 42, 134).

[81] *Retractationes* 1. 22 (21). 2 (PL 32, 619).

xii. *Contra Faustum Manichaeum* (CPL 321; PL 42, 207–518, CSEL 25:1, 257–797)

This is the most extensive of Augustine's anti-Manichaean works, composed in 397–98 in the form of a dialogue with one of the leading African advocates of Manichaeism, whom Augustine, so he tells us in his *Confessions*, had found so disappointing and inadequate (*Confs.* 5.6–10 – 7.13). Many of the thirty-three books, which vary considerably in length, display Augustine's explanations and defences of catholic Christianity's use of the OT. Faustus tirelessly charged catholics with unprincipled selectivity in their fidelity to the OT. Hence in Bk. 6 Augustine draws the essential distinction between commands that shape life ("You shall not covet") and those that signify life ("You shall circumcise").[82] What in the OT's own day was a precept is now a testimony.[83]

Much of what Augustine states about the figurative significance – of the future and the spiritual – of the OT's concern with the temporal and material is unsurprising. He is keen to insist that the godly saints of the OT, the patriarchs and prophets, knew better than the carnal masses:

> They understood by the revelation of God's Spirit what was appropriate for that era and how God determined that future realities should be symbolized and foretold through all their actions and words. Their greater longing was for the New Testament, but their present duty in the body was carried out to signify new things to come by means of ancient promises.[84]

Christians have no interest in the fulfilment of OT promises in material terms.

Bk. 14 defends the application to Christ of Deut 21:33, "Cursed is everyone who hangs on a tree". The lengthy Bk. 12 surveys prophecies of Christ throughout the OT, and the even longer Bk. 22 seeks to rebut Faustus' maligning of the horrors of the OT, whether perpetrated by God or his servants, sometimes at his command. Augustine here provides one of his fullest justifications of war – a topic on which his teaching was to be of enormous influence.[85] Polygamy was no offence when it was customary, and the licentiousness of the patriarchs did not consist simply in having many wives.[86] Bk. 22 also contains as lucid a general statement of the relation of the two Testaments as one can find in Augustine:

> Concerning the precepts and sacraments of the Old Testament we have by now repeatedly said at length that we should understand them to have contained one element which was given to be fulfilled in practice through the grace of the New Testament, and another which would be shown by its removal as having been fulfilled through the truth now made manifest. By the love of God and neighbour the command of law would be accepted for implementation, but the promise of the law would be exposed as having been accomplished by the cessation of circumcision and other sacraments of that time. The commandment made people guilty, engendering a desire for salvation, while the promise employed figures (*figuras*), arousing expecation of a saviour, so that, through the advent of the New Testament, the bestowal of grace freed the former and the actualizing of the truth abolished the latter. The very law which was given through Moses became grace and truth through Jesus Christ – grace, that is, so that,

---

82 *Contra Faustum* 6.2 (PL 42, 227–28).

83 Ibid. 6.9 (PL 42, 237).

84 Ibid. 4.2 (PL 42, 219).

85 Ibid. 22.74–78 (PL 42, 447–51).

86 Ibid. 22.47, 48 (PL 42, 428–29).

with the gift of the remission of sins, what was commanded might be observed by the gift of God, and truth, so that what was promised be realized by the faithfulness of God.[87]

In another book Augustine draws out one implication of these guidelines for exegesis: when we find something in the OT which the NT does not require or even forbids, we must seek its meaning, for the very fact of its no longer being observed proves that it has been fulfilled. What does the now obsolete requirement of levirate marriage (Deut 25:5–10) prefigure but the obligation on every evangelist to raise up seed for his deceased brother, that is, Christ, and to name that seed after Christ, which Paul fulfilled, spiritually, with the truth now accomplished (1 Cor 4:15; 2:13).[88]

xiii. *Contra adversarium legis et prophetarum* (CPL 326; PL 42, 603–66; CCL 49, 1–131)

In 420 Augustine undertook, at the urgent request of fellow-Christians in Carthage, the refutation of a book by an unnamed heretic of Marcionite or similar persuasion which was creating a stir in Carthage.[89] As justification for not devoting more than this mention to it here, we cite Augustine's own statement near the end of the work: in *Contra Faustum* and *Contra Adimantum* you will find a great deal that is applicable to this critic likewise. "And perhaps if those books were read, there would have been little or no need to write this one".[90]

xiv. *City of God* (CPL 313; PL 41, 13–804; CSEL 40; CCL 47–48)

Augustine's most celebrated treatise focuses heavily on the OT in several books. Book 11 is mostly concerned, yet again, with the Genesis creation story. Bk. 18. 26–48 surveys OT prophecies of Christ, while Bk. 20. 21–30 deals with its predictions of the final judgement. But the most extended treatment of the OT comprises most of Bks. 15–17, which ramble through what may be called the salvation-history of the OT, with an eye to the development of the city of God in its earthly pilgrimage. For the present purpose, this brief record must suffice.

2. The *De doctrina Christiana* of Augustine and His Hermeneutics

Sources: PL 34, 15–122; CSEL 80 (1963), 3–169 (W. M. Green); CCL 32 (1962), 1–167 (J. Martin); with French transl., BAug 11 (1949), 169–539 (G. Combès/J. Farges); several English translations, incl. D. W. Robertson (Library of Liberal Arts; New York: Bobbs-Merrill 1958).

In expounding the OT, as we have seen, Augustine is often remarkably explicit about the principles determining his exegesis. Yet his only discussion

87 Ibid. 22. 6 (PL 42, 403–04).

88 Ibid. 32. 9 (PL 42, 502).

89 *Retractiones* 2. 58 (84) (PL 32, 654). On the work see now T. Raveaux's entry in Augustinus-Lexikon I, 107–11.

90 *Contra adversarium* 2. 12. 41 (PL 42, 664).

devoted specifically to the task of interpreting and proclaiming the Bible is *De doctrina Christiana.* Thus in translating the title, the active sense of 'teaching' or 'instruction' is more appropriate than 'doctrine'. It is a book about the task of the Christian teacher in construing and communicating the Scriptures. When compiling his *Retractationes* in 426–27, Augustine discovered that he had earlier left *De doctrina Christiana* (*DDC*) incomplete, up to 3.25.35. Thereupon he completed the third book and added the fourth, making, as he says, three to aid the understanding of the Scriptures and the fourth their public presentation – a two-part exegetical and homiletic manual.[91]

There is general agreement that the first part of the work was completed early in Augustine's episcopate, by 397. This certainly holds for Bks. 1–2, which some scholars believe, partly on the evidence of a very early manuscript, may have first been issued separately. Others find no grounds for supposing that any of it was 'published' until it was completed in 426–27.[92] The attempt has also been made, unconvincingly to most minds, to fix the composition of the prologue in 426–27 rather than in the mid-390s.[93]

DDC has attracted an enormous literature from specialists in several disciplines. Book 4, on the proper eloquence of the Christian orator, need not concern us here, but we may note that Augustine takes Amos as an example of the eloquence of the OT prophets. He chose Amos because his prophecy allowed Augustine to concentrate on the way it was expressed, without having to bother with explaining its meaning. (The frequency of tropes in the prophets set a challenge to the expositor, although Augustine took comfort from the fact that the greater the figurative obscurity, the more delightful the enjoyment of elucidation.) And since the LXX was more enigmatic, because more figurative, than the original, he would use Jerome's Vulgate translation of Amos.[94]

Elsewhere also in *DDC*, the OT is drawn in illustratively rather than addressed exegetically in its own terms, although at a few points the OT is clearly in Augustine's sights. Having distinguished between things (or realities, *res*) and signs (*signa*), he devotes most of Book I to the former. He uses *res* here of things that do not signify something else, whereas *signa* are things used to signify something. So Book 1 deals with the realities of the Christian creed which are to be enjoyed or used or both.

In Book 2, after distinguishing various kinds of signs, he fastens on words – the main signs by which human beings express themselves, both orally and in written letters, which are thus signs of signs.[95] Scripture is

---

91 *Retractationes* 2.4 (30).1 (PL 32, 631).

92 See J. Martin's discussion in CCL 32, vii–xix.

93 C. Mayer, "'Res per signa'. Der Grundgedanke des Prologs in Augustins Schrift *De doctrina christiana* und das Problem seiner Datierung", *REAug* 20 (1974) 100–112.

94 *DDC* 4.7.15–21 (PL 34, 96–8). Cf. M. Moreau, "Sur un commentaire d'Amos 6, 1–6", *S. Augustin et la Bible* (BTT 3; 1986) 313–22.

95 Among the extensive literature, see C. Kirwan, *Augustine* (London/New York: Routledge 1989) 35–55; J. M. Rist, *Augustine* (Cambridge: Cambridge UP 1994) 23–40; B. D. Jackson, "The Theory of Signs in St. Augustine's *De doctrina Christiana*", *REAug* 15 (1969) 9–49; the massive enterprise of C. P. Mayer, *Die Zeichen in der geistigen Entwicklung und in der Theologie des jungen Augustinus* (Cassiciacum 24:1; Würzburg: Augustinus-Verlag 1969); *Die Zeichen ... in der Theo-*

composed of signs, in one language originally but dispersed in numerous translations. But the reader of the Scriptures is beset with many and varied obscurities and ambiguities. It cannot be unimportant that this is the first marker Augustine erects when he comes to speak of the Scriptures. That this is so is confirmed by his proceeding immediately to discern this state of affairs as God-given. Although hardly anything is found in Scriptures' obscurities which is not plainly expressed elsewhere, the Holy Spirit has so healthily modulated (*modificavit*) the Bible that its clarity satisfies the hungry while its lack of clarity humbles the proud, who have to work at understanding it, and counters the disdain that regards the obvious as worthless. To Augustine it is well evident that the discovery accomplished only with difficulty is the more pleasurable, and that comprehension is more readily secured through similitudes than literal directness.

Augustine's example is Cant 4:2, "Your teeth are like a flock of shorn (sheep), coming up from washing, which all bear twins and not a barren one among them". This extended similitude tells one nothing that is not conveyed in plain words elsewhere.

> Nevertheless, in a strange way, I contemplate the saints more pleasantly when I envisage them as the teeth of the Church, cutting off men from their errors and transferring them to her body after their hardness has been softened as if by being bitten and chewed. I recognize them more pleasantly as shorn sheep having put aside the burdens of the world like so much fleece, and as ascending from the washing, which is baptism, all to create twins, which are the two precepts of love, and I see no one of them sterile of this holy fruit.[96]

This whole passage is highly revealing of the true face of Augustine the interpreter of Holy Scripture. It is not so much the exquisite ingenuity (a common enough quality, after all, when expositors set to work on the Song of Songs) as the unabashed delight he takes in it and the playfulness with which he deploys it. The preference for the figurative over the literal reminds us of his exegetical apprenticeship at Ambrose's feet in Milan – "the letter kills, the spirit gives life" – and the Platonic reinforcement, in both master and pupil, of the instinctive tendency to eschew the surface meaning in favour of the depth it both points to and conceals. As he commented on Psalm 104 (105), "let us commend in the body of this psalm its soul lurking hidden, as it were, that is, the inner understanding hidden in the externals of its words".[97] Such an attitude helps to explain why Augustine expended such energy on the OT in particular, and why the often fanciful outcome so often conveys a certain spiritual gravitas – for it is expressive of a profoundly spiritual vision of heaven and earth.

Before proceeding further with Augustine's guidance in *DDC* on the deciphering of *signa*, we must touch on a couple of prolegomena which he deals with in the work, beginning with the canon of Scripture. Augustine

---

logie Augustins II. *Die Antimanichäische Epoche* (Cassiciacum 24:2; 1974); more briefly on the Stoic background, M. L. Colish, *The Stoic Tradition from Antiquity to the Early Middle Ages* 2. *Stoicism in Christian Latin Thought through the Sixth Century* (Studies in the History of Christian Thought 35; Leiden: E. J. Brill 1985) 181–86.

[96] *DDC* 2.6.7–8 (PL 34, 38–39), tr. Robertson 37–38.

[97] *En. in Ps.* 104 (105). 35 (PL 37, 1402).

endorsed an OT canon based on the LXX, including those books known today as deutero-canonical or apocryphal but which Augustine knew that the Jews did not recognize.[98] He held to this despite a change of mind about the authorship of Wisdom and Ecclesiasticus.[99] In determining canonicity the criterion is acceptance by the majority of catholic churches, especially those of apostolic origin. Acknowledging differences on the canon, Augustine gives greatest weight to books recognized by all churches, but in a case of disagreement he cannot choose between the greater number of churches and churches of greater authority.[100]

The issue of *text and translation* is more complicated. It is well known that Augustine elevated the LXX above the Hebrew of the OT. The emending of Latin versions is to be carried out by reference to the Greek, "among which as far as the Old Testament is concerned, the authority of the Seventy translators excels".[101] Although there are indications that he may not wholly credit the tradition of the seventy-two working in hermetically sealed isolation from each other,[102] his conviction that the LXX's inspiration stands on a par with the Hebrew writers' is unshaken:

> For the very same Spirit that was in the prophets when they uttered their messages was at work also in the Seventy scholars when they translated them. And the Spirit could have said something else as well, with divine authority, as if the prophet had said both things, because it was the same Spirit that said both. The Spirit could also have said the same thing in a different way. ... He could also have omitted something, or added something, so that it might be shown in this way too that the task of translation was achieved ... by the power of God which filled and directed the mind of the translator ...
>
> ... it follows that anything in the Hebrew text that is not found in that of the Seventy translations is something which the Spirit of God decided not to say through the translators but through the prophets. Conversely, anything in the Septuagint that is not in the Hebrew texts is something which the same Spirit preferred to say through the translators, instead of through the prophets, thus showing that the former and the latter alike were prophets.[103]

A reason for such a remarkable position is not to be found in Augustine's ignorance of Hebrew. (He knew some Punic, a cognate Semitic language, and occasionally used it to elucidate a Hebrew term.) For he never attained fluency in Greek either. This much is clear, although scholarly opinions have accorded him varying degrees of competence short of fluency. He could use Greek to verify a biblical text, and in his latter years he stretched himself to cope with some patristic Greek, but he never enjoyed easy access; "it is likely that

---

[98] *City of God* 18.3.6; listed in *DDC* 2.8.13 (PL 34, 41). The additional books were not to be read as church lections, *Letter* 64.3 (PL 33, 233).

[99] *DDC* 2.8.13 (PL 34, 41) with *Retract.* 2.4 (30).2 (PL 32, 631); *City of God* 17.20.1.

[100] *DDC* 2.8.12 (PL 34, 40–41). Cf. La Bonnardière, "Le Canon des divines Écritures", *S. Augustin et la Bible* (BTT 3; 1986) 287–301; R. Hennings, *Die Briefwechsel zwischen Augustinus und Hieronymus und ihr Streit um den Kanon des Alten Testaments und die Auslegung von Gal. 2, 11–14* (Suppl. to VC 21; Leiden: E. J. Brill 1994) 110–15, 200–217.

[101] *DDC* 2.15.22 (PL 34, 46).

[102] Ibid. ("they are said", "it is related", "even if they conferred"); *City of God* 18.43 ("even supposing that ... they had compared the words of their several translations").

[103] *City of God* 18.43; tr. H. Bettenson, *Augustine, City of God* (Harmondsworth: Penguin Books 1972) 821–22.

the average theology graduate today knows at least as much Greek as did the great bishop of Hippo".[104]

The authority of the LXX for Augustine rested on consensus, as well as on its inspiration. This was first "the consensus of so many venerable and learned translators" – even if they had collaborated rather than worked independently.[105] But more important was the consensus of the churches:

> The church has received this Septuagint as if it were the only translation; the Greek-speaking Christian peoples use it and most are not aware whether any other exists ... it is the judgement of the churches of Christ that no one person (i. e. Jerome) should be preferred over the authority of so large a body of men (i. e. the Seventy).[106]

In addition, Augustine was pastorally sensitive to the conservatism of congregations familiar with a translation based on the LXX and liable to be suspicious of novelty in such an important foundation of faith.[107]

All of these arguments, and others besides, featured in the correspondence between Augustine and Jerome on translating the OT that began in 395 with Augustine's *Letter* 28 and lasted a decade, giving way after *Letter* 82 of 405 to other more pressing church concerns.[108]

Yet, troubling as Augustine found Jerome's abandonment of the LXX for the *veritas hebraica*, in *DDC* he still commends the learning of Hebrew as well as Greek in order to make one's way through the number and variety of the Latin translations.[109] An alternative way of coping with divergent translations is "to consult the versions of those who have bound themselves closely to the words".[110]

At this juncture Augustine identifies no such literal or verbatim translations, but soon afterwards names the *Itala* as his preference, both for its adherence to the words and its clarity of meaning.[111] If only what Augustine meant by the *Itala* were so clear! Some scholars have emended the text to remove it, others improbably have identified it as Jerome's Vulgate, but most plausibly it was an earlier translation made in Italy, or at least current there, and brought back to Africa by Augustine.[112]

---

104 G. Bonner in CHB I (1970) 550. See Marrou, Saint Augustin (1958) 27–37, and 631–37; P. Courcelle, *Les lettres grecques en Occident de Macrobe à Cassiodore* (Paris: E. de Boccard ²1948) 137–94.

105 *DDC* 2.15.22 (PL 34, 46).

106 *City of God* 18.43.

107 Cf. Bonner in CHB I (1970) 545–46.

108 See W. J. Sparrow-Simpson, *The Letters of St Augustine* (Handbooks of Christian Literature; London: SPCK 1919) 216–39; J. N. D. Kelly, *Jerome. His Life, Writings, and Controversies* (London: Duckworth 1975) 217–20, 263–72; Hennings, Briefwechsel (1994) esp. 29–45; G. Jouassard, "Reflexions sur la position de saint Augustin relativement aux Septante dans sa discussion avec saint Jérôme", *REAug* 2 (Mémorial Gustave Bardy I; 1956) 93–9. The whole correspondence between the two is edited by J. Schmid in Florilegium Patristicum 22 (Bonn: Peter Hanstein 1930). See also now A. Fürst, "*Veritas Latina*. Augustins Haltung gegenüber Hieronymus' Bibelübersetzungen", *REAug* 40 (1994) 105–26.

109 *DDC* 2.11.16 – 13.19 (PL 34, 42–44).

110 *DDC* 2.13.19 (PL 34, 44).

111 *DDC* 2.15.22 (PL 34, 46).

112 Bonner in CHB I (1970) 545; cf. Pontet, L'exégèse (1945) 226–27; Combès/Farges *ad loc.*, BAug 11, 574–75.

We must envisage Augustine working with different texts of the Bible throughout his life. In his *Letter* 261 to Audax, of indeterminate but presumably later date, he told the *grammaticus:*

> I do not have Jerome's translation of the Psalter from the Hebrew. I myself have not made a translation but have corrected several faults of the Latin codices from Greek manuscripts. I have perhaps thereby made the text better than it was, but not what it should be. Even now when I am struck while reading by defects that escaped me at that time, I correct them by comparing the codices.[113]

De Bruyne has examined Augustine's revisions of the Psalter in detail, from which it may be concluded that he used a Milanese Psalter similar to that of Verona, and from about 415 also took account of the Gallican Psalter of Jerome.[114] But the special status of the LXX was never undermined. Although in his later works he paid more attention to Jerome's OT translations, he tended to accept Jerome's renderings alongside those based on the LXX.[115] But in a latish work such as the *Questions on the Heptateuch*, the use made of the LXX remains minimal.

In addition to the original languages, Augustine also commends in *DDC* other studies such as history and geography for the elucidation of Scripture. Yet his conclusion is characteristically limiting – and allegorical: just as what the Israelites got by spoiling the Egyptians was less than they later acquired at Jerusalem, so too "all the knowledge, which is certainly useful, collected from the books of pagan writers, when compared with the knowledge conferred by the divine Scriptures. For whatever one learns elsewhere is condemned there if it is harmful, and is found there if it is beneficial".[116] Such an attitude separated him from Jerome, and helps to explain the inconsistencies and limitations of his biblical scholarship.

Augustine's biblical expositions, especially in sermon and homily, are also animated far more than Jerome's by the need to edify the faithful. The importance of this for Augustine becomes evident in the discussion of figurative signs which occupies most of Bk. 3 of *DDC*. After touching on the typically Jewish servitude of taking signs for the realities themselves, he propounds a method for determining whether a work or expression is literal or figurative: "anything in the divine Word that can be literally referred neither to correct behaviour nor to the truth of the faith you should recognize as figurative". For "Scripture teaches nothing but love, and condemns nothing but lust (*cupiditatem*)".[117] Augustine proceeds to spell out what these criteria entail for understanding figurative signs. Interspersed with this guidance are a number of commonsense rules of thumb, bearing particularly on diversity of cultures and contexts.

---

113 *Letter* 261.5 (PL 33, 1077).

114 "Saint Augustin réviseur de la Bible", in *Miscellanea Agostiniana* II (1931) 521–606 at 544–78; A. Solignac in DictS XII (1986) 2566–7. De Bruyne also covers more briefly Ecclesiasticus (578–85), the Heptateuch (585–91) and Job (591–94).

115 So concludes La Bonnardière, "Augustin a-t-il utilisé la 'Vulgata' de Jérôme?", *S. Augustin et la Bible* (BTT 3; 1986) 303–12.

116 *DDC* 2.42.63 (PL 34, 64–65).

117 *DDC* 3.10.14, 15 (PL 34, 71).

Things which seem disreputable to the inexperienced, whether merely spoken or actually done on the part of God or of human beings whose sanctity is commended to us, are all figurative; their hidden kernels are to be extracted from the husks to nourish love.[118]

But since desire or intention is the critical factor, "what is normally shameful in other persons is, in a divine or a prophetic person, the sign of an important reality. There is every difference between union with a prostitute in moral abandon and in the foreshadowing of the prophet Hosea".[119]

Augustine arrives at the following general comment on the OT:

Therefore, although all or almost all of the things recorded in the books of the Old Testament are to be taken not only literally but also figuratively, there are those taken literally by the reader because done by individuals who are commended but which are alien to the practice of worthy people who observe God's commands after the coming of the Lord. In these cases the reader must refer the figure to his understanding but not translate the act itself into behaviour. Many things were at that time done honourably (*officiose*) which now can be done only lustfully.[120]

This judgement follows Augustine's discussion of David's condemnation for his adulterous passion for Bathsheba, but not for having many wives. It reveals again that drive to make consistent and acceptable sense of Scripture which led Augustine not only to a quasi-modern appeal to cultural relativism but also into hazardous rationalizations and above all into tireless figurative spiritualizing to save the appearances.

In completing *DDC* in the mid-420s, Augustine commended the seven rules of Tyconius as aids for penetrating the hidden recesses of Scripture.[121] This nonconformist Donatist layman, who flourished ca. 370–90, was excommunicated for his departures from Donatist orthodoxy, without, it seems, ever becoming a catholic.[122] His commentary on the Apocalypse of John, now recoverable only in fragments, was a powerful influence in Western medieval interpretation, and Augustine's indebtedness to him at a formative stage of his theological development, after his return to Africa in 388, was considerable.[123] Tyconius' *Book of Rules*, his only work to survive intact, is the first Latin (i.e. Western Christian) treatise on biblical interpretation.

Augustine is careful to stress that Tyconius remained in error as a Donatist and exaggerated the usefulness of his rules, which by no means clarified all of Scripture's obscurities (as Tyconius' own Apocalypse commentary demon-

---

[118] *DDC* 3.12.18 (PL 34,72–73).

[119] Ibid.

[120] *DDC* 3.22.32 (PL 34,78).

[121] *DDC* 3.30.42–37.56 (PL 34,81–90). For the text of Tyconius' *Liber regularum* (CPL 709), see PL 18, 15–66; F.C. Burkitt (ed.), *The Book of Rules of Tyconius* (TaS 3:1; Cambridge: UP 1894), and W.S. Babcock, *Tyconius, The Book of Rules* (SBL Texts and Translations 31, Early Christian Literature Ser. 7; Atlanta: Scholars Press 1989). Babcock reproduces Burkitt's text, with ET. I cite the work as *LR* from Burkitt's edition.

[122] On Tyconius see A. Mandouze, *Prosopographie chrétienne du Bas-Empire* 1. *Prosopographie de l'Afrique chrétienne (303–533)* (Paris: Éditions du CNRS 1982) 1122–27, and literature noted by Babcock xii. On the *Liber regularum*, P. Bright, *The Book of Rules of Tyconius. Its Purpose and Inner Logic* (Notre Dame, IN: University of Notre Dame Press 1988), C. Kannengiesser/P. Bright, *A Conflict of Christian Hermeneutics in Roman Africa: Tyconius and Augustine* (Colloquy 58; Berkeley, CA: Center for Hermeneutical Studies 1989).

[123] See, for example, Markus, Saeculum (1970) 115–22.

strated). Yet the attraction for Augustine of the seven rules is inescapable, and their importance will be immediately obvious to readers of this essay in the light of much that has been presented above. Tyconius offered

> keys and windows into the secrets of the law ... certain mystical rules which hold for the recesses of the whole law and make the treasures of the truth invisible to some people. If the rationale of these rules is accepted ..., whatever is closed will be opened and whatever is obscure made luminous, so that anyone traversing the immense forest of prophecy guided by these rules like tracks of light will be preserved from going astray.[124]

Four of the seven rules are concerned with parts and whole. The first is "Concerning the Lord and his Body", whereby, as Augustine puts it, a transition takes place from the head to the body or vice versa without change of person. When a speaker describes himself as both a bridegroom and a bride (Isa 61:10), the interpreter has to determine which applies to Christ the head and which to his body the church.[125] The counterpart to this rule is the seventh, on the devil and his body, which is given twice as much space by Augustine. The address to Lucifer in Isa 14:12 can be understood only partly of the devil himself, for it is his body that is cast down upon earth, although he is in his body.[126]

The second rule, entitled "Concerning the Bipartite Body of the Lord", points, says Augustine, to the mixed character of the church and hence should have been called "Concerning the True and Mixed (or Counterfeit) Body of the Lord". The woman speaking in Cant 1:5 says "I am black and beautiful" because of "the temporal unity of good and bad fish within the same net". Authentic and hypocrite similarly appear together in Isa 42:16-17.[127] Rule four deals with "species and genus", seen, for example, when Scripture mentions a particular city or nation in a manner applicable to the whole human race.[128] Augustine discusses at length how Scripture switches without explicit warning between carnal and spiritual Israel, requiring vigilance in the reader and affording benefit thereby.

> The elevated prophetic style, while speaking to or about the carnal Israel, imperceptibly switches to the spiritual, and while speaking of or to the latter, still seems to be speaking of or to the former – not spitefully begrudging us understanding of the Scriptures but therapeutically exercizing our understanding.[129]

---

124 *DDC* 3.30.43 (PL 34,82); *LR* prol. (Burkitt 1). Augustine's quotation varies only slightly from Burkitt's critical text of Tyconius. My translation omits *visibiles* ("make visible the treasures ..."), which virtually all the MSS lack (see CCL 32,103 *ad loc.*), but editions have generally included. Starting from the influence of this (apparent) intrusion, Kannengiesser, Conflict (1989) 3-7, exaggerates Augustine's misreading, or misrepresentation, of Tyconius. In particular, *obtinent* (here 'hold for'; cf. Babcock's 'obtain in') can hardly mean 'withhold' or the equivalent to 'make invisible', but only something like 'apply to, hold true for'. At one point (6) KANNENGIESSER uses 'govern', which is not far from the mark. His translation 'withhold' was challenged at the Colloquy; see Conflict (1989) 40,70-72.

125 *DDC* 3.31.44 (PL 34,82); *LR* I (Burkitt 1-3).

126 *DDC* 3.37.55 (PL 34,88); *LR* VII (Burkitt 70-71).

127 *DDC* 3.32.45 (PL 34,82-83); *LR* II (Burkitt 8-10).

128 *DDC* 3.34.47 (PL 34,84); *LR* IV (Burkitt 31).

129 *DDC* 3.34.49 (PL 34,85).

Or again things said about Solomon may become clear only when related to Christ or the church of which he is part.[130]

Of the three remaining rules, the fifth, "Concerning Times", still bears on parts and wholes, for one of the ways it operates is through synecdoche: by inclusive counting (as we might put it) "after six days" may be the same as "after eight days".[131] This rule also applies to special numbers 7, 10, 12 and their multiples. "Seven times a day" means "always" (cf. Ps 118 (119):164; 33:2 (34:1)). Thus the rule has much wider application than to times.[132]

Rule six, on "Recapitulation", is invoked to resolve difficulties resulting from Scripture's departure from the strict sequence of events. Thus Gen 2:9 (the bringing forth of trees for the garden) refers to something that happened before God put the man in the garden, which is recorded in the previous verse. Likewise Gen 11:1 (the earth was of one language) harks back to the situation before the division into nations chronicled in Genesis 10.[133]

Finally we must note the third rule, "Concerning Promises and Law", which Augustine disposes of fairly rapidly. It is not so much a rule to solve questions as itself a major question, perhaps better called "Concerning the Spirit and the Letter" (with explicit mention of his earlier treatise of this title) or "Concerning Grace and Command". Tyconius laboured under the disadvantage of preceding the Pelagian dispute, "which has made us", says Augustine, "much more alert and attentive" towards the Scriptures than he was. Hence the inadequacies of this rule, such as Tyconius' failure to recognize that faith is a gift of God.[134]

Augustine's presentation of Tyconius' seven rules completes the longer part of *DDC* which is devoted to finding out (*inveniendo*) what is to be rightly understood from the Scriptures. The interest of this chapter is Augustine rather than Tyconius, and hence with what the former made of the latter rather than with the latter's teaching in its own right.[135] In these terms, "the extent to which Augustine's exegesis is in debt to the Book of Rules is remarkable", for Augustine "was always in search of universal principles that might help to remove subjectivity from spiritual exegesis".[136] Not least did Augustine share with Tyconius the conviction that the obscurity of much of the Bible was a good thing—intended by the Spirit, the author of all Scripture, to exercise the intuition of the expositor and to reward the seeking of those who

---

130 *DDC* 3.34.47 (PL 34, 84); *LR* IV (Burkitt 37–39).

131 *DDC* 3.35.50 (PL 34, 86); *LR* V (Burkitt 55–59).

132 *DDC* 3.35.51 (PL 34, 86); *LR* V (Burkitt 59). Tyconius calls these numbers *legitimi*, 'lawful' or 'proper'; cf. Babcock's 'specific'.

133 *DDC* 3.36.52–3 (PL 34, 86–87). These are Augustine's, not Tyconius', illustrations, revealing again his preoccupation with early Genesis.

134 *DDC* 3.33.46 (PL 34, 83). Augustine does less than justice to Tyconius, who not only talks of faith as given "through Christ", like the Spirit and grace, but also cites that most favoured of Augustine's anti-Pelagian proof-texts, "What have you that you did not receive?" (1 Cor 4:7); see *LR* III (Burkitt 18–19).

135 See n. 124 above for a comment to this question. KANNENGIESSER unconvincingly argues that for Tyconius the *regulae* were not guidelines for interpretation but structuring principles inherent in Scripture; see also Conflict (1989) 68–69.

136 H. CHADWICK in Kannengiesser/Bright, Conflict, 49, with many examples on 49–50.

refuse to remain at the level of appearances. That is to say, Tyconius' rules were made by Augustine to subserve the requirements of his instinctively Platonic exegetical bent.

At the same time to Tyconius is due, as well as to Africa's deep-seated Catholic-Donatist divide which he to some extent straddled, the heavily ecclesiological preoccupation of much of Augustine's OT exegesis. Throughout the rules Tyconius keeps returning to the theme of the bipartite church and interprets cities as dissimilar as Jerusalem and Nineveh and Tyre, as well as nations as different as Elam and Egypt, as figures of the church's bipartite character. Augustine will locate the mixed nature of the church in less visible differences than Tyconius, focussing more on the ambiguity of the apparently holy, but the community of concern is only too evident.

A magnificent start to the scientific collection and analysis of all of Augustine's citations of the OT has been made by ANNE-MARIE LA BONNARDIÈRE in a series of volumes covering Deuteronomy (1967), Joshua to Job, with 1 Esdras, Tobit, Judith and Maccabees (1960), Proverbs (1975), Jeremiah (1972), the twelve Minor Prophets (1964) and the Wisdom of Solomon (1970).[137] The completion of such a labour will doubtless be facilitated by computer technology.[138] These inventories produce their surprises, such as Augustine's minimal interest in Jeremiah, his personality and role in the history of God's ancient people.[139] On the other hand, Augustine makes remarkably heavy use of Proverbs and the Wisdom literature in general, in a variety of liturgical, catechetical, pastoral and apologetic contexts, as well as for the prefiguring of Christ by the personified Wisdom.[140] The letters recently first published by JOHANNES DIVJAK further confirm Augustine's predilection for these books.[141]

The availability of a full set of such analyses of the OT books would not ease the challenge of formulating some final comments on Augustine's use of the former Testament. We certainly must not miss the sheer vastness of his immersion in it. "No Western theologian before him had lived so much in Scripture, or taken so much from it as he".[142] But as we have just noticed, he drew on the OT very unevenly. PONTET can even say that his recourse to the OT would be strictly limited were it not for the Psalms, but this judgement relates to Augustine's sermons, which give an inadequate impression of his preoccupation with early Genesis, and happens also to underestimate his fondness for the Wisdom books.[143]

---

[137] LA BONNARDIÈRE, *Biblia Augustiniana;* all volumes published by Études Augustiniennes in Paris.

[138] For earlier attempts see De Bruyne, S. Augustin réviseur, *Misc. Agost.* II (1931) 522.

[139] LA BONNARDIÈRE, *Bibl. August. Le Livre de Jérémie* (1972) 77. Lamentations yields no citations and deuterocanonical Baruch only two isolated texts.

[140] *Le Livre des Proverbes* (1975) 189–90; cf. LA BONNARDIÈRE, "Les sentences des Sages dans la pastorale de saint Augustin", Kannengiesser (ed.), Jean Chrysostome et Augustin (1975) 175–98.

[141] Over a third of OT references are to the four Wisdom books; ed. Divjak et al., BAug 46 B, 583.

[142] A. Harnack, *History of Dogma* (tr. N. Buchanan; 1894–99), V (repr. New York: Dover Publications 1961) 98.

[143] L'exégèse (1945) 581.

Yet uneven use does not indicate any departure on Augustine's part from the common convictions of the early Church of the plenary inspiration of the whole of Scripture and its freedom from error.[144] This persuasion of the God-given unity of the Bible is responsible for what might be called the 'butterfly method' in his exegesis – his flitting from text to text, apparently arbitrarily, in search of illumination. The connections too often seem fanciful, yet manage to elicit admiring smiles at their delightful ingenuity.

For our purposes, the unity of the Bible determines the relationship between the Testaments. Put at its boldest, "For what is the 'Old Testament' but a concealed form of the new? And what is the 'New Testament' but the revelation of the old?"[145] The OT is replete with 'figures', 'mysteries', 'sacraments', 'signs', 'shadows', 'forms' etc. of the NT. Augustine uses a rich vocabulary to portray the symbolic foreshadowing character of the OT. Indeed, he will call the whole of the Bible "the books of the divine sacraments" or "the Scripture of mysteries",[146] but it is chiefly in the expositions of the OT that the cracking of a code comes most frequently to mind in reading Augustine.[147] One repeatedly senses the expectation of the congregation waiting for their bishop to conjure up Christ and his Church in the most unpromising of OT passages.

Thus Augustine normally works with a two-level understanding of Scripture. The terms may vary – literal, historical, carnal, etc. on the one side, and allegorical, spiritual, prophetic, mystical, etc. on the other. He seems most at ease in allegorizing when the literal-historical meaning has first been affirmed. Thus he could say of his treatment of paradise in the *City of God:*

> This is the kind of thing that can be said by way of allegorical interpretation of paradise; and there may be other more valuable lines of interpretation. There is no prohibition against such exegesis, provided that we also believe in the truth of the story as a faithful record of historical fact.[148]

Precisely why the two belong together in Augustine's mind is open to further investigation. Certainly they are not related as they would be in the Reformation, in the insistence that the literal, i.e. grammatical-historical, meaning is the spiritual meaning. Nor is the common relationship between them in Augustine that of some more modern discussion, as in the Pontifical Biblical Commission's recent document, *The Interpretation of the Bible in the Church:*

> The spiritual sense can never be stripped of its connection with the literal sense. The latter remains the indispensable foundation. Otherwise, one could not speak of the "fulfilment" of Scripture. Indeed, in order that there be fulfilment, a relationship of continuity and of conformity is essential.[149]

---

[144] See Polman, Word of God (1961).

[145] *City of God* 16.26; cf. similarly 4.33, 5.18. On the unity of OT and NT, see Pontet, L'exégèse (1945) 305–84; Strauss, Schriftgebrauch (1959) 68–72.

[146] *On the Advantage of Believing* 17.35 (PL 42, 91); *Against Julian* 6.7.20 (PL 44, 834).

[147] C. Couturier, "*Sacramentum* et *mysterium* dans l'oeuvre de saint Augustin", H. Rondet et al., Études augustiniennes (1953) 161–332, esp. 195–225 on the OT.

[148] *City of God* 13.21; tr. Bettenson 535. "Like most ancient writers, Augustine assumes that even matter-of-fact narratives are polyvalent"; Chadwick in DBI 67. Cf. Strauss, Schriftgebrauch (1959) 126–48.

[149] (Rome: Libreria Editrice Vaticana 1993) 82.

It is precisely "the relationship of continuity and conformity" that one too often misses in Augustine.

Yet the spiritual meaning has experienced a minor comeback in the latter twentieth century. At a time when reaction against the aridities of the historico-critical approach has fostered, and been fostered by, what at times seems almost a free-for-all in biblical hermeneutics, marked frequently by a blatant disregard for the literal sense intended by the writer, Augustine must appear less alien. There is after all no doubting the depths of spirituality and the profoundly Christ-centred and church-centred theology that his OT exegesis served.

3. The Influence of Augustine's Old Testament Exegesis and Hermeneutics

Studies: R. E. McNally, *The Bible in the Early Middle Ages* (Woodstock Papers 4; Westminster, MD: Newman Press 1959); B. Smalley, *The Study of the Bible in the Middle Ages* (Oxford: Basil Blackwell ²1952); CHB 2 (1969; repr. 1980); H. de Lubac, *Exégèse médiévale. Les quatre sens de L'Écriture* I–IV (Paris: Aubier 1959–64); C. Spicq, *Esquisse d'une histoire de l'exégèse latine au moyen âge* (Paris 1944).

So all-pervasive was Augustine's influence on Christian thought and writing in the medieval West that in short compass one cannot avoid selectivity in identifying the impact of his handling of the OT. Its range is evident in unexpected directions. His sole extended treatment of 1 and 2 Samuel and then only of a few chapters, in *City of God* 17, has been shown to have become a source for numerous medieval commentaries on Samuel.[150] The derivation of Adam's name from the four corners of the world was probably mediated to the Middle Ages by Augustine from a Jewish apocryphal source.[151]

There is no doubting the wide dissemination of the major works – the Psalms exposition, *De Genesi ad litteram* and *Quaestiones in Heptateuchum*. André Wilmart's survey of "La tradition des grands ouvrages de saint Augustin" lists 368 MSS of the *Enarrationes in Psalmos*, compared with 258 for the *Confessions*, 233 for *On the Trinity* and 376 for the *City of God*.[152] Although many of the *Enarrationes* MSS are partial copies, it is after all by far Augustine's bulkiest work.

It continued to be copied (even into the era of printing) despite the production of numerous other Psalms commentaries which drew heavily on Augustine's. The exposition of Psalms 100–150 by Prosper of Aquitaine in the mid-fifth century is little more than a condensation of Augustine (and he may have done the same for the rest of the Psalter).[153]

[150] J. Black, "*De Civitate Dei* and the Commentaries of Gregory the Great, Isidore, Bede and Hrabanus Maurus on the Book of Samuel", *Augustinian Studies* 15 (1984) 114–27.

[151] It occurs in, e.g., *Enarr. in Ps* 95 (96). 15 (PL 37, 1236); McNally, The Bible (1959) 26–27.

[152] In *Misc. Agost.* II (1931) 257–315 at 295–315.

[153] CPL 524; new edition in CCL 68 A (1972).

Cassiodorus's *Expositio Psalmorum*[154] was compiled by "borrowing light, in my usual fashion, from Augustine's light", so he tells us in commending the latter's commentary in his programmatic manual which had a wide influence on libraries and curricula in the medieval world.[155] Despite his fulsome praise of Augustine's collection,[156] Cassiodorus's own effort is jejune, primarily a literary exercise lacking the African father's rich vein of spirituality in exegesis.[157]

Despite such later expositions, Augustine's *Enarrationes* "restait justement l'autorité suprême dans l'Église occidentale".[158] Its place as the sole complete patristic treatment of the Psalter was further strengthened by the special importance of the Psalms for the *lectio divina* and *opus Dei* of monastic culture.[159] Augustine was by far the most heavily used exegetical quarry of the Carolingian commentary compilers,[160] but more significant still was the use of material from him in the standard Bible commentary of the central and later Middle Ages, the *Glossa Ordinaria*.[161] The gloss on the Psalter was, it seems, largely the work of Anselm of Laon (d. 1117), a pupil of Anselm at Bec and the key figure in the formation of the complete *Glossa* at Laon.[162] In turn his gloss on the Psalter was expanded by Peter Lombard in his *Magna Glosatura*.[163] Peter was an ardent disciple of Augustine.

"A history of commentaries in the Middle Ages is still to be written."[164] No listing comparable to WILMART's for the other "grands ouvrages" yet exists of the MSS of Augustine's *De Genesi ad litteram*, although the job is being tackled country by country in the Vienna Academy's series, *Die Handschriftliche Überlieferung der Werke des Heiligen Augustinus*. Yet is clear that it was the Genesis commentary most exploited by the Carolingians,[165] and

---

154 CPL 900; CCL 97–98 (1958).

155 *Institutiones* 1.4.1–2 (PL 70, 1115), critical edition by R. A. B. MYNORS (Oxford: Clarendon Press 1937).

156 *Expos. Psalmorum*, praef. (CCL 97, 3).

157 P. RICHÉ, *Education and Culture in the Barbarian West, Sixth through Eighth Centuries* (1972; tr. J. J. Contreni; Columbia, SC: University of South Carolina Press 1976) 166–67.

158 Wilmart, La tradition (1931) 300.

159 On this see the fine portrait by the lamented J. LECLERCQ, *The Love of Learning and the Desire for God* (tr. C. Misrahi; New York: Fordham University Press 1961).

160 For a list of their Psalms commentaries see McNally, The Bible (1959) 100–101.

161 For an introduction see G. R. EVANS, *The Language and Logic of the Bible: the Earlier Middle Ages* (Cambridge: Cambridge UP 1984) 37–47, 173–76; also Smalley, The Study (1952) esp. 46–66, and in TRE 13 (1984) 452–57; and introduction to the facsimile reprint of edition of Strasbourg, ca. 1480, 4 vols. (ed. M. T. Gibson/K. Froehlich; Turnhout: Brepols 1992).

162 For his Psalms commentary, PL 116, 193–696; A. WILMART, "Un commentaire des Psaumes restitué à Anselme de Laon", *RTAM* 8 (1936) 325–44.

163 Psalms commentary, PL 191, 55–1296. One feature of the *Enarrationes in Psalmos* that was not influential in the medival period was its title, which was first given by Erasmus (Wilmart, La tradition (1931) 295, 313 n. 10). This was not known by N. M. HÄRING, "Commentary and Hermeneutics", R. L. BENSON/G. CONSTABLE (eds.), *Renaissance and Renewal in the Twelfth Century* (Oxford: Clarendon Press 1982) 173–200 at 174.

164 Häring, Commentary (1982) 199; cf. Smalley, The Study (1952) 185: "The later middle ages is largely unexplored territory from the point of view of Bible studies".

165 McNally, The Bible (1959) 43, 64, with listing on 95–96, including Angelomus of Luxeuil (ca. 850), on whose OT commentaries see M. L. W. LAISTNER, *The Intellectual Heritage of the Early Middle Ages* (ed. C. G. Starr; Ithaca, NY: Cornell University Press 1957) 181–201.

that the gloss on Genesis and Exodus was largely composed from *De Genesi* and Augustine's *Quaestiones in Heptateuchum* by one Gilbert the Universal, a pupil of Anselm of Laon.[166] Another medieval biblical scholar rescued from obscurity by the late BERYL SMALLEY, Andrew of St. Victor who flourished in the mid-twelfth century, also made considerable use of the two works of Augustine just mentioned.[167]

Yet Augustine has been described as "less influential as a biblical commentator than Jerome, Ambrose, and Ambrosiaster".[168] JEAN LECLERCQ regards Origen, especially as Latinized by Jerome and Rufinus, as the most important patristic source of medieval biblical learning.[169] While it is undoubtedly true that Augustine's *De doctrina Christiana* enjoyed wide and long reception in the medieval centuries,[170] and that knowledge of Tyconius' *Liber regularum* was almost entirely dependent on Augustine's presentation of it in *DDC*,[171] Augustine's book was read far more for its case for a Christian rhetoric (Bk. 4) and its bearing on the relation between secular and sacred studies than for its guidance on interpreting literal and figurative signs.

Augustine only very rarely, and in early writings, speaks of *four senses* of Scripture,[172] but he has nevertheless been credited with being the chief transmitter of this notion to the Middle Ages.[173] More securely his contribution should be discerned in the more general legacy of patristic biblical study to later centuries, namely, the superiority of the spiritual sense of Scripture, which is so pervasive as to need no illustration or documentation.[174] We may couple with this the raising of larger questions that could be the work only of an exegete with the theological, philosophical and spiritual depths of Augustine. According to SMALLEY, Augustine's *DDC* bequeathed "a philosophy of Bible study ... St. Jerome gave the medieval scholar his text and his learned apparatus; St. Augustine told him what his aim should be" – and that

[166] Smalley, The Study (1952) 60–62, 226, and her articles in *RTAM* 7 (1935) 235–62, and 8 (1936) 24–64.

[167] Smalley, The Study (1952) 112–95 (esp. 126–32), 384 n., 388 n.

[168] H. CHADWICK in DBI 68.

[169] CHB 2 (1969/80) 194–95, but see the critical comment on this chapter by J. J. CONTRENI, "Carolingian Biblical Studies", U.-R. BLUMENTHAL (ed.), *Carolingian Essays* (Washington, DC: Catholic University of America Press 1983) 71–98 at 73 n. 6. Augustine's selective coverage may have influenced the medievals – hence perhaps the meagre attention paid to the OT prophetic books in the Carolingian era, otherwise prolific for Bible commentaries: so M. L. W. LAISTNER, *Thought and Letters in Western Europe A. D. 500 to 900* (revd. edit.; Ithaca, NY: Cornell University Press 1957) 301, confirmed by the lists in McNally, The Bible (1959) 102–04.

[170] Perhaps slightly exaggerated by ROBERTSON in his translation, xii–xvii; more cautiously, I. OPELT, "Materialien zur Nachwirkung von Augustins Schrift De doctrina christiana", JAC 17 (1974) 64–73.

[171] Burkitt, xx–xxiv.

[172] *On the Advantage of Believing* 3.5–8 (PL 42, 68–71) – "One isolated text" (Chadwick in DBI 66); *De Genesi ad litteram imperf.* 2.5 (PL 34, 222), *De Genesi ad litteram* 1.1.1 (PL 34, 247).

[173] Evans, Language and Logic (1984) 114; McNally, The Bible (1959) 54: "The patristic work which furnished the Middle Ages with the most useful category of the biblical senses was Augustine's *De Genesi* ..., which provides a fourfold division".

[174] But see Smalley, The Study (1952) 303–05, for the tenacious influence of Augustine's insistence that "You shall not boil a kid in the milk of its dam" (Exod 23:19) had no literal meaning.

aim is inseparable from the reign of love of which *DDC* talks.[175] From another perspective, it was precisely the fusion of Platonic and Christian visions in *De Genesi ad litteram* that attracted medievals such as Honorius of Autun and Giles of Rome.[176]

In the words of another distinguished historian of Christian biblical wisdom, "Luther was one of the few exegetes since St. Augustine to give basic thought to the meaning of time and of history in the plan of God".[177] In that massive renewal of Bible study that was the sixteenth-century Reformation, it was Luther's continuing commitment to multiple senses, rather than Calvin's stricter historical exegesis, that could still reckon seriously with Augustine's treatment of the OT. Calvin consulted *De Genesi ad litteram*, *Quaestiones in Heptateuchum* and, most of all *Enarrationes in Psalmos*, but frequently faulted their author's speculative bent, excessive subtlety and obsession with the LXX.[178] Luther's lectures on the Psalms, on the contrary, display a sympathetic reception of the *Enarrationes* of Augustine, not least for his christological interpretation of the Psalter.[179] By comparison, Luther's use of *De Genesi ad litteram* and Augustine's other OT exegetical works is limited.

175 Ibid. 22–23. Cf., on a somewhat different level, the persisting preoccupation with his question of the relation between the two accounts of creation, ibid. 132.

176 See the papers by R. D. CROUSE and E. GIANNARELLI in *Congresso ... Atti* (see n. 179 below) III, 167–77, 179–87.

177 J. PELIKAN, *Luther the Expositor: Introduction to the Reformer's Exegetical Writings* (Luther's Works; St Louis: Concordia Publishing House 1959) 243.

178 L. SMITS, *Saint Augustin dans l'oeuvre de Jean Calvin* (Assen: Van Gorcum & Comp. N.V. 1956–58) I, 170–71, 180–81; II, 201–02, 230–38; J. M. J. LANGE VAN RAVENSWAAY, *Augustinus totus noster. Das Augustinverständnis bei Johannes Calvin* (FKDG 45; Göttingen: Vandenhoeck & Ruprecht 1990) 113–15.

179 F. HELD, "Augustins Enarrationes in Psalmos als exegetische Vorlage für Luthers erste Psalmenvorlesung", *TSK* 102 (1930) 1–30; E. G. RUPP, *The Righteousness of God. Luther Studies* (London: Hodder and Stoughton 1953) 140–57; H.-U. DELIUS, *Augustin als Quelle Luthers. Eine Materialsammlung* (Berlin: Evangelische Verlagsanstalt 1984), summarized in idem, "Zu Luthers Augustinrezeption", in *Congresso Internazionale su S. Agostino nel XVI Centenario della Conversione. Roma, 15–20 settembre 1986. Atti* (Studia Ephemeridis "Augustinianum" 26; Rome: Institutum Patristicum Augustinianum 1987) III, 241–56.

Chapter Twenty-two

Church and Synagogue as the Respective Matrix of the Development of an Authoritative Bible Interpretation An Epilogue

By Magne Sæbø, Oslo

To the modern mind *interpretation* may in the first instance mean a personal occupation. Similarly, the interpretation of the Bible has often or primarily been regarded as a work of independent individuals – no matter what their inevitable *Vorverständnis* might be.

In Antiquity, the interpreters were more dependent of their social matrix than is usually the case today. Surely there were always individual interpreters, but in comparison to the modern situation they were, to a much greater extent, integrated parts of institutions or bound by some collective body and, ideologically more heavily determined by old, received traditions.

1. Historiographically, this general state of affairs had to be considered seriously for the present History of Interpretation of the Hebrew Bible / Old Testament, in particular with regard to the beginnings and first parts of the history of biblical interpretation, among Jews as well as Christians. The aspect of ancient collectivity may open for various important perspectives. Here, three perspectives deserve special attention.

First, a History of biblical interpretation may have an appropriate *starting-point* in its own basis, which is the Hebrew Bible / Old Testament, the Holy Scripture of Jews and Christians. Since it was within the scriptures that became the Scripture that a process of *inner, scriptural interpretation* really started, a description of the interpretation history should not ignore this early beginning although it also, for certain reasons, may be called the 'pre-history' of biblical interpretation.[1] The Scripture in its final form, then, is not only to be regarded as the basis and object of all later interpretations, developed in manifold ways throughout the centuries; but to some degree, the Scripture is even in itself open to scrutiny of its own 'history of interpretation', since it in various ways involves interpretations – and reinterpretations – of traditions and, to some extent, constitutes the outcome of just the variegated 'inner-biblical exegesis'. This significant phenomenon of an initial biblical interpretation has been demonstrated by M. Fishbane, in the first chapter of the present

[1] Cf. further my discussion of this issue in the Prolegomenon, sect. 5, above.

volume. The fact of this perspective, however, actualizes another related one as well.

Second, on closer examination, it will appear that the makers of this early 'inner-biblical exegesis' for the most part were anonymous transmitters and interpreters of Israel's ancient and predominantly sacred traditions, behind which they remain indiscernible. They were but parts – though indeed most creative parts – of a dynamic and most complex process of transmission, of a *traditio,* and even more so as their transmission emerged within the framework of various institutions and different milieus in ancient Israel. What is now available as Scripture is the ultimate form, the *traditum* or the *Endgestalt,* of their anonymous and creative work, based on an immense variety of traditions, that finally were united in an authoritative *canon*, and that at about the same time had acquired a standard Hebrew – respectively Greek – *text*. This entangled process, being another part of the 'pre-history' of scriptural interpretation, has been described in the tripartite chapter two by E. Tov, J. Barton, and J. W. Wevers.

The literary documents of the textually and canonically stabilized Holy Scripture became, in other words, at the end of this initial stage, the unrivalled object and basis of all subsequent and richly varying biblical interpretation. At that very point, the history proper of 'biblical interpretation' may be said to have begun. But, at the same time, it is evident that the beginning and emergence of this early interpretation turned out to be a longer and more complex process than is commonly supposed – and not least so because of other factors that constitute yet another important perspective.

For, third, biblical interpretations implied also the question of *culture* – as they always do.[2] This significant perspective of biblical interpretation relates first to the broader socio-cultural and institutional context of the interpretations.[3] When external conditions changed considerably, the effect was often new interpretations, or at least a transformation of the traditional ones. All the time, biblical interpretations seem to have been in varying degrees dependent upon basic cultural and other environmental circumstances. On this occasion, therefore, the history of biblical interpretation has deliberately not been treated isolated or abstractly, with a biased focus on ideas, abstract notions and methodologies, but has been studied and described under due observation of its wider and varied *social and cultural setting*. At this point, the prime challenge has been to give utmost heed to an adequate balance of different indispensable factors.

The external setting of interpretation which so far has been described in

---

[2] M. Haran, "Midrashic and Literal Exegesis and the Critical Method in Biblical Research", *Studies in Bible,* ed. S. Japhet (ScrHier 31; 1986) 19–48, has paid attention to this aspect, cf. esp. 21: "The history of biblical exegesis is, in the main, a reflection of the history of western culture – the culture marked by Judeo-Christian tradition and roots of which derive from the Near East. ... While this document of faith [i. e. the Scripture], however, remained basically unchanged, ideas were not static and the methods of study also shifted with the course of time. Man's thought, therefore, constantly sought to realize itself through this sacred document".

[3] This aspect was touched upon in the Prolegomenon, sect. 7, and treated more elaborately in several chapters above.

general terms as socio-cultural and institutional in character, may be specified or differentiated somewhat further. For the cultural setting, in its widest sense, consisted not only of what might be called 'non-theological' factors, like those just mentioned, but included philosophical, ideological and theological elements as well. These elements, or 'intrinsic' cultural factors, that were most significant for the whole progress of biblical interpretation, played an important role also at the early stages of its history.

The 'intrinsic' cultural elements became not least manifest at the transition from the 'inner-biblical' interpretation to a broad 'extra-canonical' literary activity that emerged in close and partly interpretative proximity to the biblical literature. It gave rise to new forms and patterns of scriptural interpretation. In one specific way, this may be observed in the rich and multiform literature of the Qumran community, whose unique profile has been described by J. Maier in chapter three. In another and far more variegated way, it is also apparent in the vast areas of the Jewish so-called Apocryphal and Pseudepigraphical literature, with its diverse interpretations, as well as more specifically in the writings of Josephus. In the two main sections of chapter five, R. A. Kraft and S. Mason have made valuable observations on these parts of an early and most complex Jewish material, in particular regarding the question of 'scriptural – and canonical – consciousness'. These mutually different domains of early 'extra-canonical' literature display, on the one hand, a multifaceted picture of various links, or 'roots', to the Hebrew Scriptures, that were in the long process of becoming canonized, and on the other hand, a rich – both Hebrew and Greek – development of many new interpretations and creative combinations of received traditions.

Whereas it might be said that the afore-mentioned areas of Jewish 'post-biblical' literature 'carried on', to some degree, the biblical history of tradition, the case – or rather the whole cultural and spiritual situation – seemed to be nearly an opposite one for the great Jewry in Alexandria, the unsurpassed melting pot of Hellenistic culture at the time, as it also, more or less, was for Jews elsewhere in the Hellenistic Mediterranean region. For, 'looking back' on their Holy Scriptures, in particular the books of the Law, as having an unequalled religious and moral authority and so, in principle, being unchangeable as texts, the Hellenistic Jews had a very delicate problem, namely how to cope, under new and changed conditions, with their unchangeable received Scripture. Essentially, the problem was that of a proper understanding and interpreting of sacred and authorative texts, including the most intricate question of adapting an unchangeable Holy Writ in view of radical new circumstances. In other words, it was the problem of critically reflected *hermeneutics*, or, put in more popular terms, how to find a 'key' that might unlock the riddles of a sacred text without ruining its sanctity and authority.

It was, however, characteristic for the cultural situation in Alexandria that this hermeneutical problem was neither new nor unique, as F. Siegert has shown in chapter four. The problem had already been acknowledged and treated and was differently solved by Greek philosophers and their schools and by Alexandrian scholars, for whom many texts in the old and venerable works of Homer represented a similar challenging problem of understanding and explaining morally. Taught by the Greeks in various ways, Alexandrian Jewish scholars, and Philo more effectively—and selectively—than others, could *benefit from the philosophical and literary legacy of Athens*; Moses was met by Homer. Faced with various obscurities and cruces in Scripture some Jewish scholars—but not all—explored the possibility that some texts might have more than one sense: beyond their literal and historical sense they might, first of all, be read and interpreted *allegorically*; and in this and other ways, "the hermeneutics of multiple meanings" was developed and promoted.[4] As for both Greeks and Jews, their diverse hermeneutical endeavours represented an obvious *apologetic* interest.

It is, finally, a conspicuous fact that Philo, although being "one of the Sages of the Jewish community of Alexandria", became "a classic for the Christian Church",[5] and this expression of his great impact on early Christian theology is even more amazing as "the Rabbis, on the other hand, do not even record his name".[6] For the history of biblical interpretation, it may be of specific importance that the most extensive impact of his works was related to just the significant issue of *hermeneutics*—which forms the very 'heart' of the whole of this history, deeply connected with both 'interpretation', having a broader sense, as well as with the multifarious concrete 'exegesis'.[7] Through the impressive *Wirkungsgeschichte* of his works on the Christian side, Philo got to a unique position on the borderline of ancient Judaism and Christianity.

2. When the Alexandrian Jewish scholars—over some time from the 3rd century BCE onward—produced a Greek version of the Five books of the Law as well as of the other scriptures of the Hebrew Bible, they expressed through this so-called Septuagint version[8] another theological language and terminology, a new linguistic and conceptual coherence (*Begrifflichkeit*) in Greek that in many ways differed from the received Hebrew one. The duality of a Hebrew and a Greek *text* was later on paralleled by a duality in *canon* whereby the Alexandrian canon in various ways deviated from the Hebrew one.[9]

These remarkable dualities did in fact represent some grave tension in ancient Jewish culture, spirituality and theology. Yet, the deep spiritual division did not seem to cause a fundamental 'turning point' or any complete "shift of paradigm"[10] in Jewish thinking and tradition, as might be expected—and certainly not so in comparison with what soon happened through

---

[4] Cf. Siegert, chap. 4, sect. 4.0, above.

[5] So Siegert, ibid., stating that the works of Philo "would have been entirely lost had he not become a classic for the Christian Church".

[6] So Siegert, chap. 4, sect. 4.9.

[7] Cf. further the complementary essay by J. F. Procopé in chap. 12, esp. sect. 3.

[8] As for the puzzling question of Greek versions cf. above Wevers, chap. 2.3; further Siegert, chap. 4.2, on the *Epistle of Aristaeus* and its "hermeneutic programme".

[9] Regarding the complicated questions of an Alexandrian or Greek canon in relation to the Hebrew one see Barton, chap. 2.2, sect. 1 (with references to further lit.); cf. also J. Maier, "Zur Frage des biblischen Kanons im Frühjudentum im Licht der Qumranfunde", JBTh 3 (1988) 135–46.

[10] Cf. Th. S. Kuhn, *The Structure of Scientific Revolution* (Chicago 1962) x; 43–51.

the definitive 'parting of the ways' of early Judaism and rising Christianity.[11] Between these two communities of faith, an entirely new and far-reaching duality emerged – that also had a specific effect on the contrasting duality of Hebrew and Alexandrian Jewish tradition.

However, speaking only of 'Jewish' and 'Christian' in this respect is *stricte dictu* a generalization which to some degree anticipates a later situation and focuses on the two winners in the 'long run'. For, about the time of the 'parting of the ways' – beginning the main part B of the present History – there existed, as J. Fossum has shown in chapter six, a considerable plurality of 'groupings' and 'sects', among which the Samaritan community and some baptismal sects as well as various Jewish and Christian groupings may be specially mentioned.[12] This implies that around the time when the history of interpretation in a proper sense began – meaning the interpretation of the canonical Scripture of Hebrew Bible / Old Testament – it did not only take place within a context of a rich literary activity, be it 'qumranic' or 'apocryphal' or 'pseudepigraphical' in character, but its main socio-cultural and institutional framework turned out to be a most complex and variegated one, displaying a great pluriformity.

In this situation, two more factors that were of some importance for the further development deserve special notice.

First, after the catastrophy of the fall of the Second Temple, aggravated by the calamities of 'the Jewish war', resulting in the dispersion of the Jewish community from Jerusalem as their prime religious and cultural centre, the fundamental position of the Hebrew Bible – as well as that of the Synagogue as a religious and cultural meeting-place – increased considerably. The Scripture was not only the basic authority for the people, but it also became a unifying institution, being more or less a substitute for the loss of the Temple. The Jewish people became *am has-sēpher,* "the people of the Book".

Second, closely related to the increasingly central position of Scripture, also nationally and culturally, the established procedure of an accurate *transmission* of the written and not least of the oral Torah, dealt with by different schools,[13] managed to promote and develop the legacy of ancient Jewish interpretation of Scripture, combined with early rabbinic learning. As it was not bound to Jerusalem it could be pursued in the schools of the homeland as well as in Babylonia, in Alexandria as in other places of Jewish settlements. In this way, the ancient Jewish and early rabbinic tradition and learning, despite geographical and other differences, represented another unifying factor in the life of the people.

---

[11] Cf. recently J. D. G. Dunn (ed.), *Jews and Christians. The Parting of the Ways A. D. 70 to 135* (WUNT 66; Tübingen 1992).

[12] See further D. Kraemer, chap. 8, sect. 1. Cf. i. a. also L. L. Grabbe, *Judaism from Cyrus to Hadrian,* vol. 2. *Roman Period* (Minneapolis 1992 / London 1994); and, for an Israelitic perspective, idem, *Priests, Prophets, Diviners, Sages: A Socio-Historical Study of Religious Specialists in Ancient Israel* (Valley Forge, PA 1995).

[13] Cf. i. a. B. Gerhardsson, *Memory and Manuscript. Oral Tradition and Written Transmission in Rabbinic Judaism and Early Christianity* (ASNU 22; Uppsala 1961), esp. chap. 1–12; also, idem, *Tradition and Transmission in Early Christianity* (CNT 20; Lund / Copenhagen 1964).

When it comes, however, to the question of a more precise description of the bridge "from the inner-biblical interpretation to the early rabbinic exegesis", or what may be called the 'proto-rabbinic' interpretative activity, J. HARRIS has shown, in chapter seven, that there are many problems associated with this transition of tradition in ancient Jewish scriptural interpretation, not least because of a rather scanty existence of direct literary evidence in the field. Yet, in a more indirect way, some lines may be discernible, first of all with regard to the relatively similar ways and procedures in which one earlier and later responded to the challenges of "textual anomalies and irregularities" in Scripture,[14] or how one, in some adapting way, spelled out in concrete and practical details what in the Scripture was expressed in the form of short and condensed statutes and passages. It may, therefore, seem proper to assume a substantial degree of continuity between inner-biblical and later (proto-)rabbinic biblical interpretation. On this line, Hillel the Elder is usually granted a most prominent position. It will, however, remain a matter of dispute whether Hillel's renowned seven hermeneutical rules also are to be seen in dependence of other scholars or primarily as a basic innovation of his own, being then a fundamental 'turning point'. Anyway, "we cannot state definitively what Hillel's role was in the emergence of rabbinic exegesis".[15]

Harking back to the beginning of this section two and to the emerging duality of ancient Judaism and early Church, the 'parting of the ways' of Jews and Christians presented a completely new duality that generated a radical schism between them. More than a casual counterpart, representing just some theological variations, the rising Christianity 'doubled' the traditional Judaism in a way that caused a fundamental "shift of paradigm", meaning a fully different theological and cultural 'universe' and exhibiting a new referential system, grounded in a contrastive messianic faith;[16] by this it understood Jesus as Christ and his life, death, and resurrection to be in fulfilment of the Hebrew Scripture. What remains most important in this connection is that the deep break between Jews and Christians, rooted in a deep conviction of divergent faiths, was proved and expressed *hermeneutically*, by a divergent reading and interpreting of the same received Scripture.

An expression – and a characteristic token – of the ensuing theological segregation of Christians and Jews was the new Christian name of their common Holy Writ, 'Old Testament', being a term that originated in Paul's scriptural interpretation (2 Cor 3:14); it was used as a name for the Hebrew Bible for the first time by Melito of Sardis. Beyond the Hebrew canon as well as the later Alexandrian one, the Church, with some time, created a *double canon* of a fundamentally new kind that combined the 'Hebrew Bible' as the

---

[14] See Harris, chap. 7, sect. 3; cf. also D. Kraemer, chap. 8, sect. 1.

[15] So Harris, sect. 4. Summing up Harris says: "The rabbinic documents, for the most part, seek to create an image of unbroken exegetical continuity; at the same time, one transitional figure, Hillel, is associated with some form of exegetical shift, the precise nature of which seems to have been subject to dispute". Cf. Kraemer, ibid.

[16] Cf. SH. TALMON, "Typen der Messiaserwartung um die Zeitenwende", *Probleme biblischer Theologie* (G. v. Rad-FS, ed. H. W. Wolff; München 1971) 571–88; now also in idem, *Gesellschaft und Literatur in der Hebräischen Bibel. Ges. Aufsätze* 1 (Neukirchen-Vluyn 1988) 209–24.

'Old Testament' with a partly complementary and partly contrary 'New Testament'.[17] In spite of the segregation of Jews and Christians as contrastive communities of faith, the Church in this way established an integration of the Hebrew Bible / Old Testament and the New Testament.

When describing this most complex process of an emerging interpretation of the 'Old Testament' in the early Christian preaching and teaching in the various writings of the New Testament, H. Hübner, in chapter nine, makes a strong case for the essential difference between the Hebrew Bible as such and the 'Old Testament' as received in the New Testament, as *Vetus Testamentum in Novo receptum,* based on some fundamental "*theological* differences".[18] Further, focusing on the inner Jewish duality of Hebrew and Greek in the Alexandrian Septuagint, referred to above, he gives prominence to "this Greek Bible" as "*the Bible of the New Testament authors*".[19] With its New Testament the early Church added a new dimension to the previous tension between Hebrew and Greek/Hellenistic; and that impact was to have long-term effects.

By the theological shaping and selecting of the New Testament writings, the collective body of the early Church appeared as the determining context within which the emerging Christian scriptural interpretation developed. Likewise, on the other hand, the tradition of Jewish scriptural interpretation was fostered and developed within the Jewish cultural and religious community, represented first of all by the Synagogue, taken in a broad sense, including also the different 'academies' of Jewish and rabbinic learning. The respective collectivity of these two differing communities of faith became the *matrix* of their respective scriptural interpretation. Nearly from the beginning, then, the complex *history of biblical interpretation* was a *divided Jewish and Christian interpretation* – like two trees from one root.

3. Referring, in this respect, simply to the 'Jewish' or the 'rabbinic' side of the ancient scriptural interpretation might be another generalization about which one has to be cautious, since these terms to some extent are multifaceted; even a term like 'the Rabbis' is, as J. Harris has underscored, "a construct that must not be taken to mean that all Rabbis saw something in a particular way".[20] Rabbinic Judaism was indeed no homogeneous entity; and there were always individual Rabbis and different schools of Rabbis. Nevertheless, without unduly harmonization, also combining lines and specific traits of an idiosyncratic whole may be observed in the rabbinic traditions. The crucial point is, also on this occasion, the question of adequate distinctions.

The broad topic of chapter eight, focusing on the "formative growth of the tradition of rabbinic interpretation", may be examined from various signifi-

[17] See i.a. H. Frh. v. Campenhausen, *Die Entstehung der christlichen Bibel* (BHT 39; Tübingen 1968), esp. chap. 1–2; cf. also J. Roloff, *Neues Testament* (Neukirchen–Vluyn 1977) 261: "Die Schaffung des *Doppelkanons aus Altem und Neuem Testament* war wohl die wichtigste theologische Leistung des frühen Christentums".

[18] Cf. Hübner, chap. 9, sect. 2.

[19] So Hübner, sect. 3; cf. also sect. 5.

[20] See Harris, chap. 7, sect. 4.

cant angles. In the first section of the chapter, complementing chapter six above, D. KRAEMER has surveyed some socio-cultural aspects of "local conditions for a developing rabbinic tradition". As for relations of this kind, it seems probable that there were some connecting links between the Pharisees and the later Rabbis, who "turned their attention to Torah". Yet, as regards the question of pharisaic approaches to reading and interpreting Scripture, there exists no literary record that for certainty might recover them as predecessors and creators of the later rabbinic interpretative methods. On the other hand, "it is entirely conceivable that significant elements of the midrash of the Rabbis were their own very unique invention".[21]

The vast literary area of various rabbinic works, more specifically, exhibits a conspicuous shift as regards scriptural interpretation, whereby the Mishnah, as R. KALMIN says, "marks a watershed in rabbinic history". The Mishnah of the tannaitic[22] period, on the one hand, described by D. KRAEMER in section two of chapter eight, has in fact relatively few direct references to the Hebrew Bible. In question of religious authority, it shows a remarkable "independence of spirit", and it does not pretend to be a 'commentary to the Torah'. On the other hand – as R. KALMIN states, in section three of the chapter, discussing the rabbinic scriptural interpretation in Midrash – the "post-mishnaic compilations [i.e. mainly the various Midrashim and the two Talmuds] quote Scripture much more frequently than does Mishnah, a difference which may indicate a major ideological or conceptual change"; and that may be considered to be even more significant as in this late period Jewish and rabbinic exegesis were "virtually synonymous", whereas earlier "a wealth of non-rabbinic Jewish sources (for example, Philo and Josephus) comment on the Bible".[23] In the post-mishnaic growth of rabbinic tradition, the shift in the interpretive relation to Scripture may, to a great extent, be seen as an expression of the religious and hermeneutical problem, how to cope with the authority of the Mishnah, and the 'oral Torah', in relation to that of the Scripture, and the 'written Torah', including an increased weight on its 'plain meaning'.[24] In this respect, Talmud Yerushalmi and Talmud Bavli – the two most comprehensive and 'finalizing' collections of rabbinic teaching and learning in late Antiquity – seem to "occupy a middle position" between the Mishnah, on which they are commenting, and the various Midrashim.[25]

The complex relations of Mishnah – Midrash – Talmud are further investigated by J. NEUSNER, in section four of chapter eight. With special focus on the aspects of hermeneutics and methodological taxonomy, he gives an extensive and synthetic treatment of the exegetical character of these three main 'blocks' of rabbinic tradition, individually as well as in their relation to each

[21] So Kraemer, chap. 8, sect. 1.

[22] The term 'tannaitic' "designates the period between the destruction of the Jerusalem Temple in 70 CE and the publication of the Mishnah in the early third century CE", so Kalmin, chap. 8, sect. 3.

[23] Kalmin, ibid.

[24] Cf. now especially D. HALIVNI, *Peshat and Derash. Plain and Applied Meaning in Rabbinic Exegesis* (New York 1991).

[25] Kalmin, ibid.

other, and not least with regard to the dual Talmud as "a systematic commentary" of the Mishnah. As for the specific character of the Midrashim, NEUSNER deals in particular with Sifra's scripturally related "two-pronged polemic against the Mishnah".[26] In view of possible inner-rabbinic polemics, however, there are considerably divergent judgments and opinions among Jewish scholars. KALMIN, discussing with some of them, is especially opposing the view of NEUSNER, that the midrashic "compilations, qua compilations, respond to and polemicize against the Mishnah".[27]

Finally, along with this most variegated rabbinic tradition, consummated in the 'concluding' Talmuds, there was also the destinctive field of a flourishing Jewish interpretation represented by the Targums, whose various Aramaic translations often contain interpretative expansions. Their specific character has been discussed by É. LEVINE, in section five of chapter eight.

4. The 'parting of the ways' of Christians and Jews, referred to above, originated from within the Jewish community, due to Jewish-Christians' conviction of a diverging faith. Before long, however, the segregation grew deeper and broader, materialized in new literary works, institutionalized on the Christian side in the Primitive Church, that relatively early, as a counterpart to the Synagogue, was given names and designations that had been particular to Israel as the chosen people of God. This is only one aspect of the general fact that early Christian theology, to a high degree, brought about an extensive re-interpretation of the Hebrew Bible / Old Testament; and that became a vital part of its identity.

It was stated above, by HARRIS, that it is difficult to describe precisely the 'bridge' from older Jewish to later rabbinic biblical interpretation, because of a considerable lack of literary evidence from the period in question. Whether the same could be said of the 'bridge' from the New Testament authors to those of the early Church, as regards biblical interpretation, may perhaps be a matter of dispute, depending partly of how one defines the character of 'literary evidence'; but relatively early, there existed a rich patristic literature, replete with interpretative references to the Hebrew or Greek Bible.

In his study of the first stages of the development of a scriptural interpretation in the early Greek Church, O. SKARSAUNE opens his scrutiny, in chapter ten, by saying: "In many respects, Christian literature of the period 30–250 CE may be said to be one single large commentary on the Scriptures, the Hebrew Bible". This common interpretative trend and, by all details of the literary activity of the Apostolic Fathers and Christian Apologists, this unitary factor in their literature may be further substantiated by the fact of a unique

[26] Neusner, chap. 8, sect. 4.4 and 4.3.

[27] Kalmin, ibid. – When, moreover, the views of NEUSNER and other Jewish scholars in this way are presented side by side, partly in direct discussion, it should be regarded as a reflection of recent scholarly debate in the field. Further, it may generally be said that when some essays in the present volume have a bearing on the same subject or otherwise have references to each other, sometimes even with tension, it should not be looked upon as an unseemly over-lapping but rather as 'stereophonic' complementing. Also, tentatively, the stylistic and otherwise idiosyncratic flavour of the individual authors has been retained, occasionally also in orthography (and American English has been held equal to British English).

tradition of exegetical practice, in particular observable in Justin, namely the use of chosen 'proof texts' from the Old Testament, first of all 'proofs from prophecy', to prove the truth of the Christian messianic belief.[28] This 'proving' from the Old Testament, as the recognized authoritative basis, or according to an established tradition of scriptural 'testimonies',[29] occurred not only in dialogues with Jews but proved useful also on other occasions, as in encounters with pagans or even in inner-christian polemics. The specific 'proof text' or 'testimony' tradition promoted not only a new hermeneutical approach but also a special theology that, although being critical to Judaism, it fostered a greater integration of Old and New Testament in the Christian Bible, as did also the polemical reaction, especially by Irenaeus and Tertullian, against Marcion's denunciation of the Old Testament.[30] With its focus on combining *typoi* in the two testaments of Scripture, the 'proof text' dominated theology had definitely some broader influence, but it was gradually superseded by the Philonic-allegoric exegesis of Origen, which had another orientation. At the same time, there seems to have been, from Justin on, "a gradual wearing down of the distinct characteristics of the testimony tradition".[31]

By all this, the main subject was – in reference to Jews as well as to Christian heretics – the delicate question of a proper or 'right' understanding and interpretation of the received Scriptures. So was the case also for Alexandrian theologians of the early third century; but the philosophical and hermeneutical legacy from Athens, mediated first of all by Philo, caused another posing of the problems – which generated quite other solutions than those just described. In his study of the philosophical and hermeneutical background and framework of the characteristic Alexandrian theology, J. F. Procopé, in chapter twelve, has concentrated his examination on the important 'middle Platonism' as the ideological context, and on the issue of Greek and Hellenistic hermeneutics, discussing in particular the allegorical interpretation that marked the Alexandrian exegetes so strongly.[32] Thereby, he has also commented on the famed Alexandrian rule: 'Elucidating Homer from Homer',[33] which for Christian theology would mean: 'Elucidating Scripture from Scripture', or, as it later was formulated: *Sacra Scriptura sui ipsius interpres.*

In his essay on Christian exegesis of the Old Testament in the Alexandrian tradition, in chapter thirteen, J. N. B. Carleton Paget touches also on this rule of 'Scripture interpreting Scripture', as part of the context of the specific Alexandrian exegesis, where there "was a wide range of approaches to the exegesis of the OT".[34] But the main interest of his study is, of course, devoted to Clement and, above all, to Origen, as the most outstanding representatives of Alexandrian biblical interpretation. They were very much alike. First of all,

[28] Skarsaune, chap. 10, sect. 1–2.
[29] Ibid., esp. sect. 3.
[30] Ibid., sect. 4.2.
[31] So Skarsaune, chap. 11.
[32] He thus complements the study on earlier Jewish Alexandrian tradition by F. Siegert, in chap. four; see esp. sect. 1, on the Hellenistic art of interpretation, and sect. 4, on Philo.
[33] Procopé, chap. 12, sect. 3.5; also commented on by Siegert, chap. 4, sect. 1.4.
[34] See Carleton Paget, chap. 13, sect. 1.2.6.

both of them were deeply influenced by Greek philosophical and particularly by Philonic hermeneutical premises in their exegetical methodology and terminology. But there were also differences between them.[35] Clement, who has been reckoned as the first Christian writer to use the term 'Old Testament', as distinguished from the writings of the 'New Testament',[36] was not as text-related as Origen, nor did he "attempt a systematic exposition of his hermeneutical assumptions".[37] Like Philo and Origen, Clement "is primarily an allegorist of the OT"; but he focused, in different ways, on the symbolic sense of the texts, at times also on their literal one. His aim for the interpretation of the Old Testament was more that of meditation than of commentary in a technical sense.[38]

Origen, on the other hand, was in his thinking exclusively innovatory and systematic; his many, often exegetical works to the Old Testament, had an "obviously scholarly character".[39] He was the first Christian who, through his monumental *Hexapla,* attempted to establish an accurate text of the Septuagint, and he was specially engaged in the problem of the Old Testament canon. In his exegetical work on the Old Testament, he more than others before him "saw it as appropriate to *consult* Jewish exegetes". Particularly remarkable on this occasion, is that he also "was the first Christian to attempt to construct a systematic theory of hermeneutics", thanks to the philosophical legacy of Alexandria. Essential to his hermeneutical system was his conviction that all Scripture was divinely inspired and therefore also was a harmonious, self-interpreting whole.[40] He remained an *allegoricus semper interpres* who combined his commitment to philology and ancient grammatical rules and practices with his belief "in the twofold meaning of Scripture and in the supremacy of the spiritual over the literal meaning of a text",[41] although his awareness of the historical and literal sense should not be misjudged.[42] Origen's influence, finally, was immense and became far-reaching, both in view of Eusebius, Athanasius and the so-called Cappadocian Fathers[43] and far beyond them.[44]

Often, the allegorical exegesis of the Alexandrian tradition has been put in contrast with the exegetical tradition of the Antiochene school, which is described by S. Hidal, in chapter fourteen. And, indeed, the well known words of Diodore of Tarsus, from his 'fragm. 93', may apply to his successors

[35] Ibid., sect. 3.5.

[36] He had, however, a predecessor in Melito of Sardis who spoke of "the books of the Old Covenant"; see sect. 2 above.

[37] Ibid., sect. 2.3.

[38] Ibid., sect. 2.6.

[39] Cf. ibid., sect. 3.5: "He was interested in bringing order to the discipline of OT exegesis, of establishing criteria by which to distinguish a good interpretation from a bad one".

[40] Ibid., sect. 3.1.

[41] Ibid., sect. 3.5.

[42] Ibid., sect. 3.4.2.

[43] Ibid., sect. 4.

[44] Cf. ibid., sect. 3.5: "Origen did much to set in motion the forms in which later Christians would write about the OT and the methods they would use in its exposition". See further C. Jacob, in chap. 20, on the reception of the Origenist tradition in Latin exegesis.

in the so-called younger Antiochene school he founded; they run like a principle: "we much prefer the historical sense to the allegory". However, Diodore also distinguished carefully – as one differentiation among others – between *historia, theoria,* and *allegoria,* whereby the key concept *theoria,* without leaving its basis in the *sensus litteralis*, "makes it possible to see *typoi* in the OT and to proclaim Christ". In this way, the historical or literal sense "is transcended by the higher sense, the *theoria,* but it is not abolished". On the other hand, "to say *something else* than is intended in the text (or its *theoria*), that is allegory".[45] Later, John Chrysostom expressed the matter, in his Fifth homily on Isaiah 5, by saying: "allegory is allowed only when the Scripture clearly states that an allegory is intended".[46] Both John and Theodore of Mopsuestia, to mention only two outstanding Antiochenes, adhered firmly to the rule of 'Scripture interpreting Scripture',[47] for which the Christian conviction of the unity of the two testament Bible was an established and basic presupposition.

When the Antiochenes favoured the historical sense of the texts it might seem likely that they also had near contacts with Jewish scholars or circles, as has in fact been assumed. But, in this respect, Hidal has shown a rather ambiguous picture. There was some Jewish influence on the so-called older Antiochene school, but as for "the classical period with Diodore and Theodore, there is good reason for not postulating such an influence" – not to speak of John's sermons *Adversus Iudaeos.*[48] By posing the question on a more general level, moreover, G. Stemberger, in his analysis in chapter fifteen, has discussed the problem of possible exegetical contacts between Christian and Jews in the Roman Empire. He expresses great reserve and has shown how complicated the whole matter really is. There was always some literary influence, but there is only scanty evidence of more direct contacts, even in the Holy Land – with Justin born in Samaria, Origen living at Caesarea (since about 230), as was Eusebius, and Jerome in Bethlehem. It may have more general relevance, in this respect, what Stemberger says of Eusebius: "There certainly are points of contact between Eusebius' exegesis and rabbinic literature; but they are comparatively few and not clear evidence of his personal contacts with contemporary Jews".[49] Instead of direct exegetical contacts between representatives of Church and Synagogue the main trend was, as time moved on, a still stronger 'parting of the ways'.

On each side of the 'fence', furthermore, there were tendencies of an 'inner departing' in major regions: on the Jewish side, first of all in Palestine and Babylonia, with a specific Talmud in each region; on the Christian side, there was an ever deeper split between East and West – and in each of the areas, there came further 'local' ruptures, mostly of a theological character. Scrip-

---

[45] Hidal, chap. 14, sect. 2.

[46] Ibid., sect. 4, with the author's wording.

[47] Ibid., sect. 3 and 4.

[48] Ibid.

[49] Stemberger, chap. 15, sect. 7; cf. also on Jerome: "In spite of a vast literature on Jerome and the Jews, an in-depth analysis of Jerome's Jewish traditions still remains a desideratum".

tural interpretation became increasingly integrated in the development of Christian dogmas.

So was, not least, the case among Syrian Christians who experienced grave dogmatic discussions and split in the fifth century. The Syrian 'situation', however, was also earlier rather unique in its complexity, culturally and theologically. As for the Syriac translation of the Hebrew Bible, described by M. WEITZMAN, in chapter sixteen, this translation, Peshitta, was clearly influenced by other translation traditions, both by the Septuagint and, especially, by the Targums; yet, it has a most genuine character of its own, partly theologically determined.[50] The Syriac scriptural interpretation, within the framework of a rich, partly anonymous literature, described by L. VAN ROMPAY, in chapter seventeen, has first of all, and hardly unexpected, a near relation to the Antiochene tradition, especially to the works of Theodore. In the writings of well known exegetes like Aphrahat and Ephrem, of the fourth century, among others, one finds historical as well as typological and symbolic interpretations, based on the tenet of continuity in God's salvation in the Old and New Testament.[51]

In the West, too, there were close relations between Bible translation and interpretation in the Church. The development here was also related to the far-reaching impact of the Septuagint of the Greek East, first of all in the Old Latin translations, whose beginnings "still are not quite clear", as it is stated by E. SCHULZ-FLÜGEL, in chapter eighteen.[52] There were diverse corrections of the Latin versions, with the Septuagint as the exclusive standard. Jerome, however, was the first to bring about a basic and radical shift; and this he did, not as much by his revision of some Old Testament texts according to Origen's *Hexapla* (about 387), as through his own fresh translation (around 390) – the Vulgate, that he in a new way based on the Hebrew text as the 'true' text, as *veritas Hebraica.* Jerome's corrections based on *Hexapla* were highly cherished by Augustine, but his new translation from the Hebrew was heavily criticized by the bishop of Hippo,[53] as did many others. The hot issue was just the exclusiveness of the Septuagint as the authoritative version of the Old Testament for the Christian Church.[54] Through his preference of the *Hebraica veritas*, Jerome had set a problem and established a new situation that turned out to be most consequential for a long time. He did not only make considerable work on the translation of the Hebrew Bible, but he also – among still other kinds of literary activity – commented on several Old Testament books, which is the main subject in the essay by R. KIEFFER, in chapter nineteen.[55] As for the hermeneutical principles of Jerome, underlying

---

[50] See esp. Weitzman, chap. 16, sect. 5, on the theological attitudes of the translators.

[51] See esp. Van Rompay, chap. 17, sect. 3, on the exegesis of Ephrem.

[52] Schulz-Flügel, chap. 18, sect. 1.1; cf. also her opening words, sect. 0: "The very premises and problems which characterized the use of the Old Testament in the Christian East, were adopted together with the text by the Latin West".

[53] Parts of an interesting correspondence between Jerome and Augustine are on this.

[54] Ibid., esp. sect. 3.

[55] Kieffer, chap. 19, sect. 3, states that "with the exception of Augustine, there is no Latin Church Father who has left so many different kinds of writings as Jerome".

his many commentaries, he exhibits a remarkable shift – similar to his changed attitude to the Septuagint – from a fascination with the spiritual or mystical meaning of Scripture that he, influenced by Origen, displayed in his first scholarly work, to an increasing interest in the literal or historical sense of the Bible. This interest of Jerome as *vir trilinguis* may have been fostered by his broad translation work and his occupation with philological and historical aspects of the texts. At times, however, Jerome, who was concerned about an 'orthodox' Christian interpretation, distinguished also between three meanings: "the historical or literal, the tropological or allegorical, and the spiritual or mystical", and for the last one he used various names.[56]

Whereas Jerome increasingly turned away from the text of the Septuagint and the allegorical interpretation of Origen, Hilary of Poitiers and Ambrose of Milan, on the other hand, represented in their exegesis a reception and further advancement of the Origenist tradition in the Latin West; thereby they "paved the way for subsequent Latin exegesis", as CHR. JACOB says in the beginning of his essay, in chapter twenty. In this respect, the understanding and practice of the allegorical approach to the Old Testament texts would have the main attention, as it actually had. However, Hilary is generally aware of the difficulties of the allegorical interpretation, and it is his opinion that "it is not easy to discern whether a certain passage of Scripture is to be understood as a simple historical narrative or in the typical sense; the knowledge of the simple event is corrupted if treated vainly as a prophecy and its prefigurative dynamic is destroyed if it is considered as a historical fact only".[57] As for Ambrose, the allegorical techniques were used within the framework of his allusive language, his literary aesthetics, his rhetoric, and his homiletics, combining philosophy and Bible, serving "the sacramental dimension of his writings".[58]

Looking back at the many and diverse approaches and trends in view of the text and interpretation of the Hebrew Bible / Old Testament, it may be said with some right that various tendencies seem to 'coincide' in the numerous and multifaceted writings of Augustine. His comprehensive *œuvre*, described by D. F. WRIGHT, in chapter twenty-one, may represent, to some extent, a synthesis of the preceding history of biblical interpretation in the Ancient Church. It may also be maintained that whereas Origen in his literary activity combined philology and textcritical work with hermeneutical and systematic reflexion, his Latin successors did not in the same way combine all these aspects: Jerome was an eminent philologian and exegete but without a specific treatise on hermeneutic, and Augustine, on the other hand, was scarcely any great linguist but indeed a great systematic thinker. That is apparent in his many commentaries, *enarrationes*, and *sermones,*[59] but first of

[56] Ibid., sect. 2.3.

[57] Jacob, chap. 20, sect. 2.1, with the wording of the author, and with reference to Daniélou, Saint Hilaire évêque et docteur (1968) 9–18, 12.

[58] Ibid., sect. 3.2, where Jacob says of the rhetoric of Ambrose: "His orchestration of the OT narrative is directed by principles that become visible after decoding his allegorical mode of expression. His writings demonstrate a real virtuosity within this paradigm".

[59] Wright, chap. 21, sect. 1.

all, in his major hermeneutical discussion in *De doctrina Christiana* [*DDC*].[60] It is an 'instruction' (more than 'doctrine'), WRIGHT says, "about the task of the Christian teacher in construing and communicating the Scripture".

As already mentioned, Augustine favoured the Septuagint, not only as the authoritative text, but also as the canon of the Church. But, although he found Jerome's abandonment of the Septuagint troubling, "in *DDC* he still commends the learning of Hebrew as well as Greek"; and in addition he "also commends in *DDC* other studies such as history and geography for the elucidation of Scripture". In his hermeneutic – also related to the specific bipartite theology of history in his *De civitate Dei* – Augustine, says WRIGHT, "normally works with a two-level understanding of Scripture. The terms may vary – literal, historical, carnal, etc. on the one side, and allegorical, spiritual, prophetic, mystical, etc. on the other. He seems most at ease in allegorizing when the literal-historical meaning has first been affirmed". Finally, this is embedded in his theory of language, mainly related to the Stoic doctrine of *res et signa*.[61]

On the whole, Augustine, bishop and scholar, may be said to have had a consolidating function in the Church, not least in the history of Christian biblical interpretation, and even more so as his exegetical and hermeneutical, as well as his systematic, work was done in the context of the Church and for the Church. The influence of his various achievements was immense in the Church, for centuries.

5. In the end, then, a long *double way* – though just the first part of a still longer history of biblical interpretation – has been followed: from an initial 'inner-biblical' interpretation to the different stages of a more advanced and subtle interpretation of the Scripture, on the Jewish side, in the Mishnah and Midrashim of the rabbinic tradition, culminating in the Talmuds, as well as on the Christian side, in the New Testament-based patristic exegesis of different schools in the early and ancient Church, culminating in late Antiquity in the synthesis of Augustine's hermeneutics. These two main roads, with several minor deviating paths, have mostly been kept apart by the ancient Synagogue and Church – who have moved forward in relatively great isolation from one another, with only few signs of combining tracks.

By all this, it may be evident – and will be further substantiated through the subsequent volumes of this history of biblical interpretation – that the foundation of Jewish as well as of Christian scriptural interpretation, to a great extent, was laid in Antiquity. Through their many and manifold discussions and their various solving of hermeneutical and exegetical problems related to the Hebrew Bible / Old Testament, ancient Jewish and Christian scholars, in the matrix of their respective communities of faith, 'showed the way' for further development of biblical interpretation.

---

[60] Ibid., sect. 2. Cf. also the study of Schulz-Flügel, chap. 18, esp. sect. 3.

[61] Wright, ibid.; cf. Schulz-Flügel, ibid.

Contributors

Abbreviations

Indexes

Names/Topics/References

Contributors

John Barton (b. 1948) Oriel and Laing Professor of the Interpretation of Holy Scripture, University of Oxford. Selected publ.: *Amos's Oracles against the Nations* (SOTSMS 6), Cambridge 1980; *Reading the Old Testament: Method in Biblical Study,* London 1984; *Oracles of God: Perceptions of Ancient Prophecy in Israel after the Exile,* London 1986 / New York 1988; *People of the Book: The Authority of the Bible in Christianity*, London / Louisville 1988; *Isaiah 1–39* (OTG), Sheffield 1995.

Michael Fishbane (b. 1943) Nathan Cummings Professor of Jewish Studies, in the Divinity School and the College, and Chair of the Committee of Jewish Studies, The University of Chicago. Selected publ.: *Text and Texture. Studies in Biblical Literature,* New York 1979; *Biblical Interpretation in Ancient Israel,* Oxford 1985; *Judaism. Revelation and Traditions,* San Francisco 1987; *Garments of Torah. Essays in Biblical Hermeneutics,* Bloomington, IN 1989; *The Kiss of God. Mystical and Spiritual Death in Judaism*, Seattle, WA 1994.

Jarl Fossum (b. 1946) Professor of New Testament Studies, the University of Michigan. Selected publ.: *The Name of God and the Angel of the Lord* (WUNT 36), Tübingen 1985; *The Image of the Invisible God* (NTOA 30), Fribourg/Göttingen 1995.

Jay Harris (b. 1956) Professor of Jewish Studies, Harvard University. Selected publ.: *Nachman Krochmal: Guiding the Perplexed of the Modern Age* (Modern Jewish Masters Series 4), New York 1991; *"How Do We Know This?" Midrash and the Fragmentation of Modern Judaism,* Albany, NY 1995.

Sten Hidal (b. 1946) Associate Professor of Old Testament, University of Lund. Selected publ.: *Interpretatio Syriaca. Die Kommentare des heiligen Ephraem des Syrers zu Genesis und Exodus mit besonderer Berücksichtigung ihrer auslegungsgeschichtlichen Stellung* (ConBOT 6), Lund 1974; *Ephraem the Syrian, Hymns of Paradise. Translated into Swedish with a Commentary and Introduction,* Skellefteå 1985; "Den antiokenska exegetikskolan och judisk skriftlärdom", *Judendom och kristendom under de första århundradena* 2, Oslo 1986, 190–200.

Hans Hübner (b. 1930) Professor of Biblical Theology, University of Göttingen. Selected publ.: *Rechtfertigung und Heiligung in Luthers Römerbriefkommentar,* Witten 1965; *Das Gesetz in der synoptischen Tradition,* Witten 1973, Göttingen [2]1986; *Das Gesetz bei Paulus* (FRLANT 119), Göttingen 1978, [3]1982 (also in English and Italian); *Gottes Ich und Israel. Zum Schriftgebrauch des Paulus in Römer 9–11* (FRLANT 136), Göttingen 1984; *Biblische Theologie des Neuen Testaments* 1–3, Göttingen 1990–1995 (also in Italian).

Christoph Jacob (b. 1958) Privat-Dozent, University of Münster. Selected publ.: *"Arkandisziplin", Allegorese, Mystagogie. Ein neuer Zugang zur Theologie des Ambrosius von Mailand* (Theoph. 32), Frankfurt a. M. 1990; "Allegorese: Rhetorik, Ästhetik, Theologie", *Neue Formen der Schriftauslegung* (ed. T. Sternberg; QD 140) Freiburg 1992, 131–163; *Das geistige Theater. Ästhetik und Moral bei Johannes Chrysostomus* ('Habilitationsschrift'; in print).

Richard Kalmin (b. 1953) Th. R. Racoosin Professor of Talmud, Jewish Theological Seminary of America, New York. Selected publ.: *The Redaction of the Babylonian*

Talmud: Amoraic or Saboraic? (MHUC 12), Cincinnati, OH 1989; *Sages, Authors and Editors in Rabbinic Babylonia* (Brown Judaic Studies), Atlanta 1994.

René Kieffer (b. 1930) Professor of New Testament, University of Uppsala. Selected publ.: *Au delà des recensions? L'évolution de la tradition textuelle dans Jean VI, 52–71,* Uppsala 1968; *Essais de méthodologie néo-testamentaire,* Lund 1972; *Nytestamentlig teologi,* Lund 1977, [3]1990; *Foi et justification à Antioche. Interprétation d'un conflit,* Paris 1982; *Johannes-evangeliet* I–II, Uppsala 1987–88.

David Kraemer (b. 1955) Professor of Talmud and Rabbinics, Jewish Theological Seminary of America, New York. Selected publ.: *The Mind of the Talmud,* Oxford 1990; *Responses to Suffering in Classical Rabbinic Literature,* Oxford 1995; *Reading the Rabbis* (Oxford; forthcoming).

Robert A. Kraft (b. 1934) Berg Professor of Religious Studies, University of Pennsylvania. Selected publ.: *Barnabas and the Didache* (*The Apostolic Fathers: A New Translation and Commentary,* ed. by Robert M. Grant, 3), New York 1965; English edition of W. Bauer: *Orthodoxy and Heresy in Early Christianity* (co-ed. with G. Krodel), Philadelphia 1971; "The Multiform Jewish Heritage of Early Christianity", *Christianity, Judaism and Other Greco-Roman Cults* 3 (Studies for Morton Smith, ed. J. Neusner), Leiden 1975, 174–199; "Christian Transmission of Greek Jewish Scriptures: a Methodological Probe", *Paganisme, Judaisme, Christianisme: Influences et affrontements dans le Monde Antique* (Melanges M. Simon, ed. A. Benoit et al.), Paris 1978, 207–226; *Early Judaism and its Modern Interpreters* (with G. W. E. Nikkelsburg), Atlanta 1986.

Étan Levine (b. 1934) Professor of Biblical Studies, University of Haifa. Selected publ.: *The Aramaic Version of the Bible: Contents and Context* (BZAW 174), Berlin/New York 1988; *Un Judio Lee el Nuevo Testamento,* Madrid 1980; *The Aramaic Version of Ruth,* Rome 1973; *The Aramaic Version of Jonah,* Jerusalem 1975; *The Aramaic Version of Lamentations,* New York 1976; *The Aramaic Version of Qohelet,* New York 1978.

Johann Maier (b. 1933) Emer. Professor of Jewish Studies, University of Cologne. Selected publ.: *Zwischen den Testamenten. Zur Geschichte und Religion des zweiten Tempels,* Würzburg 1990; *Geschichte der jüdischen Religion* (Herder-Taschenbuch 4116), Freiburg i. Br. 1992; *Gesù Cristo e il cristianesimo nella tradizione giudaica antica* (Studi biblici 106), Brescia 1994; *Die Qumran-Essener. Die Texte vom Toten Meer* 1–2, Munich 1995; *Die Kabbalah,* Munich 1995.

Steve Mason (b. 1957) Associate Professor, Division of Humanities, York University [1995–1996: Professor and Head, Department of Classics and Ancient Mediterranean Studies, The Pennsylvania State University]. Selected publ.: *Josephus and the New Testament,* Peabody, MA 1992; *Flavius Josephus on the Pharisees: A Composition-Critical Study* (SPB 39), Leiden 1991; *An Early Christian Reader,* Peabody, MA 1996 (with Tom Robinson; forthcoming).

Jacob Neusner (b. 1932) Professor of Religious Studies, University of South Florida, Tampa, and Visiting Professor of Religion, Bard College, Annandale-on-Hudson, NY. Selected publ.: among his more than 600 books, some are listed in the Bibliography of his essay, chap. 8.4 above; recently: *The Presence of the Past, the Pastness of the Present. History, Time and Paradigm in Rabbinic Judaism,* Bethesda 1995.

James N. B. Carleton Paget (b. 1966) Assistant Lecturer in New Testament Studies, University of Cambridge. Selected publ.: *The Epistle of Barnabas: Outlook and Background* (WUNT II.64), Tübingen 1994; "Barnabas 9:4: A peculiar verse on circumcision", *VC* 45 (1991) 242–254; "The Epistle of Barnabas and St. Paul" (forthcoming in *NovT* 1996); "Jewish proselytism at the time of Christian origins: chimera or reality?" (forthcoming in *JSNT* 1996).

JOHN F. PROCOPÉ (1941–1995) was Senior member of King's College, and Member of the Faculties of Classics and Divinity, University of Cambridge. Selected publ.: "Quiet Christian courage: A topic in Clemens Alexandrinus and its philosophical background", StPatr 15 (ed. E. A. Livingstone), Berlin 1984, 489–494; "Democritus on Politics and the Care of the Soul", *CQ* 39 (1989) 307–331; "Epicureans on Anger", *Philanthropia und Eusebia: FS für A. Dihle zum 70. Geburtstag* (ed. G. M. Most, H. Petersmann and A. M. Ritter), Munich 1991, 363–386; 'Hochherzigkeit' and 'Höflichkeit', RAC XV, Stuttgart 1991, 766–795 and 930–986; "Seneca", *Moral and Political Essays: Cambridge Texts in the History of Political Thought* (with J. M. Cooper), Cambridge 1995.

LUCAS VAN ROMPAY (b. 1949) Professor of Aramaic language and literature, State University of Leiden. Selected publ.: *Théodore de Mopsueste. Fragments syriaques du Commentaire des Psaumes (Psaume 118 et Psaumes 138–148),* Louvain 1982; *Le commentaire sur Genèse-Exode 9,32 du manuscrit (olim) Diyarbakir 22,* Louvain 1986.

MAGNE SÆBØ (b. 1929) Professor of Old Testament Theology, The Norwegian Lutheran School of Theology (former: Free Faculty of Theology), Oslo. Selected publ.: *Sacharja 9–14. Untersuchungen von Text und Form* (WMANT 34), Neukirchen-Vluyn 1969; *Ordene og Ordet. Gammeltestamentlige studier,* Oslo 1979; *Salomos ordspråk, Forkynneren, Høysangen, Klagesangene* [Commentary], Oslo 1986.

EVA SCHULZ-FLÜGEL (b. 1939) Dr. theol., Vetus Latina Institute, Beuron. Selected publ.: *Quinti Septimi Florentis Tertulliani De virginibus velandis. Text, Einleitung, deutsche Übersetzung, theologischer und philologischer Kommentar,* Diss. theol. Göttingen 1977 (rev. and publ. in SC, 1996); Tyrannius Rufinus, *Historia monachorum sive de vita sanctorum patrum* (PTS 34), Berlin/New York 1990; *Vetus Latina, die Reste der altlatinischen Bibel* 10/3, *Canticum Canticorum* (1. Lief.), Freiburg 1992; "Interpretatio. Zur Wechselwirkung von Übersetzung und Auslegung im lateinischen Canticum Canticorum", *Biblische und patristische Studien für H. J. Frede und W. Thiele zu ihrem 70. Geburtstag* (ed. R. Gryson), Freiburg 1993, 131–141; Gregorius Eliberritanus, *Epithalamium sive Explanatio in Canticis Canticorum* (Vetus Latina. Aus der Geschichte der lateinischen Bibel 26), Freiburg 1994.

FOLKER SIEGERT (b. 1947) Professor of Jewish Studies and New Testament, and Director of the *Institutum Judaicum Delitzschianum*, University of Münster. Selected publ.: *Drei hellenistisch-jüdische Predigten* 1–2 (WUNT 20, 61), Tübingen 1980, 1992; *Nag-Hammadi-Register* (WUNT 26), Tübingen 1982; *Argumentation bei Paulus, gezeigt an Röm 9–11* (WUNT 34), Tübingen 1985; *Philon von Alexandrien: Über die Gottesbezeichnung "wohltätig verzehrendes Feuer" ⟨De Deo⟩* (WUNT 46), Tübingen 1988.

OSKAR SKARSAUNE (b. 1946) Professor of Church History, The Norwegian Lutheran School of Theology (former: Free Faculty of Theology), Oslo. Selected publ.: *The Proof from Prophecy. A Study in Justin Martyr's Proof-Text Tradition: Text-Type, Provenance, Theological Profile* (NovTSup LVI), Leiden 1987; *Kristendommen i Europa* 1: *Fra Jerusalem til Rom og Bysants,* Oslo 1987; *Da Skriften ble åpnet. Den første kristne tolkning av Det gamle testamente,* Oslo 1987; *Incarnation. Myth or Fact?* (Concordia Scholarship Today), St. Louis 1991.

GÜNTER STEMBERGER (b. 1940) Professor of Jewish Studies, University of Vienna. Selected publ.: *Juden und Christen im Heiligen Land. Palästina unter Konstantin und Theodosius,* Munich 1987; *Midrash. Vom Umgang der Rabbinen mit der Bibel. Einführung, Texte, Erläuterungen,* Munich 1989; *Pharisäer, Sadduzäer, Essener* (SBS 144), Stuttgart 1991 (Eng.: Minneapolis 1995); *Einleitung in Talmud und Midrasch,* Munich [8]1992 (Eng.: Edinburgh 1991).

EMANUEL TOV (b. 1941) Professor, Department of Bible, The Hebrew University, and Editor-in-chief, Dead Sea Scrolls Publication Project, Jerusalem. Selected publ.: *The text-Critical Use of the Septuagint in Biblical Researh* (Jerusalem Biblical Studies 3), Jerusalem 1981 (new ed. 1996); *A Computerized Data Base for Septuagint Studies – The Parallel Aligned Text of the Greek and Hebrew Bible , CATSS* 2 (JNSL Sup. ser. 1), Oxford 1986; With collaboration of R. A. Kraft: *The Greek Minor Prophets Scroll from Naḥal Ḥever, (8ḤevXIIgr) (The Seiyal Collection I)* (DJD VIII), Oxford 1990 (corrected ed. 1995); *Textual Criticism of the Hebrew Bible,* Minneapolis and Assen / Maastricht 1992, ^{2}1995; With collaboration of Stephen J. Pfann: *The Dead Sea Scrolls on Microfiche – A Comprehensive Facsimile Edition of the Texts from the Judean Desert* (with a Companion Vol.), Leiden 1993, rev. ed. 1995.

Michael Weitzman (b. 1946) Lecturer in Hebrew and Jewish Studies, University College London. Selected publ.: "Usage and Avoidance of the Term 'Chosen People'", *Language Studies* (Hebr. with Engl. sum.), Jerusalem 1990, 101–128; "From Judaism to Christianity: the Syriac Version of the Hebrew Bible", *The Jews among Pagans and Christians* (ed. J. Lieu/J. North/T. Rajak), London 1992, 147–173; "The Qaddish Prayer and the Peshitta of Chronicles", *Hebrew and Arabic Studies in Honour of Joshua Blau* (ed. H. Ben-Shammai), Tel Aviv/Jerusalem 1993, 261–290 (Hebr.); "Peshitta, Septuagint and Targum", OCA 247 (1994) 51–84.

John W. Wevers (b. 1919) Emer. Professor of Near Eastern Studies, University of Toronto. Selected publ.: Editions of the Pentateuch volumes of the Göttinger Septuaginta (*Septuaginta Vetus Testamentum Graecum,* I. *Genesis*, Göttingen 1974; II,1. *Exodus,* 1991; II,2. *Leviticus,* 1986; III,1. *Numeri,* 1982; III,2. *Deuteronomium,* 1977), along with the Text Histories of each volume (*Text History of the Greek Genesis, ... Exodus, ... Leviticus, ... Numeri, ... Deuteronomy* [MSU 11, 21, 19, 16, 13], Göttingen 1974, 1992, 1985, 1982, 1978).

David F. Wright (b. 1937) Senior Lecturer in Ecclesiastical History, New College, University of Edinburgh. Selected publ.: *Common Places of Martin Bucer* (transl. and ed.), Appleford 1972; *Martin Bucer. Reforming Church and Community* (ed. and contrib.), Cambridge 1994; *Dictionary of Scottish Church History and Theology* (chief gen. ed.), Edinburgh 1993; "The Manuscripts of St. Augustine's *Tractatus in Evangelium Iohannis*", RAug 8 (1972) 55–143 and 16 (1981) 59–100.

Abbreviations

As for the system of references to and abbreviations of Biblical books, the Apocrypha and Pseudepigrapha, Classical and Patristic works, Dead Sea Scroll texts, Targums, Mishnaic and other rabbinic material as well as Nag Hammadi tractates a general reference may be made to the rules and abbreviations listed in "*JBL* Instructions for Contributors" (*SBL Membership Directory and Handbook*, Decatur, GA 1994, 223–230).

1. General Abbreviations

ad loc.	ad locum
Akk	Akkadian
Ar	Arabic
Aram	Aramaic
Assyr	Assyrian
Bab	Babylonian
BCE	Before Common Era
BH	Biblia Hebraica
B/bk(s).	B/book(s)
B.M.	British Museum
ch./chap(s).	chapter(s)
ca.	circa
Can	Canaanite
CE	Common Era
cf.	confer, compare
CNRS	Centre National de la Recherche Scientifique
col(s).	column(s)
Copt	Coptic
cr.	copyright
DSS	Dead Sea Scrolls
du.	dual
ed(s).	editor(s) / edited by
Eg	Egyptian
ep(s).	epistle(s)
ET	English translation
et al.	et alii
Eth	Ethiopic
f(f).	following unit(s) [the point is left out before another punctuation mark]
fig(s).	figure(s)
frg(s).	fragment(s)
FS	Festschrift
G	Greek versions
Gk	Greek language
HB	Hebrew Bible
Heb	Hebrew
hi.	hif'il
hitp.	hitpa'el
i. a.	inter alia
ibid.	ibidem
Lat	Latin
LXX	Septuagint
MS(S)	Manuscript(s)
MT	Mas(s)oretic Text
NF	Neue Folge
ni.	nif'al
n(n).	note(s)
no(s).	number(s)
NS	New Series
NT	New Testament
obv.	obverse
OG	Old Greek
OS	Old Series
OT	Old Testament
P	Peshitta
p(p).	page(s)
Pal	Palestinian
pass.	passim
Pers	Persian
Phoen	Phoenician
pi.	pi'el
Pl(s).	plate(s)

pl.	plural	TaNaK	*T*ora, *N*ebi'im, *K*etubim ('Law, Prophets, Writings'), Hebrew Bible
Q	Qumran		
QL	Qumran Literature		
q. v.	quod vide	Tg(s).	Targum(s)
RV	Revised Version	tr.	translated/translation
Sam	Samaritan	Ug	Ugaritic
sec.	section(s)	UP	University Press
sg.	singular	v(v).	verse(s)
Sum	Sumerian	var.	variant
s. v.	sub voce	Vg	Vulgate
Syr	Syriac	VL	Vetus Latina

2. Abbreviations of Periodicals, Yearbooks, Reference Works and Series

Only abbreviations of periodicals are in italics.

AASF	Annales Academiae Scientiarum Fennicae
AB	Anchor Bible
ABD	Anchor Bible Dictionary
AcOr	*Acta Orientalia*
ACW	Ancient Christian Writers. The Works of the Fathers in Translation (ed. J. Quasten / J. C. Plumpe)
AfO	*Archiv für Orientforschung*
AfR	*Archiv für Reformationsgeschichte*
AGJU	Arbeiten zur Geschichte des antiken Judentums und des Urchristentums
AGWG	Abhandlungen der Gesellschaft der Wissenschaften zu Göttingen
AHW	*Akkadisches Handwörterbuch* (W. von Soden)
AJ	Antiquitates Judaicae
AJP	*American Journal of Philology*
AJSL	*American Journal of Semitic Languages and Literatures*
AKG	Arbeiten zur Kirchengeschichte
ALBO	Analecta Lovaniensia Biblica et Orientalia
ALGHJ	Arbeiten zur Literatur und Geschichte des Hellenistischen Judentums
ALKMA	*Archiv für Literatur- und Kirchengeschichte des Mittelalters*
ALW	*Archiv für Liturgiewissenschaft*
AnBib	Analecta Biblica
ANEP	*Ancient Near East in Pictures* (ed. J. B. Pritchard)
ANESTP	*Ancient Near East Supplementary Texts and Pictures* (ed. J. B. Pritchard)
ANET	*Ancient Near Eastern Texts* (ed. J. B. Pritchard)
ANF	The Ante-Nicene Fathers. Translation of the Writings of the Fathers down to A.D. 325
AnOr	Analecta Orientalia
ANRW	*Aufstieg und Niedergang der Römischen Welt* (II, ed. W. Haase / H. Temporini)
Anton.	*Antonianum*
AOAT	Alter Orient und Altes Testament
AOS	American Oriental Series
AOT	*The Apocryphal Old Testament* (ed. H. F. D. Sparks)

APAT	*Die Apokryphen und Pseudepigraphen des Alten Testaments* (ed. E. Kautzsch)
APOT	*Apocrypha and Pseudepigrapha of the Old Testament* (ed. R. H. Charles)
ARG	*Archiv für Reformationsgeschichte*
ArOr	*Archiv Orientální*
ARW	*Archiv für Religionswissenschaft*
ASNU	Acta seminarii neotestamentici Upsaliensis
ASP	American Studies in Papyrology
ASTI	Annual of the Swedish Theological Institute (of Jerusalem)
(A)SV	(American) Standard Version
ATA	Alttestamentliche Abhandlungen
ATANT	Abhandlungen zur Theologie des Alten und Neuen Testaments
ATD	Das Alte Testament Deutsch
ATR	*Anglican Theological Review*
AuA	Antike und Abendland
AuC	Antike und Christentum
Aug	*Augustinianum*
AUSS	*Andrews University Seminary Studies*
AzTh	Arbeiten zur Theologie
AV	Authorized Version
BA	*Biblical Archaeologist*
BASOR	*Bulletin of the American Schools of Oriental Research*
BAug	Bibliothèque Augustinienne
BBB	Bonner biblische Beiträge
BDB	*Hebrew and English Lexicon of the Old Testament* (F. Brown / S. R. Driver / C. A. Briggs)
BEATAJ	Beiträge zur Erforschung des Alten Testaments und des antiken Judentums
BETL	Bibliotheca Ephemeridum Theologicarum Lovaniensium
BEvT	Beiträge zur evangelischen Theologie
BFChrT	Beiträge zur Förderung christlicher Theologie
BGBE	Beiträge zur Geschichte der biblischen Exegese
BGBH	Beiträge zur Geschichte der biblischen Hermeneutik
BGPhMA	Beiträge zur Geschichte der Philosophie und Theologie des Mittelalter
BHEAT	Bulletin d'histoire et d'exégèse de l'Ancien Testament
BHK	*Biblia Hebraica* (ed. R. Kittel)
BHS	*Biblia Hebraica Stuttgartensia* (ed. K. Elliger / W. Rudolph)
BHT	Beiträge zur historischen Theologie
Bib.	*Biblica*
BibOr	Biblica et orientalia
BICS	*Bulletin of the Institute of Classical Studies*
BIOSCS	*Bulletin of the International Organisation for Septuagint and Cognate Studies*
BJRL	*Bulletin of the John Rylands University Library of Manchester*
BKAT	Biblischer Kommentar: Altes Testament
BKV	Bibliothek der Kirchenväter
BLE	*Bulletin de littérature ecclésiastique*
BN	*Biblische Notizen*
BP	Biblia Patristica
BPSup	Biblia Patristica, supplément
BRL^2	*Biblisches Reallexikon* (ed. K. Galling)

BSac	*Bibliotheca Sacra*
BSOAS	*Bulletin of the School of Oriental and African Studies*
BTB	*Biblical Theology Bulletin*
BThSt	Biblisch-Theologische Studien
BTT	*La Bible de tous les temps* (I–VIII)
BU	Biblische Untersuchungen
BWANT	Beiträge zur Wissenschaft vom Alten und Neuen Testament
BZ	*Biblische Zeitschrift*
BZAW	Beiheft zur ZAW
BZNW	Beiheft zur ZNW
BZRGG	Beiheft zur ZRGG
CA	Confessio Augustana
CAD	*The Assyrian Dictionary of the Oriental Institute*, University of Chicago
CAG	Commentaria in Aristotelem Graeca
CAH	Cambridge Ancient History
CAT	Commentaire de l'Ancien Testament
CBC	Cambridge Bible Commentary
CB.OTS	Coniectanea Biblica. Old Testament Series [cf. ConBOT]
CBQ	*The Catholic Biblical Quarterly*
CBQMS	CBQ-Monograph Series
CCat	Corpus Catholicorum
CCG	Corpus Christianorum, series graeca [= CChr.SG]
CChr.SG	see CCG
CChr.SL	see CCL
CCL	Corpus Christianorum, series latina [= CChr.SL]
CH	*Church History*
CHB	*The Cambridge History of the Bible* (I–III)
CII	Corpus inscriptionum Iudaicarum [= CIJ]
CIJ	see CII
CIL	Corpus inscriptionum Latinarum
CIS	Corpus inscriptionum Semiticarum
CJ	*Classical Journal*
CNT	Coniectanea Neotestamentica
ConBOT	Coniectanea biblica. OT Series [= CB.OTS]
CP	*Classical Philology*
CPG	Clavis Patrum Graecorum
CPJ	Corpus papyrorum Judaicarum
CPL	Clavis Patrum Latinorum
CQ	*Classical Quarterly*
CR	Corpus reformatorum
CRINT	Compendia rerum Iudaicarum ad Novum Testamentum
CS	*Cahiers sioniens*
CSCT	Columbia Studies in the Classical Tradition (Leiden)
CSCO	Corpus scriptorum christianorum Orientalium
CSEL	Corpus scriptorum ecclesiasticorum Latinorum
CTBT	Cuneiform Texts from Babylonian Tablets in the British Museum
CTM	*Concordia Theological Monthly*
CWS	The Classics of Western Spirituality (ed. R.J. Payne / J. Farina)
DACL	Dictionnaire d'archéologie chrétienne et de liturgie
DBI	A Dictionary of Biblical Interpretation (ed. R.J. Coggins / J.L. Houlden)

DBSup Dictionnaire de la Bible, Supplément
DCH *The Dictionary of Classical Hebrew* (D.J.A. Clines)
DHGE Dictionnaire d'histoire et de géographie ecclésiastique
DictS Dictionnaire de spiritualité ascétique et mystique
DJD Discoveries in the Judaean Desert
DS *Enchiridion symbolorum* (ed. A. Denzinger / A. Schönmetzer)
DTC Dictionnaire de théologie catholique

EA Erlanger Ausgabe der Werke M. Luthers
Ebib Etudes bibliques
EDB Encyclopedic Dictionary of the Bible (ed. L.F. Hartman)
EdF Erträge der Forschung
EEC Encyclopedia of the Early Church
EHAT Exegetisches Handbuch zum Alten Testament
EJ Encyclopaedia Judaica (Jerusalem 1972)
EKL Evangelisches Kirchenlexikon
EncBibl Encyclopaedia Biblica (Jerusalem)
EncRel Encyclopaedia of Religion (ed. M. Eliade)
EPRO Etudes préliminaires aux religions orientales dans l'Empire Romain
ERE Encyclopaedia of Religion and Ethics
ErIsr Eretz Israel
EstBib *Estudios bíblicos*
ETH Etudes de théologie historique
ETL *Ephemerides Theologicae Lovanienses*
ETS Erfurter theologische Studien
EvK Evangelische Kommentare
EvQ *Evangelical Quarterly*
EvTh *Evangelische Theologie*
EWNT *Exegetisches Wörterbuch zum Neuen Testament*

FB Forschung zur Bibel
FC Fathers of the Church
FChLDG Forschungen zur christlichen Literatur- und Dogmengeschichte
FKDG Forschungen zur Kirchen- und Dogmengeschichte
FontC Fontes Christiani. Zweisprachige Neuausgabe christlicher Quellentexte aus Altertum und Mittelalter
FRLANT Forschungen zur Religion und Literatur des Alten und Neuen Testaments
FS Franziskanische Studien
FSt Franciscan Studies
FSÖTh Forschungen zur systematischen und ökumenischen Theologie
FTS Freiburger theologische Studien
FZPhTh *Freiburger Zeitschrift für Philosophie und Theologie*

GCS Die Griechischen christlichen Schriftsteller der ersten drei Jahrhunderte
GesB *Hebräisches und aramäisches Handwörterbuch* (W. Gesenius / F. Buhl)
GesK *Hebräische Grammatik* (W. Gesenius / E. Kautzsch)
GesKC *Gesenius' Hebrew Grammar* (E. Kautzsch / A.E. Cowley)
GesMD *Hebräisches und Aramäisches Handwörterbuch* (W. Gesenius / R. Meyer / H. Donner)
GHAT Göttinger Handkommentar zum Alten Testament
GLB de Gruyter Lehrbuch
GOF Göttinger Orientforschungen

GOTR	*Greek Orthodox Theological Review*
GRBS	*Greek, Roman, and Byzantine Studies*
Greg	*Gregorianum*
GTA	Göttinger theologische Arbeiten
GTB	Van Gorcum's theologische bibliotheek
HAL	*Hebräisches und aramäisches Lexicon zum Alten Testament* (W. Baumgartner et al.; = KBL[3])
HAR	Hebrew Annual Review
HAT	Handbuch zum Alten Testament
HAW	Handbuch der Altertumswissenschaften
HBC	Harper's Bible Commentary (ed. J. L. Mays et al.)
HBT	Horizons in Biblical Theology
HDG	*Handbuch der Dogmengeschichte* (ed. M. Schmaus / J. Geiselmann / H. Rahner)
HDTG	*Handbuch der Dogmen- und Theologiegeschichte* (ed. C. Andresen)
Hen	*Henoch*
HeyJ	*Heythrop Journal*
HKAT	Handkommentar zum Alten Testament
HKG	*Handbuch der Kirchengeschichte* (ed. G. Krüger)
HNT	Handbuch zum Neuen Testament
HR	History of Religion
HSCP	Harvard Studies in Classical Philology
HSM	Harvard Semitic Monographs
HSS	Harvard Semitic Studies
HThK	Herders theologischer Kommentar zum Neuen Testament
HTR	*Harvard Theological Review*
HTS	Harvard Theological Studies
HUBP	Hebrew University Bible Project
HUCA	Hebrew Union College Annual
HWP	Historisches Wörterbuch der Philosophie
HZ	*Historische Zeitschrift*
IB	Interpreter's Bible
IBS	Irish Biblical Studies
ICC	International Critical Commentary
IDB	Interpreter's Dictionary of the Bible
IDBSup	Supplements to IDB
IEJ	*Israel Exploration Journal*
IKZ	*Internationale Kirchliche Zeitschrift*
Instr.Patr.	Instrumenta Patristica
Int	*Interpretation*
IOS	*Israel Oriental Studies*
IRT	Issues in Religion and Theology
ISBE	International Standard Bible Encyclopedia
ITQ	*Irish Theological Quarterly*
JAAR	*Journal of the American Academy of Religion*
JAC	Jahrbuch für Antike und Christentum
JANES(CU)	*Journal of the Ancient Near Eastern Society of Columbia University*
JAOS	*Journal of the American Oriental Society*
JB	Jerusalem Bible [cf. SBJ]
JBC	Jerome Biblical Commentary

JBL	*Journal of Biblical Literature*
JBR	*Journal of Bible and Religion*
JBTh	Jahrbuch für Biblische Theologie
JCS	*Journal of Cuneiform Studies*
JEH	*Journal of Ecclesiastical History*
JEOL	Jaarbericht Ex Oriente Lux
JETS	*Journal of the Evangelical Theological Society*
JHI	*Journal of the History of Ideas*
JHS	*Journal of Hellenic Studies*
JJS	*Journal of Jewish Studies*
JNES	*Journal of Near Eastern Studies*
JNSL	*Journal of Northwest Semitic Languages*
JPSV	Jewish Publication Society Version
JQR	*Jewish Quarterly Review*
JR	*Journal of Religion*
JSHRZ	Jüdische Schriften aus hellenistisch-römischer Zeit
JSJ	*Journal for the Study of Judaism in the Persian, Hellenistic and Roman Periods*
JSNTSup	Journal for the Study of New Testament. Supplement Series
JSOT	*Journal for the Study of the Old Testament*
JSOTSup	Journal for the Study of the Old Testament. Supplement Series
JSP	*Journal for the Study of Pseudepigrapha*
JSPSup	JSP. Supplement Series
JSS	*Journal of Semitic Studies*
JSSMon	JSS. Monograph
JTC	*Journal for Theology and the Church*
JTS	*Journal of Theological Studies*
KAI	*Kanaanäische und Aramäische Inschriften* (H. Donner / W. Röllig)
Kairos	*Kairos. Zeitschrift für Religionswissenschaft und Theologie*
KAT	Kommentar zum Alten Testament
KBL	*Lexicon in Veteris Testamenti libros* (L. Koehler / W. Baumgartner; cf. HAL)
KeH	Kurzgefaßtes exegetisches Handbuch zum Alten Testament
KEK	Kritisch-exegetischer Kommentar über das Neue Testament
KHC	Kurzer Hand-Commentar zum Alten Testament
KHAT	Konkordanz zum Hebräischen Alten Testament (G. Lisowsky)
KJV	King James Version
KStTh	Kleine Schriften zur Theologie
KTU	*Die Keilschriftalphabetischen Texte aus Ugarit* I (ed. M. Dietrich / O. Loretz / J. Sanmartín)
KuD	*Kerygma und Dogma*
LAPO	Littératures anciennes du Proche-Orient
LAW	Lexikon der Alten Welt
LCC	Library of Christian Classics
LCL	Loeb Classical Library
LD	Lectio Divina
LLAVT	*Lexicon linguae aramaicae Veteris Testamenti* (E. Vogt)
LM	Lexikon des Mittelalters
LPGL	*Patristic Greek Lexicon* (G. W. H. Lampe)
LTK	Lexikon für Theologie und Kirche
LUÅ	Lunds Universitet Årsskrift

Mand.	*Veteris Testamenti Concordantiae* (S. Mandelkern)
MGH	Monumenta Germaniae Historica inde ab a. C. 500 usque ad a. 1500
MGWJ	*Monatsschrift für Geschichte und Wissenschaft des Judentums*
MH	Museum Helveticum
MHUC	Monographs of the Hebrew Union College
Mikra	*Mikra. Text, Translation, Reading and Interpretation of the Hebrew* (CRINT II/1, ed. M. J. Mulder)
MS	Medieval Studies (Toronto)
MSSNTS	Monograph Series. Society for New Testament Studies (cf. SNTSMS)
MSSOTS	Monograph Series. Society for Old Testament Studies (cf. SOTSMS)
MSU	Mitteilungen des Septuaginta-Unternehmens
MThSt	Marburger theologische Studien
MTZ	*Münchener Theologische Zeitschrift für das Gesamtgebiet der katholischen Theologie*
NAB	New American Bible
NASB	New American Standard Bible
NCB	New Century Bible
NCOT	*A New Concordance of the Old Testament* (A. Even-Shoshan)
NEB	New English Bible
NEchtB	Neue Echter Bibel
NedTT	*Nederlands Theologisch Tijdschrift*
Neot	*Neotestamentica*
NAWG.PH	Nachrichten der Akademie der Wissenschaften in Göttingen, I. Philologisch-historische Klasse
NH	Nag Hammadi
NHS	Nag Hammadi Studies
NICOT	New International Commentary on the Old Testament
NIV	New International Version
NJB	New Jerusalem Bible
NJBC	The New Jerome Biblical Commentary (ed. R. E. Brown et al.)
NKZ	*Neue Kirchliche Zeitschrift*
NovT	*Novum Testamentum*
NovTSup	Supplements to NovT
NPNF	Nicene and Post-Nicene Fathers
NRSV	New Revised Standard Version
NRT	*Nouvelle revue théologique*
NTA	Neutestamentliche Abhandlungen
NTOA	Novum Testamentum et Orbis Antiquus
NTG^{26}	*Novum Testamentum Graece* (26th; ed. K. Aland et al.)
NTS	*New Testament Studies*
NTTS	New Testament Tools and Studies
Numen	*Numen: International Review for the History of Religion*
NumenSup	Supplements to *Numen*
NZSTh	*Neue Zeitschrift für systematische Theologie*
OBL	Orientalia et Biblica Lovaniensia
OBO	Orbis Biblicus et Orientalis
OCA	Orientalia Christiana Analecta
OCD	Oxford Classical Dictionary
OCP	*Orientalia Christiana Periodica*
OLD	Oxford Latin Dictionary

OLZ	*Orientalistische Literaturzeitung*
Or	Orientalia (Rome)
OrAnt	*Oriens antiquus*
OrChr	*Oriens christianus*
OTL	Old Testament Library
OTP	*The Old Testament Pseudepigrapha* (ed. J. H. Charlesworth)
OTS	Oudtestamentische Studiën
PAAJR	*Proceedings of the American Academy for Jewish Research*
PatSor	Patristica Sorbonensia
PatSt	Patristic Studies of the Catholic University of America
PCB	Peake's Commentary on the Bible (ed. M. Black / H. H. Rowley)
PCPS	Proceedings of the Cambridge Philological Society
PG	Patrologiae cursus completus. Series Graeca (ed. J.-P. Migne)
Philol	*Philologus*
PJ	*Palästina-Jahrbuch*
PL	Patrologiae cursus completus. Series Latina (ed. J.-P. Migne)
PLSup	Patrologiae Latinae supplementum
PO	Patrologia Orientalis (ed. R. Graffin / F. Nau)
PS	Patrologia Syriaca
PTA	Papyrologische Texte und Abhandlungen
PTS	Patristische Texte und Studien
PVTG	Pseudepigrapha Veteris Testamenti graece
PW	Real-Encyclopädie der classischen Altertumswissenschaft (Pauly-Wissowa)
PWSup	Supplements to PW
Qad	*Qadmoniot*
QD	Quaestiones disputatae
RA	*Revue d'Assyriologie et d'archéologie orientale*
RAC	Reallexikon für Antike und Christentum
RAug	Recherches Augustiniennes
RB	*Revue biblique*
RBén	*Revue bénédictine; de critique, d'histoire et de littérature religieuses*
RE	Realencyklopädie für protestantische Theologie und Kirche
REA	*Revue des études anciennes*
REAug	*Revue des études augustiniennes*
RechBib	Recherches bibliques
REG	*Revue des études grecques*
REJ	*Revue des études juives*
REL	*Revue des études latines*
ResQ	*Restoration Quarterly*
RevQ	*Revue de Qumran*
RevScRel	*Revue des sciences religieuses*
RevSém	*Revue sémitique*
RGG^3	Religion in Geschichte und Gegenwart (3rd ed.)
RHE	*Revue d'histoire ecclésiastique*
RHPR	*Revue d'histoire et de philosophie religieuses*
RHR	*Revue de l'histoire des religions*
RIDA	*Revue international des droits de l'antiquité*
RLA	Reallexikon der Assyriologie
RM	Rheinisches Museum

RQ	*Römische Quartalschrift für christliche Altertumskunde und Kirchengeschichte*
RR	*Review of Religion*
RS	Ras Shamra (field numbers of tablets excavated)
RSLR	*Rivista di storia e letteratura religiosa*
RSPT	*Revue des sciences philosophiques et théologiques*
RSR	*Recherches de science religieuse*
RSV	Revised Standard Version
RTAM	*Recherches de théologie ancienne et médiévale*
RTL	*Revue théologique de Louvain*
RVV	Religionsgeschichtliche Versuche und Vorarbeiten
SacEr	Sacris erudiri
SANT	Studien zum Alten und Neuen Testament
SAQ	Sammlung ausgewählter kirchen- und dogmengeschichtlicher Quellenschriften
SB	Sources bibliques
SBA	Schweizerische Beiträge zur Altertumswissenschaft
SBJ	La Sainte Bible de Jérusalem (cf. JB)
SBL	Society of Biblical Literature
SBLDS	SBL Dissertation Series
SBLMS	SBL Monograph Series
SBS	Stuttgarter Bibelstudien
SC	Sources chrétiennes
SCent	*Second Century*
SCO	Studi classici e orientali
ScrHier	Scripta Hierosolymitana
SCS	Septuagint and Cognate Studies
SEÅ	Svensk Exegetisk Årsbok
Sem	*Semitica*
SESJ	Suomen Eksegeettisen Seuran julkaisuja
SHT	Studies in Historical Theology
SJ	Studia Judaica
SJLA	Studies in Judaism in Late Antiquity
SJT	*Scottish Journal of Theology*
SKG.G	Schriften der Königsberger Gelehrter Gesellschaft. Geisteswissenschaftliche Klasse
SL	*Sumerisches Lexikon* (A. Deimel)
SNT	Schriften des Neuen Testaments
SNTSMS	Society for New Testament Studies Monograph Series (cf. MSSNTS)
SO	Sources Orientales
SOTSMS	The Society for Old Testament Study Monograph Series (cf. MSSOTS)
SPAW.PH	Sitzungsberichte der preußischen Akademie der Wissenschaften. Philosophisch-historische Klasse
SPB	Studia Post-Biblica
Spec.	*Speculum. A Journal of Mediaeval Studies*
SR	Studies in Religion / Sciences religieues
SSN	Studia Semitica Neerlandica
SSR	Studi storici religiosi
SSS	Semitic Studies Series
STDJ	Studies in the Texts of the Desert of Judah
StNT	Studien zum Neuen Testament
StPatr	Studia patristica

StTh	*Studia Theologica*
Str-B	*Kommentar zum Neuen Testament aus Talmud und Midrasch* (H. Strack / P. Billerbeck)
StudNeot	Studia Neotestamentica
StudOr	Studia Orientalia
StudPhil	*Studia Philonica*
SUNT	Studien zur Umwelt des Neuen Testaments
SVTP	Studia in Veteris Testamenti Pseudepigraphia
TaS	Texts and Studies
TDNT	Theological Dictionary of the New Testament
TDOT	Theological Dictionary of the Old Testament
TEG	Traditio Exegetica Graeca
THAT	Theologisches Handwörterbuch zum Alten Testament
ThBü	Theologische Bücherei
ThLZ	*Theologische Literaturzeitung*
ThPh	*Theologie und Philosophie*
ThR	*Theologische Rundschau*
TQ	*Theologische Quartalschrift*
TRE	Theologische Realenzyklopädie
TS	*Theological Studies*
TSAJ	Texte und Studien zum Antiken Judentum
TSK	*Theologische Studien und Kritiken*
TTK	*Tidsskrift for Teologi og Kirke*
TTZ	*Trier Theologische Zeitschrift*
TU	Texte und Untersuchungen zur Geschichte der altchristlichen Literatur
TWAT	Theologisches Wörterbuch zum Alten Testament
TWNT	Theologisches Wörterbuch zum Neuen Testament
TyE	Textos y Estudios "Cardenal Cisneros"
TynB	*Tyndale Bulletin*
TZ	*Theologische Zeitschrift*
UBSGNT	United Bible Societies *Greek New Testament*
UF	Ugarit-Forschungen
USQR	*Union Seminary Quarterly Review*
VC	*Vigiliae Christianae. Review of Early Christian Life and Language*
VD	*Verbum Domini*
VF	*Verkündigung und Forschung*
VT	*Vetus Testamentum*
VTSup	Supplements to VT
WA	Weimarer Ausgabe (M. Luther, Werke. Kritische Gesamtausgabe)
WBC	Word Biblical Commentary
WC	Westminster Commentary
WDB	Westminster Dictionary of the Bible
WdF	Wege der Forschung
WHJP	World History of the Jewish People
WMANT	Wissenschaftliche Monographien zum Alten und Neuen Testament
WO	*Welt des Orients*
WTJ	*Westminster Theological Journal*
WUNT	Wissenschaftliche Untersuchungen zum Neuen Testament
WZKM	*Wiener Zeitschrift für die Kunde des Morgenlandes*

ZA	*Zeitschrift für Assyriologie*
ZAH	*Zeitschrift für Althebraistik*
ZAW	*Zeitschrift für die alttestamentliche Wissenschaft*
ZBK	*Zürcher Bibelkommentar*
ZDGM	*Zeitschrift der Deutschen morgenländischen Gesellschaft*
ZDPV	*Zeitschrift des Deutschen Palästina-Vereins*
ZHT	*Zeitschrift für historische Theologie*
ZKG	*Zeitschrift für Kirchengeschichte*
ZKT	*Zeitschrift für katholische Theologie*
ZNW	*Zeitschrift für die neutestamentliche Wissenschaft*
ZPE	*Zeitschrift für Papyrologie und Epigraphik*
ZRGG	*Zeitschrift für Religions- und Geistesgeschichte*
ZST	*Zeitschrift für systematische Theologie*
ZTK	*Zeitschrift für Theologie und Kirche*

Indexes

Names/Topics/References

Names

1. Biblical and Classical Names

There may be minor differences in the spelling of some names

2. Modern Authors

From about 1650

Topics

Some Hebrew and Greek words are transcribed and printed in italics, some are in Hebrew and Greek characters and are placed at the end of this index

Hebrew words

See also transcribed Hebrew words

Greek words

See also transcribed Greek words

References

The references are divided into the following groups, partly in view of the plan of this volume (cf. also OTP, by Charlesworth, with regard to sect. 3, and F. García Martínez, *The Dead Sea Scrolls Translated* [1994], regarding sect. 4): 1. Hebrew Bible / Old Testament (799); 2. Hellenistic-Jewish Literature (813); 3. Apocrypha and Pseudepigrapha (820); 4. Qumran (823); 5. New Testament (825); 6. Targum (828); 7. Mishnah (829); 8. Tosefta (829); 9. Midrash and related works (830); 10. The Palestinian Talmud (830); 11. The Babylonian Talmud (830); 12. Greek and Latin Authors (831); 13. Early Christian and Medieval Writings (834); 14. Various (847). – The shift of traditional Latin and modern English names of works, especially in sect. 2–3 and 12–13, is for practical reasons. – Septuagint references when deviating from the order of the Hebrew Bible are in italics and square brackets [ ].

1. Hebrew Bible / Old Testament

2. Hellenistic-Jewish Literature

3. Apocrypha and Pseudepigrapha

4. Qumran

5. New Testament

6. Targum

7. Mishnah

8. Tosefta

9. Midrash and Related Works

10. The Palestinian Talmud

11. The Babylonian Talmud

12. Greek and Latin Authors

13. Early Christian and Medieval Writings

14. Various